EXPLANATION

I. Example of entry under artist:
    (1) **BELLOWS, George Wesley,** 1882-1925
    (2)   **Children on the porch** (On the porch)   OCo
    (3)   DN. Bellows
    (4)   Time. 300 years (col)
    (5)   **On the porch.** See Children on the porch

EXPLANATION

(1) Name of painter, surname in capitals
(2) Title used followed (in parentheses) by alternative title and by symbol
    giving location of painting. Meaning of symbol is given in Key to
    Symbols, pages 21-3.
(3)-(4) Names of books in which reproductions may be found. Full entry for
    these books is given in List of Works Indexed, pages 9-20.
(5) Reference from alternative title to title used

II. Example of title entry:
    Children on the porch by G. W. Bellows
    On the porch by G. W. Bellows

EXPLANATION

All titles entered in their alphabetical places in index, first word in boldface type

III. Example of subject entry:
    Bridges
        Moses, A. M. R.   Sunday (The covered bridge)
        Whistler, J. A. M.   Old Battersea bridge

EXPLANATION

To find books in which reproductions occur, consult the main entries under
    Moses and under Whistler

INDEX TO REPRODUCTIONS

OF

AMERICAN PAINTINGS

FIRST SUPPLEMENT

By the Same Authors

INDEX TO REPRODUCTIONS OF EUROPEAN PAINTINGS

INDEX TO REPRODUCTIONS

OF

AMERICAN PAINTINGS

FIRST SUPPLEMENT

*A guide to pictures occurring in more than
four hundred works*

BY
ISABEL STEVENSON MONRO
AND
KATE M. MONRO

THE H. W. WILSON COMPANY

NEW YORK   1964

PREFACE

This supplement to INDEX TO REPRODUCTIONS OF AMERICAN PAINT-INGS, published in 1948, continues the earlier index through 1961. It lists the paintings of artists reproduced in more than 400 general books on art, books on individual artists, and catalogs of museums and of special exhibitions.

Material indexed was chosen by the compilers and was selected because it introduced names of new and older artists and of additional reproductions. A few books issued before 1948 have been included as they were published while the original volume was in process of printing or because they were suggested for inclusion. Many small publications, even of pamphlet size, have been indexed, since otherwise the names of some newly-discovered or rather obscure artists might not appear. In fact, this index may be particularly valuable in identifying some of these less-known names.

The word *American* in the title of this index refers to artists of the United States, not only native-born, but also foreign-born who have become naturalized or who have lived and worked in the United States so that their later work is regarded as American. Artists are regarded as American when they are so identified in museum catalogs and exhibitions.

As in the foundation volume, paintings are entered (1) under name of artist, followed by his dates when obtainable, by title of picture, and by an abbreviated entry for the book in which the reproduction may be found; (2) under distinctive titles; and (3) in some cases under subjects. Locations of paintings in permanent collections have been indicated by symbols following the title of the picture whenever such information has been available.

Symbols. Symbols follow the form used in the previous index. They are usually formed by taking the first letter from the name of the state, the second from the city or town, and the third from some distinguishing letter for the museum or other institution where the original is located. For example, the letters *NUM* represent *N* for New York, *U* for Utica, *M* for Munson-Williams-Proctor Institute. A few exceptions occur in the use of *MM* for the Metropolitan Museum, New York; of *MMA* for the Museum of Modern Art, New York; and *WMAA* for the Whitney Museum of American Art, New York.

Subjects. Subjects, such as Boxers and wrestlers, Children, Circus, and place names, are given for paintings where such groupings might be helpful in identifying the pictures or interesting in themselves. Names of individuals occurring as sitters are always given as subjects. Married women have usually been entered under their married names with references from their maiden names unless such references would follow immediately under the subjects.

Titles. Titles are given in their alphabetical order if they seem distinctive enough to be brought out or if such titles might be remembered and so traced to the artist. In the case of two titles found for the same

picture, both are given under the artist with reference from the alternative title unless it follows immediately below. The alternative title is also listed in its alphabetical order followed by the name of the painter. For example, under Chase, William Merritt, the title *Turkish page* occurs, followed by the alternative title in parentheses (*Boy feeding a cockatoo*). The title *Boy feeding a cockatoo* also appears as a title under Chase with the reference See *Turkish page*. Both titles are also given in their alphabetical place in the index.

Unidentified artists. Under the entry Unidentified artists, reproductions are listed for those that have a subject value, such as names of individuals or places, or for those that have distinctive titles, as *Quilting Party*.

The compilers are very grateful to the many museums and libraries that have lent or given material for indexing. Although these organizations cannot all be listed, the compilers wish to mention the Library of the University of North Carolina for the many courtesies extended to them.

I. S. M.
K. M. M.

Winter Park, Florida

May 1964

CONTENTS

Preface 5

List of Works Indexed 9

Key to Symbols Used for Locations of Paintings 21

List of Institutions with Symbols Used in This Book 25

Explanation 30

Index to Reproductions of American Paintings 31

LIST OF WORKS INDEXED

The abbreviated forms in boldface type are those used in the index. Full name of author, or museum, publisher, place, and date follow in roman type.

Art since 1945—Art since 1945 by Marcel Brion and others. N.Y. Harry N. Abrams, 1958

Ashton. Philip Guston—Ashton, Dore. Philip Guston. N.Y. Grove press, 1960

ATeS. Collection—Arizona state college, Tempe. Collection of American art. Tempe, The college, 1954

ATU. Coll of Amer art. University of Arizona. Collection of American art. Tucson, The university, 1947

Barker. Amer ptg—Barker, Virgil. American painting, history and interpretation. N.Y. The Macmillan co. 1950

Barker. From realism—Barker, Virgil. From realism to reality in recent American painting. Lincoln, University of Nebraska press, 1959

Barr. Masters of modern art. See MMA. Masters

Barr. Painting and sculpture. See MMA. Ptg and sculpture

Barr. What is mod ptg 1956—Barr, Alfred Hamilton. What is modern painting. rev (i.e. 6th) ed. N.Y. Museum of modern art, 1956 (Introduction to the modern arts 2)

Baur. Amer ptg—Baur, John Ireland Howe. American painting in the nineteenth century: main trends and movements. N.Y. Frederick A. Praeger, 1953

Baur. Balcomb Greene—Baur, John Ireland Howe. Balcomb Greene. N.Y. American federation of arts, 1961

Baur. Bradley Walker Tomlin—Baur, John Ireland Howe. Bradley Walker Tomlin. N.Y. The Macmillan co. 1957

Baur. Charles Burchfield—Baur, John Ireland Howe. Charles Burchfield. N.Y. The Macmillan co. 1956

Baur. George Grosz—Baur, John Ireland Howe. George Grosz. N.Y. Whitney museum of American art, 1954

Baur. MacIver and Pereira—Baur, John Ireland Howe. Loren MacIver; I. Rice Pereira. N.Y. The Macmillan co. 1953

Baur. Nature—Baur, John Ireland Howe. Nature in abstraction, the relation of abstract painting and sculpture to nature in twentieth century American art. N.Y. The Macmillan co. 1958

Baur. New art—Baur, John Ireland Howe, ed. New art in America: fifty painters of the twentieth century by J. I. H. Baur, ed., Lloyd Goodrich, D. C. Miller, J. T. Soby, F. S. Wight. N.Y. New York Graphic society, 1957

Baur. Philip Evergood—Baur, John Ireland Howe. Philip Evergood. N.Y. Published for the Whitney museum of American art by Frederick A. Praeger, 1960

Baur. Revolution—Baur, John Ireland Howe. Revolution and tradition in modern American art. Cambridge, Harvard university press, 1951

Baur. William Zorach—Baur, John Ireland Howe. William Zorach. N.Y. Published for the Whitney museum of American art by Frederick A. Praeger, 1959

Baur. Young America 1957. See WMAA. Young America 1957

Bazin—Bazin, Germain. History of modern painting. N.Y. The Hyperion press, 1951

Bazin. History of art—Bazin, Germain. A history of art from prehistoric times to the present. Boston, Houghton Mifflin co. 1959

Belknap—Belknap, Waldron Phoenix. American colonial painting: materials for a history. Cambridge, Harvard university press, 1959

Benton—Benton, Thomas Hart, An artist in America. New and rev ed. N.Y. University of Kansas City press, 1951

Biddle. Yes and no—Biddle, George. The yes and no of contemporary art, an artist's evaluation. Cambridge, Harvard university press, 1957

Blesh—Blesh, Rudi. Modern art, U.S.A. men, rebellion, conquest, 1900-1956. N.Y. Alfred A. Knopf, 1956

Blesh. Stuart Davis—Blesh, Rudi. Stuart Davis. N.Y. Grove press, 1960

Bolton. Ezra Ames—Bolton, Theodore and Cortelyou, Irwin F. Ezra Ames of Albany, portrait painter, craftsman, Royal arch mason, banker. N.Y. New-York Historical society, 1955

Born—Born, Wolfgang. American landscape painting, an interpretation. New Haven, Yale university press, 1948

Breeskin. Milton Avery—Breeskin, Adelyn. Milton Avery. N.Y. The American federation of arts, 1960

Brion, Marcel. Art since 1945. See Art since 1945

Brooks. John Sloan—Brooks, Van Wyck. John Sloan, a painter's life. N.Y. E. P. Dutton & co. 1955

Brown. Amer ptg—Brown, Milton Wolf. American painting from the Armory show to the depression. Princeton, Princeton university press, 1955

Brussels. Exposition—Brussels. Exposition universelle et internationale, 1958. American art: four exhibitions. 17 April to October 18, 1958. N.Y. American federation of arts, 1958

Bywaters. Andrew Dasburg—Bywaters, Jerry. Andrew Dasburg. N.Y. American federation of arts, 1959

Canaday—Canaday, John. Mainstreams of modern art. N.Y. Simon and Schuster, 1959

CanO. Hirshhorn coll—National gallery of Canada, Ottawa. Some American paintings from the collection of Joseph H. Hirshhorn. 2d ed. Ottawa, The gallery, 1957

Carlson. Gallery—Carlson, Raymond, ed. Gallery of western paintings. N.Y. McGraw-Hill Book co. 1951

Cheney. Expressionism 1948 ed.—Cheney, Sheldon. Expressionism in art. rev ed. Liveright publishing co. 1948

Cheney. New world history—Cheney, Sheldon. A new world history of art. N.Y. The Viking press, 1956

Cheney. Primer 1958 ed—Cheney, Sheldon. A primer of modern art. 13th rev ed. N.Y. Liveright publishing corp. 1958

Cheney. Story 1958 ed—Cheney, Sheldon. The story of modern art. rev and enl mid-century ed. N.Y. The Viking press, 1958

Chew. 250 years of art—Chew, Paul A. comp. and ed. Two hundred and fifty years of art in Pennsylvania. Greensburg, Pa. The Westmoreland county museum of art, 1959

CLA. 35 ptgs—Los Angeles county museum. Thirty-five paintings from the collection of the Los Angeles county museum. n.p. 1950 (Picture book no 1)

Coates. Walter Quirt—Coates, Robert M. Walter Quirt. N.Y. The American federation of arts, 1960

Cortelyou. Ezra Ames supp—Cortelyou, Irvin W. A supplement to the catalogue of pictures by Ezra Ames of Albany, N.Y. New-York historical society, 1957

CoS. New accessions USA—Colorado Springs fine arts center. New accessions USA, 1946-1960. Colorado Springs, 1946-1960

Cowdrey—Cowdrey, Mary Bartlett. American academy of fine arts and American art-union. Exhibition record 1816-1852. N.Y. New-York historical society, 1953 2v

Craven. Rainbow book—Craven, Thomas. The rainbow book of art. Cleveland, The World publishing co. 1956

Craven. Treasury 1952 ed.—Craven, Thomas. A treasury of art masterpieces from the renaissance to the present day. rev and enl. N.Y. Simon and Schuster, 1952

CSB. Illusion—Santa Barbara museum of art. Illusion and reality in contemporary American art. Santa Barbara, The museum, 1956

CSB. Impressionism—Santa Barbara museum of art. Impressionism and its influence in American art . . . n.p. 1954

CSFP. Annual ex—California Palace of the Legion of Honor, San Francisco. Annual exhibition, 1946-1952. San Francisco, The palace, 1946-1952

CSFP. Annual exhibition of contemporary American painting. See CSFP. Annual ex, 1950/51; Annual ex, 1952

CSFP. First spring annual ex. See CSFP. Annual ex, 1946

CSFP. Handbook—California Palace of the Legion of Honor, San Francisco. Handbook of the collections. San Francisco, The palace, 1960

CSFP. Illusionism—California Palace of the Legion of Honor, San Francisco. Illusionism & trompe l'oeil, an idea illustrated by an exhibition held May 3—June 12, 1949. San Francisco, The palace, 1949

CtHW. Durrie—Wadsworth atheneum, Hartford, Conn. George Henry Durrie, Connecticut painter of American life. Special loan exhibition March 12-April 13, 1947. Hartford, The atheneum, 1947

CtHW. Handbook—Wadsworth atheneum, Hartford, Conn. Handbook. Hartford, 1958

CtHW. Thomas Cole—Wadsworth atheneum, Hartford, Conn. Thomas Cole 1801-1848: one hundred years later. A loan exhibition, Wadsworth atheneum . . . Whitney museum of American art. Hartford, The atheneum, 1949

CtHW. Trumbull—Wadsworth atheneum, Hartford, Conn. John Trumbull: painter—patriot, an exhibition organized to honor the bicentennial of the artist's birth. October 10-November 25, 1956. Hartford, The atheneum, 1956

CtY. Portrait index—Yale university, New Haven, Conn. Portrait index, 1701-1951. New Haven, Yale university press, 1951

CtY. Soc Anonyme—Yale university, New Haven, Conn. Gallery of fine arts. Collection of the Société anonyme. 1920. New Haven, 1950

CtY. Yale alumni—Yale university, New Haven, Conn. Pictures collected by Yale alumni. Exhibition May eight to June eighteen, 1956. New Haven, 1956

Davidson v1, v2.—Davidson, Marshall B. Life in America. Boston, Houghton Mifflin co. 1951 2v

DC. Amer ptrs of the South—The Corcoran gallery of art, Washington, D.C. American painters of the South, April 23-June 5, 1960. Washington, The gallery, 1960

DC. Biennial ex.—The Corcoran gallery of art, Washington, D.C. Biennial exhibition of contemporary American painting, 1947-1961. Washington, The gallery, 1947-1961

DC. De gustibus—The Corcoran gallery of art, Washington, D.C. De gustibus, an exhibition of American paintings illustrating a century of taste and criticism, January 9 through February 20, 1949. Washington, The gallery, 1949

DC. Halpert collection—The Corcoran gallery of art, Washington, D.C. A loan exhibition from the Edith Gregor Halpert collection. January 16-February 26, 1960. Washington, The gallery, 1960

DC. Masterpieces—The Corcoran gallery of art, Washington, D.C. Masterpieces of the Corcoran gallery of art. Washington, The gallery, 1959

DC. Privately owned—The Corcoran gallery of art, Washington, D.C. Privately owned, a selection of works of art from collections in the Washington area, February tenth-March thirtieth, 1952. Washington, The gallery, 1952

DC. Ryder—The Corcoran gallery of art, Washington, D.C. Albert Pinkham Ryder, April 8-May 12, 1961. Washington, The gallery, 1961

De Mare. G. P. A. Healy—De Mare, Marie. G. P. A. Healy, American artist: an intimate chronicle of the nineteenth century. N.Y. David McKay co. 1954

Dickson. John Wesley Jarvis—Dickson, Harold E. John Wesley Jarvis, American painter, 1780-1840 with a checklist of his works. N.Y. New-York historical society, 1949

DN. Amer primitive ptgs—U.S. National gallery of art, Washington, D.C. American primitive paintings from the collection of Edgar William and Bernice Chrysler Garbisch. Washington, The gallery, 1954-1957 (2 parts)

DN. Bellows—U.S. National gallery of art, Washington, D.C. George Bellows, a retrospective exhibition, January 19 through February 24, 1957. Washington, The gallery, 1957

DN. Homer—U.S. National gallery of art, Washington, D.C. Winslow Homer, a retrospective exhibition: National gallery of art, Metropolitan museum of art. Washington, The gallery, 1958

DN. Mellon collection—U.S. National gallery of art, Washington, D.C. Paintings and sculpture from the Mellon collection. Washington, The gallery, 1940

DNC. Gellatly coll, 1954—Smithsonian institution. National collection of fine arts, Washington, D.C. Catalog of American and European paintings in the Gellatly collection. 4th ed. Washington, The institution, 1954

Donahue. William Pachner—Donahue, Kenneth. William Pachner. N.Y. The American federation of arts, 1959

DP. Catalogue—The Phillips collection, Washington, D.C. Catalogue, 1952. n.p., n.d.

Ebersole. Fletcher Martin—Ebersole, Barbara. Fletcher Martin. Gainesville, University of Florida press, 1954

Eliot. Art of our time—Eliot, Alexander. Art of our time, 1950-1960: painting, architecture, sculpture. N.Y. Omicron books, 1959

Eliot. Three hundred years of American painting. See Time. 300 years

Evans—Evans, Grose. Benjamin West and the taste of his times. Carbondale, Southern Illinois university press, 1959

Faulkner. Art today, 1956—Faulkner, Ray Nelson. Art today, an introduction to the fine and functional arts. 3d ed. N.Y. Henry Holt & co. 1956

50 years of modern art—50 years of modern art, introduction by Emile Langui. N.Y. Frederick A. Praeger, 1959

Fleischman collection. See WiMiA. Amer ptg, 1760-1960

Flexner. Amer ptg—Flexner, James Thomas. The pocket history of American painting. N.Y. Pocket books, 1957

Flexner. Copley—Flexner, James Thomas. John Singleton Copley. Boston, Houghton Mifflin co. 1948

Flexner. First flowers—Flexner, James Thomas. First flowers of our wilderness. Boston, Houghton Mifflin co. 1947 (American painting v1)

Flexner. Light of distant skies—Flexner, James Thomas. The light of distant skies, 1760-1835. N.Y. Harcourt, Brace and co. 1954 (American painting v2)

Flexner. Short history—Flexner, James Thomas. A short history of American painting. Boston, Houghton Mifflin co. 1950

Foote. John Smibert—Foote, Henry Wilder. John Smibert, painter, with a descriptive catalogue of portraits and notes on the work of Nathaniel Smibert. Cambridge, Harvard university press, 1950

Ford. Edward Hicks—Ford, Alice Elizabeth. Edward Hicks, painter of The peaceable kingdom. Philadelphia, University of Pennsylvania press, 1952

Ford. Pictorial folk art—Ford, Alice Elizabeth. Pictorial folk art, New England to California. N.Y. Studio publications, 1949

Frankenstein. After the hunt—Frankenstein, Alfred. After the hunt: William Harnett and other American still life painters 1870-1900. Berkeley, University of California press, 1953

Frankenstein. Two journeyman ptrs—Frankenstein, Alfred and Healy, Arthur K. D. Two journeyman painters. Middlebury, Vt. Sheldon museum, 1950

Gardner. 1959 ed—Gardner, Helen. Art through the ages. 4th ed rev under the editorship of Sumner McK. Crosby by the Department of the history of art, Yale university. N.Y. Harcourt, Brace and co. 1959

GAtM. Holbrook collection—Georgia museum of art, Athens, Ga. The Eva Underhill Holbrook memorial collection. Athens, University of Georgia, 1953

Genauer—Genauer, Emily. Best of art. N.Y. Doubleday & co. 1948

Getlein. Abraham Rattner. Getlein, Frank. Abraham Rattner. N.Y. The American federation of arts, 1960

Goodrich. Amer art—Goodrich, Lloyd and Baur, John Ireland Howe. American art of our century. N.Y. Published for the Whitney museum of American art by F. A. Praeger, 1961

Goodrich. Edward Hopper—Goodrich, Lloyd. Edward Hopper. Baltimore Penguin books, 1949 (The Penguin modern painters)

Goodrich. John Sloan—Goodrich, Lloyd. John Sloan. N.Y. Published for the Whitney museum of American art by The Macmillan co. 1952

Goodrich. Max Weber—Goodrich, Lloyd. Max Weber. N.Y. Published for the Whitney museum of American art by The Macmillan co. 1949

Goodrich. Pioneers of modern art in America. See WMAA. Pioneers

Goodrich. Reginald Marsh. See WMAA. Marsh

Goodrich. Ryder—Goodrich, Lloyd. Albert P. Ryder. N.Y. George Braziller, 1959 (Great American artists series)

Goodrich. Winslow Homer—Goodrich, Lloyd. Winslow Homer. N.Y. George Braziller, 1959 (Great American artists series)

Goodrich. Yasuo Kuniyoshi—Goodrich, Lloyd. Yasuo Kuniyoshi. N.Y. Published for the Whitney museum of American art by The Macmillan co. 1948

Goossen. Stuart Davis—Goossen, Eugene C. Stuart Davis. N.Y. George Braziller, 1959 (Great American artists series)

Gordon. Karl Schrag—Gordon, John. Karl Schrag. N.Y. The American federation of arts, 1960

Gregory. The world of Whistler—Gregory, Horace. The world of James McNeill Whistler. N.Y. Thomas Nelson & sons, 1959

Gruskin—Gruskin, Alan D. Painting in the U.S.A. N.Y. Doubleday & co. 1946

Habasque—Habasque, Guy. Cubism. Geneva, Skira, 1959 (Taste of our time series)

Helm. John Marin—Helm, MacKinley. John Marin. Boston, Pelligrini & Cudahy in association with the Institute of contemporary art, 1948

Hess. Abstract ptg—Hess, Thomas B. Abstract painting, background and American phase. N.Y. Viking press, 1951

Hess. Willem De Kooning—Hess, Thomas B. Willem de Kooning. N.Y. George Braziller, 1959 (Great American artists series)

Hunter. Jackson Pollock. See MMA. Jackson Pollock

Hunter. Mod Amer ptg—Hunter, Sam. Modern American painting and sculpture. N.Y. Dell publishing co. 1959 (Laurel edition)

IaDa. Silver jubilee—Davenport municipal art gallery, Davenport, Iowa. Silver jubilee exhibition of 100 contemporary painters. Davenport, 1950

IaDa. 30th anniversary—Davenport municipal art gallery, Davenport, Iowa. Thirtieth anniversary exhibition of 100 contemporary American paintings. n.p., 1955

IaDa. Wood—Davenport municipal art gallery, Davenport, Iowa. Grant Wood and the American scene. February 3-24, 1957. n.p., n.d.

ICA. Abstract and surrealist art. See ICA. Annual ex, 1947/48

ICA. Amer artists paint the city—Chicago. Art institute. American artists paint the city. XXVIIIth biennale, Venice, 1956. Chicago, The institute, 1956

ICA. American exhibition: paintings, sculpture. See ICA. Annual ex.

ICA. Annual ex—Chicago, Art institute. American exhibition: paintings, sculpture. v56, 1945/46-v64, 1961 (lacking: v57, 1946/47; v59, 1949/50) Chicago, The institute, 1945-1961. 6 numbers

ICA. From colony to nation—Chicago. Art institute. From colony to nation, an exhibition of American painting, silver and architecture from 1650 to the War of 1812. Chicago, The institute, 1949

InIJ. Chase centennial—John Herron art museum, Indianapolis, Ind. Chase centennial exhibition . . . November 1-December 11, 1949 n.p., n.d.

InIJ. 105 ptgs—John Herron art museum, Indianapolis, Ind. 105 paintings in the John Herron art museum. Indianapolis, Art association of Indianapolis, 1951

InTH. Catalogue—Sheldon Swope art gallery, Terre Haute, Ind. Catalogue 1951 Terre Haute, The gallery, 1951

IU. Contemp Amer ptg—Illinois. University. College of fine and applied arts. Exhibition of contemporary American painting, 1948-1952. Urbana, The university, 1948-1952. 5 numbers

IU. Contemp Amer ptg & sculp—Illinois. University. College of fine and applied arts. Contemporary American painting and sculpture, 1953-1961. Urbana, The university, 1953-1961. 9 numbers

IU. 20th century—Illinois. University. College of fine and applied arts. 20th century works of art from the permanent collection . . . 1957. Urbana, The university, 1957

Janis—De Kooning—Janis, Harriet Grossman and Blesh, Rudi. De Kooning. N.Y. Grove press, 1960

Janson. Key monuments—Janson, Horst Woldemar, ed. Key monuments of the history of art, a visual survey ed by H. W. Janson with Dora Jane Janson. Englewood Cliffs, N.J. Prentice-Hall and Harry N. Abrams, 1959

Janson. Picture history—Janson, Horst Woldemar and Janson, Dora Jane. Picture history of painting from cave painting to modern times. N.Y. Harry N. Abrams, 1957

Jean. Surrealist ptg—Jean, Marcel. The history of surrealist painting, with the collaboration of Arpad Mezei. Tr from the French by S. W. Taylor. N.Y. Grove press, 1959

Jetté. Amer heritage collection—Jetté, Edith Kemper and Jetté, Ellerton Marcel. A group of paintings from the American heritage collection. Waterville, Me. Colby college press, 1956

John Marin—John Marin memorial exhibition with a foreword by Duncan Phillips; appreciation by William Carlos Williams and Dorothy Norman; conclusion to a biography by MacKinley Helm; John Marin—frontiersman by F. S. Wight. Los Angeles, University of California, 1955. (Organized by the Art galleries of the University of California, Los Angeles, Cleveland, Minneapolis, Boston, Phillips, San Francisco)

Jones. New-found folk art—Jones, Agnes Halsey and Jones, Louis C. New-found folk art of the young republic. Cooperstown, N.Y. State historical assn. 1960

Jones. Rediscovered ptrs—Jones, Agnes Halsey. Rediscovered painters of upstate New York 1700-1875. Utica, Munson-Williams-Proctor institute, 1958. (Exhibition sponsored by N.Y. state historical assn; Albany institute; Munson-Williams-Proctor institute; New-York historical society, 1958-1959)

Kallir. Amer primitive ptgs—Kallir, Otto. American primitive paintings. Washington, Smithsonian institution, 1958

KLU. Benton—University of Kansas. Museum of art, Lawrence. Thomas Hart Benton; a retrospective exhibition, April 12 to May 18, 1958. Lawrence, The university, 1958

KLU. Wood—University of Kansas. Museum of art, Lawrence. Grant Wood, 1891-1942, a retrospective exhibition, April 12 to May 30, 1959. Lawrence, The university, 1959

KyLS. Kentucky port gall—The J. B. Speed art museum, Louisville, Ky. A preliminary catalogue of the Kentucky portrait gallery, Louisville, 1949

Langui, Emile. See 50 years of modern art

Larkin—Larkin, Oliver W. Art and life in America. N.Y. Rinehart & co. 1949

Larkin rev ed—Larkin, Oliver W. Art and life in America. rev and enl ed. N.Y. Holt, Rinehart and Winston, 1960

Lee. Art then and now.—Lee, Kathryn Dean and Burchwood, Katharine Tyler. Art then and now. N.Y. Appleton-Century Crofts. 1949

Leepa—Leepa, Allen. The challenge of modern art. N.Y. Beechhurst press, 1949

Leeper. Everett Spruce—Leeper, John Palmer. Everett Spruce. N.Y. The American federation of arts, 1959

Lewis. Russell Smith—Lewis, Virginia E. Russell Smith, romantic realist. Pittsburgh, University of Pittsburgh press, 1956

Lewisohn—Lewisohn, Sam A. Painters and personality. N.Y. Harper & brothers, 1947

Lipman. Primitive ptrs—Lipman, Jean and Winchester, Alice, eds. Primitive painters in America 1750-1950: an anthology. N.Y. Dodd Mead & co. 1950

MB. Great Americans—Boston museum of fine arts. Great Americans from the Revolution to the Civil war. Meriden, Meriden gravure co. 1954 (Picture book no 1)

MB. Karolik coll—Boston museum of fine arts. M. and M. Karolik collection of American paintings, 1815-1865. Cambridge, Harvard university press, 1949

MB. Lane—Boston museum of fine arts. Fitz Hugh Lane. Boston, The museum, 1956 (Picture book no 8)

MB. New England miniatures—Boston museum of fine arts. New England miniatures. Boston, The museum. 1957

MB. Prendergast—Boston museum of fine arts. Maurice Prendergast by Hedley Howell Rhys. Cambridge, Harvard university press, 1960

MB. Ptgs in water color—Boston museum of fine arts. Catalogue of paintings and drawings in water color. Boston, The museum, 1949

MBIC. Jack Levine—Boston. Institute of contemporary art. Jack Levine with an essay by F. S. Wight and a foreword by Lloyd Goodrich. N.Y. Whitney museum of American art, 1955

MBIC. Salemme—Boston. Institute of contemporary art. Salemme. Boston, 1955?

MBIC. View 1960—Boston. Institute of contemporary art. View 1960. Boston, The institute, 1960

MBIC. Villon and Feininger—Boston. Institute of contemporary art. Jacques Villon. Lyonel Feininger . . . N.Y. Chanticleer press, 1949?

McCausland. A. H. Maurer—McCausland, Elizabeth. A. H. Maurer, 1868-1932. Minneapolis, Walker art center, 1949

McCausland. Marsden Hartley—McCausland, Elizabeth. Marsden Hartley. Minneapolis, University of Minnesota press, n.d.

McClintock—McClintock, Gilbert S. Valley views of northeastern Pennsylvania. Wilkes-Barre, The Wyoming historical and genealogical society, 1948

McCracken. Charles M. Russell—McCracken, Harold. The Charles M. Russell book: the life and work of the cowboy artist. Garden City, Doubleday & co. 1957

McCracken. George Catlin—McCracken, Harold. George Catlin and the old frontier. N.Y. The Dial press, 1959

McCracken. Portrait of the old west—McCracken, Harold. Portrait of the old west with a biographical check list of western artists. N.Y. McGraw-Hill book co. n.d.

McCracken. Remington—McCracken, Harold. A catalogue of the Frederic Remington collection with chronology and notes. N.Y. Knoedler galleries (for the Remington art memorial, Ogdensburg N. Y.) 1954

McCurdy—McCurdy, Charles, ed. Modern art, a pictorial anthology. N.Y. The Macmillan co. 1958

McDermott. G. C. Bingham—McDermott, John Francis. George Caleb Bingham, river portraitist. Norman, University of Oklahoma press, 1959

McDermott. Samuel Seymour—McDermott, John Francis. Samuel Seymour: pioneer artist of the plains and the Rockies. Washington, Government printing office, 1951 (Smithsonian publication 4043)

McKibben. Sargent's Boston—McKibben, David. Sargent's Boston with an essay & biographical summary & a complete checklist of Sargent's portraits. Boston, Boston museum of fine arts, 1956

McKinney—McKinney, Roland Joseph. Famous American painters. N.Y. Dodd, Mead & co. 1955 (Famous biographies for young people)

MdBMu. Rendezvous—Baltimore. Municipal museum. Rendezvous for taste: Peale's Baltimore museum, 1814 to 1830: Exhibition celebrating the 25th anniversary of the Peale museum 1931-1956. Baltimore, n.d.

MeC. Inaugural ex—Colby college art collection. Inaugural exhibition including gifts acquired through the Friends of arts at Colby. Waterville, Me. The college, 1959

Mendelowitz—Mendelowitz, Daniel Marcus. A history of American art. N.Y. Holt, Rinehart and Winston, 1960

MiA. Root coll—University of Michigan, Ann Arbor. Selection from the Edward Root collection, the Munson-Williams-Proctor institute, Utica, N.Y., Circulated by the Smithsonian institution, 1959-60. n.p. n.d.

MiC. Zoltan Sepeshy—Cranbrook academy, Bloomfield Hills, Mich. Zoltan Sepeshy, April 28-May 14, 1950. Bloomfield Hills, The academy, 1950

MiD. Coll in progress—Detroit institute of arts. Collection in progress: selections from the Lawrence and Barbara Fleischman collection of American art. Detroit, The institute, 1955

MiD. Ports of the Pitts family—Detroit institute of arts. Portraits of eight generations of the Pitts family from the seventeenth to the twentieth century. Detroit, The institute, 1959

MiD. Ptg in America—Detroit institute of arts. Painting in America, the story of 450 years [exhibition] April 23 through June 9, 1957. Detroit, The institute, 1957

MiD. Travelers in Arcadia—Detroit institute of arts. Travelers in Arcadia, American artists in Italy 1830-1875. Detroit, The institute, 1951; Toledo museum of art, 1951 (Text by E. P. Richardson and Otto Wittmann, jr.)

MiD. Treasures—Detroit institute of arts. Treasures from the Detroit institute of arts. Detroit, 1960

Middleton. Jeremiah Theus—Middleton, Margaret Simons. Jeremiah Theus, colonial artist of Charles Town. Columbia, University of South Carolina press, 1953

Miller, A. J. The West—Miller, Alfred Jacob. The West of Alfred Jacob Miller (1837) from the notes and water colors in the Walters art gallery with an account of the artist by Marvin C. Ross. Norman, University of Oklahoma press, 1951

Miller, D. David G. Blythe—Miller, Dorothy. Life and work of David G. Blythe. Pittsburgh, University of Pittsburgh press, 1950

MM. Amer ptg today—Metropolitan museum of art. N.Y. American painting today, a national competitive exhibition, 1950. N.Y. The museum, 1950

MM. 100 Amer ptrs—Metropolitan museum of art. N.Y. 100 American painters of the 20th century, works selected from the collections of the Metropolitan museum of art with an introduction by R. B. Hale. N.Y. The museum, 1950

MMA. Abstract—N.Y. Museum of modern art. Abstract painting and sculpture in America by Andrew Carnduff Ritchie. N.Y. The museum, 1951

MMA. Contemp ptrs—N.Y. Museum of modern art. Contemporary painters [by] James Thrall Soby. N.Y. The museum, 1948

MMA. Demuth—N.Y. Museum of modern art. Charles Demuth by Andrew Carnduff Ritchie. N.Y. The museum, 1950

MMA. Edward Hopper. See Goodrich, Lloyd. Edward Hopper

MMA. Ernst—N.Y. Museum of modern art. Max Ernst, ed by William S. Lieberman. N.Y. The museum, 1961

MMA. Fifteen—N.Y. Museum of modern art. 15 Americans, ed by Dorothy C. Miller. N.Y. The museum, 1952

MMA. Fourteen—N.Y. Museum of modern art. 14 Americans, ed by Dorothy C. Miller. N.Y. The museum, 1946

MMA. Jackson Pollock—N.Y. Museum of modern art. Jackson Pollock; text by Sam Hunter. N.Y. The museum. Distributed by Simon and Schuster, 1956/7

MMA. Masters—N.Y. Museum of modern art. Masters of modern art, ed by Alfred H. Barr, jr. 3d ed rev. N.Y. The museum, 1958

MMA. New Amer ptg—N.Y. Museum of modern art. The new American painting as shown in eight European countries 1958-1959. N.Y. The museum, 1959

MMA Ptg and sculpture—N.Y. Museum of modern art. Painting and sculpture collection [by Alfred H. Barr, jr.] N.Y. Erich S. Herrmann, 1950

MMA. Rothko—N.Y. Museum of modern art. Mark Rothko [by Peter Selz] N.Y. The museum, 1961

MMA. Shahn—N.Y. Museum of modern art. Ben Shahn. N.Y. The museum, 1947 (Special bulletin, summer, 1947)

MMA. Sixteen—N.Y. Museum of modern art. Sixteen Americans, ed by Dorothy C. Miller with statements by the artist and others. N.Y. The museum, 1959

MMA. Soby collection—N.Y. Museum of modern art. The James Thrall Soby collection of works of art pledged or given to the museum. N.Y. The museum, 1961

MMA. 12 Americans—N.Y. Museum of modern art. 12 Americans, ed by Dorothy C. Miller with statements by the artists and others. N.Y. The museum, 1956

MMA. Watkins—N.Y. Museum of modern art. Franklin C. Watkins by A. C. Ritchie. N.Y. The museum, 1950

MMA. What is modern painting. See Barr. What is modern painting

MMA. Yves Tanguy—N.Y. Museum of modern art. Yves Tanguy by James Thrall Soby. N.Y. The museum, 1955

MnMW. Classic tradition—Walker art center, Minneapolis, Minn. The classic tradition in contemporary art, April 24 through June 28, 1953. Minneapolis, University of Minnesota, 1953

MnMW. Contemporary—Walker art center, Minneapolis, Minn. Contemporary American painting and sculpture collected by Mr. and Mrs. Roy R. Neuberger, May 25th through August 10th, 1952. Minneapolis, The center, 1952

MnMW. Eighty works—Walker art center, Minneapolis, Minn. Eighty works from the Richard Brown Baker collection, March 12-April 16, 1961. n.p. n.d.

MnMW. Expressionism 1900-1955—Walker art center, Minneapolis, Minn. Expressionism 1900-1955: Walker art center; Institute of contemporary art; San Francisco museum of art; Cincinnati art museum and Contemporary art center; Baltimore museum of art; Albright art gallery. n.p. 1956

MnMW. Precisionist view—Walker art center, Minneapolis, Minn. The precisionist view in American art. Minneapolis, The center, 1960 (Exhibition held in cooperation with Whitney, Detroit, Los Angeles, San Francisco museums)

MnMW. Reality and fantasy—Walker art center, Minneapolis, Minn. Reality and fantasy, May 23 through July 2, 1954. Minneapolis, The center, 1954

MnMW. Roszak—Walker art center, Minneapolis, Minn. Theodore Roszak [by H. H. Arnason]. Minneapolis, The center, 1956 (In collaboration with the Whitney museum)

MnMW. 60 Amer ptrs—Walker art center, Minneapolis, Minn. 60 American painters 1960; abstract expressionist painting of the fifties, April 3-May 8, 1960. Minneapolis, The center, 1961

MnMW. Stuart Davis—Walker art center, Minneapolis, Minn. Stuart Davis, an exhibition organized by the Walker art center in collaboration with the Des Moines art center, San Francisco museum of art and the Whitney museum of American art. n.p. [1957]

MNS. Homer—Smith college museum of art, Northampton, Mass. Winslow Homer, illustrator. Catalogue of the exhibition with a checklist of wood engravings and a list of illustrated books by Mary Bartlett Cowdrey. Northampton, The college, 1951

MnU. Arnold Blanch—University of Minnesota. Department of art. Arnold Blanch, the years 1924-1949. Minneapolis, The university, 1949

MnU. 40 Amer ptrs—University of Minnesota. Department of art. 40 American painters, 1940-1950. June 4-August 30, 1951. Minneapolis, the university, 1951

MnU. Philip Guston—University of Minnesota. Department of art. Philip Guston, April 10-May 12, 1950. n.p., n.d.

Mocsanyi. Karl Knaths—Mocsanyi, Paul. Karl Knaths. Washington, The Phillips gallery, 1957

Moderns and their world—The moderns and their world, with an introduction by John Rothenstein. London, Phoenix house, 1957?

MoKN. Handbook—William Rockhill Nelson gallery of art, Kansas City, Mo. Handbook of the collections in the William Rockhill Nelson gallery of art and Mary Atkins museum of fine arts. 4th ed. Kansas City, 1959

Morgan—Morgan, Lewis Henry. The Indian journals, 1859-62. Ann Arbor, University of Michigan press, 1959

Morley. Carl Morris—Morley, Grace L. Carl Morris. N.Y. The American federation of arts, 1960

Moses—Moses, Anna Mary (Robertson) Grandma Moses, American primitive. N.Y. Doubleday & co. 1947

MoSL. Beckman—St. Louis. City art museum. Max Beckman, retrospective exhibition: City art museum of St Louis, Los Angeles county museum, Detroit institute of arts, Baltimore museum of art, Minneapolis institute of arts. n.p., n.d.

MoSL. Contemporary Amer ptg—St Louis. City art museum. Contemporary American painting, November 12 to December 10, 1951. St Louis, The museum, 1951

MoSL. 50 masterworks—St Louis. City art museum. Fifty masterworks from the City art museum of St Louis [at Wildenstein, Nov. 5, 1958] n.p., n.d.

MoSL. 40 masterpieces—St Louis. City art museum. 40 masterpieces, a loan exhibition of paintings from American museums 6 October to 10 November, 1947. Fortieth anniversary exhibiton. n.p., n.d.

MoSL. Handbook 1953—St Louis. City art museum. Handbook of the collections. St Louis, The museum, 1953

Mount. John Singer Sargent—Mount, Charles Merrill. John Singer Sargent, a biography. N.Y. W. W. Norton & co. 1955

MSE. Catalogue of ports, 1950—Essex institute, Salem, Mass. Additions to the catalogue of portraits in the Essex institute received since 1936. Compiled by R. L. Jackson. Salem, The institute, 1950?

MSM. Handbook—Springfield, Mass. Museum of fine arts. Handbook. 2d ed. Springfield, The museum, 1958

MSt. Country art—Little, Nina Fletcher. Country art in New England, 1790-1840. Sturbridge, Mass. 1960 (Old Sturbridge village booklet series)

Munsterberg—Munsterberg, Hugo. Twentieth century painting. N.Y. Philosophical library, 1951

Murphy. John James Audubon—Murphy, Robert Cushman. John James Audubon, an evaluation of the man and his work. N.Y. New-York Historical society, 1956

MWA. Checklist of portraits—Massachusetts antiquarian society, Worcester, Mass. Checklist of the portraits in the library of the American antiquarian society by F. L. Weis. Worcester, The society, 1947

MWiS. Ex 4 and 7—Sterling and Francine Clark art institute, Williamstown, Mass. Exhibit four and exhibit seven. n.p. [1958]

MWM. Georgia O'Keeffe—Worcester art museum. An exhibition by Georgia O'Keeffe. October 4 through December 4, 1960 n.p., n.d.

Myers—Myers, Bernard Samuel. Modern art in the making. N.Y. McGraw-Hill book co. 1950

Myers. Art—Myers, Bernard Samuel. Art and civilization. N.Y. McGraw-Hill book co. 1917

NAD. Amer tradition. National academy of design, N.Y. The American tradition, 1800-1900. N.Y. The academy, 1951

NAD. Annual ex—National academy of design, N.Y. Annual exhibition, v 120 (2d half) 1946-v 136, 1961. N.Y. The academy, 1946-1961. 19 numbers.

NAD. Special ex, 1956—National academy of design, N.Y. Special exhibition: contemporary prints and watercolors, November 15-December 2, 1956. N.Y. The academy, 1956

NAI. Hudson valley—Albany institute of history and art, Albany, N.Y. Hudson valley paintings 1700-1750. Albany, The institute, 1959

NBuA. Acquisitions 1954-57—Buffalo fine arts academy. Contemporary art acquisitions 1954-1957. Buffalo, The academy, 1957. 4 numbers

NBuA. Acquisitions 1957-58. Buffalo fine arts academy. Contemporary art acquisitions 1957-1958. Buffalo, The academy, 1959

NBuA. Acquisitions 1959-1961—Buffalo fine arts academy. Contemporary art acquisitions 1959-1961. Buffalo, The academy, 1961

NBuA. Catalogue of the ptgs—Buffalo fine arts academy. Catalogue of the paintings and sculpture in the permanent collection, ed by A. C. Ritchie. Buffalo, The academy, 1949

NBuA. Contemporary ptgs—Buffalo fine arts academy. Catalogue of contemporary paintings and sculpture, ed by A. C. Ritchie. Buffalo, The academy, 1949

NBuA. Eugene Speicher—Buffalo fine arts academy. Eugene Speicher, a retrospective exhibition of oils and drawings . . . 1908-1949. Held September 29-October 26, 1950. Buffalo, The academy, 1950

NBuA. Expressionism—Buffalo fine arts academy. Expressionism in American painting, May 10-June 29, 1952, Albright art gallery, Buffalo, N.Y. Buffalo, The academy, 1952

NBuA. Fifty ptgs—Buffalo fine arts academy. Fifty paintings, 1905-1913, the fiftieth anniversary exhibition May 14-June 12, 1955. Buffalo, The academy, 1955

NBuA. Still—Buffalo fine arts academy. Paintings by Clyfford Still, Nov. 5-Dec. 13, 1959. n.p., n.d.

Newmeyer—Newmeyer, Sarah. Enjoying modern art. N.Y. Reinhold publishing corporation, 1955

NHMC. Alexander James—Currier gallery of art, Manchester, N.H. Memorial exhibition: Alexander James, 1890-1946. Manchester, The gallery, 1947

NHMC. Andrew Wyeth—Currier gallery of art, Manchester, N.H. Paintings and drawings by Andrew Wyeth. Manchester, The gallery, 1951

NHMC. Paul Sample—Currier gallery of art, Manchester, N.H. Paul Sample retrospective exhibition July 15 to September 15, 1948. Manchester, The gallery, 1948

NIC. Arthur G. Dove—Cornell university, Ithaca, N.Y. Andrew Dickson White museum of art. Arthur G. Dove, 1880-1946: a retrospective exhibition, November 1954. Ithaca, The university, 1954

NJMo. Forty years—The Montclair art museum, Montclair, N.J. Forty years of collecting. An exhibition presenting the major American paintings in the permanent collection of The Montclair art museum. Montclair, The museum, 1953

NJMo. Your Montclair art museum—The Montclair art museum, Montclair, N.J. Your Montclair art museum, its collections, activities, services. Summit, N.J. John F. McKenna co. 1955

NJN. Early N.J. artists—The Newark museum of art, Newark, N.J. Early New Jersey artists, 18th and 19th centuries. March 7-May 10. Newark, The museum, 1957

NJN. Weber—The Newark museum, Newark, N.J. Max Weber retrospective exhibition October 1-November 15, 1959. Newark, The museum, 1959

NJP. Amer folk art—Princeton University. American folk art, a collection of paintings presented in 1958 by Edward Duff Balken . . . to the art museum of Princeton university. n.p., n.d.

NNHS. Lockman—The New-York historical society. De Witt McClellan Lockman memorial exhibition March 14-May 15, 1958. N.Y. The society, 1958

NNHS. Waldron Phoenix Belknap coll—The New-York historical society. The Waldron Phoenix Belknap, jr. collection of portraits and silver . . . Cambridge, Harvard university press, 1955

NNSG. Handbook—The Solomon R. Guggenheim museum, N.Y. A handbook to the collection. N.Y. The museum, 1959

NNSG. Younger Amer ptrs—The Solomon R. Guggenheim museum, N.Y. Younger American painters; a selection, May 12 to July 25, 1954. N.Y. The museum, 1954

NoCR. Catalogue—North Carolina museum of art, Raleigh. Catalogue of paintings including three sets of tapestries by W. R. Valentiner. Raleigh, The museum, 1956

NSP. Sportscapes—The Parrish art museum, Southampton, N.Y. Sportscapes: hunting—fowling—angling. A loan exhibition. July 25-August 24, 1959. Southampton, The museum, 1959

NSP. William Merritt Chase—The Parrish art museum, Southampton, N.Y. William Merritt Chase, 1849-1916: a retrospective exhibition, June 30-July 27, 1957. Southampton, The museum, 1957

NSyE. The Eight—Everson museum of art of Syracuse and Onondaga county, N.Y. The Eight. Syracuse, 1958

NUM. Art across America—Munson-Williams-Proctor institute, Utica, N.Y. Art across America, a selection of American art from collections open to the public in communities of one hundred thousand or less. Utica, The institute, 1960

NUM. Root bequest—Munson-Williams-Proctor institute, Utica, N.Y. Edward Wales Root bequest. Utica, The institute, 1961

NYG. Fine art—New York graphic society —Fine art reproductions: old and modern masters. N.Y. The society, 1946 (and supplement, 1948) Consecutively paged with 3 indexes

OCiM. Guide—Cincinnati art museum. Guide to the collections, 1950? n.p., n.d.

OCiM. Ptgs by the Peale family—Cincinnati art museum. Paintings by the Peale family [exhibited] October 1 to 31, 1954. Cincinnati, The museum, 1954

OCiM. Rediscoveries—Cincinnati art museum. Rediscoveries in American painting. Cincinnati, The museum, 1955

OCl. Feininger—Cleveland museum of art. The work of Lyonel Feininger, catalogue of an exhibition sponsored by The Print club of Cleveland and The Cleveland museum of art, November 2-December 9, 1951. Cleveland, The museum, 1951

OCl. Handbook—Cleveland museum of art. Handbook. Cleveland, The museum, 1958

OCl. Keller—Cleveland. Institute of art. The Henry G. Keller memorial exhibition . . . sponsored by The Cleveland institute of art and The Cleveland museum of art. Cleveland, The museum, 1950

OCl. Portrait miniatures—Cleveland museum of art. Portrait miniatures: the Edward B. Greene collection. Cleveland, The museum, 1951

OCl. Some contemporary works—Cleveland museum of art. Some contemporary works of art. Cleveland, The museum, 1958

OCl. Sommer—Cleveland museum of art. The William Sommer memorial exhibition . . . Cleveland, The museum, 1950

OCo. George Bellows—Columbus gallery of fine arts. Paintings by George Bellows, March 21 to April 21, 1957. n.p., n.d.

O'Hara. Jackson Pollock—O'Hara, Frank. Jackson Pollock. N.Y. George Braziller, 1959 (Great American artists series)

O'Neal—O'Neal, William B. Primitive into painter, life and letters of John Toole. Charlottesville, University of Virginia press, 1960

OrPA. C. S. Price—Portland art museum and the Walker art center. C. S. Price, a memorial exhibition . . . Portland, Ore. Portland art association, 1951

OrPA. Ptgs & sculptures—Portland art museum, Portland, Ore. Paintings and sculptures of the Pacific northwest: Oregon, Washington, British Columbia. Portland, The museum, 1959

OT. Contemp Amer ptgs—Toledo museum of art. Contemporary American paintings: The Mau collection. Toledo, The museum, 1947

OT. John Sloan—See Goodrich. John Sloan

OT. Travelers in Arcadia. See MiD. Travelers in Arcadia

OYB. Accessions—Butler institute of American art, Youngstown, Ohio. Special exhibit of accessions during the past two years. Youngstown, The institute, 1956-1958

OYB. Annual—Butler institute of American art, Youngstown, Ohio. Annual midyear show, 1948-1960. Youngstown, The institute, 1948-1960 (1948-1952 has title Annual new year show) 12 numbers

OYB. Blythe—Butler institute of American art, Youngstown, Ohio. An exhibition of the work of David G. Blythe. Youngstown, The institute, 1947

OYB. Catalogue, 1951—Butler institute of American art, Youngstown, Ohio. Catalogue of the permanent collection of American art. Youngstown, The institute, 1951

OYB. Supplement—Butler institute of American art, Youngstown, Ohio. Supplement to the collection of the permanent collection of American art, Youngstown, The institute, 1951

OYB. Supplement, 1959—Butler institute of American art. Supplement to the Catalogues of the permanent collection (published October 1951 and October 1954) Youngstown, The institute, 1959

PA. Annual ex, 1947-1961—Pennsylvania academy of the fine arts, Philadelphia. Annual exhibition of painting and sculpture, 1947-1961, Philadelphia, The academy, 1947-1961. 13 numbers

PA. Carles—Pennsylvania academy of the fine arts and the Philadelphia museum of art. Memorial exhibition, Arthur B. Carles, March 18 through April 12, 1953. n.p., n.d.

Pearson. Mod renaissance—Pearson, Ralph M. Modern renaissance in American art presenting the work and philosophy of 54 distinguished artists. N.Y. Harper & brothers, 1954

Pearson, H. The man Whistler—Pearson, Hesketh. The man Whistler. N.Y. Harper & brothers, 1952

Pierson—Pierson, William Henry and Davidson, Martha, eds. Arts of the United States, a pictorial survey. N.Y. McGraw-Hill book co. 1960

Ponente. Mod ptg, 1960—Ponente, Nello. Modern painting, contemporary trends. N.Y. Skira, 1960

Porter. Thomas Eakins—Porter, Fairfield. Thomas Eakins. N.Y. George Braziller, 1959 (The great American artists series)

Pousette-Dart. Amer ptg—Pousette-Dart, Nathaniel. American painting today. N.Y. Hastings house, 1958

PPC. Amer classics—Carnegie institute, Pittsburgh. American classics of the nineteenth century. Pittsburgh, The institute, 1957

PPC. International ex, 1950-1961/62. Carnegie institute, Pittsburgh. Dept of fine arts. The Pittsburgh international exhibition of paintings. Pittsburgh, The institute, 1950-1961. (1958 entitled: The 1958 Pittsburgh bicentennial international exhibition of contemporary painting and sculpture) 6 numbers

PPC. Ptg in the U.S. 1949—Carnegie institute, Pittsburgh. Painting in the United States, 1949. Pittsburgh, The institute, 1949

PPhM. Arensberg coll—Philadelphia museum of art. The Louise and Walter Arensberg collection: v 1: 20th century section. Philadelphia, The museum, 1954

PPhM. Gallatin coll—Philadelphia museum of art. A. E. Gallatin collection, "Museum of living art." Philadelphia, The museum, 1954

PR. Catalogue—Reading public museum and art gallery, Reading, Pa. Catalogue of paintings. 4th ed. Reading, The museum, 1953

Pulitzer—Pulitzer, Louise and Pulitzer, Joseph. Modern painting, drawing & sculpture collected by Louise and Joseph Pulitzer. Cambridge, Fogg art museum, 1958 2v

Rathbone—Rathbone, Perry Townsend, ed. Westward the way: the character and development of the Louisiana Territory as seen by artists and writers of the nineteenth century. St Louis, City art museum, 1954

Rathbun—Rathbun, Mary Chalmers and Hayes, Bartlett, H. Layman's guide to modern art: paintings for a scientific age. N.Y. Oxford university press, 1949

Raynal. History v3—Raynal, Maurice. History of modern painting, v3: from Picasso to surrealism. Geneva, Skira, 1950

Read. Art now 1948—Read, Herbert. Art now; an introduction to the theory of modern painting and sculpture. new ed. N.Y. Pitman publishing co., 1948

Read. Concise history—Read, Herbert. A concise history of modern painting. N.Y. Frederick A. Praeger, 1959

Rewald. History of impressionism—Rewald, John. The history of impressionism. 2d ed. N.Y. The museum of modern art, 1946

Richardson. Ptg in America—Richardson, Edgar Preston. Painting in America: the story of 450 years. N.Y. Thomas Y. Crowell co. 1956 (Growth of America series)

Richardson. Travelers in Arcadia. See MiD. Travelers in Arcadia

Richardson. Washington Allston—Richardson, Edgar Preston. Washington Allston, a study of the romantic artist in America. Chicago, University of Chicago press, 1948

Riley. Your art heritage—Riley, Olive Lasette. Your art heritage. N.Y. McGraw-Hill book co. 1952

Ritchie, Andrew Carnduff. Abstract ptg and sculpture. See MMA. Abstract

Ritchie, Andrew Carnduff. Demuth. See MMA. Demuth

Ritchie, Andrew Carnduff. Watkins. See MMA. Watkins

Robb. Art 1953 ed—Robb, David Metheny and Garrison, Jesse James. Art in the western world. 3d ed. Harper & brothers, 1953

Robb. Harper history—Robb, David Metheny. The Harper history of painting: the occidental tradition. N.Y. Harper & brothers, 1951

Roberts. Mark Tobey—Roberts, Colette. Mark Tobey. N.Y. Grove press, 1959

Robertson. Jackson Pollock—Robertson, Bryan. Jackson Pollock. N.Y. Harry H. Abrams, 1960

Rodman. Horace Pippin—Rodman, Selden. Horace Pippin, a Negro painter in America. N.Y. Quadrangle press, 1947

Rodman. Portrait of the artist—Rodman, Selden. Portrait of the artist as an American: Ben Shahn; a biography with pictures. N.Y. Harper & brothers, 1951

Roos—Roos, Frank John. An illustrated handbook of art history. rev ed N.Y. The Macmillan co. 1954

Rosenblum—Rosenblum, Robert. Cubism and twentieth-century art. N.Y. Harry N. Abrams, 1961

Schwabacher. Arshile Gorky—Schwabacher, Ethel K. Arshile Gorky. With a preface by Lloyd Goodrich and an introduction by Meyer Schapiro. N.Y. Published for the Whitney museum of American art by The Macmillan co. 1957

Sears. Highlights—Sears, Clara Endicott. Highlights among the Hudson river artists. Boston, Houghton Mifflin co. 1947

Seiberling—Seiberling, Frank. Looking into art. N.Y. Henry Holt and co. 1959

Sellers. C. W. Peale v2—Sellers, Charles Coleman. Charles Willson Peale, v2: later life, 1790-1827. Philadelphia. American philosophical society, 1947

Selz. Mark Rothko. See MMA. Rothko

Selz. New images—Selz, Peter. New images of man with statements by the artists. N.Y. Museum of modern art in collaboration with the Baltimore museum of art, 1959

Sewall. History of western art—Sewall, John Ives. A history of western art. N.Y. Henry Holt and co. 1953

Shahn—Shahn, Ben. Ben Shahn, his graphic art. Text by James Thrall Soby. N.Y. George Braziller, 1957

Sizer. John Trumbull—Sizer, Theodore. Works of Colonel John Trumbull, artist of the American revolution. New Haven, Yale university press, 1950

Soby. Ben Shahn—Soby, James Thrall. Ben Shahn. N.Y. Museum of modern art, 1947 (Penguin modern painters)

Sweet—Sweet, Frederick A. Sargent, Whistler and Mary Cassatt: The Art institute of Chicago. Jan. 14 through Feb. 25, 1954; the Metropolitan museum of art, March 25 through May 23, 1954. Chicago, The institute, 1954

Taylor. Fifty centuries, 1954 ed. Taylor, Francis Henry. Fifty centuries of art. N.Y. Harper & brothers, 1954

Time. 300 years—Time, the weekly news magazine. Three hundred years of American painting by Alexander Eliot. N.Y. 1957

Tolman—Tolman, Ruel Pardee. The life and works of Edward Greene Malbone. N.Y. The New-York historical society, 1958. (New-York historical society: The John Divine Jones Fund series XIII)

UNESCO. 1860-1949—United nations educational, scientific and cultural organization. Catalogue of colour reproductions of painting from 1860 to 1949. Paris, UNESCO, 1949

UNESCO. 1860-1955—United nations educational, scientific and cultural organization. Catalogue of colour reproductions of paintings—1860 to 1955. 3d ed. Paris, UNESCO, 1955

UNESCO. 1860-1959—United nations educational, scientific and cultural organization. Catalogue of colour reproductions of paintings—1860 to 1959. 5th ed. Paris, UNESCO, 1959

UNESCO. Prior to 1860—United nations educational, scientific and cultural organization. Catalogue of colour reproductions of paintings prior to 1860. Paris, UNESCO, 1950

UNESCO. Prior to 1860 3d ed.—United nations educational, scientific and cultural organization. Catalogue of colour reproductions of paintings prior to 1860, 3d ed. Paris, UNESCO, 1955

UNESCO. Prior to 1860 5th ed.—United nations educational, scientific and cultural organization. Catalogue of colour reproductions of paintings prior to 1860. 5th ed. Paris, UNESCO, 1960

Upjohn—Upjohn, Edward Miller; Wingert, P. S.; and Mahler, J. G. History of world art. N.Y. Oxford university press, 1949

U.S. National Capital sesquicentennial com —U.S. The National Capital sesquicentennial commission. American processional 1492-1900. Washington, Corcoran gallery of art, 1950

Vail. Stuyvesant ports—Vail, Robert William Glenroie. The case of the Stuyvesant portraits. N.Y. New-York historical society, 1958

VR. Amer ptg—Virginia museum of fine arts, Richmond. American painting. 1954, 1958. Richmond, The museum, 1954, 1958

VR. Biennial ex—Virginia museum of fine arts, Richmond. Biennial exhibition of contemporary American paintings, v6, 1948. Richmond, The museum, 1948

VR. Healy's sitters—Virginia museum of fine arts, Richmond. A souvenir of the exhibition entitled Healy's sitters . . . between the years 1837 and 1899. Richmond, The museum, 1950

VRV. William James Hubard—Valentine museum, Richmond. William James Hubard, 1807-1862, a concurrent survey and exhibition, January, 1948. Richmond, The museum, 1948

VWR. Amer. folk art—The Abby Aldrich Rockefeller folk art collection, Williamsburg, Va. American folk art. Williamsburg, Colonial Williamsburg, 1959

VWR. Folk art—The Abby Aldrich Rockefeller collection, Williamsburg, Va. Folk art collection, a descriptive catalogue by Nina Fetcher Little. Williamsburg, Colonial Williamsburg, 1957

Walker. Ptgs from America—Walker, John. Paintings from America. Baltimore, Penguin books, 1951 (Penguin modern painters)

Weir. Recollections—Weir, John Ferguson. Recollections, ed by Theodore Sizer. N.Y. New-York historical society, 1957

Wight. Arthur G. Dove—Wight, Frederick Stallknecht. Arthur G. Dove. Berkeley, University of California press, 1958

Wight. Hans Hofmann—Wight, Frederick Stallknecht. Hans Hofmann. Berkeley, University of California press, 1957

Wight. Hyman Bloom—Wight, Frederick Stallknecht. Hyman Bloom: Albright art gallery, Institute of contemporary art, Lowe gallery, M. H. De Young memorial museum, Whitney museum of American art. Boston, Institute of contemporary art, 1954

Wight. Milestones—Wight, Frederick Stallknecht. Milestones of American painting in our century. N.Y. Chanticleer press, 1948

Wight. Milton Avery—Wight, Frederick Stallknecht. Milton Avery: The Baltimore museum of art, The Institute of contemporary art, Loew gallery, Phillips gallery, Wadsworth atheneum. Baltimore, Baltimore museum of art, 1952?

Wight. Morris Graves—Wight, Frederick Stallknecht; Baur, John I. H.; and Phillips, Duncan. Morris Graves. Berkeley, University of California press, 1956

WiMiA. Amer ptg 1760-1960—Milwaukee art center, Milwaukee, Wis. American painting 1760-1960; a selection of 125 paintings from the collection of Mr and Mrs Lawrence A. Fleischman, Detroit. Milwaukee art center, March 3rd through April 3rd, 1960. Milwaukee, The center, 1960

WiMiA. Crawford—Milwaukee art center, Milwaukee, Wis. Ralston Crawford, February 6-March 9, 1958. Milwaukee, The center, 1958

WiMiA. Raphaelle Peale—Milwaukee art center, Milwaukee, Wis. Raphaelle Peale, exhibition January 15th, through February 15th 1959; M. Knoedler & co., N.Y. March 2nd through March 31st, 1959. n.p., n.d.

WMAA. Annual ex—Whitney museum of American art. Annual exhibition: sculpture, paintings, watercolors, drawings, 1948-1959. N.Y. The museum 1948-1959. 11 numbers

WMAA. Arshile Gorky. See Schwabacher. Arshile Gorky

WMAA. Blakelock—Whitney museum of American art. Ralph Blakelock centenary exhibition in celebration of the centennial of the City college of New York. April 22 to May 22, 1947. N.Y. The museum, 1947

WMAA. Contemp Amer ptg—Whitney museum of American art. Annual exhibition of contemporary American painting, 1955/56-1959/60. N.Y. The museum, 1956-1960. 5 numbers

WMAA. Four Amer expressionists—Whitney museum of American art. Four American expressionists: Doris Caesar; Chaim Gross; Karl Knaths; Abraham Rattner. N.Y. The museum, 1959

WMAA. George Grosz. See Baur. George Grosz

WMAA. Hyman Bloom. See Wight. Hyman Bloom

WMAA. John Sloan. See Goodrich. John Sloan

WMAA. Juliana Force—Whitney museum of American art. Juliana Force and American art, a memorial exhibition Sept. 24-Oct. 30, 1949. N.Y. The museum, 1949

WMAA. Marsh—Whitney museum of American art. Reginald Marsh. Exhibition and catalogue: Whitney, Columbus, Detroit, St Louis, Dallas, Los Angeles, Santa Barbara. N.Y. The museum, 1955 (Text by Lloyd Goodrich)

WMAA. Maurer. See McCausland. Maurer

WMAA. Max Weber. See Goodrich. Max Weber

WMAA. Museum and its friends, 1958—Whitney museum of American art. The museum and its friends: twentieth century American art from collections of the friends of the Whitney museum, 1958. N.Y. The museum, 1958

WMAA. Museum and its friends, 1959—Whitney museum of American art. The museum and its friends: eighteen living American artists selected by the friends of the Whitney museum. N.Y. The museum, 1959

WMAA. Neuberger collection—Whitney museum of American art. Roy and Marie Neuberger collection: modern American painting and sculpture. n.p. 1955?

WMAA. New decade—Whitney museum of American art. New decade: 35 American painters and sculptors. N.Y. The museum, 1955

WMAA. New images of man. See Selz. New images

WMAA. Pioneers—Whitney museum of American art. Pioneers of modern art in America. April 9-May 19, 1946. N.Y. The museum, 1946

WMAA. Ryder—Whitney museum of American art. Albert P. Ryder, Centenary exhibition October 18 to November 30, 1947. N.Y. The museum, 1947

WMAA. Sara Roby—Whitney museum of American art. The collection of the Sara Roby foundation, April 29-June 14, 1959. N.Y. The museum, 1959

WMAA. Young America 1957—Whitney museum of American art—Young American art—Young America 1957; thirty American painters and sculptors under thirty-five. N.Y. The museum, 1957

WMAA. Young America 1960—Whitney museum of American art. Young America 1960; thirty American painters under thirty-six. N.Y. The museum, 1960

WMAA. Zorach—Whitney museum of American art. William Zorach. N.Y. The museum, 1959

KEY TO SYMBOLS USED FOR LOCATIONS
OF PAINTINGS

AP — Phoenix art museum, Phoenix, Ariz.

ATeS — Arizona state college, Tempe, Ariz.

ATU — University of Arizona, Tucson, Ariz.

CanO — National gallery of Canada, Ottawa

CLA — Los Angeles county museum of history, science and art, Los Angeles, Calif.

CLAU — University of California, Los Angeles, Calif.

CLAUS — University of Southern California, Los Angeles, Calif.

CoD — Denver art museum, Denver, Colo.

CoS — Colorado Springs fine arts center, Colorado Springs, Colo.

CP — Pasadena art institute, Pasadena, Calif.

CSB — Santa Barbara museum of art, Santa Barbara, Calif.

CSC — Crocker art gallery, Sacramento, Calif.

CSD — Fine arts society of San Diego, San Diego, Calif.

CSFD — M. H. De Young memorial museum, San Francisco, Calif.

CSFM — San Francisco museum of art, San Francisco, Calif.

CSFP — California palace of the legion of honor, San Francisco, Calif.

CtHW — Wadsworth atheneum, Hartford, Conn.

CtLH — Litchfield historical society, Litchfield, Conn.

CtNB — New Britain institute, New Britain, Conn.

CtNH — New Haven colony historical society, New Haven, Conn.

CtNL — Lyman Allyn museum, New London, Conn.

CtY — Yale university, New Haven, Conn.

DC — The Corcoran gallery of art, Washington, D.C.

DCap — The Capitol, Washington, D.C.

DeW — Wilmington society of the fine arts, Wilmington, Del.

DeWin — Henry Francis Du Pont Winterthur museum, Greenville, Del.

DF — Freer gallery of art, Washington, D.C.

DN — National gallery of art, Washington, D.C.

DNC — Smithsonian institution. National collection of fine arts, Washington, D.C.

DP — Phillips collection, Washington, D.C.

DW — The White house, Washington, D.C.

ELK — Kensington palace, London, England

ELN — National gallery, London, England

ELNP — National portrait gallery, London, England

ELT — Tate gallery, London, England

FaW — Norton gallery and school of art, West Palm Beach, Fla.

FPL — The Louvre, Paris, France

FPP — Petit palais, Paris, France

GAtM — Georgia museum of art, Athens, Ga.

GST — Telfair academy, Savannah, Ga.

HaH — Honolulu academy of arts, Honolulu, Hawaii

IaDa — Davenport municipal art gallery, Davenport, Iowa

IaDM — Des Moines art center, Des Moines, Iowa

IaIU — University of Iowa, Iowa City, Iowa

IBM — International business machines corporation, New York, N.Y.

ICA — Art institute of Chicago, Chicago, Ill.

ICH — Chicago historical society, Chicago, Ill.

ICN — Newberry library, Chicago, Ill.

InBu — Indiana university, Bloomington, Ind.

InIJ — John Herron art institute, Indianapolis, Ind.

InR — Richmond art association, Richmond, Ind.

InTH — Sheldon Swope art gallery, Terre Haute, Ind.

IU — Krannert art museum, University of Illinois, Urbana, Ill.

KLU — Museum of art, University of Kansas, Lawrence, Kans.

KW — Wichita art museum, Wichita, Kans.

KyLS — J. B. Speed memorial, Louisville, Ky.

MAC — Amherst college, Amherst, Mass.

MAP — Addison gallery of American art, Phillips academy, Andover, Mass.

MB	Boston museum of fine arts, Boston, Mass.	**MoSLH**	Missouri historical society, St Louis, Mo.
MBA	Boston athenaeum, Boston, Mass.	**MoSLM**	Mercantile library association of St Louis, Mo.
MBF	Faneuil hall, Boston, Mass.	**MoSLW**	Washington university, St Louis, Mo.
MBH	Massachusetts historical society, Boston, Mass.	**MoSp**	Springfield art museum, Springfield, Mo.
MBIC	Institute of contemporary art, Boston, Mass.	**MPB**	Berkshire athenaeum and museum, Pittsfield, Mass.
MBT	Trinity church, Boston, Mass.	**MSE**	Essex institute, Salem, Mass.
MCH	Harvard university, Cambridge, Mass. Same symbol for Fogg art museum.	**MSG**	George Walter Vincent Smith art gallery, Springfield, Mass.
MCoL	Free public library, Concord, Mass.	**MSM**	Springfield museum of fine arts, Springfield, Mass.
MdAn	United States naval academy, Annapolis, Md.	**MSP**	Peabody museum, Salem, Mass.
MdBH	Maryland historical society, Baltimore, Md.	**MSt**	Old Sturbridge Village, Sturbridge, Mass.
MdBM	Baltimore museum of art, Baltimore, Md.	**MWA**	American antiquarian society, Worcester, Mass.
MdBMu	Municipal museum (Peale museum), Baltimore, Md.	**MWiC**	Williams college, Williamstown, Mass.
MdBP	Peabody institute, Baltimore, Md.	**MWiS**	Sterling and Francine Clark institute, Williamstown, Mass.
MdBW	Walters art gallery, Baltimore, Md.	**MWM**	Worcester art museum, Worcester, Mass.
MdHW	Washington county museum of fine arts, Hagerstown, Md.	**NAD**	National academy of design, New York, N.Y.
MeB	Bowdoin college, Brunswick, Me.	**NAI**	Albany institute of history and art, Albany, N.Y.
MeC	Colby college, Waterville, Me.	**NAS**	New York State capitol, Albany, N.Y.
MeR	William A. Farnsworth library and art museum, Rockland, Me.	**NBH**	Long Island historical society, Brooklyn, N.Y.
MexS	Supreme court building, Mexico, D.F.	**NBM**	Brooklyn museum, Brooklyn, N.Y.
MiA	University of Michigan, Ann Arbor, Mich.	**NBuA**	Albright-Knox art gallery, Buffalo, N.Y.
MiC	Cranbrook academy, Bloomfield Hills, Mich.	**NCa**	Canajoharie library and art gallery, Canajoharie, N.Y.
MiD	Detroit institute of fine arts, Detroit, Mich.	**NCB**	National museum of baseball, Cooperstown, N.Y.
MiM	Hackley art gallery, Muskegon, Mich.	**NCHA**	New York State historical society, Cooperstown, N.Y.
MLL	William Lane foundations, Leominster, Mass.	**NeL**	University of Nebraska, Lincoln, Nebr.
MM	Metropolitan museum of art, New York, N.Y.	**NeO**	Joslyn art museum, Omaha, Nebr.
MMA	Museum of modern art, New York, N.Y.	**NHD**	Dartmouth college, Hanover, N.H.
MnMI	Minneapolis institute of arts, Minneapolis, Minn.	**NHMC**	Currier gallery of art, Manchester, N.H.
MnMW	Walker art center, Minneapolis, Minn.	**NHP**	Warner house association, Portsmouth, N.H.
MNS	Smith college, Northampton, Mass.	**NIC**	Cornell University, Ithaca, N.Y.
MnSH	Minneapolis historical society, St Paul, Minn.	**NJF**	Monmouth county historical society, Freehold, N.J.
MnSJ	Jerome Hill reference library, St Paul, Minn.	**NJMo**	Montclair art museum, Montclair, N.J.
MnU	University of Minnesota, Minneapolis, Minn.	**NJN**	Newark museum association, Newark, N.J.
MoKN	William Rockhill Nelson gallery of art, Kansas City, Mo.	**NJP**	The Art museum, Princeton university, Princeton, N.J.
MonH	State capitol, Helena, Mont.	**NKS**	Senate house museum, Kingston, N.Y.
MoSL	City art museum, St Louis, Mo.	**NMS**	New Mexico museum of art, Santa Fe, N.M.
MoSLB	Boatmen's national bank, St Louis, Mo.		

NNAJ	American Jewish historical society, New York, N.Y.	**PA**	Pennsylvania academy of the fine arts, Philadelphia, Pa.
NNAM	American museum of natural history, New York, N.Y.	**PH**	Historical society of Pennsylvania, Philadelphia, Pa.
NNCH	New York. City Hall, New York, N.Y.	**PMB**	Barnes foundation, Merion, Pa.
NNCo	Cooper union, New York, N.Y.	**PPC**	Carnegie institute, Pittsburgh, Pa.
NNHS	New-York historical society, New York, N.Y.	**PPD**	Duquesne club, Pittsburgh, Pa.
		PPhA	American philosophical society, Philadelphia, Pa.
NNMC	Museum of the City of New York, New York, N.Y.	**PPhI**	Independence hall, Philadelphia, Pa.
NNPL	New York public library, New York, N.Y.	**PPhJ**	Jefferson medical college, Philadelphia, Pa.
NNSG	Solomon R. Guggenheim museum, New York, N.Y.	**PPhL**	Library company of Philadelphia, Philadelphia, Pa.
NNSL	St Luke's hospital, New York, N.Y.	**PPhM**	Philadelphia museum of art, Philadelphia, Pa.
NNSR	New school of social research, New York, N.Y.	**PPhU**	Union league of Philadelphia, Pa.
		PPhUn	University of Pennsylvania, Philadelphia, Pa.
NNU	Union league club, New York, N.Y.	**PR**	Reading museum, Reading, Pa.
NoCG	University of North Carolina. Greensboro, N.C.	**PW**	Westmoreland county museum of art, Greensburg, Pa.
NoCR	North Carolina museum of art, Raleigh, N.C. (Formerly North Carolina State art gallery)	**RNH**	Newport historical society, Newport, R.I.
		RNR	Redwood library and athenaeum, Newport, R.I.
NOR	Remington art memorial, Ogdensburg, N.Y.	**RPAt**	Providence athenaeum, Providence, R.I.
NR	Rochester memorial art gallery, Rochester, N.Y.	**RPB**	Brown university, Providence, R.I.
NScU	Union college, Schenectady, N.Y.	**RPHS**	Rhode Island historical society, Providence, R.I.
NSP	Parrish art museum, Southampton, N.Y.	**RPS**	Rhode Island school of design, Providence, R.I.
NStS	Suffolk museum, Stony Brook, N.Y.	**SCCG**	Gibbes art gallery, Charleston, S.C.
NSU	Syracuse university, Syracuse, N.Y.	**ScG**	Glasgow art gallery and museum, Glasgow, Scotland
NSyE	Everson museum of art of Syracuse and Onondaga county, Syracuse, N.Y.	**SwB**	Kunstmuseum, Basel, Switzerland
		TMB	Brooks memorial art gallery, Memphis, Tenn.
NUM	Munson-Williams-Proctor institute, Utica, N.Y.	**TNF**	Fisk university, Nashville, Tenn.
NWP	United States military academy, West Point, N.Y.	**TxD**	Dallas museum of fine arts, Dallas, Tex.
OCiM	Cincinnati art museum, Cincinnati, Ohio	**TxF**	Fort Worth museum of art, Fort Worth, Tex.
OCiT	Taft museum, Cincinnati, Ohio	**TxH**	Houston museum of fine arts, Houston, Tex.
OCl	Cleveland museum of art, Cleveland, Ohio	**TxSa**	Witte memorial museum, San Antonio, Tex.
OCo	Columbus gallery of fine arts, Columbus, Ohio	**VCU**	University of Virginia, Charlottesville, Va.
OCoA	Ohio state archaeological and historical society, Columbus, Ohio	**VR**	Virginia museum of fine arts, Richmond, Va.
		VRCM	Confederate memorial institute, Richmond, Va.
OkNU	University of Oklahoma, Norman, Okla.	**VRV**	Valentine museum, Richmond, Va.
OkT	Philbrook art center, Tulsa, Okla.	**VtMS**	Sheldon museum, Middlebury, Vt.
OkTT	Thomas Gilchrist institute of American history and art, Tulsa, Okla.	**VWC**	College of William and Mary, Williamsburg, Va.
OOb	Oberlin college, Oberlin, Ohio	**VWR**	The Abby Aldrich Rockefeller folk art collection, Williamsburg, Va.
OrPA	Portland art museum, Portland, Ore.	**WaS**	Seattle art museum, Seattle, Wash.
OrPH	Oregon historical society, Portland, Ore.	**WaSU**	University of Washington, Seattle, Wash.
OT	Toledo museum of art, Toledo, Ohio	**WiMiA**	Milwaukee art center, Milwaukee, Wis. Same symbol for Milwaukee art institute
OYB	Butler institute of American art, Youngstown, Ohio	**WMAA**	Whitney museum of American art, New York, N.Y.

LIST OF INSTITUTIONS WITH SYMBOLS
USED IN THIS BOOK

The Abby Aldrich Rockefeller folk art collection, Williamsburg, Va. VWR

Addison gallery of American art, Phillips academy, Andover, Mass. MAP

Albany institute of history and art, Albany, N.Y. NAI

Albright-Knox art gallery, Buffalo, N.Y. NBuA

American antiquarian society, Worcester, Mass. MWA

American Jewish historical society, New York, N.Y. NNAJ

American museum of natural history, New York, N.Y. NNAM

American philosophical society, Philadelphia, Pa. PPhA

Amherst college, Amherst, Mass. MAC

Arizona state college, Tempe, Ariz. ATeS

Art association of Indianapolis, Ind. InIJ

Art institute of Chicago, Chicago, Ill. ICA

Baltimore, Md. Municipal museum (Peale museum) MdBMu

Baltimore museum of art, Baltimore, Md. MdBM

Barnes foundation, Merion, Pa. PMB

Basel, Switzerland. Kunstmuseum. SwB

Berkshire athenaeum and museum, Pittsfield, Mass. MPB

Boatmen's national bank, St Louis, Mo. MoSLB

Boston athenaeum, Boston, Mass. MBA

Boston museum of fine arts, Boston, Mass. MB

Bowdoin college, Brunswick, Me. MeB

Brooklyn museum, Brooklyn, N.Y. NBM

Brooks memorial art gallery, Memphis, Tenn. TMB

Brown university, Providence, R.I. RPB

Buffalo fine arts academy, Buffalo, N.Y. Albright-Knox art gallery. NBuA

Butler institute of American art, Youngstown, Ohio. OYB

California palace of the legion of honor, San Francisco, Calif. CSFP

Canajoharie library and art gallery, Canajoharie, N.Y. NCa

The Capitol, Washington, D.C. DCap

Carnegie institute, Pittsburgh, Pa. PPC

Carolina art association. Gibbes art gallery, Charleston, S.C. SCCG

Chicago art institute, Chicago, Ill. ICA

Chicago historical society, Chicago, Ill. ICH

Cincinnati art museum, Cincinnati, Ohio OCiM

City art museum, St. Louis, Mo. MoSL

Cleveland museum of art, Cleveland, Ohio. OCl

Colby college, Waterville, Me. MeC

College of William and Mary, Williamsburg, Va. VWC

Colorado Springs fine arts center, Colorado Springs, Colo. CoS

Columbus gallery of fine arts, Columbus, Ohio. OCo

Concord, Mass. Free public library. MCoL

Confederate memorial institute, Richmond, Va. VRCM

Cooper union, New York, N.Y. NNCo

The Corcoran gallery of art, Washington, D.C. DC

Cornell university, Ithaca, N.Y. White art museum. NIC

Cranbrook academy, Bloomfield Hills, Mich. MiC

Crocker art gallery, Sacramento, Calif. CSC

Currier gallery of art, Manchester, N.H. NHMC

Dallas museum of fine arts, Dallas, Tex. TxD

Dartmouth college, Hanover, N.H. NHD

Davenport municipal art gallery, Davenport, Iowa. IaDa

Denver art museum, Denver, Colo. CoD

Des Moines art center, Des Moines, Iowa. IaDM

Detroit institute of arts, Detroit, Mich. MiD

De Young memorial museum, San Francisco, Calif. CSFD

Duquesne club. Pittsburgh, Pa. PPD

Essex institute, Salem, Mass. MSE

Everson museum of art of Syracuse and Onondaga county, Syracuse, N.Y. NSyE

Faneuil hall, Boston, Mass. MBF

Fine arts society of San Diego, San Diego, Calif. CSD

Fisk university, Nashville, Tenn. TNF

Fogg art museum, Harvard university, Cambridge, Mass. MCH

Fort Worth museum of art, Fort Worth, Tex. TxF

Freer gallery of art, Washington, D.C. DF

George Walter Vincent Smith gallery, Springfield, Mass. MSG

Georgia museum of art, Athens, Ga. GAtM

Gibbes art gallery, Charleston, S.C. SCCG

Glasgow art gallery and museum, Glasgow, Scotland. ScG

Guggenheim museum, New York, N.Y. NNSG

Hackley art gallery, Muskegon, Mich. MiM

Harvard university, Cambridge, Mass. MCH

Henry Francis Du Pont Winterthur museum, Greenville, Del. DeWin

Historical society of Pennsylvania, Philadelphia, Pa. PH

Honolulu academy of arts, Honolulu, Hawaii. HaH

Houston museum of fine arts, Houston, Tex. TxH

Independence hall, Philadelphia, Pa. PPhI

Indiana university, Bloomington, Ind. InBU

Institute of contemporary art, Boston, Mass. MBIC

International business machines corporation, New York, N.Y. IBM

J. B. Speed memorial, Louisville, Ky. KyLS

Jefferson medical college, Philadelphia, Pa. PPhJ

Jerome Hill reference library, St Paul, Minn. MnSJ

John Herron art institute, Indianapolis, Ind. InIJ

Joslyn art museum, Omaha, Nebr. NeO

Kensington Palace, London, England. ELK

Krannert art museum, University of Illinois, Urbana, Ill. IU

Kunstmuseum, Basel, Switzerland. SwB

Lane foundation, Leominster, Mass. MLL

Layton art gallery, Milwaukee, Wis. Milwaukee art center. WiMiA

Library company of Philadelphia, Pa. PPhL

Litchfield historical society, Litchfield, Conn. CtLH

Long Island historical society, Brooklyn, N.Y. NBH

Los Angeles county museum of history, science and art, Los Angeles, Calif. CLA

The Louvre, Paris, France. FPL

Lyman Allyn museum, New London, Conn. CtNL

M. H. De Young memorial museum, San Francisco, Calif. CSFD

Maryland historical society, Baltimore, Md. MdBH

Massachusetts antiquarian society, Worcester, Mass. MWA

Massachusetts historical society, Boston, Mass. MBH

Mercantile library association of St Louis, St Louis, Mo. MoSLM

Metropolitan Museum of art, New York, N.Y. MM

Mexico, D.F. Supreme court building. MexS

Milwaukee art center, Milwaukee, Wis. WiMiA

Milwaukee art institute, Milwaukee, Wis. WiMiA

Minneapolis institute of arts, Minneapolis, Minn. MnMi

Minnesota historical society, St Paul, Minn. MnSH

Missouri historical society, St Louis, Mo. MoSLH

Monmouth county historical society, Freehold, N.J. NJF

Montana State capitol, Helena, Mont. MonH

Montclair art museum, Montclair, N.J. NJMo

Municipal museum (Peale museum), Baltimore, Md. MdBMu

Munson-Williams-Proctor institute, Utica, N.Y. NUM

Museum of modern art, New York, N.Y. MMA

Museum of the City of New York, New York, N.Y. NNMC

National academy of design, New York, N.Y. NAD

National gallery, London, England, ELN

National gallery of art, Washington, D.C. DN

National gallery of Canada, Ottawa. CanO

National museum of baseball, Cooperstown, N.Y. NCB

National portrait gallery, London, England. ELNP

New Britain institute, New Britain, Conn. CtNB

New Haven colony historical society, New Haven, Conn. CtNH

New Mexico museum of art, Santa Fe, N.M. NMS

New school of social research, New York, N.Y. NNSR

New York. City Hall, New York, N.Y. NNCH

New York graphic society, New York, N.Y. NYG

New-York historical society, New York, N.Y. NNHS

New York public library, New York, N.Y. NNPL

New York State capitol, Albany, N.Y. NAS

New York State historical society, Cooperstown, N.Y. NCHA

Newark museum association, Newark, N.J. NJN

Newberry library, Chicago, Ill. ICN

Newport historical society, Newport, R.I. RNH

North Carolina museum of art, Raleigh, N.C. NoCR

North Carolina State art gallery. See North Carolina museum of art, Raleigh, N.C.

Norton gallery and school of art, West Palm Beach, Fla. FaW

Oberlin college, Oberlin, Ohio. OOb

Ohio State archaeological and historical society OCoA

Old Sturbridge Village, Sturbridge, Mass. MSt

Oregon historical society, Portland, Ore. OrPH

Parrish art museum, Southampton, N.Y. NSP

Pasadena art institute, Pasadena, Calif. CP

Peabody institute, Baltimore, Md. MdBP

Peabody museum, Salem, Mass. MSP

Peale museum (Municipal museum), Baltimore, Md. MdBMu

Pennsylvania academy of the fine arts, Philadelphia, Pa. PA

Petit palais, Paris, France. FPP

Philadelphia museum of art, Philadelphia, Pa. PPhM

Philbrook art center, Tulsa, Okla. OkT

Phillips academy, Andover, Mass. Addison gallery of American art. MAP

Phillips collection, Washington, D.C. DP

Phoenix art museum, Phoenix, Ariz. AP

Portland art museum, Portland, Ore. OrPA

Princeton university, Princeton, N.J. The Art museum. NJP

Providence athenaeum, Providence, R.I. RPAt

Reading museum, Reading, Pa. PR

Redwood library and athenaeum, Newport, R.I. RNR

Remington art memorial, Ogdensburg, N.Y. NOR

Rhode Island historical society, Providence, R.I. RPHS

Rhode Island school of design, Providence, R.I. RPS

Richmond art association, Richmond, Ind. InR

Rochester memorial art gallery, Rochester, N.Y. NR

St Louis, Mo. City art museum. MoSL

St Luke's hospital, New York, N.Y. NNSL

San Francisco museum of art, San Francisco, Calif. CSFM

Santa Barbara museum of art, Santa Barbara, Calif. CSB

Seattle art museum, Seattle, Wash. WaS

Senate house museum, Kingston, N.Y. NKS

Sheldon museum, Middlebury, Vt. VtMS

Sheldon Swope art gallery, Terre Haute, Ind. InTH

Smith college, Northampton, Mass. MNS

Smithsonian institution, Washington, D.C. National collection of fine arts DNC

Solomon R. Guggenheim museum, New York, N.Y. NNSG

Speed memorial, Louisville, Ky. KyLS

Springfield art museum, Springfield, Mo. MoSp

Springfield museum of fine arts, Springfield, Mass. MSM

Sterling and Francine Clark art institute, Williamstown, Mass. MWiS

Suffolk museum, Stony Brook, N.Y. NStS

Syracuse museum of art, Syracuse, N.Y. See Everson museum of Syracuse and Onondaga county, N.Y.

Syracuse university, Syracuse, N.Y. NSU

Taft museum, Cincinnati, Ohio. OCiT

Tate gallery, London, England. ELT

Telfair academy, Savannah, Ga. GST

Thomas Gilchrist institute of American history and art, Tulsa, Okla. OkTT

Toledo museum of art, Toledo, Ohio. OT

Trinity church, Boston, Mass. MBT

Union college, Schenectady, N.Y. NScU

Union league club, New York, N.Y. NNU

Union league of Philadelphia, Philadelphia, Pa. PPhU

United States military academy, West Point, N.Y. NWP

United States naval academy, Annapolis, Maryland, MdAn

University of Arizona, Tucson, Ariz. ATU

University of California, Los Angeles, Calif. CLAU

University of Illinois, Urbana, Ill. Krannert art museum. IU

University of Iowa, Iowa City, Iowa. IoIU

University of Kansas, Lawrence, Kans. Museum of art. KLU

University of Michigan, Ann Arbor, Mich. MiA

University of Minnesota, Minneapolis, Minn. MnU

University of Nebraska, Lincoln, Nebr. NeL

University of North Carolina, Woman's College, Greensboro, N.C. NoCG

University of Oklahoma, Norman, Okla. OkNU

University of Pennsylvania, Philadelphia, Pa. PPhUn

University of Southern California, Los Angeles, Calif. CLAUS

University of Virginia, Charlottesville, Va. VCU

University of Washington, Seattle, Wash. WaSU

Valentine museum, Richmond, Va. VRV

Virginia museum of fine arts, Richmond, Va. VR

Wadsworth atheneum, Hartford, Conn. CtHW

Walker art center, Minneapolis, Minn. MnMW

Walters art gallery, Baltimore, Md. MdBW

Warner house association, Portsmouth, N.H. NHP

Washington county museum of fine arts, Hagerstown, Md. MdHW

Washington university, St Louis, Mo. MoSLW

Westmoreland county museum of art, Greensburg, Pa. PW

White art museum, Cornell university, Ithaca, N.Y. NIC

The White house, Washington, D.C. DW

Whitney museum of American art, New York, N.Y. WMAA

Wichita art museum, Wichita, Kans. KW

William A. Farnsworth library and art museum, Rockland, Me. MeR

William Lane foundation, Leominster, Mass. MLL

William Rockhill Nelson gallery of art, Kansas City, Mo. MoKN

Williams college, Williamstown, Mass. MWiC

Wilmington society of the fine arts, Wilmington, Del. DeW

Winterthur museum, Greenville, Del. DeWin

Witte memorial museum, San Antonio, Tex. TxSA

Worcester art museum, Worcester, Mass. MWM

Yale university, New Haven, Conn. CtY

EXPLANATION

I. Example of entry under artist:
    (1) **BELLOWS, George Wesley,** 1882-1925
    (2)   **Children on the porch** (On the porch) OCo
    (3)   DN. Bellows
    (4)   Time. 300 years (col)
    (5)   **On the porch.** See Children on the porch

EXPLANATION

(1) Name of painter, surname in capitals
(2) Title used followed (in parentheses) by alternative title and by symbol giving location of painting. Meaning of symbol is given in Key to Symbols, pages 21-3.
(3)-(4) Names of books in which reproductions may be found. Full entry for these books is given in List of Works Indexed, pages 9-20.
(5) Reference from alternative title to title used

II. Example of title entry:
    Children on the porch by G. W. Bellows
    On the porch by G. W. Bellows

EXPLANATION

All titles entered in their alphabetical places in index, first word in boldface type

III. Example of subject entry:
    Bridges
       Moses, A. M. R. Sunday (The covered bridge)
       Whistler, J. A. M. Old Battersea bridge

EXPLANATION

To find books in which reproductions occur, consult the main entries under Moses and under Whistler

INDEX TO REPRODUCTIONS OF AMERICAN PAINTINGS
SUPPLEMENT

AACH, Herbert, 1924-
 Mesa Grande
  IU. Contemp Amer ptg & sculp, 1961
Abandoned by M. Henriksen
Abandoned quarry by L. Kroll
Abandoned treasures by Y. Kuniyoshi
Abandoned wharf by R. Vickrey
ABBE, Mrs S. B.
 Voyageur   MoSLH
 Rathbone
ABBEY, Edwin Austin, 1852-1911
 King Lear's daughters   MM
  MM. 100 Amer ptrs
 Mrs Edwin Austin Abbey   CtY
  CtY. Portrait index
Abbey, Mary Gertrude (Mead) 1851-1931
 Abbey, E. A. Mrs Edwin Austin Abbey
ABBOT, Agnes Anne, 1897-
 To the yacht races   MB
  MB. Ptgs in water color
Abeel, Maria. See Duyckinck, Maria (Abeel)
Abeel, Garret, 1734-1799
 Kilburn, L. Garret Abeel
Abeel, Mary (Byvanck) 1742-1795
 Kilburn, L. Mrs Garret Abeel
Abelard the drowned, master of the Phan-
  tom by M. Hartley
ABERCROMBIE, Gertrude, 1909-
 Message for mercy
  IU. Contemp Amer ptg, 1951
The abiding—Summer and sea by N. Sand-
  gren
Above the earth by M. Tobey
Above the excavation by N. Spencer
Above the river by E. Fiene
Abraham by B. Newman
ABRAMS, Mary Tatum, 1925-
 Paradise tree
  VR. Amer ptg, 1958
ABRAMS, Ross, 1920-
 Landscape
  VR. Amer ptg, 1958
Absence by J. Ernst
Absolom by J. W. Treiman
Abstract by G. Cavallon
Abstract by L. Schanker
Abstract composition by C. Barnes
Abstract landscape by K. Knaths
Abstract landscape by C. S. Price
Abstract portrait of Savadsky by K. S.
  Dreier
Abstraction by R. Armer
Abstraction by J. Berlandina
Abstraction by I. Bolotowsky
Abstraction by H. G. Burckhardt
Abstraction by K. Callahan
Abstraction by G. Cavallon

Abstraction by C. L. Cicero
Abstraction by B. Connelly
Abstraction by A. G. Dove
Abstraction by S. Francis
Abstraction by P. Ghikas
Abstraction by M. Hartley
Abstraction by K. Khosrovi
Abstraction by R. McChesney
Abstraction by G. J. McNeil
Abstraction by G. O'Keeffe
Abstraction by C. S. Price
Abstraction by M. L. Schamberg
Abstraction by B. W. Tomlin
Abstraction by J. Van Everen
Abstraction—storm by B. Greene
Abstraction—white iris by G. O'Keeffe
Abstraction—white rose by G. O'Keeffe
Abstraction with flowers by M. Hartley
L'académicien by R. Lindner
Academy of music, Philadelphia, Sketch for
  curtain by R. Smith
Acadia by M. B. Prendergast
Accent grave by F. J. Kline
Access by L. Bunce
Accra beach by S. M. Etnier
Acheson, Alice (Stanley)
 James, A. Mrs Dean Acheson
Acrobats
 Beckmann, M. Acrobat on trapeze
 Beckmann, M. Acrobats
 Curry, J. S. The passing leap
 De Kooning, W. Acrobat
 Demuth, C. H. Acrobats
 Demuth, C. H. Female acrobats
 Demuth, C. H. Two acrobats
 Hirsch, J. Triumph
 Kuhn, W. Acrobat in green
 Kuhn, W. Acrobat in white
 Kuhn, W. Acrobat in white and blue
 Pickens, A. Acrobat, 1947
 Weber, M. Acrobats
Acropolis—night by E. Ewing
Across four pines by W. A. Kienbusch
Across Penobscot bay by W. A. Kienbusch
Across the harbor by A. B. Davies
Across the road by A. G. Dove
Across the tracks by R. Gwathmey
Action by W. T. Murch
Actor by P. Guston
Actor and his family by A. Pickens
Actors by M. Beckmann
Actors' duel by C. R. Leslie
Actress by T. Eakins

An **actress,** Portrait of by W. M. Chase
Adam by K. Knaths
Adam by B. Newman
Adam and Eve by R. Cowles
Adam and Eve by S. G. Reinhardt
Adam and Eve by Unidentified artist
The **Adam** Lemp brewery by C. Wimar
Adams, Abigail. See Belcher, Abigail
    (Adams)
ADAMS, Cassilly, b 1843
    Custer's last fight
        McCracken. Portrait of the old west
        (col)
Adams, John, president U.S. 1735-1826
    Brown, M. John Adams
    Copley, J. S. John Adams
    Peale, C. W. John Adams
    Stuart, G. John Adams
    Trumbull, J. John Adams
Adams, John Quincy, president U.S. 1767-
    1848
    Bingham, G. C. John Quincy Adams
    Copley, J. S. John Quincy Adams
    Healy, G. P. A. John Quincy Adams
Adams, Samuel, 1722-1803
    Copley, J. S. Samuel Adams
ADAMS, Wayman, 1883-1959
    Alexander Ernestinoff   InIJ
    InIJ. 105 ptgs
    Musicos ambulantes
        PPC. International ex, 1950
Adams family, c1850
    Unidentified artist. Adams family
Adams' house by E. Hopper
Addicks, Stanley
    Eakins, T. The pianist (Stanley Addicks)
Addicks, Weda (Cook)
    Eakins, T. Concert singer (Weda Cook)
Addie by T. Eakins
Addison E. Andrews (paddle steamship)
    Bard, J. Paddle steamship Addison E.
    Andrews
Adirondack guide by W. Homer
Adirondack lake by W. Homer
Adirondack woods, guide and dog by W.
    Homer
Adirondacks by W. Homer
Adirondacks along Ausable river by J. Marin
Adit by S. Davis
Adler, Felix, 1851-1933
    Zerbe, K. Felix Adler
ADLER, Samuel M. 1898-
    Breakwater
        IU. Contemp Amer ptg & sculp, 1959
    Fortune teller
        IU. Contemp Amer ptg, 1950
    Invocation   WMAA
        IU. Contemp Amer ptg & sculp, 1953
        (col)
    Pierson
        Pousette-Dart. Amer ptg
    Juxtaposition II
        IU. Contemp Amer ptg & sculp, 1961
    The lottery
        PA. Annual ex, 1951
    Mauve still life   IU
        IU. Contemp Amer ptg, 1952
        IU. 20th century

The offering
    Pearson. Mod renaissance
To thine own self
    IU. Contemp Amer ptg, 1951
White still life
    IU. Contemp Amer ptg & sculp, 1955
Admiration of the orchestrelle for the cine-
    matograph by M. Ray
Adobe houses by C. S. Price
Adolescence by G. Wood
ADOLPHE, Albert Jean, 1865-1940
    Self-portrait
        Chew. 250 years of art
Adoration of the Magi by D. Aronson
Adoration of the moon by M. Weber
Adoration of the mother by C. W. Haw-
    thorne
Adoring angels by J. La Farge
Adrenalin hour by B. L. Culwell
Advancing sea by M. Avery
Adventure by A. B. Davies
The **advocate** by J. C. Wayne
Aegina from the Acropolis, Athens by H. B.
    Warren
Aerial gyrations by C. Sheeler
Aerograph by M. Ray
Affection by E. Cortor
Affluent surface by I. R. Pereira
African thistle by H. G. Keller
Aft deck no 2 by Z. L. Sepeshy
After all . . . , 1933 by C. H. Demuth
After an ambush by B. Perlin
After an ice storm by M. Weber
After night's study by J. F. Peto
After rain by E. Lawson
After rain by M. Sterne
After Sir Christopher Wren by C. H. De-
    muth
After sundown by R. A. Blakelock
After the bath by M. Cassatt
After the bath by Raphaelle Peale
After the fire by W. Thon
After the hunt by J. D. Chalfant
After the hunt by W. M. Harnett
After the hunt by W. Homer
After the questioning by G. Grosz
After the rain by M. Sterne
After the show by C. Prendergast
After the shower by J. E. Swinnerton
After the storm by T. H. Benton
After the storm by S. Browne
After the storm by W. M. Hart
After the storm by A. L. Ripley
After the storm by M. Sterne
After the tornado, Bahamas by W. Homer
After Titian by B. Shahn
Afterglow by G. R. Beal
Afterglow by W. Homer
Afterglow, Tautira river valley, Tahiti by
    J. La Farge
Afternoon by A. N. Wyeth
Afternoon at Tony's by M. J. Tolegian

Afternoon in August by Y. Johnston
Afternoon light by C. S. Hopkinson
Afternoon mail by W. Manning
Afternoon, Pincian hill, Rome by M. B.
  Prendergast
Afternoon sun by G. Prestopino
Afternoon wind by L. M. Eilshemius
Agate heights by E. Poe
Age of anxiety by B. Shahn
Age of reason by K. L. Seligmann
Aggressive by H. Hofmann
The **aggressor** by F. Ruvolo
Aggressors by W. Utley
Aggressors' retribution by W. Gropper
Agincourt by F. Roth
Aging actress by M. Siporin
Aging harlequin by K. Zerbe
The **agitator** by G. Grosz
Agnew clinic by T. Eakins
Agony by A. Gorky
Agrarian dishabille by W. W. Quirt
Agriculture and logging by T. H. Benton
Agrippina and her children mourning over
  the ashes of Germanicus by B. West
Agrippina landing at Brundisium with the
  ashes of Germanicus by B. West
Ahab and Abigail by K. L. Callahan
Ahko, Portrait of by A. Gorky
AHLAS, Lambro
  Jump rope
    NAD. Annual ex, 1957
Ainlee by J. D. Brooks
Ainslie, Eva Rosanna
  Theus, J. Mrs Theus (traditionally known
    as Eva Rosanna Ainslie)
Air raid by J. Hirsch
Air raid by V. Spagna
Aircraft factory by R. Crawford
Airplane synchromy in yellow and orange by
  S. MacDonald-Wright
Airplane synchromy in yellow-orange by S.
  Macdonald-Wright
Ajax by E. Melcarth
Aladjálov, Constantin. See Alajálov, Con-
  stantin
ALAJÁLOV, Constantin, 1900-
  Harlequin and woman   CtY
    CtY. Soc Anonyme
Alameda shore by J. Lee
Alaska by H. Sterne
Albany, New York
  Eights, J. East side Market street (now
    Broadway) Albany, 1805
  Eights, J. Number 1 north side of State
    street, Albany, 1806
  Eights, J. State street in 1805
The **Albany** boat by G. R. Beal
Albany Schoharie stagecoach by F. Stucker
ALBEE, Percy Frederick, 1883-1959
  The bridge
    NAD. Annual ex, 1951
ALBERS, Josef, 1888-
  b and p (B+P)   NNSG
    NNSG. Handbook
  City
    Rathbun

  Dark
    CSFP. Annual ex, 1950/51
    MMA. Abstract
  Facade
    ICA. Annual ex, 1947/48
  The gate   CtY
    CtY. Soc Anoyme
    Pierson
  Homage to the square
    Pousette-Dart. Amer ptg
  Homage to the square: Ascending
                                         WMAA
    Goodrich. Amer art (col)
    Mendelowitz
    Pierson
  Homage to the square: Dedicated
                                         NBuA
    NBuA. Acquisitions 1954-57 (col front)
  Homage to the square: Legendary pasture
    Time. 300 years (col)
  Homage to the square: Precinct (Homage
    to the square—early yellow)
    IU. Contemp Amer ptg, 1952
    MnMW. Classic tradition
  Homage to the square: Ritardando
    Ponente. Mod ptg, 1960 (col)
  Homage to the square: Yes
    DC. 25 biennial ex, 1957
  Inside and out   CtHW
    CoS. New accessions USA, 1954
  Layered
    Rathbun (col)
  Lowers
    Pearson. Mod renaissance
  Red wall
    McCurdy
  Study for an early diary
    Seiberling (col)
  Study for painting, mirage A of 1940
    Read. Concise history
  View
    Pearson. Mod renaissance
  White front   MiA
    NUM. Art across America
Albert IV the Wise, count of Hapsburg,
  d 1239
  Walker, C. H. Albert IV the Wise
Albert bridge, London by M. Lichtenberg
Albert's son by A. N. Wyeth
ALBRIGHT, Ivan Le Lorraine, 1897-
  And God created man in his own image.
    See Room 203
  And man created God in his own image.
    See Room 203
  Fleeting time, thou hast left me old   MM
    Barker. From realism
    Mendelowitz
  Harbor of dreams   OYB
    OYB. Catalogue 1951
  Heavy the oar to him who is tired,
    Heavy the coat, heavy the sea   ICA
    CoS. New accessions USA, 1950
    Gruskin (col)
  Hole in the wall gang
    NAD. Annual ex, 1954
  Hopscotch   MMA
    Barr. Masters p 160
  Into the world there came a soul called
    Ida   ICA
    Baur. New art
    Canaday
    CoS. New accessions USA, 1948
    Pierson

ALBRIGHT, I. L.—*Continued*
Maker of dreams (Man with a mallet)
    CtHW
    CtHW. Handbook
Maker of images
    Baur. New art
Man with a mallet. See Maker of dreams
The picture of Dorian Gray
    ICA. Annual ex, 1944/46
    Pearson, Mod renaissance
Poor room—There is no time, no end, no
    today, no yesterday, no tomorrow,
    only the forever, and forever, and
    forever, without end
    Baur. New Art (col)
    Eliot. Art of our time (col)
    ICA. Amer artist paints the city
    Time. 300 years (col)
The purist
    PPC. International ex, 1950
Roaring Fork, Wyoming
    WiMiA. Amer ptg 1760-1960
Room 203 (And man created God in his
    own image; And God created man in
    his own image)   ICA
    Baur. New art
    Flexner. Amer ptg
    Flexner. Short history
    McCurdy
    WMAA. Julianna Force
Self-portrait, 1935
    Baur. Revolution
Temptation of St Anthony
    MnMW. Expressionism 1900-1955
    NBuA. Expressionism
That which I should have done I did not
    do   ICA
    Baur. New art
    Newmeyer
    Pearson. Mod renaissance
    Pearson. Mod renaissance (detail)
    Pierson
    Richardson. Ptg in America
There is man in God
    PA. Annual ex, 1956
There were no flowers tonight
    DC. 20 biennial ex, 1947
    WiMiA. Amer ptg 1760-1960
Tin
    DC. 24 biennial ex, 1955
Wherefore now ariseth the illusion of a
    third dimension
    MM. Amer ptg today
The wild bunch   MMA
    Pearson. Mod renaissance
    Pousette-Dart. Amer ptg
    WiMiA. Amer ptg 1760-1960
Woman   MMA
    Barr. Masters
    MMA. Masters
Yesterday
    NAD. Annual ex, 1961

Portrait of the artist
Bohrod, A. Ivan Albright
ALBRIGHT, Malvin Marr, known as
    Zsissly, 1897-
Boothbay harbor, Maine
    PPC. International ex, 1950
Dinner table   GAtM
    GAtM. Holbrook collection
Incoming tide, Maine   OT
    OT. Contemp Amer ptgs

Summer in Maine
    PPC. Ptg in the U.S. 1949
Victoria
    Gruskin (col)
Yaquima bay, Oregon
    NAD. Annual ex, 1948
ALBRO, Maxine, 1903-
Skipping   ATU
    ATU. Coll of Amer art
ALCALAY, Albert, 1917-
Earth
    MBIC. View 1960
East end in New York
    IU. Contemp Amer ptg & sculp, 1955
Heavy industry
    WMAA. Contemp Amer ptg, 1955
Urban labyrinth
    IU. Contemp Amer ptg & sculp, 1957
Vanishing city
    IU. Contemp Amer ptg & sculp, 1959
Alden, Hannah, b 1798
    Unidentified artist. Hannah Alden
Alden, Sarah, b 1796
    Unidentified artist. Sarah Alden
The alders by C. Hassam
ALDRICH, William Truman, 1880-
Boathouse   MB
    MB. Ptgs in water color
Gasometer   MB
    MB. Ptgs in water color
A giant   MB
    MB. Ptgs in water color
Machine shop   MB
    MB. Ptgs in water color
Woodland scene   MB
    MB. Ptgs in water color
Alexander, Cicely
    Whistler, J. A. M. Cicely Alexander
ALEXANDER, Cosmo John, c 1724-1772
Alexander Grant
    Pierson
Charles Dudley
    DC. Privately owned
Mrs Charles Dudley
    DC. Privately owned
ALEXANDER, Francesca, 1837-1917
Lina Pistolesi
    MiD. Travelers in Arcadia
ALEXANDER, Francis, 1800-1880?
James Gates Percival   CtY
    CtY. Portrait index
Lydia Huntley Sigourney   NJMo
    NJMo. Forty years
Mrs Jared Sparks   MCH
    Pierson
    Richardson. Ptg in America
ALEXANDER, Fred, 1914-
Interurban   OYB
    OYB. Catalogue 1951
ALEXANDER, Henry, 1862-1895
Laboratory of Thomas Price
    Frankenstein. After the hunt
ALEXANDER, John White, 1856-1915
John Ferguson Weir   CtY
    CtY. Portrait index
    Weir. Recollections
Phyllis   InTH
    InTH. Catalogue
Study in black and green   MM
    MM. 100 Amer ptrs
Thomas Nast
    Chew. 250 years of art

Alfir's delight by A. G. Dove

Algerian scene by J. Whorf

Algerian scene: the bridge by J. Whorf

Algerian soldiers by J. Teyral

Algerian street scene by J. Whorf

Alice by W. M. Chase

Alice in grey by L. Lucioni

Alice in the Shinnecock studio by W. M. Chase

Alice with wolfhound by W. M. Chase

All soundings are referred to high water by K. Sage

All things are changing, nothing dies by P. Mangravite

ALLAN, Bill, 1936-
    Blind fish approaching summer
    PPC. International ex, 1958

Allée by S. Davis

Allegheny mountains
    Harvey, G. Amongst the Allegheny mountains

Allegorical themes. See Symbolical and allegorical themes

Allegro by M. Tobey

ALLEN, Agnes
    J. Somers Smith
    PA. Annual ex, 1947

Allen, Ann (Crawford) 1759-1808
    Malbone, E. G. Mrs Zachariah Allen

Allen, Beulah. See Clarke, Beulah (Allen)

ALLEN, Charles Curtis, 1886-
    Westwood hillside   MB
    MB. Ptgs in water color

Allen, Clara (Walker) fl 1750
    Hesselius, J. Mrs William Allen
    Wollaston, J. Mrs William Allen

Allen, Elizabeth. See Deas, Elizabeth (Allen)

ALLEN, Junius, 1898-
    North inlet
    NAD. Annual ex, 1961

Allen, Lydia, b 1784
    Malbone, E. G. Lydia Allen

Allen, Samuel, fl 1795
    Peale, J. Samuel Allen of Philadelphia

Allen, Solomon, 1751-1821
    Ames, E. Solomon Allen

ALLEN, Thomas, 1849-1924
    Portal of the mission of San José, Texas
                                           MB
    MB. Ptgs in water color

Allen, William, 1841-1849
    Prior, W. M. William Allen

Allen, Mrs William. See Allen, Clara (Walker)

Allen, Mrs Zachariah. See Allen, Ann (Crawford)

Alligators
    Sargent, J. S. Muddy alligators

Allium Sativum by G. Palazzola

Allouard-Jouan, Madame
    Sargent, J. S. Madame Allouard-Jouan

The all-seeing eye by Unidentified artist

All's well by W. Homer

Allston, Ann (Channing) See Channing, Ann

Allston, Rachel Moore. See Flagg, Rachel Moore Allston

ALLSTON, Washington, 1779-1843
    American scenery: Time, afternoon with
        a southwest haze   MB
    Canaday
    Richardson. Washington Allston
    Angel releasing St Peter from prison MB
    Richardson. Washington Allston
    Artist's mother, Mrs Henry Collins Flagg
    Richardson. Washington Allston
    Beatrice
    Richardson. Washington Allston
    Belshazzar's feast   MB
    Barker. Amer ptg
    Flexner. Light of distant skies
    Larkin
    Larkin rev ed
    NBuA. Expressionism
    Richardson. Washington Allston
    Roos
    Benjamin West   MB
    Richardson. Washington Allston
    Buck's progress, no 1: Introduction of a
        country lad to a click of town bucks
    Richardson. Washington Allston
    The buck's progress, no 3: Midnight fray
        with a watchman
    Flexner. Light of distant skies
    Christ healing the sick, first study
    Richardson. Washington Allston
    Coast scene on the Mediterranean
    NUM. Art across America
    Richardson. Washington Allston
    David playing before Saul   SCCG
    Richardson. Washington Allston
    The dead man revived by touching the
        bones of the prophet Elisha   PA
    Canaday
    Flexner. Light of distant skies
    Richardson. Ptg in America
    Richardson. Washington Allston
    Death of King John
    Richardson. Washington Allston (unfinished)
    The deluge   MM
    Baur. Amer ptg
    Bazin
    Flexner. Light of distant skies
    Larkin (detail)
    Larkin rev ed (detail)
    Mendelowitz
    Pierson
    Richardson. Washington Allston
    Walker. Ptgs from America
    Diana in the chase   MCH
    Pierson
    Richardson. Washington Allston
    Donna Mencia in the robbers' cavern MB
    MB. Karolik coll
    Richardson. Washington Allston
    Elijah fed by the ravens (Elijah in the
        desert)   MB
    Flexner. Light of distant skies
    Larkin rev ed (col)
    Lee. Art then and now
    Pierson
    Richardson. Washington Allston
    Evening hymn
    Richardson. Washington Allston
    WiMiA. Amer ptg 1760-1960

ALLSTON, Washington—*Continued*
Flight of Florimell   MiD
  MiD. Treasures
  Pierson
  Richardson. Ptg in America (col detail)
  Richardson. Washington Allston (col)
Francis Dana Channing
  Richardson. Washington Allston
Head of a Jew   MB
  Richardson. Washington Allston
Isaac of York   MBA
  Richardson. Washington Allston
Italian landscape   MAP
  Canaday
  Larkin
  Larkin rev ed
  PPC. Amer classics
  Richardson. Washington Allston
Italian landscape   MiD
  MiD. Travelers in Arcadia
  Richardson. Washington Allston
  Roos
Italian landscape   OT
  MiD. Travelers in Arcadia
Italian shepherd boy   MiD
  Richardson. Washington Allston
Jacob's dream
  Richardson. Washington Allston
Jason returning to demand his **father's**
  kingdom
  Canaday
  Richardson. Washington Allston
Jeremiah dictating his prophecy of the
  destruction of Jerusalem   CtY
  Flexner. Light of distant skies
  Richardson. Washington Allston
Landscape   MCoL
  Richardson. Washington Allston
Landscape, American scenery. See American scenery
Landscape, evening
  Richardson. Washington Allston
Landscape with a lake   MB
  MB. Karolik coll
  Richardson. Washington Allston
Lorenzo and Jessica
  Richardson. Washington Allston
Man in chains   MAP
  Richardson. Washington Allston
Mrs William Channing
  Richardson. Washington Allston
Moonlit landscape   MB
  Barker. Amer ptg
  Born
  Canaday
  Flexner. Amer ptg
  Flexner. Light of distant skies
  Flexner. Short history
  Mendelowitz
  MiD. Ptg in America
  Pierson
  Richardson. Ptg in America
  Richardson. Washington Allston
  Robb. Harper history
  Roos
  Time. 300 years (col)
Mother watching her sleeping child
  Richardson. Washington Allston
The poor author and the rich bookseller
                     MB
  Flexner. Light of distant skies
  ICA. From colony to nation
  Richardson. Washington Allston

Rebecca at the well
  Richardson. Washington Allston
Rising of a thunderstorm at sea   MB
  Pierson
  Richardson. Ptg in America
  Richardson. Washington Allston
Robert Rogers   RNR
  Richardson. Washington
Rosalie
  Flexner. Light of distant skies
  Richardson. Washington Allston
St Peter in prison, Study for head of
  Richardson. Washington Allston
Samuel Taylor Coleridge   ELNP
  Richardson. Washington Allston
Samuel Taylor Coleridge (Dana coll)
  Richardson. Washington Allston (unfinished
Samuel Williams
  MiD. Coll in progress
  Richardson. Washington Allston
  WiMiA. Amer ptg 1760-1960
Saul and the witch of Endor   MAC
  Richardson. Washington Allston
Self-portrait   MB
  Flexner. Light of distant skies
  MB. Great Americans
  Pierson
  Richardson. Washington Allston
The sisters
  Richardson. Washington Allston
Uriel in the sun
  Richardson. Washington Allston
The valentine
  Richardson. Washington Allston
William Ellery Channing   MB
  MB. Great Americans
  Richardson. Washington Allston

Portrait of the artist
Malbone, E. G. Washington Allston

Allston, Mrs Washington. See Channing, Ann

Almost airtight compartments by J. Berlandina

Almost silence by J. Ernst

Alms by C. Booth

Almy, James G. fl 1798
Malbone, E. G. James G. Almy

Alone by J. Ernst

Alone by P. Evergood

Alone by M. Weber

Along the Arno by O. M. Pleissner

Along the Borgo pass by C. L. Cicero

Along the boulevard, Paris by M. B. Prendergast

Along the coast by M. B. Prendergast

Along the coast by P. Riba

Along the Erie canal by A. B. Davies

Along the North shore by S. W. Woodward

Along the path by S. Laufman

Along the river by P. Dickinson

Along the road, Cordoba, Mexico by D. Macknight

Along the Susquehanna by J. Kane

Along the waterfront by R. Marsh

Alpine district, New Jersey by J. Marin

The **Alps** by H. G. Keller

Unidentified boy
  Courtelyou. Ezra Ames supp
Unidentified man
  Cortelyou. Ezra Ames supp
A view of Lake George and Caldwell
    village [without fort]
  Bolton. Ezra Ames
William Annesley (?)
  Bolton. Ezra Ames
William James
  Bolton. Ezra Ames
William Tully   CtY
  Bolton. Ezra Ames
Ames, Julius Rubens, 1801-1850
  Ames, E. Julius Rubens Ames
Ames, Marcia Lucretia, 1797/98-1886
  Ames, E. Marcia L. Ames
Ames, Zipporah (Wood) 1775-1836
  Ames, E. Mrs Ezra Ames
AMFT, Robert, 1916-
  Landscape   OYB
  OYB. Annual 1958
  OYB. Suplement 1959
Amidon, Mary, fl 1830
  Stock, J. W. (attributed works) Mary
    Amidon
Among the led horses by F. Remington
Amory, Elizabeth (Bowen) 1777-1857
  Malbone, E. G. Mrs Thomas Amory
Amory, Georgina Margaret. See Lowell,
    Georgia Margaret (Amory)
Amory, Katherine (Greene) 1731-1777
  Copley, J. S. Mrs John Amory
Amory, Thomas, 1722-1784
  Copley, J. S. Thomas Amory jr
Amory, Mrs Thomas. See Amory, Elizabeth
    (Bowen)
L'amour, toujours l'amour by H. Franken-
    thaler
The amulet by C. Howard
ANA by S. Davis
Anahita, the flight of night by W. M. Hunt
Anatomical man by B. Shahn
The anatomist by H. Bloom
Anatomy by J. McGarrell
Ancestor by E. Friedensohn
Anchor by I. R. Pereira
Ancient facade by P. Sarkisian
The ancient form by B. Greene
Ancient valley by R. Gleitsmann
And God created man in his own image by
    I. L. Albright
And man created God in his own image by
    I. L. Albright
". . . and the home of the brave" by C. H.
    Demuth
Andalusian garden by H. G. Keller
ANDERSEN, Andreas S. 1908-
  Susan   ATU
  ATU. Coll of Amer art
ANDERSEN, Leif
  Siesta
  NAD. Annual ex, 1957
Anderson, Miss
  Jarvis, J. W. Miss Anderson
Anderson, Alexander, 1775-1870
  Jarvis, J. W. Alexander Anderson
Anderson, Edward A. 1923-
  Delta Queen and Packet Whisper   OYB
  OYB. Annual 1955
  OYB. Supplement 1959

Anderson, Ellen Amory. See Curtis, Ellen
    Amory (Anderson)
ANDERSON, Guy, 1906-
  Sharp sea   WaS
  OrPA. Ptgs & sculptures
ANDERSON, John, 1923-
  Creation of Eve
  IU. Contemp Amer ptg & sculp, 1953
  Pousette-Dart. Amer ptg
Anderson children by O. Frazer
Andes by F. J. Kline
André, John, 1751-1780
  Durand, A. B. Capture of Major André
  Toole, J. Capture of Major André
André-Michel, Mme Robert. See Ormond,
    Rose Marie
ANDREWS, Ambrose, fl 1824-1859
  Schuyler family   NNHS
  Jones. Rediscovered ptrs
ANDREWS, Sperry, 1917-
  Mill race
  NAD. Annual ex, 1953
Anemones by James McLaughlin
Angel by K. Okada
Angel by F. C. Watkins
Angel battling demons by P. Mangravite
Angel posed by F. C. Watkins
Angel releasing St Peter from prison by
    W. Allston
Angel square by D. Kingman
The angel will turn a page in the book by
    F. C. Watkins
Angel with book by D. Aronson
Los angelitos by E. Berman
Angell, James Rowland, 1869-1949
  Johansen, J. C. James Rowland Angell
Angelo's place by G. O. Coleman
Angels administering to Christ by T. Cole
Angels at the cross by D. Aronson
Angels representing adoration, praise, thanks-
    giving and love by J. La Farge
Anglers. See Fishermen and fishing
Anglers' heaven by R. M. Mason
Angora goat by E. F. Spruce
Anguish by B. Greene
Animal and mineral by J. Ernst
Animal and young by D. Hayes
Animals
  See also Cattle, Horses, Sheep, etc.
  Curry, J. S. Sanctuary
  Field, E. S. Garden of Eden
  Hicks, E. Grave of William Penn
  Hicks, E. Noah's ark
  Hicks, E. The peaceable kingdom
  Hicks, E. The peaceable kingdom of the
    branch
  Hicks, E. Residence of David Twining
  Hidley, J. H. (attributed works) Noah's
    ark
  Keller, H. G. Returning from the Feria
  Pippin, H. The holy
  Pippin, H. Holy mountain
  Remington, F. Navajo raid
  Tait, A. F. Barnyard
  Unidentified artist. Creation scene
  Woodside, J. A. Country fair
  Zeliff, A. E. Barnyard

ANLIKER, Roger William, 1924?-
    Any moment
        DC. 22 biennial ex, 1951
        ICA. Annual ex, 1951
    Caerulea
        Chew. 250 years of art
    Remembering
        IU. Contemp Amer ptg, 1952
Ann by G. Bellows
Ann by A. Brook
Anna by R. Lebrun
Anna's garden by H. G. Keller
Anne by H. V. Poor
Anne in purple wrap by G. W. Bellows
Anne in white by G. W. Bellows
Annesley, Margaret (La Casse) 1800-1832
    Ames, E. Mrs William Annesley (?)
Annesley, William, 1793-1862
    Ames, E. William Annesley (?)
Annette by E. G. Malbone
Annis, Sarah. See Sully, Sarah (Annis)
Anonymous by A. G. Dove
Another expulsion by G. P. Du Bois
Another Sunday by C. F. McCall
ANSHUTZ, Thomas Pollock, 1851-1912
    Aunt Hannah
        MiD. Coll in progress
    Becky Sharp   PA
        PA. Annual ex, 1955
    Steamboats on the Ohio
        Chew. 250 years of art
    Steelworkers' noontime
        Chew. 250 years of art
        Davidson v 1
        PA. Annual ex, 1955
        Pierson
        Richardson. Ptg in America
        U.S. National Capital sesquicentennial
            com
        WiMiA. Amer ptg 1760-1960
    The Tanagra   PA
        PA. Annual ex, 1955
The answer is no by K. Sage
Antelao by L. C. Scarborough
Antelope
    Audubon, J. W. Prong-horned antelope
    Miller, A. J. Herd of antelope
    Miller, A. J. Pawnee Indian shooting
        antelope
    Miller, A. J. Rock of Independence
    O'Keeffe, G. Antelope
Antelope mountain by E. F. Spruce
Anthony, May. See Dyer, May (Anthony)
Antietam, Condition at by F. D. Duncan
Antinomes no 1, 1959 by W. Pachner
The antique by M. Weber
The antique cast by A. Gorky
Antiques by A. Bohrod
Antiquity by R. Courtright
ANTREASIAN, Garo Zareh, 1922-
    Early spring—South side
        IU. Contemp Amer ptg, 1948
ANUSZKIEWICZ, Richard, 1930-
    Brightness as a third dimension
        IU. Contemp Amer ptg & sculp, 1961
Any moment by R. W. Anliker

Apache village on Lake Ahrocum by G.
    Catlin
Apaches are coming by F. Remington
Apaches listening by F. Remington
Apartment house by M. Frary
Apartment no 2 by K. Zerbe
Apartment tower by N. Spencer
The Apennines by A. B. Davies
Aperitif by H. L. McFee
Apocalypse by G. Peterdi
Apocalyptic landscape by G. Grosz
The apostle by W. W. Quirt
Apotheosis by B. Shahn
Apotheosis of Marie-Henri Beyle by J.
    Wilde
Apotheosis of Mexican baroque by E. Ber-
    man
The apotheosis of Nelson by B. West
Apparition by H. Hofmann
The apparition by A. Revington
Apparition of danger by H. Bloom
The appeal of Coriolanus by B. West
Apple blossoms by M. J. Heade
Apple blossoms by J. La Farge
Apple blossoms by D. Macknight
Apple country by Joe Jones
Apple gatherers by Unidentified artist
Apple hill, Cooperstown, New York. View
    from by S. F. B. Morse
Apple of discord by T. H. Benton
Apple orchard by G. Inness
Apple trees in December by D. J. McCosh
APPLEBY, Theodore, 1923-
    Esperance
        PPC. International ex, 1958
Appleford, Thomas, fl 1736-1767
    Wollaston, J. Thomas Appleford
Apples by A. Dasburg
Apples by W. Sommer
Apples by W. Whittredge
Apples and jug by S. Davis
Apples in a basket by J. F. Francis
Apples in the hay by W. Kuhn
Appleton, Margaret (Gibbs) 1701-1771
    Copley, J. S. Mrs Nathaniel Appleton
The appointment by M. R. Barnes
Apprentice by W. M. Chase
Approaching a city by E. Hopper
Approaching night by M. Sokole
Approaching storm by L. M. Eilshemius
Approaching storm by G. Grosz
Approaching storm by C. W. Rain
Approaching storm: beach near Newport
    by M. J. Heade
Approaching storm from Alban hills by G.
    Inness
April cat by W. Sommer
April day by D. Lutz
April 1, 1957 by J. Levee
An April mood by C. E. Burchfield
April showers by A. Rattner
April snow by H. G. Keller

April snow by M. B. Prendergast
Apsaras by E. A. Donati
Apteka by J. Levine
Apthorp, Charles, 1698?-1758
Feke, R. Charles Apthorp
Apthorp, Grizzel. See Trecothick, Grizzel (Apthorp)
Apthorp, Hannah. See Bulfinch, Hannah (Apthorp)
Apthorp, Sarah Wentworth. See Morton, Sarah Wentworth (Apthorp)
Apthorp, Susan. See Bulfinch, Susan (Apthorp)
Aquarelle by G. Grosz
Aquarelle: collage by Tseng Yo-ho
Aqueduct by J. De Martini
The **aqueduct,** Pittsburgh by R. Smith
Aquitaine by J. Youngerman
Arabesque by J. Pollock
Arabesque with bull by F. Martin
Arachne by J. Sloan
Arapahos by A. J. Miller
ARBOGAST, Valentine
Mountain goats
NSP. Sportscapes
Arboretum by flashbulb by S. Davis
Arbuckle, James, fl 1766
Peale, C. W. James Arbuckle
Arbuckle, Tabitha Scarborough (Custis) fl 1776
Peale, C. W. Mrs James Arbuckle and son Edward
Arc de Triomphe, Paris by E. D. Boit
Arcadia II by F. Dzubas
An **Arcadian** by T. Eakins
Arch hotel by S. Davis
Arch of Octavius by A. Bierstadt
Arch of silence by L. Gatch
Arch of Titus, Rome by G. P. A. Healy
Arch of Triumph by B. Shahn
Archaeological treasure by H. Bloom
Archaic idol by M. Rothko
Archaic landscape by J. Gregoropoulos
Archaic rock by S. Sarkisian
Archaic tree by L. Gatch
Archangel Gabriel by B. West
Archbold, Anne
MacMonnies, F. W. Mrs Anne Archbold
ARCHER, Edmund, 1904-
Howard Patterson of the Harlem Yankees
WMAA
Goodrich. Amer art
Archer, William S. 1789-1855
Healy, G. P. A. William S. Archer
Architect's dream by T. Cole
Architectural cadences by C. Sheeler
Architecture by C. H. Demuth
Arctic cabin by J. Hultberg
The **arena** by H. Weston
Arena of civilization by M. Tobey
Arethusa by A. B. Davies
Arezzo, Street in by E. D. Boit
Argali—mountain sheep by A. J. Miller
Arguing angels by J. W. Treiman
Argula by A. Gorky

Ariadne. See Mythological themes—Ariadne
Aricara female by A. J. Miller
L'Ariccia by R. Smith
Arid land by S. Sherman
Arizona
Eilshemius, L. M. Yuma, Arizona
Macknight, D. Purple abyss, Grand Canyon, Arizona
Moran, T. Arizona sunset near the Grand Canyon
Ark of the covenant by E. S. Field
The **Arkansa** near the Rocky mountains, View on by S. Seymour
Arkansas (ship)
Hashagen, A. Ship Arkansas leaving Havana
Arkansas landscape by E. F. Spruce
ARKUSH, Jacob
Leona
NAD. Annual ex, 1948
Armchair strategists by W. Gropper
Armenian girl by W. J. Glackens
ARMER, Ruth, 1896-
Abstraction, no 270   CSFM
CSFP. Annual ex, 1948/49
Pousette-Dart. Amer ptg
Twilight hush
CSFP. Anual ex, 1948/49
Armistead, George, 1780-1818
Peale, Rembrandt. Col George Armistead
Armistice night by G. B. Luks
The **armoire** of Proteus by Y. Tanguy
Armor must change by B. W. Tomlin
ARMS, John Taylor, 1887-1953
Mont St Michel
Roos
Armstrong, Hannah
Robinson, B. Hannah Armstrong
Army of the Potomac by J. Hope
Army officer by F. Remington
ARNEST, Bernard Patrick, 1917-
Man in orange
PPC. International ex, 1952
Portrait of D   CoS
CoS. New accessions USA, 1958
Underpass
WMAA. Contemp Amer ptg, 1953
View of the city through signs   MnMW
CoS. New accessions USA, 1952
The **Arno** by O. M. Pleissner
Arnold, Miss, fl 1830
Unidentified artist. Miss Arnold knitting
Arnold, Mrs, fl 1830
Unidentified artist. Mrs Arnold holding an apple
ARNOLD, Edward, c 1824-1866
Battle of Port Hudson, 1863   DNC
U.S. National Capital sesquicentennial com
Arnold by B. Nordberg
ARONSON, David, 1923-
Adoration of the Magi
Genauer
Angel with book
VR. Amer ptg, 1954
Angels at the cross
ICA. Annual ex, 1954
Christ before Pilate
WMAA. Contemp Amer ptg, 1949

ARONSON, David—*Continued*
  Coronation of the Virgin   VR
    Baur. Revolution
    MMA. Fourteen
    Pierson
  Joseph and the Ishmaelites no 1   IU
    IU. Contemp Amer ptg & sculp, 1957
    IU. 20th century
  Joseph and the Ishmaelites no 2
    IU. Contemp Amer ptg & sculp, 1959
  Last supper   ICA
    MMA. Fourteen
  Madonna and Child with saints
    MMA. Fourteen
  The magician
    IU. Contemp Amer ptg & sculp, 1961
  Presentation of the Virgin
    IU. Contemp Amer ptg, 1952
  Resurrection
    MMA. Fourteen
    NBuA. Expressionism
  Trinity
    IU. Contemp Amer ptg, 1949
    MMA. Fourteen
  Young Christ
    MMA. Fourteen
  Young Joseph
    IU. Contemp Amer ptg & sculp, 1955
Around painting by W. Hedrick
Arrangement by A. B. Carles
Arrangement by A. H. Maurer
Arrangement by M. A. Sprague
Arrangement by B. W. Tomlin
Arrangement in black and brown by J. A. M. Whistler
Arrangement in flesh-color and black by J. A. M. Whistler
Arrangement in grey and black (Artist's mother) by J. A. M. Whistler
Arrangement in grey and black (Thomas Carlyle) by J. A. M. Whistler
Arrangement in pink and purple by J. A. M. Whistler
Arrangement on a blue table by J. Jarvaise
Arranging the tulips by G. Melchers
Arrest of Monmouth before James II by J. S. Copley
The **arrival** by C. di Marca-Relli
Arrival-departure by W. Pachner
Arrival of Nike at Panmunjom by R. L. Grilley
Art dealer Fleischmann by W. M. Chase
Art of building by T. H. Benton
Art of painting by A. Bohrod
Art on the beach by P. Evergood
Art versus law by D. G. Blythe
Arthur, Chester Alan, president U.S. 1830-1886
  Healy, G. P. A. Chester A. Arthur
ARTHUR, Revington, 1909-
  Circus family
    IU. Contemp Amer ptg, 1950
  Green pool
    Gruskin
  The last supper
    PPC. Ptg in the U.S. 1949
An **artist,** Portrait of by X. Gonzales
Artist and his model by M. Hirshfield
Artist and his mother by A. Gorky

An **artist** as a young man by P. Evergood
Artist in his studio by P. Tilyard
Artist in summer by H. V. Poor
Artist looks at nature by C. Sheeler
Artist showing his picture of a scene from "Hamlet" to his parents by W. Dunlap
The **artist** sketching his friends by P. Weber
Artist's card rack by W. M. Harnett
Artist's daughter by W. M. Chase
Artist's daughter by G. Tooker
Artist's dream by G. H. Comegys
Artist's fantasy by P. Evergood
Artist's mother by M. Beckmann
Artist's mother by W. M. Chase
Artist's mother by W. H. Cotton
Artist's mother by J. A. M. Whistler
Artists sketching by W. Homer
The **artist's** son by W. Zorach
Artist's studio by W. M. Chase
Artist's studio by R. A. Mintz
Artist's studio by J. F. Weir
Artist's studio in an afternoon fog by W. Homer
Artist's wife by A. James
Artist's window, View from by W. M. Harnett
The **arts** of life by T. H. Benton
Arts of the west by T. H. Benton
Arundel castle by F. Stella
As the sunlight bursts by H. Spiers
Ascendant by V. Candell
Ascension by J. S. Copley
Ascension by S. Goodman
Ascension by J. La Farge
The **Ascension** of our Saviour by B. West
Ascensions by C. Schucker
Ascutney mountain from Claremont, N. H. by A. Bierstadt
Ash can by L. MacIver
Ashburton, Alexander Baring, baron, 1774-1848
  Healy, G. P. A. Lord Ashburton
Ashby, Anne. See Manigault, Anne (Ashby)
Ashen gods by L. Dodd
Asheville by W. De Kooning
Ashley, Elizabeth Billings, 1745-1826
  Field, E. S. Elizabeth Billings Ashley
Asleep on the path by W. Sommer
Aspects of the harbor by L. Manso
Aspiration by A. V. Tack
Aspiring by L. Dodd
ASPLUND, Henry Martin, 1909-
  Nude
    NAD. Annual ex, autumn 1949
ASPLUND, Tore, 1903-
  Rue de Rivoli, Paris
    NAD. Special ex, 1956
  Town of Jim Thorpe, Pennsylvania
    NAD. Annual ex, 1959
Assignation by A. Salemme
Assiniboin encampment on the upper Missouri by J. M. Stanley

L'Assommoir, Illustration for by C. H. Demuth
Assorted prints by J. G. Bruff
Astle, Thomas
  West, B. Thomas Astle
Astor place by F. Criss
Astoria boulevard by M. Sievan
Astral assemblage by E. W. Day
Astral image by M. Rothko
Astronomical blessings are in order by A. Salemme
At a house in Harley street by C. H. Demuth
At Barrytown, Hudson river by D. Johnson
At close quarters by C. M. Russell
At dawn by G. D. Brush
At Golgotha by R. Breinin
At Maxie Ford's by S. E. Dickinson
At nature's mirror by R. A. Blakelock
At night by K. Zerbe
At the beach by M. Beckmann
At the beach by W. J. Glackens
At the beach by M. B. Prendergast
At the beach by L. L. Ribak
At the chestnut root by A. B. Davies
At the crossing by G. Martino
At the end of the rope by C. M. Russell
At the fair by Y. Tanguy
At the fishing grounds by F. H. Lane
At the inn by D. Burliuk
At the lake by M. Weber
At the mill by M. Weber
At the opera by M. Cassatt
At the piano by J. A. M. Whistler
At the shore by A. H. Maurer
At the shore by M. B. Prendergast
At the table by H. Baumbach
Athens by J. La Farge
Athens, U.S., View of by L. Dodd
ATHERTON, John C. 1900-1952
  Christmas eve   MMA
    Pierson
  Construction: Shaftsbury, Vermont
    CSFP. Annual ex, 1952
  Fisherman's chest
    ICA. Annual ex, 1951
    IU. Contemp Amer ptg, 1950
  Icy shore
    IU. Contemp Amer ptg & sculp, 1953
  Low tide monument
    CSFP. Annual ex, 1948/49
  Nets, boats and sea
    IU. Contemp Amer ptg, 1952
  Rocky farmyard
    NBuA. Contemporary ptgs
    Pousette-Dart. Amer ptg
    WMAA. Annual ex, 1952
  Spirals
    SCFP. Annual ex, 1947/48
  Three towers
    IU. Contemp Amer ptg, 1951
  Villa Rotunda   NBuA
    NBuA. Contemporary ptgs
  Winter Hudson
    MM. Amer ptg today

Athlete and landscape by J. Glasco
Atkins, Martha. See Barnes, Martha (Atkins)
Atkinson, Frances Deering (Wentworth) See Wentworth, Frances Deering (Wentworth) lady
Atkinson, Hannah (Wentworth) 1700-1760
  Blackburn, J. Mrs Theodore Atkinson
Atkinson, Theodore, 1698-1779
  Blackburn, J. Col Theodore Atkinson
Atkinson, Theodore, 1736-1769
  Blackburn. J. Theodore Atkinson jr
Atlantic by E. Kelly
Atlantic by H. E. Mattson
Atlantic by T. Yerxa
Atlantic cable
  Dudley, R. Splicing the cable
Atlas and Hesperides by J. S. Sargent
Atmospheric conditions by H. Bayer
Atmospheric mood by F. Ruvolo
Attack by Crow Indians by A. J. Miller
Attack on an emigrant train by C. Wimar
Attack on the supply train by F. Remington
Attacked by the stickmen by G. Grosz
Attar by P. Guston
Attic by W. De Kooning
Attic dormer by J. W. McCoy
Attic windows by R. B. Tague
Attraction by B. Connelly
Attraction by F. Ruvolo
Atwater, Edward Elias, 1816-1887
  Jocelyn, N. Edward Elias Atwater
Atwood's cove by C. F. Gaertner
Aubade by E. Kelly
Aucassin and Nicoletta by C. H. Demuth
Auction day by J. Kempsmith
Aude, Mme A. F. fl 1899
  Cassatt, M. Mme A. F. Aude and her two daughters
Audition by C. A. Morris
AUDUBON, John James, 1785-1851
  American porcupine   NNAM
    Pierson
    Murphy. John James Audubon
  Black-billed cuckoo   NNHS
    NYG. Fine art
    Pierson
  Black-tailed hare or jack-rabbit   MoSL
    Rathbone
  Blue grosbeak
    NYG. Fine art
  Blue jay
    NYG. Fine art
  Bobwhite (called Virginian partridge by the artist)   NNHS
    Time. 300 years (col)
  Brown pelican   NNHS
    Larkin
    Larkin rev ed
  California condor
    Murphy. John James Audubon
  Carolina parrot
    NYG. Fine art
  Carolina parroquet   NNHS
    Mendelowitz
  Carolina turtle-dove
    NYG. Fine art

AUDUBON, J. J.—*Continued*
Chuck-Will's widow   NNHS
  Craven. Treasury 1952 ed
Common crossbill
  NYG. Fine art
Egret. See Snowy heron
European cormorant   NNHS
  Murphy. John James Audubon
Fisher or marten
  Rathbone
Fox and goose   OYB
  Chew. 250 years of art
  OYB. Catalogue 1951
Golden plover   NNHS
  Murphy. John James Audubon
Great black-backed gull   NNHS
  Murphy. John James Audubon
Green heron   MCH
  Rathbone
Gyrfalcon   NNHS
  Pierson
Head of a buffalo calf
  Rathbone
Ivory-billed woodpecker   MCH
  Rathbone
Mockingbird (with rattlesnake robbing
  nest)   NNHS
  Murphy. John James Audubon
Natchez, Mississippi in 1822
  Pierson
Osprey and the otter and the salmon
                             ATeS
  ATeS. Collection
  NUM. Art across America
Passenger pigeon   NNHS
  Murphy. John James Audubon
Pileated woodpecker
  NYG. Fine art
Portrait of a girl
  NYG. Fine art
Purple grackle   NNHS
  Larkin rev ed (col)
  Pierson
  Richardson. Ptg in America
Red-breasted merganser
  NYG. Fine art
Red-tailed hawk   MCH
  Rathbone
Richardson's Columbian squirrel
  CtY. Yale alumni
Roseate spoonbill   NNHS
  Murphy. John James Audubon
Ruby-throated hummingbird
  NYG. Fine art
Say's or western fox squirrel   MoSLB
  Rathbone
Sea eagle (so called)   NNHS
  Murphy. John James Audubon
Shoveller duck
  NYG. Fine art
Snowy heron or white egret
  Craven. Rainbow book (col)
  Craven. Treasury 1952 ed (col)
  Murphy. John James Audubon
Snowy owl   NNHS
  Craven. Treasury 1952 ed
Snowy owl   DN
  Walker. Ptgs from America
Trumpeter swan   NNHS
  Flexner. Light of distant skies
Turkey buzzard   NNHS
  Murphy. John James Audubon

Victor Gifford Audubon
  CtY. Yale alumni
Virginia deer   NBM
  Pierson
  Roos
Wild turkey   NNHS
  Lee. Art then and now
  Murphy. John James Audubon
  NYG. Fine art
  Time. 300 years (col)
Wolverene   NNNH
  Rathbone
Woodpeckers   NNHS
  Craven. Rainbow book
  Flexner. Amer ptg
  Flexner. Short history
  Taylor. Fifty centuries, 1954 ed (col)
Yellow-breasted chat
  NYG. Fine art

Attributed works

A girl   DN
  NYG. Fine art

Portrait of the artist

Audubon, V. G. and Audubon, J. W. John
  James Audubon
Inman, H. John James Audubon

AUDUBON, John Woodhouse, 1812-1862
Common American deer   NNNH
  Rathbone
A Forty-niner
  U.S. National Capital sesquicentennial
  com
Gray wolf or white American wolf NNNH
  Rathbone
Hare
  CtY. Yale alumni
Prairie wolf or coyote   NNNH
  Rathbone
Prong-horned antelope   NNNH
  Rathbone

AUDUBON, John Woodhouse, 1812-1862
  and AUDUBON, Victor Gifford,
  1809-1860
John James Audubon   NNAM
  Murphy. John James Audubon

AUDUBON, Victor Gifford, 1809-1860

Attributed works

Hudson river view   MB
  MB. Karolik coll

Portrait of the artist

Audubon, J. J. Victor Gifford Audubon
AUDUBON, Victor Gifford, 1809-1860 **and**
  AUDUBON, John Woodhouse, 1812-
  1862
John James Audubon   NNAM
  Murphy. John James Audubon
AUERBACH-LEVY, William, 1889-
Vanity
  NAD. Annual ex, 1952
August by L. Gatch
August afternoon by C. E. Burchfield
August evening by C. E. Burchfield
August in the city by E. Hopper
August serenity by L. Kroll
Augusta, Maine by Unidentified artist
Auguste and his horse by A. J. Miller
Augustin, Robert, fl 1876
  Herff, C. A. Hanging of Bob Augustin

Aull, Mrs Robert, fl 1837
  Bingham, G. C. Mrs Robert Aull
AULT, George C. 1891-1948
  Brooklyn ice house   NJN
    Brown. Amer ptg
  Factory chimney   PPhM
    CoS. New accessions USA, 1950
  Sullivan street abstraction
    MnMW. Precisionist view
Aunt Fanny by G. W. Bellows
Aunt Hannah by T. P. Anshutz
Aunt Thankful's farm by W. Thon
Aura of a pond by A. Okamura
Aurangabad market by L. Dodd
Auratum lily by E. W. Motley
Aurelia by J. Farnsworth
Aurora by Unidentified artist
AUSTIN, Darrel, 1907-
  Beast enchanted
    Gruskin (col)
  Beautiful beast
    PPC. Ptg in the U.S. 1949
  Catamount   MMA
    Pierson
    Read. Art now, 1948 ed
  Europa and the bull   MiD
    Cheney. Story 1958 ed
  The garden
    Cheney. Expressionism 1948 ed
  Lady in the greenwood
    IU. Contemp Amer ptg & sculp, 1953
  Moon song
    Baur. Revolution
  Sorceress
    PA. Annual ex, 1950
  The tiger
    Newmeyer
  The tightrope   MM
    MM. 100 Amer ptrs
  Tigress with three cubs
    IU. Contemp Amer ptg & sculp, 1955
  Vixen
    Bazin
  White catamount
    CSFP. Annual ex, 1948/49
Austin, Elizabeth (Waldo) fl 1747
  Greenwood, J. Mrs Benjamin Austin
Austin, Warren Robinson, 1877-
  Finck, F. J. The Hon. Warren Robinson
    Austin, chief of the United States mis-
    sion to the United Nations
AUSTIN, Winnifred
  Mandarin duck
    NSP. Sportscapes
Autobiography by J. E. Levi
Autocrats by B. W. Tomlin
Automobiles
  Burchfield, C. E. Promenade
  Lee, D. E. Country wedding
  Moses, A. M. R. The old automobile
  Taylor, W. L. Electric automobile, Boston,
    1892
  Whorf, J. Winter, North end, Boston
Autumn by M. Hartley
Autumn by M. Hewes
Autumn by W. Homer
Autumn by W. Plate
Autumn convocation by W. Bailey

Autumn dance by K. L. Callahan
Autumn desert by A. Dasburg
Autumn festival by M. B. Prendergast
Autumn fruit by A. Dasburg
Autumn fruit by H. V. Poor
Autumn fruits by H. G. Keller
Autumn glory by K. Matthew
Autumn in New England, cider making by
    G. H. Durrie
Autumn in the Catskills by W. M. Hart
Autumn landscape by A. Blanch
Autumn landscape by E. Spruce
Autumn landscape by N. Takehita
Autumn leaves by K. Knaths
Autumn migration by C. A. Morris
Autumn no 3 by C. A. Morris
Autumn oaks by G. Inness
Autumn on the road to Deblois by J. Marin
Autumn outing by C. M. Williamson
Autumn piece, Maine by J. Marin
Autumn pleasures by C. C. Ross
Autumn—Ranchos de Taos by A. Dasburg
Autumn rain by D. Macknight
Autumn recollections by F. C. Watkins
Autumn rhythm by J. Pollock
Autumn scene by G. Inness
Autumn still life by W. M. Chase
Autumnal by A. M. Duca
Autumnal fantasy by C. E. Burchfield
Avalar by B. Hopkins
Ave by B. Shahn
Avegno, Judith. See Madame X
Avenue of martyrs by W. Pachner
Avenue of trees by M. Weber
AVERY, Milton, 1893-
  Advancing sea
    Breeskin. Milton Avery
  Bicycle rider by the Loire
    Breeskin. Milton Avery
  Birds over sea
    IU. Contemp Amer ptg & sculp, 1959
  Boats on Gaspé bay   GatM
    GatM. Holbrook collection
  Breaking sea   MdBM
    Breeskin. Milton Avery
  Brook bathers
    Breeskin. Milton Avery
  Brown hat
    Bazin
    Breeskin. Milton Avery
    Wight. Milton Avery (col)
  Bucolic landscape   NBuA
    CoS. New accessions USA, 1948
    NBuA. Contemporary ptgs
  Burlesque
    Breeskin. Milton Avery
  Cello player
    Breeskin. Milton Avery
  The circus
    Breeskin. Milton Avery
  Clear cut landscape   CSFM
    Breeskin. Milton Avery
    CoS. New accessions USA, 1956
    Time. 300 years (col)
  Conversation in studio
    Breeskin. Milton Avery

AVERY, Milton—*Continued*
Dark forest
  Breeskin. Milton Avery
Eilshemius
  Breeskin. Milton Avery
Flower vendor
  PPC. Ptg in the U.S. 1949
Gaspé landscape
  Pierson
  Wight. Milton Avery (col)
Gaspé-pink sky
  Breeskin. Milton Avery
  Wight. Milton Avery (col)
Harbor at night   DP
  DP. Catalogue
Interior with flowers   MdBM
  Wight. Milton Avery (col)
The letter
  Rathbun
March in brown
  Breeskin. Milton Avery
Morning sea
  Breeskin. Milton Avery
Mother and child (Cohen coll)
  Wight. Milton Avery (col)
Mother and child (Karlis coll)
  Beeskin. Milton Avery (col)
Music lesson
  Wight. Milton Avery (col)
Music maker
  Wight. Milestones (col)
My wife. See Woman with green face
Offshore island   NeL
  CoS. New accessions USA, 1960
Orange vase
  IU. Contemp Amer ptg, 1952
Ox on hillside   AP
  NUM. Art across America
Pink cock
  Breeskin. Milton Avery
Pink tablecloth   NUM
  Breeskin. Milton Avery
Poetry after breakfast
  Pousette-Dart. Amer ptg
Red sun
  Breeskin. Milton Avery
Reflections
  Breeskin. Milton Avery
Riders in the park
  Breeskin. Milton Avery
Rocky landscape
  IU. Contemp Amer ptg, 1950
Rooster's domain
  Breeskin. Milton Avery
Sand, sea and sky
  Breeskin. Milton Avery
Sea and dunes
  Breeskin. Milton Avery
Seascape
  WMAA. Museum and its friends, 1958
The Seine   WMAA
  Goodrich. Amer art
  WMAA. Contemp Amer ptg, 1953
Self-portrait
  Wight. Milton Avery (col)
Sheep
  Breeskin. Milton Avery
Spring in France
  IU. Contemp Amer ptg & sculp, 1955
Spring orchard
  IU. Contemp Amer ptg & sculp, 1961
Still life   PPhM
  CoS. New accessions USA, 1946

Still life with derby
  Wight. Milton Avery (col)
Sunset   NBM
  Breeskin. Milton Avery
Sunset on a quiet sea
  Breeskin. Milton Avery
Swimmers and sunbathers   MM
  Breeskin. Milton Avery
Tangerine moon and wine dark sea
  Breeskin. Milton Avery (col)
Three cows on hillside
  CSFP. Annual ex, 1947/48
Three friends
  MnMW. Contemporary
Trees   OYB
  OYB. Catalogue 1951
Two figures at dusk
  Pierson
  Wight. Milton Avery (col)
  WMAA. Neuberger collection (col)
Upper pasture
  Breeskin. Milton Avery
White moon
  Breeskin. Milton Avery
Woman with green face (My wife)
  Breeskin. Milton Avery
  Wight. Milton Avery (col)
Yellow jacket
  Breeskin. Milton Avery
Yellow meadow
  Breeskin. Milton Avery
  IU. Contemp Amer ptg & sculp, 1957
Yellow sky
  Breeskin. Milton Avery
AVERY, Ralph H. 1906-
Downtown fantasy
  NAD. Annual ex, 1959
The **aviary** by H. G. Keller
The **Avignon** Pieta no 2, Variation on by
  W. J. Pachner
Avocados by A. Dasburg
Avxentieff. See Pregel, Alexandra
Awakening by D. Newman
Awakening night by M. Tobey
Awalk poplars by A. G. Dove
Axtell, Margaret (De Peyster) 1728-1781
  Unidentified artist. Mrs William Axtell
    (possibly Mrs Abraham De Peyster
    jr)
  Wollaston, J. Mrs William Axtell?
Ayers, Harriet Hubbard, fl 1878
  Chase, W. M. Harriet Hubbard Ayers
Azalea tropical trails (Florida) by K.
  Matthew
Azilum, Site of by J. O. Montalant
Azoic fugue by B. Browne
The **Azores** by R. D. Gauley
Aztec III by J. Youngerman

B

b and p by J. Albers
Babbling brook by A. B. Durand
Babcock, Adam, 1740-1817
  Pelham, H. Adam Babcock
Babcock, Alice (Wyer) See Wyer, Alice

Babcock, Mrs Francis Adam. See Wyer, Alice
Babcock, Henry, 1784-1826?
  Malbone, E. G. Henry Babcock
Babcock, Martha Hubbard. See Higginson, Martha Hubbard (Babcock)
Babette by E. E. Speicher
Baby at play by T. Eakins
Baby in blue cradle by Unidentified artist
Baby in pink and white by Unidentified artist
Baby in red chair by Unidentified artist
Baby in wicker basket by J. W. Stock
Baby reclining by Unidentified artist
Baby with doll by S. J. Hambein (attributed works)
Baby with fruit by Unidentified artist
Baby's curse by A. Leslie
Bacchanalian revel by G. Hesselius
Bacchus and Ariadne by G. Hesselius
Bach by K. Knaths
Bach orchestra by M. Weber
BACHELDER, John B. fl 1865 and CHAPPEL, Alonzo, 1828-1887
  Death of Abraham Lincoln   RPB
  U.S. National Capital sesquicentennial com
Bachelor's drawer by J. Haberle
Bachelor's friend by W. M. Harnett (attributed works)
Back of a fisherman's shop by W. M. Chase
Back of Bear mountain by J. Marin
Back of beyond V by R. Ruben
Back porches by A. Janjigian
Backdrop of East Lynne by C. H. Demuth
Backrush by W. Homer
Backstage by W. Gropper
Backus, Eunice. See Trumbull, Eunice (Backus)
A backwater, Chalcot by J. S. Sargent
Backyard on Tenth street by W. De Kooning
Backyard, winter, Maine no 2 by W. A. Kienbusch
Backyards, Greenwich village by J. Sloan
Backyards in snow by C. E. Burchfield
Backyards in spring by C. E. Burchfield
Bacon, Asa, 1771-1857
  Dickinson, A. Asa Bacon
BACON, Henry, 1839-1912
  American boats in Venice harbor   MB
    MB. Ptgs in water color
  My camels resting   MB
    MB. Ptgs in water color
  Scene on the Nile   MB
    MB. Ptgs in water color
  Tomorrow we'll be sober   MB
    MB. Ptgs in water color
  Venice lacemakers   MB
    MB. Ptgs in water color
Bacon, Mrs John. See Goldthwait, Elizabeth
Bacon, Leonard, 1802-1881
  Weir, J. F. The Theological of Yale university
Bacon, Letitia Wilson Jordan, fl 1888
  Eakins, T. Letitia Wilson Jordan Bacon

BACON, Peggy, 1895-
  Blessed damosel   WMAA
  Brown. Amer ptg
  Nobody's pet
    NYG. Fine art
  Nosegay
    NYG. Fine art
  Untilled field   WMAA
    Pierson
  Wanderlust   ATU
    ATU. Coll of Amer art

Portrait of the artist

Brook, A. Peggy Bacon and Metaphysics
Badger, James, 1757-1817
  Badger, J. James Badger
BADGER, Joseph, 1708-1765
  Cornelius Waldo   MWM
    Baker. Amer ptg
    Belknap
    NNHS. Waldron Phoenix Belknap coll
  Daniel Rea   OYB
    OYB. Catalogue 1951
  Elizabeth Greenleaf   VWR
    Kallir. Amer primitive ptgs
    VWR. Folk art (col)
  Hannah Upham Haskins   NBM
    Pierson
  James Badger   MM
    Flexner. First flowers
    Pierson
  James Bowdoin   MiD
    Belknap
    MiD. Ports of the Pitts family
  Jeremiah Belknap   OCl
    Larkin
    Larkin rev ed
  John Larrabee   MWM
    Pierson
  John Pitts (after Smibert)   MiD
    MiD. Ports of the Pitts family
  Jonathan Edwards sr   CtY
    CtY. Portrait index
    Flexner. Copley
    U.S. National Capital sesquicentennial com
  Mrs Cassius Hunt   NNHS
    Belknap
  Mrs Cornelius Waldo   MWM
    Belknap
  Mrs Isaac Foster   DN
    DN. Amer primitive ptgs, pt 2
  Mrs John Edwards   MB
    Flexner. First flowers
    Pierson
    Richardson. Ptg in America
  Still life   MeC
    NUM. Art across America
  Thomas Cushing   MSE
    Belknap
  Two children   VWR
    NUM. Art across America

Attributed works

A man, Portrait of   DN
  Belknap
Badgers
  La Farge, J. Uncanny badger
BAER, Howard
  Cribbage players
    PPC. Ptg in the U.S. 1949
  Fortune hunters
    DC. 21 biennial ex, 1947
Bagnell dam on the Osage river by F. Martin

Bagshot heath, Surrey by B. West (attributed works)
The Bahamas
   Hart, G. O. The Bahamas
   Homer, W. Glass windows, Bahamas
Baigneuse by A. Katz
Les baigneuses by D. Park
Bailey, Benjamin, d 1832
   Jarvis, J. W. Benjamin Bailey
Bailey, Mrs Francis
   Peale, C. W. Mrs Francis Bailey
BAILEY, Vernon Howe, 1874-
   Metropolis
     NYG. Fine art
BAILEY, William. 1930-
   Autumn convocation
     MBIC. View 1960
   Figures in landscape
     IU. Contemp Amer ptg & sculp, 1961
Bailey's beach by C. Hassam
Bailleul: tents by J. S. Sargent
Bainbridge, William, 1774-1833
   Jarvis, J. W. Commodore William Bainbridge
BAKER, George Augustus, 1821-1880

Attributed works

Augustus Van Horne Stuyvesant, sr
                              NNHS
   Vail. Stuyvesant ports
   Mrs A. V. H. Stuyvesant   NNHS
   Vail. Stuyvesant ports
Baker, Jim, fl 1850
   Love, W. Jim Baker, a dressed-up portrait wearing a costume made by a Sioux squaw
BAKER, Roger
   Three fishermen
     NAD. Annual ex, 1960
Baking day by W. R. Leigh
Le bal Bullier by A. H. Maurer
Bal Martinique by W. J. Glackens
Bal Tabarin by E. Shinn
Balancing rock, Gloucester harbor by J. Sloan
Balcony I by K. L. Seligmann
Balcony view by L. M. Eilshemius
Bald boy by W. Sommer
Baldwin, Lucy. See Durand, Lucy (Baldwin)
BALDWIN, William, fl 1844
   Merry raftsmen
   Rathbone
Bali bazaar by M. Sterne
Baling cotton by B. Shahn
BALIS, C. fl 1850
   George and Emma Eastman   MoKN
   Jones. Rediscovered ptrs
Ball, Miss
   Jarvis, J. W. Miss Ball
Ball, Eleanor, 1731-1770
   Theus, J. Eleanor Ball
Ball, Elias, c 1675-1751
   Theus, J. Elias Ball
Ball-play of the Choctaws by G. Catlin
Ballerina and the black cat by B. Lintot
Ballet dancer by E. Shinn
Ballet girl in pink by W. J. Glackens

BALLIN, Hugo, 1879-1956
   Journey's end
     NAD. Annual ex, autumn 1949
   Reflections
     NAD. Annual ex, 1947, 2d half
   Sister Rebecca Cleaden
     NAD. Annual ex, 1949, 1st half
The balloon by M. B. Prendergast
Balloon ascension at Baltimore, 1834 by N. V. Calyo
Balsam apple and vegetable by J. Peale
Balsam apples and turnips by Raphaelle Peale
Baltic—a recollection by L. Feininger
Baltimore, Maryland
   Calyo, N. V. Balloon ascension at Baltimore, 1834
   Calyo, N. V. Baltimore in 1837
   Doughty, T. Baltimore from Beech hill, View of
   Doughty, T. Baltimore from the seat of R. Gilmor
   Guy, F. Baltimore in 1802
   Guy, F. Baltimore, 1803
   Latrobe, B. H. Roman Catholic church, Baltimore, c 1805
   Maril, H. Baltimore waterfront
   Smith, R. Old Holliday street theatre, Baltimore
   Unidentified artist. View of Baltimore, c 1840
Bamboo by W. T. Murch
Banana plant and squash by H. L. McFee
Bananas by H. Giese
Bananas and blue grapes by K. Knaths
Bananas for the attorney general by W. Homer
Bancker, Anna (Boelen) 1733-1790
   Durand, J. Mrs Adriaan Bancker
Bancker, Richard, 1728-1775
   Durand, J. Richard Bancker
Bancker, Sarah (Duyckinck) b 1732
   Durand, J. Mrs Richard Bancker
Band, Hilde. See Kayn, Hilde (Band)
Banjo lesson by H. O. Tanner
Banjo player by W. S. Mount
BANKS, Virginia, 1920-
   Basket of line and bait
     PPC. Ptg in the U.S. 1949
Banks fisherman by W. Homer
Bannister, Christian (Stelle) fl 1774
   Stuart, G. Mrs John Bannister and her son
Bannock Indian by A. J. Miller
The banquet by J. Levine
Banyar, Elizabeth (Naden) c 1739-1808
   Blackburn, J. Mrs Goldsbrow Banyar
Banyar, Goldsbrow, 1724-1815
   Ames, E. Goldsbrow Banyar
   Dickinson, A. Goldsbrow Banyar, 1808
   Trumbull, J. Goldsbrow Banyar
Banyar, Mrs Goldsbrow. See Banyar, Elizabeth (Naden)
Baptisam of our Savour by A. Johnson
Baptising at Three Wells by P. Hurd
Baptism in Kansas by J. S. Curry
Baptismal scene by M. Rothko
Bar by G. P. Du Bois
Bar and grill by M. Roberts

Bar Italia by P. Cadmus
Barber shops
Davis, S. Barber shop
Hicks, T. Barber shop, the musicale
Sample, P. S. Barber shop
BARBIER, D.

Attributed works
Chouteau's pond, St Louis   MoSLH
Born (here as Unidentified artist)
Ford. Pictorial folk art
Barbizon nymph by R. H. Colescott
Barbour, William Macleod, 1827-1899
Weir, J. F. The Theological of Yale university
Barcelona market II by Martyl
Barclay children by Unidentified artist
Bard, Isabella MacDonald (MacNichol) c 1785- c 1875
Stuart, G. Mrs James Bard
BARD, James, 1815-1897
Hudson river steamboat Daniel Drew
Lipman. Primitive ptrs
Hudson river steamboat Rip Van Winkle   MB
MB. Karolik coll
Pierson
Richardson. Ptg in America
Paddle steamship Addison E. Andrews   MeC
Jetté. Amer heritage collection
The Robert L. Stevens breaking ice in the Hudson river
Lipman. Primitive ptrs
Tugboat O. M. Pettit   NNHS
Lipman. Primitive ptrs
Bard, Mrs James. See Bard, Isabella MacDonald (MacNichol)
Bare knuckles by G. A. Hayes
Bareback rider, Paris by M. B. Prendergast
Bareback riders by W. H. Brown
Barfüsserkirche in Erfurt by L. Feininger
Bargain hunters by K. H. Miller
Bargaining for a horse by W. S. Mount
BARKER, Walter
Calle Paradiso   MCH
Pulitzer v2
Stormy sky, Venice   MB
CoS. New accessions USA, 1960
View in Forest park   MCH
Pulitzer v2
The **barker** by R. Vickrey
Barker's booth by H. Koerner
Barksdale, Thomas, 1780-1850
Malbone, E. G. Thomas Barksdale
Barn by C. E. Burchfield
Barn Bluff, Red Wing, Minnesota by Unidentified artist
Barn by the pool by W. S. Mount
Barn chair by A. Brook
Barn interior by K. Knaths
Barn reds by C. Sheeler
Barn variation by C. Sheeler
BARNARD, S. fl 1831
Charleston, South Carolina   CtY
Davidson v 1
Barnes, Abraham, fl 1753
Wollaston, J. Col Abraham Barnes

Barnes, Mrs Albert C.
Glackens, W. J. Mrs Barnes and Grover
BARNES, Charles, 1915-
Abstract composition   CtY
CtY. Soc Anonyme
Barnes, Mrs Jabez. See Barnes, Martha (Atkins)
BARNES, Lucius, fl 1834
Martha Atkins Barnes   VWR
VWR. Folk art (col)
Barnes, Martha (Atkins) 1739-1834
Barnes, L. Mrs Martha Atkins Barnes
BARNES, Matthew Rackham, 1880-1951
The appointment   CSFM
CoS. New accessions USA, 1952
High peak   MMA
Baur. Revolution
BARNES, Robert
James Joyce
ICA. Annual ex, 1961
BARNET, Will, 1911-
Creation
WMAA. Annual ex, 1957
Multiple images I
DC. 27 biennial ex, 1961
Old man's afternoon
MoSL. Contemporary Amer ptg
BARNETT, Herbert Phillip, 1910-
County fair   ATU
ATU. Coll of Amer art
Gray ruin and stone house   OCiM
CoS. New accessions USA, 1956
Lime quarry
DC. 20 biennial ex, 1947
BARNETT, Rita Wolpé
To the earth
PA. Annual ex, 1951
Barns. See Farmyards and farm buildings
Barnstable, View of by Unidentified artist
Barnwell, Mary H. See Means, Mary H. (Barnwell)
Barnyards. See Farmyards and farm buildings
Barometer falling by H. M. Mayer
Baron, Alexander, b 1777
Malbone, E. G. Dr Alexander Baron jr
Baron, Isabelle. See Barron, Isabel
Baroque landscape by T. Chambers (attributed works)
Barracks by H. Pippin
Barrell, Joseph, fl 1765
Copley, J. S. Joseph Barrell
Barrels of money by V. Dubreuil
BARRETT, Neil, 1915-
Chicago image
IU. Contemp Amer ptg & sculp, 1961
Compression
ICA. Annual ex, 1959/60
Conquered king
IU. Contemp Amer ptg & sculp, 1959
Barrett, Mrs Roger. See Barrett, Neil
The **barrier** by F. Martin
Barriers by C. Plochmann
Barron, Isabel, fl 1801
Malbone, E. G. Isabel Barron
Barrooms
Clonney, J. G. Politicians in a country bar
Knaths, K. Barroom
Sloan, J. McSorley's back room
Sloan, J. McSorley's bar
Sloan, J. McSorley's cats

BARTLETT, Gray, 1885-1951
Bart's place
Carlson. Gallery (col)
Hidden spring
Carlson. Gallery (col)
Indian camp
Carlson. Gallery (col)
Indian police
Carlson. Gallery (col)
Night herd
Carlson. Gallery (col)
Ox train
Carlson. Gallery (col)
Saddled for the first time
Carlson. Gallery (col)
BARTLETT, John Russell, fl 1850

Attributed works

Crossing the quicksand
Davidson v 1
Bartlett, Lydia. See Reynolds, Lydia (Bartlett)
Bartlett, Paul Wayland, 1865-1929
Hamilton, J. M. Paul Wayland Bartlett in his Paris studio
BARTLETT, William Henry, 1809-1894
Faneuil hall from the water
Sears. Highlights
Mt Vernon   MdBM
NYG. Fine art
Washington's tomb, Mt Vernon   MdBM
NYG. Fine art
Bartol, Barnabas, fl 1826
Cole, J. G. Capt Barnabas Bartol
BARTOLL, William Thompson, 1817-1859
Girl and cat   VWR
VWR. Folk art (col)
Barton, Samuel, 1767-1795
Gullager, C. Samuel Barton
Bart's place by G. Bartlett
BASCOM, Ruth (Henshaw) Miles, 1772-1848
Edwin Davis   MSt
Little. Country art
Eliza Jane Gay   NCHA
Jones. New-found folk art
Horatio Gates Henshaw of Leicester, Massachusetts   NCHA
Jones. New-found folk art
John White
Lipman. Primitive ptrs
Lady in a sheer white cap (possibly Mrs H. G. Henshaw)   NCHA
Jones. New-found folk art
Mr and Mrs Otis Jones of Athol, Mass.
Lipman. Primitive ptrs
Mrs H. G. Henshaw (?) See Lady in a sheer white cap
Profile of a boy   VWR
VWR. Folk art (col)
Profile of baby in orange   NCHA
Jones. New-found folk art
Self-portrait
Ford. Pictorial folk art
Lipman. Primitive ptrs
Baseball. See Games and sports—Baseball
Basement room by C. Sheeler
Bash-Bish falls, South Egremont, Massachusetts by J. F. Kensett
Basic by G. Cox
Basket bouquet by K. Knaths

Basket of clams by W. Homer
Basket of fruit by M. Bradley
Basket of fruit by Rubens Peale
Basket of fruit with parrot by A. M. Randall
Basket of line and bait by V. Banks
Basque fishing boats, Pasajes-Ancho by M. J. Patterson
Bass
Homer, W. Bass
Homer, W. Life-size black bass
Bass boats by M. Logan
Bass Rocks by S. Davis
BASSFORD, Wallace, 1900-
Gull a'winging
IU. Contemp Amer ptg, 1950
Motif de fête
IU. Contemp Amer ptg, 1951
Bastille day by M. B. Prendergast
Bateman, Margaret Creighton
Chase, W. M. Mrs Margaret Creighton Bateman
Bates, Isaac
Harding, C. Isaac Bates
Bath, Maine
Unidentified artist. Burning of Old South church, Bath, Maine
The **bath** by M. Cassatt
The **bath** by H. Katzman
Bather by E. N. Bischoff
Bather by I. Bishop
Bather by R. Haines
Bather by N. J. Oliveira
Bather by R. Reid
Bathers by C. Browning
Bathers by J. Charlot
Bathers by E. Cortor
Bathers by C. H. Demuth
Bathers by L. Feininger
Bathers by W. M. Hunt
Bathers by B. Karfiol
Bathers by J. McGarrell
Bathers by M. B. Prendergast
Bathers by P. Tchelitchew
Bathers by A. Toney
Bathers by M. Weber
Bathers in a grotto by A. Ozenfant
Bathers on rocks by J. Marin
Bathers, the cove, La Jolla by H. G. Keller
Bathers: eight foreground figures by Walkowitz
Bathers: four foreground figures by A. Walkowitz
Bathers: three foreground figures by A. Walkowitz
Bathing at Bellport by W. J. Glackens
Bathing, Marblehead by M. B. Prendergast
Bathing party in New York by W. P. Chappel
Bathing pool by C. Codman
Battell, Joseph, 1806-1874
Hovenden, T. Joseph Battell
Battell, Mrs Philip, fl 1831
Mason, B. F. Mrs Philip Battell
Battersea Reach by J. A. M. Whistler

Battery Bee by C. W. Chapman

Battery belles by R. Marsh

Battery park, New York, in winter by G. W.
  Bellows

Battle at sunset with the God of the maize
  by A. Gorky

Battle front by J. S. Sargent

Battle of lights, Coney island by J. Stella

Battle of the elks by C. M. Russell

Battle of the gods by K. L. Callahan

BAUM, Don, 1922-
  Portrait
    ICA. Annual ex, 1957

BAUM, Walter Emerson, 1884-1956
  Winter's end   OT
    OT. Contemp Amer ptgs

BAUMAN, Leila T. fl 1850
  Geese in flight   DN
    DN. Amer primitive ptgs, pt 2
  U.S. mail boat   DN
    DN. Amer primitive ptgs, pt 2

BAUMBACH, Harold, 1903-
  At the table
    IU. Contemp Amer ptg, 1952
  New England landscape   ATU
    ATU. Coll of Amer art

BAUMGARDEN, George
  Telephone habit
    Davidson v2

BAUMGARTNER, Warren W. 1894-
  Cascade waters
    NAD. Annual ex, 1960
  La push
    NAD. Annual ex, 1955
  Stonehenge
    NAD. Annual ex, 1949, 2d half

The bay by W. Farndon

The bay beyond by A. Brook

Bay bottom by L. Bunce

Bay mare and colt and a couple of others by
  C. S. Price

Bay of Panama by M. J. Heade

Bayard, Anna Maria. See Jay, Anna Maria
  (Bayard)

Bayard, Mary (Beekman) See Beekman,
  Mary

Bayard, Mrs Stephen N. See Beekman, Mary

Bayard, Pierre du Terrail, seigneur de, 1474?-
  1524
  West, B. Death of the Chevalier Bayard

BAYER, Herbert, 1900-
  Atmospheric conditions
    Rathbun
  Linear structure
    CoS. New accessions USA, 1960
  Verdure   MNS
    CoS. New accessions USA, 1952

BAYNE, Walter M. S. fl 1853
  Landscape (painted in style of Doughty)
    Sears. Highlights

Bazaar with coconut palms, Bali by M.
  Sterne

BAZIOTES, William A. 1912-
  Amazon
    OCl. Some contemporary works
  The beach   WMAA
    Baur. Nature
    Cheney. Story 1958 ed
    Goodrich. Amer art

Black night   PPC
  CoS. New accessions USA, 1956
  IU. Contemp Amer ptg & sculp, 1955

Black on white   NUM
  NUM. Root bequest

Black silhouette
  CSFP. Annual ex, 1950/51

Blue mirror
  McCurdy
  MMA. Abstract (col)

Cat
  MMA. Fifteen

Congo
  ICA. Annual ex, 1954

Desert landscape
  IU. Contemp Amer ptg & sculp, 1953

Dragon   MM
  Baur. New art
  Brussels. Exposition
  MM. 100 Amer ptrs
  Taylor. Fifty centuries, 1954 ed (col)

Dusk   NNSG
  NNSG. Handbook

Dusk   PPC
  Read. Concise history

The dwarf   MMA
  Baur. New art
  Baur. Revolution
  MMA. Contemp ptrs
  MMA. New Amer ptg (col)
  Pierson

Egyptian
  MnU. 40 Amer ptrs

Flame   NNSG
  Chew. 250 years of art
  Mendelowitz
  IU. Contemp Amer ptg & sculp, 1957
  NNSG. Younger Amer ptrs

Flesh eaters
  PPC. International ex, 1952

The fountain
  Hess. Abstract ptg

Green night
  MnMW. 60 Amer ptrs

Jungle
  Baur. New art (col)
  MMA. Fifteen
  Pousette-Dart. Amer ptg

Moby Dick
  WMAA. Contemp Amer ptg, 1955
  WMAA. Museum and its friends, 1958

Moon animal   IU
  IU. Contemp Amer ptg, 1951
  IU. 20th century
  OCl. Some contemporary works

Moon fantasy
  WMAA. New decade

Moon forms
  Baur. New art
  CSFP. Annual ex, 1948/49
  WMAA. New decade

Mummy
  Hess. Abstract ptg

Night mirror
  MMA. Fifteen

Pompeii   MMA
  Art since 1945
  MMA. New Amer ptg
  Pierson
  Time. 300 years (col)

Primeval landscape   PPhM
  MMA. New Amer ptg
  WMAA. Contemp Amer ptg, 1953

BAZIOTES, W. A.—*Continued*
Red landscape   MnMI
  Hunter. Mod Amer ptg
The sea
  Ponente. Mod ptg, 1960 (col)
  WMAA. Contemp Amer ptg, 1959/60
Sleepwalker
  Blesh
  IU. Contemp Amer ptg, 1950
Still life, 1945
  MnU. 40 Amer ptrs
Toy in the sun   CLA
  CoS. New accessions USA, 1952
Toy world
  MMA. Fifteen
Trance
  MnMW. Reality and fantasy
  WMAA. New decade
White bird   NBuA
  NBuA. Acquisitions 1957-58
  WMAA. Annual ex, 1957

The **beach** by W. A. Baziotes

The **beach** by R. Frame

The **beach** by H. Koerner

The **beach** by W. Pachner

The **beach** by E. F. Spruce

Beach at Annisquam by W. J. Glackens

Beach at Dieppe by W. J. Glackens

Beach at Gloucester by M. B. Prendergast

Beach at Miramar by C. G. Farr

Beach at St Ives, Cornwall, England by H. Lever

Beach at St Jean de Luz by W. J. Glackens

Beach at Sestri Levante, Italy by E. D. Boit

Beach grass by H. Durfee

Beach hat by R. Henri

Beach patterns by H. G. Keller

Beach patterns by C. A. Morris

Beach scene near New London by W. J. Glackens

Beach scene with a newspaper by H. Sterner

Beach scene with figures by M. B. Prendergast

Beach with blue tree by M. B. Prendergast

Beachcomber by J. E. Levi

Beachmont by M. B. Prendergast

Beacon-on-the-Hudson by Unidentified artist

BEAL, Gifford Reynolds, 1879-1956
Afterglow   ATeS
  ATeS. Collection
The Albany boat   MM
  MM. 100 Amer ptrs
  Pierson
Circus at the Hippodrome
  McCurdy
Circus parade
  NAD. Annual ex, 1956
Circus ponies   DP
  DP. Catalogue
Columbus avenue, snowy day
  NAD. Annual ex, 1947, 2d half
Dock square
  NAD. Annual ex, 1951
Dublin pool
  NAD. Annual ex, 1948
Freight yards   NSyE
  Brown. Amer ptg

Hunter, winter
  NSP. Sportscapes
Impression from Life with father   DP
  DP. Catalogue
Sunday morning
  CSB. Impressionism
Terrace, Central park
  Gruskin

The **bear** dance by G. Catlin

BEARD, James Henry, 1814-1893
Land speculator
  U.S. National Capital sesquicentennial com
The long bill   OCiM
  Barker. Amer ptg
  U.S. National Capital sesquicentennial com

BEARDEN, Romare, 1912-
Christ driving the money changers from the Temple
  Rathbun

Bearers of gifts by K. M. Martin

Bears
  Miller, A. J. Grizzly bear
  Miller, A. J. Hunting the bear
  Russell, C. M. Capturing the grizzly
  Russell, C. M. A disputed trail
  Russell, C. M. Roping a grizzly

Bear's Paw by J. M. Stanley

The **beast** by W. Millarc

Beast enchanted by D. Austin

The **beast** in the jungle, Illustrations for by C. H. Demuth

Beating a retreat by A. J. Miller

Beatrice by W. Allston

Beatrice standing by W. J. Glackens

BEATTIE, George
Pisa   OCl
  Pousette-Dart. Amer ptg

BEAUCHAMP, John W. 1906-
Painting   WMAA
  Pousette-Dart. Amer ptg

BEAUCHAMP, Robert, 1923-
Two sisters
  PPC. International ex, 1961/62

BEAUGUREAU, Francis H.
Seoul, 1952
  NAD. Annual ex, 1959

Beaulieu by M. Beckmann

Beauregard, Pierre Gustave Toutant, 1818-1893
  Healy, G. P. A. General P. G. T. Beauregard

Beautification by M. Weber

Beautiful beast by D. Austin

The **beauty** by G. P. Du Bois

Beauty is where you find it by A. A. Dehn

Beauty parlor by C. M. Russell

BEAUX, Cecilia, 1863-1942
The dreamer   OYB
  OYB. Catalogue 1951
  Fanny Travis Cochran. See A little girl— Fanny Travis Cochran
A little girl—Fanny Travis Cochran   PA
  Chew. 250 years of art
Man in white (Dr Henry S. Drinker) DN
  Pierson

Les **beaux** by L. MacIver

Beaver lake, Lost river region by M. Hartley
Beaver Meadow by P. S. Sample
BECK, Leonard
  Mahu
    IU. Contemp Amer ptg, 1948
  Memory
    IU. Contemp Amer ptg, 1948
BECK, Margit, 1915-
  Rockport harbor
    NAD. Annual ex, 1955
  Rocks and pines
    ICA. Annual ex, 1961
BECK, Rosemarie, 1923-
  House of the moon, II, 1956
    Baur. Nature
  Number 2, 1955
    WMAA. Young America 1957
  Number 3, 1954   WMAA
    Pierson
    WMAA. Young America 1957
Becker, Mrs Alfred L.
  Hawthorne, C. W. Mrs Alfred L. Becker
BECKER, Joseph, 1841-1910
  First train on the Central Pacific railroad,
    1869
    U.S. National Capital sesquicentennial
    com
BECKETT, Charles E. 1814-1866?
  Furbish's dash to Montreal   NCHA
    Jones. New-found folk art
Beckett, Marianne, fl 1829
  Peale, A. C. Marianne Beckett
BECKMANN, Max, 1884-1950
  Acrobat on trapeze
    MoSL. Beckmann
  Acrobats
    MMA. Contemp ptrs
  Actors
    MoSL. Beckmann
    Pearson. Mod renaissance
  Artist's mother
    MoSL. Beckmann
  At the beach
    Cheney. Expressionism 1948 ed
  Beaulieu
    IU. Contemp Amer ptg, 1950 (col)
  Begin the beguine   MiA
    MoSL. Beckmann
  Black lilies
    UNESCO. 1860-1955
  Blindman's buff
    MoSL. Beckmann
  The boat
    PA. Annual ex, 1951
  Boat on the Riviera
    MoSL. Beckmann
  Cabana
    MoSL. Beckmann
  Café
    MoSL. Beckmann
  Cattle in barn
    MoSL. Beckmann
  Christ and the woman taken in adultery
    MoSL. Beckmann
  Christ in Limbo
    MoSL. Beckmann
  Circus caravan
    Read. Concise history (col)
  Dancer with tambourine
    MoSL. Beckmann

Departure   MMA
  Barr. What is mod ptg
  Canaday
  50 years of mod art
  Janson. Key monuments
  Janson. Picture history (col)
  McCurdy
  MMA. Ptg and sculpture
  MoSL. Beckmann
  Myers. Art
  Newmeyer
  Robb. Harper history
Descent from the cross   MMA
  McCurdy
Double portrait
  MoSL. Beckmann
The dream
  Janson. Key monuments
  MoSL. Beckmann
Eternity
  MoSL. Beckmann
Euretta
  MoSL. Beckmann
Family picture   MMA
  MoSL. Beckmann
Fisherwomen
  MnMW. Expressionism 1900-1955
  PPC. Ptg in the U.S. 1949
  Time. 300 years (col)
Four men around a table   MoSLW
  McCurdy
  MMA. Contemp ptrs
  MoSL. Beckmann
Galleria Umberto
  MoSL. Beckmann
Genius
  MoSL. Beckmann
Girl with parrot
  MoSL. Beckmann
Hotel lobby   NBuA
  CoS. New accessions USA, 1950
  NBuA. Expressionism
  PPC. International ex, 1950
Ice floes
  Cheney. Expressionism 1948 ed
The king
  MoSL. Beckmann
Laboratory
  CSFP. Annual ex, 1948/49
Landscape with factory
  MoSL. Beckmann
Louise Pulitzer   MCH
  Pulitzer v2
Man and woman
  MoSL. Beckmann
Man with fish
  Read. Concise history
Masquerade   MCH
  Pulitzer v2
The mill
  MoSL. Beckmann
Mirror
  MoSL. Beckmann
The night
  Myers
Nude
  Read. Art now, 1948 ed
Pau de St Jannes
  MoSL. Beckmann
Portrait of the artist with a saxophone
  50 years of mod art
The prodigal son among swine   MMA
  MoSL. Beckmann

BECKMANN, Max—*Continued*
  Quappi in turban
    MoSL. Beckmann
  The rainbow
    UNESCO. 1860-1955
  Reclining woman with mandolin
    Moderns and their world (col)
  Removal of the Sphinxes
    MoSL. Beckmann
  Robbery of Europe
    Moderns and their world
  Self-portrait, 1912
    MoSL. Beckmann
  Self-portrait, 1950
    Pearson. Mod renaissance
  Self-portrait with a cigarette, 1923 MMA
    McCurdy
    MoSL. Beckmann
  The shore
    UNESCO. 1860-1955
  Skaters
    MoSL. Beckmann
  Soldier's dream
    MoSL. Beckmann
  Souvenir of Chicago   MCH
    Pulizter v 1
  Still life with fish and pinwheel
    MoSL. Beckmann
  Still life with flowers
    MoSL. Beckmann
  The street
    MoSL. Beckmann
    Pearson. Mod renaissance
  Studio corner
    CSFP. Annual ex, 1950/51
    MoSL. Beckmann
  Summer day
    UNESCO. 1860-1955
  Tightrope dancer
    IU. Contemp Amer ptg, 1949
  Tulips
    UNESCO. 1860-1955
  Two women
    50 years of mod art (col)
  Young men by the sea, 1905
    MoSL. Beckmann
  Young men by the sea, 1943   MoSL
    MoSL. Beckmann
    MoSL. Handbook 1953
  Zeretelli   MCH
    MoSL. Beckmann
    Pulitzer v 1
BECKWITH, James Carroll, 1852-1917
  Henry Parks Wright   CtY
    CtY. Portrait index
  William H. Brewer   CtY
    CtY. Portrait index
Becky Sharp by T. P. Anshutz
Bedrooms
  Benson, F. W. Fisherman's bedroom, Eastham, Massachusetts
  De Martini, J. Interior with three figures
  Pittman, H. Nine P. M.
Bee hunter by A. J. Miller
Bee keeper by E. F. Spruce
The **beech** by L. Gatch
Beecher, Lyman, 1775-1863
  Harding, C. Lyman Beecher
BEECHER, William Ward
  Collector's cabinet
    CSFP. Annual ex, 1952

Beeches by A. B. Durand
Beechwood boulevard, Pittsburgh by J. Kane
Beekman, Catharina (De Boogh) fl 1720
  Unidentified artist. Lady of the Beekman family (Mrs William Beekman?)
Beekman, Catherine, 1762-1839
  Durand, J. Catherine Beekman
Beekman, Catherine Peters (De Lanoy) 1691-1765
  Duyckinck, E. (attributed works) Mrs William Beekman
Beekman, Cornelia, 1708-1786
  Duyckinck, E. Cornelia Beekman
Beekman, Gerardus, 1684-1770
  Duyckinck, G. (attributed works) Col Gerardus Beekman
Beekman, Henry
  Unidentified artist. Henry Beekman
Beekman, James, fl 1761
  Kilburn, L. James Beekman
Beekman, Mrs James. See Beekman, Jane (Keteltas)
Beekman, Jane (Keteltas)
  Kilburn, L. Mrs James Beekman
Beekman, Magdalen
  Unidentified artist. Magdalen Beekman
Beekman, Mary, 1765-1831
  Durand, J. Mary Beekman
Beekman, William, 1623-1707
  Unidentified artist. Gentleman of the Beekman family (William Beekman?)
Beekman, William, 1653-1728
  Duyckinck, G. (attributed works) Dr William Beekman
Beekman, William, 1684-1770
  Duyckinck, E. (attributed works) Dr William Beekman
Beekman, Mrs William, 1691-1765. See Beekman, Catherine Peters (De Lanoy)
Beekman, Mrs William, fl 1720. See Beekman, Catharina (De Boogh)
Beers, Sally. See Leffingwell, Sally (Beers)
Beers, Timothy Phelps, 1789-1858
  Jocelyn, N. Timothy Phelps Beers
Beetle with red markings by C. Culver
Before the white man came by C. M. Russell
The **beggars'** dance of Teton Sioux by G. Catlin
Beggar's joys by P. Guston
Begin the beguine by M. Beckmann
Beginning by A. Osver
Beginning of a snowstorm by C. E. Burchfield
Begonias by E. E. Speicher
Behold by L. P. Smith
Behold . . . man by U. Romano
Belated wayfarers by G. C. Bingham
Belcher, Abigail (Adams) 1727-1771
  Copley, J. S. Mrs Jonathan Belcher
Belcher, Jonathan, 1710-1776
  Copley, J. S. Jonathan Belcher jr
Belfield by Rubens Peale (original by C. W. Peale)
Belgian melon by W. M. Chase
Belinda standing by A. Brook
Belisarius and the boy by B. West
Belknap, Aaron, 1789-1847
  Durand, A. B. Aaron Belknap

Belknap, Aaron Betts, 1816-1880
  Durand, A. B. Aaron Betts Belknap
Belknap, Jeremiah, b 1752
  Badger, J. Jeremiah Belknap
Belknap, Mary Josepha Lydia Stearns (Bel-
    knap) 1771-1862
  Durand, A. B. Mrs Aaron Belknap
BELKNAP, Zebakiah, 1781-1858
  Mrs Thomas Belknap   VWR
    VWR. Folk art (col)
  Thomas Harrison   VWR
    VWR. Folk art (col)
Bella Venezia by E. Berman
The Belle Creole at New Orleans by Un-
    identified artist
Belles of the Battery by R. Marsh
BELLOWS, Albert Fitch, 1829-1883
  Wayside inn   MB
    MB. Ptgs in water color
Bellows, Anna (Smith)
  Bellows, G. W. My mother
Bellows, Anne
  Bellows, G. W. Anne in purple wrap
  Bellows, G. W. Anne in white
Bellows, Emma Louise Story
  For portraits of Mrs Bellows see entries
    under Bellows, G. W. beginning with
    titles "Emma"
Bellows, George, fl 1906
  Bellows, G. W. My father
Bellows, Mrs George. See Bellows, Anna
    (Smith)
BELLOWS, George Wesley, 1882-1925
  Ann   ATeS
    ATeS. Collection
  Anne in black   MAC
    NUM. Art across America
  Anne in purple wrap   MAP
    DN. Bellows
  Anne in white   PPC
    DN. Bellows
  Aunt Fanny   IaDM
    Baur. Revolution
    DN. Bellows
    Time. 300 years (col)
  Battery park, New York, in winter. See
    Blue snow, the Battery
  Beach at Coney island
    DN. Bellows
  Big dory   CtNB
    DN. Bellows
  Blue morning
    DN. Bellows
  Blue snow, the Battery (Battery park, New
    York)
    DN. Bellows
    OCo. George Bellows
  Both members of this club   DN
    Baur. New art (col)
    Baur. Revolution
    DN. Bellows
    McCurdy
    NYG. Fine art
    Pierson
    Seiberling
    UNESCO. 1860-1949
    UNESCO. 1860-1955
    Walker. Ptgs from America
  A boy   InIJ
    InIJ. 105 ptgs

Chester Dale   DN
  DN. Bellows
Children on the porch (On the porch)
                                            OCo
  DN. Bellows
  Time. 300 years (col)
The circus   MAP
  DN. Bellows
  Lee. Art then and now
  OCo. George Bellows
Cliff dwellers   CLA
  CLA. 35 ptgs
  Craven. Treasury 1952 ed
  DN. Bellows
  Pierson
Club night
  DN. Bellows
  WMAA. Museum and its friends, 1958
Cornfield and harvest   OCo
  DN. Bellows
Crowd, polo game. See Polo scene
Crucifixion   ICA
  Brown. Amer ptg
  Cheney. Expressionism 1948 ed
Dawn of peace   OCiM
  Brown. Amer ptg
Day in June   MiD
  DN. Bellows
  MiD. Treasures
Dempsey and Firpo   WMAA
  DN. Bellows
  Goodrich. Amer art
  Larkin
  Larkin rev ed
  Mendelowitz
  NYG. Fine art
  OCo. George Bellows
  Roos
  Upjohn
Edith Cavell   MSM
  DN. Bellows
  MSM. Handbook
  OCo. George Bellows
Elinor, Jean and Anna   NBuA
  Baur. New art
  Canaday
  DN. Bellows
  Lewisohn
  NAD. Amer tradition
  NBuA. Catalogue of the ptgs
  Pierson
  Roos
Emma and her children   MB
  DC. 25 biennial ex, 1957
Emma in black (Emma at a window) DP
  DN. Bellows
  DP. Catalogue
Emma in purple dress   TxD
  DN. Bellows
Fisherman
  DN. Bellows
Fisherman's family
  DN. Bellows
Fishermen's huts
  DN. Bellows
Floating ice   WMAA
  DN. Bellows
  Goodrich. Amer art (col)
Fog breakers-sea spume   GAtM
  GAtM. Holbrook collection

BELTON, Francis S. fl 1817-34
  Rochester, New York, c1820
    WiMiA. Amer ptg 1760-1960
BEMELMANS, Ludwig, 1898-1962
  Sketch for Parsley: The end
    NSP. Sportscapes
  Sketch for Parsley: The hunter's fall
    NSP. Sportscapes
Ben Cruachan by R. Smith
Benares by M. Sterne
Benares on the Ganges by M. Sterne
BENBRIDGE, Henry, 1744-1812
  Gatling children
    Chew. 250 years of art
  Hartley family group
    Pierson
Bend at Newton Hook by C. F. Gaertner
Bend in Storm King by C. F. Gaertner
Bender, Horace, pseud. See Greenough,
    Horatio
Benham, Jonathan, fl 1710
  Unidentified artist. Jonathan Benham
BENJAMIN, Max, 1928-
  Peninsula
    OrPA. Ptgs & sculptures
Benjamin Reber's farm, View of by C. Hof-
    mann
Benjamin's house by A. N. Wyeth
BENN, Ben, 1884-
  Mother and child   WMAA
    Baur. Revolution
    Pierson
  Sea gulls
    PA. Annual ex, 1952
BENNET, F. R. fl 1875
  Dance on a Sequoia swamp   NCHA
    Jones. New-found folk art
Bennett, F. R. See Bennet, F. R.
BENNETT, Rainey, 1907-
  Blue mist
    IU. Contemp Amer ptg & sculp, 1959
  Composition
    IU. Contemp Amer ptg & sculp, 1961
  Evening light
    IU. Contemp Amer ptg, 1951
  Red studio
    IU. Contemp Amer ptg & sculp, 1957
BENNETT, William James, 1787-1844
  Broadway from Bowling Green, c 1826
    Davidson v2
  Detroit, 1836
    Davidson v2
  Packet Row, South street, New York
                                      NNPL
    Davidson v 1
BENRIMO, Thomas Duncan, 1887-1958
  Biaxial
    NNSG. Younger Amer ptrs
  Fetish
    ICA. Annual ex, 1951
  Figure in space
    WMAA. Contemp Amer ptg, 1952
  Goat song
    IU. Contemp Amer ptg & sculp, 1955
  Lute player
    IU. Contemp Amer ptg, 1951
  Mirage   OCiM
    CoS. New accessions USA, 1954
  Nostalgic migration
    ICA. Annual ex, 1947/48

Pastorale
  IU. Contemp Amer ptg, 1952
Quiescent space
  IU. Contemp Amer ptg & sculp, 1953
Reflections
  Pousette-Dart. Amer ptg
Ring around the moon
  IU. Contemp Amer ptg & sculp, 1957
BENSON, Frank Weston, 1862-1951
  The bowsprit   MB
    MB. Ptgs in water color
  Currituck marshes, North Carolina   MB
    MB. Ptgs in water color
  Danvers river, Massachusetts   MB
    MB. Ptgs in water color
  Fisherman's bedroom, Eastham, Massa-
    chusetts   MB
    MB. Ptgs in water color
  Lower reservoir, Tihonet   MB
    MB. Ptgs in water color
  Meadows in winter   MB
    MB. Ptgs in water color
  My daughters   MWM
    Roos
  Rainy day   ICA
    NYG. Fine art
  Red and gold   OYB
    OYB. Catalogue 1951
  Redhead ducks   MB
    MB. Ptgs in water color
  Still life   DC
    NYG. Fine art
Benson, Robert, 1739-1823
  Trumbull, J. Robert Benson
BENTLEY, Claude Ronald, 1915-
  Colima
    IU. Contemp Amer ptg & sculp, 1957
  Separated
    IU. Contemp Amer ptg, 1949
  Smoking mirror
    DC. 27 biennial ex, 1961
  White sands
    IU. Contemp Amer ptg, 1951
BENTLEY, Lester
  George Wyckoff jr
    PPC. Ptg in the U.S. 1949
BENTON, Thomas Hart, 1889-
  Aaron   PA
    Benton
    Craven. Treasury 1952 ed
  After the storm
    KLU. Benton
  Agriculture and logging (mural)
    Larkin (detail)
    Larkin rev ed (detail)
  America today   NNSR
    Lewisohn
  Apple of discord
    KLU. Benton
  Art of building   NNSR
    Roos
  Arts of life   CtNB
    Cheney. Story 1958 ed
  Arts of the west   CtNB
    Craven. Rainbow book
    Mendelowitz
    Pierson
  Arts of the west   WMAA
    Craven. Treasury 1952 ed
    Myers
    Upjohn

BENTON, T. H.—*Continued*
Boomtown, 1928   NR
  Baur. New art
  Pierson
Carl Ruggles. See Sun treader
Catalytic crackers
  Benton
Cattle loading, West Texas   MAP
  Wight. Milestones
Chilmark   OYB
  Baur. Revolution
  OYB. Catalogue 1951
Cradling wheat   MoSL
  KLU. Benton
  MoSL. Handbook 1953
Custer's last stand
  KLU. Benton
First crop   IBM
  Bazin
Hailstorm   NeO
  Baur. New art
  CoS. New accessions USA, 1952
Harzfeld's mural
  Benton
History of the early United States
  KLU. Benton
Hollywood
  KLU. Benton
Homestead   MMA
  Newmeyer
Jealous lover of Lone Green valley
  McCurdy
  Roos
Jessie, 17 years old
  KLU. Benton
July hay   MM
  Baur. New art (col)
  Flexner. Amer ptg
  Flexner. Short history
  Pierson
  Time. 300 years (col)
June hay   MM
  Benton
Little brown jug
  IaDa. Wood
Lord heal the child
  KLU. Benton
The Lord is my shepherd   WMAA
  Goodrich. Amer art
  KLU. Benton
Louisiana rice fields   NBM
  Baur. Revolution
  Canaday
  NYG. Fine art
The meal   WMAA
  Lee. Art then and now
Missouri mural
  Benton
Negro soldier
  Benton
  KLU. Benton
New England editor   MB
  CoS. New accessions USA, 1948
Persephone
  Benton
  KLU. Benton
Photographing the bull
  KLU. Benton
Political, business and intellectual ballyhoo
  (Ceiling panel no 6)   CtNB
  Brown. Amer ptg
Preparing the bill
  Baur. New art

Roasting ears   MM
  Craven. Rainbow book (col)
  Craven. Treasury 1952 ed (col)
  MM. 100 Amer ptrs (col)
  Taylor. Fifty centuries, 1954 ed (col)
Self-portrait
  Benton
  KLU. Benton
Silver vase
  KLU. Benton
Soldier's joy
  Benton
Sun treader—Portrait of Carl Ruggles,
  1934   MoKN
  Baur. New art
  KLU. Benton
Susanna and the elders   CSFP
  Benton
  CSFP. Handbook
Three figures
  Brown. Amer ptg
  WMAA. Pioneers
Threshing wheat   InTH
  InTH. Catalogue
  KLU. Benton
  UNESCO. 1860-1955
Weighing cotton
  Gruskin (col)
White horse
  KLU. Benton
BEN-ZION, 1899-
De profundis
  Pearson. Mod renaissance
Handwriting on the wall
  IU. Contemp Amer ptg, 1952
Large thistles
  IU. Contemp Amer ptg & sculp, 1955
Moses
  Pierson
Orchard with yellow sky
  IU. Contemp Amer ptg & sculp, 1953
The poet and the saint
  Pearson. Mod renaissance
Symbols of our time
  Pearson. Mod renaissance
Three dancers
  ICA. Annual ex, 1947/48
White pitcher with field flowers
  IU. Contemp Amer ptg, 1950
Berezov, Mrs Maurice. See Fine, Perle
Berg, Alban, 1885-1935
  Rederer, F. J. Alban Berg, Portrait of
Bergamo, Italy by J. L. Smith
BERGER, Jason, 1924-
  Marilyn at the table
  MBIC. View 1960
BERGHOFF, Jack
  Nardin park   OYB
  OYB. Annual 1953
BERGMANN, Franz, 1898-
  Circus
  CSFP. Annual ex, 1946
Berkeley, George, bp, 1685-1753
  Smibert, J. Bishop Berkeley and his family
Berkeley, Philippa Frances (Culpeper) Lady,
  1635-1690?
  Unidentified artist. Lady Berkeley
Berkeley 54, 1955 by R. Diebenkorn
Berkeley no 2 by R. Diebenkorn

Berkeley no 16 by R. Diebenkorn

Berkeley no 38 by R. Diebenkorn

Berks county almshouse, Views of the surroundings of by C. Hofman

Berkshire mountains
   Durand, A. B. Monument mountain, Berkshires

BERLANDINA, Jane, 1898-
   Abstraction, 1945   MCH
      Pulitzer v2
   Almost airtight compartments   MCH
      Pulitzer v2
   Figures in space
      IU. Contemp Amer ptg & sculp, 1955
   The garden   MCH
      Pulitzer v2
   Let's search our souls   MCH
      Pulitzer v2
   Passage a travers   MoSL
      CoS. New accessions USA, 1954
   Three clowns   CSFD
      CoS. New accessions USA, 1948

BERLIN, Bernard, 1918-
   Dance hall
      ICA. Annual ex, 1959/60

Berlin, May 3, 1945 by J. Groth

BERMAN, Eugene, 1899-
   Los angelitos
      CSFP. Annual ex, 1948/49
   Apotheosis of\ Mexican baroque
      CSFP. Annual ex, 1950/51
   Bella Venezia
      ICA. Annual ex, 1947/48
   Bridges of Paris   PPhM
      Canaday
   The cart   MMA
      MMA. Soby collection
   Courtyard   DP
      DP. Catalogue
   Dark muse
      Pearson. Mod renaissance
   Daybreak   DP
      DP. Catalogue
   Dead life, sea lion skull, driftwood and coral
      CSFP. Annual ex, 1947/48
   Devil's holiday   MMA
      MMA. Masters
   Evening in Venice
      Read. Art now, 1948 ed
   Gates of the city, nightfall   MMA
      CSFP. Illusionism
      McCurdy
      Pierson
   Hat seller   CtHW
      CtHW. Handbook (col)
   Magic circle, Venice
      Myers
   Mélancholie
      CtY. Yale alumni
   Memory of Ischia   MMA
      MMA. Soby collection
   Mexican pyramid—the living and the dead   CSFP
      CoS. New accessions USA, 1960
   Muse of the western world   MM
      MM. 100 Amer ptrs
      Pierson
   Napolitana
      Bazin
      IU. Contemp Amer ptg & sculp, 1955

Obelisks
   Pearson. Mod renaissance
Ophelia
   PPC. Ptg in the U.S. 1949
Paludes
   Wight. Milestones (col)
Panel for a mural decoration
   CSFP. Illusionism
   Janson. Picture history
Perspective Mexican hill town
   DC. 22 biennial ex, 1951
Proserpine (Persephone)   MoSL
   Genauer
   MoSL. Handbook 1953
Rico Lebrun, Portrait of   IU
   IU. Contemp Amer ptg, 1948
   IU. 20th century
   Pearson. Mod renaissance
Steep bridge
   NAD. Annual ex, 1949, 1st half
Steep bridge no 3
   WMAA. Contemp Amer ptg, 1949
Summer still life
   IU. Contemp Amer ptg, 1950
Temptation of St Anthony
   Pearson. Mod renaissance
Through the marshes
   CtY. Yale alumni
Viva Mexico
   NAD. Annual ex, spring 1950
Wall of spikes
   IU. Contemp Amer ptg, 1949

BERMAN, Fred, 1926-
   Falling sun VI
      WMAA. Young America 1960
   Floating white city
      WMAA. Contemp Amer ptg, 1959/60
   Unfinished painting
      WMAA. Young America 1960

Berman, Leonid. See Leonid

Bermuda
   Demuth, C. H. Bermuda, 1917
   Demuth, C. H. Bermuda no 2
   Homer, W. Rocky shore

Bermuda group by J. Smibert

Bermuda window in a semitropical character by M. Hartley

Bernard by L. Karp

Berry boy by J. G. Brown

Berry pickers by W. Homer

Bertagna, Carmela, fl 1884
   Sargent, J. S. Carmela Bertagna

BERTOIA, Harry, 1915-
   Quadrilaterals   NUM
      NUM. Root bequest

The **Bessie** of New York by A. G. Dove

Bethel (ship)
   Unidentified artist. Letter of marque ship Bethel of Boston

Bethlehem by L. Ford

Bethlehem, Pennsylvania by J. W. Hill

Bethlehem, Pennsylvania by Unidentified artist

Bethune, George, 1769-1859
   Malbone, E. G. George Bethune

Betrothal by A. Gorky

Betrothal I by A. Gorky

Betrothal II, 1947 by A. Gorky

BETSBERG, Ernestine, 1908-
   Roman shop
      IU. Contemp Amer ptg & sculp, 1959

BETTS, Edward Howard, 1920-
Coastal landscape   OYB
  NAD. Annual ex, 1957
  OYB. Supplement 1959
Driftwood   IaDa
  IaDa. Silver jubilee
Rocky landscape
  NAD. Annual ex, 1953
Storm tide   OYB
  OYB. Annual 1953
  OYB. Supplement
Betts, Eliza. See Rathbone, Eliza (Betts)
BETTS, Louis, 1873-
  Albert Arnold Sprague   CtY
  CtY. Portrait index
  Booth Tarkington   InIJ
  InIJ. 105 ptgs
  Frances and Judy   OYB
  OYB. Catalogue 1951
  Mary Julien Glover
  NAD. Annual ex, spring 1950
  Self-portrait   InTH
  InTH. Catalogue
Between acts by H. C. Pitz
Between Ceppo Morelli and Ponte Grande
  by F. E. Church
Between rounds by T. Eakins
Beyle, Marie-Henri, Apotheosis of by J.
  Wilde
Beyond the truth by S. Chun
Beyond white by J. Xcéron
Bianca by R. W. Weir
La **Biancheria** by J. S. Sargent
Biarritz: big sea by E. D. Boit
Biaxial by T. D. Benrimo
Bibb, Mary Lucy Pocahontas, 1818-1844
  Bush, J. H. Mary Lucy Pocahontas Bibb
Biblical and religious themes
  Allston, W. Belshazzar's feast
  Allston, W. Christ healing the sick, first
    study
  Allston, W. David playing before Saul
  Allston, W. Dead man revived by touch-
    ing the bones of the prophet Elijah
  Allston, W. Elijah fed by the ravens
  Allston, W. Jacob's dream
  Allston, W. Jeremiah dictating his proph-
    ecy
  Allston, W. Rebecca at the well
  Allston, W. Saul and the witch of Endor
  Aronson, D. Adoration of the Magi
  Aronson, D. Christ before Pilate
  Aronson, D. Coronation of the Virgin
  Aronson, D. Joseph and the Ishmaelites
  Aronson, D. Last supper
  Aronson, D. Resurrection
  Aronson, D. Young Christ
  Arthur, R. The last supper
  Bearden, R. Christ driving the money
    changers from the Temple
  Beckmann, M. Christ and the woman
    taken in adultery
  Beckmann, M. Christ in Limbo
  Beckmann, M. Descent from the cross
  Beckmann, M. The prodigal son among
    swine
  Bellows, G. W. Crucifixion
  Benton, T. H. Susanna and the elders
  Berman, E. Temptation of St Anthony
  Brewton, J. Suicide of Judas

Church, F. E. Finding of Moses
Cole, T. Angels administering to Christ
Cole, T. Dead Abel
Cole, T. Expulsion from the Garden of
  Eden
Cole, T. John the Baptist in the wilder-
  ness
Copley, J. S. The ascension
Cowles, R. Adam and Eve
Curry, J. S. Baptism in Kansas
Devoll, R. The prodigal son
Doolittle, A. Prodigal son reclaimed
Eakins, T. Crucifixion
Field, E. S. Garden of Eden
Franck, F. S. Lazarus resurrected
Greene, S. Cain and Abel
Haidt, J. V. Christ before Pilate
Haidt, J. V. Crucifixion
Hesselius, G. The last supper
Hicks, E. Peaceable kingdom
Hidley, J. H. (attributed works) Noah's
  ark
Hurd, P. Baptising at Three Wells
Johnson, A. Baptisam of our Savour spok
Kamihira, B. Lowering from the cross
La Farge, J. Adoring angels
La Farge, J. Ascension
La Farge, J. The centurion: study for a
  window in Judson memorial church,
  New York
La Farge, J. Christ and Nicodemus
La Farge, J. Christ and the psalmist
La Farge, J. Good Samaritan: design for
  a window, Trinity church, Buffalo
La Farge, J. Good shepherd
La Farge, J. St Paul: Study for a memo-
  rial window
Land, J. Passover supper
Laning, E. Moses with the tablets of the
  law
Lathrop, B. B. Japhthah's return
Lebrun, R. The centurion's horse
Lebrun, R. The Magdalene
Lebrun, R. Woman of the Crucifixion
Motherwell, R. B. Decalogue, Jacob's lad-
  der and burning bush
Nagler, F. The passion according to St
  Matthew
Oakley, V. Christ and the woman of
  Samaria
Page, W. Flight into Egypt
Philipp, R. Raising the cross
Pippin, H. Temptation of St Anthony
Pippin, H. The woman taken in adultery
Porter, R. Sacrifice of Isaac
Quirt, W. W. Descent from the cross
Reinhardt, S. G. Raising of Lazarus
Ronson, D. Marriage at Cana
Ryder, A. P. Christ appearing to Mary
Ryder, A. P. Resurrection
Ryder, A. P. Story of the cross
Shirlaw, W. Susannah and the elders
Snow, J. E. Belshazzar's feast
Terry, L. Jacob's dream
Unidentified artist. Abraham and Isaac
Unidentified artist. Adam and Eve
Unidentified artist. Adoration of the Magi
Unidentified artist. Belshazzar's feast
Unidentified artist. Christ and the woman
  of Samaria
Unidentified artist. Christ at Emmaus
Unidentified artist. Christ on the road to
  Emmaus

Unidentified artist. Creation scene
Unidentified artist. Crowning of King Jereboam
Unidentified artist. Crucifixion
Unidentified artist. Finding of Moses
Unidentified artist. Flight into Egypt
Unidentified artist. The four apostles writing the gospels
Unidentified artist. Good Samaritan
Unidentified artist. Isaac blessing Jacob
Unidentified artist. Joseph and his brethren
Unidentified artist. Joseph interpreting Pharaoh's dream
Unidentified artist. Marriage at Cana
Unidentified artist. Moses in the bulrushes
Unidentified artist. Prodigal son gambling
Unidentified artist. The prodigal son in misery
Unidentified artist. The prodigal son receiving his patrimony
Unidentified artist. The prodigal son reclaimed
Unidentified artist. The prodigal son reveling with harlots
Unidentified artist. Rebecca at the well
Unidentified artist. Ruth and Naomi
Van Duzer, C. E. Pieta
Vincent, T. Crucifixion
Watkins, F. C. Crucifixion
West, B. The angel of the Lord announcing the resurrection to the Marys at the sepulchre
West, B. The archangel Gabriel
West, B. The ascension of our Saviour
West, B. Christ healing the sick in the temple
West, B. Christ on the Mount of Olives
West, B. Christ rejected by the Jews
West, B. The conversion of St Paul
West, B. The destruction of the beast and the false prophets
West, B. Elijah convincing the false prophets of Baol
West, B. Hagar and Ishmael
West, B. Peter denying Christ
West, B. Raising of Lazarus
West, B. Return of Jephthah
West, B. St Paul persecuting the Christians
West, B. St Paul shaking off the viper
West, B. St Paul's restoration to sight by Ananias
West, B. Saul and the witch of Endor
Willson M. A. Prodigal son reclaimed by his father

Bidart, French Pyrenees by E. D. Boit
BIDDLE, George, 1885-
Cannibalism of war   MexS
  Biddle. Yes and no
  Pearson. Mod renaissance
Frankie Loper
  Gruskin
His first crossing
  Cheney. Expressionism 1948 ed
Kuniyoshi, Portrait of
  Pearson. Mod renaissance
Marguerite Zorach. See Woman with a letter
My neighbor, Al
  Pearson. Mod renaissance

Negro spiritual: Ride on, conquering king
  PPC. Ptg in the U. S. 1949
Not even he may rest
  Pearson. Mod renaissance
Raphael Soyer and his models
  Biddle. Yes and no
Tenement
  Robb. Harper history
Two Negroes
  Pearson. Mod renaissance
William Gropper
  Larkin
  Larkin rev ed
Woman with a letter (Marguerite Zorach)   MM
  MM. 100 Amer ptrs
  Pierson

Portrait of the artist
Brook, A. George Biddle playing the flute
Biddle, John, 1789?-1859
Sully, T. Major John Biddle
Biddle, Mary, 1781-1850
Malbone, E. G. Mary Biddle
Biddle, Rebecca Cornell, fl 1824
Sully, T. Rebecca Cornell Biddle
Biddle, Thomas, 1790-1831
Sully, T. Major Thomas Biddle (PA)
Sully, T. and Sully, T. W. Major Thomas Biddle (DN)
BIDNER, Robert
Rufescent idlers
  OYB. Annual 1952
BIERSTADT, Albert, 1830-1902
Ambush   MB
  MB. Karolik coll
Arch of Octavius   MBA
  MiD. Travelers in Arcadia
Ascutney mountain from Claremont, New Hampshire
  Sears. Highlights
Bison with coyotes
  McCracken. Portrait of the old west
Black horse   MB
  MB. Karolik coll
Bombardment of Fort Sumter   PPhU
  Born
  Pierson
  U. S. National Capital sesquicentennial com
Buffalo bull   NJN
  Rathbone
Buffalo trail   MB
  MB. Karolik coll
Burning ship
  Pierson
Couple driving
  Born
Fishing boats at Capri   MB
  MB. Karolik coll
Geyser, Yellowstone park   MB
  MB. Karolik coll
Giant redwood trees of California   MPB
  Davidson v 1
  NUM. Art across America
Grove of trees   MB
  MB. Karolik coll
Guerrilla warfare   NNCe
  Walker. Ptgs from America
Halt in the Rocky mountains
  McCracken. Portrait of the old west

BIERSTADT, Albert—*Continued*
  In the Yosemite valley   CtHW
    CtHW. Handbook
  Indian camp   MB
    MB. Karolik coll
  Indians near Fort Laramie   MB
    MB. Karolik coll
  Jenny lake, Wyoming
    Rathbone
  Lake Tahoe, California   MB
    MB. Karolik coll
  Last of the buffalo   DC
    Barker. Amer ptg
    DC. Masterpieces
    McCracken. Portrait of the old west
      (col)
    Pierson
    Rathbone (col)
  Marina Grande in Capri   NBuA
    MiD. Travelers in Arcadia
    NBuA. Catalogue of the ptgs
  Merced river, Yosemite valley   MM
    Bazin
    Canaday
    Larkin
    Larkin rev ed
  Moose hunters' camp, Nova Scotia MB
    MB. Karolik coll
  Mount Corcoran   DC
    McCracken. Portrait of the old west
      (col)
  Mount Whitney   MnMI
    Born
  Mountain lake   TxH
    Rathbone
  Nooning on the Platte   MoSL
    Rathbone
  Oregon trail   OYB
    OYB. Catalogue 1951
    Rathbone
  Palm trees with a domed church   MB
    MB. Karolik coll
  Rainbow over Jenny lake
    Time. 300 years (col)
  Rocky mountains   MM
    Davidson v 1
    Mendelowitz
    Pierson
  Rocky mountains   IBM
    McCracken. Portrait of the old west
  Rocky mountains, Colorado   MB
    MB. Karolik coll
  St Lawrence river from the citadel,
    Quebec   MB
    MB. Karolik coll
    Pierson
  San Rafael, California
    Sears. Highlights
  Seal rocks, Farallones   MB
    MB. Karolik coll
  Snow scene with buffaloes   MB
    MB. Karolik coll
  Starr King mountain, California   OCl
    Roos
  Storm in the mountains   MB
    MB. Karolik coll
  Surveyor's wagon in the Rockies   MoSL
    Rathbone
  Thunderstorm in the Rocky mountains
                                    MB
    MiD. Ptg in America
    NYG. Fine art
    Pierson
    Rathbone
    Richardson. Ptg in America

  Valley of the Yosemite   MB
    MB. Karolik coll
  View from the Wind river mountains,
    Wyoming   MB
    MB. Karolik coll
  Western sunset
    Rathbone
  Wind river country, Wyoming   CtNB
    Rathbone
Big apple tree by J. Sloan
Big Bend by E. F. Spruce
Big black by J. Youngerman
Big Bowl (a Crow chief) by A. J. Miller
Big business by C. Singer
Big dory by G. W. Bellows
Big horse by W. Sommer
The **big** noise by P. Evergood
Big nose George by C. M. Russell
Big red by S. Francis
Big Rock pool by H. E. Mattson
Big Sandy river, Scene on the by A. J.
    Miller
Big tree by K. E. Fortess
Bigelow, William Sturgis
    Chadwick, F. B. William Sturgis Bigelow
BIGGS, Walter, 1886-
  Night spot
    NAD. Annual ex, 1951
  Studio
    NAD. Annual ex, 1961
BIGLER, Mary Jane
  Planes in the sunflowers
    OYB. Annual 1952
Bike race by J. De Martini
Billboard by G. Hartigan
BILLINGS, Henry, 1901-
  Discovery
    Gruskin
Billings, Mabel
    Jennys, W. Mabel Billings
BINFORD, Julien, 1908-
  Crap shooter
    Gruskin (col)
  Red chair with straw flowers
    IaDa. 30th anniversary
    IU. Contemp Amer ptg & sculp, 1953
  Table with cyclamens
    IU. Contemp Amer ptg, 1952
  Woman with a purple hat
    Gruskin (col)
BINGHAM, George Caleb, 1811-1879
  Belated wayfarers
    McDermott. G. C. Bingham
    Rathbone
  Benoist Troost   MoKN
    McDermott. G. C. Bingham
  Boatmen on the Missouri (copy of origi-
    nal)   DeWin
    McDermott. G. C. Bingham
  Canvassing for a vote   MoKN
    McDermott. G. C. Bingham
    MoKN. Handbook
    OCiM. Rediscoveries
  Captured by Indians
    McDermott. G. C. Bingham
    Rathbone
  Checker players   MiD
    McDermott. G. C. Bingham

BINGHAM, G. C.—*Continued*
Raftsmen playing cards   MoSL
  Barker. Amer ptg
  DC. De gustibus
  McDermott. G. C. Bingham
  MoSL. 50 masterworks
  MoSL. Handbook 1953
  PPC. Amer classics
  Richardson. Ptg in America
  Roos
  UNESCO. Prior to 1860
  UNESCO. Prior to 1860 3d ed
  UNESCO. Prior to 1860 5th ed
  MB. Karolik coll
Raftsmen playing cards no 2. See In a
  quandary
Sallie Ann Camden
  McDermott. G. C. Bingham
Samuel Bullitt Churchill
  McDermott. G. C. Bingham
Scene on the Ohio   MoSLH
  McDermott. G. C. Bingham
Self-portrait 1835   MoSL
  DC. Amer ptrs of the South
  McDermott. G. C. Bingham
  MoSL. Handbook 1953
  PA. Annual ex, 1955
Self-portrait, 1877?
  McDermott. G. C. Bingham
Shooting for the beef   NBM
  Flexner. Amer ptg
  Flexner. Short history
  McDermott. G. C. Bingham
  Mendelowitz
  Pierson
  Rathbone
The squatters
  McDermott. G. C. Bingham
The storm   CtHW
  CtHW. Handbook
  McDermott. G. C. Bingham
  Rathbone
Stump speaking   MoSLB
  Craven. Rainbow book
  Craven. Treasury 1952 ed (col)
  McDermott. G. C. Bingham
  Rathbone
  U.S. National Capital sesquicentennial
    com
Susan Howard Hockaday and her daughter
    Susan
  McDermott. G. C. Bingham
The thread of life
  McDermott. G. C. Bingham
Trappers' return   MiD
  Baur. Amer ptg
  McDermott. G. C. Bingham
  MiD. Ptg in America (col cover)
  MiD. Treasures
  Pierson
  Richardson. Ptg in America (col detail)
Two citizens engaged in a conversation
                                          MoSLM
  Roos
Verdict of the people   MoSLB
  Barker. Amer ptg
  Davidson v2
  McDermott. G. C. Bingham
  Mendelowitz
  Rathbone
The verdict of the people no 2, 1878 DN
  McDermott. G. C. Bingham
View of a lake in the mountains
  McDermott. G. C. Bingham

Washington crossing the Delaware
  McDermott. G. C. Bingham
Watching the cargo   MoSLH
  McDermott. G. C. Bingham
The wood boat   MoSL
  Canaday
  McDermott. G. C. Bingham
  MoSL. Handbook 1953
  OCiM. Rediscoveries
  Rathbone
  Time. 300 years (col)
Wood-boatmen on a river   MB
  MB. Karolik coll

Birch, Mrs James T. fl 1877
  Bingham, G. C. Mrs James T. Birch

BIRCH, Thomas, 1779-1851
Brig in a storm   MoSL
  MoSL. Handbook 1953
City of Philadelphia from the treaty elm.
  See Penn's treaty tree
The Constitution and the Guerrière MAP
  Larkin
  Larkin rev ed
The Constitution and the Guerriere MdAn
  U.S. National Capital sesquicentennial
    com
Edward Hunt
  WiMiA. Amer ptg 1760-1960
Fairmount water works   PA
  Pierson
  U.S National Capital sesquicentennial
    com
Landing of William Penn   MB
  MB. Karolik coll
Late summer
  Chew. 250 years of art
Marine view with ships
  Chew. 250 years of art
Milford, North Wales, Pennsylvania MB
  MB. Karolik coll
New York harbor   MB
  MB. Karolik coll
Off the Maine coast
  Sears. Highlights
Penn's treaty tree (City of Philadelphia
    from the treaty elm)
  Born
  Flexner. Light of distant skies
  PA. Annual ex, 1955
  Pierson
Philadelphia from Petty Island c 1825
  MB. Karolik coll
Seascape   MB
  MB. Karolik coll
  Sears. Highlights
Seascape   MeC
  MeC. Inaugural ex
Shipwreck   NBM
  Born
  PA. Annual ex, 1955
Skating   MB
  MB. Karolik coll
Sleigh ride in the country   MB
  MB. Karolik coll
The United States and the Macedonian,
    1812   PH
  Davidson v 1
  Pierson
  Richardson. Ptg in America
Upper Hudson
  Sears. Highlights

The Wasp and the Frolic   MB
  MB. Karolik coll
Winter   PR
  NUM. Art across America
  PR. Catalogue
Winter scene outside of Bristol, Penn-
  sylvania
  Chew. 250 years of art
Birches by J. Whorf
Birckhead, Catharine A. (McEvers) 1795-
  1868
  Peale, S. M. Mrs Hugh McC Birckhead
Bird and ball by R. Ruben
Bird and roses by P. W. Roberts
Bird bath by A. Rattner
Bird cloud by L. Feininger
Bird effort by J. Pollock
Bird, fish, fruit by S. Provan
Bird harbor, Maine by A. P. Chase
Bird in the heart by J. Carroll
Bird in the spirit by M. Graves
Bird in the sun no 2 by J. Zajac
Bird Key bay by S. Solomon
Bird mountain, Castleton, Vermont by
  J. Hope
Bird rock, California by H. G. Keller
The birdcage by K. Zerbe
Birdie with straw hat by L. Rivers
Birds
  See also names of individual birds, e.g.
    Cuckoos; Woodpecker
  Avery, M. Birds over sea
  Baziotes, W. A. White bird
  Blanch, A. Woman feeding birds
  Bohrod, A. Bird and gauntlet
  Graves, M. Bird in the mist
  Graves, M. Bird in the moonlight
  Graves, M. Bird in the spirit
  Graves, M. Bird maddened by the long
    winter
  Graves, M. Bird singing in the moonlight
  Graves, M. Blind bird
  Graves, M. Guardian
  Graves, M. In the air
  Graves, M. Little-known bird of the inner
    eye
  Graves, M. Masked bird fishing in the
    golden stream
  Graves, M. Message
  Graves, M. Pink bird
  Graves, M. Shore birds
  Graves, M. Spirit bird
  Graves, M. Surf birds
  Hartley, M. Birds of the Bagaduce
  Hartley, M. Give us this day
  Homer, W. Right and left
  Keller, H. G. Birds, rocks, and the sea
  Kriesberg, I. Birds alighting
  Ludens, E. Rare birds
  Norfeldt, B. J. O. Flight of birds
  Pollock, J. Bird
  Price, C. S. Bird by the sea
  Price, C. S. Black bird
  Price, C. S. Young birds
  Runquist, Arthur. Bird
  Siegriest, L, Birds at rest
  Thon, W. Seabirds
  Woellfer, E. Birds and orange sky
  Wyeth, A. N. Soaring

Bird's-eye view of the Mandan village by
  G. Catlin
Birds flying by C. Chen
Bird's nest by C. Sheeler
Birmingham meeting house I, 1940 by H.
  Pippin
Birmington from the top of Coal hill oppo-
  site Pittsburgh, 1834 by R. Smith
Birth by J. Pollock
Birth of Cephalopods by M. Rothko
Birth of spring by F. C. Watkins
Birth of Taurus by H. Hofmann
Birth of the atom (Atomic series) by J.
  De Diego
Birthday cake by R. H. Wilt
Birthday party by E. Giobbi
Birthplace by W. Pachner
BISCHOFF, Elmer Nelson, 1916-
  Bather
    WMAA. Contemp Amer ptg, 1959/60
  Figures in garden
    IU. Contemp Amer ptg & sculp, 1959
  Seated figure in garden   WMAA
    Goodrich. Amer art
  White flower
    IU. Contemp Amer ptg & scupl, 1961
BISHOP, Isabel, 1902-
  Bather   ATU
    ATU. Coll of Amer art
  Blowing rings
    Gruskin
  Girls waiting
    NAD. Annual ex, 1957
  Homeward
    Pierson
  Interlude
    PA. Annual ex, 1953
  The kid
    NYG. Fine art
  Lunch hour
    Gruskin
  Mending   WMAA
    WMAA. Sara Roby
  Nude   WMAA
    Goodrich. Amer art
  Snack bar   OCo
    McCurdy
  Subway scene
    WMAA. Annual ex, 1958
  Two girls   MM
    Mendelowitz
    MM. 100 Amer ptrs
  Waiting   NJN
    Baur. Revolution
    Pierson
Bismarck, Otto Eduard Leopold, prince von,
  1815-1898
  Healy, G.P.A. Otto von Bismarck
Bison with coyotes by A. Bierstadt
The bistro by A. Blatas
BISTTRAM, Emil, 1895-
  Bulldogging
    Pearson. Mod renaissance
  The fleet
    Pearson. Mod renaissance
  Koshares (New Mexico Indian dance
    series)
    Pearson. Mod renaissance
  Marine patterns
    Pearson. Mod renaissance
A bit of the Cape by F. J. Waugh

BLACK, Frederick E. 1924-
  Untitled
    IU. Contemp Amer ptg & sculp, 1959
    WMAA. Contemp Amer ptg, 1959/60
Black abstraction by G. O'Keeffe
The black and the white by M. Rothko
Black & 3 whites by E. A. Donati
Black and white by C. Booth
Black and white by W. De Kooning
Black and white by A. D. F. Reinhardt
Black and white by J. De J. Smith
Black and white and read all over by H.
  Frankenthaler
Black and white no 5, 1952 by J. Pollock
Black and white painting by J. Pollock
Black angels by B. Greene
Black Ball liner by R. W. Salmon (at-
  tributed works)
Black-billed cuckoo by J. J. Audubon
Black bird by C. S. Price
Black bottle by H. Lotterman
Black bush, autumn, Dogtown by W. A.
  Kienbusch
Black city by W. G. Congdon
Black control by I. R. Pereira
Black cross by G. O'Keeffe
Black cross with red sky by G. O'Keeffe
Black dahlia by P. Jennins
Black demon by H. Hofmann
Black-eyed susans by S. Serisawa
Black freighter by J. Levine
Black Friday by W. De Kooning
Black harbor, grey moon by E. Wedin
Black hat by H. G. Dearth
Black Hawk (Sauk chief) 1767-1838
  Catlin, G. Black Hawk
Black herd by H. Nichols
Black Hills by A. J. Miller
Black horse by A. Bierstadt
Black horse by M. O. Sheets
Black horse by W. Sommer
Black horses by A. M. R. Moses
Black houses by C. E. Burchfield
Black in red by S. Francis
Black interior by R. B. Motherwell
Black iris by G. O'Keeffe
Black iron by C. E. Burchfield
Black landscape by B. J. Gardner
Black landscape by Y. Tanguy
Black lilies by M. Beckmann
Black lion by B. Browne
Black movements by L. Dodd
Black night by W. A. Baziotes
Black no 8 by Y. Ohashi
Black on white by W. A. Baziotes
Black over reds by M. Rothko
Black palace with red courtyard by Y.
  Johnston
Black patio door by G. O'Keeffe
Black place green by G. O'Keeffe
Black place III by G. O'Keeffe
Black rocks, kelp and sea by W. Brice

Black roses by G. L. K. Morris
Black silhouette by W. A. Baziotes
Black still life by R. B. Motherwell
Black sun by J. Marin
Black table by N. Vasilieff
Black target by J. Johns
Black tree in bright light by K. Schrag
Black waves by M. Graves
Black, white and grey by J. Pollock
Black widow by M. Ray
Black wires by R. Koppe
Black yawl by L. Feininger
Blackberry picker by A. N. Wyeth
A blackbird with snow-covered red hills
  by G. O'Keeffe
The blackboard by K. Davies
The blackboard by C. Marca-Relli
BLACKBURN, Joseph, c 1700-1765
  Elizabeth and James Bowdoin   MeB
    Pierson
  Isaac Winslow and his family. See Wins-
    low family
  James Pitts   MiD
    MiD. Ports of the Pitts family
    MiD. Treasures
  John Erving jr
    Belknap
  Mary (Polly) Warner   NHP
    NUM. Art across America
    Richardson. Ptg in America
  Mary Sylvester Dering   NM
    Flexner. Copley
  Mrs Goldsbrow Banyar   NNHS
    Vail. Stuyvesant ports
  Mrs James Otis jr   NBM
    Flexner. First flowers
  Mrs James Pitts   MiD
    Belknap
    MiD. Ptg in America
    MiD. Ports of the Pitts family
    MiD. Treasures
  Mrs Jonathan Warner
    ICA. From colony to nation
  Mrs Theodore Atkinson   OCl
    OCl. Handbook
    Pierson
  Theodore Atkinson   MWM
    Larkin (detail)
    Larkin rev ed (detail)
    Pierson
  Theodore Atkinson jr   RPS
    Belknap
  Winslow family (Isaac Winslow and his
    family)   MB
    Barker. Amer ptg
    Flexner. First flowers
    ICA. From colony to nation
    Larkin
    Larkin rev ed
    Mendelowitz
    Pierson
BLACKBURN, Morris Atkinson, 1902-
  Blue door   PPhM
    CoS. New accessions USA, 1952
  Nets and boats   OYB
    OYB. Annual 1953
    OYB. Supplement
Blackened monument by G. L. Mueller
The Blackfeet by A. J. Miller

Blackfoot doctor in his mystery dress endeavoring to cure his dying patient by G. Catlin

Blackfoot medicine man by G. Catlin

Blacksmith shop by E. Johnson

Blacksmiths
Brown, J. G. The blacksmith
Hunt, W. M. The forge
Johnson, E. Blacksmith shop
Mayer, F. B. Leisure and labor
Neagle, J. Pat Lyon at the forge
Neagle, J. Pat Lyon, blacksmith

Black-tailed hare or jack-rabbit by J. J. Audubon

BLAGDEN, Thomas P. 1911-
Offshore wind
CtY. Yale alumni

Blai, Boris, 1893-
Watkins, F. C. Boris Blai

Blaine, James Gillespie, 1830-1893
Healy, G. P. A. James G. Blaine

Blair, Frank P.
Bingham, G. C. Gen Nathaniel Lyon and Gen Frank P. Blair starting from the Arsenal gate in St Louis to capture Camp Jackson

BLAIR, Jeanette
Spring
OYB. Annual 1954

BLAIR, Robert N. 1912-
Light and shade   OYB
OYB. Annual 1953
OYB. Supplement

BLAIR, Streeter, 1888-
Downing house, Chester county, Pennsylvania
Kallir. Amer primitive ptgs

Blair family by D. Blythe

Blake, Eliza (Izard)
Wollaston, J. Mrs Daniel Blake

Blakelock, Cora Rebecca (Bailey) b 1836?
Blakelock, R. A. Mrs Blakelock, Portrait of

BLAKELOCK, Ralph Albert, 1847-1919
After sundown   MAP
WMAA. Blakelock
At nature's mirror   DNC
NAD. Amer tradition
WMAA. Blakelock
Brook by moonlight   OT
Barker. Amer ptg
The chase   MWM
McCracken. Portrait of the old west
WMAA. Blakelock
Evening silhouettes
CtY. Yale alumni
WMAA. Blakelock
Golden autumn   GAtM
GAtM. Holbrook collection
Indian encampment   MM
Pierson
WMAA. Blakelock
Indian madonna
WMAA. Blakelock
Landscape   MM
MM. 100 Amer ptrs
Mrs Blakelock, Portrait of
WMAA. Blakelock
Moonlight   NBM
Baur. Amer ptg
Mendelowitz
Pierson
Time. 300 years (col)
WMAA. Blakelock

Moonlight   PPC
WMAA. Blakelock
Moonlight, Indian encampment   DNC
DNC. Gellatly coll, 1954
Larkin
Larkin rev ed
McCracken. Portrait of the old west (col)
Moonlight landscape   DP
Born
Moonlight sonata   MB
WMAA. Blakelock
Nymphs
WMAA. Blakelock
Old New York: northwest corner 55th street and Seventh avenue, c 1868 (Lemle coll)
WMAA. Blakelock
Old New York, shanties at 55th street and Seventh avenue   WiMiA
NJN. Early N.J. artists
PPC. Amer classics
Peace among the nations
WMAA. Blakelock
Pink roses
WMAA. Blakelock
Pipe dance   MM
McCracken. Portrait of the old west
Rising moon   ATeS
ATeS. Collection
Rocky mountains   MPB
McCracken. Portrait of the old west
Rathbone
Sunrise   NoCR
NoCR. Catalogue
WMAA. Blakelock
Three trees
WMAA. Blakelock
Twilight   OYB
OYB. Catalogue 1951
Vision of life   ICA
Pierson
Woods at sunset   NJMo
NJMo. Forty years

BLANCH, Arnold, 1896-
Autumn landscape
IU. Contemp Amer ptg, 1952
Bull
MnU. Arnold Blanch
Cathedral
MnU. Arnold Blanch
Circus girl
MnU. Arnold Blanch
Flowermakers
MnU. Arnold Blanch
Forevermore
MnU. Arnold Blanch
Four ships   WMAA
Pierson
Garden
MnU. Arnold Blanch
Georgia landscape   MM
MnU. Arnold Blanch
Girl with cornflower
MnU. Arnold Blanch
Hooked rug
MnU. Arnold Blanch
In Colorado
MnU. Arnold Blanch
Music before winter
MnU. Arnold Blanch
New England
NYG. Fine art

BLANCH, Arnold—*Continued*
  Painter of birds
    MnU. 40 Amer ptrs
  Pleasures of spring
    MnU. Arnold Blanch
  Rodeo in the Rockies   ATU
    ATU. Coll of Amer art
  Snap shot
    MnU. Arnold Blanch
  Swamp country   NBM
    MnU. Arnold Blanch
  Swamp folk   NBM
    Gruskin
    Pierson
  Table
    MnU. Arnold Blanch
  Tampa fair
    IU. Contemp Amer ptg, 1951
  Upright trees
    IU. Contemp ptg & sculp, 1955
  The village
    MnU. 40 Amer ptrs
  Woman feeding birds
    MnU. Arnold Blanch
Blanch, Mrs Arnold. See Lee, Doris
  (Emrick)
BLANCH, Lucille, 1895-
  Outdoor circus
    NYG. Fine art
  Still life in white   ATU
    ATU. Coll of Amer art
BLANCHARD, Carol, 1919?-
  Beachcomber
    IU. Contemp Amer ptg, 1951
  Family portrait
    IU. Contemp Amer ptg, 1950
  Family portrait
    IU Contemp Amer ptg & sculp, 1957
  Late again   IU
    CoS. New accessions USA, 1952
Bland, Sarah (Fitzhugh) See Fitzhugh,
  Sarah
Bland, Mrs Theodorick. See Fitzhugh,
  Sarah
BLANEY, William, 1865-1944
  Old fish house   MB
    MB. Ptgs in water color
BLASHFIELD, Edwin Howland, 1848-1936
  Carry on   MM
    Brown. Amer ptg
  Power of the law
    Pierson

Portrait of the artist
  Lockman, D. M. Edwin Howland Blash-
    field
Blast furnace by N. Spencer
Blast II by A. Gottlieb
BLATAS, Arbit, 1908-
  The bistro
    IU. Contemp Amer ptg, 1951
  Dinner still life
    Genauer (col)
  Four figures in a bistro
    PPC. International ex, 1952
  Pont Neuf
    IU. Contemp Amer ptg & sculp, 1955
  Still life with black bottle
    IU. Contemp Amer ptg & sculp, 1957
BLAUSTEIN, Alfred, 1924?-
  Buffet supper
    NBuA. Expressionism

  Galleria, Naples
    IU. Contemp Amer ptg & sculp, 1957
  Trussed sheep
    IU. Contemp Amer ptg & sculp, 1959
Bleak weather by A. Winter
Bleecker, Frances (Wade) 1787-1856
  Malbone, E. G. Annette (probably Mrs
    Alexander Bleecker)
  Malbone, E. G. Mrs Alexander Bleecker
Bleecker, Harmanus, 1779-1849
  Ames, E. Harmanus Bleecker
Bleecker, Mrs Jan Jansen
  Unidentified artist. Mrs Jan Jansen Bleeck-
    er
Bleecker, Leonard, 1755-1844
  Ames, E. Leonard Bleecker
Bleecker street Saturday night by J. Sloan
Blessed damosel by P. Bacon
Blessing of the fleet by L. Bosa
Blind accordion player by B. Shahn
Blind beggars by J. Lawrence
Blind botanist by B. Shahn
Blind fish approaching summer by B. Allan
The **blind** one by B. Greene
Blind Spanish singer by R. Henri
Blindman's buff by M. Beckmann
Blizzard by D. Macknight
BLOCH, Albert, 1882-
  Portrait
    Cheney. Primer 1958 ed
BLOCK, Laurens, fl 1650
  New Amsterdam   NNHS
    Flexner. First flowers
Block Island by E. Kelly
Blockade of Boston, View of the by C.
  Remick
Blocks by W.T. Murch
Blonde model by J. S. Sargent
Bloodgood, Francis, 1768-1840
  Ames, E. Francis Bloodgood
BLOOM, Cynthia, 1933-
  Lowlands
    MBCI. View 1960
BLOOM, Donald S.
  Pool room
    OYB. Annual 1959
BLOOM, Hyman, 1913-
  The anatomist   WMAA
    Barker. From realism
    Baur. New art (col)
    Goodrich. Amer art (col)
    Larkin rev ed (col)
    Pierson
  Apparition of danger
    Wight. Hyman Bloom (col)
  Archaeological treasure
    Baur. New art
    Hess. Abstract ptg (col)
    MMA. Contemp ptrs
  The bride
    WMAA. Neuberger collection (col)
  Buried treasure
    Baur. Revolution
    CSFP. Annual ex, 1950/51
    IU. Contemp Amer ptg, 1952 (col)
    Wight. Hyman Bloom (col)
    Wight. Milestones (col)
  Cadaver on a table
    ICA. Annual ex, 1954

Chandelier 1
  ICA. Annual ex, 1951
Chandelier II, 1945
  NBuA. Expressionism
  Wight. Hyman Bloom
Conquest
  NNSG. Younger Amer ptrs
Corpse of an elderly female
  Pierson
  Pousette-Dart. Amer ptg
Female corpse, back view
  Baur. New art
Female leg
  IU. Contemp Amer ptg & sculp, 1957
The harpies
  Wight. Hyman Bloom
The medium
  Wight. Hyman Bloom
Slaughtered animal   CLAU
  Time. 300 years (col)
  Wight. Hyman Bloom
The stone
  Hess. Abstract ptg
The synagogue   MMA
  Baur. New art
  Pierson
  Wight. Hyman Bloom
Torso and limbs
  MnMW. Expressionism 1900-1955
Treasure map   MAP
  Pierson
Blowing leaves by J. Gernand
Blowing rings by I. Bishop
Blue abstraction by A. B. Carles
Blue amorphous by R. Pousette-Dart
Blue and black by S. Francis
Blue and black by K. R. Morris
Blue and green music by G. O'Keeffe
The **blue** and the strawberry roan by
  M. B. Watkins
Blue at night by A. Gottlieb
Blue at noon by A. Gottlieb
Blue-black by S. Francis
Blue boat by W. Homer
Blue bowl by E. W. Motley
The **blue** boy by E. S. Field
The **blue** boy by W. Pachner
Blue brook water fall by J. H. Twachtman
Blue building by D. Stoltenberg
Blue canyon by C. A. Morris
Blue chair by G. Grosz
Blue chair by W. Sommer
Blue chair by F. C. Watkins
Blue chimney by A. Osver
Blue cloud by L. Feininger
Blue clown by W. Kuhn
Blue clown by P. Tchelitchew
Blue coast by L. Feininger
Blue cradle by J. Tworkov
Blue depths by J. Guerrero
Blue Devils marching down Fifth avenue
  by G. B. Luks
Blue doll by A. Pickens
Blue door by M. A. Blackburn
Blue evolution by C. K. Sibley

Blue eyes by Unidentified artist
Blue finch by F. E. Conway
Blue gable by G. Münter
Blue garden by Y. Johnston
Blue glasses by C. Brown
The **blue** gown by W. M. Chase
Blue grosbeak by J. J. Audubon
Blue hands by H. Warshaw
Blue hole on the Little Miami river by
  R. S. Duncanson
Blue horizon by P. Ghikas
Blue horse by M. Chagall
Blue horse by W. Sommer
Blue interior by D. L. Demboski
Blue is for bass by J. Lechay
Blue jay by J. J. Audubon
Blue juggler by W. Kuhn
Blue kimono by W. M. Chase
Blue landscape by L. Calcagno
Blue lines by R. Scarlett
Blue marine by L. Feininger
Blue marine by A. P. Ryder
Blue Medicine by G. Catlin
Blue mirror by W. A. Baziotes
Blue mist by R. Bennett
Blue moon by D. Kingman
Blue morning by G. W. Bellows
Blue mountain near Taos by J. Marin
Blue necklace by E. E. Speicher
Blue New York by M. Weber
Blue night by H. E. Mattson
Blue poles by J. Pollock
Blue rectangles by I. Bolotowsky
Blue rhythm by H. Hofmann
Blue rocks by M. Kahn
Blue sea, Crotch island by J. Marin
Blue shadows by D. Macknight
The **blue** shawl by R. Soyer
Blue sky by G. Grosz
Blue snow, the Battery by G. W. Bellows
Blue space by B. Greene
Blue spruce by W. A. Kienbusch
Blue table by J. Jarvaise
Blue table by M. Yektai
Blue territory by H. Frankenthaler
Blue tiger by H. Pippin
Blue II by G. O'Keeffe
The **blue** unconscious by J. Pollock
Blue vase by W. Sommer
Blue waterfall by V. Candell
Blue, white and grey by R. L. Knipschild
Blue with china ink . . . Homage to John
  Cage by R. B. Motherwell
The **bluebird** by P. Evergood
BLUEMNER, Oscar Florianus, 1867-1938
  Moonshine fantasy
    Baur. Revolution
  Old canal port   WMAA
    Goodrich. Amer art
    Pierson

BLUEMNER, O. F.—*Continued*
Radiant night   MAP
  Pierson
Silktown on the Passaic
  Brown. Amer ptg
  Pierson
  WMAA. Pioneers
The blues singer by S. Menkès
Bluff house by H. M. Gasser
Blum, Robert Frederick, 1857-1903
  Chase, W. M. Robert Frederick Blum
BLUMBERG, Yuli, 1894-
A man, Portrait of
  PPC. Ptg in the U.S. 1949
BLUME, Peter, 1906-
The boat   MMA
  Lewisohn
  NYG. Fine art
  UNESCO. 1860-1955
The bridge
  Brown. Amer ptg
  MnMW. Precisionist view
Buoy
  MMA. Contemp ptrs
Crucifixion
  IU. Contemp Amer ptg & sculp, 1953
  Pousette-Dart. Amer ptg
  Roos (detail)
Eternal city   MMA
  Barr. What is mod ptg
  Baur. New art (col)
  Larkin
  Larkin rev ed
  MMA. Masters (col)
  Pearson. Mod renaissance
  Pierson
  Robb. Harper history
  WMAA. Juliana Force
Excavation
  CSFP. Annual ex, 1947/48
  MMA. Contemp ptrs
Half-way house
  Chew. 250 years of art
  WiMiA. Amer ptg 1760-1960
Home for Christmas   OCo
  Brown. Amer ptg
Key West beach   MMA
  Baur. Revolution
  MMA. Soby collection
Landscape with poppies   MMA
  CSB. Illusion
  Gruskin
Light of the world   WMAA
  Baur. New art
  Goodrich. Am art
  Mendelowitz
  MnMW. Reality and fantasy
Lilies   MB
  MB. Ptgs in water color
Maine coast
  Baur. New art
Man of sorrows   WMAA
  Goodrich. Amer art
  Pierson
Parade   MMA
  Baur. New art
  MMA. Ptg and sculpture
  McCurdy
  Pierson
Passage to Etna   MCH
  Pierson

The rock   ICA
  Baur. New art
  Baur. Revolution
  Pearson. Mod renaissance
  Pierson
  PPC. International ex, 1950
The shrine
  Pearson. Mod renaissance
South of Scranton   MM
  Baur. New art
  Biddle. Yes and no
  MM. 100 Amer ptrs
  Pearson. Mod renaissance
  Taylor. Fifty centuries, 1954 ed (col)
  Time. 300 years (col)
  Wight. Milestones
Underpass
  WMAA. Contemp Amer ptgs, 1953
White factory   NeL
  Barker. From realism
  Pierson
BLUMENSCHEIN, Ernest Leonard, 1874-
1960
Enchanted forest
  NAD. Annual ex, 1947, 2d half
The pass   ATeS
  ATeS. Collection
BLUNT, John S. 1800?-1835
Boston harbor   MB
  MB. Karolik coll
Topsail schooner in sheltered waters
  Flexner. Light of distant skies
Winter scene   MB
  MB, Karolik coll
Blunt, Martha (Garsed) 1803-1885
  R, M. Mrs George William Blunt
BLYTH, Benjamin, fl 1746-1787
Samuel Curwen   MSE
  Pierson

Attributed works
Samuel McIntire   MSE
  MSE. Cat of ports, 1950
BLYTHE, David Gilmor, 1815-1865
Art versus law   NBM
  Mendelowitz
  Miller, D. David G. Blythe
  Pierson
  Richardson. Ptg in America
Blair family
  Miller, D. David G. Blythe
Courtroom scene
  Miller, D. David G. Blythe
Dry goods and notions   PPD
  Miller, D. David G. Blythe
  OCiM. Rediscoveries
  PPC. Amer classics
Farm scene
  Chew. 250 years of art
Gen Doubleday watching his troops cross
  the Potomac   NCB
  Miller, D. David G. Blythe
  Pierson
  U.S. National Capital sesquicentennial
  com
Gouty fisherman   ATeS
  ATeS. Collection
Hideout
  Miller, D. David G. Blythe
In the Pittsburgh post office   MB
  MB. Karolik coll
James McDonald   OYB
  OYB. Catalogue 1951

Libby prison   MB
  MB. Karolik coll
  Miller, D. David G. Blythe
Lincoln crushing the dragon of rebellion   MB
  MB. Karolik coll
Mrs Jeremiah Webber and son
  Miller, D. David G. Blythe
On the sly
  Miller, D. David G. Blythe
Pittsburgh horsemarket
  Miller, D. David G. Blythe
Post office   PPG
  Barker. Amer ptg
  Miller, D. David G. Blythe
  OYB. Blythe
President Lincoln writing the Emancipation proclamation
  Miller, D. David G. Blythe
Prospecting
  Miller, D. David G. Blythe
Recruits wanted
  Miller, D. David G. Blythe
The runaway   PPD
  OCiM. Rediscoveries
Shoremen
  Miller, D. David G. Blythe
Silas Gault
  OYB. Blythe
Stagecoach   PPD
  Miller, D. David G. Blythe
Street urchins   OYB
  OYB. Blythe
  OYB. Catalogue 1951
Thomas Coburn
  Miller, D. David G. Blythe
Tramps hideout
  OYB. Blythe
Trial scene   NR
  Miller, D. David G. Blythe
Whoa, Emma
  Larkin
  Larkin rev ed
  Miller, D. David G. Blythe
Young musician   PW
  Chew. 250 years of art
  NUM. Art across America
BMT, Fourteenth street by R. Marsh
Boardley, Elizabeth Beale, 1777-1862
  Stuart, G. Elizabeth Boardley
Boardman, Daniel Sherman, 1768-1864
  Earl, R. Daniel Boardman
Boardman, Elijah, 1760-1823
  Earl, R. Elijah Boardman
Boardwalk in moonlight by L. Jackson
The boat by M. Beckmann
The boat by P. Blume
The boat by Y. Tanguy
Boat and grain elevator #2 by R. Crawford
Boat and grain elevators by R. Crawford
Boat dock on the Riviera by M. Beckmann
Boat fantasy, Deer isle, Maine series, no 30 by J. Marin
Boat landing by M. B. Prendergast
Boat landing, Dinard by M. B. Prendergast
Boat off Deer isle by J. Marin
Boat race, Boston harbor by A. A. Lawrence
Boat, sky and sea, Small Point, Maine by J. Marin

Boat with blue by J. Marin
Boathouse by W. T. Aldrich
Boathouse, winter, Harlem river by E. Lawson
Boating party by A. Pickens
Boating party in Central park by W. Whittredge
Boating party on the Thames by G. P. A. Healy
Boats by J. E. Heliker
Boats at anchor by J. S. Sargent
Boats drying their sails, Sestri Levante, Italy by E. D. Boit
Boats off the coast of Devonshire by W. Homer
Boats on Gaspé bay by M. Avery
Boats, sea and rocks by J. Marin
Boca by S. Solomon
BOCCIA, Edward E. 1921-
  Lyric yellow
    IU. Contemp Amer ptg & sculp, 1957
  Suspended forms   MoSL
    CoS. New accessions USA, 1954
BODMER, Karl, 1809-1893
  Buffalo coming to drink in the upper Missouri
    Morgan
  Buffalo dance of the Mandan
    Morgan (col)
  Crow Indians
    Morgan
  Fort Clark
    Morgan
  Fort Pierre
    Morgan
  Funeral scaffold of a Sioux chief
    Morgan (col)
  Indian bull boats on the Missouri
    Morgan (detail)
  Interior of the hut of a Mandan chief
    Morgan (col)
  A Mandan village
    Morgan (col)
  Mato-topé, with the marks of his exploits
    Morgan (col)
  The Minnetaree scalp dance
    Morgan
  Noapeh, an Assiniboin Indian; Psihdja-sahpa, a Yanktonai Indian
    Morgan (col)
  Travelers meeting Minnetaree Indians
    Morgan
  The Yellowstone and Missouri rivers
    Morgan
Boelen, Anna. See Bancker, Anna (Boelen)
BOESE, Henry, 1744-1860
  Delaware Water Gap
    McClintock
  Stage coach seventy-six of the Knickerbocker line   NNMC
    U.S. National Capital sesquicentennial com
Boeuf by K. Knaths
Bogardus, Magdalena
  Unidentified artist. Magdalena Bogardus
Bogart, Joseph Outen, fl 1820
  Peale. Rembrandt. Lt Col Joseph Outen Bogart
BOGGS, Frank, 1855-1926
  Le Havre
    CSB. Impressionism

Boheme girl by R. Soyer

The **Bohemian** by T. Eakins

BOHROD, Aaron, 1907-
Antiques
PPC. Ptg in the U.S. 1949
The art of painting. See Self-portrait
Bird and gauntlet
OYB. Annual 1957
Human comedy
IU. Contemp Amer ptg & sculp, 1959
Ivan Albright (Through a glass darkly)
WiMiA. Amer ptg 1760-1960
Landscape near Chicago   WMAA
Baur. Revolution
McCurdy
NYG. Fine art
Pierson
Wight. Milestones
Merry-go-round   IaDa
IaDa Silver jubilee
IaDa. 30th anniversary
Military necessity
Time. 300 years (col)
Oak street platform   MB
Larkin
Larkin rev ed
Paper storm   ATU
ATU. Coll of Amer art
Pillar
MnMW. Reality and fantasy
Rainy night
Gruskin (col)
Sacred and profane
IU. Contemp Amer ptg & sculp, 1957
Self-portrait (The art of painting)
WiMiA. Amer ptg 1760-1960
Street in Peoria   OYB
OYB. Catalogue 1951
Through a glass darkly. See Ivan Albright
West park, Pittsburgh
IU. Contemp Amer ptg, 1948

Boiler synthesis by R. Crawford

Bois de Sioux river by J. M. Stanley

BOIT, Edward Darley, 1840-1915
Arc de Triomphe   MB
MB. Ptgs in water color
Beach at Sestri Levante, Italy   MB
MB. Ptgs in water color
Biarritz, a big sea   MB
MB. Ptgs in water color
Bidart, French Pyrenees   MB
MB. Ptgs in water color
Boats drying their sails, Sestri Levante,
Italy   MB
MB. Ptgs in water color
Bologna: A bright morning   MB
MB. Ptgs in water color
Bordighera, Italy   MB
MB. Ptgs in water color
The Capitol, Washington   MB
MB. Ptgs in water color
East river, New York   MB
MB. Ptgs in water color
Florence   MB
MB. Ptgs in water color
Florence from San Miniato   MB
MB. Ptgs in water color
Genoa: A hillside   MB
MB. Ptgs in water color
Genoa: The port   MB
MB. Ptgs in water color

Lake Orta, Italy   MB
MB. Ptgs in water color
Lake Maggiore, Italy   MB
MB. Ptgs in water color
London: A bend of the Thames at Chelsea
MB
MB. Ptgs in water color
Morning at Gargagno, Lake of Garda
MB
MB. Ptgs in water color
Morning at Rive, Lake of Garda   MB
MB. Ptgs in water color
Morning near Paris   MB
MB. Ptgs in water color
Old mill near St Enogat, Britanny   MB
MB. Ptgs in water color
On the Consuma pass, Tuscany   MB
MB. Ptgs in water color
Ouchy, Lake Geneva, Switzerland   MB
MB. Ptgs in water color
Park avenue, New York   MB
MB. Ptgs in water color
Piccadilly, London   MB
MB. Ptgs in water color
Place de l'Opéra, Paris   MB
MB. Ptgs in water color
Place du Carrousel, Paris, 1911   MB
MB. Ptgs in water color
Poppi in the Casentino, Tuscany   MB
MB. Ptgs in water color
Rio di San Barnaba, Venice   MB
MB. Ptgs in water color
Rio di San Lorenzo, Venice   MB
MB. Ptgs in water color
Rough sea at Portofino, Italy   MB
MB. Ptgs in water color
St Malo from Dinard, low tide, Brittany
MB
MB. Ptgs in water color
St Peter's, Rome   MB
MB. Ptgs in water color
Street in Arezzo   MB
MB. Ptgs in water color
Venice: Afternoon on the Campo San
Trovaso   MB
MB. Ptgs in water color
Venice: Afternoon on the Grand canal
MB
MB. Ptgs in water color
Venice: Fisherman's quarter on the Giudecca   MB
MB. Ptgs in water color
Venice: Looking toward the Giudecca
MB
MB. Ptgs in water color
Venice: Morning on the Grand canal
MB
MB. Ptgs in water color
Venice: Off San Giorgio   MB
MB. Ptgs in water color
Venice: Showery morning on the Zattere
MB
MB. Ptgs in water color

Boit, Mary Louise (Cushing) fl 1888
Sargent, J. S. Mrs Edward D. Boit

Boit children
Sargent, J. S. Daughters of Edward D. Boit

Bolling, Mary (Randolph) 1775?-1845
Hubard, W. J. Mrs William Bolling

Bologna: A bright morning by E. D. Boit

BOLOTOWSKY, Ilya, 1907-
 Abstraction, 1939   CtY
  CtY. Soc Anonyme
 Blue rectangles   WMAA
  Pierson
 Diamond shaped
  CSEP. Annual ex, 1950/51
 Large vertical   WMAA
  Goodrich. Amer art
 Sombre vertical with lines
  VR. Amer ptg 1958
The **bolter** by C. M. Russell
Bolton by F. Guy
Bolton landing by W. De Kooning
BOMAR, Bill, 1919-
 Lilacs and glasses
  IU. Contemp Amer ptg & sculp, 1955
 Melon   TxF
  CoS. New accessions USA, 1952
Bombardment of Fort Sumter by A. Bierstadt
Bombardment of Tripoli under Commodore Preble, 1804 by M. F. Corné
Bomber by R. Crawford
Bond, Gorham
 Goodridge, E. Gorham Bond
Bondsville fair by A. M. R. Moses
Bone, Richard
 Robinson, B. Richard Bone
Bone player by W. S. Mount
Bonfire by R. Cowles
BONHAM, Horace, 1835-1892
 Nearing the issue at the cockpit, 1870
            DC
  Davidson v2
  Mendelowitz
Bonjean, Mme
 Tchelitchew, P. Madame Bonjean
The **book** by W. M. Chase
Book, beerstein and corncob pipe by J. F. Peto
Book of life by L. Pershing
Book, shell and ship by K. Knaths
BOOKATZ, Samuel, 1910-
 Gate watch   OYB
  OYB. Annual 1958
  OYB. Supplement 1959
 Steel town madonna
  IU. Contemp Amer ptg & sculp, 1953
The **bookcase** by K. Davies
Books by J. F. Peto
Books on a shelf by J. F. Peto
Boomtown by T. H. Benton
Boon by J. D. Brooks
Boon companions by E. H. Garrett
Boone, Daniel, 1735-1820
 Bingham, G. C. Daniel Boone escorting a band of pioneers into western country
 Cole, T. Daniel Boone and cabin on Great Osage lake
 Harding, C. Daniel Boone
 Harding, C. (attributed works) Daniel Boone
The **bootblack** by G. H. Yewell
BOOTH, Cameron, 1892-
 Alms
  ICA. Annual ex, 1951

 Black and white   MnMW
  MnMW. 60 Amer ptrs
 Clam bay farm
  Cheney. Expressionism 1948 ed
 Evening
  Pousette-Dart. Amer ptg
 Painting, 1951
  MnU. 40 Amer ptrs
 Regal personages
  MnU. 40 Amer ptrs
 Street in Stillwater   DP
  DP. Catalogue
 The winters passed
  MnMW. Classic tradition
Boothbay harbor, Maine by M. M. Albright
Boots by M. Hartley
BORDER limner, fl 1815
 Alice Slade   DN
  DN. Amer primitive ptgs, pt 1
  Jones. Rediscovered ptrs
 Harriet Leavens
  ICA. From colony to nation
  Jones. Rediscovered ptrs
 Joseph Slade   DN
  DN. Amer primitive ptgs, pt 1
  Jones. Rediscovered ptrs
 Philip Slade   DN
  DN. Amer primitive ptgs, pt 2
 Robert Lockridge Dorr   VWR
  Ford. Pictorial folk art
Bordighera, Italy by E. D. Boit
Bordley, John Beale, 1727-1804
 Peale, C. W. John Beale Bordley
Bordley, Sarah Fishbourne, fl 1782
 Peale, C. W. Sarah Fishbourne Bordley
BORDUAS, Paul Émil, 1905-
 Morning candelabra   MMA
  Art since 1945
BORIE, Adolphe, 1877-1934
 Betty Campbell Madeira
  Chew. 250 years of art
BORIS, Bessie
 Old man with umbrella
  PA. Annual ex, 1961
Borland, Francis, 1691-1763
 Copley, J. S. Francis Borland
BORTIN, Dora
 Russian tea service
  PA. Annual ex, 1954
BOSA, Louis, 1905-
 Blessing of the fleet
  NAD. Annual ex, 1947, 1st half
 Carnival on ice
  DC. 22 biennial ex, 1951
  MM. Amer ptg today
 End of the festival   IU
  IU. Contemp Amer ptg, 1949
  IU. 20th century
 Fish story
  IU. Contemp Amer ptg, 1951
 Golden palace
  NAD. Annual ex, 1952
 Hallowe'en   MWM
  CoS. New accessions USA, 1950
  IU. Contemp Amer ptg, 1950
 Monks fishing, Venice   OYB
  OYB. Annual 1960
 Monks of Burano
  IU. Contemp Amer ptg & sculp, 1959
 My family reunion   WMAA
  Pierson
 Ponte Vecchio, Florence
  OYB. Annual 1956

BOSA, Louis—*Continued*
Procession of the Savior
IU. Contemp Amer ptg & sculp, 1953
San Barnaba
NAD. Annual ex, 1954
Spring on Ninth avenue
Gruskin
Welcome home
IU. Contemp Amer ptg, 1948
Boston, Massachusetts
Brown, G. L. Public gardens, Boston
Chambers, T. Boston harbor, c 1840
Fransioli, T. A. Louisburg square
Hardy, P. Tremont street, Boston
Harvey, G. Reaping on Boston Common, 1835-1840
Harvey, G. State House and Boston Common, 1830
Harvey, G. Tremont house, Boston
Hassam, C. Boston Common at twilight
Hassam, C. Columbus avenue, Boston: rainy day
Hassam, C. Rainy day
Hubbard, C. The National Lancers with the reviewing officers on Boston Common
Marston, J. B. State street and old State House, Boston, 1801
Paine, L. G. Copley square
Prendergast, M. B. South Boston
Prendergast, M. B. Street scene, Boston
Prendergast, M. B. Tremont street, Boston
Prendergast, M. B. West church, Boston
Ricci, J. Louisburg square, winter
Salmon, R. W. Boston harbor from Constitution wharf
Salmon, R. W. Boston harbor: Long and Central wharves, 1832
Savory, T. C. National Lancers on Boston Common
Sharp, W. Railroad jubilee on Boston Common
Zerbe, K. Park street, Boston
Boston daily by K. Zerbe
Boston harbor by J. S. Blunt
BOSWORTH, Sala
Jonathan Sprague   OCoA
Ford. Pictorial folk art
Melissa Sprague   OCoA
Ford. Pictorial folk art
Botafogo by R. S. Du Casse
Botafogo bay, Rio de Janeiro by J. Lavalle
Both members of this club by G. W. Bellows
BOTHWELL, Dorr, 1902-
Idea and forms
CSFP. Annual ex, 1947/48
Keepsake from Mallorca
CSFP. Annual ex, 1952
BOTKIN, Henry Albert, 1896-
The ceremony   MB
CoS. New accessions USA, 1956
IU. Contemp Amer ptg, 1951
Performer
Gruskin
Botsford, Polly, 1754-1813
Unidentified artist. Mourning picture—Polly Botsford and her children
BOTT, Emil, fl 1849-1880
Scene on the Monongahela
Chew. 250 years of art

BOTTON, Jean de, 1898-
The four horsemen of the Apocalypse
PPC. Ptg in the U.S. 1949
BOUCHÉ, Louis, 1896-
County home
WiMiA. Amer ptg 1760-1960
Fire
IU. Contemp Amer ptg, 1949
High street bus barn
Pousette-Dart. Amer ptg
Long Island sound
Gruskin (col)
Mural assistant   CLA
Time. 300 years (col)
New Lebanon railroad station
PPC. Ptg in the U.S. 1949
Peppercombe porch
PPC. International ex, 1950
Piermont, New York
NAD. Annual ex, 1959
Self-portrait
WiMiA. Amer ptg 1760-1960
Stamford harbor   WMAA
Goodrich. Amer art
NYG. Fine art
Ten cents a ride   MM
MM. 100 Amer ptrs
Pierson
Unpainted horses   ATeS
ATeS. Collection
BOUCHÉ, René
Saul Steinberg
IU. Contemp Amer ptg & sculp, 1957
Boudé, Samuel, fl 1755
West, B. Samuel Boudé
Boudé, Mrs Samuel, fl 1755
West, B. Mrs Samuel Boudé
Boudoir by W. De Kooning
BOUDRO(U), Alexandr, fl 1851
A. Dickson entering Bristol in 1819 VWR
VWR. Amer folk art
VWR. Folk art (col)
Bounetheau's aunt by E. G. Malbone
The bountiful board by Unidentified artist
Bouquet by H. Hofmann
Bouquet by R. Philipp
Bouquet by S. Serisawa
Bouquet abstraction by A. B. Carles
Bouquet in blue vase by A. B. Carles
Bouquet in Quimper pitcher by W. J. Glackens
Bouquet of flowers by H. G. Keller
Bourgouis W—r and his squaw by A. J. Miller
Bourne, Mercy (Gorham) 1695-1782
Copley, J. S. Mrs Sylvanus Bourne
Bours, Peter, 1783-1860
Malbone, E. G. Peter Bours
BOUTELLE, De Witt Clinton, 1820-1884
Indian surveying a landscape   MB
MB. Karolik coll
Bovard, Mrs James M.
Trebilcock, P. Mrs James M. Bovard
BOVÉ, Richard John, 1920-
Classic still life
NAD. Annual ex, 1954
New York scene
NAD. Annual ex, spring 1950
Steeplechase horses
NAD. Annual ex, 1956

BOWDEN, H.
View of the bay
  CSFP. Annual ex, 1948/49
Bowditch, Nathaniel, 1773-1838
  Stuart, G. Nathaniel Bowditch
Bowdoin, Elizabeth, fl 1760
  Blackburn, J. Elizabeth and James Bowdoin
Bowdoin, Elizabeth, 1750-1809. See Temple, Elizabeth (Bowdoin) lady
Bowdoin, Elizabeth, fl 1754-1762. See Pitts, Elizabeth (Bowdoin)
Bowdoin, Elizabeth (Erving) 1731-1803
  Feke, R. Mrs James Bowdoin
  Malbone, E. G. Mrs James Bowdoin
Bowdoin, James, 1676-1747
  Badger, J. James Bowdoin
Bowdoin, James, 1726-1790
  Feke, R. James Bowdoin II
Bowdoin, James, 1752-1811
  Malbone, E. G. Hon James Bowdoin
Bowdoin, James, fl 1760
  Blackburn, J. Elizabeth and James Bowdoin
Bowdoin, Mrs James. See Bowdoin, Elizabeth (Erving)
Bowdoin, Phoebe (Murdock) d 1772
  Feke, R. Mrs William Bowdoin
Bowdoin, William, fl 1748
  Feke, R. William Bowdoin
Bowdoin, Mrs William. See Bowdoin, Phoebe (Murdock)
Bowen, Elizabeth. See Amory, Elizabeth (Bowen)
Bowen, Lydia. See Clark, Lydia (Bowen)
BOWER, John, fl 1809-1819
  View of bombardment of Fort McHenry
                                        ICH
    U. S. National Capital sesquicentennial com
BOWERS, Edward, fl 1855-1867
  Fruit and wine   MB
    MB. Karolik coll
Bowers, Mrs Jerathmael. See Bowers, Mary (Sherburne)
Bowers, Mary (Sherburne) 1735-1799
  Copley, J. S. Mrs Jerathmael Bowers
The **Bowery** by R. Marsh
The **Bowery** at night by W. L. Sonntag
Bowery at Pell street by R. Marsh
Bowery drunks by R. Marsh
The **bowl** by R. Marsh
Bowl of apples by W. Sommer
Bowl of fruit by Unidentified artist
Bowl of wild roses by J. La Farge
Bowne, Walter, 1770-1846
  Malbone, E. G. Walter Bowne
The **bowsprit** by F. W. Benson
Box of tricks by C. H. Demuth
Box party by K. H. Miller
Boxers and wrestlers
  Bellows, G. W. Both members of this club
  Bellows, G. W. Club night
  Bellows, G. W. Dempsey and Firpo
  Bellows, G. W. Ringside seats
  Eakins, T. Between rounds
  Eakins, T. Wrestlers
  Hayes, G. A. Bare knuckles

  Luks, G. B. Wrestlers
  Martin, F. The glory
  Martin, F. Lullaby
  Martin, F. The undefeated
Boy by G. W. Bellows
Boy by B. Karfiol
Boy by M. B. Prendergast
Boy by B. Shahn
Boy and girl by R. Soyer
Boy bathers by B. Karfiol
Boy carrying deer by W. Homer
Boy eating an apple by W. M. Chase
Boy feeding a cockatoo by W. M. Chase
Boy fishing by W. Homer
Boy from Stalingrad by P. Evergood
Boy from the plains by P. Hurd
Boy holding dog by J. Bradley (attributed works)
Boy holding lamb's head by W. Stein
Boy in beaver hat by A. M. Von Phul
Boy in blue coat by Unidentified artist
Boy in Mexico by C. L. Casebier
Boy in plaid by Unidentified artist
Boy in the grass by B. Perlin
Boy on stenciled carpet by E. S. Field (attributed works)
Boy picking apples by W. Homer
Boy picking flowers by F. Martin
Boy smoking by W. M. Chase
Boy stealing fruit by Y. Kuniyoshi
Boy with a cigar by W. M. Chase
Boy with a toy drum by Unidentified artist
Boy with birds by D. Jameson
Boy with chalice by C. A. Morris
Boy with cow by Y. Kuniyoshi
Boy with doves by S. Menkès
Boy with finch by Unidentified artist
Boy with guitar by H. Lotterman
Boy with hammer and iron pot by Unidentified artist
Boy with machine by R. Lindner
Boy with squirrel by J. S. Copley
Boy with still life by S. Roesen
Boy with the anchor by W. Homer
Boy with whip by Unidentified artist
Boylston, Nicholas, 1716-1771
  Copley, J. S. Nicholas Boylston
Boylston, Sarah (Morecock) 1696-1774
  Copley, J. S. Mrs Thomas Boylston
Boynton, Emeline, b 1813?
  Walton, H. Emeline Boynton, age 32
Boynton, Harriet Elizabeth, b 1843?
  Walton, H. Harriet Elizabeth Boynton, age 2 years
Boynton, Henry, b 1806?
  Walton, H. Henry Boynton, age 39
BOYNTON, James W. 1929?
  Bright stalk
    WMAA. Young America 1957
  Cove
    NNSG. Younger Amer ptrs
  Image and space
    WMAA. Young America 1957

BOYNTON, J. W.—*Continued*
  Limestone Edge   TxD
    Pierson
  Sun trap   OYB
    Brussels. Exposition
Boys bathing by W. Homer
Boys beaching a dory by W. Homer
Boys caught napping in a field by W. S.
    Mount
Boys fishing by J. Kane
Boys in a pasture by W. Homer
Boys on the beach by J. S. Sargent
Boys skating by G. H. Durrie
Boys wading by W. Homer
Brace's rock, Eastern point, Gloucester by
    F. H. Lane
Brackett, Albert Gallatin, 1829-1896
  Healy, G. P. A. Albert G. Brackett
BRACKMAN, Robert, 1898-
  Junior
    NAD. Annual ex, 1949, 1st half
  Lighthouse keeper
    NAD. Annual ex, 1947, 2d half
    NAD. Annual ex, 1961
  Peter Freuchen
    PA. Annual ex, 1958
    PPC. International ex, 1950
  Portrait in studio light
    NAD. Annual ex, 1959
  Sailor's holiday   MM
    MM. 100 Amer ptrs
  Self-portrait
    NAD. Annual ex, 1953
  Still life in gray
    IU. Contemp Amer ptg, 1952
  Still life with figure   IaDa
    Gruskin
    IaDa. Silver jubilee
  Unmasked
    PPC. Ptg in the U.S. 1949
  Young woman with bird
    NAD. Annual ex, spring 1950
BRADFORD, Howard, 1919-
  Hanging bird
    ICA. Annual ex, 1957
BRADFORD, William, 1823-1892
  Ship Dashing Wave off Boston Light
                                              MSP
    NUM. Art across America
Bradley, Mr, fl 1835
  Philips (attributed works) Mr Bradley
Bradley, Mrs, fl 1835
  Phillips (attributed works). Mrs Bradley
BRADLEY, I. J. H. fl 1830-1855
  The cellist   DP
    Barker. Amer ptg
    Baur. Amer ptg
    DP. Catalogue
    Pierson
BRADLEY, J. C.
  Still life with red plush and thistle
    CSFP. Annual ex, 1946
BRADLEY, John, fl 1836-1847
  Emma Homan   DN
    DN. Amer primitive ptgs, pt 2
  Little girl in lavender   DN
    DN. Amer primitive ptgs, pt 1
        Attributed works
  Boy holding dog   VWR
    VWR. Folk art (col)

  Girl with flower basket   VWR
    VWR. Folk art (col)
Bradley, Lucy
  Earl, R. Lucy Bradley
BRADLEY, Mary, fl 1830
  Basket of fruit   VWR
    Pierson
    VWR. Amer folk art (col)
BRADSHAW, Glenn R.
  Factory no 1
    NAD. Annual ex, 1957
BRADSHAW, J. W.
  An Indian   DN
    DN. Amer primitive ptgs, pt 2
Brailsford, Dr, fl 1802
  Malbone, E. G. Dr Brailsford
Brailsford, Samuel, b 1729
  Theus, J. Col Samuel Brailsford
Branch bank of the United States by R.
    Smith
Brandegee, Mary Bryant (Pratt)
  Sargent, J. S. Mrs Edward D. Brandegee
Brandywine by W. Sommer
Brandywine landscape by W. Sommer
The Brandywine, View on by J. Peale
Branford, William, 1756-1776
  Theus, J. Young William Branford
Brant, Joseph (Thayendanegea) 1742-1807
  Ames, E. Joseph Brant, Thayendanegea
BRANTZ, Lewis
  Pittsburgh, 1790   PPC
    Davidson v2
Brasher, Miss, fl 1804
  Malbone, E. G. Miss Brasher
Brass, Catherine. See Yates, Catherine
    (Brass)
Brass band by J. Covert
Brattle, William, 1702-1776
  Copley, J. S. William Brattle
The bravado by A. J. Miller
The brave's return by C. M. Russell
Bread and circuses by R. Gwathmey
The breadline by G. B. Luks
Breadmakers by M. Sterne
Breaker by P. Busa
The breaker boy by G. B. Luks
Breakers by L. B. La Farge
Breakers, Maine coast by J. Marin
Breakfast at sunrise by A. J. Miller
The breakfast table by J. S. Sargent
Breaking down the wild horse by G. Catlin
Breaking sea by M. Avery
Breaking the home ties by T. Hovenden
Breaking up camp at sunrise by A. J. Miller
Breaking up the ice in spring by F. Reming-
    ton
Breaking wave by W. Homer
Breakwater by S. M. Adler
Breakwater by Y. Johnston
Breakwater by J. Kaplan
Breakwater, Tynemouth by W. Homer
Breathitt, Jane. See Sappington, Jane
    (Breathitt)
BRECKNER, George, 1914-
  Mill entrance   OYB
    OYB. Annual 1954
    OYB. Supplement

Breeches buoy by A. Winter
Breezing up by W. Homer
BREININ, Raymond, 1908-
  At Golgotha   OYB
    OYB. Supplement
  City view
    CSFP. Annual ex, 1952
  He walks alone
    Gruskin
  In a garden of ancient loves
    IU. Contemp Amer ptg, 1948
  Jean Piccard
    Genauer
    PA. Annual ex, 1948
  The magicians
    NAD. Annual ex, 1947, 1st half
  The night   MB
    MB. Ptgs in water color
    Pierson
  They guard the night
    Baur. Revolution
  White house   MMA
    Cheney. Primer 1958 ed
Breintall, Mary. See Peters, Mary (Brein-tall)
BREREWOOD, Francis, fl 1730
  Benedict Leonard Calvert, Governor of
    Maryland   MdBW
    DC. Amer ptrs of the South
BRETT, Dorothy Eugenie, 1883-
  Women's dance
    IU. Contemp Amer ptg & sculp, 1953

Portrait of the artist

Ray, R. D. The Honorable Dorothy
  Eugenie Brett
Brewer, Nicholas
  Peale, C. W. Nicholas Brewer I
Brewer, William Henry, 1828-1910
  Beckwith, J. C. William H. Brewer
BREWSTER, Anna Richards, 1870-1952
  Clovelly street, Devon   OYB
    OYB. Supplement
BREWSTER, John, 1766-1854?
  Child with a peach   MB
    MB. Karolik coll
  Francis O. Watts with bird   NCHA
    Jones. New-found folk art
  One shoe off   NCHA
    Jones. New-found folk art

Attributed works

Eliphaz Thayer and his wife, Deliverance
                        NCHA
  Jones. New-found folk art
Gentleman in a landscape   NCHA
  Jones. New-found folk art
Lady in a landscape   NCHA
  Jones. New-found folk art
BREWTON, James
  Suicide of Judas
    PA. Annual ex, 1959-60
Brewton, Rebecca. See Motte, Rebecca
  (Brewton)
The **briarwood** pipe by W. Homer
BRICE, William, 1921-
  Black rocks, kelp and sea
    IU. Contemp Amer ptg & sculp, 1955
  Fragments of roses
    IU. Contemp Amer ptg & sculp, 1953

Ocean and cliffs   CLA
  CoS. New accessions USA, 1956
  ICA. Annual ex, 1957
Ocean and rocks
  PPC. International ex, 1955
Rose picture   MCH
  Pulitzer v2
Rose sequence
  Pousette-Dart. Amer ptg
Roses
  NBuA. Expressionism
Young woman with gloves
  PPC. Ptg in the U.S. 1949
Bridal veil and El Capitan, Yosemite valley
  by T. Hill
The **bride** by H. Bloom
The **bride** by A. Rattner
The **bride** by F. Robbins
Bride and owl by G. Hartigan
The **bridge** by C. Schucker
Bridge and steps, Venice by M. B. Prender-gast
Bridge for fishing by L. M. Eilshemius
Bridge sign by E. Hicks
BRIDGES, Charles, fl 1725-1750
  Anne Byrd   VWR
    NUM. Art across America
  Maria Taylor Byrd of Westover, Virginia
                        MM
    Belknap
    Mendelowitz
    Pierson
    Richardson. Ptg in America
  Mrs William Byrd (?) (Stewart coll)
    Flexner. First flowers
  Wilhelmina Byrd (?)
    Belknap

Attributed works

Mann Page the second (?)   VWC
  Barker. Amer ptg
Bridges
  Albee, P. F. The bridge
  Berman, E. Bridges of Paris
  Blatas, A. Pont Neuf
  Blume, P. The bridge
  Bosa, L. Ponte Vecchio, Florence
  Burliuk, D. Harlem river bridge
  Cook, H. N. The bridge
  Crawford, R. Whitestone bridge
  Crimi, A. D. Brooklyn bridge
  Davis, S. Bridge at Courbevoie
  Dickinson, P. Bridge
  Dickinson, P. Harlem
  Dove, A. G. Holbrook's bridge, northwest, 1938
  Duveneck, F. The bridges, Florence
  Drumlevitch, S. Bronx bridge
  Feininger, L. Bridge
  Glackens, W. J. La Villette
  Goodwin, A. C. High bridge, New York
  Guglielmi, L. The bridge
  Halpert, S. Brooklyn bridge
  Hill, J. W. Hudson river bridge near
    Waterford
  Howard, W. Le Pont Neuf
  Kane, J. Juniata river
  Katzman, H. Brooklyn bridge
  Koch, J. The bridge
  Koerner, H. The bridge
  Lawson, E. High bridge

Bridges—*Continued*
  Lawson, E. Spring night, Harlem river
  Lichtenberg, M. Albert bridge, London
  Moses, A. M. R. Sunday (The covered bridge)
  Prendergast, M. B. Bridge in Venice
  Prendergast, M. B. Ponte della Paglia
  Pucci, A. J. Ponte Vecchio
  Ranger, H. W. High bridge
  Rufty, E. M. Bridge over Dock street
  Schucker, C. The bridge
  Sheeler, C. Golden Gate
  Smith, R. Monongahela bridge after the freshet in 1832
  Smith, W. H. Hell Gate bridge
  Spencer, N. Two bridges
  Stella, J. The bridge
  Stella, J. Brooklyn bridge
  Stuempfig, W. The railroad bridge
  Toney, A. Bridge
  Unidentified artist. Town bridge
  Watson, R. The bridge
  Whistler, J. A. M. Last of old Westminster
  Whistler, J. A. M. Old Battersea bridge
Bridle path, Tahiti by J. La Farge
Bridle path, White mountains by W. Homer
Bridlington quay by W. Homer
Brig Antelope in Boston harbor by F. H. Lane
Brig Charles of Boston by M. F. Corné
Brig in a storm by T. Birch
Briggs, Mr, fl 1840
  Unidentified artist. Mr Briggs
Briggs, Mrs, fl 1840
  Unidentified artist. Mrs Briggs
BRIGGS, Ernest, 1923-
  Painting, 1954
    MMA. 12 Americans
  Painting, 1955 [1]
    MMA. 12 Americans
  Painting, 1955 [2]
    MMA. 12 Americans
  Painting, 1955 [3]
    MMA. 12 Americans
  Painting, 1955 [4]
    MMA. 12 Americans
  Painting, 1956
    MMA. 12 Americans (col)
Briggs, Mary, fl 1840
  Unidentified artist. Mary Briggs
Brigham's yard, Kingston by E. E. Speicher
Bright beyond by I. R. Pereira
Bright stalk by J. W. Boynton
Brightening Seine by J. Whorf
Brightness as a third dimension by R. Anuszkiewicz
Brighton, England by R. Smith
Brine, Augustus, 1770-1840
  Copley, J. S. Midshipman Augustus Brine
Bringing home the cattle—coast of Florida by T. Moran
Bringing home the moose by T. Eakins
Bringing home the new cook by F. Remington
Bringing home the scalp by C. M. Russell
Bringing in the Christmas tree by A. M. R. Moses
Brinton, John H. 1832-1907
  Eakins, T. Dr John H. Brinton

Bristol mills by B. Miller
British fleet forcing the Hudson river passage, 1776 by D. Serres
British privateers with French prizes in New York harbor by Unidentified artist
British troops at Concord by R. Earl
Broadway, night by J. Marin
Broadway, 1936 by M. Tobey
Broadway restaurant by G. Hartigan
BRODERSON, Morris, 1928-
  Chicken market
    WMAA. Young America 1960
  Sound of flowers
    WMAA. Young America 1960
BRODIE, Gandy, 1925-
  Momentous vision of spring
    WMAA. Annual ex, 1957
Brodnax, Edward, d 1746
  Unidentified artist. Edward Brodnax
Broe and McDonald listen in by K. Schmidt
Broken life by A. Refregier
Broken pot with blue vase by H. L. McFee
Broken tree by M. Weber
A **bronc** to breakfast by C. M. Russell
Bronson, Catherine. See Townsend, Catherine
Bronx bridge by S. Drumlevitch
Bronx light by B. Weiner
BROOK, Alexander, 1898-
  Amalia   OT
    OT. Contemp Amer ptgs
  Ann   MM
    Lewisohn
    MM. 100 Amer ptrs
  Barn chair
    PPC. Ptg in the U.S. 1949
  The bay beyond
    ICA. Annual ex, 1951
  Belinda standing   MoSL
    MoSL. Handbook 1953
  Clifford Tallulah Maddox
    IU. Contemp Amer ptg, 1949
  Frogtown lady
    IU. Contemp Amer ptg, 1948
  George Biddle playing the flute   MMA
    Brown. Amer ptg
  Georgia jungle   PPC
    Gruskin (col)
    Time. 300 years (col)
  Introspection
    CSFP. Annual ex, 1948/49
  The intruder
    WMAA. Juliana Force
  Mood   WMAA
    Goodrich. Amer art
  Mother and daughter
    NAD. Annual ex, 1957
  My wife   DC
    NYG. Fine art
  Peggy Bacon and metaphysics   NeL
    Gruskin
    Pierson
  Remnants   ATeS
    ATeS. Collection
    Pousette-Dart. Amer ptg
    PPC. International ex, 1950
  Rosa Maria
    NAD. Annual ex, 1959
  The sentinels   WMAA
    Goodrich. Amer art (col)
    NYG. Fine art
    Pierson

Serafina
  NAD. Annual ex, 1956
The shore
  NAD. Annual ex, 1952
Sleeping girl
  Brown. Amer ptg
Southern belle
  DC. 22 biennial ex, 1951
  NAD. Annual ex, 1948
Summer wind
  Baur. Revolution
Which way to Sunbury?
  DC. 20 biennial ex, 1947
The yellow fan   NUM
  NUM. Root bequest
Young pianist
  NAD. Annual ex, spring 1950
  PA. Annual ex, 1948

Brook, Mrs Alexander. See Knee, Gina
Brook, Gina (Knee) See Knee, Gina
Brook among rocks by J. S. Sargent
Brook bathers by M. Avery
Brook by moonlight by R. A. Blakelock
Brook in Vermont by G. H. Hallowell
Brook, Montclair by G. Inness
Brook Watson and the shark by J. S. Copley
BROOKES, Samuel Marsden, b 1816
  Salmon trout and smelt   CSFD
  Frankenstein. After the hunt
Brooklyn, New York
  Guy, F. Brooklyn, 1816-1820
  Unidentified artist. Street in Brooklyn
    c 1840-1860
Brooklyn bridge by A. D. Crimi
Brooklyn bridge by S. Halpert
Brooklyn bridge by H. Katzman
Brooklyn bridge by J. Stella
Brooklyn bridge—Variation on an old theme
    by J. Stella
Brooklyn ice house by G. Ault
Brooklyn Navy yard by J. W. Martens
BROOKS, James D. 1906-
  Ainlee   MM
    Art since 1945
    Pierson
  Altoon
    MMA. 12 Americans (col)
  Boon
    WMAA. Annual ex, 1958
  Cauthunda
    Seiberling
  Denain
    IU. Contemp Amer ptg & sculp, 1961
  Dolamen   NNSG
    NNSG. Handbook
  E—1953
    WMAA. New decade
  Flight
    MnU. 40 Amer ptrs
  Gant   NBuA
    MMA. 12 Americans
    NBuA. Acquisitions 1954-57
  Gordian
    Hunter. Mod Amer ptg
  Holdan
    MMA. 12 Americans
  Jackson
    MMA. New Amer ptg
  Jondol
    PPC. International ex, 1961/62

Karrig   MnMW
  Art since 1945 (col)
  MMA. New Amer ptg (col)
  MnMW. 60 Amer ptrs (col)
Larpolo
  ICA. Annual ex, 1961
Loring
  Ponente. Mod ptg, 1960 (col)
M—1951
  PPC. International ex, 1952
M—1953
  NNSG. Younger Amer ptrs
Number 18, 1949
  Hess. Abstract ptg
Number 27, 1950   WMAA
  Cheney. New world history
  Cheney. Story 1958 ed
  Hess. Abstract ptg
  McCurdy
  MMA. Abstract
  WMAA. New decade
Number 38, 1951
  MnU. 40 Amer ptrs
Number 44
  IU. Contemp Amer ptg, 1952
  Pousette-Dart. Amer ptg
Q—1952
  IU. Contemp Amer ptg & sculp, 1955
Qualm   MMA
  MMA. New Amer ptg
  MMA. 12 Americans
Quatic
  MMA. 12 Americans
R—1953
  Eliot. Art of our time (col)
  MMA. 12 Americans
  Time. 300 years (col)
Rasalus   WMAA
  Goodrich. Amer art (col)
S—1951
  IU. Contemp Amer ptg & sculp, 1953
T—1954
  WMAA. New decade
BROOKS, Nicholas A. fl 1880-1904
  Still life with playbill   OOb
  Frankenstein. After the hunt
Brother and sister sharing a book by W. M.
    Prior (manner of)
Brothers by A. G. Dove
Brothers by B. Shahn
BROUDY, Miriam
  Douarnenez
    NAD. Annual ex, 1961
Broughton, Mrs Alexander. See Ravenel,
    Elizabeth Damaris
Broughton, Anne, d 1755?
  Johnston, H. Anne Broughton (Mrs John
    Gibbes)
Broughton, Charlotte. See Izard, Charlotte
    (Broughton)
Broughton, Nicholson
  Unidentified artist. Captain Nicholson
    Broughton
Brower, Catherine, fl 1791
  MacKay. Catherine Brower
BROWERE, Alburtis Del Orient, 1814-1887
  Catskills   NBM
    Born
  Crossing the Isthmus, c 1852
    U.S. National Capital sesquicentennial
    com
  Falls of San Joaquin, California   ICA
    Born

BROWERE, A. D.—*Continued*
Mrs McCormick's general store, Catskill,
 N.Y.   NCHA
  Davidson v2
  Jones. Rediscovered ptrs
Stockton, California, 1856   CSFD
  Born

Attributed works
Hudson river landing   NAI
  Jones, Rediscovered ptrs
Brown, Mrs Abiah, fl 1804
Malbone, E. G. Mrs Abiah Brown
BROWN, Carlyle, 1919-
Blue glasses
  DC. 27 biennial ex, 1961
Red cabinet   WMAA
  Goodrich. Amer art
  McCurdy
  Pierson
  WMAA. New decade
Red still life
  IU. Contemp Amer ptg & sculp, 1957
The round table
  PPC. International ex, 1952
Round table with fiasco and landscape
  ICA. Annual ex, 1954
  WMAA. New decade
Shelf still life
  ICA. Annual ex, 1957
Still life with bottles
  WMAA. Annual ex, 1954
Still life with glasses and roses   IU
  Pierson
Still life with landscape
  IU. Contemp Amer ptg & sculp, 1953
Table with fish and scales
  ICA. Annual ex, 1951
Table with glasses and napkin
  CSFP. Annual ex, 1952
  WMAA. Contemp Amer ptg, 1951
Table with glasses and roses   IU
  IU. Contemp Amer ptg, 1952
  IU. 20th century
  Pousette-Dart. Amer ptg
BROWN, Douglas, 1899-
Haunted house (Suburban development,
 Mexico city)   MB
  MB. Ptgs in water color
BROWN, Douglas Edwin, 1904-
Decadence in Guatemala   CtY
  CtY. Soc Anonyme
Brown, Elizabeth (Byles) 1737-1763
Copley, J. S. Mrs Gawen Brown
BROWN, George Loring, 1814-1889
Castello Dell'ovo, Bay of Naples   MB
  MB. Karolik coll
Leatherstocking kills the panther   MB
  MB. Karolik coll
Medford marshes   MB
  MB. Karolik coll
Olneyville, Rhode Island
  Sears. Highlights
Public gardens, Boston   MB
  MB. Karolik coll
View of Norwalk island   MAP
  Born
BROWN, J. fl 1808
Laura Hall   NCHA
  Jones. Rediscovered ptrs
  NUM. Art across America
Mrs Calvin Hall   VWR
  Jones. Rediscovered ptrs

Attributed works
Clarissa Partridge Childs   VWR
  VWR. Amer folk art (col)
Brown, Jacob Jennings, 1775-1827
Jarvis, J. W. General Jacob Jennings
 Brown
Brown, Mrs Jacob Jennings. See Brown,
 Pamela (Williams)
BROWN, Joan, 1938-
Steam room at Boyes Hot Springs
  IU. Contemp Amer ptg & sculp, 1961
The sun blew up in Salinas
  WMAA. Young America 1960
Things and mess in classroom
  WMAA. Young America 1960
Brown, John, 1800-1859
Hovenden, T. Last moments of John
 Brown
Pippin, H. John Brown going to his
 hanging
Pippin, H. John Brown reading his Bible
Pippin, H. Trial of John Brown
Brown, Mrs John Ball. See Brown, Rebecca
 (Warren)
BROWN, John George, 1831-1913
Berry boy   MSG
  Larkin
  Larkin rev ed
The blacksmith   NoCR
  NoCR. Catalogue
County gallants   OT
  Pierson
Longshoremen's noon   DC
  Davidson v 1
BROWN, Mather, 1761-1831
Charles Bulfinch   MCH
  Pierson
John Adams   MBA
  ICA. From colony to nation
Self-portrait   MWA
  MWA. Checklist of portraits
William Van Murray   DN
  DN. Mellon coll
Brown, Nicholas(?) 1769-1841
Malbone, E. G. Nicholas(?) Brown
Brown, Pamela (Williams) 1785-1878
Ames, E. Mrs Jacob Jennings Brown
Brown, Rebecca (Warren)
Harding, C. Mrs John Ball Brown
BROWN, Roy Henry, 1879-1956
Early autumn snow
  NAD. Annual ex, 1947, 2d half
Harbinger of spring
  NYG. Fine art
Brown, Sarah, 1773-1846
Malbone, E. G. Sarah Brown
BROWN, W. H. fl 1886
Bareback riders   DN
  DN. Amer primitive ptgs, pt 2
Brown and black on plum by M. Rothko
Brown and white by W. De Kooning
Brown figure by R. B. Motherwell
Brown hat by M. Avery
Brown painting by C. A. Morris
Brown pelican by J. J. Audubon
Brown sweater by R. Soyer
Brown Swiss by A. N. Wyeth
BROWNE, Byron, 1907-
Azoic fugue
  Pousette-Dart. Amer ptg

Black lion
ICA. Annual ex, 1947/48
The dancers
IU. Contemp Amer ptg, 1950
Still life in primary colors
Larkin
Summer night   IU
IU. Contemp Amer ptg, 1951
IU. 20th century
Two figures
IU. Contemp Amer ptg
Variations on a still life
MMA. Abstract
Woman with bird   WMAA
Pierson

Browne, Jane. See Livermore, Jane
(Browne)

Browne, Katherine (Winthrop) 1711-1781
Unidentified artist. Mrs Samuel Browne
jr

BROWNE, Syd, 1907-
After the storm
NAD. Annual ex, 1952

BROWNELL, Charles De Wolf, 1822-1901
The Charter Oak   CtHW
CtHW. Handbook

BROWNING, Colleen, 1923-
The bathers
NAD. Annual ex, 1957
Film studio   OYB
OYB. Annual 1954
OYB. Supplement
Fire escape
MnMW. Reality and fantasy
Holiday
PPC. International ex, 1952
Iberian landscape
IU. Contemp Amer ptg & sculp, 1953
Out   CSFP
CSB. Illusion
Telephones
IU. Contemp Amer ptg & sculp, 1955
OYB. Annual 1955
OYB. Supplement 1959
The window
IU. Contemp Amer ptg & sculp, 1959

BRUCE, Edward, 1879-1943
Landscape of Provence
Baur. Revolution
Tuscan landscape
Lewisohn

BRUCE, Patrick Henry, 1880-1937
Composition II   CtY
Baur. Revolution
Brown. Amer ptg
CtY. Soc Anonyme
McCurdy
MMA. Abstract
Pierson
Painting   WMAA
Goodrich. Amer art
Pierson

Bruce, William, 1779-1845
Malbone, E. G. William Bruce

BRUCKMAN, Lodewÿk Karel, 1903-
Memories
IU. Contemp Amer ptg, 1952

BRUFF, Joseph Goldsborough, 1804-1889
Assorted prints
CSFP. Illusionism
The rack
Hess. Abstract ptg

BRUSH, George De Forest, 1855-1941
At dawn
McCracken. Portrait of the old west
In the garden   MM
MM. 100 Amer ptrs
Pierson
Mother and child   MB
Larkin
Larkin rev ed
Roos
Silence broken
McCracken. Portrait of the old west
Thea   OYB
OYB. Catalogue 1951

Brushy hillside by E. F. Spruce

Bruyn, Severyn
Vanderlyn, J. Severyn Bruyn

Bryan, Jennie Byrd
Healy, G. P. A. Jennie Bryan

Bryan, Thomas B. fl 1857
Healy, G. P. A. The Bryan family

Bryant, William Cullen, 1794-1878
Gray, H. P. William Cullen Bryant
Morse, S. F. B. William Cullen Bryant

Bryant square by J. Marin

Buchanan, James, president U.S. 1791-1868
Healy, G. P .A. James Buchanan

Buchanan, Mildred. See Knowles, Mildred
(Buchanan)

Buchenwald cart by R. Lebrun

BUCK, Bennett, 1900-
Circus scene   ATU
ATU. Coll of Amer art

BUCK, Claude, 1890-
Leslie   InTH
InTH. Catalogue

BUCK, Lewis
Iotrio
Pousette-Dart. Amer ptg

Bucking bronco by C. M. Russell

Buckland, William, 1734-1774
Peale, C. W. William Buckland

Bucklin, Amelia. See Cornwall, Amelia
(Bucklin)

Bucks county barn by C. Sheeler

The buck's progress by W. Allston

Bucolic landscape by M. Avery

Budd children, fl 1825
Unidentified artist. Five children of the
Budd family

BUDINGTON, Jonathan, fl 1800-1812
Father and son   DN
DN. Amer primitive ptgs, pt 2

BUDNICK, Sidney J. 1921-
Number 23
ICA. Annual ex, 1947/48

Buehr, Mrs George Frederick. See Hoff,
Margo

Buen Retiro, Madrid by W. J. Glackens

Buffalo, New York
Sellstedt, L. G. Buffalo harbor from the
foot of Porter avenue
Walsh, E. Fort Erie from Buffalo creek,
site of the city of Buffalo, c 1810

Buffalo Bill's traps by G. Cope

Buffalo dance of the Mandan by K. Bodmer

Buffalo hunting in summer by P. Rindisbacher

Buffalo newsboy by T. Le Clear

Buffaloes
  Audubon, J. J. Head of a buffalo calf
  Bierstadt, A. Buffalo bull
  Bierstadt, A. Buffalo trail
  Bierstadt, A. Last of the buffalo
  Bierstadt, A. Snow scene with buffaloes
  Bodmer, K. Buffalo coming to drink in the upper Missouri
  Catlin, G. Buffalo chase
  Catlin, G. Buffalo chase of the Sioux
  Catlin, G. Buffalo chase, upper Missouri
  Catlin, G. Buffalo crossing Yellowstone in winter
  Catlin, G. Buffalo hunt on snow shoes
  Catlin, G. Buffalo hunt, under the wolf mask
  Catlin, G. Buffalo stampede
  Catlin, G. Catlin hunting buffalo
  Catlin, G. Sioux Indians hunting buffalo
  Darley, F. O. C. Hunting buffaloes
  Eastman, S. Hunting buffalo in winter
  Miller, A. J. Approaching buffalo
  Miller, A. J. The bravado
  Miller, A. J. Buffalo at bay
  Miller, A. J. Buffalo chase—by a female
  Miller, A. J. Buffalo hunting near Independent rock
  Miller, A. J. Buffalo turning on his pursuers
  Miller, A. J. Buffaloes drinking and bathing at night
  Miller, A. J. Hunting buffalo
  Miller, A. J. Killing buffalo with the lance
  Miller, A. J. Pawnee running buffalo
  Miller, A. J. Running buffalo
  Miller, A. J. Surround of buffalo by Indians
  Miller, A. J. Wounded buffalo
  Miller, A. J. Yell of triumph
  Pippin, H. Buffalo hunt
  Remington, F. Recruit from civilization
  Rindisbacher, P. Buffaloes in winter
  Rindisbacher, P. Indians hunting buffalo
  Russell, C. M. Buffalo crossing the Missouri
  Russell, C. M. The buffalo drive
  Russell, C. M. Buffalo hunt
  Russell, C. M. Wild man's meat
  Russell, C. M. Wounded buffalo
  Stanley, J. M. Buffalo hunt on the southern plains
  Tait, A. F. Buffalo hunt
  Trotter, N. H. Held up by buffalo
  Unidentified artist. Buffalo hunter
  Wimar, C. Buffalo dance
  Wimar, C. Buffalo hunt
  Wimar, C. Buffaloes crossing the Yellowstone
Buffet supper by A. Blaustein
Bugbee family by B. F. Mason
BUHALIS, Nicholas
  Horse
    PA. Annual ex, 1959-60
Building a dam, Shetucket by J. A. Weir
Building in a park by A. Ozenfant
Buildings at night by B. Currie
Buildings, Lancaster by C. H. Demuth
Buildings of Lebanon by C. Sheeler
The **bulb** by W. T. Murch

Bulfinch, Charles, 1763-1844
  Brown, M. Charles Bulfinch
  Dunkerley, J. (attributed works) Charles Bulfinch
Bulfinch, Hannah (Apthorp) fl 1787
  Dunkerley, J. (attributed works) Mrs Charles Bulfinch
Bulfinch, Susan (Apthorp) 1734-1815
  Smibert, J. Mrs Thomas Bulfinch
Bulkley, Ellen. See Ruggles, Ellen (Buckley)
Bull-boating by A. J. Miller
Bull dance of the Mandans by G. Catlin
Bull Durham by S. Davis
The **bull** ring by R. Lebrun
Bulldogging by E. Bisttram
BULLER, Audrey, 1902-
  Comedy
    NYG. Fine art
  Nude in doorway
    Baur. Revolution
Bullfights and bullfighters
  Keller, H. G. Impressions of a bull fight
  Marco-Relli, C. di. Bull fight
  Martin, F. Killer in costume
  Martin, F. The toss
  Ulbricht, J. La Veronica
Bullard, Robert Lee, 1861-1947
  Lockman, D. M. Lt Gen Robert Lee Bullard
Bulls
  See also Cattle
  Austin, D. Europa and the bull
  Benton, T. H. Photographing the bull
  Blanch, A. Bull
  Corbino, J. Stampeding bulls
  Nelson, R. A. Soldier and bull
  Poor, H. V. The bull
  Stevens, E. J. Mad bull
  Tchelitchew, P. Bull fight
Buloz, Christine Blaze de Bury, fl 1879
  Sargent, J. S. Mme Buloz
BULTMAN, Fritz, 1919-
  Sleeper   WMAA
    Pousette-Dart. Amer ptg
  Sleeper no 2
    WMAA. Contemp Amer ptg, 1952
  Via Porta Romana II
    IU. Contemp Amer ptg & sculp, 1953
Bulwer-Lytton, Edward Robert, 1st earl of Lytton. See Lytton, Edward Robert Bulwer-Lytton, 1st earl of
BUMPAS, Rosemary Harley, 1922-
  Lumber for the Argo
    VR. Amer ptg, 1958
BUNCE, Louis, 1907-
  Access
    OrPA. Ptgs & sculpture (col)
  Bay bottom no 1   WaS
    CoS. New accessions USA, 1952
BUNDY, Horace, 1814-1883
  Vermont lawyer   DN
    DN. Amer primitive ptgs, pt 1
Bunker, Anna Hardaway
  Harding, C. Anna Hardaway Bunker
Bunker Hill, Battle of, 1775
  Trumbull, J. Battle of Bunker's Hill
Bunkerhill (steamboat)
  Huge, J. F. Steamboat Bunkerhill
BUNTING, J. D.
  Darby, Pennsylvania, after the burning of Lord's mill
    Baur. Amer ptg (detail)
  Pierson

Buoy by P. Blume
BURBANK, Elbridge Ayer, 1858-1949
  Hopi snake dance   OYB
    OYB. Catalogue 1951
BURCHFIELD, Charles Ephraim, 1893-
  An April mood   WMAA
    Baur. Charles Burchfield (col)
    Baur. New art (col)
    Goodrich. Amer art (col)
    Larkin rev ed (col)
    Pierson
  April woods
    OYB. Catalogue 1951
  August afternoon   MM
    NYG. Fine art
  August evening
    IU. Contemp Amer ptg & sculp, 1959
  Autumnal fantasy
    Flexner. Amer ptg
    Flexner. Short history
  Backyards in snow   ATeS
    ATeS. Collection
  Backyards in spring   PPhM
    Canaday
  Barn   DP
    DP. Catalogue
  Beginning of a snowstorm   WMAA
    Myers
  Black houses
    Baur. Charles Burchfield
  Black iron
    Baur. Charles Burchfield
    MiD. Coll in progress
    Pierson
    WiMiA. Amer ptg 1760-1960
    WMAA. Museum and its friends, 1958
  Church bells ringing, rainy winter night
                             OCl
    Baur. Charles Burchfield (col)
    Baur. New art
    Cos. New accession USA, 1950
    Craven. Treasury 1952 ed
    MMA. Contemp ptrs
    OCl. Handbook
    Pierson
  The cicada
    Baur. Charles Burchfield
  Clatter of crows in spring woods
    Baur. Charles Burchfield
    Baur. Revolution
  Coming of spring   MM
    Baur. Charles Burchfield
    Baur. New art
    MM. 100 Amer ptrs
  Cricket chorus in the arbor
    Baur. Charles Burchfield (col)
  Dandelion seed balls and trees   MM
    Baur. Charles Burchfield
    WMAA. Pioneers
  Day in midwinter   NJMo
    NJMo. Forty years
  Dusty road in July
    WMAA. Annual ex, 1958
  Edge of town   MoKN
    Baur. Charles Burchfield
  End of day   PA
    Baur. Charles Burchfield
  Evening   NJN
    Baur. Charles Burchfield
    Larkin
    Larkin rev ed

Evening peace
    CanO. Hirshhorn coll
  February thaw   NBM
    Brown. Amer ptg
  First hepaticas   MMA
    Larkin
    Larkin rev ed
  The four seasons
    IU. Contemp Amer ptg & sculp, 1961
  Freight cars
    MMA. Contemp ptrs
  Freight cars under a bridge   MiD
    MiD. Treasures
  Garden of memories   MMA
    Baur. Charles Burchfield
  Ghost plants
    Baur. Charles Burchfield
  Glory of spring
    Baur. Charles Burchfield
  Great elm   PPC
    Bazin
  Haunted evening
    Baur. Charles Burchfield
  Hot September wind
    Baur. Charles Burchfield (col)
    MiD. Coll in progress (col)
  House of mystery   ICA
    Baur. Charles Burchfield
    Baur. Revolution
    Brown. Amer ptg
    Pierson
  Hush before the storm   KW
    Baur. Charles Burchfield
  Ice glare   WMAA
    Goodrich. Amer art
    Lee. Art then and now
    Mendelowitz
    NYG. Fine art
  In May   MB
    MB. Ptgs in water color
  Insects at twilight   MMA
    Baur. Charles Burchfield
    Pierson
  Interurban line   MMA
    Newmeyer
  July clouds
    Baur. Charles Burchfield
  June radiance
    PA. Annual ex, 1958
  Lace gables   NUM
    MiA. Root coll
    NUM. Root bequest
  Lavender and old lace   CtNB
    Baur. Charles Burchfield
  March
    Cheney. Story 1958 ed
  March sunlight   MCH
    Baur. Charles Burchfield
  March wind   OCl
    Baur. Charles Burchfield
    Craven. Treasury 1952 ed
  Mid-June   NBuA
    NBuA. Contemporary ptgs
  Moonflowers at dusk
    Baur. Charles Burchfield (col)
  Mysterious bird   DeW
    Baur. Charles Burchfield
  Night of the equinox
    Baur. Charles Burchfield
    WMAA. Sara Roby

BURCHFIELD, C. E.—*Continued*
Night wind
   Barr. What is mod ptg
   Baur. Charles Burchfield
   Baur. New art
   Baur. Revolution
   Brown. Amer ptg
   McCurdy
   Rathbun
Noonday heat
   Baur. Charles Burchfield
Noontide in late May   WMAA
   Goodrich. Amer art (col)
November evening   MM
   Baur. Charles Burchfield
   Craven. Rainbow book
   Craven. Treasury 1952 ed (col)
   Wight. Milestones
October   OCo
   Brown. Amer ptg
Old house by creek   WMMA
   Baur. Charles Burchfield
   Bazin. History of art (col)
   Goodrich. Amer art
Old meetinghouse and locust trees
   Baur. Charles Burchfield
Oncoming spring
   PPC. International ex, 1955
   Time. 300 years (col)
The parade
   Baur. Charles Burchfield
   MiD. Coll in progress
Pippin house, East Liverpool, Ohio MMA
   MMA. Masters
Poplar trees
   Baur. Charles Burchfield
Poplars in June
   Baur. Charles Burchfield
Portrait study in a doorway   DP
   Baur. Charles Burchfield
Promenade
   Baur. New art
   Brown. Amer ptg
   Lewisohn
   McCurdy
   NYG. Fine art
Quiet pond   ATU
   ATU. Coll of Amer art
Radiant springtime
   IU. Contemp Amer ptg & sculp, 1957
Railroad in spring
   WiMiA. Amer ptg 1760-1960
Rainy night   CSD
   Baur. Charles Burchfield
   Gruskin
Red barn
   CtY. Yale alumni
Road in early spring   InIJ
   InIJ. 105 ptgs
Rogues' gallery   MMA
   Baur. Charles Burchfield
September wind and rain   OYB
   OYB. Annual 1953
   OYB. Supplement
Six o'clock   NSyE
   Baur. Charles Burchfield
   Baur. New art
   Time. 300 years
Song in the rain   CtHW
   CtHW. Handbook
   Pierson

Song of the katydids
   Baur. Charles Burchfield
   WiMiA. Amer ptg 1760-1960
Song of the marsh
   Baur. Charles Burchfield
   VR. Amer ptg, 1954
Song of the telegraph
   Baur. Charles Burchfield
The sphinx and the Milky way   NUM
   Baur. Charles Burchfield
   NUM. Art across America
   Pierson
   Richardson. Ptg in America
The star
   PPC. Ptg in the U.S. 1949
   WiMiA. Amer ptg 1760-1960
Still life in winter
   PPC. International ex, 1952
Sulphurous evening   MoSL
   Baur. Charles Burchfield
   MoSL. Handbook 1953
Summer afternoon
   Baur. Charles Burchfield
   Time. 300 years (col)
   WMAA. Annual ex, 1949
Sun and rocks   NBuA
   Baur. Charles Burchfield
   CoS. New accessions USA, 1954
   Mendelowitz
   NBuA. Expressionism
   Pierson
   Pousette-Dart. Amer ptg
   PPC. International ex, 1950
   Time. 300 years (col)
Sun setting through the catalpas   OCl
   Baur. Charles Burchfield
Three days of rain   DP
   DP. Catalogue
Three trees
   Baur. Charles Burchfield
Thunderclap
   Baur. Charles Burchfield
White violets and abandoned coal mine
      NBuA
   NBuA. Acquisitions 1954-57
White violets and coal mine   OCl
   Baur. Charles Burchfield
Window by the alley
   Baur. Charles Burchfield
Winter bouquet   MB
   Baur. Charles Burchfield
   MB. Ptgs in water color
Winter moonlight   KW
   Baur. Charles Burchfield
   Eliot. Art of our time (col)
Winter solstice   OCo
   Roos
Winter twilight   WMAA
   Roos
Wires down   PPC
   Baur. Charles Burchfield
Woman in doorway   DP
   DP. Catalogue
Burckhardt, Rudolph
De Kooning, W. Rudolph Burckhardt
   (unfinished painting and detail)
The **Burden** family enjoying the Hudson
   river near Troy by J. M. Hart and
   A. F. Tait (attributed works)

BURG, Copeland Charles, 1895-
  Flowers in the city
    IU. Contemp Amer ptg, 1952
  Mexican landscape
    CSFP. Annual ex, 1946
Burgoyne, John, 1722-1792
  Trumbull, J. Surrender of Gen Burgoyne
    at Saratoga
Burial by H. G. Burkhardt
Burial by S. Greene
Burial by B. W. Tomlin
Burial of a young man by R. Kent
Burial of an acrobat by M. Beckmann
Burial of the Queen of Sheba by P. Ever-
    good
Buried treasure by H. Bloom
BURKHARDT, Hans Gustave, 1904-
  Abstraction
    WMAA. Annual ex, 1958
  Burial
    IU. Contemp Amer ptg, 1951
  One monent of silence
    ICA. Annual ex, 1951
  Studio of G.
    WMAA. Contemp Amer ptg, 1951
BURKHART, Emerson, 1905-
  Dead duck
    OYB. Annual 1952
  Spiritual decadence
    MnMW. Reality and fantasy
  Spiritual decay   OYB
    OYB. Catalogue 1951
Burlesque by M. Avery
BURLIN, Paul, 1886-
  Calypso
    IU. Contemp Amer ptg & sculp, 1953
  Composition
    MnU. 40 Amer ptrs
  Corridors of time
    VR. Biennial ex, 1948
  Ephiphany of a hero
    NBuA. Expressionism
  Homunculus
    Pierson
  In the shadow of a mystery
    MnU. 49 Amer ptrs
  The magnificence
    Pousette-Dart. Amer ptg
  New England landscape   WMAA
    Pearson. Mod renaissance
    WMAA. Pioneers
  Nude figure
    Myers. Art
  Pool player
    MoSL. Contemporary Amer ptg
  Red, red, not the same   WMAA
    Goodrich. Amer art
  Red theme
    Pearson. Mod renaissance
  Soda jerker
    Pearson. Mod renaissance
  Street scene
    NYG. Fine art
  Wandering Jew
    Myers
  Witness the whatless
    Genauer (col)
  Young man alone with his face
    Pearson. Mod renaissance
BURLIUK, David, 1882-
  At the inn   DP
    DP. Catalogue

Harlem river bridge   CtY
  Pierson
White cow   WMAA
  Pierson
         Portrait of the artist
  Soyer, M. David Burliuk in his studio
Burned over by M. Tobey
Burnet, William, 1688-1729
  Watson, J. Gov William Burnet
Burnham, Caroline Matilda (Wood) d 1832
  Ames, E. Mrs Eleazer Burnham
Burnham, Eleazer, b 1780
  Ames, E. Eleazer Burnham
Burnham, Mrs Eleazer. See Burnham, Caro-
    line Matilda (Wood)
Burnham, T. O. H. P. See Burnham, Thom-
    as Mickell
BURNHAM, Thomas Mickell, 1818-1866
  First state election in Detroit, Michigan,
    1837   MiD
    U.S. National Capital sesquicentennial
      com
  First state election in Michigan
    Pierson
Burning of Charles Town by Unidentified
    artist
Burning of Old South church, Bath, Maine
    by Unidentified artist
Burning of the hearts by L. Siegriest
Burning of the Tombs, New York city by
    Unidentified artist
Burning ship by A. Bierstadt
The **Burnish** sisters by W. M. Prior
Burnt man by L. A. Golub
Burnt spinner by R. Lebrun
BURPEE, Sophia, fl 1806
         Attributed works
  Morning   VWR
    VWR. Folk art (col)
         Portrait of the artist
  Unidentified artist. Sophia Burpee
Burr, Thaddeus, 1735-1801
  Copley, J. S. Thaddeus Burr
Burr, Theodosia, 1783-1812?
  Vanderlyn, J. Theodosia Burr
Burrill, James, 1772-1820
  Malbone, E. G. James Burrill jr
BURROUGHS, Bryson, 1869-1934
  The consolation of Ariadne   MM
    MM. 100 Amer ptrs
Burroughs family by H. Dawkins
Burst by A. Gottlieb
Burst into life by H. Hofmann
Bursting flowers by W. Reiss
Burtis, Betsy, d 1813
  Jarvis, J. W. Betsey Burtis
BURTON, Charles, fl 1820-1832
  The Capitol, Washington, 1824   MM
    Davidson v2
    U.S. National Capital sesquicentennial
      com
  Governor's room, City hall, New York,
    c 1830
    Dickson. John Wesley Jarvis
Bus stop by S. Shawkey
Bus view by G. O. Coleman
BUSA, Peter, 1915-
  Breaker
    WMAA. Contemp Amer ptg, 1959/60

Bush, Hannah(?) c 1767-1807
  MacKay. Mrs John Bush
Bush, John, 1755-1816
  MacKay. John Bush
  Pratt, M. John Bush
Bush, Mrs John. See Bush, Hannah(?)
BUSH, Joseph H. 1794-1865
  Mary Lucy Pocahontas Bibb   KyLS
  KyLS. Kentucky port gall
The Bushkill, View on by T. Doughty
Business by C. H. Demuth
Bussey, Eliza. See Davis, Eliza (Bussey)
Buswell, Mrs Leslie
  Hailman, J. K. W. Mrs Leslie Buswell
Butcher boy by G. B. Luks
Butcher shop by C. Semser
Butler, Edward, 1762-1803
  Malbone, E. G. Capt Edward Butler
Butler, Henry Audubon, 1872-1934
  Olinsky, I. G. Henry Audubon Butler
Butler, Joseph Green, 1840-1927
  Olinsky, I. G. Joseph Green Butler jr
  Watkins, F. C. Joseph C. Butler
Butler, Nicholas Murray, 1862-1947
  Lockman, D. M. Dr Nicholas Murray
    Butler
Butler, Sara Grace Heath
  Speicher, E. E. Sara Grace Heath Butler
Butte, Utah by A. A. Dehn
Butterflies
  Peale, T. R. Still life with flowers and
    insects
Buttersworth, James E. See Butterworth,
  James E.
BUTTERWORTH, James E. 1817-1894
  Defense of America's cup, 1870
    Davidson v2
  Hudson river sloop Phillip R. Paulding
    DC. Privately owned
  The yacht America leaving Boston harbor
    for England   RPS
    U.S. National Capital sesquicentennial
    com
Buttes on the Missouri by C. Wimar
Button falls by H. E. Schnakenberg
Buttonwood farm by N. C. Wyeth
Buzzards
  Audubon, J. J. Turkey buzzards
  Phillips, M. A. Landscape: Buzzard
By the fireside by Unidentified artist
By the sea by R. Haines
By the sea by W. H. Holmes
By the shore by W. Homer
By the tomb of the prophet by A. P. Ryder
BYFIELD, Nathaniel, b 1676?
  Richard Middlecott
    Belknap

          Portrait of the artist
  Smibert, J. Nathaniel Byfield
BYGRAVE, William
  American clipper bark Zephyr in Messina
    harbor, Sicily
    Davidson v 1
Byles, Elizabeth. See Brown, Elizabeth
  (Byles)
Byles, Mather, 1706-1788
  Pelham, P. Mather Byles

Byrd, Anne, fl 1735
  Bridges, C. Anne Byrd
Byrd, Maria (Taylor) 1674-1744
  Bridges, C. Maria Taylor Byrd of West-
    over, Virginia
  Bridges, C. Mrs William Byrd (?)
Byrd, Wilhelmina, d 1716
  Bridges, C. Wilhelmina Byrd (?)
Byrd, Mrs William. See Byrd, Maria (Tay-
  lor)
BYRUM, Ruthven H.
  Grand view
    NYG. Fine art
  Newfound gap (Smoky mountains)
    NYG. Fine art
  Peaceful valley (Blue Ridge mountains)
    NYG. Fine art
Byvanck, Mary. See Abeel, Mary (Byvanck)
BYWATERS, Jerry, 1906-
  On the ranch   TxD
    Gruskin

                    C

Cabana by M. Beckmann
Cabbage head by P. Tchelitchew
Cabell, Agnes S. B. (Gamble) 1783-1863
  Jarvis, J. W. Mrs William Henry Cabell
Cabell, William Henry, 1772-1853
  Jarvis, J. W. William Henry Cabell II
Cabin in the cotton I by H. Pippin
Cabin in the cotton III, by H. Pippin
Cabot, Mary (Fitch) 1723?-1756
  Greenwood, John. Mrs Francis Cabot
CABRAL, Flavio, 1918-
  Quiet day, Lisbon
    IU. Contemp Amer ptg & sculp, 1961
Cabs for hire by L. M. Eilshemius
Cactus by C. Sheeler
Cactus and sundry by J. W. Treiman
Cadaver on a table by H. Bloom
The cadium sound by A. Gottlieb
Cadiz at dusk by D. W. Ellis
CADMUS, Paul, 1904-
  Bar Italia
    Pierson
  Fantasia on a theme by Dr S.   WMAA
    Goodrich. Amer art (col)
    Gruskin
  The nap
    CSB. Illusion
  Night in Bologna   WMAA
    WMAA. Sara Roby (col)
  Playground
    Baur. Revolution
    McCurdy
    Pierson
  Point o' view
    Gruskin
  Reflections
    ICA. Annual ex, 1945/46
  The shower
    Bazin
  Sunday sun
    WMAA. Contemp Amer ptg, 1959/60
Cadwalader, George
  Sully, T. Gen George Cadwalader

Cadwalader, John, 1742-1787
  Peale, C. W. Gen John Cadwalader
Cadwalader, Thomas, 1779-1841
  Malbone, E. G. Gen Thomas Cadwalader
Cadwalader, Mrs Thomas. See Biddle, Mary
CADY, Walter H.
  In old Kentucky
    NYG. Fine art

Caerulea by R. W. Anliker
Café by Y. Kuniyoshi
Café by J. Mitchell
Café de la Paix by W. J. Glackens
Café Florian, Venice by M. B. Prendergast
Café Lafayette by W. J. Glackens
Café on Riva degli Schiavoni, Venice by J. S.
  Sargent
Café, Place des Vosges by S. Davis
Café scene by J. Lawrence
CAFFERTY, James H. 1819-1869 and
  ROSENBERG, Charles D. fl 1858
  Wall street, half past 2 o'clock, Oct. 13,
  1857   NNMC
    Davidson v2
    U.S. National Capital sesquicentennial
    com

Cain and Abel by S. Greene
CALCAGNO, Lawrence, 1916-
  Blue landscape
    Baur. Nature
  Earth legend VII
    PPC. International ex, 1958
  Pacific series, no IX—Sierra   NBuA
    NBuA. Acquisitions 1954-57
  Sapaque
    PPC. International ex, 1955
  Sapaque II   WMAA
    Brussels. Exposition
  Vertical black
    VR. Amer ptg, 1958
  White painting no 3, 1958
    MnMW. 60 Amer ptrs
  White painting no 11, 1958
    IU. Contemp Amer ptg & sculp, 1959
Calcutta by W. A. Smith
CALDER, Alexander, 1898-
  Octopus
    Read. Art now, 1948 ed
  Spiny
    MMA. Abstract
  Untitled   IU
    IU. 20th century
  Untitled   MMA
    MMA. Soby collection
Calendars by A. Gorky
Calhoun, John Caldwell, 1782-1850
  Healy, G. P. A. John C. Calhoun
  Hubard, W. J. John C. Calhoun
  Trumbull, J. John C. Calhoun
CALIFANO, Frank
  Evening usualty
    Baur. Revolution
California condor by J. J. Audubon
California farm by L. H. Lebduska
California landscape by J. F. Cole
California mission by J. F. Cole
Call of the law by C. M. Russell
Call of the west wind by C. H. Davis
Calla with roses by G. O'Keeffe

CALLAHAN, Kenneth L. 1907-
  Abstraction I, 1950
    MMA. Abstract
  Ahab and Abigail. See Autumn dance
  Autumn dance (Ahab and Abigail)
    OrPA. Ptgs & sculptures
  Battle of the gods   KW
    Cheney. Story 1958 ed
    ICA. Annual ex, 1957
  Challenge and response   WaSU
    CoS. New accessions USA, 1950
  Conversation   NBM
    Baur. Revolution
  Fiery night
    Time. 300 years (col)
  Interwoven, thread
    PPC. Ptg in the U. S. 1949
  Northwest landscape
    Cheney. Story 1958 ed
  Rock landscape no 2
    IU. Contemp Amer ptg & sculp, 1959
  The search
    DC. 22 biennial ex, 1951
  The seed was in itself   WaS
    CoS. New accessions USA, 1954
  Shadows on the rock   WaS
    Pousette-Dart. Amer ptg
  Transition   WMAA
    Pierson
  The trapped
    WMAA. Contemp Amer ptg, 1952
  Vital storm
    Cheney. Expressionism 1948 ed
Callahan, Rose
  Sharrer, H. Rose Callahan and child
Callender, John, 1706-1748
  Feke, R. Rev John Callender
Calligraphic by M. Tobey
Calligraphy of rhythms by P. Fine
Calling of St Matthew by G. H. Hallowell
Calling the moose by P. R. Goodwin
Calm horizon by C. A. Morris
Cal-Sag by E. Lanyon
Calvert, Benedict Leonard, fl 1727
  Brerewood, F. Benedict Leonard Calvert,
  Governor of Maryland
Calvert, Charles, 1756-1777
  Hesselius, J. Charles Calvert and his
  Negro slave
Calvert, Elizabeth
  Hesselius, J. Elizabeth Calvert
CALVIN, Perry, 1924-
  Hucksters   OYB
    OYB. Annual 1950
    OYB. Catalogue 1951
CALYO, Nicolino Vicomte, 1799-1884
  Balloon ascension at Baltimore, 1834
    Davidson v2
  Baltimore in 1837   MdBH
    DC. Amer ptrs of the South
  The great fire in New York, 1835
    U.S. National Capital sesquicentennial
    com
  Hot corn girl
    Davidson v2
  Ice cart, c 1840
    Davidson v2
  Milk man, c 1840
    Davidson v2
  Soap-locks or Bowery boys, New York,
  c 1840
    Davidson v2

CALYO, N. V.—*Continued*
  View of New York city, c 1835
    WiMiA. Amer ptg 1760-1960
  View of the Merchants' exchange and
    Girard's bank, Philadelphia
    WiMiA. Amer ptg 1760-1960
  The volante at Habana   VWR
    VWR. Folk Art (col)

Attributed works
  New York—Hoboken ferry, c 1838
    Davidson v2
Calypso by P. Burlin
Calypso by K. Martin
Cambridge, New York by A. M. R. Moses
Cambridge valley by A. M. R. Moses
Camden, Sallie Ann, fl 1840
    Bingham, G. C. Sallie Ann Camden
Camden hills from Baker's island, Penobscot
    bay by M. Hartley
Camels
    Bacon, H. My camels resting
Camel's Hump by E. Hopper
Camp Butler, Maryland, 1861 by Unidenti-
    fied artist
Camp fire, preparing the evening meal by
    A. J. Miller
Camp meeting by W. Whittredge
Camp receiving a supply of meat by A. J.
    Miller
Camp scene (Sioux) by A. J. Miller
Campo Santa Maria Formosa, Venice by
    M. B. Prendergast
Canadian Mounted Police with prisoners by
    C. M. Russell
Canal street no 2 by K. Zerbe
Canals
    Delbos, J. Canal
    Harvey, G. Afternoon, dead calm: View
      on the Erie Canal near Pittsford, New
      York
    Hill, J. W. Scene on the Erie canal
    Pickett, J. Lehigh canal, sunset, New
      Hope, Pennsylvania
    Ryder, A. P. The canal
    Smith, R. Aqueduct in the Pennsylvania
      canal over the Juniata
    Tobey, M. Canals
    Woodbury, C. H. Canal scene, Holland
Canandaigua, New York
    Jeffrey, A. Main street, Canandaigua, N.Y.
      1830-40
CANDELL, Victor, 1903-
  Ascendant   WMAA
    Pierson
    WMAA. Contemp Amer ptg, 1952
  Blue waterfall
    PPC. International ex, 1952
  Contact
    IU. Contemp Amer ptg & sculp, 1955
  Conversation piece
    IU. Contemp Amer ptg & sculp, 1957
  Percussion
    DC. 26 biennial ex, 1959
  Summer
    DC. 27 biennial ex, 1961
  Village dog
    IU. Contemp Amer ptg & sculp, 1953
  Yule log
    IU. Contemp Amer ptg, 1952

Candide by A. James
Canfield, Ithamar, 1764-1848
    Jennys, R. Ithamar Canfield
Canfield, Richard
    Whistler, J. A. M. Richard Canfield
Cannabin by X. Gonzalez
Cannibalism of war by G. Biddle
Cannon, Mrs Daniel. See Trusler, Mary
Canoes and canoeing
    Brush, G. De F. At dawn
    Brush, G. De F. Silence broken
    Catlin, G. Down the Mississippi in a
      birch-bark canoe
    Catlin, G. Excavating a canoe, British
      Columbia
    Homer, W. Canoe in rapids
    Homer, W. Canoeing in the Adirondacks
    Homer, W. Entering the first rapid
    Homer, W. Guide fishing
    Homer, W. Under the falls, grand dis-
      charge
    Koerner, W. H. D. City man's vacation
Cantey, Margaret. See Sinkler, Margaret
    (Cantey)
Canticle by M. Tobey
Canton street by G. Martino
Canvassing for a vote by G. C. Bingham
The **canyon** by G. C. Delano
Canyon mosaic by C. A. Morris
Cape Ann by M. B. Prendergast
Cape Ann landscape by S. Davis
Cape Cod dunes by G. Grosz
Cape Cod evening by E. Hopper
Cape Cod marsh and sky by D. Macknight
Cape Cod morning by E. Hopper
Cape fog by R. G. Hamilton
Cape landscape by R. G. Hamilton
Cape May wharf by F. Yost
Cape Nedick by H. Strater
Cape Porpoise harbor by E. O'Hara
Cape still life by H. Maril
Cape Trinity, Saguenay river by W. Homer
Cape Trinity, Saguenay river, moonlight by
    W. Homer
El **Capitan** by T. Hill
The **Capitol,** Washington by E. D. Boit
Capitol reflections by K. Matthew
Capri, A corner in by E. Vedder
Capri cliffs by F. Crowninshield
Capri girl by J. S. Sargent
Capriccioso by H. Hofmann
Captain and crew by K. Knaths
Captain of the fishing fleet by W. M. Chase
The **captive** by H. F. Farny
Captive charger by C. Wimar
The **captive** Gaul by F. Remington
The **captives** by P. Trevigno
Capture of Major André by J. Toole
Capture of the Hessians at Trenton by J.
    Trumbull
Capture of wild horses by Indians by A. J.
    Miller
Captured by Indians by G. C. Rathbone
Capturing the grizzly by C. M. Russell

Car with dark top by E. Ewing
Caravan en route by A. J. Miller
Caravan on the Platte by A. J. Miller
Caravan on the prairies by W. T. Ranney
Caravan taking to the water by A. J. Miller
Caravan theater minstrels by J. De Martini
Caravan: trappers crossing the river by
   A. J. Miller
CARBONE, Francesco, 1923-
  War among the arthropods
   MBIC. View 1960
Carcass by J. Hirsch
Carcass by T. Roszak
Card players by J. Levine
Card players by R. C. Woodville
Card rack with oval photograph of Abraham
   Lincoln by J. F. Peto
Cardinal by F. J. Kline
A **cardinal**, Portrait of by T. B. Read
The **cardinal's** portrait by T. E. Rosenthal
Caresse enfantine by M. Cassatt
Cargo by C. di Marca-Relli
Caribbean cornucopia by A. A. Dehn
Caribbean moon by S. M. Etnier
CARLES, Arthur Becker, 1882-1952
  Arrangement   ICA
   PA. Annual ex, 1955
   PA. Carles (cover)
   Pierson
  Blue abstraction
   PA. Carles
  Bouquet abstraction   WMAA
   Goodrich. Amer art
   Pierson
  Bouquet in blue vase   PPhM
   Chew. 250 years of art
  Composition III, 1931-32   MMA
   McCurdy
   MMA. Abstract
  Composition no 6, 1936
   PA. Annual ex, 1955
   PA. Carles
  Flower piece
   PA. Annual ex, 1955
  French village church
   PA. Carles
  Glass and flowers
   Cheney. Primer 1958 ed
  Painting, 1935-40
   Hess. Abstract ptg
  Summer flowers
   PA. Carles
  Turkey   PPhM
   Hess. Abstract ptg
   PA. Carles
  White callas
   PA. Carles
  White nude with apple
   PA. Annual ex, 1955
CARLIN, A. B. fl 1871
  Sherman's march through Georgia, 1864
   U.S. National Capital sesquicentennial
   com
CARLIN, John, 1813-1891
  Sparking
   Chew. 250 years of art

CARLSEN, Emil 1853-1932
  Entrance to the harbor of St Thomas
                              PR
   PR. Catalogue
  The surf   OYB
   OYB. Catalogue 1951
Carlton, Linda Dietz
  Chase, W. M. Linda Dietz Carlton
Carlyle, Thomas, 1795-1881
  Whistler, J. A. M. Thomas Carlyle
CARMEN, Cicero, 1926-
  Near Tibidabo
   ICA. Annual ex, 1959/60
Carmencita, by W. M. Chase
Carmencita by J. S. Sargent
Carmer, Rachel. See Lenox, Rachel (Car-
  mer)
Carmick, Stephen, fl 1760
  West, B. Stephen Carmick
Carmine theater by J. Sloan
Carnation Lily, Lily Rose, Sketch for by
  J. S. Sargent
Carnes, Captain of Salem
  Unidentified artist. Capt Carnes of Salem
Carnival of autumn by M. Hartley
Carnival time by J. Kempsmith
Carnivals. See Fairs and festivals
The **carob** tree by A. M. Duca
Carol I, king of Rumania, 1839-1914
  Healy, G. P. A. Charles I
Carolina parroquet by J. J. Audubon
Carolina parrot by J. J. Audubon
Carolina turtle-dove by J. J. Audubon
Caroline Augusta by H. R. Rittenberg
Carolus-Duran (Charles Émile Auguste
  Durand) 1838-1917
  Sargent, J. S. Carolus Duran
CARONE, Nicolas, 1917-
  Member of a city cast no 9
   ICA. Amer artists paint the city
  Monk in white
   IU. Contemp Amer ptg & sculp, 1955
  Reflecting poet
   ICA. Annual ex, 1951
  Reverse image
   IU. Contemp Amer ptg & sculp, 1957
  St Francis of Assisi
   IU. Contemp Amer ptg & sculp, 1953
  Satyr
   MnMW. 60 Amer ptrs
  Self-portrait: head
   PPC. International ex, 1952
  Sound of blue light
   Brussels. Exposition
  Untitled
   IU. Contemp Amer ptg & sculp, 1961
Carousel, by A. H. Maurer
Carousel by M. B. Prendergast
Carousel by the sea by C. H. Carter
Carpenter, Mr, fl 1810
  Unidentified artist. Mr Carpenter
CARPENTER, Francis Bicknell, 1830-1900
         Attributed works
  A. Lincoln reception at the White house,
   1863
    U.S. National Capital sesquicentennial
    com
Carpenter, William, 1767-1823
  Earl, R. William Carpenter

CARR, Lyell
Remington's studio
McCracken. Remington

CARR, William, fl 1833
Harbor scene with fish market near Philadelphia
U.S. National Capital sesquicentennial
com

Carrara: a little quarry by J. S. Sargent
Carrara: a quarry by J. S. Sargent
Carrara: in a quarry by J. S. Sargent

Carrara: Lizzatori I by J. S. Sargent
Carrara: Lizzatori II by J. S. Sargent
Carrara: M. Derville's quarry by J. S.
Sargent
Carrara: marmo statuario by J. S. Sargent
Carrara: quarry I by J. S. Sargent
Carrara: quarry II by J. S. Sargent
Carrara: Trajan's quarry by J. S. Sargent
Carrara: wet quarries by J. S. Sargent
Carrara: workmen by J. S. Sargent

Carroll, Charles, 1737-1832
Harding, C. Charles Carroll of Carrollton

Carroll, Mrs Charles. See Chew, Harriet
Carroll, Mrs Daniel. See Darnall, Eleanor
CARROLL, Edward
Fairfield Osborn   MM
CoS. New accessions USA, 1960

CARROLL, John, 1892-1959
Bird in her heart
IU. Contemp Amer ptg, 1948
Claire Luce as Camille
NAD. Annual ex, 1948
Evening   MiD
Cheney. Story 1958 ed
Jean
Gruskin (col)
Little sheep
CSFP. Annual ex, 1948/49
Lois
OYB. Annual 1953
Mrs Carroll
NAD. Annual ex, 1947, 1st half
Red roses
PPC. Ptg in the U.S. 1949
Sleeping
NYG. Fine art
Spring bonnet
Bazin
IU. Contemp Amer ptg, 1950
Truth is upward
NAD. Annual ex, 1960
White flower
IU. Contemp Amer ptg, 1951
Roos
White lace   OT
Baur. Revolution
Cheney. Story 1958 ed
Pierson
Young girl
Cheney. Expressionism 1948 ed
Carroll, Mrs John
Carroll, J. Mrs Carroll
CARROLL, Leon, 1887-1937
Three gold diggers   CtY
CtY. Soc Anonyme

Carry on by E. H. Blashfield
Cars in sleet storm by A. G. Dove
Carson's men by C. M. Russell
The cart by E. Berman
CARTER, Clarence Holbrook, 1904-
Carousel by the sea
Gruskin
Jane Reed and Dora Hunt   MMA
McCurdy
Pierson
Stew   OT
ICA. Annual ex, 1945/46
OT. Contemp Amer ptgs
Tide water
IU. Contemp Amer ptg, 1948
Yellow blinds   OYB
OYB. Catalogue 1951
Carter, Mrs James Otis, b 1780
Malbone, E. G. Mrs James Otis Carter
CARTER, Mrs Robert, fl 1833
Napoleon's army crossing the Alps   MB
MB. Karolik coll
CARTNEY, Mary Elizabeth, fl 1840
Court house and Centre square, Easton
McClintock
Court house, Easton
McClintock
CARTON, Norman, 1908-
Ocean brilliance
IU. Contemp Amer ptg & sculp, 1961
CARY, Samuel, 1742-1812
Copley, J.S. Samuel Cary
Cary, Sarah (Gray) 1742-1825
Copley, J. S. Mrs Samuel Cary
La casa de Dios by S. Raffo
Cascade in the forest by J. F. Kensett
Cascade waters by W. W. Baumgartner
CASEBIER, Cecil Lang, 1922-
Boy in Mexico   TxD
CoS. New accessions USA, 1956
Casey, Mrs John, fl 1840
Unidentified artist. Mrs John Casey and
daughter
Cashmere shawl by J. S. Sargent
CASILEAR, John William, 1811-1893
Moonlight
Sears. Highlights
Reminiscence of the Genesee river
Sears. Highlights
Cass, Lewis, 1782-1866
Tuthill, A. G. D. Lewis Cass
Cassatt, Alexander
Cassatt, M. Alexander Cassatt and his son
Cassatt, Lydia, fl 1881
Cassatt, M. Lydia Cassatt reading
CASSATT, Mary, 1845-1926
After the bath (La sortie du bain) OCl
OCl. Handbook
Pierson
Sweet
Alexander Cassatt and his son
PA. Annual ex, 1955
At the opera   MB
Cheney. Story 1958 ed
Rewald. History of impressionism
The bath   FPP
Sweet

The bath (La toilette)   ICA
  Flexner. Amer ptg
  Flexner. Short history
  Mendelowitz
  MiD. Ptg in America
  Newmeyer
  PA. Annual ex, 1955
  Pierson
  Riley. Your art heritage
  Sweet
Caresse enfantine   DNC
  DC. 25 biennial ex, 1957
Child holding a dog   CtHW
  CtHW. Handbook
Child with red hat   MWiS
  MWiS. Ex 4 and 7
A cup of tea   MB
  Bazin
  Sweet
  Time. 300 years (col)
The cup of tea   MM
  McKinney
  Sweet
In the box
  Sweet
In the garden   MdBM
  Sweet
In the loge   DN
  Lee. Art then and now
Lady at the tea table   MM
  McCurdy
  Sweet
La loge (Midy coll)
  Sweet
  Time. 300 years (col)
The loge (The opera box)   DN
  Rewald. History of impressionism
  UNESCO. 1860-1955
Lydia Cassatt reading   NEO
  CSB. Impressionism
Mme A. F. Aude and her two daughters
  Sweet
Mrs Havemeyer and her daughter
  Sweet
Mrs John Howard Whittemore. See Por-
  trait of a grand lady
Mrs Peter Frelinghuysen
  DC. Privately owned
Morning toilet   DN
  Rewald. History of impressionism
  Walker. Ptgs from America (col)
Mother and child   PPhM
  Canaday
Mother and child   OYB
  Chew. 250 years of art
  OYB. Catalogue 1951
Mother and child   OCiM
  OCiM. Guide
Mother and child   KW
  Pierson
  Sweet (col front)
  Time. 300 years (col)
Mother and child   MWM
  Roos
Mother and child   FPL
  UNESCO. 1860-1955
Mother and children   MCH
  PPC. Amer classics
Mother holding child
  Sweet
On the balcony   PPhM
  Sweet

The opera box. See The loge (DN)
Portrait of a grand lady (Mrs John
  Howard Whittemore)
  Sweet
Reading Le Figaro
  Sweet
Self-portrait
  Sweet
La sortie du bain. See After the bath
La toilette. See The bath
Torero and young girl   MWiS
  MWiS. Ex 4 and 7
Under the horse-chestnut tree   MMA
  MMA. Masters
Woman and child driving   PPhM
  Pierson
  Sweet (col)
  Taylor. Fifty centuries, 1954 ed (col)
  Walker. Ptgs from America
Woman arranging her veil   PPhM
  Canaday
  Pierson
  Sweet
Woman in black   MoSL
  MoSL. Handbook 1953
  MoSL. Masterworks
Woman reclining
  NUM. Art across America
Woman with a dog   DC
  DC. Masterpieces (col)
Women admiring a child   MiD
  MiD. Treasures
Women picking fruit (Young women pick-
  ing fruit)   PPC
  Pierson
  Richardson. Ptg in America
A young girl   MM
  MM. 100 Amer ptrs
Young girl in green bonnet   DNC
  DNC. Gellatly col, 1954
Young girls   InIJ
  InIJ. 105 ptgs
Young woman reading (Woman reading)
                                          MB
  Rewald. History of impressionism
  Sweet
Young women picking fruit. See Women
  picking fruit
CASSILL, R. V.
Small town evening   IaDa
  IaDa. Silver jubilee
Castel Gandolfo by G. Innes
Castello Dell'ovo, Bay of Naples by G. L.
  Brown
CASTELLÓN, Federico, 1914-
Dark figure   WMAA
  Baur. Revolution
  Goodrich. Amer Art
  Pierson
Return of the prodigal
  ICA. Annual ex, 1947/48
Supplication   ATU
  ATU. Coll of Amer Art
Casting in the falls by W. Homer
Casting the fly by W. Homer
The **castle** by R. Eshoo
Castle Garden, New York
  Ulrich, C. F. In the land of promise:
  Castle Garden
A **castle** in England or Ireland by T.
  Doughty

Cat boats, Newport by C. Hassam
Cataclysm by H. Hofmann
Catalyst by H. Hofmann
Catalytic crackers by T. H. Benton
Catamount by D. Austin
Catching the Thanksgiving turkey by A. M. R. Moses
Catching up by A. J. Miller
Catfish row by J. Lawrence
Cathedral entrance by D. W. Ellis
Cathedral in the woods by J. Lam
Cathedrals
  Blanch, A. Cathedrals
  Chavez, E. A. Cathedral
  Feininger, L. Cathedral, Cammin
  Feininger, L. The east choir of Halle cathedral
  Freibert, J. Urban cathedral
  Halpert, S. Cathedral interior
  Halpert, S. Notre Dame, Paris
  Lewis, N. Cathedral
  Pach, W. Cathedral
  Pollock, J. Cathedral
  Prendergast, M. P. Notre Dame, Paris
  Sargent, J. S. Cordova: interior of the cathedral
Catlin, Clara Bartlett (Gregory) 1808?-1845
  Catlin, G. Mrs George Catlin
CATLIN, George, 1796-1872
  Ah-mou-a, The Whale, Kee-o-kuk warrior DNC
    McCracken. George Catlin (col)
  Apache village on Lake Ahrocum NNAM
    Bazin
  Archery of the Mandans or game of the arrow
    Morgan (col)
  Ba-da-ah-chon-du, a Crow chief NNAM
    McCracken. George Catlin (col)
  Ball-play of the Choctaws DNC
    Davidson v 1
    McCracken. George Catlin
  The bear dance DNC
    McCracken. George Catlin
    Morgan (col)
  The beggars' dance of Teton Sioux DNC
    McCracken. George Catlin
  Bi-eets-ee-cure, The Very Sweet Man, Crow warrior DNC
    McCracken. George Catlin
    Morgan
  Bird's eye view of the Mandan village DNC
    Mendelowitz
    Time. 300 years (col)
  Black Hawk DNC
    Rathbone
  Blackfoot doctor in his mystery dress endeavoring to cure his dying patient NNAM
    Flexner. Amer ptg
    Flexner. Short history
  Blackfoot medicine man DNC
    McCracken. George Catlin (col)
  Blue Medicine
    Rathbone
  Breaking down the wild horse PPhUn
    Chew. 250 years of art

Buffalo chase NNAM
  McCracken. Portrait of the old west (col)
  Rathbone
Buffalo chase in snowdirft DNC
  Pierson
Buffalo chase of the Sioux DNC
  McCracken. George Catlin
Buffalo chase, upper Missouri DNC
  McCracken. George Catlin (col)
Buffalo crossing Yellowstone in winter
  McCracken. George Catlin
Buffalo hunt on snow shoes
  Larkin rev ed
Buffalo hunt, under the wolf mask DNC
  Rathbone
  Time. 300 years (col)
Buffalo stampede
  McCracken. George Catlin
Bull dance of the Mandans NNAM
  McCracken. Portrait of the old west
Catlin hunting buffalo for food
  McCracken. George Catlin
Catlin painting the Four Bears NNAM
  McCracken. George Catlin (col)
Champion Choctaw ball-player DNC
  McCracken. George Catlin
Chin-cah-pee, The Fire Bug DNC
  McCracken. George Catlin
Clara Gregory Catlin DNC
  McCracken. George Catlin
Clermont, first chief of the Osages DNC
  McCracken. George Catlin
  Time. 300 years (col)
Col-lee, chief of the Cherokees DNC
  McCracken. George Catlin
Comanche feats of horsemanship DNC
  McCracken. George Catlin
Comanche village in Texas DNC
  McCracken. George Catlin
Comanche war party meeting dragoons DNC
  McCracken. George Catlin (col)
Crow chief at his toilet NNAM
  McCracken. George Catlin (col)
A Crow tepee DNC
  McCracken. George Catlin
Crow warriors bathing in Yellowstone NNAM
  McCracken. George Catlin (col)
Crow woman DNC
  McCracken. George Catlin
Dance of the berdash of the Sauk and Fox Morgan
DeWitt Clinton NNHS
  McCracken. George Catlin
The Double Walker, Nom-ba-mon-nee, a brave of the Omaha tribe
  Morgan
Down the Mississippi in a birch-bark canoe DNC
  McCracken. George Catlin
Ee-ah-sa-pa, The Black Rock, a Sioux chief DNC
  McCracken. George Catlin
Encounter with buffalo on Missouri DNC
  McCracken. George Catlin
The evil spirit, O-ke-pa
  McCracken. George Catlin
Excavating a canoe, British Columbia NNAM
  McCracken. George Catlin (col)

Fort Pierre with Sioux camped around
DNC
McCracken. George Catlin
Fort Snelling on the upper Mississippi
OkTT
McCracken. George Catlin
Fort Union, mouth of the Yellowstone
DNC
McCracken. George Catlin
Ha-na-ta-nu-maik, The Wolf Chief, head
of the Mandans   DNC
McCracken. George Catlin
The handsome dance, Venezuela, South
America   NNAM
McCracken. George Catlin (col)
Haw-che-ke-sug-ga, chief of the Missouris
DNC
McCracken. George Catlin
Ha-won-je-tah, The One Horn, first chief
of the Sioux   DNC
McCracken. George Catlin
Roos
He who drinks the juice of the stone
DNC
Rathbone
Hill of death, upper Missouri   DNC
McCracken. George Catlin (col)
His-oo-san-chees, The Little Spaniard,
Comanche warrior   DNC
McCracken. George Catlin
Indian boy   MoKN
MoKN. Handbook
Indians atacking grizzly bears   NNHS
McCracken. George Catlin
Kee-mo-ra-nia, a beau of the Peorias DNC
McCracken. George Catlin
Kee-o-kuk on horseback   DNC
McCracken. George Catlin (col)
Morgan
Kee-o-kuk, the Running Fox   DNC
McCracken. George Catlin (col)
Kiowa girl and boy   DNC
McCracken. George Catlin
Konza warriors, woman and child NNAM
McCracken. George Catlin (col)
La-doo-ke-a, the Buffalo Bull, Grand
Pawnee warrior   DNC
McCracken. George Catlin (col)
Lay-law-she-kaw, chief of the Shawnees
DNC
McCracken. George Catlin
Mah-to-he-ha, The Old Bear   DNC
Morgan
Time. 300 years (col)
Mandan medicine man   DNC
McCracken. George Catlin (col)
Mandan O-kee-pa, the bull dance   DNC
McCracken. George Catlin (col)
Mandan torture ceremony   NNAM
McCracken. George Catlin (col)
Mandan village   DNC
McCracken. George Catlin
Morgan
The medicine bag dance of the Sauk and
Fox
Morgan
Mew-hew-she-kaw, The White Cloud,
chief of the Ioways
McCracken. George Catlin (col)
Minnetaree village   DNC
McCracken. George Catlin

Mix-ke-móte-skin-na, The Iron Horn,
Blackfoot warrior   DNC
McCracken. George Catlin
Moving camp   DNC
McCracken. George Catlin
Muk-a-tah-mish-o-kah-kiak, The Black
Hawk   DNC
McCracken. George Catlin (col)
Notch-ee-ming-a, No Heart, chief of the
Iowas   DNC
McCracken. George Catlin
Morgan
No-way-ke-sug-gah, an Oto warrior DNC
McCracken. George Catlin (col)
Ojibway (Chippewa) woman and baby
DNC
McCracken. George Catlin
Oliver Wolcott
McCracken. George Catlin
Om-pah-ton-ga, Big Elk, Chief of the
Omahas   DNC
McCracken. George Catlin (col)
One Horn, a Dakota (Sioux) chief   ICH
Pierson
Richardson. Ptg in America
Osceola
McCracken. George Catlin
Osceola   NNAM
Roos
Osceola, The Black Drink   DNC
McCracken. George Catlin
Prairie bluffs burning, upper Missouri
DNC
McCracken, George Catlin (col)
Prairie fire   DNC
Rathbone
Pshan-shaw, Arikara girl   DNC
McCracken. George Catlin
The sacred red pipe—stone quarry OkTT
McCracken. George Catlin
Sah-ko-ka, The Mint Mandan girl   DNC
McCracken. George Catlin
St Louis, 1836   DNC
Davidson v 1
Sam Houston
McCracken. George Catlin
Sam Perryman   DNC
Rathbone
The Sauk and Fox slave dance
Morgan
Scalp dance of the Sioux   DNC
McCracken. Portrait of the old west
(col)
Rathbone
Seehk-hee-da, The White Eyebrows, Man-
dan man   DNC
McCracken. George Catlin
Self-portrait   OkTT
McCracken. George Catlin
Se-non-ti-yak, The Blistered Foot, Ioway
medicine man   NNAM
McCracken. George Catlin (col)
Sioux beggars' dance
Morgan
Sioux Indians hunting buffalo   DNC
McCracken. George Catlin
Sioux Indians pursuing a stag in their
canoes   DNC
Time. 300 years (col)
A Sioux village   NNAM
McCracken. Portrait of the old west
(col)

CATLIN, George—*Continued*
Sky-se-ro-ka. a chief of the Pawnee Picks
                                        DNC
  McCracken. George Catlin
Snowshoe dance of the Chippewas DNC
  McCracken. George Catlin
Snowshoe dance of the Ojibbeway
                                        DNC
  Rathbone
Steamboat Yellowstone leaving St Louis
                                        DNC
  McCracken. George Catlin
Stee-tcha-ko-me-co, The Great King, chief
  of the Creeks   DNC
  McCracken. George Catlin
Stu-mick-o-sucks, The Buffalo's Back
  Fat, chief of the Blackfeet   DNC
  McCracken. George Catlin (col)
The sun dance
  Morgan
Tah-teck-a-da-hair, The Steep Wind, a
  Sioux warrior   DNC
  McCracken. George Catlin (col)
Tal-lee, Osage warrior   DNC
  McCracken. George Catlin (col)
Ta-wah-que-nah, The Mountain of Rocks,
  Comanche chief   DNC
  McCracken. George Catlin
Tcha-aes-ka-ding, Barefoot Boy   DNC
  McCracken. George Catlin
Tcha-kauks-o-ko-maugh, The Great Chief
                                        DNC
  McCracken. George Catlin
Tchan-dee, Tobacco, second chief of
  Oglala Sioux   DNC
  McCracken. George Catlin
Ten-squat-a-way, Shawnee prophet   DNC
  McCracken. George Catlin
  Morgan
Tis-se-woo-na-tis, wife of a Cheyenne chief
                                        DNC
  McCracken. George Catlin (col)
Toh-to-wah-kon-da-pee, The Blue Medi-
  cine   DNC
  McCracken. George Catlin
Ud-je-jock, the Pelican   DNC
  Baur. Amer ptg
United States Military Academy, West
  Point, N.Y.   CtY
  Davidson v2
Upper Missouri: the grand detour NNAM
  Pierson
  U.S. National Capital sesquicentennial
  com
Uruguay medicine man, South America
                                        NNAM
  McCracken. George Catlin (col)
View on the upper Missouri   DNC
  Rathbone
    Time. 300 years (col)
Village of the dead   OkTT
  McCracken. George Catlin
Virginia constitutional convention of 1829-
  30   NNHS
  Davidson v2
  McCracken. George Catlin
  U.S. National Capital sesquicentennial
  com
Wah-pa-ko-las-kuk, The Bear's Track
                                        DNC
  McCracken. George Catlin
Wah-pe-kee-suck, The White Cloud DNC
  McCracken. George Catlin (col)

Wa-nah-de-tunk-ah, The Black Dog, East-
  ern Sioux   DNC
  McCracken. George Catlin
Wee-ta-ra-sha-ro, chief of Pawnee Picks
                                        DNC
  McCracken. George Catlin
Wife of Kee-o-kuk   DNC
  McCracken. George Catlin
Wi-jun-jon, The Pigeon's Egg Head DNC
  McCracken. George Catlin (col)
  William Clark
  McCracken. George Catlin
Winter hunting on upper Missouri DNC
  McCracken. George Catlin
Wun-nee-tow, the White Buffalo, Black-
  foot medicine man
  McCracken. George Catlin
          Portrait of the artist
  Fisk, W. H. George Catlin
Catlin, John Mortimer, 1801-1881
  Inman, H. John M. Catlin
Catlin, Mrs George. See Catlin, Clara Bart-
  lett (Gregory)
Catlin, Nicholas
  Walters, S. Memorial to Nicholas Catlin
Cats
  Abercrombie, G. Message for mercy
  Bacon, P. Nobody's pet
  Bacon, P. Wanderlust
  Bartoll, W. T. Girl and cat
  Brook, A. Peggy Bacon and Metaphysics
  Clemens, P.L. Ruth with cat
  Cortor, E. Affection
  De Diego, J. Guilty cats
  Fransioli, T. A. The cat
  Koch, J. Nude with cat
  Lindner, R. Paul Verlaine [with cat]
  Lintot, B. Ballerina
  Luks, G. B. Cat and kittens
  Luks, G. B. Woman with black cat
  Philipp, R. Xmas morning
  Pickens, A. Card players
  Schnakenberg, H. E. Cat and kittens
  Sloan, J. Backyards, Greenwich Village
  Sloan, J. McSorley's cats
  Tomlin, B. W. Outward preoccupation
  Toole, J. Nannie Toole (with cat)
  Unidentified artist. The cat
  Unidentified artist. Cat and kittens
  Unidentified artist. Caught in the act
  Unidentified artist. Lydia and Tabitha
  Unidentified artist. Picking flowers
  Vasilieff, N. Girl with cat
Cat's cradle by J. Kearns
Cat's cradle in blue by B. Shahn
Catskill Clove by A. B. Durand
Catskill mountains
  Browere, A. D. Catskills
  Church, F. E. Catskill mountains, 1852
  Cole, T. Catskill mountains
  Cole, T. In the Catskills
  Cole, T. Prometheus bound
  Cole, T. River in the Catskills
  Doughty, T. In the Catskills
  Durand, A. B. Catskill mountains near
    Shandaken
  Hart, J. M. Catskill creek, New York
  Hart, W. M. Autumn in the Catskills
A **Catskill** stream by A. B. Durand
Cattel, Mary (Ladson) fl 1801
  Malbone, E. G. Mrs William Cattel

Cattle

See also Bulls

Avert, M. Three cows on a hillside
Beckmann, M. Cattle in barn
Bingham, G. C. Landscape with cattle
Burliuk, D. White cows
Casilaer, J. W. Reminiscence of the Genesee river
Dove, A. G. Cows in pasture
Fisher, A. The watering place
Hart, W. M. Cattle in a stream
Hicks, E. Cornell farm
Hinckley, T. H. Cows and sheep in pasture
Hinckley, T. H. Great Blue hill and Neponset river
Hinckley, T. H. Noon
Homer, W. Weaning the calf
Innis, G. Landscape with cattle
Nichols, H. Black herd
Palmer, W. C. Cows in the corn
Price, C. S. Cattle
Price, C. S. Cattle by the river
Price, C. S. Cow with calf
Price, C. S. Cows going to pasture
Price, C. S. The dream
Russell, C. M. The bolter
Russell, C. M. Heads or tails
Russell, C. M. Heeling a bad one
Russell, C. M. Jerked down
Russell, C. M. A loose cinch
Russell, C. M. Roping a wild one
Russell, C. M. The roundup
Russell, C. M. A serious predicament
Russell, C. M. Waiting for a chinook
Ryder, A. P. Evening glow—the old red cow
Ryder, A. P. Pastoral study
Ryder, A. P. The pasture
Ryder, A. P. Summer's faithful pasture
Sommer, W. Cows
Sommer, W. Cows resting
Sommer, W. Pink cow
Spruce, E. F. White cow
West, B. Landscape with cow

Cattle loading, West Texas by T. H. Benton

Caucus by W. Kuhn

Caught in net by M. Freedman

Caught in the equinox by A. Salemme

Cavalcade by A. J. Miller

CAVALLON, Giorgio, 1904-
Abstract no 6, 1952
  Pousette-Dart. Amer ptg
Abstraction, 1950
  McCurdy
  MMA. Abstract
Untitled   NBuA
  NBuA. Acquisitions 1959-1961
  ICA. Annual ex, 1959/60

Cavalry charge on the western plain by F. Remington

CAVANAUGH, Tom
American errant   NeO
  CoS. New accessions USA, 1954

CAVAT, Irma, 1928-
White morning
  IU. Contemp Amer ptg & sculp, 1959

Cavell, Edith Louise, 1865-1915
Bellows, G. W. Edith Cavell

Cayambe by F. E. Church

Celebration by S. Magada

Celebration by F. Martin

Celestral by J. Grillo

The **'cellist** by I. J. H. Bradley

Cello player by E. W. Dickinson

Cemeteries

Chambers, S. Mount Auburn cemetery, Cambridge
Cloar, C. Gibson bayou anthology
Herron, D. St Louis cemetery, New Orleans

Centaur by J. Kinigstein

Centaurs by S. Sherman

Central park by G. Grosz

Central park by M. B. Prendergast

Central park at night by G. Grosz

Central park, winter by W. J. Glackens

Centurion by J. Corbino

Centurion by J. La Farge

Centurion's horse by R. Lebrun

Century plant by E. F. Spruce

Ceracchi, Giuseppe, 1751-1802
Trumbull, J. Giuseppe Ceracchi

Ceremonial bronze taking the form of a bird by M. Graves

Ceremony by H. A. Botkin

Ceremony by P. Guston

Cerulean sea and isle by J. Marin

CHADWICK, fl 1854
Placer mining, 1854
  Davidson v 1

CHADWICK, Francis Brooks, 1850-1943
William Sturgis Bigelow   MB
  MB. Ptgs in water color

Portrait of the artist

Sargent, J. S. Francis Brooks Chadwick

CHAET, Bernard, 1924-
Pastoral
  MBIC. View 1960
Remains II
  IU. Contemp Amer ptg & sculp, 1961
White table
  IU. Contemp Amer ptg & sculp, 1953

CHAIKEN, William, 1921-
Dusk
  IU. Contemp Amer ptg & sculp, 1957
Vase with flowers
  IU. Contemp Amer ptg & sculp, 1959

Chair by R. D'Arista

Chair by M. Goldberg

Chair with apples by W. Kuhn

La **Chaise-longue** by W. Gay

Chakwa tea plantation by W. Gropper

CHALFANT, Jefferson David, 1856-1931
After the hunt
  Frankenstein. After the hunt
Old flintlock
  Frankenstein. After the hunt
Old violin
  Frankenstein. After the hunt
Which is which?
  CSFP. Illusionism
  Frankenstein. After the hunt

Chalice by M. Graves

Chalice and lyre by M. Graves

The **challenge** by C. M. Russell

Challenge and response by K. L. Callahan

Chalmers, Lionel, 1715-1777
  Theus, J. Dr Lionel Chalmers
Chalmers, Martha (Logan) (?) 1721-1765
  Theus, J. Mrs Lionel Chalmers
Chama running red by J. Sloan
Chamber music by J. De Botton
Chambered nautilus by A. N. Wyeth
CHAMBERLAIN, Elwyn, 1928-
  Icarus
    MnMW. Reality and fantasy
Chamberlayne, Mrs Thomas. See Byrd, Wilhelmina
Chamberlayne, Wilhelmina (Byrd). See Byrd, Wilhelmina
CHAMBERS, Thomas, b 1808?
  Boston harbor   DN
    DN. Amer primitive ptgs, pt 1
  Connecticut river valley   DN
    DN. Amer primitive ptgs, pt 1
  Hudson river valley, sunset   DN
    DN. Amer primitive ptgs, pt 2
  Mount Auburn cemetery, Cambridge   DN
    DN. Amer primitive ptgs, pt 2
  Old Sleepy Hollow church   DN
    DN. Amer primitive ptgs, pt 2

Attributed works

  Baroque landscape   NCHA
    Jones. New-found folk art
CHAMBERS, Thomas, 1815-1866?
  Capture of H. B. M. frigate Macedonian
    by U.S. frigate United States. See
    The United States and the
    Macedonian
  Delaware Water Gap   NCHA
    Jones. Rediscovered ptrs
  Hudson river landscape
    Lipman. Primitive ptrs
  Hudson river scene   RPS
    Ford. Pictorial folk art
  Looking north to Kingston (View of
    Kingston, New York)   MNS
    Barker. Amer ptg
    Larkin (detail)
    Larkin rev ed
  Niagara Falls   CtHW
    Brussels. Exposition
    Ford. Pictorial folk art
  River scene
    Lipman. Primitive ptrs
  Under Cliff, seat of Gen G. P. Morris   RPS
    Born
  The United States and the Macedonian
    Ford. Pictorial folk art
    Lipman. Primitive ptrs
  View of Kingston, New York. See Looking north to Kingston
  View of West Point   MnMI
    Ford. Pictorial folk art
  View of the Hudson river at West Point   NR
    Jones. Rediscovered ptrs

Attributed works

  Landscape—probably a Hudson river
    scene   MeC
    Jetté. Amer heritage collection
Champion Choctaw ball-player by G. Catlin
Champs-Elysées by M. B. Prendergast

Chandelier 1 by H. Bloom
Chandler, Elizabeth. See Plummer, Elizabeth (Chandler)
CHANDLER, Joseph G. fl 1850
  Charles H. Sisson   DN
    DN. Amer primitive ptgs, pt 1
Chandler, Samuel, fl 1780
  Chandler, W. Capt Samuel Chandler
Chandler, Mrs Samuel, fl 1780
  Chandler, W. Mrs Samuel Chandler
CHANDLER, Winthrop, 1747-1790
  Ebenezer and Samuel Crafts
    Lipman. Primitive ptrs
  Ebenezer Devotion
    Davidson v 1
    Larkin
    Larkin rev ed
    Pierson
  Mrs Ebenezer Devotion
    Pierson
  Mrs Gleason and Bethia   OCoA
    Ford. Pictorial folk art
  Mrs Samuel Chandler   DN
    Brussels. Exposition
    DN. Amer primitive ptgs, pt 2
    Richardson. Ptg in America
  Samuel Chandler   DN
    DN. Amer primitive ptgs, pt 2
    Larkin (detail)
    Larkin rev ed (detail)
  View of a city
    Flexner. Light of distant skies
  William Glysson (William Gleason)   OCoA
    Davidson v 1
    Flexner. Light of distant skies
    Ford. Pictorial folk art
Changes of time by J. Haberle
Changing seasons by T. Ochikubo
Chanler, Elizabeth
  Sargent, J. S. Miss Elizabeth Chanler
Channing, Ann, 1778-1815
  Malbone, E. G. Ann Channing
Channing, Francis Dana, b 1775
  Allston, W. Francis Dana Channing
Channing, Lucy Ellery, 1752-1834
  Allston, W. Mrs William Channing
Channing, William Ellery, 1780-1842
  Allston, W. William Channing
  Stuart, G. William Ellery Channing
The chant by J. Ernst
Chantet lane by A. Dasburg
CHAPIN, Francis, 1899-
  Harbor at Edgartown
    IU. Contemp Amer ptg, 1950
    PPC. Ptg in the U.S. 1949
  House of the dogs
    IU. Contemp Amer ptg, 1952
  Oak creek canyon, Arizona
    IU. Contemp Amer ptg & sculp, 1957
  Regatta at Edgartown
    DC. 23 biennial ex, 1952
CHAPIN, James, 1887-
  Ruby Green singing   FaW
    Time. 300 years (col)
CHAPIN, Joshua Bicknell, 1814-1881
  Old mill, Hanover, N.H.   MB
    MB. Ptgs in water color
  Young woman
    OYB. Annual 1954

CHAPIN, Moses Thompson, 1814-1836
Stone cottage, Hanover, New Hampshire
MB
MB. Ptgs in water color
CHAPMAN, Charles Shepard, 1879-
Last parable
NYG. Fine art
White water ahead
NAD. Annual ex, 1947, 2d half
CHAPMAN, Conrad Wise, 1842-1913
Battery Bee   VRCM
U.S. National Capital sesquicentennial
com
Confederate submarine torpedo boat H. L.
Hunley   VRCM
Pierson
U.S. National Capital sesquicentennial
com
Fort Sumter, December 8, 1863
Pierson
Lady on a balcony in Rome   VRV
MiD. Travelers in Arcadia
Panorama: the valley of Mexico   VRV
Born
Pierson
CHAPMAN, F. A. fl 1875
The day we celebrate, the fourth of July
CtY
Davidson v2
Chapman, George, fl 1850
Mason, B. F. George Chapman
Chapman, Mrs George, fl 1850
Mason, B. F. Mrs George Chapman
CHAPMAN, John Gadsby, 1808-1889
Drawing a bead on a woodchuck   OYB
OYB. Catalogue 1951
Landing of Columbus
Ford. Edward Hicks
Looking for good scenery   VRV
MiD. Travelers in Arcadia
Pines in the Villa Barberini   MB
MB. Karolik coll
Scenery found   VRV
MiD. Travelers in Arcadia
Chapman, Mrs John Jay. See Chanler,
Elizabeth
CHAPPEL, Alonzo, 1828-1887
Surrender at Appomattox, 1865
U.S. National Capital sesquicentennial
com
CHAPPEL, Alonzo, 1828-1887 **and BACH-
ELDER, John B.** fl 1865
Death of Abraham Lincoln
U.S. National Capital sesquicentennial
com
CHAPPEL, William P. fl 1807-1810
Bathing party in New York
Davidson v2
Citizens supplying a fire engine with water
from a pump, New York, c 1809
Davidson v2
City watchman and his watch box, New
York, 1809
Davidson v2
Lamp lighter
Davidson v2 (detail)
Old tea water pump and cart, New York,
1807
Davidson v2
Raising a house, New York, 1810
Davidson v2 (detail)

Charash, Mrs Jack. See Rosenthal, Doris
Charge of the Rough Riders at San Juan
hill by F. Remington
Charles I, king of Great Britain, 1600-1649
Copley, J.S. Charles I demanding im-
peachment of five members of House
of Commons
Charles II, king of Great Britain, 1620-1685
West, B. Gen Monk receiving Charles II
on the beach of Dover
Charles of Boston (brig)
Corné, M. F. The Brig Charles of Boston
Charleston, South Carolina
Barnard, S. Charleston, South Carolina,
1831
Elliott, P. C. Charleston, South Carolina
Roberts, B. Charleston, View of
Walker, W.A. Charleston harbor from the
Battery during the bombardment of
Fort Sumter, April 13, 1861
Zerbe, K. St Philip's, Charleston
Charlestown, Massachusetts
Unidentified artist. Burning of Charles
Town
CHARLOT, Jean, 1898-
Bathers   PPhM
CoS. New accessions USA, 1958
Charlotte W. White (sailing vessel)
Sanborn, P. Ship Charlotte W. White
Charred beloved by A. Gorky
The **Charter** Oak by C. D. Brownell
Chartiers creek near Pittsburgh, 1840 by
R. Smith
Chartiers creek on the Ohio river, 1872 by
R. Smith
CHASE, A. P. fl 1850
Bird harbor, Maine   MeC
Jetté. Amer heritage collection
Chase, Alice
Chase, W. M. Alice in the mirror
Chase, W. M. Alice in the Shinnecock
studio
Chase, W. M. Alice with wolfhound
Chase, W. M. My daughter Alice
Chase, Alice (Gerson)
Chase, W. M. Mrs Chase and Cosy
Chase, W. M. Mrs Chase as a Spanish
girl
Chase, W. M. Mrs Chase in Prospect
park
Chase, David H.
Chase, W. M. My father (David H.
Chase)
Chase, Dieudonnée
Chase, W. M. Dieudonnée (Dieudonnée
Chase)
Chase, W. M. Feather boa (Dieudonnée
Chase)
Chase, Dorothy
Chase, W. M. Dorothy Chase
Chase, W. M. My little daughter Dorothy
Chase, W. M. Sketch of a child (Dorothy
Chase)
Chase, Dorothy Bremond
Chase, W. M. Girl in a red embroidered
jacket
Chase, Eliza Grover, fl 1852
Mason, B. F. Eliza Grover Chase
Chase, Harry Woodburn, 1883-1955
Lockman, D. M. Chancellor Harry Wood-
burn Chase

CHASE, W. M.—*Continued*
Still life   InBU
  NSP. William Merritt Chase
Still life   OkT
  NSP. William Merritt Chase
Still life   TxD
  NSP. William Merritt Chase
Still life   PA
  PA. Annual ex, 1955
Still life, fruit and pottery   OCiM
  NSP. William Merritt Chase
Still life—Striped bass   MoKN
  NSP. William Merritt Chase
Still life with brushes and pottery OCiM
  NSP. William Merritt Chase
Still life with cockatoo (White cockatoo)
                           NSP
  NSP. William Merritt Chase
Still life with fish   MoSL
  NSP. William Merritt Chase
Still life with fish   NSP
  NSP. William Merritt Chase
Still life with fish   OkT
  NSP. William Merritt Chase
Still life with fish   VCU
  NSP. William Merritt Chase
Still life with fish (A skate)   PA
  InIJ. Chase centennial
  NSP. William Merritt Chase
Still life with fish, brass kettle, lemon
  and onions
  NSP. William Merritt Chase (col)
Study in curves. See Reclining nude
Study of an old woman
  NSP. William Merritt Chase
Summertime
  NSP. William Merritt Chase
Sunlight and shadow
  NSP. William Merritt Chase
Tea time   MiM
  NSP. William Merritt Chase
The Tenth street studio   PPC
  InIJ. Chase centennial
The Tenth street studio   MoSL
  MoSL. Handbook 1953
  NSP. William Merritt Chase
Thomas Dewing   NAD
  NSP. William Merritt Chase
Turkish page (Boy feeding a cockatoo)
                         OCiM
  InIJ. Chase centennial
  NSP. William Merritt Chase
Unknown Dane   PPhM
  NSP. William Merritt Chase
View of Fiesole   MNS
  NSP. William Merritt Chase
View of Venice   RPS
  NSP. William Merritt Chase
Whistling boy   MiD
  NSP. William Merritt Chase
White bench   NSP
  NSP. William Merritt Chase
White cockatoo. See Still life with cockatoo
William A. Clark   DC
  InIJ. Chase centennial
  NSP. William Merritt Chase
William Clyde Fitch   MAC
  NSP. William Merritt Chase
William Gutley Munson
  InIJ. Chase centennial
William Rockhill Nelson   MoKN
  MoKN. Handbook

William Worthington Scranton NAD
  NSP. William Merritt Chase
A woman   CtHW
  NSP. William Merritt Chase
Woman in black   MNS
  NSP. William Merritt Chase
Woman in white   NUM
  PPC. Amer classics
Yellow roses   NSP
  NSP. William Merritt Chase
Chase, Mrs. William Merritt. See Chase, Alice (Gerson)
Chase homestead by W. M. Chase
A **Chase** student by W. M. Chase
The **chase** by R. A. Blakelock
Chasm of the Colorado by T. Moran
Chassidic dance by M. Weber
Chateau Argol, Environment of by K. L. Seligmann
Chateau-Thierry by W. J. Glackens
Chatham, William Pitt, 1st earl of. See Pitt, William, 1st earl of Chatham
CHAVEZ, Edward Arcenio, 1917-
Cathedral
  IU. Contemp Amer ptg & sculp, 1955
Mirage
  WMAA. Annual ex, 1957
Processional
  IU. Contemp Amer ptg, 1952
Taxidermist's window
  IU. Contemp Amer ptg, 1949
  NBuA. Expressionism
The **checkered** house by A. M. R. Moses
Checkers. See Games and sports—Checkers
Cheese factory by Unidentified artist
Cheever's mill on the St Croix by H. Lewis
Chelsea, Massachusetts
  Unidentified artist. Marine hospital, Chelsea
Chelsea girl by J. A. M. Whistler
Chelsea lady and Bouvardia by R. P. R. Neilson
Chelsea shop by J. A. M. Whistler
CHEN, Chi, 1912-
Birds flying   OYB
  OYB. Annual 1955
  OYB. Supplement 1959
Chuang tze
  PA. Annual ex, 1961
The good earth
  NAD. Annual ex, 1960
River flowing . . . flowing
  IU. Contemp Amer ptg & sculp, 1957
Cheney family, fl 1795
  Unidentified artist. Cheney family
Cherbourg, Port of by M. Jamieson
CHERMAYEFF, Serge, 1900-
Conference of great powers
  IU. Contemp Amer ptg, 1950
Emerging figure
  IU. Contemp Amer ptg, 1951
Yellow, plus and minus
  IU. Contemp Amer ptg, 1949
CHERNEY, Marvin, 1925-
Classical nude
  PA. Annual ex, 1959-60
Cherry orchard by J. Marin
Cherry twice by F. Martin

Cherubs and children by B. Shahn

CHESNEY, Lee, 1920-
Night sea no 2
OYB. Annual 1959
OYB. Supplement 1959

Chess. See Games and sports—Chess

Chestnut-sided warbler on barberry by C. E. Heil

Chestnut stallion, Discovery by V. Flannery

Cheves, Mary Elizabeth (Dulles) See Dulles, Mary Elizabeth

Cheves, Mrs Langdon. See Dulles, Mary Elizabeth

Chew, Harriet, 1775-1861
Trumbull, J. Harriet Chew

Chew, Samuel Lloyd, b 1737?
Hesselius, J. Samuel Lloyd Chew

Chew house by R. Smith

Chez le fleuriste by C. Hassam

Chez Mouquin by W. J. Glackens

Chicago, Illinois
Cuthbert, V. I. Environs of Chicago
Shahn, B. Chicago

Chicago image by N. Barrett

Chicago space no 7, 1941 by L. Moholy-Nagy

Chicken market by M. Broderson

The **chief** by F. J. Kline

Child, Elizabeth (Jarvis) 1782-1854
Jarvis, J. W. Mrs Lewis Child

A **child** by M. B. Prendergast

Child acrobats by L. P. Harmon

Child of an Idumean night by A. Gorky

Children
Ames, E. Children of Gov Daniel D. Tomkins
Balis, C. George and Emma Eastman
Bascom, R. H. M. Profile of baby in orange
Benbridge, H. Gatling children
Blanchard, C. Late again
Brewster, J. Child with a peach
Cassatt, M. Child holding a dog
Christopher, W. The child
Clonney, J. G. Sleigh ride
Copley, J. S. Child of the Greenleaf family
Copley, J. S. Children of George III
Corbino, J. A child
Durand, J. Rapalje children
Eakins, T. Baby at play
Ellsworth, J. S. Children
Emery, E. Child in sitting room of Matthew Cushing house
Evergood, P. The future belongs to them
Goodwin, E. W. Christmas presents
Grant, J. Two children
Gwathmey, R. Children dancing
Harmon, L. P. Nursery school
Herzog, H. Grandfather's lesson
Homer, W. Children on a fence
Homer, W. Children playing under a Gloucester wharf
Johnston, J. Edward and Sarah Rutter
Karfiol, B. Child holding apple
Mason limner. David, Joanna, and Abigail Mason
Myers, J. Playground pleasures
Paul, J. Four children playing in a courtyard
Peale, J. Jane and James Peale jr

Prendergast, M. B. Children playing on the beach
Prendergast, M. B. Fishing party
Prior, W. M. (attributed works) Two children with dog
Prior, W. M. (manner of) Brother and sister sharing a book
Quirk, T. C. Vigil at the beach
Ruellan, A. Children's mardi gras
Sachs, L. The Herbert children
Sargent, J. S. The Pailleron children
Sloan, J. Dust storm, Fifth avenue
Stearns, J. B. Children fishing
Stock, J. W. Child in a wicker basket
Stock, J. W. Wilcox children
Toole, J. Toole children
Tuthill, A. G. D Jackson, Solon, Elizabeth and Anna Miretta Vail
Tuthill, A. G. D. Sylvester, Julia, Jane and Catherine Larned
Unidentified artist. Angeline Eliza Shepard and her brother, Elisha Henry Shepard
Unidentified artist. Baby in blue cradle
Unidentified artist. Baby in pink and white
Unidentified artist. Baby in red chair
Unidentified artist. Baby reclining
Unidentified artist. Baby with fruit
Unidentified artist. Barclay children
Unidentified artist. Boy and girl
Unidentified artist. Child and doll
Unidentified artist. Child in blue
Unidentified artist. Child with rocking horse
Unidentified artist. Child with wheelbarrow
Unidentified artist. Children of Jacob Franks
Unidentified artist. Dover baby
Unidentified artist. Five children of the Budd family
Unidentified artist. George and Jane Bigelow
Unidentified artist. Hobby horse
Unidentified artist. Innocence
Unidentified artist. Mary and David Dalzell of South Egremont, Massachusetts
Unidentified artist. Raymond children
Unidentified artist. That's my doll!
Unidentified artist. Two children with a deer
Unidentified artist. Woodward children
Wollaston, J. Children of Warner Lewis
Woodside, J. A. Children in a courtyard

Boys
Allston, W. Italian shepherd boy
Badger, J. His son James
Badger, J. Jeremiah Belknap
Bascom, R. H. Profile of a boy
Bellows, G. B. Forty-two kids
Bingham, G. C. The mill boy
Blythe, D. G. On the sly
Blythe, D. G. Silas Gault
Blythe, D. G. Street urchins
Blythe, D. G. Young musician
Border limner. Robert Lockridge Dorr
Bradley, J. (attributed works) Boy holding dog
Brewster, J. Francis O. Watts with bird
Brackman, R. Junior
Brown, J. G. Berry boy
Casebier, C. L. Boy in Mexico

Children—Boys—_Continued_

Catlin, G. Indian boy
Chandler, J. G. Charles H. Sisson
Chase, W. M. Boy eating an apple
Chase, W. M. Master Roland Dana Chase
Chase, W. M. Turkish page
Chase, W. M. Whistling boy
Cook, N. Little dandy
Copley, J. S. Jonathan Mountfort
Davis, G. R. Sea sounds
Davis, G. R. Study
Dinnerstein, S. Magnolia
Durrie, G. H. William J. Conover as a boy
Duveneck, F. A boy
Duveneck, F. Whistling boy
Field, E. S. Boy on stenciled carpet
Francis, J. F. Three children
Frazer, O. Anderson children
Freake limner. Henry Gibbs
Freake limner. Robert Gibbs
Goodridge, E. Gorham Bond
Goodridge, E. Stephen Salisbury
Greene, S. Ischia
Henri, R. Dutch Joe
Henri, R. Laughing child
Hesselius, J. Charles Calvert and his Negro slave
Homer, W. Boy picking apples
Homer, W. Boys bathing
Homer, W. Boys wading
Homer, W. Children on the beach
Homer, W. The seesaw
Homer, W. Snap the whip
Hubard, W. J. William A. Shafer
Inman, H. The newsboy
Inman, H. Young fishermen
James, A. Danny
Jameson, D. Boy with kite
Jamieson, M. Children of Rome
Johnston, J. The Westwood children
Kane, J. Boys fishing
Karfiol, B. Boy bathers
Knight, F. Portrait of a young artist
Kuniyoshi, Y. Boy stealing fruit
Kuniyoshi, Y. Little Joe with cow
Le Clear, T. Buffalo newsboy
Luks, G. B. Butcher boy
Luks, G. B. Flyweight champ of Jumel place
Luks, G. B. The gamin
Luks, G. B. Sulking boy
Malbone, E. G. James McPherson
Malbone, E. G. Jeremiah Kahler
Mason, B. F. Rufus and Gardner Wainwright
Matson, G. W. City child
Otis, B. Seated boy
Perlin, B. Orthodox boys
Phillips, J. C. Future admiral
Pickering, H. D. Some grow up
Prendergast, J. D. Young American artist
Prior, W. M. William Allen
Reeder, D. Walter Martin
Refregier, A. Boy drawing
Ruellan, A. Boy and gull
Sargent, J. S. Boys on the beach
Sargent, J. S. Gordon Fairchild holding a guinea-pig
Sargent, J. S. Peter Augustus Jay at the age of three
Sheffield, I. James Francis Smith
Sommer, W. Bald boy
Sommer, W. A boy
Sommer, W. One of the Dominskies
Sommer, W. Pensive boy

Sommer, W. Pompous boy
Sommer, W. Ray
Sommer, W. Seated boy in lavender overalls
Speicher, E. E. Greek boy
Stock, J. W. Horace Wilson Eddy
Stock, J. W. William Howard Smith
Stock, J. W. Young hammerer
Sully, T. Torn hat
Theus, J. Charles Burnham Cochran
Theus, J. Hutchinson boy
Theus, J. Maurice Keating
Tilyard, P. Charles Slade Tilyard
Toole, J. George Toole
Unidentified artist. Abraham Clark and his children
Unidentified artist. Boy in blue coat
Unidentified artist. Boy in plaid
Unidentified artist. Boy of the De Peyster family
Unidentified artist. Boy with a toy drum
Unidentified artist. Boy with finch
Unidentified artist. Boy with hammer and iron pot
Unidentified artist. Boy with whip
Unidentified artist. De Peyster boy with deer
Unidentified artist. Henry Gibbs
Unidentified artist. Henry Wells
Unidentified artist. John Van Cortlandt
Unidentified artist. John Whorf with bow and arrow
Unidentified artist. Little boy in red
Unidentified artist. Master Willoughby
Unidentified artist. Mrs Starke's brother of Troy
Unidentified artist. Negro child
Unidentified artist. Rhode Island choir boy
Unidentified artist. Schoolmaster and boys
Unidentified artist. Two boys in green tunics
Unidentified artist. Warren Crosby
Unidentified artist. Young man in a gray linen suit
Vanderlyn, J. Severyn Bruyn
Von Phul, A. M. Boy in beaver hat
Walton, H. De Mott Smith, aged 8
Zorach, W. The artist's son

Girls

Albro, M. Skipping
Ames, E. Ann Walsh
Ames, E. Katharine Barber James (?)
Bartoll, W. T. Girl and cat
Bellows, G. W. Children on the porch
Bellows, G. W. Emma and her children
Bellows, G. W. Jean with blue book and apple
Bellows, G. W. Lady Jean
Betts, L. Frances and Judy
Bingham, G. C. Little Red Riding Hood
Bingham, G. C. Sallie Ann Camden
Bradley, J. Emma Homan
Bradley, J. Little girl in lavender
Brewster, J. One shoe off
Brook, A. Belinda standing
Cassatt, M. Child holding a dog
Cassatt, M. Child with red hat
Cassatt, M. Young girl in green bonnet
Cassatt, M. Young girls
Chase, W. M. Dorothy Chase
Chase, W. M. Girl with doll
Chase, W. M. Helen Chase

Chase, W. M. My little daughter Dorothy
Chase, W. M. Sketch of a child (Dorothy Chase)
Copley, J. S. Mary Elizabeth Martin
Copley, J. S. Mary Warner
Copley, J. S. Three princesses
Darling, R. Child in a yellow chair
Dasburg, A. Ramoncita
Davis, G. R. Deborah and Nietzsche
De Peyster manner. Eva and Katherine De Peyster
Durand, J. Mary Beekman
Earl, R. Nathaniel Shaw Woodbridge and his daughter Mary
Earl, R. Stryker sisters
Eichholtz, J. Margaret Adelia Leman
Eichholtz, J. The Ragan sisters
Evergood, P. Girl with sunflowers
Fadden, M. French child on train
Farnsworth, J. The amateur
Field, E. S. Ellen Virtue Field
Field, E. S. Girl holding rattle
Field, E. S. Girl in yellow with a red doll
Glackens, W. J. Artist's daughter in Chinese costume
Hamblin, S. J. (attributed works) Baby with doll
Hesselius, J. Elizabeth Calvert
Hubard, W. J. Elizabeth and Anna Deans
Janicki, H. Weavers of a spell
Johnson, J. Letitia McCurdy
Karfiol, B. Child holding apple
Kühn, J. E. Eleanor Darnall
Lasker, J. Little match girl
Lewin, C. L. Girl with bird
Luks, G. B. The spielers
MacKay. Catherine Brower
Malbone, E. G. Perkins children
Malbone, E. G. Sarah Reeve Ladson
Mason, B. F. Julia, Ann and Harriet Tilden
Mason limner. Alice Mason
Morse, S. F. B. Little Miss Hone
Nura. News and soda pop
Paul, J. Children at play
Peckham, R. Memorial portrait of Mary L. Edgell
Prendergast, M. B. A child
Prendergast, M. B. Evening on a pleasure boat, Boston
Prendergast, M. B. Girl in blue
Prior, W. M. The Burnish sisters
Prior, W. M. Little child with big dog
Prior, W. M. Three sisters of the Coplan family
Prior, W. M. (attributed works) Girl seated on bench
Prior, W. M. (attributed works) Little girl holding apple
Prior, W. M. (manner of) Three children
Rosenthal, D. Girl and bananas
Sargent, J. S. Daughters of Edward D. Boit
Sommer, W. June
Sommer, W. Little girl with apple
Sommer, W. Tess
Stock, J. W. Mary Jane Smith
Stuart, G. Henrietta Elizabeth Frederica Vane
Theus, J. Col Jones' grandchild (Sarah Jones)
Theus, J. Elizabeth Damaris Ravenel and her sister

Theus, J. Little Alice Hayne
Thompson, C. Girl with dove
Toole, J. Jennie Toole
Unidentified artist. Abigail Hall
Unidentified artist. Catalinja Post
Unidentified artist. Charlotte Marsteller
Unidentified artist. Child holding eyeglasses
Unidentified artist. Child in blue dress
Unidentified artist. Child in red dress
Unidentified artist. Child with dog
Unidentified artist. Curls and scallops
Unidentified artist. Eva and Catherina De Peyster
Unidentified artist. Girl by the waterfall
Unidentified artist. Girl in black pinafore
Unidentified artist. Girl in green
Unidentified artist. Girl of the Ten Eyck family
Unidentified artist. Girl on balcony
Unidentified artist. Girl with hoop
Unidentified artist. Henrietta Frances Cuthbert
Unidentified artist. Jean Macdonald Lee Myers
Unidentified artist. Little girl and the cat
Unidentified artist. Little girl of the Schuyler family
Unidentified artist. Little girl with a flower book
Unidentified artist. Little girl with a snowberry
Unidentified artist. Lydia and Tabitha
Unidentified artist. Margaret Gibbs
Unidentified artist. Mary Briggs
Unidentified artist. Picking flowers
Unidentified artist. The Pool sisters
Unidentified artist. Sisters in red
Unidentified artist. Twin sisters
Unidentified artist. Two little girls in blue
Unidentified artist. Walking the puppy
Unidentified artist. Young girl in white
Walton, H. Harriet Elizabeth Boynton
Walton, H. Sarah Louisa Spencer
Watkins, F. C. Fanciful meeting long ago
Watkins, F. C. Prudence
Wetherby, I. A. Mary Eliza Jenkins
Whistler, J. A. M. The Chelsea girl
Whistler, J. A. M. Cicely Alexander
Whistler, J. A. M. Little Rose of Lyme Regis
Wood, G. Susan Angevine Shaffer
Children of Frejus by S. Gechtoff
Children on the porch by G. W. Bellows
Children's mardi gras by A. Ruellan
Children's prison by W. Pachner
Children's theatre by J. Myers
Childs, Mrs Asa. See Childs, Clarissa (Partridge)
Childs, Clarissa (Partridge) fl 1810
    Brown, J. (attributed works) Clarissa Partridge Childs
Child's skull by H. Warshaw
Child's toy by D. Richardson
Chilmark by T. H. Benton
Chimborazo by F. E. Church
Chimera by H. Hofmann
Chimney rock by A. J. Miller
Chimneys by B. Wigfall
Chimneys and buildings by A. Osver
China Town no 1 by K. Zerbe

Chinatown, Maw Wah by J. Lechay
Chinese restaurant by J. Sloan
Chinese restaurant by M. Weber
Chinook burial grounds by J. M. Stanley
Chinook Indian by A. J. Miller
CHIPMAN, fl 1840
  Melons and grapes   DN
    DN. Amer primitive ptgs, pt 2
Chittenden, Russell Henry, 1856-1943
  Weir, J. F. Russell H. Chittenden
Choate, Sarah. See Sears, Sarah Choate
Chocorua's curse by T. Cole
The choice of Hercules by B. West
Cholmondeley, Lady
  Sargent, J. S. Lady Cholmondeley
Choose your partner by A. James
Chop suey by E. Hopper
Chouteau's Point, St Louis, Missouri by
  D. Barbier (attributed works)
Christ by H. Pippin
Christ and the psalmist by J. La Farge
Christ and the woman of Samaria by V.
  Oakley
Christ and the woman of Samaria by Un-
  identified artist
Christ and the woman taken in adultery by
  M. Beckmann
Christ at Emmaus by Unidentified artist
Christ before Pilate by D. Aronson
Christ before Pilate by J. V. Haidt
Christ driving the money changers from the
  Temple by R. Bearden
Christ healing the sick, first study by W.
  Allston
Christ in Limbo by M. Beckmann
Christ in thorns by J. Probst
Christ on the road to Emmaus by Unidenti-
  fied artist
Christ rejected by B. West
Christening by A. De Leon
Christianbury crags, Scotland, from the road
  to Langholm by A. Pope
CHRISTIE, E. A. fl 1870
  Wyoming valley
    McClintock
Christie, Gabriel, 1722-1799
  Earl, R. Gen Gabriel Christie
Christina's world by A. N. Wyeth
Christmas at the line camp by C. M. Russell
Christmas eve by J. C. Atherton
Christmas eve by G. Inness
Christmas eve by A. M. R. Moses
Christmas morning breakfast by H. Pippin
Christmas party by Unidentified artist
Christmas presents by E. W. Goodwin
Christmas tree by E. D. Lewandowski
CHRISTOPHER, William, 1924-
  The child
    MBIC. View 1960
Christy, Samuel Cartmill, fl 1821
  Harding, C. Samuel Cartmill Christy
Chrysanthemums by W. M. Chase
Chuang tze by Chi Chen
Chuck-Will's-widow by J. J. Audubon

CHUN, Sungwoo, 1935-
  Beyond the truth
    IU. Contemp Amer ptg & sculp, 1961
  Hyang-to (Homeland) no 2
    WMAA. Young America 1960
  Spring harvest
    WMAA. Young America 1960
CHUNG, Kim, 1930-
  Altar of silence
    IU. Contemp Amer ptg & sculp, 1961
CHURCH, Frederick Edwin, 1826-1900
  Between Ceppo Morelli and Ponte Grande
                                    NNCo
    MiD. Travelers in Arcadia
  Catskill mountains   MnMW
    Barker. Amer ptg
    NYG. Fine art
  Cayambe   MB
    MB. Karolik coll
  Chimborazo
    Born
  Cotopaxi, Ecuador   PR
    Born
    NUM. Art across America
    PR. Catalogue
  Finding of Moses   MB
    MB. Karolik coll
  Grand Manan, sunrise off the Maine coast
                                      CtHW
    Pierson
  Harp of the winds   MB
    MB. Karolik coll
  Heart of the Andes   MM
    Bazin
    Flexner. Amer ptg
    Flexner. Short history (detail)
  Hooker's party coming to Hartford CtHW
    Baur. Amer ptg
    CtHW. Handbook
    Pierson
  Housetop in Ecuador   NNCo
    Richardson. Ptg in America
  The iceberg
    Larkin
    Larkin rev ed
  Mountains of Ecuador   CtHW
    Pierson
  Niagara Falls   DC
    DC. De gustibus
    Pierson
    Richardson. Ptg in America
    Time. 300 years (col)
  The Parthenon   MM
    Mendelowitz
  Scene in the Catskills   MNS
    Pierson
  Scene on the Magdalene   NAD
    NAD. Amer tradition
  Sunset   NUM
    NYG. Fine art
  Tropical sunset
    Sears. Highlights
  View of Cotopaxi   ICA
    Pierson
Church bells ringing, rainy weather night by
  C. E. Burchfield
Church street el by C. Sheeler
Churches
  Carles, A. B. French village church
  Chambers, T. Old Sleepy Hollow church
  Cole, J. F. California mission
  Crane. S. W. Church at Willow

Crowninshield, F. Church in Rome

Dreier, D. New York: the Little church around the corner

Feininger, L. The church

Feininger, L. Church in Halle

Feininger, L. Church of the Minorites, II, 1926

Feininger, L. Church on the hill

Feininger, L. Village church (Nieder-Reissen)

Fletcher, A. Communion service, First Presbyterian church

Fransioli, T. A. St Andrew's church, Roanoke

Garber, D. Old church, Carversville

Halpert, S. Church interior

Hassam, C. Church at Old Lyme, Connecticut

Harvey, G. St Thomas church, Broadway, New York

Hicks, E. Grave of William Penn

Hirsch, S. Nuremberg

Kingman, D. Old mission, San Diego

Kramer, P. S. St Thomas church

Latrobe, B. H. Roman Catholic church, Baltimore, c 1805

Lee, D. E. Country wedding

Lutz, D. Mountain church, San Cristobal

Middleton, T. Interior of the Second street church, Charleston, South Carolina

Moses, A. M. R. Going to church

Moses, A. M. R. Picnic

Moses, A. M. R. The Whiteside church

O'Keeffe, G. Ranchos church

Perlin, B. Santa Maria della Salute

Pippin, H. Birmingham meetinghouse I, 1940

Prendergast, M. B. St Mark's, Venice

Prendergast, M. B. Santa Maria Formosa, Venice

Prendergast, M. B. West church, Boston

Rosenthal, D. Mexican church

Santo, P. A ray of hope

Spencer, N. Pike county church

Unidentified artist. Burning of Old South church, Maine

Unidentified artist. Twenty-two houses and a church

Whitaker, F. Pro Deo, pro populo

Wyeth, A. N. Tolling bell

Zerbe, K. St Philip's, Charleston

Zerbe, K. Terror

Churchill, Samuel Bullitt, fl 1837
Bingham, G. C. Samuel Bullitt Churchill

The **cicada** by C. E. Burchfield

CICERO, Carmen L. 1926-
Abstraction   NJN
   WMAA. Young America 1957
Along the Borgo Pass
   WMAA. Contemp Amer ptg, 1959/60
Courtship
   DC. 26 biennial ex, 1959
The fall   NeL
   CoS. New accessions USA, 1958
Leonardo
   ICA. Annual ex, 1961
The mandarin
   WMAA. Young America 1957
Odradek   NNSG
   NNSG. Handbook

Cider making by W. M. Davis

Cigar box by K. Knaths

Cigarette papers by S. Davis

CIKOVSKY, Nicolai, 1894-
Flowers in a garden
   NAD. Annual ex, 1958
Fruit, vase and mandolin
   Gruskin
Girl in bue
   IU. Contemp Amer ptg, 1948
Landscape with sunflower
   IU. Contemp Amer ptg, 1950
Spring melody   DC
   DC. 21 biennial ex, 1949
Wisconsin landscape   ATU
   ATU. Coll of Amer art

Cin Zin by K. Knaths

The **cinch** ring by C. M. Russell

Cincinnati, 1835 by J. C. Wild

Cincinnati Enquirer by W. M. Harnett

Cinerarias and fruit by M. B. Prendergast

Circa 1880 by J. A. Oneto

The **circle** by W. T. Murch

Circle image by L. Schanker

Circle painting, 4 by W. Hedrick

Circles in rectangles by L. Schanker

Circular forms by P. Strand

Circus

   See also Clowns and jesters

Avery, M. The circus

Beal, G. R. Circus at the Hippodrome

Beal, G. R. **Circus parade**

Beal, G. R. **Circus ponies**

Bellows, G. W. The circus

Bennett, B. Circus scene

Bergmann, F. Circus

Blanch, L. Outdoor circus

Brown, W. H. Bareback riders

Demuth, C. H. The circus

Kamihira, B. Circus performers

Keller, H. G. Circus folk

Keller, H. G. First show at two

Kingman, D. Circus and the lady

Kopman, B. Circus

Logan, A. The circus

Marin, J. Circus forms

Marin, J. Circus horses

Marin, J. In the ring

Prendergast, M. B. Bareback rider

Prendergast, M. B. Nouveau cirque

Schwartz, L. O. Circus fantasy

Shinn, E. Saturday night, Sarasota, Florida

Shinn, E. Trapeze, Winter garden, New York

Stahl, Ben. Rehearsal under the big top

Wilt, R. Circus triptych

Circus caravan by M. Beckmann

Circus elephants by J. Marin

Circus family by A. Revington

Circus girl by A. Blanch

Circus horses by A. De Knight

Circus is coming by C. C. Ward

Circus mirror by J. Corbino

Citta della torre by R. O. Pozzatti

The **city** by J. Albers

The **city** by X. Gonzales

The **city** by H. Hofmann

The **city** by E. Hopper

The **city** by L. MacIver

The **city** by C. di Marca-Relli
City at night by L. Feininger
City builders by M. Hoff
City child by G. W. Matson
City child by T. Yerxa
City construction by J. Marin
City evening by A. Jones
The **city** from Greenwich village by J. Sloan
City interior by C. Sheeler
City life by G. Hartigan
City man's vacation by W. H. D. Koerner
City moon by A. G. Dove
City movement, downtown Manhattan by J. Marin
City National bank by D. Nichols
The **city**—no 2 by R. Gleitsmann
City of dreadful night by B. Shahn
A **city** of fantasy by Unidentified artist
City of spires by R. Gleitsmann
City people in the country by P. Mangravite
City Point, Virginia
Henry, E. L. City Point, Virginia, headquarters of General Grant
City radiance by M. Tobey
City scene by J. Gannam
City-shape by L. Lozowick
City shapes by N. Spencer
City still life by A. Rattner
City sunlight by E. Hopper
City view by R. Breinin
City walls by N. Spencer
City watchman and his watch box, New York by W. P. Chappel
Ciudad de Dos Corazones by R. S. Neuman
Civic center, San Francisco by F. J. Rederer
Civil war, United States. See Historical themes—United States—Civil war
Civilization by W. Gropper
Civita Vecchia by R. Smith
Clam bay farm by C. Booth
Clam-diggers by K. Knaths
Clam-diggers, Provincetown by K. Knaths
Clark, Abraham, fl 1820
Unidentified artist. Abraham Clark and his children
Clark, Agnes
Speicher, E. E. Agnes Clark
CLARK, Eliot Candee, 1883-
Tuscany
NAD. Annual ex, 1958
Clark, Emily J.
Chase, W. M. The opera cloak (Miss Emily J. Clark)
Clark, Mrs Innes. See Clark, Lydia (Bowen)
Clark, Jane, b 1723
Smibert, J. (attributed works) Jane Clark
Clark, Mrs Joseph S.
Watkins, F. C. Mrs Joseph S. Clark jr
Clark, Lucy. See Croghan, Lucy (Clark)
Clark, Lydia (Bowen) 1752-1831?
Malbone, E. G. Mrs Innes Clark
Clark, Margo. See Veres
Clark, Mary Rebecca, b 1843
Heade, M. J. Mary Rebecca Clark

Clark, Sheldon, 1785-1840
Morse, S. F. B. Sheldon Clark
Clark, William, 1770-1838
Catlin, G. Gen William Clark
Russell, C. M. Lewis and Clark meeting Flathead Indians
Russell, C. M. Lewis and Clark meeting Mandans
Clark, William Andrews, 1839-1928
Chase, W. M. Senator William A. Clark
Clarke, Anne (Furneaux) 1715-1784
Greenwood, J. Anne Furneaux Clarke
Clarke, Beulah (Allen) c 1787-1827
Ames, E. Mrs William Clarke
Clarke, John, 1702-1764
Greenwood, J. John Clarke
Clarke, Mrs William. See Clarke, Beulah (Allen)
Classic and romantic art by J .S. Singer
Classic landscape by C. Sheeler
Classic male by W. De Kooning
Classic still life by R. J. Bové
Classical nude by M. Cherney
Classical still life by B. Greene
Classical still life by J. Jarvaise
Clatter of crows in spring woods by C. E. Burchfield
Clay, Henry, 1777-1852
Healy, G. P. A. Henry Clay
Hubard, W. J. Henry Clay
Inman, H. Henry Clay
Jarvis, J. W. Henry Clay
Neagle, J. Henry Clay
Peale, C. W. Henry Clay
Clayton's pasture by S. Laufman
Clear cut landscape by M. Avery
Clearing by R. Gwathmey
Clearing up by G. Inness
CLEARY, Joseph S.
Prior to
CSFP. Annual ex, 1950/51
Clematis henryi by W. C. Palmer
CLEMENS, Paul Lewis, 1911-
Ruth with cat
Gruskin (col)
Clemens, Samuel Langhorne, 1835-1910
Shinn, E. Mark Twain
Cleombrotus II, king of Sparta, 212-240, B.C.
West, B. Cleombrotus ordered into banishment by Leonidas II, king of Sparta
Cleophas, master of the Gilda Gray by M. Hartley
Clermont, first chief of the Osages, by G. Catlin
Cleveland, Arthur
Wyeth, A. N. Arthur Cleveland
Cleveland, Ohio
Heine, S. Southwest portion of the public square, Cleveland
Cliché by S. Davis
The **cliff** by E. F. Spruce
Cliff at Montauk by B. Greene
Cliff dwellers by G. W. Bellows
Cliff dwellings by R. Jonson
Cliff rock, Appledore by C. Hassam
Cliffs and the sea by L. Dodd
Cliffs at Manayunk by F. Speight

Cliffs at Newport, Rhode island by J. F. Kensett

Cliffs beyond Abiquiu, dry waterfall by G. O'Keeffe

Cliffs of red sandstone near the Rocky mountains by S. Seymour

Cliffs of the Green river, Wyoming by T. Moran

Cliffs of the Upper Colorado river by T. Moran

Cliffs, Soames sound by J. Heliker

Clinton, Catherine (Jones) 1783-1855
  Ames, E. Mrs DeWitt Clinton

Clinton, DeWitt, 1769-1828
  Ames, E. Dewitt Clinton, 1818
  Catlin, G. DeWitt Clinton
  Jarvis, J. W. De Witt Clinton

Clinton, Mrs DeWitt. See Clinton, Catherine (Jones)

Clinton, Elizabeth. See Tallmadge, Elizabeth (Clinton)

Clinton, George, 1739-1812
  Ames, E. Governor George Clinton

Clinton, George Washington, 1778-1818
  Ames, E. George W. Clinton

Clinton square, Syracuse, N.Y. by J. M. Culverhouse

CLOAR, Carroll, 1913-
  Forbidden thicket   OYB
    OYB. Annual 1956
    OYB. Supplement 1959
  Gibson bayou anthology
    IU. Contemp Amer ptg & sculp, 1957
  Promenade
    PPC. International ex, 1955
  Sun sinking in Tyrzona
    CanO. Hirshhorn coll (col)
  Where will you spend eternity
    IU. Contemp Amer ptg & sculp, 1959
  Wrecked building
    ICA. Annual ex, 1961

Clock by P. Guston

Clock by J. Haberle

Clock by J. D. McClusky

Clock by W. T. Murch

Clock and bottle by K. Knaths

Clock II, 1957 by P. Guston

The **cloister** by A. N. Wyeth

Cloistered island by L. O. Schwartz

The **Cloisters** by W. M. Chase

The **Cloisters** by A. N. Wyeth

CLONNEY, James Goodwyn, 1812-1867
  Happy moment   MB
    MB. Karolik coll
  Pierson
  In the cornfield   MB
    MB. Karolik coll
  In the woodshed   MB
    MB. Karolik coll
  Interior
    Jones. Rediscovered ptrs
  Politicians in a country bar   NCHA
    Jones. Rediscovered ptrs
  Sleigh ride   MB
    MB. Karolik coll
    Time. 300 years (col)
  Waking up   MB
    MB. Karolik coll
  What a catch!   MB
    Jones. Rediscovered ptrs
    MB. Karolik coll

Closed sea, wide world by Y. Tanguy

Closet door by J. F. Peto

Closing days by Y. Tanguy

CLOSSON, William Baxter Palmer, 1848-1929
  Pine tree and snow storm   MB
    MB. Ptgs in water color

Clothesline by G. F. Pucci

Cloud study by R. Smith

Clouded sun by G. Inness

Cloudy day, Rhode Island by M. J. Heade

Clovelly street, Devon by A. R. Brewster

Clowns and jesters
  See also Circus
  Bennett, B. Circus scene
  Brackman, R. Unmasked
  Chase, W. M. Jester
  Chase, W. M. The king's jester
  Berlandina, J. Three clowns
  Evergood, P. The jester
  Hensel, H. Clown with rooster
  Kuhn, W. Blue clown
  Kuhn, W. Clown in his dressing room
  Kuhn, W. Young clown
  Kuniyoshi, Y. The clown
  Lockman, D. M. Coco the clown
  Luks, G. B. The clown
  Martin, F. Clown act
  Moller, H. Clown
  Parshall, D. E. Clowns
  Rattner, A. Clowns and kings
  Romano, U. Green clown
  Shahn, B. Clown
  Sloan, J. Old clown making up
  Tchelitchew, P. Blue clown
  Tschacbasov, N. Clown

Club night by G. W. Bellows

Clump of trees, Study of a by J. F. Cropsey

Coaching through New Jersey by M. Klepper

Coal carrier by A. G. Dove

Coal mine by H. B. McCarter

Coast guard station by E. Hopper

Coast in winter by W. Homer

Coast of Brittany: alone with the tide by J. A. M. Whistler

Coast of Cornwall by G. Inness

Coast of Crete by R. D. Gauley

The **coast** of fog by R. Tam

The **coast** of Maine by F. J. Waugh

Coast of nevermore by L. Feininger

Coast of Sardinia by R. D. Gauley

Coast scene by J. H. Twachtman

Coast scene on the Mediterranean by W. Allston

Coast town by M. Frary

Coastal landscape by E. H. Betts

Coastal scene by J. F. Kensett

Coastline by C. S. Price

Coates, Samuel, 1748-1830
  Sully, T. Samuel Coates

Coats, David
  Gullager, C. Capt David Coats

COBB, Darius, 1834-1919
  Mary Abigail Dodge (known as Gail Hamilton)   MSE
    MSE. Cat of ports, 1950

Cobblers by M. Jules
Cobb's house by E. Hopper
Coburn, Thomas, fl 1853
  Blythe, D. G. Thomas Coburn
COCCO, Francesco di, 1900-
  Composition
    CSFP. Annual ex, 1946
Cochran, Charles Burnham, 1766-1833
  Malbone, E. G. Charles B. Cochran
  Theus, J. Charles Burnham Cochran
Cochran, Fanny Travis
  Beaux, C. A little girl—Fanny Travis
    Cochran
Cochran, William, 1754?-1833
  Trumbull, J. Rev William Cochran
The cock by Unidentified artist
Cock and glove by K. Knaths
Cock fight by H. Moller
Cockatoos
  Chase, W. M. Still life with cockatoo
  Chase, W. M. Turkish page
Cocke, John Hartwell, 1780-1866
  Hubard, W. J. Gen John H. Cocke, of
    Bremo
Cockfight, Mexico by G. O. Hart
Coco the clown by D. M. Lockman
CODMAN, Charles, 1800-1842
  Bathing pool   MB
    MB. Karolik coll
  Encampment and entertainment of the
    Boston rifle company by the Portland
    rifle company, 1830
    U.S. National Capital sesquicentennial
    com
  The hayfield
    Sears. Highlights
  View near Portland, Maine
    Sears. Highlights
  Wounded deer
    Sears. Highlights
Codwise, James, b 1772
  Trumbull, J. Capt James Codwise
Codwise, Rebecca (Rodgers) fl 1797
  Trumbull, J. Mrs James Codwise
COE, Elias V. fl 1837
  Mrs Phebe Houston   DN
    DN. Amer primitive ptgs, pt 2
Coenties slip by J. Youngerman
Coeymans, Ariaantje. See Verplanck,
  Ariaantje (Coeymans)
Coffee line by J. Sloan
Coffin, Sir Isaac, 1759-1852
  Stuart, G. Admiral Sir Isaac Coffin
Coffin, Martha. See Derby, Martha (Coffin)
COGGESHALL, Calvert, 1907-
  Landscape
    NYG. Fine art
  Nightscape
    MMA. Abstract
Cohen, Mendes
  Peale, R. Col Mendes Cohen
COHOON, Hannah, fl 1854
  Tree of life
    Pierson
COLBURN, Francis Peabody, 1909-
  Lonely places
    CSFP. Annual ex, 1946
Cold day by D. Macknight
Cold day by E. F. Spruce
Cold gray day by D. Macknight

COLDEN, Cadwallader, 1688-1776
  Pratt, M. Cadwallader Colden and Warren
    de Lancey
Colden, Cadwallader David, 1769-1834
  Jarvis, J. W. Cadwallader D. Colden
Colden family, c 1780
  Unidentified artist. Cadwallader Colden
    family
COLE, Joseph Foxcroft, 1837-1892
  A brook, Montecito, California   MB
    MB. Ptgs in water color
  California landscape   MB
    MB. Ptgs in water color
  California mission   MB
    MB. Ptgs in water color
  Mystic lake, Massachusetts   MB
    MB. Ptgs in water color
COLE, Joseph Greenleaf, 1803-1858
  Barnabas Bartol
    Frankenstein. Two journeyman ptrs
  Clement Storer
    Frankenstein. Two journeyman ptrs
              Attributed works
  Samuel Mountfort Pitts sr (possibly by
    L. E. Cole)   MiD
    MiD. Ports of the Pitts family
COLE, Thomas, 1801-1848
  American lake scene   MiD
    MiD. Treasures
  Angels administering to Christ
    CtHW. Thomas Cole
  Architect's dream   OT
    CtHW. Thomas Cole
    MiD. Travelers in Arcadia
    Pierson
    Richardson. Ptg in America (col detail)
  Catskill mountains   OCl
    OCl. Handbook
    Pierson
    Time. 300 years (col)
  Chocorua's curse
    CtHW. Thomas Cole
  Consummation   NNHS
    Larkin
    Larkin rev ed
  Daniel Boone and cabin on Great Osage
    lake   MAC
    CtHW. Thomas Cole
  Dead Abel   NAI
    MiD. Travelers in Arcadia
  The departure   DC
    DC. Masterpieces
  Destruction of empire (Course of empire)
                                           NNHS
    Born
    Pierson
    Roos
  Distant view of the Falls of Niagara
    CtHW. Thomas Cole
  Dream of Arcadia   NNHS
    Cowdrey v2
    CtHW. Thomas Cole
  Dream of Arcadia   MoSL
    CtHW. Thomas Cole
    MoSL. Handbook 1953
  Dream of Arcadia   OT
    Myers. Art
  Evening in Arcady   CtHW
    CtHW. Thomas Cole
    MiD. Travelers in Arcadia

Expulsion from the Garden of Eden   MB
  Barker. Amer ptg
  Larkin rev ed (col)
  MB. Karolik coll
  Mendelowitz
  Pierson
Expulsion from the Garden of Eden   MiD
  CtHW. Thomas Cole
Garden of Eden   MiD
  CtHW. Thomas Cole
Hartford, Connecticut
  CtHW. Thomas Cole
Head waters of Juniata
  CtHW. Thomas Cole
In the Catskills   MM
  Pierson
  Richardson. Ptg in America
Italian landscape   OYB
  CtHW. Thomas Cole
  OYB. Catalogue 1951
Italian scenery
  CtHW. Thomas Cole
John the Baptist in the wilderness   CtHW
  CtHW. Handbook
Landscape
  Chew. 250 years of art
Landscape with tree trunks   RPS
  Born
  Pierson
Last of the Mohicans   CtHW
  Robb. Harper history
Maid of the mist
  Born
Monte Video, summer home of Daniel
  Wadsworth   CtHW
  CtHW. Handbook
  CtHW. Thomas Cole
Mount Aetna from Taormina, Sicily
                                     CtNL
  CtHW. Thomas Cole
Mountain ford
  Sears. Highlights
Mountain landscape with waterfall   RPS
  Born
  Pierson
Notch of the White mountains
  CtHW. Thomas Cole
Old mill at sunset   NBM
  CtHW. Thomas Cole
Oxbow of the Connecticut   MM
  Born
  Canaday
  Flexner. Amer ptg
  Flexner. Short history
  Larkin
  Larkin rev ed
  Mendelowitz
  Pierson
  Time. 300 years (col)
Prometheus bound
  NUM. Art across America
The return   DC
  DC. De gustibus
River in the Catskills   MB
  MB. Karolik coll
Roman aqueduct   MM
  MiD. Travelers in Arcadia
The Roman Campagna   CtHW
  MiD. Travelers in Arcadia
Romantic landscape   NoCR
  NoCR. Catalogue
Salvator Rosa sketching banditti
  CtHW. Thomas Cole

Sunny morning on the Hudson river MB
  MB. Karolik coll
Temple of Segesta with the artist sketch-
  ing   MB
  MB. Karolik coll
Titan's goblet   MM
  Baur. Amer ptg
  Bazin
  CtHW. Thomas Cole
The tornado   DC
  CtHW. Thomas Cole
Tree sketch from nature   NNHS
  CtHW. Thomas Cole
View near Conway, New Hampshire
  CtHW. Thomas Cole
View near Tamworth; In the White moun-
  tains   MiD
  CtHW. Thomas Cole
View near Ticonderoga or Mount Defiance
  CtHW. Thomas Cole
View of the White mountains   CtHW
  CtHW. Thomas Cole
Voyage of life: Childhood   NNSL
  CtHW. Thomas Cole
  Pierson
Voyage of life: Manhood   NUM
  Canaday
  Pierson
  Richardson. Ptg in America
Voyage of life: Old age   NUM
  Pierson
Voyage of life: Youth   NNSL
  Canaday
  CtHW. Thomas Cole
Voyage of life: Youth   NUM
  Pierson

          Portrait of the artist
Cummings, T. S. Thomas Cole
Coleman, Constance. See Richardson, Con-
  stance (Coleman)
COLEMAN, Glenn O. 1887-1932
  Angelo's place   MMA
    Pierson
  Bus view
    Brown. Amer ptg
  Downtown street   WMAA
    Brown. Amer ptg
    Goodrich. Amer art
    McCurdy
    Pierson
  Fort Lee ferry   NBM
    Pierson
COLEMAN, Loring W.
  Rural pattern   OYB
    OYB. Annual 1959
    OYB. Supplement 1959
  Shelter of longing
    NAD. Annual ex, 1961
  Warmth of memory
    NAD. Annual ex, 1956
Coleridge, Samuel Taylor, 1772-1834
  Allston, W. Samuel Taylor Coleridge
Coles, Hannah. See Neilson, Hannah (Coles)
COLESCOTT, Robert H. 1925-
  Barbizon nymph
    OrPA. Ptgs & sculptures
Colford, Eleanor. See Jones, Eleanor (Col-
  ford)
Colima by C. R. Bentley
The collect or fresh water pond by A. Rob-
  ertson (attributed works)

A **collection** of things by R. Koppe

Collection X, no 2 by K. Zerbe

Collector's cabinet by W. W. Beecher

College on the hill by W. Lester

Colles, Christopher, 1738-1816
  Jarvis, J. W. Christopher Colles

Colleti, Kathleen
  Speicher, E. E. Kathleen Colleti

Collins, Edward, 1704-1753
  Pierpont limner. Edward Collins

Collins, Henry, fl 1729
  Feke, R. Henry Collins (formerly called Gershom Flagg III)
  Smibert, J. Henry Collins

COLLINS, John, fl 1846
  Mauch Chunk
    McClintock

Colman, Benjamin
  Pelham, P. Rev Benjamin Colman

Colman, Benjamin, 1673-1747
  Smibert, J. Benjamin Colman

COLMAN, Samuel, 1832-1920
  Covered wagons crossing Medicine Bow creek (Emigrant train fording Medicine Bow creek)
    Davidson v 1 (col front)
    Rathbone
    U.S. National Capital sesquicentennial com
  Emigrant train fording Medicine Bow creek. See Covered wagons crossing Medicine Bow creek
  Ships of the plains   NNU
    Pierson
    Rathbone

COLOMB, Christophe, fl 1790
  White Hall plantation, Louisiana c 1790
    U.S. National Capital sesquicentennial com

Colonial cubism by S. Davis

Color analogy by M. Hartley

Color isolation by J. Ernst

Color poem by H. Hofmann

Color symphony by A. Walkowitz

Colorado river
  Moran, T. Chasm of the Colorado

Colossal bust at low water mark, used as metre by the aborigines by J. J. Egan

Colossal head by L. A. Golub

Colossal luck by W. M. Harnett

Colossal owls and eagles of the inner eye by M. Graves

Colosseum by B. Perlin

Colosseum no 2 by W. G. Congdon

Colts at Soda Springs by H. Strater

Columbia by Unidentified artist

Columbus, Christopher, 1446?-1506
  Chapman, J. G. Landing of Columbus
  Hicks, E. Columbus
  Kemmelmeyer, F. First landing of Christopher Columbus

Columbus avenue, Boston: rainy day by C. Hassam

Columbus avenue, snowy day by G. R. Beal

Columbus circle by D. Kingman

Columbus circle, New York by M. B. Prendergast

COLYER, Vincent, 1825-1888
  Fort Arbuckle, Oklahoma territory
    Rathbone

Comanche feats of horsemanship by G. Catlin

Comanche village in Texas by G. Catlin

Comanche war party meeting dragoons by G. Catlin

The **comb** by M. Weber

Combination concrete no 2 by S. Davis

Combing the ridges by W. R. Leigh

Comedy by A. Buller

COMEGYS, George H. fl 1838
  Artist's dream
    Cowdrey v 1

Comer, Sarah. See Dolbeare, Sarah (Comer)

Coming into port by L. J. Liberté

Coming of spring by C. E. Burchfield

Coming storm by W. Homer

Coming storm by G. Inness

Coming storm by Unidentified artist

Coming to the point by W. S. Mount

Common crossbill by J. J. Audubon

Communion by R. Gikow

Communion service, First Presbyterian church by A. Fletcher

Company for supper by D. Nichols

Competitor (ship)
  Wales, G. C. Clipper ship Competitor

Composed from my window by J. Marin

Composite harbor scene with volcano by Unidentified artist

Composition by K. L. Seligmann

Composition around red by C. Sheeler

Composition, Cape Split, Maine, 1933 by J. Marin

Composition—Farmscape no 3, 1955 by A. Rattner

Composition, head and flowers by A. Rattner

Composition in an oval by T. Roszak

Composition in black and ochre by A. Yunkers

Composition in blue by B. Parker

Composition in red, yellow and blue by A. Leepa

Composition in white by I. R. Pereira

Composition in white by T. J. Roszak

Composition on green by H. Ferren

Composition: the storm by B. Greene

Composition—three figures by M. Weber

Composition, tree branch by R. Conover

Composition with clarinet and tin horn by B. Shahn

Composition with fried egg by W. Sanderson

Composition with head by A. Gorky

Composition with old shoes by A. Rattner

Composition with still life by E. W. Dickinson

Composition with three figures by A. Rattner

Composition with three figures by M. Weber

Composition with violet by B. Gonzales

Compression by N. Barrett

CONANT, Lucy Scarborough, 1867-1921
Antelao   MB
  MB. Ptgs in water color
Concealed enemy by G. C. Bingham
Concentrated pine top by M. Graves
Conception by S. MacDonald-Wright
Conception synchromy by S. MacDonald-Wright
Concert singer by T. Eakins
Concord by B. Newman
Concord, Massachusetts
  Earl, R. View of the town of Concord, Massachusetts, c 1775
Concord, Battle of, 1775
  Earl, R. Battle of Concord
Concretion by G. L. K. Morris
A **condition** of New England by F. D. Duncan
Condors
  Audubon, J. J. California condor
CONDUIT (Contoit), Louis
  Pointer and quail
    NSP. Sportscapes
CONE, Marvin, 1891-
  Habitation
    ICA. Annual ex, 1945/46
  Silent watcher
    IU. Contemp Amer ptg & sculp, 1957
  Three doorways
    ICA. Annual ex, 1951
Coney Island, New York
  Bellows, G. W. Beach at Coney Island, N.Y.
  Davis, N. Coney Island: summer labyrinth
  Marsh, R. Coney Island
  Marsh, R. Coney Island beach
  Stella, J. Battle of lights, Coney Island
Confederate submarine torpedo boat H. L. Hunley by C. W. Chapman
Conference at night by E. Hopper
Conference of great powers by S. Chermayeff
Conference of the treaty of peace with England by B. West
Confidants by G. Gluckman
The **confidence** by J. Hirsch
Conflagration at the museum by M. Siporin
Conflict by T. Egri
CONGDON, William Grosvenor, 1912-
  Black city
    WMAA. New decade
  Colosseum no 2
    IU. Contemp Amer ptg & sculp, 1953
  Istanbul no 6, 1953
    MnMW. Expressionism 1900-1955
  Notre Dame
    IU. Contemp Amer ptg & sculp, 1957
  Orvieto
    NBuA. Expressionism
  Piazza Navona   NUM
    MiA. Root coll
  Piazza San Marco
    CtY. Yale alumni
    IU. Contemp Amer ptg & sculp, 1959
    WMAA. Contemp Amer ptg, 1953
  Piazza, Venice
    DC. 23 biennial ex, 1952

St Germaine   WMAA
McCurdy
Pierson
  WMAA. New decade
Taj Mahal no 3
  IU. Contemp Amer ptg & sculp, 1955
Venice no 1   MoSL
  Faulkner. Art today, 1956
  MoSL. Handbook 1953
  Pousette-Dart. Amer ptg
  WMAA. New decade
Venice no 2
  PA. Annual ex, 1951
Conglomeration by J. Haberle
Congo by W. A. Baziotes
Congregation by Z. Sepeshy
Congress voting independence by R. E. Pine and E. Savage
Conjurer by J. Kirschenbaum
Connecticut clock by K. Knaths
Connecticut farm by M. Varga
Connecticut farm buildings by C. Sheeler
Connecticut field by W. Kienbusch
Connecticut river by A. G. Dove
Connecticut river valley by T. Chambers
Connecticut rocks by R. Cowles
Connecticut sea captain by I. Sheffield
Connecticut stream by R. Cowles
Connecticut woods by H. W. Ranger
CONNELLY, Brian, 1926-
  Abstraction   ICA
    ICA. Annual ex, 1951
    Pousette-Dart. Amer ptg
  Rosa gallica   NSyE
    CoS. New accessions USA, 1956
  The spectrum, a painting in four acts
    PPC. International ex, 1952
  Window with flowers
    MnMW. Reality and fantasy
Connelly, John, fl 1813
  Sully, T. John Connelly
Conner's rock, Cape Eliza, Maine by G. B. Luks
Conover, Rebecca (Crawford) fl 1842
  Durrie, G. H. Mrs Tunis V. Conover
CONOVER, Robert, 1920-
  Composition, 1951
    MnMW. Classic tradition
  Composition, tree branch
    Baur. Nature
  Gray abstraction
    MMA. Abstract
Conover, Tunis V. fl 1842
  Durie, G. H. Tunis V. Conover
Conover, William J. fl 1842
  Durrie, G. H. William J. Conover as a boy
Conquered king by N. Barrett
Conquest by H. Bloom
The **consolation** of Ariadne by B. Bryson
Constance by A. P. Ryder
Constant by E. W. Dickinson
Constellation by M. Tobey
The **Constitution (frigate)**
  Birch, T. The Constitution and the Guerrière

The **Constitution** (frigate)—*Continued*
  Corné, M. F. The Constitution and the Guerrière
  Salmon, R. W. The Constitution in Boston harbor
Construction by B. Diller
Construction by N. Gabo
Construction by H. Hofmann
Construction by R. B. Motherwell
Construction in blue by P. Gaulois
Construction no 2 by G. Steele
Construction: Shaftsbury, Vermont by J. C. Atherton
Constructions by V. I. Cuthbert
Consuela by E. E. Speicher
Consummation by T. Cole
Contact by V. Candell
Contemplation by C. M. Russell
Contemporary American sculpture by B. Shahn
Contentment by L. Eilshemius
Continence of Scipio (copy of Poussin) by J. Smibert
Continuum number 16 by E. M. Smith
Contrada by F. J. Kline
Convention by B. Shahn
Convergence by J. Pollock
Converging disks by G. L. K. Morris
Conversation by K. L. Callahan
Conversation by J. Floch
Conversation by H. Pittman
Conversation by H. E. Schnakenberg
Conversation by Y. Tanguy
Conversation by R. Vickrey
Conversation by M. Weber
Conversation in studio by M. Avery
Conversation piece by V. Candell
Conversation piece by W. Williams
Conversations by B. Shahn
Conversing by signs by A. J. Miller
The **conversion** of St Paul by B. West
CONWAY, Frederick E. 1900-
  Blue finch
    IU. Contemp Amer ptg & sculp, 1955
  Dancer
    IU. Contemp Amer ptg, 1949
  Green bird   MoSL
    MoSL. Handbook 1953
  Mystery
    IU. Contemp Amer ptg, 1948
    IU. Contemp Amer ptg, 1951
  Red object
    IU. Contemp Amer ptg & sculp, 1957
  Witchery   DC
    DC. 21 biennial ex, 1949
Conway, New Hampshire, View near by T. Cole
Conway castle, North Wales by B. West (attributed works)
Cook, Alvah, fl 1825
  Unidentified artist. Dr Alvah Cook
COOK, Howard Norton, 1901-
  The bridge no 1   PPhM
    Pousette-Dart. Amer ptg

  Magical city
    IU. Contemp Amer ptg & sculp, 1957
  White structures
    IU. Contemp Amer ptg, 1952
Cook, James W. fl 1810
  Jarvis, J. W. James W. Cook
Cook, Maud
  Eakins, T. Maud Cook (Young woman in pink dress)
COOK, Nelson, fl 1840
  Little dandy   VtMS
    NUM. Art across America
Cook, Weda. See Addicks, Weda (Cook)
Cooke, Elisha
  Pollard limner (attributed works) Elisha Cooke
Cooke, Sir George, bart
  Copley, J. S. Sir George Cooke, bart
COOKE, L. M. fl 1875
  Salute to Gen Washington in New York harbor   DN
    DN. Amer primitive ptgs, pt 1
Cool doll in pool by P. Evergood
Coolidge, Calvin, president U.S. 1872-1933
  Lockman, D. M. President Calvin Coolidge
  Salisbury, F. O. Calvin Coolidge
Coolidge, Cornelius, fl 1804
  Malbone, E. G. Cornelius Coolidge
Coolidge, Joseph, 1747-1821
  Stuart, G. Joseph Coolidge
Coon hunt by Unidentified artist
COOPER, Colin Campbell, 1856-1937
  Lotus pool, El Encanto, Santa Barbara
                                          PR
    PR. Catalogue
Cooper, Elizabeth (Fenimore) fl 1816
  Freeman, Mr. Mrs William Cooper
  Unidentified artist. Elizabeth Fenimore Cooper
COOPER, J. fl 1714
  Allegorical figures   CtNL
    Flexner. First flowers
  Eighteenth-century gentleman   NNHS
    Barker. Amer ptg
  Gentleman with violin   NNHS
    NNHS. Waldron Phoenix Belknap coll
Cooper, James Fenimore, 1789-1851
  Jarvis, J. W. James Fenimore Cooper
COOPER, Mario Ruben, 1905-
  East river dock
    NAD. Annual ex, 1954
  Peace memorial, Hiroshima   OYB
    OYB. Supplement 1959
COOPER, Peter, fl 1720
  Southeast prospect of the city of Philadelphia, c 1720   PPhL
    U.S. National Capital sesquicentennial com
Cooper, Richard Fenimore, 1776-1813
  Ames, E. Richard Fenimore Cooper
COOPER, W. B. fl 1840?
  Mrs John Cornwall   KyLS
    KyLS. Kentucky port gall
Cooper, William, 1754-1809
  Stuart, G. William Cooper of Cooperstown
Cooper, Mrs William. See Cooper, Elizabeth (Fenimore)
Cooperstown, New York
  Morse, S. F. B. View from Apple hill, Cooperstown, New York
Coot hunter by A. N. Wyeth

COPE, George, 1855-1929
Buffalo Bill's traps
  Frankenstein. After the hunt
Fisherman's accoutrements   OYB
  OYB. Supplement 1959
Hunter's equipment
  Chew. 250 years of art
Professor Hunter Worrell's pipe
  Frankenstein. After the hunt
Still life, 1902
  Frankenstein. After the hunt
Still life, 1911
  Frankenstein. After the hunt

Coplan sisters
Prior, W. M. Three sisters of the Coplan
  family

COPLEY, John Singleton, 1737-1815
Ann Tyng   MB
  Flexner. Copley
  Larkin
  Larkin rev ed
  Pierson
Arrest of Monmouth before James II
                                             MCH
  Pierson
The ascension   MB
  Flexner. Copley
Augustus Brine   MM
  Flexner. Copley
Benjamin Pickman
  Flexner. Copley
Boy with squirrel (Henry Pelham)
  Barker. Amer ptg
  Flexner. Copley (col front)
  Flexner. First flowers
  Mendelowitz
  Pierson
  Walker. Ptgs from America
Brook Watson   InIJ
  InIJ. 105 ptgs
Brook Watson and the shark. See Watson
  and the shark
Brother and sisters of Christopher Gore
  (The Gore children)
  Flexner. Copley
  Pierson
Charles I demanding impeachment of five
  members of House of Commons
                                             MCH
  Pierson
Child of the Greenleaf family
  Belknap
Children of George III
  Walker. Ptgs from America (col)
Colonels Hugo and Schleppengull   MCH
  Flexner. Copley
Copley family   DN
  Barker. Amer ptg
  Flexner. Copley
  Larkin
  Larkin rev ed
  Walker. Ptgs from America
Death of Chatham   ELT
  Flexner. Copley
  Flexner. Light of distant skies
Death of Major Pierson   ELN
  Flexner. Copley
Deborah Scollay   MWM
  Flexner. Copley
  MB. New England miniatures
  Pierson

Elizabeth Allen Stevens   NJMo
  NJMo. Your Montclair art museum
Elizabeth Pitts   MiD
  MiD. Ports of the Pitts family
Elizabeth Ross   MB
  Flexner. Copley
Elkanah Watson   NJP
  Bolton. Ezra Ames
An engraver, known as Henry Pelham
  Flexner. First flowers
Epes Sargent   DN
  Flexner. Copley
  Flexner. Copley (detail)
  ICA. From colony to nation
  Pierson
  Walker. Ptgs from America
Ezekiel Goldthwait   MB
  Pierson
  Richardson. Ptg in America
Francis Borland
  MB. New England miniatures
Galatea   MB
  Pierson
George Green   MB
  MB. New England miniatures
The Gore children. See Brother and sis-
  ters of Christopher Gore
Isaac Smith   CtY
  CtY. Portrait index
  Pierson
Jacob Fowle   DC
  Barker. Amer ptg
  DC. Masterpieces
  U.S. National Capital sesquicentennial
  com
James Otis
  Flexner. Copley
James Tilley, New England merchant
  Davidson v 1
James Warren   MB
  MB. Great Americans
Jane Browne   DN
  Flexner. First flowers
Jeremiah Lee   CtHW
  Pierson (detail)
Jeremiah Lee (Lee coll)
  Upjohn
John Adams   MCH
  Roos
John Gray   MiD
  MiD. Treasures
John Greene   NHMC
  NUM. Art across America
John Hancock   MB
  Craven. Rainbow book
  Flexner. Short history (col)
  MB. Great Americans
  Roos
John Montresor (William? Montresor)
                                             MiD
  MiD. Treasures
  Richardson. Ptg in America
John Quincy Adams   MB
  MB. Great Americans
  Roos
John Winthrop   MCH
  Flexner. Copley
Jonathan Belcher
  Belknap
  NNHS. Waldron Phoenix Belknap coll
Jonathan Jackson
  MB. New England miniatures

COPLEY, J. S.—*Continued*
Jonathan Mountfort   MiD
   MiD. Ports of the Pitts family
Joseph Barrell   MWM
   Pierson
Joseph Mann   MB
   Flexner. First flowers
Joseph Sherburne   MM
   Flexner. First flowers
Joseph Warren   MB
   MB. Great Americans
Joshua Henshaw   CSFP
   CSFP. Handbook
Joshua Winslow
   Belknap
Lady Frances Wentworth   NNPL
   UNESCO. Prior to 1860
   UNESCO. Prior to 1860 3d ed
   UNESCO. Prior to 1860 5th ed
Mars, Venus, and Vulcan
   Flexner. First flowers
Mary and Elizabeth Royall   MB
   Richardson. Ptg in America
Mary Elizabeth Martin   MAP
   Flexner. Light of distant skies
Mary Warner
   Flexner. Copley
   Flexner. First flowers
   MiD. Ptg in America
Mr and Mrs Isaac Winslow   MB
   Flexner. First flowers
   Larkin
   Larkin rev ed
Mr and Mrs Ralph Izard   MB
   Flexner. Copley
Mr and Mrs Thomas Mifflin   PH
   Flexner. Copley
   Flexner. First flowers (col)
   Pierson
   Richardson. Ptg in America (col)
   Robb. Harper history
   Roos
Mrs Benjamin Pickman
   CtY. Yale alumni
   Flexner. Copley
Mrs Daniel Rea and child   OYB
   OYB. Catalogue 1951
Mrs Ezekiel Goldthwait   MB
   Flexner. Copley
   Pierson
Mrs Gawen Brown   CtY
   CtY. Portrait index
Mrs Gawen Brown (pastel, Lockwood coll)
   Flexner. First flowers
Mrs George Watson   CtY
   MB. New England miniatures
Mrs Isaac Smith   CtY
   CtY. Portrait index
   Pierson
Mrs James Warren   MB
   MB. Great Americans
Mrs Jerathmael Bowers   MM
   Belknap
   Flexner. First flowers
   Pierson
Mrs Jeremiah Lee   CtHW
   Pierson
Mrs John Amory   MB
   Flexner. First flowers

Mrs John Bacon   NBM
   NYG. Fine art
   UNESCO. Prior to 1860
   UNESCO. Prior to 1860 3d ed
   UNESCO. Prior to 1860 5th ed
Mrs John Greene   OCl
   Belknap
   OCl. Handbook
Mrs John Winthrop   MM
   Flexner. First flowers
Mrs Jonathan Belcher
   Belknap
Mrs Joseph Mann   MB
   Belknap
   Flexner. Copley
   Flexner. First flowers
   NNHS. Waldron Phoenix Belknap coll
Mrs Michael Gill
   Flexner. First flowers
Mrs Nathaniel Appleton   MCH
   Flexner. Copley
   Flexner. First flowers
Mrs Paul Richard
   Flexner. Copley
   Flexner. First flowers
Mrs Roger Morris
   MiD. Coll in progress
   WiMiA. Amer ptg 1760-1960
Mrs Samuel Cary
   Flexner. Copley
   MB. New England miniatures (col)
Mrs Samuel Waldo   CtY
   MB. New England miniatures
Mrs Seymour Fort   CtHW
   Craven. Treasury 1952 ed (col)
   CtHW. Handbook
   Janson. Picture history
   Lee. Art then and now
   MoSL. 40 masterpieces
   Pierson
   Robb. Art 1953 ed
   Time. 300 years (col)
Mrs Sylvanus Bourne   MM
   Richardson. Ptg in America
Mrs Thomas Boylston   MCH
   Barker. Amer ptg
   Bazin. History of art
   Gardner 1959 ed
   ICA. From colony to nation
   Janson. Key monuments
   Mendelowitz
   Walker. Ptgs from America
Mrs Thomas Greene
   WiMiA. Amer ptg 1760-1960
Mrs William Whipple
   Belknap
Nathaniel Hurd   OCl
   Barker. Amer ptg
   Larkin rev ed (col detail)
   Myers. Art
   OCl. Handbook
   Pierson
Nathaniel Hurd (miniature)
   Flexner. Copley
Nathaniel Hurd (unfinished)   NR
   Flexner. First flowers
Nathaniel Sparhawk
   Flexner. First flowers
Nicholas Boylston   MB
   Roos
   Time. 300 years (col)

Paul Revere   MB
  Flexner. First flowers
  MB. Great Americans
  McKinney
  Pierson
  Time. 300 years (col)
Richard, Earl Howe   DN
  DN. Mellon coll
Samuel Adams   MB
  Flexner. First flowers
  Larkin
  Larkin rev ed
  MB. Great Americans
Samuel Cary
  Flexner. Copley
  MB. New England miniatures (col)
Samuel Fayerweather   CtY
  CtY. Portrait index
  MB. New England miniatures
Samuel Pitts   MiD
  MiD. Ports of the Pitts family
Samuel Verplanck   MM
  Davidson v 1
Self-portrait (Du Pont coll)
  Flexner. Copley
  Pierson
Self-portrait (Greene coll)
  Craven. Treasury 1952 ed
  Flexner. Copley
  MB. New England miniatures (col)
  Time. 300 years (col)
Self-portrait (Hammond coll)
  Flexner. Copley
Sir George Cooke, bart   MoKN
  MoKN. Handbook (col)
Sir William Pepperrell and his family
                                    NoCR
  NoCR. Catalogue
Sketch for the Knatchbull family
  Flexner. Copley
Thaddeus Burr   MoSL
  MoSL. 50 masterworks
  MoSL. Handbook 1953
Thomas Amory jr
  Flexner. Copley
Thomas Hancock   MCH
  Flexner. Copley
Thomas Mifflin and Mrs Mifflin   PH
  ICA. From colony to nation
Three princesses
  Flexner. Copley
  Flexner. Light of distant skies
Watson and the shark (Brook Watson
  and the shark)   MB
  Barker. Amer ptg
  Craven. Treasury 1952 ed
  Flexner. Amer ptg
  Flexner. Copley
  Flexner. Light of distant skies
  Flexner. Short history
  Janson. Key monuments
  Janson. Picture history
  Mendelowitz
  MiD. Treasures
  Pierson
  Richardson. Ptg in America
  Roos
  Time. 300 years (col)
William Brattle
  Flexner. Copley
William Welsteed   CtY
  Flexner. First flowers

Attributed works
Daniel D. Rogers
  MB. New England miniatures (col)
Henry Pelham (?)   MB
  MB. New England miniatures (col)
Peter Oliver jr
  MB. New England miniatures
Whitehead Hicks   NNMC
  Belknap

Portrait of the artist
Copley, J. S. Self-portrait
Copley family by J. S. Copley
Copley square by L. G. Paine
Copper kettle by K. Knaths
Copper light by I. R. Pereira
Coppet (Lake Geneva) by W. S. Haseltine
Copyist by C. Locke
Coq d'Or by K. Knaths
Coral necklace by T. Eakins
Corazziere by E. Martinelli
CORBETT, Edward, 1919-
  New Mexico number 34
    IU. Contemp Amer ptg & sculp, 1955
  Newcomb college   NBuA
    NBuA. Acquisitions 1957-58
  Number 15   MMA
    Pierson
  Provincetown II
    ICA. Annual ex, 1959-60
  Provincetown no 6   NJN
    CoS. New accessions USA, 1960
CORBINO, Jon, 1905-
  Centurion
    MM. Amer ptg today
  A child
    IU. Contemp Amer ptg, 1949
  Circus mirror
    NAD. Annual ex, 1957
    PPC. Ptg in the U.S. 1949
  Crucifixion
    PPC. International ex, 1950
  Equestrian sunrise
    NAD. Annual ex, 1961
  Eve
    IU. Contemp Amer ptg, 1951
  Family
    Gruskin
  Flood refugees   MM
    MM. 100 Amer ptrs
    Pierson
  Flowers   MAP
    Rathbun
  The meeting   MoKN
    CoS. New accessions USA, 1946
  Moonlight
    Genauer (col)
  Race track   NJMo
    NJMo. Forty years
  Stampeding bulls   OT
    Pierson
  Summer holiday
    NAD. Annual ex, 1948
  Three horsemen
    IU. Contemp Amer ptg, 1948
Corcoran, William Wilson, 1798-1888
  Healy, G. P. A. William W. Corcoran
Corder, Rose
  Whistler, J. A. M. Rose Corder

Cordova: interior of the cathedral by J. S. Sargent

Coren, Susan. See Towers, Mrs Susan (Coren)

Corfu
Sargent, J. S. Corfu: cypresses
Sargent, J. S. Corfu: lights and shadows
Sargent, J. S. Corfu: the terrace
Corinth no 3, 1959 by T. Stamos

Cormorants
Audubon, J. J. European cormorant
Corn belt city by E. Hopper
Corn dance, New Mexico by J. Marin
Corn, dark by G. O'Keeffe
Corn field by D. Macknight
Corn husking by W. Homer
Corn husking by E. Johnson
Corn husking at Nantucket by E. Johnson
CORNÉ, Michele Felice, 1752-1832
Bombardment of Tripoli, 1804   RPHS
Davidson v 1
ICA. From colony to nation
U.S. National Capital sesquicentennial com
Brig Charles of Boston   MB
MB. Ptgs in water color
Constitution and the Guerrière   CtNH
Davidson v 1
Letter-of-Marque ship Mount Vernon of Salem
Davidson v 1
Ship America hand lining on the Grand Bank   MSP
Davidson v 1
Cornee, William, fl 1836
Peckham, R. William Cornee with flute
Cornee, Mrs William, fl 1836
Peckham, R. Mrs William Cornee with music
Cornelia street by J. Sloan
CORNELL, John V. fl 1830
Iron witch   NNHS
Davidson v 2
View of the Highlands from Ruggles house, Newburgh, New York   NNHS
NNHS. Waldron Phoenix Belknap coll
CORNELL, Joseph, 1903-
Pavilion
Hunter. Mod Amer ptg
Cornell, Katharine, 1898-
Speicher, E. E. Katharine Cornell as Candida, 1926
Cornell family, A gentleman of by J. W. Jarvis
Cornell farm by E. Hicks
Corner café by S. Davis
Corner of a pasture by E. Glannon
Corner saloon by E. Hopper
Cornfield and harvest by G. W. Bellows
Cornwall, Amelia (Bucklin) 1825-1891
Cooper, W. B. Mrs John Cornwall
Coronation by J. Levine
Coronation of the Virgin by D. Aronson
Corporation shed by N. Spencer
Corpse of elderly female by H. Bloom
Corpus Christi, Santa Fe by J. Sloan
Corpus delicti by G. Grosz
Corridors by M. B. Prendergast

Corridors of time by P. Burlin
Corroded implement by D. W. Ellis
Cortlandt, Mrs Pierre. See Van Cortlandt, Anne (Stevenson)
CORTOR, Eldzier, 1915-
Affection
Pearson. Mod renaissance
Americana
IU. Contemp Amer ptg, 1948
The bathers
ICA. Annual ex, 1945/46
Room number VI
IU. Contemp Amer ptg, 1951
Pearson. Mod renaissance
Southern souvenir
Pearson. Mod renaissance
Two nudes
Pearson. Mod renaissance
CORWINE, Aaron Houghton, 1802-1830
Samuel Hildreth
OCiM. Rediscoveries
Thomas J. Matthews
OCiM. Rediscoveries
Coryell's ferry by J. Pickett
Cos Cob by G. O'Keeffe
Cosmic synchromy by M. Russell
COSTIGAN, John Edward, 1888-
Springtime   NJMo
NJMo. Forty years
Costume figure with mask by A. Rattner
The cot by J. Sloan
Cotopaxi, View of by F. E. Church
Cotopaxi, Ecuador by F. E. Church
Cottage, Cape Cod by E. Hopper
Cottage landscape, Hawarden, Wales by M. B. Prendergast
Cotter, Joanna. See Somerby, Joanna (Cotter)
The cotters' Saturday night by E. G. H. Pinney
Cotton, Mrs Leslie, fl 1888
Chase, W. M. Lady in black (Mrs Leslie Cotton)
COTTON, William Henry, 1880-
Artist's mother
NAD. Annual ex, 1958
Cotton from field to mill by P. Evergood
Cotton picker by R. Gwathmey
Cotton pickers by W. Homer
Cotton picker's home by W. A. Walker
Cotton plantation by C. Giroux
Cottonwoods on the Missouri by C. Wimar
The couch by B. Kamihira
Cougars
Miller, A. J. Shooting a cougar
Counterpoint by T. Ochikubo
Country dance by M. E. Ferrill
Country dance by F. Martin
Country dance by W. S. Mount
Country fair by H. Sharrer
Country fair by J. A. Woodside
Country fair in Pennsylvania, 1824 by J. A. Woodside
Country flowers by E. Isenberger
Country gallants by J. G. Brown
Country girl by A. P. Ryder

Country horse show by P. S. Sample
A country house by W. S. Mason
Country in winter by D. Macknight
Country lass by G. Fuller
Country road by W. D. Fausett
Country school by W. Homer
Country wedding by J. L. Krimmel
Country wedding by D. E. Lee
County election by G. C. Bingham
County fair by H. P. Barnett
County fair by W. Peirce
County home by L. Bouché
The couple by G. Grosz
The couple by J. Hirsch
Couple driving by A. Bierstadt
Courbet at Trouville, Harmony in blue and
    silver by J. A. M. Whistler
Course of empire by E. Leutze
Court of death by Rembrandt Peale
The courtesan by S. Post
COURTRIGHT, Robert
    Antiquity   OCo
        CoS. New accessions USA, 1960
Courtroom scenes
    Bingham, G. C. The puzzled witness
    Blythe, D. G. Courtroom scene
    Blythe, D. G. Trial scene
    Levine, J. Courtroom study
    Matteson, T. H. Justice's court in the
        backwoods
    Pippin, H. Trial of John Brown
    Wighe, A. Rural court scene, 1849
Courtship by C. L. Cicero
Courtyard by E. Berman
Courtyard, Tetuan by J. S. Sargent
COUSE, Eanger Irving, 1866-1936
    Making medicine
        OYB. Catalogue 1951
COUTURIER, Hendrick, fl 1660

        Attributed works
    Governor Stuyvesant   NNHS
        Mendelowitz
The cove by J. W. Boynton
The cove by W. Farndon
The cove by L. Kester
The cove by J. Marin
The cove by M. B. Prendergast
Cove at sunset by E. Isenburger
The covered bridge by A. M. R. Moses
Covered wagons
    Bartlett, G. Ox train
    Bierstadt, A. Nooning on the Platte
    Colman, S. Covered wagons crossing
        Medicine Bow creek
    Colman, S. Ships of the plains
    Eastman, S. Emigrants attacked by the
        Comanches
    Remington, F. Attack on the supply train
    Ranney, W. T. Pioneers
    Russell, C. M. Covered wagons
    Russell, C. M. The jerk line
    Russell, C. M. Wagon boss
    Scott, J. W. A. Old covered wagon
    Unidentified artist. Pennsylvania mill with
        conestoga wagon

COVERT, John, 1882-
    Brass band   CtY
        Baur. Revolution
        Brown. Amer ptg
        CtY. Soc Anonyme
        Hunter. Mod Amer ptg
        McCurdy
        MMA. Abstract
        Pierson
        Rathbun
    Temptation of St Anthony   CtY
        MMA. Abstract
        Pierson
    Vocalization   CtY
        Blesh
The covey by T. Hill
CORVILLE, H. E.
    Ye Boston baked beans   NNHS
        Ford. Pictorial folk art
Cow and bird II by N. D. Daly
Cow and calf by N. Daly
Cow at play by A. G. Dove
Cow I, 1935 by A. G. Dove
Cowboys
    Bartlett, G. Night herd
    Dasburg, A. Portrait of a cowboy
    Dixon, M. Cowboy and packhorse
    Eakins, T. Cowboys in the Bad Lands
    Hurd, P. José Herrera
    Megargee, L. Cowboy and his lady
    Price, C. S. Cowboys at moonlight
    Russell, C. M. At the end of the rope
    Russell, C. M. Cowboy life
    Russell, C. M. Heads or tails
    Russell, C. M. A serious predicament
    Russell, C. M. The strenuous life
    Russell, C. M. Tight dally and loose latigo
Cowgirl by Y. Kuniyoshi
COWLES, Russell, 1887-
    Adam and Eve
        IU. Contemp Amer ptg, 1949
    Bonfire
        VR. Amer ptg, 1954
    Connecticut rocks
        Gruskin
    Connecticut stream
        DC. 22 biennial ex, 1951
    Forest boundary
        Pearson. Mod renaissance
    Parade   InTH
        Pearson. Mod renaissance
    Prodigal son
        Pearson. Mod renaissance
Cows. See Cattle
Cow's skull: red, white, and blue by G.
    O'Keeffe
Cow's skull with calico roses by G. O'Keeffe
Cox, David
    Peale, Rembrandt. David Cox
COX, Gardner, 1906-
    Basic
        IU. Contemp Amer ptg, 1950
    Basic no 2
        ICA. Annual ex, 1947-48
    Basic no 12   MB
        CoS. New accessions USA, 1952
        IU. Contemp Amer ptg, 1951
    Maine study
        MMA. Amer ptg today

COX, Jan, 1919-
  Maenades, Study for
    MBIC. View 1960
COX, Joe
  Room interior no 1
    IU. Contemp Amer ptg, 1948
COX, John Rogers, 1915-
  Gray and gold   OCl
    CSB. Illusion
    UNESCO. 1860-1949
    UNESCO. 1860-1955
  The meadow   OYB
    CSFP. Annual ex, 1947/48
    OYB. Annual 1956
    OYB. Supplement 1959
  White cloud
    Gruskin (col)
COX, Kenyon, 1856-1919
  Augustus Saint-Gaudens   MM
    MM. 100 Amer ptrs
    Pierson
  The light of learning
    Pierson
Coxe, Sara (Cox) fl 1813
  Sully, T. Mrs John Redman Coxe
Coyotes
  Audubon, J. W. Prairie wolf or coyote
  Price, C. S. Coyotes
Cradle by J. Tworkov
Cradling wheat by T. H. Benton
CRAFFT, R. B. fl 1836
  The merchant   VWR
    VWR. Folk art (col)
CRAFTS, Ebenezer, fl 1781
  Chandler, W. Col Ebenezer and Col Sam-
    uel Crafts
CRAIG, Nancy Ellen, 1928-
  Study in brown
    NAD. Annual ex, 1957
CRAMER, Konrad, 1888-
  Improvisation no 1
    Brown. Amer ptg
  Improvisation no 2
    Pierson
    WMAA. Pioneers
Cranberry bogs: bright weather by R. W.
  Gray
Cranberry bogs: gray skies by R. W. Gray
Cranberry pickers by E. Johnson
Cranberry pickers in Nantucket by E. John-
  son
CRANE, Bruce, 1857-1937
  Winter idyl
    NYG. Fine art
Crane, Kent
  Sloan, J. Kent Crane
Crane, Louisa. See Meads, Louisa (Crane)
CRANE, Stanley W. 1905-
  Church at Willow
    IU. Contemp Amer ptg, 1950
  Handel still life
    PPC. Ptg in the U.S. 1949
Cranes by A. Osver
Crap shooter by J. Binford
Crary, Albert, fl 1825
  Unidentified artist. Capt Albert Crary
Crawford, Ann. See Allen, Ann (Crawford)
CRAWFORD, John S. 1838-1876
  Gov David Tod   OYB
    OYB. Catalogue 1951

CRAWFORD, Ralston, 1906-
  Aircraft factory (Aircraft plant)   OCiM
    CoS. New accessions USA, 1950
    WiMiA. Crawford
  Boat and grain elevator #2, 1941-42 DP
    WiMiA. Crawford
  Boat and grain elevators   DP
    DP. Catalogue
  Boiler synthesis
    MnMW. Precisionist view
  Bomber
    IU. Contemp Amer ptg, 1949
  Bomber, 1944
    WiMiA. Crawford
  Elevated with black and white
    WiMiA. Crawford
  Fishing boats #2, 1955
    WiMiA. Crawford
  Fishing boats #3, 1955-56
    WiMiA. Crawford
  Freight cars, Minneapolis, 1949
    WiMiA. Crawford
  From the bridge
    McCurdy
    MMA. Abstract
    Rathbun
  The glass, 1954
    WiMiA. Crawford
  Grain elevator from the bridge
    WiMiA. Crawford
  Grain elevators, Minneapolis   MnMW
    WiMiA. Crawford
  Havana harbor
    CSFP. Annual ex, 1948/49
  Havana harbor #3, 1948
    WiMiA. Crawford
  Maitland bridge no 2
    MnU. 40 Amer ptrs
  Minneapolis grain elevators
    ICA. Annual ex, 1951
    MnMW. Classic tradition
  Mountain bird maru   OT
    CoS. New accessions USA, 1952
  Nacelles, 1945
    WiMiA. Crawford
  Nacelles under construction
    CSFP. Annual ex, 1947/48
  Net, 1955
    WiMiA. Crawford
  Nets with blue, 1955-56
    WiMiA. Crawford
  New Orleans #2
    WiMiA. Crawford
  New Orleans #4
    WiMiA. Crawford
  New Orleans #5   NeL
    WiMiA. Crawford
  New Orleans still life
    MnU. 40 Amer ptrs
  Red barge #1, 1942
    WiMiA. Crawford
  S. S. Del Sud, 1954
    WiMiA. Crawford
  Sails #2, 1955
    WiMiA. Crawford
  Shaw's propellers no 2, 1960
    MnMW. Precisionist view
  Test-able   GAtM
    GAtM. Holbrook collection
  Third avenue el, 1949   MnMW
    MnMW. Precisionist view
    WiMiA. Crawford

Tour of inspection
  ICA. Annual ex, 1947/48
U.S.S. Pensacola, 1946
  WiMiA. Crawford
Whitestone bridge   NR
  Larkin
  Larkin rev ed
  Pierson
Crawford, Rebecca. See Conover, Rebecca
  (Crawford)
Crazy Nora by W. E. Winner
Creation by W. Burnet
Creation of Eve by J. Anderson
Creation scene by Unidentified artist
Crécy, Battle of, 1346
  West, B. The battle of Crécy
The **creeks**: interior by G. Hartigan
Cremorne gardens by J. A. M. Whistler
Crenshaw, Alfred Valentine, fl 1850
  Hubard, W. J. Alfred V. Crenshaw
Creole child by Unidentified artist
Crescendo by A. B. Davies
Crest by J. Tworkov
Cret, Paul Philippe, 1876-1945
  Watkins, F. C. Paul P. Cret
Cribbage players by H. Baer
Cricket chorus in the arbor by C. E. Burchfield
CRIMI, Alfred Di Giorgio, 1900-
  Brooklyn bridge
    NAD. Annual ex, 1955
The **crimson** gown by F. Duveneck
CRISS, Frances, 1901-
  Astor place, 1932   WMAA
    CSB. Illusion
The **critic** by J. Tester
Critics: San Giorgio degli Schiavoni, Venice
  by J. L. Smith
Crocky, Davy Emmet. See Kelly, Emmett
Croghan, George, 1791-1849
  Jarvis, J. W. Col George Croghan
Croghan, Lucy (Clark) 1765-1838
  Jarvis, J. W. Mrs William Croghan
Croghan, William, 1752-1822
  Jarvis, J. W. Major William Croghan
Croghan, Mrs William. See Croghan, Lucy
  (Clark)
Crolius, Clarkson, 1773-1843
  Ames, E. Clarkson Crolius
Crooke, Kitty. See Dudley, Kitty (Crooke)
CROOME, William, 1790-1860
  Crystal valley farm, a view of the Hudson
    river at the Overslaugh   NAI
    Jones. Rediscovered ptrs
CROPSEY, Jasper Francis, 1823-1900
  Clump of trees, Study of   MB
    MB. Karolik coll
  Eagle cliff, Franconia Notch, New Hampshire   NoCR
    NoCR. Catalogue
  Eagle cliff, New Hampshire   MB
    MB. Karolik coll
    Pierson
  Hasting-on-the-Hudson, going fishing
    NSP. Sportscapes
  The Isle of Capri
    MiD. Travelers in Arcadia

Italian landscape   MB
  MB. Karolik coll
Lake of Nemi   NAD
  NAD. Amer tradition
Mountain lakes
  NYG. Fine art (col)
Niagara Falls   NBM
  Born
Niagara Falls from the foot of Goat island
                        MB
  MB. Karolik coll
Schatacook mountain, Housatonic valley,
  Connecticut   MB
  MB. Karolik coll
Starrucca viaduct, Susquehanna valley OT
  Pierson
Upper Hudson
  Sears. Highlights
View of the Kaaterskill house   MnMI
  Barker. Amer ptg
  Born
  Pierson
White mountains in autumn   GAtM
  GAtM. Holbrook collection
Winter scene on the Hudson   CtHW
  CtHW. Handbook
  Jones. Rediscovered ptrs
Woodland stream
  NYG. Fine art
Wyoming valley   MM
  McClintock
Youle's shot tower, East river shore
                    NNHS
  Born
Croquet. See Games and sports—Croquet
Crosby, Warren
  Unidentified artist. Warren Crosby
CROSS, Bernice, 1912-
  Stone angel   DP
    DP. Catalogue
CROSS, Henry H. 1837-1918
  Geronimo   OkPP
    Time. 300 years (col)
  Red Cloud and Burning Heart   OkPP
    Time. 300 years (col)
Cross by S. Francis
Cross-section, plant life by C. Seliger
Crossbills
  Audubon, J. J. Common crossbill
Crossing the Divide by A. J. Miller
Crossing the ford by H. G. Keller
Crossing the ford, Platte river, Colorado by
  W. Whittredge
Crossing the Kansas by A. J. Miller
Crossing the North fork of the Platte by
  A. J. Miller
Crossing the pasture by W. Homer
Crossing the river: moonlight by A. J.
  Miller
Crossing the river—trapper trying its depth
  by A. J. Miller
Crotch island derricks by J. De Martini
CROTEAU, Wilfred, 1930-
  Composition no 136, 1960
    MBIC. View 1960
Crouching figure by B. Greene
Crow chief at his toilet by G. Catlin
Crow encampment by A. J. Miller
A **crow** flew by by A. N. Wyeth

Crow Indian on the lookout by A. J. Miller
Crow Indians by K. Bodmer
Crow scouts in winter by C. M. Russell
A Crow teepee by G. Catlin
Crow warriors bathing in Yellowstone by G. Catlin
Crow woman by G. Catlin
Crowd, polo scene by G. W. Bellows
Crowell, Edward Payson, 1830-1911
Unidentified artist. Edward P. Crowell
CROWLEY, Harry
Illuminations
IU. Contemp Amer ptg, 1952
Crown of thorns by H. Moller
CROWINSHIELD, Frederic, 1845-1918
Capri cliff   MB
MB. Ptgs in water color
Church in Rome   MB
MB. Ptgs in water color
From my studio   MB
MB. Ptgs in water color
Mt Etna from Taormina   MB
MB. Ptgs in water color
St Peter's, Rome, from the Palatine   MB
MB. Ptgs in water color
Spring blossoms   MB
MB. Ptgs in water color
A street, Perugia   MB
MB. Ptgs in water color
Taormina   MB
MB. Ptgs in water color
Crowninshield's wharf, Salem by G. Ropes
Crows
Burchfield, C. E. Clatter of crows in spring woods
Graves, M. Moon and crow in surf
Heil, C. E. Young crow
Keller, H. G. Crows in winter
McFee, H. L. Crow with peaches
Crow's nest by W. Whittredge
Crow's nest from Bull hill, Hudson river by Unidentified artist
Crucifixion by P. Blume
Crucifixion by J. Corbino
Crucifixion by T. Eakins
Crucifixion by J. V. Haidt
Crucifixion by R. Lebrun
Crucifixion by H. Pippin
Crucifixion by L. Schanker
Crucifixion by Unidentified artist
Crucifixion by T. Vincent
Crucifixion by J. Wolfe
Crucifixion, Sketch for by Z. L. Sepeshy
Crucifixion, Study for by T. Eakins
Crucifixion in yellow by A. Rattner
Crucifixion triptych by R. Lebrun
Cruger, Anna, fl 1740
Unidentified artist. Anna Cruger
Cruger, John, 1677-1744
Unidentified artist. John Cruger
Cruger, Mrs John Church, fl 1842
Healy, G. P. Mrs John Church Cruger
Crumbs of comfort by J. F. Peto
Crystal valley farm, a view of the Hudson river at the Overslaugh by W. Croome

CSOKA, Stephen, 1897-
Sorrow
NAD. Special ex, 1956
El cuadro de los Abanicos by E. Francés
Cuautla, Mexico by D. Macknight
"Cuba Si" by J. Youngerman
Cuban nude by B. Karfiol
Cuckoos
Audubon, J. J. Black-billed cuckoo
Cuernavaca by W. D. Fausett
Culpeper, Philippa Frances. See Berkeley, Philippa Frances (Culpeper) lady
CULVER, Charles, 1908-
Beetle with red markings   OYB
OYB. Annual 1957
OYB. Supplement 1959
CULVERHOUSE, Johann Mongels, fl 1849-1891
Clinton square, Syracuse, N.Y.
Jones. Rediscovered ptrs
CULWELL, Ben L. 1918-
Adrenalin hour
MMA. Fourteen
Death by burning
MMA. Fourteen
Figment of erotic torture
MMA. Fourteen
Me and the battle of Tassafaronga, Guadalcanal
MMA. Fourteen
Men fighting and stars in the Solomons
MMA. Fourteen
Where sun and rain mate: landscape near Pali, Oahu, Hawaii
MMA. Fourteen
Cumming, Mrs Alexander. See Goldthwait, Elizabeth
CUMMINGS, Thomas Seir, 1804-1894
Thomas Cole   CtY
CtY. Portrait index
Cunningham, Mrs Nathaniel. See Cunningham, Sarah (Kilby)
Cunningham, Ruth. See Otis, Ruth (Cunningham)
Cunningham, Sarah (Kilby) 1732-1759
Greenwood, J. Sarah Kilby
Smibert, J. Mrs Nathaniel Cunningham
A cup of tea by P. Evergood
Cup of tea by M. Cassatt
Cup of tea by M. Weber
Cupid. See Mythological themes—Cupid
Curfew by R. Rauschenberg
Curfew hour by A. P. Ryder
Curls and scallops by Unidentified artist
CURRAN, Charles Courtney, 1861-1942
Dewdrops and roses
NYG. Fine art
Currants by G. Wood
CURRIE, Bruce, 1911-
Buildings at night   OYB
OYB. Annual 1954
OYB. Supplement
Girl drying her hair
IU. Contemp Amer ptg & sculp, 1959
Girl in yellow skirt   OYB
OYB. Annual 1958
OYB. Supplement 1959

Seated woman
  IU. Contemp Amer ptg & sculp, 1961
Woman watering plant
  NAD. Annual ex, 1960
CURRIER, Frank, 1843-1909
  Whistling boy   InIJ
    InIJ. 105 ptgs
Currituck marshes, North Carolina by F. W.
  Benson
CURRY, John Steuart, 1897-1946
  Baptism in Kansas   WMAA
    Baur. Revolution
    Canaday
    DC. 25 biennial ex, 1957
    Goodrich. Amer art (col)
    Larkin
    Larkin rev ed
    McCurdy
    Wight. Milestones
  Flying Codonas   WMAA
    NYG. Fine art
  Hog killing a rattlesnake
    Craven. Treasury 1952 ed
  Hogs killing a snake   ATU
    ATU. Coll of Amer art
  Hogs killing rattlesnakes   ICA
    Baur. Revolution
    Pierson
    Time. 300 years (col)
  John Brown   MM
    MM. 100 Amer ptrs
  Line storm
    Craven. Treasury 1952 ed (col)
  The Mississippi   MoSL
    Gruskin (col)
  The passing leap
    IaDa. Wood
  Sanctuary   OYB
    OYB. Catalogue 1951
  The tornado   MiM
    DC. De gustibus
    Pierson
    Roos
    WMAA. Juliana Force
  Wisconsin landscape   MM
    Craven. Rainbow book
    Time. 300 years (col)
Curse of gold by Unidentified artist
Curtain call by E. Shinn
Curtis, Ariana (Wormeley) fl 1882
  Sargent, J. S. Mrs Daniel Sargent Curtis
Curtis, Ellen Amory (Anderson) fl 1903
  Sargent, J. S. Mrs Charles Pelham Curtis
Curtis, Mrs Daniel Sargent. See Curtis,
  Ariana (Wormeley)
Curtis, Ralph Wormeley, 1854-1922
  Sargent, J. S. Ralph Curtis on the beach
    at Scheveningen, Holland
Curved composition in yellow, red and blue
  by A. Leepa
Curwen, Joseph, 1778-1848
  Malbone, E. G. Joseph Curwen
Curwen, Mrs Joseph. See Curwen, Selina
  Fenwick (Gadsden)
Curwen, Samuel, 1715-1802
  Blyth, B. Samuel Curwen
Curwen, Selina Fenwick (Gadsden) d 1819
  Malbone, E. G. Mrs Joseph Curwen
Curwin, George, 1610-1685
  Unidentified artist. Capt George Curwin

Cushing, Alice, fl 1878
  Emery, E. Alice Cushing in the west par-
    lor of Peter Cushing house, Hingham,
    Massachusetts
Cushing, Frank Hamilton, 1857-1900
  Eakins, T. Frank Hamilton Cushing
Cushing, Mrs Frank Hamilton
  Eakins, T. Mrs Frank Hamilton Cushing
Cushing, Margaret Eleanor (Norwood)
  fl 1815
  Ames, E. Mrs Thomas Humphrey Cush-
    ing
Cushing, Mary Louise. See Boit, Mary
  Louise (Cushing)
Cushing, Thomas, 1696-1746
  Badger, J. Thomas Cushing
Cushing, Thomas Humphrey, 1755-1822
  Ames, E. Thomas Humphrey Cushing
Cushing, Mrs Thomas Humphrey. See Cush-
  ing, Margaret Eleanor (Norwood)
Cushing house, Child in sitting room of by
  E. Emery
Custance, John, fl 1778
  West, B. Mr and Mrs John Custance
Custance, Mrs John, fl 1778
  West, B. Mr and Mrs John Custance
Custer's last fight by C. Adams
Custer's last stand by T. H. Benton
Custer's last stand by C. M. Russell
Custis, Eleanor Parke, 1779-1852
  Trumbull, J. Eleanor Parke Custis, 1792
Custis, Frances Parke, b 1709
  Unidentified artist. Frances Parke Custis
Custis, Tabitha Scarborough. See Arbuckle,
  Tabitha Scarborough (Custis)
Custom house, Santiago de Cuba by W.
  Homer
Cut-out by J. Pollock
Cuthbert, Henrietta Frances, 1813-1889
  Unidentified artist. Henrietta Frances
    Cuthbert
Cuthbert, James Alexander Ross, 1767-1849
  Malbone, E. G. James Alexander Ross
    Cuthbert
CUTHBERT, Virginia Isobel, 1908-
  Alex Fletcher   PW
    Chew. 250 years of art
  Environs of Chicago
    DC. 22 biennial ex, 1951
  Factory no 1, 1953
    VR. Amer ptg, 1954
  Office building   NBuA
    NBuA. Contemporary ptgs
  Our classic heritage
    CSFP. Annual ex, 1950-51
  Talpa graveyard
    IU. Contemp Amer ptg, 1950
Cutt, Catherine. See Moffatt, Catherine
  (Cutt)
Cut-Taa-Tas-Tia, a Fox chief by J. O. Lewis
Cutts, Rose Adèle. See Williams, Rose
  Adèle (Cutts) Douglas
Cuyler, Anna (Wendell), fl 1780
  Unidentified artist. Anna Wendell Cuyler
Cuyler, Catalina (Schuyler) 1705-1759
  Unidentified artist. Catalina Schuyler
Cuyler, Mrs Cornelius, 1705-1759. See Cuy-
  ler, Catalina (Schuyler)
Cuyler, Mrs Cornelius, fl 1780. See Cuyler,
  Anna (Wendell)

Cybernetics by B. Shahn
Cycladic light by D. Lund
The cycle by M. Tobey
The cyclists by L. Feininger
Cylinder and orange by W. T. Murch
Cypresses by J. S. Sargent
Cyrus liberating the family of Astyges by
      B. West

D

DABO, Leon, 1868-1960
   Rhythms   InTH
      InTH. Catalogue
Dachau chamber, Study for by R. Lebrun
Dad's coming by W. Homer
Daggett, Miss, c 1785
   Unidentified artist. Miss Daggett
Daggett, David, 1764-1851
   Tenney, U. D. David Daggett
Daggett, Mrs Henry
   Bellows, G. W. Aunt Fanny
Dague, Paul B.
   Pippin, H. Paul B. Dague, deputy sheriff
      Chester county
Daily news by Y. Kuniyoshi
Daisies by C. H. Demuth
Daisies by G. B. Klitgaard
Daisies by M. Graves
Dakota encampment by S. Eastman
A Dakota village by S. Eastman
Dale, Chester, 1883-1962
   Bellows, G. W. Chester Dale
Dale, Maud (Murray)
   Bellows, G. W. Mrs Chester Dale
A Dallas night by G. Grosz
Dally, Christiana. See De Peyster, Chris-
      tiana (Dally)
DALY, Norman David, 1911-
   Cow and bird II
      IU. Contemp Amer ptg, 1950
   Cow and calf
      IU. Contemp Amer ptg & sculp, 1953
Dalzell children, fl 1845
   Unidentified artist. Mary and David Dal-
      zell of South Egremont, Massachu-
      setts
Damaged man by L. A. Golub
Dame à l'absence by Y. Tanguy
Der dampfer Odin by L. Feininger
Danaïdes by J. S. Sargent
The dance by J. Hirsch
The dance by S. Rosenberg
Dance hall by B. Perlin
Dance marathon by P. Evergood
Dance of the haymakers by W. S. Mount
Dance of the San Domingo Indians by J.
      Marin
Dance rhythm by E. Geller
Dancer by F. E. Conway
Dancer by G. Dante
Dancer by M. Soyer

Dancer dressing by F. Martin
Dancer in white by E. Shinn
Dancer with tambourine by M. Beckmann
Dancers by A. B. Davies
Dancers by the clock by M. Siporin
Dancers resting by M. Greenwood
Dancing dryads by A. P. Ryder
Dancing nuns by H. V. Olson
Dancing tree by A. G. Dove
Dandelion seed balls and trees by C. E.
      Burchfield
The dandy by Unidentified artist
Dangerous territory by C. M. Russell
DANIEL, Lewis C. 1901-1952
   Prayer makers
      IU. Contemp Amer ptg, 1950
Daniel Drew (steamboat)
   Bard, J. Hudson river steamboat Daniel
      Drew
Daniel in the lion's den by M. Hirshfield
DANIELL, George
   Oregon rocks
      PA. Annual ex, 1947
Daniell, Sarah Proctor. See Wilson, Sarah
      Proctor (Daniell)
Daniels, Josephus, 1862-1948
   Lockman, D. M. Josephus Daniels
Danny by A. James
DANTE, Giglio, 1916-
   The dancer   MSM
      CoS. New accessions USA, 1946
DANTON, F. fl 1894
   Time is money   CtHW
      Frankenstein. After the hunt
Danvers river, Massachusetts by F. W. Ben-
      son
Danville by G. E. Doudera
Daphne by J. De Feo
Daphne by J. McLarty
Daphne by J. S. Sargent
DAPHNIS, Nassos, 1914-
   Forward but beyond
      PPC. International ex, 1955
   3-61-MT
      NBuA. Acquisitions 1959-1961
Dappled with damson by O. E. L. Graves
Darby, Mrs John, fl 1852
   Bingham, G. C. Mrs John Darby
Darby, Pennsylvania, after the burning of
      Lord's mill by J. D. Bunting
D'ARISTA, Robert, 1929-
   The chair
      NNSG. Younger Amer ptrs
   Kitchen table   OT
      CoS. New accessions USA, 1956
   Still life with coffee pot
      IU. Contemp Amer ptg & sculp, 1955
   Table with bottles and cheese
      PPC. International ex, 1955
Dark by J. Albers
Dark and light by F. Hillsmith
Dark anonymity by J. G. Haley
Dark figure by F. Castellón
Dark forest by M. Avery
Dark green painting by A. Gorky
Dark harbor by L. J. Liberté

Dark hills and white horses by E. J. Kosa
Dark in the forest by J. Kirschenbaum
Dark mountain by M. Hartley
Dark muse by E. Pearson
Dark night by A. A. Dehn
Dark pond by W. De Kooning
Dark rain by A. Rattner
Dark red leaves on white by G. O'Keeffe
Dark river by E. Magafan
Dark sky—dark water by J. Lechay
Dark stretch by H. Weber
Dark trees and sunny meadow by K. Schrag
Dark wave by R. Tam
Darkly, soft darts by A. Okamura
Darkness and light by B. Greene
DARLEY, Felix Octavius Carr, 1822-1888
  Emigrants crossing the plains
    McCracken. Portrait of the old west
    (col)
  Hunting buffaloes
    McCracken. Portrait of the old west
Darley, Francis Thomas Sully
  Sully, T. Mother and child (Mrs William
    H. W. Darley and Francis Thomas
    Sully Darley)
Darley, Jane Cooper (Sully) 1807-1877
  Sully, T. Mother and child (Mrs William
    H. W. Darley and Francis Thomas
    Sully Darley)
DARLING, Robert, fl 1835
  Child in a yellow chair   NCHA
    Jones. New-found folk art
Darnall, Eleanor, 1704-1796
  Kühn, J. E. Eleanor Darnall
Darnall, Henry, 1702-1788?
  Kuhn, J. E. Henry Darnall III
Darrah, Mrs Robert K. See Darrah, Sophia
  Towne
DARRAH, Sophia Towne, 1830?-1881
  Seascape   MB
    MB. Ptgs in water color
DASBURG, Andrew, 1887-
  Apples   WMAA
    Bywaters. Andrew Dasburg
    Pierson
  Autumn desert
    Bywaters. Andrew Dasburg (col)
  Autumn fruit
    Bywaters. Andrew Dasburg
    Pierson
  Autumn—Ranchos de Taos
    Bywaters. Andrew Dasburg
  Avocados
    Bywaters. Andrew Dasburg
  Chantet lane   CoD
    Bywaters. Andrew Dasburg (col)
  Ducks   MM
    Bywaters. Andrew Dasburg
  Fields of Llano   TxD
    Bywaters. Andrew Dasburg
  Gothic
    Bywaters. Andrew Dasburg
  Improvisation to form
    Brown. Amer ptg
    McCurdy
  Jo Bakos
    Bywaters. Andrew Dasburg

Judson Smith   TxD
  Bywaters. Andrew Dasburg
Landscape
  Larkin
  Larkin rev ed
  WMAA. Pioneers
Llano Quemado
  Bywaters. Andrew Dasburg
New Mexican landscape
  Bywaters. Andrew Dasburg
New Mexican village   NMS
  Bywaters. Andrew Dasburg
November, New Mexico   TxD
  Bywaters. Andrew Dasburg
Portrait of a cowboy
  Bywaters. Andrew Dasburg
Portrait of Ida
  Bywaters. Andrew Dasburg
Ramoncita   OCiM
  Bywaters. Andrew Dasburg
Road into Ranchos de Taos
  Bywaters. Andrew Dasburg
Road to Lamy   MM
  Bywaters. Andrew Dasburg
Sermon on the Mount
  Brown. Amer ptg
Still life, 1918
  Brown. Amer ptg
  Bywaters. Andrew Dasburg
Still life, 1924
  Bywaters. Andrew Dasburg
Talpa
  Bywaters. Andrew Dasburg
Taos plaza
  Bywaters. Andrew Dasburg
Tulips (1)
  Bywaters. Andrew Dasburg
Tulips (2)   CLA
  Bywaters. Andrew Dasburg
White morning
  Bywaters. Andrew Dasburg
DAUGHERTY, James Henry, 1889-
  Mural decoration   CtY
    CtY. Soc Anonyme
Daughter of the mines by G. B. Luks
Daughters of revolution by G. Wood
Dauntless bird by M. Weber
Davenport, John, 1597-1669?
  Foster, J. (attributed works) John Daven-
    port
Davenport, Iowa
  Wild, J. C. View of Davenport, Iowa and
    the Mississippi
DAVEY, Randall, 1887-
  Girl in a hunting cap
    NAD. Annual ex, 1951
  Harness horse stables—Cape Girardeau
    PPC. Ptg in the U.S. 1949
  Jockey in red silk
    NAD. Annual ex, 1961
David, Jean Terford, 1792-1839
  Sully, T. Capt Jean T. David
David, Mrs Jean Terford. See David, Mary
  (Sicard)
David, Mary (Sicard) fl 1813
  Sully, T. Mary Sicard David
David playing before Saul by W. Allston
David playing to King Saul by P. Evergood
David the king by M. Schwartz

DAVIES, Arthur Bowen, 1862-1928
Across the harbor   InIJ
  InIJ. 105 ptgs
Adventure   MM
  Brown. Amer ptg
Along the Erie canal   DP
  Born
  DP. Catalogue
  Richardson. Ptg in America
The Apennines   NUM
  NUM. Art across America
Arethusa   OYB
  OYB. Catalogue 1951
At the chestnut root   NSyE
  NSyE. The eight
Crescendo   WMAA
  Baur. Revolution
  Goodrich. Amer art
  Larkin (detail)
  Larkin rev ed (detail)
  NBuA. Fifty ptgs
Dancers   MiD
  Brown. Amer ptg
  Pierson
Day of good fortune
  WMAA. Museum and its friends, 1958
The dream   MM
  Mendelowitz
  Pierson
Evensong   DNC
  DNC. Gellatly coll, 1954
Every Saturday   NBM
  McCurdy
Facade
  Cheney. Primer 1958 ed
The flood   DP
  DP. Catalogue
  Pierson
Inland tempest   NUM
  NUM. Root bequest
Interior   MnMI
  Cheney. Expressionism 1948 ed
Italian landscape, the Apennines
  NYG. Fine art
Maya, mirror of illusions   ICA
  Roos
Mother of dawn   ATeS
  ATeS. Collection
Passing of dreams   MB
  MB. Ptgs in water color
Springtime of delight   DP
  Born
  DP. Catalogue
Twilight travelling
  Lewisohn
Unicorns   MM
  Cheney. Story 1958 ed
  MM. 100 Amer ptrs
  Pierson
DAVIES, Kenneth, 1925-
The blackboard
  Frankenstein. After the hunt
  IU. Contemp Amer ptg, 1952
The bookcase   CtHW
  CoS. New accessions USA, 1952
Pocusmania   MSM
  CoS. New accessions USA, 1952
  IU. Contemp Amer ptg, 1951 (col)
  MSM. Handbook (col)
The sword   MiD
  MiD. Treasures

DAVIES, Thomas, 1737?-1812
View of Green Bush on the Hudson's river
  near Albany   MiD
  Jones. Rediscovered ptrs
Davis, Charles, 1772-1821
  Stuart, G. Charles Davis
Davis, Mrs Charles. See Davis, Eliza (Bussey)
DAVIS, Charles Harold, 1856-1933
Call of the west wind   OYB
  OYB. Catalogue 1951
Northwest wind   ICA
  NYG. Fine art
DAVIS, Eben Parsons, 1818-1902
Eben Davis' horse   VWR
  VWR. Folk art (col)
Mr and Mrs Eben P. Davis   VWR
  VWR. Folk art (col)
Davis, Mrs Eben Parsons. See Davis, Rhoda
  Ann (Thatcher)
Davis, Mrs Edward Livingston. See Davis,
  Maria Louisa (Robbins)
Davis, Edwin, fl 1838
  Bascom, R. H. M. Edwin Davis
Davis, Eliza (Bussey) 1783-1825
  Stuart, G. Mrs Charles Davis
DAVIS, Gladys Rockmore, 1901-
Deborah and Nietzsche
  Gruskin (col)
  NYG. Fine art
End of summer   OT
  OT. Contemp Amer ptgs
Pink tights   IaDa
  IaDa. 30th anniversary
Sea sounds
  NAD. Annual ex, autumn 1949
Study   ATU
  ATU. Coll of Amer art
Study of an old woman
  PA. Annual ex, 1952
Les sylphides
  Gruskin (col)
Davis, Isaac P. 1771-1855
  Malbone, E. G. Isaac P. Davis
DAVIS, Jerrold, 1926-
Figure before a field
  PPC. International ex, 1958
Painting of the ocean no 8
  IU. Contemp Amer ptg & sculp, 1961
Standing figure
  IU. Contemp Amer ptg & sculp, 1959
DAVIS, Joseph Hilliard, fl 1820-1837
Bartholomew Van Dame
  Lipman. Primitive ptrs
Esther Tuttle   NNHS
  Lipman. Primitive ptrs
Henry Laurens Roberts
  Lipman. Primitive ptrs
James and Sarah Tuttle   NNHS
  Ford. Pictorial folk art
  Mendelowitz
  Pierson
Joseph and Sarah Ann Emery
  Lipman. Primitive ptrs
Levi B. Tasker   MSt
  Little. Country art
A man and a lady
  Ford. Pictorial folk art
Separate tables   NCHA
  Jones. New-found folk art

Tilton family   VWR
  Flexner. Light of distant skies
  VWR. Folk art (col)
York family   MMA
  Baur. Amer ptg
  Attributed works
Frugal housewife   VWR
  VWR. Folk art (col)
Hannah Goodwin Whitehouse Moulton
                                             MeC
  Jetté. Amer heritage collection
James Roberts Moulton   MeC
  Jetté. Amer heritage collection
Mrs Tuttle
  Ford. Pictorial folk art
DAVIS, Lew E. 1910-
Market   ATeS
  ATeS. Collection
Davis, Livingston, fl 1890
  Sargent, J. S. Mrs Edward Livingston
    Davis and her son Livingston Davis
Davis, Maria Louisa (Robbins) fl 1890
  Sargent, J. S. Mrs Edward Livingston
    Davis and her son Livingston
DAVIS, Noel
Coney Island: summer labyrinth
  OYB. Annual 1959
Davis, Rhoda Ann (Thatcher) 1819-1877
  Davis, E. P. Mr and Mrs Eben P. Davis
DAVIS, Stuart, 1894-1964
Adit no 2, 1928
  Goossen. Stuart Davis
Allée
  MnMW. Stuart Davis (col)
ANA   MiC
  NUM. Art across America
Apples and jug   MLL
  Goossen. Stuart Davis
Arboretum by flashbulb
  Blesh. Stuart Davis
  Cheney. Primer 1958 ed
  Goossen. Stuart Davis
Arch hotel   NeL
  Barker. From realism
  CoS. New accessions USA, 1948
Bass Rocks no 1   KW
  Goossen. Stuart Davis (col)
  Pierson
Bass Rocks no 2   KW
  MnMW. Stuart Davis
Barber shop
  MnMW. Contemporary
  WMAA. Neuberger collection
Bridge at Courbevoie
  Goossen. Stuart Davis
Bull Durham
  WMAA. Pioneers
Café, Place des Vosges
  Goossen. Stuart Davis
  MnMW. Stuart Davis
Cape Ann landscape
  Larkin
  Larkin rev ed
Cigarette papers, 1921
  Goossen. Stuart Davis
Cigarette papers, 1933 (Cahill coll)
  Goossen. Stuart Davis
Cliché   NNSG
  Goossen. Stuart Davis
  NNSG. Handbook
  Read. Concise history

Cliché, Detail study for
  MnMW. Stuart Davis
Colonial cubism   MnMW
  Goossen. Stuart Davis (col)
  PA. Annual ex, 1956
  Rosenblum (col)
  WMAA. Annual ex, 1955
Combination concrete, 1957
  Blesh. Stuart Davis (col)
Combination concrete no 2, 1958
  Goossen. Stuart Davis (col)
  WMAA. Museum and its friends, 1959
Corner café   DP
  DP. Catalogue
Deuce   CSFM
  Blesh. Stuart Davis
  Goossen. Stuart Davis
  IU. Contemp Amer ptg & sculp, 1955
  MnMW. Stuart Davis
Eggbeater no 1, 1927   DP
  Blesh. Stuart Davis
  Brown. Amer ptg
  Pierson
Eggbeater no 2, 1927   WMAA
  Blesh. Stuart Davis (col)
  Goodrich. Amer art
  MnMW. Stuart Davis
Eggbeater no 3, 1927   MLL
  Blesh. Stuart Davis
  Goossen. Stuart Davis
  Time. 300 years (col)
Eggbeater no 4, 1927
  Blesh. Stuart Davis
Eggbeater no 5, 1930   MMA
  CoS. New accessions USA, 1946
  Goossen. Stuart Davis
  MMA. Ptg and sculpture
Eye level   MLL
  Goossen. Stuart Davis
  MnMW. Stuart Davis
Famous firsts   NBM
  Goossen. Stuart Davis
Feasible no 2, 1952   MoSL
  Goossen. Stuart Davis
  MnMW. Stuart Davis
Flying carpet   MMA
  Biddle. Yes and no
  MnMW. Stuart Davis
For internal use only
  Genauer (col)
  Goossen. Stuart Davis (col)
  MMA. Abstract (col)
  MnMW. Stuart Davis
Garage lights   NR
  Blesh. Stuart Davis
  Richardson. Ptg in America
Gloucester street   MLL
  Blesh. Stuart Davis
  Goossen. Stuart Davis
Gloucester sunset
  MnMW. Stuart Davis
Havana plaza
  Goossen. Stuart Davis
History of communication
  Blesh. Stuart Davis
Hot stillscape
  Munsterberg
Hot stillscape for six colors
  Cheney. Story 1958 ed
  DC. Halpert collection
  Goossen. Stuart Davis (col)

DAVIS, Stuart—*Continued*
Hotel de France
  Blesh. Stuart Davis
House and street   WMAA
  Blesh. Stuart Davis
  Brown. Amer ptg
  Goossen. Stuart Davis
  Lee. Art then and now
  MnMW. Stuart Davis
House, tree shapes
  Blesh. Stuart Davis
Industry   ATU
  ATU. Coll of Amer art
Interior
  Goossen. Stuart Davis
Iris   MM
  MM. 100 Amer ptrs
Itlksez   MLL
  Goossen. Stuart Davis
Landscape
  Goossen. Stuart Davis
Landscape with drying sails
  Blesh. Stuart Davis
Lawn and sky
  Blesh. Stuart Davis
Leroy's shift
  MnMW. Stuart Davis
Lesson I, 1956
  Goossen. Stuart Davis
  PPC. International ex, 1958
Little giant still life   VR
  CoS. New accessions USA, 1950
  Goossen. Stuart Davis
  MnMW. Classic tradition
  MnMW. Stuart Davis
  MnU. 40 Amer ptrs
Lobby wall
  DC. 27 biennial ex, 1961
Lucky strike   MMA
  Baur. New art
  Blesh. Stuart Davis
  Goossen. Stuart Davis (col)
  McCurdy
  MMA. Abstract
  Pierson
A man   MLL
  Goossen. Stuart Davis
Matches no 2, 1927
  Blesh. Stuart Davis
Max no 1, 1949
  MnMW. Stuart Davis
Max no 2, 1949
  Goossen. Stuart Davis
Medium still life
  Blesh. Stuart Davis
  Goossen. Stuart Davis
  MnMW. Stuart Davis
Mellow pad
  Blesh. Stuart Davis (col)
  Goossen. Stuart Davis
  MnMW. Stuart Davis
Memo   WMAA
  MnMW. Stuart Davis (col)
  WMAA. Sara Roby
Men without women
  Blesh. Stuart Davis
Midi   CtHW
  CtHW. Handbook
  Goossen. Stuart Davis
  ICA. Annual ex, 1954
  MnMW. Stuart Davis

Multiple views
  Blesh. Stuart Davis
  Goossen. Stuart Davis
Mural, Drake university
  Pierson
Music hall
  Blesh. Stuart Davis
Myopic vista   MLL
  Goossen. Stuart Davis
New Mexican landscape   WMAA
  Goossen. Stuart Davis
New York mural
  MnMW. Stuart Davis
New York, 1932
  MnU. 40 Amer ptrs
New York-Paris no 1, 1931   IaIU
  Blesh. Stuart Davis
  Goossen. Stuart Davis
New York-Paris no 2, 1931   OrPA
  MnMW. Stuart Davis
New York-Paris no 3, 1931
  Blesh. Stuart Davis
  Goossen. Stuart Davis
New York under gaslight
  Flexner. Amer ptg
  Flexner. Short history
  Goossen. Stuart Davis
New York waterfront   NBuA
  Bazin
  NBuA. Contemporary ptgs
Nu
  Goossen. Stuart Davis
The outside
  Goossen. Stuart Davis
  MnMW. Stuart Davis
Owh! in San Paó   WMAA
  Art since 1945
  Baur. New art (col)
  Blesh. Stuart Davis (col)
  Goodrich. Amer art (col)
  IU. Contemp Amer ptg, 1952 (col)
  MnMW. Stuart Davis (col)
  Pierson
  WMAA. Contemp Amer ptg, 1951
Package deal
  Goossen. Stuart Davis
Pad no 1, 1946   HaH
  Goossen. Stuart Davis
  MnMW. Stuart Davis
Pad no 4, 1947
  MnMW. Stuart Davis
Pajarite
  Goossen. Stuart Davis
The Paris bit   WMAA
  Goodrich. Amer art (col)
Percolator   MM
  Blesh. Stuart Davis
Place des Vosges no 1, 1928   NJN
  Goossen. Stuart Davis
Place des Vosges no 2, 1928
  Blesh. Stuart Davis (col)
  Goossen. Stuart Davis
Place Pasdeloup   WMAA
  Baur. New art
  Goodrich. Amer art (col)
  Goossen. Stuart Davis (col)
  Pierson
  WMAA. Juliana Force

Pochade
  Chew. 250 years of art
  Eliot. Art of our time (col)
  Goossen. Stuart Davis
  ICA. Annual ex, 1961
  WMAA. Annual ex, 1958
Première   CLA
  Blesh. Stuart Davis (col)
  DC. 26 biennial ex, 1959
The President
  Hess. Abstract ptg
Radio tubes   ATeS
  ATeS. Collection
Rapt at Rappaport's
  IU. Contemp Amer ptg & sculp, 1953
Rapt at Rappaport's (Hirshhorn coll)
  Goossen. Stuart Davis
Rapt at Rappaport's (Wolf coll)
  MnMW. Stuart Davis (col)
Ready-to-wear   ICA
  Blesh. Stuart Davis (col)
  Goossen. Stuart Davis
  PPC. International ex, 1955
Ready to wear, Study for
  MnMW. Stuart Davis
Red cart   MAP
  Robb. Harper history
  Roos
  Wight. Milestones (col)
Report from Rockport
  Baur. New art
  Blesh. Stuart Davis
  Gardner 1959 ed
  Goossen. Stuart Davis
  Gruskin (col)
  Hess. Abstract ptg
  Pierson
  Rosenblum
Rockport beach
  Blesh. Stuart Davis
  Goossen. Stuart Davis (col)
Rocky neck, Gloucester
  Blesh. Stuart Davis
Rue de L'Echaude
  Blesh. Stuart Davis
  Goossen. Stuart Davis (col)
Rue des Rats no 2, 1929
  Goossen. Stuart Davis
Rue Vercingetorix
  Goossen. Stuart Davis
Sail loft
  Blesh. Stuart Davis
  MnMW. Stuart Davis
Salt shaker   MMA
  Baur. New art
  Goossen. Stuart Davis (col)
  McCurdy
  Rosenblum
Salt shaker (Halpert coll)
  MMA. Abstract
  Read. Art now, 1948 ed
Semé
  Blesh. Stuart Davis (col)
  Goossen. Stuart Davis
  Pearson. Mod renaissance
Shapes of landscape space
  Goossen. Stuart Davis
Smith's cove
  Goossen. Stuart Davis

Snow on the mountain   GAtM
  GAtM. Holbrook collection
Something on the eight ball   PPhM
  Blesh. Stuart Davis (col)
  Goossen. Stuart Davis (col)
  ICA. Amer artists paint the city (col)
  Mendelowitz
  Myers. Art
  Pierson
Standard with still life
  IU. Contemp Amer ptg & sculp, 1959
Stele
  MnMW. Stuart Davis
  WMAA. Museum and its friends, 1958
Still life—three objects   CtHW
  Blesh. Stuart Davis
  Goossen. Stuart Davis
Still life with flowers
  Pearson. Mod renaissance
Still life with saw   DP
  Goossen. Stuart Davis
Street and bridge
  Myers
Summer landscape   MMA
  Barr. What is mod ptg
  Baur. Revolution
  Blesh. Stuart Davis
  Goossen. Stuart Davis
  UNESCO. 1860-1955
Summer landscape no 2, 1940 (Alan coll)
  Goossen. Stuart Davis
Summer twilight
  Goossen. Stuart Davis
  MiD. Coll in progress
  WiMiA. Amer ptg 1760-1960
Sunrise
  Blesh. Stuart Davis
  Goossen. Stuart Davis (col)
Super table
  Goossen. Stuart Davis
  MnMW. Stuart Davis
Swing landscape   InBu
  Blesh. Stuart Davis
  Goossen. Stuart Davis
Television
  Goossen. Stuart Davis
The terminal
  Goossen. Stuart Davis
  MnMW. Stuart Davis
Tournos   NUM
  Goossen. Stuart Davis (col)
  MnMW. Stuart Davis
  Pousette-Dart. Amer ptg
Town square   NJN
  Blesh. Stuart Davis
Triatic
  MnMW. Stuart Davis
Tropes de teens
  Blesh. Stuart Davis (col)
  IU. Contemp Amer ptg & sculp 1957
Ultra marine   PA
  Baur. Revolution
  Blesh. Stuart Davis
  Goossen. Stuart Davis
  MnMW. Stuart Davis
U.N. conference room 3, 1956, Study for
  Goossen. Stuart Davis
  MnMW. Stuart Davis
Underpass no 2, 1955
  MnMW. Stuart Davis

DAVIS, Stuart—*Continued*
    Ursine park
        Baur. Nature (col)   IBM
        Blesh. Stuart Davis (col)
        Goossen. Stuart Davis (col)
        Hunter. Mod Amer ptg (col)
        Pearson. Mod renaissance
    Visa   MMA
        Baur. New art
        Blesh. Stuart Davis (col)
        Goossen. Stuart Davis (col)
        MMA. Masters (col)
        MnMW. Stuart Davis
        PPC. International ex, 1952
    Ways and means
        IU. Contemp Amer ptg & sculp, 1961
    Yellow hills
        Goossen. Stuart Davis
DAVIS, William M. 1836?-1927
    Cider making   NCHA
        Davidson v 1
D'Avouille, Camille
    Whistler, J. A. M. Mme Camille D'Avouille
DAWKINS, Henry, fl 1754-1776
    Burroughs family
        Flexner. First flowers
        Ford. Pictorial folk art
Dawn by P. Evergood
Dawn by M. J. Heade
Dawn by H. Mattson
Dawn by J. Sloan
Dawn by M. Tobey
Dawn by R. S. Turner
Dawn at Culebra by J. Lie
Dawn II by A. G. Dove
Dawn III by A. G. Dove
Dawn in Pennsylvania by E. Hopper
Dawn light by H. E. Mattson
Dawn of peace by G. W. Bellows
Dawn over Fordham by A. Mosca
Dawson, Matilda Washington
    Neagle, J. Matilda Washington Dawson
Day, George Edward, 1815-1905
    Weir, J. F. The Theological of Yale uni-
        versity
Day, Jeremiah, 1773-1867
    Morse, S. F. B. Jeremiah Day
Day, Philo, fl 1810
    Unidentified artist. Mourning picture—
        Philo Day
DAY, Worden, 1916-
    Astral assemblage
        IU. Contemp Amer ptg, 1950
    Prima Materia
        MMA. Abstract
    The wanderer
        ICA. Annual ex, 1951
Day family, fl 1823
    Goldsmith, D. Mr and Mrs Lyman Day
        and daughter, Cornelia
A day at the race by R. Diebenkorn
Day in bed by P. S. Sample
Day in June by G. W. Bellows
Day in June by L. Kroll
Day in midwinter by C. E. Burchfield
Day in the country by M. B. Prendergast
Day of good fortune by A. B. Davies

Day of mountain flowers by T. Meehan
Daybreak by E. Berman
Daybreak by E. Magafan
Daymare by C. W. Rain
A day's catch by S. A. Mount
Day's end by W. R. Derrick
Day's end by S. Menkès
Day's end by W. W. Quirt
De mains pâles aux cieux lassés by Y. Tan-
    guy
De profundis by Ben-Zion
De profundis by W. S. Schwartz
Dead Abel by T. Cole
Dead bird by A. P. Ryder
Dead cottonwood tree by G. O'Keeffe
Dead duck by E. Burkhart
Dead end by D. Kingman
Dead leaves by E. K. Schwabacher
Dead life, sea lion skull, driftwood and coral
    by E. Berman
Dead man by J. Kinigstein
Dead man revived by touching the bones of
    the prophet Elijah by W. Allston
Dead men by F. Remington
Dead opossum by J. S. Eisenstat
Dead plover by M. Hartley
Deadline on the range by C. M. Russell
Dean, Barbara
    Unidentified artist. Barbara Dean
Deans, Anna Maria
    Hubard, W. J. Elizabeth and Anna Deans
Deans, Elizabeth Patterson
    Hubard, W. J. Elizabeth and Anna Deans
DEARTH, Henry Golden, 1864-1918
    Black hat   InIJ
        InIJ. 105 ptgs
Deas, Anne (Izard) 1779-1863
    Malbone, E. G. Mrs William Allen Deas
DEAS, Charles, 1818-1867
    The death struggle
        Pierson
    The devil and Tom Walker
        DC. Privately owned
    Long Jakes. See The trapper
    Prairie fire   NBM
        Baur. Amer ptg
        McCracken. Portrait of the old west
            (col)
        Pierson
    The trapper (Long Jakes)   CtY
        Davidson v 1
        McCracken. Portrait of the old west
        Rathbone
    Voyageurs   MB
        Davidson v 1
        MB. Karolik coll
Deas, Elizabeth (Allen) 1742-1803
    Theus, J. Elizabeth Allen
Deas, Mrs John. See Deas, Elizabeth (Allen)
Deas, Mary (Somers) fl 1801
    Malbone, E. G. Mrs David Deas
Deas, Mrs William Allen. See Deas, Anne
    (Izard)
Death by F. C. Watkins
Death, Study for by F. C. Watkins
Death by burning by B. L. Culwell

Death cry by B. W. Tomlin
Death in the orchard by F. C. Watkins
Death of a man by W. De Kooning
Death of a miner by B. Shahn
Death of Chatham by J. S. Copley
Death of Europe by E. F. Savage
Death of General Montgomery at Quebec by J. Trumbull
Death of Jane McCrea by J. Vanderlyn
Death of King John by W. Allston
Death of Major Pierson by J. S. Copley
Death of Socrates by B. West
Death of the general by F. Dzubas
Death on a pale horse by A. P. Ryder
Death on a pale horse by B. West
Death on the beach by B. Shahn
The **death** struggle by C. Deas
Death wish by J. De Feo
Death whoop by S. Eastman
Deathrose by J. De Feo
De Boogh, Catharina. See Beekman, Catharina (De Boogh)
Deborah and Nietzsche by G. R. Davis
DE BOTTON, Jean
  Chamber music
    NAD. Annual ex, 1948
Debris of summer by P. Perkins
Debuke, Jemima. See Winslow, Jemima (Debuke)
Decadence in Guatemala by D. E. Brown
Decalogue, Jacob's ladder and burning bush by R. B. Motherwell
Decatur, Stephen, 1779-1820
  Unidentified artist. Commodore Stephen Decatur
Decay and resurrection by K. Merrild
December by P. Horiuchi
Deciduous circumstance by R. Ruben
DECKER, Joseph, b 1853?
  Hard lot
    Frankenstein. After the hunt
Declaration of Independence by E. Hicks
Declaration of Independence by J. Trumbull
DECOMBES, Emilie, d 1906
  Surf at Ogunquit, Maine   MB
    MB. Ptgs in water color
  Swiss mountains   MB
    MB. Ptgs in water color
  Young girl   MB
    MB. Ptgs in water color
Decoration with cloud by M. Weber
DE DIEGO, Julio, 1900-
  Altitude 2000
    IU. Contemp Amer ptg, 1951
  Birth of the atom (Atomic series)
    Pearson. Mod renaissance
  Elements of reconstruction
    Gruskin (col)
  Forces against violent attack
    Rathbun
  Guilty cats   IBM
    Genauer
  Heroic figures
    Pearson. Mod renaissance

Italy: historical town
  IU. Contemp Amer ptg & sculp, 1953
Perplexity of what to do
  Pearson. Mod renaissance
Phantom boat   NJMo
  NJMo. Forty years
Prodigious industrial phenomenon
  VR. Biennial ex, 1948
They shall sail the seven seas
  Larkin
  Larkin rev ed
Trojan horse
  IU. Contemp Amer ptg, 1949
Unexpected encounter
  IU. Contemp Amer ptg, 1948
What are they going to do next (Disasters of the soul series)
  Pearson. Mod renaissance
The **deep** by J. Pollock
Deep orange on black by S. Francis
Deep river by J. Lie
Deep-sea trawlers, Maine by J. Marin
Deep vision by I. R. Pereira
Deer
  Audubon, J. W. Common American deer
  Audubon, J. J. Virginia deer
  Codman, C. Wounded deer
  Homer, W. Deer drinking
  Homer, W. Fallen deer
  Knaths, K. Deer at sunset
  Knaths, K. Frightened deer in moonlight
  Morse, H. D. Deer in a thicket
  Price, C. S. Mule deer
  Rungius, C. Moose
  Russell, C. M. Battle of the elks
  Russell, C. M. White tails
  Ryder, A. P. Stag and two does
  Ryder, A. P. Stag drinking
  Sample, P. S. Winter visitor
  Tait, A. F. Saved—a hard chase
  Tait, A. F. Young buck and doe
  Tait, A. F. and Gay, E. Deer at the lake
  Unidentified artist. Deer hunt
  Unidentified artist. De Peyster boy with deer
  Unidentified artist. Two children with a deer
  Whittredge, W. Deer, Mount Storm park, Cincinnati
Deer hunter by R. Huck
Deer island, Maine: Stonington waterfront by J. Marin
Deer isle, boats, and pertaining thereto by J. Marin
Deer isle islets, Maine by J. Marin
Deer isle, Maine, series no 30—Boat fantasy by J. Marin
Deer isle, Stonington, Maine by J. Marin
Deer Tongue lane by S. Laufman
DE ERDELY, Francis, 1904-
  Red sweater   CoD
    CoS. New accessions USA, 1946
  Sevastopol
    ICA. Annual ex, 1945/46
Deer's skull with pedernal by G. O'Keeffe
DEEZIK, Val, 1914-
  V. J. day   OYB
    OYB. Annual 1948
    OYB. Catalogue 1951

Defaced portrait by B. Shahn
The defendants by B. Shahn
Defending the stockade by C. Schreyvogel
Defense of America's cup, 1870 by J. E. Butterworth
DE FEO, Jay, 1929-
  Daphne
    MMA. Sixteen
  Death wish
    MMA. Sixteen
  Deathrose
    MMA. Sixteen
  Origin
    MMA. Sixteen
  The Veronica
    MMA. Sixteen
Defiance: Inviting a shot before Petersburg, Virginia by W. Homer
Defiant culprit by C. M. Russell
De Forest, David Curtis, 1774-1825
  Morse, S. F. B. David C. De Forest
DE GRAILLY, Victor
  View of Niagara Falls
    Sears. Highlights
  Washington's headquarters, Newburgh-on-the-Hudson
    Sears. Highlights
DE GRAILLY, Walter
  View from West Point
    Sears. Highlights
  Washington's tomb at Mount Vernon
    Sears. Highlights
De Haas, John Philip
  Peale, C. W. John Philip de Haas
DEHN, Adolph Arthur, 1895-
  Beauty is where you find it   WMAA
    Pierson
  Butte, Utah   MMA
    Gruskin
  Caribbean cornucopia
    IU. Contemp Amer ptg, 1952
  Dark night
    Pearson. Mod renaissance
  Garden of the gods
    Pearson. Mod renaissance
  Haitian heaven
    Pousette-Dart. Amer ptg
    PPC. International ex, 1952
  Haitian Mardi Gras   IaDa
    IaDa. Silver jubilee
  Jimmy Savo and rope   WMAA
    Goodrich. Amer art
    Pierson
  Jungle in Venezuela
    Pearson. Mod renaissance
  Market, Port-au-Prince, Haiti   ATeS
    ATeS. Collection
  Minnesota in August
    NYG. Fine art
  Sentinels of the west   ATU
    ATU. Coll of Amer art (col)
  Shower in Colorado   MB
    MB. Ptgs in water color
  The sisters   WMAA
    Brown. Amer ptg
  Spring in Central park   MM
    MM. 100 Amer ptrs
  Sunday painters
    Pearson. Mod renaissance
DeKay, Sidney G. 1880-1949
  Lockman, D. M. Col Sidney G. DeKay

DE KNIGHT, Avel
  Circus horses
    NAD. Annual ex, 1954
DE KOONING, Willem, 1904-
  Acrobat
    Hess. Willem De Kooning
    Janis. De Kooning
  Asheville   DP
    Baur. New art
    DP. Catalogue
    Hess. Abstract ptg (col)
    Hess. Willem De Kooning (col)
    Janis. De Kooning
    Larkin rev ed
    Pierson
  Attic
    Hess. Willem De Kooning
    Janis. De Kooning
  Backdrop for a dance recital, Study for
    Hess. Willem De Kooning
  Backyard on Tenth street   MdBM
    Hess. Willem De Kooning
  Black and white
    CSFP. Annual ex, 1950/51
  Black Friday, 1949 no 1 (Lloyd coll)
    Hess. Willem De Kooning
  Black Friday, 1949 no 2 (Lloyd coll)
    Hess. Willem De Kooning
  Bolton landing
    Hess. Willem De Kooning
  Boudoir   MoKN
    Hess. Willem De Kooning
  Boudoir (Tishler coll)
    Hess. Willem De Kooning
  Brown and white
    Hess. Willem De Kooning
  Classic male. See Seated figure
  Composition   NNSG
    Hunter. Mod Amer ptg (col)
    NNSG. Handbook
    Read. Concise history
  Dark pond
    WMAA. New decade
  Death of a man
    Hess. Willem De Kooning (detail)
  Detour
    Canaday
  Door to the river   WMAA
    Goodrich. Amer art (col)
  Duck pond
    Hess. Willem De Kooning
  Easter Monday   MM
    Art since 1945
    Hess. Willem De Kooning
    Janis. De Kooning (col)
  Elegy
    Hess. Willem De Kooning (col)
  Excavation   ICA
    Baur. New art
    CoS. New accessions USA, 1952
    Hess. Willem De Kooning (col)
    Janis. De Kooning (col)
    MMA. Abstract
    Pousette-Dart. Amer ptg
  February
    Baur. Nature
    Eliot. Art of our time (col)
    Hess. Willem De Kooning (col)
    Hess. Willem De Kooning (detail)
    Janis. De Kooning (col)
    Janis. De Kooning (detail)
    MMA. New Amer ptg

Woman as landscape
  Hess. Willem De Kooning
Woman in landscape I
  Janis. De Kooning
Woman (Green)
  Hess. Willem De Kooning
Woman (Ocher)
  Hess. Willem De Kooning
Woman sitting
  Hess. Willem De Kooning
Yellow river
  MnMW. 60 Amer ptrs
Delancey, Alice. See Izard, Alice (Delancey)
De Lancey, Mrs Oliver. See De Lancey,
  Phila (Franks)
De Lancey, Phila (Franks) 1722-1811
  Duyckinck, G. (attributed works) Chil-
    dren of Jacob Franks
  Duyckinck, G. (attributed works) Phila
    Franks
De Lancey, Warren, fl 1775
  Pratt, M. Cadwallader Colden and War-
    ren de Lancey
DELANEY, Joseph, 1904-
  His last address   ATU
  ATU. Coll of Amer art
  Innocence   ATU
  ATU. Coll of Amer art
DELANO, Gerard Curtis, 1890-
  The canyon
    Carlson. Gallery (col)
  Desert thunderhead
    Carlson. Gallery (col)
  Moonlight stampede
    Carlson. Gallery (col)
  Navajo
    Carlson. Gallery (col)
  Navajo boy
    Carlson. Gallery (col)
  Sheep on the desert
    Carlson. Gallery (col)
  Vermillion cliffs
    Carlson. Gallery (col)
DELANOY, Abraham, 1742-1795
  Benjamin West   NNHS
  Pierson
De Lanoy, Catherine Peters. See Beekman,
  Catherine Peters (De Lanoy)
Delaware meadows by G. Inness
Delaware river and valley
  Chambers, T. Delaware Water Gap
  Eakins, T. On the Delaware
  Inness, G. Delaware valley
  Inness, G. Delaware Water Gap
  Inness, G. View on the Delaware, Water
    Gap in the distance
  McIlvaine, W. Delaware Water Gap
Delaware (river) country, Pennsylvania by
  J. Marin
Delaware Water Gap village by L. M. Eil-
  shemius
DELBOS, Julius, 1879-
  Canal   InTH
    InTH. Catalogue
  Haiti
    NAD. Annual ex, 1953
  Martha's Vineyard
    NAD. Annual ex, 1947, 2d half
DE LEON, Amanda, 1908-
  Christening   OYB
    OYB. Supplement

Delfina by J. Youngerman
Delicate board by S. Provan
Delight by H. Hofmann
Delirium is our best deceiver by P. S.
  Sample
Deliverance by Y. Kuniyoshi
Delmores, Aimée
  Lockman, D. M. Aimée Delmores
De Long, Mehitabel Preston, fl 1865
  Mason, B. F. Mehitabel Preston de Long
Delta Queen and the packet Whisper by
  E. A. Anderson
The **deluge** by W. Allston
A **demand** of estimation by K. Nack
De Mare, Agnes (Healy) b 1842
  Healy, G. P. A. Agnes de Mare and her
    son
De Mare, Jeanne, fl 1889
  Healy, G. P. A. Jeanne de Mare
De Mare, Marie, fl 1882
  Healy, G. P. A. Marie de Mare
DE MARTINI, Joseph, 1896-
  Aqueduct
    PA. Annual ex, 1952
  Bike race no 2
    NAD. Annual ex, 1952
  Caravan theater minstrels   ATU
    ATU. Coll of Amer art
  Crotch Island derricks   MnMW
    Pierson
  Foggy night
    Genauer
  Interior with three figures
    CSFP. Annual ex, 1948/49
    IU. Contemp Amer ptg, 1949
  Lighthouse point   NeL
    Gruskin
  Moonlight   ICA
    NYG. Fine art
  Mountain village
    IU. Contemp Amer ptg, 1950
  The promontory   IU
    IU. Contemp Amer ptg, 1948
    IU. 20th century
  Quarry pool   MAP
    Cheney. Expressionism 1948 ed
    Cheney. Story 1958 ed
    Rathbun
  Self-portrait
    Cheney. Expressionism 1948 ed
  The wreck of the St Christopher   MM
    MM. 100 Amer ptrs
DEMBOSKI, Dorothy L.
  Blue interior   OYB
    OYB. Annual 1960
Democracies fear peace offensive by B.
  Shahn
Demonstration in Paris by B. Shahn
Dempsey and Firpo by G. W. Bellows
DEMUTH, Charles Henry, 1883-1935
  Acrobats, 1916   PMB
    MMA. Demuth
  Acrobats, 1918
    MMA. Demuth
  Acrobats, 1919   MMA
    Baur. New art
    Biddle. Yes and no
    Larkin (detail)
    Larkin rev ed (detail)
    MM. Contemp ptrs

DEMUTH, C. H.—*Continued*
  MMA. Demuth (col)
  MMA. Masters (col)
  Pierson
  Richardson. Ptg in America
After all . . . , 1933   FaW
  MMA. Demuth
  MnMW. Precisionist view
  WMAA. Juliana Force
After Sir Christopher Wren
  Brown. Amer ptg
  MMA. Demuth
. . . and the home of the brave   ICA
  MMA. Demuth
  Rosenblum
Architecture
  MiD. Coll in progress
  WiMiA. Amer ptg 1760-1960
L'Assommoir, Illustration for   PPhM
  MMA. Demuth
At a house in Harley street   MMA
  MMA. Demuth
  PA. Annual ex, 1955
  Pierson
Aucassin and Nicoletta   OCo
  Moderns and their world
Backdrop of East Lynne   NeL
  MMA. Demuth
Bathers
  Chew. 250 years of art
The beast in the jungle, Illustrations for
  MMA. Demuth
Bermuda, 1917   PPhM
  PPhM. Arensberg coll
Bermuda no 2 (The schooner)   MMA
  MMA. Demuth
Box of tricks   PPhM
  Chew. 250 years of art
Buildings, Lancaster   WMAA
  Goodrich. Amer art
Business   ICA
  Hunter. Mod Amer ptg
  MMA. Demuth
The circus   OCo
  MMA. Demuth
  Pierson
Daisies   WMAA
  MMA. Demuth
Dunes   OCo
  MMA. Demuth
Early houses, Provincetown   MMA
  MMA. Demuth
Eggplant   DP
  Bazin
  DP. Catalogue
Eggplant and plums   ICA
  Mendelowitz
  PA. Annual ex, 1955
Eggplant and summer squash   CtHW
  CtHW. Handbook
Eggplant and tomatoes
  MMA. Demuth
End of the parade: Coatsville, Pennsylvania
  Baur. New art (col)
  MMA. Demuth
Erdgeist, Illustration for
  MMA. Demuth
Factory
  CtY. Yale alumni

Female acrobats   MMA
  MMA. Soby collection
Flower piece
  MMA. Demuth
Flower study   OCl
  MMA. Demuth
Flower study no 1   ICA
  NYG. Fine art
Flower study no 4
  NYG. Fine art
Flowers   MB
  MB. Ptgs in water color
Flowers (Fleischman coll)
  MiD. Coll in progress
  MMA. Demuth
  WiMiA. Amer ptg 1760-1960
Flowers, cyclamen   ICA
  MMA. Demuth
Gloucester   RPS
  MMA. Demuth
Golden Swan (Hell Hole)
  MMA. Demuth
The governess first sees the ghost of
    Peter Quint
  PA. Annual ex, 1955
Grapes and turnips
  Chew. 250 years of art
Green dancer
  MMA. Demuth
Green pears
  MMA. Demuth
Hell Hole. See Golden Swan
Houses   OCo
  MMA. Contemp ptrs
I saw the figure 5 in gold   MM
  Baur. New art
  MM. 100 Amer ptrs (col)
  MMA. Demuth (col)
  Pierson
  Taylor. Fifty centuries, 1954 ed (col)
In vaudeville   PPhM
  PPhM. Gallatin coll
In vaudeville (White coll)
  Baur. New art
  MMA. Contemp ptrs
Incense of a new church   OCo
  Brown. Amer ptg
  WMAA. Pioneers
Kiss-me-over-the-fence
  MiD. Coll in progress
  WiMiA. Amer ptg 1760-1960
Lancaster   PPhM
  PPhM. Arensberg coll
Lancaster, Pennsylvania, View of   NBuA
  MMA. Demuth
  Sewall. History of western art
Man and woman
  MMA. Demuth
Many brave hearts are asleep in the deep
  MMA. Demuth
Miles and the governess
  PA. Annual ex, 1955
Modern conveniences   OCo
  DC. De gustibus
  Roos
My Egypt   WMAA
  Gardner 1959 ed
  Goodrich. Amer art (col)
  Janson. Picture history
  Mendelowitz

MMA. Demuth
MnMW. Precisionist view (col)
PA. Annual ex, 1955
Pierson
Roos
Time. 300 years (col)
Wight. Milestones (col)
Nana, Illustrations for   MMA
  MMA. Demuth
Nana, Illustrations for   PMB
  MMA. Demuth
New Hope, Pennsylvania
  MMA. Demuth
Nospmas M. Egiap, Lancaster, Pennsyl-
  vania
  Chew. 250 years of art
On stage
  MiD. Coll in progress
  WiMiA. Amer ptg 1760-1960
Pandora's box, Illustration for   PMB
  MMA. Demuth
Pansies
  MMA. Demuth
Paquebot, Paris   OCo
  Baur. Revolution
  Brown. Amer ptg
  MMA. Demuth
  Pierson
Poe's The masque of the red death, Illus-
  tration for   PMB
  MMA. Demuth
Poppies   NUM
  NUM. Root bequest
Poppies (Halpert coll)
  Baur. New art
  MMA. Demuth
  Pierson
Poster portrait of O'Keeffe
  MnMW. Precisionist view
Purple pup
  Baur. New art
Red chimneys   DP
  Born
  DP. Catalogue
Rue du Singe qui Pêche
  MMA. Demuth
  MnMW. Classic tradition
Sails   CSB
  MMA. Demuth
The schooner. See Bermuda no 2
Sky after El Greco   ATeS
  ATeS. Collection
Stairs, Provincetown   MMA
  MMA. Demuth
  MnMW. Precisionist view
  Rosenblum
Still life   PPhM
  Robb. Harper history
Still life, no 2, 1922   OCo
  MMA. Demuth
Strolling   MMA
  MMA. Demuth
Studio interior
  MMA. Demuth
The tower   OCo
  McCurdy
Trees   OCo
  Brown. Amer ptg
Trees and barns, Bermuda   KLU
  MMA. Demuth
  Pierson

Tuberoses   MWiC
  MMA. Demuth
The turn of the screw, Illustration for
  Baur. Revolution
  Lewisohn
  MMA. Demuth
Two acrobats
  MMA. Demuth
Vaudeville
  MMA. Demuth
Vaudeville musicians   MMA
  MMA. Demuth
Waiting   ICA
  MMA. Demuth
  PA. Annual ex, 1955
White architecture   MLL
  MnMW. Precisionist view
Woman with walking stick
  MMA. Demuth
Zinnias, larkspur and daisies
  MMA. Demuth
The den by H. Pippin
Denain by J. D. Brooks
The denial by R. O. Pozzatti
Denison, Mr. c 1785
  Unidentified artist. Mr Denison
Denison, Mrs. c 1785
  Unidentified artist. Mrs Denison
Denison, Edward, 1778-1845
  Peale, Rembrandt. Edward Denison
Denison, Eunice. See Hatch, Eunice (Deni-
  son)
Denning family, fl 1772
  Williams, W. The Denning family
Dennis, Aaron Chase, fl 1803
  Malbone, E. G. Aaron Chase Dennis
DENNISON, Dorothy D.
  Professional painters
    OYB. Annual 1949
Dennison, Miss, fl 1775
  Unidentified artist. Miss Dennison
Dennison hill, Southbridge, Massachusetts
  by Unidentified artist
Departing boat by Z. Sepeshy
Departing guests by W. Thompson
Departure by M. Beckmann
Departure by T. Cole
Departure by J. Hirsch
Departure of Regulus by B. West
De Peyster, Abraham B. 1763-1801
  Peale, C. W. Abraham B. De Peyster
De Peyster, Catherine, 1771-1799
  Vanderlyn, P. (attributed works) Cath-
  erine De Peyster
De Peyster, Christiana (Dally) 1748-1813
  Peale, C. W. Mrs William De Peyster jr
De Peyster, Elizabeth, 1765-1804. See Peale,
  Elizabeth (De Peyster)
De Peyster, Elizabeth, 1787-1826. See Rem-
  sen, Elizabeth (De Peyster)
De Peyster, Elizabeth (Haring) 1743-1821
  Peale, C. W. Mrs John De Peyster
De Peyster, Gerard, 1776-1824
  Unidentified artist. Gerard De Peyster
De Peyster, Isaac, 1662-1728
  Unidentified artist. Isaac De Peyster
De Peyster, James A. fl 1720
  Unidentified artist. James A. De Peys-
  ter (?)

De Peyster, James W. 1745-1812
  Peale, C. W. James W. De Peyster
De Peyster, Johannes, 1694-1789
  Unidentified artist. Johannes De Peyster III
De Peyster, John, 1731-1807
  Peale, C. W. John De Peyster
De Peyster, Mrs John. See De Peyster, Elizabeth (Haring)
De Peyster, John B. 1765-1846?
  Peale, C. W. John B. De Peyster
De Peyster, Margaret, 1728-1781. See Axtell, Margaret (De Peyster)
De Peyster, Margaret (De Peyster) 1774-1815
  Peale, C. W. Mrs Gerard De Peyster
De Peyster, William, 1709-1780?
  Peale, C. W. William De Peyster (copy after John Durand)
De Peyster, William, 1735-1803
  Peale, C. W. William De Peyster jr
De Peyster, Mrs William jr. See De Peyster, Christiana (Dally)
De Peyster children, 1730?
  Unidentified artist. Eva and Catherina De Peyster
De Peyster family, Member of
  Unidentified artist. Boy of the De Peyster family
  Unidentified artist. De Peyster boy with deer
  Unidentified artist. De Peyster girl with lamb (Margaret or Catherine)
Deposition by S. Greene
Deposition by W. Pachner
Depression by J. Lawrence
Derby, John, 1762-1831
  Malbone, E. G. John Derby
Derby, Martha (Coffin) fl 1802
  Malbone, E. G. Mrs Richard C. Derby
Derby hill theme: Hiawatha by P. Tchelitchew
Derby view by W. D. Fausett
The derelict by M. Roberts
Derelicts by F. Gill
Dering, Mary Sylvester, 1725-1794
  Blackburn, J. Mary Sylvester Dering
DERRICK, William Rowell, b 1857
  Day's end
    NSP. Sportscapes
  Duckblind
    NSP. Sportscapes
Descension by M. C. Morgan
Descent by F. C. Watkins
Descent from the cross by M. Beckmann
Descent from the cross by W. Quirt
Desdemona by A. P. Ryder
The desert by E. F. Spruce
Desert at night by E. F. Spruce
Desert domain by P. Grimm
Desert landscape by W. A. Baziotes
Desert landscape by L. Siegriest
Desert ranges by M. Dixon
Desert song by L. Megargee
Desert sun by R. F. Gates
Desert thunderhead by G. C. Delano
Desert twilight by L. Goldin

Deserted farm by M. Hartley
Deserted farm by M. Weber
Deserted Navajo home by J. E. Swinnerton
Deserted Navajo trading post by J. E. Swinnerton
Design for color by L. Lucioni
Design for the memory by A. Rattner
Desire by M. Jules
The desk by N. Spencer
Desperate stand by C. M. Russell
Destination unknown by T. Egri
The destruction of the beast and the false prophets by B. West
Destruction of the empire by T. Cole
Detour by W. De Kooning
Detour by K. Sage
Detroit, Michigan
  Bennett, W. J. Detroit, 1836
  Burnham, T. O. H. P. First state election in Detroit, Michigan
  H., E. Detroit, 1794
DÉTRÉ, Roland, 1903-
  Nude in grisaille
    IU. Contemp Amer ptg & sculp, 1959
Deuce by S. Davis
DEUTSCH, Boris, 1892-
  What atomic war will do to you
    IU. Contemp Amer ptg, 1949
Deutsche presse by W. M. Harnett
Deux personnages by G. Vass
The devil and Tom Walker by C. Deas
The devil and Tom Walker by J. Quidor
Devil's gate by A. J. Miller
Devil's holiday by E. Berman
DEVLAN, Francis Daniel, 1835-1870
  Gibraltar forge   PR
    PR. Catalogue
DEVOLL, Ruby, fl 1830
  The prodigal son   VWR
    VWR. Folk art (col)
Devotion, Ebenezer, 1684-1771
  Chandler, W. Rev Ebenezer Devotion
De Wandelaer, Catherine. See Gansevoort, Catherine (De Wandelaer)
De Wandelaer, Pau, fl 1725
  Gansevoort limner. Pau de Wandelaer
Dewdrops and roses by C. C. Curran
Dewees, William Potts, 1768-1841
  Neagle, J. Dr William Potts Dewees
Dewey, Thomas Edmund, 1902-
  Shahn, B. Dewey, Vandenberg and Taft
DEWING, Thomas Wilmer, 1851-1938
  Lady in yellow   MBI
    Richardson. Ptg in America
  The letter   MM
    MM. 100 Amer ptrs
  Music
    DC. Privately owned
  Orange and rose
    WiMiA. Amer ptg 1760-1960
  The recitation   MiD
    Pierson
  The spinet   DNC
    DNC. Gellatly coll, 1954
    Pierson

  Portrait of the artist
  Chase, W. M. Thomas Dewing

Dexter, Franklin Bowditch, 1842-1920
  Thomas, P. M. Franklin Bowditch Dexter
Dial by P. Guston
Dialogue 1 by A. Gottlieb
Diamond shaped by I. Bolotowsky
Diamond shoal by W. Homer
Diana by A. P. Ryder
Diana and Callisto by A. Russell
Diana in the chase, or Swiss scenery by W.
  Allston
Diary of a seducer by A. Gorky
Dice players by K. F. Roesch
DICKINSON, Anson, 1779-1852
  Asa Bacon   CtY
    CtY. Portrait index
  Goldsbrow Banyar   NNHS
    Vail. Stuyvesant ports
  Goldsbrow Banyar (replica)
    Vail. Stuyvesant ports
  Man with a harelip   OCl
    OCl. Portrait miniatures

Attributed works
  Sarah Pierce
    MB. New England miniatures
DICKINSON, Edwin Walter, 1891-
  Cello player   WMAA
    WMAA. Sara Roby
  Composition with still life, 1933-37 MMA
    Baur. New art
  Constant
    NAD. Annual ex, 1952
    PPC. Ptg in the U.S. 1949
  Finger lakes
    MMA. Fifteen
  Fossil hunters   WMAA
    Goodrich. Amer art (col)
  Ruin at Daphne   MM
    Baur. New art
    McCurdy
    Pousette-Dart. Amer ptg
  Self-portrait
    Baur. New art
    MMA. Fifteen
  Surf, Point Lookout
    IU. Contemp Amer ptg & sculp, 1955
  Unfinished composition
    MMA. Fifteen
  View from window, Paris
    NAD. Annual ex, 1958
  Villa la Mouette   MM
    MM. 100 Amer ptrs
  Windows, Paris
    ICA. Annual ex, 1954
  Woodland scene   NIC
    Baur. New art
    MMA. Fifteen
    Pierson
DICKINSON, Eleanor C.
  My father   OYB
    OYB. Annual 1960
DICKINSON, Preston, 1891-1930
  Along the river   DP
    DP. Catalogue
  Bridge   NJN
    Larkin
    Larkin rev ed
    Mendelowitz

  The factory   MB
    Baur. Revolution
    McCurdy
  The factory   OCo
    Precisionist view
  Harlem river   WMAA
    Born
    NYG. Fine art
  High bridge   OCl
    Brown. Amer ptg
  Industry   WMAA
    Goodrich. Amer art
    Pierson
    Roos
  Mountain farm
    WMAA. Pioneers
  Old quarter, Quebec   DP
    Wight. Milestones
  Quebec   OCiM
    Born
  The ramparts—Quebec   MM
    MM. 100 Amer ptrs
  Still life   OCl
    OCl. Handbook
  Still life with yellow green chair   OCo
    Brown. Amer ptg
    MnMW. Precisionist view
    NYG. Fine art
    Pierson
DICKINSON, Sidney Edward, 1890-
  At Maxie Ford's
    NAD. Annual ex, autumn 1949
  Mary   IaDa
    IaDa. 30th anniversary
    NAD. Annual ex, 1956
  Our son, Thorn
    NAD. Annual ex, 1949, 1st half
    PPC. Ptg in the U.S. 1949
  Peter Juley and son
    NAD. Annual ex, 1951
  Raphael Soyer
    NAD. Annual ex, 1961
  The search
    PPC. International ex, 1950
Dickinson, Thorn
  Dickinson, S. E. Our son, Thorn
Di Cocco, Francesco. See Cocco, Frances-
  co di
DIEBENKORN, Richard, 1922-
  Berkeley no 2, 1953
    NNSG. Younger Amer ptrs
    Read. Concise history
  Berkeley no 7, 1953   MCH
    Pulitzer v2
  Berkeley no 16
    IU. Contemp Amer ptg & sculp, 1955
  Berkeley no 38
    PPC. International ex, 1955
  Berkeley no 54, 1955
    VR. Amer ptg, 1958
  A day at the race   PPC
    CoS. New accessions USA, 1954
  Girl on a terrace
    Brussels. Exposition
    Selz. New images (col)
  Girl with three coffee cups (Girl with
    cups)
    MnMW. Eighty works
    Selz. New images
  Man and woman in a large room
    Selz. New images

DIEBENKORN, Richard—*Continued*
Man and woman seated
  Selz. New images
Number 4, 1951
  Pulitzer v 1
Pouring coffee
  PPC. International ex, 1958
Two nudes
  PPC. International ex, 1961/62
Woman and checkerboard   CSB
  NUM. Art across America
Woman in a window   NBuA
  NBuA. Acquisitions 1957-58
Yellow seascape
  IU. Contemp Amer ptg & sculp, 1961
Dieppe by M. B. Prendergast
Dies, Jane (Goelet) See Goelet, Jane
DIETZ, fl 1830
Milford, North Wales, Pennsylvania   MB
  MB. Karolik coll
Digger by J. Hirsch
DI GIOIA, Frank, 1900-
Fish market   ATU
  ATU. Coll of Amer art
  Gruskin (col)
DIKE, Philip Latimer, 1906-
Echo from the sea   OYB
  OYB. Annual 1959
  OYB. Supplement 1959
Flags and fishes
  IU. Contemp Amer ptg, 1951
Golden light
  NAD. Special ex, 1956
Orchards and hills
  IU. Contemp Amer ptg, 1948
Shore tapestry
  NAD. Annual ex, 1955
Valley ranch   ATeS
  ATeS. Collection
Victorian tapestry
  IU. Contemp Amer ptg, 1950
View of Los Angeles
  ICA. Annual ex, 1945/46
Dilemma by W. W. Quirt
DILLER, Burgoyne A. 1906-
Composition
  McCurdy
  MMA. Abstract
Construction   CtY
  CtY. Soc Anonyme
Number 10
  CSFP. Annual ex, 1950/51
Dimock, Edith. See Glackens, Edith (Dimock)
Dinard by M. B. Prendergast
Dining rooms
Clonney, J. G. Interior
Koch, J. Interior—dining room
Sargent, J. S. The breakfast table
Sargent, H. Dinner party
Dinner still life by A. Blatas
Dinner table by M. M. Albright
DINNERSTEIN, Harvey
Magnolia
  NAD. Annual ex, 1954
Noah-Wolf
  PA. Annual ex, 1950
Diomed and his horses stopped by the lightning of Jupiter by B. West

Diptych by E. M. Smith
Directional multiplicity by R. O. Preusser
Directions yellow by I. R. Pereira
Dirigo island by W. Kienbusch
Discarded treasures by W. M. Harnett (attributed works)
Discharge of cargo at pier by R. Marsh
Discovery by H. Billings
Discovery by G. Faddis
Dish of blackberries by Raphaelle Peale
Disintegrated and reanimated by M. Graves
Dismissal of school on an October afternoon by H. Inman
Dismounted: 4th troopers moving by F. Remington
Disorder by R. Soyer
A **disputed** trail by C. M. Russell
Disrobing figure by L. Johnson
Distant sail by K. Knaths
Distant view of lake by A. J. Miller
Distant view of the Rocky mountains by J. J. Egan
Distraction by A. G. Dove
Distributing goods to the Gros Ventres by J. M. Stanley
DI VALENTIN, Louis, 1908-
Neither yet have you faith
  Genauer
  NAD. Annual ex, 1947, 1st half
Divisibilité indéfinie by Y. Tanguy
DIXON, James Budd
Untitled
  CSFP. Annual ex, 1948/49
DIXON, Maynard, 1875-1946
Cowboy and packhorse
  Carlson. Gallery (col)
Desert ranges
  Carlson. Gallery (col)
Drought and downpour
  Carlson. Gallery (col)
Katchinamaker
  Carlson. Gallery (col)
Lonesome road
  Carlson. Gallery (col)
Peace in October
  Carlson. Gallery (col)
Red gateway
  Carlson. Gallery (col)
The wise men
  Carlson. Gallery (col)
Dobbin, Mrs George W. See Pue, Rebecca
Dock by C. A. Morris
Dock square by G. R. Beals
Docks, East Boston by M. B. Prendergast
Doctrine of the Trinity by J. S. Sargent
DODD, Lamar, 1909-
Ashen gods
  DC. 21 biennial ex, 1949
Aspiring
  IU. Contemp Amer ptg & sculp, 1955
Athens [U.S.] View of   IBM
  Gruskin
Aurangabad market
  IU. Contemp Amer ptg & sculp, 1961
Black movements
  IU. Contemp Amer ptg, 1950

Cliffs and the sea
  IU. Contemp Amer ptg, 1951
  MM. Amer ptg today
Crucifixion no 2
  NAD. Annual ex, 1956
Granite city   NAD
  Cheney. Story 1958 ed
Italian sunlight
  IU. Contemp Amer ptg & sculp, 1959
Madonnas of the rain
  IU. Contemp Amer ptg, 1948
Monhegan theme   MM
  Pierson
  Pousette-Dart. Amer ptg
Objects on table
  IU. Contemp Amer ptg, 1949
A rainy ride   GAtM
  GAtM. Holbrook collection
Savannah   NJMo
  NJMo. Forty years
Sicily
  NAD. Annual ex, 1960
Winter road
  VR. Biennial ex, 1948
Dodd, William Lamar. See Dodd, Lamar
Dodge, Mrs James Mapes
  Eakins, T. Portrait of a lady (Mrs James
    Mapes Dodge)
Dodge, Mary Abigail, 1833-1896
  Cobb, D. Mary Abigail Dodge (known as
    Gail Hamilton)
Dodging an arrow by A. J. Miller
Dog dance of the Dakotahs by S. Eastman
Dog dance of the Kansas Indians by S. Sey-
    mour
Dogs
  Bradley, J. (attributed works) Boy hold-
    ing dog
  Cassatt, M. Woman with a dog
  Chase, W. M. Alice with wolfhound
  Chase, W. M. Girl with dog
  Clonney, J. G. Sleigh ride
  Conduit, L. Pointer and quail
  Copley, J. S. Mary Warner [with dog]
  Eakins, T. Lady with a setter dog
  Evergood, P. Juju and her dog Copelia
  Glackens, W. J. Lenna and Imp
  Homer, W. Hunting dog among dead
    trees
  Homer, W. Huntsman and dogs
  Marsden, T. On a point
  Miller, A. J. Indians watching a canoe
  Osthaus, E. H. On the points
  Poore, H. R. Hound
  Prior, W. M. Little child with big dog
  Tracy, J. M. Grouse shooting
  Tracy, J. M. Pointers
  Unidentified artist. Two brown and white
    puppies
  Unidentified artist. Walking the puppy
  Woolworth, C. A. Little dog
  Wyeth, A. N. Raccoon
  Zorach, M. T. Hound
Dolamen by J. D. Brooks
Dolbeare, Sarah (Comer)
  Pollard limner. Mrs John Dolbeare
The doll by M. Siporin
The doll and the monster by G. P. Du Bois
Dollar bill and playbill by W. M. Harnett
    (attributed works)

Dollarfish and sheepshead by W. A. Walker
Dolores in blue costume by H. A. Sawyer
Domain by C. A. Hall
The domino girl by Unidentified artist
Dominoes. See Games and sports—Dominoes
DONAGHY, John, 1838-1931
  Three balls for five cents
    Chew. 250 years of art
Donaldson, Althea (Lenox) 1807-1878
  Thibault, A. Althea Lenox (?)
DONATI, Enrico A. 1909-
  Apsaras
    IU. Contemp Amer ptg & sculp, 1959
  Black & 3 whites
    NNSG. Younger Amer ptrs
  Ego et l'aurore
    IU. Contemp Amer ptg, 1948
  Electric eye
    IU. Contemp Amer ptg, 1951
  Gore et mandra   WMAA
    Goodrich. Amer art
  Guirson
    IU. Contemp Amer ptg & sculp, 1961
  Habbaku dancers   NBuA
    NBuA. Acquisitions 1959-1961
  Meteorite
    WMAA. Contemp Amer ptg, 1951
  Moss agate
    IU. Contemp Amer ptg, 1950
  Naram-Sin
    MnMW. 60 Amer ptrs
Donkeys
  Megargee, L. Donkey business
  Weir, J. A. Visiting neighbors
Donna Mencia in the robbers' cave by W.
    Allston
DONNELLY, Thomas, 1893-
  Valhalla bridge   WMAA
    NYG. Fine art
Don Pasquale by D. Rosenthal
Don Quixote
  Folinsbee, J. F. Don Quixote
  Gonzalez, X. Don Quixote
  Meeker, D. J. Don Quixote
  Rattner, A. Composition: Don Quixote
Don't cry, little mother by P. Evergood
DOOLITTLE, Amos, 1754-1832
  Prodigal son reclaimed   VWR
    Ford. Pictorial folk art
      Portrait of the artist
    Earl, R. Amos Doolittle
Doomsday by K. Knaths
Door to the river by W. De Kooning
Doorway by R. Vickrey
Doorway, Venice by J. A. M. Whistler
Doreau, Clara C.
  Lockman, M. D. Mrs Clara C. Doreau
Dorian Gray, Picture of by I. L. Albright
Dorr, Henrietta, fl 1818
  Unidentified artist. Henrietta Dorr,
    Chatham Center, New York
Dorr, Robert Lockridge, 1810-1815
  Border limner. Robert Lockridge Dorr
The dory by W. Homer
Douarnenez by M. Broudy
Double disparate by R. Lebrun
Double feature by R. Rauschenberg
Double indemnity by W. W. Quirt

Double portrait by M. Beckmann
Double portrait by C. S. Hopkinson
Double portrait of Berdie by L. Rivers
Doubleday, Abner, 1819-1893
  Blythe, D. G. Gen Doubleday watching
    his troops cross the Potomac
Doubt by W. W. Quirt
The **doubter** by Y. Tanguy
A **doubtful** guest by C. M. Russell
DOUDERA, Gerard E. 1932-
  Danville   OYB
    OYB. Annual 1958
    OYB. Supplement 1959
Doughboy's equipment by C. A. Meurer
Doughty, Mrs Thomas. See Trusler, Mary
DOUGHTY, Thomas, 1793-1856
  Anglers
    NSP. Sportscapes
  Baltimore from Beech hill, View of MB
    MB. Karolik coll
  Baltimore from the seat of R. Gilmor
                                        MdBM
    MdBMu. Rendezvous
  A castle in England or Ireland
    Sears. Highlights
  Echo lake   GAtM
    GAtM. Holbrook collection
  Fishing by a waterfall   MB
    MB. Karolik coll
  Fishing pool
    Sears. Highlights
  A home on the Hudson
    Sears. Highlights
  Ideal landscape   ATeS
    ATeS. Collection
  In nature's wonderland   MiD
    MiD. Treasures
    Pierson
    Richardson. Ptg in America
    Roos
  In the Catskills   MAP
    Canaday
    Larkin
    Larkin rev ed
    Pierson
  Landscape   MM
    Bazin
  Landscape, house on cliff above pool PA
    Pierson
  Landscape, the ferry   MoKN
    MoKN. Handbook
  Landscape with fisherman   MB
    MB. Karolik coll
  Landscape with fisherman and sailboat
    WiMiA. Amer ptg 1760-1960
  Mountain torrent
    Sears. Highlights
  Naval home, Gray's ferry, Philadelphia
    MB. Karolik coll
  On the banks of the Susquehanna
    Born
  The raft   RPS
    Barker. Amer ptg
    Born
  Summer in the Catskills
    Sears. Highlights
  View from Stacey hill, Stoddard, New
    Hampshire   MB
    MB. Karolik coll

  View on the Bushkill
    Chew. 250 years of art
  Winter landscape   MB
    MB. Karolik coll
Douglas, Mrs Stephen Arnold. See Williams,
    Rose Adèle (Cutts) Douglas
DOUGLASS, Lucy, fl 1810
  Royal psalmist
    Flexner. Light of distant skies
Douw, Magdalena
  Unidentified artist. Magdalena Douw
DOVE, Arthur G. 1880-1946
  A. S. 1925, Portrait of   MMA
    Wight. Arthur G. Dove
  Abstraction, 1941
    NIC. Arthur G. Dove
    Wight. Arthur G. Dove
  Abstraction no 1, 1910
    NIC. Arthur G. Dove
  Abstraction no 1-6, 1910
    Wight. Arthur G. Dove
  Abstraction no 2, 1910
    NIC. Arthur G. Dove
  Time. 300 years (col)
    Wight. Arthur G. Dove (col)
  Across the road
    Wight. Arthur G. Dove
  Alfir's delight
    NIC. Arthur G. Dove
    Wight. Arthur G. Dove
    WMAA. Museum and its friends, 1958
  Anonymous, 1942   MM
    Wight. Arthur G. Dove (col)
  A walk poplars
    Wight. Arthur G. Dove (col)
  The Bessie of New York   MdBM
    Wight. Arthur G. Dove (col)
  Brothers
    Hess. Abstract ptg
  Cars in sleet storm
    NIC. Arthur G. Dove
  City moon
    Wight. Arthur G. Dove
  Coal carrier   DP
    Wight. Arthur G. Dove (col)
  Connecticut river
    Wight. Arthur G. Dove
  Cow I, 1935
    Wight. Arthur G. Dove
  Cow at play   IBM
    Baur. New art
  Cows in pasture   DP
    DP. Catalogue
    NIC. Arthur G. Dove
    Wight. Arthur G. Dove (col)
  Dancing tree
    Wight. Arthur G. Dove
  Dawn II
    NIC. Arthur G. Dove
  Dawn III
    NIC. Arthur G. Dove
    Wight. Arthur G. Dove
  Distraction   WMAA
    Mendelowitz
  Electric peach orchard   DP
    DP. Catalogue
  Ferry boat wreck   WMAA
    Goodrich. Amer art (col)
    Wight. Arthur G. Dove (col)
  Fields of grain as seen from train NBuA
    NBuA. Acquisitions 1957-58
    Wight. Arthur G. Dove

Flour mill II, 1938 (Flour mill abstraction)
    DP
  Baur. Revolution
  DP. Catalogue
  NIC. Arthur G. Dove
  Wight. Arthur G. Dove (col)
Fog horns   CoS
  Baur. New art
  NUM. Art across America
  Pierson
  Rathbun
  Wight. Arthur G. Dove
Frank Dusenberg, Portrait of
  Read. Art now, 1948 ed
George Gershwin's Rhapsody in blue
  part I, 1927
  Wight. Arthur G. Dove
Goat   MM
  Wight. Arthur G. Dove (col)
Gold, green and brown   DP
  Baur. Revolution
Golden storm   DP
  DP. Catalogue
Graphite and blue
  NIC. Arthur G. Dove
Green, gold and brown   DP
  NIC. Arthur G. Dove
  Pierson
Hand sewing machine, 1927   MM
  MM. 100 Amer ptrs
  Wight. Arthur G. Dove
Hand sewing machine, 1941
  NIC. Arthur G. Dove
Hardware store
  Wight. Arthur G. Dove
High noon   KW
  Wight. Arthur G. Dove (col)
Holbrook's bridge, northwest, 1938
  Wight. Arthur G. Dove (col)
Huntington harbor   DP
  DP. Catalogue
Huntington harbor no 2
  Wight. Arthur G. Dove
The inn
  Wight. Arthur G. Dove (col)
Landscape, c 1908
  NIC. Arthur G. Dove
Landscape, 1908-09
  NIC. Arthur G. Dove
Landscape in five flats
  NIC. Arthur G. Dove
Life goes by   DP
  DP. Catalogue
The lobster
  Wight. Arthur G. Dove
Long Island (oil)
  Wight. Arthur G. Dove
Long Island (water color)
  Wight. Arthur G. Dove
Mars, orange and green
  NYG. Fine art
  UNESCO. 1860-1949
  UNESCO. 1860-1955
Moon, 1935 (Zurier coll)
  Baur. New art (col)
  NBuA. Expressionism
  Wight. Arthur G. Dove
Moon, 1940 (Solinger coll)
  NIC. Arthur G. Dove
Naples yellow morning
  NIC. Arthur G. Dove

Nature symbolized, no 2, 1911   ICA
  Baur. Nature
  Baur. Revolution
  Pierson
  Wight. Arthur G. Dove
No feather pillow   NUM
  Wight. Arthur G. Dove (col)
October, 1935
  Wight. Arthur G. Dove
Out over the Sound
  NIC. Arthur G. Dove
Pagan philosophy
  WMAA. Pioneers
Parabola
  NIC. Arthur G. Dove
  Wight. Arthur G. Dove
Pieces of red, green & blue   MLL
  Wight. Arthur G. Dove (col)
Plant forms   WMAA
  Goodrich. Amer art
  Hunter. Mod Amer ptg
  Wight. Arthur G. Dove (col)
Pozzuoli red   DP
  NIC. Arthur G. Dove
Rain or snow   DP
  DP. Catalogue
  NIC. Arthur G. Dove
  Pierson
  Wight. Arthur G. Dove
Reaching waves   MM
  Brown. Amer ptg
Rise of the full moon   DP
  DP. Catalogue
  NIC. Arthur G. Dove
  Read. Concise history
Rising moon
  Wight. Arthur G. Dove (col)
Rising tide
  McCurdy
  MMA. Abstract
  Wight. Arthur G. Dove
Rooftops   MLL
  NIC. Arthur G. Dove
  Wight. Arthur G. Dove (col)
Sails
  Wight. Arthur G. Dove
Sand barge   DP
  MMA. Abstract
  Wight. Arthur G. Dove (col)
  Wight. Milestones (col)
Silver tanks and moon   PPhM
  Wight. Arthur G. Dove
Snow thaw   DP
  Larkin
  Larkin rev ed
  NIC. Arthur G. Dove
Square on the pond   MLL
  Wight. Arthur G. Dove
Storm clouds in silver
  Cheney. Primer 1958
Summer, 1935   MLL
  Wight. Arthur G. Dove (col)
Summer orchard   NUM
  NUM. Root bequest
Sunrise I, 1937   MLL
  Baur. Nature (col)
  Wight. Arthur G. Dove (col)
Sunrise II, 1937
  Wight. Arthur G. Dove
Sunset III, 1937   CtY
  CtY. Soc Anonyme
  Wight. Arthur G. Dove

DOVE, A. G.—*Continued*
Tanks   MLL
  Wight. Arthur G. Dove (col)
Team of horses
  Baur. New art
That red one   MLL
  NIC. Arthur G. Dove
  Wight. Arthur G. Dove (col)
Team of horses
  Wight. Arthur G. Dove
Telegraph pole   ICA
  Wight. Arthur G. Dove
Through a frosty moon
  DC. Privately owned
Waterfall   DP
  Wight. Arthur G. Dove (col)
Weather vane
  NIC. Arthur G. Dove
Willow tree   FaW
  Wight. Arthur G. Dove
Wind, clouds and water
  Cheney. Expressionism 1948 ed
Woodpecker   DP
  DP. Catalogue
Dove love by C. Howard
Dove of the inner eye by M. Graves
Dover baby by Unidentified artist
Doves
  Audubon, J. J. Carolina turtle-dove
  Thompson, C. Girl with dove
  Unidentified artist. Venus drawn by doves
Dowager in a wheelchair by P. Evergood
Dowdall, Eliza Hopkins (Nicoll) fl 1809
  Jarvis, J. W. Mrs George Robert Dowdall
Dowdall, George Robert. 1783-1820
  Jarvis, J. W. George Robert Dowdall
Down the ways by J. Schoener
Down to earth by A. James
Down the Mississippi in a birch-bark canoe
  by G. Catlin
Downing house, Chester county, Pennsyl-
  vania by S. Blair
Downing the nigh leader by F. Remington
Downtown fantasy by R. H. Avery
Downtown street by G. O. Coleman
Dowse, Relief. See Gill, Relief (Dowse)
Doyer by P. Guston
DOZIER, Otis, 1904-
  Fishermen
    MM. Amer ptg today
  Passage to the sea   TxF
    Pousette-Dart. Amer ptg
  Pelicans
    IU. Contemp Amer ptg, 1952
  Summer   TxD
    Pierson
Drachenfels by W. Whittredge
Dragon by W. A. Baziotes
Dragonwyck, Costumes for by D. E. Lee
Dramatis personae by J. Levine
Drapeau by M. Weber
Draped head by M. Weber
Drawing a bead on a woodchuck by J. G.
  Chapman
Drayton, Charlotte. See Manigault, Char-
  lotte (Drayton)
Drayton, Maria Miles (Heyward) See Hey-
  ward, Maria Miles

Drayton, Mrs William. See Heyward, Maria
  Miles
The **dream** by M. Beckmann
The **dream** by A. B. Davies
The **dream** by C. S. Price
Dream catch by P. Evergood
Dream of a good life by M. Siporin
Dream of Arcadia by T. Cole
Dream of Columbus by W. J. Hubard
Dream of flying by M. Hoff
Dream ride by W. J. Glackens
The **dreamer** by C. Beaux
DREIER, Dorothea A. 1870-1923
  Flower market at Geneva   CtY
    CtY. Soc Anonyme
  New York: the Little church around the
    corner   CtY
    CtY. Soc Anonyme
  Portrait of the artist
  Shirlaw, W. Dorothea A. Dreier
DREIER, Katherine Sophie, 1877-
  Abstract portrait of Marcel Duchamp
                                                           MMA
    MMA. Abstract
  Abstract portrait of Savadsky
    Cheney. Expressionism 1948 ed
  Explosion   CtY
    CtY. Soc Anonyme

          Portrait of the artist
  Goldthwaite, A. Katherine S. Dreier
Dress rehearsal by M. B. Prendergast
Dressing room by W. Kuhn
Dressmaker's shop by R. Soyer
DREWES, Werner, 1899-
  Night fantasy   CtY
    CtY. Soc Anonyme
  Re-awakening   WMAA
    CoS. New accessions USA, 1948
  Still life, New York   IBM
    Bazin (col)
Drift for summer by M. Tobey
Driftwood by E. H. Betts
Driftwood by W. Homer
Driftwood by F. James
Driftwood by Z. L. Sepeshy
Driftwood, Monegan by E. Fiene
Driftwood, North Pacific by B. J. O. Nord-
  feldt
DRIGGS, Elsie, 1898-
  Pittsburgh, 1927   WMAA
    MnMW. Precisionist view
The **drive,** Central Park by W. J. Glackens
Drought and downpour by M. Dixon
Drought-stricken area by A. Hogue
Drowsy company by H. G. Keller
Drugstore by S. Wilson
DRUMLEVITCH, Seymour, 1923-
  Bronx bridge   NBuA
    CoS. New accessions USA, 1952
  Roman aqueduct   OYB
    OYB. Annual 1954
    OYB. Supplement
  Ruins
    WMAA. Annual ex, 1955
  Synagogue
    CanO. Hirshhorn coll (col)

Drums, Indian and word of God by M. Tobey

Dry goods and notions by D. G. Blythe

Dry nets by L. W. Quanchi

Drying codfish in Brittany by Leonid

Duane, Anthony, fl 1725
  Unidentified artist. Anthony Duane

DU BACK, Charles Steven
  Summer
    WMAA. Contemp Amer ptg, 1959/60

DUBIN, Ralph, 1918-
  Plaster
    VR. Amer ptg, 1954

Dublin by G. Hartigan

Dublin and environs by L. MacIver

Dublin pool by G. R. Beal

Dubocq, Mme, fl 1807
  Peale, J. Mme Dubocq and her four children

DU BOIS, Guy Pène, 1884-1958
  Americans in Paris   MMA
    Lewisohn
  Another expulsion
    NAD. Annual ex, spring 1950
  Bar
    Brown. Amer ptg
  The beauty
    PPC. Ptg in the U. S. 1949
  The doll and the monster   MM
    MM. 100 Amer ptrs
    Pierson
    WMAA. Juliana Force
  Glitter
    OYB. Annual 1954
  Morning, Paris cafe   WMAA
    NYG. Fine art
    Pierson
  Opera box   WMAA
    Larkin rev ed
  Restaurant
    Gruskin
  Shovel hats   WMAA
    WMAA. Sara Roby
  Waiter
    Cheney. Story 1958 ed
  Window in the Union club
    Baur. Revolution
  Woman with cigarette   WMAA
    Goodrich. Amer art

Du Bosc, Mary. See Wragg, Mary (du Bosc)

DUBREUIL, V.
  Barrels of money
    Frankenstein. After the hunt

Dubuque, Iowa by J. C. Wild

DUCA, Alfred Milton, 1920-
  Autumnal
    IU. Contemp Amer ptg, 1951
  The carob tree
    IU. Contemp Amer ptg & sculp, 1953

DU CASSE, Ralph Saule, 1916-
  Botafogo
    IU. Contemp Amer Ptg & sculp, 1957
  The grandest of Noo
    IU. Contemp Amer ptg & sculp, 1961
  The kiss
    IU. Contemp Amer ptg & sculp, 1953
  St George and the calla lillies
    VR. Amer ptg, 1958

San Francisco bay
    IU. Contemp Amer ptg & sculp, 1955   NNSG
    Strahmutchi
    NNSG. Handbook
    NNSG. Younger Amer ptrs

Duchamp, Marcel, 1887-
  Dreier, K. S. Abstract portrait of Marcel Duchamp

Duché, Jacob, 1737?-1798
  Duché, T. S. Rev Jacob Duché and Thomas Spence Duché

DUCHÉ, Thomas Spence, 1763-1790
  Jacob and Thomas Spence Duché   PH
    Chew. 250 years of art

Duck decoy by K. Knaths

Duck hunters on the Hoboken marshes by W. T. Ranney

Duck pond by W. De Kooning

Duck shooting by E. Moran

Duck shooting by A. F. Tait

Duckblind by W. R. Derrick

Ducks
  Audubon, J. J. Red-breasted merganser
  Audubon, J. J. Shoveller duck
  Austin, W. Mandarin duck
  Benson, F. W. Currituck marshes, North Carolina
  Benson, F. W. Redhead ducks
  Dasburg, A. Ducks
  Derrick, W. R. Duckblind
  Earle, L. C. Escape
  Graves, M. Wounded scoter
  Hartley, M. Labrador ducks
  Knap, N. D. The flight
  Knaths, K. Duck flight
  Scott, P. M. Pintails

Duclair on Seine by H. D. Martin

Dudley, Charles, 1737-1797
  Alexander, C. J. Charles Dudley

Dudley, Kitty (Crooke)
  Alexander, C. J. Mrs Charles Dudley

DUDLEY, Robert, fl 1866
  Awaiting the reply over the trans-Atlantic cable   MM
    Davidson v 1
  Splicing the cable   MM
    U.S. National Capital sesquicentennial com

Duel and pantomime by L. Michael

Duel of the entomologist by F. Ruvolo

DUGMORE, Edward, 1915-
  Number six
    PPC. International ex, 1955
  Painting 1960-D   NBuA
    NBuA. Acquisitions 1959-1961

Dull lecture by G. S. Newton

Dull story by G. C. Bingham

Dulles, Mary Elizabeth, fl 1806
  Malbone, E. G. Mary Elizabeth Dulles

Dummy by D. W. Ellis

Dummy by C. Maringer

DU MOND, Frank Vincent, 1865-1951
  Fishing companions
    NSP. Sportscapes

DUNCAN, Frank Davenport, 1915-
  Condition at Antietam
    PPC. International ex, 1950
  A condition of New England
    PPC. Ptg in the U.S. 1949

DUNCAN, F. D.—*Continued*
Le Faou
    IU. Contemp Amer ptg & sculp, 1955
Mallorca III
    PA. Annual ex, 1954
Through the window
    IU. Contemp Amer ptg, 1952
Through to the sea
    IU. Contemp Amer ptg, 1948
Within autumn
    Pousette-Dart. Amer ptg
Duncan, Isadora, 1877-1927
    Walkowitz, A. Three dance abstractions:
        Isadora Duncan
DUNCANSON, Robert S. 1821-1871
Blue hole on the Little Miami river
                                        OCiM
    OCiM. Rediscoveries
    Pierson
Uncle Tom and Little Eva   MiD
    OCiM. Rediscoveries
Dunes by C. H. Demuth
Dunes and breakwaters by L. Feininger
Dunes and marshes by D. Macknight
Dunes at Marshfield by W. Homer
Dunes, Baltic by L. Feininger
Dunes with ray of light II by L. Feininger
DUNKERLEY, Joseph, fl 1783-1787
Ebenezer Storer (possibly after Copley)
                                        CtY
    CtY. Portrait index

Attributed works

Charles Bulfinch   MB
    MB. New England miniatures
Mrs Charles Bulfinch   MB
    MB. New England miniatures
DUNLAP, William, 1766-1839
Artist showing his picture of a scene from
    "Hamlet" to his parents   NNHS
    Richardson. Ptg in America
David Van Horne   MiD
    Pierson
Dunlap family   NNHS
    ICA. From colony to nation
    Pierson
Samuel Griffin   DN
    DN. Amer primitive ptgs, pt 1
Scene from the dramatization of James
    Fenimore Cooper's novel "The Spy"
                                        NCHA
    Davidson v2
Self-portrait   CtY
    CtY. Portrait index
Dunlap family, fl 1788
    Dunlap, W. Dunlap family
Dunn, Mary. See Thorp, Mary (Dunn)
DUNN, Robert, 1932-
Figures and still life
    IU./ Contemp Amer ptg & sculp, 1959
Duo I by J. Tworkov
Duograph by I. R. Pereira
Duran, Carolus. See Carolus-Duran
DURAND, Asher Brown, 1796-1886
Aaron Belknap   NNHS
    NNHS. Waldron Phoenix Belknap coll
Aaron Betts Belknap   NNHS
    NNHS. Waldron Phoenix Belknap coll

Andrew Jackson   NNHS
    U.S. National Capital sesquicentennial
        com
Babbling brook   MB
    MB. Karolik coll
Beeches   MM
    Bazin
Capture of Major André   MWM
    Cowdrey v 1
    Pierson
Catskill Clove   NNCe
    Pierson
Catskill mountains near Shandaken
    NYG. Fine art
A Catskill stream   NBM
    Mendelowitz
Early morning, Cold Spring, New York
                                        NJMo
    NJMo. Forty years
    NJMo. Your Montclair art museum
Hudson at Rhinebeck   GAtM
    GAtM. Holbrook collection
Hunter   ATeS
    ATeS. Collection
In the woods   MAC
    NUM. Art across America
In the woods   MM
    Upjohn
Kindred spirits   NNPL
    Barker. Amer ptg
    Born
    Canaday
    Craven. Rainbow book
    CtHW. Thomas Cole
    Flexner. Amer ptg
    Flexner. Short history
    Larkin
    Larkin rev ed
    Pierson
    Richardson. Ptg in America
    Roos
    Time. 300 years (col)
    Walker. Ptgs from America
Lake George, New York   MB
    MB. Karolik coll
Landscape   InIJ
    InIJ. 105 ptgs
Landscape   NJN
    NJN. Early N. J. artists
Mrs Aaron Belknap   NNHS
    NNHS. Waldron Phoenix Belknap coll
Mrs Durand and her sister   NJN
    Pierson
Mrs Nicholas William Stuyvesant NNHS
    Vail. Stuyvesant ports
Monument mountain, Berkshires   MiD
    NYG. Fine art
    UNESCO. Prior to 1860
    UNESCO. Prior to 1860 3d ed
Morning of life   NAD
    NAD. Amer tradition
Mountain valley
    Sears. Highlights
North Mountain reservation, South Orange,
    New Jersey
    Sears. Highlights
The old oak   NNHS
    Pierson
Roman head   NNHS
    MiD. Travelers in Arcadia
Sunday morning   NNHS
    Born
    NYG. Fine art (col)

DURRIE, G. H.—*Continued*
Winter landscape; gathering wood   MB
  MB. Karolik coll
  Mendelowitz
Winter scene (Fleischman coll)
  WiMiA. Amer ptg 1760-1960
Winter scene (Hoppin coll)
  CtHW. Durrie
Winter scene in New England   CtY
  CtHW. Durrie
Winter scene, Jones' inn
  CtHW. Durrie
Wood for winter   NNHS
  Born
  CtHW. Durrie
  Pierson
Woodsman in winter
  CtHW. Durrie
Durrie, John, 1792-1857
  Durrie, G. H. John Durrie
Dusenberg, Frank
  Dove, A. G. Frank Dusenberg
Dusk by W. A. Baziotes
Dusk by W. Chaiken
Dusk by K. Knaths
Dusk at Fuji by P. Evergood
Dust bowl by A. Hogue
Dust, drought and destruction by W. C.
  Palmer
Dust storm, Fifth avenue by J. Sloan
Dusty road in July by C. E. Burchfield
Dutch girl in white by R. Henri
Dutch Joe by R. Henri
Dutch lunch by S. Rosen
DUVENECK, Frank, 1848-1919
  A boy   OYB
  OYB. Catalogue 1951
  The bridges, Florence   MoSL
  MoSL. Handbook 1953
  The crimson gown (Mrs Mary Goddard
    Williams   NoCR
  NoCR. Catalogue
  Georg von Hoesslin   MiD
  Canaday
  Head of an old man   DNC
  DNC. Gellatly coll, 1954
  Henry James
  NAD. Amer tradition
  Mary Cabot Wheelwright   NBM
  Pierson
  Mrs Mary Goddard Williams. See The
    crimson gown
  Music master
  Baur. Revolution
  Old town brook, Polling, Bavaria   OCiM
  Born
  Turkish page   PA
  Pierson
  Richardson. Ptg in America
  Venetian girl   OCl
  OCl. Handbook
  Whistling boy   OCiM
  Bauer. Amer ptg
  Brown. Amer ptg
  DC. De gustibus
  OCiM. Guide
  Pierson
  Roos

Woman with forget-me-nots   OCiM
  Pierson
Young man   NBM
  Mendelowitz
Young man (Nichols coll)
  Larkin
    Portrait of the artist
Chase, W. M. Duvenek in the studio
Chase, W. M. Duveneck painting the
  Turkish page
Duyckinck, Anna (Rapalje) 1733-1811
  Kilburn, L. Mrs Gerardus Duyckinck II
DUYCKINCK, Evert, 1667-1724?
  Mrs Gerardus Beekman (Magdalen
    Abeel) (1)
  Belknap
    Attributed works
  Cornelia Beekman
  Belknap
  Mrs Gerardus Beekman (Magdalen
    Beekman) (2)
  Belknap
  Mrs William Beekman (1)
  Belknap
  Mrs William Beekman (2)
  Belknap
  William Beekman
  Belknap
DUYCKINCK, Gerardus, 1695-1745?
    Attributed works
  Children of Jacob Franks (Phila and
    David Franks)   NNAJ
  Belknap
  Flexner. First flowers (here as De
    Peyster manner)
  Elizabeth Van Brugh   NNHS
  Flexner. First flowers (here as De
    Peyster manner)
  Gerardus Beekman
  Belknap
  Joseph(?) Hallett   NNHS
  Belknap
  Mrs Henry Van Rensselaer   NNHS
  Belknap
  Mrs Jacob Franks   NNAJ
  Belknap
  Mrs Joseph(?) Hallett   NNHS
  Belknap
  Mrs Moses Levy   NNMC
  Belknap
  Phila Franks   NNAJ
  Belknap
  William Beekman
  Belknap

    Portrait of the artist
  Kilburn, L. Gerardus Duyckinck II
Duyckinck, Mrs Gerardus. See Duyckinck,
  Anna (Rapalje)
DUYCKINCK, Gerrit, 1660-c 1710
  Mrs Augustus Jay   NNHS
  Belknap
  Vail. Stuyvesant ports
  Mrs Gerrit Duyckinck   NNHS
  Barker. Amer ptg
  Belknap
  Flexner. First flowers
  Larkin
  Larkin rev ed
  Mendelowitz
  Pierson

DUYCKINCK, Gerrit—*Continued*
Self-portrait   NNHS
 Belknap
 Flexner. First flowers
 Pierson
Attributed works
Young lady   DN
 Belknap
 DN. Amer primitive ptgs, pt 1
Duyckinck, Maria (Abeel) 1666-1738
 Duyckinck, Gerrit. Mrs Gerrit Duyckinck
Duyckinck, Sarah. See Bancker, Sarah
 (Duyckinck)
Dwarf by W. A. Baziotes
Dwelling by C. A. Morris
Dwight, Christiana (Broughton) fl 1747
 Theus, J. Christiana Broughton (copy of
  pastel by Henrietta Johnston)
Dwight, Mrs Daniel. See Dwight, Christiana
 (Broughton)
Dwight, Theodore, 1764-1846
 Ames, E. Theodore Dwight
Dwight, Timothy, 1752-1817
 Trumbull, J. Timothy Dwight
Dwight, Timothy, 1828-1916
 Tarbell, E. C. Timothy Dwight
 Weir, J. F. The Theological of Yale uni-
  versity
DYER, Briggs, 1911-
 Tabletop   ATU
  ATU. Coll of Amer art
Dyer, Mrs Charles Gifford. See Dyer, May
 (Anthony)
Dyer, May (Anthony) 1850-1914
 Sargent, J. S. Mrs Charles Gifford Dyer
Dying Hercules by S. F. B. Morse
Dying steer by R. Lebrun
Dynasty by K. Okada
Dysart, Winifred
 Fuller, G. Winifred Dysart
DZUBAS, Friedelbald, 1915-
 Arcadia II
  WMAA. Annual ex, 1958
 Death of the general   CtY
  CtY. Soc Anonyme

E

E, 1915 by M. Hartley
E—1953 by J. D. Brooks
E pluribus unum by M. Tobey
EADES, Luis, 1923-
 War prisoners   OYB
  OYB. Annual 1958
  OYB. Supplement 1959
Eagle cliff, Franconia Notch, New Hamp-
 shire by J. Cropsey
Eagle cliff, New Hampshire by J. F.
 Cropsey
Eagle in the rock by M. Graves
Eagles
 Audubon, J. J. Sea eagle (so called)
 Graves, M. Eagle
 Unidentified artist. Eagle and snake
 Unidentified artist. Screaming eagle

Eakins, Benjamin, 1818-1899?
 Eakins, T. Benjamin Eakins
Eakins, Susan Hannah (MacDowell) 1852-
 1938
 Eakins, T. Lady with a setter dog
EAKINS, Thomas, 1844-1916
 A. W. Lee
  Porter. Thomas Eakins
  WiMiA. Amer ptg 1760-1960
 The actress   PPhM
  Bazin (col detail)
 Addie   PPhM
  Baur. Amer ptg
  Baur. Revolution
 Agnew clinic   PPhUn
  Barker. Amer ptg
  Canaday
  Canaday (detail)
  Craven. Rainbow book
  Craven. Treasury 1952 ed
  Flexner. Amer ptg
  Flexner. Short history
  PA. Annual ex, 1955
  Pierson
  Porter. Thomas Eakins
  Robb. Harper history
  Roos
  U.S. National Capital sesquicentennial
  com
 An Arcadian
  Porter. Thomas Eakins
 Arthur B. Frost   PPhM
  Robb. Art 1953 ed
 Baby at play
  CtY. Yale alumni
  Porter. Thomas Eakins
 Baseball players, 1875   RPS
  Davidson v2
  NYG. Fine art
  Porter. Thomas Eakins
  U.S. National Capital sesquicentennial
  com
 Beatrice Fenton. See Coral necklace
 Benjamin Eakins   PPhM
  Cheney. Story 1958 ed
  Porter. Thomas Eakins
 Benjamin Howard Rand PPhJ
  Porter. Thomas Eakins
 Between rounds   PPhM
  Pierson
  Porter. Thomas Eakins (col)
  Robb. Art 1953 ed
  Taylor. Fifty centuries, 1954 ed (col)
  Time. 300 years (col)
  U.S. National Capital sesquicentennial
  com
 The Bohemian (Franklin Schenk) PPhM
  Porter. Thomas Eakins
 Bringing home the moose
  NSP. Sportscapes
 Cardinal Martinelli
  Porter. Thomas Eakins
 Cello player   PA
  PA. Annual ex, 1955
 Charles Haseltine   NJMo
  NJMo. Forty years
  NJMo. Your Montclair art museum
 Charles Lewis Fussel   PR
  PR. Catalogue
 Charles Linford, the artist IBM
  Porter. Thomas Eakins

EAKINS, Thomas—*Continued*

Chess players   MM
  Pierson
  Porter. Thomas Eakins
Concert singer (Weda Cook)   PPhM
  Craven. Treasury 1952 ed (col)
  DC. 25 biennial ex, 1957
  Larkin (detail)
  Larkin rev ed
  PA. Annual ex, 1955
  Pierson
  Porter. Thomas Eakins
  Time. 300 years (col)
Coral necklace (Beatrice Fenton)   OYB
  OYB. Accessions
  OYB. Supplement 1959
Cowboys in the Bad Lands
  Rathbone
  U.S. National Capital sesquicentennial com
Crucifixion   PPhM
  Porter. Thomas Eakins
Crucifixion, Study for
  Chew. 250 years of art
Elinor S. F. Pue   VR
  Porter. Thomas Eakins
Elizabeth at the piano   MAP
  Porter. Thomas Eakins
Ernest Lee Parker
  Porter. Thomas Eakins
Fairman Rogers four-in-hand   PPhM
  Porter. Thomas Eakins (col)
  Time. 300 years (col)
  U.S. National Capital sesquicentennial com
Frank Hamilton Cushing   OkTT
  Porter. Thomas Eakins
Frank Jay St John
  WiMiA. Amer ptg 1760-1960
Franklin Schenk. See The Bohemian
George Cadwalader   OYB
  OYB. Catalogue 1951
Gross clinic   PPhJ
  Canaday
  Janson. Key monuments
  Janson. Picture history
  Larkin
  Larkin rev ed
  Myers. Art
  PA. Annual ex, 1955
  Pierson
  Porter. Thomas Eakins
  Richardson. Ptg in America
Gross clinic, Sketch for   PPhM
  Chew. 250 years of art
  Porter. Thomas Eakins
Harrison S. Morris
  PA. Annual ex, 1953
Head of young woman
  Porter. Thomas Eakins
Henry A. Rowland   MAP
  Pierson
  Porter. Thomas Eakins
Home scene   NBM
  Porter. Thomas Eakins
Horatio C. Wood   MiD
  Porter. Thomas Eakins
Hunting
  MiD. Coll in progress
  WiMiA. Amer ptg 1760-1960

John Biglen in a single scull   CtY
  NYG. Fine art
  Robb. Harper history (col)
John Biglen in a single scull   MM
  Davidson v2
  McCurdy
  Porter. Thomas Eakins
John H. Brinton
  Porter. Thomas Eakins
John McClure Hamilton   CtHW
  CtHW. Handbook
John McClure Hamilton   GAtM
  GAtM. Holbrook collection
Joseph Leidy jr. See Man with red necktie
Katherine
  Porter. Thomas Eakins
Lady with a setter dog (Mrs Eakins)   MM
  Lee. Art then and now
  Pierson
  Porter. Thomas Eakins
Letitia Wilson Jordan Bacon   NBM
  MoSL. 40 masterpieces
  PA. Annual ex, 1955
  Pierson
  Porter. Thomas Eakins
Louis N. Kenton. See The thinker
Man with red necktie (Dr Joseph Leidy jr)   NJN
  Porter. Thomas Eakins
Margaret
  Porter. Thomas Eakins
Marguerite in skating costume   PPhM
  Porter. Thomas Eakins
Maud Cook (Young woman in pink dress)
  Porter. Thomas Eakins
Max Schmitt in a single scull   MM
  Barker. Amer ptg
  Canaday
  Lewisohn
  Mendelowitz
  NBuA. Expressionism
  PA. Annual ex, 1955
  Pierson
  Porter. Thomas Eakins (col)
  Roos
  Taylor. Fifty centuries, 1954 ed (col)
  Time. 300 years (col)
Maybelle
  Porter. Thomas Eakins (col)
Mending the net   PPhM
  Canaday
  Canaday (detail)
Miss Parker. See Old-fashioned dress
Miss Van Buren   DP
  Canaday (col)
  DP. Catalogue
  Pierson
  Porter. Thomas Eakins
  Walker. Ptgs from America (col)
Mrs Anna M. Kershaw
  Porter. Thomas Eakins
Mrs Eakins. See Lady with a setter dog
Mrs Edith Mahon   MNS
  Larkin
  Larkin rev ed
Mrs Frank Hamilton Cushing   PPhM
  Porter. Thomas Eakins
Mrs Gilbert Parker   MB
  Porter. Thomas Eakins

Mrs M. S. Stokes   NCa
   Porter. Thomas Eakins
Mrs S   NCa
   NUM. Art across America
Mrs Thomas Eakins
   PA. Annual ex, 1955
Mrs William D. Frishmuth   PPhM
   Canaday
   Craven. Treasury 1952 ed
Mrs William Shaw Word
   Porter. Thomas Eakins
Monsignor Diomede Falconio   DN
   Porter. Thomas Eakins (col)
Music   NBuA
   Porter. Thomas Eakins
   PPC. Amer classics
Musicians rehearsing   PPhM
   Canaday
Nude back
   Porter. Thomas Eakins
Oarsmen   PPhM
   Chew. 250 years of art
   Porter. Thomas Eakins
Oarsmen on the Schuylkill   NBM
   Porter. Thomas Eakins
Oboe player (Benjamin Sharp)   PPhM
   Chew. 250 years of art
Old-fashioned dress (Miss Parker)
       PPhM
   Porter. Thomas Eakins
On the Delaware
   Porter. Thomas Eakins
Pathetic song   DC
   Barker. Amer ptg
   DC. De gustibus
   DC. Masterpieces
   Gardner 1959 ed
   Mendelowitz
   MiD. Ptg in America
   Pierson
   Richardson. Ptg in America
The pianist (Stanley Addicks)   InIJ
   InIJ. 105 ptgs
Portrait of a lady (Mrs James Mapes
   Dodge)   PPhM
   Porter. Thomas Eakins
Professionals at rehearsal   PPhM
   Porter. Thomas Eakins
Pushing for rail   MM
   NYG. Fine art
Rail shooting. See Will Schuster and
   black man going shooting for rail
Riter Fitzgerald, Sketch for portrait
   (Fleischman coll)
   MiD. Coll in progress
   WiMiA. Amer ptg 1760-1960
Robert M. Lindsay, the print collector
       MiD
   MiD. Treasures
   Porter. Thomas Eakins
Robert M. Lindsay, Sketch for portrait
       MiD
   Porter. Thomas Eakins
Sailboats racing on the Delaware   PPhM
   Porter. Thomas Eakins
Sailing   PPhM
   Craven. Treasury 1952 ed
   NYG. Fine art

Sailing boats   PPhM
   Richardson. Ptg in America
Salutat   MAP
   Canaday
   Hunter. Mod Amer ptg
   Porter. Thomas Eakins (col)
   Roos
Samuel Murray
   Porter. Thomas Eakins
Self-portrait, c 1902   NAD
   NAD. Amer tradition
   PA. Annual ex, 1955
   Porter. Thomas Eakins
Signora Gomez d'Arza   MM
   McKinney
   MM. 100 Amer ptrs
   Porter. Thomas Eakins (col)
Stanley Addicks. See The pianist
Starting out after rail   MB
   PA. Annual ex, 1955
Starting out after rail   KW
   Pierson
   Porter. Thomas Eakins (col)
Street scene in Seville
   Porter. Thomas Eakins
Study of a girl's head
   Porter. Thomas Eakins   PPhM
The swimming hole   TxF
   PA. Annual ex, 1955
   Pierson
   Porter. Thomas Eakins (col)
   Time. 300 years (col)
Taking the count   CtY
   Seiberling
Taking the count, Study for head of
   referee
   Porter. Thomas Eakins (col)
The thinker (Louis N. Kenton)   MM
   Myers. Art
   PA. Annual ex, 1955
   Pierson
Thomas Sharp. See Oboe player
Turning the stake boat   OCl
   OCl. Handbook
   Pierson
   Porter. Thomas Eakins
   Walker. Ptgs from America
The violinist
   Porter. Thomas Eakins
Walt Whitman   PA
   Craven. Rainbow book
   Craven. Treasury 1952 ed
   Mendelowitz
   Pierson
   Porter. Thomas Eakins (col)
   Robb. Harper history
   Roos
   Time. 300 Years (col)
Weda Cook. See Concert singer
Will Schuster and black man going shoot-
   ing for rail (Rail shooting)
   Craven. Treasury 1952 ed (col)
   CtY. Yale alumni
   Porter. Thomas Eakins
   UNESCO. 1860-1949
   UNESCO. 1860-1955
William McDowell
   Porter. Thomas Eakins
William Rush and his model   HaH
   Porter. Thomas Eakins

EAKINS, Thomas—*Continued*
William Rush carving his allegorical figure
    of the Schuylkill river   NBM
  Bazin
  CtY. Yale alumni
  NBuA. Fifty ptgs
  Pierson
  Porter. Thomas Eakins (col)
William Rush carving his allegorical figure
    of the Schuylkill river   PPhM
  Larkin rev ed (col detail)
  Pierson
  Porter. Thomas Eakins (col)
  Time. 300 years (col)
  Walker. Ptgs from America
William Smith Forbes   PPhJ
  Porter. Thomas Eakins
A woman   ATeS
  ATeS. Collection
Wrestlers, 1889   NAD
  Porter. Thomas Eakins
Wrestlers, 1898   PPhM
  Chew. 250 years of art
Wrestlers, Sketch for   PPhM
  Porter. Thomas Eakins
Young man   PPhM
  Porter. Thomas Eakins
Young woman in pink dress. See Maud
  Cook
Youth playing fife
  Porter. Thomas Eakins
Eakins, Mrs Thomas. See Eakins, Susan
  Hannah (MacDowell)
EARL, Ralph, 1751-1801
Amos Doolittle   CtNL
  NUM. Art across America
Andrew Jackson   CtY
  Larkin (detail)
Baron von Steuben   CtY
  Pierson
  Roos
Battle of Concord   NNPL
  Davidson v 1
Battles of Lexington and Concord. See
  British troops at Concord
Benjamin Tallmadge and his son William
    CtLH
  Pierson
British troops at Concord (Battles of Lex-
  ington and Concord)
  Flexner. Light of distant skies
  Ford. Pictorial folk art
Daniel Boardman   DN
  Flexner. Light of distant skies
Elijah Boardman
  Larkin
  Larkin rev ed
Gabriel Christie   MoKN
  MoKN. Handbook
Lady Williams and child   MM
  Flexner. Light of distant skies
Looking east from Denny hill
  Barker. Amer ptg
  Pierson
Lucy Bradley   MiD
  MiD. Treasures
Mrs Benjamin Tallmadge and son and
  daughter   CtLH
  ICA. From colony to nation
  Pierson

Mrs Moses Seymour and her son Epaphro-
  ditus   MoSL
  MoSL. 50 masterworks
  MoSL. Handbook 1953
Mrs William Moseley and her son Charles
    CtY
  Larkin
  Larkin rev ed
  Pierson
Mrs William Taylor and child   NBuA
  NBuA. Catalogue of the ptgs
  Pierson
  OCiM. Rediscoveries
Nathaniel Shaw Woodbridge and his
  daughter Mary
  CtY. Yale alumni
Oliver Ellsworth and his wife   CtHW
  CtHW. Handbook (col)
  Pierson
  Robb. Harper history
Roger Sherman   CtY
  Barker. Amer ptg
  Canaday
  CtY. Portrait index
  Davidson v2
  Flexner. Amer ptg
  Flexner. Light of distant skies
  Flexner. Short history
  ICA. From colony to nation
  Mendelowitz
  MoSL. 40 masterpieces
  Pierson
  Richardson. Ptg in America
  Time. 300 years (col)
Stryker sisters   OYB
  OYB. Catalogue 1951
View of the town of Concord, Massa-
  chusetts, c 1775
  Lipman. Primitive ptrs
William Austin   CtY
  Roos
William Carpenter   MWM
  NYG. Fine art
  Pierson
William Taylor   NBuA
  Barker. Amer ptg
  Born
  ICA. From colony to nation
  NBuA. Catalogue of the ptgs
  OCiM. Rediscoveries
  Pierson
EARL, Ralph Eleasar Whitesides, 1788-
  1837
Andrew Jackson (Lee coll)   ·
  DC. Privately owned
Andrew Jackson   PH
  Ford. Edward Hicks
Andrew Jackson   CtY
  Larkin rev ed
Andrew Jackson   NoCR
  NoCR. Catalogue
Family portrait   DN
  DN. Amer primitive ptgs, pt 1
EARLE, Lawrence Carmichael, 1845-1921
Escape
  NSP. Sportscape
Earle, Ralph. See Earl, Ralph
Early by L. MacIver
Early American abstract by M. Weber
Early autumn by M. Peck

Early autumn snow by R. H. Brown
Early evening by M. B. Prendergast
Early houses, Provincetown by C. H. Demuth
Early Italy by H. B. McCarter
Early morning after a storm at sea by W. Homer
Early morning, Cold Spring, New York by A. B. Durand
Early morning, Paris by O. M. Pleissner
Early morning, Paris by E. Shinn
Early spring by E. Lawson
Early spring by T. C. Steele
Early spring—South side by G. Z. Antreasian
Early spring tree by G. O'Keeffe
Early springtime on the farm by A. M. R. Moses
Early summer by M. B. Prendergast
Early summer, Vermont by E. Lawson
Early Sunday morning by E. Hopper
Early thaw by A. Obrosey
Earth by A. Alcalay
Earth and green by M. Rothko
Earth glow by K. Okada
Earth legend by L. Calcagno
Earth machines by F. Martin
Earth rhythms by R. Jonson
The easel by R. B. Motherwell
East barrier by J. Tworkov
East Charleston school by P. S. Sample
East field by T. Stamos
East Hampton, Long Island by W. Homer
East New York by H. Rose
East of Easter by R. Ruben
East of Lexington by K. Zerbe
East of the Bowery by J. Myers
East Riding of Yorkshire yeomanry disembarking from H. M. S. Cressy by R. A. Parker
East river by E. D. Boit
East river by J. E. Heliker
East river by J. Marin
East river by M. B. Prendergast
East river dock by M. R. Cooper
East river from Brooklyn by W. J. Glackens
East river nocturne by G. L. K. Morris
East river rooftops by G. A. Picken
East river, snow by R. Henri
East rock from the south by G. H. Durrie
East rock, New Haven by G. H. Durrie
East Sandwich marshes by D. Macknight
East Tenth street jungle by R. Marsh
East Twelfth street by B. Shahn
East wind by S. Wilson
East wind over Weehawken by E. Hopper
Easter and the totem by J. Pollock
Easter bonnet by G. Layton
Easter morning by W. De Kooning
Easter morning on Eye street by R. F. Lahey

Eastern elegy by M. Greenwood
Eastern memory by M. Greenwood
Eastern point, Prout's neck by W. Homer
Eastern tranquillity by C. C. Ross
Eastern twilight by R. Iwamoto
Eastman, Constance
  Lockman, D. M. Constance Eastman
EASTMAN, Seth, 1808-1875
  Dakota encampment   MnSJ
    Rathbone
  Dakota village   MnSJ
    Morgan
    Rathbone
  Death whoop
    McCracken. Portrait of the old west
  Dog dance of the Dakotahs
    McCracken. Portrait of the old west
  Emigrants attacked by the Comanches   MnSJ
    Rathbone
  Falls of St Anthony   MnSJ
    Rathbone
  Hunting buffalo in winter
    McCracken. Portrait of the old west
  Indian attack   MM
    Davidson v 1
  Indian sugar camp   MnSJ
    Rathbone
  Indians traveling   MnSJ
    Morgan
    Rathbone
  Lacrosse playing among the Sioux Indians   DC
    DC. Masterpieces
    McCracken. Portrait of the old west (col)
    Pierson
    Rathbone (col)
  Laughing waters   MnSJ
    Rathbone
  Mourning for the dead
    Pierson
  Sioux Indians breaking up camp   MB
    MB. Karolik coll
    Pierson
  Squaws playing ball on the prairie   MCH
    Pierson
  View of Fort Snelling   MnMI
    Born
    Davidson v 1
    U.S. National Capital sesquicentennial com
  Wenona's leap   MnSJ
    Rathbone
EASTMAN, William
  Studio table   OCl
    OCl. Handbook
Eastman children, fl 1850
  Balis, C. George and Emma Eastman
Easton, Pennsylvania
  Cartney, M. E. M. Court house and Centre square, Easton
  Cartney, M. E. M. Court house, Easton
  Unidentified artist. Easton
  Weygandt, C. E. Easton
Easy by L. Lewitin
Eaton family memorial by S. Jordan
L'eau nue by Y. Tanguy
Eau Sucre river by A. J. Miller

Ebsworth, Elizabeth. See Swinton, Elizabeth (Ebsworth)

Ecce Homo by U. Romano

Echo by J. Pollock

Echo by T. Stamos

Echo from the sea by P. L. Dike

Echo lake by T. Doughty

Echo of a dream by A. Salemme

Ecke, Mrs Gustav. See Tseng Yu-ho

Ecstasy by P. Mangravite

Ecstatic gander by M. Graves

Ecuador
Church, F. E. Cotopaxi, Ecuador
Church, F. E. Housetop in Ecuador

Eddy, Arthur Jerome, 1859-1920
Whistler, J. A. M. Arthur Jerome Eddy

Eddy, Horace Wilson, 1840-1850
Stock, J. W. Horace Wilson Eddy

EDDY, Oliver Tarbell, 1799-1868
Four youngest children of William Rankin and Abigail Ogden Rankin   NJN
NJN. Early N. J. artists

Eden by H. Frankenthaler

Edgartown, Massachusetts
Chapin, F. Harbor at Edgartown

Edge of August by M. Tobey

Edge of evening by N. Meitzler

Edge of the east water by J. Whorf

Edge of the field by A. N. Wyeth

Edge of the grove by M. B. Prendergast

Edge of town by C. E. Burchfield

Edgehill by R. Smith

Edgehill road, Philadelphia by R. Smith

Edgell, Mary L. fl 1830
Peckham, R. Memorial portrait of Mary L. Edgell

EDIE, Stuart Carson, 1908-
Still life   ATU
ATU. Coll of Amer art

Editorial by J. Hirsch

EDMONDS, Francis William 1806-1863
New scholar
Cowdrey v 1
Real estate agent offering valuable lots
Davidson v2
Sparking
Cowdrey v 1

EDMONDSON, Leonard, 1916-
Equivalent restraint
IU. Contemp Amer ptg & sculp, 1953
Experience of meaning
WMAA. Annual ex, 1952
External dictation
IU. Contemp Amer ptg & sculp, 1955
Fashion and purport
NNSG. Younger Amer ptrs
Passage   VR
CoS. New accessions USA, 1958
VR. Amer ptg, 1958

Edwards, Abigail (Fowles)
Badgar, J. Mrs John Edwards

EDWARDS, Ethel
Landscape in ivory
IU. Contemp Amer ptg & sculp, 1955

Edwards, Mrs John. See Edwards, Abigail (Fowle)

Edwards, John Cummings, fl 1844
Bingham, G. C. John Cummings Edwards

Edwards, Jonathan, 1703-1758
Badger, J. Jonathan Edwards

EDWARDS, Thomas, fl 1822-1856

Attributed works
Franklin Haven   MB
MB. New England miniatures

Eel spearing at Setauket by W. S. Mount

Eeling by K. Knaths

Effervescence by K. L. Seligmann

Effort at speech between two people by E. Friedensohn

EGAN, John J. 19th cent
Colossal bust at low water mark, used as metre by the aborigines   PPhUn
Born (panorama detail)
Distant view of the Rocky mountains   PPhUn
Born (panorama detail)
Lake Concordia and aboriginal tumuli   PPhUn
Born (panorama detail)
Terraced mound in a snow storm at sunset   PPhUn
Born (panorama detail)

Egberts, Cornelius, fl 1826
Ames, E. Cornelius Egberts

Egg and rock by W. T. Murch

Egg salad by Unidentified artist

Eggbeater no 1 by S. Davis

Eggbeater no 2 by S. Davis

Eggbeater no 3 by S. Davis

Eggbeater no 4 by S. Davis

Eggbeater no 5 by S. Davis

Eggington, Elizabeth, b 1656
Unidentified artist. Elizabeth Eggington

Eggplant by C. H. Demuth

Eggplant and plums by C. H. Demuth

Eggplant and summer squash by C. H. Demuth

Eggplant and tomatoes by C. H. Demuth

Eggplants by C. H. Demuth

Eggs and carafe by M. Sterne

Ego et l'aurore by E. A. Donati

EGRI, Ted, 1913-
Bicycle riders
IU. Contemp Amer ptg, 1952
Conflict
IU. Contemp Amer ptg & sculp, 1953
Destination unknown
IU. Contemp Amer ptg & sculp, 1955

Egyptian by W. A. Baziotes

Egyptian girl by J. S. Sargent

EHNINGER. John Whetton, 1827-1889
October
Davidson v 1
Turkey shoot   MB
Davidson v2
MB. Karolik coll
Yankee peddler   NJN
Larkin
Larkin rev ed

EICHHOLTZ, Jacob, 1776-1842
An incident of the Revolution   MB
  MB. Karolik coll
Man in a yellow waistcoat   MB
  MB. Karolik coll
Margaret Adelia Leman   DN
  DN. Amer primitive ptgs, pt 1
Mr Kline   DN
  DN. Amer primitive ptgs, pt 1
Mrs Christopher B. Mayer   PR
  PR. Catalogue
The Ragan sisters   DN
  DC. Amer ptrs of the South
Rebecca Trissler Eichholtz
  Chew. 250 years of art
Self-portait
  Pierson
  Richardson. Ptg in America

Eichholtz, Rebecca Trissler, fl 1841
  Eichholtz, J. Rebecca Trissler Eichholtz

Eiger from Mürren by J. S. Sargent

Eight allegories of fate by C. Von Wiegand

Eight bathers by M. B. Prendergast

Eight bells by W. Homer

Eight bells' folly: memorial for Hart Crane
  by M. Hartley

Eight figures by M. Weber

Eight girls by the sea by M. B. Prendergast

Eighteenth-century gentleman by J. Cooper

EIGHTS, James, 1798-1882
East side market (now Broadway) Al-
  bany   NAI
  Jones. Rediscovered ptrs
Number 1 north side of State street, Al-
  bany, 1806   NAI
  Jones. Rediscovered ptrs
State street, Albany, 1805   NAI
  Bolton. Ezra Ames

EILSHEMIUS, Louis Michel, 1864-1943
Afternoon wind   MMA
  Baur. New art (col)
  Baur. Revolution
  Pierson
Approaching storm   DP
  Larkin rev ed
  Loring
Balcony view   DP
  DP. Catalogue
Bridge for fishing   DP
  Baur. New art
  Born
  DP. Catalogue
  Pierson
Cabs for hire   DP
  Bazin
  DP. Catalogue
Contentment
  Wight. Milestones
Delaware Water Gap village   MM
  MM. 100 Amer ptrs
Don Quixote
  Baur. New art
Falls
  CanO. Hirshhorn coll
Figures in landscape   WMAA
  Goodrich. Amer art
Flying Dutchman   WMAA
  McCurdy

Haunted house   MM
  Cheney. Story 1958 ed
  Walker. Ptgs from America
Jealousy
  Baur. New art
Madge in the morning   DP
  DP. Catalogue
Niagara Falls   MiD
  Richardson. Ptg in America
The pool   CtY
  CtY. Soc Anonyme
Rejected suitor   DP
  DP. Catalogue
Skater   ATeS
  ATeS. Collection
Tragedy or Found drowned   MM
  Baur. New art
  Pierson
Tranquility   MB
  MB. Ptgs in water color
Two bathers   OYB
  OYB. Catalogue 1951
West Point, New York
  NYG. Fine art
Yuma, Arizona   DP
  DP. Catalogue
      Portrait of the artist
Avery, M. Eilshemius

EISENSTAT, Jane Sperry
Dead opossum
  PA. Annual ex, 1958

The **el** and the snow by D. Kingman

Eldorado by R. Marsh

Election day at the State House by J. L.
  Krimmel

An **election** day bonfire, Fifth and Chestnut
  streets, Philadelphia by B. Uhle

Election night by J. Levine

Election scene, Catonsville, Baltimore county
  by A. J. Miller

Election scene during the Harrison—Van
  Buren campaign, 1840 by F. H. Schell

Electric automobile, Boston, 1892 by W. L.
  Taylor

Electric eye by E. A. Donati

Electric peach orchard by A. G. Dove

Elegy by H. Hofmann

Elegy by M. Kawabata

Elegy to the Spanish republic XXXIV by
  R. B. Motherwell

Elegy to the Spanish republic LVIII by
  R. B. Motherwell

Elements of reconstruction by J. De Diego

Elements of structure by C. A. Morris

Elephants
  Marin, J. Circus elephants

Elevated railway, Berlin by H. Post

Elevated with black and white by R. Crawford

Eleventh street by G. Vass

Eli Whitney gun factory by W. G. Munson

Elijah convincing the false prophets of Baol
  by B. West

Elijah fed by the ravens by W. Allston

Elijah in the desert by W. Allston

Elinor, Jean and Anna by G. W. Bellows

Eliphaz by K. Knaths

Elizabeth, consort of Albert I of Austria, king of Germany, fl 1300
    Walker, C. H. Elizabeth of Tirol
Elizabeth, queen of Rumania, 1843-1916
    Healy, G. P. A. Elizabeth, queen of Rumania
Elizabeth by F. J. Kline
Elizabeth at the piano by T. Eakins
Elizabeth, New Jersey
    Opper, E. Fire engine, Elizabeth, New Jersey, c 1880
Elk
    Miller, A. J. Elk swimming the Platte
    Miller, A. J. Hunting elk
    Miller, A. J. Hunting elk among the Black hills
Elle viendra by Y. Tanguy
Elliott, Barnard, 1740-1778
    Theus, J. Col Barnard Elliott jr
ELLIOTT, Charles Loring, 1812-1868
    Daniel Stanton   NNHS
        Cowdrey v 1
    John Wakefield Francis   NNHS
        Cowdrey v 1
    Mrs Thomas Goulding (Mary Anne Goulding)   NAD
        Larkin
        Larkin rev ed
        NAD. Amer tradition
        NJN. Early N. J. artists
        Pierson
    Prosper M. Wetmore   NNHS
        Cowdrey v 1
    Sanford Thayer   MB
        MB. Karolik coll
Elliott, Mary Bellinger (Elliott) d 1774
    Theus, J. Mrs Barnard Elliott jr
ELLIOTT, Philip Clarkson, 1903-
    Charleston, South Carolina   NBuA
        NBuA. Acquisitions 1954-57
    Shelocta, Pennsylvania   NBuA
        NBuA. Contemporary ptgs
Elliott, Mrs Philip Clarkson. See Cuthbert, Virginia Isobel
ELLIS, A. fl 1830
    Gentleman with high collar   NCHA
        Jones. New-found folk art
    Lady with a nosegay
        Jones. New-found folk art
ELLIS, Dean W. 1922?-
    Cadiz at dusk
        NAD. Annual ex, 1956
    Cathedral entrance   MSM
        CoS. New accessions USA, 1952
    Corroded implement
        OYB. Annual 1952
    The dummy   OCl
        CoS. New accessions USA, 1948
    Fortifications of Elba
        NAD. Annual ex, 1960
    Fragments from yesterday
        IU. Contemp Amer ptg, 1950
    Intimate conversation   OYB
        OYB. Annual 1949
        OYB. Catalogue 1951
    Scrap   OCl
        Pousette-Dart. Amer ptg
Ellis, Maria (Wilcocks) b 1871
    Jarvis, J. W. Mrs John French Ellis
Ellison, Thomas, 1773-1820
    Jarvis, J. W. Col Thomas Ellison

Elliston, Mary (Perot) 1687-1775
    Unidentified artist. Mrs Robert Elliston
Ellsworth, Abigail (Wolcott) 1756-1818
    Earl, R. Oliver Ellsworth and his wife
ELLSWORTH, James Sanford, 1802-1874
    Children
        Lipman. Primitive ptrs
    Couple
        Lipman. Primitive ptrs
    Mrs Jennie Post
        Lipman. Primitive ptrs
    Red-haired gentleman and his wife
        Lipman. Primitive ptrs
    Unidentified boy
        Lipman. Primitive ptrs
Ellsworth, Oliver, 1745-1807
    Earl, R. Chief Justice Oliver Ellsworth and his wife
    Trumbull, J. Oliver Ellsworth
Ellsworth, Mrs Oliver. See Ellsworth, Abigail (Wolcott)
Elm fruit by L. McIver
ELMER, Edwin Romanzo, 1850-1923
    A lady of Baptist Corner, Ashfield, Massachusetts
        U.S. National Capital sesquicentennial com
    Magic glass
        Frankenstein. After the hunt
    Mourning picture   MNS
        Baur. Amer ptg
ELSHIN, Jacob, 1892-
    Iconostas
        MoSL. Contemporary Amer ptg
Emancipation proclamation by A. A. Lamb
Embarkation by C. A. Morris
Embattled farmer by A. James
Ember tree by J. H. Fitzgerald
Emblem of peace by Unidentified artist
Emblems of peace by W. M. Harnett
Embrace by H. Hofmann
The embryo by I. R. Pereira
Emerald by H. Moller
Emerald pool by J. H. Twachtman
Emergency by H. S. Gillette
Emerging figure by S. Chermayeff
Emerging forms by C. A. Morris
EMERY, Ella, fl 1870
    Alice Cushing in the west parlor of Peter Cushing house, Hingham, Massachusetts
        Pierson
    Child in the sitting room of Matthew Cushing house
        Ford. Pictorial folk art
Emery, Joseph, fl 1834
    Davis, J. H. Joseph and Sarah Ann Emery
Emery, Sarah Ann, fl 1834
    Davis, J. H. Joseph and Sarah Ann Emery
Emes. See also Ames
Emes, Fanny, fl 1819
    Ames, E. Mrs Jesse Emes
Emes, Henry, 1783-1833
    Ames, E. Henry Emes
Emes, Jesse, 1739-1839
    Ames, E. Jesse Emes
Emigrant train fording Medicine Bow creek, Rocky mountains by S. Colman

Emigrants attacked by the Comanches by S. Eastman

Emigrants crossing the plains by F. O. C. Darley

The emigration of Daniel Boone by G. C. Bingham

Emma and her children by G. W. Bellows

Emma at a window by G. W. Bellows

Emma in black by G. W. Bellows

Emma in purple dress by G. W. Bellows

Emmet, Elizabeth. See Leroy, Elizabeth (Emmet)

EMMONS, Alexander Hamilton
Nathaniel William Taylor   CtY
CtY. Portrait index

EMMONS, Nathaniel, 1703-1740
Andrew Oliver
Belknap
Flexner. First flowers
NNHS. Waldron Phoenix Belknap coll
Samuel Sewall   MBH
Belknap

The emperor by A. Rattner

Emperor ploughs the fields by T. Stamos

Emperor's garden by C. R. Holty

Employment agency by I. Soyer

Emporium of Indian curiosities by J. F. Richardt

The empress by G. W. McLaughlin

Empty mansion by E. O'Hara

Empty town in desert by Y. Kuniyoshi

Encampment by A. J. Miller

Encampment and entertainment of the Boston rifle company by the Portland rifle company, 1830 by C. Codman

Encampment of Indians by A. J. Miller

Enchanted forest by E. L. Blumenschein

End of an era by M. Siporin

End of day by C. E. Burchfield

End of day by R. Gwathmey

End of day by Z. L. Sepeshy

End of day by W. Stuempfig

The end of Dover Beach by R. B. Motherwell

End of Fourteenth street crosstown line by R. Marsh

End of summer by G. R. Davis

End of summer by M. Tobey

End of the act by H. G. Keller

End of the day by H. G. Keller

End of the day by F. Remington

End of the day by V. P. Solomon

End of the festival by L. Bosa

End of the game by A. Salemme

End of the hunt by D. Nichols

End of the parade: Coatesville, Pa., 1920 by C. H. Demuth

End of the street by J. Myers

End of the war: starting home by H. Pippin

End of the world by G. Grosz

End of winter by J. H. Twachtman

Endeavor II and Ranger by J. W. Golinkin

ENDERS, Cleade
Subway
NAD. Annual ex, 1955

Endicott, Ellen (Peabody) 1833-1927
Sargent, J. S. Mrs William Crowninshield Endicott

ENGEL, Harry, 1901-
Theatre
IU. Contemp Amer ptg & sculp, 1955

ENGEL, Irma
Landscape
CSFP. Annual ex, 1948/49

Engineer Heartfield by G. Grosz

English, James Edward, 1812-1890
Flagg, J. B, James Edward English

English cod by W. M. Chase

English cottage by S. P. R. Triscott

An English gentleman by B. West

English landscape by W. Groombridge

Enigma of the collective American soul by P. Evergood

Enigmatic combat by A. Gorky

Enigmatical section by A. Nepote

ENNIS, George Pearse, 1884-1936
Tapping a furnace   OYB
OYB. Supplement

Ennui and tranquillity by Y. Tanguy

Ensor, James, baron, 1860-1949
Katzman, H. Ensor seated before The Entry of Christ into Brussels

Entering the first rapid by W. Homer

The entertainers III by R. Markman

The entombment by J. Foote

The entombment by M. Rothko

Entrance by K. E. Fortess

Entrance by R. Gleitsmann

Entrance by D. Thrall

Entrance to a coal mine near Wheeling, Virginia by G. Harvey

Entrance to the harbor of St Thomas by E. Carlsen

Entretat, le Cabestan Capstan by Leonid

Envelopment (Rubezahl) by K. L. Seligmann

Epaminondas, d 326 B. C.
West, B. Death of Epaminondas

Ephiphany of a hero by P. Burlin

Epoch by T. George

Epoch by B. Shahn

Equestrian by C. R. Holty

Equestrian sunrise by J. Corbino

Equestrians by J. Marin

Equestrienne by J. Marin

Equinox by J. McGarrell

Equinox by C. W. Rain

Equivalent restraint by L. Edmondson

Erdgeist, Illustration for by C. H. Demuth

Erewhon by R. J. Wolff

ERICKSON, John, 1919-
The wall
NNSG. Younger Amer ptrs

Erie Canal
Harvey, G. Afternoon, dead calm: View on the Erie canal near Pittsford, New York
Hill, J. W. Scene on the Erie Canal

Erie Canal—*Continued*
  Imbert, A. Erie canal celebration, New
    York, 1825
  Keys, M. Lockport on the Erie canal
Erie street boys by C. F. Gaertner
Erie underpass by N. Spencer
Ernestinoff, Alexander
  Adams, W. Alexander Ernestinoff
ERNST, Jimmy, 1920-
  Absence
    ICA. Amer artists paint the city
  Almost silence   MM
    CoS. New accessions USA, 1954
  Alone   NNSG
    Mendelowitz
    NNSG. Handbook
    NNSG. Younger Amer ptrs
  Animal and mineral
    IU. Contemp Amer ptg & sculp, 1953
  The chant   NBuA
    NBuA. Acquisitions 1954-57
    PPC. International ex, 1955
  Color isolation
    IU. Contemp Amer ptg, 1952
  Flying Dutchman   MMA
    Read. Art now, 1948 ed
  Laboratory report
    PPC. Ptg in the U.S. 1949
  Narrative
    IU. Contemp Amer ptg & sculp, 1957
  Night flight
    WMAA. Annual ex, 1951
  Personal appearance
    Pousette-Dart. Amer ptg
  Personal history   WMAA
    Goodrich. Amer art
    McCurdy
    Pierson
    WMAA. New decade
  Polar space   NUM
    NUM. Root bequest
  Rock painting
    IU. Contemp Amer ptg & sculp, 1961
  Speculation   NBM
    CoS. New accessions USA, 1952
  Stillness
    Brussels. Exposition
  Time for fear   MMA
    MMA. Abstract
    Read. Concise history
  Timescape   WMAA
    Pierson
    WMAA. Sara Roby
  Tomorrow morning
    VR. Amer ptg, 1958
  Tropic
    WMAA. Museum and its friends, 1958
    WMAA. New decade
Ernst, Mrs Max. See Tanning, Dorothea
Erving, Elizabeth. See Bowdoin, Elizabeth
    (Erving)
Erving, John, 1728-1816
  Blackburn, J. John Erving jr
Erving, Mrs John, fl 1732
  Smibert, J. Mrs John Erving
Escape by L. C. Earle
Escape by P. Evergood
Escape by X. Gonzales
Escape by J. W. Treiman
Escape from Blackfeet by A. J. Miller

Escudier, Mme Paul (Le Fevre) fl 1885
  Sargent, J. S. Mme Paul Escudier
ESHOO, Robert, 1926-
  The castle
    IU. Contemp Amer ptg & sculp, 1957
  Evolution of a day
    WMAA. Young America 1957
  Herkimer
    WMAA. Young America 1957
  Summer day
    MBIC. View 1960
  Verdant rise
    IU. Contemp Amer ptg & sculp, 1959
Esperance by T. Appleby
Essex market by G. Hartigan
Eternal city by P. Blume
Eternal dictation by L. Edmondson
Eternal pageant by W. W. Quirt
Eternal world by F. Puma
Eternity by M. Beckmann
ETHEROVICH, Anthony, 1916-
  Merry bench   OYB
    OYB. Catalogue 1951
  The merry table   OYB
    OYB. Annual 1951
Ethiopia saluting the colors by B. Robinson
Etna, Mount
  Crowninshield, F. Mt Etna from Taormina
  Silsbee, M. Taormina and Mt Aetna
Etnier, Mrs C. E.
  Watkins, F. C. Mrs C. E. Etnier
ETNIER, Stephen Morgan, 1903-
  Accra beach   OYB
    OYB. Annual 1953
    OYB. Supplement
  Caribbean moon
    NAD. Annual ex, 1955
  Jamaica noon
    NAD. Annual ex, 1953
  Lighthouse service dock, Nassau
    NAD. Annual ex, 1958
  Port of call
    IU. Contemp Amer ptg & sculp, 1957
  Sea cross
    Gruskin
  The seiner
    NSP. Sportscapes
Etretat by G. Innes
ETTING, Emlen Pope, 1905-
  Spring song
    Gruskin (col)
Etting, Solomon, 1764-1847
  Jarvis, J. W. Solomon Etting
Etting, Mrs Solomon, 1764-1831
  Jarvis, J. W. Mrs Solomon Etting
Euclid avenue by J. Levine
Euretta by M. Beckmann
Europa and the bull by D. Austin
European cormorant by J. J. Audubon
EVANS, J. G. fl 1840-1859
  Commodore Perry carrying the gospel of
    God to the heathen, 1853   ICH
    U.S. National Capital sesquicentennial
    com
EVANS, James, fl 1825-1854
  The white squall   DN
    DN. Amer primitive ptg, pt 2

EVANS, John T. fl 1815
    Attributed works
Man with a whip   MeC
    Jetté. Amer heritage collection
Evans, William T.
    Rouland, O. William T. Evans
Evaporating night by I. R. Pereira
Evarts, William Maxwell, 1818-1901
    Hunt, W. M. William Maxwell Evarts
Eve by J. Corbino
Evening by C. Booth
Evening by C. E. Burchfield
Evening by J. Carroll
Evening by K. Schrag
Evening by J. Schueler
Evening garden by A. Rattner
Evening glow—the old red cow by A. P.
    Ryder
Evening hymn by W. Allston
Evening image by K. R. Morris
Evening in Arcady by T. Cole
Evening in Keene valley by W. M. Hart
Evening in the country by D. Nichols
Evening in Venice by E. Berman
Evening landscape by R. Frame
Evening light by R. Bennett
Evening, Montauk by K. R. Morris
Evening on a pleasure boat, Boston by
    M. B. Prendergast
Evening on the road to Granada by H. G.
    Keller
Evening peace by C. E. Burchfield
Evening radiance by K. Schrag
Evening reading by P. Evergood
Evening shower, Paris by M. B. Prender-
    gast
Evening silhouettes by R. A. Blakelock
Evening sky by K. Schrag
Evening song by W. Allston
Evening star by J. Jones
Evening storm. Schoodic, Maine by M.
    Hartley
Evening usualty by F. Califano
Evensong by A. B. Davies
Eventide by M. Friedman
Eventide by R. Haines
Eventide by H. E. Mattson
Everett, Edward, 1794-1865
    Healy, G. P. A. Edward Everett
Everett, Hannah (Vincent)
    Jarvis, J. W. Mrs James Everett
Everett, James
    Jarvis, J. W. Rev James Everett
EVERGOOD, Philip, 1901-
Alone   MNM
    Baur. Philip Evergood
American shrimp girl
    Baur. Philip Evergood
    Time. 300 years (col)
American tragedy
    Baur. Philip Evergood
    Time. 300 years (col)
Art on the beach
    Baur. Philip Evergood

An artist as a young man
    Baur. Philip Evergood
Artist's fantasy
    Baur. Philip Evergood (col)
The big noise
    Baur. Philip Evergood
The bluebird
    Baur. Philip Evergood
Boy from Stalingrad
    Baur. Philip Evergood
Burial of the Queen of Sheba
    Baur. Philip Evergood
Cool doll in pool
    Baur. Philip Evergood
Cotton from field to mill
    Baur. Philip Evergood
A cup of tea
    Baur. Philp Evergood
Dance marathon
    Baur. Philip Evergood
David playing to King Saul
    Baur. Philip Evergood
Dawn
    Baur. Philip Evergood
Don't cry, mother   MMA
    Biddle. Yes and no
    Mendelowitz
    Myers
    Riley. Your art heritage
Dowager in a wheelchair   WMAA
    Baur. Philip Evergood
    ICA. Annual ex, 1954
    PPC. International ex, 1955
    WMAA. Sara Roby
Dream catch
    Baur. New art
    Baur. Philip Evergood
    CanO. Hirshhorn coll
    Genauer
    Pierson
Dusk at Fuji
    Baur. Philip Evergood
Enigma of the collective American soul
    Baur. Philip Evergood (col)
Escape
    IU. Contemp Amer ptg & sculp, 1961
Evening reading
    Baur. Philip Evergood
Everybody wants to live   CLA
    CLA. 35 ptgs
Farmer's daughter
    Baur. Philip Evergood
Fascist company
    Baur. Philip Evergood
Flight of fancy   MdBM
    Baur. Philip Evergood
Flowers by the lake
    Baur. Philip Evergood
The forgotten man
    Baur. Philip Evergood
The future
    IU. Contemp Amer ptg & sculp, 1955
The future belongs to them
    Baur. Philip Evergood
Garden of Betty Mae
    Baur. Philip Evergood
Girl with sunflowers
    Baur. Philip Evergood (col)
Happy entrance
    Baur. Philip Evergood

Treadmill
  Baur. Philip Evergood
Turmoil
  Baur. Philip Evergood
Twilight landscape
  Baur. Philip Evergood
Vase and flowers
  Baur. Philip Evergood
Virginia in the grotto   WMAA
  Baur. Philip Evergood
  Goodrich. Amer art
Wheels of victory
  Baur. Philip Evergood
Woman at piano
  Baur. Philip Evergood
Woman of Iowa
  Baur. Philip Evergood (col)
Worker's victory
  Baur. Philip Evergood
Every Saturday by A. B. Davies
Everybody wants to live by P. Evergood
Everyday sovereign by C. Howard
Everyman by B. Shahn
EVETT, Kenneth, 1913-
  Rodeo   ATU
    ATU. Coll of Amer Art
  Trio   NJMo
    IU. Contemp Amer ptg, 1951
    NJMo. Your Montclair art museum
The evil of drink by W. W. Quirt
Evil omen by A. Gottlieb
Evolution of a day by R. Eshoo
Evora, Portugal by J. S. Sargent
Evocation by J. Ferren
EWING, Edgar, 1913-
  Acropolis—night
    IU. Contemp Amer ptg & sculp, 1961
  Car with dark top
    ICA. Annual ex, 1951
  Parabolic San Francisco
    IU. Contemp Amer ptg & sculp, 1957
  St Cyr
    ICA. Annual ex, 1959/60
    IU. Contemp Amer ptg & sculp, 1959
  The sergeant's coat
    ICA. Annual ex, 1957
  View of Mt Wilson
    PPC. Ptg in the U. S. 1949
Excavating a canoe, British Columbia by
  G. Catlin
Excavation by P. Blume
Excavation by W. De Kooning
Exclamation by A. Gottlieb
Execution by J. Strombotne
Exhibition by B. Greene
Exhuming the mastodon by C. W. Peale
Exit by Y. Kuniyoshi
Exit in color by F. Martin
Expanding elements by C. A. Morris
Expanse of sky 1 by L. Feininger
Expedition to capture wild horses—Sioux by
  A. J. Miller
Experience of meaning by L. Edmondson
Experience of tragedy yet to come by W.
  W. Quirt
Explosion by K. S. Dreier
Expression of an impression by M. Sterne

Expulsion from the Garden of Eden by
  T. Cole
Expulsion of possessions in a danger of
  being gained by K. Nack
Extinction of the species by Y. Tanguy
Extinction of useless lights by Y. Tanguy
Exuberance by H. Hofmann
Exultation by S. Reinhardt
Eye level by S. Davis
Eye witness by C. E. Pickhardt
The eyes have it by W. W. Quirt
Eyes in the heat by J. Pollock
Eyes tested by R. Marsh

F

The fabulous crustacean by L. E. Kupfer-
  man
Facade by J. Albers
Facade by A. B. Davies
Facade by H. Frankenthaler
Face of a rabbi by W. Pachner
Factory by G. R. Bradshaw
Factory by V. I. Cuthbert
Factory by C. H. Demuth
Factory by P. Dickinson
Factory by G. McConnell
Factory chimney by G. C. Ault
Factory window in Manhattan by L. Fein-
  inger
FADDEN, Marie-Celeste
  French child on train
    PA. Annual ex, 1950
FADDIS, George, 1920-
  Discovery   OYB
    OYB. Supplement 1959
Fading light by H. Holt
FAGNANI, Giuseppe, 1819-1873
  Mrs A. V. H. Stuyvesant
  Vail. Stuyvesant ports
Die fahne hoch! by F. Stella
A fair wind by W. Homer
Fairchild, Gordon, 1822-1832
  Sargent, J. S. Gordon Fairchild holding
    a guinea pig
Fairchild, Sally, fl 1885
  Sargent, J. S. Lady with a blue veil
Fairman Rogers four-in-hand by T. Eakins
Fairmont water works by T. Birch
Fairmount and Schuylkill river by W.
  Groombridge
Fairport harbor by C. F. Gaertner
Fairs and festivals
  Barnett, H. County fair
  Bosa, L. Carnival on the ice
  Garrett, A. W. Western festival
  Hallowell, G. H. Italian fiesta, night
  Harrison, B. J. Fair of the American
    institute of New York, held at Niblo's
    garden, c 1845
  Higgins, V. Fiesta day
  Holty, C. R. Carousel
  Homer, W. The carnival

Fairs and festivals—*Continued*
Kempsmith, J. Carnival time
Kuniyoshi, Y. Carnival
Moses, A. M. R. Bondsville fair
Peirce, W. County fair
Pickens, A. Carnival
Prendergast, M. B. Autumn festival
Prendergast, M. B. Carnival
Prendergast, M. B. Festival day, Venice
Prendergast, M. B. Festival night, Venice
Prendergast, M. B. May day, Central park
Sample, P. S. Country horse show
Sawyer, H. A. Carnival
Shahn, B. Carnival
Sharrer, H. Country fair
Siporin, M. Fiesta in Trastevere
Sloan, J. Corpus Christi, Santa Fe
Varga, M. Country carnival
Wilson, S. Fisherman's festival
Woodside, J. A. Country fair in Pennsylvania, 1824

Fairy tale by H. Hofmann

Faith, hope and charity by W. Sommer

The **faithful** Colt by W. M. Harnett

Fakirs by Y. Kuniyoshi

Falcon by S. W. Hayter

Falcon by E. Kelly

Falconio, Diomede, 1842-1917
Eakins, T. Monsignor Diomede Falconio

Falcons
Audubon, J. J. Gyrfalcon

The **fall** by C. L. Cicero

Fall of old houses by E. Fiene

Fallen angels by K. L. Seligmann

Fallen deer by W. Homer

Fallen pine, Camp island by W. A. Kienbusch

Fallen rider by P. Tchelitchew

Falling rocket by J. A. M. Whistler

Falling sun VI by F. Berman

Fallout red by R. G. Hamilton

Falls by L. Eilshemius

Falls of Niagara taken from the road two miles below Chippawa by J. Trumbull

Falls of St Anthony by S. Eastman

Falls of San Joaquin, California by A. D. Browere

Falls of the Ohio and Louisville by A. H. Wyant

Family burying ground by Unidentified artist

Family groups
Ames, E. The Fondey family
Andrews, A. Schuyler family
Beckmann, M. Family picture
Bellows, G. W. Fisherman's family
Benbridge, H. Hartley family group
Blackburn, J. Winslow family
Blanchard, C. Family portrait
Bosa, L. My family reunion
Cassatt, M. Mme. A. F. Aude and her two daughters
Copley, J. S. Copley family
Copley, J. S. Sir William Pepperrell and his family
Copley, J. S. Sketch for the Knatchbull family
Corbino, J. Family
Davis, J. H. Separate tables
Davis, J. H. Tilton family
Dawkins, H. Burroughs family
Dunlap, W. Dunlap family
Earl, R. E. W. Family portrait
Evergood, P. Kleinholz family
Feke, R. Isaac Royall and his family
Field, E. S. Joseph Moore and his family
Glackens, W. J. Family group: Irene Dimock, Edith Glackens, Ira Glackens, Grace Dwight Morgan
Goldsmith, D. Mr and Mrs Lyman Day and daughter Cornelia
Goldsmith, D. Talcott family
Greene, S. Family portrait
Greenwood, J. Greenwood and Lee families
Healy, G. P. A. Bryan family
Johnson, E. Family group (Hatch family)
Johnston, J. The James McCormick family of Baltimore, c 1804
Kuniyoshi, Y. Maine family
Morse, S. F. B. Morse family
Peale, C. W. Peale family
Peale, J. James Peale and his family
Peale, J. Mme Dubocq and her four children
Peale, J. Self-portrait with his family
Pickens, A. Henry Hope and family
Rockmore, N. Family group
Rogoway, A. The family
Savage, E. The Washington family
Smibert, J. Bishop Berkeley and his family
Stettheimer, F. Family portrait
Stock, J. W. Parsons family
Trumbull, J. John Vernet and his family
Trumbull, J. Jonathan Trumbull jr and his family
Unidentified artist. Adams family
Unidentified artist. Cheney family
Unidentified artist. George Washington family
Unidentified artist. Gerard Stuyvesant family group
Unidentified artist. Hunter family of Germantown, Pennsylvania
Unidentified artist. Maryland family
Unidentified artist. Nathan Hawley and family
Unidentified artist. New England family group
Unidentified artist. Sargent family
Unidentified artist. Victorian family
Unidentified artist. Walker family
Walkowitz, A. Family group
Weber, M. Family reunion
West, B. The Adrian Hope family group
Williams, W. John Wiley, his mother and sisters
Williams, W. William Denning family
Wright, J. Self-portrait of the artist with his family

Family rooms. See Living rooms

Family tree by G. Palazzola

Famous firsts by S. Davis

Fanciful meeting long ago by F. C. Watkins

Fancy picture. Fishing with waterfall by Unidentified artist

The **fandango** by C. C. Nahl

Faneuil, Peter, 1700-1743
  Smibert, J. Peter Faneuil
Faneuil hall from the water by W. H. Bartlett
Fantasia on a theme by Dr S. by P. Cadmus
Fantasy by M. Golubov
Le Faou by F. D. Duncan
Far country—Synchromy by S. MacDonald-Wright
Faraway by C. W. Rain
The farewell by B. Perlin
Farewell to Pisa by E. Laning
Farewell to Union square by M. Kantor
Farley, Eben, 1775-1826
  Malbone, E. G. Eben Farley
Farm composition by A. Rattner
Farm machine by R. Lebrun
Farm machinery by C. Peake
Farm news by E. E. Speicher
Farm road by M. A. Phillips
Farm scene by Unidentified artist
Farm still life by A. Rattner
Farmer, Hannah. See Peck, Hannah (Farmer)
Farmer by B. Shahn
Farmer by E. E. Speicher
Farmer's daughter by P. Evergood
Farmers nooning by W. S. Mount
Farmer's wife by R. Gwathmey
Farmhouse in Mahantango valley by Unidentified artist
Farming
  Benton, T. H. Cradling wheat
  Benton, T. H. First crop
  Benton, T. H. June hay
  Benton, T. H. July hay
  Benton, T. H. Louisiana rice fields
  Benton, T. H. Threshing wheat
  Benton, T. H. Weighing cotton
  Codman, C. The hayfield
  Homer, W. Corn husking
  Homer, W. Harvest scene
  Homer, W. Haymaking
  Homer, W. Springtime in Virginia
  Homer, W. Veteran in a new field
  Johnson, E. Corn husking
  Jones, J. Harvest
  Jones, J. Wheat farmers
  Krans, O. Planting corn
  Krans, O. Sowing grain at Bishop hill
  Martin, F. Rural family
  Moses, A. M. R. Haying time
  Mount, W. S. Farmers nooning
  Nichols, D. Summer bounty
  Pleissner, O. M. Stacking alfalfa
  Price, C. S. Plowing
  Sterne, M. Reapers
  Thompson, J. B. Harvest in Vermont
  Unidentified artist. Haymakers
  Unidentified artist. Making hay
  Williams, V. Winnowing grain in California
  Wood, G. Iowa cornfield
Farmyards and farm buildings
  Blythe, D. G. Farm scene
  Burchfield, C. E. Barn
  Burchfield, C. E. Red barn
  Durrie, G. H. Farm scene, summer
  Durrie, G. H. Farmstead in winter
  Durrie, G. H. Farmyard, winter
  Durrie, G. H. Farmyard in winter, selling corn
  Durrie, G. H. New England farm scene
  Durrie, G. H. New England winter scene
  Durrie, G. H. Returning to the farm
  Durrie, G. H. Sunday in the country
  Durrie, G. H. Winter farm scene
  Durrie, G. H. Winter in the country, a cold morning
  Hartley, M. Deserted farm
  Hewes, M. Hollow hill pastoral
  Hicks, E. Hillborn farm
  Hofmann, C. View of Benjamin Reber's farm
  Kroll, L. Farm in Maine
  Lebduska, L. H. California farm
  Moses, A. M. R. Bringing in the Christmas tree
  Moses, A. M. R. Early springtime on the farm
  Moses, A. M. R. Grandma goes to the city
  Moses, A. M. R. Haying time
  Moses, A. M. R. Home of Hezekiah King
  Moses, A. M. R. In the springtime
  Moses, A. M. R. McDonell farm
  Moses, A. M. R. Mount Nebo in winter
  Moses, A. M. R. The old oaken bucket
  Moses, A. M. R. Our barn
  Moses, A. M. R. Over the river to grandma's house
  Moses, A. M. R. Wash day
  Moses, A. M. R. A winter's day
  Mount, W. S. Long Island farmhouse
  O'Keeffe, G. Lake George barns
  O'Keeffe, G. Stables
  O'Keeffe, G. White Canadian barn
  Palmer, F. F. American farm scene
  Park, L. Flax-scutching, 1847
  Richardson, C. C. French Canadian barn
  Ryder, A. P. Barnyard
  Sample, P. S. Maple sugaring in Vermont
  Seigert, P. Wisconsin farm scene
  Sepeshy, Z. L. January, Michigan farm
  Sheeler, C. Barn variation
  Sheeler, C. Bucks county barn
  Sheeler, C. Connecticut farm buildings
  Spangler, C. D. Old Hager farm
  Tait, A. F. Barnyard
  Thon, W. Aunt Thankful's farm
  Unidentified artist. Farmhouse in Mahantango valley
  Unidentified artist. New England farm in winter
  Unidentified artist. Thrifty farm
  Unidentified artist. A valley farm
  Unidentified artist. Victorian dairy farm, study in green
  Varga, M. Connecticut farm
  Wheat, J. September harvest
  Woodwell, J. R. Farmhouse at Scalp Level
  Wyeth, A. N. McVey's barn
  Zeliff, A. E. Barnyard
Farnam, Henry, 1803-1888
  Healy, G. P. A. Henry Farnam
FARNDON, Walter, 1876-
  The bay
    NAD. Annual ex, 1949, 1st half

FARNDON, Walter—*Continued*
The cove
  NAD. Annual ex, autumn 1949
The inlet
  NAD. Annual ex, 1947, 2d half
Farnham, Captain, fl 1850
  Unidentified artist.   Capt Farnham of
    Farnham, Maine
FARNSWORTH, Jerry, 1895-
The amateur   OT
  OT. Contemp Amer ptgs
Aurelia
  IU. Contemp Amer ptg, 1949
  NAD. Annual ex, spring 1950
Naked in the city
  IU. Contemp Amer ptg, 1948
Standing with reluctant feet where brook
    and river meet
  NAD. Annual ex, 1952
Young man from Arkansas
  MM. Amer ptg today
Farnsworth, Mrs Jerry. See Sawyer, Helen
  Alton
FARNY, Henry F. 1847-1916
The captive   OCiM
  McCracken. Portrait of the old west
    (col)
Song of the talking wire   OCiT
  McCracken. Portrait of the old west
FARR, Charles Griffin, 1908-
Beach at Miramar
  CSFP. Annual ex, 1952
Figures in a hallway
  CSFP. Annual ex, 1948/49
Street in Knoxville   CSFM
  Pousette-Dart. Amer ptg
Farr, Elizabeth, d 1813
  Unidentified artist. Mourning picture—
    Elizabeth Farr
Farrington, Peter, fl 1781
  Unidentified artist. Peter Farrington
FARRUGGIO, Remo M. 1906-
Monhegan
  MM. Amer ptg today
Renaldo and the enchanted garden
  IU. Contemp Amer ptg & sculp, 1957
Fascist company by P. Evergood
Fashion and purport by L. Edmondson
The fat and the thin by G. Grosz
Father and child by B. Shahn
Father and son by J. Budington
Fatma by P. Tchelitchew
FAULKNER, Barry, 1881-
Young Daniel Webster and the Constitu-
    tion
  NAD. Annual ex, 1946, 2d half
Fauré, Gabriel Urbain, 1845-1924
  Sargent, J. S. Gabriel Fauré
FAUSETT, William Dean, 1913-
Country road
  NYG. Fine art
Cuernavaca   ATU
  ATU. Coll of Amer art (col)
Derby view   MMA
  Barr. What is mod ptg
The lake
  NYG. Fine art
A favorite by J. Haberle

Fay, Samuel Prescott Phillips, fl 1834
  Mason, B. F. Judge Samuel Prescott Phil-
    lips Fay
Fay, Mrs Samuel Prescott Phillips, fl 1834
  Mason, B. F. Mrs S. P. P. Fay
Fayerweather, Hannah. See Winthrop, Han-
    nah Fayerweather
Fayerweather, Samuel, 1724-1781
  Copley, J. S. Samuel Fayerweather
Fear by Y. Tanguy
Fear by R. Vickrey
FEARING, Kelly, 1918-
The place of the angel and Tobias
  IU. Contemp Amer ptg & sculp, 1957
Saint Rose
  IU. Contemp Amer ptg & sculp, 1955
Feasible by S. Davis
Feast of pure reason by J. Levine
Feather boa by W. M. Chase
February by W. De Kooning
February by L. Goldin
February thaw by C. E. Burchfield
February's sun by F. J. Mulhaupt
Fedalma by G. Fuller
Feeding the hungry by A. Refregier
Feeding the pigeons by W. M. Chase
FEININGER, Lyonel, 1871-1956
Baltic—a recollection   OT
  OCl. Feininger
Barfüsserkirche in Erfurt
  Rosenblum
Bathers
  MBIC. Villon and Feininger
Bicycle riders
  Rosenblum
Bird cloud   MCH
  OCl. Feininger
Black yawl   MCH
  Pulitzer v 1
Blue cloud
  MBIC. Villon and Feininger
Blue coast   OCo
  IU. Contemp Amer ptg, 1950
  UNESCO. 1860-1955
Blue marine   NUM
  UNESCO. 1860-1955
Bridge no 3
  McCurdy
Bridge V, 1919   PPhM
  Baur. New art
  MM. Abstract
  OCl. Feininger
Cathedral, Cammin, 1942
  MBIC. Villon and Feininger
The church   MM
  Gruskin (col)
  MM. 100 Amer ptrs (col)
Church (Wuppertal)
  UNESCO. 1860-1955
Church in Halle
  Moderns and their world (col)
Church of the Minorites II, 1926 MnMW
  Baur. New art
  McCurdy
  Pierson
  UNESCO. 1860-1955
Church on the hill
  MBIC. Villon and Feininger

City at night, 1941
  Baur. New art
  Pierson
Coast of nevermore
  IU. Contemp Amer ptg, 1951
  OCl. Feininger
The cyclists
  Moderns and their world
Der dampfer Odin   GAtM
  GAtM. Holbrook collection
Dunes and breakwaters
  MBIC. Villon and Feininger
Dunes, Baltic   MCH
  Pulitzer v2
Dunes with ray of light II, 1944   NBuA
  MBIC. Villon and Feininger
  NBuA. Contemporary ptgs
  Rathbun
  Rosenblum
East choir of Halle cathedral
  50 years of mod art
  Read. Concise history (col)
Expanse of sky 1   NBuA
  NBuA. Acquisitions 1954-57
Factory windows in Manhattan
  CSFP. Annual ex, 1950/51
  ICA. Amer artists paint the city
  ICA. Annual ex, 1951
  MnU. 40 Amer ptrs
Fisher off the coast
  Bazin
Gaberndorf II   MoKN
  MoKN. Handbook p 149
Gables I, 1925
  MBIC. Villon and Feininger
  OCl. Feininger
Gables IV
  OCl. Feininger
Gateway and tower I, 1924-26
  Raynal. History v3 (col)
Gelmeroda, 1927   NNSG
  NNSG. Handbook
Gelmeroda IV, 1915   NNSG
  NNSG. Handbook
  Time. 300 years (col)
Gelmeroda VIII, 1921   WMAA
  Baur. New art (col)
  Goodrich. Amer art (col)
Gelmeroda XIII, 1936   MM
  OCl. Feininger
The glorious victory of the sloop Maria
                                       MoSL
  Gruskin
  MoSL. Handbook 1953
  OCl. Feininger
  Pierson
  Rosenblum
  Sewall. History of western art
  Wight. Milestones (col)
Gothic spire
  UNESCO. 1860-1949
  UNESCO. 1860-1955
Her majesty the Barque II   OCl
  OCl. Feininger
High houses
  MnMW. Contemporary
  WMAA. Neuberger collection
Houses by the river
  Baur. New art
  PPC. International ex, 1950
Jagged clouds   CtHW
  CtHW. Handbook

Locomotive
  OCl. Feininger
Locomotive with big wheel
  Baur. New art
Lonesome shores   CSFL
  OCl. Feininger
Longueil, Normandy
  OCl. Feininger
Luminosity
  OCl. Feininger
Lunar web
  Baur. Nature (col)
  Cheney. Story 1958 ed
  Pousette-Dart. Amer ptg
Lüneburg II   NNSG
  NNSG. Handbook
Manhattan architecture
  Munsterberg
Manhattan canyon   MdBM
  OCl. Feininger
Manhattan, dawn
  OCl. Feininger
Manhattan, dusk
  MM. Amer ptg today
Manhattan, moonwake
  MBIC. Villon and Feininger
Manhattan, night 1941
  MBIC. Villon and Feininger
Marine, 1927
  MBIC. Villon and Feininger
Marine II, 1925
  OCl. Feininger
Old American locomotive
  MBIC. Villon and Feininger
On the Baltic I, 1941
  MBIC. Villon and Feininger
Portentous sunset
  MBIC. Villon and Feininger
Quimper at night
  OCl. Feininger
Racing skerry cruisers (Yacht race)
  OCl. Feininger
The river   MWM
  OCl. Feininger
  Pierson
Side wheeler   MiD
  Baur. Revolution
  Lee. Art then and now
  MiD. Treasures
  NBuA. Fifty ptgs
  OCl. Feininger
  Pierson
Spell
  PPC. International ex, 1952
Steamer Odin II, 1927   MMA
  Canaday
  MMA. Masters (col)
  OCl. Feininger
  Read. Art now, 1948 ed
  Roos
Storm brewing
  MBIC. Villon and Feininger
Street in Paris
  Baur. Revolution
  McCurdy
Study in space V   ATeS
  ATeS. Collection
Sunset   MB
  OCl. Feininger
Sunset fires
  PPC. International ex, 1955

FEININGER, Lyonel—*Continued*
Town gate tower II, 1925
  OCl. Feininger
Town hall (Zottelstedt)
  MBIC. Villon and Feininger
Town hall of Cammin
  OCl. Feininger
Trumpeter in the village
  MnMW. Expressionism 1900-1955
Tug   NNSG
  Mendelowitz
Umpferstedt II   PPhM
  PPhM. Arensberg coll
Village   DP
  Read. Concise history
Village church, 1937
  MnU. 40 Amer ptrs
Village church (Nieder-Reissen) 1924
  MBIC. Villon and Feininger
Vita nova
  MMA. Abstract
Vollersroda
  Cheney. Primer 1958 ed
The voyage
  UNESCO. 1860-1955
Western roadstead
  MBIC. Villon and Feininger
Western sea   MSM
  OCl. Feininger
Windclouds at sundown
  Baur. Revolution
Yacht
  Pierson
Yacht race. See Racing skerry cruisers
Zirchow V   NBM
  CoS. New accessions USA, 1954
Zirchow VII
  MMA. Abstract
FEININGER, Theodore Luke, 1910-
Ghosts of engines   MMA
  Baur. Revolution
  CoS. New accessions USA, 1948
FEITELSON, Lorser, 1898-
Genesis, first version   CSFM
  Baur. Revolution
  Pierson
Magical forms
  IU. Contemp Amer ptg, 1950
Mirabilia
  IU. Contemp Amer ptg, 1951
Painting
  IU. Contemp Amer ptg, 1949
FEKE, Robert, c 1705-1760
Charles Apthorp   OCL
  Belknap
  Flexner. First flowers
  OCl. Handbook
Henry Collins (formerly called Gershom
    Flagg III)
  Belknap
Isaac Royall and family   MCH
  Flexner. First flowers
  ICA. From colony to nation
  Mendelowitz
  Pierson
Isaac Winslow   MB
  Flexner. First flowers
  Pierson
James Bowdoin II   MeB
  Flexner. First flowers
  MiD. Ptg in America
  Pierson
  Roos

John Callender   RPHS
  Flexner. First flowers
Mary McCall   PA
  OCiM. Rediscoveries
Mrs Barlow Trecothick   KW
  Belknap
  NNHS. Waldron Phoenix Belknap coll
Mrs Charles Willing
  Flexner. First flowers
Mrs Gershom Flagg IV
  Flexner. First flowers
Mrs James Bowdoin   MeB
  Belknap
  Flexner. Copley
  Pierson
Mrs John Vinal (?) See Unknown lady
    (Mrs John Vinal?)
Mrs Josiah Martin   MiD
  Belknap
  Flexner. First flowers
  MiD. Treasures
Mrs William Bowdoin   MeB
  Belknap
  Pierson
Mrs William Peters   PH
  Flexner. First flowers
Samuel Waldo   MeB
  Barker. Amer ptg
  Flexner. First flowers
  NUM. Art across America
  Pierson
  Richardson. Ptg in America
  Roos
Self-portrait, c 1750   RPHS
  Mendelowitz
  Pierson
Self-portrait, 1730 (Foote coll)
  Flexner. First flowers
  Pierson
Thomas Hiscox
  Flexner. First flowers
  Pierson
  Time. 300 years (col)
Unknown lady (Mrs John Vinal?) NBM
  Flexner. Amer ptg
  Flexner. Short history
  ICA. From colony to nation
  Larkin
  Larkin rev ed
  Pierson
  Robb. Harper history
William Bowdoin   MeB
  Flexner. Light of distant skies
Young colonial   ATeS
  ATeS. Collection
Young girl in flower   NBM
  Flexner. First flowers (col)

Attributed works

Mrs Ralph Inman (also attributed to
    Blackburn)
  Belknap
FELDMAN, Walter, 1925-
Once upon the past
  MBIC. View 1960
Female corpse, back view by H. Bloom
Female figure by R. Soyer
Female figure with turban by H. C. Peale
Female leg by H. Bloom
Female of the species by W. R. Leigh

Femme avec fourrures by J. S. Sargent

Fence builders by E. F. Spruce

Fence on the hill by W. S. Mount

Fencing master by G. Melchers

Fenno, Eliza, d 1817
Malbone, E. G. Eliza Fenno

Fenton, Beatrice, 1887-
Eakins, T. Coral necklace

FENTON, P. fl 1815
Miranda E. Lord from Connecticut   MeC
Jetté. Amer heritage collection

FERBER, Herbert, 1906-
Number 1, 1959
WMAA. Contemp Amer ptg, 1959/60

Ferguson, James
Peale, Raphaelle. Major James Ferguson

Fernandez, Alice
Chase, W. M. Alice Fernandez

FERREN, Herbert, 1906-
Composition on green
MMA. Abstract

FERREN, John, 1905-
Evocation
MnU. 40 Amer ptrs
Figuration
MnU. 40 Amer ptrs
Fire vase
Cheney. Story 1958 ed
The garden   WMAA
Baur. Nature (col)
CSFP. Annual ex, 1952
Goodrich. Amer art (col)
Pierson
WMAA. Contemp Amer ptg, 1951
WMAA. Contemp Amer ptg, 1955
Medianus
IU. Contemp Amer ptg & sculp, 1957
Mojave no 1
PPC. International ex, 1955
Painting, 1950
McCurdy
MMA. Abstract
Red and blue   NeL
CoS. New accessions USA, 1956
Eliot. Art of our time (col)
Time. 300 years (col)

FERRILL, M. E. fl 1869-1883
Country dance
Jones. Rediscovered ptrs
Sleighing scene, Lansingburgh   MiD
Jones. Rediscovered ptrs
Pierson

Ferry boat wreck by A. G. Dove

Festa della regatta, Palazzo Barbaro by J. S.
Sargent

Festivals. See Fairs and festivals

Fête champêtre by S. Sherman

Fête champêtre by D. Tanning

Fête du Suquet by W. J. Glackens

Fetish by T. Benrimo

FEUERHERM, Kurt Karl, 1926-
Golden tree
ICA. Annual ex, 1957
Mexican meat market
MM. Amer ptg today
NBuA. Expressionism

Field, Eliza Willing Spring (Peters) 1820-
1902
Sargent, J. S. Mr and Mrs John W. Field

Field, Ellen Virtue, 1835-1916
Field, E. S. Ellen Virtue Field

FIELD, Erastus Salisbury, 1805-1900
Ark of the covenant   DN
DN. Amer primitive ptgs, pt 1
The blue boy   VWR
Flexner. Amer ptg
Flexner. Short history
Boy on stenciled carpet   VWR
VWR. Folk art (col)
Elizabeth Billings Ashley   MSM
Lipman. Primitive ptrs
Ellen Virtue Field   MSM
Lipman. Primitive ptrs
Garden of Eden   MB
Barker. Amer ptg
Baur. Amer ptg
Ford. Pictorial folk art
Lipman. Primitive ptrs
MB. Karolik coll
Pierson
Girl holding rattle   VWR
Pierson
Historical monument of the American re-
public   MSM
Ford. Pictorial folk art
Larkin
Larkin rev ed
Lipman. Primitive ptrs
Mendelowitz
MSM. Handbook (col)
Pierson
Roos
Time. 300 years (col)
Joseph Moore and his family   MB
Pierson
A lady   DN
DN. Amer primitive ptgs, pt 1
A man   DN
DN. Amer primitive ptgs, pt 1
Mr Pearce (?)   VWR
Brussels. Exposition
Ford. Pictorial folk art
VWR. Folk art (col)
Mrs Joseph Moore
Pierson
Mrs Pearce ? (A woman)   VWR
Brussels. Exposition
Ford. Pictorial folk art
Larkin
Larkin rev ed
VWR. Folk art (col)
The Taj Mahal   DN
DN. Amer primitive ptgs, pt 2

Attributed works

Girl in yellow with a red doll   NCHA
Jones. New-found folk art

Field, Hannah (Gladding) 1768-1848
Malbone, E. G. Mrs John Field

Field, Mrs John. See Field, Hannah (Gladding)

Field, John White, fl 1882
Sargent, J. S. Mr and Mrs John W. Field

Field, Mrs John White. See Field, Eliza
Willing Spring (Peters)

Field II by T. Stamos

Field III, 1954 by T. Stamos

Field flowers by S. Menkès

Fields of grain as seen from train by A. G.
Dove

Fields of Llano by A. Dasburg

FIENE, Alicia
Sleep
  NAD. Annual ex, 1958
FIENE, Ernest, 1894-
Above the river   ATeS
  ATeS. Collection
Driftwood, Monegan
  NAD. Annual ex, 1952
Fall of old houses   DP
  NYG. Fine art
Hudson navigation boat   WMAA
  Pierson
Lobsterman's gear no 2
  IU. Contemp Amer ptg, 1951
Razing old post office, New York
  Gruskin
Second variation
  IU. Contemp Amer ptg, 1950
Self-portrait
  Larkin
  Larkin rev ed
Variations on a theme: the wreck no 2,
  1948   WMAA
  Goodrich. Amer art
  Pierson
Fiery night by K. L. Callahan
Fiesole, View of by W. M. Chase
Fiestas. See Fairs and festivals
Fifth avenue by J. Sloan
Fifth avenue and Forty-second street by J.
  Marin
Fifth avenue nocturne by C. Hassam
Fifth vision of Queen Vaidehi by R. Gor-
  chov
Fifty-seventh street by R. Henri
Fight for the waterhole by F. Remington
Figment of erotic torture by B. L. Culwell
Figural composition by W. Pachner
Figuration by J. Ferren
Figure by C. di Marca-Relli
Figure by R. B. Motherwell
Figure and mask by A. Rattner
Figure before a field by J. Davis
Figure in blue by R. Soyer
Figure in landscape by W. De Kooning
Figure in pictorial space by S. Menkès
Figure in pink and green by R. B. Mother-
  well
Figure in prayer by W. Pachner
Figure in space by T. D. Benrimo
Figure in the rain by R. Lebrun
Figure lost in the light by B. Greene
Figure study by J. S. Sargent
Figure study by F. Taubes
Figure study by M. Weber
Figure with bird by M. Weber
Figure with wings and mask by A. Rattner
Figures and still life by R. Dunn
Figures in a hallway by C. G. Farr
Figures in a park by M. B. Prendergast
Figures in garden by E. N. Bischoff
Figures in landscape by W. Bailey
Figures in landscape by L. M. Eilshemius

Figures in landscape by J. Glasco
Figures in space by J. Berlandina
Figures on the cross with lantern by R.
  Leburn
Figures waiting by A. Rattner
Figures with mobiles by H. J. Teyral
Fillmore, Millard, president U.S. 1800-1874
  Healy, G. P. A. Millard Fillmore
Film studio by C. Browning
FILMUS, Tully, 1903-
  Gladys   WMAA
  CSB. Illusion
The final veteran by L. Rivers
FINCH, Keith, 1920?-
  Locomotive   CLA
  Pousette-Dart. Amer ptg
Locust
  ICA. Annual ex, 1951
Standing figure
  PPC. International ex, 1955
Suburban figure
  IU. Contemp Amer ptg & sculp, 1959
FINCK, Furman Joseph, 1900-
I've got nothing to wear   OT
  OT. Contemp Amer ptgs
Warren Robinson Austin
  PPC. Ptg in the U. S. 1949
Finding of Moses by F. E. Church
Finding of Moses by M. Schwartz
Finding of Moses by Unidentified artist
Finding of Queen Zenobia by A. Russell
FINE, Perle, 1908-
Calligraphy of rhythms
  IU. Contemp Amer ptg, 1951
In the beginning
  Rathbun
Pink harlequin
  VR. Biennial ex, 1948
Storm departs
  Baur. Nature
Tolling bell
  WMAA. Annual ex, 1955
Finger lakes by E. W. Dickinson
FINK, Don
The wild one
  ICA. Annual ex, 1961
FINKELSTEIN, Louis
Green, green, I love you green
  WMAA. Contemp Amer ptg, 1959/60
FIORE, Joseph, 1925-
Poland Spring, Maine   WMAA
  IU. Contemp Amer ptg & sculp, 1961
Fir tree, Deer Isle, Maine by J. Marin
Fire by A. Refregier
Fire eater by F. C. Watkins
Fire engine by E. Opper
Fire engine, Elizabeth, New Jersey by E.
  Opper
Fire escape by C. Browning
Fire in the woods by A. M. R. Moses
Fire Island by W. De Kooning
Fire Island landing by B. Mitchell
Fire of the warehouse of Henry Webb and
  company, Baltimore, 1827 by Unidenti-
  fied artist
Fire vase by J. Ferren
Fire wheel by J. A. M. Whistler

Firecrackers sold here by W. T. Wiley
Fireflies by H. G. Keller
Fireman by W. M. Prior (manner of)
Fireworks by G. O. Hart
FIRKS, Henry, fl 1849
  San Francisco, 1849   RNH
    Davidson v 1
First branch of the White river, Vermont
    by E. Hopper
First child by L. P. Harmon
First crop by T. H. Benton
First envoy from Santo Domingo by P.
    Tilyard
First frost by K. Knaths
First hepaticas by C. E. Burchfield
The **first** hypothesis by C. Howard
First landing of Christopher Columbus by
    F. Kemmelmeyer
First of January by W. De Kooning
First row, orchestra by E. Hopper
First show at two by H. G. Keller
The **first** skating by A. M. R. Moses
First snow by D. Macknight
First step by R. C. Woodville
First Texas Central railroad by C. M.
    Williamson
Fish, Hamilton, 1808-1893
  Hicks, T. Hamilton Fish
Fish, Nicholas, 1758-1833
  Malbone, E. G. Nicholas Fish
Fish by W. M. Chase
Fish by J. D. McClusky
Fish and birds by E. F. Spruce
Fish and lobsters by W. M. Chase
The **fish** and the man by C. W. Hawthorne
Fish bowl by P. Tchelitchew
Fish cleaner by V. Vytlacil
Fish composition by V. Vytlacil
Fish forms by V. Schreckengost
Fish house door by J. F. Peto
Fish house, New England by M. Hartley
Fish houses, Newfoundland by D. Macknight
Fish in bottle by M. H. Visser't Hooft
Fish in sea and stars by M. Graves
The **fish** is on the other side by Unidentified
    artist
Fish kite by Y. Kuniyoshi
Fish market by F. Di Gioia
Fish market by L. Gatch
Fish reflected upon outer and mental space
    by M. Graves
Fish: Study for glass by J. La Farge
Fish weir, Maine by Leonid
Fish weir near Sprucehead by Leonid
Fisher, Alexander Metcalf, 1794-1822
  Morse, A. F. B. Alexander Metcalf Fisher
FISHER, Alvan, 1792-1863
  The Hudson pool
    Sears. Highlights
  Niagara
    Pierson
  Sugar loaf mountain   MB
    MB. Karolik coll

  The watering place
    Sears. Highlights
  White mountains
    Sears. Highlights
          Attributed works
  Lakes and mountains   MB
    MB. Karolik coll
       Portrait of the artist
  Fraser, C. Alvan Fisher
Fisher, James, fl 1802
  Malbone, E. G. James Fisher
FISHER, Jonathan, 1768-1847
  Building at Harvard college, c 1810   MeC
    Jetté. Amer heritage collection
  Self-portrait
    Larkin
    Larkin rev ed
Fisher, Samuel, 1814-1899
  Weir, J. F. The Theological of Yale uni-
    versity
Fisher off the coast by L. Feininger
Fisher or marten by J. J. Audubon
Fisherfolk in a boat by W. Homer
Fisherfolk on the beach at Tynemouth by
    W. Homer
Fisherman and the djinn by J. La Farge
Fisherman's accoutrements by G. Cope
Fisherman's bedroom, Eastham, Massachu-
    setts by F. W. Benson
Fisherman's bride by T. Roszak
Fisherman's chest by J. C. Atherton
A **fisherman's** day by W. Homer
Fisherman's family by G. W. Bellows
Fisherman's morning by Z. L. Sepeshy
Fisherman's still life by J. B. Stearns
Fishermen and fishing
  Baker, R. Three fishermen
  Bellows, G. W. Fisherman
  Cropsey, J. F. Hasting-on-the Hudson,
    going fishing
  Doughty, T. Anglers
  Dozier, O. Fishermen
  Etnier, S. M. The seiner
  Goodwin, P. R. Trout fishing
  Hartley, M. Nova Scotia fishermen
  Hassam, C. Montauk fisherman
  Homer, W. Boy fishing
  Homer, W. Casting the fly
  Homer, W. The dory
  Homer, W. Fisherfolk in a boat
  Homer, W. A fisherman's day
  Homer, W. Fishing
  Homer, W. Guide fishing
  Homer, W. Herring net
  Homer, W. Ouananiche fishing: Lake St
    John, Quebec
  Homer, W. Shark fishing
  Homer, W. Sunrise fishing in the
    Adirondacks
  Homer, W. Trout fishing, Lake St John,
    Quebec
  Luks, G. Conner's rock, Cape Eliza, Maine
  Marin, J. Fishermen and boats
  Mason, R. M. Anglers heaven
  Mason, R. M. Fishing at the Spillway
  Michelson, L. Fishermen on the Seine

Fishermen and fishing—*Continued*
Price, C. S. Fisherman
Price, C. S. Fishermen
Rattner, A. Fisherman
Sample, P. S. Iceland fishermen
Sample, P. S. Two trout fishermen
Spruce, E. F. Fisherman
Spruce, E. F. Surf fisherman
Stock, J. W. Fisherman with his dog
Sword, J. B. The strike—trout fishing
Tait, A. F. Striped-bass fishing
Terrell, E. Fisherman
Wertz, H. Fisherman in red hat and shirt
Whorf, J. Edge of the east water
Zajac, J. Anglers
Fishermen on shore by W. Homer
Fishermen's festival by S. Wilson
Fishermen's huts by G. W. Bellows
Fishermen's huts by A. P. Ryder
Fishermen's last supper by M. Hartley
The **fisherwoman** by Leonid
Fisherwomen by M. Beckmann
Fishes with red stripes by R. B. Motherwell
Fishing at the spillway by R. M. Mason
Fishing boat by J. Marin
Fishing boat and white sun by M. Kahn
Fishing boats by R. Crawford
Fishing boats at Capri by A. Bierstadt
Fishing by a waterfall by T. Doughty
Fishing companions by F. V. Du Mond
Fishing on the Mississippi by G. C. Bingham
Fishing party by M. B. Prendergast
Fishing party in the mountains by T. Hill
Fishing pool by T. Doughty
Fishing shrimps at Boulogne by Leonid
Fishing village by F. Martin
Fishing village by C. S. Price
Fishkill, New York, View from by W. G. Wall
FISK, William H.
George Catlin   DN
McCracken. George Catlin (col)
Morgan
Fitch, Eleazer Thompson, 1791-1871
Stone, W. O. Eleazer Thompson Fitch
Fitch, John, fl 1725
Unidentified artist. John Fitch
Fitch, Mary. See Cabot, Mary (Fitch)
Fitch, William Clyde
Chase, W. M. William Clyde Fitch
The **fitting** room by K. H. Miller
FitzGerald, Charles
Glackens, W. J. Charles FitzGerald
FITZGERALD, James Herbert, 1910-
Ember tree
OrPA. Ptgs & sculptures
The witness tree   WaS
ICA. Annual ex, 1951
Fitzgerald, Riter, d 1911
Eakins, T. Riter Fitzgerald, Sketch for portrait of
Fitzhugh, Sarah, 1746-1793
Hesselius, J. Sarah Fitzhugh
Fitzwilliam by A. James
Five in the afternoon by R. B. Motherwell

Five islands, Maine by W. Zorach
Five-master by Unidentified artist
Five strangers by Y. Tanguy
Flag carried at the Siege of Louisburg by Unidentified artist
The **flagellants** by S. Fogel
Flagellation by S. Greene
The **flagellators** by S. Greene
FLAGG, George Whiting, 1816-1897
Rebecca   NNHS
MiD. Travelers in Arcadia
Flagg, Mrs Gershom IV. See Flagg, Hannah (Pitson)
Flagg, Hannah (Pitson) 1711-1784
Feke, R. Mrs Gershom Flagg IV
FLAGG, Jared Bradley, 1820-1899
James Edward English   CtY
CtY. Portrait index
Samuel Johnson Hitchcock   CtY
CtY. Portrait index
Seth Perkins Staples (after S. L. Waldo and William Jewett)   CtY
CtY. Portrait index
Flagg, Rachel Moore Allston
Allston, W. Artist's mother, Mrs Henry Collins Flagg
Flagging antelope by C. M. Russell
Flags and fishes by P. Dike
Le **flambeau** by C. R. Holty
Flame by W. A. Baziotes
Flame by L. Gatch
Flame by J. Pollock
Flame and winter tree by K. Schrag
FLANNERY, Vaughn, 1898-
Chestnut stallion, Discovery
PPC. International ex, 1950
The governor's cup   DP
DP. Catalogue
Swan island   OT
OT. Contemp Amer ptgs
Flatboatmen by night by G. C. Bingham
Flax-scutching bee by L. Park
Flayed arm by H. Tovish
Flayed hills by D. V. Schlegell
Fleecing the priest by C. M. Russell
Fleeting time, thou hast left me old by I. L. Albright
Flesh eaters by W. A. Baziotes
FLETCHER, Alex, 1866-1952
Communion service, First Presbyterian church   PW
Chew. 250 years of art
Portrait of the artist
Cuthbert, V. I. Alex Fletcher
Fletcher, Levi
Sully, T. Levi Fletcher
Flight by J. D. Brooks
Flight by E. Harris
Flight by R. D. King
Flight by N. D. Knap
Flight into Egypt by W. Page
Flight into Egypt by Unidentified artist
Flight into morning by J. Gelb
Flight of birds by B. J. O. Nordfeldt
Flight of fancy by P. Evergood

Flight of Florimell by W. Allston
Flight of night by W. M. Hunt
Flight of plover by M. Graves
Flight of the clowns by E. Shinn
Flintlock by S. Martin
Float at low tide, Revere beach by M. B. Prendergast
Float on the Schuylkill by W. Stuempfig
Floating ice by G. W. Bellows
Floating island by G. G. Russell
Floating white city by F. Berman
Floats and markers by S. Wilson
FLOCH, Joseph, 1894-
 Conversation
  NAD. Annual ex, 1947, 1st half
 Girl looking out of window   NJMo
  NJMo. Forty years
 Near the sea
  NAD. Annual ex, 1960
 Still life with nude
  NAD. Annual ex, 1958
 Terrace
  NAD. Annual ex, 1954
Flock of sheep by W. Homer
Flood by A. B. Davies
Flood by B. J. O. Nordfeldt
Flood refugees by J. Corbino
Floral composition by H. Hofmann
Florence by T. Roszak
Florence, Italy
 Boit, E. D. Florence
 Boit, E. D. Florence from San Miniato
 Bosa, L. Ponte Vecchio, Florence
 Duveneck, F. The bridges, Florence
 Pucci, A. J. Ponte Vecchio
 Sargent, J. S. Florence: Boboli gardens
 Sargent, J. S. Florence: Torre Galli
Florence protecting the arts by A. H. Thayer
Florentines by A. H. Maurer
Florida
 Harvey, G. White pelicans in Florida
 Heade, M. J. On the Sebastian river, Florida
 Homer, W. Homosassa river
 Homer, W. Indian in Florida swamps
 Homer, W. Thornhill bar, Florida
 Martin, F. Florida landscape
 Matthew, K. Azalea tropical trails, Florida
 Pleissner, O. M. Florida landscape
Florinsky, Michael T.
 Evergood, P. M. T. Florinsky, D. S. Mirsky and the pidget
Florist's window by J. Lawrence
FLORSHEIM, Richard Aberle, 1916-
 Night city
  Time. 300 years (col)
 Wharves   MiD
  CoS. New accessions, USA, 1960
Flounder by R. Tam
Flour mill by A. G. Dove
Flower abstraction by M. Hartley
Flower eruption by T. Stamos
Flower forms by C. Sheeler
Flower market at Geneva by D. A. Dreier
Flower piece by A. B. Carles

Flower piece by C. H. Demuth
Flower piece by M. Weber
Flower still life by N. Tschacbasov
Flower study by C. H. Demuth
Flower study by N. L. Murphy
Flower vendor by M. Avery
Flower vendor by R. Soyer
Flower vendors by R. Gwathmey
Flower women by I. Rose
Flowered hat by H. V. Poor
Flowering branch by H. Hofmann
Flowering white by J. Tworkov
Flowermakers by A. Blanch
Flowers by J. Corbino
Flowers by C. H. Demuth
Flowers by A. H. Maurer
Flowers by F. J. Rederer
Flowers and fruit by Unidentified artist
Flowers, butterfly, and book by Unidentified artist
Flowers by the lake by P. Evergood
Flowers, cyclamen by C. H. Demuth
Flowers from Claire Spencer's garden by M. Hartley
Flowers from my garden by B. Klonis
Flowers in a garden by N. Cikovsky
Flowers in Pennsylvania Dutch teapot by F. C. Watkins
Flowers in the city by C. C. Burg
Flowers in vase by F. Papsdorf
Flowers on a window ledge by J. La Farge
Flowers with four doilies by H. Pippin
Flowers with hat and cane by H. Pippin
Floyd, Mary. See Tallmadge, Mary (Floyd)
Flutes. See Musicians and musical instruments—Flutes
Fluttering fowl by R. Koppe
Fluttering pendant by K. R. Morris
Flying box by J. Hultberg
Flying carpet by S. Davis
Flying Codonas by J. S. Curry
Flying Dutchman by L. M. Eilshemius
Flying Dutchman by J. Ernst
Flying Dutchman by A. P. Ryder
Flying horses by M. B. Prendergast
Flying kites, Montmartre by W. J. Glackens
Flying trapeze by A. Rattner
Flyweight champ of Jumel place by G. B. Luks
Fog horns by A. G. Dove
Fog lifts by J. Marin
Fog warning by W. Homer
FOGEL, Seymour, 1911-
 Driftwood structure
  Pearson. Mod renaissance
 The flagellants
  Pearson. Mod renaissance
 Genesis
  Pearson. Mod renaissance
 Icarian flight   TxF
  Pousette-Dart. Amer ptg
 Labyrinth
  Pearson. Mod renaissance

Foggy night by J. De Martini

Foggy pasture by D. W. Gorsline

Foissin, Elizabeth. See Trapier, Elizabeth (Foissin)

Folding chair by A. Katz

FOLINSBEE, John Fulton, 1892-
Don Quixote
    NAD. Annual ex, 1953
Night
    NAD. Annual ex, spring 1950
Quarry pool
    NAD. Annual ex, 1955

FOLLETT, Jean, 1917-
Untitled, 1950
    NNSG. Younger Amer ptrs

Fondey family, fl 1803
Ames, E. The Fondey family

Football. See Games and sports—Ball

Footbridge at Bridgeport by J. H. Twackman

FOOTE, John, 1921-
The entombment
    IU. Contemp Amer ptg, 1951

For God must have loved them by E. Melcarth

For internal use only by S. Davis

For service rendered by W. Hedrick

For Thanksgiving by H. G. Keller

FORBES, Donald, 1905-
Landscape with bird's nest   ATU
    ATU. Coll of Amer art

FORBES, Hannah Lucinda, fl 1820
Mourning piece
    Ford. Pictorial folk art

Forbes, William Smith, 1831-1905
Eakins, T. Professor William Smith Forbes

Forbidden blossom by W. Pachner

Forbidden fruit by Y. Kuniyoshi

Forbidden thicket by C. Cloar

Force in space by C. G. Shaw

Forces against violent attack by J. De Diego

FORD, Lauren, 1891-
Bethlehem   InIJ
    InIJ. 105 ptgs
Nativity
    PC. Ptg in the U.S. 1949

The ford by H. G. Keller

Foreboding by H. M. Mayer

Forest by W. Homer

Forest by E. Magafan

Forest by S. Sherman

Forest by V. Vytlacil

Forest by M. Weber

Forest boundary by R. Cowles

Forest city by A. Friedman

Forest hill—the Nelson homestead near Boonville by G. C. Bingham

Forest of Arden by A. P. Ryder

Forest of Zogbaum by W. De Kooning

Forest park, View in by W. Barker

Forest stream, a study from nature by A. H. Wyant

Forevermore by A. Blanch

The forge by W. M. Hunt

Forget it by L. Lewitin

Forging the shaft, replica by J. F. Weir

Forgotten cabin by A. James

The forgotten man by P. Evergood

Forlorn one by R. S. Neuman

FORMAN, Alice, 1931-
Untitled landscape no 6, 1960
    WMAA. Young America 1960
Untitled landscape no 11, 1959
    WMAA. Young America 1960

Forman, David
Peale, C. W. Gen David Forman

Formation of rock by A. J. Miller

Forms by A. E. Gallatin

Forms abstracted by M. Hartley

Forms follow man by M. Tobey

FORST, Miles, 1923-
Cell
    NNSG. Younger Amer ptrs

Forsythias by H. Moller

Fort, Mrs Seymour, fl 1776
Copley, J. S. Mrs Seymour Fort

Fort Arbuckle, Oklahoma territory by V. Colyer

Fort Clark by K. Bodmer

Fort Harker, Kansas by H. Stieffel

Fort Keough, Montana by H. Stieffel

Fort Laramie by A. J. Miller

Fort Laramie, Interior of by A. J. Miller

Fort Lee ferry by G. O. Coleman

Fort McHenry, Star Spangled Banner over by Unidentified artist

Fort Montgomery, View near by W. G. Wall

Fort Pierre by K. Bodmer

Fort Pierre with Sioux camped around by G. Catlin

Fort Plain, New York by J. H. Hidley

Fort St Jean, Marseilles by R. Smith

Fort Snelling by Unidentified artist

Fort Snelling by J. C. Wild

Fort Snelling on the upper Mississippi by G. Catlin

Fort Snelling, View of by S. Eastman

Fort Sumter by C. W. Chapman

Fort Ticonderoga, Ruins of by R. Smith

Fort Union, mouth of the Yellowstone by G. Catlin

Fort Vancouver by H. J. Warre

FORTESS, Karl Eugene, 1907-
Big tree
    Pearson. Mod renaissance
Entrance
    Pearson. Mod renaissance
Group of trees
    Pearson. Mod renaissance
Landscape
    NYG. Fine art
Portrait
    IU. Contemp Amer ptg, 1949
Rockhill special   ATU
    ATU. Coll of Amer art
Upright 3
    IU. Contemp Amer ptg & sculp, 1955

Fortifications of Elba by D. W. Ellis

Fortune hunters by H. Baer

Fortune seller by K. Zerbe

Fortune teller by S. M. Adler
Fortune teller by W. J. Gordon
A Forty-niner by J. W. Audubon
Forty-second street by T. Roszak
Forty-two kids by G. W. Bellows
Forward but beyond by N. Daphnis
FOSBURGH, James Whitney, 1910-
  The kite
    CSFP. Annual ex, 1952
FOSS, Oliver, 1920-
  Paris under snow
    IU. Contemp Amer ptg, 1952
  Relaxation
    MoSL. Contemporary Amer ptg
Fossil hunters by E. W. Dickinson
Fossils by M. Tobey
Foster, Mrs Isaac, fl 1755
  Badger, J. Mrs Isaac Foster
FOSTER, John, 1648-1681
  John Wheelwright (?)   MBS
    Barker. Amer ptg

Attributed works

John Davenport   CtY
  CtY. Portrait index
  Flexner. First flowers
  Ford. Pictorial folk art
  Pierson
Foul weather, Percé by H. G. Keller
FOUNTAIN, Albert J. 1862-1936
  Celebration of the Gadsden purchase
    NUM. Art across America
The fountain by W. A. Baziotes
The fountain by W. Thon
Fountains at night, World's Columbian exposition, Chicago by W. Homer
Fountains of Europe by M. Tobey
Four and a half out of every five by B. Shahn
The four apostles writing the Gospels by Unidentified artist
Four children playing in a street by J. Paul
Four dancers by M. Soyer
Four figures in a bistro by A. Blatas
Four girls in meadow by M. B. Prendergast
The four horsemen of the Apocalypse by J. de Botton
Four houses by A. P. Martino
Four-master off the Cape by J. Marin
Four men by D. Park
Four men around a table by M. Beckmann
Four o'clock in summer: hope by T. Tanguy
Four o'clock on the Seine by J. Marin
Four opposites by J. Pollock
Four-panel green by A. Leslie
Four part synchromy, no 7, 1914-15 by M. Russell
Four piece orchestra by B. Shahn
The four seasons by C. E. Burchfield
4 September 1960 by K. R. Morris
Fourcaud, Louis de, 1851-1914
  Sargent, J. S. Louis de Fourcaud
Fourteenth street by R. Marsh
Fourteenth street by K. H. Miller

Fourteenth street promenade by G. L. K. Morris
Fourth dimension by P. Sullivan
Fourth of July by L. Guglielmi
Fourth of July by C. W. Hare
Fourth of July celebration in Centre square, Philadelphia, 1819 by J. L. Krimmel
Fourth of July in Centre square, Philadelphia, c 1810 by J. L. Krimmel
Fourth of July orator by B. Shahn
Fourth of July picnic by S. Merrett
Fourth Pennsylvania Cavalry by Unidentified artist
Fowle, Jacob, 1704-1778?
  Copley, J. S. Jacob Fowle
Fowler, Samuel Stevenson, 1799-1850
  Ames, E. Samuel Stevenson Fowler
Fowles, Abigail. See Edwards, Abigail (Fowles)
FOWLER, O. R. fl 1838
  A gentleman   MeC
    Jetté. Amer heritage collection
  A lady   MeC
    Jetté. Amer heritage collection
Fox island, Maine by M. Hartley
Fox hunter by K. Knaths
Foxes
  Audubon, J. J. Fox and goose
  Darrel, A. Vixen
  Graves, M. Fox with phoenix wing
  Hazel, S. M. Fox
  Hinkley, T. Fox in West Virginia
  Homer, W. Fox hunt
  Hope, J. Winter scene: the red fox
  Pippin, H. The getaway
Fragment of an empire by F. Roth
Fragment of peace by M. Tobey
Fragment: three heads by H. J. Teyral
Fragment: two figures by H. J. Teyral
Fragments and reconstruction by U. Romano
Fragments from yesterday by D. W. Ellis
Fragments of elegance by W. Lockwood
Fragments of roses by W. Brice
Fragrance of fear by M. Tomkins
Fragrance of grasses by K. Schrag
FRAME, Robert, 1924-
  Beach no 1
    IU. Contemp Amer ptg & sculp, 1961
  Evening landscape
    IU. Contemp Amer ptg & sculp, 1957
FRANCES, Esteban, 1914-
  El cuadro de los Abanicos
    IU. Contemp Amer ptg, 1952
  Salto mortal
    CSP. Annual ex, 1947/48
Frances and Judy by L. Betts
Francis, John, 1763-1796
  Malbone, E. G. John Francis
FRANCIS, John F. 1810-1885
  Apples in a basket
    Chew. 250 years of art
    WiMiA. Amer ptg 1760-1960
  Grapes in a bowl
    CSFP. Illusionism
  Iris and snowballs
    Frankenstein. After the hunt

FRANCIS, J. F.—*Continued*
Still life NJP
Barker. Amer ptg
Still life, 1867 MB
Frankenstein. After the hunt
Still life with apples and chestnuts, 1859 MB
MB. Karolik coll
Still life with wine bottles and basket of fruit MB
MB. Karolik coll
Three children MB
MB. Karolik coll

Francis, John Wakefield, 1810-1885
Elliott, C. L. John Wakefield Francis

FRANCIS, Sam, 1923?-
Abstraction WaS
CoS. New accessions USA, 1958
Big red MMA
MMA. New Amer ptg (col)
MMA. 12 Americans (col)
Black in red MMA
MMA. New Amer ptg
MMA. 12 Americans
Blue and black (Power coll)
MMA. New Amer ptg
Ponente. Mod ptg, 1960 (col)
Blue—black NBuA
MMA. 12 Americans
NBuA. Acquisitions 1954-57
Cross
PPC. International ex, 1961/62
Deep orange on black
MMA. 12 Americans
Gray
MMA. 12 Americans
Red and black NNSG
NNSG. Handbook
PPC. International ex, 1955
Red in red, 1955
McCurdy
MMA. 12 Americans
Summer no 1
50 years of mod art
Read. Concise history (col)
Summer no II
Art since 1945
Two worlds
MnMW. 60 Amer ptrs
Watercolour
Read. Concise history
The white line
WMAA. Contemp Amer ptg, 1959/60

FRANCK, Frederick Sigfred, 1909-
From my attic
NBuA. Expressionism
Lazarus resurrected
IU. Contemp Amer ptg, 1949
New York from Hoboken
IU. Contemp Amer ptg, 1950 (col)
New York with roller coaster
IU. Contemp Amer ptg & sculp, 1953
The soothsayer
IU. Contemp Amer ptg, 1952
Still life enters death
IU. Contemp Amer ptg, 1951

Franconia range—mist and rain by J. Marin
FRANK, Eugene C. d 1914
Wyalusing
McClintock
Frankenberg, Mrs Lloyd. See MacIver, Loren

FRANKENSTEIN, John Peter, 1816-1881
The artist in his studio
Chew. 250 years of art
WiMiA. Amer ptg 1760-1960

FRANKENTHALER, Helen, 1928-
L'amour, toujours l'amour
IU. Contemp Amer ptg & sculp, 1959
Black and white and read all over
ICA. Annual ex, 1961
Blue territory WMAA
Goodrich. Amer art
WMAA. Young America 1957
Eden
Hunter. Mod Amer ptg (col)
The facade
PPC. International ex, 1955
Italian beach
PPC. International ex, 1961/62
Loreli
Baur. Nature (col)
Las Mayas
MnMW. 60 Amer ptrs
Round trip NBuA
NBuA. Acquisitions 1957-58
Trojan gates MMA
Cheney. Story 1958 ed

FRANKFURTER, Jack, 1929-
Reconstruction
VR. Amer ptg, 1958

Franklin, Benjamin, 1706-1790
Healy, G. P. A. Benjamin Franklin at the court of Louis XVI
Peale, C. W. Benjamin Franklin
West, B. Benjamin Franklin drawing electricity from the sky
Wright, J. (attributed works) Benjamin Franklin

Franklin, Maud
Whistler, J. A. M. Arrangement in black and white (The young American, Maud Franklin)

Franklin park, Boston by M. B. Prendergast
Franks, Bilhah Abigail (Levy)
Duyckinck, G. (attributed works) Mrs Jacob Franks

Franks, David, 1720-1793
Duyckinck, G. (attributed works) Children of Jacob Franks

Franks, Jacob, 1688-1769
Unidentified artist. Jacob Franks
Franks, Mrs Jacob. See Franks, Bilhah Abigail (Levy)
Franks, Phila. See De Lancey, Phila (Franks)
FRANKS, Seymour, 1916-
Kaleidoscopic journey
ICA. Annual ex, 1947/48
Vibration
IU. Contemp Amer ptg, 1952

FRANSIOLI, Thomas Adrian, 1906-
The cat
PPC. International ex, 1952
Interior number 2
IU. Contemp Amer ptg & sculp, 1957
Louisburg square
IU. Contemp Amer ptg, 1951
St Andrew's church, Roanoke
IU. Contemp Amer ptg, 1952
Way to Penobscot
IU. Contemp Amer ptg, 1950

FRARY, Michael, 1918-
Apartment house   TxD
  Pousette-Dart. Amer ptg
Coast town   OYB
  OYB. Annual 1959
Oil construction on the beach   OYB
  OYB. Annual 1955
  OYB. Supplement 1959
Still life with thistles
  IU. Contemp Amer ptg & sculp, 1953
FRASCONI, Antonio, 1919-
Warwick mine, exit no 1
  WMAA. Annual ex, 1956
Fraser, Alexander, 1722-1791
  Theus, J. Alexander Fraser
FRASER, Charles, 1782-1860
Alvan Fisher   MM
  MM. New England miniatures (col)
Rice Hope   SCCG
  Davidson v 1
The fratellini by L. MacIver
FRAZER, Oliver, 1808-1864
Anderson children   KyLS
  KyLS. Kentucky port gall
Freake, Elizabeth (Clarke) 1642-1713
  Freake limner. Mrs Freake and baby
    Mary
FREAKE limner, fl 1668-1723
Henry Gibbs
  Flexner. First flowers
  Ford. Pictorial folk art (col)
  ICA. From colony to nation
    Larkin rev ed
Margaret Gibbs
  Barker. Amer ptg
  Flexner. Amer ptg
  Flexner. First flowers
  Flexner. Short history
  Mendelowitz
  Time. 300 years (col)
Mrs Freake and baby Mary   MWM
  NYG. Fine art p211
  Richardson. Ptg in America
  Robb. Art 1953 ed
  Robb. Harper history
Robert Gibbs
  Flexner. First flowers
  Pierson
FREDENTHAL, David, 1914-
The immigrant
  WMAA. Annual ex, 1956
The people   ATU
  ATU. Coll of Amer art
Requiem
  Genauer
Veni, vidi, vici
  IU. Contemp Amer ptg, 1949
The free trader by C. M. Russell
Free trappers in trouble by A. J. Miller
FREEDMAN, Maurice, 1904-
Caught in net
  PPC. Ptg in the U. S. 1949
Pemaquid lobster
  Gruskin (col)
Squall off Christmas cove
  Cheney. Primer 1958 ed
FREEMAN, Mr. fl 1816
Mrs William Cooper (Elizabeth Feni-
  more Cooper)   NCHA
  Jones. Rediscovered ptrs
  Pierson

Peter Volo   NCHA
  Jones. New-found folk art
  Attributed works
Catherine A. Russell
  Jones. Rediscoverd ptrs
Rensselaer W. Russell (in his thirteenth
  year)
  Jones. Rediscovered ptrs
FREEMAN, Don, 1908-
Carl Sandburg   ATU
  ATU. Coll of Amer art
Freeman, Mrs Joseph. See Von Wiegand,
  Charmion
Freight cars by C. E. Burchfield
Freight cars in desert by P. S. Sample
Freight cars, Minneapolis by R. Crawford
Freight cars under a bridge by C. E. Burch-
  field
Freight yards by G. R. Beal
Frelinghuysen, Mrs Peter
  Cassatt, M. Mrs Peter Frelinghuysen
FRENCH, Jared, 1905-
The rope   WMAA
  Goodrich. Amer art
  MnMW. Reality and fantasy
  Pierson
  WMAA. Contemp Amer ptg, 1955
French Canadian barn by C. C. Richardson
French child on train by M. Fadden
French village church by A. B. Carles
Fresh water cove from Dolliver's neck,
  Gloucester by F. H. Lane
Freuchen, Peter, 1886-
  Brackman, R. Peter Freuchen
FRIEBERT, Joseph, 1908-
Synagogue   ICA
  Pousette-Dart. Amer ptg
Urban cathedral
  ICA. Amer artists paint the city
FRIED, Theodore, 1902-
Nursing mother
  PPC. Ptg in the U.S. 1949
FRIEDENSOHN, Elias, 1924-
Ancestor
  IU. Contemp Amer ptg & sculp, 1961
Effort at speech between two people
  WMAA. Young America 1957
Jeune fille en fleur   IU
  IU. Contemp Amer ptg & sculp, 1957
  IU. 20th century
Prometheus
  IU. Contemp Amer ptg & sculp, 1959
Secret
  WMAA. Young America 1957
FRIEDMAN, Arnold, 1873-1946
Forest city
  Baur. Revolution
Unemployable   MM
  Cheney. Story 1958 ed
FRIEDMAN, Martin, 1896-
Eventide
  IU. Contemp Amer ptg, 1948
The grotto
  PPC. Ptg in the U.S. 1949
Metropolitan nocturne
  IU. Contemp Amer ptg & sculp, 1953
Pink flower
  IU. Contemp Amer ptg & sculp, 1955

FRIEDMAN, Martin—*Continued*
The quarry   ATU
    ATU. Coll of Amer art
Sawtooth Falls   MMA
    Pierson
A **friendly** call by W. M. Chase
Friends or enemies by C. M. Russell
Friendship by M. Weber
FRIESEKE, Frederick Carl, 1874-1939
    Yellow room   InIJ
    InIJ. 105 ptgs
Frieze by J. Pollock
Frightened deer in moonlight by K. Knaths
FRINCK, O. E. S. fl 1845
    Landscape
        Sears. Highlights
Frishmuth, Mrs William D.
    Eakins, T. Mrs William D. Frishmuth
Frog monster by B. Shahn
Frogman by J. Pollock
Frogtown lady by A. Brook
From a cathedral by B. Margo
From afar by F. Nagler
From an ivory tower by J. L. Lasker
From Arkansas by G. Schreiber
From Avenue A by H. Rose
From Cranberry isle by J. F. Heliker
From elements of evening by B. Margo
From February by B. Margo
From my attic by F. S. Franck
From my studio by F. Crowninshield
From my studio window by J. Kane
From my window by C. C. Ross
From nature in the garden by Rubens Peale
From one night to the other by Y. Tanguy
From seeing Cape Split by J. Marin
From shipwrecks by B. Margo
From that day on by B. Shahn
From the bridge by R. Crawford
From the bridge, New York city by J. Marin
From the pelvis series by G. O'Keeffe
From the plain by G. O'Keeffe
From the plains no 1, 1953 by G. O'Keeffe
From the terrace by S. Laufman
From the town beyond the river by G. Grosz
From the upper terrace by J. H. Twachtman
From Weehawken heights by J. Marin
From Williamsburg bridge by E. Hopper
The **fronfroneur** by K. J. Priebe
Front face by W. M. Harnett
Front porch by R. Gwathmey
Front street by C. S. Price
Frontier by K. M. Martin
Frontiersman, Head of a by F. Remington
FROST, Arthur Burdett, 1851-1928
    Hunting deer   MB
        MB. Ptgs in water color
    Hunting the moose
        NSP. Sportscapes

        Portrait of the artist
    Eakins, T. Arthur B. Frost

FROST, John O. J.
    Marblehead harbor
        Lipman. Primitive ptrs
Frothingham, Abby Langdon. See Wales,
    Abby Langdon (Frothingham)
Frowning cliff, Watkins glen, New York
    by J. Hope
Frozen sounds by A. Gottlieb
Frozen station by J. Hultberg
Frugal housewife by J. H. Davis (attribu-
    ted works)
Fruit by J. Peale
Fruit by H. V. Poor
Fruit and daisies by A. Pregel
Fruit and flowers by M. B. Prendergast
Fruit and flowers by Unidentified artist
Fruit and goldfinch by Wagguno
Fruit and melon by Unidentified artist
Fruit and table by K. Knaths
Fruit and wine by E. Bowers
Fruit bowl by H. Hofmann
Fruit bowl by W. Sommer
Fruit bowl with mirror by S. Menkès
Fruit in a white bowl by B. A. Sawyer
Fruit in yellow bowl by M. R. Wilson
Fruit on table by S. Roesen
Fruit, vase and mandolin by N. Cikovsky
Fruit with striped pottery by W. J.
    Glackens
Fruits of autumn by J. Peale
Fruits of Belfield by C. W. Peale
Fry, Catherine, 1780-1858
    Malbone, E. G. Catherine Fry
Full fathom five by J. Pollock
Full moon by H. B. Schleeter
Full white by L. P. Smith
FULLER, Augustus, 1812-1873
    Fanny Negus Fuller and twins
        Ford. Pictorial folk art
    A gentleman   MeC
        Jetté. Amer heritage collection
    A lady   MeC
        Jetté. Amer heritage collection
    Lady wearing a red pompon   MSM
        Ford. Pictorial folk art
        MSM. Handbook
FULLER, C. Sue, 1914-
    String construction no 30
        IU. Contemp Amer ptg, 1952
    String composition no 50
        IU. Contemp Amer ptg & sculp, 1955
Fuller, Fanny Negus, fl 1840
    Fuller, A. Mrs Fanny Negus Fuller and
        twins
FULLER, George, 1822-1884
    Country lass   MNS
        Larkin
        Larkin rev ed
    Fedalma   DNC
        DNC. Gellatly coll, 1954
    Gold and old lace   OYB
        OYB. Catalogue 1951
    Ideal head   DP
        DP. Catalogue
        Pierson
    Mrs Weatherbee. See Old age (Mrs
        Weatherbee)

Nydia   MM
  NAD. Amer tradition
Old age (Mrs Weatherbee)   MoSL
  MoSL. Handbook 1953
The quadroon   MM
  Barker. Amer ptg
Tomato patch   MiD
  Pierson
  Richardson. Ptg in America
Winifred Dysart   MWM
  Pierson
Fuller, Margaret. See Ossoli, Sarah Mar-
  garet (Fuller) marchesa d'
Fuller, Sue. See Fuller, C. Sue
Fully developed escutcheon by C. Howard
FULTON, Robert, 1765-1815
  Mrs Oliver H. Perry
  MB. New England miniatures (col)

  Portrait of the artist
  Leroy, E. E. Robert Fulton
  Peale, Rembrandt. Robert Fulton
Fulton and Nostrand by J. Lawrence
Fulton street, New York by S. Pierson
La fumée d'ambre-gris by J. S. Sargent
Fun by W. W. Quirt
Funeral coach by B. Kamihira
Funeral of the poet Panizza by G. Grosz
Funeral scaffold of a Sioux chief by K.
  Bodmer
The fur jacket by J. A. M. Whistler
Fur traders descending the Misouri by G. C.
  Bingham
Fur trappers' rendezvous by A. J. Miller
Furbish, Dependence H.
  Beckett, C. E. Furbish's dash to Mon-
  treal
Furling the foresail by C. R. Patterson
Furlough by G. Grosz
Furneaux, Anne. See Clarke, Anne
  (Furneaux)
FURNESS, John Mason, 1763-1804
  John Vinal   NBM
  Flexner. Light of distant skies
  Pierson
The furniture of time by Y. Tanguy
Furniture shop and warehouse of Duncan
  Phyfe, Fulton street, New York by
  Unidentified artist
Further festivities at the Contessa Sanse-
  verini's by J. Wilde
Fury by H. Hofmann
Fusion by W. Kamys
Fussel, Charles Lewis, 1840-1909
  Eakins, T. Charles Lewis Fussel
The future by P. Evergood
Future admiral by J. C. Phillips
The future belongs to them by P. Evergood

G

G-5, 1923-26 by L. Moholy-Nagy
Gaberndorf II by L. Feininger
Gables I, 1925 by L. Feininger
Gables IV by L. Feininger

GABO, Naum, 1890-
  Blue construction in space—kinetic
                                     CtHW
  CtHW. Handbook
  Construction
  Read. Art now, 1948 ed
  Linear construction no 2, variation no 1,
  1950   MAP
  MnMW. Classic tradition
Gabriel by F. C. Watkins
Gabrielle by A. H. Maurer
Gadsden, Selina Fenwick. See Curwen, Se-
  lina Fenwick (Gadsden)
Gadsden purchase, Celebration of by A. J.
  Fountain
GAERTNER, Carl Frederick, 1898-1952
  Atwood's cove
  IU. Contemp Amer ptg, 1950
  PPC. Ptg in the U. S. 1949
  Bend at Newton hook   OYB
  OYB. Supplement
  Bend in Storm King   OCl
  Pousette-Dart. Amer ptg
  Erie street boys
  NAD. Annual ex, spring 1950
  Fairport harbor
  MM. Amer ptg today
  Lands end road
  IU. Contemp Amer ptg, 1949
  Pidge, Blink and the sea   IaDa
  IaDa. Silver jubilee
  IaDa. 30th anniversary
  Population—3000
  VR. Biennial ex, 1948
  River view and the plaza
  IU. Contemp Amer ptg, 1948
  The St Clair fire   OCl
  OCl. Handbook
  Wharf players, moonlight
  CSFP. Annual ex, 1952
Galatea by J. S. Copley
Gallagher, Mary
  Henri, R. Mary Gallagher
GALLAGHER, Sears, b 1869
  Landscape with a farmhouse   MB
  MB. Ptgs in water color
GALLATIN, Albert Eugene, 1881-1952
  Composition, 1942   PPhM
  PPhM. Gallatin coll
  Forms
  McCurdy
  MMA. Abstract
Galleria, Naples by A. Blaustein
Galleria Umberto by M. Beckmann
Gallery of the Louvre by S. F. B. Morse
Gallond, Almira. See Moore, Almira (Gal-
  lond)
GALLOWAY, 1940-
  Sea coming into the land
  MBIC. View 1960
Galloway, Jane, 1745-1801
  West, B. Jane Galloway
Galloway, Mrs Richard
  Hesselius, J. Mrs Richard Galloway jr of
  Cedar Park, Maryland
Gambetta, Léon, 1838-1882
  Healy, G. P. A. Léon Gambetta
Gamble, Agnes S. B. See Cabell, Agnes
  S. B. (Gamble)
The gamblers by E. Higgins
The game by B. Kamihira

The **game** by M. Schapiro
Game of chance by G. Ortman
Game of pretend by A. Pickens
Games and sports
    See also Boxers and wrestlers; Fisher-
    men and fishing; Hunters and hunting
Bosa, L. Hallowe'en
Cadmus, P. Playground
Kirschenbaum, J. Playground
Unidentified artist. Winter sports on the
    farm

Archery
Catlin, G. Archery of the Mandans or
    game of the arrow

Badminton
Lee, D. E. Badminton

Ball
    See also other ball games below, e.g.
    Croquet; Pool; Tennis
Catlin, G. Ball-play of the Choctaws
Catlin, G. Champion Choctaw ball-player
Eakins, T. Baseball players
Eastman, S. Lacrosse playing among the
    Sioux
Phillips, M. A. Night baseball
Schanker, L. Football
Shahn, B. Handball
Warren, F. E, Night baseball game
    Cardinals vs. Dodgers

Bicycling
Avery, M. Bicycle rider
De Martini, J. Bike race no 2
Egri, T. Bicycle riders
Egri, T. Destination unknown
Feininger, L. Bicycle riders
Wyeth, A. N. Young America

Cards
Baer, H. Cribbage players
Bingham, G. C. In a quandary
Higgins, E. The gamblers
Johnson, E. Card playing at Fryeburg,
    Maine
Levine, J. Card players
Pickens, A. Card players
Stanley, J. M. Indians playing cards
Watkins, F. C. Solitaire
Woodville, R. C. Card players

Checkers
Bingham, G. C. Checker players

Chess
Eakins, T. Chess players
Lawrence, J. Chess on Broadway
Moller, H. Chess players
Poor, H. V. Chess game
Tooker, G. Chess game

Croquet
Homer, W. Croquet match
Homer, W. Croquet players
Sample, P. S. Roque

Dice
Binford, J. Crap shooter

Dominoes
Pippin, H. Domino players
Unidentified artist. The domino girl

Hopscotch
Albright, I. L. Hopscotch
MacIver, L. Hopscotch
Vickrey, R. Hopscotch

Kite flying
Glackens, W. J. Flying kites, Montmartre
Kester, L. Kite fliers

Polo
Bellows, G. W. Polo at Lakewood
Bellows, G. W. Polo scene
Hurd, P. Landscape with polo players

Pool
Bloom, D. S. Pool room
Burlin, P. Pool player

Quoits
Homer, W. Pitching quoits

Rowing
Eakins, T. John Biglen in a single scull
Eakins, T. Oarsmen

Skating
Beckmann, M. Skaters
Birch, T. Skating
Bosa, L. Carnival on the ice
Durrie, G. H. Boys skating
Eilshemius, L. Skater
Gignoux, F. R. (attributed works) Winter
    landscape with skaters
Glackens, W. J. Roller skating rink
Homer, W. Skating at Central park
Kuniyoshi, Y. Skating
Maril, H. Skaters
Moses, A. M. R. The first skating
Moses, A. M. R. The trappers II
Pepper, C. H. Skating
Schuessele, C. and Weber, P. Skating at
    Kelley's dam, Germantown
Smith, M. Skating at the wide waters
    on the canal
Stuart, G. The skater
Toole, J. Skating scene

Skiing
Evergood, P. Men and mountain
Pike, J. Kids skiing

Skipping rope
Ahlas, L. Jump rope
Albro, M. Skipping
Prendergast, M. B. Skipping rope

Swimming
Bellows, G. W. Forty-two kids

Tennis
Bellows, G. W. Tennis tournament
The **gamin** by G. B. Luks
Gangster funeral by J. Levine
GANNAM, John
    City scene
        NAD. Annual ex, 1952
GANSEVOORT limner
    Leonard Gansevoort
        Flexner. First flowers
    Mrs Leonard Gansevoort
        Flexner. First flowers

INDEX TO REPRODUCTIONS OF PAINTINGS 177

Pau De Wandelaer NAI
Belknap
Flexner. First flowers (col)
Jones. Rediscovered ptrs
NAI. Hudson valley

Gansevoort, Catherine (De Wandelaer)
Gansevoort limner. Mrs Leonard Gansevoort

Gansevoort, Catherine (Van Schaick) 1752-1830
Ames, E. Mrs Peter Gansevoort

Gansevoort, Leonard, 1751-1810
Gansevoort limner. Leonard Gansevoort

Gansevoort street by W. De Kooning

GANSO, Emil, 1895-1941
Village church
NYG. Fine art

Gant by J. Brooks

Garage lights by S. Davis

GARBER, Daniel, 1880-1958
Old church, Carversville
NAD. Annual ex, 1959
Pioneer's house InIJ
InIJ. 105 ptgs

Garden by D. Austin
Garden by J. Berlandina
Garden by A. Blanch
Garden by J. Ferren
Garden by J. E. Levi
Garden frieze by S. Amato
Garden in Sochi by A. Gorky
Garden in Sochi motif by A. Gorky
A garden is a sea of flowers by R. S. Turner
Garden of Betty Mae by P. Evergood
Garden of Eden by T. Cole
Garden of Eden by E. S. Field
Garden of memories by C. E. Burchfield
Garden of the Generalife, Granada by R. D. Gauley
Garden of the gods by A. A. Dehn
Garden wall by M. Kahn
Garden wall by J. S. Sargent

Gardiner, Emma Jane (Tudor) 1785-1865
Malbone, E. G. Mrs Robert Hallowell Gardiner

Gardiner, Robert Hallowell, 1782-1864
Malbone, E. G. Robert H. Gardiner

GARDNER, Byron J. 1930-
Black landscape
OrPA. Ptgs & sculptures

Gardner, Isabella (Stewart) 1840-1924
Sargent, J. S. Mrs John Lowell Gardner

Gargoyles no 5, Paris by A. Rattner
Gargoyles of Notre Dame by W. Homer
Garland, Elizabeth. See Richard, Elizabeth (Garland)
Garlics by P. Ruta
Garmisch-Partenkirchen by M. Hartley

GARNERAY, Ambroise Louis, 1783-1857
Lake Erie, Battle of ICH
U.S. National Capital sesquicentennial com

GARRETT, Adams Wirt, 1908-
Western festival
ICA. Annual ex, 1945/46

GARRETT, Edmund Henry, 1853-1929
Boon companions MB
MB. Ptgs in water color

GARVER, Walter R. 1927-
Half a man
NAD. Annual ex, 1956
Symbols OYB
OYB. Annual 1955
OYB. Supplement 1959

Gas by E. Hopper
Gas tank by J. Stella
Gasometer by W. T. Aldrich
Gaspé fishermen by J. Lonergan
Gaspé landscape by M. Avery
Gaspé-pink sky by M. Avery

GASSER, Henry Martin, 1909-
Bluff house
NAD. Annual ex, 1949, 2d half
Michel's house
NAD. Annual ex, 1947, 1st half
Pennsylvania
NAD. Annual ex, autumn 1949

GATCH, Lee, 1902-
Arch of silence
ICA. Annual ex, 1959/60
Archaic tree
IU. Contemp Amer ptg & sculp, 1961
August NeL
Hess. Abstract ptg
The beech
DC. 27 biennial ex, 1961
Fish market
PA. Annual ex, 1959-60
The flame MAP
Hess. Abstract ptg (col)
ICA. Annual ex, 1954
IU. Contemp Amer ptg, 1951
Pousette-Dart. Amer ptg
Ghost club
CSFP. Annual ex, 1950/51
Gothic night MB
OCl. Some contemporary works
Pierson
Greenhouse
Baur. Nature (col)
Pierson
PPC. International ex, 1950
WMAA. Neuberger collection
High tension tower NUM
NUM. Root bequest
OCl. Some contemporary works
Industrial night DP
DP. Catalogue
ICA. Amer artists paint the city
Time. 300 years (col)
Jumping joy WMAA
Goodrich. Amer art
McCurdy
The lamb
PPC. International ex, 1955
Lambertville pietà
ICA. Annual ex, 1959/60
Marching Highlanders DP
DP. Catalogue
Night fishing DP
OCl. Some contemporary works
Pennsylvania farm MoSL
MoSL. Handbook 1953
Pierson
Pleasure garden
CSFP. Annual ex, 1952

GATCH, Lee—*Continued*
Steeplechase
MnU. 40 Amer ptrs
Studio tapestry
PPC. International ex, 1961/62
Three candidates for election   DP
DP. Catalogue
Winter wood
IU. Contemp Amer ptg & sculp, 1959
Yaddo gardens
MnU. 40 Amer ptrs
The gate by J. Albers
The gate by W. Pachner
Gate watch by S. Bookatz
Gates, Horatio, 1728-1806
Stuart, G. Horatio Gates
GATES, Robert Franklin, 1906-
Desert sun   MdBM
CoS. New accessions, USA, 1960
Kitty Hawk   DC
CoS. New accessions USA, 1954
South window
IU. Contemp Amer ptg & sculp, 1961
Sunflower   DP
DP. Catalogue
Sunflowers and goldfinches
MM. Amer ptg today
Gates of the city, nightfall by E. Berman
Gateway and tower I by L. Feininger
Gatfield, Elizabeth. See Rogers, Elizabeth (Gatfield)
The gathering by W. Pachner
Gatling children, fl 1870
Benbridge, H. Gatling children
GAULEY, Robert David, 1875-1943
Amalfi   MB
MB. Ptgs in water color
The Azores   MB
MB. Ptgs in water color
Coast of Crete   MB
MB. Ptgs in water color
Coast of Sardinia   MB
MB. Ptgs in water color
Garden of the Generalife, Granada   MB
MB. Ptgs in water color
Mediterranean coast   MB
MB. Ptgs in water color
Mt Vesuvius from the bay of Naples   MB
MB. Ptgs in water color
Naples   MB
MB. Ptgs in water color
GAULOIS, Paul, 1901-1943
Construction in blue   CtY
CtY. Soc Anonyme
Gault, Silas
Blythe, D. G. Silas Gault
Gautier, Judith, 1846-1917
Sargent, J. S. Judith Gautier
Gautreau, Mme
Sargent, J. S. Madame X (Madame Gautreau)
GAW, William A. 1895-
Surviving trace of something
CSFP. Annual ex, 1952
GAY, Edward, 1837-1928 and **TAIT, Arthur Fitzwilliam,** 1819-1905
Deer at the lake
NSP. Sportscapes

Gay, Eliza Jane, fl 1840
Bascom, R. H. M. Eliza Jane Gay
GAY, Walter, 1865-1937
La chaise-longue   MB
MB. Ptgs in water color
Statue at Vaux-le-Vicomte   MB
MB. Ptgs in water color
Gay head by A. P. Ryder
Gay philosopher—why worry by H. Major
Gay table cloth by J. M. Hanson
GEAR, J.
Cook enrag'd at the steerage passengers being late with their breakfast   ICH
Davidson v 1
Gear by K. Knaths
GECHTOFF, Sonia, 1926-
Children of Frejus
WMAA. Young America 1960
Love at high noon
Brussels. Exposition
Untitled, 1953
NNSG. Younger Amer ptrs
Geese
Bauman, L. T. Geese in flight
Bellows, G. W. Geese and stormy sky
Graves, M. Ecstatic gander
Graves, M. Young gander ready for flight
Homer, W. Wild geese
Hunt, L. B. Northeaster—Canada geese
Wilson, B. Ross snow geese
GELB, Jan, 1906-
Flight into morning
Baur. Nature
Gellatly, John, 1853-1931
Wiles, I. R. John Gellatly
GELLER, Esther, 1921-
Dance rhythm   MAP
Rathbun
Lady with slouched hat
IU. Contemp Amer ptg, 1951
Mountain landscape   MB
MB. Ptgs in water color
Gelmeroda by L. Feininger
Gelmeroda IV by L. Feininger
Gelmeroda VIII, 1921 by L. Feininger
Gelmeroda XIII by L. Feininger
Gelston, David, 1744-1828
Jarvis, J. W. David Gelston
General Knox mansion by A. N. Wyeth
Genesee river and valley
Casilear, J. W. Reminiscence of the Genesee river
Genesis by S. Fogel
Genesis by L. E. Kupferman
Genesis by Y. Tanguy
Genesis by M. Tobey
Genesis by M. Tomkins
Genesis by J. Xcéron
Genesis, first version by L. Feitelson
Genet, Edmond Charles, 1763-1834
Ames, E. Edmond Charles Genet
Genie by M. Resnick
Genius by M. Beckmann
The genius of America encouraging the emancipation of the blacks by S. Jennings

Genoa, Italy
Boit, E. D. Genoa: A hillside
Boit, E. D. Genoa: The port
Sargent, J. S. Genoa: the university
Gentleman farmer by Unidentified artist
Gentleman hunter by S. Steinberg
Gentleman in a landscape by J. Brewster
(attributed works)
Gentleman with high collar by A. Ellis
George, Captain, fl 1820
Unidentified artist. Capt George of Haver-
hill, Massachusetts
George, Mrs, fl 1820
Unidentified artist. Wife of Capt George.
Haverhill, Massachusetts
GEORGE, Thomas, 1918-
Epoch   NBuA
NBuA. Acquisitions 1959-1961
George Fryer's still life by W. M. Harnett
George Gershwin's Rhaposody in blue part I,
1927 by A. G. Dove
George Tilyou's steeplechase by R. Marsh
George went swimming at Barnes hole, but
it got too cold by J. Mitchell
Georgia jungle by A. Brook
Georgia landscape by A. Blanch
Geraniums
Knaths, K. Geraniums in night window
Peale, Rembrandt. Rubens Peale with the
first geranium brought to America
Weber, M. Geranium
GERARD, Joseph
High tide   DP
DP. Catalogue
GERARDIA, Helen, 1913-
Third avenue el
IU. Contemp Amer ptg & sculp, 1959
GERASSI, Fernando, 1900?-
Magic mountains
Time. 300 years (col)
Germain by W. G. Congdon
German girl, Head of by W. M. Harnett
German officer, 1914 by M. Hartley
German train by W. Pachner
Germania by H. Hofmann
GERNAND, John, 1913-
Blowing leaves   DP
DP. Catalogue
Geronimo by H. H. Cross
Gerrish, Abigail, fl 1750
Greenwood, J. Abigail Gerrish and her
grandmother
GERRY, Peggy
Whelan's pier, Roslyn
NSP. Sportscapes
GERRY, Samuel, 1813-1891
Mount Washington, New Hampshire
                                             NoCR
NoCR. Catalogue
Gerson, Alice. See Chase, Alice (Gerson)
Gertrude II by B. Greene
Gertrude III by B. Greene
Gesture by M. Weber
Gesturing figures by M. Russo
The **getaway** by H. Pippin
Getting ready by Martyl

Gettysburg, Battle of, 1863
Richards, J. Battle of Gettysburg, 1863
Geyser, Yellowstone park by A. Bierstadt
GHIKAS, Panos, 1919-
Abstraction no 1
ICA. Annual ex, 1947/48
Blue horizon
MBIC. View 1960
Ghost club by L. Gatch
Ghosts of engines by T. L. Feininger
Ghost plants by C. E. Burchfield
Ghost stories by F. Remington
GIACOMETTI, Alberto, 1901-
The studio   PPC
CoS. New accessions USA, 1958
A **giant** by W. T. Aldrich
Giant blue spring, Yellowstone region by
T. Moran
Giant redwood trees of California by A.
Bierstadt
Gibbes, Mrs John. See Broughton, Anne
Gibbes, Robert Morgan, 1796-1864
Hubard, W. H. Robert Morgan Gibbes
Gibbs, George, 1776-1833
Malbone, E. G. George Gibbs III
Gibbs, Henry, 1668-1723
Freake limner. Henry Gibbs
GIBBS, Howard, 1904-
Hearthstone
MBIC. View 1960
Gibbs, Margaret, fl 1670
Freake limner. Margaret Gibbs
Gibbs, Margaret, 1701-1771. See Appleton,
Margaret (Gibbs)
Gibbs, Robert, 1665-1702
Freake limner. Robert Gibbs
Gibraltar forge by F. D. Devlan
GIBRAN, Kahlil, 1881-1931
Nude figure kneeling among clouds   MB
MB. Ptgs in water color
Gibson bayou anthology by C. Cloar
GIESE, Harold
Bananas   DP
DP. Catalogue
GIFFORD, Robert S. 1840-1905
Island of Mount Desert from the mainland
NUM. Art across America
GIFFORD, Sanford Robinson, 1823-1880
In the wilderness   OT
Pierson
Richardson. Ptg in America
Kaaterskill Falls   MM
Pierson
Tivoli   MM
MiD. Travelers in Arcadia
Gift bearer by M. O. Sheets
Gifts from the sea by B. J. O. Nordfeldt
Gignilliat, Jane Elizabeth. See Heyward,
Jane Elizabeth (Gignilliat)
GIGNOUX, François Régis, 1816-1882
Mountain valley
Sears. Highlights
Winter scene in New Jersey   MB
MB. Karolik coll
Winter sports
Born
                   Attributed works
Winter landscape with skaters
Sears. Highlights

Gignoux, Régis François. See Gignoux, François Régis

GIKOW, Ruth, 1914-
Communion
IU. Contemp Amer ptg, 1950
Golden canopy
IU. Contemp Amer ptg, 1949
Muted city
IU. Contemp Amer ptg & sculp, 1957
Roman street scene
WMAA. Annual ex, 1948
Teenagers
IU. Contemp Amer ptg & Sculp, 1955
Gila river
Pratt, H. C. Rio Gila, View on the
GILL, Frederick
Derelicts
NAD. Annual ex, 1961
Gill, Relief (Dowse) 1676-1759
Copley, J. S. Mrs Michael Gill
GILLETTE, Henry S.
Emergency
NAD. Annual ex, 1949, 2d half
Gilmor, Robert, 1774-1848
Hubard, W. J. Robert Gilmor II
Jarvis, J. W. Robert Gilmor II
Woodville, R. C. Robert Gilmor II
Gilmor, Mrs Robert. See Ladson, Sarah Reeve
Gilmor, Sarah Reeve (Ladson) See Ladson, Sarah Reeve
GIOBBI, Edward, 1926-
Birthday party
IU. Contemp Amer ptg & sculp, 1957
Kitchen still life
WMAA. Young America 1960
The voyage
WMAA. Young America 1960
Giorgione book by K. Knaths
Giotto's tower by H. Katzman
Gipsies' camp by J. W. Jarvis (after Morland)
Girard by D. Lord
A girl by J. J. Audubon (attributed works)
A girl by J. Levine
A girl by W. M. Prior (attributed works)
Girl against a tree by B. Karfiol
Girl and bananas by D. Rosenthal
Girl and cat by W. T. Bartoll
Girl at the piano by T. Robinson
Girl at the Tuileries by J. Phillips
Girl by the waterfall by Unidentified artist
Girl crocheting by E. C. Tarbell
Girl drying her hair by B. Currie
Girl holding a dog by S. Menkès
Girl holding rattle by E. S. Field
Girl in a hunting cap by R. Davey
Girl in a mirror by M. Hirschfield
Girl in a red embroidered jacket by W. M. Chase
Girl in a white blouse by R. Soyer
Girl in black and white by W. J. Glackens
Girl in black pinafore by Unidentified artist
Girl in blue by N. Civosky
Girl in blue by M. B. Prendergast
Girl in blue dress by M. Sterne

Girl in blue dress by Unidentified artist
Girl in blue kimono by W. M. Chase
Girl in fur hat by J. Sloan
Girl in green and rose by J. Pascin
Girl in orange sweater by M. Soyer
Girl in white and silver by W. Kuhn
Girl in window by J. Sloan
Girl in yellow jacket by C. Ruthenberg
Girl in yellow skirt by B. Currie
Girl in yellow with a red doll by E. S. Field
Girl jumping rope by B. Shahn
Girl looking out of window by J. Floch
Girl of the Ten Eyck family by Unidentified artist
Girl on a terrace by R. Diebenkorn
Girl on balcony by Unidentified artist
Girl on sofa by Y. Kuniyoshi
Girl playing a pe-pa by S. Moy
Girl resting by M. S. Wilkes
Girl seated on bench by W. M. Prior (attributed works)
Girl waiting by Y. Kuniyoshi
Girl with a cat by W. Sutton (attributed works)
Girl with a hand mirror by W. M. Paxton
Girl with a letter by W. Homer
Girl with bird by C. L. Lewin
Girl with bird by L. Rossbach
Girl with cornflower by A. Blanch
Girl with cups by R. Diebenkorn
Girl with dog by W. M. Chase
Girl with doll by W. M. Chase
Girl with dove by C. Thompson
Girl with flower basket by J. Bradley (attributed works)
Girl with fruit bowl by S. Menkès
Girl with hoop by Unidentified artist
Girl with laurel by W. Homer
Girl with parrot by M. Beckmann
Girl with pigeons by M. Hirshfield
Girl with red hair by Y. Tanguy
Girl with pitchfork by W. Homer
Girl with sunflowers by P. Evergood
Girl with the red shoes (Magdalena Douw) by Unidentified artist
Girl with three coffee cups by R. Diebenkorn
Girls and bananas by D. Rosenthal
Girls from Fleugel street by J. Levine
Girls on a cliff by W. Homer
Girls on esplanade by M. B. Prendergast
Girls playing on the beach by W. M. Chase
Girls preparing kava, Samoa by J. La Farge
Girls waiting by I. Bishop
Girls with lobster by W. Homer
Girod, Mme. See Poirson, Suzanne
GIROUX, C. fl 1850
Cotton plantation   MB
Davidson v 1
MB. Karolik coll

GISH, Peter M.
Toledo I
NAD. Annual ex, 1959
Gist, Mordecai, 1743-1792
Peale, C. W. Mordecai Gist
Give us this day by M. Hartley
GIVLER, William H. 1908-
Interior
OrPA. Ptgs & sculptures
Glacier streams—the Simplon by J. S.
Sargent
GLACKENS, Edith (Dimock) 1876-1955
The Sunday walk PMB
Glackens

Portrait of the artist
Glackens, W. J. Artist's wife
Glackens, W. J. Artist's wife and son
GLACKENS, Lenna
William and Imp
Glackens

Portrait of the artist
Glackens, W. J. Artist's daughter in
Chinese costume
Glackens, W. J. Lenna and Imp
GLACKENS, William James, 1870-1938
Armenian girl PMB
Glackens
Artist's daughter in Chinese costume
Glackens
Artist's wife CtHW
CtHW. Handbook
Glackens
NAD. Amer tradition
Artist's wife and son
Glackens
At the beach PA
Glackens
Bal Martinique
Glackens
Ballet girl in pink
Glackens
Bathing at Bellport
Glackens
Beach at Dieppe PMB
Glackens
Beach at Annisquam
NYG. Fine art
Beach at St Jean de Luz
Glackens
Beach scene near New London OCo
Glackens
Beatrice standing
Glackens
Bouquet in Quimper pitcher
PA. Annual ex, 1955
Buen Retiro, Madrid
Glackens
WMAA. Juliana Force
Café de la Paix
Glackens
Café Lafayette
Glackens
Central park, winter MM
Bauer. New art
Glackens
Charles FitzGerald
Glackens
Chateau-Thierry
Glackens

Chez Mouquin ICA
Baur. New art
Brown. Amer ptg
Glackens (col)
Hunter. Mod Amer ptg
NBuA. Fifty ptgs
PA. Annual ex, 1955
Pierson
Richardson. Ptg in America
Roos
Walker. Ptgs from America
Dream ride
NYG. Fine art
The drive, Central park OCl
Glackens
OCl. Handbook
PA. Annual ex, 1955
East river from Brooklyn
Glackens
Family group: Irene Dimock, Edith
Glackens, Ira Glackens, Grace Dwight
Morgan
Glackens (col)
Ferdinand Sinzig
Glackens
Fête du Suquet WMAA
Glackens
Flying kites, Montmartre MB
CSB. Impressionism
Glackens
Fruit with striped pottery ATeS
ATeS. Collection
Girl in black and white WMAA
Chew. 250 years of art
Green car MM
Bazin
Glackens (col)
MM. 100 Amer ptrs
George B. Luks
Glackens
Hammerstein's roof garden WMAA
Baur. New art
Glackens
Goodrich. Amer art
McCurdy
Pierson
A holiday in the park. See Washington
square
Jetties at Bellport NBuA
NBuA. Catalogue of the ptgs
Lenna and Imp
Glackens
Luxembourg gardens DC
DC. Masterpieces
Glackens
Mahone bay NeL
Born
NSyE. The eight
March day, Washington square
Glackens (col)
WMAA. Museum and its friends, 1958
(col)
Mrs Barnes and Grover
Glackens
Night after San Juan
Brown. Amer ptg
U.S. National Capital sesquicentennial
com
Nude dressing hair
NUM. Art across America

GLACKENS, W. J.—*Continued*
Nude with apple   NBM
  Glackens (col)
  PA. Annual ex, 1955
  Time. 300 years (col)
Outside the Guttenburg race track
  Glackens
Park by the river   NBM
  Baur. Revolution
  Glackens (col)
  Time. 300 years (col)
Pony ballet   PMB
  Glackens
Race track   PMB
  Glackens
Roller skating rink
  Glackens
  Larkin
  Larkin rev ed
Shoppers (Mrs L. E. Travis, Edith
  Glackens, Florence Scovel Shinn)
  Glackens
  PA. Annual ex, 1955
Soda fountain   PA
  Baur. New art (col)
  Glackens
  Pierson—
Still life—Crabapples in blue bowl
  CtY. Yale alumni
Still life with three glasses   OYB
  OYB. Accessions
  OYB. Supplement 1959
The swing
  Brown. Amer ptg
Temple gold medal nude
  Glackens
La Villette   PPC
  Glackens
Washington square (A holiday in the
  park)   MMA
  Brown. Amer ptg
West Hartford
  Glackens
Woman on sofa
  Glackens

Portrait of the artist
Henri, R. William Glackens, 1904
Glackens, Mrs William James. See Glack-
  ens, Edith (Dimock)
Gladding, Hannah. See Field, Hannah
  (Gladding)
Gladiators by P. Guston
Gladys by T. Filmus
The **glance** of amber by Y. Tanguy
GLANNON, Edward, 1911-
Corner of a pasture
  NYG. Fine art
GLARNER, Fritz, 1899-
Composition, 1942
  MnU. 40 Amer ptrs
Relational painting, 1943   CtY
  CtY. Soc Anonyme
Relational painting, 1947-48   MMA
  Biddle. Yes and no
  MMA. Abstract (col)
  MMA. 12 Americans (col)
  Read. Concise history

Relational painting, 1949-51   WMAA
  Baur. New art (col)
  Goodrich. Amer art (col)
  MMA. 12 Americans
  Pierson
  WMAA. Contemp Amer ptg, 1951
Relational painting, 1950
  CSFP. Annual ex, 1950/51
Relational painting 53, 1950
  MMA. 12 Americans
Relational painting 55, 1951
  MMA. 12 Americans
Relational painting 61, 1953
  Baur. New art
Relational painting 64, 1953
  MMA. 12 Americans
Relational painting 67, 1953
  NNSG. Younger Amer ptrs
Relational painting 68, 1954
  McCurdy
Relational painting 79, 1956
  DC. 25 biennial ex, 1957
  VR. Amer ptg, 1958
Relational painting, tondo 6, 1948
  MMA. 12 Americans
Relational painting—tondo 18
  MnU. 40 Amer ptrs
  Pousette-Dart. Amer ptg
Relational painting, tondo 20, 1951-54
  Baur. New art
Relational painting, tondo 40, 1956
                     MnMW
  CoS. New accessions USA, 1958
  MMA. 12 Americans
Tondo no 15   MdBM
  Pierson
Tondo no 21
  IU. Contemp Amer ptg, 1952
GLASCO, Joseph, 1925-
Athlete and landscape
  MMA. Fifteen
Figures in landscape
  Mendelowitz
  NNSG. Younger Amer ptrs
  WMAA. New decade
Head
  NBuA. Expressionism
Interior with standing man
  IU. Contemp Amer ptg & sculp, 1959
Male head
  IU. Contemp Amer ptg, 1952
Marvello
  WMAA. Contemp Amer ptg, 1953
  WMAA. New decade
Portrait of a poet   WMAA
  Goodrich. Amer art
  Pierson
Salome
  Pierson
  WMAA. New decade
Sleepers
  MMA. Fifteen
Sleeping figure
  Pierson
Sun bath
  CanO. Hirshhorn coll
  IU. Contemp Amer ptg, 1951
Two figures   MMA
  MMA. Fifteen
The **glass** by R. Crawford
Glass and flowers by A. B. Carles

Glass house lake by J. H. Hidley
Glass windows, Bahamas by W. Homer
Glazier by W. De Kooning
Gleason, Bethia, fl 1785
 Chandler, W. Mrs Gleason and Bethia
Gleason, William. See Glysson, William
GLEITSMANN, Raphael, 1910-
 Ancient valley
  IU. Contemp Amer ptg, 1949
 The city—no 2
  PPC. International ex, 1950
 City of spires
  PPC. Ptg in the U. S. 1949
 An entrance
  IU. Contemp Amer ptg, 1950 (col)
 Green wall   OYB
  OYB. Annual 1950
  OYB. Catalogue 1951
 The wall   IaDa
  IaDa. Silver jubilee
 Winter trees
  NAD. Annual ex, 1949, 1st half
Glen, Mrs John. See Jones, Sarah
Glimpse of Lake George by J. F. Kensett
Glitter by G. P. Du Bois
Glitter by G. Prestopino
Glittering moonlight by F. K. M. Rehn
The glorious victory of the sloop Maria by
  L. Feininger
The glory by F. Martin
Glory of spring by C. E. Burchfield
Gloucester, Massachusetts
 Davis, S. Gloucester street
 Demuth, C. H. Gloucester
 Lane, F. H. Gloucester from Brookbank
 Lane, F. H. View of Gloucester from
  Rocky Neck
 Prendergast, M. B. Gloucester
 Sloan, J. Balancing rock, Gloucester har-
  bor
 Sloan, J. Hill, Main street, Gloucester
 Zerbe, K. Gloucester alley
Gloucester boats by K. Matthew
Gloucester docks by E. Horter
Gloucester farm by W. Homer
Gloucester schooners and sloop by W.
  Homer
Gloucester sunset by S. Davis
Gloucester trolley by J. Sloan
Glover, Mary Julien
 Betts, L. Miss Mary Julien Glover
GLUCKMAN, Grigory, 1898-
 Confidants
  DC. 21 biennial ex, 1949
 Nu
  PPC. Ptg in the U. S. 1949
Glysson, William, fl 1780
 Chandler, W. Dr William Glysson
Goat song by T. D. Benrimo
Goats
 Arbogast, V. Mountain goats
 Dove, A. G. Goat
 Keller, H. G. Goats among the peaks
 Spruce, E. F. Angora goat
 Spruce, E. F. Goat
The goblet by W. Sommer
The goblet by B. W. Tomlin

GODDELL, J. G. fl 1830
 Attributed works
 Young lady of the Nathaniel Johnson
  family   MeC
 Jetté. Amer heritage collection
Godfrey of Bouillon, 1061?-1100
 Walker, C. H. Godfrey of Bouillon
God's day by C. F. McCall
GOEDIKE, Shirl, 1923-
 Race in the sun
  IU. Contemp Amer ptg & sculp, 1961
Goelet, Jane, 1720-1799
 Unidentified artist. Jane Goelet
Going through the thoroughfare by J.
  Marin
Going to church by G. H. Durrie
Going to church by A. M. R. Moses
Going to town by P. S. Sample
Going up by A. Osver
GOLD, Albert, 1906-
 Nicetown
  PA. Annual ex, 1950
Gold and old lace by G. Fuller
Gold, green and brown by A. G. Dove
Gold scab by J. A. M. Whistler
GOLDBERG, Michael, 1924-
 Chair   MnMW
  MnMW. 60 Amer ptrs
 Old Zip Coon
  PPC. International ex, 1961/62
 Still life
  WMAA. Young America 1957
 Still life with onion rolls
  WMAA. Young America 1957
 Summer house   NBuA
  NBuA. Acquisitions 1957-58
Golden afternoon, Oregon by C. Hassam
Golden autumn by R. A. Blakelock
Golden canopy by R. Gikow
Golden carnival by W. L. Metcalf
Golden dawn by R. Pousette-Dart
Golden gardens by M. Tobey
Golden Gate by C. Sheeler
Golden hat by K. Zerbe
The golden lady by W. M. Chase
Golden leaves by H. L. McFee
Golden light by P. L. Dike
Golden palace by L. Bosa
Golden plover by J. J. Audubon
Golden reverie by R. Pousette-Dart
Golden screen: caprice in purple and gold
  no 2, 1865 by J. A. M. Whistler
Golden splendor by H. Hofmann
Golden storm by A. G. Dove
Golden Swan by C. H. Demuth
Golden tree by K. K. Feuerherm
GOLDIN, Leon, 1923-
 Desert twilight
  IU. Contemp Amer ptg & sculp, 1957
 February
  IU. Contemp Amer ptg & sculp, 1961
 Gray beach
  PA. Annual ex, 1959-60
 Hill town
  IU. Contemp Amer ptg & sculp, 1959

GOLDRING, Milton, 1919?-
Morning hour
WMAA. Annual ex, 1957
Goldsborough, Henrietta Maria (Tilghman)
1707-1771
Unidentified artist. Mrs William Goldsborough and grandson
GOLDSMITH, Deborah, 1808-1836
George Addison Throop
Lipman. Primitive ptrs
Lady and gentleman   NCHA
Jones. Rediscovered ptrs
Mr and Mrs Lyman Day and daughter, Cornelia
Jones. Rediscovered ptrs
Self-portrait
Lipman. Primitive ptrs
Talcott family   VWR
Lipman. Primitive ptrs
VWR. Amer folk art
Goldthwait, Elizabeth, 1733-1861
Copley, J. S. Mrs John Bacon
Goldthwait, Elizabeth (Lewis) 1714-1794
Copley, J. S. Mrs Ezekial Goldthwait
Goldthwait, Ezekial, 1710-1782
Copley, J. S. Ezekial Goldthwait
GOLDTHWAITE, Anne, 1873-1944
Katherine S. Dreier   CtY
CtY. Soc Anonyme
Golf course, East Gloucester by M. B. Prendergast
GOLINKIN, Joseph Webster, 1896-
Endeavor II and Ranger
NYG. Fine art
The Hambletonian
NYG. Fine art
GOLUB, Leon Albert, 1922-
Burnt man
NNSG. Younger Amer ptrs
Colossal head
Selz. New images
Damaged man
Selz. New images
Head XXVI
IU. Contemp Amer ptg & sculp, 1961
Horseman
Selz. New images
Orestes
Selz. New images (col)
Parturition
IU. Contemp Amer ptg & sculp, 1957
Reclining youth
Selz. New images
GOLUBOV, Maurice, 1905-
Fantasy
MMA. Abstract
Gomez d'Arza, Signora
Eakins, T. Signora d'Arza
Gondolas, Venice by M. B. Prendergast
Gondolier by J. S. Sargent
GONZALES, Boyer, 1909-
Composition with violet
OrPA. Ptgs & sculptures
GONZALEZ, Xavier, 1899-
Cannabin
PPC. International ex, 1952
The city
ICA. Amer artists paint the city
Don Quixote
NAD. Annual ex, 1958

Escape
IU. Contemp Amer ptg, 1949
PPC. Ptg in the U.S. 1949
Landscape
Pousette-Dart. Amer ptg
Landscape no 9   WMAA
Pierson
WMAA. Annual ex, 1951
Landscape in construction
DC. 22 biennial ex, 1951
Landscape in grey
IU. Contemp Amer ptg & sculp, 1955
The offering
Pearson. Mod renaissance
Portrait of an artist
Pearson. Mod renaissance
Ram's head
IU. Contemp Amer ptg, 1950
Pearson. Mod renaissance
Terminal
ICA. Annual ex, 1954
Zen Buddist
NAD. Annual ex, 1960
Gonzales, Mrs Xavier. See Edwards, Ethel
Good angel tenanted by K. Zerbe
A good day's work—return from duck hunt by J. B. Sword
The good earth by C. Chen
Good Friday by K. Zerbe
Good intent by J. Peters
Good keeper C. R. Holty
Good news by M. Weber
Good Samaritan by Unidentified artist
Good Samaritan: Design for a window, Trinity church, Buffalo by J. La Farge
Good shepherd by J. La Farge
Good time by A. Salemme
Goodman, Mrs Nelson. See Sturgis, Katharine
GOODMAN, Sidney
Ascension
PA. Annual ex, 1961
GOODNOUGH, Robert, 1917-
Movement of horses II
PPC. International ex, 1961/62
Seated figure with gray   WMAA
Goodrich. Amer art
The struggle   NBuA
NBuA. Acquisitions 1957-58
Tree in the field
Baur. Nature
Goodrich, Mr, fl 1818
Unidentified artist. Mr Goodrich, Hancock, Massachusetts
Goodrich, Chauncey Allen, 1790-1800
Jocelyn, N. Chauncey Allen Goodrich
GOODRIDGE, E.
Gorham Bond
MB. New England miniatures
Stephen Salisbury
MB. New England miniatures
GOODRIDGE, Sarah, 1788-1853
Gilbert Stuart   MB
MB. New England miniatures
John Lowell jr
MB. New England miniatures
Mrs Abel Peirson
MB. New England miniatures
Mrs John Lowell jr
MB. New England miniatures (col)

Mrs Thomas B. Wales
 MB. New England miniatures
Mrs Timothy Pickering (after Stuart)
 MB. New England miniatures
Timothy Pickering
 MB. New England miniatures
GOODWIN, Arthur Clifton, 1866-1929
High bridge, New York
 Born
Landscape with brook
 Born
GOODWIN, Edwin Weyburn, 1800-1845
Christmas presents
 Jones. Rediscovered ptrs
GOODWIN, Philip R. 1882-1935
Calling the moose
 NSP. Sportscapes
Rainbow trout
 NSP. Sportscapes
Trout fishing
 NSP. Sportscapes
GOODWIN, Richard LaBarre, 1840-1910
Hunter's cabin door   MSM
 Frankenstein. After the hunt
Kitchen piece
 Frankenstein. After the hunt
Theodore Roosevelt's cabin door MSM
 Frankenstein. After the hunt
 MSM. Handbook
Goodyear, Anson Conger, 1877-
 Speicher, E. E. A. Conger Goodyear,
 1942
Goodyear, Charles, 1800-1860
 Healy, G. P. A. Charles Goodyear
Goose river, by A. N. Wyeth
GORCHOV, Ron, 1930-
Fifth vision of Queen Vaidehi
 WMAA. Young America 1960
Sorcerer's gear
 WMAA. Young America 1960
Gordian by J. Brooks
GORDON, Maxwell, 1910-
Parade
 IU. Contemp Amer ptg, 1952
Pose downtown
 IU. Contemp Amer ptg, 1951
GORDON, William J.
Fortune tellers
 IU. Contemp Amer ptg, 1948
Gore, Christopher, 1785-1827
 Trumbull, J. Christopher Gore
Gore children
 Copley, J. S. Brother and sisters of Chris-
 topher Gore
Gore et mandra by E. A. Donati
Gorge of the St Croix river by H. Lewis
Gorham, Mercy. See Bourne, Mercy (Gor-
 ham)
GORKY, Arshile, 1904-1948
Agony   MMA
 Art since 1945 (col)
 Barr. What is mod ptg
 Baur. New art
 Baur. Revolution
 CoS. New accessions USA, 1950
 McCurdy
 MMA. Abstract (col)
 MMA. Masters (col)
 MMA. New Amer ptg (col)
 Pierson
 Read. Concise history (col)
 Schwabacher. Arshile Gorky (col)

Ahko, Portrait of
 Schwabacher. Arshile Gorky
The antique cast
 Schwabacher. Arshile Gorky
Argula   MMA
 Schwabacher. Arshile Gorky
Artist and his mother   WMAA
 Baur. New art
 Goodrich. Amer art (col)
 Schwabacher. Arshile Gorky (col)
Battle at sunset with the god of the maize
 Schwabacher. Arshile Gorky
Betrothal I
 OCl. Some contemporary works
 Schwabacher. Arshile Gorky
Betrothal II, 1947   WMAA
 Baur. New Art
 50 years of mod art
 Goodrich. Amer art (col)
 Hess. Abstract ptg (col)
 MnMW. 60 Amer ptrs
 Pierson
 Pousette-Dart. Amer ptg
 Read. Concise history
 Schwabacher. Arshile Gorky (col)
The calendars   WMAA
 MMA. New Amer ptg
 Schwabacher. Arshile Gorky (col)
 WMAA. Juliana Force
Charred beloved
 Blesh
 Schwabacher. Arshile Gorky
Child of an Idumean night
 Schwabacher. Arshile Gorky
Composition, 1932-33
 MMA. Abstract
Composition with head, c 1935
 Schwabacher. Arshile Gorky
Dark green painting
 MMA. New Amer ptg
 Ponente. Mod ptg, 1960 (col)
 Schwabacher. Arshile Gorky
Diary of a seducer
 Hess. Abstract ptg
 Janson. Key monuments
 Janson. Picture history
 MMA. Fourteen
 Schwabacher. Arshile Gorky
Enigmatic combat   CSFM
 Pierson
 Schwabacher. Arshile Gorky
Garden in Sochi, c 1938-41
 Schwabacher. Arshile Gorky
Garden in Sochi, 1941 (1)   MMA
 MMA. Fourteen
 Schwabacher. Arshile Gorky
 Time. 300 years (col)
Garden in Sochi, c 1941 (2)
 Schwabacher. Arshile Gorky
Garden in Sochi motif
 Schwabacher. Arshile Gorky
How my mother's embroidered apron un-
 folds in my life
 Schwabacher. Arshile Gorky
Image in Xhorkom   MMA
 Hess. Abstract ptg
 Schwabacher. Arshile Gorky
Image in Xhorkom (Raynal coll)
 Schwabacher. Arshile Gorky
Impatience
 Read. Art now, 1948 ed

GORKY, Arshile—*Continued*
Landscape table
  MMA. Fourteen
  Ponente. Mod ptg, 1960 (col)
  Schwabacher. Arshile Gorky
Last painting, 1948
  Schwabacher. Arshile Gorky
The leaf of the artichoke is an owl
  Schwabacher. Arshile Gorky
The limit
  Schwabacher. Arshile Gorky (col)
Liver is the cock's comb   NBuA
  Baur. New art (col)
  Jean. Surrealist ptg
  Larkin rev ed (col)
  NBuA. Acquisitions 1954-57
  OCl. Some contemporary works
  Pierson
  Schwabacher. Arshile Gorky
Myself and my imaginary wife, Portrait of
  Schwabacher. Arshile Gorky
Newark airport murals, Panel of
  Schwabacher. Arshile Gorky
Nighttime enigma and nostalgia
  NBuA. Expressionism
  Schwabacher. Arshile Gorky
Nude, 1946
  Schwabacher. Arshile Gorky
The orators
  Schwabacher. Arshile Gorky
Organization
  Schwabacher. Arshile Gorky
Painting, 1936-37   WMAA
  Goodrich. Amer art
  Schwabacher. Arshile Gorky
The pirate II
  Schwabacher. Arshile Gorky
The plow and the song   OOb
  OCl. Some contemporary works
  Schwabacher. Arshile Gorky
The plow and the song (Gordon coll)
  Schwabacher. Arshile Gorky (col)
  WMAA. Museum and its friends, 1958
    (col)
Portrait
  Schwabacher. Arshile Gorky
Self-portrait, c 1937
  Schwabacher. Arshile Gorky
Soft night
  Schwabacher. Arshile Gorky
Still life, 1929
  Schwabacher. Arshile Gorky
Still life with palette
  Schwabacher. Arshile Gorky
Still life with skull
  Schwabacher. Arshile Gorky
Three roses
  Schwabacher. Arshile Gorky
The unattainable
  MMA. Fourteen
  Schwabacher. Arshile Gorky
Vartoosh, Portrait of
  Schwabacher. Arshile Gorky
Water of the flowery mill   MM
  Cheney. Story 1958 ed
  Schwabacher. Arshile Gorky
Waterfall
  Baur. Nature (col)
  Hess. Abstract ptg
  Hunter. Mod Amer ptg (col)
  Schwabacher. Arshile Gorky (col)

GORSLINE, Douglas Warner, 1913-
Foggy pasture
  NAD. Annual ex, 1949
Thomas Wolfe
  Gruskin
GORSON, Aaron Harry, 1872-1933
Steel mill at night
  Chew. 250 years of art
Gosier II by A. Yunkers
Gosman family, A gentleman of by J. W.
  Jarvis
Gosse, Sir Edmund William, 1849-1928
  Sargent, J. S. Sir Edmund Gosse
The **gossips** by H. Pittman
Gotham news by W. De Kooning
Gothic by A. Dasburg
Gothic by J. Pollock
Gothic by M. Tobey
Gothic enflamed by A. Rattner
Gothic light by L. Gatch
Gothic sentinels by P. Trivigno
Gothic spire by L. Feininger
Gothic woods and nymph by G. Grosz
GOTO, Joseph, 1916-
Landscape
  IU. Contemp Amer ptg & sculp, 1957
GOTTLIEB, Adolph, 1903-
Blast II
  PPC. International ex, 1958
  Read. Concise history
Blue at night
  VR. Amer ptg, 1958
Blue at noon
  Eliot. Art of our time (col)
  Time. 300 years (col)
Burst
  MMA. New Amer ptg (col)
The cadium sound
  IU. Contemp Amer ptg & sculp, 1955
Dialogue 1   NBuA
  NBuA. Acquisitions 1959-1961
Evil omen
  MnMW. Contemporary
  Pierson
  WMAA. Neuberger collection
Exclamation
  MnMW. 60 Amer ptrs (col)
Frozen sounds no 1, 1951   WMAA
  Goodrich. Amer art (col)
  IU. Contemp Amer ptg & sculp, 1953
  Pierson
  Pousette-Dart. Amer ptg
Frozen sounds no 2, 1952   NBuA
  Hunter. Mod Amer ptg
  NBuA. Acquisitions 1954-57
Hot horizon
  Pierson
Labyrinth
  WMAA. New decade
Links of memory
  CSFP. Annual ex, 1947/48
Man and arrow
  MnU. 40 Amer ptrs
Man looking at woman
  CSFP. Annual ex, 1950/51
Pictograph   CLA
  CoS. New accessions USA, 1960
  CSFP. Annual ex, 1948/49
  IU. Contemp Amer ptg, 1950
  Wight. Milestones (col)

Red sky
  Baur. Nature
Romanesque façade
  Hess. Abstract ptg (col)
  IU. Contemp Amer ptg, 1951 (col)
Sea and tide
  WMAA. New decade
The seer   DP
  DP. Catalogue
  Larkin rev ed
Side pull
  MMA. New Amer ptg
Souvenirs of the sea
  MnU. 40 Amer ptrs
Spectre of the sea
  IU. Contemp Amer ptg, 1948
  Roos
T
  ICA. Annual ex, 1951
  Hess. Abstract ptg
Tournament
  IU. Contemp Amer ptg, 1952
  MMA. New Amer ptg
Transfiguration no 2
  Pierson
Voyager's return   MMA
  Art since 1945
  MMA. Contemp ptrs
W. 1954   NNSG
  NNSG. Handbook
  NNSG. Younger Amer ptrs
Waiting
  PPC. International ex, 1952
Watching
  NUM. Art across America
GOTTLIEB, Harry, 1895-
  Their only roof, 1930   ATU
  ATU. Coll of Amer art
Gould, James, 1770-1838
  Waldo, S. L. James Gould
GOULD, L. A.
  Niagara seen with different eyes (after
    a print by Lumley)   NCHA
  Jones. New-found folk art
Goulding, Mary Anne, fl 1858
  Elliott, C. L. Mrs Thomas Goulding
Gourds by J. S. Sargent
Gouty fisherman by D. G. Blythe
Gouverneur, Abram, 1671-1740
  Unidentified artist. Abram Gouverneur
Gouverneur, Mary (Leisler) d 1747
  Unidentified artist. Mrs Abram Gouver-
    neur
Gouverneur, Mrs Samuel, fl 1750
  Wollaston, J. Mrs Samuel Gouverneur
Government bureau by G. Tooker
Government house, Bowling Green, New
    York, 1797 by C. Milbourne
Governess and children by Unidentified
    artist
Governor II by W. T. Murch
The governor's cup by V. Flannery
Governor's room, City hall, New York,
    c 1830 by C. Burton
Goyescas, Study for by B. Shahn
GRABACH, John R. 1886-
  Pedestrians in village
    NAD. Annual ex, spring 1950
Grackles
  Audubon, J. J. Purple grackle

GRAHAM, Elwood
  Spanish lace   CSFM
  Pousette-Dart. Amer ptg
Graham, Frances (Wickham) fl 1857
  Healy, G. P. A. Mrs James Graham
Graham, Mrs James Duncan. See Graham,
    Frances (Wickham)
GRAHAM, John D. 1888-
  Vox humana   CtY
  CtY. Soc Anonyme
GRAHAM, Robert M.
  New Guinea beer party
    IU. Contemp Amer ptg, 1948
Grain elevator from the bridge by R. Craw-
    ford
Grain elevators, Minneapolis by R. Craw-
    ford
GRAMATKY, Hardie, 1907-
  Throughway
    NAD. Special ex, 1956
Gramercy park by G. W. Bellows
Gramercy park by F. W. Howell
Granada by R. B. Motherwell
Granada gardens by V. Vytlacil
Grand Canyon by J. E. Swinnerton
Grand Canyon, Arizona by P. Wenck
Grand Canyon of the Yellowstone river by
    T. Moran
Grand central terminal by M. Weber
Grand finale by L. Pitts
Grand Manan, sunrise off the Maine coast
    by F. E. Church
Grand street brides by G. Hartigan
Grand view by R. H. Byrum
Granda flora by H. G. Keller
The grandest of Noo by R. S. Du Casse
Grandfather by H. Sterne
Grandfather's lesson by H. Herzog
Grandma goes to the big city by A. M. R.
    Moses
Grandma's hearthstone by J. Haberle
Granite city by L. Dodd
Granny Ames' house by G. W. Bellows
GRANT, Catharine Harley, 1897-
  Villa Maria
    PA. Annual ex, 1949
GRANT, Gordon, 1875-
  Harbor traffic
    NYG. Fine art
Grant, Ida M. (Honoré) fl 1874
  Healy, G. P. A. Mrs Frederick Dent
    Grant
GRANT, J. fl 1843
  Two children   MB
  MB. Karolik coll
Grant, Ulysses Simpson, president U.S. 1822-
    1885
  Healy, G. P. A. Ulysses Simpson Grant
  Lambdin, J. R. Gen Ulysses S. Grant
Grape hill, Manayunk by G. Martino
Grapes and turnips by C. H. Demuth
Grapes in a bowl by J. F. Francis
Graphite and blue by A. G. Dove
Grass path in spring by M. A. Phillips
Gratz, Rachel, 1783-1823
  Malbone, E. G. Rachel Gratz

Gratz, Rebecca, 1781-1869
  Malbone, E. G. Rebecca Gratz
Grave of William Penn by E. Hicks
Gravel by R. Vickrey
Gravel bar, White river by E. Hopper
Gravel pit by W. T. Turman
Graves, Henry, 1806-1892
  Whistler, J. A. M. Henry Graves, the
    printseller
GRAVES, Morris, 1910-
  Bird in the mist
    Wight. Morris Graves
  Bird in the moonlight (Ross coll)
    Wight. Morris Graves
  Bird in the spirit   WMAA
    Goodrich. Amer art (col)
    MM. 100 Amer ptrs
  Bird maddened by the long winter
    IU. Contemp Amer ptg & sculp, 1953
    Pierson
  Bird singing in the moonlight   MMA
    Baur. Revolution
    Faulkner. Art today, 1956
    McCurdy
    MMA. Contemp ptrs
    Pierson
  Black waves   NBuA
    ICA. Annual ex, 1947/48
    NBuA. Contemporary ptgs
  Blind bird   MMA
    Baur. New art
    Hunter. Mod Amer ptg (col)
    Larkin
    Larkin rev ed
    MMA. Masters (col)
    Rodman. Portrait of the artist
    Wight. Morris Graves (col)
  Blind bird no 2, 1940 (Markson coll)
    Wight. Morris Graves (col)
  Ceremonial bronze taking the form of a
    bird   WaS
    Wight. Morris Graves
  Chalice   DP
    DP. Catalogue
    Wight. Morris Graves
  Chalice and lyre
    Wight. Morris Graves
  Colossal owls and eagles of the inner eye
    NBuA. Expressionism
  Concentrated pine top
    Wight. Morris Graves
  Daisies
    Wight. Morris Graves (col)
  Disintegrated and reanimated
    Wight. Morris Graves
  Dove of the inner eye
    Wight. Morris Graves
  Eagle   DP
    DP. Catalogue
    Wight. Morris Graves
  Eagle in the rock
    Wight. Morris Graves
  Ecstatic gander
    Wight. Morris Graves
  Fish in sea and stars   WaS
    50 years of mod art
  Fish reflected upon outer and mental space
    Wight. Morris Graves (col)
  Flight of plover   WMAA
    Goodrich. Amer art
    Pierson
    Wight. Morris Graves

  Fox with phoenix wing   PPhM
    CoS. New accessions USA, 1956
  Guardian   IU
    Canaday
    IU. Contemp Amer ptg & sculp, 1955
    IU. 20th century
    Larkin rev ed (col)
    Wight. Morris Graves (col)
    WMAA. Museum and its friends, 1959
  Guardian (Willis coll)
    OrPA. Ptgs & sculptures
  In the air
    Wight. Morris Graves
  Individual state of the world   MMA
    Wight. Morris Graves (col)
  Journey   WaS
    CoS. New accessions USA, 1948
  Journey   WMAA
    Baur. New art
    WMAA. Juliana Force
  Journey no 2, 1943   WMAA
    Wight. Morris Graves
  Journey (Baldwin coll)
    Wight. Milestones
  Joyous young pine   MMA
    Baur. New art
    IU. Contemp Amer ptg, 1951
    MMA. Contemp ptrs
  Joyous young pine   CSB
    CoS. New accessions USA, 1958
  Joyous young pine (Ludington coll)
    CtY. Yale alumni
  Joyous young pine (Wolf coll)
    Wight. Morris Graves (col)
  Little bird alone
    Cheney. Story 1958 ed
  Little-known bird of the inner eye MMA
    Baur. New Art (col)
    Cheney. Primer 1958 ed
    Flexner. Amer ptg
    Flexner. Short history
    Read. Art now, 1948 ed
    Wight. Morris Graves (col)
  Masked bird fishing in the golden stream
    Cheney. Story 1958 ed
    Wight. Morris Graves
  Message
    Wight. Morris Graves
  Moon and crow in the surf
    Wight. Morris Graves
  Moor swan   WaS
    Wight. Morris Graves
  Pink bird
    Wight. Morris Graves (col)
  Preening sparrows   WaS
    Pousette-Dart. Amer ptgs
    Time. 300 years (col)
  Purification series
    Wight. Morris Graves
  Ritual vessel-mirror
    Wight. Morris Graves
  Sea and the morning redness   ICA
    Wight. Morris Graves
  Sea, fish, and constellation   WaS
    Time. 300 years
    Wight. Morris Graves
  Shore birds no 1, c 1940
    Wight. Morris Graves
  Shore birds no 2, 1940
    Baur. New art
    Wight. Morris Graves
  Shore birds submerged in moonlight
    Wight. Morris Graves

Snake and moon   MMA
  Barr. What is mod ptg
Spirit bird no 6, 1953
  Wight. Morris Graves
Spring   WaS
  Read. Concise history
Surf birds   MiD
  Wight. Morris Graves
Surf birds (Laughton coll)
  Wight. Morris Graves
Surf reflected upon higher space   NUM
  NUM. Root bequest
Time of change
  UNESCO. 1860-1949
Trout in a stream
  MiD. Coll in progress
  Wight. Morris Graves
  WiMiA. Amer ptg 1760-1960
Woodpeckers   WaS
  UNESCO. 1860-1957
  Wight. Morris Graves
Wounded gull   DP
  Cheney. New world history
  DP. Catalogue
  Wight. Morris Graves
Wounded gull (Newberry coll)
  Munsterberg
Wounded gull (Tannahill coll)
  Baur. New art
  UNESCO. 1860-1949
  UNESCO. 1860-1955
Wounded ibis
  MnU. 40 Amer ptrs
Wounded scoter   OCl
  OCl. Handbook
  Wight. Morris Graves (col)
Wounded sea gull
  MnMW. Expressionism 1900-1955
Young forest pine tree in bloom   DP
  MnU. 40 Amer ptrs
  Wight. Morris Graves
Young gander ready for flight   DP
  NNSG. Younger Amer ptrs
  Wight
Young owl and moth   CoS
  NUM. Art across America
GRAVES, O. E. L. 1897-
  Dappled with damson   OYB
  OYB. Supplement 1959
GRAY, Cleve, 1918-
  Hipparchus   IU
  IU. Contemp Amer ptg, 1951
  IU. 20th century
  Man and the northern lights   MAP
  CoS. New accessions USA, 1952
  Mosque, Cordova: no 2, 1959   WMAA
  Goodrich. Amer art
  The wool winder
  ICA. Annual ex, 1961
GRAY, Henry Peters, 1819-1877
  William Cullen Bryant   NNHS
  Cowdrey v 1
Gray, John, 1713-1782
  Copley, J. S. John Gray
GRAY, Ralph Weld, 1880-1944
  Cranberry bogs: bright weather   MB
  MB. Ptgs in water color
  Cranberry bogs: gray skies   MB
  MB. Ptgs in water color
  Home camp in March   MB
  MB. Ptgs in water color
Gray, Sarah. See Cary, Sarah (Gray)

Gray by S. Francis
Gray abstraction by R. Conover
Gray and gold by J. R. Cox
Gray beach by L. Goldin
Gray day on the lagoon by W. M. Chase
Gray desert by G. Peirce
The gray man dances by G. Grosz
Gray rocks and gray trees by M. Kantor
Gray ruin and stone house by H. P. Barnett
Graziana by E. E. Speicher
Grazing horse by A. P. Ryder
The great barrier by E. Magafan
Great black-backed gull by J. J. Audubon
Great Blue hill and Neponset river by T. H.
  Hinckley
Great elm by C. E. Burchfield
The Great Goot by M. Wilson
The great mystery 11 by A. J. Jensen
Great seas by F. J. Waugh
The great waters by K. L. Seligmann
Great Western (steamship)
  Walter, J. Arrival of the Great Western
GREBENAK, Louis
  Wall
    MM. Amer ptg today
Greek boy by E. E. Speicher
Greek island by T. Stamos
Greek love token by J. La Farge
Greek orison by T. Stamos
Green, George, 1742-1814
  Copley, J. S. George Green
Green, Rebecca (Spooner) 1743-1806
  Unidentified artist. Mrs Timothy Green
Green, Ruby
  Chapin, J. Ruby Green singing
GREEN, Samuel M. 1909-
  Woodshed interior   MNS
  Time. 300 years (col)
Green by B. W. Tomlin
Green and lavender horse by W. W. Quirt
Green apples by W. Homer
Green apples and scoop by W. Kuhn
Green ballet by E. Shinn
Green bird by F. E. Conway
The green bodice by J. A. Weir
Green bottle by H. Hofmann
Green burst by K. R. Morris
Green car by W. J. Glackens
Green composition by B. Greene
Green dancer by C. H. Demuth
Green depth by I. R. Miller
Green depth by I. R. Pereira
Green dory by W. Homer
Green, gold and brown by A. G. Dove
Green, green, I love you green by L. Finkel-
  stein
Green hat by E. E. Speicher
Green Head, Deer Isle, Maine by J. Marin
Green heron by J. J. Audubon
Green landscape by J. Tworkov
The green lion by P. Tchelitchew
Green night by W. A. Baziotes

Green on blue by M. Rothko
The green one by W. P. Morehouse
Green patio door by G. O'Keeffe
Green pears by C. H. Demuth
Green peppers by J. Wilde
Green pool by R. Arthur
Green premonitions by A. Lunak
Green river, Oregon by A. J. Miller
Green sea by H. E. Mattson
Green shore by M. B. Prendergast
Green silver by J. Pollock
Green squash by K. Knaths
Green striped bowl by A. H. Maurer
Green table by N. Spencer
Green target by J. Johns
Green wall by R. Gleitsmann
Green woods by B. J. O. Nordfeldt
Greene, Mr., fl 1810
  Jarvis, J. W. Mr Greene
Greene, Mrs, fl 1810
  Jarvis, J. W. Mrs Greene
GREENE, Balcomb, 1904-
  Abstraction—Storm
    Baur. Balcomb Greene
  Ancient form   MMA
    Baur. Balcomb Greene
    Baur. Revolution
    Pierson
    Read. Concise history
  Anguish
    Baur. Balcomb Greene
    Selz. New images
  Black angels
    Baur. Balcomb Greene
    Leepa
  The blind one
    IU. Contemp Amer ptg, 1952
  Blue space
    MMA. Abstract
  Classical still life
    ICA. Annual ex, 1961
  Cliff at Montauk
    Baur. Balcomb Greene
  Composition, 1940   NNSG
    Baur. Balcomb Greene
  Composition, 1958
    Baur. Balcomb Greene
    WMAA. Annual ex, 1958
  Composition: the storm   WMAA
    Baur. Nature (col)
    Goodrich. Amer art (col)
    Pierson
    Time. 300 years (col)
  Crouching figure
    Baur. Balcomb Greene
  Darkness and light
    Baur. Balcomb Greene
  Exhibition
    Baur. Balcomb Greene
  Figure lost in the light
    Baur. Balcomb Greene
    WMAA. Museum and its friends, 1958
  Gertrude II
    Selz. New images (col)
  Gertrude III
    Baur. Balcomb Greene
  Green composition
    Baur. Balcomb Greene

The heirloom man
  Baur. Balcomb Greene
Interior
  Baur. Balcomb Greene
Joan by the sea
  Baur. Balcomb Greene
The magistrate
  Baur. Balcomb Greene
Monument to light
  Baur. Balcomb Greene
The necklace
  Baur. Balcomb Greene (col)
Nude in yellow ochre
  Pousette-Dart. Amer ptg
  PPC. International ex, 1952
Olympia
  Baur. Balcomb Greene
Portrait, 1955-56
  Baur. Balcomb Greene
The sea
  Baur. Balcomb Greene
Seated figure
  Baur. Balcomb Greene
Seated woman
  Selz. New images
The studio
  Baur. Balcomb Greene
This architectural world   WMAA
  Baur. Balcomb Greene
  Read. Art now, 1948 ed
Three women
  Baur. Balcomb Greene
Tragic actor
  Baur. Balcomb Greene
Two heads
  Baur. Balcomb Greene
Two men
  Baur. Balcomb Greene
Two women
  Baur. Balcomb Greene (col)
Waiting figure
  Hess. Abstract ptg
  ICA. Annual ex, 1951
The white space
  ICA. Annual ex, 1947/48
Youth
  Baur. Balcomb Greene
Woman and man
  Baur. Balcomb Greene
Woman dressing
  Baur. Balcomb Greene
Woman with folded arms
  Baur. Balcomb Greene
The wreck, no 2, 1958
  Baur. Balcomb Greene
Yvanka
  IU. Contemp Amer ptg & sculp, 1959
Greene, Catherine (Greene) 1735-1785
  Copley, J. S. Mrs John Greene
GREENE, Gertrude, 1911-
  Monumentality
    MMA. Abstract
Greene, John, fl 1770
  Copley, J. S. John Greene
Greene, Mrs John. See Greene, Catherine
  (Greene)
Greene, Katherine. See Amory, Katherine
  (Greene)
Greene, Martha (Coit) 1706-1784
  Sargent, J. S. Mrs Thomas Greene
Greene, Martha Washington. See Night-
  ingale, Martha Washington (Greene)
Greene, Ray, 1765-1849
  Malbone, E. G. Hon Ray Greene

GREENE, Stephen, 1917-
  The burial   WMAA
    Bazin
    CSFP. Annual ex, 1948/49
    Goodrich. Amer art
    IU. Contemp Amer ptg, 1950
  Cain and Abel
    IU. Contemp Amer ptg & sculp, 1957
  The deposition   WMAA
    Genauer
    Mendelowitz
    WMAA. New decade
    MMA. Contemp ptrs
    Pierson
  Deposition from the cross   MCH
    Pulitzer v2
  Family portrait   MiD
    WMAA. Juliana Force
  Flagellation   MoKN
    CoS. New accessions USA, 1952
  The flagellators   MoSL
    CoS. New accessions USA, 1948
    MoSL. Handbook 1953
  Howl
    IU. Contemp Amer ptg & sculp, 1961
  Ischia
    CSFP. Annual ex, 1950/51
  Limbo
    CSFP. Annual ex, 1947/48
  The performance
    WMAA. New decade
  The sentinel
    VR. Amer ptg, 1954
  The studio
    IU. Contemp Amer ptg & sculp, 1955
  Tulips   MCH
    Pulitzer v2
Greene, Mrs Thomas. See Greene, Martha
  (Coit)
Greenhouse by L. Gatch
GREENLEAF, Benjamin
  Anna Hammond Pope   MSt
    Little. Country art
Greenleaf, Elizabeth, b 1748
  Badger, J. Elizabeth Greenleaf
Greenleaf, Stephen, 1652-1743
  Unidentified artist. Stephen Greenleaf jr
Greenleaf family, Child of by J. S. Copley
Greenough, Horatio, 1805-1852
  Hubard, W. J. Horatio Greenough, the
    American sculptor, in his studio in
    Florence
Greenville, South Carolina
  Tucker, J. South east view of Greenville,
    South Carolina, 1825
Greenville, Treaty of, 1795
  Unidentified artist. The Indian treaty of
    Greenville, 1795
GREENWOOD, Ethan Allen, 1779-1856
  Isaiah Thomas   MWA
    MWA. Checklist of portraits
  Rebecca Tufts Whittemore   MSt
    Little. Country art
GREENWOOD, John, 1727-1792
  Abigail Gerrish and her grandmother
                       MSE
    NUM. Art across America
  Alice Furneaux Clarke   MSE
    MSE. Catalogue of ports, 1950
  American sea captains carousing at Suri-
    nam. See Sea captains carousing at
    Surinam

  Elizabeth Moffatt
    Belknap
  Greenwood and Lee families
    Flexner. First flowers
    Pierson
  John Clarke   MSE
    MSE. Catalogue of ports, 1950
  John Moffatt
    Belknap
  Judith Pickman   NNHS
    Belknap
  Lois (Pickering) Orne   MSE
    MSE. Catalogue of ports, 1950
  Mrs Benjamin Austin   DeWin
    Belknap
  Mrs Francis Cabot
    Flexner. Copley
  Mrs John Moffatt
    Belknap
  Sarah Kilby
    Belknap
  Sea captains carousing at Surinam (Amer-
    ican sea captains carousing at Suri-
    nam)   MoSL
    Davidson v 1
    Flexner. First flowers
    ICA. From colony to nation
    Mendelowitz
    MoSL. 50 masterworks
    MoSL. Handbook 1953
    Pierson
    Richardson. Ptg in America
    Robb. Harper history
    Time. 300 years (col)
    U. S. National Capital sesquicentennial
    com
GREENWOOD, Marion, 1909-
  Dancers resting
    Gruskin
    Pearson. Mod renaissance
  Eastern elegy   OYB
    OYB. Annual 1956
    OYB. Supplement 1959
  Eastern memory
    Pearson. Mod renaissance
  Invocation
    NAD. Annual ex, 1951
    PA. Annual ex, 1951
  Mississippi girl
    Pearson. Mod renaissance
  Rice line
    Pearson. Mod renaissance
  Simple confession   ATU
    ATU. Coll of Amer art
Greenwood and Lee families by J. Green-
  wood
The greeting by A. J. Miller
Greeting the trappers by A. J. Miller
GREGOROPOULOS, John, 1921-
  Archaic landscape
    MBIC. View 1960
GREGORY, A. V.
  The ship Ringleader   MSP
    Davidson v 1
Gregory, Clara Bartlett. See Catlin, Clara
  Bartlett (Gregory)
Gregory, Dudley Sanford
  Linen, G. Margaret Henderson Gregory
    and Dudley Sanford Gregory
Gregory, Margaret Henderson
  Linen, G. Margaret Henderson Gregory
    and Dudley Sanford Gregory

Grey and gold by J. R. Cox
Grey and green by G. J. Vander Sluis
Grey and silver, Battersea reach by J. A. M. Whistler
Grey day, Goochland by G. Inness
Grey day in Adirondacks by J. N. Rosenberg
Grey hills by G. O'Keeffe
Grey note—mouth of the Thames by J. A. M. Whistler
Grey numbers by J. Johns
Grey on blue and brown by H. H. Holbrook
Grey rose by C. W. Hare
Grey sea by J. Marin
Greyed rainbow by J. Pollock
Griffin, Samuel, fl 1809
  Dunlap, W. Samuel Griffin
GRIFFITH, E. N. fl 1894
  Still life, 1894
    Frankenstein. After the hunt
GRILLEY, Robert L. 1920-
  Arrival of Nike at Panmunjom   IU
    IU. Contemp Amer ptg & sculp, 1953
    IU. 20th century
GRILLO, John, 1917-
  Celestral   MnMW
    MnMW. 60 Amer ptrs
Grimball, Mary Magdalen (Prioleau) 1742-1813
  Theus, J. Mrs Thomas Grimball
Grimball, Thomas, 1745-1783
  Theus, J. Col Thomas Grimball
GRIMM, Paul
  Desert domain
    NYG. Fine art
  Pleasant retreat
    NYG. Fine art
Griswold, Eunice. See Pinney, Eunice (Griswold) Holcombe
Griswold family
  Johnson, Mr. Mr and Mrs Sherman Griswold and their three favorite sheep
Grizzly bear by A. J. Miller
GRODE, Shearly Mae, 1925-
  Two musicians   LaN
    CoS. New accessions USA, 1956
GROOMBRIDGE, William, 1748-1811
  English landscape   MdBH
    Flexner. Light of distant skies
  Fairmount and Schuylkill river   PH
    ICA. From colony to nation
    Pierson
  Woodlands, seat of William Hamilton, near Philadelphia
    Chew. 250 years of art
GROPPER, William, 1897-
  Aggressors' retribution   OYB
    OYB. Catalogue 1951
  Armchair strategists
    CanO. Hirshhorn coll
  Backstage
    PPC. Ptg in the U.S. 1949
  Chakwa tea plantation
    IU. Contemp Amer ptg, 1952
  Civilization
    Rathbun
  Headless horseman
    CSFP. Annual ex, 1947/48

Homeless   MM
  MM. 100 Amer ptrs
  Pierson
Horseman   ATU
  ATU. Coll of Amer art
Incumbent
  Cheney. Expressionism 1948 ed
Isolationist
  Wight. Milestones
Joe Magarac
  Bazin
Migration   ATeS
  ATeS. Collection
  Mendelowitz
The opposition
  Larkin
  Larkin rev ed
The Senate   MMA
  Barr. What is mod ptg
  Baur. Revolution
  Cheney. Story 1958 ed
  McCurdy
  NYG. Fine art
  Pierson
  Robb. Harper history
  UNESCO. 1860-1949
The speaker   ATU
  ATU. Coll of Amer art
Talmudic student
  IU. Contemp Amer ptg & sculp, 1955
Time
  IU. Contemp Amer ptg, 1949
  Roos
Upper House   PA
  Gruskin

Portrait of the artist
Biddle, G. William Gropper
Grosbeak
Audubon, J. J. Blue grosbeak
GROSS, Sidney, 1921-
Industrial variations no 1
  PPC. Ptg in the U.S. 1949
El motif
  NAD. Annual ex, 1948
Untitled no 6
  DC. 27 biennial ex, 1961
Gross clinic by T. Eakins
Gross clinic, Sketch for by T. Eakins
GROSZ, George, 1893-1959
After the questioning
  Baur. George Grosz
  Craven. Treasury 1952 ed
The agitator
  Biddle. Yes and no
The ambassador of good will   MM
  Baur. George Grosz
  MM. 100 Amer ptrs
Apocalyptic landscape   IU
  IU. 20th century
Approaching storm   WMAA
  Baur. George Grosz (col)
  Gruskin (col)
Aquarelle
  UNESCO. 1860-1955
  UNESCO. 1860-1959
Attacked by the stickmen
  Baur. George Grosz
Blue chair   KW
  Baur. George Grosz
Blue sky
  CanO. Hirshhorn coll

Cape Cod dunes
  Baur. George Grosz
Central park
  NYG. Fine art
Central park at night   ICA
  Baur. George Grosz
Corpus delicti
  Baur. George Grosz
Couple   WMAA
  Baur. George Grosz
  Baur. New art
  Goodrich. Amer art
  Mendelowitz
  Pierson
A Dallas night
  Pousette-Dart. Amer ptg
Dr Neisse. See Max Hermann-Neisse
End of the world
  Baur. George Grosz
Engineer Heartfield   MMA
  Baur. George Grosz
  MMA. Masters
The fat and the thin
  Baur. George Grosz
From the town beyond the river
  PPC. Ptg in the U.S. 1949
Funeral of the poet Panizza
  McCurdy
Furlough
  Baur. George Grosz
Gothic woods and nymph
  VR. Biennial ex, 1948
The gray man dances
  Baur. George Grosz
  Newmeyer
Homage to Oskar Panizza (Nightmare)
  50 years of mod art
I am glad I came back   ATeS
  ATeS. Collection
  Baur. George Grosz
I was always present   MiC
  Baur. George Grosz
I woke one night and saw a burning
  house
  ICA. Annual ex, 1947/48
  Pearson. Mod renaissance
Landscape, Bornholm
  Baur. George Grosz
Little murderer
  Baur. George Grosz
  MnMW. Expressionism 1900-1955
Maid arranging hair of corpulent woman
                                     PPhM
  Canaday
  Canaday (detail)
A man of opinion
  Craven. Treasury 1952 ed ,col)
Manhattan harbour
  UNESCO. 1860-1959
Max Hermann-Neisse (Dr Neisse) MMA
  Baur. George Grosz
  Cheney. Story 1958 ed
  Craven. Rainbow book
  Craven. Treasury 1952 ed
  McCurdy
Metropolis   MMA
  McCurdy
  Myers
  Read. Concise history
Model in the studio
  Pearson. Mod renaissance
Night club whoopee   GAtM
  GAtM. Holbrook collection

Nightmare. See Homage to Oskar Pa-
  nizza
No let up
  Wight. Milestones
Nude with bath towel
  Baur. George Grosz
Painter of the hole
  Baur. George Grosz
  Pearson. Mod renaissance
Peace II, 1946   WMAA
  Baur. George Grosz
  Goodrich. Amer art (col)
  WMAA. Juliana Force
A piece of my world no 1, c 1938   NJN
  Baur. New art (col)
  Genauer
  Pearson. Mod renaissance
A piece of my world no 2, c 1938
  Baur. George Grosz
The pit   KW
  Baur. George Grosz (col)
  Baur. New art
  Baur. Revolution
  Cheney. Story 1958 ed
  Pierson
Punishment   MMA
  Gruskin
Rainbow fiend
  IU. Contemp Amer ptg, 1949
  NBuA. Expressionism
Republican automatons   MMA
  McCurdy
Self-portrait, 1938
  Baur. George Grosz
Shoeshine   MB
  MB. Ptgs in water color
Street scene
  Baur. George Grosz
  Baur. Revolution
The survivor   PPC
  Baur. George Grosz
  Pearson. Mod renaissance
  Pierson
Table-talk
  Read. Art now, 1948 ed
Theatrical dummy in Iwan Goll's Me-
  thusalem, design for
  Baur. George Grosz
The tortured ham
  Baur. George Grosz
Waiting for a job   ATU
  ATU. Coll of Amer art
Waving the flag   WMAA
  Baur. George Grosz
  Baur. New art
  Goodrich. Amer art
  Pierson
GROTH, John, 1908-
  Berlin, May 3, 1945
  NAD. Annual ex, spring 1950
The grotto by M. Friedman
Ground-air control by D. L. Weismann
Ground swell by E. Hopper
The group by J. Strombotne
Group of artists by R. Soyer
Group of figures by M. Weber
Grouse
  Peale, Rubens. Two grouse in under-
    brush of laurel
Grouse shooting by J. M. Tracy
Grove by P. Guston
Grove by E. Ludins

Grove of trees by A. Bierstadt
Grove of trees by S. Laufman
Growth by M. Kantor
Growth by E. Vicente
The grudge by R. Thompson
GRUNEWALD, Gustavus, 1805-1878
    Wyoming valley (1)
        McClintock
    Wyoming valley (2)
        McClintock
Grymes, Alice. See Page, Alice (Grymes)
Guard room in the palace of Fontainebleau
    by W. P. P. Longfellow
Guardian by M. Graves
Guardian by R. Watson
Guardians of the secret by J. Pollock
Guerrilla warfare by A. Bierstadt
GUERIN, Jean
    Water waltz
        PPC. Ptg in the U.S. 1949
GUERIN, John William, 1921?-
    Meadow
        IU. Contemp Amer ptg & sculp, 1957
    Ship channel
        IU. Contemp Amer ptg & sculp, 1959
GUERRERO, José, 1914-
    Blue depths
        PPC. International ex, 1961/62
    Presence of black no 1   NBuA
        NBuA. Acquisitions 1959-1961
    Signs and portents   NNSG
        NNSG. Handbook
    Three blues
        NNSG. Younger Amer ptrs
GUGLIELMI, Louis, 1906-1956
    The bridge
        Gruskin
    Fourth of July
        CSFP. Annual ex, 1952
    Job's tears
        IU. Contemp Amer ptg, 1948
    Mental geography
        McCurdy
    A muted street
        MnMW. Precisionist view
    New York 21
        IU. Contemp Amer ptg, 1950
        MM. Amer ptg today
        PA. Annual ex, 1952
    Night windows
        IU. Contemp Amer ptg, 1951
    An odyssey for moderns
        Larkin
    Rampart street
        ICA. Annual ex, 1951
    The river   ICA
        Pierson
    Solitudes
        CSFP. Annual ex, 1948/49
    The temptation of St Anthony
        Genauer
        IU. Contemp Amer ptg, 1949
    Terror in Brooklyn   WMAA
        Baur. Revolution
        Cheney. Primer 1958 ed
        Goodrich. Amer art (col)
        Pierson
Guide and mountains and sky by W. Homer
Guide carrying deer by W. Homer

Guide fishing by W. Homer
Guide to Croaghan by R. Henri
Guilty cats by J. De Diego
Guinan, Texas, 1886-1956
    Marsh, R. Texas Guinan and her gang
Guirson by E. A. Donati
The guitar by G. B. Luks
Guitar player by M. Weber
Guizot, François Pierre Guillaume, 1787-1874
    Healy, G. P. A. François Pierre Guillaume
        Guizot
Gulch mine, Central city, Colorado by E.
    Leutze
Gulf coast shipyard by E. D. Lewandowski
Gulf stream by W. Homer
Gull a'winging by W. Bassford
GULLAGER, Christian, 1762-1826
    David Coats   MoSL
        MoSL. Handbook 1953
    John May   MWA
        Larkin
        Larkin rev ed
        MWA. Checklist of portraits
    Samuel Barton
        ICA. From colony to nation
Gulls
    Audubon, J. J. Great black-backed gull
    Benn, B. Sea gulls
    Evergood, P. American shrimp girl
    Graves, M. Wounded gull
    Graves, M. Wounded sea gull
    Keller, H. G. Gulls feeding
    Marin, J. Gulls, Cape Split, Maine
    Marin, J. Sea and gulls
    Marin, J. Sea gulls
    Mattson, H. E. Gulls and sea
    Ruellan, A. Boy and gull
    Spruce, E. F. Gull
    Spruce, E. F. Sea gulls
Gun foundry, Cold Spring, New York by
    J. F. Weir
GUSTON, Philip, 1912-
    Actor
        Ashton. Philip Guston
    Attar
        Ashton. Philip Guston (col)
    Beggar's joys
        Ashton. Philip Guston (col)
        MMA. New Amer ptg (col)
        MMA. 12 Americans (col)
    Ceremony
        Genauer
        MnU. Philip Guston
    The clock   MMA
        Ashton. Philip Guston (col)
        Hunter. Mod Amer ptg (col)
        MMA. New Amer ptg
    Clock II, 1957
        Ashton. Philip Guston
    Dial   WMAA
        Ashton. Philip Guston (col)
        Goodrich. Amer art (col)
    Doyer II, 1958
        Ashton. Philip Guston
    Fable, 1956   MoSLW
        Ashton. Philip Guston
    Fable II, 1957
        Ashton. Philip Guston (col)
    Gladiators
        MnU. Philip Guston
    Gouache
        Ashton. Philip Guston

Grove
  Ashton. Philip Guston (col)
Holiday
  NAD. Annual ex, 1947, 1st half
If this be not I   MoSLW
  Gruskin (col)
  MnU. Philip Guston
Martial memory   MoSL
  Larkin
  Larkin rev ed
  MnU. Philip Guston
  Pierson
  Roos
The mirror
  Art since 1945 (col)
  Read. Concise history
Musa Mckim
  MnU. Philip Guston
Native's return   DP
  Ashton. Philip Guston
Night children
  Bazin
  MnU. Philip Guston
Nile
  WMAA. Museum and its friends, 1959
Number 5, 1952
  Ashton. Philip Guston
Number 6, 1952
  Ashton. Philip Guston
Painter's city
  Ashton. Philip Guston (col)
  Canaday
Painting, 1950
  Ashton. Philip Guston
Painting, 1952
  Ashton. Philip Guston (col)
  MMA. 12 Americans
Painting, 1954   MMA
  McCurdy
  MMA. New Amer ptg
  MMA. 12 Americans
  NNSG. Younger Amer ptrs
Performers   MM
  MM. 100 Amer ptrs
  MnU. Philip Guston
Poet
  Ashton. Philip Guston (col)
The porch no 1   IU
  IU. Contemp Amer ptg, 1948
  IU. 20th century
Porch no 2, 1946-47   NUM
  Ashton. Philip Guston
  MnU. Philip Guston
  NBuA. Expressionism
Review, 1948-49
  Ashton. Philip Guston
Review, 1950
  MnU. 40 Amer ptrs
The room
  Ashton. Philip Guston
  MMA. 12 Americans
  MnMW. 60 Amer ptrs
Sanctuary
  IU. Contemp Amer ptg, 1949
  MnU. Philip Guston
The sculptor   VR
  CoS. New accessions USA, 1946
Sentimental moment
  Gruskin (col)
Shanah
  MnU. 40 Amer ptrs
  MnU. Philip Guston

Sleeper
  Ashton. Philip Guston
The street
  Pierson
Summer
  Eliot. Art of our time (col)
  Time. 300 years (col)
To B. W. T. 1951-52
  MMA. 12 Americans
To Fellini
  Ashton. Philip Guston
  Ponente. Mod ptg, 1960 (col)
The tormentors
  Ashton. Philip Guston
  PPC. International ex, 1950
Untitled painting, 1955-56
  Ashton. Philip Guston
  Baur. Nature (col)
Untitled painting, 1958
  Ashton. Philip Guston (col)
The visit
  MMA. 12 Americans
Voyage   NBuA
  Ashton. Philip Guston (col)
  NBuA. Acquisitions 1954-57
White painting
  Ashton. Philip Guston
Zone
  Art since 1945
  Ashton. Philip Guston (col)
  WMAA. Museum and its friends, 1958
GUTMANN, Gerrie
  The uninvited
  CSFP. Annual ex, 1952
GUY, Francis, c 1760-1820
  Baltimore, 1803   NBM
    Davidson v2
    DC. Amer ptrs of the South
  Bolton
    Flexner. Light of distant skies
  Brooklyn, 1816-1820 (Winter scene in
    Brooklyn)   NBM
  Born
    Davidson v2
    Flexner. Light of distant skies
    Mendelowitz
    Pierson
  Pennington mills, Baltimore, view down-
    stream   MdBP
    Barker. Amer ptg
  Pennington mills, Baltimore, view up-
    stream   MdBP
    Davidson v 1
  Tontine coffee house, New York c 1798
                                          NNHS
    Davidson v2
    Larkin
    Larkin rev ed
    Pierson
  View of Baltimore, basin and Federal hill
    MdBMu. Rendezvous
  Washington's tomb   MdBH
    ICA. From colony to nation
  Winter scene in Brooklyn. See Brooklyn,
    1816-1820
GUY, James
  Composition no 6—50
    MM. Amer ptg today
GUYOL DE GUIRAN, François-Marie,
  fl 1815
  Marie Elise Provenchere   MoSLH
    Pierson

GWATHMEY, Robert, 1903-
Across the tracks
Larkin
Larkin rev ed
Bread and circuses   MSM
Pierson
Children dancing   OYB
OYB. Catalogue 1951
Clearing
DC. 25 biennial ex, 1957
Cotton picker
IU. Contemp Amer ptg, 1951
End of day   IBM
Mendelowitz
Farmer's wife
CanO. Hirshhorn coll
IU. Contemp Amer ptg & sculp, 1953
Flower vendors
CSFP. Annual ex, 1950/51
Front porch
PPC. International ex, 1950
Hoeing   PPC
Bazin
Gruskin (col)
McCurdy
Hoeing tobacco   GAtM
GAtM. Holbrook collection
Painting of a smile   NeL
CoS. New accessions USA, 1954
Pierson
Pick 'till the rain hits
ICA. Annual ex, 1954
Poll tax country
DC. 20 biennial ex, 1947
Singing and mending
CSFP. Annual ex, 1948/49
Southern community
IU. Contemp Amer ptg, 1950
Southern scene
MM. Amer ptg today
Sowing   WMAA
Goodrich. Amer art
Vacationist
Pierson
Winter's playground
Pousette-Dart. Amer ptg
The **gypsy** by G. Tooker
Gypsy with a cigarette by R. Henri
Gypsy's house by M. Hoff
Gyrfalcon by J. J. Audubon

H

H., E.
Detroit, 1794 (Detroit public library)
Davidson v2
H. L. Hunley (submarine)
Chapman, C. W. Confederate submarine
torpedo boat H. L. Hunley, 1863
Habbaku dancers by E. A. Donati
HABERLE, John, 1856-1933
Bachelor's drawer
Frankenstein. After the hunt
Changes of time
CSFP. Illusionism
Frankenstein. After the hunt
Clock
Frankenstein. After the hunt

Conglomeration
Frankenstein. After the hunt
A favorite   MSM
Frankenstein. After the hunt
Grandma's hearthstone   MiD
Frankenstein. After the hunt
Pierson
Richardson. Ptg in America
Time and eternity   CtNB
Frankenstein. After the hunt
Pierson
Torn in transit
CSFP. Illusionism
Frankenstein. After the hunt
Habersham, James, 1712-1775
Theus, J. Gov James Habersham
Habitation by M. Cone
HACKER, Gerte F.
White pitcher
OYB. Annual 1951
HADDOCA, A. fl 1830
Red Jacket   DN
DN. Amer primitive ptgs, pt 1
Hadley, Arthur Twining, 1856-1930
Kendall, W. S. Arthur Twining Hadley
Hagar and Ishmael by B. West
HAHN, Walter H. 1927-
Satan
IU. Contemp Amer ptg & sculp, 1953
HAHN, William, 1840?-1890?
Yosemite valley
U.S. National Capital sesquicentennial
com
HAIDT, John Valentin, 1700-1780
Christ before Pilate
ICA. From colony to nation
Crucifixion
ICA. From colony to nation
Timothy Horsfield jr
Chew. 250 years of art
HAILMAN, Johanna Knowles (Woodwell)
1871-
Happy morning
PPC. International ex, 1950
Mrs Leslie Buswell
PPC. Ptg in the U.S. 1949
My house   PPC
Chew. 250 years of art
Hailstorm by T. H. Benton
Haines, Charles Richard. See Haines, Rich-
ard
HAINES, Richard, 1906-
The bather
IU. Contemp Amer ptg & sculp, 1961
By the sea
MM. Amer ptg today
Eventide
IU. Contemp Amer ptg, 1950
Mesa Verde
IU. Contemp Amer ptg, 1951
Morning sea   MoKN
CoS. New accessions USA, 1952
Night of return
CSFP. Annual ex, 1952
Pousette-Dart. Amer ptg
The prodigal son   DC
CoS. New accessions USA, 1952
DC. 22 biennial ex, 1951
PPC. Ptg in the U.S. 1949
Town meeting   ATeS
ATeS. Collection
Hairdresser's window by J. Sloan
Haiti by J. Delbos

Haitian heaven by A. A. Dehn
Haitian Mardi Gras by A. A. Dehn
HAKLHUBER, F. fl 1860
 Herndon hotel, Omaha, Nebraska **MoSLH**
 Rathbone
Hale, Edward Everett, 1822-1909
 Chase, W. M. Edward Everett Hale
 Hale, P. L. Edward Everett Hale
HALE, Philip Leslie, 1865-1931
 Edward Everett Hale
 Larkin
 Larkin rev ed
HALEY, John Charles, 1905-
 Dark anonymity
  IU. Contemp Amer ptg & sculp, 1953
 Myriad
  IU. Contemp Amer ptg, 1952
 Monument valley
  IU. Contemp Amer ptg, 1951
HALEY, Sally, 1908-
 Red chair
  OrPA. Ptgs and sculptures (col)
 Robed figures in ambulatory
  MnMW. Reality and fantasy
Half a man by W. R. Garver
Halfway house by D. G. Blythe
Halibut fishing by W. Homer
Hall, Abigail, 1795-1878
 Unidentified artist. Abigail Hall
Hall, Mrs Calvin. See Hall, Mercy (Barnes)
HALL, Carl A. 1921-
 The dance
  IU. Contemp Amer ptg, 1948
 Domain
  PPC. Ptg in the U.S. 1949
 Junction
  OrPA. Ptgs & sculptures
 Vagrants
  IU. Contemp Amer ptg, 1951
Hall, David, fl 1775
 Williams, W. David Hall
Hall, Deborah, fl 1776
 Williams, W. Deborah Hall
Hall, Laura, fl 1808
 Brown, J. Laura Hall
Hall, Mercy (Barnes) fl 1808
 Brown, J. Mrs Calvin Hall
Hall, William
 Williams, W. William Hall
Hall at Shinnecock by W. M. Chase
Halle cathedral, East choir by L. Feininger
Les **halles** by W. A. Smith
Hallett, Joseph, 1678-1750
 Duyckinck, G. (attributed works)
  Joseph(?) Hallett
 Unidentified artist. Gentleman of the Hallett family (probably Joseph Hallett)
Hallett, Mrs Joseph. See Hallett, Mary (Lawrence) Greenoak
Hallett, Maria. See Tallmadge, Maria (Hallett)
Hallett, Mary (Lawrence) Greenoak, fl 1728
 Duyckinck, G. Mrs Joseph(?) Hallett
 Unidentified artist. Lady of the Hallett family (probably Mrs Joseph Hallett)
Hallett family, Member of
 Unidentified artist. Boy of the Hallett family
 Unidentified artist. Son of Capt **Samuel** Hallett
Hallowe'en by L. Bosa

Hallowe'en mask by R. Vickrey
HALLOWELL, George Hawley, 1871-1926
 Brook in Vermont   MB
  MB. Ptgs in water color
 Calling of St Matthew (copy after Carpaccio)   MB
  MB. Ptgs in water color
 Italian fiesta, night   MSM
  MSM. Handbook
 Mountains in Dalmatia   MB
  MB. Ptgs in water color
 Snow drapery   MB
  MB. Ptgs in water color
 The tree   MB
  MB. Ptgs in water color
 Trees in winter   MB
  MB. Ptgs in water color
HALPERT, Samuel, 1884-1930
 Brooklyn bridge   WMAA
  Goodrich. Amer art
  Pierson
 Cathedral interior
  WMAA. Pioneers
 Church interior
  Brown. Amer ptg
 Notre Dame, Paris   MM
  Brown. Amer ptg
HALSEY, William Melton, 1915-
 The onlookers
  Pousette-Dart. Amer ptg
Halt—dismount by F. Remington
Halt in the Rocky mountains by A. Bierstadt
Halt of the wise men by J. LaFarge
HAMBLEN, Sturtevant J. fl 1856
 Attributed works
 Baby with doll   VWR
  VWR. Folk art (col)
 Unknown woman   MSt
  Little. Country art
The **Hambletonian** by J. W. Golinkin
Hamblin, Sturtevant J. See Hamblen, Sturtevant J.
Hamilton, Alexander, 1757-1804
 Ames, E. Alexander Hamilton
 Peale, C. W. Alexander Hamilton
 Trumbull, J. Alexander Hamilton
Hamilton, Gail. See Dodge, Mary Abigail
HAMILTON, James, 1819-1878
 Monitor and Merrimac   PH
  Chew. 250 years of art
HAMILTON, John McLure
 Paul Wayland Bartlett in his Paris studio
  Chew. 250 years of art
HAMILTON, Robert G. 1920?-
 Cape fog
  IU. Contemp Amer ptg & sculp, 1959
 Cape landscape
  NUM. Art across America
 Fallout red
  MBIC. View 1960
 Landscape with a mirror
  PPC. International ex, 1958
 Mayflower
  IU. Contemp Amer ptg & sculp, 1961
Hamlet and Horatio by J. Miller
HAMMER, John J. 1842-1906
 Peaceful day in the Mohawk valley MB
  MB. Karolik coll
 Sculptor's studio   MB
  MB. Karolik coll

Hammersley, Mrs Hugh
  Sargent, J. S. Mrs Hugh Hammersley
Hammerstein's roof garden by W. J. Glackens
Hammond, Anna. See Pope, Anna (Hammond)
Hancock, John, 1737-1793
  Copley, J. S. John Hancock
HANCOCK, Nathaniel, fl 1805
  Jedidiah Morse   CtY
    CtY. Portrait index
  Self-portrait   CtY
    CtY. Portrait index
Hancock, Thomas, 1703-1764
  Copley, J. S. Thomas Hancock
Hand sewing machine by A. G. Dove
Handball by B. Shahn
Handel still life by S. W. Crane
Handkerchief point by M. B. Prendergast
The **handsome** dance, Venezuela, South America by G. Catlin
Handwriting on the wall by Ben-Zion
Handy, John, 1756?-1828
  Malbone, E. G. Major John Handy
Hanging bird by H. Bradford
Hanging clothes by J. Koch
Hanging of Bob Augustin by C. A. Herff
HANSON, Joseph Mellor, 1900-
  Composition
    Pousette-Dart. Amer ptg
  Gay table cloth
    WMAA. Contemp Amer ptg, 1950
  Red dominant
    CSFP. Annual ex, 1952
Happy entrance by P. Evergood
Happy family in Virginia by W. Homer
Happy moment by J. G. Clonney
Happy morning by J. K. W. Hailman
HARARI, Hananiah, 1912-
  Man's boudoir no 1 (realism)   ATU
    ATU. Coll of Amer art
  Man's boudoir no 2 (abstraction) ATU
    ATU. Coll of Amer art
  Old valentine
    CSFP. Illusionism
Harbinger of spring by R. Brown
Harbor by M. B. Prendergast
Harbor by J. W. Schulein
Harbor by P. Wescott
Harbor at Edgartown by F. Chapin
Harbor at night by M. Avery
Harbor at night by M. Jackson
Harbor festivity by J. G. F. Von Wicht
Harbor of dreams by I. L. Albright
Harbor scene with fish market near Philadelphia by W. Carr
Harbor traffic by G. Grant
Harbor with red for Mary Lou by J. Lechay
Hard lot by J. Decker
HARDING, Chester, 1792-1866
  Amos Lawrence   DN
    Mendelowitz
    Pierson
  Andrew Jackson
    DC. Privately owned

  Anna Hardaway Bunker   InIJ
    Barker. Amer ptg
    InIJ. 105 ptgs
  Benjamin Pickman   MB
    MB. Karolik coll
  Charles Carroll of Carrollton   DN
    DC. Amer ptrs of the South
  Chester Harding Krum   MoSL
    MoSL. Handbook 1953
  Daniel Boone   MoSLH
    Davidson v 1
  Isaac Bates
    Larkin
    Larkin rev ed
  John Marshall   MBA
    Time. 300 years (col)
  John Randolph of Roanoke   CtY
    CtY. Portrait index
  John Randolph of Roanoke   DN
    DN. Mellon coll
  Lyman Beecher   CtY
    CtY. Portrait index
  Mrs John Ball Brown   MB
    Pierson
  Samuel Cartmill Christy
    Flexner. Light of distant skies

Attributed works

  Daniel Boone (Filson club, Louisville)
    Ford. Pictorial folk art
Hardware store by A. G. Dove
Hardy, Catherine Sears (Wheeler) 1806-1876
  Hardy, J. P. Catherine Wheeler Hardy and her daughter
HARDY, Jeremiah Pearson, 1800-1888
  Catherine Wheeler Hardy and her daughter   MB
    MB. Karolik coll
    Pierson
    Richardson. Ptg in America
  Mary Ann Hardy   MB
    MB. Karolik coll
  New England picnic, 1855   MB
    Davidson v2
  Pic Nic, Camden, Maine   MB
    MB. Karolik coll
Hardy, Mrs Jeremiah Pearson. See Hardy, Catherine Sears (Wheeler)
Hardy, Mary Ann, 1809-1887
  Hardy, J. P. Mary Ann Hardy
HARDY, Philip, fl 1843-1847
  Tremont street, Boston   MB
    MB. Karolik coll
HARE, Channing Weir, 1899-
  Fourth of July
    IU. Contemp Amer ptg, 1950
  The grey rose   IaDa
    IaDa. 30th anniversary
  John Horton
    PPC. Ptg in the U.S. 1949
  Passementerie
    IU. Contemp Amer ptg, 1952
  Young hunter
    NAD. Annual ex, 1948
HARE, David, 1917-
  Two
    Read. Art now, 1948 ed
The **harem** by M. Weber
Hares
  Audubon, J. J. Black-tailed hare or jackrabbit
  Audubon, J. W. Hare

Haring, Elizabeth. See De Peyster, Elizabeth (Haring)

Harkness tower (Yale) by K. Matthew

Harlem by K. Zerbe

Harlem river by P. Dickinson

Harlem river by E. Lawson

Harlem river bridge by D. Burliuk

Harlequin by W. Kuhn

Harlequin by K. Zerbe

Harlequin and woman by C. Alajálov

HARMON, Lily (Perelmutter) 1913-
  Child acrobats
    IU. Contemp Amer ptg & sculp, 1955
  First child
    PPC. Ptg in the U.S. 1949
  Nursery school
    IU. Contemp Amer ptg, 1952
  Pink dunes
    IU. Contemp Amer ptg & sculp, 1957
  Provincetown
    IU. Contemp Amer ptg & sculp, 1959
  Sunset and white trees
    CanO. Hirshhorn coll

Harmony in blue and silver by J. A. M. Whistler

Harmony in grey and green by J. A. M. Whistler

Harmony in red: Lamplight by J. A. M. Whistler

Harness horse stables—Cape Girardeau by R. Davey

HARNETT, William Michael, 1848-1892
  After the hunt   CSFP
    CSFP. Handbook (col)
    CSFP. Illusionism
    Faulkner. Art today, 1956
    Flexner. Amer ptg
    Flexner. Short history
    Frankenstein. After the hunt (col)
    McCurdy
    Mendelowitz
    Pierson
    Richardson. Ptg in America (col)
    Time. 300 years (col)
  After the hunt   OCo
    Frankenstein. After the hunt
    PA. Annual ex, 1955
  After the hunt   OYB
    OYB. Supplement
  Artist's card rack
    Frankenstein. After the hunt
    WiMiA. Amer ptg 1760-1960 (col)
  Artist's window, View from
    Frankenstein. After the hunt
  Cincinnati Enquirer
    Frankenstein. After the hunt
  Colossal luck
    DC. Halpert coll
    Frankenstein. After the hunt
  Deutsche presse
    Frankenstein. After the hunt
  Emblems of peace   MSM
    Baur. Revolution
    CSFP. Illusionism
    MSM. Handbook
    PA. Annual ex, 1955
    Pierson
  The faithful Colt   CtHW
    CtHW. Handbook
    Frankenstein. After the hunt
    Pierson

  Front face
    Frankenstein. After the hunt
  George Fryer's still life
    Frankenstein. After the hunt
  German girl, Head of a   MCH
    Frankenstein. After the hunt
  Head of Minerva
    Frankenstein. After the hunt
  Job lot, cheap
    Frankenstein. After the hunt
  London Times
    Frankenstein. After the hunt
  Meerschaum pipe
    Frankenstein. After the hunt
  Merganser duck
    OYB. Catalogue 1951
  Mortality and immortality
    Frankenstein. After the hunt
  Music and good luck
    Frankenstein. After the hunt
  Music and literature   NBuA
    Frankenstein. After the hunt
    NBuA. Catalogue of the ptgs
    UNESCO. 1860-1955
    UNESCO. 1860-1959
  Oil sketch, 1874
    Frankenstein. After the hunt
  Old Cremona   MM
    Bazin
  Old cupboard door
    Frankenstein. After the hunt
  Old models   MB
    Baur. Amer ptg
    CSFP. Illusionism
    Frankenstein. After the hunt
    Janson. Picture history
    Larkin
    Larkin rev ed
    OCiM. Rediscoveries
    Pierson
    Roos
    Walker. Ptgs from America
  Old North Carolina
    OCiM. Rediscoveries
  The old refrain
    UNESCO. 1860-1955
    UNESCO. 1860-1959
  Old violin   OCiM
    Barker. Amer ptg
    CSFP. Illusionism
    Frankenstein. After the hunt
    PA. Annual ex, 1955
    Pierson
  Searching the Scriptures
    Frankenstein. After the hunt
  The secretary's table
    Chew. 250 years of art
  Social club
    Frankenstein. After the hunt
  Solace
    CSFP. Illusionism
  Still life, 1877
    Frankenstein. After the hunt
  Still life, 1887
    Frankenstein. After the hunt
  Still life, 1888
    Frankenstein. After the hunt
  Still life: salt glaze pot, pipe and Le Figaro
    Chew. 250 years of art
  Still life with bric-a-brac   MCH
    Frankenstein. After the hunt

HARNETT, W. M.—*Continued*
Still life with letter to Thomas B. Clarke
                                 MAP
  Frankenstein. After the hunt
Still life with tankard
  Frankenstein. After the hunt
Study table   NUM
  Frankenstein. After the hunt
  NUM. Art across America
Thieves in the pantry
  Frankenstein. After the hunt
Toledo blade
  Frankenstein. After the hunt
With the Staatszeitung   MoSL
  MoSL. Handbook 1953
Wooden box of catawba grapes
  Frankenstein. After the hunt
Ye knights of old
  Frankenstein. After the hunt

Attributed works

Bachelor's friend   MAP
  Frankenstein. After the hunt
Discarded treasures   MNS
  Frankenstein. After the hunt
Dollar bill and playbill
  Frankenstein. After the hunt
Old friends
  Frankenstein. After the hunt
Old reminiscences   DP
  Frankenstein. After the hunt
Old scraps   MMA
  Frankenstein. After the hunt
Old souvenirs
  Frankenstein. After the hunt
Protection
  Frankenstein. After the hunt
Still life with violin   OYB
  OYB. Catalogue 1951
To Edwin Booth
  Frankenstein. After the hunt
Harp of the winds by F. E. Church
Harp of the winds by H. D. Martin
Harpie by B. Shahn
The **harpies** by H. Bloom
Harris, Charles, b 1784
  Malbone, E. G. Charles Harris
HARRIS, Eleanor, 1899-
Flight
  ICA. Annual ex, 1947/48
Harris, Mrs Lebdeus, fl 1831
  Mason, B. F. Mrs Lebdeus Harris
Harris, Richard D. b 1780
  Malbone, E. G. Richard D. Harris
Harris, Samuel, 1814-1899
  Weir, J. F. The Theological of Yale university
HARRISON, B. J.
Fair of the American institute of New York, held at Niblo's garden, c 1845
  Davidson v 1
Harrison, John fl 1823
  Mayhew, N. John Harrison
Harrison, Mrs John, fl 1823
  Mayhew, N. Mrs John Harrison and her daughter Maria
Harrison, Thomas, fl 1815
  Belknap, Z. Capt Thomas Harrison
Harrison, Mrs Thomas, fl 1815
  Belknap, Z. Mrs Thomas Harrison

HART, George Overbury, 1868-1933
The Bahamas   WMAA
  NYG. Fine art
  Pierson
Cockfight, Mexico   NJN
  Pierson
Fireworks   OCl
  OCl. Handbook
Palisade amusement park   MB
  MB. Ptgs in water color
Sultan's tomb, Fez, Morocco   MB
  MB. Ptgs in water color
HART, James MacDougal, 1828-1901
Catskill creek, New York   NBuA
  NBuA. Catalogue of the ptgs
On the lake shore   MB
  MB. Karolik coll
Picnic on the Hudson   NBM
  Born
View on the Hudson   NCHA
  NYG. Fine art
HART, James McDougal, 1828-1901 **and Tait, Arthur Fitzwilliam,** 1819-1905

Attributed works

The Burden family enjoying the Hudson river near Troy   NAI
  Jones. Rediscovered ptrs
Hart, John, fl 1795
  Polk, C. P. John Hart
Hart, Mrs John, fl 1795
  Polk, C. P. Mrs John Hart and her daughter
Hart, Pop. See Hart, George Overbury
Hart, Samuel, fl 1806
  Unidentified artist. Dr Samuel Hart
HART, William M. 1823-1894
After the storm   MB
  Jones. Rediscovered ptrs
  MB. Karolik coll
Autumn in the Catskills
  Sears. Highlights
Cattle in a stream
  Sears. Highlights
Evening in Keene valley, Adirondacks
  Sears. Highlights
Hartford, Connecticut
  Cole, T. Hartford, Connecticut
Hartford (steamship)
  Smith, J. B. Steamer Hartford, 1849
HARTIGAN, Grace, 1922-
Billboard   MnMI
  Art since 1945
  Hunter. Mod Amer ptg (col)
Bride and owl
  MMA. 12 Americans
Broadway restaurant   MoKN
  Brussels. Exposition
  Eliot. Art of our time (col)
City life
  MMA. New Amer ptg
  MMA. 12 Americans
The creeks: interior
  Read. Concise history
Dublin
  MnMW. 60 Amer ptrs
Essex market
  MMA. New Amer ptg
Grand street brides
  Goodrich. Amer art
  Pierson
Interior—the creeks
  MMA. New Amer ptg (col)

New England, October NBuA
  NBuA. Acquisitions 1957-58
Ocean bathers
  MMA. 12 Americans
Persian jacket MMA
  MMA. 12 Americans
River bathers MMA
  McCurdy
  MMA. 12 Americans (col)
St Valentine
  PPC. International ex, 1961/62
Shinnecock canal MMA
  MMA. Soby collection
The showcase
  WMAA. Contemp Amer ptg, 1955

HARTL, Leon, 1889-
Still life with red fish CtHW
  CoS. New accessions USA, 1960

HARTLEY, Marsden, 1877-1943
Abelard the drowned, master of the Phantom
  McCausland. Marsden Hartley
Abstraction, 1911
  McCausland. Marsden Hartley
Abstraction, 1916 MnU
  MMA. Abstract
Abstraction with flowers
  McCausland. Marsden Hartley
  McCurdy
Albert Pinkham Ryder
  Baur. New art
  Cheney. Story 1958 ed
  Riley. Your art heritage
Autumn
  McCausland. Marsden Hartley
Beaver lake, Lost river region
  McCausland. Marsden Hartley
Bermuda window in a semitropical character
  McCausland. Marsden Hartley
Birds of the Bagaduce OYB
  OYB. Accessions
  OYB. Supplement 1959
Boots MMA
  MMA. Masters
Camden hills from Baker's island, Penobscot bay
  McCausland. Marsden Hartley
Carnival of autumn
  McCausland. Marsden Hartley
Cleophas, master of the Gilda Gray
  McCausland. Marsden Hartley
Color analogy OCo
  Brown. Amer ptg
Dark mountain ICA
  Brown. Amer ptg
Dead plover
  McCausland. Marsden Hartley
Deserted farm
  McCausland. Marsden Hartley
"E," 1915
  Hunter. Mod Amer ptg (col)
  McCurdy
  Read. Concise history
Eight bells' folly: memorial for Hart Crane
  McCausland. Marsden Hartley
Evening storm, Schoodic, Maine, MMA
  McCurdy
  Read. Concise history

Fishhouse, New England
  NYG. Fine art
  UNESCO. 1860-1949
  UNESCO. 1860-1955
  UNESCO. 1860-1959
Fishermen's last supper
  Baur. New art
  DC. De gustibus
  Flexner. Amer ptg
  Flexner. Short history
  McCausland. Marsden Hartley
  MnMW. Contemporary
  MnMW. Expressionism 1900-1955
  Pierson
  WMAA. Neuberger collection
Flower abstraction
  UNESCO. 1860-1955
  UNESCO. 1860-1959
Flowers from Claire Spencer's garden NBuA
  NBuA. Contemporary ptgs
  Time. 300 years (col)
Forms abstracted
  Larkin
  Larkin rev ed
Fox island, Maine MAP
  Cheney. Story 1958 ed
  Wight. Milestones (col)
Garmisch-Partenkirchen
  McCausland. Marsden Hartley
A German officer 1914 MM
  Baur. New art (col)
  Baur. Revolution
  Pierson
  Time. 300 years (col)
Give us this day
  McCausland. Marsden Hartley
  WMAA. Museum and its friends, 1958
Himmel MoKN
  MoKN. Handbook p 149
Hurricane island, Vinal Haven, Maine PPhM
  Canaday
In the moraine, Dogtown common, Cape Ann
  McCausland. Marsden Hartley
Labrador ducks
  McCausland. Marsden Hartley
Landscape no 29, 1907?
  McCausland. Marsden Hartley
Landscape, no 32, 1911
  McCausland. Marsden Hartley
Landscape no 56, 1909
  McCausland. Marsden Hartley
Landscape, New Mexico OCl
  OCl. Handbook
Landscape, Venice
  McCausland. Marsden Hartley
Last of New England—the beginning of New Mexico ICA
  Baur. Revolution
Lighthouse
  Baur. Revolution
Lincoln, Portrait of
  CtY. Yale alumni
Lobster buoys and nets
  McCausland. Marsden Hartley
Lobster fishermen MM
  MM. 100 Amer ptrs
  Taylor. Fifty centuries, 1954 ed (col)
Lobster pots and buoy
  NUM. Art across America

HARTLEY, Marsden—*Continued*
Log jam, Penobscot bay   MiD
  Mendelowitz
  MiD. Treasures
  Richardson. Ptg in America
Maine landscape, autumn   TNF
  Brown. Amer ptg
Maine snowstorm
  McCausland. Marsden Hartley
Marie St Esprit
  McCausland. Marsden **Hartley**
Military
  McCausland. Marsden Hartley
Mount Katahdin
  CanO. Hirshhorn coll
  McCausland. Marsden Hartley
Mount Katahdin, autumn no 1   NeL
  Barker. From realism (col)
  Baur. New art
  Pierson
  Roos
Mount Katahdin, Maine (Lowenthal coll)
  NBuA. Expressionism
Movement
  Cheney. Primer 1958 ed
Movement no 9, 1916
  McCausland. Marsden Hartley
Movements, 1915   ICA
  Brown. Amer ptg
New England fishhouse. See Fishhouse,
  New England
New Mexico
  Cheney. Primer 1958 ed
New Mexico: landscape
  McCausland. Marsden Hartley
New Mexico recollections   OCo
  Brown. Amer ptg
Nova Scotia fishermen   IBM
  Bazin (col)
  WMAA. Juliana Force
Number 48   NBuA
  NBuA. Fifty ptgs
Off to the Banks   DP
  DP. Catalogue
Old bars, Dogtown   WMAA
  Goodrich. Amer art
  Munsterberg
Painting no 5, 1914-15   WMAA
  Goodrich. Amer art (col)
  Pierson
Paysage
  McCausland. Marsden Hartley
Pears
  McCausland. Marsden Hartley
Peasants' paradise
  McCausland. Marsden Hartley
Portrait
  McCausland. Marsden Hartley
Red cross
  WMAA. Pioneers
Robin Hood cove, Georgetown, Maine
  McCausland. Marsden Hartley
  Time. 300 years (col)
Roses
  McCausland. Marsden Hartley
Rubber plant   CtY
  CtY. Soc Anonyme
Smelt brook falls   MoSL
  Born
  Gruskin (col)
  Larkin
  Larkin rev ed
  MoSL. Handbook 1953

Still life, 1912
  McCausland. Marsden Hartley
Still life, 1923
  McCausland. Marsden Hartley
Still life, 1929   ATeS
  ATeS. Collection
Still life no 3, 1916
  McCausland. Marsden Hartley
Still life no 12, 1910
  McCausland. Marsden Hartley
Still life: fruit
  McCausland. Marsden Hartley
Storm clouds, Maine
  McCausland. Marsden Hartley
Waterfall, Morse pond
  McCausland. Marsden Hartley
The wave   MWM
  Baur. New art
  Pierson
Wild roses   DP
  Baur. New art
  DP. Catalogue
  UNESCO. 1860-1955
  UNESCO. 1860-1959
Young worshipper of the truth
  McCausland. Marsden Hartley

Hartley family
  Benbridge, H. Hartley family group

Harvard college
  Fisher, J. Building at Harvard college,
    c 1810

Harvest by J. Jones

Harvest by K. Knaths

Harvest by J. Penney

Harvest by M. Tobey

Harvest in Vermont by J. B. Thompson

Harvest scene by W. Homer

HARVEY, George, fl 1840-1878
  Afternoon, dead calm: View on the Erie
    canal near Pittsford, New York (Late
    afternoon—Calm on the Erie canal)
    Jones. Rediscovered ptrs
    U.S. National Capital sesquicentennial
    com
  Amongst the Allegheny mountains   NBM
    Born
  Entrance to a coal mine near Wheeling,
    Virginia
    U.S. National Capital sesquicentennial
    com
  Extra-curricular activity under the Apostle
    oak, 1841
    Davidson v2
  Hastings landing—Palisade rocks in shad-
    ow   NNHS
    Jones. Rediscovered ptrs
  Houses on a tobacco plantation   NNHS
    Davidson v 1
  Late afternoon—Calm on the Erie canal.
    See Afternoon, dead calm: View on
    the Erie canal near Pittsford, New
    York
  Portland pier, Lake Erie   NNHS
    Davidson v2
  Reaping on Boston common, 1835-1840
    (Blair coll)
    Davidson v2
  St Thomas church, Broadway, New York,
    c1835
    Davidson v2

Spring: burning up fallen trees, a girdled clearing, Canada   NBM
Pierson
State House and Boston Common, 1830
Tolman
Tremont house, Boston   MBA
Larkin
View on the Hudson   MB
MB. Karolik coll
White pelicans in Florida   MB
MB. Karolik coll
Winter: an impediment in travelling   MB
MB. Ptgs in water color
HARVEY, James V. 1929-
Helmund II
WMAA. Young America 1960
Yaddo
DC. 27 biennial ex, 1961
Harvey, Rachel. See Montgomery, Rachel (Harvey)
HARVEY, Sarah E. fl 1877
Winstead, Connecticut   NJP
NJP. Amer folk art
The Harvey breaker, West Nanticoke by T. Hill
Harwood, Adeline, fl 1820
Unidentified artist. Adeline Harwood
Harwood, Margaret (Strachan) fl 1772
Peale, C. W. Mrs Thomas Harwood
Harzfeld's mural by T. H. Benton
Haseltine, Charles F. 1840-1915
Eakins, T. Charles Haseltine
HASELTINE, William Stanley, 1835-1900
Coppet (Lake Geneva)   OYB
OYB. Supplement
Seascape
Chew. 250 years of art
HASEN, Burton, 1921-
Night watch, New Guinea
IU. Contemp Amer ptg & sculp, 1961
Hasey, Susanna. See Lindall, Susanna (Hasey)
HASHAGEN, A. fl 1847
Ship Arkansas leaving Havana   DN
DN. Amer primitive ptgs, pt 1
Hasidic dance by M. Weber
Haskell's house by E. Hopper
Haskins, Hannah Upham, fl 1759
Badger, J. Hannah Upham Haskins
HASSAM, Childe, 1859-1935
The alders
NAD. Amer tradition
Bailey's beach   ICA
NYG. Fine art
Boston Common at twilight   MB
McCurdy
Canterbury, 1889   MB
MB. Ptgs in water color
Cat boats, Newport   PA
CSB. Impressionism
Chez la fleuriste
PPC. Amer classics
Church at Old Lyme   NBuA
NBuA. Catalogue of the ptgs
NBuA. Expressionism
NBuA. Fifty ptgs
Roos
Church at Old Lyme, Connecticut   NSP
Time. 300 years (col)
Cliff rock, Appledore   InIJ
InIJ. 105 ptgs

Columbus avenue, Boston: rainy day   MWM
Pierson
Fifth avenue nocturne   OCl
OCl. Handbook
Golden afternoon, Oregon   MM
NYG. Fine art
July 14, Rue Daunou   MM
MM. 100 Amer ptrs
Laurel in the ledges   ATeS
ATeS. Collection
Little cobbler's shop   MAP
Pierson
Melting snow, Fifth avenue, 1905   OYB
OYB. Catalogue 1951
Montauk fisherman
NSP. Sportscapes
New York window   DC
DC. 25 biennial ex, 1957
Rainy day, Boston   OT
Pierson
Southwest wind   MWM
Pierson
Richardson. Ptg in America
Street scene in winter   MM
Mendelowitz
Sunny blue sea   DNC
Born
DNC. Gellatly coll, 1954
Union square in spring   MNS
Larkin
Larkin rev ed
Washington arch, spring   DP
Bazin
DP. Catalogue
Winter nightfall in the city
NYG. Fine art
Hassam, Frederick Childe. See Hassam, Childe
Hastings landing—Palisade rocks in shadow by G. Harvey
Hastings-on-the-Hudson, going fishing by J. F. Cropsey
Hat display by R. Marsh
Hat seller by E. Berman
Hat, umbrella and bag by J. F. Peto
Hatch, Eunice (Denison)
Jennys, W. Mrs Reuben Hatch
Hatch, Reuben
Jennys, W. Major Reuben Hatch
Hatch family
Johnson, E. Family group (Hatch family)
HATHAWAY, Rufus, 1770-1822
Joseph Robertson Tolman   DN
DN. Amer primitive ptgs, pt 2
Hauling in the gill net by F. Remington
Haunted evening by C. E. Burchfield
Haunted house by D. Brown
Haunted house by L. M. Eilshemius
Haunted house by M. Kantor
Haunted house by W. Peirce
Havana bandana by K. Knaths
Havana harbor by R. Crawford
Havana plaza by S. Davis
HAVELL, Robert, 1793-1878
Pendennis castle, Falmouth, Cornwall   MB
MB. Ptgs in water color
Sing Sing, 1856   NScU
NYG. Fine art

HAVELL, Robert—*Continued*
View of the Hudson river from Horton's road near Croton   MnMI
Born
Attributed works
Mohawk valley   NCHA
Jones. Rediscovered ptrs
U.S. National Capital sesquicentennial com
Havemeyer, Louisine (Waldron)
Cassatt, M. Mrs Havemeyer and her daughter
Haven, Franklin, fl 1830
Edwards, T. (attributed works) Franklin Haven
HAVILAND, Matilda A. fl 1825
Tilted bowl   VWR
VWR. Folk art (col)
Hawaii
Culwell, B. L. Where sun and rain mate: landscape near Pali, Oahu, Hawaii
Hawks
Audubon, J. J. Red-tailed hawk
Spruce, E. F. The hawk
Wilson, B. Hawk and quail
Hawley, Jesse, 1773-1842
Ames, E. Jesse Hawley
Hawley family, fl 1801
Unidentified artist. Nathan Hawley and family
Ha-won-je-tah, The One Horn, first chief of the Sioux by G. Catlin
HAWTHORNE, Charles Webster, 1872-1930
Adoration of the mother   OYB
OYB. Accessions
OYB. Supplement 1959
The fish and the man   TxD
CoS. New accessions USA, 1948
Mrs Alfred L. Becker   InIJ
InIJ. 105 ptgs
Hawthorne, New York by G. A. Picken
Hay ledge by A. N. Wyeth
Hay wagon by C. S. Price
HAYES, David, 1931-
Animal and young   NNSG
NNSG. Handbook
HAYES, George A. fl 1860
Bare knuckles   DN
DN. Amer primitive ptgs, pt 1
Time. 300 years (col)
Hayes, Patrick, abp, 1867-1938
Lockman, D. M. Patrick Cardinal Hayes
HAYES, William Jacob, 1830-1875
Wapiti
Rathbone
The **hayfield** by C. Codman
Haying time by A. M. R. Moses
Haymakers by Unidentified artist
Haymaking by W. Homer
Hayne, Alice, fl 1750
Theus, J. Little Alice Hayne
HAYS, William Jacob, 1872-1934
Westchester hills
NYG. Fine art
Haystack: Belle-ile, Brittany by D. Macknight
HAYTER, Stanley William, 1901-
Falcon
DC. 20 biennial ex, 1947

Leaping figure
ICA. Annual ex, 1947/48
Red figure   MoSL
CoS. New accessions USA, 1960
Seated witness
Read. Art now, 1948 ed
Victim   MoSL
CoS. New accessions USA, 1950
Hayter, William. See Hayter, Stanley William
Hazard, Mrs Benjamin. See Lyman, Harriet
Hazard, Harriet (Lyman) See Lyman, Harriet
HAZELL, S. M. fl 1890
Fox
NSP. Sportscapes
Hazeltine, William Stanley. See Haseltine, William Stanley
Hazy sunrise at sea by M. J. Heade
He did what he wanted by Y. Tanguy
He walks alone by R. Breinin
He who drinks the juice of the stone by G. Catlin
HEAD, Josef, 1921-
Impressions of Milan
IU. Contemp Amer ptg & sculp, 1953
Head by J. Glasco
Head by A. H. Maurer
Head by W. Pachner
Head by C. S. Price
Head in landscape by A. H. Maurer
Head in motion by A. H. Maurer
Head of a cretin by B. Shahn
Head of an old man by F. Duveneck
Head of Stevie by L. Rivers
Head of winter by P. Tchelitchew
Head XXVI by L. A. Golub
Head waters of Juniata by T. Cole
Head with yellow ground by K. Khosrovi
HEADE, Martin Johnson, 1819-1904
Apple blossoms
WiMiA. Amer ptg 1760-1960
Approaching storm: beach near Newport   MB
MB. Karolik coll
Pierson
Time. 300 years (col)
Bay of Panama   MB
MB. Karolik coll
Cloudy day, Rhode Island   MB
MB. Karolik coll
Dawn   MB
MB. Karolik coll
Hazy sunrise at sea   VtMS
NUM. Art across America
High tide on the marshes   OCl
OCl. Handbook
Hummingbirds and gold and purple orchids
Chew. 250 years of art
Hummingbirds and orchids   MiD
Pierson
Richardson. Ptg in America
Hunters resting   MB
MB. Karolik coll
Lake George
Baur. Amer ptg

Magnolia grandiflora   MB
  MB. Karolik coll
Magnolias   MB
  MB. Karolik coll
Mary Rebecca Clark   MB
  MB. Karolik coll
Off shore: after the storm   MB
  MB. Karolik coll
On the Sebastian river, Florida
  Born
Orchids and hummingbird   MB
  Larkin
  Larkin rev ed
  MB. Karolik coll
Orchids and spray orchids with humming-
  birds   MB
  MB. Karolik coll
Passion flowers and hummingbirds   MB
  MB. Karolik coll
Rocks in New England   MB
  MB. Karolik coll
Rocky shore   MB
  MB. Karolik coll
Roses on a palette   MB
  MB. Karolik coll
Salt marshes, Newport, Rhode Island MB
  MB. Karolik coll
South American river   MB
  MB. Karolik coll
  Pierson
Spring shower, Connecticut valley   MB
  Baur. Revolution
  MB. Karolik coll
  Pierson
Storm approaching Narragansett bay
  Mendelowitz
Storm over Narragansett bay   OYB
  OYB. Supplement 1959
Stranded boat   MB
  MB. Karolik coll
Sunset   MiD
  MiD. Treasures
Sunset, Black rock, Connecticut   MB
  MB. Karolik coll
Sunset: Lake Champlain   MB
  MB. Karolik coll
Sunset on Long beach   MB
  MB. Karolik coll
Sunset over the marshes   MB
  MB. Karolik coll
Sunset: tropical marshes   MB
  MB. Karolik coll
Tropical landscape
  Born
Vase of mixed flowers   MB
  MB. Karolik coll
Water lily   MB
  MB. Karolik coll
Headed for Boston by J. Marin
Headland by H. E. Mattson
Headless horse who wants to jump by Y.
  Kuniyoshi
Headless horseman by W. Gropper
Heads by A. Rattner
Heads by M. Weber
Heads or tails by C. M. Russell
Healy, Agnes
  Healy, G. P. A. Agnes and Mary Healy
Healy Edith, b 1848?
  Healy, G. P. A. Mrs Healy and Edith:
    The Healy garden in Paris

HEALY, George Peter Alexander, 1813-
  1894   DC
Abraham Lincoln   DC
  DC. Masterpieces
  Time. 300 years (col)
Abraham Lincoln   DN
  U.S. National Capital sesquicentennial
  com
  VR. Healy's sitters
Agnes and Mary Healy   KyLS
  VR. Healy's sitters
Albert G. Brackett   DN
  VR. Healy's sitters
Albert J. Myer   DNC
  VR. Healy's sitters
Alice Tyler
  VR. Healy's sitters
Andrew Jackson   DC
  VR. Healy's sitters
Arch of Titus   NJN
  Larkin
  Larkin rev ed
  MiD. Travelers in Arcadia
  Pierson (Here as by Church, Healy
    and McEntee)
  U.S. National Capital sesquicentennial
  com
  VR. Healy's sitters
Asher, B. Durand (?)   NNHS
  VR. Healy's sitters
Ave de Pennedegie
  VR. Healy's sitters
Benjamin Franklin at the court of Louis
  XVI   PPhA
  VR. Healy's sitters
Boating party on the Thames, excursion
  of the Healy and Whitehouse families
  VR. Healy's sitters
Bryan family   VR
  VR. Healy's sitters
Cardinal McCloskey   ICN
  Barker. Amer ptg
  VR. Healy's sitters
Charles I, king of Roumania   ICN
  De Mare. G. P. A. Healy
  VR. Healy's sitters
Charles Goodyear
  VR. Healy's sitters
Chester A. Arthur   DC
  VR. Healy's sitters
Daniel Webster   VR
  De Mare. G. P. A. Healy
  VR. Healy's sitters
Edward Everett   ICN
  VR. Healy's sitters
Elizabeth, queen of Roumania   ICN
  De Mare. G. P. A. Healy
  VR. Healy's sitters
Emma Thrusby   NNHS
  VR. Healy's sitters
Ferdinand de Lesseps   ICN
  VR. Healy's sitters
François Pierre Guillaume Guizot   DNC
  De Mare. G. P. A. Healy
  VR. Healy's sitters
Franklin Pierce   MB
  MB. Karolik coll
Franklin Pierce   DC
  VR. Healy's sitters
Franz Liszt   ICN
  De Mare. G. P. A. Healy
  VR. Healy's sitters

HEATH, James, 1757-1834
George Washington (after G. Stuart)
Frankenstein. Two journeyman ptrs

Portrait of the artist
Stuart, G. James Heath
Heathcote, Caleb, 1666-1721
Unidentified artist. Caleb Heathcote
HEATON, William, 1918-
Heraldic hedge
IU. Contemp Amer ptg & sculp, 1959
The **heavens** by R. Tamayo
Heavy, heavy by R. Kent
Heavy industry by A. Alcalay
Heavy sea, Manchester by M. R. Sturgis
Heavy the oar to him who is tired, heavy
the coat, heavy the sea by I. L. Al-
bright
Hebrew books, holy day books by B. Shahn
Hector parting with his wife and child at
the Scæan gate by B. West
HEDRICK, Wally, 1928-
Around painting
MMA. Sixteen
Circle painting, 4
MMA. Sixteen
For service rendered
MMA. Sixteen
Heroic image
MMA. Sixteen
Spirit
MMA. Sixteen
Heeling a bad one by C. M. Russell
HEGELHEIMER, William, 1928-
Landscape
MBIC. View 1960
HEIDEL, Frederick, 1915-
OrPA. Ptgs & sculptures   OrPA
Height by K. Okada
HEIL, Charles Emile, 1870-
Bay-breasted warbler on apple blossom
MB
MB. Ptgs in water color
Chestnut-sided warbler on barberry   MB
MB. Ptgs in water color
Field sparrow on blackberry   MB
MB. Ptgs in water color
Lotus   MB
MB. Ptgs in water color
Ovenbird and pink lady's slipper   MB
MB. Ptgs in water color
Young crow   MB
MB. Ptgs in water color
HEINE, Sebastian
Southwest portion of the public square,
Cleveland
Barker. Amer ptg
Heir to the future by A. Refregier
The **heirloom** man by B. Greene
HEITLAND, Wilmot Emerton, 1893-
Road to Bonao   ICA
NYG. Fine art
Sheepshead shore
NAD. Annual ex, spring 1950
Held up by N. H. Trotter
Helen by J. Sloan
Heliker, Edward. See Heliker, John Edward
HELIKER, Jacob, 1917-
Cliffs, Soames sound
WMAA. Annual ex, 1960

HELIKER, John Edward, 1909-
Boats   ATeS
ATeS. Collection
East river
Cheney. Story 1958 ed
WMAA. New decade
From Cranberry isle   WMAA
Goodrich. Amer art
Imaginary landscape   IU
IU. Contemp Amer ptg, 1949
IU. 20th century
Maine coast
Gruskin
IU. Contemp Amer ptg & sculp, 1955
Maine rocks
CSFP. Annual ex, 1948/49
Mediterranean landscape   NeL
CoS. New accessions USA, 1950
Monreale   PPhM
IU. Contemp Amer ptg, 1951
Pierson
WMAA. New decade
Nova Scotia landscape   OCl
CoS. New accessions USA, 1958
Of Maine   WMAA
Baur. Nature
Old factory   ATU
ATU. Coll of Amer art
Palazzo
Pousette-Dart. Amer ptg
Perilous night
NAD. Annual ex, 1948
Scava
MMA. Abstract
Self-portrait, 1957
VR. Amer ptg, 1958
Self-portrait, 1958
WiMiA. Amer ptg 1760-1960
Spring
IU. Contemp Amer ptg & sculp, 1961
Tarquinia
IU. Contemp Amer ptg, 1950
Viterbo
IU. Contemp Amer ptg & sculp, 1953
White rocks, Nova Scotia   WMAA
Pierson
WMAA. Sara Roby (col)
Helios in the lead by H. G. Keller
Hell Gate bridge by W. H. Smith
Hell Gate tie by G. Vass
Hell hole by C. H. Demuth
Helleu, Paul César, 1859-1927
Sargent, J. S. Paul Helleu
Sargent, J. S. Paul Helleu sketching and
his wife
Helmund II by J. V. Harvey
Hemenway, Harriet (Lawrence) fl 1890
Sargent, J. S. Mrs Augustus Hemenway
Hemlock by J. Mitchell
Hemlock pool by J. H. Twachtman
Henderson, John, 1747-1785
Stuart, G. John Henderson
Hendrickson, Catharine, fl 1770
Unidentified artist. Catharine Hendrick-
son
Henka. See Sawyer, Helen Alton
HENNESSEY, Timothy
Madonna enthroned   MCH
Pulitzer v2

HENRI, Robert, 1865-1929
Beach hat   MiD
  PA. Annual ex, 1955
Blind Spanish singer
  NBuA. Fifty ptgs
Dutch girl in white   MM
  MM. 100 Amer ptrs
Dutch Joe   WiMi
  Roos
East river, snow
  Brown. Amer ptg
  PA. Annual ex, 1955
Eva Green   KW
  PA. Annual ex, 1955
  Pierson
Fifty-seventh street. See West 57th street
  in 1902
George Luks   CanO
  PA. Annual ex, 1955
  Pierson
Guide to Croaghan
  PA. Annual ex, 1955
Gypsy with a cigarette   IBM
  Bazin
Herself   ICA
  NYG. Fine art
Himself   ICA
  NYG. Fine art
Indian girl   InIJ
  InIJ. 105 ptgs
Irish girl   ATeS
  ATeS. Collection
Jimmie O'D   NJMo
  NJMo. Forty years
John Sloan, 1906
  Brooks. John Sloan
Laughing child   WMAA
  Chew. 250 years of art
Little dancer   OYB
  OYB. Catalogue 1951
La Madrilenita   GST
  NUM. Art across America
Mary   MAP
  Larkin
  Larkin rev ed
Mary Gallagher   NJN
  Mendelowitz
Moira
  NSyE. The eight
New York street in winter
  Walker. Ptgs from America
Old model and her daughter
  Time. 300 years (col)
Picnic at Menhoppen, Pennsylvania, July
  4, 1902   PW
  Chew. 250 years of art
Sea and cliffs
  McKinney
Sissy   GAtM
  GAtM. Holbrook collection
Storm tide
  Goodrich. Amer art
West 57th street in 1902 (Fifty-seventh
  street)   CtY
  Brown. Amer ptg
  PA. Annual ex, 1955
  Pierson
William Glackens, 1904
  Glackens
Willie Gee   NJN
  Brown. Amer ptg

Young woman in white   DN
  McCurdy
  PA. Annual ex, 1955
  Robb. Harper history
Zenka of Bohemia
  NAD. Amer tradition
HENRIKSEN, Mae
Abandoned
  NAD. Special ex, 1956
HENRY, Edward Lamson, 1841-1919
City point, Virginia, headquarters of Gen-
  eral Grant   MAP
  U.S. National Capital sesquicentennial
  com
The 9:45 accommodation, Stratford, Conn.,
  1867   MM
  Barker. Amer ptg
  Davidson v2
  Pierson
The old Westover mansion   DC
  U.S. National Capital sesquicentennial
  com
Henry, William, fl 1755
  West, B. William Henry
HENSEL, Hopkins, 1921-
Clown with rooster   MB
  CoS. New accessions USA, 1946
Drummers
  IU. Contemp Amer ptg, 1948
Ice cream parlor   OT
  PPC. Ptg in the U.S. 1949
The widow
  IU. Contemp Amer ptg, 1949
Henshaw, Horatio Gates, fl 1839
  Bascom, R. H. M. Horatio Gates Hen-
  shaw
Henshaw, Mrs Horatio Gates (?) fl 1839
  Bascom, R. H. M. Lady in a sheer white
  cap (possibly Mrs Horatio Gates Hen-
  shaw)
Henshaw, Joshua, 1703-1777
  Copley, J. S. Joshua Henshaw
Henshaw, Ruth. See Bascom, Ruth (Hen-
  shaw) Miles
Her majesty the Barque II by L. Feininger
Her world by P. Evergood
Heraldic ground by J. Muller
Heraldic hedge by W. Heaton
Herbert, George Hubert, 1872-1949
  Lockman, D. M. Coco the clown
Herbert, Jane. See Vanderveer, Jane (Her-
  bert)
The **Herbert** children by L. Sachs
Hercules (ship)
  Unidentified artist. Ship Hercules of Sa-
  lem, 1809
Hérédité des caractères by Y. Tanguy
HERFF, Charles Adelbert, 1853-1943
  Hanging of Bob Augustin
  Ford. Pictorial folk art
HERFORD, Oliver, 1863-1935
Spider's nightmare   MB
  MB. Ptgs in water color
HERING, Harry, 1887-
  Woodstock art conference
  PPC. Ptg in the U.S. 1949
HERIOT, George
The Capitol after the British assault on
  Washington, 1815   NNHS
  Davidson v 1

Herkimer by R. Eshoo
Hermann-Neisse, Max
  Grosz, G. Max Hermann-Neisse (Dr Neisse)
Hermitage, Talavera by H. G. Keller
Herndon hotel, Omaha, Nebraska by F. Haklhuber
Hero by K. Okada
Heroic figures by J. De Diego
Heroic image by W. Hedrick
Herons
  Audubon, J. J. Green heron
  Audubon, J. J. Snowy heron or white egret
Herrera, José
  Hurd, P. José Herrera
Herreshoff, Carl Frederick, 1763-1819
  Malbone, E. G. Carl F. Herreshoff
Herreshoff, Sarah (Brown) See Brown, Sarah
Herring net by W. Homer
Herriot, Mary (Ouldfield) fl 1761
  Theus, J. Polly Ouldfield of Winyah
Herriot, Mrs Robert. See Herriot, Mary (Ouldfield)
HERRON, Davis, 1908-
  St Louis cemetery, New Orleans   ATU
    ATU. Coll of Amer art
HERSCH, Lee, 1896-
  Number 3G
    ICA. Annual ex, 1947/48
Herself by R. Henri
HERZOG, Hermann, 1832-
  Grandfather's lesson
    NSP. Sportscapes
HESS, J. N.
  Rail shooting
    NSP. Sportscapes
HESS, James, fl 1879
  University of Kansas, c 1879   KLU
    U.S. National Capital sesquicentennial com
HESS, Leta English
  Still life
    DC. 26 biennial ex, 1959
HESSELIUS, Gustavus, 1682-1755
  Bacchanalian revel
    Flexner. First flowers
  Bacchus and Ariadne   MiD
    MiD. Ptg in America
    MiD. Treasures
    Pierson
    Richardson. Ptg in America
  Lapowinsa   PH
    Flexner. Amer ptg
    Flexner. First flowers
    Flexner. Short history
    Mendelowitz
    Pierson
    Roos
  The last supper
    Flexner. First flowers
  Mrs Lydia Hesselius   PH
    Pierson
  Self-portrait   PH
    Flexner. First flowers
    Pierson
    Roos

Tishcohan
  Barker. Amer ptg
  Flexner. First flowers
  U.S. National Capital sesquicentennial com
Hesselius, Mrs Gustavus. See Hesselius, Lydia (Addison)
HESSELIUS, John, 1728-1778
  Abraham Keteltas
    Pierson
  Charles Calvert and his Negro slave   MdBM
    Barker. Amer ptg
    Flexner. First flowers
    ICA. From colony to nation (col cover detail)
    NYG. Fine art
    Pierson
    Roos
    Time. 300 years (col)
    UNESCO. Prior to 1860
    UNESCO. Prior to 1860 3d ed
  Elizabeth Calvert   MdBM
    Larkin
    Larkin rev ed
  Margaret Robins   DN
    DN. Amer primitive ptgs, pt 2
  Mrs Abraham Keteltas
    Pierson
  Mrs Richard Galloway jr of Cedar Park, Maryland   MM
    Mendelowitz
    Pierson
    Roos
  Mrs William Allen   MiD
    Belknap
  Samuel Lloyd Chew
    Chew. 250 years of art
  Sarah Fitzhugh   MdBH
    Belknap
Hesselius, Lydia (Addison) d 1745?
  Hesselius, G. Mrs Lydia Hesselius
HETZEL, George, 1826-1899
  Sunshine and shadow
    Chew. 250 years of art
HEWES, Madeline, 1910-
  Autumn
    VR. Amer ptg, 1954
  Hollow hill pastoral
    PPC. Ptg in the U.S. 1949
  The outing
    PPC. International ex, 1952
Hewitt, Mr
  Jennys, W. Mr Hewitt
Hewitt, Mrs
  Jennys, W. Mrs Hewitt
Heyward, Daniel, 1720-1778
  Theus, J. Col Daniel Heyward
Heyward, Mrs Daniel. See Heyward, Jane Elizabeth (Gignilliat)
Heyward, Elizabeth (Savage) 1770-1833
  Malbone, E. G. Mrs Thomas Heyward jr
Heyward, Hannah Miles, 1773-1867
  Malbone, E. G. Hannah Miles Hayward
Heyward, Jane Elizabeth (Gignilliat)
  Theus, J. Mrs Daniel Heyward
Heyward, Maria Miles, 1784-1862
  Malbone, E. G. Maria Miles Heyward
Hialeah by A. Leslie
HICKS, Edward, 1780-1849
  Bridge sign
    Ford. Edward Hicks

HICKS, Edward—*Continued*
Columbus
  Ford. Edward Hicks
Cornell farm   DN
  Brussels. Exposition
  DN. Amer primitive ptgs, pt 2
  Lipman. Primitive ptrs
Cornell farm (Lee coll)
  Ford. Edward Hicks (col)
Declaration of Independence   DN
  DN. Amer primitive ptgs, pt 2
  Ford. Edward Hicks
Declaration of Independence (Lipman
  coll)
  Lipman. Primitive ptrs
Falls of Niagara
  Ford. Edward Hicks
  Lipman. Primitive ptrs
Grave of William Penn   VWR
  VWR. Folk art (col)
Grave of William Penn (Garbisch coll)
  Ford. Edward Hicks pl 26
Grave of William Penn (Hicks coll)
  Ford. Edward Hicks
Hillborn farm
  Ford. Edward Hicks
Innocence, meekness, liberty
  Ford. Edward Hicks
Landscape
  Ford. Edward Hicks pl 33
Noah's ark   PPhM
  Ford. Edward Hicks (col)
  Ford. Pictorial folk art
Peaceable kingdom   NBuA
  Baur. Amer ptg
  Ford. Edward Hicks
  Ford. Edward Hicks pl 34
  NBuA. Catalogue of the ptgs
Peaceable kingdom   PPhM
  Canaday
  Canaday (detail)
  Ford. Edward Hicks
Peaceable kingdom   DP
  DP. Catalogue
Peaceable kingdom   MWM
  Flexner. Light of distant skies
  Ford. Edward Hicks pl 21
  Janson. Picture history
Peaceable kingdom   NCHA
  Ford. Edward Hicks (col)
  Taylor. Fifty centuries, 1954 ed (col)
  Time. 300 years (col)
Peaceable kingdom   NNHS
  Ford. Edward Hicks
  OCiM. Rediscoveries
Peaceable kingdom   NBM
  Ford. Pictorial folk art
  Larkin
  Larkin rev ed
  Newmeyer
  NYG. Fine art
  Riley. Your art heritage
Peaceable kingdom   OCl
  OCl. Handbook
Peaceable kingdom   MMA
  UNESCO. Prior to 1860 3d ed
  UNESCO. Prior to 1860 5th ed
  UNESCO. 1860-1949
  Walker. Ptgs from America
Peaceable kingdom   VWR
  VWR. Amer folk art (col)
  VWR. Folk art (col)

Peaceable kingdom (Cahill coll)
  Flexner. Short history (col detail)
  Ford. Edward Hicks pl 24
  Lipman. Primitive ptrs (col)
  Pierson
  Richardson. Ptg in America (col)
  Robb. Harper history (col)
Peaceable kingdom (Carle coll)
  Ford. Edward Hicks pl 1
  Ford. Edward Hicks pl 3
The peaceable kingdom (Carlen coll)
  Ford. Edward Hicks pl 35
Peaceable kingdom (Grossman coll)
  Ford. Edward Hicks
Peaceable kingdom (Halpert coll)
  Chew. 250 years of art
  DC. Halpert collection
The peaceable kingdom (Kirk coll)
  Ford. Edward Hicks pl 23
Peaceful kingdom   DN
  DN. Amer primitive ptgs, pt 1
Penn's treaty with the Indians   DN
  DN. Amer primitive ptgs, pt 1
Penn's treaty with the Indians (1)
  Ford. Edward Hicks
Penn's treaty with the Indians (2)
  OCiM. Rediscoveries
Penn's treaty with the Indians (Carle coll)
  Flexner. Light of distant skies
Residence of David Twining   MMA
  Barker. Amer ptg
  Davidson v 1
  Ford. Edward Hicks
  Ford. Pictorial folk art
Residence of David Twining   VWR
  Larkin rev ed (col)
  Pierson
  VWR. Folk art (col)
Washington crossing the Delaware
  Lipman. Primitive ptrs

Attributed works
The lion family
  Ford. Pictorial folk art
Portrait of the artist
  Hicks, T. Edward Hicks
HICKS, Thomas, 1823-1890
Barber shop, the musicale   NoCR
  NoCR. Catalogue
Edward Hicks
  Ford. Edward Hicks
Gerard Stuyvesant   NNHS
  Vail. Stuyvesant ports
Hamilton Fish   NNCH
  Barker. Amer ptg
  Larkin
  Larkin rev ed
Sarah Margaret Fuller, Marchioness Ossoli
  MiD. Travelers in Arcadia
Hicks, Whitehead, 1728-1770
  Copley, J. S. (attributed works) White-
    head Hicks
Hicks, Zechariah, 1755-1842
  Pelham, H. (attributed works) Zechariah
    Hicks (?)
The **hidden** apple by P. Evergood
Hidden spring by G. Bartlett
Hide-and-seek by W. M. Chase
Hide-and-seek by P. Tchelitchew
Hideout by D. G. Blythe
HIDLEY, Joseph H. 1830-1872
Fort Plain, New York, c 1865
  Lipman. Primitive ptrs

Glass house lake
  Lipman. Primitive ptrs
Poestenkill, New York   NCHA
  Born
  Ford. Pictorial folk art
  Jones. Rediscovered ptrs
Poestenkill, New York, summer
  Lipman. Primitive ptrs
Poestenkill, New York, winter
  Lipman. Primitive ptrs
West Sand lake
  Lipman. Primitive ptrs

Attributed works

Noah's ark   VWR
  VR. Amer folk art
Higby, J. fl 1800
  Malbone, E. G. J. Higby
HIGGINS, Eugene, 1874-1958
The gamblers   MM
  Pierson
Les pauvres
  Brown. Amer ptg
Share croppers
  NAD. Annual ex, autumn 1949
Weary
  Baur. Revolution
HIGGINS, Victor, 1884-1949
Fiesta day   OYB
  OYB. Catalogue 1951
Holy week procession   InIJ
  InIJ. 105 ptgs
Indian fields   MB
  MB. Ptgs in water color
Higgins pier by M. Sterne
Higginson, Mrs George. See Higginson,
  Martha Hubbard (Babcock)
Higginson, Henry Lee, 1834-1919
  Sargent, J. S. Maj Henry Lee Higginson
Higginson, Martha Hubbard (Babcock)
  1781-1863
  Malbone, E. G. Mrs George Higginson
High bridge by P. Dickinson
High bridge by E. Lawson
High bridge by H. W. Ranger
High bridge, New York by A. C. Goodwin
High cliff, coast of Maine by W. Homer
High houses by L. Feininger
High noon by A. G. Dove
High noon by E. Hopper
High peak by M. R. Barnes
High priest by K. L. Seligman
High snow—low sun by T. Stamos
High street bus barn by L. Bouché
High tension tower by L. Gatch
High tide by J. Gerard
High tide (detail) by W. Homer
High tide on the marshes by M. J. Heade
High water in the Bayou country by Un-
  identified artist
High yaller by R. Marsh
Highland light by M. Kantor
Highland light by J. Kaplan
The **Highlands** from West Point, View of
  by J. F. Weir
Highway by G. Tooker
Hilda by B. Karfiol

HILDEBRANDT, Lily
Horses   CtY
  Rathbun
Hildreth, Samuel
  Corwine, A. H. Dr Samuel Hildreth
HILL, John William, 1812-1897
Bethlehem, Pennsylvania   NNPL
  McClintock
Hudson river bridge near Waterford
      NNHS
  Jones. Rediscovered ptrs
Scene on the Erie canal
  Davidson v2
  WiMiA. Amer ptg 1760-1960
Schenectady, N.Y.   NNHS
  Jones. Rediscovered ptrs
HILL, Thomas, 1829-1908
Bridal veil and El Capitan, Yosemite val-
  ley
  Sears. Highlights
El Capitan, Yosemite valley near Mirror
  lake
  Born
The covey
  NSP. Sportscapes
Fishing party in the mountains   CSFD
  Born
The Harvey breaker, West Nanticoke
  McClintock
Wyoming valley (1)
  McClintock
Wyoming valley (2)
  McClintock
Hill beyond the bridge by P. S. Sample
Hill in winter by D. Macknight
Hill, Main street, Gloucester by J. Sloan
Hill of death, upper Missouri by G. Catlin
Hill town by L. Goldin
Hill town by C. Prendergast
Hill town in Campania by R. Morgan
Hillborn farm by E. Hicks
Hillside by J. S. Sargent
Hillhouse, James, 1754-1832
  Vanderlyn, J. James Hillhouse
Hillhouse, James Abraham, 1789-1841
  Jocelyn, N. James Abraham Hillhouse
Hillhouse, Thomas, 1766-1834
  Ames, E. Thomas Hillhouse
Hills, Huldah (Mulford) 1806-1878
  Ames, E. Mrs John Hills
Hills by B. Karfiol
Hills of the Trap formation by S. Seymour
Hills, South Truro by E. Hopper
HILLSMITH, Fannie, 1911-
Dark and light
  IU. Contemp Amer ptg & sculp, 1959
The house
  ICA. Annual ex, 1947/48
Interior at Honfleur
  IU. Contemp Amer ptg & sculp, 1961
Midnight
  IU. Contemp Amer ptg & sculp, 1955
Queen's gambit
  PPC. International ex, 1955
Signs of the city
  NNSG. Younger Amer ptrs
Town house
  IU. Contemp Amer ptg & sculp, 1957
HILTON, Roy, 1892-
Ivory tower
  IU. Contemp Amer ptg, 1952

Himmel by M. Hartley

Himself by R. Henri

HINCHEY, William J. 1829-1893
Dedication of the Eads bridge at St
Louis, Missouri, 1874
U.S. National Capital sesquicentennial
com

HINCKLEY, Thomas Hewes, 1813-1896
Cows and sheep in pasture
Sears. Highlights
Great Blue hill and Neponset river
Sears. Highlights
Noon
Sears. Highlights
Rotherham, Yorkshire, **England**   **MB**
MB. Karolik coll

HINKLE, Clarence K. 1880-
Spring landscape
CSFP. Annual ex, 1952

HINKLEY, Thomas, 1879-
Fox in West Virginia
NSP. Sportscapes

Hipparchus by C. Gray

Hiroshima by E. Reindel

HIRSCH, Joseph, 1910-
Air raid   **MM**
MM. 100 Amer ptrs
Carcass
IU. Contemp Amer ptg, 1952
NAD. Annual ex, 1954
The confidence
Baur. Revolution
The couple   **MSM**
CoS. New accessions USA, 1958
WMAA. Contemp Amer ptg, 1955
Dance
ICA. Annual ex, 1959/60
Departure
PPC. International ex, 1950
Digger
Genauer (col)
Editorial   **ATU**
ATU. Coll of Amer art
The iceman
NAD. Annual ex, 1947, 1st half
Memorial
NAD. Annual ex, 1957
Nine men
MM. Amer ptg today
PPC. Ptg in the U.S. 1949
An old man   **MB**
Wight. Milestones
Politicians   **WMAA**
Larkin
Prisoner   **WMAA**
CSB. Illusion
The senator   **WMAA**
Larkin rev ed
Pierson
Singing man
CSFP. Annual ex, 1947/48
Triumph
IU. Contemp Amer ptg, 1950

HIRSCH, Stefan, 1899-
Lower Manhattan (New York, Lower
Manhattan   **DP**
Brown. Amer ptg
Cheney. Story 1958 ed
MnMW. Precisionist view
Nurenberg
Genauer
Pic of Orizaba   **WMAA**
Pierson

HIRSHFIELD, Morris, 1872-1946
Artist and his model
50 years of mod art
Daniel in the lion's den
Read. Art now 1948
Girl in a mirror   **MMA**
Pierson
Girl with pigeons
Rathbun
Nude at window
Read. Art now 1948
Wight. Milestones
Tiger   **MMA**
Baur. Revolution
Lipman. Primitive ptrs
McCurdy
Two women in front of a mirror
Jean. Surrealist ptg

HIRST, Claude Raguet, d 1942
An interesting book
Frankenstein. After the hunt

His first crossing by G. Biddle

Hiscox, Thomas, 1686-1773
Feke, R. Rev Thomas Hiscox

Historical monument of the American re-
public by E. S. Field

Historical themes

Great Britain
14th century
West, B. King Edward III entertain-
ing his prisoners after the battle of
Calais
West, B. Queen Philippa interceding for
the burgesses of Calais
17th century
West, B. General Monk receiving
Charles II on the beach at Dover
18th century
Trumbull, J. Sortie from Gibraltar

Rome
West, B. Agrippina and her children
mourning the ashes of Germanicus
West, B. Agrippina landing at Brundi-
sium with the ashes of Germanicus
West, B. The appeal of Coriolanus

Sparta
West, B. Cleombrotus ordered into ban-
ishment by Leonidas II, king of
Sparta

United States
See also Indians of North America—
Wars
Colonial period
Hicks, E. Penn's treaty with the Indians
Pine, R. E. and Savage, E. Congress
voting independence, July, 1776
West, B. Penn's treaty with the Indians
Revolutionary period
See also names of battles, e.g. Bunker
Hill, Battle of; Concord, Battle of;
Princeton, Battle of
Bingham, G. C. Washington crossing the
Delaware
Earl, R. British troops at Concord
Hicks, E. Declaration of independence
Kemmelmeyer, F. George Washington
reviewing the western army at Fort
Cumberland

Leutze, E. Washington crossing the Delaware
Peale, J. Washington and his generals at Yorktown
Pine, R. E. and Savage, E. Congress voting independence, July, 1776
Reed, R. L. Washington and Lafayette at the battle of Yorktown
Remick, C. Blockade of Boston, View of
Rivers, L. Washington crossing the Delaware
Serres, D. British fleet forcing the Hudson river passage, 1776
Toole, J. Capture of Major André
Trumbull, J. Attack on Quebec
Trumbull, J. Capture of the Hessians at Trenton
Trumbull, J. Death of General Mercer at the battle of Princeton
Trumbull, J. Declaration of Independence
Trumbull, J. Resignation of General Washington at Annapolis
Trumbull, J. Signing the Declaration of Independence
Trumbull, J. Surrender of General Burgoyne at Saratoga
Trumbull, J. Surrender of Lord Cornwallis at Yorktown
Tucker, A. Washington crossing the Delaware
West, B. Conference of the treaty of peace with England
White, J. B. Gen Marion in his swamp encampment inviting a British officer to dinner

1800-1860

Birch, T. The Constitution and the Guerrière
Catlin, G. Virginia constitutional convention of 1829-30
Corné, M. F. Bombardment of Tripoli under Commodore Preble, 1804
Corné, M. F. The Constitution and the Guerrière
Myers, W. H. Battle of the plains of Mesa, 1847
Unidentified artist. Privateer schooner Surprise of Baltimore capturing the British ship Star, 1815

Civil war

Bierstadt, A. Bombardment of Fort Sumter
Bingham, G. C. Gen Nathaniel Lyon and Gen Frank P. Blair starting from the Arsenal gate in St Louis to capture Camp Jackson
Bingham, G. C. Order no 11, 1869
Carlin, A. B. Sherman's march through Georgia
Chapman, C. W. Fort Sumter, December 8, 1863
Chappel, A. Surrender at Appomattox
Hamilton, J. Monitor and Merrimac
Homer, W. Defiance: Inviting a shot before Petersburg, Virginia, 1864
Homer, W. Prisoners from the front
Homer, W. Skirmish in The Wilderness
Hopper, E. Light battery at Gettysburg
O'Neil, M. Civil war encampment
Siporan, M. Order No 11

Unidentified artist. Attack of the rebel ram Manassas on the U.S.S. Pensacola
Unidentified artist. Camp Butler, Maryland, 1861
Unidentified artist. Civil war battle scene
Unidentified artist. Civil war—Symbolic panorama
Unidentified artist. Fourth Pennsylvania cavalry

Spanish-American war

Glackens, W. J. The night after San Juan: tending the wounded
Remington, F. Charge of the Rough Riders at San Juan Hill
Remington, F. The scream of shrapnel at San Juan hill, Cuba, July 1, 1898
Zogbaum, R. F. Admiral Dewey at Manila bay, 1898

History of communication by S. Davis
History of the early United States by T. H. Benton
Hitchcock, Samuel Johnson, 1786-1845
Flagg, J. B. Samuel Johnson Hitchcock
Hite, Mrs Isaac, fl 1790
Polk, C. P. Mrs Isaac Hite and James Madison Hite
Hnizdovsky, Jacques. See Hnizdovsky, Yakiv
HNIZDOVSKY, Yakiv, 1915-
New housing
IU. Contemp Amer ptg & sculp, 1961
New York subway OYB
OYB. Annual 1960
Passage Denfert
IU. Contemp Amer ptg & sculp, 1959
Hobbs, Sarah, fl 1830
Unidentified artist. Sarah Hobbs
Hobby horse by Unidentified artist
Hockaday, Susan Howard, fl 1859
Bingham, G. C. Susan Howard Hockaday and her daughter Susan
Hoeing by R. Gwathmey
Hoeing tobacco by R. Gwathmey
HOENER, Arthur, 1929-
Seated figure, Yakshi
MBIC. View 1960
HOFF, Margo
City builders
IU. Contemp Amer ptg & sculp, 1959
Dream of flying
IU. Contemp Amer ptg, 1951
Gypsy's house
IU. Contemp Amer ptg, 1950
Mosque
IU. Contemp Amer ptg & sculp, 1955
Surprise party
IU. Contemp Amer ptg & sculp, 1953
Wind rose
IU. Contemp Amer ptg & sculp, 1961
Woman in a white room
IU. Contemp Amer ptg & sculp, 1957
Hoffman, Eliza, 1779-1857
Hubard, W. J. Eliza Hoffman
Hoffman, Harriet Emily, 1815-1892
Hubard, W. J. Jeremiah Hoffman and daughter
Hoffman, Jeremiah, 1777-1845
Hubard, W. J. Jeremiah Hoffman and his daughter
Hoffman, John, 1772-1837
Hubard, W. J. John Hoffman

Hoffman, William Henry, 1813-1865
  Sully, T. William Henry Hoffman
    (replica)
Hoffman's slough by A. N. Wyeth
HOFMANN, Charles, fl 1872-78
  View of Benjamin Reber's farm   DN
    DN. Amer primitive ptgs, pt 1
    Time. 300 years (col)
  View of the Schuylkill county almshouse
    property, Pennsylvania, 1876   DN
    DN. Amer primitive ptgs, pt 2
  Views of the buildings and surroundings
    of the Berks county almshouse, 1878
                                          DN
  U.S. National Capital sesquicentennial
    com
HOFMANN, Hans, 1880-1957
  Aggressive
    Wight. Hans Hofmann
  Ambush   MMA
    Biddle. Yes and no
  Apparition
    IU. Contemp Amer ptg, 1950
  Birth of Taurus
    Wight. Hans Hofmann (col)
  Black demon   MAP
    CoS. New accessions USA, 1948
  Blue enchantment
    IU. Contemp Amer ptg, 1952
    Pousette-Dart. Amer ptg
  Blue rhythm   ICA
    CoS. New accessions USA, 1954
  Bouquet
    Wight. Hans Hofmann (col)
  Burst into life
    IU. Contemp Amer ptg & sculp, 1953
      (col)
    Wight. Hans Hofmann (col)
  Capriccioso
    IU. Contemp Amer ptg & sculp, 1957
  Cataclysm
    Rathbun
  Catalyst
    IU. Contemp Amer ptg, 1949
  Chimera
    IU. Contemp Amer ptg & sculp, 1961
  The city
    ICA. Annual ex, 1959/60 (col cover)
  Color poem
    Hess. Abstract ptg
  Composition no I, 1951
    MnMW. Classic tradition
  Construction   WMAA
    Mendelowitz
    WMAA. Annual ex, 1950
  Delight   MMA
    Wight. Hans Hofmann (col)
  Elegy   MnMW
    MnMW. 60 Amer ptrs
    Wight. Hans Hofmann
  Embrace   MLL
    Wight. Hans Hofmann (col)
  Exuberance   NBuA
    Art since 1945 (col)
    Hunter. Mod Amer ptg
    NBuA. Acquisitions 1954-57 (col)
    Read. Concise history
    Wight. Hans Hofmann (col)
  Fairy tale
    Hess. Abstract ptg
  Floral composition
    Wight. Hans Hofmann (col)

  Flowering branch
    Wight. Hans Hofmann (col)
  Fruit bowl   NeL
    Barker. From realism
    CoS. New accessions USA, 1952
  Fruit bowl, 1950 (Neuberger coll)
    Wight. Hans Hofmann (col)
  Fury no 1
    ICA. Annual ex, 1947/48
  Germania, 1951   MdBM
    Wight. Hans Hofmann
  Germania: version 6
    CSFP. Annual ex, 1952
  Golden splendor
    IU. Contemp Amer ptg & sculp, 1959
  Green bottle   MLL
    Wight. Hans Hofmann
  Idolatress, 1944
    Wight. Hans Hofmann
  Idolatress, 1949
    MnU. 40 Amer ptrs
  Interior
    Wight. Hans Hofmann (col)
  Joy
    CSFP. Annual ex, 1950/51
  Libration
    Wight. Hans Hofmann
  Magenta and blue   WMAA
    Cheney. Story 1958 ed
    CoS. New accessions USA, 1952
    Goodrich. Amer art (col)
    Pierson
    Wight. Hans Hofmann (col)
  The magician
    Ponente. Mod ptg, 1960 (col)
  Mrs Hans Hofmann
    Wight. Hans Hofmann
  Morning mist
    DC. 27 biennial ex, 1961
  Mosaics, 1956 (Northeast corner, 711
    Third avenue, New York)
    Wight. Hans Hofmann (col)
  Mosaics, 1956 (Southwest corner, 711
    Third avenue, New York)
    Wight. Hans Hofmann (col)
  Orange vase
    Wight. Hans Hofmann (col)
  Orchestral dominance in yellow
    Wight. Hans Hofmann (col)
  Phoenix
    Blesh
  The pond
    ICA. Annual ex, 1959/60
    MnMW. Eighty works
  Provincetown wharves
    Wight. Hans Hofmann
  Push and pull no 3
    ICA. Annual ex, 1951
  Radiant space
    Baur. Nature (col)
  The ravine
    WMAA. Museum and its friends, 1958
  The red cap
    PA. Annual ex, 1954
  Red lift
    PPC. International ex, 1952
  Red trickle
    Time 300 years (col)
    Wight. Hans Hofmann (col)
  Reminiscence
    IU. Contemp Amer ptg, 1951
  Rising sun
    Ponente. **Mod ptg, 1960 (col)**

Scotch and Burgundy
  Wight. Hans Hofmann (col)
Seated girl
  MnU. 40 Amer ptrs
Self-portrait, 1902
  Wight. Hans Hofmann
Serpentine
  Cheney. Story 1958 ed
Sommernachtstraum   NBuA
  NBuA. Acquisitions 1957-58
Studio number 1, in grey
  IU. Contemp Amer ptg & sculp. 1955
Submerged
  Wight. Hans Hofmann
The third hand
  IU. Contemp Amer ptg, 1948
Visione nobilissima
  NBuA. Expressioniam
Voices of spring
  ICA. Annual ex, 1961
The window   MM
  McCurdy
  MMA. Abstract
X—1955
  Wight. Hans Hofmann (col)
Hofmann, Mrs Hans
  Hofmann, H. Mrs Hans Hofmann
Hogs killing a snake by J. S. Curry
Hogs killing rattlesnake by J. S. Curry
HOGUE, Alexander, 1898-
  Drought-stricken area   TxD
  Pierson
  Dust bowl   IBM
  Baur. Revolution
HOLBROOK, Hollis Howard, 1909-
  Grey on blue and brown
  IU. Contemp Amer ptg & sculp, 1961
Holbrook's bridge, northwest by A. G.
  Dove
Holcombe, Eunice (Griswold) See Pinney,
  Eunice (Griswold) Holcombe
Holding up the payroll by F. Remington
Holding up the sheriff by C. M. Russell
Holding up the stage by C. M. Russell
Hole in the wall gang by I. L. Albright
Holiday by C. Browning
Holiday by C. K. Sibley
Holiday in the park by W. J. Glackens
Holiday on the Hudson by G. B. Luks
Holidays by M. B. Prendergast
Hollingsworth, Anna Maria. See Morris,
  Anna Maria (Hollingsworth)
Hollingsworth, Mary. See Morris, Mary
  (Hollingsworth)
Hollow hill pastoral by M. Hewes
Holly house, Cos Cob, Connecticut by J. H.
  Twachtman
Hollyhocks by E. Johnson
Hollywood by T. H. Benton
Holme, Isaac, 1702-1751
  Theus, J. Hon Isaac Holme
HOLMEAD (Holmead Phillips) 1889-
  St George and the dragon   CtY
  CtY. Soc Anonyme
Holmes, Abiel, 1763-1837
  Savage, E. Abiel Holmes
Holmes, Oliver Wendell, 1841-1935
  Hopkinson, C. S. Oliver Wendell Holmes

HOLMES, William Henry, 1864-1933
  By the sea
  Born
  Maryland landscape
  Born
HOLT, Henry, 1889-1941
  Fading light, Stowe valley   MB
  MB. Ptgs in water color
HOLTY, Carl Robert, 1900-
  Carousel
  Pierson
  Emperor's garden
  VR. Amer ptg, 1958
  Equestrian
  MMA. Abstract
  Le flambeau   IU
  IU. Contemp Amer ptg, 1948
  IU. 20th century
  Good keeper
  Rathbun
  Still life
  IU. Contemp Amer ptg, 1950
  Suspension of forms
  Baur. Revolution
HOLTZMAN, Harry, 1912-
  Sculpture   CtY
  CtY. Soc Anonyme
The holy by H. Pippin
Holy mountain I, 1944 by H. Pippin
Holy mountain II, 1944 by H. Pippin
Holy mountain IV, 1946 by H. Pippin
Holy Name mission by R. Marsh
Holy week procession by V. Higgins
Holyoke, Edward, 1689-1769
  Pelham, H. (after Copley) Edward Holy-
  oke
Holyoke, Mrs Edward Augustus. See Pick-
  man, Judith
Holyoke, Judith (Pickman) See Pickman,
  Judith
Homage to Boston by J. Levine
Homage to John Cage by R. B. Motherwell
Homage to Rome by E. Isenburger
Homage to the square: Ascending by J.
  Albers
Homage to the square: Precinct by J. Al-
  bers
Homage to the square: Yes by J. Albers
Homan, Emma, fl 1843
  Bradley, J. Emma Homan
Home at Montclair by G. Inness
Home by the sea by W. Whittredge
Home camp in March by R. W. Gray
Home for Christmas by P. Blume
Home for Thanksgiving by A. M. R.
  Moses
Home of Hezekiah King by A. M. R.
  Moses
Home of the heron by G. Inness
A **home** on the Hudson by T. Doughty
Home on the ranch by L. Megargee
Home scene by T. Eakins
Home, sweet home by W. Homer
Home, sweet home by W. R. Leigh
Home, sweet home by C. Sheeler
Homeless by W. Gropper

HOMER, Winslow, 1836-1910
  Adirondack guide   MB
    Goodrich. Winslow Homer (col)
    MB. Ptgs in water color
    Pierson
  Adirondack lake   MB
    MB. Ptgs in water color
  Adirondack woods, guide and dog
    CtY. Yale alumni
    DN. Homer
  Adirondacks   MCH
    Goodrich. Winslow Homer (col)
    Pierson
    Robb. Art 1953 ed
  After the hunt   CLA
    DN. Homer
  After the tornado, Bahamas (After the
      hurricane, Bahamas)   ICA
    Barker. Amer ptg
    Goodrich. Winslow Homer (col)
    Larkin rev ed (col detail)
    Pierson
  Afterglow (Boats off the coast of Devon-
      shire)   MB
    MB. Ptgs in water color
  Afternoon fog   NR
    Goodrich. Winslow Homer
  All's well. See The lookout—All's well
  Artists sketching
    Goodrich. Winslow Homer
  Artist's studio in an afternoon fog   NR
    DN. Homer
  Autumn
    Goodrich. Winslow Homer
  Backrush
    Goodrich. Winslow Homer
  Bananas for the attorney general
    DN. Homer
  Banks fishermen. See Herring net
  A basket of clams
    Goodrich. Winslow Homer
  Bass   ATeS
    ATeS. Collection
    Craven. Treasury 1952 ed
  Berry pickers   MeC
    Goodrich. Winslow Homer
    MNS. Homer
  Blue boat   MB
    MB. Ptgs in water color
  Boats off the coast of Devonshire. See
      Afterglow
  Boy carrying deer
    CtY. Yale alumni
  Boy fishing
    DN. Homer
    Goodrich. Winslow Homer
  Boy picking apples
    MiD. Coll in progress
    WiMiA. Amer ptg 1760-1960
  Boy with the anchor   OCl
    OCl. Handbook
  Boys bathing   MWiC
    Goodrich. Winslow Homer
  Boys beaching a dory   OT
    Goodrich. Winslow Homer
  Boys in a pasture   MB
    Goodrich. Winslow Homer
  Boys wading   MeC
    Goodrich. Winslow Homer
    MeC. Inaugural ex
  Breaking wave   MB
    Goodrich. Winslow Homer
    MB. Ptgs in water color

  Breakwater, Tynemouth
    DN. Homer
  Breezing up (A fair wind)   DN
    DN. Homer (col cover)
    Goodrich. Winslow Homer
    Janson. Picture history
    MoSL. 40 masterpieces
    Roos
    Walker. Ptgs from America (col)
  The briarwood pipe   OCl
    OCl. Handbook
  Bridle path, White mountains   MWiS
    Goodrich. Winslow Homer
    Larkin (detail)
    Larkin rev ed
    MWiS. Ex 4 and 7
    Pierson
  Bridlington quay   MB
    MB. Ptgs in water color
  By the shore
    DN. Homer
  Canoe in rapids   MCH
    Pierson
  Canoeing in the Adirondacks
    MiD. Coll in progress
    WiMiA. Amer ptg 1760-1960
  Cape Trinity, Saguenay river
    DN. Homer
  Cape Trinity, Saguenay river, moonlight
    Goodrich. Winslow Homer
  The carnival   MM
    Goodrich. Winslow Homer (col)
  Casting in the falls
    Goodrich. Winslow Homer
  Casting the fly
    DN. Homer
  Children on a fence   KLU
    Pierson
  Children on the beach
    Goodrich. Winslow Homer
  Children playing under a Gloucester wharf
                                             MB
    DN. Homer
    MB. Ptgs in water color
  Coast in winter   MWM
    Walker. Ptgs from America
  Coming storm   NBM
    DN. Homer
    Goodrich. Winslow Homer (col)
    NYG. Fine art
  Corn husking   ATeS
    ATeS. Collection
  Cotton pickers
    DN. Homer
    Goodrich. Winslow Homer
    U.S. National Capital sesquicentennial
      com
  Country school   MoSL
    Davidson v2
    MoSL. 50 masterworks
    MoSL. Handbook 1953
    Pierson
    Richardson. Ptg in America (col de-
      tail)
    U.S. National Capital sesquicentennial
      com
  Croquet match
    Barr. What is mod ptg
    DN. Homer
    Goodrich. Winslow Homer
    MNS. Homer

Croquet players   NBuA
  NBuA. Catalogue of the ptgs
Croquet scene   ICA
  Davidson v 2
  Goodrich. Winslow Homer
  Pierson
  UNESCO. 1860-1949
  UNESCO. 1860-1955
  UNESCO. 1860-1959
Crossing the pasture
  DN. Homer
  Goodrich. Winslow Homer
Custom house, Santiago de Cuba
  Goodrich. Winslow Homer
Dad's coming
  Goodrich. Winslow Homer
Deer drinking
  DN. Homer
  Goodrich. Winslow Homer
Defiance: Inviting a shot before Peters-
  burg, Virginia, 1864   MiD
  MiD. Treasures
Diamond shoal   IBM
  Baur. Amer ptg
The dinner horn   MiD
  MiD. Treasures
The dory   MB
  MB. Ptgs in water color
Driftwood
  DN. Homer
  NBuA. Fifty ptgs
Dunes at Marshfield. See Sand dune
Early morning after a storm at sea OCl
  Baur. Amer ptg
  Baur. Revolution
  Goodrich. Winslow Homer
  OCl. Handbook
East Hampton, Long Island
  DN. Homer
Eastern point, Prout's neck   MWiS
  MWiS. Ex 4 and 7
Eight bells   MAP
  Goodrich. Winslow Homer (col)
  Larkin
  Larkin rev ed
  Pierson
  Time. 300 years (col)
Entering the first rapid
  Goodrich. Winslow Homer
A fair wind. See Breezing up
Fallen deer   MB
  Larkin (detail)
  Larkin rev ed (detail)
  MB. Ptgs in water color
Fisherfolk in a boat   MCH
  Goodrich. Winslow Homer
Fisherfolk on the beach at Tynemouth
                                   DP
  Goodrich. Winslow Homer
A fisherman's day   DF
  Born
Fishing
  NSP. Sportscapes
Flock of sheep, Houghton farm
  Goodrich. Winslow Homer
Fog warning (Halibut fishing)   MB
  Bazin. History of art
  Goodrich. Winslow Homer
The forest. See Hunting dog among dead
  trees

Fox hunt   PA
  DC. De gustibus
  DN. Homer
  Goodrich. Winslow Homer (col)
  McCurdy
  Pierson
  Robb. Harper history
Gargoyles of Notre Dame
  Goodrich. Winslow Homer
Girl with a letter
  Goodrich. Winslow Homer
Girl with laurel   MiD
  DN. Homer
Girl with pitchfork   DP
  DN. Homer
Girls on a cliff   MB
  MB. Ptgs in water color
Girls with lobster   OCl
  DN. Homer
  MNS. Homer
Glass windows, Bahamas   NBM
  DN. Homer
Gloucester farm   PPhM
  Canaday
Gloucester schooners and sloop   PPhM
  DN. Homer
Green apples
  MNS. Homer
Green dory   MB
  MB. Ptgs in water color
  Pierson
Guide and mountains and sky. See Woods-
  man and fallen tree
Guide carrying deer
  Lewisohn
Guide fishing   InIJ
  InIJ. 105 ptgs
Gulf stream   MM
  Craven. Rainbow book (col)
  Craven. Treasury 1952 ed (col)
  Flexner. Amer ptg (col)
  Flexner. Short history (col)
  Goodrich. Winslow Homer (col)
  MM. 100 Amer ptrs
  MM. 100 Amer ptrs (col detail)
  NYG. Fine art
  Pierson
  Taylor. Fifty centuries, 1954 ed (col)
  Time. 300 years (col)
  UNESCO. 1860-1949
  UNESCO. 1860-1955
  UNESCO. 1860-1959
Halibut fishing. See Fog warning
Harvest scene   NCa
  DN. Homer
Haymaking   OCo
  Goodrich. Winslow Homer
Herring net (Banks fishermen)   ICA
  Lee. Art then and now
  McKinney
  NYG. Fine art
  Roos
  U.S. National Capital sesquicentennial
    com
High cliff, coast of Maine   DNC
  Goodrich. Winslow Homer
High tide   MM
  Bazin (col detail)
  Goodrich. Winslow Homer
Home, sweet home
  DN. Homer
  Goodrich. Winslow Homer

HOMER, Winslow—*Continued*
Homosassa river   NBM
    NYG. Fine art
Hound and hunter   DN
    DN. Homer
The Houses of Parliament
    DN. Homer
Hudson river (River scene, lumberman,
    and logs in river)   MB
    Goodrich. Winslow Homer
    MB. Ptgs in water color
Hudson river, logging   DC
    DC. Masterpieces
    DN. Homer
    NYG. Fine art (col)
The hunter   PPhM
    Canaday
Hunting dog among dead trees (On the
    track; The forest)   MB
    MB. Ptgs in water color
Huntsman and dogs   PPhM
    DN. Homer
    Goodrich. Winslow Homer (col)
    Mendelowitz
    MiD. Ptg in America
    Pierson
    Richardson. Ptg in America
Hurricane, Bahamas
    Taylor. Fifty centuries, 1954 ed (col)
In charge of the baby
    Goodrich. Winslow Homer
In the mountains   NBM
    Goodrich. Winslow Homer
Indian camp   MB
    MB. Ptgs in water color
Indian hunter in the Everglades (Indian
    in Florida swamps; Young hunter in
    woods)   MB
    MB. Ptgs in water color
Indian woman at oven. See Native wom-
    an cooking
The initials
    DN. Homer
    Goodrich. Winslow Homer
    MiD. Coll in progress
    WiMiA. Amer ptg 1760-1960
Inland water, Bermuda
    Goodrich. Winslow Homer
Inside the bar, Tynemouth   MM
    DN. Homer
    Pierson
Kissing the moon   MAP
    DN. Homer
    Goodrich. Winslow Homer
Leaping trout   MB
    DN. Homer
    Goodrich. Winslow Homer
    MB. Ptgs in water color
The life line   PPhM
    Canaday
    Goodrich. Winslow Homer
    Pierson
Life-size black bass
    Goodrich. Winslow Homer
Light on the sea   DC
    DC. Masterpieces
Long Branch, New Jersey   MB
    Barker. Amer ptg
    Goodrich. Winslow Homer (col)
    Pierson
    Richardson. Ptg in America
The lookout   MCH
    Robb. Harper history

The lookout—All's well   MB
    Craven. Rainbow book
    Craven. Treasury 1952 ed
    DN. Homer
    Goodrich. Winslow Homer
    Mendelowitz
    Roos
Lost on the Grand Banks   CLA
    DN. Homer
Maine coast
    Rosenblum
Milking time
    DN. Homer
    Goodrich. Winslow Homer
The morning bell at a New England fac-
    tory (Clark coll)
    CtY. Yale alumni
    Davidson v 1
    DN. Homer
    Goodrich. Winslow Homer
    Janson. Key monuments
    MNS. Homer
Morning-glories
    DN. Homer
Mussel gatherers   MdBM
    DN. Homer
Nassau   MM
    DN. Homer
Nassau, woman at campfire. See Native
    woman cooking
Native woman cooking (Negro woman
    cooking; Indian woman at oven; Nas-
    sau, woman at campfire)   MB
    MB. Ptgs in water color
Negro woman cooking. See Native woman
    cooking
The new novel   MSM
    DN. Homer
The nooning   CtHW
    CtHW. Handbook
    Goodrich. Winslow Homer
Northeaster   MM
    Canaday
    NAD. Amer tradition
    NYG. Fine art
    Pierson
    Upjohn
Old friends   MWM
    DN. Homer
Old settlers, Adirondacks   MB
    DN. Homer
    MB. Ptgs in water color
On a lee shore   RPS
    Born
    DN. Homer
    Goodrich. Winslow Homer (col)
On guard
    Goodrich. Winslow Homer
On the beach   NCa
    DN. Homer
On the beach at Marshfield
    MNS. Homer
On the stile   MeC
    Goodrich. Winslow Homer
On the track. See Hunting dog among
    dead trees
Orange tree and gate, Nassau
    MiD. Coll in progress
Ouananiche fishing: Lake St John, Quebec
    MB
    MB. Ptgs in water color
Palm tree
    CanO. Hirshhorn coll

Palm tree, Nassau   MM
  Bazin. History of art (coll)
  DN. Homer (col)
  NYG. Fine art
  Time. 300 years (col)
  UNESCO. 1860-1959
Palm trees, Florida   MB
  DN. Homer
  Goodrich. Winslow Homer
Pitching quoits   MCH
  U.S. National Capital sesquicentennial
  com
Playing old soldier   MB
  U.S. National Capital sesquicentennial
  com
The portage
  NYG. Fine art
Prisoners from the front   MM
  Canaday
  Pierson
  Richardson. Ptg in America
  Time. 300 years (col)
Promenade on the beach   MSM
  MSM. Handbook
Prospect rock, Essex county, N.Y.   DNC
  DNC. Gellatly coll, 1954
  Goodrich. Winslow Homer
Prout's Neck, breakers   ICA
  DN. Homer
The rapids, Hudson river, Adirondacks
                                      ICA
  NYG. Fine art
Reading in the sun
  Goodrich. Winslow Homer
Return of the gleaner
  Goodrich. Winslow Homer
Right and left   PPhM
  Bazin
Right and left   DN
  DN. Homer
  Goodrich. Winslow Homer
Right and left (Morgan coll)
  Walker. Ptgs from America
River scene, lumberman, and logs in river.
  See Hudson river
Rocky coast   CtHW
  DN. Homer
Rocky shore, Bermuda   MB
  MB. Ptgs in water color
Rowing home   DP
  DP. Catalogue
Royal palm trees
  DN. Homer
Rum cay   MWM
  Goodrich. Winslow Homer
The rustics
  Goodrich. Winslow Homer
Saguenay river, lower rapids   MWM
  Goodrich. Winslow Homer
  Richardson. Ptg in America
Sailing a dory
  DN. Homer
Sailing boats in a watering trough
  MNS. Homer
Sailing the catboat
  DN. Homer
Sand dune (Dunes at Marshfield)
  DN. Homer
Santiago de Cuba
  DN. Homer
Schooners at anchor, Key West
  DN. Homer

Searchlight, harbor entrance, Santiago de
  Cuba   MM
  DN. Homer
  Goodrich. Winslow Homer
  Pierson
The seesaw   NCa
  MNS. Homer
Shark fishing
  DN. Homer
  Goodrich. Winslow Homer
The shell heap   NBM
  DN. Homer
  NYG. Fine art
Shepherdess of Houghton farm
  MiD. Coll in progress
Ship unfurling sails   PPhM
  Canaday
Shipbuilding at Gloucester   MNS
  MNS. Homer
Shooting the rapids, Saguenay river   MM
  Goodrich. Winslow Homer
Shore and surf, Nassau   MM
  DN. Homer
The sick chicken   MeC
  DN. Homer
  Goodrich. Winslow Homer
Skating at Central park
  NYG. Fine art
Skating in Central park, New York, 1860
                                      MoSL
  Davidson v2
  MoSL. Handbook 1953
Sketch in Florida. See Thornhill bar,
  Florida
Skirmish in The Wilderness   CtNB
  DN. Homer
  U.S. National Capital sesquicentennial
  com
Sloop, Bermuda   MM
  Mendelowitz
  NYG. Fine art
  Roos
Snap-the-whip   OYB
  Goodrich. Winslow Homer (col)
  MNS. Homer
  OYB. Catalogue 1951
  Pierson
  Time. 300 years (col)
Sponge diver   MB
  MB. Ptgs in water color
Sponge fishermen, Bahamas
  DN. Homer
Spring
  DN. Homer
Spring blossoms
  MNS. Homer
Springtime in Virginia
  Richardson. Ptg in America
Startled
  MiD. Coll in progress
  WiMiA. Amer ptg 1760-1960
Storm in the Bahamas   MM
  Myers. Art
  Riley. Your art heritage
Stowing sails, Bermuda   ICA
  DN. Homer
  NYG. Fine art
Summer night
  DN. Homer
  Goodrich. Winslow Homer (col)

HOMER, Winslow—*Continued*
Summer squall   MWiS
  Goodrich. Winslow Homer
  MWiS. Ex 4 and 7
  Time. 300 years (col)
Sunday morning in Virginia   OCiM
  DN. Homer
Sunlight on the coast   OT
  DN. Homer
Sunrise fishing in the Adirondacks
  DN. Homer
Sunset, Saco bay   MWiS
  MWiS. Ex 4 and 7
Taking sunflower to teacher   GAtM
  GAtM. Holbrook collection
Thornhill bar, Florida (Sketch in Florida)
                    MB
  MB. Ptgs in water color
Three boys on the shore
  Goodrich. Winslow Homer
Three men in a canoe
  Goodrich. Winslow Homer
To the rescue   DP
  DP. Catalogue
Trout fishing, Lake St John, Quebec MB
  MB. Ptgs in water color
The turtle pound (Turtle pond)   NBM
  Goodrich. Winslow Homer (col)
  Pierson
Two boats
  DN. Homer
Two guides   MWiS
  Goodrich. Winslow Homer (col)
  MWiS. Ex 4 and 7
  Pierson
Two trout   IBM
  DN. Homer
Tynemouth sands   MB
  MB. Ptgs in water color
Under the coco palm   MCH
  DN. Homer
  Goodrich. Winslow Homer
Under the falls, grand discharge
  Goodrich. Winslow Homer
Undertow   MWiS
  Goodrich. Winslow Homer
  MWiS. Ex 4 and 7
Unruly calf
  DN. Homer
  MiD. Coll in progress
Veteran in a new field
  DN. Homer
A voice from the cliffs
  DN. Homer
Water fan
  Goodrich. Winslow Homer
Weaning the calf   NoCR
  Goodrich. Winslow Homer
  NoCR. Catalogue
  UNESCO. 1860-1959
Weary
  DN. Homer
Weatherbeaten, or Stormbeaten
  CtY. Yale alumni
  Goodrich. Winslow Homer
West point, Prout's neck   MWiS
  Goodrich. Winslow Homer (col)
  MWiS. Ex 4 and 7
  Pierson
The west wind   MAP
  Goodrich. Winslow Homer
Wild geese
  DN. Homer

Winter coast
  Barker. Amer ptg
  DN. Homer
  Goodrich. Winslow Homer
Woman driving geese   AP
  NUM. Art across America
Woman sewing   DC
  DC. Masterpieces
Woman with flower
  DN. Homer
The woodchopper
  Born
The woodcutter
  DN. Homer
  Goodrich. Winslow Homer
Woodsman and fallen tree (Guide and
  mountains and sky)   MB
  MB. Ptgs in water color
World's Columbian exposition—the foun-
  tains at night   MeB
  DN. Homer
  U.S. National Capital sesquicentennial
  com
The wreck   PPC
  Goodrich. Winslow Homer
  PPC. Amer classics
The wreck of the Iron Crown
  DN. Homer
  Goodrich. Winslow Homer
The wreck, or girl with red stockings MB
  Goodrich. Winslow Homer
The wrecked schooner   MoSL
  MoSL. Handbook 1953
Young hunter in woods. See Indian hunter
  in the Everglades
Homeric struggle by B. Shahn
Homestead by T. H. Benton
Homestead by J. Kane
Homestead mill near Pittsburgh by W. C.
  Wall
Homeward by I. Bishop
Homeward bound by A. P. Ryder
Hommage à Albert Camus by F. Roth
Hommage à Andrés Segovia by R. J. Stein
Homosassa river by W. Homer
Homunculus by P. Burlin
Hooft, Martha Visser 't. See Visser 't Hooft,
  Martha
Hooked rug by A. Blanch
Hooker, Mary. See Pierpont, Mary (Hooker)
Hooker, Thomas, 1586?-1647
  Church, F. E. Thomas Hooker's party
  coming to Hartford
Hoosick Falls in winter by A. M. R. Moses
HOPE, James, 1818?-1892
  Army of the Potomac   MB
  MB. Karolik coll
  Bird mountain, Castleton, Vermont   MB
  MB. Karolik coll
  Frowning cliff, Watkins glen, New York
                    MB
  MB. Karolik coll
  Winter scene: the red fox   MB
  MB. Karolik coll
Hope family
  West, B. The Adrian Hope family group
Hopi snake dance by E. A. Burbank
HOPKINS, Budd, 1931-
  Avalar
  WMAA. Young America 1960
  Number 1
  WMAA. Young America 1960

Hopkins, Eliza. See Page, Eliza (Hopkins)
HOPKINSON, Charles Sydney, 1869-
  Afternoon light   MB
    MB. Ptgs in water color
    Pierson
  Double portrait
    PPC. Ptg in the U.S. 1949
  Oliver Wendell Holmes
    Time. 300 years (col)
  Rocks and sea   MB
    MB. Ptgs in water color
HOPKINSON, Francis, 1737-1791
  Self-portrait   MdBH
    MdBMu. Rendezvous
HOPPER, Edward, 1882-
  Adams' house
    Goodrich. Edward Hopper (col)
  Approaching a city   DP
    DP. Catalogue
    Goodrich. Edward Hopper
  August in the city   FaW
    Goodrich. Edward Hopper (col)
    ICA. Annual ex, 1951
  Camel's Hump   NUM
    Goodrich. Edward Hopper (col)
    NUM. Root bequest
  Cape Cod evening
    Baur. New art
    Goodrich. Edward Hopper (col)
  Cape Cod morning   WMAA
    Time. 300 years (col)
    WMAA. Sara Roby (col)
  Chop suey
    Goodrich. Edward Hopper
  The city   ATU
    ATU. Coll of Amer art
    Larkin
    Larkin rev ed
    NUM. Art across America
  City sunlight
    PPC. International ex, 1955
  Coast Guard station   NJMo
    NJMo. Forty years
    NJMo. Your Montclair art museum
  Cobb's house   MWM
    Goodrich. Edward Hopper
  Conference at night
    MnU. 40 Amer ptrs
    PPC. Ptg in the U.S. 1949
  Cornbelt city
    MMA. Contemp ptrs
  Corner saloon   MMA
    Goodrich. Edward Hopper (col)
    Pierson
    WMAA. Juliana Force
  Cottage, Cape Cod   ATeS
    ATeS. Collection
  Cottages at Wellfleet
    MiD. Coll in progress
  Dawn in Pennsylvania
    Baur. Revolution
    Goodrich. Edward Hopper (col)
    Wight. Milestones
  Early Sunday morning   WMAA
    Baur. New art
    Brown. Amer ptg
    Canaday
    DC. De gustibus
    Faulkner. Art today, 1956
    Gardner 1959 ed
    Goodrich. Amer art (col)

    Goodrich. Edward Hopper (col)
    Hunter. Mod Amer ptg (col)
    ICA. Amer artists paint the city
    Mendelowitz
    MiD. Ptg in America
    Pierson
    Richardson. Ptg in America
    Time. 300 years (col)
  East wind over Weehawken
    Goodrich. Edward Hopper
  First branch of the White river, Vermont
                    MB
    MB. Ptgs in water color
  First row, orchestra
    CanO. Hirshhorn coll
    WMAA. Contemp Amer ptg, 1951
  From Williamsburg bridge   MM
    MM. 100 Amer ptrs
  Gas   MMA
    Baur. New art
    Goodrich. Edward Hopper (col)
    MMA. Contemp ptrs
    Pierson
  Gravel bar, White river
    Goodrich. Edward Hopper (col)
  Ground swell   DC
    Goodrich. Edward Hopper
    NYG. Fine art
  Haskell's house
    Goodrich. Edward Hopper
  High noon
    PPC. International ex, 1950
  Hills, South Truro   OCl
    OCl. Handbook
  Hotel lobby
    ICA. Annual ex, 1945/46
  Hotel room   MMA
    Seiberling
  House by the railroad   MMA
    Barr. What is mod ptg
    Brown. Amer ptg
    MMA. Masters (col)
    Goodrich. Edward Hopper (col)
    Pierson
    Seiberling
  House of the foghorn no 3
    CtY. Yale alumni
  House on Pamet river   WMAA
    Goodrich. Amer art
    Goodrich. Edward Hopper
    NYG. Fine art
    Pierson
    UNESCO. 1860-1949
  Lee shore   WMAA
    CSB. Illusion
  Light battery at Gettysburg   MoKN
    CoS. New accessions USA, 1948
  Lighthouse
    Upjohn
  Lighthouse at Two Lights
    Baur. New art
    Goodrich. Edward Hopper (col)
    Taylor. Fifty centuries, 1954 ed (col)
    WiMiA. Amer ptg 1760-1960
  Manhattan bridge and Lily apartments
    Goodrich. Edward Hopper
    MiD. Coll in progress
    WiMiA. Amer ptg 1760-1960
  Manhattan bridge loop   MAP
    Goodrich. Edward Hopper
    Rathbun
    Time. 300 years (col)

HOPPER, Edward—*Continued*
Methodist church, Provincetown   CtHW
  CtHW. Handbook
Morning in a city
  Goodrich. Edward Hopper
  WMAA. Museum and its friends, 1958
New York movie   MMA
  50 years of mod art
  Goodrich. Edward Hopper (col)
  Mendelowitz
  Newmeyer
New York, New Haven and Hartford
                        InIJ
  InIJ. 105 ptgs
New York pavements
  MiD. Coll in progress
Night windows   MMA
  Goodrich. Edward Hopper
Nighthawks   ICA
  Baur. New art (col)
  Baur. Revolution
  Craven. Rainbow book
  Flexner. Amer ptg
  Flexner. Short history
  Goodrich. Edward Hopper
  McCurdy
  Pierson
  Time. 300 years (col)
Office at night   MnMW
  Goodrich. Edward Hopper
Pennsylvania coal town   OYB
  DC. 21 biennial ex, 1949
  Larkin rev ed (col)
  OYB. Catalogue 1951
  Pierson
Room in Brooklyn   MB
  Goodrich. Edward Hopper
Room in New York   NeL
  Goodrich. Edward Hopper
Room on the sea
  Eliot. Art of our time (col)
  Time. 300 years (col)
  WMAA. Museum and its friends
Rooms by the sea
  Pousette-Dart. Amer ptg
Rooms for tourists
  Goodrich. Edward Hopper (col)
Route 6, Eastham   InTH
  Goodrich. Edward Hopper
Saltillo rooftops
  Goodrich. Edward Hopper (col)
Second-story sunlight   WMAA
  Goodrich. Amer art
Seven A. M. 1948   WMAA
  CSFP. Annual ex, 1952
  Goodrich. Amer art (col)
  MnU. 40 Amer ptrs
Sheridan theatre   NJN
  Gruskin (col)
Shoshone cliffs   OYB
  OYB. Annual 1954
  OYB. Supplement
Sierra Madre at Saltillo
  WiMiA. Amer ptg 1760-1960
Skylights
  Baur. New art
  Goodrich. Edward Hopper (col)
Sunday   DP
  Bazin
  Cheney. Primer 1958 ed
  Cheney. Story 1958 ed
Sunlight on brownstones
  Time. 300 years (col)

Tony's house   NBuA
  NBuA. Acquisitions 1954-57
Two on the aisle   OT
  Brown. Amer ptg
White river at Sharon   WMAA
  Pierson
  WMAA. Sara Roby
Hopscotch. See Games and sports—Hopscotch
Horace Tuttle's livery stable by Unidentified artist
HORIUCHI, Paul, 1906-
December no 1
  OrPA. Ptgs & sculptures
Horizon conditions by R. Tam
Horizontal arrangement by C. W. Smith
Horizontal illusion by I. R. Pereira
Horn pipe by M. Tobey
Horner, William Edmonds, fl 1836
Sully, T. Dr William Edmonds Horner (detail)
Horry, Daniel, d 1785?
Theus, J. Col Daniel Horry
Horse mackerel by K. Knaths
Horse power by R. Strang
Horseman by L. A. Golub
Horseman by W. Gropper
Horseneck brook, winter by J. H. Twachtman
Horses
Bartlett, G. Hidden spring
Bartlett, G. Indian police
Bartlett, G. Night herd
Bartlett, G. Saddled for the first time
Beal, G. R. Circus ponies
Bellows, G. W. Polo at Lakewood
Bellows, G. W. Sand team
Bellows, G. W. White horse
Bennett, B. Circus scene
Benton, T. H. White horse
Bierstadt, A. Black horse
Bingham, G. C. The mill boy
Blythe, D. G. Pittsburgh horsemarket
Blythe, D. G. The runaway
Boudro(u), A. A. Dickson entering Bristol in 1819
Buhalis, N. Horse
Catlin, G. Breaking down wild horses
Catlin, G. Comanche feats of horsemanship
Catlin, G. Keokuk on horseback
Davis, E. P. Eben Davis' horse
De Knight, A. Circus horses
Delano, G. C. Moonlight stampede
Delano, G. C. Navajo
Dixon, M. Cowboy and packhorse
Dixon, M. Peace in October
Dixon, M. Red gateway
Eakins, T. Fairman Rogers four-in-hand
Evett, K. Rodeo
Flannery, V. Chestnut stallion, Discovery
Flannery, V. The governor's cup
Freeman. Peter Volo
Gropper, W. Horseman
Hewes, M. Hollow hill pastoral
Hildebrandt, L. Horses
Homer, W. Bridle path, White mountains
Johnson, F. T. Mountain trail
Keller, H. G. End of the act
Keller, H. G. Storm-frightened animals

Keyes, C. A. Geo. S. Howe driving Rough and Ready
Kosa, E. J. Dark hills and white horses
Lebrun, R. Centurion's horse
Leigh, W. R. Combing the ridges
Leigh, W. R. Female of the species
Leigh, W. R. A lowdown trick
Leigh, W. R. The rescue
Miller, A. J. Approaching buffalo
Miller, A. J. Arapahos
Miller, A. J. Auguste and his horse
Miller, A. J. Beating a retreat
Miller, A. J. The Blackfeet
Miller, A. J. Camp scene (Sioux)
Miller, A. J. Capture of wild horses by Indians
Miller, A. J. Crow encampment
Miller, A. J. Crow Indian on the lookout
Miller, A. J. Dodging an arrow
Miller, A. J. Escape from Blackfeet
Miller, A. J. Indian certificate
Miller, A. J. Indian girls racing
Miller, A. J. Indian oracle
Miller, A. J. Indian woman on horseback in the vicinity of the Cut rocks
Miller, A. J. Indians in a storm: night scene
Miller, A. J. Indians returning to camp with game
Miller, A. J. Pawnee running buffalo
Miller, A. J. Picketing horses
Miller, A. J. Shoshone female catching a horse
Miller, A. J. Shoshone Indian and his pet horse
Miller, A. J. Snake Indians
Miller, A. J. Stampede of wild horses
Miller, A. J. Wild horses
Palmer, W. C. Horses in landscape
Prendergast, M. B. Bareback rider, Paris
Prendergast, M. B. Dress rehearsal
Prendergast, M. B. Horse and wagon
Prendergast, M. B. The rider
Price, C. S. Bay mare and colt and a couple of others
Price, C. S. Horses
Price, C. S. Horses in a barnyard
Price, C. S. Mare and foal
Price, C. S. Mare with colt
Price, C. S. White mare with foal
Quidor, J. Tom Walker's flight
Quirt, W. W. Horses and man
Ranney, W. T. The lasso
Ray, R. Survivors
Remington, F. Among the led horses
Remington, F. Apaches are coming
Remington, F. Apaches listening
Remington, F. Dismounted: 4th troopers moving
Remington, F. Downing the nigh leader
Remington, F. End of the day
Remington, F. General Leonard A. Wood on horseback
Remington, F. Halt—dismount
Remington, F. The last march
Remington, F. An old time plains fight
Remington, F. On the southern plains in 1860
Remington, F. Pioneer and the Indian
Remington, F. The scout: friends or enemies?
Remington, F. The snow trail
Remington, F. Snowbound on the overland stage
Remington, F. United States cavalry defending a position
Russell, C. M. The bolter
Russell, C. M. Bucking bronco
Russell, C. M. Capturing the grizzly
Russell, C. M. Caught with the goods
Russell, C. M. The challenge
Russell, C. M. The cinch ring
Russell, C. M. Cowboy life
Russell, C. M. A dangerous cripple
Russell, C. M. The free trader
Russell, C. M. Heeling a bad one
Russell, C. M. Holding up the sheriff
Russell, C. M. In without knocking
Russell, C. M. Jerked down
Russell, C. M. A loose cinch
Russell, C. M. Roping a grizzly
Russell, C. M. Sagebrush sport
Russell, C. M. The scout
Russell, C. M. Smoke of a .45
Russell, C. M. Smoking them out
Russell, C. M. Stampeded
Russell, C. M. Surprise attack
Russell, C. M. An unscheduled stop
Russell, C. M. When law dulls the edge of chance
Russell, C. M. When Sioux and Blackfeet meet
Russell, C. M. Wild horse hunters
Russell, C. M. Wild men's meat
Ryder, A. P. Grazing horse
Ryder, A. P. Hunter's rest
Ryder, A. P. In the stable
Ryder, A. P. Lone scout
Ryder, A. P. Racetrack
Ryder, A. P. Roadside meeting
Ryder, A. P. White horse
Saalburg, A. R. Wild horses
Sample, P. S. Going to town
Schreyvogel, C. My bunkie
Sheets, M. O. Black horse
Simkhovitch, S. Two horses
Sommer, W. Big horse
Sommer, W. Black horse
Sommer, W. Blue horse
Sommer, W. Horses in the snow
Sommer, W. Languid leisure
Sommer, W. Three horses in alarm
Sommer, W. Two yellow horses
Strang, R. Horse power
Strang, R. Slow poke
Strang, R. Spring
Strang, R. Water
Strater, H. Colts at Soda Springs
Troye, E. Edward Troye and an unidentified boy
Troye, E. Richard Singleton
Unidentified artist. Buffalo hunter
Unidentified artist. General Washington on white charger
Unidentified artist. Horses in a stream
Unidentified artist. Lady Suffolk
Unidentified artist. Runaway horse
Unidentified artist. Start of the hunt
Unidentified artist. The trotter
Unidentified artist. War horses
Van Zandt, T. K. Judge Van Arbam in his sleigh
Watkins, M. B. The blue and the strawberry roan
Wimar, C. Captive charger

Horse's skull on blue by G. O'Keeffe

Horsfield, Timothy
Haidt, J. V. Timothy Horsfield jr

HORTER, Earl, 1881-1940
Gloucester docks
NYG. Fine art

Horton, John
Hare, C. W. John Horton

Hortus occlusus by G. Kepes

The host by G. W. McLauchlin

Hostiles by C. M. Russell

Hot corn girl by N. V. Calyo

Hot horizon by A. Gottlieb

Hot house by W. Plate

Hot September wind by C. E. Burchfield

Hot springs near the Yellowstone by T. Moran

Hot stillscape by S. Davis

Hot stillscape for six colors by S. Davis

HOTCHKISS, Thomas Hiram, c 1834-1869
Old aqueduct   MB
MB. Ptgs in water color
Taormina, the island of Sicily   NNHS
MiD. Travelers in Arcadia

Hotel corridor by R. B. Motherwell

Hotel corridor by D. Rosenthal

Hotel lobby by M. Beckmann

Hotel lobby by E. Hopper

Hotel lobby by H. C. Pitz

Hotels, restaurants, etc
Bellows, A. F. Wayside inn
Boudro(u), A. A. Dickson entering Bristol
Cropsey, J. F. View of Kaaterskill house
Davis, S. Hotel de France
Du Bosi, G. P. Restaurant
Durrie, G. H. Jones' inn
Durrie, G. H. Winter scene, Jones' inn
Guy, F. Tontine coffee house, New York
Haklhuber, F. Herndon hotel, Omaha, Nebraska
Harvey, G. Tremont house, Boston
Krimmel, J. L. Interior of an American inn
Lawrence, J. Cafe scene
Sloan, J. Chinese restaurant
Sloan, J. Lafayette hotel
Sloan, J. Renganeschi's, Saturday night
Sloan, J. Soula's Rathskeller
Sloan, J. Yeats at Petitpas
Unidentified artist. Fashionable inn, New York
Unidentified artist. Judd's hotel, Philadelphia

HOUMÈRE, Walter, 1895-
Lute, flute and dance
Robb. Art 1953 ed

Hound by H. R. Poore

Hound by M. T. Zorach

Hound and hunter by W. Homer

The hours by E. G. Malbone (copy of miniature by Samuel Shelley)

The house by F. Hillsmith

The house by E. Laning

House and street by S. Davis

House by the railroad by E. Hopper

House in the pines by S. Laufman

House in the woods by S. Laufman

House maid by W. M. Paxton

House of cards by S. Serisawa

House of mystery by C. E. Burchfield

House of the dogs by F. Chapin

House of the foghorn by E. Hopper

House of the moon by R. Beck

House on Pamet river by E. Hopper

House on Teel's island by A. N. Wyeth

House on the sea by W. Whittredge

House, tree shapes by S. Davis

Houseman, Jacob, fl 1809
Jarvis, J. W. Jacob Houseman

Houses by C. H. Demuth

Houses by the river by L. Feininger

The Houses of Parliament by W. Homer

Housetop in Ecuador by F. E. Church

Houston, Henry W. fl 1837
Coe, E. V. Henry W. Houston

Houston, Phebe, fl 1837
Coe, E. V. Mrs Phebe Houston

Houston, Samuel, 1793-1863
Catlin, G. Gen Sam Houston
Unidentified artist. Samuel Houston as Marius

HOVENDEN, Thomas, 1840-1895
Breaking the home ties   PPhM
Chew. 250 years of art
DC. De gustibus
Joseph Battell   CtY
CtY. Portrait index
Last moments of John Brown   MM
Davidson v2
U.S. National Capital sesquicentennial com
Old version
WiMiA. Amer ptg 1760-1960
Self-portrait
Chew. 250 years of art

How my mother's embroidered apron unfolds in my life by A. Gorky

How order no 6 came through by F. Remington

HOWARD, Charles, 1899-
The amulet
Read. Concise history
California
Genauer (col)
Dove love
CSFP. Annual ex, 1946
Everyday sovereign
CSFP. Annual ex, 1950/51
The first hypothesis
CSFP. Annual ex, 1947/48
IU. Contemp Amer ptg, 1949
Fully-developed escutcheon
IU. Contemp Amer ptg, 1950
The matement
PPC. International ex, 1952
Prescience   MM
MM. 100 Amer ptrs
Pierson
The progenitors
CSFP. Annual ex, 1948/49
Rumour
Read. Art no, 1948 ed

Trinity   ICA
  ICA. Anual ex, 1945/46
  McCurdy
  MMA. Abstract
Howard, Mrs Henry. See Berlandina, Jane
Howard, John Eager, 1752-1827
  Peale, C. W. Gov John Eager Howard
  (after Rembrandt Peale)
HOWARD, John Langley
  Spring cleaning
    ICA. Annual ex, 1951
  Storm coming
    CSFP. Annual ex, 1952
Howard, Mrs Robert Boardman. See Kent, Adaline
HOWARD, Wing
  Le Pont Neuf
    NAD. Annual ex, 1947, 1st half
Howarden, Margaret. See Livingston, Margaret (Howarden)
Howe, George S. fl 1860
  Keys, C. A. Geo. S. Howe driving Rough and Ready
Howe, Richard, 1st earl, 1726-1799
  Copley, J. S. Richard, Earl Howe
HOWELL, Felicie Waldo, 1897-
  Gramercy park   InIJ
    InIJ. 105 ptgs
Howl by S. Greene
Howl of the weather by F. Remington
Hubard, Maria Mason (Tabb) 1813-1888
  Hubard, W. J. Mrs William James Hubard
HUBARD, William James, 1807-1862
  Alfred V. Crenshaw   VRV
    VRV. William James Hubard
  Dream of Columbus   VRV
    VRV. William James Hubard
  Eliza Hoffman
    VRV. William James Hubard
  Elizabeth and Anna Deans
    VRV. William James Hubard
  Henry Clay   VCU
    VRV. William James Hubard
  Horatio Greenough in his studio in Florence   VRV
    MiD. Travelers in Arcadia
    Pierson
    Richardson. Ptg in America
    VRV. William James Hubard
  Jeremiah Hoffman and daughter
    VRV. William James Hubard
  John C. Calhoun   DC
    Time. 300 years (col)
    VRV. William James Hubard
  John H. Cocke, of Bremo   VCU
    VRV. William James Hubard
  John Hoffman
    VRV. William James Hubard
  John Marshall
    VRV. William James Hubard
  Mann S. Valentine   VRV
    VRV. William James Valentine
  Mann S. Valentine, 2nd, and the artist   VRV
    MiD. Travelers in Arcadia
    VRV. William James Hubard
  Milk man and the maid
    VRV. William James Hubard
  Mrs Henry Wythe Tabb
    VRV. William James Hubard
  Mrs John C. Rutherfoord
    VRV. William James Hubard

  Mrs John Tabb
    VRV. William James Hubard
  Mrs William Bolling
    VRV. William James Hubard
  Mrs William James Hubard
    VRV. William James Hubard
  Rebecca Pue
    VRV. William James Hubard
  Robert Gilmor II   MdBM
    DC. Amer ptrs of the South
  Robert Morgan Gibbes   MdBH
    VRV. William James Hubbard
  Self-portrait
    VRV. William James Hubard
  Thomas Williamson
    VRV. William James Hubard
  William A. Shafer
    VRV. William James Hubard
Hubbard, Bradford
  Moulthrop, R. Bradford Hubbard
HUBBARD, Charles, fl 1837
  The National Lancers with the reviewing officers on Boston Common   MB
    MB. Lane
Hubbard, Elbert Green, 1856-1915
  Chase, W. M. Elbert Hubbard
Hubbard, Henry, 1769-1844
  Malone, E. G. Henry Hubbard
Hubbell, Anna Gibbon (Johnson) 1809-1895
  Neagle, J. Anna Gibbon Johnson
HUCK, Robert, 1923-
  Deer hunter
    OrPA. Ptgs & sculptures
Huckleberry pickers by C. S. Price
The hucksters by P. Calvin
HUDSON, Charles William, 1871-1943
  Spruce tree in a landscape   MB
    MB. Ptgs in water color
Hudson, Eliza, fl 1820
  Ames, E. Mrs Robert Hudson
HUDSON, John Bradley, 1832-1903
  View in Maine   MB
    MB. Karolik coll
Hudson, Maria (Mackie) 1795-1862
  Sully, T. Mrs Edward Hudson
Hudson, Robert, c 1785-1825
  Ames, E. Robert Hudson
HUDSON, William, fl 1850
  Political debate between two Irishmen
    Davidson v2
Hudson autumn by B. Mitchell
Hudson Bay fur company by R. Marsh
Hudson burlesk chorus by R. Marsh
Hudson burlesk, Union City, New Jersey by R. Marsh
Hudson navigation boat by E. Fiene
Hudson river and valley
  Audubon, V. G. (attributed works) Hudson river view
  Bellows, G. W. Floating ice [Hudson river] 1910
  Bellows, G. W. Morning snow [The Hudson from Riverside park]
  Bellows, G. W. Rain on the river [Hudson river from Riverside drive, 1908]
  Bellows, G. W. Up the Hudson
  Birch, T. Upper Hudson
  Browere, A. D. (attributed works) Hudson river landing
  Chambers, T. Hudson river landscape
  Chambers, T. Hudson river scene
  Chambers, T. Hudson river valley, sunset

Hudson river and valley—*Continued*
Chambers, T. View of the Hudson river at West Point
Chambers, T. (attributed works) Landscape—probably a Hudson river scene
Cornell, J. V. View of the Highlands from Ruggles house, Newburgh, New York
Croome, W. Crystal valley farm, a view of the Hudson river at the Overslaugh
Cropsey, J. F. Upper Hudson
Cropsey, J. F. Winter scene on the Hudson
Davies, T. View of Green Bush on the Hudson's river near Albany
De Grailly, W. View from West Point
Durand, A. B. Hudson at Rhinebeck
Fisher, A. The Hudson pool
Hart, J. M. View on the Hudson
Hart, J. M. and Tait. A. F. (attributed works) The Burden family enjoying the Hudson river near Troy
Harvey, G. View on the Hudson
Havell, R. View of the Hudson river from Horton's road near Croton
Hill, J. W. Hudson river bridge near Waterford
Homer, W. Hudson river
Homer, W. Hudson river logging
Homer, W. The rapids, Hudson river, Adirondacks
Johnson. D. At Barrytown, Hudson river
Lechay, J. Hudson river
Mitchell, B. Hudson autumn
Moore, C. H. Down the Hudson to West Point
Porter, R. Hudson river highlands
Unidentified artist. Beacon-on-the Hudson
Unidentified artist. Crow's nest, from Bull hill, Hudson river looking toward West Point
Unidentified artist. Hudson river landscape
Unidentified artist. Hudson river landscape with sailboats
Unidentified artist. Hudson river view
Unidentified artist. Outing on the Hudson
Unidentified artist. Palisades
Unidentified artist. Sunset by the river
Wall, W. G. Hudson river from West Point
Wall, W. G. View near Fishkill, N.Y.
Wall, W. G. View near Fort Montgomery
Weir, J. F. View of the Highlands from West Point
Wheelock, M. G. On the Hudson
Wyant, A. H. On the upper Hudson
Hudson river bridge near Waterford by J. W. Hill
Hudson river school series, 30 by J. Jarvaise
Hudson river school series, 59 by J. Jarvaise
Hudson river school series, 86 by J. Jarvaise
Hudson river schooner Robert Knapp by J. Bard
Hudson river sloop Phillip R. Paulding by J. E. Butterworth
Hudson river steamboat Rip Van Winkle by J. Bard
HUGE, J. Frederick
Steamboat Bunkerhill
Ford. Pictorial folk art

Huger, Daniel Elliott, 1779-1854
Malbone, E. G. Judge Daniel E. Huger
Hughes, John, abp, 1797-1865
Healy, G. P. A. Archbishop John Hughes
Hugo, Colonel
Copley, J. S. Colonels Hugo and Schleppengull
Hull, Isaac, 1773-1843
Jarvis, J. W. Commodore Isaac Hull
HULTBERG, John, 1922-
Arctic cabin   IU
  CoS. New accessions USA, 1958
  IU. Contemp Amer ptg & sculp, 1957
  IU. 20th century
Flying box   MM
  CoS. New accessions USA, 1956
Frozen station
  IU. Contemp Amer ptg & sculp, 1959
Italian journey   NBuA
  NBuA. Acquisitions 1954-57
  PPC. International ex, 1955
The lake
  VR. Amer ptg, 1958
Night still life   WMAA
  Pierson
  WMAA. Annual ex, 1955
Number 1, 1960
  IU. Contemp Amer ptg & sculp, 1961
Tilted horizon   NeL
  NUM. Art across America
Yellow sky   DC
  DC. Masterpieces
  DC. 24 biennial ex, 1955
Human comedy by A. Bohrod
The **human** fold—flowering by J. W. Treiman
Human pool tables by R. Marsh
Hummingbirds
Audubon, J. J. Ruby-throated hummingbird
Heade, M. J. Hummingbirds and gold and purple orchids
Heade, M. J. Hummingbirds and orchids
Heade, M. J. Orchids and hummingbird
Heade, M. J. Orchids and spray orchids with hummingbirds
Heade, M. J. Passion flowers and hummingbirds
Humphreys, David, 1752-1818
Stuart, G. David Humphreys
Hunger by B. Shahn
Hunt, Mrs Cassius, fl 1760
Badger, J. Mrs Cassius Hunt
Hunt, Edward, fl 1810
Birch, T. Edward Hunt
HUNT, H. P. fl 1848
Lady holding a book   MeC
  Jetté. Amer heritage collection
HUNT, Lynn Bogue
Northeaster—Canada geese
  NSP. Sportscapes
Hunt, Mrs Richard Morris
Hunt, W. M. Mrs Richard Morris Hunt and child
HUNT, William Morris, 1824-1879
Anahita, the flight of night   MB
  Pierson
Bathers   MWM
  DC. De gustibus
  Roos

Flight of night   PA
  Barker. Amer ptg
  Larkin rev ed
  Pierson
  Richardson. Ptg in America
  Roos
Flight of night (mural)
  Larkin
The forge   OYB
  OYB. Supplement
Gloucester harbor   MB
  Pierson
Ida Mason   MB
  Pierson
Ideal head   InIJ
  InIJ. 105 ptgs
Lemuel Shaw
  Larkin rev ed (col detail)
  Pierson
Marguerite   MB
  Pierson
Mrs Richard Morris Hunt and child
  Pierson
Self-portrait   MB
  Larkin
  Larkin rev ed
  Mendelowitz
  Pierson
William Maxwell Evarts   CtY
  CtY. Portrait index
The hunt by W. W. Quirt
Hunted sky by Y. Tanguy
Hunter, Mary (Smyth)
  Sargent, J. S. Mrs Charles Hunter
Hunter family, fl 1835
  Unidentified artist. Hunter family of Ger-
    mantown, Pennsylvania
Hunter in the hills by L. Kroll
Hunters and hunting
  Beal, G. R. Hunter, winter
  Bingham, G. B. Shooting for the beef
  Catlin, G. Buffalo chase
  Catlin, G. Buffalo chase of the Sioux
  Catlin, G. Buffalo chase, upper Missouri
  Catlin, G. Winter hunting on upper Mis-
    souri
  Chapman, J. G. Drawing a bead on a
    woodchuck
  Darley, F. O. C. Hunting buffaloes
  Durant, A. B. Hunter
  Eakins, T. Hunting
  Eakins, T. Pushing for rail
  Eakins, T. Will Schuster and black man
    going shooting (Rail shooting)
  Eastman, S. Hunting buffalo in winter
  Evergood, P. The hunters
  Frost, A. B. Hunting deer
  Frost, A. B. Hunting the moose
  Goodwin, P. R. Calling the moose
  Hess, J. N. Rail shooting
  Homer, W. Hound and hunter
  Homer, W. Huntsman and dogs
  Homer, W. Indian hunter in the Ever-
    glades
  Kuhn, R. Wounded wolves
  Mason, R. M. The moment that makes
    duck hunting
  Miller, A. J. Argali—mountain sheep
  Miller, A. J. Buffalo at bay
  Miller, A. J. Buffalo hunting near Inde-
    pendence rock
  Miller, A. J. Grizzly bear
  Miller, A. J. Head of antelope
  Miller, A. J. Hunters in search of game
  Miller, A. J. Hunting buffalo
  Miller, A. J. Hunting elk
  Miller, A. J. Hunting the bear
  Miller, A. J. Killing buffalo with the
    lance
  Miller, A. J. Running buffalo
  Miller, A. J. Shooting a cougar
  Miller, A. J. Trappers starting for the
    beaver hunt
  Miller, A. J. Trapping beaver
  Miller, A. J. Wounded buffalo
  Miller, A. J. Yell of triumph
  Moran, E. Duck shooting
  Osthaus, E. H. On the points
  Ranney, W. T. Duck hunters on the
    Hoboken marshes
  Russell, C. M. When meat was plentiful
  Russell, C. M. When tracks spell meat
  Russell, C. M. Wild horse hunters
  Ryder, A. P. Hunter's rest
  Stanley, J. M. Buffalo hunt on the south-
    ern plains
  Sword, J. B. A good day's work—return
    from duck hunt
  Tait, A. F. Buffalo hunt
  Tait, A. F. Duck shooting
  Tracy, J. M. Grouse shooting
  Tracy, J. M. Hunter and two dogs
  Tracy, J. M. Pointers
  Unidentified artist. Buffalo hunter
  Unidentified artist. Coon hunt
  Unidentified artist. End of the hunt
  Unidentified artist. Hunting scene
  Unidentified artist. Start of the hunt
  Williamson, C. M. Night hunters
  Wyeth, A. C. Coot hunter
Hunter's cabin door by R. L. Goodwin
Hunter's equipment by G. Cole
Hunter's rest by A. P. Goodrich
Hunters resting by M. J. Heade
Hunting dog among dead trees by W.
  Homer
HUNTINGTON, Daniel, 1816-1906
  George Peabody   CtY
    CtY. Portrait index
  Martha Washington's reception
    NYG. Fine art
HUNTINGTON, Daniel, 1816-1906, and
  KENSETT, John Frederick, 1816-
  1872
  Seascape, Newport
    MB. Karolik coll
Huntington, Jabez, 1719-1786
  Trumbull, J. Major General Jabez Hunt-
    ington
Huntington, Jabez, 1767-1848
  Trumbull, J. Jabez Huntington
Huntington harbor by A. G. Dove
Hurd, Nathaniel, 1730-1777
  Copley, J. S. Nathaniel Hurd
HURD, Peter, 1904-
  Baptising at Three Wells   GAtM
    GAtM. Holbrook collection
  Boy from the plains
    McCurdy
    Pierson
  Gerald Marr   CoS
    CoS. New accessions USA, 1954

HURD, Peter—*Continued*
  José Herrera   MoKN
    Eliot. Art of our time (col)
    MoKN. Handbook
    Time. 300 years (col)
  Landscape with polo players
    Gruskin (col)
  Rainy season   NBM
    Baur. Revolution
Hurdy-gurdy by G. S. Ratkai
Hurricane, Bahamas by W. Homer
Hurricane island by W. A. Kienbusch
Hurricane island, Vinal Haven, Maine by
  M. Hartley
Husband and wife in a landscape by W.
  Williams
Hush before the storm by C. E. Burchfield
Hutchinson, Edwin, fl 1846
  Mason, B. F. Edwin Hutchinson
Hutchinson, Sally. See Oliver, Sally (Hutch-
  inson)
Hutchinson boy by J. Theus
Huts, Newfoundland by D. Macknight
Hutson, Mary (Woodward) 1717-1785
  Theus, J. Mrs William Hutson
Hutson, Richard, 1747-1793
  Earl, J. (attributed works) Richard Hut-
  son
Hyacinth by L. MacIver
Hyang-to (Homeland) by S. Chun
Hybrid by F. Ruvolo
Hyde, Richard, 1783-1854
  Malbone, E. G. Richard Hyde
Hydrant water conveyed through wooden
  pipes, 1816, York, Pennsylvania by
  L. Miller

I

I.R.T. by G. L. K. Morris
I am glad I came back by G. Grosz
I bear the children of tomorrow by U.
  Romano
I got a harp by D. Lutz
I looked into a dream by J. Thecla
I, my own keeper by N. Tschacbasov
I saw the letter 5 in gold by C. H. Demuth
I think so by Y. Kuniyoshi
I was always present by G. Grosz
I woke up one night and saw a house burn-
  ing by G. Grosz
Iberia by P. Trivigno
Iberian landscape by C. Browning
Icarian flight by S. Fogel
Icarus by E. Chamberlain
Icarus by J. Molzahn
Icarus descended by R. Lytle
Ice cart, c 1840 by N. V. Calyo
Ice cream parlor by H. Hensel
Ice cream vendor by C. W. Rain
Ice floes by M. Beckmann
Ice glare by C. E. Burchfield

Iceberg by F. E. Church
Iceland fishermen by P. S. Sample
The iceman by J. Hirsch
Ices by J. Lawrence
Ichabod Crane at a ball at the Van Tassel
  mansion by J. Quidor
Ichabod Crane pursued by the Headless
  Horseman by J. Quidor
Iconostas by J. Elshin
Icy shore by J. Atherton
Ida, Portrait of by A. Dasburg
Ide, Mrs Gregory. See Childs, Clarissa
  (Partridge)
Idea and forms by D. Bothwell
Ideal head by G. Fuller
Ideal head by W. M. Hunt
Ideal head by E. Vedder
Ideal landscape by T. Doughty
The ides by P. Jenkins
Idolatress by H. Hoffman
The idols by C. Wells
If this be not I by P. Guston
Ikon no 386 by J. Xceron
Île de la cité by R. Kuntz
I'll take the high road by E. J. Kosa
Illimited sequences by Y. Tanguy
Illumination by R. Pousette-Dart
Illuminations by H. Crowley
Ilsley, Silas, fl 1834
  Unidentified artist. Rev Silas Ilsley
I'm glad I came back by G. Grosz
I'm tired by Y. Kuniyoshi
Image and space by J. W. Boynton
Image in Xhorkom by A. Gorky
Images of Pompeii by V. Vytlacil
Imaginary landscape by J. E. Heliker
Imagined music by K. F. Roesch
IMBERT, Anthony, fl 1824-1836
  Erie canal celebration, New York, 1825
                          NNMC
    Davidson v2
    U.S. National Capital sesquicentennial
    com
The immigrant by D. Fredenthal
Immigrants' arrival at New York, 1847 by S.
  B. Waugh
Impatience by A. Gorky
Imploring dead by R. Lebrun
Impressionism by C. Sheeler
Imprisoned force by C. A. Morris
Improvisation no 1 by K. Cramer
Improvisation no 2 by K. Cramer
Improvisation in a Greek key by J. Levine
Improvisation on a mill town by C. Sheeler
Improvisation to form by A. Dasburg
In a garden of ancient loves by R. Breinin
In a quandary by G. C. Bingham
In biege with sand by R. B. Motherwell
In charge of the baby by W. Homer
In Colorado by A. Blanch
In Fairmont by N. Spencer
In May by C. E. Burchfield

In my own time by W. Pachner
In nature's wonderland by T. Doughty
In old Kentucky by W. H. Cady
In the air by M. Graves
In the beginning by P. Fine
In the beginning by M. Morgan
In the box by M. Cassatt
In the cabin by N. Spencer
In the Catskills by J. F. Kensett
In the cornfield by J. G. Clonney
In the fields by E. Johnson
In the forest by R. Pousette-Dart
In the garden by G. D. Brush
In the garden by M. Cassatt
In the garden by L. Kester
In the Generalife by J. S. Sargent
In the hollow of the hill by D. Macknight
In the library by M. B. Prendergast
In the loge by M. Cassatt
In the Luxembourg gardens by M. B. Prendergast
In the Luxembourg gardens by J. S. Sargent
In the moraine, Dogtown common, Cape Ann by M. Hartley
In the mountains by W. Homer
In the park by A. M. R. Moses
In the park by M. B. Prendergast
In the parlor by H. Sharrer
In the patio by G. O'Keeffe
In the ring by J. Marin
In the Rockies by W. Whittredge
In the shadow of a mystery by P. Burlin
In the springtime by A. M. R. Moses
In the stable by A. P. Ryder
In the studio by J. Ricci
In the studio by R. Soyer
In the summerhouse by G. Tooker
In the swamp opposite Bayou Sara by J. R. Meeker
In the third sleep by K. Sage
In the valley by D. Macknight
In the wake of the buffalo hunters by C. M. Russell
In the wake of the ferry by J. Sloan
In the wilderness by S. R. Gifford
In the woods by A. B. Durand
In the woodshed by J. G. Clonney
In vaudeville by C. H. Demuth
In without knocking by C. M. Russell
Inauguration by J. Levine
Incantation by C. Sheeler
Incantation no 2 by G. Johanson
Incense of a new church by C. H. Demuth
Inches, Louise (Pomeroy) fl 1887
  Sargent, J. S. Mrs Charles Edward Inches
An incident of the Revolution by J. Eichholtz
Incoming tide by M. M. Albright
Incumbent by W. Gropper
Indefinite divisibility by Y. Tanguy

Independence, Missouri
  Warren, F. E. Town square, Independence
Independence hall, Philadelphia by K. Matthew
Independence hall, Philadelphia by E. Shinn
India by B. Shahn
Indian blanket by K. Knaths
Indian bull boats on the Missouri by K. Bodmer
Indian camp by G. Bartlett
Indian camp by A. Bierstadt
Indian camp by W. Homer
Indian campfire by C. Wimar
Indian encampment by G. C. Bingham
Indian encampment by R. A. Blakelock
Indian encampment by Unidentified artist
Indian fields by V. Higgins
Indian penny by W. W. Quirt
Indian sugar camp by S. Eastman
Indian telegraph by J. M. Stanley
Indian village of Alpuyeca by E. Isenburger
Indians of North America
  See also Medicine man; Tepees; also names of Indian chiefs, e.g., Black Hawk (Sauk chief), Red Jacket (Sagoyewatha) (Seneca Indian chief)
  Bartlett, G. Indian camp
  Bartlett, G. Indian police
  Bierstadt, A. Indians near Fort Laramie
  Bingham, G. C. Concealed enemy
  Birch. T. Landing of William Penn
  Blakelock, R. A. Indian madonna
  Bodmer, K. Crow Indians
  Bodmer, K. Interior of the hut of a Mandan chief
  Bodmer, K. Mato-topé with the marks of his exploits
  Bodmer, K. Noapeh, an Assiniboin Indian; Psihdja-Sahpa, a Yanktonai Indian
  Boutelle, D. C. Indian surveying a landscape
  Bradshaw, J. W. An Indian
  Brush, G. D. At dawn
  Brush, G. D. Silence broken
  Catlin, G. See titles under name of artist
  Couse, E. I. Making medicine
  Cross, H. H. Red Cloud and Burning Heart
  Delano, G. C. Navajo
  Delano, G. C. Navajo boy
  Dixon, M. Katchinamaker
  Eastman, S. Death whoop
  Eastman, S. Indian attack
  Eastman, S. Indians travelling
  Eastman, S. Lacrosse playing among the Sioux
  Eastman, S. Sioux Indians breaking up camp
  Eastman, S. Squaws playing ball on the prairie
  Farny, H. F. Song of the talking wire
  Henri, R. Indian girl
  Hesselius, G. Tishcohan
  Hesselius, G. Lapowinsa
  Hicks, E. Penn's treaty with the Indians
  Homer, W. Indian camp
  Homer, W. Indian hunter in the Everglades

Indians of North America—*Continued*

Homer, W. Indian woman at oven

King, C. B. No Heart—Ioway

King, C. B. Shaumonekusse, chief of the Otoes

King, C. B. Young Omahaw, War Eagle, Little Missouri and Pawnees

King, G. B. No-way-ke-sug-ga, an Oto

King, G. B. Tah-ro-hon, an Iowa warrior

King, G. B. (attributed works) Le Soldat du Chêne, an Osage chief

Krans, O. Indians

Krieghof, C. Indians portaging furs

Leigh, W. R. Baking day

Leigh, W. R. The mystic

Lewis, J. O. Cut-Taa-Tas-Tia, a Fox chief

Lewis, J. O. Me-no-quet, a Pottawattomie chief

Lewis, J. O. Nabu-Naa-Kee-Shick, a Chippewa chief

Lewis, J. O. Pe-che-co, a Pottawattomie chief

Lewis, J. O. Sun-a-get, a Pottawattomie chief

Lewis, J. O. Tens-qua-ta-wa, the Shawnee prophet

Lewis, J. O. Waa-Na-Taa, chief of the Sioux

Mathies, J. L. D. Seneca veterans of the war of 1812

Miller, A. J. See titles under name of artist

Neagle, J. Indian heads

Neagle, J. Knife Chief of the Pawnee Loups

Remington, F. Apaches listening

Remington, F. The outlier

Remington, F. Pioneer and the Indian

Rindisbacher, P. Indians hunting buffalo

Rindisbacher, P. Indians returning from war

Russell, C. M. See titles under name of artist

Schreyvogel, C. The silenced war whoop

Seymour, S. Indians

Seymour, S. Oto council

Seymour, S. Pawnee council

Sharp, J. H. Young chief's mission

Shaw, J. Indians sighting a ship

Stanley, J. M. Indians playing cards

Stanley, J. M. Ko-kak-koo-kiss, a Towoccono warrior

Stevens, J. Sioux Indians attacking a Minnesota farm

Unidentfiied artist. Buffalo hunter

Unidentified artist. Indian chief

Unidentified artist. Murder of Jane Mc-Crea

Vanderlyn, J. Death of Jane McCrea

West, B. William Penn's treaty with the Indians

Wilgus, W. J. Ut-Ha-Wah (Capt Cole)

Wimar, C. Attack on an emigrant train, 1856

Wimar, C. Buffalo hunt

Wimar, C. Captive charger

Wimar, C. Indians approaching Fort Benton

Wimar, C. On the warpath

Dancers and dancing

Bodmer, K. Buffalo dance of the Mandan

Bodmer, K. The Minnetaree scalp dance

Burbank, E. A. Hopi snake dance

Catlin, G. The bear dance

Catlin, G. The beggars' dance of Teton Sioux

Catlin, G. Bull dance of the Mandans

Catlin, G. Dance of the berdash of the Sauk and Fox

Catlin, G. Mandan O-kee-pa, the bull dance

Catlin, G. The medicine bag dance of the Sauk and Fox

Catlin, G. The Sauk and Fox slave dance

Catlin, G. Scalp dance of the Sioux

Catlin, G. Sioux beggar's dance

Catlin, G. Snowshoe dance of the Chippewas

Catlin, G. Snowshoe dance of the Ojibbeway

Catlin, G. The sun dance

Eastman, S. Dog dance of the Dakotahs

Marin, J. Corn dance, New Mexico

Marin, J. Dance of the San Domingo Indians

Rindisbacher, P. Indian dance

Rindisbacher, P. War dance of the Sauks and Foxes

Seymour, S. Dog dance of the Kansas Indians

Stanley, J. M. Osage scalp dance

Wimar, C. Buffalo dance

Wars

Adams, C. Custer's last fight

Catlin, G. Comanche war party meeting dragoons

Mathies, J. L. D. Seneca veterans of the war of 1812

Miller, A. J. Threatened attack

Remington, F. Cavalry charge on the southern plains

Russell, C. M. Custer's last stand

Russell, C. M. Desperate stand

Russell, C. M. Indian warfare

Schreyvogel, C. Defending the stockade

Schreyvogel, C. The silenced war whoop

Indians of South America

Catlin, G. The handsome dance, Venezuela, South America

Catlin, G. Uruguay medicine man, South America

Individual state of the world by M. Graves

Industrial by R. L. Ochs

Industrial composition by E. D. Lewandowski

Industrial façade by C. A. Morris

Industrial landscape by G. L. K. Morris

Industrial night by L. Gatch

Industrial scene by H. D. Sharrer

Industrial town by A. Rattner

Industrial variations by S. Gross

Industrial worker by B. Shahn

Industry by S. Davis

Industry by P. Dickinson

An **infanta** (Souvenir of Velásquez) by W. M. Chase

Infernal machine at dawn by J. W. McCullough

Infinite divisibility by Y. Tanguy
Inflation means depression by B. Shahn
The **informer** by F. Ruvolo
Ingersoll, R. Sturgis, 1891-
  Watkins, F. C. R. Sturgis Ingersoll
INGHAM, Charles Cromwell, 1796-1863
  Katherine Sedgwick
    MB. New England miniatures
Ingraham, Solomon, d 1806?
  Verstille, W. Capt Solomon Ingraham
Ingram mansion, Pittsburgh by J. Kane
Initial by F. J. Kline
Initials by W. Homer
Inland pool by L. Kroll
Inland tempest by A. B. Davies
Inland water, Bermuda by W. Homer
The **inlet** by W. Farndon
INMAN, Henry, 1801-1846
  David Sproat Kennedy   NNHS
    NNHS. Waldron Phoenix Belknap coll
  Dismissal of school on an October after-
    noon   MB
    MB. Karolik coll
  Georgianna Buckham and her mother MB
    Larkin (detail)
    Larkin rev ed (detail)
    Pierson
  Henry Clay
    Time. 300 years (col)
  John James Audubon
    CtY. Yale alumni
  John M. Catlin   CtY
    CtY. Portrait index
  John Marshall
    MB. Great Americans
  John Wesley Jarvis   MCH
    Dickson. John Wesley Jarvis
  Mrs Robert Lenox   NNHS
    NNHS. Waldron Phoenix Belknap coll
  The newsboy   MAP
    NJN. Early N.J. artists
  Picnic in the Catskills   NBM
    Born
    Pierson
  Richard Varick   NHMC
    NUM. Art across America
  Rural happiness
    NYG. Fine art
  Samuel Jones   CtY
    CtY. Portrait index
  Self-portrait   PA
    Richardson. Ptg in America
  Young fishermen   MM
    Bazin
Inman, Mrs Ralph, 1725-1761
  Feke, R. (attributed works) Mrs Ralph
    Inman (also attributed to Blackburn)
The **inn** by A. G. Dove
INNESS, George, 1825-1894
  Apple orchard   MiD
    MiD. Treasures
  Approaching storm from Alban hills OCl
    OCl. Handbook
  Autumn oaks   MM
    Barker. Amer ptg
    NYG. Fine art
    Pierson
    Taylor. Fifty centuries, 1954 ed (col)
    Upjohn

  Autumn scene   GAtM
    GAtM. Holbrook collection
  Brook, Montclair   PR
    PR. Catalogue
  Castel Gandolfo   OrPA
    PPC. Amer classics
  Christmas eve   NJMo
    NJMo. Forty years
  Clearing up   MSG
    Baur. Amer ptg
  Clouded sun   PPC
    Pierson
  Coast of Cornwall
    Cheney. Story 1958 ed
  Coming storm, 1878   NBuA
    Larkin
    Larkin rev ed
    NBuA. Catalague of the ptgs
  Coming storm, 1880   MAP
    Larkin rev ed (col)
    Pierson
    Time. 300 years (col)
  Delaware meadows   MnMW
    Larkin
  Delaware valley   MM
    McClintock
    Robb. Harper history
  Delaware Water Gap   MM
    Born
    Flexner. Amer ptg
    Flexner. Short history
    McClintock
    Pierson
  Delaware Water Gap   NJMo
    McClintock
    NJMo. Your Montclair art museum
    Time. 300 years (col)
  Etretat   CtHW
    CtHW. Handbook
  Evening at Medfield   MM
    Cheney. New world history
  Grey day, Goochland   DP
    Pierson
    Richardson. Ptg in America
  Harvest scene in the Delaware valley
              MnMW
    Larkin rev ed
  Home at Montclair   MWiS
    MWiS. Ex 4 and 7
  Home of the heron   ICA
    Gardner 1959 ed
    Lee. Art then and now
    Mendelowitz
    Pierson
  June   NBM
    Mendelowitz
    Pierson
    Time. 300 years (col)
  Lackawanna valley   DN
    Born
    McClintock
    Pierson
    U.S. National Capital sesquicentennial
      com
    Walker. Ptgs from America
  Lake Albano   DP
    DP. Catalogue
  Late afternoon, Montclair, New Jersey
              ATeS
    ATeS. Collection
  March of the crusaders
    Sears. Highlights

INNESS, George—*Continued*
The monk   MAP
  NUM. Art across America
  Pierson
Moonlight on Passamaquoddy bay   ICA
  McKinney
Moonlight, Tarpon Springs   DP
  DP. Catalogue
Near the village, October   OCiM
  OCiM. Guide
Old mill   ICA
  Barker. Amer ptg
Painting at Montclair   InTH
  InTH. Catalogue
Passing shower
  NYG. Fine art
Peace and plenty   MM
  NYG. Fine art
  Pierson
  Richardson. Ptg in America
  Roos
The rainbow   InIJ
  InIJ. 105 ptgs
Roman Campagna   MoSL
  Born
  MoSL. Handbook 1953
Sacred grove near Rome
  MiD. Travelers in Arcadia
Tiber below Perugia   OT
  MiD. Travelers in Arcadia
Under the greenwood
  NAD. Amer tradition
Venice: S. Giorgio Maggiore   KLU
  Pierson
View on the Delaware, Water Gap in the
  distance
  McClintock
Woodgatherers: autumn afternoon MWiS
  MWiS. Ex 4 and 7
Woodland vista   MB
  MB. Karolik coll

Portrait of the artist
  Chase, W. M. George Inness
INNESS, George, 1853-1926
  Landscape with cattle   NJMo
  NJMo. Forty years
Innocence by J. Delaney
Innocence, meekness, liberty by E. Hicks
The **innocents** by C. L. Martin
Inns. See Hotels, restaurants, etc.
Inquisition by A. Salemme
Insects at twilight by C. E. Burchfield
Inside and out by J. Albers
Inside looking out by B. Shahn
Inside of an Indian tent by P. Rindisbacher
Inside—outside by I. R. Pereira
Inside the bar by W. Homer
Interchange by W. De Kooning
An **interesting** book by C. R. Hirst
Interior by A. B. Davies
Interior by S. Davis
Interior by W. H. Givler
Interior by B. Greene
Interior by H. Hofmann
Interior by L. Kroll
Interior by T. McKibben

Interior by R. M. Pollack
Interior by M. Ray
Interior by C. Sheeler
Interior by B. Swan
Interior by R. Watson
Interior and bay by J. C. Lewis
Interior and exterior by W. Zorach
Interior at Honfleur by F. Hillsmith
Interior of Fort Laramie by A. J. Miller
Interior of the fourth dimension by M.
  Weber
Interior—the creeks by G. Hartigan
Interior with figure by R. Soyer
Interior with figures by M. Weber
Interior with flowers by M. Avery
Interior with men by M. Weber
Interior with standing figure by J. Glasco
Interior with three figures by J. Martini
Interlude by I. Bishop
Interlude by Z. L. Sepeshy
Interlunar sea by C. Wells
Intersection by M. Tobey
Interurban by F. Alexander
Interurban line by C. E. Burchfield
Interwoven thread by K. Callahan
Intimate conversation by D. W. Ellis
Into Dogtown, autumn by W. Kienbusch
Into the world there came a soul called Ida
  by I. L. Albright
Introspection by A. Brook
The **intruder** by A. Brook
The **intruder** by H. Janicki
Invasion by B. Kopman
Invasion by E. Millman
Invention—dance by M. Ray
Invention on a microscopic theme by L. E.
  Kupferman
The **inventor** by K. Zerbe
Invitation by G. J. McNeil
Invocation by S. M. Adler
Invocation by M. Greenwood
Ionian sea by C. Oscar
Iotrio by L. Buck
Iowa (battleship)
  Aldrich, W. T. A giant
Iowa cornfield by G. Wood
IPPOLITO, Angelo, 1922-
  Morning
    WMAA. Young America 1957
  Storm   WMAA
    Baur. Nature (col)
    Goodrich. Amer art (col)
    WMAA. Young America 1957
  West
    WMAA. Annual ex, 1958
Ipswich bay by F. H. Lane
Ipswich sand dunes by A. T. Roberts
Iris by K. Schrag
Iris, Study of by J. La Farge
Iris and snowballs by J. E. Francis
Irish girl by R. Henri
Irish landscape by L. McIver

The **Iron Crown (ship)**
Homer, W. Wreck of the Iron Crown
Iron dragon by J. E. Levi
Iron witch by J. V. Cornell
The **ironers** by Unidentified artist
Iroquois Indian by A. J. Miller
Irving, Washington, 1783-1859
Jarvis, J. W. Washington Irving
Isaac blessing Jacob by Unidentified artist
Isaac of York by W. Allston
Ischia by S. Greene
Iselin, Eleanora (O'Donnell) 1821-1897
Sargent, J. S. Mrs Adrian Iselin
ISENBURGER, Eric, 1902-
Amalfi
IU. Contemp Amer ptg, 1951
Country flowers
VR. Biennial ex, 1948
Cove at sunset
IU. Contemp Amer ptg, 1948
Homage to Rome
NAD. Annual ex, 1951
Indian village of Alpuyeca
IU. Contemp Amer ptg & sculp, 1959
Jimmy Savo
NAD. Annual ex, 1960
Roar of the wooden horse
PPC. Ptg in the U.S. 1949
Romantic figure   DC
DC. 21 biennial ex, 1949
Sea and wharf at Provincetown
NAD. Annual ex, 1957
Self-portrait
ICA. Annual ex, 1945/46
Still life
NAD. Annual ex, 1956
Island of happiness by Y. Kuniyoshi
Island of Mount Desert from the mainland by R. S. Gifford
Island, Small point, Maine by J. Marin
The **Isle** of Capri by J. F. Cropsey
Isle of the gods by E. J. Stevens
Isolationist by W. Gropper
Isotopes by W. T. Murch
Israel by W. Pachner
Israel by S. Rosenberg
Istanbul by W. G. Congdon
It was blue and green by G. O'Keeffe
It will soon be here by O. Kraus
Italian beach by H. Frankenthaler
Italian farmyard by G. Wood
Italian fiesta, night by G. H. Hallowell
Italian flower market by M. B. Prendergast
Italian girl by M. B. Prendergast
Italian head by J. S. Sargent
Italian journey by J. Hultberg
Italian shepherd boy by W. Allston
Italian sunlight by L. Dodd
Italy
See also Florence; Rome; Venice
Allston, W. Italian landscape
Bierstadt, A. Marina Grande in Capri
Boit, E. D. See titles under name of artist
Bruce, E. Tuscan landscape

Church, F. E. Between Ceppo Morelli and Ponte Grande
Cole, T. Italian landscape
Cole, T. Italian scenery
Cole, T. Roman aqueduct
Cropsey, J. F. The Isle of Capri
Cropsey, J. F. Italian landscape
Cropsey, J. F. Lake of Nemi
Davies, A. B. The Apennines
Davies, A. B. Italian landscape, the Apennines
De Diego, J. Italy: historical town
McCarter, H. B. Early Italy
Prendergast, M. B. Roman Campagna
Shahn, B. Italian landscape
Toole, J. Vesuvius
Vedder, E. Bed of the Torrent Mugnone, near Florence
Vedder, E. Italian landscape
Weiss, H. Italian village
Ithaca, New York
Walton, H. View of Ithaca, Tompkins county, N.Y. in November 1838
Itlksez by S. Davis
I've got nothing to wear by F. J. Furman
Ives, Eli, 1779-1861
Jocelyn, N. Eli Ives
IVEY, William, 1919-
White painting
OrPA. Ptgs & sculptures (col)
Ivory-billed woodpecker by J. J. Audubon
Ivory tower by R. Hilton
IWAMOTO, Ralph, 1927-
Eastern twilight   OYB
OYB. Annual 1957
OYB. Supplement 1959
Izard, Alice (Delancey)
Copley, J. S. Mr and Mrs Ralph Izard
Izard, Anne. See Deas, Anne (Izard)
Izard, Charlotte (Broughton) c 1729-1801
Theus, J. Mrs Henry Izard
Izard, Eliza, 1784-1862
Malbone, E. G. Eliza Izard
Izard, Eliza (Mrs Daniel Blake) See Blake, Eliza (Izard)
Izard, George, 1776-1828
Malbone, E. G. Capt George Izard
Izard, Mrs Henry. See Izard, Charlotte (Broughton)
Izard, Margaret. See Manigault, Margaret (Izard)
Izard, Ralph, 1742-1804
Copley, J. S. Mr and Mrs Ralph Izard
Malbone, E. G. Capt Ralph Izard
Theus, J. Ralph Izard as a boy
Turnbull, J. Ralph Izard
Izard, Mrs Ralph. See Izard, Alice (Delancey)

J

J by J. McGarrell
The **jacket** by B. Perlin
Jack-in-the-pulpit by G. O'Keeffe
Jackman, Gracie Beardsley Jefferson, fl 1835
Unidentified artist. Gracie Beardsley Jefferson Jackman and her daughter

Jackson, Andrew, president U.S. 1767-1845
  Durand, A. B. Andrew Jackson
  Earl, R. Andrew Jackson
  Earl, R. E. W. Andrew Jackson
  Harding, C. Andrew Jackson
  Healy, G. P. A. Andrew Jackson
  Jarvis, J. W. Gen Andrew Jackson
  Peale, A. C. Andrew Jackson
  Peale, C. W. Andrew Jackson
  Sully, T. Andrew Jackson
  Waldo, S. L. Andrew Jackson
Jackson, Jonathan, 1743-1810
  Copley, J. S. Jonathan Jackson
JACKSON, Lee, 1909-
  Boardwalk in moonlight
    NAD. Annual ex, spring 1950
JACKSON, Martin, 1919-
  Harbor at night   DC
    CoS. New accessions USA, 1950
    DC. 21 biennial ex, 1949
  Night fair
    NAD. Annual ex, 1952
  Tintype, 1948
    IU. Contemp Amer ptg, 1949
    NAD. Annual ex, 1948
  Toy battle   OYB
    OYB. Annual 1953
    OYB. Supplement
Jackson by J. D. Brooks
JACOBI, Rudolf, 1889-
  Landscape   CtY
    CtY. Soc Anonyme
Jacob's dream by W. Allston
Jacob's dream by L. Terry
Jacquelin, Edward, fl 1722
  Unidentified artist. Edward Jacquelin the
    second
Jagged clouds by L. Feininger
El Jaleo by J. S. Sargent
Jamaica noon by S. M. Etnier
JAMES, Alexander, 1890-1946
  Artist's wife   KW
    NHMC. Alexander James
  Candide   MSM
    MSM. Handbook
  Choose your partner
    NHMC. Alexander James
  Danny
    NHMC. Alexander James
  Down to earth
    Gruskin (col)
  Embattled farmer
    NHMC. Alexander James
  Fitzwilliam
    NHMC. Alexander James
  Forgotten cabin
    NHMC. Alexander James
  Heart of darkness
    NHMC. Alexander James
  Joan
    NHMC. Alexander James
  John P. Marquand
    NHMC. Alexander James
  Luther Smith
    NHMC. Alexander James
  Mrs Dean Acheson
    NHMC. Alexander James
  Sandy   MoKN
    NHMC. Alexander James
  Selectmen
    NHMC. Alexander James

  Self-portrait, 1940
    NHMC. Alexander James
  A solitary
    NHMC. Alexander James
James, Alexander Robertson
  James, A. Sandy
James, Catharine (Barber) 1782-1859
  Ames, E. Mrs William James
JAMES, Frederic
  Driftwood
    NAD. Annual ex, 1949, 2d half
James, Frederika
  James, A. Artist's wife
James, Henry, 1843-1916
  Duveneck, F. Henry James, 1882
  Sargent, J. S. Henry James
James, Katharine Barber, 1834-1890
  Ames, E. Katharine Barber James (?)
James, Marcia Lucretia (Ames) See Ames,
  Marcia Lucretia
James, William, 1771-1782
  Ames, E. William James
James, Mrs William, 1782-1854. See James,
  Catharine (Barber)
James, Mrs William, 1797/98-1886. See
  Ames, Marcia Lucretia
JAMESON, Demetrios, 1919-
  Boy with birds
    OrPA. Ptgs & sculptures
  Boy with kite
    NNSG. Younger Amer ptrs
JAMIESON, Mitchell, 1915-
  Children of Rome
    MM. Amer ptg today
  Convoy entering Mers-el-Kebir
    NYG. Fine art
  Maelstrom   WaS
    Pousette-Dart. Amer ptg
  Off Hatteras   TxF
    CoS. New accessions USA, 1956
  Port of Cherbourg
    PPC. Ptg in the U.S. 1949
Jane Reed and Dora Hunt by C. H. Carter
JANICKI, Hazel, 1918-
  The intruder
    IU. Contemp Amer ptg & sculp, 1953
  Weavers of a spell   OYB
    OYB. Annual 1951
    OYB. Catalogue 1951
Janitor's holiday by P. S. Sample
JANJIGIAN, Anahid
  Back porches
    NAD. Annual ex, 1959
January by W. De Kooning
January, Michigan farm by Z. L. Sepeshy
Japanese peasants by J. La Farge
Japanese toy tiger and odd objects by Y.
  Kuniyoshi
Japhthah's return by B. B. Lathrop
JARVAISE, James, 1925-
  Arrangement on a blue table   OYB
    OYB. Annual 1955
    OYB. Supplement 1959
  Blue table
    IU. Contemp Amer ptg & sculp, 1953
  Classical still life
    IU. Contemp Amer ptg & sculp, 1957

JARVIS, J. W.—*Continued*
Nathan Starr jr (of Middletown, Conn.)
    NNHS
  Dickson. John Wesley Jarvis
Oliver Hazard Perry   NNCH
  Dickson. John Wesley Jarvis
  Dickson. John Wesley Jarvis (detail)
  Larkin
  Larkin rev ed
  Pierson
Peter Scoyen   NJF
  Dickson. John Wesley Jarvis
The pirate Laffite   LaNM
  Dickson. John Wesley Jarvis
Robert Gilmor jr   PA
  Dickson. John Wesley Jarvis
Samuel Chester Reid   MnMI
  Dickson. John Wesley Jarvis
Self-portrait (Giskra coll)
  Dickson. John Wesley Jarvis
Self-portrait (Lambert coll)
  Dickson. John Wesley Jarvis
Self-portrait   MdBW
  MdBMu. Rendezvous
Solomon Etting   MdBH
  Dickson. John Wesley Jarvis
Thomas Ellison   NNHS
  Dickson. John Wesley Jarvis
Thomas Macdonough
  Dickson. John Wesley Jarvis
  Dickson. John Wesley Jarvis (detail)
Thomas Paine
  U.S. National Capital sesquicentennial com
Unknown man   MM
  Dickson. John Wesley Jarvis
Washington Irving   CtY
  CtY. Portrait index
Washington Irving (Sunnyside restoration coll)
  Dickson. John Wesley Jarvis
William Bainbridge   NNCH
  Dickson. John Wesley Jarvis
William Croghan
  Dickson. John Wesley Jarvis
William Henry Cabell II
  Dickson. John Wesley Jarvis
William Johnston   NNHS
  Dickson. John Wesley Jarvis
William Leffingwell   CtY
  CtY. Portrait index
  Dickson. John Wesley Jarvis
William Linn
  Dickson. John Wesley Jarvis
William Neilson
  Dickson. John Wesley Jarvis
William Samuel Johnson
  Dickson. John Wesley Jarvis
  Flexner. Light of distant skies
William W. Van Ness   NNHS
  Dickson. John Wesley Jarvis
Young boy
  WiMiA. Amer ptg 1760-1960

Attributed works

Sailor's head (reputed self-portrait of Jarvis)
  Dickson. John Wesley Jarvis

Portrait of the artist

Inman, H. John Wesley Jarvis
Otis, B. John Wesley Jarvis (after Jarvis' self-portrait)

Jarvis, Lydia (Liscome) 1799-1848
  Jarvis, J. W. Lydia Liscome
Jarvis, Mrs John Wesley, d 1813. See Burtis, Betsey
Jarvis, Mrs John Wesley, 1799-1848. See Jarvis, Lydia (Liscome)
Jason by R. Morrow
Jason returning to demand his father's kingdom by W. Allston
Jaudennes y Nebot, Joseph de, fl 1795
  Stuart, G. Joseph de Jaudennes y Nebot
Jaudenes y Nebot, Louise Carolina Matilde (Stoughton) de, 1778-1822?
  Stuart, G. Matilde de Jaudenes y Nebot
Jay, Anna Maria (Bayard) b 1670
  Duyckinck, Gerret. Mrs Augustus Jay
Jay, Augustus, 1665-1751
  Unidentified artist. Augustus Jay
Jay, John, 1745-1829
  Ames, E. John Jay (after Stuart)
Jay, Peter Augustus, 1877-1933
  Sargent, J. S. Peter Augustus Jay at the age of three
Jazz by M. Ray
Jazz band by B. Perlin
Je t'aime, II, 1955 by R. B. Motherwell
Jealous lover of Lone Green valley by T. H. Benton
Jealousy by L. M. Eilshemius
Jean by G. W. Bellows
Jean by J. Carroll
Jean, Anne and Joseph by G. W. Bellows
Jean in blue by E. E. Speicher
Jean with blue book and apple by G. W. Bellows
Jeanne by A. H. Maurer
Jeanne d'Arc, Saint, 1412-1431
  Ryder, A. P. Joan of Arc
Jefferson, Joseph, 1829-1905
  Leslie, C. R. Actors' duel: Mr Jefferson and Mr Blissett
Jefferson, Thomas, president U.S. 1743-1826
  Peale, C. W. Thomas Jefferson, c 1791
  Peale, Raphaelle. Thomas Jefferson
  Peale, Rembrandt. Thomas Jefferson
  Pyle, H. Thomas Jefferson
  Stuart, G. Thomas Jefferson
  Sully, T. Thomas Jefferson
  Trumbull, J. Thomas Jefferson, detail from the Declaration of Independence
JEFFREY, Agnes, 1806-1896
  Main street, Canandaigua
  Jones. Rediscovered ptrs
Jenkins, Mary Eliza
  Wetherby, I. A. Mary Eliza Jenkins
JENKINS, Paul, 1923-
  Black dahlia
    Baur. Nature
  The ides
    Cheney. Story 1958 ed
    WMAA. Young America 1957
  Phenomena—with nitrogen before
    IU. Contemp Amer ptg & sculp, 1961
  St George
    IU. Contemp Amer ptg & sculp, 1959
  To Queequeg
    Read. Concise history

JENNINGS, Samuel, fl 1789-1834
Liberty displaying the arts and sciences (The genius of America encouraging the emancipation of the blacks)
Davidson v2
ICA. From colony to nation
U.S. National Capital sesquicentennial com

Jenny lake, Wyoming by A. Bierstadt

Jennys, J. William. See Jennys, William

JENNYS, Richard, fl 1774-1832
Ithamar Canfield
Lipman. Primitive ptrs

JENNYS, William, fl 1802
Constant Storrs   PA
Pierson
Eneas Munson   CtY
CtY. Portrait index
Gentleman of the Brewer family (Man in the coonskin hat)
Pierson
Mabel Billings
Larkin
Larkin rev ed
Member of the Smith family of Suffield, Connecticut and Rutland, Vermont
Lipman. Primitive ptrs
Mr Hewitt   MSM
MSM. Handbook
Mrs Constant Storrs   PA
Richardson. Ptg in America
Pierson
Mrs Hewitt   MSM
MSM. Handbook
Mrs Reuben Hatch   CtNL
Pierson
Reuben Hatch   CtNL
Pierson
William Stoddard Williams
ICA. From colony to nation
Woman with a fan   DC
DC. Masterpieces

Attributed works

Young girl   MeR
NUM. Art across America

Jensen, Alfred Julio, 1903-
The great mystery 11   NBuA
NBuA. Acquisitions 1959-1961

Jereboam, King
Unidentified artist. Crowning of King Jereboam

Jeremiah dictating his prophecy by W. Allston

The **jerk** line by C. M. Russell

Jerked down by C. M. Russell

Jersey hills by J. Marin

Jersey shore by J. J. Jones

Jersey turnpike, View from by R. A. Parker

Jessie, 17 years old by T. H. Benton

JESSUP, Jared, fl 1800-1810
Overmantel, Burk tavern, Bernardston
Flexner. Light of distant skies

Jesters. See Clowns and jesters

Jesus exalted in song by B. Shahn

Jet and turquoise by W. Lockwood

Jetties at Bellport by W. J. Glackens

Jeune fille en fleur by E. Friedensohn

A **Jew,** Head of by W. Allston

JEWETT, William, 1795-1873 and WALDO, Samuel Lovett, 1783-1861
Frederick Wolcott   CtY
CtY. Portrait index
John Trumbull   CtY
CtY. Portrait index

Jimmie O'D by Henri

Jimmy Savo and rope by A. Dehn

Jo by J. A. M. Whistler

Jo Bakos by A. Dasburg

Joan by A. James

Joan by the sea by B. Greene

Joan of Arc. See Jeanne d'Arc, Saint

Job lot, cheap by W. M. Harnett

Job no 2, 1958 by A. Rattner

Job no 9, 1959 by A. Rattner

Job's tears by L. Guglielmi

JOCELYN, Nathaniel, 1796-1881
Augustus Russell Street   CtY
CtY. Portrait index
Chauncey Allen Goodrich   CtY
CtY. Portrait index
Edward Elias Atwater   CtY
CtY. Portrait index
Eli Ives   CtY
CtY. Portrait index
James Abraham Hillhouse   CtY
CtY. Portrait index
James Luce Kingsley   CtY
CtY. Portrait index
Jonathan Knight   CtY
CtY. Portrait index
Timothy Phelps Beers   CtY
CtY. Portrait index

Portrait of the artist

Munger, G. Nathaniel Jocelyn

Jockey in red silk by R. Davey

JOE, Dale, 1928-
Pocket
WMAA. Young America 1960
Profile
WMAA. Young America 1960

Joe Magarac by W. Gropper

Joel by W. Meyerowitz

Joel's cave by M. Weber

JOHANSEN, John Christen, b 1876
James Rowland Angell   CtY
CtY. Portrait index

JOHANSON, George, 1928-
Incantation no 2
OrPA. Ptgs & sculptures

John Biglen in a single scull by T. Eakins

John street, New York by J. B. Smith

John the Baptist in the wilderness by T. Cole

Johnny Appleseed by K. Knaths

JOHNS, Jasper, 1930-
Black target
MMA. Sixteen
Green target   MMA
MMA. Sixteen
Grey numbers
PPC. International ex, 1958
Large white flag
MMA. Sixteen
Numbers in color   NBuA
MMA. Sixteen
NBuA. Acquisitions 1959-1961

JOHNS, Jasper—*Continued*
Target with four faces   MMA
  MMA. Sixteen
Tennyson
  MMA. Sixteen
Two flags
  WMAA. Contemp Amer ptg, 1959-60
White numbers   MMA
  MMA. Sixteen
White target   MMA
  MMA. Soby collection
JOHNSON, Mr. fl 1825-1837
Mr and Mrs Sherman Griswold and their
  three favorite sheep
  Jones. Rediscovered ptrs
JOHNSON, Ann, fl 1840
Baptisam of our Savour   VWR
  VWR. Folk art (col)
Johnson, Anna Gibbon. See Hubbell, Anna
  Gibbon (Johnson)
Johnson, Catharine Livingston Thorn,
fl 1796
  Sharples, J. Catharine Livingston Thorn
  Johnson
JOHNSON, David, 1827-1908
At Barrytown, Hudson river
  DC. Privately owned
Mount Marcy
  Born
Old mill, West Milford, New Jersey
                                 NBM
  Born
JOHNSON, Eastman, 1824-1906
Blacksmith shop   NoCR
  NoCR. Catalogue
Blacksmith shop   NCHA
  U.S. National Capital sesquicentennial
  com
Card playing at Fryeburg, Maine
  MiD. Coll in progress
  WiMiA. Amer ptg 1760-1960
Corn husking   NSyE
  Davidson v2
  Pierson
Corn husking at Nantucket   MM
  Davidson v 1
Cranberry pickers
  CSB. Impressionism
Cranberry pickers in Nantucket   ATeS
  ATeS. Collection
Family group (The Hatch family)   MM
  Mendelowitz
  Pierson
  Roos
Hollyhocks   CtNB
  NUM. Art across America
In the fields   MiD
  MiD. Treasures
  Pierson
  Richardson. Ptg in America
Letter home   MB
  MB. Karolik coll
Maple sugar campfire, Fryeburg, Maine
                                 CtY
  Davidson v 1
Measurement and contemplation   MB
  MB. Karolik coll
Nantucket school of philosophy   MdBW
  Mendelowitz
Noah Porter   CtY
  CtY. Portrait index

Not at home   NBM
Larkin
Larkin rev ed
Old Kentucky home, life in the South
                                NNHS
  Cheney. Expressionism 1948 ed
  NAD. Amer tradition
  Pierson
  Roos
The old stage coach   WiMi
  Time. 300 years (col)
The pension agent   CSFP
  CSFP. Handbook
A ride for liberty: the fugitive slave NBM
  U.S. National Capital sesquicentennial
  com
Study in red—morning news at the camp
  Baur. Amer ptg
Sugaring off   OYB
  OYB. Catalogue 1951
Two men (Samuel W. Rowse and Robert
  Rutherford)   MM
  Barker. Amer ptg
  Pierson
  Richardson. Ptg in America
Winnowing grain   MB
  MB. Karolik coll
Johnson, Edward, 1767-1829
  Peale, Rembrandt. Mayor Edward John-
  son
JOHNSON, Frank Tenney, 1874-1939
Mountain trail   ATeS
  ATeS. Collection
On Salt Lake trail   IaDa
  IaDa. 30th anniversary
Johnson, Guy, 1740?-1788
  West, B. Col Guy Johnson
Johnson, Jonathan Eastman, See Johnson,
  Eastman
JOHNSON, Larry, 1935-
Disrobing figure
  WMAA. Young America 1960
Landscape with still life
  WMAA. Young America 1960
JOHNSON, Lester, 1919-
Self-portrait in ochre
  PPC. International ex, 1961/62
Johnson, Thomas, 1732-1819
  Peale, C. W. Gov Thomas Johnson and
  family
Johnson, Sir William, bart, 1715-1774
  Wollaston, J. Sir William Johnson
Johnson, William Samuel, 1727-1819
  Jarvis, J. W. William Samuel Johnson
Johnson family member, c 1830
  Goddell, J. G. (attributed works) Young
  lady of the Nathaniel Johnson family
JOHNSTON, David Claypoole, 1799-1865
Early New England schoolroom scene
                                MWA
  Davidson v2
Militia muster   MWA
  Pierson
  Richardson. Ptg in America
Ship smashing against rocks
  WiMiA. Amer ptg 1760-1960
Sound asleep and wide awake
  WiMiA. Amer ptg 1760-1960
Termination of a militia sham fight MWA
  Pierson
View near Milton, Massachusetts with Flat
  pond and buildings
  WiMiA. Amer ptg 1760-1960

JOHNSTON, Henrietta, fl 1707-1729
  Anne Broughton   CtY
    CtY. Portrait index
    Flexner. First flowers (detail)
  Mrs Samuel Wragg   SCCG
    Pierson
  William Rhett   SCCG
    Flexner. First flowers
    Pierson
JOHNSTON, Joshua, c 1770-1830
  Edward and Sarah Rutter   DN
    DN. Amer primitive ptgs, pt 2
  The James McCormick family of Balti-
    more   MdBH
    Lipman. Primitive ptrs
  Letitia McCurdy
    Larkin
    Larkin rev ed
  Westwood children   DN
    DN. Amer primitive ptgs, pt 2
JOHNSTON, William, 1732-1777
  Thomas Mumford V   NBM
    Mendelowitz
Johnston, William, 1769-1848
  Jarvis, J. W. William Johnson
JOHNSTON, Ynez, 1920-
  Afternoon in August
    IU. Contemp Amer ptg & sculp, 1957
  Black palace with red courtyard   CtHW
    Pousette-Dart. Amer ptg
  Blue garden
    IU. Contemp Amer ptg, 1952
  Breakwater   WMAA
    Pierson
  Reflections in a Roman river
    IU. Contemp Amer ptg & sculp, 1955
  Steps to the lighthouse   IU
    CoS. New accessions USA, 1954
    IU. Contemp Amer ptg & sculp, 1953
  Summer storm
    WMAA. Annual ex, 1956
Jolly flatboatmen by G. C. Bingham
Jolly flatboatmen in port by G. C. Bingham
Jonah by A. P. Ryder
Jondol by J. Brooks
JONES, Amy, 1899-
  City evening
    NAD. Annual ex, 1949, 2d half
Jones, Catherine. See Clinton, Catherine
  (Jones)
Jones, Mrs D. Blair. See Jones, Amy
Jones, Eleanor (Colford) 1755-1824
  Jarvis, J. W. Mrs John Jones III
Jones, Henry, b 1790
  Ames, E. Henry Jones aged 20 years
Jones, Mrs John. See Jones, Eleanor (Col-
  ford)
Jones, John Paul, 1747-1792
  Peale, C. W. John Paul Jones
JONES, John Paul, 1924-
  The table   CSB
    CoS. New accessions USA, 1960
Jones, Joe. See Jones, Joseph J.
JONES, Joseph J. 1909-
  American farm   WMAA
    Pierson
  Apple country
    Gruskin
  Evening Star   NJMo
    NJMo. Your Montclair art museum
  Harvest   ATU
    ATU. Coll of Amer art

Jersey shore
  CSFP. Annual ex, 1952
Landscape with houseboat
  IU. Contemp Amer ptg, 1951
Landscape with swans
  IU. Contemp Amer ptg, 1952
Regatta
  PPC. International ex, 1952
Rockport   MoKN
  UNESCO. 1860-1959
Wheat farmers
  Larkin
  Larkin rev ed
Jones, Mrs Otis, fl 1831
  Bascom, R. H. M. Mr and Mrs Otis Jones
    of Athol, Massachusetts
JONES, Prescott Merrill M. 1904-
  Lubec, Maine   MB
    MB. Ptgs in water color
Jones, Samuel, 1770-1853
  Inman, H. Samuel Jones
Jones, Sarah, fl 1775
  Theus, J. Col Jones' grandchild (Sarah
    Jones)
Jones, Thomas Pascal, 1774-1848
  Malbone, E. G. Dr Thomas Pascal Jones
Jones' inn by G. H. Durrie
JONSON, Raymond, 1891-
  Cliff dwellings no 3
    Cheney. Primer 1958 ed
    Cheney. Story 1958 ed
  Composition eleven
    Cheney. Expressionism 1948 ed
  Earth rhythms no 9
    Cheney. Expressionism 1948 ed
  Earth rhythms no 11
    Cheney. Primer 1958 ed
Jordan, Ambrose Latting, 1789-1865
  Ames, E. Ambrose Latting Jordan
JORDAN, Samuel, b 1804?
  Eaton family memorial   DN
    DN. Amer primitive ptgs, pt 1
Joseph and his brethren by Unidentified
  artist
Joseph and the Ishmaelites by D. Aronson
Joseph interpreting Pharaoh's dream by Un-
  identified artist
Josephine and Mercie by E. C. Tarbell
Joslin, Mrs Milton, fl 1840
  Peckham, R. (attributed works) Widow
    Milton Joslin
JOUETT, Matthew Harris, 1787-1827
  Edward Shippen
    Flexner. Light of distant skies
  Mrs Rufus Somerby   KyLS
    KyLS. Kentucky port gall
  Principal building of Transylvania univer-
    sity
    Davidson v2
  Robert Llewellyn Todd   KyLS
    KyLS. Kentucky port gall
Jourdain, Mlle
  Sargent, J. S. Mlle Jourdain
Journey by M. Graves
Journey in white by M. Tobey
Journey's end by H. Ballin
The joust by C. di Marca-Relli
Joy by H. Hofmann

Joyce, James
  Barnes, R. James Joyce
Joyce by E. E. Speicher
Joyous landscape by A. P. Russo
Joyous young pine by M. Graves
Juana, called La Loca, queen of Castile, 1479-1555
  Walker, C. H. Joanna of Castile, the mad
JUDD, De Forrest
  Maguey   TxD
    CoS. New accessions USA, 1952
Judd's hotel, Philadelphia, c 1825 by Unidentified artist
Judd's house, Southold, Long Island by Unidentified artist
The judge by J. Levine
The Judith roundup by C. M. Russell
Judson Stoddard by R. Robinson
Jugglers
  Evergood, P. Juggler of doom
  Kuhn, W. Juggler
  Kuniyoshi, Y. Amazing juggler
Juju and her dog Copelia by P. Evergood
Juju as a wave by P. Evergood
Juke box by D. Tanning
JULES, Mervin, 1912-
  Cobblers
    NYG. Fine art
  Desire   ATU
    ATU. Coll of Amer art
  Museum of Modern art
    Larkin
Juley, Peter
  Dickinson, S. E. Peter Juley and son
Julia by P. Evergood
Juliet by F. Martin
July by W. De Kooning
July clouds by C. E. Burchfield
July 4th, 5th, and 6th by F. Martin
July 14, Rue Daunou by C. Hassam
July hay by T. H. Benton
Jump rope by L. Ahlas
Jumping joy by L. Gatch
Junction by C. A. Hall
Junction by J. W. McCoy
June by G. Inness
June by W. Sommer
June day by W. T. Richards
June hay by T. H. Benton
June night by H. Koerner
June radiance by C. E. Burchfield
Jungle by W. A. Baziotes
Jungle by E. J. Stevens
Jungle in Venezuela by A. A. Dehn
Juniata river by J. Kane
Junior by R. Brackman
Junk yard by H. Koerner
Juno receiving the cestus from Venus by B. West
Justice's court in the backwoods by T. H. Matteson
Juxtaposition by S. M. Adler

K

Kaaterskill Falls by S. R. Gifford
Kaaterskill house, View of by J. F. Cropsey
KABAK, Robert, 1930-
  New York harbor
    IU. Contemp Amer ptg & sculp, 1959
KACHADOORIAN, Zubel, 1924-
  Matriarch and the prodigal son
    IU. Contemp Amer ptg & sculp, 1961
  Romanscape
    IU. Contemp Amer ptg & sculp, 1959
KACHMER, George, 1911-
  Winter along the mills   OYB
    OYB. Annual 1956
    OYB. Supplement 1959
KAEP, Louis Joseph, 1903-
  Men of Nazare
    NAD. Annual ex, 1958
Kahler, Jeremiah, 1795-1881
  Malbone, E. G. Jeremiah Kahler
Kahler, Jeremiah J. 1749-1830
  Malbone, E. G. Jeremiah Kahler
KAHN, Max, 1903-
  Blue rocks
    PA. Annual ex, 1959-60
  Fishing boat and white sun
    ICA. Annual ex, 1961
  Garden wall
    IU. Contemp Amer ptg & sculp, 1959
  Village in the mountains
    IU. Contemp Amer ptg, 1952
  We gather together
    DC. 26 biennial ex, 1959
KAHN, Wolf, 1927-
  Large olive grove   WMAA
    WMAA. Young America 1960
  September light
    IU. Contemp Amer ptg & sculp, 1959
  Silver sea
    WMAA. Young America 1960
  Summer 1954
    IU. Contemp Amer ptg & sculp, 1957
Kalamazoo cove by D. Lutz
Kaleidoscopic journey by S. Franks
Kaleidoscopic journey by F. Ruvolo
KALF, Willem, 1622-1693
  Still life   MSM
    Rathbun
KALLEM, Henry, 1913?-
  Rococo table
    DC. 26 biennial ex, 1959
KAMIHIRA, Ben, 1925-
  Circus performers
    NAD. Annual ex, 1954
  The couch   WMAA
    Goodrich. Amer art
  Funeral coach
    WiMiA. Amer ptg 1760-1960
    WMAA. Young America 1960
  The game
    WMAA. Annual ex, 1958
  Interior
    WMAA. Young America 1960
  Lowering from the cross
    PA. Annual ex, 1958
  Segment of Spain
    NAD. Annual ex, 1959
  Wedding dress
    DC. 27 biennial ex, 1961

Kamperman, George
  Watkins, F. C. Dr George Kamperman
KAMROWSKI, Gerome, 1917-
  Open twist
    IU. Contemp Amer ptg, 1950
  Urgent hour
    IU. Contemp Amer ptg, 1952
    MMA. Abstract
KAMYS, Walter, 1917-
  Fusion
    MBIC. View 1960
  Seaquake   CtY
    CtY. Soc Anonyme
Kane, John, 1734-1808
  Ames, E. John Kane
KANE, John, 1860-1934
  Along the Susquehanna
    Cheney. Story 1958 ed
  Beechwood boulevard, Pittsburgh
    Kallir. Amer primitive ptgs
  Boys fishing
    NSP. Sportscapes
  From my studio window
    Baur. New art (col)
  Homestead   MM
    Cheney. Story 1958 ed
  Ingram mansion, Pittsburgh
    CtY. Yale alumni
  Juniata river   NBuA
    NBuA. Contemporary ptgs
  Panther Hollow   WMAA
    Goodrich. Amer art
  Prosperity's increase
    Wight. Milestones
  Scotch day at Kennywood   MMA
    Baur. New art
    Pierson
  Self-portrait   MMA
    Barr. What is mod ptg
    Baur. New art
    Baur. Revolution
    Lipman. Primitive ptrs
    McCurdy
    Mendelowitz
    MMA. Masters (col)
    Pierson
    Time. 300 years (col)
    Walker. Ptgs from America
  Through Coleman Hollow up the Alle-
    gheny valley   MMA
    Chew. 250 years of art
  Turtle creek valley   KW
    Baur. New art
    Pierson
Kane, John Kintzing, 1795-1858
  Neagle, J. John Kintzing Kane
Kansas, University of
  Hess, J. University of Kansas, c 1879
KANTOR, Morris, 1896-
  Farewell to Union square   NJN
    Brown. Amer ptg
    Wight. Milestones
  Gray rocks and gray trees
    ICA. Annual ex, 1947/48
  Growth   IU
    IU. Contemp Amer ptg, 1951
    IU. 20th century
  Haunted house   ICA
    Pierson
  Highland light
    Lewisohn

  On the beach   MM
    MM. 100 Amer ptrs
  Orchestra
    Brown. Amer ptg
  Pines and fog   ATU
    ATU. Coll of Amer art
  Skyrocket   WMAA
    Goodrich. Amer art
  Still life (1)
    Cheney. Expressionism 1948 ed
  Still life (2)
    NYG. Fine art
  Still life (Phillips coll)
    Gruskin
  Storm   WMAA
    Pierson
  Summertime
    Pousette-Dart. Amer ptg (col)
  Tranquility
    IU. Contemp Amer ptg, 1950
  Union square, night   DP
    DP. Catalogue
KAPLAN, Joseph, 1900-
  Breakwater
    IU. Contemp Amer ptg, 1950
  Highland light
    IU. Contemp Amer ptg, 1951
  Interior
    IU. Contemp Amer ptg & sculp, 1953
KARFIOL, Bernard, 1886-1952
  Bathers
    Roos
  Boy   DP
    DP. Catalogue
    Wight. Milestones
  Boy bathers   WMAA
    Baur. Revolution
    Goodrich. Amer art (col)
    Pierson
    WMAA. Pioneers
  Child holding apple
    Brown. Amer ptg
  Christina   ICA
    Baur. Revolution
  Christina   PPC
    Pierson
  Cuban nude   MM
    Pierson
  Girl against a tree
    PPC. Ptg in the U.S. 1949
  Hilda
    Cheney. Expressionism 1948 ed
  Hills
    Cheney. Expressionism 1948 ed
  Laurent pony cart
    NYG. Fine art
  Nude on red couch
    IU. Contemp Amer ptg & sculp, 1953
  Repose
    Pousette-Dart. Amer ptg
  Seated nude   MMA
    Brown. Amer ptg
  Standing nude   WMAA
    Larkin
    Larkin rev ed
  Summer   DC
    DC. 25 biennial ex, 1957
  Two bathers
    Gruskin
  Two standing figures
    Brown. Amer ptg
Karl by A. Wyeth

KARP, Leon, 1903-1951
Bernard
  VR. Biennial ex, 1948
Spring flowers
  PPC. Ptg in the U.S. 1949
Still life with banjo
  IU. Contemp Amer ptg, 1950
Karrig by J. D. Brooks
Kasson, Mrs Ambrose. See Hall, Laura
Katchinamaker by M. Dixon
Katharine by E. E. Speicher
Katherine by T. Eakins
Kathryn by J. L. King
KATZ, Alex, 1927-
Baigneuse
  WMAA. Young America 1960
Folding chair
  WMAA. Young America 1960
KATZMAN, Herbert, 1923-
The bath
  PPC. International ex, 1952
Brooklyn bridge
  ICA. Amer artists paint the city
  MMA. Fifteen
  MnMW. Expressionism 1900-1955
Ensor seated before The Entry of Christ
    into Brussels
  IU. Contemp Amer ptg & sculp, 1959
Giotto's tower
  MMA. Fifteen
Horse butcher
  MMA. Fifteen
New York skyline
  IU. Contemp Amer ptg & sculp, 1961
Red coffee pot
  WMAA. New decade
Two nudes before Japanese screen
                    WMAA
  Goodrich. Amer art
  PA. Annual ex, 1953
  Pierson
Woman drying her hair
  WMAA. New decade
Zinnias   KLU
  Pierson
KAWABATA, Minoru, 1911-
Elegy
  PPC. International ex, 1961/62
KAYN, Hilde (Band) 1903-1950
New moon   OT
  OT. Contemp Amer ptgs
Swingtime   NJMo
  NJMo. Forty years
KEANE, William, fl 1880
Still life
  Frankenstein. After the hunt
KEARNS, James, 1925?-
Cat's cradle
  WMAA. Contemp Amer ptg, 1959/60
Self-portrait
  WiMiA. Amer ptg 1760-1960
Keating, Maurice, b 1747?
  Theus, J. Maurice Keating
KEEFE, W. Ranford, fl 1850
Tree of foreboding
  Born
Kee-oh-mee by C. M. Russell
Kee-o-kuk, chief of the Sauk and Foxes,
    fl 1790-1848
  Catlin, G. Kee-o-kuk on horseback

Catlin, G. Kee-o-kuk, the Running Fox
Lewis, J. O. Kee-o-kuk, chief of the Sauk
Keeper of the bell by J. Whorf
Keepsake from Mallorca by D. Bothwell
Keith, Mrs. Boudinot. See Wheeler, Dora
KELLER, Henry George, 1870-1949
Abstract impressions of surf
  OCl. Keller
African thistle
  OCl. Keller
The Alps
  OCl. Keller
Andalusian garden
  OCl. Keller
Anna's garden
  OCl. Keller
April snow   OCl
  OCl. Keller
Autumn fruits   DP
  OCl. Keller
The aviary   OCl
  OCl. Keller
Bathers, the cove, La Jolla
  OCl. Keller
Beach patterns
  OCl. Keller
Bird rock, California   WMAA
  OCl. Keller
Birds, rocks, and the sea
  OCl. Keller
Bouquet of flowers   OCl
  OCl. Keller
Circus folk
  OCl. Keller
Crossing the ford
  OCl. Keller
Crows in winter
  OCl. Keller
Drowsy company
  OCl. Keller
End of the act
  OCl. Keller
End of the day
  OCl. Keller
Evening on the road to Granada
  OCl. Keller
Fireflies
  OCl. Keller
First show at two   OCl
  OCl. Keller
Fog banks, Tyrol
  OCl. Keller
For Thanksgiving
  OCl. Keller
The ford   OCl
  OCl. Keller
Foul weather, Percé
  OCl. Keller
Goats among the peaks
  OCl. Keller
Granda flora
  OCl. Keller
Gulls feeding   OCl
  OCl. Keller
Helios in the lead
  OCl. Keller
Hermitage, Talavera   OCl
  OCl. Keller
Impressions of a bull fight
  OCl. Keller
In the park
  OCl. Keller

In the path of the sun
  OCl. Keller
Kelp gatherers   MAP
  OCl. Keller
Land's end, Golden gate, California
  OCl. Keller
Memories of Andalusia
  OCl. Keller
Morning, Upper Frazer river
  OCl. Keller
Mountains, Puget sound
  OCl. Keller
Peacock
  OCl. Keller
Percé rock, Gaspe
  OCl. Keller (col)
Pescaderia, Malaga
  OCl. Keller
Ranch life, western Texas
  OCl. Keller
Ready to clean the catch, Percé   OYB
  OYB. Catalogue 1951
Returning from the Feria
  OCl. Keller
Rhythms
  OCl. Keller
San Diego zoo
  OCl. Keller
Snails
  OCl. Keller
Spell of Italy
  OCl. Keller
Still life with fruit
  OCl. Keller
Still life with fruit and flowers   MB
  MB. Ptgs in water color
Storm-frightened animals   OCl
  OCl. Handbook
  OCl. Keller
Storm-frightened horses   MB
  MB. Ptgs in water color
Sudden windstorm over the Vega
  OCl. Keller
Sunday morning in Gordon park, Cleve-
  land
  OCl. Keller
Sunflower patterns
  OCl. Keller
Sunflowers
  OCl. Keller
Sun's path
  OCl. Keller
Torment, Puerto Rico
  OCl. Keller
White horses at the sand pit
  OCl. Keller
Winter landscape   ICA
  OCl. Keller
Wisdom and destiny   OCl
  OCl. Keller
KELLEY, Donald, 1928-
Old god
  MBIC. View 1960
KELLY, Ellsworth, 1923-
Atlantic
  WMAA. Young America 1957
Aubade
  PPC. International ex, 1958
Block Island no 2
  PPC. International ex, 1961/62
Falcon
  MMA. Sixteen

New York   NBuA
  Brussels. Exposition
  NBuA. Acquisitions 1959-1961
Rebound
  MMA. Sixteen
Slip
  MMA. Sixteen
Wave motif
  MMA. Sixteen
York
  MMA. Sixteen
Kelly, Emmett
  MacIver, L. Emmett Kelly
  Veres. Davy Emmet Crocky (Emmett
    Kelly)
KELLY, Marie Tuiccillo, 1916-
Parade
  Chew. 250 years of art
  PPC. International ex, 1952
Three kings no 11   OYB
  OYB. Annual 1953
Kelp gatherers by H. G. Keller
Kemble, Fanny. See Kemble, Frances Anne
Kemble, Frances Anne, 1809-1893
  Sully, T. Fanny Kemble as Beatrice
  Sully, T. Fanny Kemble as Bianca
KEMMELMEYER, Frederick, fl 1790-1810
First landing of Christopher Columbus
                                   DN
  DN. Amer primitive ptgs, pt 2
George Washington reviewing the west-
  ern army at Fort Cumberland   DN
  DN. Amer primitive ptgs, pt 1
  Flexner. Light of distant skies
  U.S. National Capital sesquicentennial
    com
KEMPSMITH, Joan
Auction day
  OYB. Annual 1950
Carnival time   OCl
  CoS. New accessions USA, 1952
Kempton, Caleb, fl 1830
  Unidentified artist. Capt Caleb Kempton
KENDALL, William Sergeant, 1869-1938
Arthur Twining Hadley   CtY
  CtY. Portrait index
William Howard Taft   CtY
  CtY. Portrait index
KENISTON, George A. 1850-1932
Table of fruit
  DN. Amer primitive ptgs, pt 2
KENNEDY, D. J. fl 1840
View of Broad and Cherry streets above
  Arch street
  Chew. 250 years of art
Kennedy, David Sproat, 1791-1853
  Inman, H. David Sproat Kennedy
Kennedy, John Pendleton, fl 1827
  Tilyard, P. John Pendleton Kennedy
KENNEDY, Terence J. 1820-1879?
Symbolical painting   NCHA
  Jones. Rediscovered ptrs
KENSETT, John Frederick, 1816-1872
Bash-Bish Falls, South Egremont, Massa-
  chusetts   MB
  MB. Karolik coll
Cascade in the forest   MiD
  MiD. Treasures
  Pierson
Cliffs at Newport, Rhode Island   MB
  MB. Karolik coll
Coast scene with figures   CtHW
  Pierson

KENSETT, J. F.—_Continued_
Coastal scene   CtHW
  Baur. Amer ptg
Glimpse of Lake George
  Sears. Highlights
In the Catskills
  Sears. Highlights
Lake George
  Taylor. Fifty centuries, 1954 ed (col)
Mountain stream   NAD
  NAD. Amer tradition
Newport harbor, Rhode Island (Kesler
  coll)
  Born
Newport harbor, Rhode Island (Sturges
  coll)
  DC. De gustibus
  Larkin
  Larkin rev ed
Niagara Falls and the rapids   MB
  MB. Karolik coll
Paradise rock, Newport   NJM
  Mendelowitz
River scene   MM
  Pierson
  Richardson. Ptg in America
  Time. 300 years (col)
Rydal Falls, England   MSG
  Barker. Amer ptg
Sea and rocky shore   MM
  Bazin
Third beach, Newport   ICA
  Pierson
Trenton Falls, New York   MB
  MB. Karolik coll
View near Newport   OCl
  OCl. Handbook
KENSETT, John Frederick, 1816-1872, and
  HUNTINGTON, Daniel, 1816-1906
Seascape, Newport   MB
  MB. Karolik coll
KENT, Adaline, 1900-1957
Untitled   CSFM
  CoS. New accessions USA, 1954
Kent, James, 1763-1847
  Ames, E. James Kent
  Jarvis, J. W. James Kent
KENT, Rockwell, 1882-
Burial of a young man   DP
  DP. Catalogue
Heavy, heavy
  PPC. Ptg in the U.S. 1949
Mount Equinox, winter   ICA
  Pierson
Road roller   DP
  Brown. Amer ptg
Shadows of evening   WMAA
  Goodrich. Amer art
  Pierson
Toilers of the sea   CtNB
  Baur. Revolution
The trapper   WMAA
  Cheney. Story 1958 ed
Winter   MM
  MM. 100 Amer ptrs
  NYG. Fine art
Kenton, Louis N.
  Eakins, T. The thinker
Keokuk. See Kee-o-kuk, chief of the Sauk
  and Foxes

KEPES, Gyorgy, 1906-
Hortus occlusus
  IU. Contemp Amer ptg & sculp, 1961
Landscape number 3
  IU. Contemp Amer ptg & sculp, 1955
Random pattern
  MBIC. View 1960
Kershaw, Anna M.
  Eakins, T. Mrs Anna M. Kershaw
KESTER, Lenard, 1913-
The cove
  NAD. Annual ex, 1952
In the garden
  IU. Contemp Amer ptg, 1949
Kite fliers
  MoSL. Contemporary Amer ptg
November 7th
  NAD. Annual ex, 1958
Picnickers
  IU. Contemp Amer ptg, 1948
Rehearsal
  IU. Contemp Amer ptg, 1950
Keteltas, Abraham, fl 1758
  Hesselius, J. Rev Abraham Keteltas
Keteltas, Jane. See Beekman, Jane (Ketel-
  tas)
Keteltas, Sarah (Smith) fl 1757
  Hesselius, J. Mrs Abraham Keteltas
The **key** by J. Pollock
Key West beach by P. Blume
KEYES, Charles A. fl 1856
  Geo. S. Howe driving Rough and Ready
                  NCHA
  Jones. New-found folk art
KEYS, Mary, fl 1832
Lockport on the Erie canal   NUM
  Jones. Rediscovered ptrs
Keys and feather by W. T. Murch
KEYSER, Robert, 1924-
Lyric piece
  IU. Contemp Amer ptg & sculp, 1961
KHOSROVI, Karim, 1925-
Abstraction
  IU. Contemp Amer ptg & sculp, 1955
Head with yellow ground
  NNSG. Younger Amer ptrs
The **kid** by I. Bishop
Kids skiing by J. Pike
KIENBUSCH, William Austin, 1914-
Across four pines (Hurricane island)
                  WMAA
  WMAA. Sara Roby
Across Penobscot bay   TxH
  Eliot. Art of our time (col)
Backyard, winter, Maine no 2
  PPC. International ex, 1955
Barns and fences no 1   CtNB
  Pierson
Black bush, autumn, Dogtown
  Pierson
Blue spruce   TxF
  CoS. New accessions USA, 1952
Connecticut field
  WMAA. Annual ex, 1954
Dirigo island
  WMAA. New decade
Fallen pine, Camp island   NBuA
  NBuA. Acquisitions 1954-57
Hurricane island. See Across four pines
Into Dogtown, autumn
  VR. Amer ptg, 1958

Low tide   MMA
  McCurdy
  MMA. Abstract
New England stove
  WMAA. New decade
Red vine, autumn, Dogtown, 1954
  WMAA. New decade
Red vine, autumn, Dogtown, 1956
  Baur. Nature
  Goodrich. Amer art
Rocky field, Camp island, Maine
  NBuA. Expressionism
Through the pines, the ocean
  Brussels. Exposition
Twin pine   WMAA
  Pousette-Dart. Amer ptg
The weir and the island   MM
  Time. 300 years (col)
Winter, Dirigo island
  WMAA. Museum and its friends, 1958
KILBURN, Lawrence, fl 1761
  Garret Abeel   NNHS
  Belknap
  Gerardus Duyckinck II   NNHS
  Belknap
  James Beekman
  Belknap
  Mrs Garret Abeel   NNHS
  Belknap
  Mrs Gerardus Duyckinck II   NNHS
  Belknap
  Mrs James Beekman
  Flexner. First flowers
Kilby, Sarah. See Cunningham, Sarah (Kil-
  by)
Kildeer by E. F. Spruce
Killer in costume by F. Martin
Killing buffalo with the lance by A. J.
  Miller
Kindred spirits by A. B. Durand
Kine no 1 by K. Okada
KING, Charles Bird, 1785-1862
  No Heart—Ioway   DNC
  Rathbone
  The poor artist's cupboard   DC
  DC. Masterpieces
  Mendelowitz
  Rope walk interior   NCHA
  Jones. New-found folk art
  Shaumonekusse, chief of the Otoes
  Rathbone
  Vanity of an artist's dream   MCH
  Barker. Amer ptg
  Pierson
  Richardson. Ptg in America
  Young Omahaw, War Eagle, Little Mis-
  souri and Pawnees   DNC
  Pierson
  Rathbone
  U.S. National Capital sesquicentennial
  com
King, Edith
  Prendergast, M. B. La Rouge: Edith King
King, Ellen (James) 1800-1823
  Ames, E. Mrs James King
King, Frederic Gore, 1801-1829
  Morse, S. F. B. Dr Frederic Gore King
KING, George Bird, fl 1837
  No-way-ke-sug-ga, an Oto
  Morgan (col)
  Tah-ro-hon, an Iowa warrior
  Morgan (col)

Attributed works
  Le Soldat du Chêne, an Osage chief
  Morgan (col)
KING, Henrietta (Campbell)
  10:00 P.M.
  NYG. Fine art
King, Mrs. James. See King, Ellen (James)
KING, John Lord, 1909-
  Kathryn
  PA. Annual ex, 1954
King, Mrs Mitchell. See King, Henrietta
  (Campbell)
KING, Paul, 1867-
  Mystery of the East
  NYG. Fine art
KING, Robert D.
  The flight
  OYB. Annual 1949
  Landscape no 3
  OYB. Annual 1951
The king by M. Beckmann
The king by G. W. McLaughlin
King cock by K. Knaths
King Cophetua and the beggar maid by
  A. P. Ryder
King Lear by B. West
King Lear's daughters by E. A. Abbey
King of spades by J. Mitchell
King Saul by J. Levine
The king visits his paramour by S. Moy
KINGMAN, Dong, 1911-
  Angel square
  IU. Contemp Amer ptg, 1952
  Time. 300 years (col)
  Blue moon   MB
  MB. Ptgs in water color
  Circus and the lady
  IU. Contemp Amer ptg & sculp, 1953
  Columbus circle
  Gruskin (col)
  Dead end
  NAD. Annual ex, 1951
  The el and snow   WMAA
  Pierson
  Lighthouse   OYB
  OYB. Catalogue 1951
  Mile drive, California
  NAD. Annual ex, 1954
  Moon and locomotive
  Pousette-Dart. Amer ptg
  Old Mission—San Diego   IaDa
  IaDa. Silver jubilee
  IaDa. 30th anniversary
  Washington square, New York
  NAD. Annual ex, 1961
KINGMAN, Helen M. fl 1845
  Mississippi river landing   DN
  DN. Amer primitive ptgs, pt 2
The king's jester by W. M. Chase
King's joke by D. J. Meeker
Kingsley, James Luce, 1778-1852
  Jocelyn, N. James Luce Kingsley
Kingston, New York
  Chambers, T. Looking north to Kings-
  ton
KINIGSTEIN, Jonah, 1924-
  The centaur   OYB
  OYB. Annual 1954
  OYB. Supplement
  Dead man
  IU. Contemp Amer ptg & sculp, 1959

KINIGSTEIN, Jonah—*Continued*
Old lady
　IU. Contemp Amer ptg & sculp, 1957
Old man
　WMAA. Young America 1957
Pastry window
　WMAA. Young America 1957
Piazza di Spagna
　MnMW. Expressionism 1900-1955
Sicilian altar
　IU. Contemp Amer ptg & sculp, 1955
Kinlock, Mrs Frederick. See Lowndes, Mary I'On
Kinlock, Mary I'On (Lowndes) See Lowndes, Mary I'On
Kioto, View of by J. La Farge
Kiowa encampment by S. Seymour
KIRKLAND, Vance H. 1904-
Phantasy
　IU. Contemp Amer ptg, 1952
KIRSCHENBAUM, Jules, 1929?-
Conjurer
　IU. Contemp Amer ptg & sculp, 1959
Dark in the forest
　NAD. Annual ex, 1955
Playground　　　　　　　　　　　OYB
　ICA. Annual ex, 1957
　OYB. Annual 1957
　OYB. Supplement 1959
Portrait of my father
　NAD. Annual ex, 1953
Still life with skulls
　ICA. Annual ex, 1959/60
Woman with fighting dogs
　NAD. Annual ex, 1961
The **kiss** by R. S. Du Casse
The **kiss** by C. Seliger
Kiss-me-over-the-fence by C. H. Demuth
Kissing the moon by W. Homer
Kit and kin by K. Knaths
Kitchell, Harvey, fl 1865
　Mason, B. F. Harvey Kitchell
Kitchen ball at White Sulphur Springs, Virginia, 1838 by C. Mayr
Kitchen piece by R. L. Goodwin
Kitchen table by R. D'Arista
Kitchens
　Edmonds, F. W. Real estate agent offering valuable lots
　Giobbi, E. Kitchen still life
　Lee, D. E. Thanksgiving
　Lee, D. E. Thanksgiving day
　Mintz, R. A. The kitchen
　Pippin, H. Christmas morning breakfast
　Pippin, H. Quaker mother and child
　Pippin, H. Saturday night bath
　Pippin, H. Saying prayers
　Pippin, H. Sunday morning breakfast
　Rosenfeld, E. Kitchen sink
　Sommer, W. Kitchen
The **kite** by J. W. Fosburgh
Kite fliers by L. Kester
Kitty Hawk by R. F. Gates
Eine **kleine** nachtmusik by D. Tanning
KLEINHOLZ, Frank, 1901-
Rendezvous
　IU. Contemp Amer ptg, 1952

Spring is in the air
　Cheney. Expressionism 1948 ed
Kleinholz family
　Evergood, P. Kleinholz family
KLEPPER, Max
Coaching through New Jersey, 1903
　　　　　　　　　　　　　　　　NNHS
　Davidson v2
Kline, Mr. fl 1825
　Eichholz, J. Mr Kline
KLINE, Franz Josef, 1910-
Accent grave
　MMA. New Amer ptg
　MMA. 12 Americans
　Read. Concise history
Andes
　WMAA. Annual ex, 1958
Cardinal
　Hess. Abstract ptg
　MMA. New Amer ptg
　MMA. 12 Americans
The Chief　　　　　　　　　　　　MMA
　Biddle. Yes and no
　Hess. Abstract ptg
　McCurdy
　MMA. 12 Americans
　Newmeyer
　Pousette-Dart. Amer ptg
Contrada
　PPC. International ex, 1961-62
Cross-section
　Time. 300 years
Elizabeth
　Chew. 250 years of art
Initial
　Ponente. Mod ptg, 1960
Laureline
　Baur. Nature
Leda
　PPC. International ex, 1952
Mahoning　　　　　　　　　　　WMAA
　Goodrich. Amer art
　MnMW. 60 Amer ptrs
　Pierson
New Year wall: Night
　Ponente. Mod ptg, 1960 (col)
New York　　　　　　　　　　　NBuA
　ICA. Amer artists paint the city
　NBuA. Acquisitions 1954-57
Number 2, 1954
　Cheney. Story 1958 ed
Painting, 1951
　Blesh
Painting no 2, 1954
　WMAA. New decade
Painting no 7, 1952　　　　　　　NNSG
　NNSG. Handbook
　NNSG. Younger Amer ptrs
　Pierson
　Read. Concise history
　WMAA. New decade
Painting no 11, 1953
　PPC. International ex, 1955
Requiem
　NBuA. Acquisitions 1959-1961
Siegfried　　　　　　　　　　　　PPC
　Mendelowitz
　PPC. International ex, 1958
　WMAA. Museum and its friends, 1959
Third avenue
　Hunter. Mod Amer ptg

Wanamaker block
Art since 1945
Eliot. Art of our time
MMA. New Amer ptg
MMA. 12 Americans
MnMW. Eighty works
White forms
50 years of mod art
MMA. 12 Americans

KLITGAARD, Georgina (Berrian) 1893-
Daisies
NYG. Fine art

KLONIS, Bernard, 1906-1957
Flowers from my garden   ATU
ATU. Coll of Amer art

KNAP, N. D.
The flight
NSP. Sportscapes

Knatchbull family
Copley, J. S. Sketch for the Knatchbull
family

KNATHS, Karl, 1891-
Abstract landscape
IU. Contemp Amer ptg, 1949
Adam
PPC. Ptg in the U.S. 1949
Autumn leaves   NBM
Mocsanyi. Karl Knaths
Pierson
Bach
Mocsanyi. Karl Knaths
Bananas and blue grapes   DP
Mocsanyi. Karl Knaths
Barn interior
Mocsanyi. Karl Knaths
WMAA. Four Amer expressionists
Barroom   DP
Mocsanyi. Karl Knaths
Basket bouquet
MM. Amer ptg today
Mocsanyi. Karl Knaths
Boeuf
OCl. Some contemporary works
Book, shell and ship   IaDM
CoS. New accessions USA, 1954
Mocsanyi. Karl Knaths
Captain and crew
IU. Contemp Amer ptg & sculp, 1961
Cigar box
Mocsanyi. Karl Knaths
Cin Zin   DP
Mocsanyi. Karl Knaths
UNESCO. 1860-1959
Clam-diggers   DP
DP. Catalogue
Clam-diggers, Provincetown   MM
MM. 100 Amer ptrs
Clock and bottle   IU
IU. Contemp Amer ptg, 1948
IU. 20th century
Cock and glove   DP
DP. Catalogue
Mocsanyi. Karl Knaths
Pierson
Roos
Connecticut clock   DP
DP. Catalogue
Mocsanyi. Karl Knaths (col)
Copper kettle
MnU. 40 Amer ptrs
Coq d'Or
MnMW. Classic tradition

Deer at sunset   DP
Mocsanyi. Karl Knaths (col)
Distant sail
OCl. Some contemporary work
Doomsday   NBuA
ICA. Annual ex, 1947/48
NBuA. Acquisitions 1954-57
WMAA. Four Amer expressionists
Duck decoy, 1951   DP
Mocsanyi. Karl Knaths
Duck decoy, 1954   DP
Mocsanyi. Karl Knaths (col)
Duck flight   WMAA
Baur. Revolution
Goodrich. Amer art (col)
IU. Contemp Amer ptg, 1950
Mocsanyi. Karl Knaths
Pierson
WMAA. Four Amer expressionists (col)
Dusk
Mocsanyi. Karl Knaths
WMAA. Museum and its friends, 1958
Eeling
Mocsanyi. Karl Knaths
Eliphaz   PA
Mocsanyi. Karl Knaths
First frost
OCl. Some contemporary works
Fox hunter   MoSL
MoSL. Handbook 1953
Frightened deer in moonlight   DP
DP. Catalogue
Mocsanyi. Karl Knaths
WMAA. Four Amer expressionists
Fruit and table
Leepa
Gear   InBu
Mocsanyi. Karl Knaths
NUM. Art across America
WMAA. Four Amer expressionists
Geraniums in night window   DP
Mocsanyi. Karl Knaths
Giorgione book   MMA
Mocsanyi. Karl Knaths
Green squash   DP
Mocsanyi. Karl Knaths
Harvest   DP
Bazin
DP. Catalogue
MnU. 40 Amer ptrs
Mocsanyi. Karl Knaths (col)
Read. Concise history
Havana bandana   MdBM
CoS. New accessions USA, 1956
Head of young woman   ATeS
ATeS. Collection
Horse mackerel   MoSL
Eliot. Art of our time (col)
Time. 300 years (col)
Hunters   NHMC
CoS. New accessions USA, 1960
Indian blanket   NeL
DC. 21 biennial ex, 1949
Mocsanyi. Karl Knaths
Johnny Appleseed
Mocsanyi. Karl Knaths
King cock   DP
Mocsanyi. Karl Knaths
Kit and kin   DP
DP. Catalogue
Mocsanyi. Karl Knaths

KNATHS, Karl—*Continued*
Lady
  WMAA. Four Amer expressionists
Lilacs   DP
  Mocsanyi. Karl Knaths
Lilacs and books   NR
  Mocsanyi. **Karl Knaths**
Maritime   DP
  McCurdy
  MMA. Abstract
  Mocsanyi. Karl Knaths
  Wight. Milestones
Mexican platter   WMAA
  CoS. New accessions USA, 1958
  WMAA. Four Amer expressionists
Mexican platter   DP
  DC. De gustibus
  Mocsanyi. Karl Knaths
Moby Dick
  Mocsanyi. Karl Knaths
The moon   MWM
  CoS. New accessions USA, 1952
  CSFP. Annual ex, 1950/51
  Hess. Abstract ptg
  Mocsanyi. Karl Knaths
Moonlight, harbour town   DP
  Mocsanyi. Karl Knaths
The moors   DP
  Mocsanyi. Karl Knaths (col)
Net mender   DP
  Mocsanyi. Karl Knaths
  WMAA. Four Amer expressionists
Number seven—Saul
  WMAA. Four Amer expressionists
Number zero—Adam   NBuA
  CoS. New accessions USA, 1952
  Mocsanyi. Karl Knaths
  NBuA. Expressionism
Orarian   DP
  Mocsanyi. Karl Knaths
Overhauling the trawl   DP
  Mocsanyi. Karl Knaths (col)
Pennsylvania landscape   DP
  Mocsanyi. Karl Knaths
Picasso book
  IU. Contemp Amer ptg & sculp, 1957
Pine bough   MB
  Mocsanyi. Karl Knaths
Pine timber (Pine tree)   DP
  Mocsanyi. Karl Knaths (col)
  Richardson. Ptg in America
  WMAA. Four Amer expressionists
  (col)
Pink lustre
  Mocsanyi. Karl Knaths
Provincetown jamboree
  PCC. International ex, 1950
Queen of clubs
  CSFP. Annual ex, 1948/49
  Mocsanyi. Karl Knaths
Red clock
  OCl. Some contemporary works
  Mocsanyi. Karl Knaths
  Pousette-Dart. Amer ptg
  WMAA. Four Amer expressionists
Red table   DP
  Mocsanyi. Karl Knaths
Ruined wharf   NUM
  Mocsanyi. Karl Knaths
Rye bread
  Mocsanyi. Karl Knaths

Salt flats   MnMW
  CoS. New accessions USA, 1952
  Mocsanyi. Karl Knaths
Sculling
  DC. 27 biennial ex, 1961
Sou'easter interim
  Mocsanyi. Karl Knaths
Still life (1)
  Cheney. Expressionism 1948 ed
Still life (2)   PPhM
  Mocsanyi. Karl Knaths
Store and gear   ICA
  Mocsanyi. Karl Knaths
The sun   DP
  Mocsanyi. Karl Knaths (col)
  WMAA. Four Amer expressionists
  (col)
Sunflower
  Mocsanyi. Karl Knaths
Table top
  Mocsanyi. Karl Knaths
Time, tide and town
  Mocsanyi. Karl Knaths
Tired violin
  Mocsanyi. Karl Knaths
The tower
  ICA. Annual ex, 1951
Two fishermen
  WMAA. Four Amer expressionists
White vase
  IU. Contemp Amer ptg & sculp, 1955
Winter wharf
  Baur. Nature
  Mocsanyi. Karl Knaths
KNEE, Gina, 1898-
Saturday, again
  VR. Biennial ex, 1948
        Portrait of the artist
  Brook, A. My wife
Knife Chief of the Pawnee Loups by J.
  Neagle
KNIGHT, Frederic, 1898-
Portrait of a young artist   ATU
  ATU. Coll of Amer art
Knight, Jonathan, 1789-1864
  Jocelyn, N. Jonathan Knight
KNIPSCHILD, Robert L. 1927-
Blue, white and grey
  PPC. International ex, 1952
Knockout by L. Lewitin
Knoedler's, 34th street by E. Shinn
KNOLL, Charles
        Attributed works
Panic of 1869   MeC
  Jette. Amer heritage collection
Knowles, Mildred (Buchanan)
  Sargent, J. S. Mrs Knowles and her
    children
Knox, Henry, 1750-1806
  Stuart, G. Henry Knox
Knoxville, Street in by C. G. Farr
KOCH, John, 1909-
The American boy   GAtM
  GAtM. Holbrook collection
The bridge   CSFP
  CSFP. Annual ex, 1952
  Time. 300 years (col)
Hanging clothes
  NAD. Annual ex, 1951
Interior—dining room
  NAD. Annual ex, 1957

Manuscript
  CSB. Illusion
The movers
  NAD. Annual ex, 1955
Nude with cat
  Gruskin
Stairway
  NAD. Annual ex, 1948
10 A.M.
  NAD. Annual ex, 1960
The visit
  ICA. Annual ex, 1961
KOCH, Samuel, 1887-
Orchard street, New York city   ATU
  ATU. Coll of Amer art
KOERNER, Henry, 1915-
Barker's booth
  IU. Contemp Amer ptg, 1950
The beach
  CSFP. Annual ex, 1948/49
The bridge
  PPC. Ptg in the U.S. 1949
June night
  Time. 300 years (col)
Junk yard
  PA. Annual ex, 1949
Monkey bars
  Baur. Revolution
The monument
  DC. 21 biennial ex, 1949
Mountain top
  DC. 22 biennial ex, 1951
My parents
  Time. 300 years (col)
The prophet
  IU. Contemp Amer ptg, 1949
Subway
  NAD. Annual ex, 1949, 1st half
Vanity Fair   WMAA
  Bazin
  CoS. New accessions USA, 1948
  Goodrich. Amer art
  McCurdy
  Pierson
  WMAA. Juliana Force
Winter journey
  Eliot. Art of our time (col)
KOERNER, William Henry Dethlef, 1878-
    1938
City man's vacation
  NSP. Sportscapes
KOESTER, Frederic, 1924-
Street corner, Paris
  IU. Contemp Amer ptg, 1952
KOFFLER, Mary Mintz, 1906-
Mementos
  NAD. Annual ex, 1958
Ko-kak-koo-kiss, a Towoccono warrior by
    J. M. Stanley
Konza warriors, woman and child by G.
    Catlin
KOPF, Maxim, 1892-
The star
  Genauer
KOPMAN, Benjamin, 1887-
Circus
  Brown. Amer ptg
Invasion   ATU
  ATU. Coll of Amer art
The lynching
  Cheney. Expressionism 1948 ed

Meditation
  Baur. Revolution
Portrait—Bear
  Pierson
KOPPE, Richard, 1916-
Black wires
  IU. Contemp Amer ptg, 1950
A collection of things
  IU. Contemp Amer ptg, 1948
  Roos
Fluttering fowl
  IU. Contemp Amer ptg, 1951
Primitive dance
  WMAA. Annual ex, 1953
Winged web
  PPC. International ex, 1952
Kormendi, Mrs Laszlo. See Varga, Margit
KOSA, Emil Jean, 1903-
Dark hills and white horses
  NAD. Annual ex, 1953
I'll take the high road   OT
  OT. Contemp Amer ptgs
Stepping out
  NAD. Annual ex, 1948
Summit of Antelope valley
  ICA. Annual ex, 1945/46
Kosciusko, Thaddeus. 1746-1817
  West, B. General Kosciusko
Koshares (New Mexico Indian dance series)
    by E. Bisttram
KOSKI, Ray J. 1910-
Performers   OYB
  OYB. Catalogue 1951
KOZLOW, Richard, 1926-
Palermo   OYB
  OYB. Annual 1951
  OYB. Catalogue 1951
KRAMER, Jack, 1923-
Three figures
  MBIC. View 1960
KRAMER, Paul S.
St Thomas church
  NAD. Annual ex, 1953
The scullers
  NAD. Annual ex, 1955
Krans, Beta, fl 1900
  Krans, O. Mrs Beta Krans
KRANS, Olof, 1838-1916
Indians
  Lipman. Primitive ptrs
It will soon be here
  Ford. Pictorial folk art
Mrs Beta Krans
  Lipman. Primitive ptrs
Planting corn
  Ford. Pictorial folk art
Self-portrait, c 1900
  Lipman. Primitive ptrs
Sowing grain at Bishop hill
  Lipman. Primitive ptrs
  U.S. National Capital sesquicentennial
    com
KRAUSKOPF, Bruno, 1892-
Sun on the lake
  PPC. International ex, 1952
KREIDER, Stanton, 1922-
Plexus counterplexus
  MoSL. Contemporary Amer ptg
KRIEGHOF, Cornelius, 1812-1872
Indians portaging furs
  U.S. National Capital sesquicentennial
    com

KRIESBERG, Irving, 1919-
  Birds alighting
    MMA. Fifteen
  Yellow sheep
    MMA. Fifteen
KRIMMEL, John Lewis, 1787-1821
  Country wedding   PA
    Chew. 250 years of art
    Flexner. Light of distant skies
  Election day at the State house   NNHS
    Pierson
  Election scene in front of the State house
      in Philadelphia (Independence hall)
      about 1818   PH
    Davidson v2
  Fourth of July celebration in Centre
      square, Philadelphia, 1819   PH
    Pierson
    Richardson. Ptg in America
    U.S. National Capital sesquicentennial
      com
  Fourth of July in Centre square, Philadel-
      phia, c 1810   PA
    Davidson v2
    Pierson
  Interior of an American inn   OT
    Pierson
  Parade passing Independence hall, Phila-
      delphia   MoSp
    Chew. 250 years of art
    U.S. National Capital sesquicentennial
      com
  Quilting party   DeWin
    Pierson
KROLL, Leon, 1884-
  Abandoned quarry
    NAD. Annual ex, 1960
  August serenity
    PPC. International ex, 1950
  The bridge
    Brown. Amer ptg
  Day in June
    PPC. Ptg in the U.S. 1949
  Farm in Maine   WMAA
    Larkin
    Larkin rev ed
  Hunter in the hills
    Gruskin (col)
  In the country   MiD
    Baur. Revolution
    Pierson
  Inland pool
    NAD. Annual ex, 1956
  Interior
    NAD. Annual ex, autumn 1949
  Naiad
    NAD. Annual ex, 1947, 2d half
  Nude   MM
    MM. 100 Amer ptrs
    Pierson
  Nude in rocky background
    IU. Contemp Amer ptg, 1952
  Odalisque
    NAD. Annual ex, 1958
  Reverie
    NAD. Annual ex, 1948
  Road from the cove
    Lewisohn
    Time. 300 years (col)
  Road through willows   WMAA
    Goodrich. Amer art
    McCurdy

Krum, Chester Harding
  Harding, C. Chester Harding Krum
KRUSE, Alexander Z. 1890-
  Mayor La Guardia as conductor   ATU
    ATU. Coll of Amer art
KÜHN, Justus Engelhardt, fl 1708-1717
  Eleanor Darnall   MdBH
    Barker. Amer ptg
    Flexner. First flowers
    ICA. From colony to nation
    Larkin
    Larkin rev ed
    Pierson
    Robb. Harper history
  Henry Darnall III   MdBH
    Pierson
KUHN, Robert
  Wounded wolf
    NSP. Sportscapes
KUHN, Walt, 1880-1949
  Acrobat in green   MAP
    Brown. Amer ptg
  Acrobat in white
    Cheney. Expressionism 1948 ed
    Cheney. Story 1958 ed
  Acrobat in white and blue
    CanO. Hirshhorn coll
  Apples in the hay   MMA
    Pierson
  Blue clown   WMAA
    Baur. Revolution
    Goodrich. Amer art (col)
    McCurdy
    Pierson
    Robb. Harper history
    UNESCO. 1860-1955
    UNESCO. 1860-1959
    Wight. Milestones
  Blue juggler   MoKN
    Bazin
  Caucus
    Brown. Amer ptg
  Chair with apples   NUM
    NUM. Art across America
  Clown in his dressing room   WMAA
    Pierson
  Dressing room   NBM
    Pierson
  Girl in white and silver   MM
    MM. 100 Amer ptrs
    Pierson
  Green apples and scoop
    CtY. Yale alumni
  Harlequin
    Brown. Amer ptg
  Juggler   MoKN
    MoKN. Handbook p 150
  Man with ship model
    WMAA. Pioneers
  Peaches
    IU. Contemp Amer ptg, 1948
  Roberto
    Genauer
    Larkin
    Larkin rev ed
  Trio   CoS
    Time. 300 years (col)
  Tulip buds   DP
    DP. Catalogue
  Victoria
    Brown. Amer ptg
  White clown
    Cheney. Primer 1958 ed

Young clown ATeS
 ATeS. Collection
 Mendelowitz
Young clown CoD
 Gruskin
KUNIYOSHI, Yasuo, 1893-1953
Abandoned treasures GAtM
 Goodrich. Yasuo Kuniyoshi
Amazing juggler IaDM
 Baur. New art
 IU. Contemp Amer ptg & sculp, 1953
 Pierson
 Pousette-Dart. Amer ptg
 Time. 300 years (col)
Bouquet and stove (Stove and bouquet)
 KW
 Goodrich. Yasuo Kuniyoshi
 Larkin
 Larkin rev ed
 Wight. Milestones
Bow with cow
 Lewisohn
Boy stealing fruit OCo
 Brown. Amer ptg
 Riley. Your art heritage
Café WMAA
 Goodrich. Yasuo Kuniyoshi
Carnival
 CSFP. Annual ex, 1950/51
 IU. Contemp Amer ptg, 1950
 PPC. Ptg in the U. S. 1949
The clown OYB
 OYB. Catalogue 1951
Cowgirl ATU
 ATU. Coll of Amer art
Daily news OCiM
 CoS. New accessions USA, 1960
 Goodrich. Yasuo Kuniyoshi
 Grushkin (col)
Deliverance WMAA
 Goodrich. Amer art (col)
 Goodrich. Yasuo Kuniyoshi (col)
 Myers
The dream
 Goodrich. Yasuo Kuniyoshi
Empty town in desert
 Goodrich. Yasuo Kuniyoshi
Exit MM
 MM. 100 Amer ptrs (col)
Fakirs WMAA
 CSFP. Annual ex, 1952
 NBuA. Expressionism
 WMAA. Sara Roby
Festivities ended
 Goodrich. Yasuo Kuniyoshi
Fish kite
 Baur. New art (col)
 MM. Amer ptg today
Forbidden fruit
 MnU. 40 Amer ptrs
 Pearson. Mod renaissance
 PPC. International ex, 1950
Girl on sofa ATeS
 ATeS. Collection
Girl waiting
 Cheney. Story 1958 ed
Headless horse who wants to jump MiC
 Baur. New art
 ᴅaur. Revolution
 Goodrich. Yasuo Kuniyoshi
 ICA. Annual ex, 1945/46
 McCurdy
 NUM. Art across America
 Pierson

I think so NBuA
 NBuA. Contemporary ptgs
I'm tired WMAA
 Bazin
 Goodrich. Amer art (col)
 Goodrich. Yasuo Kuniyoshi
 NYG. Fine art
 Pierson
Island of happiness WMAA
 Baur. New art
 Goodrich. Yasuo Kuniyoshi
 Pearson. Mod renaissance
Japanese toy tiger and odd objects
 Goodrich. Yasuo Kuni~oshi
 NYG. Fine art
Lay figure MnMW
 Goodrich. Yasuo Kuniyoshi
 MnU. 40 Amer ptrs
Little girl run for your life
 Goodrich. Yasuo Kuniyoshi
Little Joe with cow DC
 Baur. New art
 DC. Halpert collection
 Goodrich. Yasuo Kuniyoshi
 Pierson
Look, it flies
 CanO. Hirshhorn coll
 Goodrich. Yasuo Kuniyoshi
 Pierson
Lover's pike
 CSFP. Annual ex, 1947/48
 Goodrich. Yasuo Kuniyoshi
 IU. Contemp Amer ptg, 1948
Maine family DP
 DP. Catalogue
The mirror WMAA
 Goodrich. Yasuo Kuniyoshi
 Pearson. Mod renaissance
Mr Ace
 PPC. International ex, 1952
Mother and daughter PPC
 Goodrich. Yasuo Kuniyoshi
 MnMW. Expressionism 1900-1955
Nude
 Cheney. Primer 1958 ed
Revelation KW
 Pearson. Mod renaissance
 Pierson
Room 110 NeL
 Barker. From realism
 Goodrich. Yasuo Kuniyoshi
 Pearson. Mod renaissance
Rotting on the shore
 CSFP. Annual ex, 1948/49
 Goodrich. Yasuo Kuniyoshi
 IU. Contemp Amer ptg, 1949
Season ended
 Goodrich. Yasuo Kuniyoshi
Self-portrait as a golf player MMA
 Goodrich. Yasuo Kuniyoshi
 Roos
She mourns GAtM
 GAtM. Holbrook collection
She walks among the ruins
 Genauer
 Goodrich. Yasuo Kuniyoshi
Skating
 Cheney. Expressionism 1948 ed
Somebody tore my poster
 Baur. New art
 Goodrich. Yasuo Kuniyoshi
 WMAA. Museum and its friends, 1958
 (col)

KUNIYOSHI, Yasuo—*Continued*
Squash
  Brown. Amer ptg
Stove and bouquet. See Bouquet and stove
Strong woman and child   WMAA
  Goodrich. Yasuo Kuniyoshi
  Pierson
  WMAA. Juliana Force
Summer storm   MiD
  Goodrich. Yasuo Kuniyoshi
This is my playground
  Goodrich. Yasuo Kuniyoshi
To the ball
  ICA. Annual ex, 1951
Upside down table and mask   MMA
  Goodrich. Yasuo Kuniyoshi
Weather vane and sofa   CSB
  Goodrich. Yasuo Kuniyoshi
  Portrait of the artist
Biddle, G. Kuniyoshi, Portrait of, 1938
KUNTZ, Roger, 1927?-
Île de la Cité
  IU. Contemp Amer ptg & sculp, 1955
Los Angeles freeway
  IU. Contemp Amer ptg & sculp, 1957
KUPFERMAN, Lawrence Edward, 1909-
The fabulous crustacean   MB
  CoS. New accessions USA, 1950
Genesis
  IU. Contemp Amer ptg & sculp, 1961
Invention on a microscopic theme
  Baur. Revolution
Microscopic
  IU. Contemp Amer ptg, 1950
The tempest   IU
  IU. Contemp Amer ptg & sculp, 1953
  IU. 20th century
Walden pond
  Pousette-Dart. Amer ptg
Worship at Eleusis
  MBIC. View 1960
KURZ, Friedrich, b 1818
Minnetarees on Upper Missouri   MCH
  McCracken. Portrait of the old west
  (col)
KUUSI, Helmi, 1913-
Shepherd's eve
  UNESCO. 1860-1949
Kwaunon by J. La Farge

L

L., H. B. fl 1861
Conflagration in a city on the eastern
  seaboard, 1861
  U.S. National Capital sesquicentennial
  com
Laboratory by M. Beckmann
Laboratory of Thomas Price by H. Alexan-
  der
Laboratory report by J. Ernst
Labrador ducks by M. Hartley
Labyrinth by S. Fogel
Labyrinth by A. Gottlieb
Labyrinth by J. O'Neil
Labyrinth by B. Shahn
Labyrinth by R. Vickrey
La Casse, Margaret. See Annesley, Mar-
  garet (La Casse)

Lace cap by S. F. B. Morse
Lace gables by C. E. Burchfield
LACHOWICZ, William, 1925?-
Signal   OYB
  OYB. Annual 1956
  OYB. Supplement 1959
Lackawanna valley by G. Inness
Lacrosse playing among the Sioux by S.
  Eastman
A **lad** from the fleet by F. Martin
The **ladder** by J. C. Wayne
Ladies in waiting by H. Mandel
Ladies of the evening by R. Philipp
The **ladle** by J. Marin
Ladson, James, 1753-1812
  Malbone, E. G. Major James Ladson
Ladson, Judith (Smith) 1762-1820
  Malbone, E. G. Mrs James Ladson
Ladson, Mary. See Cattel, Mary (Ladson)
Ladson, Sarah Reeve, 1790-1866
  Malbone, E. G. Sarah Reeve Ladson
Lady and gentleman by D. Goldsmith
Lady and her son by J. Vanderlyn
Lady at the tea table by M. Cassatt
Lady holding a book by H. P. Hunt
Lady in a dark blue dress by S. L. Waldo
  and W. Jewett
Lady in a fine scarf by W. M. Prior (man-
  ner of)
Lady in a landscape by J. Brewster (at-
  tributed works)
Lady in a sheer white cap by R. H. M.
  Bascom
Lady in black by W. M. Chase
Lady in pink skirt by M. B. Prendergast
Lady in purple by M. B. Prendergast
Lady in the greenwood by D. Austin
Lady in white bonnet by Unidentified artist
Lady in yellow by T. W. Dewing
Lady Jean by G. W. Bellows
Lady of eleven by Y. Tanguy
Lady of the lake by H. Pippin
Lady of the lake by Unidentified artist
Lady of the Lange Lijsen by J. A. M.
  Whistler
Lady on a balcony in Rome by C. W. Chap-
  man
Lady on a wet day by M. B. Prendergast
Lady playing guitar by W. M. Chase
Lady wearing a red pompon by A. Fuller
Lady with a blue veil by J. S. Sargent
Lady with a harp by T. Sully
Lady with a nosegay by A. Ellis
Lady with a rose by Unidentified artist
Lady with a setter dog by T. Eakins
Lady with a white shawl by W. M. Chase
Lady with brown eyes by Unidentified artist
Lady with curls by Unidentified artist
Lady with fan by W. M. Chase
Lady with fan by N. Tschacbasov
Lady with lavender ribbons by Unidentified
  artist
Lady with plumed headdress by Unidentified
  artist

LA FARGE, John—*Continued*
Uncanny badger
  WiMiA. Amer ptg 1760-1960
View of Kioto   MB
  MB. Ptgs in water color
LA FARGE, John, 1835-1910 and **LOW,
  Will H.,** 1853-1932
Decorative panel   MB
  MB. Ptgs in water color
LA FARGE, Louis Bancel, 1866-1938
Breakers   MB
  MB. Ptgs in water color
Seashore   MB
  MB. Ptgs in water color
Lafayette, Marie Joseph Paul Yves Roch
  Gilbert du Motier, marquis de, 1757-
  1834
Morse, S. F. B. Lafayette
Peale, C. W. Washington, Lafayette, and
  Tench Tilghman
Reed, R. L. Washington and Lafayette at
  the battle of Yorktown
Lafayette hotel by J. Sloan
Laffite, Jean, c 1780-c 1825
Jarvis, J. W. The pirate Laffite
The Lagoon, Venice by M. B. Prendergast
The Lagoon, Venice by J. A. M. Whistler
La Guardia, Fiorello Henry, 1882-1947
Kruse, A. Z. Mayor La Guardia as con-
  ductor
LAHEY, Richard Francis, 1893-
Easter morning on Eye street
  DC. 22 biennial ex, 1951
Paula
  NAD. Annual ex, 1947, 1st half
Ruth Ann
  PPC. Ptg in the U. S. 1949
Laight, Edward, fl 1802
Malbone, E. G. Edward Laight
Lair of the sea serpent by E. Vedder
The lake by W. D. Fausett
The lake by J. Hultberg
Lake Albano by G. Inness
Lake and mountain scene by A. J. Miller
Lake Concordia and aboriginal tumuli by
  J. J. Egan
Lake Erie, Battle of, 1812
Garneray, A. L. Battle of Lake Erie
Lake George by A. B. Durand
Lake George by M. J. Heade
Lake George by J. K. Kensett
Lake George by A. H. Wyant
Lake George and Caldwell village, A view
  by E. Ames
Lake George barns by G. O'Keeffe
Lake George, coat and red by G. O'Keeffe
Lake George near Caldwell, New York by
  R. Smith
Lake George, Perspective painting of by E.
  Ames
Lake George window by G. O'Keeffe
A lake in the mountains, View of by G. C.
  Bingham
Lake in wooded country: sunset by B. West
  (attributed works)
Lake landscape by A. Rattner
Lake Lure by J. Pike
Lake Maggiore, Italy by E. D. Boit

Lake of Nemi by J. F. Cropsey
Lake Orta, Italy by E. D. Boit
Lake Sanford in the Adirondacks by H. D.
  Martin
Lake scene—Mountains of the winds by A.
  J. Miller
Lake scene, Rocky mountains by A. J. Mil-
  ler
Lake scene, Wind river mountains by A. J.
  Miller
Lake Tahoe, California by A. Bierstadt
Lake, Tunk mountain by J. Marin
Lakes and mountains by A. Fisher (attrib-
  uted works)
LAM, Jennette, 1911-
Cathedral in the woods
  IU. Contemp Amer ptg & sculp, 1961
LAMB, A. A. fl 1865
Emancipation proclamation   DN
  DN. Amer primitive ptgs, pt 1
The lamb by L. Gatch
LAMBDIN, George Cochran, 1830-1896
The pruner   MB
  Chew. 250 years of art
  MB. Karolik coll
LAMBDIN, James Reid, 1807-1889
John Penn (copy of ptg by Pine)   PH
  Chew. 250 years of art
Ulysses S. Grant   PA
  Chew. 250 years of art
Lambertville pietà by L. Gatch
Laming, Benjamin
Peale, C. W. Benjamin Laming and wife
LA MORE, Chet, 1908-
Segment of the garden
  PPC. Ptg in the U. S. 1949
LAMOTTE, Bernard, 1903-
Nogent-le-Rotrou
  IU. Contemp Amer ptg, 1949
Rue de Crimée
  CSFP. Annual ex, 1947/48
Lamplight by R. Soyer
The lamplight portrait by C. W. Peale
Lamplighter, New York, 1806 by **W. P.**
  Chappel
LANCASTER, Robert L.
Staccato for dormers   OYB
  OYB. Annual 1953
Lancaster by C. H. Demuth
LAND, Jerome
Passover supper
  OYB. Annual 1948
Land and seawater scape by Unidentified
  artist
Land of Evangeline by J. R. Meeker
Land of promise, Castle garden, New York
  by C. F. Ulrich
Land of the bright sun by R. Rosenborg
Land speculator by J. H. Beard
Landing the charettes by A. J. Miller
Lands End, Cornwall by W. T. Richards
Land's end, Golden gate, California by H.
  G. Keller
Lands end road by C. F. Gaertner
Landscape by R. Abrams
Landscape by R. Amft
Landscape by R. A. Blakelock
Landscape by W. M. Chase

Landscape by T. Cole
Landscape by A. Dasburg
Landscape by S. Davis
Landscape by T. Doughty
Landscape by A. G. Dove
Landscape by A. B. Durand
Landscape by I. Engel
Landscape by K. E. Fortess
Landscape by O. E. S. Frinck
Landscape by W. Hegelheimer
Landscape by E. Hicks
Landscape by R. Jacobi
Landscape by R. King
Landscape by H. E. Mattson
Landscape by A. H. Maurer
Landscape by W. Pachner
Landscape by C. Sheeler
Landscape by J. H. Twachtman
Landscape by M. Weber
Landscape, Bornholm by G. Grosz
Landscape, evening by 'W. Allston
Landscape for contemplation by L. Manso
Landscape forms by R. Rosenborg
Landscape from above by C. Wells
Landscape, house on cliff above pool by T. Doughty
Landscape in construction by S. Laufman
Landscape in five flats by A. G. Dove
Landscape in grey by X. Gonzáles
Landscape in ivory by E. Edwards
Landscape in Maine by J. Marin
Landscape near Chicago by A. Bohrod
Landscape, New Mexico by M. Hartley
Landscape no 29, 1907? by M. Hartley
Landscape no 32, 1911 by M. Hartley
Landscape no 36 by M. Hartley
Landscape of Provence by E. Bruce
Landscape of the absolute by I. R. Pereira
Landscape table by A. Gorky
Landscape, the ferry by T. Doughty
Landscape II, 1953 by P. Wonner
Landscape, Venice by M. Hartley
Landscape with a broken tree by K. H. Miller
Landscape with a farmhouse by S. Gallagher
Landscape with a lake by W. Allston
Landscape with a mirror by R. Hamilton
Landscape with bird's nest by D. Forbes
Landscape with blue-violet by W. Rakocy
Landscape with brook by A. C. Goodwin
Landscape with cattle by G. C. Bingham
Landscape with cattle by G. H. Durrie
Landscape with cattle by G. Inness jr
Landscape with cow by B. West
Landscape with drying sails by S. Davis
Landscape with factory by M. Beckmann
Landscape with farm by A. H. Maurer
Landscape with figures by R. L. Loftin
Landscape with figures by W. S. Mount

Landscape with fisherman and sailboat by T. Doughty
Landscape with fishermen by T. Doughty
Landscape with flowers by P. Blume
Landscape with houseboat by J. J. Jones
Landscape with houses by H. L. McFee
Landscape with letters by K. Zerbe
Landscape with mansion and white mantel by H. Pittman
Landscape with mountains by H. W. Rice
Landscape with polo players by P. Hunt
Landscape with poppies by P. Blume
Landscape with potted plant in foreground by Zalmar
Landscape with rider by J. Pollock
Landscape with scrap metal III by K. Zerbe
Landscape with still life by L. Johnson
Landscape with sunflowers by N. Cikovsky
Landscape with swans by J. Jones
Landscape with tree trunks by T. Cole
LANE, Fitz Hugh, 1804-1865
  At the fishing grounds   MB
    MB. Lane
  Brace's rock, Eastern point, Gloucester
                            MB
    MB. Karolik coll
    MB. Lane
  Brig Antelope in Boston harbor   MB
    MB. Karolik coll
    MB. Lane
  Fresh water cove from Dolliver's neck, Gloucester   MB
    MB. Karolik coll
    MB. Lane
    Pierson
  Gloucester from Brookbank   MB
    MB. Karolik coll
    MB. Lane
  Ipswich bay   MB
    MB. Lane
  Maine inlet   MB
    MB. Karolik coll
    MB. Lane
    Pierson
  New England coast shipping
    OCiM. Rediscoveries
  New York harbor   MB
    MB. Karolik coll
    MB. Lane
  Off Mount Desert island   NBM
    Baur. Amer ptg
  Owl's head, Penobscot bay, Maine   MB
    MB. Karolik coll
    MB. Lane
    Time. 300 years (col)
  Ships in ice off Ten Pound island, Gloucester   MB
    MB. Karolik coll
    MB. Lane
    Mendelowitz
    Pierson
  View of Gloucester from Rocky Neck
    NUM. Art across America
Lang, Florence O. R.
  Seyffert, L. Florence O. R. Lang
Lang, Mrs Henry. See Lang, Florence O. R.

Langhorne, Pennsylvania, c 1845
  Hicks, E. Residence of David Twining, 1787
Langsdorf, Mrs Alexander jr. See Martyl (Suzanne Schweig)
Languid leisure by W. Sommer
LANING, Edward, 1906-
  Farewell to Pisa
    ICA. Annual ex, 1945/46
  The house
    WMAA. Contemp Amer ptg, 1952
  Learning to read   NNPL
    Gruskin (col)
  Medieval scribe   NNPL
    Gruskin (col)
  Moses with the tablets of the law NNPL
    Gruskin (col)
  Mural   NNPL
    NAD. Annual ex 1946, 2d half
Lansing, John, 1754-1829
  Ames, E. John Lansing jr
LANYON, Ellen, 1926-
  Cal-Sag
    IU. Contemp Amer ptg & sculp, 1957
  Terminal
    IU. Contemp Amer ptg & sculp, 1953
Lapowinsa by G. Hesselius
Laramie, Fort. See Fort Laramie
Large collage by R. B. Motherwell
Large encampment north of the Cut rocks by A. J. Miller
Large olive grove by W. Kahn
A **large** picture which is a landscape by Y. Tanguy
Large vertical by I. Bolotowsky
Large white flag by J. Johns
Large white nude by J. Sloan
Larned, George, fl 1825
  Tuthill, A. G. D. Col George Larned
Larned children, fl 1825
  Tuthill, A. G. D. Sylvester, Julia, Jane and Catherine Larned
Larpolo by J. D. Brooks
Larrabee, John, 1686-1762
  Badger, J. Capt John Larrabee
Larry's creek, West branch, Susquehanna by R. Smith
Lasher, Caim
  Speicher, E. E. Caim Lasher
LASKER, Joseph L. 1919-
  From an ivory tower
    IU. Contemp Amer ptg, 1952
  Little match girl
    IU. Contemp Amer ptg, 1951
  Naples   WMAA
    Goodrich. Amer art
  Sticks and stones
    CSFP. Annual ex, 1952
  Wallscape
    NAD. Annual ex, 1957
The **lasso** by W. T. Ranney
The **last** days by Y. Tanguy
The **last** Don Quixote by A. Rattner
The **last** king by J. Levine
Last of New England—beginning of New Mexico by M. Hartley
Last of old Westminster by J. A. M. Whistler
Last of the buffalo by A. Bierstadt

Last of the herd by C. M. Russell
Last of the lighthouse by J. E. Levi
Last of the Mohicans by T. Cole
Last parable by C. S. Chapman
Last snow by W. C. Palmer
Last stop by S. Wilson
The **last** supper by D. Aronson
The **last** supper by R. Arthur
The **last** supper by G. Hesselius
Late afternoon by R. Vickrey
Late afternoon—Calm on the Erie canal by G. Harvey
Late afternoon, Montclair, New Jersey by G. Inness
Late again by C. Blanchard
Late edition by C. Osver
Late summer by T. Birch
Latest news by M. Weber
Lathom, Lady Wilma (Radnor) countess of, 1869-1931
  Sargent, J. S. The countess of Lathom
LATHROP, Betsy B. fl 1812
  Japhthah's return   VWR
    VWR. Folk art (col)
LATHROP, William Langson, 1859-1938
  Muskrat hunter   PR
    PR. Catalogue
LATROBE, Benjamin Henry, 1766-1820
  East front of the President's house, with the addition of the North and South porticos, 1807   DLC
    Davidson v2
  Roman Catholic church, Baltimore, c 1805
    Davidson v2
LAUFMAN, Sidney, 1891-
  Along the path
    NAD. Annual ex, 1953
  Clayton's pasture
    IU. Contemp Amer ptg, 1948
  Deer Tongue lane   InIJ
    InIJ. 105 ptgs
  From the terrace
    MM. Amer ptg today
  Grove of trees
    NAD. Annual ex, 1958
  House in the pines   OT
    OT. Contemp Amer ptgs
  House in the woods
    DC. 22 biennial ex, 1951
  The path
    PA. Annual ex, 1951
  Pines   OYB
    OYB. Annual 1954
    OYB. Supplement
  Plowed field
    NYG. Fine art
  Spring landscape
    Gruskin
  Through the woods
    IU. Contemp Amer ptg & sculp, 1957
  Trees
    IU. Contemp Amer ptg, 1951
  Vernal
    NAD. Annual ex, 1960
  View from the terrace
    NAD. Annual ex, 1952
Laughing child by R. Henri
Laughing waters by S. Eastman
Laughing worker by P. Evergood

Laughton, Charles, 1899-1962
  Martin, F. Charles Laughton as Captain
    Kidd
Launching by G. W. Bellows
Laurel blossoms in vase by J. Marin
Laurel in the ledges by C. Hassam
Laurel run by E. W. Redfield
Laureline by F. J. Kline
Laurens, Eleanor (Ball) See Ball, Eleanor
Laurens, Mrs Henry. See Ball, Eleanor
Laurens, Tryntje. See Provost, Tryntje
    (Laurens)
LAURENT, John, 1921-
  From Mount Agamenticus—fall
    IU. Contemp Amer ptg & sculp, 1959
Laurent pony cart by B. Karfiol
LAVALLE, John, 1896-1940?
  Botafogo bay, Rio de Janeiro   MB
    MB. Ptgs in water color
Lavender and old lace by C. E. Burchfield
Lavender mist by J. Pollock
Law court by J. C. Wayne
LAWMAN, Jasper Holman, 1825-1906
  Snyder's Hollow   PPC
    Chew. 250 years of art
Lawn and sky by S. Davis
Lawrence, Mr, fl 1803
  Malbone, E. G. Mr Lawrence
LAWRENCE, A. A. fl 1852
  Boat race, Boston harbor (Boat race be-
    tween Harvard boat clubs in Boston
    harbor)   MB
    MB. Karolik coll
Lawrence, Amos, fl 1845
  Harding, C. Amos Lawrence
Lawrence, Harriet, 1793-1870. See Peirson,
    Harriet (Lawrence)
Lawrence, Harriet, fl 1890. See Hemenway,
    Harriet (Lawrence)
LAWRENCE, Jacob, 1917-
  Blind beggars   MM
    MM. 100 Amer ptrs
  Café scene   ATU
    ATU. Coll of Amer art
    Gruskin (col)
  Catfish row
    Pearson. Mod renaissance
  Chess on Broadway
    ICA. Amer artists paint the city
  Depression, 1950
    Baur. New art
  Florist's window
    IU. Contemp Amer ptg, 1952
  Fulton and Nostrand
    WMAA. Annual ex, 1958
  Ices
    IU. Contemp Amer ptg & sculp, 1961
  Magic man
    IU. Contemp Amer ptg & sculp, 1959
  Masks
    IU. Contemp Amer ptg & sculp, 1955
  Migration of the Negro   MMA
    McCurdy
  Most of the people are very poor
    Larkin
    Larkin rev ed
  Seamstress
    Baur. New art

Sedation   MMA
  Pierson
Shipping out   WMAA
  Goodrich. Amer art
Slums, 1951
  Baur. New art (col)
Tombstones   WMAA
  Baur. New art
  Bazin
  Pierson
Vaudeville
  Eliot. Art of our time (col)
  Pearson. Mod renaissance
  Time. 300 years (col)
War series: another patrol   WMAA
  Goodrich. Amer art
  Pierson
Woman at work (Migration of the Negro
    series)   DP
  DP. Catalogue
You can buy whiskey for twenty-five
    cents a quart
  Pearson. Mod renaissance
Lawrence, Rachel (Longfield) 1689-1768
  Unidentified artist. Mrs Thomas Lawrence
Lawrence, Thomas, 1689-1754
  Unidentified artist. Thomas Lawrence
Lawrence, William Augustus
  Morse, S. F. B. William Augustus Law-
    rence
LAWSON, Ernest, 1873-1939
  After rain   DP
    DP. Catalogue
    Glackens
  Boat house, winter, Harlem river   DC
    Larkin
    Larkin rev ed
  Early spring
    NSyE. The eight
  Early summer, Vermont   OCo
    Pierson
  Harlem river   NJN
    NBuA. Fifty ptgs
  High bridge   WMAA
    Bazin
    Goodrich. Amer art
  May in the mountains   DP
    DP. Catalogue
  Misty day in March   OYB
    OYB. Catalogue 1951
  Old mill   InIJ
    InIJ. 105 ptgs
  Spring night, Harlem river   DP
    Born
    CSB. Impressionism
    DP. Catalogue
    McCurdy
    Pierson
  Sunset, High bridge   DP
    Cheney. Story 1958 ed
    DP. Catalogue
  The valley   OCo
    Brown. Amer ptg
  Winter   MM
    MM. 100 Amer ptrs
  Winter, Central park, New York   ATeS
    ATeS. Collection
  Winter on the river   WMAA
    Pierson
Lay figure by Y. Kuniyoshi
Layered by J. Albers

LAYTON, Gloria
Easter bonnet
NAD. Annual ex, 1954
The **leader** by W. M. Chase
The **leaf** of the artichoke is an owl by A.
Gorky
Leaning figure by M. Weber
Leaping figure by S. W. Hayter
Leaping trout by W. Homer
Learning to read by E. Laning
Leatherstocking kills the panther (il for
Cooper's Pioneers) by G. L. Brown
Leave it to the experts by P. Evergood
Leavens, Harriet, fl 1815
Border limner. Harriet Leavens
Leaves in Weehawken by W. De Kooning
Leaving the manor house by Unidentified
artist
LEAVITT, Joseph Warren, fl 1825
At Loudon, New Hampshire
Ford. Pictorial folk art
House of Moses Morse, Loudon, New
Hampshire
Pierson
Lebanon, Buildings at by C. Sheeler
LEBDUSKA, Lawrence H. 1894-
California farm   ATU
ATU. Coll of Amer art (col)
Lebrun, Federico. See Lebrun, Rico
LEBRUN, Rico, 1900-1964
Anna
NYG. Fine art
Buchenwald cart   PA
OCl. Some contemporary works
The bull ring   MM
MM. 100 Amer ptrs
Burnt spinner
IU. Contemp Amer ptg, 1951
Centurion's horse
MM. Amer ptg today
Pearson. Mod renaissance
Crucifixion   NSyE
IU. Contemp Amer ptg & sculp, 1957
Mendelowitz
Crucifixion triptych
Baur. New art
Dachau chamber, Study for
Selz. New images (col)
Double disparate
Selz. New images
Dying steer
IU. Contemp Amer ptg & sculp, 1959
Farm machine no 1, 1947
MnU. 40 Amer ptrs
Figure in the rain   MMA
Baur. New art (col)
Figures on the cross with lantern   CoD
CoS. New accessions USA, 1958
PA. Annual ex, 1953
Imploring dead
IU. Contemp Amer ptg & sculp, 1961
The Magdalene
Pearson. Mod renaissance
Migration to nowhere
Baur. New art
Mocking soldier   IU
IU. Contemp Amer ptg, 1949
IU. 20th century
Pilgrim with flowered hat
PPC. International ex, 1955

Rooster on arm of the cross   MoSL
Baur. New art
MnMW. Expressionism 1900-1955
NBuA. Expressionism
Pousette-Dart. Amer ptg
PPC. International ex, 1952
VR. Amer ptg, 1954
Shell of Mary
Baur. Revolution
Still life, melons   CSB
CoS. New accessions USA, 1946
Study for a soldier   CLA
CoS. New accessions USA, 1950
Vertical composition
Pearson. Mod renaissance
Wight. Milestones
Woman of the crucifixion   NeL
Barker. From realism
CoS. New accessions USA, 1952
ICA. Annual ex, 1951
MnU. 40 Amer ptgs
Wood of the holy cross   WMAA
Goodrich. Amer art
Pierson

Portrait of the artist
Berman, E. Rico Lebrun
LECHAY, James, 1907-
Blue is for bass
CSFP. Annual ex, 1952
IU. Contemp Amer ptg, 1951
Chinatown, Maw Wah
WMAA. Annual ex, 1955
Dark sky—dark water
VR. Biennial ex, 1948
Harbor with red for Mary Lou   OCl
CoS. New accessions USA, 1954
Hudson river   ATU
ATU. Coll of Amer art
LE CLEAR, Thomas, 1818-1882
Buffalo newsboy   NBuA
Baur. Amer ptg
NBuA. Catalogue of the ptgs
NJN. Early N.J. artists
Pierson
Leda by F. J. Kline
Leda in high places by P. Evergood
Lee, A. W.
Eakins, T. A. W. Lee
Lee, Anne (Theus) b 1750
Theus, J. Mrs William Lee
LEE, Doris (Emrick) 1905-
Badminton
IU. Contemp Amer ptg, 1952
Pearson. Mod renaissance
Costumes for Dragonwyck
Pearson. Mod renaissance
Country wedding   NBuA
Gruskin (col)
NBuA. Contemporary ptgs
The runaway   ATU
ATU. Coll of Amer art (col)
Sappho
IU. Contemp Amer ptg & sculp, 1955
Shelves
PPC. International ex, 1952
Siesta   PPC
Pearson. Mod renaissance
Summer   NBuA
NBuA. Acquisitions 1957-58
Thanksgiving   ICA
NYG. Fine art

Thanksgiving day
  Pearson. Mod renaissance
Winter in the Catskills
  NYG. Fine art
Lee, Geraldine
  Bellows, G. W. Geraldine Lee
Lee, Jeremiah, 1721-1775
  Copley, J. S. Jeremiah Lee
Lee, Mrs Jeremiah, fl 1769
  Copley, J. S. Mrs Jeremiah Lee
LEE, Joseph, fl 1870
  Alameda shore   CSFD
  Born
  Oak Knoll, Napa   CSFD
  Born
  Pierson
Lee, Robert Edward, 1807-1870
  Healy, G. P. A. Robert E. Lee
LEE, Robert J.
  Trombone player   MSM
  CoS. New accessions USA, 1956
Lee, Vernon, pseud. See Paget, Violet
Lee, Mrs William. See Lee, Anne (Theus)
Lee shore by E. Hopper
Leeds, Lucy (Orcutt) fl 1840
  Unidentified artist. Lucy Orcutt Leeds
    and her son
LEEPA, Allen, 1919-
  Composition in red, yellow and blue
    Leepa
  Curved composition in yellow, red and
    blue
    Leepa
  Nude
    Leepa
  Still life in green
    Leepa
  Still life in red, yellow, white and blue
    Leepa
  Tree
    Leepa
LEE-SMITH, Hughie
  Old man and youth
    NAD. Annual ex, 1959
Leffingwell, Sally (Beers) fl 1807
  Jarvis, J. W. Mrs William Leffingwell
Leffingwell, William, 1765-1834
  Jarvis, J. W. William Leffingwell
Lefort, Henri, b 1852
  Sargent, J. S. Henri Lefort
Legareville, South Carolina by P. A. Tren-
  holm
Le Havre by F. Boggs
Lehigh canal, sunset, New Hope, Pennsyl-
  vania by J. Pickett
Leidy, Joseph, 1866-1942
  Eakins, T. Man with red necktie (Dr
    Joseph Leidy jr)
LEIGH, William Robinson, 1866-1955
  Baking day
    Carlson. Gallery (col)
  Combing the ridges
    Carlson. Gallery (col)
  Female of the species
    Carlson. Gallery (col)
  Home sweet home
    Carlson. Gallery (col)
  A lowdown trick
    Time. 300 years (col)
  The mystic
    Carlson. Gallery (col)

The rescue
  Carlson. Gallery (col)
Voice of the desert
  Carlson. Gallery (col)
Leila by A. K. Stoddard
Leisler, Hester. See Rynders, Hester
  (Leisler)
Leisler, Mary. See Gouverneur, Mary
  (Leisler)
Leisure and labor by F. B. Mayer
Leman, Margaret Adelia, fl 1825
  Eichholtz, J. Margaret Adelia Leman
Lemons and sugar by Rubens Peale
Lenna and Imp by W. J. Glackens
Lenox, Althea. See Donaldson, Althea
  (Lenox)
Lenox, Elizabeth Sproat. See Maitland,
  Elizabeth Sproat (Lenox)
Lenox, James, 1772-1839
  Jarvis, J. W. James Lenox
Lenox, James, 1800-1880
  Unidentified artist. James Lenox
Lenox, Rachel (Carmer) 1763-1843
  Inman, H. Mrs Robert Lenox
  Trumbull, J. Mrs Robert Lenox
  Unidentified artist. Mrs Robert Lenox
  Unidentified artist. Mrs Robert Lenox
    (possibly a copy of Inman portrait)
Lenox, Robert, 1759-1839
  Thibault, A. Robert Lenox
  Trumbull, J. Robert Lenox
  Unidentified artist. Robert Lenox (after
    Jarvis)
Lenox, Mrs Robert. See Lenox, Rachel
  (Carmer)
Lenox family, Member of
  Thibault, A. Lady of the Lenox family
Leona by J. Arkush
Leonardo by C. L. Cicero
LEONID (Leonid Berman) 1896-
  Drying codfish in Brittany
    ICA. Annual ex, 1951
  Entretat, le Cabestan Capstan   CtHW
    Pierson
  Fish weir, Maine
    ICA. Annual ex, 1954
  Fish weir near Sprucehead
    WMAA. Contemp Amer ptg, 1953
  The fisherwoman   MMA
    MMA. Soby collection
  Fishing shrimps at Boulogne   NJN
    CoS. New accessions USA, 1956
  Malamocco   MMA
    McCurdy
    Pierson
  Mussel gatherers at high tide   MMA
    MMA. Soby collection
  Narragansett bay
    VR. Amer ptg, 1954
  Port Jefferson   MoKN
    MoKN. Handbook p 150
  Portuguese sea
    CSFP. Annual ex, 1948/49
  Provincetown
    IU. Contemp Amer ptg, 1952
    Pousette-Dart. Amer ptg
  Rice field near Milan
    WMAA. Annual ex, 1955
LeRoy, Daniel, 1761-1791
  Unidentified artist. Daniel LeRoy

LEROY, Elizabeth (Emmet) fl 1815-1830
Robert Fulton   MWA
    MWA. Checklist of portraits
Le Roy, New York by Unidentified artist
Leroy's shift by S. Davis
LESLIE, Alfred, 1928-
Baby's curse   MnMW
    MMA. Sixteen
    MnMW. 60 Amer ptrs
Four-panel green
    MMA. Sixteen
Hialeah   NBuA
    NBuA. Acquisitions 1959-1961
Money
    PPC. International ex, 1961/62
Number 25
    WMAA. Contemp Amer ptg, 1959/60
The second two-panel horizontal
    MMA. Sixteen
Soldier's medal   NBuA
    NBuA. Acquisitions 1959-1961
LESLIE, Charles Robert, 1794-1859
Actors' duel: Mr Jefferson and Mr. Blis-
    sett
    Flexner. Light of distant skies
Murder of Rutland   PA
    Flexner. Light of distant skies
Personification of murder   MdBMu
    MdBMu. Rendezvous
Sophia Western   PA
    Flexner. Light of distant skies
Leslie by C. Buck
Lesseps, Ferdinand Marie, viscount de, 1805-
    1894
    Healy, G .P. A. Ferdinand de Lesseps
The **lesson** by J. S. Sargent
Lesson I, 1956 by S. Davis
LESTER, William, 1910-
College on the hill
    CSFP. Annual ex, 1952
Old Fort Davis   TxF
    Pousette-Dart. Amer ptg
Lesueur, Charles Alexandre
    Peale, C. W. Charles Alexandre Lesueur
Let us pray by W. Pachner
Let's search our souls by J. Berlandina
The **letter** by M. Avery
The **letter** by T. W. Dewing
The **letter** by R. L. Newman
Letter home by E. Johnson
Letter rack with jack of hearts by J. F.
    Peto
Letter rack with Lerado postmark by J. F.
    Peto
Letty in leghorn by R. Philipp
LEUTZE, Emanuel, 1816-1868
Course of empire
    Barker. Amer ptg
Gulch mine, Central city, Colorado CoDP
    Rathbone
Washington crossing the Delaware
    Davidson v 1
Westward the course of empire takes its
    way   DN
    Pierson
Levant for E. W. R. by T. Stamos
Levant no 7 by T. Stamos
LEVEE, John, 1924-
April 1, 1957
    Read. Concise history

May 2, 1956
    WMAA. Young America 1957
Painting
    PPC. International ex, 1955
September 1, 1956
    WMAA. Young America 1957
The **levee** by J. W. Taylor
LEVER, Hayley, 1876-1958
Beach at St Ives, Cornwall, England
                          NJMo
    NJMo. Forty years
Still life
    NAD. Annual ex, 1959
Lever, Richard Hayley. See Lever, Hayley
LEVI, Julian Edwin, 1900-
Autobiography
    CSFP. Annual ex, 1947/48
Beachcomber
    Gruskin (col)
The garden
    ICA. Annual ex, 1961
Iron dragon
    IU. Contemp Amer ptg & sculp, 1955
    NAD. Annual ex, 1956
Last of the lighthouse   NJN
    Pierson
Margaret Boni playing the recorder NBuA
    NBuA. Contemporary ptgs
Poseidon
    IU. Contemp Amer ptg & sculp, 1959
Red pastoral   MiD
    CoS. New accessions USA, 1958
Sand and sky
    PPC. Ptg in the U.S. 1949
Ship graveyard
    Baur. Revolution
Strata
    IU. Contemp Amer ptg & sculp, 1961
Tarring nets   ATU
    ATU. Coll of Amer art
Tidewater shapes
    IU. Contemp Amer ptg, 1948
Weir
    IU. Contemp Amer ptg, 1951
The widow
    IU. Contemp Amer ptg, 1949
LEVINE, David, 1927?-
Preliminary examination
    ICA. Annual ex, 1961
LEVINE, Jack, 1915-
Apteka
    DC. 20 biennial ex, 1947
    ICA. Amer artists paint the city
    MBIC. Jack Levine
    PA. Annual ex, 1948
The banquet
    MBIC. Jack Levine
    WMAA. Neuberger collection
Black freighter
    IU. Contemp Amer ptg & sculp, 1959
Card players
    Lewisohn
City lights
    MnU. 40 Amer ptrs
Coronation
    MnU. 40 Amer ptrs
Courtroom study
    IU. Contemp Amer ptg & sculp, 1955
Dramatis personae   ATU
    ATU. Coll of Amer art

Election night   MMA
  CoS. New accessions USA, 1956
  PPC. International ex, 1955
  Time. 300 years (col)
Euclid avenue
  WMAA. Contemp Amer ptg, 1950
Feast of pure reason   MMA
  Baur. New art
  Cheney. Story 1958 ed
  Larkin
  Larkin rev ed
  MBIC. Jack Levine
  McCurdy
  MMA. Masters
  Myers
  Read. Concise history
  Roos
  Seiberling
Gangster funeral   WMAA
  Baur. New art
  Goodrich. Amer art (col)
  Larkin rev ed (col detail)
  Pierson
Gangster's funeral, Study for
  NUM. Art across America
A girl
  CanO. Hirshhorn coll
Girls from Fleugel street
  DC. 26 biennial ex, 1959
Homage to Boston
  IU. Contemp Amer ptg, 1951
  MBIC. Jack Levine
  PPC. International ex, 1950
Improvisation in a Greek key
  IU. Contemp Amer ptg, 1950
Inauguration   WMAA
  WMAA. Sara Roby
The judge
  PA. Annual ex, 1956
King Josiah
  Munsterberg
King Saul
  Eliot. Art of our time (col)
  Time. 300 years (col)
The last king
  DC. 21 biennial ex, 1949
Love, oh careless love
  ICA. Annual ex, 1959/60
  OYB. Annual 1959
Magician
  CSFP. Annual ex, 1948/49
  IU. Contemp Amer ptg, 1948
Medicine show IV   KW
  CoS. New accessions USA, 1960
Neighborhood physician   MnMW
  MnMW. Expressionism 1900-1955
The passing scene   MMA
  MBIC. Jack Levine
Pawnshop
  MBIC. Jack Levine
Pensionnaire   NeL
  Barker. From realism
  CoS. New accessions USA, 1946
Reception in Miami
  IU. Contemp Amer ptg, 1949
  MBIC. Jack Levine
Self-portrait with muse
  IU. Contemp Amer ptg & sculp, 1961
The street
  Pierson

String quartette   MM
  Gruskin (col)
  MM. 100 Amer ptrs
  Taylor. Fifty centuries, 1954 ed (col)
  Wight. Milestones
Tombstone cutter
  MBIC. Jack Levine
  MiD. Coll in progress
  NBuA. Expressionism
  WiMiA. Amer ptg 1760-1960
The trial   ICA
  Baur. New art (col)
  Pierson
  WMAA. Museum and its friends, 1959
The trial   OCo
  CoS. New accessions USA, 1956
The turnkey
  IU. Contemp Amer ptg & sculp, 1957
Under the el   DP
  Pousette-Dart. Amer ptg
Welcome home   NBM
  Baur. New art
  Baur. Revolution
  CoS. New accessions USA, 1948
  Genauer
  MBIC. Jack Levine
  Mendelowitz
  MMA. Contemp ptrs
  Pierson
Woodstock pastorale   CSFP
  CoS. New accessions USA, 1952
  CSFP. Annual ex, 1952
  CSFP. Handbook
Levine, Mrs Jack. See Gikow, Ruth
LEVINSON, Abraham Frater, 1883-1946
  Mexican vase with flowers   MB
  MB. Ptgs in water color
Levy, Bilhah Abigail. See Franks, Bilhah
  Abigail
Levy, Grace (Mears)
  Duyckinck, G. (attributed works) Mrs
  Moses Levy
Levy, Moses, 1665?-1728
  Unidentified artist. Moses Levy
LEWANDOWSKI, Edmund D. 1914-
  Christmas tree
    ICA. Annual ex, 1951
    MMA. Abstract
  Gulf coast shipyard
    Pousette-Dart. Amer ptg
  Industrial composition   NBM
    Baur. Revolution
  Ore freighter   WiMi
    MnMW. Precisionist view
  White sails
    WMAA. Annual ex, 1950
  Winter port   MB
    MB. Ptgs in water color
LEWIN, C. L. fl 1850
  Girl with bird
    Ford. Pictorial folk art
LEWIS, Edmund Darch, 1837-1910
  Wyoming valley
    McClintock
Lewis, Eleanor Parke (Custis). See Custis,
  Eleanor Parke
Lewis, Elizabeth. See Goldthwait, Elizabeth
  (Lewis)
LEWIS, Henry, 1819-1904
  Cheever's mill on the St Croix, 1847
                     MnMI
  U.S. National Capital sesquicentennial
    com

LEWIS, Henry—*Continued*
Gorge of the St Croix river, 1847 MnMI
Davidson v2
A street in St Louis   MoSL
MoSL. Handbook 1953
Attributed works
St Louis after the great fire
Born
Lewis, Isaac, 1746-1840
Jarvis, J. W. Dr Isaac Lewis
LEWIS, James Otto, fl 1820-1835
Cut-Taa-Tas-Tia, a Fox chief
McCracken. Portrait of the old west
(col)
Kee-o-kuk, chief of the Sauk
McCracken. Portrait of the old west
(col)
Me-no-quet, a Pottawattomie chief
Morgan (col)
Nabu-Naa-Kee-Shick, a Chippewa chief
McCracken. Portrait of the old west
(col)
Pe-che-co, a Pottawattomie chief
Morgan (col)
Sun-a-get, a Pottawattomie chief
Morgan
Tens-qua-ta-wa, the Shawnee prophet
Morgan (col)
Waa-Na-Taa, chief of the Sioux
McCracken. Portrait of the old west
(col)
Lewis, Jane (Clark). See Clark, Jane
Lewis, Mrs John. See Clark, Jane
LEWIS, John Chapman, 1920-
Interior and bay   DC
CoS. New accessions USA, 1956
Penthesilean trawler
IU. Contemp Amer ptg, 1952
Lewis, John L.
Noxon, H. R. John L. Lewis
Lewis, Meriwether, 1774-1809
Russell, C. M. Lewis and Clark meeting
Flathead Indians
Russell, C. M. Lewis and Clark meeting
the Mandans
LEWIS, Norman, 1909-
Cathedral
ICA. Amer artists paint the city
Newer grounds
CSFP. Annual ex, 1952
Night walk
Baur. Nature
Urban
MMA. Abstract
Lewis, Rebecca
Wollaston, J. Warner Lewis II and
Rebecca
Lewis, Warner, fl 1756
Wollaston, J. Warner Lewis
Wollaston, J. Warner Lewis II and Re-
becca
Lewis, Mrs Warner, fl 1756
Wollaston, J. Mrs Warner Lewis
LEWIS, William A. 1918-
Winter's day   OYB
OYB. Annual 1958
OYB. Supplement 1959
Lewis children
Wollaston, J. Children of Warner Lewis
LEWITIN, Landès, 1892-
Easy
MMA. Sixteen

Forget it
MMA. Sixteen
Knockout
MMA. Sixteen
Think of me, dear
MMA. Sixteen
Lexington and Concord, Battles of, 1775
Earl, R. Battles of Lexington and Con-
cord
Lexington battle monument by Unidentified
artist
Leyland, Frederick R.
Whistler, J. A. M. Arrangement in black
LIBBY, William Charles, 1919-
Nonconformists   OYB
OYB. Catalogue 1951
Libby prison by D. G. Blythe
Liberation by B. Shahn
LIBERMAN, Alexander, 1912-
Two circles
NNSG. Younger Amer ptrs
Liberté, Jean. See Liberté, Lewis Jean
LIBERTÉ, Lewis Jean, 1895-
Coming into port   ATU
ATU. Coll of Amer art
Dark harbor
IU. Contemp Amer ptg, 1950
Lighthouse at night   GAtM
GAtM. Holbrook collection
Monhegan hill
Gruskin
Sunset, Gloucester
IU. Contemp Amer ptg, 1949
Libration by H. Hofmann
LICHTENBERG, Manes
Albert bridge, London
NAD. Annual ex, 1961
LIE, Jonas, 1880-1940
Dawn at Culebra
U.S. National Capital sesquicentennial
com
Deep river   WMAA
Larkin
Larkin rev ed
Old ships drawn to home again   NBM
Pierson
LIEBMAN, Marjorie
Number 9—1953
IU. Contemp Amer ptg & sculp, 1955
Lieutenant Bulkley's PT boats at Bataan
by G. A. Picken
Life goes by by A. G. Dove
The **life** line by W. Homer
Life-size black bass by W. Homer
Life with father, Impression from by G. R.
Beal
Lifting night by C. A. Morris
The **light** by W. T. Murch
Light and shade by R. N. Blair
Light battery at Gettysburg by E. Hopper
Light, earth and blue by M. Rothko
Light in August by W. De Kooning
Light in autumn by W. Thon
Light is gold by I. R. Pereira
The **light** of learning by K. Cox
Light of the world by P. Blume
Light on the sea by W. Homer
Light wells by A. Osver

Lighter relieving a steamboat aground by G. C. Bingham
Lighthouse keeper by R. Brackman
Lighthouse service dock, Nassau by S. M. Etnier
Lighthouses
  De Martini, J. Foggy night
  De Martini, J. Lighthouse point
  Hartley, M. Lighthouse
  Hopper, E. Lighthouse at Two Lights
  Kantor, M. Highland light
  Kaplan, J. Highland light
  Kingman, D. Lighthouse
  Liberté, L. J. Lighthouse at night
  Thon, W. The outpost
Lightning at sea by G. O'Keeffe
Lights by C. A. Morris
Lilacs by K. Knaths
Lilacs and books by K. Knaths
Lilacs and glasses by B. Bomar
Lilies by P. Blume
Lilies by H. Pippin
Lily and the sparrows by P. Evergood
Lilya by E. E. Speicher
Limbo by S. Greene
Lime quarry by H. P. Barnett
Limestone edge by J. W. Boynton
Limestone quarry by R. O. Pozzatti
The limit by A. Gorky
Lincoln, Abraham, president U.S. 1809-1865
  Bachelder, J. B. and Chappel, A. Death of Abraham Lincoln
  Blythe, D. G. Lincoln crushing the dragon of rebellion
  Blythe, D. G. President Lincoln writing the Emancipation proclamation
  Hartley, M. Portrait of Lincoln
  Healy, G. P. A. Abraham Lincoln
  Healy, G. P. A. The peacemakers
  Peto, J. F. Lincoln and the Pfleger stretcher
  Peto, J. F. Rack picture with portrait of Lincoln
  Pippin, H. Abe Lincoln, the great emancipator
  Pippin, H. Abraham Lincoln and his father building their cabin on Pigeon creek
  Unidentified artist. Lincoln and his Cabinet, c 1860
A Lincoln reception at the White house by F. B. Carpenter (attributed works)
Lind, Jenny, 1820-1887
  Healy, G. P. A. Jenny Lind
Lindall, Elizabeth. See Pitts, Elizabeth (Lindall)
Lindall, Susanna (Hasey) 1660-1733
  Smibert, J. Mrs James Lindall
LINDNER, Richard, 1901-
  L'académicien
    ICA. Annual ex, 1954
    IU. Contemp Amer ptg & sculp, 1955
  Boy with machine
    ICA. Annual ex, 1957
  Paul Verlaine
    MnMW. Reality and fantasy
Lindsay, Robert M. d 1908
  Eakins, T. Robert M. Lindsay
Linear pattern by W. Saltzman

Linear structure by H. Bayer
LINEN, George, 1802-1888
  Margaret Henderson Gregory and Dudley Sanford Gregory
    DC. Privately owned
Linford, Charles, 1846-1897
  Eakins, T. Charles Linford, the artist
Links of memory by A. Gottlieb
Linn, William, 1752-1808
  Jarvis, J. W. Dr William Linn
LINTOT, Barbara
  Ballerina and the black cat
    NAD. Annual ex, 1947, 1st half
Lions
  Browne, B. Black lion
  Hicks, E. (attributed works) The lion family
  Marin, J. The lions in the ring
Lisbeth's painting by W. De Kooning
Liscome, Lydia. See Jarvis, Lydia (Liscome)
Listening to the voice of stone by G. Mofchum
Liszt, Franz, 1811-1886
  Healy, G. P. A. Franz Liszt
Litter by E. Melcarth
Little attic by W. De Kooning
Little Big Horn, Battle of, 1876
  Benton, T. H. Custer's last stand
Little bird alone by M. Graves
Little bouquet by M. A. Phillips
Little boy in red by Unidentified artist
Little canyon by E. F. Spruce
Little captain by P. Evergood
Little child with big dog by W. M. Prior
Little coat and fur shop by K. H. Miller
Little cobbler's shop by C. Hassam
Little dancer by R. Henri
Little dandy by N. Cook
Little dog by C. A. Woolworth
Little Falls, New York by Unidentified artist
Little giant still life by S. Davis
Little girl and the cat by Unidentified artist
A little girl—Fanny Travis Cochran by C. Beaux
Little girl holding apple by W. M. Prior (attributed works)
Little girl in lavender by J. Bradley
Little girl run for your life by Y. Kuniyoshi
Little girl with a snowberry by Unidentified artist
Little girl with apple by W. Sommer
Little Joe with cow by Y. Kuniyoshi
Little king by J. Pollock
Little-known bird of the inner eye by M. Graves
Little madonna by G. B. Luks
Little maid of Arcady by A. P. Ryder
Little match girl by J. L. Lasker
Little Miss Hone by S. F. B. Morse
Little movie theater by J. Sloan
Little murderer by G. Grosz
Little Red Riding Hood by G. C. Bingham
Little Rose of Lyme Regis by J. A. M. Whistler

Little sailboat by J. Marin
Little Scheveningen: grey note by J. A. M. Whistler
Little Scotch girl by E. G. Malbone
Little sheep by J. Carroll
The little white girl by J. A. M. Whistler
Littleton, New Hampshire by Unidentified artist
The liver is the cock's comb by A. Gorky
Livermore, Jane (Browne) 1734-1803
    Copley, J. S. Jane Browne
Livermore, Mrs Samuel. See Livermore, Jane (Browne)
Living rooms
    Benson, F. W. Rainy day
    Carlin, J. Sparking
    Pippin, H. Victorian interior
    Pittman, H. Reflections
    Sargent, H. Tea party
    Sharrer, H. D. In the parlor
Livingston, Eliza, 1786-1860
    Malbone, E. G. Eliza Livingston
Livingston, Mrs Jasper H. See Livingston, Eliza
Livingston, John W. 1778-1860
    Malbone, E. G. John W. Livingston
Livingston, Margaret, 1681-1758. See Vetch, Margaret (Livingston)
Livingston, Margaret, 1738-1818. See Stuyvesant, Margaret (Livingston)
Livingston, Margaret (Howarden) fl 1717
    Unidentified artist. Mrs Robert Livingston
Livingston, Robert, 1654-1728
    Unidentified artist. Robert Livingston
Livingston, Robert R. 1746-1813
    Vanderlyn, J. Robert R. Livingston
Llano Quemado by A. Dasburg
Lloyd, Henry, 1685-1763
    Mare, J. Henry Lloyd I (copy after Wollaston)
Lobby wall by S. Davis
The lobster by A. G. Dove
Lobster boat by J. Marin
Lobster boat, Cape Split, Maine by J. Marin
Lobster buoys and nets by M. Hartley
Lobster fishermen by M. Hartley
Lobster pots and buoy by M. Hartley
Lobster traps by S. J. Twardowicz
Lobsterman's gear by E. Fiene
The lock by W. T. Murch
Lock Haven, Pennsylvania by Unidentified artist
LOCKE, Charles, 1899-
    Copyist
        NAD. Annual ex, 1949, 1st half
LOCKMAN, DeWitt McClellan, 1870-1957
    Aimée Delmores
        NNHS. Lockman
    Calvin Coolidge   NNHS
        NNHS. Lockman
    Clara C. Doreu
        NNHS. Lockman
    Coco the clown (George Hubert Herbert)
                                                       NNHS
        NNHS. Lockman
    Constance Eastman (1)
        NNHS. Lockman

Constance [Eastman] (2)
    NNHS. Lockman
    Edwin Howland Blashfield   NNHS
        NNHS. Lockman
    Harry Woodburn Chsae   NNHS
        NNHS. Lockman
    I. N. Phelps Stokes   NNHS
        NNHS. Lockman
    Josephus Daniels   NNHS
        NNHS. Lockman
    Maxwell D. Taylor   NWP
        NNHS. Lockman
    Mrs DeWitt M. Lockman. See The porphyry jar
    Mrs George Perkins
        NAD. Annual ex, autumn 1949
    Nicholas Murray Butler   NNHS
        NNHS. Lockman
    Patrick Cardinal Hayes   NNHS
        NNHS. Lockman
    The porphyry jar (Mrs DeWitt M. Lockman)
        NNHS. Lockman
    Robert Lee Bullard   NNHS
        NNHS. Lockman
    Samuel Montgomery Roosevelt
        NNHS. Lockman
    Self-portrait
        NNHS. Lockman
    Sidney G. DeKay
        NNHS. Lockman
    William Sowden Sims   NNHS
        NNHS. Lockman
Lockman, Mrs DeWitt McClellan. See Lockman, Evelyn Clair Walker
Lockman, Evelyn Clair Walker
    Lockman, D. M. The porphyry jar
Lockport on the Erie canal by M. Keys
LOCKWOOD, Ward, 1894-
    Fragments of elegance
        MM. Amer ptg today
    Jet and turquoise
        IU. Contemp Amer ptg, 1952
    Restrained flow
        IU. Contemp Amer ptg & sculp, 1959
    Southwest no 4   WMAA
        Pierson
    Southwest no 9—riders
        IU. Contemp Amer ptg & sculp, 1955
    Valley below
        IU. Contemp Amer ptg, 1951
Locomotives
    Feininger, L. Locomotive with big wheel
    Feininger, L. Old American locomotive
    Feininger, T. L. Ghosts of engines
    Finch, K. Locomotives
    Marsh, R. Locomotives watering
    Sintzenich, E. Train leaving Auburn station at Rochester, New York
    Unidentified artist. Railroad engine, the Star
Locust by K. Finch
Loeffler, Charles Martin, 1861-1935
    Sargent, J. S. Charles M. Loeffler
Loftus, Edward
    Stuart, G. Edward Loftus
Log jam, Penobscot bay by M. Hartley
LOGAN, A. fl 1874
    The circus   DN
        DN. Amer primitive ptgs, pt 1
Logan, Martha. See Chalmers, Martha (Logan) (?)

LOGAN, Maurice, 1886-
  Bass boats
    NAD. Annual ex, 1955
La loge by M. Cassatt
Logging camp by H. D. Martin
Logs drifting by B. J. O. Nordfeldt
Lois by J. Carroll
The **Loma**, New Mexico by H. C. Smith
London, England
  Boit, E. D. London: a bend of the
    Thames at Chelsea
  Boit, E. D. Piccadilly, London
  Homer, W. The Houses of Parliament
London Hippodrome by E. Shinn
London Music Hall by E. Shinn
London omnibus by J. Marin
London Times by W. M. Harnett
Lone cowboy by W. W. Quirt
Lone fisherman by W. M. Chase
Lone horseman by A. P. Ryder
Lone scout by A. P. Ryder
Lone tenement by G. W. Bellows
Loneliness by H. Weston
Lonely places by F. P. Colburn
Lonely ways by H. Lundeberg
The **loner** by W. W. Quirt
LONERGAN, John, 1896-
  Gaspé fisherman   ATU
    ATU. Coll of Amer art
  Peggy's cove   ATU
    ATU. Coll of Amer art
Lonesome road by M. Dixon
Lonesome shores by L. Feininger
Lonesome valley by E. Magafan
The **long** bill by J. H. Beard
Long Branch, New Jersey by W. Homer
Long Island by A. G. Dove
Long Island farmhouses by W. S. Mount
Long Island scene by W. S. Mount
Long Island Sound by L. Bouché
Long Island sunset by G. O'Keeffe
Long Jakes by C. Deas
The **long** story by W. S. Mount
Longeuil, Normandy by L. Feininger
Longfellow, Henry Wadsworth, 1807-1882
  Healy, G. P. A. Henry W. Longfellow
LONGFELLOW, William Pitt Preble,
  1836-1913
  Guard room in the palace of Fontaine-
    bleau   MB
    MB. Ptgs in water color
  On the Normandy coast   MB
    MB. Ptgs in water color
  Sala del Collegio, Ducal palace, Venice
                                         MB
    MB. Ptgs in water color
Longfield, Rachel. See Lawrence, Rachel
  (Longfield)
Long's Peak, Colorado by W. Whittredge
Longshoremen's noon by J. G. Brown
Look homeward, America by D. Nichols
Look, it flies by Y. Kuniyoshi
Looking east from Denny hill by R. Earl

Looking for scenery by J. G. Chapman
Looking north to Kingston by T. Chambers
Looking out to Washington square by J.
  Sloan
Looking up the Monongahela river from
  Coal hill by R. Smith
The **lookout** by W. Homer
The **lookout**—All's well by W. Homer
The **lookout**, Vermont by A. M. R. Moses
A **loose** cinch by C. M. Russell
Loper, Frankie
  Biddle, G. Frankie Loper
LORAN, Erle, 1905-
  Navajo desert camp
    IU. Contemp Amer ptg, 1949
  Rock fluorescence
    IU. Contemp Amer ptg, 1952
  Sea depth
    IU. Contemp Amer ptg & sculp, 1953
  Under sea   CSFM
    Pousette-Dart. Amer ptg
LORD, Don, 1929-
  Girard   OYB
    OYB. Annual 1955
    OYB. Supplement 1959
  Tattle tale grey
    OYB. Annual 1948
  Tree house   OYB
    OYB. Annual 1960
Lord, Miranda E. fl 1815
  Fenton, P. Miranda E. Lord from Connec-
    ticut
Lord heal the child by T. H. Benton
The **Lord** is my shepherd by T. H. Benton
Lord Ullin's daughter by A. P. Ryder
The **Lorelei** by A. P. Ryder
Loreli by H. Frankenthaler
Lorenzo and Jessica by W. Allston
Loring by J. A. Brooks
Los Angeles, California
  Dike, P. L. View of Los Angeles
  Kuntz, R. E. Los Angeles Freeway
  Sicard, P. Night over Los Angeles
Lost greenhorn by A. J. Miller
The **lost** mind by E. Vedder
Lost on the Grand Banks by W. Homer
Lost warrior by F. Remington
Lothrop, John, fl 1770
  Durand, J. John Lothrop
LOTTERMAN, Hal, 1920-
  Black bottle
    PPC. International ex, 1952
  Boy with guitar
    NAD. Annual ex, 1954
The **lottery** by S. M. Adler
Lotus by C. E. Heil
Lotus pool, El Encanto, Santa Barbara by
  C. C. Cooper
Louis Philippe, king of the French, 1773-1850
  Healy, G. P. A. Louis Philippe, king of
    France
Louisburg square by T. A. Fransioli
Louisburg square, winter by J. Ricci
Louisiana
  See also New Orleans
  Benton, T. H. Louisiana rice fields

Louisiana—*Continued*
  Colomb, C. White Hall plantation, Louisiana, c 1790
  Meeker, J. R. Land of Evangeline
  Persac, A. Shadows-on-the-Teche
  Persac, A. Sugar mill on Bayou Teche, Oliver plantation
The **Louvre** by S. F. B. Morse
LOVE, Waldo
  Jim Baker, dressed-up portrait wearing a costume made by a Sioux squaw   **CoDH**
    Davidson v 1
Love at high noon by S. Gechtoff
Love note by H. Pippin
Love, oh careless love by J. Levine
The **lovers** by P. Mangravite
The **lovers** by B. Perlin
The **lovers** by A. P. Ryder
The **lovers** by Y. Tanguy
The **lovers'** boat by A. P. Ryder
Lover's pike by Y. Kuniyoshi
Low, Mary Anne (Whittemore) 1800-1867
  Unidentified artist. Mrs Henry Somes Low
LOW, Will H. 1853-1912, and **LA FARGE, John,** 1835-1910
  Decorative panel   **MB**
    MB. Ptgs in water color
Low tide by W. A. Kienbusch
Low tide by H. Maril
Low tide by E. F. Spruce
Low tide, Beachmont by M. B. Prendergast
Low tide monument by J. C. Atherton
A **lowdown** trick by W. R. Leigh
Lowell, Abbott Lawrence, 1865-1943
  Sargent, J. S. A. Lawrence Lowell, president of Harvard
Lowell, Georgina Margaret (Amory) d 1830
  Goodridge, S. Mrs John Lowell jr
Lowell, John, 1799-1836
  Goodridge, S. John Lowell jr
The **Lowell** committee by Ben Shahn
Lowell house (Harvard university) by K. Matthew
Lower Manhattan by S. Hirsch
Lower Manhattan, 1920 by J. Marin
Lower Manhattan, 1922 by J. Marin
Lower Manhattan from Communipaw by T. Moran
Lower Manhattan from the river by J. Marin
Lower reservoir, Tihonet by F. W. Benson
Lowering from the cross by B. Kamihira
Lowlands by C. Bloom
Lowndes, Mrs James, fl 1801
  Malbone, E. G. Mrs James Lowndes
Lowndes, Mary I'On, fl 1802
  Malbone, E. G. Mary I'On Lowndes
Lowndes, Sarah (Jones) b 1757?
  Theus, J. Mrs Rawlins Lowndes
Lowndes, Thomas, 1765-1843
  Malbone, E. G. Thomas Lowndes
LOWRIE, Agnes Potter (van Ryn) 1892-
  To the dock, Tadoussac
    ICA. Annual ex, 1945/46

Lowrie, Mrs Selden Gale. See Lowrie, Agnes Potter (van Ryn)
LOZOWICK, Louis, 1892-
  City-shape   **CtY**
    CtY. Soc Anonyme
  New York, 1926-27
    MnMW. Precisionist view
  Oklahoma
    Brown. Amer ptg
Lubec, Maine by P. M. M. Jones
Luce, Claire, 1905-
  Carroll, J. Claire Luce as Camille
LUCIONI, Luigi, 1900-
  Alice in grey
    MM. Amer ptg today
  Design for color   **OT**
    CoS. New accessions USA, 1946
    OT. Contemp Amer ptgs
  Tracery of leaves
    NAD. Annual ex, 1951
    PPC. International ex, 1950
  Victorian still life   **WMAA**
    CSB. Illusion
Lucky strike by S. Davis
LUDINS, Eugene, 1904-
  Grove
    IU. Contemp Amer ptg & sculp, 1957
  Maze
    PPC. International ex, 1955
  Rare birds
    VR. Amer ptg, 1954
  The valley
    PA. Annual ex, 1948
  Water front
    IU. Contemp Amer ptg, 1949
LUKS, George Benjamin, 1867-1933
  Armistice night   **WMAA**
    Chew. 250 years of art
    Goodrich. Amer art
    Pierson
  Blue devils marching down Fifth avenue   **DP**
    Brown. Amer ptg
  The breadline
    U.S. National Capital sesquicentennial com
  The breaker boy
    NSyE. The eight
  Butcher boy
    Brown. Amer ptg
  Cat and kittens
    Chew. 250 years of art
  The clown   **MB**
    PA. Annual ex, 1955
  Conner's rock, Cape Eliza, Maine
    NSP. Sportscapes
  Daughter of the mines   **NUM**
    NUM. Root bequest
  Flyweight champ of Jumel place **OYB**
    OYB. Supplement
  The gamin   **ATeS**
    ATeS. Collection
  The guitar
    NYG. Fine art
  Hester street   **NBM**
    Baur. Revolution
    McCurdy
  Holiday on the Hudson   **OCl**
    OCl. Handbook
  Little madonna   **MAP**
    Baur. Revolution
  Man with violin   **NJMo**
    NJMo. Forty years

Mrs Gamley   WMAA
  Goodrich. Amer art
  Mendelowitz
  PA. Annual ex, 1955
  Roos
  Walker. Ptgs from America
The old duchess   MM
  MM. 100 Amer ptrs
  Pierson
Otis Skinner as Col Bridau   DP
  Bazin
  Brown. Amer ptg
  DP. Catalogue
  PA. Anual ex, 1955
Roundhouses at High Bridge   NUM
  NUM. Art across America
The spielers   MAP
  Brown. Amer ptg
  Canaday
  Chew. 250 years of art
  Larkin
  Larkin rev ed
  NBuA. Fifty ptgs
  Pierson
  Roos
  Time. 300 years (col)
  Wight. Milestones
Sulking boy   DP
  DP. Catalogue
Telling fortunes   DP
  DP. Catalogue
West side docks
  Brown. Amer ptg
Widow Magee
  Glackens
Woman with black cat   DC
  DC. 25 biennial ex, 1957
Wrestlers   MB
  Brown. Amer ptg
  PA. Annual ex, 1955
  Pierson

Portrait of the artist
Glackens, W. J. George B. Luks, c 1899
Lullaby by F. Martin
Lumber for the Argo by R. H. Bumpas
Luminosity by L. Feininger
Luminous loot by L. Mullican
LUNAK, Alan, 1915-
  Green premonitions
    ICA. Annual ex, 1959-60
Lunar binge by A. Salemme
Lunar magic by F. E. Warren
Lunar voyage by A. Salemme
Lunar web by L. Feininger
Lunch hour by I. Bishop
Luncheon scene by R. Petersen
LUND, David, 1925-
  Cycladic light
    WMAA. Young America 1960
LUNDEBERG, Helen, 1908-
  Lonely ways
    IU. Contemp Amer ptg & sculp, 1959
  Micro-macrocosmic landscape
    ICA. Annual ex, 1947/48
  The mirror   CLA
    IU. Contemp Amer ptg, 1952
    Pousette-Dart. Amer ptg
  Peaches
    IU. Contemp Amer ptg & sculp, 1957

  Season of mists
    IU. Contemp Amer ptg, 1951
  Spring
    IU. Contemp Amer ptg, 1950
  Winter sun
    IU. Contemp Amer ptg & sculp, 1955
Lüneburg II by L. Feininger
Lupton, Mrs Francis P. fl 1803
  Malbone, E. G. Mrs Francis P. Lupton
Lure of the waters by P. Evergood
Lute, flute and dance by W. Houmère
Lutes. See Musicians and musical instru-
    ments—Lutes
LUTZ, Dan, 1906-
  April day   ATeS
    ATeS. Collection
  I got a harp
    Gruskin
  Kalamazoo cove
    IU. Contemp Amer ptg, 1949
  Mountain church, San Cristobal
    IU. Contemp Amer ptg & sculp, 1957
  Sylvan episode
    IU. Contemp Amer ptg, 1950
Luxembourg gardens by W. J. Glackens
Luxembourg gardens at twilight by J. S.
  Sargent
Lydia and Tabitha by Unidentified artist
Lyell, Fenwick, fl 1807
  Jarvis, J. W. Fenwick Lyell
Lyman, Harriet, 1784-1875
  Malbone, E. G. Harriet Lyman
Lynch, Mrs Scolley. See Bibb, Mary Lucy
  Pocahontas
The **lynching** by B. Kopman
Lyon, Nathaniel, 1818-1861
  Bingham, G. C. Gen Nathaniel Lyon and
    Gen Frank P. Blair starting from the
    Arsenal gate in St Louis to capture
    Camp Jackson
Lyon, Patrick, 1779?-1829
  Neagle, J. Pat Lyon at his forge
Lyons, Richard Bickerton Pemell Lyons, 1st
  earl, 1817-1887
  Healy, G. P. A. Lord Richard Bickerton
    Pemell Lyons
Lyric by M. Tobey
Lyric piece by R. Keyser
Lyric yellow by E. E. Boccia
LYTLE, Richard, 1935-
  Icarus descended   MMA
    MMA. Sixteen
  The possessed
    MMA. Sixteen
  Prometheus
    MMA. Sixteen
  Verge
    MMA. Sixteen
Lytton, Edward Robert Bulwer-Lytton, 1st
  earl of, 1831-1891
  Healy, G. P. A. Lord Lytton

M

M—1951 by J. D. Brooks
M. R. D. by H. Sterne
Ma vie blanche et noire by Y. Tanguy

Macbeth and the witches by A. P. Ryder

Macbraire, Robert
Unidentified artist. Robert Macbraire

Macbraire, Mrs Robert
Unidentified artist. Mrs Robert Macbraire

McCALL, Charles Ford
Another Sunday
OYB. Annual 1950
God's day
PPC. Ptg in the U.S. 1949

McCall, Mary. See Plumsted, Mary (McCall)

McCARTER, Henry Bainbridge, 1864-1942
Coal mine   PA
PA. Annual ex, 1955
Early Italy
PA. Annual ex, 1955
Still life
PA. Annual ex, 1955
Sunset in the fields
PA. Annual ex, 1955

McCHESNEY, Robert, 1913-
Abstraction 2A
ICA. Annual ex, 1947/48

McCloskey, John, cardinal, 1810-1885
Healy, G. P. A. John McCloskey

McClurg, Elizabeth S. See Wickham, Elizabeth S. (McClurg)

McCLUSKY, John D. 1914-
Clock
IU. Contemp Amer ptg & sculp, 1959
Fish
IU. Contemp Amer ptg & sculp, 1961

McCONNELL, G. fl 1871
Factory   NCHA
Jones. New-found folk art

The **McConney** flats by P. Evergood

McCord, David, 1797-1855
Jarvis, J. W. David McCord

McCormick, Leander James, 1819-1900
Healy, G. P. A. Leander James McCormick

McCormick family
Johnston, J. The James McCormick family of Baltimore, c1804

McCOSH, David J. 1903-
Apple trees in December
OrPA. Ptgs & sculptures

McCOY, John W. 1910-
Attic dormer
NAD. Annual ex, 1954
The junction
NAD. Annual ex, 1946, 2d half

McCrea, Jane, fl 1846
Unidentified artist. Murder of Jane McCrea

McCULLOUGH, Joseph W. 1922-
Infernal machine at dawn
IU. Contemp Amer ptg & sculp, 1957

McCurdy, Letitia Grace, 1797-1875
Johnston, J. Letitia McCurdy

McDonald, James, fl 1855
Blythe, D. G. Col James McDonald

MacDONALD-WRIGHT, Stanton, 1890-
Airplane synchromy in yellow and orange   PPhM
Baur. New art
Airplane synchromy in yellow-orange   MM
Baur. Revolution

Conception synchromy   WMAA
Baur. New art
Brown. Amer ptg
Hunter. Mod Amer ptg
McCurdy
MMA. Abstract
Pierson
Far country—Synchromy   MiD
Larkin
Larkin rev ed
Organization 5
Cheney. Primer 1958 ed
Oriental: synchromy in blue-green   WMAA
Baur. New art (col)
Goodrich. Amer art (col)
Pierson
Sacrifice of the hair
IU. Contemp Amer ptg, 1950
Synchromy (Shawan coll)
Brown. Amer ptg
Synchromy, 1917-   MMA
MMA. Abstract
Read. Concise history
Synchromy in green and orange, 1916
MnMW. Classic tradition
Synchromy no 3   PPhM
WMAA. Pioneers
Two women   CP
CoS. New accessions USA 1946

McDonell farm by A. M. R. Moses

Macdonough, Thomas, 1783-1825
Jarvis, J. W. Capt Thomas Macdonough
Stuart, G. Commodore Thomas Macdonough

Macdougal alley by C. Sheeler

McDowell, William H.
Eakins, T. William McDowell

McEvers, Catharine A. See Birckhead, Catharine A. (McEvers)

McFEE, Henry Lee, 1886-1953
Aperitif   InIJ
InIJ. 105 ptgs
Banana plant and squash
PPC. International ex, 1950
Broken pot with blue vase
Pearson. Mod renaissance
Crow with peaches   WMAA
Pierson
Golden leaves
CSFP. Annual ex, 1947/48
Landscape with houses
Pearson. Mod renaissance
Painting no 3—still life
MM. Amer ptg today
The skull   MM
MM. 100 Amer ptrs
Still life
Brown. Amer ptg
Still life   OCo
Baur. Revolution
WMAA. Pioneers
Still life: apples
NYG. Fine art
Still life: oranges   WMAA
Gruskin
Larkin
Larkin rev ed
Still life with a green jar   FIPN
Pearson. Mod renaissance
Still life with decanter
Baur. Revolution

Still life with ivy
  NAD. Annual ex, 1951
Still life with white cloth
  IU. Contemp Amer ptg, 1948
Things on a table
  Pousette-Dart. Amer ptg
Wild flowers and grasses   GAtM
  GAtM. Holbrook collection
Yellow pitcher
  CSFP. Annual ex, 1948/49
McGARRELL, James, 1930-
Anatomy   OrPA
  CoS. New accessions USA, 1960
  OrPA. Ptgs & sculptures
Bathers
  Selz. New images (col)
Equinox
  Selz. New images
J
  IU. Contemp Amer ptg & sculp, 1961
Reflection, self-portrait
  WMAA. Contemp Amer ptg, 1959-60
Rest in air
  IU. Contemp Amer ptg & sculp, 1959
  Selz. New images
Machias, Maine by J. Marin
Machine by G. W. McLaughlin
Machine by C. A. Morris
Machine by M. L. Schamberg
Machine oil by M. L. Schamberg
Machine shop by W. T. Aldrich
McIlhenny, Henry P.
  Watkins, F. C. Henry P. McIlhenny
McILVAINE, William, fl 1857
  Delaware Water Gap
  McClintock
McILWORTH, Thomas, fl 1758-1769
  Gerardus Stuyvesant   NNHS
  Vail. Stuyvesant ports
  Nicholas William Stuyvesant   NNHS
  Vail. Stuyvesant ports
McIntire, Samuel, 1757-1811
  Blyth, B. (attributed works) Samuel Mc-
    Intire
MacIVER, Loren, 1909-
Ashcan
  MMA. Fourteen
  MnU. 40 Amer ptrs
Les beaux   ICA
  Baur. Nature
  Baur. New art
The city
  Baur. MacIver and Pereira
  MMA. Fourteen
Dublin and environs
  Baur. MacIver and Pereira
  IU. Contemp Amer ptg, 1951
Early
  Baur. MacIver and Pereira
Elm fruit
  WMAA. Annual ex, 1958
Emmett Kelly
  Baur. MacIver and Pereira
  Baur. New art
  MMA. Contemp ptrs
  Pierson
  WMAA. Neuberger collection
The fratellini   MWiC
  Baur. MacIver and Pereira
  NUM. Art across America

Hearth
  ICA. Annual ex, 1959-60
Hopscotch   MMA
  Barr. What is mod ptg
  Baur. MacIver and Pereira
  Baur. New art
  Baur. Revolution
  Mendelowitz
  MMA. Fourteen
  MMA. Masters
  Pierson
Hyacinth
  MnU. 40 Amer ptrs
Irish landscape
  IU. Contemp Amer ptg & sculp, 1957
Jimmy Savo
  Genauer
  MMA. Fourteen
Jimmy Savo's shoes
  Baur. MacIver and Pereira
Moonlight
  Baur. MacIver and Pereira
Mountain laurel
  MMA. Fourteen
Naples aquarium
  Baur. MacIver and Pereira
New York, 1952
  Baur. MacIver and Pereira
Night shadows   NBuA
  NBuA. Acquisitions 1959-1961
Oil splatters and leaves
  Baur. MacIver and Pereira
  Baur. New art (col)
Paris   MM
  MM. 100 Amer ptrs
Paris night meanders
  ICA. Annual ex, 1959/60
The poet
  Baur. MacIver and Pereira
Puddle
  Baur. MacIver and Pereira
Red votive lights   MMA
  Baur. MacIver and Pereira
  McCurdy
  MMA. Contemp ptrs
  MMA. Fourteen
  Read. Concise history
Rue Daguerre   NUM
  CoS. New accessions USA, 1956
Shack   MMA
  Myers
Sidewalk   MAP
  Rathbun
  Wight. Milestones
Skylight   MMA
  MMA. Soby collection
Snowscape
  Cheney. Story 1958 ed
Splatters and leaves
  Pousette-Dart. Amer ptg
The street   DC
  DC. 25 biennial ex, 1957
  Time. 300 years (col)
The street is young with spring
  PPC. International ex, 1952
Strunsky house
  Baur. MacIver and Pereira
Subway lights
  IU. Contemp Amer ptg & sculp, 1961
Taxi   CtHW
  Baur. MacIver and Pereira
  CtHW. Handbook

McLAUGHLIN, James
Anemones   DP
DP. Catalogue
McLAUGHLIN, John, 1898-
Untitled, 1955
VR. Amer ptg, 1958
Macmillan, Mrs Floyd. See Davis, Gladys
(Rockmore)
MacMONNIES, Frederick William, 1863-
1937
Mrs Anne Archbold
DC. Privately owned
McNEIL, George Joseph, 1909-
Abstraction, 1949
MMA. Abstract
Abstraction, 1951
PPC. International ex, 1952
Invitation
MnMW. 60 Amer ptrs
Painting
Pousette-Dart. Amer ptg
MacNUTT, Glenn Gordon, 1906-
Scallop fleet
NAD. Annual ex, 1958
Macomb, Mary Cornell (Pell). See Pell,
Mary Cornell
Macomb, Robert, 1783-1832
Malbone, E. G. Robert Macomb
Macomb, Mrs Robert. See Pell, Mary Cor-
nell
Macphaedris, Mary. See Warner, Mary
(Macphaedris)
McPherson, James, fl 1801
Malbone, E. G. James McPherson
McPherson, John, fl 1801
Malbone, E. G. Gen John McPherson
McSorley's back room by J. Sloan
McSorley's bar by J. Sloan
McSorley's cats by J. Sloan
McVey's barn by A. N. Wyeth
Mad bull by E. J. Stevens
Madam X by A. Salemme
Madame X (Madame Gautreau) by J. S.
Sargent
Maddox, Clifford Tallulah
Brook, A. Clifford Tallulah Maddox
Madeira, Betty Campbell
Borie, A. Mrs Betty Campbell Madeira
Madge in the morning by L. M. Eilshemius
Madison, Dorothea (Payne) Todd, 1768-1849
Ames, E. Dolly Madison
Madison, James, president U.S. 1751-1836
Peale, C. W. James Madison
Madison, Mrs James. See Madison, Doro-
thea (Payne) Todd
Madison square, New York by M. B. Pren-
dergast
Madonna by G. Melchers
Madonna by W. W. Quirt
Madonna and child by R. L. Newman
Madonna and child with saints by D. Aron-
son
Madonna enthroned by T. Hennessy
Madonna of the mines by P. Evergood
Madonnas of the rain by L. Dodd
Madrigal by J. Madson
La Madrilenita by R. Henri

MADSON, Jack, 1928-
Madrigal
WMAA. Young America 1957
Pursuit no 3
WMAA. Young America 1957
Maelstrom by M. Jamieson
Maenades, Study for by J. Cox
MAGADA, Stephen, 1925-
Celebration   OYB
OYB. Annual 1954
OYB. Supplement
MAGAFAN, Ethel, 1916-
Dark river
IU. Contemp Amer ptg, 1952
Daybreak
NAD. Annual ex, 1953
Forest
NAD. Annual ex, 1956
The great barrier
NAD. Annual ax, 1959
Lonesome valley
MM. Amer ptg today
Near the mountain
IU. Contemp Amer ptg & sculp, 1961
Summer
NAD. Annual ex, 1960
The Magdalene by R. Lebrun
Magenta and blue by H. Hofmann
Magic circle, Venice by E. Berman
Magic glass by E. R. Elmer
Magic man by J. Lawrence
Magic mirror by J. Pollock
Magic mountains by F. Gerassi
Magical city by H. N. Cook
Magical forms by L. Feitelson
The magician by D. Aronson
The magician by H. Hofmann
The magician by J. Levine
The magician by R. Rauschenberg
The magicians by R. Breinin
The magistrate by B. Greene
Magnetic mountain by K. L. Seligmann
The magnificence by P. Burlin
The magnificent by R. Pousette-Dart
Magnolia by H. Dinnerstein
Magnolia grandiflora by M. J. Heade
Magnolia grandiflora by J. LaFarge
Magnolias by M. J. Heade
Maguey by D. Judd
Mahantango valley farm by Unidentified
artist
Mahatmas of the lunar shore by A. Salemme
Mahon, Edith
Eakins, T. Mrs Edith Mahon
Mahone bay by W. J. Glackens
Mahoning by F. J. Kline
Mah-to-he-ha, the old bear by G. Catlin
Mahu by L. Beck
Maid arranging hair of corpulent woman
by G. Grosz
The maid of the grove by Unidentified artist
Maid of the mist by T. Cole
Mail coach by C. S. Price
Main street, Gloucester by J. Sloan

Maine
Albright, M. M. Boothbay harbor, Maine
Blume, P. Maine coast
Hartley, M. Hurricane island, Vinal Haven, Maine
Hartley, M. Maine landscape, autumn
Hartley, M. Mount Katahdin, Maine
Heliker, J. E. Maine coast
Heliker, J. E. Maine rocks
Homer, W. Maine coast
Hudson, J. B. View in Maine
Inness, G. Moonlight on Passamaquoddy bay
Kienbusch, W. A. Across Penobscot bay
Lane, F. H. Maine inlet
Marin, J. See titles under name of artist
Rosenberg, S. Maine
Spencer, N. The cove, Ogunquit
Sterne, M. Maine coast
Zorach, W. Popham beach no 1, Maine

Maine family by Y. Kuniyoshi

Maine night by C. L. Nelson

Maine snowstorm by M. Hartley

Maine study by G. Cox

Maine swimming hole by W. Peirce

Maitland, Elizabeth Sproat (Lenox) 1785-1864
Mooney, E. L. Mrs Robert Maitland
Thibault, A. Mrs Robert Maitland

Maitland, Robert, 1768-1846
Mooney, E. L. Robert Maitland

Maitland bridge no 2 by R. Crawford

Majestic tenement by A. Osver

MAJOR, Henry, 1889-1948
American frolic
NYG. Fine art
Gay philosopher—why worry
NYG. Fine art
Philosopher's heir
NYG. Fine art
Philosopher's offspring
NYG. Fine art
Philosopher's wife
NYG. Fine art

Major Dean in jail by G. C. Bingham

Maker of dreams by I. L. Albright

Maker of images by I. L. Albright

Mal du pays by G. A. Walker

Malamocco by Leonid

MALBONE, Edward Greene, 1777-1807
Aaron C. Dennis   MB
Tolman
Alexander Baron jr
Tolman
Alexander von Pfister
Tolman
Alice Wyer
Tolman
Alicia Hopton Russell
Tolman
Ann Channing   MoSL
Tolman
Ann Elizabeth Ryan
Tolman
Anne-Louis de Tousard
Tolman
Annette (probably Mrs Alexander Bleecker)   MB
Tolman

Archibald Taylor   CtY
Tolman
Asher Marx   PA
Tolman
Augusta G. Temple
Tolman
Benjamin West
Tolman
Benjamin Winslow
Tolman
Bounetheau's aunt (Young lady in pink)
                                      DNC
Tolman
Carl F. Herreshoff
Tolman
Catherine Fry   RNH
Tolman
Charles B. Cochran
Tolman
Charles C. Pinckney
Tolman
Charles Fenton Mercer
Tolman
Charles Harris
Tolman
Charles Sinkler (?)
Tolman
Cornelius Coolidge
Tolman
Daniel E. Huger
Tolman
David Moses
Tolman
Dr Brailsford
Tolman
Eben Farley   MWM
Tolman
Edward Butler
Tolman
Edward Laight
Tolman
Edward Martin
Tolman
Edward Perry
Tolman
Elisha Poinsett
Tolman
WiMiA. **Amer ptg 1760-1960**
Eliza Fenno
Tolman
Eliza Izard, 1801   SCCG
Tolman
Eliza Izard, 1802 **(Pinckney coll)**
Tolman
Eliza Livingston
Tolman
Eliza Mason
Tolman
Eye of Maria Miles Heyward
Tolman
G. Patten
Tolman
George Bethune
Tolman
George Gibbs III, **c** 1796
Tolman
George Gibbs III, **c** 1804
Tolman
George Izard   MM
Tolman
Hannah Miles Heyward
Tolman

MALBONE, E. G.—*Continued*
Mrs John L. Sullivan
 Tolman
Mrs John Nightingale
 Tolman
Mrs Joseph Curwen
 Tolman
Mrs Joseph Manigault
 Tolman
Mrs Moses Poor
 Tolman
Mrs Richard C. Derby   MM
 Tolman
Mrs Richard Sullivan   CtY
 CtY. Portrait index
 Tolman
Mrs Robert H. Gardiner
 Tolman
Mrs Robert Means
 Tolman
Mrs Thomas Amory
 Tolman
Mrs Thomas Heyward jr
 Tolman
Mrs William Allen Deas
 Tolman
Mrs William Cattel
 Tolman
Mrs William Montgomery
 Tolman
Mrs Zachariah Allen   RPS
 Tolman
Nathaniel Pearce
 Tolman
Nicholas (?) Brown   NNHS
 Tolman
Nicholas Fish
 Tolman
Nicholas Power   RPAt
 Tolman
Perkins children   MBH
 Tolman
Peter Bours
 Tolman
Rachel Gratz (Hunter coll)
 Tolman
Ralph Izard II
 Tolman
Ray Greene
 Tolman
Rebecca Gratz (?) (Bortman coll)
 Tolman
Rebecca Gratz (Nathan coll)
 Tolman
Rebecca Power
 Tolman
Richard D. Harris
 Tolman
Richard Hyde
 Tolman
Robert H. Gardiner
 Tolman
Robert Mackay
 Tolman
Robert Macomb
 CtY. Yale alumni
 Time. 300 years (col)
 Tolman (col)
Samuel Wragg   MAC
 Tolman
Sarah Alicia Shubrick
 Tolman

Sarah Brown
 Tolman
Sarah Reeve Ladson   SCCG
 Tolman
Self-portrait   DC
 DC. Amer ptrs of the South (col)
 Tolman (col)
Self-portrait c 1800   RPAt
 Tolman
Shakespeare on the lap of the muse of
  inspiration
 Tolman
Solomon Moses
 Tolman
Susan Poinsett (formerly called Anna
  Frances Poinsett)
 Tolman
 WiMiA. Amer ptg 1760-1960
Thomas Barksdale
 Tolman
Thomas Cadwalader
 Tolman
Thomas L. Winthrop
 Tolman
Thomas Lowndes
 Tolman
Thomas Means
 Tolman
Thomas Pascal Jones
 Tolman
Thomas Pinckney
 Tolman
Thomas Pinckney jr   SCCG
 Tolman
Thomas Radcliffe   CtY
 Tolman
Thomas Russell c 1796   MBH
 Tolman
Thomas Russell (Fearing coll)
 MB. New England miniatures (col)
Unknown gentleman   DNC
 Tolman
Unknown gentleman   RPS
 Tolman
Unknown young lady   SCCG
 Tolman
Walter Bowne
 Tolman
Washington Allston   MB
 MB. New England miniatures
 Pierson
 Time. 300 years (col)
 Tolman
William Bruce
 Tolman
Young lady in pink. See Bounetheau's
  aunt
Malbone, Francis, d 1809
 Stuart, G. Francis and Saunders Malbone
Malbone, Saunders, d 1784
 Stuart, G. Francis and Saunders Malbone
Male and female by J. Pollock
Male head by J. Glasco
Le **malheur** adoucit les pierres by Y. Tanguy
MALICOAT, Philip Cecil, 1908-
 November gale
  NAD. Annual ex, 1954
The **Mall,** Central park by M. B. Prender-
  gast
Mallarme's swan by R. B. Motherwell
Mallorca III by F. D. Duncan
Mama, Papa is wounded by Y. Tanguy

Mamout, Yarrow
Peale, C. W. Yarrow Mamout
Man Ray. See Ray, Man
A **man** by W. M. Chase
A **man** by S. Davis
Man by W. De Kooning
A **man** by J. Peale
A **man** by W. M. Prior (attributed works)
A **man**, Portrait of by Y. Blumberg
A **man**, Portrait of by J. Van der Pool (attributed works)
A **man** and a lady by J. H. Davis
Man and arrow by A. Gottlieb
Man and fish by M. Beckmann
Man and machine by I. R. Pereira
Man and the northern lights by C. Gray
Man and woman by M. Beckmann
Man and woman in a large room by R. Diebenkorn
Man and woman seated by R. Diebenkorn
Man building bridge by C. Ruhtenburg
Man from Maine by A. N. Wyeth
Man in a blue coat by Unidentified artist
Man in a yellow waistcoat by J. Eichholtz
Man in black coat by N. Rogers
Man in chains by W. Allston
Man in gray coat by Raphaelle Peale
Man in orange by B. P. Arnest
Man in red by Unidentified artist
Man looking at woman by A. Gottlieb
Man-made man, bewildered by nature by C. A. Morris
Man meets woman, tips hat by W. W. Quirt
A **man** of opinion by G. Grosz
Man of sorrows by P. Blume
Man of sorrows by W. W. Quirt
Man reading by J. S. Sargent
Man walking by N. J. Oliveira
Man with a harelip by A. Dickinson
Man with a mallet by I. L. Albright
Man with a watch fob by S. L. Waldo
Man with a whip by J. T. Evans (attributed works)
Man with blue eyes by Unidentified artist
Man with red necktie by T. Eakins
Man with ship model by W. Kuhn
Man with the glove by W. M. Chase
Man with violin by G. B. Luks
Man with wild flowers by B. Shahn
Manassas (ram)
Unidentified artist. Attack of the rebel ram Manassas on the U.S.S. Pensacola, 1862
Manayunk winter by A. P. Martino
MANCHESTER, M. M. fl 1834
Conversation piece: a Yates family portrait   NR
Jones. Rediscovered ptrs
Manchester by C. Sheeler
Manchester valley by J. Pickett
Mandan medicine man by G. Catlin
Mandan O-kee-pa, the bull dance by G. Catlin
Mandan torture ceremony by G. Catlin

A **Mandan** village by K. Bodmer
A **Mandan** village by G. Catlin
The **mandarin** by C. L. Cicero
Mandarin duck by W. Austin
MANDEL, Howard, 1917-
Ladies in waiting
WMAA. Contemp Amer ptg, 1950
Midnight
Pearson. Mod renaissance
Saints deposed
Pearson. Mod renaissance
Walled village
NAD. Annual ex, 1956
Maneuver for position by B. W. Tomlin
MANGRAVITE, Peppino, 1896-
All things are changing, nothing dies
WMAA. Annual ex, 1953
Angel battling demons
MM. Amer ptg today
City people in the country   WMAA
Pierson
Ecstasy
Pearson. Mod renaissance
Incubus
IU. Contemp Amer ptg, 1952
The lovers
IU. Contemp Amer ptg, 1948
Mountain bouquet
Pearson. Mod renaissance
Of sin and error
Pearson. Mod renaissance
Passions and feverishness
Pearson. Mod renaissance
Recollections
Gruskin
Succubus
Pearson. Mod renaissance
Young couple drinking   NUM
NUM. Root bequest
Young lovers
IU. Contemp Amer ptg, 1950
Manhattan by S. Hirsch
Manhattan architecture by L. Feininger
Manhattan bridge and Lily apartments by E. Hopper
Manhattan bridge loop by E. Hopper
Manhattan canyon by L. Feininger
Manhattan, dawn by L. Feininger
Manhattan, dusk by L. Feininger
Manhattan harbour by G. Grosz
Manhattan, moonwake by L. Feininger
Manhattan, night 1941 by L. Feininger
Manhattan, St Paul's by J. Marin
Manhattan tops by H. Rose
Manigault, Anne (Ashby) d 1782
Theus, J. Mrs Gabriel Manigault
Manigault, Charlotte (Drayton) 1781-1855
Malbone, E. G. Mrs Joseph Manigault
Manigault, Elizabeth (Wragg) b 1736
Theus, J. Mrs Peter Manigault
Manigault, Gabriel, 1704-1781
Theus, J. Gabriel Manigault
Manigault, Mrs Gabriel, d 1782. See Manigault, Anne (Ashby)
Manigault, Mrs Gabriel, 1762-1824. See Manigault, Margaret (Izard)
Manigault, Joseph, 1763-1843
Malbone, E. G. Joseph Manigault
Manigault, Mrs Joseph. See Manigault, Charlotte (Drayton)

Manigault, Margaret (Izard) 1768-1824
  Malbone, E. G. Mrs Gabriel Manigault
MANIGAULT, Middleton, 1887-1922
  Procession   OCo
  Pierson
  Source
  Baur. Revolution
  Wooden Indian
  WMAA. Pioneers
Manigault, Mrs Peter. See Manigault, Eliza-
  beth (Wragg)
Manila no 4 by F. Vidar
Mann, Bethia (Torrey) 1731-1798
  Copley, J. S. Mrs Joseph Mann
Mann, John P. fl 1850
  Toole, J. John Mann
Mann, Joseph, 1717?-1807
  Copley, J. S. Joseph Mann
Mann, Mrs Joseph. See Mann, Bethia (Tor-
  rey)
MANNING, Wray, 1898-
  Afternoon mail   OYB
  OYB. Annual 1950
  OYB. Catalogue 1951
Man's boudoir no 1 (realism) by H. Harari
Man's boudoir no 2 (abstraction) by H.
  Harari
Man's child by M. Peterson
Mansion doorway by P. F. Samuelson
MANSO, Leo, 1914-
  Aspects of the harbor
    IU. Contemp Amer ptg, 1951
    IU. 20th century
  Landscape for contemplation
    IU. Contemp Amer ptg & sculp, 1955
  Morning
    IU. Contemp Amer ptg & sculp, 1957
Mantel arrangement by H. Pittman
Manuscript by J. Koch
MANVILLE, Elsie, 1922-
  Yellow hat
    PA. Annual ex, 1953
Many brave hearts are asleep in the deep by
  C. H. Demuth
Maple sugar campfire, Fryeburg, Maine by
  E. Johnson
Maple sugaring in Vermont by P. S. Sample
Marblehead harbor by J. O. J. Frost
Marca-Relli, Conrad. See Marca-Relli, Cor-
  rado di
MARCA-RELLI, Corrado di, 1913-
  The arrival
    PPC. International ex, 1958
  The blackboard
    PPC. International ex, 1961/62
  Bull fight
    OCl. Some contemporary works
  Cargo
    WMAA. Contemp Amer ptg, 1959/60
  The city
    Cheney. Story 1958 ed
  Collage, 1954   ICA
    OCl. Some contemporary works
  Collage, 1955
    OCl. Some contemporary works
  Collage, 1957
    OCl. Some contemporary works
  Figure
    PA. Annual ex, 1958

The joust   MnMW
  MnMW. 60 Amer ptrs
New York City, 1953
  ICA. Amer artists paint the city
Ochre building
  IU. Contemp Amer ptg & sculp, 1955
Odalisque   NBuA
  NBuA. Acquisitions 1957-58
Sleeping figure   MMA
  Pierson
Strategist
  Brussels. Exposition
The tenant
  PPC. International ex, 1955
23 September 1959
  IU. Contemp Amer ptg & sculp, 1961
27 December 1959
  ICA. Annual ex, 1961
Warrior   NNSG
  NNSG. Handbook
March by C. E. Burchfield
March day, Washington square by W. J.
  Glackens
March in brown by M. Avery
March of the crusaders by G. Inness
March sunlight by C. E. Burchfield
March wind by C. E. Burchfield
March wind by C. F. Ryder
March woodlands by J. H. Twachtman
Marching Highlanders by L. Gatch
MARCUS, Marcia, 1928-
  Seated self-portrait
    WMAA. Young America 1960
  Still life with dead leaves
    WMAA. Young America 1960
MARE, John, 1739-1795?
  Henry Lloyd I (copy after Wollaston)
    DC. Privately owned
  John Keteltas
    Pierson
Mare, Tiburce de, 1840-1900
  Healy, G. P. A. Tiburce de Mare
Mare and foal by C. S. Price
Mare with colt by C. S. Price
Margaret by T. Eakins
Margaret Boni playing the recorder by J. E.
  Levi
MARGO, Boris, 1902-
  From a cathedral
    Pousette-Dart. Amer ptg
  From elements of evening   NBuA
    NBuA. Acquisitions 1957-58
  From February
    Baur. Nature
  From shipwrecks
    IU. Contemp Amer ptg, 1952
  Matrix of an unfathomable
    Rathbun
  Number 5
    IU. Contemp Amer ptg, 1950
  Number 7, 1945
    Baur. Revolution
  Pulsation of light
    IU. Contemp Amer ptg & sculp, 1961
  Reflections no 6
    IU. Contemp Amer ptg, 1951
Marguerite by W. M. Hunt
MARGULES, De Hirsh, 1899-
  Lower Fifth avenue   ATU
    ATU. Coll of Amer art

Painter in the landscape
  Cheney. Expressionism 1948 ed
Waterbury bridge: number one   MB
  MB. Ptgs in water color
Margulis, Max
  De Kooning, W. Max Margulis
Maria by R. B. Motherwell
Maria with dog under a tree by Unidentified
  artist
Marianna by E. E. Speicher
Marie St Esprit by M. Hartley
Marietta earth works by C. Sullivan
MARIL, Herman, 1908-
  Baltimore waterfront   DP
    DP. Catalogue
  Cape still life   MdBM
    CoS. New accessions USA, 1958
  Low tide   DC
    CoS. New accessions USA, 1960
  Rocks and water
    Cheney. Story 1958 ed
  Skaters
    OYB. Annual 1952
  3 A.M.
    NAD. Annual ex, 1960
Marilyn at the table by J. Berger
MARIN, John, 1870-1953
  Adironacks along Ausable river
    UNESCO. 1860-1955
    UNESCO. 1860-1959
  Alpine district, New Jersey
    MiD. Coll in progress
  American telephone building, New York
    city
    ICA. Amer artists paint the city
  Autumn on road to Deblois   TxH
    CoS. New accessions USA, 1954
  Autumn piece, Maine
    PA. Annual ex, 1955
  Back of Bear mountain   DP
    DP. Catalogue
    John Marin
  Bathers on rocks
    Helm. John Marin
  The black sun. See Movement no 2—re-
    lated to downtown New York
  Blue mountain near Taos
    Helm. John Marin
  Blue sea, Crotch island   MAP
    Rathbun (col)
  Boat fantasy, Deer isle
    Helm. John Marin
    John Marin
  Boat off Deer isle   PPhM
    Read. Concise history (col)
  Boat, sky, and sea, Small point, Maine
    Cheney. Story 1958 ed
  Boat with blue
    Helm. John Marin
  Boats, sea and rocks
    Helm. John Marin (col)
  Breakers, Maine coast   OCo
    Seiberling
  Broadway, night
    Helm. John Marin
  Bryant square   DP
    DP. Catalogue
  Cape Split, Maine   ICA
    NYG. Fine art
    UNESCO. 1860-1949
    UNESCO. 1860-1955
    UNESCO. 1860-1959

Cerulean sea and isle
  Lewisohn
Cherry orchard
  CtY. Yale alumni
Circus elephants   ICA
  John Marin
  UNESCO. 1860-1949
  UNESCO. 1860-1955
  UNESCO. 1860-1959
Circus forms
  Helm. John Marin (col)
Circus horses
  Helm. John Marin
City construction   NBuA
  Moderns and their world
City movement, downtown Manhattan
  no 2, 1936
  WiMiA. Amer ptg 1760-1960
Composed from my window   InIJ
  InIJ. 105 ptgs
Composition, Cape Split, Maine, no 2, 1933
  Baur. New art
  Helm. John Marin
  John Marin (col)
  WiMiA. Amer ptg 1760-1960
Corn dance, New Mexico   MM
  John Marin (col)
The cove   OCo
  Roos
Dance of the San Domingo Indians
  Helm. John Marin
Deep-sea trawlers, Maine
  Helm. John Marin
Deer island, Maine: Stonington waterfront
      CtY
  CtY. Soc Anonyme
  Mendelowitz
Deer isle, boats, and pertaining thereto
  Wight. Milestones
Deer isle islets, Maine
  NYG. Fine art
  UNESCO. 1860-1949
  UNESCO. 1860-1955
  UNESCO. 1860-1959
Deer isle, Maine   MoSL
  MoSL. Handbook 1953
Deer isle, Maine series no 30—Boat fan-
  tasy
  MnU. 40 Amer ptrs
Deer isle, Stonington, Maine
  Helm. John Marin
Delaware (river) country, Pennsylvania
  Helm. John Marin
East river no 3, 1934
  Helm. John Marin
Equestrians
  UNESCO. 1860-1955
Equestrienne
  Helm. John Marin
Fifth avenue and Forty-second street DP
  Bazin
  DP. Catalogue
  PA. Annual ex, 1955
Fir tree, Deer isle, Maine   NJN
  Baur. New art
Fishermen and boats
  UNESCO. 1860-1955
  UNESCO. 1860-1959
Fishing boat no 2, 1933
  Helm. John Marin
Fog lifts
  John Marin (col)
  MMA. Abstract
  MnU. 40 Amer ptrs

MARIN, John—*Continued*
Four-master off the Cape   DP
  DP. Catalogue
Four o'clock on the Seine
  Helm. John Marin
Franconia range—mist and rain
  Cheney. Expressionism 1948 ed
From seeing Cape Split
  Helm. John Marin
From the bridge, New York city   CtHW
  CoS. New accessions USA, 1950
  CtHW. Handbook
  Pierson
From Weehawken heights
  Pearson. Mod renaissance
Going through the thoroughfare
  UNESCO. 1860-1955
  UNESCO. 1860-1959
Green Head, Deer isle, Maine
  CanO. Hirshhorn coll
Grey rock, blue-grey sea and boat
  Baur. Revolution
Grey sea   DP
  DP. Catalogue
  John Marin (col)
Gulls, Cape Split, Maine
  PA. Annual ex, 1955
Headed for Boston   ICA
  Helm. John Marin (col)
  Taylor. Fifty centuries, 1954 ed (col)
In the ring
  Helm. John Marin
Island, Small point, Maine   PPhM
  Born
Jersey hills
  PA. Annual ex, 1954
The ladle
  John Marin
Lake, Tunk mountain, Maine series no 12,
  1934
  Helm. John Marin
Landscape in Maine   ICA
  Cheney. Expressionism 1948 ed
Laurel blossoms in vase
  Helm. John Marin
Lions in the ring
  UNESCO. 1860-1955
  UNESCO. 1860-1959
Little sailboat
  John Marin
Lobster boat
  Helm. John Marin
  John Marin
Lobster boat, Cape Split, Maine
  John Marin (col)
London omnibus   MM
  Helm. John Marin
  John Marin
Looking up Fifth avenue from Thirtieth
  street
  Helm. John Marin
  Raynal. History v3 (col)
Lower Manhattan from the river   MM
  Helm. John Marin
  John Marin (col)
  UNESCO. 1860-1949
  UNESCO. 1860-1955
  UNESCO. 1860-1959
Lower Manhattan, 1920
  Barr. What is mod ptg
  Baur. New art
  Cheney. Primer 1958 ed
  Cheney. Story 1958 ed (col)
  Craven. Rainbow book

  Gruskin
  Janson. Picture history (col)
  John Marin (col)
  Robb. Art 1953 ed
Lower Manhattan, 1922   MMA
  Canaday
  Hunter. Mod Amer ptg (col)
  McCurdy
  MMA. Abstract
  MMA. Contemp ptrs
  MMA. Masters (col)
  MMA. Ptg and sculpture
  Pierson
  Read. Art now 1948
  Rosenblum
Lower New York
  Cheney. Expressionism 1948 ed
Machias, Maine, 1945
  Helm. John Marin
  John Marin (col)
Machias, Maine, 1952
  John Marin (col)
Maine coast
  Riley. Your art heritage
Maine islands   DP
  Baur. New art (col)
  Bazin. History of art
  Cheney. Story 1958 ed
  DP. Catalogue
  Faulkner. Art today, 1956
  Gardner 1959 ed
  John Marin
  MMA. Contemp ptrs
  NYG. Fine art
  Pierson
  Richardson. Ptg in America
  Robb. Harper history
  Roos
  Rosenblum
  UNESCO. 1860-1955
  UNESCO. 1860-1959
Maine, 1928
  Cheney. Expressionism 1948 ed
Maine—the sail boat
  Cheney. Primer 1958 ed
Manhattan, St Paul's
  WMAA. Pioneers
Marin island, Small point, Maine   PPhM
  Brown. Amer ptg
  Helm. John Marin
  Larkin
  Larkin rev ed
Mid-Manhattan II, 1932
  MnMW. Classic tradition
Midtown, New York, 1928
  Helm. John Marin
Mount Chocorua   OYB
  OYB. Supplement
Mountain top   OCl
  Larkin
  Larkin rev ed
  Myers
  OCl. Handbook
The mountain, Tyrol
  Helm. John Marin
Movement, boat and sea, Deer isle, Maine
  Helm. John Marin
Movement—boat and sea in grey
  John Marin
Movement, boat, sea, rocks and sky, Maine
                 WMAA
  PA. Annual ex, 1955
Movement—Fifth avenue   ICA
  John Marin
  Pierson

Movement—green, red and black
  PPC. Ptg in the U.S. 1949
Movement in grey, green and red no 2,
  1949
  John Marin
Movement in paint ₁1₎
  Helm. John Marin
Movement in paint ₂2₎
  Helm. John Marin
Movement in paint ₃3₎
  Helm. John Marin
Movement in paint ₄4₎
  Helm. John Marin
Movement no 2—related to downtown
  New York (The black sun)   MM
  50 years of mod art
  Helm. John Marin (col)
  John Marin
  WMAA. Juliana Force
Movement, sea and rocks, Cape Split,
  Maine
  PPC. International ex, 1952
Movement, sea and sky   MLL
  DC. 21 biennial ex, 1949
  John Marin (col)
  Pierson
  WMAA. Museum and its friends, 1958
  (col)
Movement—sea or mountain, as you will
  Baur. Nature
  IU. Contemp Amer ptg, 1949
Movement: Tunk mountains
  CSFP. Annual ex, 1952
My Hell raising sea
  John Marin
Near Great Barrington   DP
  DP. Catalogue
Near Santa Fe, New Mexico
  MiD. Coll in progress
  WiMiA. Amer ptg 1760-1960
New Mexico
  Cheney. Expressionism 1948 ed
New York at night no 3, 1950
  John Marin (col)
New York, downtown
  Helm. John Marin
New York, East river
  Helm. John Marin
New York harbor, 1920   MB
  MB. Ptgs in water color
Off Cape Split, Maine   MM
  Helm. John Marin
  Newmeyer
Off Stonington   OCo
  Munsterberg
Off York island, Maine   PPhM
  Canaday
  John Marin
The old salt   MM
  50 years of mod art
  Pearson. Mod renaissance
On Morse mountain, Maine
  Cheney. Expressionism 1948 ed
  Helm. John Marin (col)
On Morse mountain, Small point, Maine
  Helm. John Marin (col)
  John Marin
  Lee. Art then and now
Peach trees in blossom
  UNESCO. 1860-1955
  UNESCO. 1860-1959

Pertaining to Deer isle, the harbor   MM
  Brown. Amer ptg
  Helm. John Marin
  John Marin
Pertaining to Nassau street, New York
                                   NeL
  Barker. From realism
Pertaining to Stonington harbor, Maine,
  no 4   MM
  John Marin
  Pierson
Phippsburg, Maine
  Helm. John Marin (col)
Pine tree, Small point, Maine   ICA
  Pierson
  UNESCO. 1860-1959
Pont Alexandre
  Helm. John Marin
The Pont Neuf
  UNESCO. 1860-1955
Pueblo and mesa, Taos mountains
  Helm. John Marin
Quoddy Head, Maine coast   DP
  DP. Catalogue
Ramapo river near Suffern, New York
  UNESCO. 1860-1955
  UNESCO. 1860-1959
Red sun—Brooklyn bridge   ICA
  John Marin
Region of Brooklyn bridge fantasy
                                   WMAA
  Goodrich. Amer art (col)
  John Marin
  Pierson
Region Weehawken, New Jersey
  MiD. Coll in progress
River effect, Paris   PPhM
  Cheney. Story 1958 ed
  PPhM. Gallatin coll
River movement—downtown
  John Marin
Rocks and sea, Small point, Maine   OCl
  Cheney. Primer 1958 ed
  Helm. John Marin
  OCl. Handbook
Sea after hurricane   CSFM
  Cheney. Story 1958 ed
Sea and gulls   MM
  Helm. John Marin
  MM. 100 Amer ptrs
Sea and rocks
  MnMW. Contemporary
  WMAA. Neuberger collection
Sea and sky
  IU. Contemp Amer ptg, 1948
Sea gulls
  Helm. John Marin
Sea horses—sea movement off Deer
  island, Maine   WMAA
  McCurdy
Sea piece   WMAA
  Cheney. Story 1958 ed
  Goodrich. Amer art (col)
  WMAA. Contemp Amer ptg, 1952
Sea piece (Fleischman coll)
  MiD. Coll in progress
  Richardson. Ptg in America
Sea piece—Boat fantasy
  Time. 300 years (col)
Sea piece, 1951 (Schulte coll)
  John Marin
Sea with red sky
  Helm. John Marin

MARIN, John—*Continued*

Seascape   CLA
  CLA. 35 ptgs
Seascape fantasy, Maine
  Time. 300 years (col)
Ships
  Lewisohn
Singer building   PPhM
  Canaday
A southwester
  Helm. John Marin
Speed—Lake Champlain   NUM
  John Marin
Spring no 1   DP
  Eliot. Art of our time (col)
  John Marin
  Time. 300 years (col)
Stock exchange, New York city
  John Marin (col)
Stonington and the harbor, Maine
  MiD. Coll in progress
  WiMiA. Amer ptg 1760-1960
Stonington harbor
  Helm. John Marin
Storm over Taos   DN
  Helm. John Marin (col)
  John Marin
  Pierson
Street crossing, New York   DP
  Helm. John Marin
  John Marin
Street movement, abstraction, New York
  MiD. Coll in progress
A street seeing
  Helm. John Marin (col)
Sun, isles and sea   MdB
  John Marin (col)
  Time. 300 years (col)
Sunset   WMAA
  Goodrich. Amer art
  Mendelowitz
  NYG. Fine art
  UNESCO. 1860-1949
  UNESCO. 1860-1955
  UNESCO. 1860-1959
Sunset (Halpert coll)
  DC. Halpert collection
  John Marin (col)
  Pierson
  Pousette-Dart. Amer ptg (col)
Sunset, Casco bay
  Baur. Revolution
  Helm. John Marin
Taos
  Biddle. Yes and no
Taos landscape, New Mexico
  Helm. John Marin
The three-master
  UNESCO. 1860-1955
  UNESCO. 1860-1959
Three nudes
  Helm. John Marin
Tree and sea, Maine   ICA
  Brown. Amer ptg
  PA. Annual ex, 1955
Tree, Cape Split
  CtY. Yale alumni
Tree forms
  MMA. Abstract
Tree no 1, Cape Split, Maine coast
  Helm. John Marin

Tunk mountains, autumn, Maine   DP
  Baur. New art (col)
  DP. Catalogue
  Larkin rev ed (col)
  Pierson
  UNESCO. 1860-1959
Tunk mountains, Maine
  NBuA. Expressionism
Two-master becalmed, Maine   MM
  Baur. New art
  Helm. John Marin
Tyrol at Kufstein, Tyrol series, no 3, 1910
  Helm. John Marin
Tyrolean mountains   OCo
  Brown. Amer ptg
Village, Maine
  Helm. John Marin
White mountain country   OCl
  John Marin
White mountain country, Dixville Notch
  no 1, 1927
  Cheney. Story 1958 ed
  John Marin
White mountain country, New Hampshire
         ATeS
  ATeS. Collection
White mountains, autumn
  Helm. John Marin
Wind on land and sea, Maine
  Cheney. New world history
  Cheney. Story 1958 ed
Women and sea
  UNESCO. 1860-1955
  UNESCO. 1860-1959
Women forms and sea
  Helm. John Marin
  John Marin
Woolworth building
  Baur. Revolution
  Flexner. Amer ptg
  Flexner. Short history
Woolworth building in construction
  NBuA. Fifty ptgs
Woolworth building no 31, 1912
  Baur. New art
  Brown. Amer ptg
  Helm. John Marin
  John Marin
  Rosenblum
Young man of the sea, Maine series no 10,
  1934   MM
  Helm. John Marin
  John Marin
Marin island, Small point, Maine by J.
  Marin
Marina Grande in Capri by A. Bierstadt
Marine by L. Feininger
Marine by A. P. Ryder
Marine by J. A. M. Whistler
Marine hospital, Chelsea, Massachusetts,
  1835-40 by Unidentified artist
Marine Sampson by A. Polonsky
Marine view with ships by T. Birch
Marine with shipping by J. Peale jr
A **mariner** by Unidentified artist
MARINGER, Carol
  Dummy
    NAD. Annual ex, 1956
MARIO, Alessandro, fl 1858-1868
  Construction work in New York, 1868
         NNHS
    Davidson v2

Marion, Francis, 1732-1795
  White, J. B. Gen Marion in his swamp
    encampment inviting a British officer
    to dinner
MARISOL (Marisol Escobar) 1930?-
  Purgatorio
    IU. Contemp Amer ptg & sculp, 1959
Maritime by K. Knaths
MARK, George Washington, fl 1817-1879
  Mountains
    Ford. Pictorial folk art
Market basket, hat, and umbrella by J. F.
  Peto
Market place, Venice by M. B. Prendergast
Markets
  Davis, L E. The market
  Dehn, A. A. Market, Port-au-Prince
  Di Gioia, F. Fish market
  Prestopino, G. The market
MARKMAN, Ronald, 1931-
  The entertainers III
    WMAA. Young America 1960
  Parade figure
    WMAA. Young America 1960
Marlin by J. Mitchell
Marmaduke, Meredith M. fl 1834
  Bingham, G. C. Meredith M. Marmaduke
Maroon on blue by M. Rothko
Marquand, John Phillips, 1893-
  James, A. John P. Marquand
Marr, Gerald
  Hurd, P. Gerald Marr
Marriage by M. Tobey
Marriage at Cana by Unidentified artist
The marriage of Heaven and Hell, Study for
  by B. Shahn
Marriage of reason and squalor by F. Stella
Mars, orange and green by A. G. Dove
Mars, Venus, and Vulcan by J. S. Copley
MARSDEN, Thomas
  On a point
    NSP. Sportscapes
Marseilles, night by R. A. Parker
Marsh, Charles, fl 1846
  Mason, B. F. Charles Marsh
Marsh, Molly. See Seymour, Molly (Marsh)
MARSH, Reginald, 1898-1954
  Along the waterfront   OYB
    OYB. Catalogue 1951
  Belles of the Battery (Battery belles)
                                           OYB
    OYB. Accessions
    OYB. Supplement 1959
    WMAA. Marsh
  BMT, Fourteenth street
    WMAA. Marsh
  The Bowery   MM
    Brown. Amer ptg
    Craven. Rainbow book
    Larkin
    Larkin rev ed
    MM. 100 Amer ptrs
  Bowery at Pell street
    WMAA. Marsh
  Bowery drunks
    IU. Contemp Amer ptg, 1951
    WMAA. Marsh
  The bowl   NBM
    Baur. Revolution
    Pierson
    WMAA. Marsh

  Coney island beach   CtHW
    CtHW. Handbook
  Coney island beach, 1934
    WMAA. Marsh
  Coney island beach, 1943   WMAA
    Mendelowitz
  Coney island beach, 1947
    WMAA. Marsh
  Coney island beach, 1951   WMAA
    WMAA. Marsh
    WMAA. Sara Roby
  Coney island, 1939
    CtY. Yale alumni
  Discharge of cargo at pier
    Pierson
  East Tenth street jungle
    WMAA. Marsh
  Eldorado
    WMAA. Marsh
  End of Fourteenth street crosstown line
                                            PA
    WMAA. Marsh
  Eyes tested
    WiMiA. Amer ptg 1760-1960
    WMAA. Marsh
  Fourteenth street
    WMAA. Marsh
  George Tilyou's steeplechase   PMB
    WMAA. Marsh
  Hat display
    WMAA. Marsh
  High yaller
    Craven. Treasury 1952 ed
    NYG. Fine art
    Roos
    WMAA. Marsh
  Holy Name mission   IBM
    ICA. Amer artists paint the city
  Hudson Bay fur company
    WMAA. Marsh
  Hudson burlesk chorus (Hudson bur-
    lesque chorus)
    NAD. Annual ex, 1955
    WMAA. Marsh
  Hudson burlesk, Union City, New Jersey
    WMAA. Marsh
  Human pool tables   WMAA
    Goodrich. Amer art (col)
    WMAA. Marsh (col)
  Locomotives watering
    WMAA. Marsh
  Martial spirit
    Bazin
  Matinee
    WMAA. Marsh (detail)
  Memories of the Stork club
    WMAA. Marsh
  Merry-go-round
    MM. Amer ptg today
    WMAA. Marsh
  Mink and mannequin
    WMAA. Marsh (col)
  Minsky's chorus
    WMAA. Marsh
  Monarch of Bermuda   ATeS
    ATeS. Collection
  Monday night at the Metropolitan   ATU
    ATU. Coll of Amer art (col)
    WMAA. Marsh
  Morning in May
    WMAA. Marsh
  Naked over New York
    WMAA. Marsh

MARSH, Reginald—_Continued_
Negroes on Rockaway beach
  Time. 300 years (col)
  WMAA. Marsh
New dodgem   WMAA
  WMAA. Marsh
No turns permitted
  WMAA. Marsh
Park bench   NeL
  Barker. From realism
Pip and Flip
  WMAA. Marsh
Prometheus in Rockefeller center
  WMAA. Marsh
Pursuit   OT
  Gruskin
  OT. Contemp Amer ptgs
Steel structure   MB
  MB. Ptgs in water color
Steeplechase park
  WMAA. Marsh
  WMAA. **Museum and its friends, 1958**
Street scene   ATU
  ATU. Coll of Amer art
Strip tease
  WMAA. Marsh
Stripper
  WMAA. **Marsh**
Swimming off West Washington **market**
                                         NBuA
  NBuA. Contemporary ptgs
  Pierson
  WMAA. Marsh
Swinging chairs
  WMAA. Marsh
Tattoo and haircut   ICA
  McCurdy
  Pierson
  WMAA. Marsh
Taxi dance hall
  WMAA. Marsh
Ten shots ten cents   MoSL
  MoSL. Handbook 1953
Texas Guinan and her gang   NUM
  NUM. Root bequest
They pay to be seen   PPhM
  Canaday
Twenty-cent movie   WMAA
  WMAA. Marsh
Under the el   MM
  Lewisohn
Why not use the el   WMAA
  Craven. Treasury 1952 ed
  Goodrich. Amer art
  Robb. Harper history
  Time. 300 years (col)
  Wight. Milestones
  WMAA. Marsh
Wooden horses
  Craven. Treasury 1952 ed (col)
Marsh in winter by D. Macknight
Marshall, John, 1755-1835
  Harding, C. Chief Justice John Marshall
  Hubard, W. J. John Marshall
  Inman, H. John Marshall
  Jarvis, J. W. John Marshall
The **marshes** by W De Kooning
Marshland by D. Macknight
Marsteller, Charlotte, c 1790
  Unidentified artist. Charlotte Marsteller

MARSTON, James B.
  State street and the old State House,
    Boston, 1801   MBH
  Davidson v2
MARTENS, J. W.
  Brooklyn Navy yard (Frigate USS United
    States)
  Pierson
Martha by Unidentified artist
Martha Washington's reception by D. Hunt-
  ington
Martha's Vineyard by J. Delbos
Martial memory by P. Guston
Martial spirit by R. Marsh
MARTIN, Caroline Louise, 1903-
  The innocents
  CSFP. Annual ex, 1952
Martin, Edward, 1782-1860
  Malbone, E. G. Edward Martin
MARTIN, Fletcher, 1904-
  Arabesque with bull
  Ebersole. Fletcher Martin
Bagnell dam on the Osage river
  Ebersole. Fletcher Martin
The barrier
  Ebersole. Fletcher Martin
Boy picking flowers
  Ebersole. Fletcher Martin
Celebration   MoKN
  Ebersole. Fletcher Martin
Charles Laughton as Captain Kidd
  Ebersole. Fletcher Martin
Cherry twice   WMAA
  Ebersole. Fletcher Martin
  NAD. Annual ex, 1949, 1st half
  Pierson
Clown act
  Ebersole. Fletcher Martin
Country dance
  Ebersole. Fletcher Martin
Dancer dressing
  Ebersole. Fletcher Martin
  PA. Annual ex, 1947
Earth machines
  Ebersole. Fletcher Martin
Exit in color
  Ebersole. Fletcher Martin
Fishing village
  Ebersole. Fletcher Martin
Florida landscape
  Ebersole. Fletcher Martin
The glory
  Ebersole. Fletcher Martin
Helen
  Ebersole. Fletcher Martin
Juliet   MM
  Ebersole. Fletcher Martin
July 4th, 5th, and 6th   IBM
  Ebersole. Fletcher Martin
Killer in costume
  Ebersole. Fletcher Martin
A lad from the fleet
  Ebersole. Fletcher Martin
Lullaby
  Ebersole. Fletcher Martin
  Gruskin (col)
Out at home
  Baur. Revolution
  Ebersole. Fletcher Martin
Picador
  Ebersole. Fletcher Martin

Quarry at night
  Ebersole. Fletcher Martin
Ruby
  Ebersole. Fletcher Martin
Rural family
  Ebersole. Fletcher Martin
Shooting gallery
  Cheney. Story 1958 ed
  Ebersole. Fletcher Martin
Still life with skull
  Ebersole. Fletcher Martin
Temptation in Tonopah
  Ebersole. Fletcher Martin
'Tis me O Lord
  Ebersole. Fletcher Martin
Tomorrow and tomorrow
  Ebersole. Fletcher Martin
The toss
  Ebersole. Fletcher Martin
Toy birds
  Ebersole. Fletcher Martin
Trouble in Frisco   MMA
  Ebersole. Fletcher Martin
  Pierson
The undefeated
  Ebersole. Fletcher Martin
Urchin's game
  Ebersole. Fletcher Martin
Vacation
  Ebersole. Fletcher Martin
Weeping girl
  Ebersole. Fletcher Martin
Wonderful object
  Ebersole. Fletcher Martin
  IU. Contemp Amer ptg & sculp, 1953
MARTIN, Homer Dodge, 1836-1897
Duclair on Seine   MB
  MB. Ptgs in water color
Harp of the winds (View of the Seine)
                                         MM
  NYG. Fine art
  Pierson
  Richardson. Ptg in America
  Roos
Lake Sanford in the Adirondacks   NNCe
  Larkin
  Larkin rev ed
  Pierson
Logging camp   MB
  Pierson
Newport landscape   OYB
  OYB. Catalogue 1951
Preston ponds, Adirondacks   MnMI
  Born
Sand dune, Lake Ontario   MM
  Pierson
View of the Seine. See Harp of the winds
Martin, Mrs Josiah. See Martin, Mary
  (Yeamans)
MARTIN, Keith Morrow, 1911-
Bearers of gifts
  WMAA. Contemp Amer ptg, 1955
Frontier   OYB
  OYB. Annual 1958
  OYB. Supplement 1959
MARTIN, Knox, 1923-
Calypso
  IU. Contemp Amer ptg & sculp, 1955
Martin, Mary Elizabeth, b 1763?
  Copley, J. S. Mary Elizabeth Martin
Martin, Mary (Yeamans) 1720-1805
  Feke, R. Mrs Josiah Martin

MARTIN, Silas, 1841-1906
Flintlock
  Frankenstein. After the hunt
Martin, Walter
  Reeder, D. Walter Martin
MARTINELLI, Ezio, 1912-
Corazziere
  ICA. Annual ex, 1947/48
Martinelli, Sebastiano, b 1848
  Eakins, T. His Eminence Cardinal Martinelli
MARTINO, Antonio Pietro, 1902-
Four houses
  NAD. Annual ex, 1951
Manayunk winter
  NAD. Annual ex, 1955
MARTINO, Giovanni, 1908-
At the crossing
  NAD. Annual ex, 1947, 1st half
Canton street
  OYB. Annual 1956
Grape hill, Manayunk   OYB
  OYB. Supplement
MARTYL (Suzanne Schweig) 1918-
Barcelona market II
  IU. Contemp Amer ptg & sculp, 1957
Getting ready   ATU
  ATU. Coll of Amer art
Northern lights
  IU. Contemp Amer ptg & sculp, 1959
South of Taxco
  IU. Contemp Amer ptg, 1951
Sun valley   ATU
  ATU. Coll of Amer art
View of Oxford
  IU. Contemp Amer ptg & sculp, 1961
Martyr by A. Rattner
Marvello by J. Glasco
Marx, Asher, fl 1803
  Malbone, E. G. Asher Marx
Marx, Joseph, fl 1806
  Malbone, E. G. Joseph Marx
Mary by S. E. Dickinson
Mary by R. Henri
Mary by S. Serisawa
Maryland family
  Unidentified artist. Maryland family
Maryland, View into by M. Reinhardt
Maryland landscape by W. H. Holmes
Masked bird fishing in the golden stream
  by M. Graves
Masks by J. Lawrence
Mason, Alice, b 1668
  Mason limner. Alice Mason
Mason, Alice, fl 1885
  Sargent, J. S. Mrs Alice Mason
MASON, Alice Trumbull, 1904-
Staff, distaff and rod
  NNSG. Younger Amer ptrs
MASON, Benjamin Franklin, 1804-1871
Bugbee family
  Frankenstein. Two journeyman ptrs
Charles K. Williams
  Frankenstein. Two journeyman ptrs
Charles Marsh
  Frankenstein. Two journeyman ptrs
Edwin Hutchinson
  Frankenstein. Two journeyman ptrs
Eliza Grover Chase
  Frankenstein. Two journeyman ptrs

MASON, B. F.—*Continued*
Elizabeth de Long Rockwell
    Frankenstein. Two journeyman ptrs
George Chapman
    Frankenstein. Two journeyman ptrs
Halsey Wing
    Frankenstein. Two journeyman ptrs
Harvey Kitchell
    Frankenstein. Two journeyman ptrs
Horatio Seymour
    Frankenstein. Two journeyman ptrs
Ira Stewart
    Frankenstein. Two journeyman ptrs
John Godfrey Saxe
    Frankenstein. Two journeyman ptrs
Julia, Mary Ann and Harriet Tilden
    Frankenstein. Two journeyman ptrs
Mehitabel Preston de Long
    Frankenstein. Two journeyman ptrs
Mrs George Chapman
    Frankenstein. Two journeyman ptrs
Mrs Halsey Wing
    Frankenstein. Two journeyman ptrs
Mrs John Godfrey Saxe
    Frankenstein. Two journeyman ptrs
Mrs Lebdeus Harris   VtMS
    Frankenstein. Two journeyman ptrs
Mrs Philip Battell
    Frankenstein. Two journeyman ptrs
Mrs Rufus Wainwright
    Frankenstein. Two journeyman ptrs
Mrs Samuel P. P. Fay
    Frankenstein. Two journeyman ptrs
Mrs Simeon Rockwell
    Frankenstein. Two journeyman ptrs
Rufus and Gardner Wainwright
    Frankenstein. Two journeyman ptrs
Rufus Wainwright
    Frankenstein. Two journeyman ptrs
Samuel Prescott Phillips Fay
    Frankenstein. Two journeyman ptrs
Simeon Rockwell
    Frankenstein. Two journeyman ptrs
Thomas E. Powers
    Frankenstein. Two journeyman ptrs

Attributed works

Norman Williams
    Frankenstein. Two journeyman ptrs
Mason, Eliza, 1784-1826
Malbone, E. G. Eliza Mason
Mason, Elizabeth Champlin. See Perry,
    Elizabeth Champlin (Mason)
Mason, Elizabeth (Heltzhoover)
Stuart, G. Mrs John Thompson Mason
Mason, Ida
Hunt, W. M. Miss Ida Mason
Mason, Lowell, 1792-1872
Unidentified artist. Lowell Mason
MASON, Roy Martell, 1886-
Anglers heaven
    NSP. Sportscapes
Fishing at the Spillway
    NSP. Sportscapes
The moment that makes duck hunting
    NSP. Sportscapes
MASON, William Sanford, fl 1838-1865
A country house   MB
    Chew. 250 years of art
    MB. Karolik coll
Venus and Cupid   MB
    MB. Karolik coll

MASON limner, fl 1670
Alice Mason
    Flexner. First flowers
    Ford. Pictorial folk art
    NUM. Art across America
Alice Mason   MQ
    Roos
David, Joanna, and Abigail Mason
    Flexner. First flowers
    Ford. Pictorial folk art
Mason children
    Mason limner. David, Joanna, and Abigail
    Mason
Masonic memorial by E. G. H. Pinney
Masqued image by J. Pollock
Masquerade by M. Beckmann
Master Willoughby by Unidentified artist
Masterpiece by W. Williams
Matau-Tathonca, Bull Bear—an Ogillalah,
    Head of by A. J. Miller
Matchbook by W. De Kooning
Matches no 2, 1927 by S. Davis
The **matement** by C. Howard
Maternità, 1943 by W. Pachner
Maternità, 1954-55 by W. Pachner
Maternità, 1956 by W. Pachner
Maternità no 1, 1957 by W. Pachner
Mather, Cotton, 1663-1728
    Pelham, P. Rev Cotton Mather
Mather, Elias, 1776-1843
    Ames, E. Elias Mather
Mather, Increase, 1639-1723
    Vanderspritt, J. Increase Mather
MATHIES, John Lee Douglas, 1780-1834
Jemima Wilkinson: the Publick Universal
    Friend
    Jones. Rediscovered ptrs
Red Jacket
    Jones. Rediscovered ptrs
Seneca veterans of the war of 1812
    Jones. Rediscovered ptrs
Wreck of the steamer Walk-in-the-water
                   MiD
    Jones. Rediscovered ptrs
Matinee by R. Marsh
Matlack, Timothy, fl 1795
    Peale, C. W. Timothy Matlack
Mato-tope with the marks of his exploits by
    K. Bodmer
Matriarch and the prodigal son by Z. Kacha-
    doorian
Matriarchy by M. Tomkins
Matrix by D. R. Stuart
Matrix of an unfathomable by B. Margo
MATSON, Greta Wilhelmina, 1915-
City child
    OYB. Annual 1948
MATTERN, Karl, 1892-
Winter shapes   IaDM
    CoS. New accessions USA, 1956
MATTESON, Thompkins Harrison, 1813-
    1884
Justice's court in the backwoods   NCHA
    Jones. Rediscovered ptrs
Sculptor's studio   NAI
    Larkin
    Larkin rev ed
Turkey shoot (from Cooper's The pio-
    neer)   NCHA
    Jones. Rediscovered ptrs

MATTHEW, K.
Autumn glory
  NYG. Fine art
Azalea tropical trails, Florida
  NYG. Fine art
Capitol reflections
  NYG. Fine art
Charming New Orleans
  NYG. Fine art
Gloucester boats
  NYG. Fine art
Harkness tower (Yale)
  NYG. Fine art
Independence hall (Philadelphia)
  NYG. Fine art
Lowell house (Harvard university)
  NYG. Fine art
Nassau hall (Princeton university)
  NYG. Fine art
Rocky neck (Gloucester)
  NYG. Fine art
Skyline (New York)
  NYG. Fine art
Spring idyll
  NYG. Fine art
Summer vista
  NYG. Fine art
Tropical surf (Florida)
  NYG. Fine art
Waterfront (New York)
  NYG. Fine art
Winter's dreamland
  NYG. Fine art
Matthews, Thomas J.
Corwine, A. H. Thomas J. Matthews
MATTSON, Henry Elis, 1887-
Atlantic
  NAD. Annual ex, 1951
Big Rock pool   OT
  OT. Contemp Amer ptgs
Blue night
  IU. Contemp Amer ptg 1948
Dawn
  IU. Contemp Amer ptg & sculp, 1961
Dawn light
  Cheney. Primer 1958 ed
Eventide   WMAA
  Goodrich. Amer art
Green sea   NBM
  Baur. Revolution
Gulls and sea   ATeS
  ATeS. Collection
Headland
  Pousette-Dart. Amer ptg
Landscape   MAP
  NYG. Fine art
Moonlit landscape   WMAA
  Pierson
Self-portrait
  Cheney. Story 1938 ed
  PA. Annual ex, 1950
Spring   WMAA
  Gruskin
Wings of the morning   MM
  Cheney. New world history
  Cheney. Story 1958 ed
  Pierson
  Wight. Milestones
Maua, our boatman by J. LaFarge
Mauch Chunk, Pennsylvania by J. Collins
Mauch Chunk, Pennsylvania by B. Mitchell

MAURER, Alfred Henry, 1868-1932
Abstraction   DP
  Larkin
  Larkin rev ed
An arrangement   WMAA
  McCausland. A. H. Maurer
At the shore
  Brown. Amer ptg
Le bal Bullier   MNS
  Baur. New art
Carousel   NBM
  McCausland. A. H. Maurer
Florentines   DP
  McCausland. A. H. Maurer
Flowers, c 1912   WMAA
  McCausland. A. H. Maurer
  McCurdy
Flowers, c 1925
  McCausland. A. H. Maurer
Gabrielle
  McCausland. A. H. Maurer
George Washington
  McCausland. A. H. Maurer
Green striped bowl
  McCausland. A. H. Maurer
Head in landscape
  MnMW. Contemporary
  WMAA. Neuberger collection
Head in motion
  Rathbun
Jeanne
  McCausland. A. H. Maurer
Landscape, c 1912
  Baur. Revolution
Landscape in the Vineyard
  Pierson
Landscape with farm
  Brown. Amer ptg
Nude
  McCausland. A. H. Maurer
Self-portrait, 1897
  McCausland. A. H. Maurer
Self-portrait with hat   MnMW
  Baur. New art
  Baur. Revolution
  McCausland. A H. Maurer (col front)
  Pierson
Still life
  NBuA. Expressionism
Still life: pear
  UNESCO. 1860-1955
  UNESCO. 1860-1959
Still life with ashtray
  Brown. Amer ptg
Still life with doily   DP
  Baur. New art (col)
  DP. Catalogue
  McCausland. A. H. Maurer
  Pierson
  UNESCO. 1860-1955
  UNESCO. 1860-1959
Still life with pears   MAP
  Hess. Abstract ptg
  McCausland. A. H. Maurer
Twin heads   WMAA
  Baur. New art
  Goodrich. Amer art
  McCausland. A. H. Maurer
  Pierson
Two girls
  WMAA. Pioneers
Two heads
  Brown. Amer ptg

MAURER, A. H.—*Continued*
Two heads (Godsoe and Knox coll)
  McCausland. A. H. Maurer
Two heads (Neumann coll)
  McCausland. A. H. Maurer
Two sisters
  McCausland. A. H. Maurer
Young girl   MeC
  MeC. Inaugural ex
MAURICE, E. Ingersoll, 1901-
Wood rose
  OYB. Annual 1955
Mauve recession by G. L. K. Morris
Mauve still life by S. M. Adler
Ma-wo-ma by A. J. Miller
Max by S. Davis
Max Schmidt in a single scull by T. Eakins
Maxon, Polly, fl 1815
  Unidentified artist. Polly Maxon of Ste-
    phentown, New York
MAXWELL, John, 1905-
Winter forms   OYB
  OYB. Annual 1957
  OYB. Supplement 1959
May, John, 1748-1812
Gullager, C. Col John May
May day, Central park by M. B. Prendergast
May 5 by B. Shahn
May in the mountains by E. Lawson
May: making soap, washing sheep by A. M.
    R. Moses
May night by W. L. Metcalf
May 2, 1956 by J. Levee
Maya, mirror of illusion by A. B. Davies
Las Mayas by H. Frankenthaler
Maybank, Susannah, b 1745
  Theus, J. Susannah Maybank
Maybelle by T. Eakins
Mayer, Mrs Christopher B. 1761-1848
  Eichholtz, J. Mrs Christopher B. Mayer
MAYER, Frank Blackwell, 1827-1899
Leisure and labor   DC
  DC. Amer ptrs of the South
MAYER, Henrik Martin, 1908-
Barometer falling   OYB
  OYB. Annual 1949
Foreboding
  OYB. Annual 1952
Mayer, Susan B. See Mayer, Mrs Christo-
    pher B.
Mayflower by R. G. Hamilton
MAYHEW, Nathaniel, fl 1823
John Harrison   DN
  DN. Amer primitive ptgs, pt 2
Mrs John Harrison and her daughter
    Marie   DN
  DN. Amer primitive ptgs, pt 2
MAYR, Christian, 1805-1850
Kitchen ball at White Sulphur Springs,
    Virginia, 1838   NoCR
  Davidson v 1
  NoCR. Catalogue
Mazatlan women by M. O. Sheets
Maze by E. Ludins
Mazyck, Mary (Mazyck)
  Theus, J. Mrs William Mazyck
Mazyck, Stephen, 1718-1770
  Theus, J. Stephen Mazyck

Mazyck, Susanne (Ravenel)
  Theus, J. Mrs Stephen Mazyck
Mazyck, William, 1739-1775
  Theus, J. William Mazyck
Me and the battle of Tassafaronga, Guadal-
    canal by B. L. Culwell
Mead, Mary Gertrude. See Abbey, Mary
    Gertrude (Mead)
MEADOR, Joshua Lawrence, 1911-
Remnants of an era
  NAD. Annual ex, 1955
The meadow by J. R. Cox
The meadow by J. W. Guerin
Meadow and hills: sunset by B. West (at-
    tributed works)
Meadows in winter by F. W. Benson
Meads, John, 1777-1859
  Ames, E. John Meads
Meads, Louisa (Crane) b 1785
  Ames, E. Mrs John Meads
The meal by T. H. Benton
Means, Mary H. (Barnwell) 1781-1849
  Malbone, E. G. Mrs Robert Means
Means, Thomas, 1767-1828
  Malbone, E. G. Thomas Means
Mears, Grace. See Levy, Grace (Mears)
Measurement and contemplation by E. John-
    son
Mechanical abstraction by M. L. Schamberg
MECHAU, Frank Albert, 1904-1946
Tom Kenney comes home
  Taylor. Fifty centuries, 1954 ed (col)
Medfield, Evening at by G. Inness
Medford marshes by G. L. Brown
Medianus by J. Ferren
Medicine bag by C. Wimar
Medicine bag dance of the Sauk and Fox by
    G. Catlin
Medicine circles by A. J. Miller
Medicine man
  Catlin, G. Blackfoot doctor in his mystery
    dress endeavoring to cure his dying
    patient
  Catlin, G. Blackfoot medicine man
  Catlin, G. Mandan medicine man
  Catlin, G. Se-non-ti-yak, the Blistered
    Foot, Ioway medicine man
  Catlin, G. Uruguay medicine man, South
    America
  Catlin, G. Wun-nee-tow, the White Buf-
    falo, Blackfoot medicine man
  Russell, C. M. The medicine man
Medicine show IV by J. Levine
Medieval scribe by E. Laning
Meditation by B. Kopman
Meditation by C. M. Russell
Meditation by A. H. Thayer
Meditation by the sea by Unidentified artist
Meditation in space by W. Sommer
Meditative series no 9, 1954 by M. Tobey
Mediterranean coast by R. D. Gauley
Mediterranean landscape by J. E. Heliker
The medium by H. Bloom
Medium still life by S. Davis
MEEHAN, Thomas, 1923-
Day of mountain flowers   OYB
  OYB. Annual 1953
  OYB. Supplement

MEEKER, Dean Jackson, 1920-
Don Quixote
  IU. Contemp Amer ptg & sculp, 1953
King's joke   WiMiA
  CoS. New accessions USA, 1956
MEEKER, Joseph Rusling, 1827-1889
In the swamp opposite Bayou Sara
  Rathbone
Land of Evangeline   MoSL
  Baur. Amer ptg
  Born
  MoSL. Handbook 1953
  Pierson
Meerschaum pipe by W. M. Harnett
MEERT, Joseph John Paul, 1905-
Motif in pink
  IU. Contemp Amer ptg & sculp, 1955
Still life on a sewing machine
  PA. Annual ex, 1950
The meeting by J. Corbino
Meeting of the three by F. Ruvolo
MEGARGEE, Lon, 1886-
Cowboy and his lady
  NYG. Fine art
Desert song
  NYG. Fine art
Donkey business
  NYG. Fine art
Home on the ranch
  NYG. Fine art
Saturday night on the ranch
  NYG. Fine art
MEIGS, Walter, 1918-
Still life with milk bottle
  IU. Contemp Amer ptg & sculp, 1953
White mist to greens
  ICA. Annual ex, 1961
MEITZLER, Neil, 1930-
Edge of evening
  IU. Contemp Amer ptg & sculp, 1959
Time of change
  OrPA. Ptgs & sculptures
Melancholia by K. Zerbe
Mélancholie by E. Berman
MELCARTH, Edward, 1915-
Ajax
  ICA. Annual ex, 1945/46 (cover)
For God must have loved them
  Genauer
Litter
  PPC. Ptg in the U.S. 1949
The sleepers
  ICA. Annual ex, 1951
String of pearls
  PPC. International ex, 1952
Washerwomen
  WMAA. Contemp Amer ptg, 1952
MELCHERS, Gari, 1860-1932
Arranging the tulips   DNC
  DNC. Gellatly coll, 1954
Fencing master   MiD
  MiD. Treasures
  Pierson
In my garden   OYB
  OYB. Catalogue 1951
Madonna   MM
  MM. 100 Amer ptrs
Mrs Samuel Mountfort Pitts   MiD
  MiD. Ports of the Pitts family
Mother and child   ICA
  NYG. Fine art

Penelope   DC
  NYG. Fine art
Thomas Pitts   MiD
  MiD. Ports of the Pitts family
Thomas Pitts, Head of   MiD
  MiD. Ports of the Pitts family
Mellow pad by S. Davis
Melon by B. Bomar
Melon, peaches and grapes by Rubens Peale
Melons and grapes by Chipman
Melons and morning glories by Raphaelle
  Peale
Melons and other fruit by Unidentified
  artist
Melting horizon by I. R. Pereira
Melville, Deborah (Scollay). See Scollay,
  Deborah
Melville, Mrs John. See Scollay, Deborah
Melville, Maria (Gansevoort) 1791-1872
  Ames, E. Mrs Allan Melville
Member of a city cast no 9 by N. Carone
Mementos by M. M. Koffler
Memo by S. Davis
Memorial by J. Hirsch
Memorial day by A. N. Wyeth
Memories by L. K. Bruckman
Memories by K. Okada
Memories by W. Quirt
Memories of Andalusia by H. G. Keller
Memories of the Stork club by R. Marsh
Memory by L. Beck
Memory of Ischia by E. Berman
Men and mountain by P. Evergood
Men fighting and stars in the Solomons by
  B. L. Culwell
Men of progress: American inventors, 1861
  by J. Sartain (after Christian Schus-
  sele)
Men of the docks by G. W. Bellows
Men of the open range by C. M. Russell
Men without women by S. Davis
Men working by K. Sage
Mending by I. Bishop
Mending fence by E. F. Spruce
Mending the harness by A. P. Ryder
Mending the nets by A. P. Ryder
MENG, John, 1734-c 1754
Self-portrait   PH
  Chew. 250 years of art
MENKÈS, Sigmund, 1896-
The blues singer
  NAD. Annual ex, 1953
Boy playing harmonica   MMA
  Pousette-Dart. Amer ptg
Boy with doves no 3
  PPC. International ex, 1952
Day's end
  DC. 20 biennial ex, 1947
  IU. Contemp Amer ptg, 1948
  UNESCO. 1860-1949
  UNESCO. 1860-1955
Field flowers
  CSFP. Annual ex, 1948/49
Figure in pictorial space
  PPC. Ptg in the U.S. 1949

MENKÈS, Sigmund—*Continued*
Fruit bowl with mirror
IU. Contemp Amer ptg, 1949
Girl holding a dog
IU. Contemp Amer ptg & sculp, 1953
Girl with fruit bowl   MnMW
CoS. New accessions USA, 1950
The painter   WMAA
Pierson
Repose
Genauer (col)
Self-portrait
NAD. Annual ex, 1948
Still life in gold and green
CanO. Hirshhorn coll
Still life with blue vase
PA. Annual ex, 1956
White lilac
NAD. Annual ex, 1959
Menkès, Zygmund. See Menkès, Sigmund
Me-no-quet, a Pottawattomie chief by J. O. Lewis
Mental geography by L. Guglielmi
Merced river, Yosemite valley by A. Bierstadt
Mercer, Charles Fenton, 1778-1858
Malbone, E. G. Charles Fenton Mercer
Mercer, Hugh, c 1725-1777
Trumbull, J. Death of Gen Mercer at the Battle of Princeton
MERCER, William, 1773?-1850?
Battle of Princeton, 1777   NJP
Davidson v 1
Battle of Princeton, 1777   PH
U.S. National Capital sesquicentennial com
The **merchant** by R. B. Crafft
Merchants' exchange and Girard's bank, Philadelphia, View of by N. V. Calyo
Merganser duck by W. M. Harnett
Mermaid by M. A. Willson
MERRETT, Susan, fl 1848
Fourth of July picnic
Born
Ford. Pictorial folk art
MERRILD, Knud, 1894-1954
Decay and resurrection
IU. Contemp Amer ptg, 1952
MERRILL, Sarah, fl 1810
Mourning picture
Ford. Pictorial folk art
Merrill, Sarah, 1813-1896. See Pitts, Sarah (Merrill)
Merritt parkway by W. De Kooning
Merry bench by A. Etherovich
Merry-go-rounds
Bohrod, A. Merry-go-round
Carter, C. H. Carousel by the sea
Marsh, R. Merry-go-round
Prendergast, M. B. Flying horses
Prendergast, M. B. Merry-go-round
Mesa Grande by H. Aach
Mesa Verde by R. Haines
Message by M. Graves
Message for mercy by G. Abercrombie
The **messenger** by R. Ray
The **messenger** by J. C. Wayne
Metamorphosis by F. Ruvolo
Metamorphosis by T. Takai

METCALF, Willard Leroy, 1858-1925
Golden carnival   NR
NYG. Fine art
May night   DC
DC. 25 biennial ex, 1957
North country   MM
NYG. Fine art
November mosaic   CtNB
NYG. Fine art
October morning, Deerfield, Massachusetts   DF
Born
Meteorite by E. A. Donati
Methodist church, Provincetown by E. Hopper
Metope by C. Oscar
Metronome by W. T. Murch
Metropolis by G. Grosz
The **Metropolitan** museum in Fourteenth street, 1881 by F. Waller
Metropolitan nocturne by M. Friedman
MEURER, Charles Alfred, b 1865
Doughboy's equipment
Frankenstein. After the hunt
The pen is mightier than the sword
Frankenstein. After the hunt
Mexican meat market by K. F. Feuerherm
Mexican news by R. C. Woodville
Mexican platter by K. Knaths
Mexican ruin by H. Sternberg
Mexican vase with flowers by A. F. Levinson
Mexico
Berman, E. Apotheosis of Mexican baroque
Berman, E. Mexican pyramid—the living and the dead
Berman, E. Perspective of Mexican hill town
Burg, C. C. Mexican landscape
Chapman, C. W. Panorama; the valley of Mexico
Fausett, W. D. Cuernavaca
Hirsch, S. Pic of Orizaba
Macknight, D. Along the road, Cordoba, Mexico
Macknight, D. Cuautla, Mexico
Macknight, D. Environs of Jalapa, Mexico
Macknight, D. In the valley
Ray, R. D. Manzanillo, Mexico
Rosenthal, D. Mexican church
Zerbe, K. Street in Tepoztlan, Mexico
Meyer de Schauensee sisters
Watkins, F. C. Misses Maude and Maxine Meyer de Schauensee
MEYEROWITZ, William, 1893-
Joel
NAD. Annual ex, 1949, 1st half
MEYR, Christian
Fire masters and officers of volunteer fire companies of Charleston, 1840
Davidson v2
MICHAEL, Lily, 1912-
Duel and pantomime
IU. Contemp Amer ptg, 1952
Michel's house by H. M. Gasser
MICHELSON, Leo, 1887-
Fishermen on the Seine
NSP. Sportscapes
Michigan landscape by L. Ritman
Micro-macrocosmic landscape by H. Lundeberg

Microscopic by L. E. Kuperman

Middlecott, Richard, fl 1713
Byfield, N. Richard Middlecott

Middleton, Alicia Hopton (Russell) See Russell, Alicia Hopton

Middleton, Arthur, fl 1771
West, B. Arthur Middleton, his wife and son

Middleton, Mrs Arthur. See Russell, Alicia Hopton

MIDDLETON, John Izard, 1785-1849
General view of the site of the ancient city of Norba   MCH
Richardson. Ptg in America

MIDDLETON, Thomas, 1797-1863
Interior of the Second street Philip's church, Charleston, South Carolina, 1836
U.S. National Capital sesquicentennial com

Midi by S. Davis

Mid-June by C. E. Burchfield

Midnight by F. Hillsmith

Midnight by H. Mandel

Midnight quarry by W. Thon

Midnight ride of Paul Revere by G. Wood

Midsummer phlox by H. Pittman

Midtown, New York by J. Marin

Midwest by C. Sheeler

MIFFLIN, Lloyd, 1846-1921
View of the Susquehanna, below Wrightsville, Pennsylvania
Chew. 250 years of art
View of the Susquehanna, Wrightsville, Pennsylvania
Chew. 250 years of art

Mifflin, Sarah (Morris) 1747?-1790
Copley, J. S. Mr and Mrs Thomas Mifflin

Mifflin, Thomas, 1744-1800
Copley, J. S. Mr and Mrs Thomas Mifflin
West, B. Thomas Mifflin

Migration by W. Gropper

Migration of the Negro by J. Lawrence

Migration to nowhere by R. Lebrun

Mike and the chart by W. Peirce

Milan, Italy
Heade, J. Impressions of Milan

MILBOURNE, Charles, fl 1790
Government house, Bowling Green, New York, 1797   NNHS
Dickson. John Wesley Jarvis

Mile drive, California by D. Kingman

Mile high by G. Peirce

Miles, Ruth (Henshaw) See Bascom, Ruth (Henshaw) Miles

Miles and the governess by C. H. Demuth

Miles City, Montana by H. Steiffel

Milford, North Wales, Pennsylvania by T. Birch

Milford, North Wales, Pennsylvania by Dietz

Military by M. Hartley

Military necessity by A. Bohrod

Militia muster by D. C. Johnston

Milk sledge by P. S. Sample

Milking time by W. Homer

Milkman by N. V. Calyo

Milkman and the maid by W. J. Hubard

Milkman of Goshen by H. Pippin

The mill by Unidentified artist

The mill boy by G. C. Bingham

Mill entrance by G. Breckner

Mill race by S. Andrews

Mill stream by W. L. Stevens

Mill wheel by L. Powell

MILLARC, William, 1920-
The beast
IU. Contemp Amer ptg, 1950

MILLER, Alfred Jacob, 1810-1874
American fur company caravan en route to Wyoming, 1837   MdBW
Davidson v 1
Antoine Clement   MdBW
Miller, A. J. The West
Approaching buffalo [1]   MdBW
Miller, A. J. The West
Approaching buffalo [2]   MdBW
Miller, A. J. The West
Arapahos   MdBW
Miller, A. J. The West
Argali—mountain sheep   MdBW
Miller, A. J. The West
Aricara female   MdBW
Miller, A. J. The West
Attack by Crow Indians   MdBW
Miller, A. J. The West
Auguste and his horse   MdBW
Miller, A. J. The West
Bannock, Indian   MdBW
Miller, A. J. The West
Beating a retreat   MB
MB. Karolik coll
Pierson
Beating a retreat   MdBW
Miller, A. J. The West
Bee hunter   MdBW
Miller, A. J. The West
Big Bowl (a Crow chief)   MdBW
Miller, A. J. The West
Black Hills   MdBW
Miller, A. J. The West
The Blackfeet   MdBW
Miller, A. J. The West
Bourgouis W---r and his squaw   MdBW
Miller, A. J. The West
The bravado   MdBW
Baum. Amer ptg
Miller, A. J. The West
Breakfast at sunrise   MdBW
Miller, A. J. The West
Breaking up camp at sunrise   MdBW
Miller, A. J. The West
Buffalo at bay   MdBW
Miller, A. J. The West
Buffalo chase—by a female   MdBW
Miller, A. J. The West
Buffalo hunting near Independence rock   MdBW
Miller, A. J. The West
Buffalo turning on his pursuers   MdBW
Miller, A. J. The West
Buffaloes drinking and bathing at night   MdBW
Miller, A. J. The West
Rathbone
Bull-boating   MdBW
Miller, A. J. The West
Rathbone

MILLER, Barse, 1904-
Bristol mills
OYB. Catalogue 1951   OYB
Mud hook
NAD. Annual ex, 1958
Parish playground
NAD. Annual ex, autumn 1949
Waterfall
NAD. Annual ex, 1951
MILLER, Charles F. fl 1850
Seven Sisters mountain
Chew. 250 years of art
MILLER, Kenneth Hayes, 1876-1952
Albert P. Ryder   DP
DP. Catalogue
Bargain hunters   WMAA
WMAA. Sara Roby
Box party   WMAA
McCurdy
Pierson
The fitting room   MM
MM. 100 Amer ptrs
Pierson
Fourteenth street
Brown. Amer ptg
Landscape with a broken tree
NAD. Annual ex, 1948
Little coat and fur shop
NYG. Fine art
Reverie
ICA. Annual ex, 1945/46
Shopper   WMAA
Goodrich. Amer art
Larkin
Larkin rev ed
Wight. Milestones
Show window no 2
Gruskin
MILLER, Lewis
Hydrant water conveyed through wooden
pipes, 1816, York, Pennsylvania
Davidson v2
MILLER, William R. fl 1853-1869
Old mill by waterfall
Sears. Highlights
MILLMAN, Edward, 1907-
Invasion
Pousette-Dart. Amer ptg
Night chant
MM. Amer ptg today
Mills
Boit, E. D. Old mill near St Enogat, Brit-
tany
Breckner, G. Mill entrance
Chapin, J. B. Old mill, Hanover, New
Hampshire
Cole, T. Old mill at sunset
Durrie, G. H. Old mill, winter
Durrie, G. H. Sunset, Mount Carmel,
Connecticut
Durrie, G. H. Winter in the country, the
old grist mill
Inness, G. Old mill
Johnson, D. Old mill, West Milford, New
Jersey
Kachmer, G. Winter along the mills
Lawson, E. Old mill
Miller, B. Bristol mills
Miller, W. R. Old mill by waterfall
Moses, A. M. R. The red mill
Unidentified artist. Mill of C. J. Hill &
Son

Unidentified artist. Old mill
Unidentified artist. Pennsylvania mill
with Conestoga wagon
Unidentified artist. Red mill
Wall, W. C. Homestead mill near Pitts-
burgh
Mills residence, Ames, New York by Un-
identified artist
MILNE, A. 19th cent
Smithtown, Long Island, c 1860   MSM
Davidson v 1
Milnor, Joseph Kirkbride, 1775-1828
Malbone, E. G. Joseph K. Milnor II
Milton, Massachusetts with Flat pond and
buildings, View near by D. C. John-
ston
Mime by M. Ray
Mine disaster by P. Evergood
Mine disaster by B. Shahn
Miners resting by P. S. Sample
Miners' wives by B. Shahn
Minerva, Head of by W. M. Harnett
MINGLE, fl 1878
Victorian building   MeC
Jetté. Amer heritage collection
Mink and mannequin by R. Marsh
Minneapolis grain elevator by R. Crawford
Minnehaha, Death of by F. Remington
Minnesota in August by A. A. Dehn
The Minnetaree scalp dance by K. Bodmer
Minnetarees on the Upper Missouri by F.
Kurz
Minot, Mrs Stephen, fl 1805
Trumbull, J. Mrs Stephen Minot
Minot, Mrs William. See Sedgwick, Kath-
erine
Minsky's chorus by R. Marsh
Minstrel banjo player by D. Morrill
Minstrel show by C. Winter
Minthorne, Hannah. See Tomkins, Hannah
(Minthorne)
MINTZ, Harry, 1907-
One day in spring
IU. Contemp Amer ptg, 1948
Self-portrait
CSFP. Annual ex, 1946
View of Toledo, Spain
IU. Contemp Amer ptg & sculp, 1961
MINTZ, Raymond August, 1925-
Artist's studio
CSFP. Annual ex, 1952
The kitchen
IU. Contemp Amer ptg, 1952
The sink
ICA. Annual ex, 1951
Window
IU. Contemp Amer ptg & sculp, 1959
MIRA, Alfred S. 1900-
Washington monument, Washington
square, N.Y.
PPC. Ptg in the U.S. 1949
Mirabilia by L. Feitelson
The miracle by S. G. Reinhardt
Mirage by T. D. Benrimo
Mirage by E. A. Chavez
Mirage of time by Y. Tanguy
Mirage—ships at night by W. Zorach
The mirror by M. Beckmann

The **mirror** by W. M. Chase
The **mirror** by P. Guston
The **mirror** by Y. Kuniyoshi
The **mirror** by H. Lundeberg
The **mirror** by P. Tchelitchew
Mirsky, D. S.
  Evergood, P. M. T. Florinsky, D. S. Mirsky and the pidget
Miss C. Parsons as the Lady of the Lake by T. Sully
Miss Liberty by Unidentified artist
Mississippi girl by M. Greenwood
Mississippi river and valley
  Curry, J. S. The Mississippi
  Kingman, H. M. Mississippi river landing
  Palmer, F. F. Champions of the Mississippi
  Palmer, F. F. Wooding up on the Mississippi
  Sebron, V. V. Sugar levee, New Orleans
  Walker, W. A. Scene along the lower Mississippi
  Wild, J. C. Dubuque, Iowa
  Wild, J. C. View of Davenport, Iowa and the Mississippi
Missouri mural by T. H. Benton
Missouri river and valley
  Bingham, G. C. Fur traders descending the Missouri
  Bingham, G. C. Missouri landscape
  Catlin, G. Upper Missouri: grand detour
  Catlin, G. View on the upper Missouri—Riccaree village
Mist by D. Macknight
Mist in the Yellowstone by T. Moran
Mr Ace by Y. Kuniyoshi
Mr River's garden by A. N. Wyeth
Mrs Besant takes action by G. Russell
Mrs Gamley by G. B. Luks
Mrs McCormick's general store, Catskill, N.Y. by A. Del O. Browere
Mrs S by T. Eakins
Mrs Starke's brother of Troy by Unidentified artist
Mrs T in cream silk by G. W. Bellows
Mrs T in wine silk by G. W. Bellows
Misty day in March by E. Lawson
Misty ocean by G. Peterdi
MITCHELL, Bruce, 1908-1963
  Fire island landing   MM
    NYG. Fine art
  Hudson autumn   ATU
    ATU. Coll of Amer art
    Gruskin (col)
  Mauch Chunk, Pennsylvania   ATU
    ATU. Coll of Amer art
MITCHELL, Fred, 1923-
  White, black and red
    NNSG. Younger Amer ptrs
MITCHELL, Joan, 1926-
  Cafe
    OCl. Some contemporary works
  George went swimming at Barnes hole, but it got too cold   NBuA
    NBuA. Acquisitions 1957-58
  Hemlock
    Baur. Nature
  King of spades
    OCl. Some contemporary works

Marlin
  PPC. International ex, 1961/62
Painting, 1953   MnMW
  MnMW. 60 Amer ptrs
Ste Hilaire
  DC. 26 biennial ex, 1959
To the harbourmaster   PPC
  Read. Concise history
Mitchell, Margaret. See Sewall, Margaret (Mitchell)
MITCHELL, Wallace, 1911-
Processional
  MnMW. Classic tradition
Mix, John, fl 1788
  Unidentified artist. John Mix
Mix, Ruth (Stanley) b 1756
  Unidentified artist. Mrs Ruth Stanley Mix
Moby Dick. by W. A. Baziotes
Moby Dick by K. Knaths
Moby Dick by B. Robinson
Mocking soldier by R. Lebrun
Mockingbird with rattlesnake robbing nest by J. J. Audubon
MODEL, Evsa, 1900-
Uptown
  MMA. Abstract
The **model** by W. M. Chase
The **model** by I. Soyer
Model in dressing room by J. Sloan
Model in the studio by G. Grosz
Modern classic by C. Sheeler
Modern conveniences by C. H. Demuth
Modern inquisitor by P. Evergood
MOFCHUM, Gerald
Listening to the voice of stone
  NAD. Annual ex, 1958
Shadow and substance
  NAD. Annual ex, 1957
Moffatt, Catherine (Cutt) 1700-1769
  Greenwood, J. Mrs John Moffatt
Moffatt, Elizabeth, b 1725
  Greenwood, J. Elizabeth Moffatt
Moffatt, John, 1692-1786
  Greenwood, J. John Moffatt
Moffatt, Mrs John. See Moffatt, Catherine (Cutt)
Mohawk valley
  Hammer, J. J. Peaceful day in the Mohawk valley
  Havell, R. (attributed works) Mohawk valley
  Unidentified artist. Mohawk valley
  Wyant, A. H. Mohawk valley
MOHOLY-NAGY, László, 1895-1946
  Ch Beata 1, 1939   NNSG
    50 years of mod art
  Chicago space no 7, 1941   NNSG
    MnMW. Classic tradition
  G-5, 1923-26   CtY
    CtY. Soc Anonyme
  Space modulator   WMAA
    Goodrich. Amer art
    Pierson
Mojave by J. Ferren
MOLLER, Hans, 1905-
  Chess players
    Genauer (col)
  Clown
    DC. 22 biennial **ex, 1951**

Cock fight
  IU. Contemp Amer ptg, 1949
Composition
  IU. Contemp Amer ptg, 1952
Crown of thorns
  Pierson
  WMAA. Annual ex, 1958
Emerald
  IU. Contemp Amer ptg & sculp, 1957
Flutes
  IU. Contemp Amer ptg & sculp, 1953
Forsythias
  Baur. Nature (col)
Music
  IU. Contemp Amer ptg & sculp, 1955
Reflections
  NBuA. Expressionism
Station of the Cross
  IU. Contemp Amer ptg & sculp, 1959
Still life with hourglass
  DC. 20 biennial ex, 1947
Towards Monhegan
  DC. 27 biennial ex, 1961
Winter
  VR. Biennial ex, 1948
Woodpile
  IU. Contemp Amer ptg, 1950
MOLZAHN, Johannes, 1892-
Icarus
  Rathbun
Phenomena   CtY
  CtY. Soc Anonyme
Moment in time by S. Rosenberg
The moment that makes duck hunting by
  R. M. Mason
Momentous vision of spring by G. Brody
MOMMER, Paul, 1899-1963
Studio interior no 2
  Pousette-Dart. Amer ptg
Mom's cathedral by P. Evergood
Monarch of Bermuda by R. Marsh
Monday night at the Metropolitan by R.
  Marsh
Money by A. Leslie
Money diggers by J. Quidor
Monhegan by R. M. Farruggio
Monhegan hill by L. J. Liberté
Monhegan theme by L. Dodd
Monitor and Merrimac by J. Hamilton
The monk by G. Inness
Monk in white by N. Carone
Monkey bars by H. Koerner
Monkeys
  Trivigno, P. Captives
  Tschacbasov, N. The monkey
  Watkins, F. C. Make the monkey jump
Monks fishing, Venice by L. Bosa
Monks of Burano by L. Bosa
Monmouth, James Scott, duke of, 1649-1685
  Copley, J. S. Arrest of Monmouth before
    James II
The Monongahela, Scene on by E. Bott
Monongahela bridge after the freshet in 1832
  by R. Smith
Monongahela river opposite Pittsburgh by
  R. Smith
Monreale by J. E. Heliker
Monroe, James, president U.S. 1758-1831
  Stuart, G. James Monroe

Monroe, Marilyn, 1926-1962
  De Kooning, W. Marilyn Monroe
Mont St Michel by J. T. Arms
Montague, Massachusetts, Gentleman from,
  by Unidentified artist
Montague, Massachusetts, Lady from, by
  Unidentified artist
MONTALANT, Joseph O. fl 1855
Site of Azilum
  McClintock
The Susquehanna
  McClintock
Tioga point valley
  McClintock
Wyalusing
  McClintock
Montauk fisherman by C. Hassam
Montauk highway by W. De Kooning
Montauk montage by R. B. Motherwell
Monte Video, summer home of Daniel Wads-
  worth by T. Cole
Monte Video, View of by T. Cole
Montesquiou-Fezensac, Robert, Comte de,
  1797-1850
  Whistler, J. A. M. Comte Robert de
    Montesquiou-Fezensac
Montezuma alarmed by evil signs by L. Sie-
  griest
Montgomery, Mrs James
  Sully, T. Mrs James Montgomery
Montgomery, Mrs John, fl 1800
  Peale, Raphaelle. Mrs John Montgomery
Montgomery, Rachel (Harvey) fl 1781
  Malbone, E. G. Mrs William Montgomery
Montgomery, Richard, 1736?-1775
  Trumbull, J. Death of Gen Montgomery
    at Quebec
Montmartre by O. M. Pleissner
Montmartre impasse by W. A. Smith
Montparnasse, Paris by M. B. Prendergast
Montresor, John, fl 1772
  Copley, J. S. Col John Montresor (Wil-
    liam? Montresor)
Montserrat by K. Schrag
The monument by H. Koerner
Monument in the plaza by J. Sloan
Monument mountain, Berkshires by A. B.
  Durand
Monument to light by B. Greene
Monument valley by J. C. Haley
Monumentality by G. Greene
Mood by A. Brook
Mood indigo by C. Seliger
The mood of now by Y. Tanguy
Moon by A. G. Dove
Moon by K. Knaths
Moon and locomotive by D. Kingman
Moon and shoals by R. Tam
Moon animal by W. A. Baziotes
Moon bathers by F. Puma
Moon fantasy by W. A. Baziotes
Moon forms by W. A. Baziotes
Moon mad crow in the surf by M. Graves
Moon maiden by P. Evergood
Moon song by D. Austin
Moon vibrations by J. Pollock
Moon woman cuts a circle by J. Pollock

MOONEY, Edward Ludlow, 1813-1887
Mrs Robert Maitland   NNHS
NNHS. Waldron Phoenix Belknap coll
Robert Maitland   NNHS
NNHS. Waldron Phoenix Belknap coll
Mooney, Thomas J. Zechariah, 1885-1942
Shahn, B. Rena and Tom Mooney
Moonflowers at dusk by C. E. Burchfield
Moonlight by R. A. Blakelock
Moonlight by J. W. Casilear
Moonlight by Corbino
Moonlight by J. De Martini
Moonlight by L. MacIver
Moonlight by A. P. Ryder
Moonlight at sea by A. P. Ryder
Moonlight—camp scene by A. J. Miller
Moonlight, harbour town by K. Knaths
Moonlight, Indian encampment by R. A.
Blakelock
Moonlight landscape by R. A. Blakelock
Moonlight marine by A. P. Ryder
Moonlight on Passamaquoddy bay by G.
Innes
Moonlight on the sea by A. P. Ryder
Moonlight on the waters by A. P. Ryder
Moonlight scene by G. C. Bingham
Moonlight sonata by R. A. Blakelock
Moonlight stampede by G. C. Delano
Moonlight, Tarpon Springs by G. Inness
Moonlit cove by A. P. Ryder
Moonlit landscape by W. Allston
Moonlit landscape by H. E. Mattson
Moonrise, marine by A. P. Ryder
Moonrise—northern Arizona by J. E. Swin-
nerton
Moonset and sunrise by M. T. Zorach
Moonshine fantasy by O. F. Bluemner
Moor swan by M. Graves
Moore, Almira (Gallond) fl 1840
Field, E. S. Mrs Joseph Moore
MOORE, Charles Herbert, 1840-1930
Down the Hudson to West Point   NPV
Born
Old bridge   NJP
Baur. Revolution
Born
Moore, Elizabeth (Vander Horst) 1737-1790
Theus, J. Mrs John Moore
Moore, Hannah. See Peale, Hannah (Moore)
MOORE, Harriet, b 1812
Richardson memorial   NCHA
Time. 300 years (col)
Moore, Joseph, fl 1840
Field, E. S. Joseph Moore and his family
Moore, Mrs John. See Moore, Elizabeth
(Vander Horst)
Moore, Mrs Joseph. See Moore, Almira
(Gallond)
Moorland landscape by B. West (attributed
works)
The moors by K. Knaths
Moose. See Deer
Moose hunters' camp, Nova Scotia by A.
Bierstadt

Mopp, Maximilian. See Oppenheimer, Max
MORAN, Edward, 1829-1901
Duck shooting
NSP. Sportscapes
Unveiling the statue of Liberty, 1886
U. S. National Capital sesquicentennial
com
MORAN, Thomas, 1837-1926
Arizona sunset near the Grand Canyon
OYB
OYB. Supplement 1959
Bringing home the cattle—coast of Florida
NBuA
NBuA. Catalogue of the ptgs
Chasm of the Colorado   DCap
Born
Cliffs of the Green river, Wyoming DNC
Rathbone
Cliffs of the Upper Colorado river, Wyo-
ming territory   DNC
Born
Pierson
Giant blue spring, Yellowstone region
Rathbone
Grand Canyon of the Yellowstone river
DN
Pierson
Hot Springs near the Yellowstone
Rathbone
Lower Manhattan from Communipaw
MdHW
NJN. Early N. J. artists
Mist in the Yellowstone
McCracken. Portrait of the old west
(col)
Spirit of the Indian   OkT
McCracken. Portrait of the old west
Teton range   MM
Bazin
Davidson v2
Mendelowitz
Myers. Art
View of Venice   DC
Chew. 250 years of art
Western landscape   CtNB
Barker. Amer ptg
Rathbone
MORE, Hermon, 1887-
Rocky hillside   WMAA
Goodrich. Amer art
Morehouse, Henry A. b 1816
Unidentified artist. Henry A. Morehouse
MOREHOUSE, William P. 1929-
The green one
WMAA. Contemp Amer ptg, 1959/60
Number 509—blue
IU. Contemp Amer ptg & sculp, 1961
Vertical
NNSG. Younger Amer ptrs
Morgan, Charles S. 1799-1859
Unidentified artist. Morgan addressing his
friends
Morgan, Daniel, c 1736-1802
Trumbull, J. Daniel Morgan
MORGAN, Maud (Cabot) 1903-
Descension
IU. Contemp Amer ptg, 1951
Pousette-Dart. Amer ptg
In the beginning
Rathbun
Morgan, Mrs Patrick Henry. See Morgan,
Maud (Cabot)

MORGAN, Randall, 1920-
 Hill town in Campania
  MnMW. Contemporary
  WMAA. Neuberger collection
 Mediterranean night
  MMA. Abstract
 Port at night   WMAA
  Pierson
 Ravello
  WMAA. Contemp Amer ptg, 1949
 Warehouse
  McCurdy
Morning by S. Burpee (attributed works)
Morning by A. Ippolito
Morning by L. Manso
Morning by E. K. Schwabacher
Morning by Z. L. Sepeshy
Morning by B. Shahn
Morning at Gargagno, Lake of Garda by E. D. Boit
Morning at Riva, Lake of Garda by E. D. Boit
Morning bell at a New England factory by W. Homer
Morning candelabra by P. É. Borduas
Morning-glories by W. Homer
Morning glow, autumn by W. Zorach
Morning hour by C. A. Morris
Morning in a city by E. Hopper
Morning in May by R. Marsh
Morning in the Blue Ridge mountains by W. L. Sonntag
Morning mist by H. Hofmann
Morning near Paris by E. D. Boit
Morning of life by A. B. Durand
Morning of November first by J. E. Wagner
Morning, Paris café by G. P. Du Bois
Morning sea by M. Avery
Morning snow by G. W. Bellows
Morning toilet by M. Cassatt
Morning, Upper Frazer river by H. G. Keller
Morocco
 Macknight, D. Outside the walls, Marrakech, Morocco
 Macknight, D. Palms with ripe dates, Morocco
 Macknight, D. White town, Azemmour, Morocco
MORRILL, D.
 Minstrel banjo player   CtHW
  Ford. Pictorial folk art
Morris, Anna Maria (Hollingsworth) 1783-1847
 Sully, T. Mrs John Boucher Morris
MORRIS, Carl A. 1911-
 Audition
  Morley. Carl Morris
 Autumn
  Pierson
 Autumn migration
  IU. Contemp Amer ptg & sculp, 1959
 Beach patterns
  Morley. Carl Morris
 Blue canyon
  Morley. Carl Morris
 Boy with chalice   CSFM
  Morley. **Carl Morris**

Brown painting   NNSG
  NNSG. Handbook
  NNSG. Younger Amer ptrs
  Read. Concise ptg
 Calm horizon
  Morley. Carl Morris
 Canyon mosaic
  Morley. Carl Morris
 Dock
  Morley. Carl Morris
 Dwelling
  ICA. Annual ex, 1951
 Elements of structure
  Morley. Carl Morris
 Embarkation
  Morley. Carl Morris
 Emerging forms
  Morley. Carl Morris
 Expanding elements no 1, 1958
  Morley. Carl Morris
 Expanding elements no 2, 1958
  Morley. Carl Morris
 Five panels
  WMAA. Annual ex, 1955
 Imprisoned force
  Morley. Carl Morris
 Industrial facade   MM
  Morley. Carl Morris
 Lifting night
  Morley. Carl Morris
 Lights
  WMAA. Annual ex, 1957
 Machine no 2, 1951   CSFM
  Morley. Carl Morris
 Man-made man, bewildered by nature
  Morley. Carl Morris
 New shores
  Morley. Carl Morris
 Night figures
  Morley. Carl Morris
 Night image
  ICA. Annual ex, 1961
 Night river   CSFP
  Morley. Carl Morris
 Out of the Coulee   WaS
  Morley. Carl Morris
 Quiet river
  Morley. Carl Morris
 Red forest   WaS
  Morley. Carl Morris
 Reflected verticals   CSB
  Morley. Carl Morris
 Restless horizon
  Morley. Carl Morris
 Riders no 10   WaS
  Pousette-Dart. Amer ptg
 Rising city
  Morley. Carl Morris (col)
 River night   CSFP
  CoS. New accessions USA, 1958
 Rockbound forms
  Morley. Carl Morris
 Seawall
  IU. Contemp Amer ptg & sculp, 1957
 Seed
  WMAA. Contemp Amer ptg, 1949
 Solids into blue
  Morley. Carl Morris (col)
 Still harbor
  Morley. Carl Morris
 Stone matrix   WMAA
  Morley. Carl Morris
 Striated forest
  Morley. Carl Morris

MORRIS, C. A.—*Continued*
Suede and tiger stripe no 2, 1957
  Morley. Carl Morris
Time enclosure
  Morley. Carl Morris
Tower
  Morley. Carl Morris
Turbulent forest   NBuA
  Morley. Carl Morris
Vertical
  Morley. Carl Morris
The wave
  Morley. Carl Morris
White tablet
  Morley. Carl Morris
Written in stone   OrPa
  CoS. New accessions USA, 1956
  Morley. Carl Morris
Yellow arc
  IU. Contemp Amer ptg & sculp, 1961
Yellow light   IU
  Morley. Carl Morris
  OrPa. Ptgs & sculptures (col)

MORRIS, George Lovett Kingsland, 1905-
Black roses
  CSFP. Annual ex, 1948/49
Composition, 1940   PPhM
  PPhM. Gallatin coll
Concretion
  McCurdy
  MMA. Abstract
Converging disks
  MnMW. Classic tradition
East river nocturne
  IU. Contemp Amer ptg & sculp, 1953
Fourteenth street promenade
  ICA. Annual ex, 1954
I.R.T.
  Pearson. Mod renaissance
Industrial landscape
  Pousette-Dart. Amer ptg
Mauve recession
  CtY. Yale alumni
Nautical composition   WMAA
  Goodrich. Amer art
  Pierson
Orvieto   IBM
  Pearson. Mod renaissance
Percussion
  NNS. Younger Amer ptrs
Precision bombing
  Read. Art now, 1948 ed
Pursuit in depth
  IU. Contemp Amer ptg & sculp, 1959
Recessional
  ICA. Annual ex, 1951
Saks Fifth Avenue window
  Pearson. Mod renaissance
String trio
  Rathbun
Suspended discs
  Cheney. Story 158 ed
  MMA. Abstract

Morris, Gouverneur, 1752-1816
Ames, E. Gouverneur Morris
Morris, Harrison S. 1856-1948
Eakins, T. Harrison S. Morris
Morris, Israel W. 1778-1870
Malbone, E. G. Israel W. Morris
Morris, Mrs John Boucher. See Morris,
  Anna Maria (Hollingsworth)

MORRIS, Kyle R. 1918-
Blue and black   NNSG
  NNSG. Handbook
  NNSG. Younger Amer ptrs
Evening image
  WMAA. Annual ex, 1958
Evening, Montauk no 2, 1957
  Brussels. Exposition
Fluttering pendant
  IU. Contemp Amer ptg & sculp, 1955
4 September 1960
  IU. Contemp Amer ptg & sculp, 1961
Green burst   NBuA
  NBuA. Acquisitions 1957-58
Number 2, 1956
  Baur. Nature
Number 5
  IU. Contemp Amer ptg & sculp, 1957
Red flow
  MnMW. 60 Amer ptrs
Morris, Lewis, 1671-1746
Watson, J. Gov Lewis Morris of New
  Jersey
Morris, Lewis, 1752-1824
Malbone, E. G. Col Lewis Morris IV
Morris, Mary (Hollingsworth) 1776-1820
Malbone, E. G. Mrs Israel W. Morris
Morris, Mary (Philipse) 1730-1825
Copley, J. S. Mrs Roger Morris
Morris, Sarah. See Mifflin, Sarah (Morris)
MORRISON, George, 1919-
Structural landscape   NeO
  CoS. New accessions USA, 1956
MORROW, Robert, 1917-
Jason   OYB
  OYB. Annual 1950
  OYB. Catalogue 1951
MORSE, Henry D. 1826-1888
Deer in a thicket
  NSP. Sportscapes
Morse, Isaac Edward, 1809-1866
Jarvis, J. W. Isaac Edward Morse
Morse, Jedidiah, 1761-1826
Hancock, N. Jedidiah Morse
Morse, Lucretia Pickering (Walker) d 1825
Morse, S. F. B. Artist's family
MORSE, Samuel Finley Breese, 1791-1872
Alexander Metcalf Fisher   CtY
  Baur. Amer ptg
Allegorical landscape   NNHS
  Born
Artist's family
  Flexner. Light of distant skies
Benjamin Silliman   CtY
  CtY. Portrait index
Congress hall. See Old House of Repre-
  sentatives
David C. De Forest   CtY
  CtY. Portrait index
Dying Hercules   CtY
  Flexner. Light of distant skies
Eli Whitney   CtY
  CtY. Portrait index
Frederic Gore King   NAD
  NAD. Amer tradition
Gallery of the Louvre   NSU
  Barker. Amer ptg
  Larkin
  Larkin rev ed
  Pierson
  Roos
Jeremiah Day   CtY
  CtY. Portrait index

Katherine Munro of Charleston, South
  Carolina   GAtM
  GAtM. Holbrook collection
Lace cap   OYB
  OYB'. Catalogue 1951
Lafayette   NNCH
  Flexner. Amer ptg
  Flexner. Short history
  Larkin (detail)
  Larkin rev ed
  Pierson
Lafayette   NNPL
  Gardner 1959 ed
Little Miss Hone   MB
  MB. Karolik coll
Mrs David Mussey   MNS
  Larkin
Mrs Jane Robinson   ATeS
  AteS. Collection
Morse family   DNC
  Flexner. Light of distant skies
The muse, Susan Walker Morse   MM
  Mendelowitz
  Pierson
Nathan Smith   CtY
  CtY. Portrait index
Niagara Falls from Table Rock   MB
  MB. Karolik coll
  Pierson
Old House of Representatives, 1821-22
  (Congress hall)   DC
  Davidson v2
  DC. Masterpieces
  Mendelowitz
  Pierson
  Richardson. Ptg in America (col)
  Roos
  Time. 300 years (col)
  U.S. National Capital sesquicentennial
    com. 7 (col front)
Sheldon Clark   CtY
  Bazin
  CtY. Portrait index
The shrine
  MiD. Travelers in Arcadia
Susan Walker Morse. See The muse
Thomas Harvey Skinner   MB
  MB. Karolik coll
View from Apple hill, Cooperstown, N.Y.
  Barker. Amer ptg
  Born
  CtY. Yale alumni
  Pierson
William Augustus Lawrence   NJMo
  NJMo. Forty years
  NUM. Art across America
William Cullen Bryant   NAD
  NAD. Annual ex. 1947, 1st half
  PPC. Amer classics

Portrait of the artist
Stone, W. O. Samuel F. B'. Morse
Morse, Mrs Samuel Finley Breese. See
  Morse, Lucretia Pickering (Walker)
Morse, Susan Walker, 1819-1885
  Morse, S. F. B. The muse: Susan Walker
  Morse
Morse family by S. F. B. Morse
Mortality and immortality by W. M. Har-
  nett
Morton, Sarah Wentworth (Apthorp) 1759-
  1846
  Stuart, G. Mrs Perez Morton

Mosaics, 1956 (Northeast corner, 711 Third
  avenue, New York) by H. Hofmann
Mosaics, 1956 (Southwest corner, 711 Third
  avenue, New York) by H. Hofmann
MOSCA, August, 1909-
  Dawn over Fordham
    CSFP. Annual ex, 1946
Moseley, Laura (Wolcott) 1761-1814
  Earl, R. Mrs William Moseley and her
    son Charles
MOSES, Anna Mary (Robertson) 1860-1961
  Black horses
    Moses
  Bondsville fair
    Moses
  Bringing in the Christmas tree
    Lipman. Primitive ptrs
    Moses (col)
  Bringing in the maple sugar
    Moses
  Cambridge, New York
    Moses
  Cambridge valley
    Moses
  Catching the Thanksgiving turkey
    Cheney. Story 1958 ed
    Moses
  The checkered house
    Moses (col)
  Christmas at home
    Time. 300 years (col)
  Christmas eve
    Moses
  The covered bridge. See Sunday
  Early springtime on the farm
    Moses (col)
  Fire in the woods
    Moses
  The first skating
    Moses
  Going to church
    Moses
  Grandma goes to the big city
    Ford. Pictorial folk art (col)
    Moses (col)
  Haying time
    Moses
  Home for Thanksgiving
    Moses
  Home of Hezekiah King
    Moses
  Hoosick Falls in winter
    Moses
  In harvest time
    Moses
  In the park
    Moses
  In the springtime
    Moses
  The lookout, Vermont, 1777
    Moses
  McDonell farm   DP
    Born
    Moses
  May: making soap, washing sheep
    Moses
  Mount Nebo in winter
    Moses
  The old automobile
    Moses
  The old oaken bucket
    Moses (col)
  Our barn
    Moses

MOSES, A. M. R.—*Continued*
  Out for the Christmas tree
    Time. 300 years (col)
  Over the bridge to grandma's house
    Cheney. Primer 1958 ed
  Over the river
    Moses
  Over the river to grandma's house
    Moses
  Picnic
    Moses
  The red mill
    Moses
  Shenandoah valley
    Moses
  Spring in the valley
    Ford. Pictorial folk art
  Sugaring-off
    Moses (col)
  Sugaring-off in maple orchard
    Moses
  Sunday (The covered bridge)
    Moses
  A tramp on Christmas day
    McCurdy
  The trappers II
    Moses
  Wash day
    Moses
  Whiteside church
    Moses
  Williamstown
    Kallir. Amer primitive ptgs
  A winter's day
    Moses

Moses, David, 1776-1858
  Malbone, E. G. David Moses

Moses, Grandma. See Moses, Anna Mary
  (Robertson)

Moses, Rachel (Gratz) See Gratz, Rachel

Moses, Solomon, 1774-1857
  Malbone, E. G. Solomon Moses

Moses, Mrs Solomon. See Gratz, Rachel

Moses by Ben-Zion

Moses by A. Rattner

Moses in the bulrushes by Unidentified artist

Moses, the Baltimore news vendor by T. W.
  Wood

Moses with the tablets of the law by E.
  Laning

Mosque by M. Hoff

Mosque, Cordova by C. Gray

Mosquito net by J. S. Sargent

Moss agate by E. A. Donati

Most of the people are very poor by J.
  Lawrence

The **mother** by A. Vellanti

Mother and child
  Allston, W. Mother watching her sleeping
    child
  Avery, M. Mother and child
  Bellows, G. W. Emma and her children
  Benn, B. Mother and child
  Bingham, G. C. Susan Howard Hockaday
    and her daughter Susan
  Brush, G. D. Mother and child
  Cassatt, M. Mrs Havemeyer and her
    daughter
  Cassatt, M. Mother and child
  Cassatt, M. Mother and children

  Cassatt, M. Mother holding child
  Catlin, G. Ojibway (Chippewa) woman
    and baby
  Chase, W. M. Mother and child
  Copley, J. S. Mrs Daniel Rea and child
  Earl, R. Lady Williams and child
  Earl, R. Mrs Moses Seymour and her
    son
  Earl, R. Mrs William Moseley and her
    son Charles
  Earl, R. Mrs William Taylor and child
  Evergood, P. Mother and child
  Freake limner. Mrs Freake and Baby
    Mary
  Fried, T. Nursing mother
  Glackens, W. J. Artist's wife and son
  Hardy, J. P. Catherine Wheeler Hardy
    and her daughter
  Harmon, L. P. First child
  Hawthorne, C. Adoration of the mother
  Hunt, W. M. Mrs Richard Morris Hunt
    and child
  Jennys, W. Member of the Smith family
    of Suffield, Connecticut and Rutland,
    Vermont, c 1800
  Kopf, M. The star
  La Farge, J. Mother and child
  Mayhew, N. Mrs John Harrison and her
    daughter Maria
  Melchers, G. Mother and child
  Newman, R. L. Mother and son
  Palmer, C. B. R. Mother and child
  Peale, C. W. Hannah Moore Peale and
    stepdaughter
  Peale, C. W. Mrs James Arbuckle and
    son Edward
  Peale, J. Mme Dubocq and her four chil-
    dren
  Polk, C. P. Mrs Isaac Hite and James
    Madison Hite jr
  Polk, C. P. Mrs John Hart and her
    daughter
  Rattner, A. Mother and child
  Sargent, J. S. Mrs Edward Livingston
    Davis and her son Livingston
  Sargent, J. S. Mrs Fiske Warren and her
    daughter Rachel
  Sargent, J. S. Mrs Knowles and her chil-
    dren
  Sharrer, H. Rose Callahan and child
  Sterne, M. Mother and child
  Stuart, G. Mrs John Bannister and her son
  Sully, T. Mother and son
  Unidentified artist. American madonna
    and child
  Unidentified artist. Aphia Salisbury Rich
    and baby Edward
  Unidentified artist. Gracie Beardsley Jef-
    ferson Jackman and her daughter
  Unidentified artist. Mrs John Casey and
    daughter
  Unidentified artist. Mrs Mann Page II
    and baby John
  Unidentified artist. Mother and child in
    white
  Unidentified artist. Mother and child in
    Windsor chair
  Vanderlyn, J. Mrs Marinus Willett and
    child
  Vellanti, A. The mother
  Weber, M. Mothers and children
  West, B. Mrs West and her son Raphael
Mother and daughter by A. Brook

Mother and daughter by Y. Kuniyoshi
Mother Archie's church by A. N. Wyeth
Mother earth by B. Stahl
Mother of dawn by A. B. Davies
MOTHERWELL, Robert Burns, 1915-
  Black interior
    IU. Contemp Amer ptg, 1952
  Black still life
    WMAA. Contemp Amer ptg, 1951
  Blue with china ink (Homage to John
    Cage) Abstraction
    CtY. Yale alumni
    MnMW. Eighty works
  Brown figure
    IU. Contemp Amer ptg, 1949
  Construction
    MMA. Contemp ptrs
  Decalogue, Jacob's ladder and burning
    bush
    IU. Contemp Amer & sculp, 1953
  The easel
    IU. Contemp Amer ptg & sculp, 1955
  Elegy to the Spanish republic XXXIV
                                   NBuA
    MMA. New Amer ptg
    NBuA. Acquisitions 1954-57
    Pierson
    Ponente. Mod ptg, 1960 (col)
  Elegy to the Spanish republic LVIII
    PPC. International ex, 1961/62
  The end of Dover Beach
    PPC. International ex, 1958
  Figure
    Read. Art now, 1948 ed
  Figure in pink and green
    MMA. Fourteen
  Fishes with red stripe
    Baur. New art
    WMAA. New decade
  Five in the afternoon
    Baur. Revolution
  Granada
    Hess. Abstract ptg
    MoSL. Contemporary Amer ptg
  Homage to John Cage. See Blue with
    china ink
  Hotel corridor
    IU. Contemp Amer ptg, 1951
  In beige with sand   MCH
    Pulitzer v2
  Je t'aime II
    PPC. International ex, 1955
    WMAA. Museum and its friends, 1958
  Large collage
    MMA. Fourteen
  Mallarme's swan
    MnU. 40 Amer ptrs
  Maria
    MMA. Fourteen
  Montauk montage
    CSFP. Annual ex, 1948/49
  Mural fragment   MnU
    MnMW. 60 Amer ptrs
  Orange personage
    MnU. 40 Amer ptrs
  Painting
    CSFP. Annual ex, 1950-51
  Pancho Villa, dead and alive, 1943 MMA
    Baur. New art
    MMA. Fourteen
    Read. Concise history

Person with orange
  Leepa
Personage with yellow ochre and white
                                     MMA
  MMA. New Amer ptg
Red skirt   WMAA
  Goodrich. Amer art
La résistance
  IU. Contemp Amer ptg, 1950
Room 8, Hotel Flora, Cannes
  ICA. Annual ex, 1951
  VR. Amer ptg, 1954
Small personage
  MMA. Fourteen
The voyage   MMA
  Art since 1945 (col)
  Baur. New art (col)
  Hunter. Mod Amer ptg (col)
  MMA. New Amer ptg (col)
  Pierson
  WMAA. New decade
Wall painting, 1950
  Mendelowitz
Wall painting III
  Pousette-Dart. Amer ptg
Wall painting IV, 1954
  Brussels. Exposition
  NNSG. Younger Amer ptrs
Western air   MMA
  Biddle. Yes and no
  McCurdy
  MMA. Abstract
  Time. 300 years (col)
El motif by S. Gross
Motif de fête by W. Bassford
Motif in pink by J. J. P. Meert
MOTLEY, Eleanor Warren, 1847-1942
  Auratum lily   MB
    MB. Ptgs in water color
  Blue bowl   MB
    MB. Ptgs in water color
  Purple petunias   MB
    MB. Ptgs in water color
Motley, Mrs Thomas. See Motley, Eleanor
  Warren
The motor by W. T. Murch
Motorists by D. Richardson
Motte, Isaac, fl 1740
  Theus, J. Isaac Motte (?)
Motte, Mrs Jacob jr. See Motte, Rebecca
  (Brewton)
Motte, Rebecca (Brewton) 1729-1781
  Theus, J. Rebecca Motte
MOULTHROP, Reuben, 1763-1814
  Ammi Ruhamah Robbins   CtY
    Flexner. Light of distant skies
    Pierson
  Bradford Hubbard   CtNH
    Pierson
    Richardson. Ptg in America
  Elisha Williams   CtY
    CtY. Portrait index
  Ezra Stiles   CtY
    CtY. Portrait index
  Thomas Robbins   CtHH
    ICA. From colony to nation
  Timothy Pitkin   CtY
    CtY. Portrait index
Moulton, Hannah Goodwin (Whitehouse)
  fl 1838
  Davis, J. H. (attributed works) Hannah
    Goodwin (Whitehouse) Moulton

Moulton, James Roberts, fl 1838
Davis, J. H. (attributed works) James
Roberts Moulton
Moulton, Mrs James Robert. See Moulton,
Hannah Goodwin (Whitehouse)
Moultrie, William, 1731-1805
Fraser, C. William Moultrie
MOUNT, Shepard Alonzo, 1804-1868
A day's catch
NSP. Sportscapes
MOUNT, William Sidney, 1807-1868
Banjo player   MiD
MiD. Treasures
OCiM. Rediscoveries
Pierson
Roos
Time. 300 years (col)
Banjo player   NStS
NUM. Art across America
Bargaining for a horse   NNHS
Flexner. Amer ptg
Flexner. Short history
Mendelowitz
Pierson
UNESCO. Prior to 1860 3d ed
Barn by the pool   MB
MB. Karolik coll
Bone player   MB
MB. Karolik coll
Boys caught napping in a field   NBM
DC. De gustibus
Pierson
Coming to the point   NNPL
Davidson v2
Country dance. See Rustic dance
Dance of the haymakers. See Music is
contagious
Eel spearing at Setauket   NNHS
Barker. Amer ptg
Baur. Amer ptg
Pierson
Richardson. Ptg in America
Farmers nooning   NStS
PPC. Amer classics (col front)
Fence on the hill   MB
MB. Karolik coll
Landscape with figures   PA
Pierson
Long Island farmhouses   MM
Bazin
Born
OCiM. Rediscoveries
Pierson
UNESCO. Prior to 1860 3d ed
Walker. Ptgs from America
Long Island scene
CtY. Yale alumni
The long story   DC
DC. Masterpieces
U.S. National Captial sesquicentennial
com
The Mount brothers' music stand   MStS
CSFP. Illusionism
Music is contagious (Dance of the hay-
makers)   NStS
NAD. Amer tradition
News from the gold diggings (Melville
coll)
Davidson v 1

Painter's triumph   PA
Larkin (detail)
Larkin rev ed (detail)
Pierson
Richardson. Ptg in America
Power of music
Larkin
Larkin rev ed
Larkin rev ed (col detail)
Pierson
Ringing the pig   NNHS
PPC. Amer classics
Rustic dance (Rustic dance after a sleigh-
ride; Country dance)   MB
Davidson v 1
MB. Karolik Coll
MOUNT, William Sidney, 1807-1868 **and
RANNEY, William Tylee,** 1813-1857
Pipe of friendship   NJN
NJN. Early N. J. artists
Mount Aetna from Taormina, Sicily by T.
Cole
Mount Auburn cemetery, Cambridge by T.
Chambers
The **Mount** brothers' music stand by W. S.
Mount
Mount Chocorua by J. Marin
Mount Corcoran by A. Bierstadt
Mount Equinox. winter by R. Kent
Mount Katahdin, autumn by M. Hartley
Mount Katahdin, Maine by M. Hartley
Mount Lassen by L. Siegriest
Mount Marcy by D. Johnson
Mount Nebo in winter by A. M. R. Moses
Mount Overlook by F. J. Reilly
Mount Vernon
Bartlett, W. H. Mt Vernon
Bartlett, W. H. Washington's tomb, Mt
Vernon
Guy, F. Washington's tomb
Prior, W. M. Washington's tomb at
Mount Vernon
Unidentified artist. Mount Vernon (after
aquatint by Francis Jukes)
Whitcomb, S. Mount Vernon
Mount Vesuvius from the bay of Naples
by R. D. Gauley
Mount Washington, New Hampshire by S.
Gerry
Mount Whitney by A. Bierstadt
Mount Wilson, View of by E. Ewing
The **mountain** by S. Serisawa
Mountain bird maru by R. Crawford
Mountain brook, Adirondacks by A. H.
Wyant
Mountain church, San Cristobal by D. Lutz
Mountain farm by P. Dickinson
Mountain ford by T. Cole
Mountain goats by V. Arbogast
Mountain gorge by G. C. Bingham
Mountain gorge near Dambulla, Ceylon by
J. La Farge
Mountain lake by A. Bierstadt
Mountain lakes by J. F. Cropsey
Mountain landscape by E. Geller
Mountain landscape with cattle by B. West
(attributed works)
Mountain landscape with waterfall by T.
Cole

Mountain laurel by L. MacIver
Mountain of the Winds by A. J. Miller
Mountain pores by A. Okamura
Mountain scene with deer by G. C. Bingham
Mountain scene with fisherman by G. C. Bingham
Mountain sea by R. Haines
Mountain stream by J. F. Kensett
Mountain top by H. Koerner
Mountain top by J. Marin
Mountain torrent by T. Doughty
Mountain torrent by A. J. Miller
Mountain trail by F. T. Johnson
The mountain, Tyrol by J. Marin
Mountain valley by A. B. Durand
Mountain valley by F. R. Gignoux
Mountain village by J. De Martini
The mountaineer by E. E. Speicher
A mountaineer and Kansas Indians, Group of by A. J. Miller
Mountains by G. W. Mark
Mountains and trees by K. Schrag
Mountains in Dalmatia by G. H. Hallowell
Mountains of Ecuador by F. E. Church
Mountains, Puget sound by H. G. Keller
The mountebanks by Y. Tanguy
Mountfort, Jonathan, 1746-1785
  Copley, J. S. Jonathan Mountfort
Mounting of the Guard by Unidentified artist
Mourning pictures
  Elmer, E. R. Mourning picture
  Jordan, S. Eaton family memorial
  Merrill, S. Mourning picture
  Unidentified artist. Mourning picture—Elizabeth Farr
  Unidentified artist. Mourning picture—left behind
  Unidentified artist. Mourning picture—Polly Botsford and her children
  Unidentified artist. Mourning picture—Philo Day
  Unidentified artist. Mourning picture sacred to the memory of Jerhusha Williams
  Unidentified artist. Mourning scene
  Unidentified artist. Smith memorial
  Unidentified artist. Tomb in memory of Richard Newhall
  Walters, S. Memorial to Nicholas Catlin
  Warner, C. T. Mourning picture—George Washington
Mourning piece by H. L. Forbes
Mourning the child by J. Schwarz
Movement by M. Hartley
Movement by B. J. O. Nordfeldt
Movement, boat and sea, Deer isle, Maine by J. Marin
Movement—boat and sea in grey by J. Marin
Movement—Fifth avenue by J. Marin
Movement in grey, green and red by J. Marin
Movement in paint by J. Marin
Movement no 9, 1916 by M. Hartley
Movement no 2, related to downtown New York by J. Marin
Movement of horses II by R. Goodnough

Movement, sea and rocks, Cape Split, Maine by J. Marin
Movement, sea and sky by J. Marin
Movement—sea or mountain—as you will by J. Marin
Movement: Tunk mountains by J. Marin
Movements, 1915 by M. Hartley
Movements and acts by Y. Tanguy
The movers by J. Koch
Moving camp by G. Catlin
Moving camp by A. J. Miller
MOY, Seong, 1921-
  Girl playing a pe-pa
    VR. Amer ptg, 1954
  The king visits his paramour
    IU. Contemp Amer ptg & sculp, 1953
    MM. Amer ptg today
  Recipe for bouillabaisse
    IU. Contemp Amer ptg & sculp, 1959
  Spring song
    IU. Contemp Amer ptg & sculp, 1955
Mud hook by B. Miller
Muddy alligators by J. S. Sargent
MUELLER, George Ludwig, 1929-
  Blackened monument
    IU. Contemp Amer ptg & sculp, 1955
  Night
    ICA. Amer artists paint the city
  Numena
    PPC. International ex, 1955
  Spad
    WMAA. Young America 1957
  Stage fragment: Faust   NNSG
    NNSG. Handbook
    NNSG. Younger Amer artists
  The study   WMAA
    Goodrich. Amer art
    Pierson
  Stuka
    Brussels. Exposition
  Wayout—side   NJN
    WMAA. Young America 1957
Mug, pipe, and newspaper by J. F. Peto
Mulberry Bend park, New York by M. B. Prendergast
Mule deer by C. S. Price
Mulford, Betsy. See Sutliff, Betsy (Mulford)
Mulford, Huldah. See Hills, Huldah (Mulford)
Mulford, Sally (Emes) 1773-1861
  Ames, E. Mrs Ezekiel Mulford
MULHAUPT, Frederick John, 1871-1938
  February's sun   PR
    PR. Catalogue
MULLER, Jan, 1923-1958
  Hamlet and Horatio
    Selz. New images
  Hanging piece
    Selz. New images
  Heraldic ground
    Selz. New images
  Of this time, of that place
    WMAA. Young America 1957
  Temptation of St Anthony
    Selz. New images (col)
  The virgins
    PPC. International ex, 1958
MULLICAN, Lee, 1919-
  Luminous loot
    IU. Contemp Amer ptg & sculp, 1953

MULLICAN, Lee—*Continued*
Salt fire
　Pousette-Dart. Amer ptg
Solstice rider
　IU. Contemp ptg & sculp, 1955
Weights of the Pacific
　IU. Contemp Amer ptg & sculp, 1957
Multiform by J. Xcéron
Multiple images I by W. Barnet
Multiple portrait by M. Weber
Multiple views by S. Davis
Multiplication of the arcs by Y. Tanguy
Mumford, Thomas, fl 1776
　Johnston, W. Thomas Mumford V
Mummy by W. A. Baziotes
MUNGER, George, 1781-1825
　Nathaniel Jocelyn　　　　　　　CtY
　　CtY. Portrait index
Munich head. W. M. Chase
Munro, Katherine
　Morse, S. F. B. Katherine Munro of Charleston, South Carolina
Munson, Eneas, 1734-1826
　Jennys, W. Eneas Munson
Munson, Israel, 1764-1844
　Unidentified artist. Israel Munson
MUNSON, William Giles, fl 1826
　Eli Whitney's gun factory　　　　CtY
　Davidson v 1
　U.S. National Capital sesquicentennial com
Munson, William Gurley, fl 1868
　Chase, W. M. William Gurley Munson
MÜNTER, Gabriele, 1877-
　Blue gable　　　　　　　　　　　IU
　　IU. 20th century
Mural by J. Pollock
Mural assistant by L. Bouché
Mural decoration by J. H. Daugherty
Murals at Roosevelt, New Jersey, Community center by B. Shahn
MURCH, Walter Tandy, 1907-
　Action
　　CSFP. Annual ex, 1952
　Bamboo
　　IU. Contemp Amer ptg & sculp, 1961
　Blocks
　　Pousette-Dart. Amer ptg
　The bulb　　　　　　　　　　　WMAA
　　MoSL. Contemporary Amer ptg
　　Pierson
　The circle　　　　　　　　　　　NBM
　　Baur. Revolution
　The clock
　　WMAA. New decade
　Cylinder and orange
　　WiMiA. Amer ptg 1760-1960
　Egg and rock
　　ICA. Annual ex, 1961
　Governor II, 1952　　　　　　　WMAA
　　Goodrich. Amer art
　　Pierson
　Isotopes
　　IU. Contemp Amer ptg, 1951
　Keys and feather
　　ICA. Annual ex, 1947/48
　The light　　　　　　　　　　　NBuA
　　NBuA. Acquisitions 1959-1961
　The lock
　　IU. Contemp Amer ptg, 1949

Metronome
　MMA. Contemp ptrs
The motor　　　　　　　　　　　　IU
　IU. Contemp Amer ptg, 1952
　IU. 20th century
Perspective
　CSB. Illusion
Sewing machine
　WMAA. New decade
Taking off　　　　　　　　　　　　OT
　ICA. Annual ex, 1954
Time clock
　ICA. Amer artists paint the city
The wall
　WiMiA. Amer ptg 1760-1960
Murder of Jane McCrea by Unidentified artist
Murder of Rutland by C. R. Leslie
Murdock, Phoebe. See Bowdoin, Phoebe (Murdock)
MURPHY, Gerald
　Watch
　　Blesh
Murphy, Mrs H. Dudley. See Murphy, Nelly Littlehale
MURPHY, Nelly Littlehale, 1867-1941
　Flower study　　　　　　　　　　MB
　　MB. Ptgs in water color
　Peonies　　　　　　　　　　　　MB
　　MB. Ptgs in water color
Murray, Mr, fl 1820
　Unidentified artist. Mr Murray
Murray, Mrs, fl 1820
　Unidentified artist. Mrs Murray
MURRAY, Albert K. 1906-
　Chester W. Nimitz
　　PPC. Ptg in the U.S. 1949
Murray, Samuel, b 1870
　Eakins, T. Samuel Murray
Murray, William Vans, 1762-1803
　Brown, M. William Vans Murray
Murray Bay landscape by E. E. Speicher
The **muse:** Susan Walker Morse by S. F. B. Morse
Muse of the western world by E. Berman
Muses by M. Weber
Muses of painting, poetry and music by W. E. West
Music by T. W. Dewing
Music by H. Moller
Music and good luck by W. M. Harnett
Music and literature by W. M. Harnett
Music before winter by A. Blanch
Music—black, blue and green by G. O'Keeffe
Music hall by S. Davis
Music lesson by M. Avery
Music maker by M. Avery
Music master by F. Duveneck
Music of the Orient by M. Weber
Music room by J. A. M. Whistler
Musical evening by M. Weber
Musicians and musical instruments
　Adams, W. Musicos ambulantes
　Allston, W. Evening hymn
　Blythe, D. G. Young musician
　Demuth, C. H. Vaudeville musicians
　Dewing, T. W. Music
　Eakins, T. Musicians rehearsing
　Eakins, T. Street scene in Seville

Evergood, P. Music
Evett, K. Trio
Grode, S. M. Two musicians
Harnett, W. M. Music and good luck
Harnett, W. M. Old models
Hicks, T. Barber shop, the musicale
Perlin, B. Jazz band
Philipp, R. Request number
Platt, G. W. Relics of a den
Sexton, F. Musical instruments
Shahn, B. Composition with clarinets and tin horn
Shahn, B. Four piece orchestra
Shahn, B. Portrait of myself when young
Unidentified artist. Musicians in the snow
Watkins, F. C. Musician
Weber, M. Bach orchestra
Weber, M. Music
Weber, M. Musical evening
Weber, M. Solo
Weber, M. String music
Weber, M. The trio
Weber, M. Two musicians
Weber, M. Wind orchestra

Accordions

Shahn, B. Blind accordion player

Bagpipes

Kane, J. Scotch day at Kennywood

Banjos

Karp, L. Still life with banjo
Mount, W. S. Banjo player

Cellos

Avery, M. Cello player
Bradley, I. J. H. The 'cellist
Dickinson, E. W. Cello player

Clarinets

Crane, S. W. Handel still life
Shahn, B. Composition with clarinet and tin horn

Drums

Hensel, H. Drummers

Fifes

Eakins, T. Youth playing fife

Flutes

Moller, H. Flutes
Peckham, R. William Cornee with flute
Weber, M. Flute soloist

Guitars

Benton, T. H. Jessie, 17 years old
Brackman, R. Sailor's holiday
Chase, W. M. Lady playing guitar
Gwathmey, R. Singing and mending
Henri, R. Blind Spanish singer
Lotterman, H. Boy with guitar
Luks, G. B. The guitar
Roszak, T. Self-portrait
Sargent, J. S. El Jaleo
Shahn, B. The song
Tooker, G. Guitar
Weber, M. Guitar player

Harmonicas

Menkès, S. Boy playing harmonica

Harps

Douglass, L. Royal psalmist
La Farge, J. Harpist

Lutz, D. I got a harp
Sully, T. Lady with a harp: Eliza Ridgely

Hurdy-gurdies

Myers, J. The tambourine

Lutes

Benrimo, T. D. Lute player
Shahn, B. Lute no 2, 1957

Mandolins

Cikovski, N. Fruit, vase and mandolin
Cikovsky, N. Spring melody
Lucioni, L. Design for color

Oboes

Eakins, T. Oboe player (Benjamin Sharp)

Organs

Sample, P. S. Sweet hour of prayer

Pianos

Benton, T. H. Sun treader—Portrait of Carl Ruggles
Eakins, T. Elizabeth at the piano
Eakins, T. Home scene
Robinson, T. Girl at the piano
Sample, P. S. Spring song
Watkins, F. C. Rosemary Thompson
Whistler, J. A. M. At the piano
Whistler, J. A. M. Gold scab
Zorach, W. Leo Ornstein (Piano concert)

Recorders

Levi, J. E. Margaret Boni playing the recorder

Saxophones

Beckmann, M. Portrait of the artist with a saxophone

Singers

Eakins, T. Concert singer
Eakins, T. Pathetic song

Spinets

Dewing, T. W. The spinet

Tambourines

Beckmann, M. Dancer with tambourine
Myers, J. The tambourine

Trombones

Lee, R. J. Trombone

Violins

Avery, M. Music maker
Chalfant, J. D. Old violin
Eakins, T. Music
Eakins, T. The violinist
Evergood, P. Nude with violin
Harnett, W. M. Old Cremona
Harnett, W. M. Old violin
Harnett, W. M. Still life, 1888
Harnett, W. M. (attributed works) Still life with violin
James, A. Choose your partner
Knaths, K. Tired violin
Levine, J. String quartette
Shahn, B. Violin player
Spruce, E. F. Fiddler
Von Wicht, J. G. F. Paganini

Musidora by B. West
Muskrat hunter by W. L. Lathrop

Mussel gatherers by W. Homer
Mussel gatherers at high tide by Leonid
Mussey, Mrs David
    Morse, S. F. B. Mrs David Mussey
Mutation by W. Quirt
Muted city by R. Gikow
A **muted** street by L. Guglielmi
My bunkie by C. Schreyvogel
My daughters by F. W. Benson
My Egypt by C. H. Demuth
My family reunion by L. Bosa
My father by G. W. Bellows
My father by W. M. Chase
My father by E. C. Dickinson
My forebears were pioneers by P. Evergood
My heart by G. O'Keeffe
My Hell raising sea by J. Marin
My house by J. K. W. Hailman
My life white and black by Y. Tanguy
My little daughter Dorothy by W. M. Chase
My mother by G. W. Bellows
My mother by P. Evergood
My mother by M. S. Parcell
My neighbor Al by G. Biddle
My parents by H. Koerner
My son is innocent by B. Shahn
My wife by M. Avery
Myer, Albert James, 1829-1880
    Healy, G. P. A. Albert J. Myer
Myers, Jacob, fl 1833
    Unidentified artist. Jacob Myers
Myers, Mrs Jacob, fl 1833
    Unidentified artist. Mrs Myers with baby
Myers, Jean Macdonald Lee, fl 1850
    Unidentified artist. Jean Macdonald Lee
        Myers
MYERS, Jerome, 1867-1940
    Children's theatre   MiD
        Richardson. Ptg in America
    East of the Bowery   NJMo
        NJMo. Forty years
    End of the street
        Pierson
    Night mission   MM
        Brown. Amer ptg
    Playground pleasures   DNC
        DNC. Gellatly coll, 1954
    Self-portrait
        WiMiA. Amer ptg 1760-1960
    Summer night, East side park   WMAA
        Goodrich. Amer art
        Pierson
    The tambourine   DP
        Brown. Amer ptg
        DP. Catalogue
        McCurdy
    Windy corner
        Baur. Revolution
Myers, John, d 1844
    Sully, T. John Myers
MYERS, William H. fl 1847
    Battle of the plains of Mesa, 1847
        U.S. National Capital sesquicentennial
        com
Myopic vista by S. Davis
Myriad by J. S. Haley

Myself and my imaginary wife, Portrait of
    by A. Gorky
Mysterious bird by C. E. Burchfield
Mystery by F. E. Conway
Mystery of the East by P. King
The **mystic** by W. R. Leigh
Mystic lake, Massachusetts by J. F. Cole
Mythological themes
    Austin, D. Europa and the bull
    Copley, J. S. Mars, Venus, and Vulcan
    Hesselius, G. Bacchus and Ariadne
    Mason, W. S. Venus and Cupid
    Morse, S. F. B. Dying Hercules
    Page, W. Cupid and Psyche
    Russell, A. Venus Anadyomene no 2
    Sargent, J. S. Atlas and the Hesperides
    Sargent, J. S. The Danaïdes
    Unidentified artist. Venus drawn by doves
    Vanderlyn, J. Ariadne
    West, B. The choice of Hercules
    West, B. Cupid and Psyche
    West, B. Diomed and his horses stopped
        by the lightning of Jupiter
    West, B. Hector parting with his wife and
        child at the Scæan gate
    West, B. Juno receiving the cestus from
        Venus
    West, B. Thetis bringing the armor to
        Achilles
    West, B. Una and the lion
    West, B. Venus lamenting the death of
        Adonis
Mythomania by K. Seligmann

N

Nabu-Naa-Kee-Shick, a Chippewa chief by
    J. O. Lewis
Nacelles by R. Crawford
Nacelles under construction by R. Crawford
NACK, Kenneth, 1923-
    A demand of estimation
        IU. Contemp Amer ptg & sculp, 1955
    Expulsion of possessions in a danger of
        being gained
        NNSG. Younger Amer ptrs
Naden, Elizabeth. See Banyar, Elizabeth
    (Naden)
NAGLER, Fred, 1891-
    From afar
        NAD. Annual ex, 1952
NAHL, Charles Christian, 1818-1875
    The fandango   CSC
        Davidson v 1
    Passion according to St Matthew
        Gruskin (col)
    Sunday morning in the mines   CSC
        Davidson v 1
        Mendelowitz
Naiad by L. Kroll
Naked in the city by J. Farnsworth
Naked over New York by R. Marsh
Nana by R. Ray
Nana, Illustrations for by C. H. Demuth
Nancy (ship)
    Thomas, J. The ship Nancy, homeward
        bound

Nancy by E. E. Speicher
NANGERONI, Carlo, 1922-
  Picnic
    IU. Contemp Amer ptg & sculp, 1959
Nantucket school of philosophy by E. Johnson
The nap by P. Cadmus
Naples by R. D. Gauley
Naples by J. L. Lasker
Naples aquarium by L. MacIver
Naples yellow morning by A. G. Dove
Napoleon's army crossing the Alps by Mrs
    Robert Carter
Napoli forio by E. S. Woelffer
Napolitana by E. Berman
Naram-Sin by E. A. Donati
Narcissus by B. West
Nardin park by J. Berghoff
Narragansett bay by Leonid
Narragansett light from northeast by Capt
    "Phindoodle"
Narrative by J. Ernst
The Narrows from Fort Hamilton, New
    York Harbor by Unidentified artist
Nassau
  Homer, W. Nassau
  Homer, W. Scene in Nassau
  Homer, W. Shore and surf, Nassau
Nassau hall (Princeton university) by K.
    Matthew
Nassau, woman at campfire by W. Homer
Nast, Thomas, 1840-1902
  Alexander, J. W. Thomas Nast
Natchez, Mississippi in 1822 by J. J. Audubon
National Lancers on Boston Common by
    T. C. Savory
National Lancers with the reviewing officers
    on Boston Common by C. Hubbard
Native house by J. La Farge
Native woman cooking by W. Homer
Natives beaching a boat, Samoa by J. La
    Farge
Natives cooking poi, Tahiti by J. La Farge
Native's return by P. Guston
Native's return by R. Strang
Nativity by L. Ford
NATKIN, Robert, 1930-
  Summer
    WMAA. Young America 1960
Nature symbolized by A. G. Dove
Nature without man by P. Evergood
Nausicaa by J. Tworkov
Nautical by L. Phillips
Nautical composition by G. L. K. Morris
Navajo by G. C. Delano
Navajo boy by G. C. Delano
Navajo desert camp by E. Loran
Navajo land by R. Ray
Navajo land by J. E. Swinnerton
Navajo raid by F. Remington
Naval home, Gray's ferry, Philadelphia by
    T. Doughty
The navigator by Unidentified artist
The navigator's wife by Unidentified artist

Naxos by J. Youngerman
NEAGLE, John, 1796-1865
  Anna Gibbon Johnson   PA
    PA. Annual ex, 1955
  George Peabody   MB
    MB. Great Americans
    MB. Karolik coll
  Gilbert Stuart   MB
    MB. Great Americans
    Pierson
  Henry Clay   PPhU
    Pierson
  Indian heads   PH
    Chew. 250 years of art
    PA. Annual ex, 1955
  John Kintzing Kane   NJP
    NUM. Art across America
  Joseph Tagert   OYB
    OYB. Supplement
  Knife Chief of the Pawnee Loups   PH
    MdBMu. Rendezvous
  Matilda Washington Dawson   PA
    Pierson
  Pat Lyon at the forge (Pat Lyon, black-
    smith)   MBA
    Davidson v 1
    Flexner. Light of distant skies
    Larkin
    Larkin rev ed
  Pat Lyon at the forge (Pat Lyon, black-
    smith)   PA
    PA. Annual ex, 1955
    Pierson
    Robb. Harper history
    Roos
    Time. 300 years (col)
  Patrick Lyon at the forge, Study for PH
    Chew. 250 years of art
  The Schuylkill, View on the   ICA
    Baur. Amer ptg
    Larkin
    Larkin rev ed
    Pierson
  William Potts Dewees   PPhUn
    PA. Annual ex, 1955
  William Strickland   CtY
    CtY. Portrait index
    Pierson
Near Avenue A by N. Spencer
Near Great Barrington by J. Marin
Near Manayunk by R. Smith
Near Paradise, Newport, Rhode island by
    W. T. Richards
Near the beach, Shinnecock by W. M. Chase
Near the mountain by E. Magafan
Near the sea by J. Floch
Near the village, October by G. Inness
Near Tibidabo by C. Carmen
Nearing the issue at the cock pit by H. Bonham
Nearly everybody reads the Bulletin by B.
    Shahn
Nebraska landscape by R. O. Pozzatti
The necklace by B. Greene
The necklace by J. Sloan
Negro Pietà by W. Pachner
Negro spiritual: Ride on conquering king by
    G. Biddle

Negroes
Anshutz, T. P. Aunt Hannah
Archer, E. Howard Patterson of the Harlem Yankees
Benton, T. H. Negro soldier
Biddle, G. Two Negroes
Brook, A. Frogtown lady
Brook, A. Southern belle
Carter, C. H. Stew
Chapin, J. Ruby Green singing
Clonney, J. G. In the cornfield
Clonney, J. G. In the woodshed
Clonney, J. G. Waking up
Curry, J. S. The Mississippi
Delaney, J. Innocence
Dinnerstein, H. Magnolia
Eakins, T. Will Shuster and black man going shooting
Evergood, P. Her world
Greenwood, M. Dancers resting
Greenwood, M. Invocation
Gwathmey, R. Hoeing
Harnett, W. M. Front face
Henri, R. Willie Gee
Hesselius, J. Charles Calvert and his Negro slave
Hirsch, J. Singing men
Homer, W. The carnival
Homer, W. Happy family in Virginia
Homer, W. Native woman cooking
Homer, W. Rum cay
Homer, W. Shark fishing
Homer, W. Sponge diver
Homer, W. Sunday morning in Virginia
Homer, W. Taking sunflowers to teacher
Homer, W. Under the coco palm
Homer, W. Unruly calf
James, A. Heart of darkness
Johnson, E. A ride for liberty: the fugitive slave
Lawrence, J. Migration of the Negro
Lawrence, J. Most of the people are very poor
Lawrence, J. Woman at work
Lawrence, J. You can buy whiskey for twenty-five cents a quart
Marsh, R. High yaller
Marsh, R. Negroes on Rockaway beach
Martin, F. Ruby
Martin, F. 'Tis me O Lord
Morrill, D. Minstrel banjo player
Mount, W. S. Bone player
Mount, W. S. Power of music
Pachner, W. Negro Pietà
Pippin, H. Sunday morning breakfast
Pippin, H. Uncle Tom
Prior, W. M. (manner of) Lady in a fine scarf
Prior, W. M. (manner of) William Whipper
Robinson, B. Ethiopia saluting the colors
Sepeshy, Z. L. Negro meeting
Shahn, B. Three men
Tanner, H. O. Banjo lesson
Turnbull, J. B. Son of a sharecropper
Unidentified artist. Enigmatic foursome
Unidentified artist. Negro child
Unidentified artist. The old plantation
Walker, G. A. Mal du pays
Watkins, F. C. Negro spiritual
Wood, T. W. Negress
Wyeth, A. N. A crow flew by

NEGUS, Caroline, fl 1837
Mrs James Page   MB
    MB. New England miniatures
Neighborhood physician by J. Levine
Neilson, Hannah (Coles) fl 1810
Jarvis, J. W. Mrs William Neilson
NEILSON, Raymond Perry Rodgers, 1881-
Chelsea lady and Bouvardia
    NAD. Annual ex, spring 1950
Hayley Lever
    NAD. Annual ex, 1947, 2d half
Hobart Nichols
    NAD. Annual ex, 1949, 1st half
Neilson, William, 1774-1852
Jarvis, J. W. William Neilson
NEIMAN, LeRoy, 1921-
Toro
    ICA. Annual ex, 1961
Neisse, Max Hermann-. See Hermann-Neisse, Max
Neither yet have you faith by L. Di Valentin
NELSON, Carl L.
Maine night no 2
    Pousette-Dart. Amer ptg
Nelson, Elizabeth (Tailer) 1667-1734
Unidentified artist. Mrs John Nelson
Nelson, Horatio Nelson, viscount, 1758-1805
West, B. The apotheosis of Nelson
West, B. Death of Lord Nelson
West, B. Project for a monument. The apotheosis of Nelson
Nelson, Mrs John. See Nelson, Elizabeth (Tailer)
Nelson, Mary Gay (Wyan) fl 1862
Bingham, G. C. Mrs Thomas W. Nelson
Nelson, Mrs Merlin. See Craig, Nancy Ellen
NELSON, Robert A.
Soldier and bull
    DC. 27 biennial ex, 1961
Nelson, Mrs Thomas W. See Nelson, Mary Gay (Wyan)
Nelson, William Rockhill, 1841-1915
Chase, W. M. William Rockhill Nelson
Nelson's island showing Monument hill and Allegheny waterfront by R. Smith
Neon thoroughfare by M. Tobey
Neponset bay by M. B. Prendergast
Neponset river, Milton by J. Wagner
NEPOTE, Alexander, 1913-
Enigmatical section
    IU. Contemp Amer ptg, 1951
Ominous
    IU. Contemp Amer ptg, 1952
Secluded   CSFM
    CoS. New accessions USA, 1950
A **nervous** woman by W. W. Quirt
The **nest** by J. Pollock
Nests of lightning by K. Sage
Net mender by K. Knaths
The **Netherlands** by W. De Kooning
Nets and boats by M. A. Blackburn
Nets, boats and sea by J. C. Atherton
Nets with blue by R. Crawford
Neue Weinsteige by R. S. Neuman
NEUMAN, Robert S. 1926-
Ciudad de Dos Corazones
    MBIC. View 1960
Forlorn one
    IU. Contemp Amer ptg, 1952

Neue Weinsteige
  PPC. International ex, 1961/62
The struggle
  IU. Contemp Amer ptg & sculp, 1953
Un vista
  IU. Contemp Amer ptg & sculp, 1961
New, 1955 by R. Crawford
New Amsterdam by L. Block
New Bedford in 1807 by W. A. Wall
New costume by M. Sawyer
New death by P. Evergood
New dodgem by R. Marsh
New England
  See also names of New England states,
    e.g., Maine; and of cities, e.g., Boston
  Baumbach, H. New England landscape
  Blanch, A. New England
  Burlin, P. New England landscape
  Durrie, G. H. Autumn in New England,
    cider making
  Durrie, G. H. New England winter scene
  Durrie, G. H. Winter scene in New Eng-
    land
  Hartigan, G. New England, October
  Heade, M. J. Rocks in New England
  Prendergast, M. B. New England village
  Unidentified artist. New England farm in
    winter
  Unidentified artist. New England hillside
  Unidentified artist. New England village
New England coast shipping by F. H. Lane
New England editor by T. H. Benton
New England faces: husband and wife by
  Unidentified artist
New England family group by Unidentified
  artist
New England goddess by Unidentified artist
New England picnic by J. P. Hardy
New England stove by W. A. Kienbusch
New Guinea beer party by R. M. Graham
New Hampshire
  Bierstadt, A. Ascutney mountain from
    Claremont, New Hampshire
  Cole, T. View near Conway, New Hamp-
    shire
  Cole, T. View near Tamworth; In the
    White mountains
  Cropsey, J. Eagle cliff, Franconia notch
  Gerry, S. Mount Washington, New Hamp-
    shire
  Leavitt, J. W. At Loudon, New Hamp-
    shire
  Macknight, D. Shelburne woods, New
    Hampshire
  Marin, J. Mountain top
  Unidentified artist. In the heart of New
    Hampshire
  Unidentified artist. Silver lake, New
    Hampshire
New Hope, Pennsylvania
  Demuth, C. H. New Hope, Pennsylvania
  Pickett, J. Lehigh canal, sunset, New
    Hope, Pennsylvania
New housing by Y. Hnizdovsky
New Jersey
  See also Delaware river and valley;
    Newark, New Jersey
  Durand, A. B. North mountain reserva-
    tion, Orange, New Jersey

Inness, G. Late afternoon, Montclair, New
  Jersey
Marin, J. Alpine district, New Jersey
The **new** Lazarus by P. Evergood
New Lebanon railroad station by L. Bouché
New life (Resurrection) by M. Tobey
New Mexico
  Dasburg, A. Autumn—Ranchos de Taos
  Dasburg, A. New Mexican landscape
  Dasburg, A. New Mexican village
  Dasburg, A. November, New Mexico
  Dasburg, A. Road into Ranchos de Taos
  Dasburg, A. Taos plaza
  Davis, S. New Mexican landscape
  Hartley, M. Landscape, New Mexico
  Hartley, M. New Mexico
  Hartley, M. New Mexico: landscape
  Marin, J. Blue mountain near Taos
  Marin, J. Near Santa Fe, New Mexico
  Marin, J. New Mexico
  Marin, J. Pueblo and mesa, Taos moun-
    tains
  Marin, J. Storm over Taos, New Mexico
  Marin, J. Taos
  Marin, J. Taos landscape, New Mexico
New Mexico number 34 by E. Corbett
New Mexico recollections by M. Hartley
New moon by H. B. Kayn
The **new** novel by W. Homer
New Orleans
  Crawford, R. New Orleans #2, 1953
  Crawford, R. New Orleans #4, 1953
  Crawford, R. New Orelans #5, 1954
  Herron, D. St Louis cemetery, New Or-
    leans
  Matthew, K. Charming New Orleans
  Philipp, R. Patio Royale, New Orleans
  Woiseri, L. J. B. de. New Orleans, 1803
New Orleans still life by R. Crawford
New scholar by F. W. Edmonds
New shores by C. A. Morris
New world a' coming by I. R. Pereira
New Year wall: Night by F. J. Kline
New York (city)
  Alcalay, A. East end in New York
  Beal, G. R. Terrace, Central park
  Bellows, G. W. Blue snow, the Battery
  Bellows, G. W. Cliff dwellers
  Bellows, G. W. Gramercy park
  Bellows, G. W. Men of the docks
  Bellows, G. W. Riverfront no 1
  Bellows, G. W. Summer night, Riverside
    drive
  Bennett, W. J. Broadway from Bowling
    Green, c 1826
  Bennett, W. J. Packet Row, South street,
    New York
  Birch, T. New York harbor
  Blakelock, R. A. Old New York: north-
    west corner 55th street and Seventh
    avenue, c 1868
  Blakelock, R. A. Old New York, shanties
    at 55th street and 7th avenue
  Block, L. New Amsterdam
  Boit, E. D. East river, New York
  Boit, E. D. Park avenue, New York
  Bové, R. J. New York scene
  Burton, C. Governor's room, City hall,
    New York, c 1830

New York (city)—*Continued*

Cafferty, J. H. and Rosenberg, C. D. Wall street half past 2 o'clock, Oct 13, 1857

Calyo, N. V. The great fire in New York, 1835

Calyo, N. V. View of New York city, c 1835

Chappel, W. P. Citizens supplying a fire engine with water from a pump, New York, 1809

Chappel, W. P. City watchman and his watch box, New York, 1809

Chappel, W. P. Old tea water pump and cart, New York, 1807

Criss, F. Astor place, 1932

Davis, S. New York, 1932

Davis, S. New York under gaslight

Davis, S. New York waterfront

Dehn, A. A. Spring in Central park

De Kooning, W. Gansevoort street

Dreier, D. A. New York: the Little church around the corner

Feininger, L. Factory windows in Manhattan

Feininger, L. Manhattan, dawn

Feininger, L. Manhattan, dusk

Feininger, L. Manhattan, moonwake

Feininger, L. Manhattan, night 1941

Fiene, E. Razing Old post office, New York

Franck, F. S. New York from Hoboken

Franck, F. S. New York with roller coaster

Glackens, W. J. Central park, winter

Glackens, W. J. The drive, Central park

Glackens, W. J. March day, Washington square

Grosz, G. Central park

Grosz, G. Central park at night

Grosz, G. Manhattan harbour

Guglielmi, L. New York 21

Guy, F. Tontine coffee house, New York, c 1798

Harvey, G. St Thomas church, Broadway, New York

Hassam, C. Fifth avenue nocturne

Hassam, C. Melting snow, Fifth avenue

Hassam, C. Union square in spring

Hassam, C. Washington arch, spring

Henri, R. Fifty-seventh street

Henri, R. New York street in winter

Henri, R. West 57th street in 1902

Hirsch, S. Lower Manhattan

Hirsch, S. Manhattan

Hnizdovsky, Y. New York subway

Hofmann, H. Mosaics, 1956 (Northeast corner, 711 Third avenue, New York)

Hofmann, H. Mosaics, 1956 (Southwest corner, 711 Third avenue, New York)

Homer, W. Skating in Central park, New York, 1860

Hopper, E. From Williamsburg bridge

Hopper, E. Manhattan bridge and Lily apartments

Hopper, E. New York pavements

Howell, F. W. Gramercy park

Imbert, A. Celebrating the opening of the Erie canal, New York harbor, Nov 4, 1825

Kabak, R. New York harbor

Kantor, M. Farewell to Union Square

Kantor, M. Union square, night

Kelly, E. New York

Kingman, D. Columbus circle

Kingman, D. Washington square, New York

Kline, F. J. New York

Koch, S. Orchard street, New York city

Lane, F. H. New York harbor

Lawson, E. Winter, Central park, New York

Lozowick, L. New York, 1926-27

Luks, G. B. Blue Devils marching down Fifth avenue

MacIver, L. New York

Marca-Relli, C. di. New York City

Margules, D. Lower Fifth avenue

Marin, J. American telephone building, New York City

Marin, J. Broadway night

Marin, J. Bryant square

Marin, J. Fifth avenue and Forty-second street

Marin, J. Looking up Fifth avenue from Thirtieth street

Marin, J. Lower Manhattan, 1920

Marin, J. Lower Manhattan, 1922

Marin, J. Lower Manhattan from the river

Marin, J. Manhattan, St Paul's

Marin, J. Mid-Manhattan II, 1932

Marin, J. Midtown, New York, 1928

Marin, J. Movement—Fifth avenue

Marin, J. New York at night

Marin, J. New York, downtown

Marin, J. New York, East river

Marin, J. New York harbor, 1920

Marin, J. Pertaining to Nassau street, New York

Marin, J. Singer building

Marin, J. Stock exchange, New York city

Marin, J. Street crossing, New York

Marin, J. Street movement, abstraction, New York

Marin, J. Woolworth building in construction

Marin, J. Woolworth building, no 31, 1912

Mario, A. Construction work in New York, 1868

Marsh, R. BMT, Fourteenth street

Marsh, R. The Bowery

Marsh, R. The Bowery at Pell street

Marsh, R. East Tenth street jungle

Marsh, R. End of Fourteenth street crosstown line

Marsh, R. Fourteenth street

Marsh, R. Monday night at the Metropolitan

Marsh, R. Naked over New York

Marsh, R. Prometheus in Rockefeller center

Marsh, R. Under the el

Matthew, K. Skyline (New York)

Matthew, K. Waterfront (New York)

Milbourne, C. Government house, Bowling Green, New York, 1797

Mira, A. S. Washington monument, Washington square, New York

Moran, T. Lower Manhattan from Communipaw

Myers, J. East of the Bowery

O'Keeffe, G. American Radiator building

O'Keeffe, G. New York, night

Pierson, S. Fulton street, New York, 1821

Pollard, C. Residence of Hendrick Remsen, c 1820

Prendergast, M. B. Central park in 1903
Prendergast, M. B. Columbus circle, New York
Prendergast, M. B. East river
Prendergast, M. B. Madison square, New York
Prendergast, M. B. The Mall, Central park
Prendergast, M. B. May day, Central park
Prendergast, M. B. Mulberry Bend park, New York
Robertson, A. New York city from North river
Rose, H. East New York
Rose, H. From Avenue A
Rose, H, Manhattan tops
Roszak, T. Forty-second street
Searle, J. Interior of Park theater, New York, 1822
Shahn, B. East Twelfth street
Shahn, B. New York
Shawkey, S. Saturday night in New York city
Sheeler, C. Macdougal alley
Shinn, E. Knoedler's, 34th street
Sloan, J. Backyards, Greenwich village
Sloan, J. Bleecker street Saturday night
Sloan, J. The city from Greenwich village, 1922
Sloan, J. Cornelia street
Sloan, J. Dust storm, Fifth avenue
Sloan, J. Fifth avenue
Sloan, J. Lafayette hotel
Sloan, J. Looking out on Washington square
Sloan, J. Roofs: 23rd street, sunset
Sloan, J. Sixth avenue and Third street
Sloan, J. Sixth avenue and Thirteenth street
Sloan, J. Sixth avenue and 30th street
Sloan, J. Sixth avenue elevated at Third street, 1928
Sloan, J. Sunday in Union square
Sloan, J. The White way
Smith, J. B. John street, c 1768
Sonntag, W. L. The Bowery at night, c 1895
Stella, J. American landscape
Tiffany, L. C. Old New York, c 1878
Tobey, M. Broadway, 1936
Tobey, M. New York
Unidentified artist. Burning of the Tombs
Unidentified artist. Fashionable inn, New York, c 1825
Unidentified artist. Five points, New York, c 1829
Unidentified artist. Furniture shop and warehouse of Duncan Phyfe, Fulton street
Unidentified artist. High bridge across the Harlem river, c 1840
Unidentified artist. Southeast prospect of the city of New York c 1850
Walkowitz, A. New York
Walkowitz, A. New York, improvisation, 1913
Waller, F. Interior of the Metropolitan museum of art, 1881
Waller, F. The Metropolitan Museum in Fourteenth street
Weber, M. Grand central terminal
Weber, M. New York
Weber, M. New York at night
Weber, M. Rush hour, New York, 1915

New York city Susannah by P. Evergood
New York—Hoboken ferry by N. V. Calyo
New York movie by E. Hopper
New York mural by S. Davis
New York, New Haven and Hartford by E. Hopper
New York-Paris no 1, 1931, by S. Davis
New York-Paris no 2, 1931 by S. Davis
New York-Paris no 3, 1931 by S. Davis
New York skyline by H. Katzman
New York subway by Y. Hinzdovsky
New York tablet by M. Tobey
New York 21 by L. Guglielmi
New York (state) Senate
    Unidentified artist. The Senate, Albany, 1850
New York window by C. Hassam
Newark, New Jersey
    Unidentified artist. David Alling house and shop
Newark airport murals, Panel of A. Gorky
Newcomb college by E. Corbett
Newer grounds by N. Lewis
Newfound gap (Smoky mountains) by R. H. Byrum
Newhall, Richard, fl 1829
    Unidentified artist. Tomb in memory of Richard Newhall
NEWMAN, Barnett, 1905-
Abraham
    MMA. New Amer ptg
Adam
    MMA. New Amer ptg
Concord
    MMA. New Amer ptg
Ulysses
    WMAA. Contemp Amer ptg, 1959/60
NEWMAN, Daniel, 1929-
Awakening
    WMAA. Young America 1960
Tempest
    WMAA. Young America 1960
Newman, Henry, 1780-1875
    Ames, E. Henry Newman
NEWMAN, Henry Roderick, 1833?-1918
Pont de Minimes, Chartres   MB
    MB. Ptgs in water color
Temple at Philae   MB
    MB. Ptgs in water color
Wild flowers   MB
    MB. Ptgs in water color
NEWMAN, Robert Loftin, 1827-1912
Landscape with figures   NBM
    Pierson
The letter   DP
    Larkin
    Larkin rev ed
Madonna and child
    Pierson
Mother and son   GAtM
    GAtM. Holbrook collection
Newport, Rhode Island
    Hassam, C. Bailey's beach
    Heade, M. J. Salt marshes, Newport, Rhode Island
    Kensett, J. F. Newport, View near
    Kensett, J. F. Newport harbor, Rhode Island

Newport Rhode Island—*Continued*
  Kensett, J. F. and Huntington, D. Seascape, Newport
  Martin, H. D. Newport landscape
  Richards, W. T. Near Paradise, Newport, Rhode Island
News and soda pop by Nura
News from the gold diggings by W. S. Mount
The newsboy by H. Inman
Newsboys by B. Riley
NEWTON, Gilbert Stuart, 1794-1835
  Dull lecture
  Flexner. Light of distant skies
NEY, Lancelot, 1900-
  Composition   MWM
    CoS. New accessions USA, 1958
Nez-Percés Indian by A. J. Miller
Niagara Falls
  Chambers, T. Niagara Falls
  Church, F. E. Niagara Falls
  Cole, T. Distant view of the Falls of Niagara
  Cropsey, J. F. Niagara Falls
  Cropsey, J. F. Niagara Falls from the foot of Goat island
  De Grailly, V. View of Niagara Falls
  Eilshemius, L. M. Niagara Falls
  Fisher, A. Niagara
  Hicks, E. Falls of Niagara, c 1825
  Gould, L. A. Niagara seen with different eyes (after a print by Lumley)
  Kensett, J. F. Niagara Falls and the rapids
  Morse, S. F. B. Niagara Falls from Table rock
  Trumbull, J. Panoramas of Niagara Falls
  Trumbull, J. View of Niagara from upper bank on British side
  Unidentified artist. Suspension bridge at Niagara
  Vanderlyn, J. Falls of Niagara
  Vanderlyn, J. Falls of Niagara taken from under the Table rock
  Vanderlyn, J. Niagara
Nice drums by J. Robinson
Nicetown by A. Gold
Nicholas by A. N. Wyeth
Nicholl, Mr, fl 1809
  Jarvis, J. W. Mr Nicholl
NICHOLS, Dale, 1904-
  City National bank   ATU
    ATU. Coll of Amer art
  Company for supper
    NYG. Fine art
  End of the hunt   MM
    NYG. Fine art
  Evening in the country
    NYG. Fine art (col)
  Look homeward, America
    NYG. Fine art
  Summer bounty
    NYG. Fine art (col)
Nichols, Francis
  Peale, C. W. Gen Francis Nichols
NICHOLS, Hobart, b 1869
  Black herd
    NAD. Annual ex, autumn 1949
  Northwest wind   NJMo
    NJMo. Forty years
  Shifting shadows
    NAD. Annual ex, 1947, 2d half

Portrait of the artist
  Neilson, R. P. R. Hobart Nichols
NICHOLS, Spencer Baird, 1875-1950
  Tumbling waters
    NAD. Annual ex, 1947, 2d
Nicoll, Eliza Hopkins. See Dowdall, Eliza Hopkins (Nicoll)
Nicot, Georges
  O'Hara, E. Georges Nicot
NIESE, Henry E. 1924-
  The ambry   WMAA
    WMAA. Young America 1960
  The red room
    WMAA. Young America 1960
  The window
    DC. 24 biennial ex, 1955
Night by M. Beckmann
Night by R. Breinin
Night by J. F. Folinsbee
Night by G. L. Mueller
Night by C. S. Price
Night by A. J. Pucci
Night by K. Zerbe
Night after San Juan by W. J. Glackens
Night and clouds by A. P. Ryder
Night and prophecy by N. Rubington
Night baseball by M. A. Phillips
Night baseball game Cardinals vs. Dodgers by F. E. Warren
Night ceremony by J. Pollock
Night chant by E. Millman
Night children by P. Guston
Night city by R. A. Florsheim
Night clouds by A. P. Ryder
Night club whoopee by G. Grosz
Night event no 2, 1958 by W. Pachner
Night fair by M. Jackson
Night fantasy by W. Drewes
Night figures by C. A. Morris
Night fisherman by E. F. Spruce
Night fishing by L. Gatch
Night flight by J. Ernst
Night herd by G. Bartlett
Night hunters by C. M. Williamson
Night image by C. A. Morris
Night in Bologna by P. Cadmus
Night journey by C. Oscar
Night mirror by W. A. Baziotes
Night mission by J. Myers
Night music by G. Ratkai
Night of return by R. Haines
Night of the equinox by C. E. Burchfield
Night of the ritual by A. Salemme
Night over Buffalo by W. C. Palmer
Night passage by W. Thon
Night river by C. A. Morris
Night scene by W. Pachner
Night sea by L. Chesney
Night shadows by L. MacIver
Night sounds by J. Pollock
Night spot by W. Biggs
Night square by W. De Kooning
Night still life by J. Hultberg
Night study of flowers by M. B. Prendergast

Night walk by N. Lewis
Night watch, New Guinea by B. Hasen
Night wind by C. E. Burchfield
Night windows by L. Guglielmi
Night windows by E. Hopper
Night worker by J. Teyral
Nighthawks by E. Hopper
Nightingale, Martha Washington (Greene) fl 1796
    Malbone, E. G. Mrs John Nightingale
Nightmare by G. Grosz
Nightscape by C. Coggeshall
Nighttime, enigma and nostalgia by A. Gorky
Nile by P. Guston
Nile river, Egypt
    Bacon, H. Scene on the Nile
Nimitz, Chester William, 1885-
    Murray, A. K. Fleet Admiral Chester W. Nimitz, U.S.N.
The 9:45 accommodation by E. L. Henry
Nine men by J. Hirsch
Nine P. M. by H. Pittman
1951 by M. Tobey
Nisus and Scylla by J. W. Treiman
Nixon, John, 1733-1808
    Malbone, E. G. John Nixon
Nixtamal y postole by D. Rosenthal
No feather pillow by A. G. Dove
No Heart—Ioway by C. B. King
No let up by G. Grosz
No one heard the thunder by K. Sage
No passing by K. Sage
No turns permitted by R. Marsh
Noah-Wolf by H. Dinnerstein
Noah's ark by E. Hicks
Noah's ark by J. H. Hidley
Nobody's pet by P. Bacon
Nocturne by B. Shahn
Nocturne in black and gold by J. A. M. Whistler
Nocturne in blue and green by J. A. M. Whistler
Nocturne in blue and silver by J. A. M. Whistler
Nogent-le-Rotrou by B. Lamotte
Nolan, Daniel J. d 1920
    Sargent, J. S. Daniel J. Nolan
Noncomformist by W. C. Libby
Nooka sound, View of by J. Webber
Noon by W. De Kooning
Noon by T. H. Hinckley
Noon on the reef by R. Tam
Noonday heat by C. E. Burchfield
Noonday rest by A. J. Miller
The nooning by W. Homer
Nooning on the Platte by A. Bierstadt
Noontide in late May by C. E. Birchfield
Norba, General view of by J. I. Middleton
NORDBERG, Barbara
    Arnold
        NAD. Annual ex, 1954

NORDFELDT, Bror Julius Olsson, 1878-1955
    Driftwood, North Pacific
        IU. Contemp Amer ptg, 1949
    Flight of birds   ATeS
        ATeS. Collection
    Flood   DC
        DC. 21 biennial ex, 1949
    Gifts from the sea
        ICA. Annual ex, 1945/46
    Green woods
        NBuA. Expressionism
    Logs drifting
        Cheney. Story 1958 ed
    Movement   MM
        MM. 100 Amer ptrs
    Pietà
        PPC. International ex, 1953
    Sea and rocks
        Cheney. Primer 1958 ed
        Cheney. Story 1958 ed
    Shore birds, Tomales Bay   IaDM
        CoS. New accessions USA, 1958
    Willow-Swamp, Minnesota
        Gruskin
NORDFELDT, Iris E. 1913-
    Surf, ten mile
        VR. Amer ptg, 1954
Norma by I. G. Olinsky
NORMAN, Irving, 1910-
    Rush hour
        IU. Contemp Amer ptg & sculp, 1957
Normandie by O. M. Pleissner
NORRIS, Ben, 1910-
    The pali
        MM. Amer ptg today
North, William, 1755-1836
    Peale, C. W. Gen William North
North country by W. L. Metcalf
North inlet by J. Allen
North mountain reservation, South Orange, N.J. by A. B. Durand
North river by G. W. Bellows
North river shad by W. M. Chase
Northeaster by W. Homer
Northeaster—Canada geese by L. B. Hunt
Northern lights by Martyl
Northern point by A. N. Wyeth
Northern seascape by R. Rosenborg
Northwest landscape by K. L. Callahan
Northwest wind by C. H. Davis
Northwest wind by H. Nichols
Northwestern town by Unidentified artist
Northwood, New Hampshire
    Unidentified artist. New England village, possibly Northwood, New Hampshire
Norwalk island, View of by G. L. Brown
Norwood, Margaret Eleanor. See Cushing, Margaret Eleanor
Nosegay by P. Bacon
Nospmas M. Egiap, Lancaster, Pennsylvania by C. H. Demuth
Nostalgia migration by T. D. Benrimo
Nostalgic night by M. Sokole
Not at home by E. Johnson
Not even he may rest by G. Biddle
Notch of the White mountains by T. Cole

The **note** by C. Sebree
Notre Dame, Paris by W. G. Congdon
Notre Dame, Paris by S. Halpert
Notre Dame, Paris by M. B'. Prendergast
Nott, Eliphalet, 1773-1866
  Ames, E. Eliphalet Nott
Notte Napolitana by A. Osver
Nouveau Cirque, Paris by M. B. Prendergast
Nova Scotia fishermen by M. Hartley
Nova Scotia landscape by J. E. Heliker
November evening by C. E. Burchfield
November gale by P. C. Malicoat
November mosaic by W. L. Metcalf
November, New Mexico by A. Dasburg
November 1951 by C. E. Spohn
November 7th by L. Kester
NOVOTNY, Elmer L. 1909-
  Wingaersheek beach   OYB
  OYB. Annual 1958
  OYB. Supplement 1959

Norwalk island, View of by G. L. Brown
No-way-ke-sug-ga, an Oto by G. B. King
NOXON, Herbert R.
  John L. Lewis
  NAD. Annual ex, 1953
Noyes, Sarah. See Tibbits, Sarah (Noyes)
NOYES, Wilbur Fiske, 1897-
  Alden Perley White (copy)   MSE
  MSE. Catalogue ports, 1950
Nu by S. Davis
Nu by G. Gluckmann
Nude by H. M. Asplund
Nude by M. Beckmann
Nude by I. Bishop
Nude by L. Kroll
Nude by Y. Kuniyoshi
Nude by A. Leepa
Nude by A. H. Maurer
Nude by R. Philipp
Nude by J. A. M. Whistler
Nude and nine apples by J. Sloan
Nude at foot of stairs by J. Sloan
Nude at window by M. Hirshfield
Nude back by T. Eakins
Nude back by E. E. Speicher
Nude by the el by P. Evergood
Nude combing her hair by R. Philipp
Nude dressing hair by W. J. Glackens
Nude figure by P. Burlin
Nude figure kneeling among clouds by
  E. Geller
Nude image no 5 by N. Rubington
Nude in doorway by A. Buller
Nude in grisaille by R. Détré
Nude in profile by R. Soyer
Nude in rocky background by L. Kroll
Nude in yellow ocre by B. Greene
Nude on red couch B. Karfiol
Nude on the roof by J. Sloan
Nude reclining by B. Shahn
Nude with apple by W. J. Glackens

Nude with bath towel by G. Grosz
Nude with cat by J. Koch
Nude with fan by G. W. Bellows
Nude with flowers by D. Park
Nude with red hair by G. W. Bellows
Nude with violin by P. Evergood
Number zero—Adam by K. Knaths
Numbers in color by J. Johns
Numena by G. L. Mueller
NURA (Nura [Woodson] Ulreich) 1900?-
  1950
  News and soda pop
  PPC. Ptg in the U.S. 1949
Nuremberg by S. Hirsch
Nursery school by L. P. Harmon
Nursing mother by T. Fried
Nydia by G. Fuller
Nymphs by R. A. Blakelock

O

Oak creek canyon, Arizona by F. Chapin
Oak Knoll, Napa by J. Lee
Oak street platform by A. Bohrod
OAKLEY, Violet, 1874-1960
  Christ and the woman of Samaria
  PA. Annual ex, 1948
The **oarsmen** by T. Eakins
Oarsmen on the Schuylkill by T. Eakins
Obelisks by E. Berman
Objects on table by L. Dodd
Oblique illusion by I. R. Pereira
Oblique progression by I. R. Pereira
Oboe player by T. Eakins
OBROSEY, Arthur
  Early thaw
  PA. Annual ex, 1959-60
Occasion by J. Stefanelle
Ocean and cliffs by W. Brice
Ocean and rocks by W. Brice
Ocean bathers by G. Hartigan
Ocean brilliance by N. Carton
Ocean greyness by J. Pollock
OCHIKUBO, Tetsuo, 1928-
  Changing seasons
  DC. 27 biennial ex, 1961
  Counterpoint   NBuA
  NBuA. Acquisitions 1957-58
Ochre building by C. di Marca-Relli
OCHS, Robert L.
  Industrial   OYB
  OYB. Annual 1952
October by C. E. Burchfield
October by J. W. Ehninger
October, 1935 by A. G. Dove
October morning, Deerfield, Massachusetts
  by W. L. Metcalf
Octopus by A. Calder
Odalisk by K. F. Roesch
Odalisque by L. Kroll
Odalisque by C. di Marca-Relli

O'Donnell, Eleanora. See Iselin, Eleanora (O'Donnell)
Odradek by C. L. Cicero
An odyssey for moderns by L. Guglielmi
Oedipus at Colonos by E. K. Schwabacher
OERTEL, Johannes Adam Simon, 1823-1909
  The Shed, Woodruff stables, Jerome avenue, the Bronx, 1848   NNMC
    NJN. Early N.J. artists
Of Maine by J. Heliker
Of sin and error by P. Mangravite
Of the resistance by A. Rattner
Of this time, of that place by J. Muller
Off Cape Split by J. Marin
Off Hatteras no 2 by M. Jamieson
Off Mount Desert island by F. H. Lane
Off Stonington by J. Marin
Off the Maine coast by T. Birch
Off to the Banks by M. Hartley
Off York island, Maine by J. Marin
The offering by S. M. Adler
The offering by X. Gonzales
The offering by N. Tschacbasov
Office at night by E. Hopper
Office board for Smith Brothers coal company by J. F. Peto
Office building by V. I. Cuthbert
Office girls by I. Soyer
Offices by C. Sheeler
Offshore island by M. Avery
Offshore wind by T. P. Blagden
Oganda by P. Wieghardt
OGDEN, Frederick, D.
  Silvery night
    NYG. Fine art
  Winter silence
    NYG. Fine art
Ogden, William Butler, 1805-1877
  Healy, G. P. A. William B. Ogden
Ogdensburg, New York
  Wall, W. G. View of Ogdensburg
Oglethorpe, James Edward, 1696-1785
  Verelst, W. Oglethorpe presenting Tomo-Chi-Chi and the Indians to the Lord Trustees of the colony of Georgia
O'HARA, Eliot, 1890-
  Cape Porpoise harbor   OYB
    OYB. Catalogue 1951
  Empty mansion
    NAD. Annual ex, autumn 1949
  Georges Nicot
    NAD. Annual ex, 1949, 2d half
OHASHI, Yutaka, 1923-
  Black no 8
    IU. Contemp Amer ptg & sculp, 1961
  Stone garden   NNSG
    NNSG. Handbook
  Stone garden IV
    VR. Amer ptg, 1958
  Untitled painting
    NUM. Art across America
Ohio evening by R. Roberts
Ohio magic by B. Shahn
Ohio river and valley
  Bingham, G. C. Scene on the Ohio
  Smith, R. Scene on the Ohio
Ohio skyline by B. Shahn
Oil construction on the beach by M. Frary

Oil splatters and leaves by L. MacIver
OKADA, Frank S. 1931-
  Taurus
    OrPA. Ptgs & sculptures
OKADA, Kenzo, 1902-
  Angel
    VR. Amer ptg, 1958
  Dynasty   NBuA
    NBuA. Acquisitions 1954-57
  Earth glow
    WMAA. Annual ex, 1958
  Height
    Ponente. Mod ptg, 1960 (col)
  Hero
    WMAA. Contemp Amer ptg, 1959/60
  Kine no 1   OCo
    NUM. Art across America
  Memories   WMAA
    Goodrich. Amer art (col)
  Painting on 23
    CtY. Yale alumni
  Silver
    MnMW. 60 Amer ptrs
  Snow mountain
    Baur. Nature
  Solstice   NNSG
    NNSG. Handbook
    NNSG. Younger Amer ptrs
    Read. Concise history
  Tanabata   MB
    Pierson
  White and gold   NBuA
    NBuA. Acquisitions 1959-1961
    PPC. International ex, 1961/62
OKAMURA, Arthur, 1932-
  Aura of a pond
    ICA. Annual ex, 1959-60
  Darkly, soft darts
    IU. Contemp Amer ptg & sculp, 1959
  Mountain pores
    IU. Contemp Amer ptg & sculp, 1961
O'KEEFFE, Georgia, 1887-
  Abstraction, 1926   WMAA
    Goodrich. Amer art
    MnMW. Precisionist view
  Abstraction—white iris
    Cheney. Expressionism 1948 ed
  Abstraction, White rose
    MWM. Georgia O'Keeffe
  American Radiator building   TNF
    Brown. Amer ptg
    Richardson. Ptg in America
  Antelope
    IU. Contemp Amer ptg & sculp, 1955
    MWM. Georgia O'Keeffe
  Black abstraction, 1927   MM
    Baur. New art
  Black cross   ICA
    McCurdy
  Black cross with red sky
    MWM. Georgia O'Keeffe
  Black iris   MM
    Baur. New art (col)
    Cheney. Story 1958 ed
    Pierson
  Black patio door
    IU. Contemp Amer ptg & sculp, 1959
    MWM. Georgia O'Keeffe
  Black place III
    MWM. Georgia O'Keeffe
  Black place green
    MWM. Georgia O'Keeffe

O'KEEFFE, Georgia—*Continued*
A blackbird with snow-covered red hills
  MWM. Georgia O'Keeffe
Blue II
  WMAA. Contemp Amer ptg, 1959/60
Blue and green music   ICA
  Brown. Amer ptg
  Pierson
Calla with roses
  Brown. Amer ptg
Cliffs beyond Abiquiu, dry waterfall
  MM. Georgia O'Keeffe
Corn, dark   MM
  Baur. Revolution
Cos Cob
  Cheney. Primer 1958 ed
Cow's skull
  Taylor. Fifty centuries, 1954 ed (col)
Cow's skull, red, white and blue   MM
  Baur. New art
  MM. 100 Amer ptrs (col)
  Pierson
Cow's skull with calico roses
  Gruskin
Dark red leaves on white   DP
  DP. Catalogue
Dead cottonwood tree   CSB
  CoS. New accessions USA, 1952
  MWM. Georgia O'Keeffe
Deer's skull with pedernal
  WMAA. Museum and its friends, 1958
    (col)
Early spring tree
  Pousette-Dart. Amer ptg
From the pelvis series
  MMA. Abstract
From the plains
  Baur. Nature (col)
  WMAA. Pioneers
From the plains no 1, 1953
  Time. 300 years (col)
Green patio door   NBuA
  NBuA. Acquisitions 1957-58
Grey hills   InIJ
  InIJ. 105 ptgs
Horse's skull on blue   ATeS
  ATeS. Collection
  Mendelowitz
In the patio no 1
  MWM. Georgia O'Keeffe
In the patio no 5
  CSFP. Annual ex, 1952
In the patio no 9, 1950   DC
  DC. Halpert collection
It was blue and green
  MWM. Georgia O'Keeffe
Jack-in-the-pulpit
  Cheney. Expressionism 1948 ed
Lake George barns   MnMW
  MnMW. Precisionist view
  MnMW. Reality and fantasy
Lake George, coat and red
  MnMW. Precisionist view
Lake George window   MMA
  Baur. New art
Lightning at sea   MLL
  MWM. Georgia O'Keeffe
Long island sunset   IBM
  Lee. Art then and now
Music—black, blue and green
  Cheney. Primer 1958 ed
My heart
  MWM. Georgia O'Keeffe

New York, night   NeL
  Barker. From realism
  ICA. Amer artists paint the city
  MnMW. Precisionist view (col)
  Time. 300 years (col)
Patio with black door   MLL
  WMAA. Museum and its friends, 1959
Patio with cloud   WiMi
  MnMW. Precisionist view
Pedernal form the ranch no 1
  DC. 27 biennial ex, 1961
Pelvis series, red and yellow
  MWM. Georgia O'Keeffe
Pelvis series, red with blue
  MnMW. Precisionist view
Pelvis with shadows and the moon
  MWM. Georgia O'Keeffe
Pelvis with the moon, New Mexico
  WMAA. Juliana Force
Pink vase and green leaves
  Cheney. Expressionism 1948 ed
Piñons with cedar
  IU. Contemp Amer ptg & sculp, 1957
Poppies   CtMS
  MWM. Georgia O'Keeffe
Ram's head, hollyhock, little hills
  Myers
Ram's head with pedernal
  Lewisohn
Ram's skull with brown leaves
  NUM. Art across America
Ranchos church   DP
  Cheney. Story 1958 ed
Ranchos church, front
  MWM. Georgia O'Keeffe
Seaweed
  MWM. Georgia O'Keeffe
Skunk cabbage   WMAA
  Larkin
  Larkin rev ed
Stables   MiD
  MiD. Treasures
  MnMW. Precisionist view
Summer days
  MWM. Georgia O'Keeffe
Wall with green door
  MWM. Georgia O'Keeffe
The wave   MAP
  Rathbun
White Canadian barn no 2, 1932   MMA
  Baur. New art
  UNESCO. 1860-1949
  UNESCO. 1860-1955
  UNESCO. 1860-1959
White flower   WMAA
  Goodrich. Amer art
White iris
  Cheney. Expressionism 1948 ed
The white place in shadow   DP
  DP. Catalogue
  Pierson
Winter cottonwoods east, V
  MWM. Georgia O'Keeffe

        Portrait of the artist
Speicher, E. E. Georgia O'Keeffe
OKIMOTO, Jerry, 1924-
Study no 3   NBuA
  NBuA. Acquisitions 1957-58
Oklahoma by L. Lozowick
Old age by G. Fuller
Old American locomotive by L. Feininger
Old aqueduct by T. H. Hotchkiss

The old automobile by A. M. R. Moses
Old barn door by J. M. Shinn
Old bars, Dogtown by M. Hartley
Old Battersea bridge by J. A. M. Whistler
Old black pot by W. M. Chase
Old boats and beach by S. Wilson
Old bridge by C. H. Moore
Old canal port by O. F. Bluemner
Old church, Carversville by D. Garber
An old clearing by A. H. Wyant
Old clown making up by J. Sloan
Old companions by J. F. Peto
Old cottager by W. M. Chase
Old courthouse in Philadelphia, 1835 by R. Smith
Old Cremona by W. M. Harnett
Old cupboard door by W. M. Harnett
The old duchess by G. B. Luks
Old factory by J. E. Heliker
Old-fashioned girl by T. Eakins
Old fish house by W. Blaney
Old flintlock by J. D. Chalfant
Old Fort Davis by W. Lester
Old friends by W. M. Harnett (attributed works)
Old friends by W. Homer
Old god by D. Kelley
Old Holliday street theatre, Baltimore by R. Smith
Old homestead by the sea by W. Whittredge
Old horizon by Y. Tanguy
Old house by creek by C. E. Burchfield
Old House of Representatives by S. F. B. Morse
Old Kentucky home, life in the South by E. Johnson
Old lady with a Bible by Unidentified artist
Old lady with a plaid shawl by Unidentified artist
Old man and youth by H. Lee-Smith
Old man with umbrella by B. Boris
Old man's afternoon by W. Barnet
Old meetinghouse and locust trees by C. E. Burchfield
Old mill by G. Inness
Old mill by E. Lawson
Old mill by Unidentified artist
Old mill at sunset by T. Cole
Old mill by waterfall by W. R. Miller
Old mill, Hanover, New Hampshire by J. B. Chapin
Old mill near St Enogat, Brittany by E. D. Boit
Old mill, West Milford, New Jersey by D. Johnson
Old mill, winter by G. H. Durrie
Old mission, San Diego by D. Kingman
Old model and her daughter by R. Henri
Old models by W. M. Harnett
Old New York, c 1878 by L. C. Tiffany
Old North Carolina by W. M. Harnett
The old oaken bucket by A. M. R. Moses
The old order changeth by C. E. Heaney

The old plantation by Unidentified artist
Old quarter, Quebec by P. Dickinson
The old refrain by W. M. Harnett
Old reminiscences by W. M. Harnett (attributed works)
The old salt by J. Marin
Old scraps by W. M. Harnett (attributed works)
Old scraps by J. F. Peto
Old settlers by W. Homer
Old sexton's place by G. Wood
Old ships drawn to home again by J. Lie
Old shipyard by M. B. Prendergast
The old shop window by P. W. Roberts
Old Sleepy Hollow church by T. Chambers
Old South wharf by J. Sharp
Old souvenirs by W. M. Harnett (attributed works)
The old stage coach by E. Johnson
An old time plains fight by F. Remington
Old town brook, Polling, Bavaria by F. Duveneck
Old tree by E. F. Spruce
Old trees at Ormsby farm by R. Smith
Old valentine by H. Harari
Old version by T. Hovenden
Old violin by J. D. Chalfant
Old violin by W. M. Harnett
Old Walnut street prison, Philadelphia in 1835 by R. Smith
The old Westover mansion by E. L. Henry
Old woman, Paris by M. B. Prendergast
Old Zip Coon by M. Goldberg
Oldest house at foot of Coal hill, opposite Market street by R. Smith
OLINSKY, Ivan Gregorewitch, 1878-1962
  Henry Audubon Butler   OYB
    OYB. Supplement 1959
  Joseph Green Butler jr   OYB
    OYB. Catalogue 1951
  Norma
    NAD. Annual ex, autumn 1949
  Red ribbon
    NAD. Annual ex, 1961
  Rosalind
    NAD. Annual ex, 1947, 2d half
Oliphant, Robert
  Peale, Raphaelle. Robert Oliphant
OLIVEIRA, Nathan J. 1928-
  Bather II
    IU. Contemp Amer ptg & sculp, 1961
  Bridge
    IU. Contemp Amer ptg & sculp, 1957
  Man walking
    Selz. New images
  Seated man with object
    PPC. International ex, 1958
    Selz. New images
  Standing man and stick   MMA
    Selz. New images (col)
  Standing woman
    ICA. Annual ex, 1959/60
  Standing woman with hat
    Selz. New images
  X-1000
    MnMW. Eighty works
Oliver, Andrew, 1707-1774
  Emmons, N. Andrew Oliver

Oliver, Daniel, 1664-1732
    Smibert, J. Daniel Oliver
Oliver, Mrs Daniel, fl 1731
    Smibert, J. Mrs Daniel Oliver
Oliver, Elizabeth. See Watson, Elizabeth
    (Oliver)
Oliver, Griselda. See Waldo, Griselda
    (Oliver)
Oliver, Peter, 1741-1821
    Copley, J. S. (attributed works) Peter
        Oliver jr
Oliver, Sally (Hutchinson) fl 1773
    Pelham, H. (attributed works) Mrs Peter
        Oliver jr
Oliver family
    Smibert, J. Daniel, Peter and Andrew
        Oliver
Olmstead, Sarah Ingersoll. See Sanford,
    Sarah Ingersoll (Olmstead)
Olneyville, Rhode island by G. L. Brown
Olsen, Christina
    Wyeth, A. N. Christina Olsen
Olsen, Herb. See Olson, Herbert Vincent
Olsen, John
    Wyeth, A. N. John Olsen's funeral
OLSON, Herbert Vincent, 1905-
    Dancing nuns
        NAD. Annual ex, 1961
    Stella
        NAD. Annual ex, 1949, 2d half
Olson, Olof. See Krans, Olof
Olympia by B. Greene
Omaha, Nebraska
    Haklhuber, F. Herndon hotel, Omaha,
        Nebraska
Ominous by A. Nepote
Omnia vincit amor by B. West
On a lee shore by W. Homer
On a point by T. Marsden
On a Shaker theme by C. Sheeler
On day herd by C. M. Russell
On deck by Z. L. Sepeshy
On guard by W. Homer
On many levels by A. Osver
On Morse mountain, Maine by J. Marin
On Salt lake trail by F. T. Johnson
On stage by C. H. Demuth
On the Ammonoosuc river by H. C. Pratt
On the balcony by M. Cassatt
On the Baltic by L. Feininger
On the banks of the Susquehanna by T.
    Doughty
On the beach by W. M. Chase
On the beach by W. Homer
On the beach by M. Kantor
On the beach by M. B. Prendergast
On the beach by E. F. Spruce
On the Consuma pass, Tuscany by E. D.
    Boit
On the Corso, Rome by M. B. Prendergast
On the Hudson by M. G. Wheelock
On the lake shore by J. M. Hart
On the Normandy coast by W. P. P. Long-
    fellow
On the points by E. H. Osthaus
On the porch by G. W. Bellows

On the porch by N. Vasilieff
On the ranch by J. Bywaters
On the road by T. Otter
On the sly by D. G. Blythe
On the southern plains in 1860 by F. Rem-
    ington
On the stile by W. Homer
On the track by W. Homer
On the warpath by A. F. Tait
On the warpath by C. Wimar
Once upon the past by W. Feldman
Oncoming spring by C. E. Burchfield
One by J. Pollock
One day in spring by H. Mintz
One-eyed creature by K. L. Seligmann
One Horn, a Dakota (Sioux) chief by G.
    Catlin
One moment of silence by H. G. Burkhardt
One of the Dominskis by W. Sommer
One shoe off by J. Brewster
O'NEIL, John, 1915-
    Labyrinth
        IU. Contemp Amer ptg, 1948
O'NEIL, M.
    Civil war encampment   DN
        DN. Amer primitive ptgs, pt 2
Oneness by H. Saslow
ONETO, Joseph Americus, 1911-
    Circa 1880
        CSFP. Annual ex, 1950/51
    White portico
        PPC. International ex, 1952
The onlookers by W. M. Halsey
ONSLOW-FORD, Gordon
    Untitled, 1960
        ICA. Annual ex, 1961
Open air breakfast by W. M. Chase
Open road by W. De Kooning
Open sea by F. J. Waugh
Open twist by G. Kamrowski
Opening of the wilderness by T. P. Rossiter
The opera box by M. Cassatt
The opera box by G. P. Du Bois
The opera cloak by W. M. Chase
Ophelia by E. Berman
OPPENHEIMER, Max, 1885-1954
    Symphony
        NYG. Fine art
OPPER, E. fl 1880
    Fire engine, Elizabeth, New Jersey, c 1880
                                              RPS
        Davidson v2
        NYG. Fine art
The opposition by W. Gropper
Opposition within a circle by T. Roszak
The oracle by A. Salemme
Orange and rose by T. W. Dewing
Orange and yellow by M. Rothko
Orange door by W. Sommer
Orange market by M. B. Prendergast
Orange over yellow by M. Rothko
Orange personage by R. B. Motherwell
Orange tree and gate, Nassau by W. Homer
Orange vase by M. Avery

Orange vase by H. Hofmann

Orange, wine glass and pansies by Maria Peale

Orarian by K. Knaths

The orators by A. Gorky

Orchard lane by R. Lane

Orchard lane road, Woodstock by J. Pike

Orchard scene by R. Porter

Orchard street, New York city by S. Koch

Orchard with yellow sky by Ben-Zion

Orchards and hills by P. L. Dike

Orchestra by M. Kantor

Orchestral dominance in yellow by H. Hofmann

Orchids and hummingbirds by M. J. Heade

Orchids and spray orchids with hummingbirds by M. J. Heade

Order no 11 by M. Siporin

Order no 11, 1868 by G. C. Bingham

Ordinary objects in the artist's creative mind by J. F. Peto

Ore freighter by E. Lewandowski

OREAR, Lucinda Redmon, 1823-1852
Permelia Redmon Wheeler   MoSL
MoSL. Handbook 1953

Oregon rocks by G. Daniell

Oregon trail by A. Bierstadt

Orestes by L. A. Golub

Organization by A. Gorky

Organization 5 by S. MacDonald-Wright

Oriental beggar by T. Stamos

Oriental camp by A. P. Ryder

Oriental head by A. Walkowitz

Oriental simplicity by C. C. Ross

Oriental: synchromy in blue-green by S. MacDonald-Wright

Origin by J. De Feo

Origin of life by W. Quirt

Ormond, Mrs Francis. See Ormond, Violet (Sargent)

Ormond, Rose Marie, 1893-1918
Sargent, J. S. Cashmere shawl (Rose Marie Ormond)
Sargent, J. S. Nonchaloire (Sargent's niece, Rose Marie Ormond)

Ormond, Violet (Sargent) 1870-1955
Sargent, J. S. The breakfast table: Sargent's sister Violet
Sargent, J. S. Violet Sargent

Ornamatique by W. Sommer

Orne, Lois (Pickering) 1684-1753
Greenwood, J. Lois Pickering Orne

Ornstein, Leo, 1895-
Zorach, W. Leo Ornstein (Piano concert)

Oropesa by K. Schrag

Orpheus by M. Tobey

ORR, Elliot, 1904-
Arrangement
IU. Contemp Amer ptg, 1950
Storm   NBM
Baur. Revolution

Orthodox boys by B. Perlin

ORTMAN, George, 1926-
Game of chance
WMAA. Young America 1960
Tales of love
WMAA. Young America 1960

Orvieto by W. G. Congdon

Orvieto by G. L. K. Morris

Osage scalp dance by J. M. Stanley

Osborn, Fairfield
Carroll, E. Fairfield Osborn

Osborn, Mrs James M.
Schnakenberg, H. E. Mrs James M. Osborn

OSCAR, Charles, 1924?-
Ionian sea
WMAA. Annual ex, 1956
Metope
WMAA. Contemp Amer ptg, 1959/60
Night journey
IU. Contemp Amer ptg & sculp, 1955
Pousette-Dart. Amer ptg

Osceola, Seminole chief, 1804-1838
Catlin, G. Osceola

OSGOOD, Charles, 1809-1890
Joseph Gilbert Waters   MSE
MSE. Catalogue of ports, 1950

Osprey and the otter and the salmon by J. J. Audubon

Ossining, New York
Havell, R. Sing Sing, 1856

Ossoli, Sarah Margaret (Fuller) marchesa d', 1810-1850
Hicks, T. Sarah Margaret Fuller

OSTHAUS, Edmund H. 1858-1928
On the points
NSP. Sportscapes

OSVER, Arthur, 1912-
Beginning
IU. Contemp Amer ptg & sculp, 1959
Blue chimney
VR. Biennial ex, 1948
Chimneys and buildings   IU
IU. Contemp Amer ptg, 1949
IU. 20th century
Cranes
MM. Amer ptg today
Going up
DC. 22 biennial ex, 1951
Light wells
CSFP. Annual ex, 1952
Majestic tenement   PA
Cheney. Expressionism 1948 ed
Genauer
PA. Annual ex, 1947
Notte Napolitana
Cheney. Story 1958 ed
On many levels   NJMo
NJMo. Your Montclair art museum
The tall red
IU. Contemp Amer ptg & sculp, 1961
Two ventilators   MM
IU. Contemp Amer ptg, 1950
MM. 100 Amer ptrs
Pierson
Villa dei misteri
IU. Contemp Amer ptg & sculp, 1955
Winter rooftops
ICA. Amer artists paint the city
World of wires
IU. Contemp Amer ptg, 1951

Osver, Mrs Arthur. See Betsberg, Ernestine

OSVER, Charles, 1923-
Late edition
ICA. Amer artists paint the city

OTIS, Bass, 1784-1861
  John Wesley Jarvis (after Jarvis' self-por-
    trait)   NNHS
    Dickson. John Wesley Jarvis
  Seated boy
    Chew. 250 years of art
Otis, James, 1702-1778
  Copley, J. S. James Otis
Otis, Mercy. See Warren, Mercy (Otis)
Otis, Ruth (Cunningham) 1728-1789
  Blackburn, J. Mrs James Otis jr
Oto council by S. Seymour
O'Toole, John. See Toole, John
OTTER, Thomas, fl 1860
  On the road   MoKN
    Rathbone
Otters
  Audubon, J. J. Osprey and the otter and
    the salmon
Ouananiche fishing: Lake St John, Quebec
    by W. Homer
Ouchy, Lake of Geneva, Switzerland by
    E. D. Boit
Ouldfield, Polly. See Herriot, Mary (Ould-
    field)
Our barn by A. M. R. Moses
Our camp by A. J. Miller
Our classic heritage by V. I. Cuthbert
Our flag is there by Unidentified artist
Our son Thorn by S. E. Dickinson
Out at home by F. Martin
Out back by W. A. Smith
Out by C. Browning
Out for a drive by Unidentified artist
Out for the Christmas tree by A. M. R.
    Moses
Out of the Coulee by C. A. Morris
Out of the web by J. Pollock
Out over the Sound by A. G. Dove
Outdoor circus by L. Blanch
The outing by M. Hewes
The outlier by F. Remington
The outpost by W. Thon
Outside by S. Davis
Outside the Guttenberg race track by W. J.
    Glackens
Outside the walls, Marrakech, Morocco by
    D. Macknight
Outskirts of the forest by W. Whittredge
Outward bound by A. P. Ryder
Outward preoccupation by B. W. Tomlin
Ovenbird and pink lady's-slipper by C. E.
    Heil
Over the bridge to grandma's house by A.
    M. R. Moses
Over the river by A. M. R. Moses
Over the river to grandma's house by A. M.
    R. Moses
Overhauling the trawl by K. Knaths
Owh! in San Paó by S. Davis
Owls
  Audubon, J. J. Snowy owl
  Graves, M. Young owl and moth
  Parker, R. A. Some owls at night
  Price, C. S. Owl
Owl's head by W. Thon

Owl's head, Penobscot bay, Maine by F. H.
    Lane
The Oxbow by T. Cole
The Oxbow by Unidentified artist
Oxen
  Avery, M. Ox on hillside
  Bartlett, G. Ox train
  Ranney, W. T. Pioneers
Oxford, England
  Martyl. View of Oxford
Oyster gatherers of Cancale by J. S. Sar-
    gent
OZENFANT, Amédée, 1886-
  Bathers in a grotto
    Read. Art now 1948
  Building in a park
    Pousette-Dart. Amer ptg
  Still life (L'esprit nouveau II)   NNSG
    NNSG. Handbook
    Read. Concise history
  Theme and variations
    Rosenblum
  Vases   MMA
    McCurdy

                        P

PACE, Stephen, 1918-
  Prophecy
    PPC. International ex, 1955
PACH, Walter, 1883-1958
  The cathedral
    WMAA. Pioneers
  St Patrick's at night
    MMA. Abstract
PACHNER, William, 1915-
  Antinomes no 1, 1959
    Donahue. William Pachner
  Arrival-departure
    Donahue. William Pachner
  Avenue of martyrs
    Donahue. William Pachner
  The beach
    Donahue. William Pachner
  The beach no 4. See Landscape
  Birthplace
    Donahue. William Pachner
  Blue boy
    Donahue. William Pachner
  Children's prison
    Donahue. William Pachner
  Deposition
    Donahue. William Pachner
  Face of a rabbi. See Head
  Figural composition
    Donahue. William Pachner
  Figure in prayer
    Donahue. William Pachner
  Forbidden blossom
    Donahue. William Pachner
  The gate
    Donahue. William Pachner
  The gathering
    Donahue. William Pachner
  German train
    Donahue. William Pachner
  Head (Face of a rabbi)
    Donahue. William Pachner
  In my own time
    Donahue. William Pachner

Israel
  Donahue. William Pachner
Landscape (The beach no 4)
  Donahue. William Pachner
Let us pray
  Donahue. William Pachner
Maternità, 1943
  Donahue. William Pachner
Maternità, 1954-55 (Theme of earth)
  Donahue. William Pachner
Maternità, 1956
  Donahue. William Pachner
Maternità no 1, 1957
  Donahue. William Pachner
Negro Pietà
  Donahue. William Pachner
Night event no 2, 1958
  Donahue. William Pachner
Night scene, 1958
  Donahue. William Pachner
Night scene, 1959
  Donahue. William Pachner
Rosh Hashana
  Donahue. William Pachner
Scholar
  Donahue. William Pachner
Space, time, embrace
  Donahue. William Pachner
Theme of earth. See Maternità, 1954-55
The truck
  Donahue. William Pachner (col)
Variation on the Avignon Pietà no 1, 1958
  Donahue. William Pachner (col)
Variation on the Avignon Pietà no 2, 1959
                                    OYB
  Donahue. William Pachner
  OYB. Annual 1959
  OYB. Supplement 1959
The Pacific by J. A. M. Whistler
Pacific circle by M. Tobey
Pacific landscape by B. Shahn
Pacific series, no 1X—Sierra by L. Calcagno
Pacific transition by M. Tobey
Package deal by S. Davis
PACKMAN, Harry
  Sunday morning   OYB
  OYB. Annual 1952
Pad by S. Davis
Pa-da-he: Wa-con-da—Elk Horn:—a Crow
  Indian by A. J. Miller
Paddle boats. See Side-wheelers
Paddy, Elizabeth. See Wensley, Elizabeth
  (Paddy)
Padre by G. W. Bellows
Padre island by E. F. Spruce
Padre Paolo of Pisa by W. Thon
Padre Sebastiano by J. S. Sargent
Pagan philosophy by A. G. Dove
Paganini by J. G. F. Von Wicht
Page, Alice (Grymes) fl 1744
  Unidentified artist. Mrs Mann Page II
    and baby John
Page, Eliza (Hopkins) fl 1837
  Negus, C. Mrs James Page
Page, Harlan, fl 1815
  Unidentified artist. Harlan Page
Page, Mrs James. See Page, Eliza (Hop-
  kins)

Page, Mann
  Bridges, C. (attributed works) Mann Page
    the second (?)
Page, Mrs Mann II. See Page, Alice
  (Grymes)
Page, Sophie Candace (Stevens) fl 1860
  Page, W. Portrait of his wife, Sophie
    Candace Stevens
PAGE, William, 1811-1885
  Cupid and Psyche
    MiD. Travelers in Arcadia
    Pierson
    Richardson. Ptg in America
    WiMiA. Amer ptg 1760-1960
  Flight into Egypt
    MiD. Travelers in Arcadia
  Portrait of his wife, Sophie Candace
    Stevens   MiD
    Baur. Amer ptg
    DC. De gustibus
    Mendelowitz
    MiD. Travelers in Arcadia
    Pierson
    Richardson. Ptg in America
  Self-portrait   MiD
    MiD. Travelers in Arcadia
    MiD. Treasures
  Young merchants   PA
    Barker. Amer ptg
    MiD. Travelers in Arcadia
    NJN. Early N.J. artists
    Pierson
Page, Mrs. William. See Page, Sophie Can-
  dace (Stevens)
Page, 1959 by M. Resnick
Paget, Violet, 1856-1935
  Sargent, J. S. Vernon Lee
Paige, Helen Maria (Yates) 1797-1829
  Ames, E. Mrs John Keyes Paige
Paige, John Keyes, 1788-1857
  Ames, E. John Keyes Paige
Pailleron children, fl 1880
  Sargent, J. S. Pailleron children
PAINE, L. Gerard, 1905-
  Copley square   MB
    MB. Ptgs in water color
Paine, Thomas, 1737-1809
  Jarvis, J. W. Thomas Paine
The painter by S. Menkès
The painter by K. Schrag
A painter, Portrait of by F. Taubes
Painter in the landscape by De H. Margules
Painter of birds by A. Blanch
Painter of the hole by G. Grosz
Painter's triumph by W. S. Mount
Painting at Montclair by G. Inness
Painting of a smile by R. Gwathmey
Painting of the ocean by J. Davis
Painting with red letter S by R. Rauschen-
  berg
Pajarito by S. Davis
Palace of the windowed rocks by Y. Tanguy
Palaestra by D. Tanning
Palazzo by J. E. Heliker
PALAZZOLA, Guy, 1920?-
  Allium sativum   MiD
    CoS. New accessions USA, 1950
    ICA. Annual ex, 1951

PALAZZOLA, Guy—*Continued*
Family tree						OYB
  OYB. Annual 1957
Prometheus rebound					OYB
  OYB. Annual 1958
  OYB. Supplement 1959
Palermo by R. Kozlow
The **pali** by B. Norris
Palisade amusement park by G. O. Hart
Palisades by Unidentified artist
The **palm** leaf shade by G. C. Bingham
Palm tree by W. Homer
Palm tree, Nassau by W. Homer
Palm trees, Florida by W. Homer
Palm trees with a domed church by A. Bierstadt
PALMER, Charles B. R. fl 1826
Mother and child					VWR
  VWR. Folk art (col)
Palmer, Elsie
  Sargent, J. S. Miss Elsie Palmer
PALMER, F. F.
American farm scene, 1853
  Davidson **v** 1
Champions of the Mississippi, 1866
  Davidson v2
Wooding up on the Mississippi, 1861
  Davidson v2
PALMER, Walter Launt, 1854-1932
Woods in winter					MB
  MB. Ptgs in water color
PALMER. William
Hovering twilight
  IaDa. 30th anniversary
PALMER, William Charles, 1906-
Clematis henryi					NUM
  NUM. Root bequest
Cows in the corn
  MoSL. Contemporary Amer ptg
Dust, drought and destruction		WMAA
  Pierson
Horses in landscape
  Gruskin
Last snow						WMAA
  Pierson
Night over Buffalo
  WMAA. Annual ex, 1957
Palms with ripe dates, Marrakech, Morocco by D. Macknight
Paludes by E. Berman
Pan and the wolf by J. A. Weir
Panama, Isthmus of
  Browere, A. Del O. Crossing the Isthmus
Pancho Villa, dead and alive by R. B. Motherwell
Pancoast, Ella. See Widener, Ella (Pancoast)
Pandora's box, Illustration for by C. H. Demuth
Panic of 1869 by C. Knoll (attributed works)
Panizza, Oskar
  Grosz, G. Homage to Oskar Panizza
Panorama, Penobscot bay islands by W. A. Kienbusch
Panorama; the valley of Mexico by C. W. Chapman
Panoramic view of the palace and gardens of Versailles by J. Vanderlyn
Pansies by C. H. Demuth
Panther Hollow by J. Kane

Papa, maman est blessée by Y. Tanguy
Paper flowers and paper by C. Vinson
Paper storm by A. Bohrod
PAPSDORF, Frederick, 1883-
Flowers in vase					OYB
  OYB. Supplement
Paquebot, Paris by C. H. Demuth
The **parable** by B. Shahn
Parabola by A. G. Dove
Parabolic San Francisco by E. Ewing
Parade by P. Blume
Parade by C. E. Burchfield
Parade by R. Cowles
Parade by M. Gordon
Parade by W. T. Kelly
Parade figure by R. Markman
Parade for repeal with Jimmy Walker by B. Shahn
Parade passing Independence hall, Philadelphia by J. L. Krimmel
PARADISE, John Wesley, 1809-1862
Mrs Elizabeth Oakes Smith
  NJN. Early N.J. artists
Paradise rock, Newport by J. F. Kensett
Paradise tree by M. T. Abrams
Paradise valley, Newport by J. La Farge
The **parallels** by Y. Tanguy
Parcell, Emma (Minor)
  Parcell, M. S. My mother
PARCELL, Malcolm Stevens, 1896-1921
F. E. Richardson jr.
  PPC. Ptg in the U.S. 1949
My mother						OYB
  OYB. Catalogue 1951
PARELLA, Albert
Roof pattern
  OYB. Annual 1952
Paris, France
  Asplund, T. Rue de Rivoli, Paris
  Berman, E. Bridges of Paris
  Boit, E. D. Arc de Triomphe
  Boit, E. D. Place de l'Opera
  Boit, E. D. Place du Carrousel, 1911
  Foss, O. Paris under snow
  Glackens, W. J. Luxembourg gardens
  Hassam, C. July 14, rue Daunou
  Kuntz, R. Île de la Cité
  MacIver, L. Paris
  Morse, S. F. B. Gallery of the Louvre
  Pleissner, O. M. Early morning, Paris
  Prendergast, M. B. Montparnasse
  Prendergast, M. B. Notre Dame, Paris
  Prendergast, M. B. Paris boulevard in rain
  Prendergast, M. B. Sketch of Paris
  Prendergast, M. B. Tuileries gardens
  Sargent, J. S. In the Luxembourg gardens
  Sargent, J. S. Luxembourg gardens at twilight
  Shinn, E. Early morning, Paris
The **Paris** bit by S. Davis
Paris café, morning by G. P. Du Bois
Paris music hall by E. Shinn
Paris night meanders by L. MacIver
Parish playground by B. Miller
La **Parisienne** by M. Weber
PARK, David, 1911-1960
Les baigneuses
  DC. 27 biennial ex, 1961

Four men   WMAA
  Goodrich. Amer art (col)
Nude with flowers
  IU. Contemp Amer ptg & sculp, 1959
The patio
  VR. Amer ptg, 1958
Riverbank
  IU. Contemp Amer ptg & sculp, 1957
Standing couple
  IU. Contemp Amer ptg & sculp, 1961
Three bathers
  PA. Annual ex, 1959-60
PARK, Linton, 1826-1870?
  Flax-scutching bee   DN
    Chew. 250 years of art
    Davidson v2
    DN. Amer primitive ptgs, pt 1
    Ford. Pictorial folk art
    U.S. National Capital sesquicentennial
      com
Park avenue, New York by E. D. Boit
Park bench by W. M. Chase
Park bench by R. Marsh
Park bench by H. Pippin
Park by the river by W. J. Glackens
Park by the sea by M. B. Prendergast
The park, Salem by M. B. Prendergast
Park Rosenberg by W. De Kooning
Park street, Boston by K. Zerbe
Park theater, Interior of, by J. Searle
Parke, Frances, d 1715
  Unidentified artist. Miss Parke (possibly
    Frances Parke)
PARKER, Bill, 1922-
  Composition in blue
    IU. Contemp Amer ptg & sculp, 1957
Parker, Eliza (Mason) See Mason, Eliza
Parker, Ernest Lee
  Eakins, T. Ernest Lee Parker
Parker, Helen, fl 1908
  Eakins, T. Old-fashioned dress (Miss
    Parker)
Parker, Mary A. (Cox)
  Eakins, T. Mrs Gilbert Lafayette Parker
PARKER, Raymond, 1922-
  Summer afternoon
    CoS. New accessions USA, 1960
  Untitled   NBuA
    IU. Contemp Amer ptg & sculp, 1961
    MnMW. 60 Amer ptrs
    NBuA. Acquisitions 1959-1961
PARKER, Robert Andrew, 1927-
  East Riding of Yorkshire yeomanry dis-
    embarking from H.M.S. Cressy
    WMAA. Young America 1957
  Marseilles, night   WMAA
    Pierson
  Red ship
    WMAA. Annual ex, 1956
  Some owls at night
    WMAA. Annual ex, 1958
  View from the Jersey turnpike, no 2
    WMAA. Young America 1957
Parker, Mrs Samuel Dunn. See Mason,
  Eliza
Parkland and trees by B. West (attributed
  works)
Parrish, Sarah Redwood
  Chase. W. M. Sarah Redwood Parrish

Parrots
  Audubon, J. J. Carolina parrot
  Beckmann, M. Girl with parrot
  Randall, A. M. Basket of fruit with par-
    rot
  Zerbe, K. The parrot and decanter
PARSHALL, Douglass Ewell, 1899-
  Clowns
    CSEP. Annual ex, 1952
Parsley, Sketch for by L. Bemelmans
Parson Weems' fable by G. Wood
PARSONS, Jackson
  Number 30, 1950
    MMA. Fifteen
Parsons family, fl 1850
  Stock, J. W. Parsons family
Parthenon
  Church, F. The Parthenon
  Walker, C. H. Section of the Parthenon
  Warren, H. B. Corner of the Parthenon,
    Athens
  Warren, H. B. The Parthenon, Athens
Partitions of the city by M. Tobey
Parturition by L. A. Golub
Pa's brainstorm by W. Sommer
PASCIN, Jules, 1885-1930
  Child with cat
    Cheney. Expressionism 1948 ed
  Girl in green and rose
    Brown. Amer ptg
  Reclining model   MMA
    Pierson
Pasiphae by J. Pollock
The pass by E. L. Blumenschein
Passacaglia by A. V. Tack
Passage by L. Edmondson
Passage à travers by J. Berlandina
Passage of the Delaware by T. Sully
Passage to Etna by P. Blume
Passage to the sea by O. Dozier
Passementerie by C. W. Hare
Passenger pigeon by J. J. Audubon
The passing leap by J. S. Curry
Passing of dreams by A. B. Davies
The passing scene by J. Levine
Passing show by P. Evergood
Passing shower by G. Inness
Passion according to St Matthew by F.
  Nagler
Passion flowers and hummingbirds by M. J.
  Heade
Passion of Sacco and Vanzetti by B. Shahn
Passions and feverishness by P. Mangravite
Passover supper by J. Land
Pastor De Segovia by D. Pond
Pastoral by B. Chaet
Pastoral study by A. P. Ryder
Pastorale by T. D. Benrimo
Pastorale by A. Pickens
Pastorale by K. Zerbe
Pastry window by J. Kinigstein
The pasture by A. P. Ryder
Pat Lyon at his forge by J. Neagle
Patch picture for Dr Physick by Raphaelle
  Peale
Patchwork cows by W. Sommer

Paterson by B. Shahn

The **path** by S. Laufman

Path in motion by F. Ruvolo

Pathetic song by T. Eakins

The **patio** by D. Park

Patio Royale by R. Philipp

Patio with black door by G. O'Keeffe

Patio with cloud by G. O'Keeffe

The **patriarch** by S. Rosenberg

Patten, G. fl 1798
    Malbone. E. G. Dr G. Patten

Patterns by Z. Sepeshy

PATTERSON, Charles Robert, 1878-
    Furling the foresail
    NYG. Fine art

Patterson, Elizabeth De Peyster (Peale)
    fl 1818
    Peale, C. W. Elizabeth De Peyster Peale
        Patterson

Patterson, Howard
    Archer, E. Howard Patterson of the Harlem Yankees

Patty by E. E. Speicher

Pau de St Jannes by M. Beckmann

PAUL, Jeremiah, fl 1791-1820
    Four children playing in a courtyard
        (Children at play)
    Flexner. Light of distant skies
    Richardson. Ptg in America
    WiMiA. Amer ptg 1760-1960

Paul and Virginia by Unidentified artist

Paula by R. F. Lahey

Les **pauvres** by E. Higgins

Pavilion by J. Cornell

Pawnee chief by C. M. Russell

Pawnee council by S. Seymour

Pawnee Indian shooting antelope by A. J. Miller

Pawnee Indians migrating by A. J. Miller

Pawnee Indians watching the caravan by A. J. Miller

Pawnee running buffalo by A. J. Miller

Pawnshop by J. Levine

PAXTON, William McGregor, 1869-1941
    Girl with a hand mirror   PR
    PR. Catalogue
    House maid   DC
    DC. De gustibus
    Sylvia   OYB
    OYB. Catalogue 1951

Payne, Dorothea. See Madison, Dorothea (Payne) Todd

Payne, Jennie (Bryan) See Bryan, Jennie

Payne, John Howard, 1792-1852
    Bingham, G. C. John Howard Payne

Payne, Mrs John Barton. See Bryan, Jennie

Paysage by M. Hartley

Peabody, Ellen. See Endicott, Ellen (Peabody)

Peabody, George, 1795-1869
    Healy, G. P. A. George Peabody
    Huntington, D. George Peabody
    Neagle, J. George Peabody

Peabody, Mrs Stephen, fl 1809
    Stuart, G. Mrs Stephen Peabody

Peace II, 1946 by G. Grosz

Peace among the nations by R. A. Blakelock

Peace and plenty by G. Inness

Peace in October by M. Dixon

Peace memorial, Hiroshima by M. R. Cooper

The **peace** pipe by C. M. Russell

The **peaceable** kingdom by E. Hicks

Peaceable kingdom by W. T. Wiley

The **peaceable** kingdom of the branch by E. Hicks

Peaceful day in the Mohawk valley by J. J. Hammer

Peaceful valley (Blue ridge mountains) by R. H. Byrum

The **peacemakers** by G. P. A. Healy

Peach jacket by E. E. Speicher

Peach trees in blossom by J. Marin

Peaches by W. Kuhn

Peaches by H. Lundeberg

Peacocks
    Davis, J. H. (attributed works) Mrs Tuttle
        (with peacock)
    Keller, H. G. Peacock
    Roberts, P. W. Plumage

Peak of Maua Roa, Moorea, Society islands by J. La Farge

PEAKE, Channing, 1910-
    Farm machinery
    IU. Contemp Amer ptg & sculp, 1955

PEALE, Anna Claypoole, 1791-1878
    Andrew Jackson   CtY
    CtY. Portrait index
    Marianne Beckett   PH
    Chew. 250 years of art
    Rubens Peale
    WiMiA. Amer ptg 1760-1960
    Still life   MAC
    OCiM. Ptgs by the Peale family
    Still life with strawberries
    MdBMu. Rendezvous

Peale, Benjamin Franklin. See Peale, Franklin

Peale, Charles Linnaeus, 1794-1832
    Peale, C. W. Charles Linnaeus Peale

PEALE, Charles Willson, 1741-1827
    Abraham B. De Peyster
    Belknap
    Alexander and Angelica Robinson
    Sellers. C. W. Peale v2
    Alexander Hamilton   PPhI
    Time. 300 years (col)
    Andrew Jackson
    Sellers. C. W. Peale v2
    Artist in his museum (Self-portrait in his museum)   PA
    Mendelowitz
    OCiM. Ptgs by the Peale family
    PA. Annual ex, 1955
    Pierson
    Robb. Harper history
    Roos
    Sellers. C. W. Peale v2
    Benjamin Franklin   PA
    Lee. Art then and now
    Robb. Harper history
    Roos
    Benjamin Franklin   PH
    OCiM. Ptgs by the Peale family
    Pierson
    U.S. National Capital sesquicentennial com
    Benjamin Laming and wife
    OCiM. Ptgs by the Peale family

Benjamin Rush
  Flexner. Light of distant skies
Charles Alexandre Lesueur
  OCiM. Ptgs by the Peale family
Charles Linnaeus Peale   MdBH
  Sellers. C. W. Peale v2
Charles Waterton   ELNP
  Sellers. C. W. Peale v2
Coleman Sellers
  Sellers. C. W. Peale v2
David Forman   MPB
  NUM. Art across America
Elizabeth De Peyster Peale Patterson
  Sellers. C. W. Peale v2
Exhuming the mastodon   MdBMu
  Barker. Amer ptg
  Flexner. Amer ptg
  Flexner. Light of distant skies
  Flexner. Short history
  Larkin
  Larkin rev ed
  MdBMu. Rendezvous (detail)
  OCiM. Ptgs by the Peale family
  Pa. Annual ex, 1955
  Pierson
  Roos
  Sellers. C. W. Peale v2
  Time. 300 years (col)
  U.S. National Capital sesquicentennial
    com
Family group. See Peale family
Francis Bailey
  OCiM. Ptgs by the Peale family
Francis Nichols   MoKN
  MoKN. Handbook
Fruits of Belfield
  Sellers. C. W. Peale v2
George Washington   OCl
  Chew. 250 years of art
George Washington, 1776   NBM
  U.S. National Capital sesquicentennial
    com
George Washington, 1779   PA
  OCiM. Ptgs by the Peale family
  Pierson
  Roos
George Washington at the Battle of
    Princeton   CtY
  CtY. Portrait index
Hannah Moore Peale and step-daughter
                                  MdBH
  Sellers. C. W. Peale v2
Henry Clay   PH
  OCiM. Ptgs by the Peale family
  Sellers. C. W. Peale v2
James Arbuckle
  Flexner. First flowers
James Madison
  Time. 300 years (col)
James Peale (The lamplight portrait)
                                  MiD
  Flexner. Light of distant skies
  MiD. Treasures
  OCiM. Ptgs by the Peale family
  Pierson
  Richardson. Ptg in America
  Sellers. C. W. Peale v2
James Peale painting a miniature MAC
  DC. Amer ptrs of the South
  OCiM. Ptgs by the Peale family
James W. De Peyster   NNHS
  Belknap

John Adams
  Time. 300 years (col)
John B. De Peyster   NNHS
  Belknap
John Beale Bordley   NNHS
  OCiM. Ptgs by the Peale family
John Cadwalader
  WiMiA. Amer ptg 1760-1960
John De Peyster   NNHS
  Belknap
  Larkin
  Larkin rev ed
John Eager Howard (after Rembrandt
    Peale)
  MdBMu. Rendezvous
John Paul Jones   PPhI
  Time. 300 years (col)
John Philip de Haas   DN
  DN. Mellon coll
The lamplight portrait. See James Peale
Mary Tilghman
  Sellers. C. W. Peale v2
Mrs Charles Willson Peale   NNHS
  Belknap
Mrs Elizabeth De Peyster Peale
  Sellers. C. W. Peale v2
Mrs Francis Bailey
  OCiM. Ptgs by the Peale family
Mrs Gerard De Peyster   NNHS
  Belknap
  NNHS. Waldron Phoenix Belknap coll
Mrs James Arbuckle and son Edward
  Flexner. First flowers
Mrs John De Peyster   NNHS
  Belknap
Mrs Thomas Harwood   MM
  PA. Annual ex, 1955
Mrs William De Peyster jr   NNHS
  Belknap
Mordecai Gist
  WiMiA. Amer ptg 1760-1960
Nicholas Brewer I
  OCiM. Ptgs by the Peale family
Peale family   NNHS
  Larkin
  Larkin rev ed
  PA. Annual ex, 1955
  Pierson
  Richardson. Ptg in America
  Roos
Pleasure party by a mill
  MiD. Ptg in America
  WiMiA. Amer ptg 1760-1960
Rachel weeping
  Flexner. Light of distant skies
Richard Tilghman
  Sellers. C. W. Peale v2
Samuel B. Webb
  MB. New England miniatures
Sarah Fishbourne Bordley   NJMo
  NJMo. Your Montclair art museum
Self-portrait   NNHS
  MdBMu. Rendezvous
Self-portrait   PA
  Roos
  Sellers. C. W. Peale v2
Self-portrait in his museum. See The artist
    in his museum
Self-portrait in uniform
  OCiM. Ptgs by the Peale family
Sophonisba Peale Sellers
  Sellers. C. W. Peale v2

PEALE, C. W.—*Continued*
Staircase group PPhM
  Barker. Amer ptg
  ICA. From colony to nation
  Larkin
  Larkin rev ed (front)
  PA. Annual ex, 1955
  Pierson
  Richardson. Ptg in America
  Roos
  Sellers. C. W. Peale
  Taylor. Fifty centuries, 1954 ed (col)
  Time. 300 years (col)
  Walker. Ptgs from America
Thomas Jefferson PPhI
  Pierson
  U.S. National Capital sesquicentennial
    com
Thomas Johnson and family
  Flexner. Light of distant skies
Timothy Matlack DN
  Mendelowitz
Titian Ramsay Peale II: in the uniform of
  a naturalist MdBH
  Sellers. C. W. Peale v2
Washington, Lafayette and Tilghman at
  Yorktown
  ICA. From colony to nation
  Pierson
  Roos
  Time. 300 years (col)
William Buckland CtY
  CtY. Portrait index
  Pierson
William De Peyster (copy after John
  Durand) NNHS
  Belknap
William De Peyster jr NNHS
  Belknap
  NNHS. Waldron Phoenix Belknap coll
William North MiD
  MiD. Treasures
William Smallwood
  MdBMu. Rendezvous
Worthy of liberty, Mr Pitt scorns to in-
  vade the liberties of other people IU
  Roos
Yarrow Mamout PH
  Sellers. C. W. Peale v2

Portrait of the artist
West, B. Charles Willson Peale

**PEALE, Charles Willson, 1741-1827 and
PEALE, Rembrandt, 1778-1870**
Gilbert Stuart NNHS
  Sellers. C. W. Peale v2
Peale, Mrs Charles Willson, 1765-1804. See
  Peale, Elizabeth (De Peyster)
Peale, Mrs Charles Willson, d 1821. See
  Peale, Hannah (Moore)
Peale, Elizabeth (De Peyster) 1765-1804
  Peale, C. W. Mrs Charles Willson Peale
Peale, Franklin, 1795-1870
  Peale, Rembrandt. Franklin Peale
Peale, Hannah (Moore) d 1821
  Peale, C. W. Hannah Moore Peale
PEALE, Harriet (Cany) 1800-1869
  Female figure with turban
  Chew. 250 years of art
PEALE, James, 1749-1831
  Bailey Washington
  DC. Privately owned
  Balsam apple and vegetable MM
  Mendelowitz

Edmond Rouvert
  Chew. 250 years of art
Fruit DC
  DC. Masterpieces
Fruits of autumn WMAA
  Barker. Amer ptg
James Peale and his family PA
  Flexner. Light of distant skies
  OCiM. Ptgs by the Peale family
  Richardson. Ptg in America
Jane and James Peale jr
  MiD. Coll in progress
  WiMiA. Amer ptg 1760-1960
Jane Rouvert
  Chew. 250 years of art
Mme Dubocq and her four children
                            KyLS
  OCiM. Ptgs by the Peale family
  KyLS. Kentucky port gall
A man MoKN
  MoKN. Handbook
Mrs Susan Coren Towers OCl
  OCl. Portrait miniatures
Ramsay-Polk family at Carpenter's point,
  Maryland
  MiD. Coll in progress
  Pierson
  WiMiA. Amer ptg 1760-1960
Rembrandt Peale CtY
  CtY. Portrait index
  OCiM. Ptgs by the Peale family
  Seller. C. W. Peale v2
Samuel Allen of Philadelphia
  WiMiA. Amer ptg 1760-1960
Self-portrait with his family PA
  Pierson
Still life ATeS
  ATeS. Collection
Still life MWM
  Flexner. Light of distant skies
Still life DeWin
  Pierson
Still life with fish bowl
  WiMiA. Amer ptg 1760-1960
Still life with fruit
  Chew. 250 years of art
Still life with grapes OYB
  OYB. Catalogue 1951
Still life with watermelon
  DC. Privately owned
View on the Brandywine
  WiMiA. Amer ptg 1760-1960
Washington and his generals at Yorktown
                            MdBH
  MdBMu. Rendezvous
  Pierson
  U.S. National Capital sesquicentennial
    com

Attributed works
Watermelon and fruit MB
  MB. Karolik coll

Portrait of the artist
Peale, C. W. James Peale (the lamplight
  portrait)
Peale, C. W. James Peale painting a
  miniature
PEALE, James, 1789-1876
  Marine with shipping
  OCiM. Ptgs by the Peale family

Portrait of the artist
Peale, J. James Peale jr
Peale, J. Jane and James Peale jr

Peale, Jane
  Peale, J. Jane and James Peale jr
PEALE, Margaretta Angelica, 1795-1882
  Still life
    Chew. 250 years of art
  Still life with cake, raisins and nuts
    WiMiA. Amer ptg 1760-1960
  Strawberries and cherries   PA
    OCiM. Ptgs by the Peale family
PEALE, Maria, 1787-1866
  Orange, wine glass and pansies
    WiMiA. Amer ptg 1760-1960
  Rubens Peale at his easel (Interior show-
    ing Rubens Peale painting)
    Chew. 250 years of art
    WiMiA. Amer ptg 1760-1960
PEALE, Mary Jane, 1827-1902
  Still life, fruit in a monogrammed bowl,
    "R.P."
    Chew. 250 years of art
PEALE, Raphaelle, 1774-1825
  After the bath   MoKN
    Janson. Picture history
    Larkin
    Larkin rev ed
    Mendelowitz
    MoKN. Handbook
    OCiM. Ptgs by the Peale family
    Pierson
    Richardson. Ptg in America
    Roos
    Time. 300 years (col)
    WiMiA. Raphaelle Peale
  Balsam apples and turnips
    WiMiA. Amer ptg 1760-1960
    WiMiA. Raphaelle Peale
  Dish of blackberries
    OCiM. Ptgs by the Peale family
    WiMiA. Raphaelle Peale
  Fox grapes and peaches   PA
    WiMiA. Raphaelle Peale
  James Ferguson   MdBH
    WiMiA. Raphaelle Peale
  Man in gray coat   WiMiA
    WiMiA. Raphaelle Peale
  Melons and morning glories
    WiMiA. Amer ptg 1760-1960
  Mrs John Montgomery   MM
    WiMiA. Raphaelle Peale
  Nathan Towson   MdBH
    MdBMu. Rendezvous
  Otho Holland William
    MdBMu. Rendezvous
  Patch picture for Dr Physick
    Frankenstein. After the hunt
    OCiM. Ptgs by the Peale family
  Robert Oliphant   DNC
    WiMiA. Raphaelle Peale
  Rubens Peale: mascot of the Macpher-
    son's Blues   DNC
    Sellers. C. W. Peale v2
    WiMiA. Raphaelle Peale
  Still life   CtHW
    Baur. Amer ptg
  Still life   MiD
    Flexner. Light of distant skies
  Still life   PH
    Frankenstein. After the hunt
  Still life c 1810   CtHW
    WiMiA. Raphaelle Peale
  Still life, 1813 (Stuempfig coll)
    ICA. From colony to nation

  Still life, 1815   PH
    CSFP. Illusionism
  Still life, 1818 (Graham coll)
    OCiM. Ptgs by the Peale family
    WiMiA. Raphaelle Peale
  Still life, c 1820   OT
    Larkin rev ed (col)
    Pierson
    WiMiA. Raphaelle Peale
  Still life: balsam apples and turnips. See
    Balsam apples and turnips
  Still life—Fruit and nuts
    CtY. Yale alumni
  Still life with cake   NBM
    Barker. Amer ptg
    DC. Amer ptrs of the South (col)
    Larkin
    Larkin rev ed
    Time. 300 years (col)
  Still life with herring   PH
    MdBMu. Rendezvous
    WiMiA. Raphaelle Peale
  Still life with peaches   NBM
    WiMiA. Raphaelle Peale
  Still life with raisin cake
    WiMiA. Raphaelle Peale
  Still life with steak   NUM
    WiMiA. Raphaelle Peale
  Still life with vegetables   CtHW
    Roos
  Still life with watermelon   MSM
    Chew. 250 years of art
    WiMiA. Raphaelle Peale
  Still life with watermelon (Stralem coll)
    WiMiA. Raphaelle Peale (col cover)
  Thomas Jefferson
    MdBMu. Rendezvous
  Watermelon and fruit
    CtY. Yale alumni
  Young man   PPC
    WiMiA. Raphaelle Peale
PEALE, Rembrandt, 1778-1860
  Court of death   MiD
    Barker. Amer ptg
    Richardson. Ptg in America
  Court of death (Sellers coll)
    Larkin
    Larkin rev ed
  David Cox   InIJ
    InIJ. 105 ptgs
  Edward Denison
    MdBMu. Rendezvous
  Edward Johnson   MdBMu
    MdBMu. Rendezvous
  Franklin Peale
    Sellers. C. W. Peale v2
  George Armistead   MdBMu
    MdBMu. Rendezvous
  George Washington   MdBP
    MdBMu. Rendezvous
  George Washington (porthole portrait)
    Chew. 250 years of art
                                               PW
  George Washington (porthole portrait)
                                               OYB
    OYB. Accessions
    OYB. Supplement 1959
  George Washington (porthole portrait)
                                               PA
    Pierson
  Joseph Outen Bogart   DC
    DC. Masterpieces

PEALE, Rembrandt—*Continued*
Mendes Cohen   MoSL
  MoSL. Handbook 1953
Robert Fulton   MiD
  MiD. Treasures
  Pierson
Rubens Peale with the first geranium
  brought to America, 1801
  MdBMu. Rendezvous
  Sellers. C. W. Peale
Samuel Smith   MdBMu
  MdBMu. Rendezvous
  OCiM. Ptgs by the Peale family
Self-portrait   MiD
  MiD. Treasures
  Pierson
Self-portrait   PA
  OCiM. Ptgs by the Peale family
Self-portrait 1791, age 13
  Sellers. C. W. Peale v2
Thomas Jefferson   NNHS
  Larkin
  Larkin rev ed
  Mendelowitz
  Pierson
  Roos
  Time. 300 years (col)

Portrait of the artist

Peale, J. Rembrandt Peale
PEALE, Rembrandt, 1778-1870 and
  PEALE, Charles Willson, 1741-1827
Gilbert Stuart   NNHS
  Sellers. C. W. Peale v2
PEALE, Rubens, 1784-1865
Basket of fruit   MB
  Chew. 250 years of art
  MB. Karolik coll
Belfield (original by C. W. Peale)
  Sellers. C. W. Peale v2
From nature in the garden
  WiMiA. Amer ptg 1760-1960
Lemons and sugar   PR
  PR. Catalogue
Melon, peaches and grapes
  WiMiA. Amer ptg, 1760-1960
Peale's museum
  OCiM. Ptgs by the Peale family
Still life 1860
  Larkin
  Larkin rev ed
Still life with fruit   MAP
  Chew. 250 years of art
Two grouse in underbrush of laurel   MiD
  OCiM. Ptgs by the Peale family
  Pierson

Portrait of the artist

Peale, A. C. Rubens Peale
Peale, Maria. Rubens Peale at his easel
Peale, Raphaelle. Rubens Peale, mascot
  of the Macpherson's Blues
Peale, Rembrandt. Rubens Peale with
  the first geranium brought to Amer-
  ica, 1801
PEALE, Sarah Miriam, 1800-1885
Mrs Hugh McC Birckhead
  MdBMu. Rendezvous
Still life
  OCiM. Ptgs by the Peale family
Still life with melon and grapes
  MdBMu. Rendezvous

Peale, Sophonisba. See Sellers, Sophonisba
  Angusciola (Peale)
PEALE, Titian Ramsay, 1799-1885
Bright house, Rehoboth beach, Delaware
  WiMiA. Amer ptg 1760-1960
Still life with flower and insects
  Chew. 250 years of art
Peale, Titian Ramsay, d 1846
  Peale, C. W. Titian Ramsay Peale II:
  in the uniform of a naturalist
Peale family
  Peale, C. W. Peale family
Peale family (James Peale)
  Peale, J. James Peale and his family
Peale's museum by Rubens Peale
Pear tree in winter by D. Macknight
Pearce, Mr, fl 1835
  Field, E. S. Mr Pearce
Pearce, Mrs fl 1835
  Field, E. S. Mrs Pearce (?)
Pearce, Nathaniel, 1770-1851
  Malbone, E. G. Nathaniel Pearce
PEARLSTEIN, Philip, 1924-
Uprooted tree
  ICA. Annual ex, 1959/60
Peasant girl by M. Sterne
Peasant woman by T. Roszak
Peasants' paradise by M. Hartley
Pe-che-co, a Pottawattomie chief by J. O.
  Lewis
Peck, Mrs Benjamin. See Peck, Hannah
  (Farmer)
Peck, Hannah (Farmer) fl 1770
  Durand, J. Mrs Benjamin Peck
PECK, Miriam, 1910-
Early autumn   OYB
  OYB. Annual 1951
  OYB. Catalogue 1951
PECKHAM, Robert, 1785-1877
Memorial portrait of Mary L. Edgell
      DN
  DN. Amer primitive ptgs, pt 2
Mrs William Cornee with music   NCHA
  Jones. New-found folk art
William Cornee with flute   NCHA
  Jones. New-found folk art

Attributed works

Widow Milton Joslin
  Ford. Pictorial folk art
Peddlers
  Ehninger, J. W. Yankee peddler
Pedernal form the ranch no 1 by G.
  O'Keeffe
Pedestrians in village by J. R. Grabach
Peel, Elizabeth, fl 1757
  West, B. Elizabeth Peel
Peep show by J. B. Thompson
Pegasus by D. Porter
Pegasus by A. P. Ryder
Peggy's cove by J. Lonergan
PEIRCE, Gerry, 1900-
Gray desert   MB
  MB. Ptgs in water color
Mile high   ATU
  ATU. Coll of Amer art
Timber line, Estes park, Colorado   MB
  MB. Ptgs in water color

PEIRCE, Waldo, 1884-
County fair
  Gruskin (col)
  Time. 200 years (col)
Haircut by the sea   MM
  Pierson
Halldis Prince   ATU
  ATU. Coll of Amer art (col)
Haunted house   OYB
  OYB. Catalogue 1951
Maine swimming hole
  Bazin
Mike and the chart
  Gruskin (col)
Sun bathers
  PPC. Ptg in the U.S. 1949
Peirson, Harriet Lawrence, 1793-1870
Goodridge, S. Mrs Abel Lawrence Peirson
PELHAM, Henry, 1749-1806
Adam Babcock
  MB. New England miniatures
Edward Holyoke (after Copley)
  MB. New England miniatures

Attributed works
Mrs Peter Oliver jr   CtY
  MB. New England miniatures
Zechariah Hicks (?)
  MB. New England miniatures

Portrait of the artist
Copley, J. S. Boy with squirrel (Henry Pelham)
Copley, J. S. An engraver, known as Henry Pelham
Copley, J. S. (attributed works) Henry Pelham)
PELHAM, Peter, 1684-1751
Benjamin Colman   MB
  Larkin
  Larkin rev ed
Cotton Mather   MWA
  Flexner. Copley
  MWA. Checklist of portraits
  Pierson
Mather Byles   MWA
  Flexner. First flowers
Pelicans
Audubon, J. J. Brown pelican
Dozier, O. Pelicans
Willson, M. A. Pelican
Pell, Mary Cornell, 1785-1854
Malbone, E. G. Mary Cornell Pell
PELLEW, John C. 1903-
Wingaersheek marsh
  NAD. Special ex, 1956
Pelvis series, red and yellow by G. O'Keeffe
Pelvis series, red with blue by G. O'Keeffe
Pelvis with shadows and the moon by G. O'Keeffe
Pelvis with the moon, New Mexico by G. O'Keeffe
Pemaquid lobster by M. Freedman
The **pen** is mightier than the sword by C. A. Meurer
Pendennis castle, Falmouth, Cornwall by R. Havell
Penelope by G. Melchers
Peninsula by M. Benjamin
Penitente by C. Wells

Penn, John, 1760-1834
Lambdin, J. R. John Penn (copy of ptg by Pine)
Penn, William, 1621-1670
Birch, T. Landing of William Penn
Hicks, E. Grave of William Penn
Hicks, E. Penn's treaty with the Indians
West, B. Penn's treaty with the Indians
PENNEY, James, 1910-
Harvest
  IU. Contemp Amer ptg, 1951
Pines, night, 1956
  Baur. Nature
Pennington mills, Baltimore, view downstream by F. Guy
Pennington mills, Baltimore, view upstream by F. Guy
Penn's treaty tree by T. Birch
Pennsylvania
  See also Philadelphia; Pittsburgh; Susquehanna river; Wyoming valley
Birch, T. Milford, North Wales, Pennsylvania
Birch, T. Winter scene outside Bristol, Pennsylvania
Blair, S. Downing house, Chester county, Pennsylvania
Gasser, H. M. Pennsylvania
Gatch, L. Pennsylvania farm
Hopper, E. Pennsylvania coal town
Knaths, K. Pennsylvania landscape
Mitchell, B. Mauch Chunk, Pennsylvania
Pickett, J. Lehigh canal, sunset, New Hope, Pennsylvania
Pennsylvania Dutch lady by Unidentified artist
Pennsylvania excavation by G. W. Bellows
Pennsylvania hospital by Unidentified artist
The **pension** agent by E. Johnson
Pensionnaire by J. Levine
Pensive boy by W. Sommer
Pensive girl by R. Soyer
Penthesilean trawler by J. C. Lewis
The **people** by D. Fredenthal
People in the park by A. Walkowitz
People on 6th avenue by A. Rattner
Peoria, Illinois
Bohrod, A. Street in Peoria
PEPPER, Charles Hovey, 1864-
Skating   MB
  MB. Ptgs in water color
The statesman   MB
  MB. Ptgs in water color
Peppercombe porch by L. Bouché
Pepperrell, Mary (Hirst) lady, 1703-1789
Smibert, J. Lady Pepperrell
Pepperrell, Sir William, 1st bart, 1696-1759
Smibert, J. Sir William Pepperrell
Pepperrell, Sir William, 2d bart, originally William Pepperrell Sparhawk, b 1746?
Copley, J. S. Sir William Pepperrell and his family
Percé rock, Gaspe by H. G. Keller
Percival, James Gates, 1795-1856
Alexander, F. James Gates Percival
Percolator by S. Davis
Percussion by V. Candell
Percussion by G. L. K. Morris

PEREIRA, Irene Rice, 1907-
Affluent surface
  Baur. MacIver and Pereira
Anchor
  Baur. MacIver and Pereira
Black control   MdBM
  CoS. New accessions USA, 1952
Bright beyond
  Baur. MacIver and Pereira
Composition in white   NJN
  MMA. Abstract
  MMA. Fourteen
  Pearson. Mod renaissance
Copper light
  Baur. MacIver and Pereira
Deep vision
  WMAA. Neuberger collection
Direction yellow
  ICA. Annual ex, 1951
  Robb. Art 1953 ed
Duograph
  CSFP. Annual ex, 1948/49
  DC. 21 biennial ex, 1949
The embryo
  Pearson. Mod renaissance
Evaporating night   TxD
  Baur. MacIver and Pereira
  Baur. New art
  CoS. New accessions USA, 1954
  Pearson. Mod renaissance
  Pierson
Green depth   MM
  McCurdy
  Mendelowitz
  MM. 100 Amer ptrs
  MMA. Fourteen
  Wight. Milestones
Horizontal illusion
  Genauer
Inside—outside
  Baur. MacIver and Pereira
Inverted light
  MnU. 40 Amer ptrs
Landscape of the absolute   WMAA
  Cheney. Story 1958 ed
  Goodrich. Amer art
  Pierson
Light is gold   WMAA
  Pearson. Mod renaissance
Man and machine
  Baur. MacIver and Pereira
Melting horizon
  Baur. MacIver and Pereira
New world a'coming
  Pearson. Mod renaissance
Oblique illusion   ATeS
  ATeS. Collection
Oblique progression   WMAA
  Baur. MacIver and Pereira (col)
  Goodrich. Amer art (col)
Projecting planes   OT
  WMAA. Juliana Force
Quadrigraph
  MMA. Contemp ptrs
  MMA. Fourteen
Receding red
  Roos
Rectangles   ATU
  ATU. Coll of Amer art
Red and blue
  Baur. MacIver and Pereira
Red, yellow and blue
  Baur. MacIver and Pereira
  IU. Contemp Amer ptg, 1948

Reflection
  MMA. Fourteen
The riddle
  Baur. MacIver and Pereira
Ruby flux
  Pousette-Dart. Amer ptg
Seven red squares
  Baur. MacIver and Pereira
Somewhere today
  Baur. MacIver and Pereira
Soul of space
  WMAA. Annual ex, 1958
Spirit of air
  Read. Concise history
Spring, twelve o'clock, 1952
  Baur. MacIver and Pereira
  Baur. Nature
  Baur. New art (col)
Transfluent lines
  Baur. New art
  Riley. Your art heritage
Transforming gold
  VR. Amer ptg, 1954
Transparent planes
  Baur. MacIver and Pereira
Transverse parallels
  Baur. MacIver and Pereira
Transversion   DP
  Baur. Revolution
  DP. Catalogue
  MMA. Fourteen
Two up
  Baur. MacIver and Pereira
Undulating arrangement   CtHW
  Larkin rev ed (col)
  Pierson
View, 1942
  MnU. 40 Amer ptrs
White lines   MMA
  Baur. MacIver and Pereira
  Baur. New art
  MMA. Fourteen
  Pierson
  Read. Art now, 1948 ed
White rectangle no 1
  Baur. MacIver and Pereira
The wind of the sun
  IU. Contemp Amer ptg & sculp, 1955
Yellow lines
  CSFP. Annual ex, 1947/48
Yellow oblongs
  Larkin
  Larkin rev ed
The performance by S. Greene
Performer by H. A. Botkin
Performers by P. Guston
Performers by R. J. Koski
Perfume counter by W. Y. Stamper
Perilous night by J. E. Heliker
Perkins, Mrs George
  Lockman, D. M. Mrs George Perkins
PERKINS, Philip
  Debris of summer
  Genauer
Perkins, Thomas Handasyd, 1764-1854
  Sully, T. Col Thomas Handasyd Perkins
Perkins children, fl 1806
  Malbone, E. G. Perkins children
PERLIN, Bernard, 1918-
  After an ambush
  Time. 300 years (col)
  Boy in the grass
  CSB. Illusion

Colosseum
  IU. Contemp Amer ptg & sculp, 1955
  McCurdy
  WMAA. New decade
The farewell   WMAA
  Pierson
  PPC. International ex, 1952
  WMAA. Sara Roby
The jacket   WMAA
  Faulkner. Art today, 1956
  Goodrich. Amer art
  IU. Contemp Amer ptg, 1952
  Pousette-Dart. Amer ptg
  WMAA. New decade
Jazz band
  ICA. Annual ex, 1959/60
The lovers   MMA
  Pierson
Orthodox boys   ELT
  ICA. Amer artists paint the city
  PPC. Ptg in the U. S. 1949
Potatoes and onions
  CSFP. Annual ex, 1952
Santa Maria della Salute
  Brussels. Exposition
The shore
  Mendelowitz
  WMAA. New decade
The street   MSM
  CoS. New accessions USA, 1950
  IU. Contemp Amer ptg, 1949
  MSM. Handbook
Street dance   VR
  CoS. New accessions USA, 1960
  IU. Contemp Amer ptg & sculp, 1959
Perot, Mary. See Elliston, Mary (Perot)
Perplexity of what to do by J. De Diego
Perrette by A. P. Ryder
Perrin, John, fl 1835
  Unidentified artist. Rev John Perrin
Perry, Edward, 1774-1800
  Malbone, E. G. Edward Perry
Perry, Elizabeth Champlin (Mason) fl 1811
  Fulton, R. Mrs Oliver Hazard Perry
Perry, Matthew Calbraith, 1794-1858
  Evans, J. G. Commodore Perry carrying
    the Gospel of God to the heathen
Perry, Oliver Hazard, 1785-1819
  Jarvis, J. W. Commodore Oliver Hazard
    Perry
  Wood, J. (attributed works) Commodore
    Oliver Hazard Perry
Perry, Mrs Oliver Hazard. See Perry,
  Elizabeth Champlin (Mason)
PERSAC, Adrien
  Shadows-on-the-Teche
    Larkin
    Larkin rev ed
  Sugar mill on Bayou Teche, Oliver planta-
    tion
    Davidson v 1
Persephone by T. H. Benton
Persephone by E. Berman
PERSHING, Louise, 1904-
  Book of life
    PPC. International ex, 1950
Person with orange by R. B. Motherwell
Personage with yellow ochre and white by
  R. B. Motherwell
Personal appearance by J. Ernst
Personal history by J. Ernst

Personification of murder by C. R. Leslie
Perspective by W. T. Murch
Perspective of Mexican hill town by E.
  Berman
Pertaining to Deer isle, the harbor by J.
  Marin
Pertaining to harbour by J. G. F. Von Wicht
Pertaining to Nassau street, New York by
  J. Marin
Pertaining to Stonington harbor, Maine by
  J. Marin
Pertaining to yachts and yachting by C.
  Sheeler
Pescaderia, Malaga by H. G. Keller
Pet rooster by R. Wilson
Peter, Saint
  Allston, W. Angel releasing St Peter from
    prison
  Allston, W. St Peter in prison, Study for
    head of
  West, B. Peter denying Christ
Peter and the wolf by B. Shahn
Peter Volo by Freeman
PETERDI, Gabor, 1915-
  Apocalypse
    ICA. Annual ex, 1954
  Misty ocean   NBM
    Pierson
  Summer IV
    PA. Annual ex, 1958
  Tidal   WMAA
    Baur. Nature (col)
    Goodrich. Amer ptg (col)
  White landscape   MiA
    NUM. Art across America
PETERS, J. fl 1800
  Good intent
  Born
Peters, Mary (Breintall) d 1789?
  Feke, R. Mrs William Peters
PETERSEN, Martin, 1870-
  Stevedores in the hole   MB
    MB. Ptgs in water color
PETERSEN, Roland, 1926-
  Luncheon scene
    IU. Contemp Amer ptg & sculp, 1961
PETERSON, Margaret, 1903-
  Man's child   CSFM
    Pousette-Dart. Amer ptg
  Sun King and merganser
    VR. Amer ptg, 1958
PETO, John Frederick, 1854-1907
  After night's study   MiD
    Pierson
  Book, beerstein and corncob pipe
    PA. Annual ex, 1955
  Books
    Frankenstein. After the hunt
  Books on a shelf
    Frankenstein. After the hunt
  Card rack with oval photograph of
    Abraham Lincoln
    CSFP. Illusionism
  Closet door
    Frankenstein. After the hunt
  Crumbs of comfort
    OCiM. Rediscoveries
  Fish house door
    Frankenstein. After the hunt
  Hat, umbrella and bag
    PA. Annual ex, 1955

PETO, J. F.—*Continued*
Letter rack with jack of hearts
  Frankenstein. After the hunt
Letter rack with Lerado postmark
  Frankenstein. After the hunt
Lincoln and the Pfleger stretcher
  Frankenstein. After the hunt
Market basket, hat, and umbrella
  Frankenstein. After the hunt
Mug, pipe, and newspaper
  Frankenstein. After the hunt
Office board for Christian Faser
  Frankenstein. After the hunt
Office board for Smith Brothers coal company
  Frankenstein. After the hunt
Old companions
  PA. Annual ex, 1955
Old scraps   MMA
  Barr. What is mod ptg
  OCiM. Redscoveries
  PA. Annual ex, 1955
Ordinary objects in the artist's creative mind
  PA. Annual ex, 1955
Pistol, gate latch, and powder horn
  Frankenstein. After the hunt
Poor man's store   MB
  Frankenstein. After the hunt
  Pierson
  Richardson. Ptg in America
The rack   ATeS
  ATeS. Collection
Rack picture with portrait of Lincoln
  Frankenstein. After the hunt
Self-portrait with rack picture
  Frankenstein. After the hunt
Still life: book, pipe, beer stein
  Chew. 250 years of art
Still life: pipe, beer stein, book
  Chew. 250 years of art
Still life with lanterns   NBM
  Baur. Revolution
  Frankenstein. After the hunt
Still life with portrait of the artist's daughter
  Frankenstein. After the hunt
PETROV, Dimitri
Poet's pipe
  ICA. Annual ex, 1951
Phantasy by V. H. Kirkland
Phantom boat by J. De Diego
Pharmaceutic cabinet by B. Utter
Phelps, William Lyon, 1865-1943
  Wickwire, J. R. William Lyon Phelps
Phenomena by J. Molzahn
Phenomena—with nitrogen before by P. Jenkins
Philadelphia
Birch, T. Penn's treaty tree
Birch, T. Philadelphia from Petty island, c 1825
Caly, N. V. View of the Merchants' exchange and Girard's bank, Philadelphia, c 1835
Cooper, P. Southeast prospect of the city of Philadelphia, c 1720
Doughty, T. Naval home, Gray's ferry, Philadelphia
Kennedy, D. J. View of Broad and Cherry street above Arch street, 1842
Krimmel, J. L. Election scene in front of the State house in Philadelphia

Krimmel, J. L. Fourth of July in Centre Square, Philadelphia, c 1810
Matthew, K. Independence hall
Shinn, E. Independence hall
Sloan, J. East entrance, City hall, Philadelphia, 1901
Smith, R. Edgehill road, Philadelphia
Smith, R. Old courthouse in Philadelphia
Smith, R. Old Walnut street prison, Philadelphia in 1835
Uhle, B. An election day bonfire, Fifth and Chestnut streets, Philadelphia
Unidentified artist. Judd's hotel, Philadelphia, c 1825
Unidentified artist. Pennsylvania hospital
Unidentified artist (after William Henry Bartlett) View of the Schuylkill waterworks, Philadelphia
Unidentified artist. Waterworks, Centre square, Philadelphia c 1810
Philemon and Baucis by K. L. Seligmann
Philip the Good, duke of Burgundy, 1396-1467
Walker, C. H. Philip the Good
PHILIPP, Robert, 1895-
Bouquet
  IU. Contemp Amer ptg, 1952
Ladies of the evening
  PPC. International ex, 1950
Letty in leghorn   ATU
  ATU. Coll of Amer art
Nude
  NAD. Annual ex, 1958
Nude combing her hair
  IU. Contemp Amer ptg, 1948
Patio Royale, New Orleans
  NAD. Annual ex, 1948
Raising the cross
  Genauer
  NAD. Annual ex, 1947, 1st half
Rendezvous   IaDa
  Gruskin
  IaDa. Silver jubilee
Request number
  NAD. Anual ex, spring 1950
Rochelle
  NAD. Annual ex, 1956
Summer breezes
  NAD. Annual ex, 1961
Xmas morning
  PPC. Ptg in the U. S. 1949
Philipse, Adolphus, 1665-1702
Unidentified artist. Adolphus Philipse
Philipse, Philip
Wollaston, J. Philip Philipse
Philipse manor at Yonkers, New York by Unidentified artist
PHILLIPS, fl 1835

Attributed works

Mr Bradley   DN
  DN. Amer primitive ptgs, pt 2
Mrs Bradley   DN
  DN. Amer primitive ptgs, pt 2
Phillips, Anna Lewis. See Phoenix, Anna Lewis (Phillips)
Phillips, Mrs Duncan. See Phillips, Marjorie (Acker)
Phillips, George, 1664-1739
Unidentified artist. Rev George Phillips
Phillips, Holmead. See Holmead

PHILLIPS, J. Campbell, b 1873
  Future admiral
  NYG. Fine art
PHILLIPS, James, 1930?-
  Girl at the Tuileries
    WMAA. Young America 1957
  Self-portrait, Versailles
    WMAA. Young America 1957
Phillips, John, 1770-1823
  Malbone, E. G. John Phillips
Phillips, John, fl 1793
  Steward, J. John Phillips
PHILLIPS, Laughlin
  Nautical   DP
    DP. Catalogue
PHILLIPS, Marjorie (Acker) 1894-
  Farm road   DP
    DP. Catalogue
  Grass path in spring
    PPC. International ex, 1950
  Landscape: buzzard   CtY
    CtY. Soc Anonyme
  Little bouquet   DP
    DP. Catalogue
  Night baseball   DP
    DP. Catalogue
  Poppies   DP
    DP. Catalogue
  Sun after rain   DP
    DP. Catalogue
The philosopher by E. Vedder
Philosopher's camp in the Adirondacks by
    W. J. Stillman
Philosopher's heir by H. Major
Philosopher's offspring by H. Major
Philosopher's wife by H. Major
"PHINDOODLE," Captain
  Narragansett light from northeast   CtNL
    Ford. Pictorial folk art
Phinney, Elihu, 1756-1813
  Ames, E. Elihu Phinney
Phipps, Mrs Ogden
  Speicher, E. E. Mrs Ogden Phipps
Phippsburg, Maine by J. Marin
Phoenix, Anna Lewis (Phillips) 1765-1854
  Unidentified artist. Mrs Daniel Phoenix
Phoenix by H. Hofmann
Phoenix by A. Urban
Photographing the bull by T. H. Benton
PHUL, Anna Maria
  St Louis belle   MoSLH
    Rathbone
Phyllis by J. W. Alexander
The pianist by T. Eakins
Piano concert by W. Zorach
Piazza di San Marco, Venice by M. B.
    Prendergast
Piazza di Spagna by J. Kinigstein
Piazza Navona by W. G. Congdon
Piazza Navona, Rome by J. S. Sargent
Piazza San Marco by W. G. Congdon
Pic of Orizaba by S. Hirsch
Pica Cotto by R. Scarlett
Picador by F. Martin
Picasso book by K. Knaths
Piccadilly, London by E. D. Boit
Piccard, Jean
  Breinin, R. Dr Jean Piccard
Pick 'till the rain hits by R. Gwathmey

PICKEN, George Alexander, 1898-
  East river rooftops
    Pousette-Dart. Amer ptg
  Hawthorne, New York
    NYG. Fine art
  Lieutenant Bulkley's PT boats at Bataan
                                             ATU
    ATU. Coll of Amer art
PICKENS, Alton, 1917-
  Acrobat
    Baur. New art
    Baur. Revolution
    MMA. Contemp ptrs
  Actor and his family
    MMA. Fourteen
    WMAA. New decade
  Blue doll   MMA
    Baur. New art
    MMA. Fourteen
    Pierson
  Boating party
    IU. Contemp Amer ptg, 1951
  Card players
    ICA. Annual ex, 1945/46
  Carnival   MMA
    Baur. New art (col)
    Flexner. Amer ptg
    Flexner. Short history
  Game of pretend
    Miller. Fourteen
  Henry Hope family
    Baur. New art
    ICA. Annual ex, 1954
    WMAA. New decade
  Pastorale
    MMA. Fourteen
  The send-off
    ICA. Annual ex, 1951
    WMAA. New decade
  Under the river
    MMA. Fourteen
PICKERING, H. Douglas, 1921-
  Some grow up   OYB
    OYB. Annual 1949
    OYB. Catalogue 1951
Pickering, Lois. See Orne, Lois (Pickering)
Pickering, Rebecca (White) 1754-1828
  Goodridge, S. (after Stuart) Mrs Timothy
    Pickering
Pickering, Timothy, 1745-1829
  Goodridge, S. (after Stuart) Timothy
    Pickering
Picketing horses by A. J. Miller
PICKETT, Joseph, 1848-1918
  Coryell's ferry, 1776   WMAA
    Baur. New art
    Chew. 250 years of art
    Ford. Pictorial folk art
    Goodrich. Amer art (col)
    Pierson
  Lehigh canal, sunset, New Hope, Pennsyl-
    vania
    Born
    Kallir. Amer primitive ptgs
  Manchester valley   MMA
    Baur. New art
    Baur. Revolution
    Ford. Pictorial folk art (col)
    McCurdy
    Mendelowitz

PICKETT, Joseph—*Continued*
  MMA. Masters (col)
  MMA. Ptg and sculpture
  Pierson
  Roos
  UNESCO. 1860-1949
  Washington under the council tree,
    Coryell's ferry, New Hope, Pennsylvania   NJN
  Baur. New Art
  Pierson
PICKHARDT, Carl E. 1908-
  Eye witness
    IU. Contemp Amer ptg, 1951
Picking cotton by B. Shahn
Pickman, Benjamin, 1740-1819
  Copley, J. S. Benjamin Pickman
Pickman, Benjamin, 1763-1843
  Harding, C. Benjamin Pickman
Pickman. Judith, 1735-1756
  Greenwood, J. Judith Pickman
Pickman, Mary (Toppan) 1744-1818
  Copley, J. S. Mrs Benjamin Pickman
Picnic by G. W. Bellows
Picnic by G. C. Bingham
Picnic by A. M. R. Moses
Picnic by C. Nangeroni
Picnic by M. B. Prendergast
Picnic by F. C. Watkins
Picnic at Menhoppen, Pennsylvania by R.
  Henri
Picnic grounds by J. Sloan
Picnic grove by M. B. Prendergast
Picnic in the Catskills by H. Inman
Picnic on the Hudson by J. M. Hart
Picnic on the Hudson by T. P. Rossiter
Picnic on the ridge by J. Sloan
Picnic with red umbrella by M. B. Prendergast
Picnickers by L. Kester
Pictograph by A. A. Gottlieb
Picture hat by H. V. Poor
Picture of Dorian Gray by I. L. Albright
Picture of my young son by A. Refregier
Pidge, blink and the sea by C. F. Gaertner
A **piece** of my world by Grosz
Pieces of red, green & blue by A. G. Dove
The **pier** by S. Wilson
Pier composition by A. Rattner
Pierce, Franklin, president U. S. 1804-1869
  Healy, G. P. A. Franklin Pierce
Pierce, Sarah, 1767-1852
  Dickinson, A. (attributed works) Sarah
    Pierce
Piermont, New York by L. Bouché
Pierpont, James, fl 1711
  Pierpont limner. Rev James Pierpont
Pierpont, Mary (Hooker) fl 1711
  Pierpont limner. Mrs James Pierpont
PIERPONT limner
  Edward Collins   NAI
    Belknap
    NAI. Hudson valley
  James Pierpont
    Flexner. First flowers
    Larkin
    Pierson

  Mrs James Pierpont
    Flexner. First flowers
    Pierson
Pierre by A. J. Miller
Pierson, Francis, d 1781
  Copley, J. S. Death of Major Pierson
PIERSON, Sarah, fl 1821
  Fulton street, New York, 1821
    U.S. National Capital sesquicentennial
      com
Pietà by J. O. Nordfeldt
Pietà by S. G. Reinhardt
Pietà by C. E. Van Duzer
Pigeon cove, Rockport, Massachusetts by
  K. Sturgis
Pigeons
  Audubon, J. J. Passenger pigeon
  Hirshfield, M. Girl with pigeons
  Sloan, J. Pigeons
  Spruce, E. F. Pigeons on a roof
Pigs
  Curry, J. S. Hogs killing a snake
  Mount, W. S. Ringing the pig
Pigtails by E. E. Speicher
PIKE, John, 1911-
  Kids skiing
    NAD. Annual ex, spring 1950
  Lake Lure
    NYG. Fine art
  Orchard lane road, Woodstock
    NAD. Annual ex, 1947, 2d half
Pike county church by N. Spencer
Pike's peak, View of by G. C. Bingham
Pileated woodpecker by J. J. Audubon
Pilgrim with flowered hat by R. Lebrun
Pillar by A. Bohrod
The **pillow** by W. Stein
Pincian hill, Rome by M. B. Prendergast
Pinckney, Charles Cotesworth, 1746-1825
  Malbone, E. G. Maj Gen Charles C.
    Pinckney
Pinckney, Eliza (Izard) See Izard, Eliza
Pinckney, Thomas, 1750-1828
  Malbone, E. G. Gen Thomas Pinckney
Pinckney, Thomas, 1780-1830
  Malbone, E. G. Thomas Pinckney jr
Pinckney, Mrs Thomas. See Izard, Eliza
PINE, Robert Edge, 1730-1788 and **SAVAGE, Edward,** 1761-1817
  Congress voting independence, July, 1776
                                              PH
    Davidson v 1   PH
  Pierson
  Richardson. Ptg in America
  U.S. National Capital sesquicentennial
    com
Pine bough by K. Knaths
Pine timber by K. Knaths
Pine tree by K. Knaths
Pine tree and snowstorm by W. B. P.
  Closson
Pine tree, Small point, Maine by J. Marin
Pine trees by K. Steinitz
Pineapple by Unidentified artist
Pines by S. Laufman
Pines and fog by M. Kantor
Pines in the Villa Barberini by J. G. Chapman

Pines, night by J. Penney
Pink angels by W. De Kooning
Pink bird by M. Graves
Pink cock by M. Avery
Pink cow by W. Sommer
The **pink** dismissal slip by P. Evergood
Pink dress by J. S. Sargent
Pink dunes by L. Harmon
Pink fan by F. Serger
Pink flower by M. Friedman
Pink harlequin by P. Fine
Pink lustre by K. Knaths
Pink masks by A. Ruellan
Pink Mississippi by J. Tworkov
Pink roses by R. A. Blakelock
Pink roses by Unidentified artist
Pink tablecloth by M. Avery
Pink tablecloth by H. V. Poor
Pink tablecloth by N. Vasilieff
Pink tights by G. R. Davis
Pink vase and green leaves by G. O'Keeffe
PINNEY, Eunice (Griswold) Holcombe,
    1770-1849
  The cotters' Saturday night
    Lipman. Primitive ptrs
  Masonic memorial
    Lipman. Primitive ptrs
  Plenty
    Lipman. Primitive ptrs
  Two women   NCHA
    Barker. Amer ptg
    Flexner. Light of distant skies
    Lipman. Primitive ptrs
    Pierson
  Undedicated memorial
    Lipman. Primitive ptrs
Piñons with cedar by G. O'Keeffe
Pintails by P. M. Scott
Pioneer and the Indian by F. Remington
Pioneers by W. T. Ranney
Pioneers by W. E. Russell
Pioneer's camp by Unidentified artist
Pioneer's house by D. Garber
Pip and Flip by R. Marsh
Pipe and bowl by P. W. Roberts
Pipe of friendship by W. T. Ranney and
    W. S. Mount
Pipe of peace by A. J. Miller
Pipe of peace by C. M. Russell
PIPPIN, Horace, 1888-1946
  Abe Lincoln, the great emancipator
    Rodman. Horace Pippin
  Abraham Lincoln and his father building
    their cabin on Pigeon creek   PMB
    Rodman. Horace Pippin
  After supper, Westchester
    Bazin
    McCurdy
  Artist's wife
    Rodman. Horace Pippin
  The barracks   DP
    DP. Catalogue
    Rodman. Horace Pippin
  The barracks, Sketch for
    Rodman. Horace Pippin

Birmingham meeting house I, 1940
  Rodman. Horace Pippin
Blue tiger
  Rodman. Horace Pippin
Buffalo hunt   WMAA
  Chew. 250 years of art
  Rodman. Horace Pippin
  Pierson
Cabin in the cotton I, 1935
  Rodman. Horace Pippin
Cabin in the cotton III, 1944
  Rodman. Horace Pippin
Christ
  Rodman. Horace Pippin
Christian Brinton   PPhM
  Rodman. Horace Pippin
Christmas morning breakfast
  Rodman. Horace Pippin
Crucifixion
  Rodman. Horace Pippin
The den
  Rodman. Horace Pippin
Domino players   DP
  DP. Catalogue
  Rodman. Horace Pippin (col)
End of the war: starting home PPhM
  Ford. Pictorial folk art
  Rodman. Horace Pippin
Flowers with four doilies
  Rodman. Horace Pippin
Flowers with hat and cane
  Rodman. Horace Pippin
The getaway
  Rodman. Horace Pippin (col)
Harmonizing
  Rodman. Horace Pippin
The holy
  CanO. Hirshhorn coll
Holy mountain I, 1944
  Rodman. Horace Pippin
Holy mountain II, 1944
  Rodman. Horace Pippin (col)
  Wight. Milestones
Holy mountain IV, 1946
  Rodman. Horace Pippin
John Brown going to his hanging PA
  Brussels. Exposition
  Rodman. Horace Pippin
  Time. 300 years (col)
John Brown reading his Bible
  Rodman. Horace Pippin
Lady of the lake
  Rodman. Horace Pippin
Lilies
  Rodman. Horace Pippin
Love note
  Rodman. Horace Pippin
Milkman of Goshen
  Rodman. Horace Pippin
Park bench
  Rodman. Horace Pippin
Paul B. Dague, deputy sheriff Chester
  county
  Rodman. Horace Pippin
Quaker mother and child   RPS
  Rodman. Horace Pippin
Red, yellow and white roses
  Rodman. Horace Pippin
Roses with red chair
  Rodman. Horace Pippin
Saturday night bath
  Rodman. Horace Pippin
Saying prayers
  Rodman. Horace Pippin

PIPPIN, Horace—*Continued*
Self-portrait I, 1941   NBuA
  NBuA. Contemporary ptgs
  Rodman. Horace Pippin
Shell holes and observation balloon
  Rodman. Horace Pippin
Summer flowers with two chairs
  Rodman. Horace Pippin
Sunday morning breakfast
  Rodman. Horace Pippin
Temptation of St Anthony
  Rodman. Horace Pippin
Trial of John Brown
  Larkin
  Larkin rev ed
  Rodman. Horace Pippin
Uncle Tom
  Rodman. Horace Pippin
Victorian interior I, 1945
  Rodman. Horace Pippin
Victorian interior II, 1945
  Rodman. Horace Pippin (col)
West Chester courthouse
  Rodman. Horace Pippin
West Chester, Pennsylvania   KW
  Rodman. Horace Pippin
Woman at Samaria   PMB
  Rodman. Horace Pippin
The woman taken in adultery
  Rodman. Horace Pippin

Pippin, Mrs Horace
  Pippin, H. Artist's wife

Pippin house, East Liverpool, Ohio by C. E.
  Burchfield

The **pirate** by A. Gorky

The **pirate** Laffite by J. W. Jarvis

Pirates' island by A. P. Ryder

Pisa by G. Beattie

Pistol, gate latch, and power horn by J. F.
  Peto

Pistolesi, Lina, fl 1878
  Alexander, F. Lina Pistolesi

The **pit** by G. Grosz

Pitching quoits by W. Homer

Pitkin, Timothy, 1726-1812
  Moulthrop, R. Timothy Pitkin

Pitson, Hannah. See Flagg, Hannah (Pitson)

Pitt, William, 1st earl of Chatham, 1708-
  1778
  Copley, J. S. Death of Chatham
  Peale, C. W. Worthy of liberty, Mr Pitt
    scorns to invade the liberties of other
    people

PITTMAN, Hobson, 1900-
  The conversation
    DC. 20 biennial ex, 1947
  The gossips
    Gruskin (col)
  Landscape with mansion and white mantel
    CSFP. Annual ex, 1952
  Mantel arrangement   OYB
    CSFP. Annual ex, 1947/48
    Genauer
    OYB. Annual 1955
    OYB. Supplement 1959
  Midsummer phlox
    OYB. Annual 1950
  Nine P.M.   DP
    DP. Catalogue

Nine P.M.   OYB
    OYB. Catalogue 1951
  Reflection
    Chew. 250 years of art
    PPC. International ex, 1950
  Spring festival
    PPC. Ptg in the U.S. 1949
  Studio in Charleston
    NAD. Annual ex, 1954
  Veiled bouquet
    DC. 23 biennial ex, 1953
  The widow   WMAA
    Baur. Revolution
  Yellow chair
    IU. Contemp Am ptg. 1948

Pitts, Elizabeth, 1734-1810
  Copley, J. S. Elizabeth Pitts
Pitts, Elizabeth (Bowdoin) fl 1754-1762
  Blackburn, J. Mrs James Pitts
Pitts, Elizabeth (Lendall) 1680-1763
  Smibert, J. Mrs John Pitts
PITTS, Elizabeth (McCord) 1880-
  Maida in our Paris studio   MiD
    MiD. Ports of the Pitts family
      Portrait of the artist
  Roper, M. M. Elizabeth McCord
Pitts, James, 1710-1776
  Blackburn, J. James Pitts
Pitts, Mrs James. See Pitts, Elizabeth
  (Bowdoin)
Pitts, John, 1668-1731
  Badger, J. (after Smibert) John Pitts
Pitts, Mrs John. See Pitts, Elizabeth
  (Lendall)
PITTS, Lendall, 1875-1938
  Grand finale   MiD
    MiD. Ports of the Pitts family
  Source of the Romanche   MiD
    MiD. Ports of the Pitts family
      Portrait of the artist
  Shumacher, W. E. Lendall Pitts
Pitts, Mrs Lendall. See Pitts, Elizabeth
  (McCord)
Pitts, Samuel, 1745-1805
  Copley, J. S. Samuel Pitts
Pitts, Samuel Mountfort, b 1835?
  Unidentified artist (possibly J. G. or L. E.
    Cole) Samuel Mountford Pitts sr
Pitts, Samuel Mountfort, d 1868
  Stanley, J. M. Samuel Mountfort Pitts
    jr
Pitts, Mrs Samuel Mountfort. See Pitts,
  Sarah (Merrill)
Pitts, Sarah (Merrill) 1813-1896
  Melchers, G. Mrs Samuel Mountfort Pitts
Pitts, Thomas, 1841-1907
  Melchers, G. Thomas Pitts
  Melchers, G. Thomas Pitts, Head of
Pittsburgh, Pennsylvania
  Blythe, D. G. In the Pittsburgh post
    office
  Bohrod, A. West park, Pittsburgh
  Brantz, L. Pittsburgh, 1790
  Driggs, E. Pittsburgh, 1927
  Kane, J. Beechwood boulevard, Pittsburgh
  Smith, R. The aqueduct, Pittsburgh, 1829
  Smith, R. North avenue, Pittsburgh
  Smith, R. Oldest house at foot of Coal
    hill, opposite Market street
  Smith, R. Powder magazine, Fort Du-
    quesne, Pennsylvania
  Smith, R. View of Pittsburgh from the
    salt works on Saw mill run

Wall, W. G. Homestead mill near Pittsburgh
Wall, W. C. Pittsburgh after the fire of 1845
Pittsburgh horsemarket by D. G. Blythe
PITZ, Henry Clarence, 1895-
  Between acts
    NAD. Special ex, 1956
  Hotel lobby   OYB
    OYB. Annual ex, 1953
    OYB. Supplement
Place de l'Opéra, Paris by E. D. Boit
Place des Vosges, by S. Davis
Place du Carrousel, Paris by E. D. Boit
The **place** of the angel and Tobias by K. Fearing
Place Pasdeloup by S. Davis
A **place** to swim by H. E. Schnakenberg
Placer mining, 1854 by Chadwick
Planes in the sunflowers by M. J. Bigler
Planning the attack by C. M. Russell
Plant forms by A. G. Dove
The **plantation** by Unidentified artist
Planting corn by O. Krans
Plaster by R. Dubin
PLATE, Walter, 1925-
  Autumn
    Baur. Nature
  Hot house
    DC. 26 biennial ex, 1959
  Interior no 1
    IU. Contemp Amer ptg & sculp, 1959
  Salmon river
    PPC. International ex, 1955
  Still life   WMAA
    WMAA. Young America 1957
  Untitled
    WMAA. Young America 1957
PLATT, George W. 1839-1899
  Quail
    Frankenstein. After the hunt
  Relics of a den
    Frankenstein. After the hunt
  Wild West
    Frankenstein. After the hunt
Platt, Mrs Nathaniel, fl 1820
  Tuthill, A. G. D. Mrs Nathaniel Platt
Platte river
  Whittredge, W. On the Platte
Playfair, Edith Hammond (Russell) lady, fl 1884
  Sargent, J. S. Lady Playfair
Playground by P. Cadmus
Playground by J. Kirschenbaum
Playground by B. Shahn
Playground pleasures by J. Meyers
Playing old soldier by W. Homer
Pleasant retreat by P. Grimm
Pleasure garden by L. Gatch
Pleasure party by a mill by C. W. Peale
Pleasures of spring by A. Blanch
Pleasures of summer by M. Weber
PLEISSNER, Ogden Minton, 1905-
  Along the Arno   MM
    MM. 100 Amer ptrs
    Pierson

The Arno   OT
  CoS. New accessions USA, 1952
  IU. Contemp Amer ptg, 1950
  PPC. Ptg in the U. S. 1949
  Early morning, Paris
    NAD. Annual ex, 1949, 1st half
  Florida landscape   IaDa
    IaDa. Silver jubilee
  Montmartre   NJMo
    NAD. Annual ex, autumn 1949
    NJMo. Forty years
    NJMo. Your Montclair art museum
  Normandie
    NAD. Annual ex, 1952
  The portal
    MM. Amer ptg today
  The Ramparts, St Malo   MWM
    CoS. New accessions USA, 1952
  Rue Gabrielle
    NAD. Annual ex, 1955
  Stacking alfalfa
    Gruskin
  The tower, Avallon
    Time. 300 years (col)
Plenty by E. G. H. Pinney
Plexus counterplexus by S. Kreider
PLOCHMANN, Carolyn, 1926-
  Barriers   OYB
    OYB. Annual 1952
    OYB. Supplement
Ploughland and distant hills by B. West (attributed works)
Plovers
  Audubon, J. J. Golden plover
  Hartley, M. Dead plover
The **plow** and the song by A. Gorky
Plowed field by S. Laufman
Plowing by C. S. Price
Plum girl by M. Sterne
Plumage by P. W. Roberts
PLUMMER, Edwin, b 1802
  Mrs Elizabeth Chandler Plummer VWR
    VWR. Folk art (col)
Plummer, Elizabeth (Chandler) 1760-1839
  Plummer, E. Mrs Elizabeth Chandler Plummer
Plummer, Mrs Thomas. See Plummer, Elizabeth (Chandler)
Plumstead, Anna Helena Amelia (Ross) 1776-1846
  Stuart, G. Mrs George Plumstead
Plumstead, Mary (McCall) b 1725
  Feke, R. Miss Mary McCall
Plumstead, Mrs William. See Plumstead, Mary (McCall)
Plymouth Sound, England by R. W. Salmon
Pochade by S. Davis
Pocket by D. Joe
Pocusmania by K. Davies
POE, Elisabeth, 1888-1947
  Agate heights   DP
    DP. Catalogue
Poem—2 by M. D. Simpson
Poestenkill, New York by J. H. Hidley
The **poet** by P. Guston
The **poet** by L. MacIver
The **poet** on Pegasus entering the realm of the Muses (Pegasus) by A. P. Ryder

Poetry after breakfast by M. Avery

Poet's pipe by D. Petrov

Poinsett, Elisha, 1723-1804
Malbone, E. G. Dr Elisha Poinsett

Poinsett, Elizabeth. See Richardson, Elizabeth (Poinsett)

Poinsett, Joel Roberts, 1779-1851
Jarvis, J. W. Joel Roberts Poinsett
Malbone, E. G. Joel Roberts Poinsett

Poinsett, Susan, 1782-1804
Malbone, E. G. Susan Poinsett (formerly called Anna Frances (Poinsett)

Point o' view by P. Cadmus

Pointer and quail by L. Conduit

Pointers by J. M. Tracy

Poirson, Suzanne, fl 1884
Sargent, J. S. Mlle Suzanne Poirson

Poland Spring, Maine by J. Fiore

Polar space by J. Ernst

Police gazette by W. De Kooning

Political, business and intellectual ballyhoo (Ceiling panel no 6) by T. H. Benton

Political debate between two Irishmen by W. Hudson

Political scene in early Bloomington by T. A. Wylie

Politicians by J. Hirsch

Politicians in a country bar by J. G. Clonney

Politics in an oyster house by R. C. Woodville

POLK, Charles Peale, 1767-1822
John Hart   DN
   DN. Amer primitive ptgs, pt 2
Mrs Isaac Hite and James Madison Hite
   jr   MdBH
   Flexner. Light of distant skies
Mrs John Hart and her daughter   DN
   DN. Amer primitive ptgs, pt 2

Polk, James Knox, president U.S. 1795-1849
Healy, G. P. A. James K. Polk

Poll tax country by R. Gwathmey

POLLACK, Reginald Murray, 1924-
Interior I
   WMAA. Annual ex, 1958
Still life I
   IU. Contemp Amer ptg & sculp, 1957

Pollard, Ann, fl 1700
Pollard limner. Ann Pollard

POLLARD, Calvin, fl 1823-1843?
Residence of Hendrick Remsen   NNHS
   NNHS. Waldron Phoenix Belknap coll

POLLARD limner
Ann Pollard   MBH
   Barker. Amer ptg
   Flexner. Amer ptg
   Flexner. First flowers
   Flexner. Short history
   Ford. Pictorial folk art
   Larkin
   Larkin rev ed
   Mendelowitz
   Pierson
   Time. 300 years (col)
Mrs John Dolbeare
   Flexner. First flowers
Thomas Thatcher (?)
   Flexner. First flowers
   Pierson
         Attributed works
Elisha Cooke
   Flexner. First flowers

POLLOCK, Jackson, 1912-1956
Arabesque
   MnMW. Eighty works
Autumn rhythm   MM
   Mendelowitz
   O'Hara. Jackson Pollock (col)
   Pierson
   Robertson. Jackson Pollock
Bird
   Robertson. Jackson Pollock (col)
Bird effort
   Hess. Abstract ptg
Birth
   O'Hara. Jackson Pollock
   Robertson. Jackson Pollock
Black and white no 5, 1952
   O'Hara. Jackson Pollock
   Robertson. Jackson Pollock
Black and white painting 1951-52
   O'Hara. Jackson Pollock
   Robertson. Jackson Pollock
   Selz. New images
Black, white and grey
   O'Hara. Jackson Pollock
Blue poles
   Robertson. Jackson Pollock (col)
Blue poles (Heller coll)
   O'Hara. Jackson Pollock (col)
   Ponente. Mod ptg, 1960 (col)
Blue poles (Olsen coll)
   Baur. New art (col)
   WMAA. New decade
The blue unconscious
   MMA. Jackson Pollock
   O'Hara. Jackson Pollock (col)
   Robertson. Jackson Pollock
Cathedral   TxD
   Art since 1945 (col)
   McCurdy
   MMA. Jackson Pollock
   O'Hara. Jackson Pollock
   Robertson. Jackson Pollock (col)
Circumcision
   Robertson. Jackson Pollock
Convergence   NBuA
   ICA. Amer artists paint the city
   Larkin rev ed (col)
   NBuA. Acquisitions 1954-57
   O'Hara. Jackson Pollock (col)
   Pierson
   Robertson. Jackson Pollock
Cut out
   O'Hara. Jackson Pollock
   Robertson. Jackson Pollock
The deep
   O'Hara. Jackson Pollock (col)
   Robertson. Jackson Pollock
   WMAA. New decade
Drawing, c 1938
   Robertson. Jackson Pollock
Drawing, c 1938-43
   Robertson. Jackson Pollock
Drawing, 1943
   O'Hara. Jackson Pollock
Drawing, c 1943-45
   Robertson. Jackson Pollock (col)
Drawing c 1944
   Robertson. Jackson Pollock
Drawing, 1945
   Robertson. Jackson Pollock
Drawing, c 1946-49
   Robertson. Jackson Pollock (col)
Drawing, 1950
   O'Hara. Jackson Pollock

Easter and the totem
  O'Hara. Jackson Pollock
  PPC. International ex, 1955
  Robertson. Jackson Pollock **(col)**
Echo
  MMA. Jackson Pollock
  O'Hara. Jackson Pollock
  Robertson. Jackson Pollock
Eyes in the heat I, 1946
  Hess. Abstract ptg
  O'Hara. Jackson Pollock
  Robertson. Jackson Pollock (col)
Eyes in the heat II, 1947
  O'Hara. Jackson Pollock
The flame
  O'Hara. Jackson Pollock
  Robertson. Jackson Pollock (col)
Four opposites
  Art since 1945
  O'Hara. Jackson Pollock
  Robertson. Jackson Pollock (col)
Frieze
  Robertson. Jackson Pollock (col)
Frogman. See Number 32, 1951
Full fathom five   MMA
  Biddle. Yes and no
  O'Hara. Jackson Pollock (col)
  Robertson. Jackson Pollock (col)
Gothic
  O'Hara. Jackson Pollock
  Robertson. Jackson Pollock (col)
Green silver
  O'Hara. Jackson Pollock
Greyed rainbow   ICA
  O'Hara. Jackson Pollock
  Robertson. Jackson Pollock
Guardians of the secret   CSFM
  Baur. New art
  MMA. Jackson Pollock
  O'Hara. Jackson Pollock
  Robertson. Jackson Pollock (col)
The key
  ICA. Annual ex, 1947/48
  O'Hara. Jackson Pollock
  Robertson. Jackson Pollock (col)
Landscape with rider
  Robertson. Jackson Pollock
Lavender mist
  MMA. Jackson Pollock
  O'Hara. Jackson Pollock (col)
  Robertson. Jackson Pollock (col)
Little king
  Robertson. Jackson Pollock
Magic mirror
  O'Hara. Jackson Pollock
  Robertson. Jackson Pollock
Male and female
  O'Hara. Jackson Pollock (col)
  Robertson. Jackson Pollock (col)
Masqued image
  Robertson. Jackson Pollock
Mixed media, 1944
  Robertson. Jackson Pollock
Moon vibrations
  O'Hara. Jackson Pollock
  Robertson. Jackson Pollock
Moon woman cuts a circle
  O'Hara. Jackson Pollock
  Robertson. Jackson Pollock
Mural, 1943   IaIU
  O'Hara. Jackson Pollock
  Robertson. Jackson Pollock

The nest
  Robertson. Jackson Pollock
Night ceremony
  O'Hara. Jackson Pollock
  Robertson. Jackson Pollock
Night sounds
  Robertson. Jackson Pollock
Number 1, 1948   MMA
  Baur. New art
  Cheney. Story 1958 ed
  MMA. Abstract
  MMA. Jackson Pollock
  MMA. Masters (col)
  Newmeyer
  O'Hara. Jackson Pollock
  Pierson
  Robertson. Jackson Pollock
Number 1, 1949
  Cheney. Story 1958 ed (col)
  Hess. Abstract ptg (col)
  O'Hara. Jackson Pollock
  Robertson. Jackson Pollock (col)
Number 2, 1949   NUM
  50 years of mod art
  MnMW. 60 Amer ptrs (col)
  O'Hara. Jackson Pollock
  Robertson. Jackson Pollock
Number 2, 1951
  WMAA. Contemp Amer ptg, 1951
  WMAA. New decade
Number 3, 1951
  Baur. New art
  ICA. Annual ex, 1951
  MMA. Fifteen
  Selz. New images
Number 3, 1952
  Robertson. Jackson Pollock
Number 4, 1949
  IU. Contemp Amer ptg, 1951
  O'Hara. Jackson Pollock
Number 4, 1952
  Robertson. Jackson Pollock
Number 5, 1948
  IU. Contemp Amer ptg & sculp, 1953
  O'Hara. Jackson Pollock
Number 5, 1950   MMA
  Hess. Abstract ptg (col)
  Seiberling (col)
Number 5, 1951
  Robertson. Jackson Pollock
Number 6, 1949
  O'Hara. Jackson Pollock
Number 6, 1952
  O'Hara. Jackson Pollock
  Selz. New images
Number 7, 1950
  Barr. What is mod ptg
  MMA. Fifteen
  Robertson. Jackson Pollock
Number 7, 1952
  Robertson. Jackson Pollock
Number 8, 1949
  MMA. New Amer ptg
  O'Hara. Jackson Pollock
Number 8, 1950
  Cheney. Primer 1958 ed
  O'Hara. Jackson Pollock
  WMAA. Neuberger collection
Number 8, 1952   CtHW
  Robertson. Jackson Pollock (col)
Number 10, 1949
  OHara. Jackson Pollock
  Robertson. Jackson Pollock

POLLOCK, Jackson—*Continued*

Number 10, 1950
  Baur. Revolution
  Robertson. Jackson Pollock
Number 10, 1951
  Robertson. Jackson Pollock
Number 11, 1951
  IU. Contemp Amer ptg, 1950
  O'Hara. Jackson Pollock
  Robertson. Jackson Pollock
Number 12, 1949   MMA
  Robertson. Jackson Pollock
Number 12, 1950
  MnU. 40 Amer ptrs
Number 12, 1952
  Cheney. Story 1948 ed
  Hunter. Mod Amer ptg (col)
  MMA. Jackson Pollock
  MMA. New Amer ptg (col)
  O'Hara. Jackson Pollock
  Pousette-Dart. Amer ptg
  Robertson. Jackson Pollock (col)
Number 14, 1948
  MMA. Jackson Pollock
  O'Hara. Jackson Pollock
  Robertson. Jackson Pollock
Number 14, 1951
  MMA. Jackson Pollock
  O'Hara. Jackson Pollock
  Robertson. Jackson Pollock
Number 16, 1950
  Robertson. Jackson Pollock
Number 17, 1949
  Robertson. Jackson Pollock
Number 22A, 1948
  MnU. 40 Amer ptrs
Number 23, 1949
  Time. 300 years (col)
Number 23, 1951
  Selz. New images
Number 24, 1948
  O'Hara. Jackson Pollock
  Robertson. Jackson Pollock
Number 26, 1951
  O'Hara. Jackson Pollock
Number 27, 1950   WMAA
  Goodrich. Amer art (col)
  O'Hara. Jackson Pollock
Number 27, 1951
  MMA. New Amer ptg
  O'Hara. Jackson Pollock
  PPC. International ex, 1952
  Robertson. Jackson Pollock
Number 28, 1950
  O'Hara. Jackson Pollock
  Robertson. Jackson Pollock (col)
Number 28, 1951
  Robertson. Jackson Pollock
Number 29, 1950
  Gardner 1959 ed
  MMA. Jackson Pollock
  O'Hara. Jackson Pollock
  Robertson. Jackson Pollock
Number 32, 1950
  Janson. Key monuments
  MMA. Jackson Pollock
  O'Hara. Jackson Pollock
  Robertson. Jackson Pollock
Number 32 (Frogman) 1951
  O'Hara. Jackson Pollock
Number 34, 1949   NUM
  Faulkner. Art today, 1956
  NUM. Root bequest

Ocean greyness   NNSG
  Baur. Nature
  Baur. New art
  MMA. Jackson Pollock
  NNSG. Handbook
  NNSG. Younger Amer ptrs
  O'Hara. Jackson Pollock
  Robertson. Jackson Pollock
One
  MMA. Jackson Pollock (col)
  O'Hara. Jackson Pollock
  Ponente. Mod ptg, 1960 (col)
  Robertson. Jackson Pollock (col)
Out of the web
  MMA. Jackson Pollock
  O'Hara. Jackson Pollock (col)
  Robertson. Jackson Pollock (col)
Painting, 1933
  MMA. Jackson Pollock
Painting, c 1944
  Robertson. Jackson Pollock
Painting, 1946
  Robertson. Jackson Pollock
Painting, 1948
  O'Hara. Jackson Pollock
  Robertson. Jackson Pollock (col)
Painting, 1951 (1)
  MMA. Jackson Pollock
  Robertson. Jackson Pollock
Painting, 1951 (2)
  MMA. Jackson Pollock
  O'Hara. Jackson Pollock
  Robertson. Jackson Pollock
Painting, 1956
  Robertson. Jackson Pollock
Panel, c 1936
  Robertson. Jackson Pollock
Pasiphaë
  O'Hara. Jackson Pollock (col)
  Robertson. Jackson Pollock (col)
Phosphorescence   MAP
  NUM. Art across America
Portrait and a dream
  O'Hara. Jackson Pollock
  Read. Concise history (col)
  Robertson. Jackson Pollock (col)
Ritual
  O'Hara. Jackson Pollock
Scent
  Eliot. Art of our time (col)
  O'Hara. Jackson Pollock
  O'Hara. Jackson Pollock (col detail)
  Robertson. Jackson Pollock (col)
  Time. 300 years (col)
Search
  O'Hara. Jackson Pollock (col)
  Robertson. Jackson Pollock
Seascape
  O'Hara. Jackson Pollock
  Robertson. Jackson Pollock (col)
Shadows
  Bazin
  Robertson. Jackson Pollock
The she-wolf   MMA
  MMA. Contemp ptrs
  O'Hara. Jackson Pollock
  Read. Concise history
  Robertson. Jackson Pollock (col)
Shimmering substance
  Art since 1945
  MMA. Jackson Pollock
  O'Hara. Jackson Pollock
  Robertson. Jackson Pollock

Silver square
  O'Hara. Jackson Pollock
Sleeping effort   MoSLW
  O'Hara. Jackson Pollock
  Robertson. Jackson Pollock
Summertime
  O'Hara. Jackson Pollock
  Robertson. Jackson Pollock
There were seven in eight
  O'Hara. Jackson Pollock
  Robertson. Jackson Pollock.
Three
  O'Hara. Jackson Pollock
Totem I, 1944
  MMA. Jackson Pollaok
  O'Hara. Jackson Pollock
  Robertson. Jackson Pollock
Totem II, 1945
  Leepa
  O'Hara. Jackson Pollock
Totem (lesson I) 1945
  Read. Art now, 1948 ed
Two
  Robertson. Jackson Pollock
Unformed figure
  O'Hara. Jackson Pollock
  Robertson. Jackson Pollock
Untitled
  CSFP. Annual ex, 1950/51
Untitled, c 1936
  O'Hara. Jackson Pollock
  Robertson. Jackson Pollock
Untitled, 1937
  O'Hara. Jackson Pollock
  Robertson. Jackson Pollock
Untitled, 1945 (Bareiss coll)
  Robertson. Jackson Pollock
Untitled, 1945 (Stuart coll)
  Robertson. Jackson Pollock
Untitled, 1950
  O'Hara. Jackson Pollock
  Robertson. Jackson Pollock
White cockatoo
  O'Hara. Jackson Pollock
  Robertson. Jackson Pollock (col)
White horizontal
  O'Hara. Jackson Pollock
White light
  O'Hara. Jackson Pollock
  Ponente. Mod ptg, 1960 (col)
  Robertson. Jackson Pollock
White on black I, 1949
  O'Hara. Jackson Pollock
White on black II, 1949
  Robertson. Jackson Pollock
Wounded beast (Wounded animal)
  CtY. Yale alumni
  O'Hara. Jackson Pollock
Polly by E. E. Speicher
Polo. See Games and sports—Polo
POLONSKY, Arthur, 1925-
Marine Sampson
  MBIC. View 1960
Pomeroy, Asahel, 1749-1833
  Unidentified artist. Asahel Pomeroy
Pomeroy, Louise. See Inches, Louise (Pomeroy)
Pompeii by W. A. Baziotes
Pompous boy by W. Sommer
POND, Dana
  Pastor De Segovia
    NAD. Annual ex, 1956

The pond by H. Hofmann
The pond by A. P. Ryder
Pont Alexandre by J. Marin
Pont de Minimes, Chartres by H. R. Newman
Le Pont Neuf by A. Blatas
Le Pont Neuf by W. Howard
Ponte della Paglia by M. B. Prendergast
Ponte Margherita by J. Stefanelli
Ponte Vecchio by L. Bosa
Ponte Vecchio by A. J. Pucci
Pony ballet by W. J. Glackens
Pool sisters, fl 1845
  Unidentified artist. The Pool sisters
Pool. See Games and sports—Pool
The pool by L. Eilshemius
The pool by B. Shahn
Pool room by D. S. Bloom
Poor, Charlotte (White) 1782-1863
  Malbone, E. G. Mrs Moses Poor
POOR, Henry Varnum, 1888-
  Anne
    NYG. Fine art
  Artist in summer
    PA. Annual ex, 1951
  Autumn fruit   WMAA
    Goodrich. Amer art
  The bull
    PPC. Ptg in the U.S. 1949
  Chess game
    Gruskin
  Flowered hat
    Genauer
  Fruit   MM
    MM. 100 Amer ptrs
  Picture hat
    Genauer
  Pink tablecloth   OCl
    Baur. Revolution
  Pierson
  Summer bouquet   ATeS
    ATeS. Collection
  White cloud
    IU. Contemp Amer ptg, 1948
Poor, Mrs Moses. See Poor, Charlotte (White)
The poor artist's cupboard by C. B. King
The poor author and the rich bookseller by W. Allston
Poor man's store by J. F. Peto
Poor room—There is no time, no end, no today, no yesterday, no tomorrow, only the forever and forever and forever without end by I. L. Albright
POORE, Henry Rankin, 1859-1940
  Hound
    NSP. Sportscapes
POPE, Alexander, 1849-1924
  Pups in transit
    Frankenstein. After the hunt
  Sportman's still life
    Frankenstein. After the hunt
  Still life
    Frankenstein. After the hunt
Pope, Anna (Hammond) fl 1800
  Greenleaf, B. Mrs Anna Hammond Pope
POPE, Arthur, 1880-
  Christianbury crags, Scotland, from the road to Langholm   MB
    MB. Ptgs in water color

Pope, Mrs Joseph. See Pope, Anna (Hammond)
Poperinghe: two soldiers by J. S. Sargent
Popham beach, Maine by W. Zorach
Poplar trees by C. E. Burchfield
Poppi in the Casentino, Tuscany, E. D. Boit
Poppies by C. H. Demuth
Poppies by G. O'Keeffe
Poppies by M. A. Phillips
Poppies by M. Silverman
Poppies in blue vase by M. B. Prendergast
Population—3000 by C. F. Gaertner
The porch by P. Guston
Porch no 2 by J. W. Treiman
Porch no 2, 1946-47 by P. Guston
Porcupine
   Audubon, J. J. American porcupine
The porphyry jar by D. M. Lockman
Port at night by R. Morgan
The port from New York interpreted by
   J. Stella
Port Hudson, Battle of, 1863
   Arnold, E. Battle of Port Hudson, 1863
Port Jefferson by Leonid
Port of call by S. M. Etnier
The portage by W. Homer
The portal by O. M. Pleissner
Port-au-Prince, Haiti
   Dehn, A. A. Market, Port-au-Prince, Haiti
Portentous sunset by L. Feininger
Porter, David, 1780-1843
   Unidentified artist. Commodore David
      Porter
PORTER, David, 1912-
   Pegasus
      IU. Contemp Amer ptg & sculp, 1953
   Sunrise in the stratosphere
      IU. Contemp Amer ptg & sculp, 1961
Porter, Noah, 1811-1892
   Johnson, E. Noah Porter
PORTER, Rufus, 1792-1884
   Hudson river highlands
      Lipman. Primitive ptrs
   Orchard scene
      Lipman. Primitive ptrs
   Rural scene
      Lipman. Primitive ptrs
   Sacrifice of Isaac
      Lipman. Primitive ptrs
Portland, Maine, View near by C. Codman
Portland pier, Lake Erie by G. Harvey
Portrait and a dream by J. Pollock
Portrait—Bear by B. Kopman
Portrait in studio light by R. Brackman
Portrait of a grand lady by M. Cassatt
Portrait of a poet by J. Glasco
Portrait of A. S. 1925 by A. G. Dove
Portrait of myself when young by B. Shahn
Portrait study in a doorway by C. E. Burchfield
Portuguese sea by Leonid
Pose downtown by M. Gordon
Poseidon by J. E. Levi
The possessed by R. Lytle
Post, Catalynje, fl 1730
   Unidentified artist. Catalynje Post

POST, Herman, 1873?-1939
   Elevated railway, Berlin   CtY
   CtY. Soc Anonyme
Post, Jennie, fl 1835
   Ellsworth, J. S. Mrs Jennie Post
POST, Shelly
   The courtesan
      NAD. Annual ex, 1949, 1st half
Post office by D. G. Blythe
The poster by R. Vickrey
Poster portrait of O'Keeffe by C. H. Demuth
Potatoes and onions by B. Perlin
Poultry market by Walter Williams
Pounding surf by F. J. Waugh
Pouring coffee by R. Diebenkorn
POUSETTE-DART, Nathaniel J. 1886-
   Renaissance
      Pousette-Dart. Amer ptg
POUSETTE-DART, Richard, 1916-
   Blue amorphous
      WMAA. New decade
   Golden dawn
      Baur. Nature
   Golden reverie
      IU. Contemp Amer ptg, 1952
      NBuA. Expressionism
   Illumination
      PPC. International ex, 1958
   In the forest   NBuA
      NBuA. Acquisitions 1957-58
   The magnificent   WMAA
      Cheney. Story 1958 ed
      Goodrich. Amer art
      Pierson
      Pousette-Dart. Amer ptg
      WMAA. New decade
   Number 11: a presence   MMA
      MMA. Abstract
   Subterranean
      IU. Contemp Amer ptg, 1951
   White garden
      IU. Contemp Amer ptg & sculp, 1953
   White reverie
      WMAA. New decade
Powder magazine, Fort Duquesne, Pennsylvania by R. Smith
POWELL, H. M. T. fl 1849-1858
   J. M. Studebaker in his wagon tire shop
      at Hangtown, California, 1853   DN
   U.S. National Capital sesquicentennial
      com
POWELL, Leslie, 1906-
   Mill wheel   ATU
      ATU. Coll of Amer art
Power, Nicholas, 1771-1844
   Malbone, E. G. Nicholas Power
Power, Rebecca, fl 1803
   Malbone, E. G. Rebecca Power
Power line by C. F. Ryder
Power of music by W. S. Mount
Power of the law by E. H. Blashfield
POWERS, Marilyn, 1925-
   Still life
      MBIC. View 1960
Powers, Thomas E. fl 1858
   Mason, B. F. Dr Thomas E. Powers
POZZATTI, Rudy O. 1925-
   Citta della torre
      WMAA. Young America 1960
   The denial   OYB
      OYB. Annual 1952

Limestone quarry
  WMAA. Annual ex, 1956
Nebraska landscape
  IU. Contemp Amer ptg & sculp, 1957
Red rocks
  WMAA. Young America 1960
Yesterday   OYB
  OYB. Annual 1951
  OYB. Catalogue 1951
Pozzuoli red by A. G. Dove
Prairie by A. J. Miller
Prairie bluffs burning, upper Missouri by G. Catlin
Prairie burial by W. T. Ranney
Prairie encampment by J. M. Stanley
Prairie fire by G. Catlin
Prairie fire by C. Deas
Prairie fire by W. T. Ranney
Prairie landscape by A. Rattner
Prairie on fire by A. J. Miller
Prairie scene: mirage by A. J. Miller
Prairie sky by A. Rattner
PRATT, Henry Cheever, 1803-1880
  On the Ammonoosuc river   MB
    MB. Karolik coll
  View on the Rio Gila, 1855
    U.S. National Capital sesquicentennial com
Pratt, Hiram, fl 1839
  Tuthill, A. G. D. Hiram Pratt
Pratt, Mary Bryant. See Brandegee, Mary Bryant (Pratt)
PRATT, Matthew, 1734-1805
  American school   MM
    Barker. Amer ptg
    Davidson v 1
    ICA. From colony to nation
    Pierson
    Richardson. Ptg in America
    Roos
    Taylor. Fifty centuries, 1954 ed (col)
    U.S. National Capital sesquicentennial com
  Benjamin West   PA
    Chew. 250 years of art
    Pierson
  Cadwallader Colden and Warren de Lancey
    Flexner. Light of distant skies
  John Bush   MWA
    Larkin
    Larkin rev ed
  Mrs Benjamin West   PA
    Pierson
Prayer makers by L. Daniel
Precipice by E. F. Spruce
Precision bombing by G. L. K. Morris
Preening sparrow by M. Graves
PREGEL, Alexandra (Avxentieff) 1907-
  Fruit and daisies
    NAD. Annual ex, 1947, 1st half
Pregel, Mrs Boris. See Pregel, Alexandra (Avxentieff)
Prehistoric construction by A. Russell
Prehistoric playground by M. Tobey
Preliminary examination by D. Levine
Première by S. Davis

PRENDERGAST, Charles, 1868-1948
  After the show
    CtY. Yale alumni
  Hill town   MAP
    Glackens
PRENDERGAST, James Donald, 1907-
  Young American artist   ATU
    ATU. Coll of Amer art
PRENDERGAST, Maurice Brazil, 1859-1924
  Acadia   MMA
    Hunter. Mod Amer ptg (col)
    MMA. Masters (col)
  Afternoon, Pincian hill, Rome   DP
    Canaday
    DP. Catalogue
  Along the boulevard, Paris   NBuA
    MB. Prendergast
    NBuA. Contemporary ptgs
  Along the coast
    MB. Prendergast
  April snow (DP). See Snow in April
  April snow, Salem   MMA
    MB. Prendergast (col)
    Pierson
  At the beach
    Lewisohn
  At the shore   MAP
    Cheney. Story 1958 ed
  Autumn festival   DP
    Baur. New art (col)
    DP. Catalogue
    Pierson
  The balloon   MAP
    MB. Prendergast (col)
  Bareback rider, Paris   OCl
    MB. Prendergast
  Bartol church. See West church, Boston
  Bastille day (Le quatorze juillet) 1892   OCl
    MB. Prendergast
  The bathers
    MB. Prendergast
  Bathing, Marblehead   MB
    MB. Ptgs in water color
  Beach at Gloucester
    MB. Prendergast
  Beach late afternoon, Maine   MB
    MB. Prendergast
  Beach, St Malo
    MB. Prendergast
  Beach scene with figures
    MB. Prendergast
  Beach with blue tree
    MB. Prendergast
  Beachmont   CtNB
    McKinney
  Boat landing   CtHW
    CtHW. Handbook
  Boat landing, Dinard
    MB. Prendergast
  A boy   MoKN
    MB. Prendergast
  Bridge and steps, Venice   FaW
    Baur. New art
  Bridge in Venice   OCl
    MB. Prendergast
  Café Florian, Venice
    MB. Prendergast
  Campo Santa Maria Formosa, Venice
    MB. Prendergast (col)
  Cape Ann   MB
    MB. Prendergast

PRENDERGAST, M. B.—*Continued*
  Straw bridge   DP
    UNESCO. 1860-1955
    UNESCO. 1860-1959
  Street scene, Boston
    MB. Prendergast
  Summer
    WMAA. Museum and its friends, 1958
  Summer day
    MB. Prendergast
  Summer in the park
    MB. Prendergast (col)
  Summer outing on the rocks
    MB. Prendergast (col)
  Sunday promenade
    MB. Prendergast
  Sunlight on the Piazzetta, Venice
    MB. Prendergast (col)
  Sunset
    MB. Prendergast
  Sunset and sea fog   OYB
    MB. Prendergast
    OYB. Supplement 1959
    Pierson
    Time. 300 years (col)
  The swans   MAP
    MB. Prendergast
  Tremont street, Boston   MAP
    MB. Prendergast
  Tuileries gardens
    MB. Prendergast
  Two girls in New England woodland
    MB. Prendergast
  Umbrellas in the rain, Venice   MB
    MB. Prendergast (col)
  Venice
    CtY. Yale alumni
  Via delle Corso, Rome. See On the Corso, Rome
  Waterfall
    MB. Prendergast
  West church, Boston, 1909   MB
    MB. Prendergast (col)
  West church, Boston (Bartol church)
    MB. Prendergast
  Wet day, Paris. See Paris boulevard in rain
  Woman arranging her hair
    MB. Prendergast
Preparing for a buffalo hunt by A. J. Miller
Preparing the bill by T. H. Benton
Prescience by C. Howard
Prescott, Harry, fl 1804
  Malbone, E. G. Harry Prescott
Presence of black no 1 by J. Guerrero
The **present** by S. Rosenberg
Presentation of the Virgin by D. Aronson
Presents to Indians by A. J. Miller
The **President,** 1922 by S. Davis
Preston, William C. 1794-1860
  Healy, G. P. A. William C. Preston
Preston ponds, Adirondacks by H. D. Martin
PRESTOPINO, Gregorio, 1907-
  Afternoon sun   OYB
    OYB. Annual 1958
    OYB. Supplement 1959
  Glitter no 3   WMAA
    Pierson

  The market   IU
    IU. Contemp Amer ptg, 1951
    IU. 20th century
  Railroad center
    IU. Contemp Amer ptg, 1959
  Roots
    IU. Contemp Amer ptg, 1952
    Pousette-Dart. Amer ptg
  Summer
    IU. Contemp Amer ptg & sculp, 1955
  Sunset
    IU. Contemp Amer ptg & sculp, 1953
  Trolley car
    Genauer
  Winter   WMAA
    Gruskin
    Pierson
Pretty girl milking the cow by B. Shahn
Pretty ships by M. B. Prendergast
PREUSSER, Robert Ormerod, 1919-
  Directional multiplicity
    Pearson. Mod renaissance
  Prismatic refractions
    Pearson. Mod renaissance
  Twentieth century baroque
    Pearson. Mod renaissance
Priam returning the body of Hector by J. Trumbull
PRICE, Clayton S. 1874-1950
  Abstract landscape
    OrPA. C. S. Price (col)
  Abstraction, 1949
    OrPA. C. S. Price
  Abstraction IV, 1943-45
    OrPA. C. S. Price
  Adobe houses
    MMA. Fourteen
    OrPA. C. S. Price
  Bay mare and colt and a couple of others
    OrPA. C. S. Price
  Bird by the sea   MM
    MM. 100 Amer ptrs
    OrPA. C. S. Price
  Black bird
    OrPA. C. S. Price
  Cattle
    OrPA. C. S. Price
  Cattle by the river
    OrPA. C. S. Price
  Coastline
    OrPA. C. S. Price
  Cow with calf
    OrPA. C. S. Price
  Cowboys at moonlight
    OrPA. C. S. Price
  Cows going to pasture
    OrPA. C. S. Price
  Coyotes
    OrPA. C. S. Price
  The dream
    MMA. Fourteen
    OrPA. C. S. Price (col)
  Fisherman   MiD
    Baur. Revolution
    MMA. Fourteen
    OrPA. C. S. Price
    Pierson
  Fishing village
    OrPA. C. S. Price
  Front street   OrPA
    MMA. Fourteen
    OrPA. C. S. Price

Hay wagon
  OrPA. C. S. Price
Head
  OrPA. C. S. Price
Head (self-portrait)
  OrPA. C. S. Price
Horses   OrPA
  OrPA. C. S. Price
Horses in a barnyard
  OrPA. C. S. Price
Huckleberry pickers   OrPA
  OrPA. C. S. Price
In the mountains
  OrPA. C. S. Price
Mail coach
  OrPA. C. S. Price
Mare and foal
  OrPA. C. S. Price
Mare with colt
  OrPA. C. S. Price
Mule deer
  OrPA. C. S. Price
Night
  OrPA. C. S. Price
Owl
  OrPA. C. S. Price (col)
Plowing   NUM
  OrPA. C. S. Price (col)
The river   OrPA
  CoS. New accession USA, 1950
Self-portrait. See Head
Two birds
  OrPA. C. S. Price
Two heads, c 1935
  OrPA. C. S. Price
Two heads, 1940-42
  OrPA. C. S. Price
Vase of flowers, 1943-45
  OrPA. C. S. Price
Vase of flowers, c 1948
  OrPA. C. S. Price
White mare and foal
  OrPA. C. S. Price
Wolves
  MMA. Fourteen
  OrPA. C. S. Price
Young birds
  OrPA. C. S. Price
PRIEBE, Karl John, 1914-
Early immigrants
  IU. Contemp Amer ptg, 1950
The fronfroneur
  IU. Contemp Amer ptg, 1948
Roos
The socialite
  IU. Contemp Amer ptg, 1949
Priestley, Flora, b 1859
  Sargent, J. S. Flora Priestley
Prima materia by W. Day
Primeval landscape by W. A. Baziotes
Primitive dance by R. Koppe
Prince, Halldis
  Peirce, W. Halldis Prince
La princesse du pays de la porcelaine by
  J. A. M. Whistler
Princeton, Battle of, 1777
  Mercer, W. Battle of Princeton, 1777
  Sanford, M. M. Washington at Princeton
  Trumbull, J. Death of General Mercer
    at the Battle of Princeton

PRINGLE, James, 1788-1847
  Smith and Dimon shipyard, New York,
    1833   NCHA
  U.S. National Capital sesquicentennial
  com
Prioleau, Mary Magdalen. See Grimball,
  Mary Magdalen (Prioleau)
PRIOR, William Matthew, 1806-1873
  The Burnish sisters   DN
    DN. Amer primitive ptgs, pt 1
  Ford. Pictorial folk art (col)
  A gentleman   MeC
  Jetté. Amer heritage collection
  Little child with big dog   NCHA
  Jones. New-found folk art
  Three sisters of the Coplan family MB
  Lipman. Primitive ptrs
  MB. Karolik coll
  Unidentified portrait (of a man) c 1846
  Lipman. Primitive ptrs
  Washington's tomb at Mount Vernon
                    VWR
  VWR. Folk art (col)
  William Allen with greyhounds MB
  Lipman. Primitive ptrs
  MB. Karolik coll
  A young man
  Ford. Pictorial folk art

        Attributed works
  A girl   RPS
  Ford. Pictorial folk art
  Girl seated on bench   VWR
  VWR. Folk art (col)
  Little girl holding apple   DN
  DN. Amer primitive ptgs, pt 2
  A man   NJN
  Ford. Pictorial folk art
  Two children with their dog Minny MSt
  Little. Country art
  NUM. Art across America
  Unknown woman   MSt
  Little. Country art
  A woman   NJN
  Ford. Pictorial folk art

         Manner of
  Brother and sister sharing a book
                   NCHA
  Jones. New-found folk art
  Fireman   NCHA
  Jones. New-found folk art
  Lady in a fine scarf   NCHA
  Jones. New-found folk art
  Three children   NCHA
  Jones. New-found folk art
  William Whipper   NCHA
  Jones. New-found folk art
Prior to by J. S. Cleary
Prize flowers by C. C. Ross
Prismatic refractions by R. O. Preusser
Prisoner by J. Hirsch
Prisoners from the front by W. Homer
Pro Deo, pro populo by F. Whitaker
PROBST, Joachim, 1913-
  Christ in thorns
  IU. Contemp Amer ptg & sculp, 1959
Procession by M. Manigault
Procession of the Savior by L. Bosa
Procession, Venice by M. B. Prendergast
Processional by E. A. Chavez

Processional by W. Mitchell

The processional by H. Saslow

Prodigal son by R. Cowles

Prodigal son by R. Devoll

Prodigal son by R. Haines

Prodigal son by B. West

The prodigal son among swine by M. Beckmann

The prodigal son gambling by Unidentified
artist

The prodigal son in misery by Unidentified
artist

The prodigal son receiving his patrimony by
Unidentified artist

The prodigal son reclaimed by A. Doolittle

The prodigal son reclaimed by Unidentified
artist

The prodigal son reclaimed by his father
by M. A. Willson

The prodigal son reveling with harlots by
Unidentified artist

Prodigious industrial phenomenon by J.
De Diego

Profanation of the host by D. Tanning

Professional painters by D. D. Dennison

Professionals at rehearsal by T. Eakins

Professor Hunter Worrell's pipe by G. Cope

Profile by D. Joe

Profile of a boy by R. H. M. Bascom

Profile of baby in orange by R. H. M.
Bascom

Profiles no 8 by N. Tschacbasov

The progenitors by C. Howard

PROHASKA, Ray, 1901-
Space between
IU. Contemp Amer ptg & sculp, 1953

Project for a monument: the apotheosis of
Nelson by B. West

Projecting planes by I. R. Pereira

Promenade by C. E. Burchfield

Promenade by C. Cloar

Promenade by M. B. Prendergast

Promenade by M. Ray

Promenade, France by M. B. Prendergast

Promenade, Gloucester by M. B. Prendergast

Promenade on the beach by W. Homer

Promenade on the pier, Nantasket by M. B.
Prendergast

Prometheus by E. Friedensohn

Prometheus by R. Lytle

Prometheus bound by T. Cole

Prometheus in Rockefeller center by R.
Marsh

Prometheus rebound by G. Palazzola

Promise of immortality by J. La Farge

The promontory by J. De Martini

Prong-horned antelope by J. W. Audubon

Prophecy by S. Pace

The prophet by H. Koerner

Prophetic light by M. Tobey

The proposal by C. M. Russell

Proposal on horseback by P. Evergood

The Propylaea, Athens by H. B. Warren

Proserpina by E. Berman

Prospect park, Brooklyn by W. M. Chase

Prospect rock, Essex county, N.Y. by W.
Homer

Prospecting by D. G. Blythe

Prospectors by Unidentified artist

Prosser, Evelina Matilda. See Tabb, Mrs
John

Protection by W. M. Harnett (attributed
works)

Proudfit, Alexander, 1770-1843
Jarvis, J. W. Rev Alexander Proudfit

Proudfit, Susan (Williams) 1780-1852
Jarvis, J. W. Mrs Alexander Proudfit

Prout's Neck, breakers by W. Homer

PROVAN, Sara, 1917-
Bird, fish, fruit
MM. Amer ptg today
Delicate board
IU. Contemp Amer ptg & sculp, 1953

Provincetown, Massachusetts
Corbett, E. Provincetown no 2
Corbett, E. Provincetown no 6
Harmon, L. Provincetown
Isenburger, E. Sea and wharf at Prov-
incetown
Knaths, K. Provincetown jamboree
Leonid. Provincetown
Sterne, M. Provincetown seascape

Provoost, David, 1642-1720?
Unidentified artist. David Provoost (?)

Provoost, Margareta. See Van Brugh, Margareta (Provoost)

Provost, George, fl 1805
Ames, E. Major George Provost

Provost, Tryntje (Laurens) b 1650
Unidentified artist. Mrs David Provoost
(?)

Prudence by F. C. Watkins

The pruner by G. C. Lambdin

The pseudolucànus reconsidered by J. Wilde

Public gardens, Boston by G. L. Brown

PUCCI, Albert John
Night
NAD. Annual ex, 1951
Ponte Vecchio
NAD. Annual ex, 1955

PUCCI, Gigi Ford
Clothesline
NAD. Annual ex, 1949, 1st half

Puddle by L. MacIver

Pue, Elinor S. F.
Eakins, T. Miss Elinor S. F. Pue

Pue, Rebecca, 1812-1884
Hubard, W. J. Rebecca Pue

Pueblo and mesa, Taos mountains by J.
Marin

Pulitzer, Joseph, 1847-1911
Sargent, J. S. Joseph Pulitzer

Pulitzer, Louise
Beckmann, M. Louise Pulitzer

Pulsation of light by B. Margo

PUMA, Fernando, 1919-1955
Eternal world
IU. Contemp Amer ptg, 1952
Moon bathers
Cheney. Primer 1958 ed

Punishment by G. Grosz

Puppet and child by S. Serisawa

Puppets by G. S. Ratkai

Pups in transit by A. Pope
Purification series by M. Graves
The purist by I. L. Albright
Purlieu by J. Wolfe
Purple abyss, Grand canyon, Arizona by
    D. Macknight
Purple brook by D. Macknight
Purple grackle by J. J. Audubon
Purple petunias by E. W. Motley
Purple pup by C. H. Demuth
Pursuer and pursued by W. Rimmer
Pursuit by J. Madson
Pursuit by R. Marsh
Pursuit in depth by G. L. K. Morris
La push by W. W. Baumgartner
Push and pull by H. Hofmann
Pushing for rail by T. Eakins
PUSHMAN, Hovsep, 1877-
    When autumn is here   IU
      NYG. Fine art (col)
Putnam, Israel, 1718-1790
    Unidentified artist. General Putnam
    Unidentified artist. General Putnam's leap
Putnam, Rufus, 1738-1824
    Turnbull, J. Rufus Putnam
PUTNAM, Wallace B. 1899-
    Sheep in fog   CtY
      CtY. Soc Anonyme
The puzzled witness by G. C. Bingham
PYLE, Howard, 1853-1911
    Thomas Jefferson
      Larkin (detail)
PYTLAK, Leonard, 1910-
    Winter rhythm
      NAD. Annual ex 1946, 2d half

Q

Q—1952 by J. D. Brooks
Quadrigraph by I. R. Pereira
Quadrilaterals by H. Bertoia
Quail
    Hill, T. The covey
    Platt, G. W. Quail
Quaker mother and child by H. Pippin
Qualm by J. D. Brooks
QUANCHI, Leon William, 1892-
    Dry nets
      IU. Contemp Amer ptg, 1951
Quappi in turban by M. Beckmann
The quarantined citadel by P. Evergood
The quarrel by F. Remington
The quarry by J. De Martini
The quarry by M. Friedman
Quarry pool by J. F. Folinsbee
Quarry pool by J. De Martini
Quatic by J. D. Brooks
Le quatorze juillet by M. B. Prendergast
Quebec by P. Dickinson

Quebec, Battle of, 1775
    Trumbull, J. Attack on Quebec
    Trumbull, J. Death of General Montgom-
      ery at Quebec
Queen of clubs by K. Knaths
Queen Philippa interceding for the burgesses
    of Calais by B. West
Queen's gambit by F. Hillsmith
QUIDOR, John, 1801-1881
    Battle scene from Knickerbocker's His-
      tory of New York   MB
      MB. Karolik coll
      Pierson
    The devil and Tom Walker
      MiD. Coll in progress
      Richardson. Ptg in America
      WiMiA. Amer ptg 1760-1960
    Ichabod Crane at a ball at the Van Tassel
      mansion
      NUM. Art across America
    Ichabod Crane pursued by the Headless
      Horseman   CtY
      Larkin
      Larkin rev ed
    Leatherstocking defies the law   NCHA
      Davidson v2
    Money diggers   NBM
      Baur. Amer ptg
      DC. De gustibus
      Pierson
    Paul Revere   ATeS
      AteS. Collection
    Return of Rip Van Winkle   DN
      Davidson v 1
      Mendelowitz
      OCiM. Rediscoveries
    Rip Van Winkle at Nicholas Vedder's
      tavern   MB
      MB. Karolik coll
      Time. 300 years (col)
    Tom Walker's flight
      MiD. Coll in progress
      WiMiA. Amer ptg 1760-1960
    Voyage to Hell Gate from Communipaw
                         KW
      Pierson
    Wolfert's will   NBM
      Barker. Amer ptg
      Flexner. Amer ptg
      Flexner. Short history
      Pierson
      Roos
Quiescent space by T. Benrimo
A quiet day in Utica by C. M. Russell
Quiet day, Lisbon, F. Cabral
Quiet pond by C. E. Burchfield
Quiet river by C. A. Morris
Quiet street by D. A. White
Quilting party by J. L. Krimmel
Quilting party by Unidentified artist
Quimper at night by L. Feininger
QUINCY, Edmond, 1903-
    View from my window   ATU
      ATU. Coll of Amer art
Quincy, Eliza Susan (Morton) 1775-1850
    Stuart, G. Mrs Josiah Quincy
Quincy, Josiah, 1772-1864
    Stuart, G. Josiah Quincy
QUIRK, Thomas Charles, 1922-
    Vigil at the beach   OYB
      OYB. Annual 1957
      OYB. Suppplement 1959

QUIRT, Walter Wellington, 1902-
Agrarian dishabille
Coates. Walter Quirt
The apostle
Coates. Walter Quirt
Carnival   MAP
Rathbun
Day's end
Coates. Walter Quirt
Descent from the cross no 3, 1957/58
Coates. Walter Quirt
Descent from the cross no 5, 1958
Coates. Walter Quirt
Dilemma
Coates. Walter Quirt
Double indemnity
Coates. Walter Quirt
Doubt
Coates. Walter Quirt
Eternal pageant
Coates. Walter Quirt
The evil of drink
Coates. Walter Quirt
Experience of tragedy yet to come
MnU. 40 Amer ptrs
The eyes have it
Coates. Walter Quirt
Fun
Coates. Walter Quirt
Green and lavender horse
Coates. Walter Quirt
Horses and man
Coates. Walter Quirt
The hunt
Coates. Walter Quirt
Indian penny
Coates. Walter Quirt
Lone cowboy
Coates. Walter Quirt
The loner
Coates. Walter Quirt
Madonna
Coates. Walter Quirt
Man meets woman, tips hat
MM. Amer ptg today
Man of sorrows no 3, 1958
Coates. Walter Quirt
Memories
Coates. Walter Quirt
Mutation   WMAA
Pierson
A nervous woman
Coates. Walter Quirt
Old man
Coates. Walter Quirt
Origin of life
Coates. Walter Quirt
ICA. Annual ex, 1947/48
Leepa
Race against time
Coates. Walter Quirt
Radiance
Coates. Walter Quirt
Reflection
Coates. Walter Quirt
The road with no turn
Coates. Walter Quirt
Rush the wind
Coates. Walter Quirt
Separate worlds
Coates. Walter Quirt
Shipwrecks
Coates. Walter Quirt

Sleeping man
Coates. Walter Quirt
Song of the guitar
Coates. Walter Quirt
The soul leaving the body
Coates. Walter Quirt
Talk
Coates. Walter Quirt
Tittering female
Coates. Walter Quirt (col)
Tragedy is self-contained
MnU. 40 Amer ptrs
Tranquillity of previous existence   MMA
Larkin
Larkin rev ed
Triumphant child
MnMW. Classic tradition
Two-figure composition
Coates. Walter Quirt
Two women
Coates. Walter Quirt
The very great lion hunters
Coates. Walter Quirt
White light
Coates. Walter Quirt
Woman
Coates. Walter Quirt
Woman of sorrows no 1, 1958
Coates. Walter Quirt (col)
Quoddy Head, Maine coast by J. Marin

R

R-1953 by J. Brooks
R, M. fl 1821
Mrs George William Blunt
MB. New England miniatures
The **rabbi** by M. Weber
Raccoon by A. N. Wyeth
Race against time by W. W. Quirt
Race in the sun by S. Goedike
Race track by J. Corbino
Race track by W. J. Glackens
Race track by A. P. Ryder
Rachel weeping by C. W. Peale
Racing skerry cruisers by L. Feininger
The **rack** by J. G. Bruff
The **rack** by J. F. Peto
Rack picture with portrait of Lincoln by J. F. Peto
Radar by J. Xceron
Radcliffe, Thomas, 1776-1806
Malbone, E. G. Thomas Radcliffe
Radiance by W. W. Quirt
Radiant night by O. F. Bluemner
Radiant space by H. Hofmann
Radiant springtime by C. E. Burchfield
Radio tubes by S. Davis
RADOMSKI, Alphonse F.
Things I loved and did not keep
NAD. Annual ex, 1949, 1st half
RADULOVIC, Savo, 1911-
Surgery
Time. 300 years (col)

RAFFO, Steve
La casa de Dios
  PA. Annual ex, 1948
Vote for me
  PPC. Ptg in the U.S. 1949
The **raft** by T. Doughty
Raft on the river by Unidentified artist
Raftsmen at night by G. C. Bingham
Raftsmen playing cards by G. C. Bingham
The **Ragan** sisters by J. Eichholtz
Rogers, Daniel Denison, fl 1780
  Copley, J. S. (attributed works) Daniel
    D. Rogers
Rail shooting by T. Eakins
Rail shooting by J. N. Hess
The **railroad** bridge by W. Stuempfig
Railroad center by G. Prestopino
Railroad engine, the Star by Unidentified
    artist
Railroad jubilee on Boston common by W.
    Sharp
Railroad men by P. Evergood
Railroads
  Becker, J. First train on the Central
    Pacific railroad, 1869
  Burchfield, C. E. Railroad in spring
  Henry, E. L. The 9:45 accommodation,
    Stratford, Connecticut, 1867
  Moses, A. M. R. Hoosick falls in winter
  Pachner, W. German train
  Pickett, J. Manchester valley
  Russell, C. M. Trail of the iron horse
  Sample, P. S. Freight cars in desert
  Sintzenich, E. Train leaving Auburn sta-
    tion at Rochester, New York
  Williamson, C. M. First Texas Central
    railroad
RAIN, Charles Wheldon, 1911-
  Approaching storm
    IU. Contemp Amer ptg & sculp, 1957
  Daymare   ATeS
    ATeS. Collection
    IU. Contemp Amer ptg, 1951
  Equinox
    CSEP. Annual ex, 1948/49
    IU. Contemp Amer ptg, 1949
  Faraway
    IU. Contemp Amer ptg, 1950 (col)
  Ice cream vendor
    IU. Contemp Amer ptg & sculp, 1953
  Summer's end
    VR. Amer ptg, 1954
Rain on Park south by F. Wong
Rain on the river by G. W. Bellows
Rain or snow by A. G. Dove
Rainbow fiend by G. Grosz
Rainbow trout by P. R. Goodwin
Rainbows
  Beckmann, M. The rainbow
  Bierstadt, A. Jenny lake, Wyoming
  Bierstadt, A. Rainbow over Jenny lake
  Inness, G. The rainbow
Rainsford's island, Boston harbor by R. W.
    Salmon
Rainstorm by K. Schrag
Rainstorm on the moors by B. West (at-
    tributed works)
Rainy day by F. W. Benson
Rainy day, Boston by C. Hassam

Rainy morning by C. M. Russell
Rainy night by A. Bohrod
Rainy night by C. E. Burchfield
A **rainy** ride by L. Dodd
Rainy season by P. Hurd
Raising a house, New York by W. P.
    Chappel
Raising of Lazarus by S. G. Reinhardt
Raising of Lazarus by B. West
Raising the cross by R. Philipp
RAKOCY, William, 1914-
  Landscape with blue-violet
    OYB. Annual 1954
Ram by J. Youngerman
Ramapo river near Suffern, New York by
    J. Marin
Ramoncita by A. Dasburg
Rampart street by L. Guglielmi
The **ramparts** by J. W. Taylor
The **ramparts**—Quebec by P. Dickinson
The **ramparts**, St Malo by O. M. Pleissner
Ram's head by X. Gonzalez
Ram's head, hollyhock, little hills by G.
    O'Keeffe
Ram's skull with brown leaves by G.
    O'Keeffe
Ramsay-Polk family at Carpenter's Point,
    Maryland by J. Peale
RAMSEY, Milne, 1846-
  Still life, 1911
  Frankenstein. After the hunt
Ranch life, western Texas by H. G. Keller
Ranchos church by G. O'Keeffe
Ranchos church, front by G. O'Keeffe
Rand, Benjamin Howard
  Eakins, T. Benjamin Howard Rand
Rand, Jasper Raymond, fl 1845
  Stock, J. W. Jasper Raymond Rand
RANDALL, A. M. fl 1777
  Basket of fruit with parrot   DN
    DN. Amer primitive ptgs, pt 2
Randolph, John, 1773-1833
  Harding, C. John Randolph of Roanoke
  Jarvis, J. W. John Randolph
  Stuart, G. John Randolph
Randolph, Mary. See Bolling, Mary (Ran-
    dolph)
Random pattern by G. Kepes
RANGER, Henry Ward, 1858-1916
  Connecticut woods   DNC
  Born
  High bridge   MM
  Born
Rankin children
  Eddy, O. T. Four youngest children of
    William Rankin and Abigail Ogden
    Rankin
RANNEY, William Tylee, 1813-1857
  Caravan on the prairies
    Rathbone
  Duck hunters on the Hoboken marshes
                                             MB
    MB. Karolik coll
  The lasso
    Rathbone
  Pioneers
    Rathbone

RANNEY, W. T.—*Continued*
Prairie burial
Rathbone
Prairie fire
McCracken. Portrait of the old west
Rathbone
Retreat
Rathbone
Scouting party
Rathbone
Trappers
Rathbone

RANNEY, William Tylee, 1813-1857 and **MOUNT, William Sidney,** 1807-1868
Pipe of friendship   NJN
NJN. Early N.J. artists

Rapalje, Anna. See Duyckinck, Anna (Rapalje)

Rapalje children
Durand, J. Children of Helena Nyse Rapalje of New York city

Rapidity of sleep by Y. Tanguy

The **rapids,** Hudson river, Adirondacks by W. Homer

Rapt at Rappaport's by S. Davis

Rare birds by E. Ludens

Rasalus by J. D. Brooks

Rathbone, Elijah, 1792-1849
Rowley, R. Elijah Rathbone

Rathbone, Eliza (Betts) 1803-1873
Rowley, R. Eliza Betts Rathbone

Rathbone, Mrs Elijah. See Rathbone, Eliza (Betts)

The **Rathskeller** by J. Sloan

RATKAI, George Stephen, 1907-
Altar boys
IU. Contemp Amer ptg & sculp, 1957
Hurdy-gurdy
IU. Contemp Amer ptg, 1951
Night music
IU. Contemp Amer ptg & sculp, 1955
Puppets
PPC. Ptg in the U. S. 1949
Revelers   OYB
OYB. Annual 1956
OYB. Supplement 1959
Wise bird
IU. Contemp Amer ptg & sculp, 1953

RATTNER, Abraham, 1895-
April showers
MnMW. Contemporary
Pierson
Riley. Your art heritage
Wight. Milestones (col)
WMAA. Four Amer expressionists
WMAA. Neuberger collection
Bird bath   NBuA
NBuA. Contemporary ptgs
The bride
CanO. Hirshhorn coll
City still life   MnMW
Larkin
Clowns and kings
Genauer
WMAA. Four Amer expressionists
Composition
Getlein. Abraham Rattner
Composition: Don Quixote
PPC. Ptg in the U. S. 1949
Composition—Farmscape no 3, 1955
Baur. Nature

Composition, head and flowers
Getlein. Abraham Rattner
Composition with old shoes
Getlein. Abraham Rattner
Composition with three figures
Cheney. Story 1958 ed
DC. 23 biennial ex, 1953
Time. 300 years (col)
Costume figure with mask
Getlein. Abraham Rattner
Crucifixion   IaDM
CoS. New accessions USA, 1952
Crucifixion in yellow
WMAA. Four Amer expressionists
Dark rain   NJN
Getlein. Abraham Rattner
Design for the memory
Getlein. Abraham Rattner
The emperor   WMAA
Baur. Revolution
Mendelowitz
Myers
Pierson
Evening garden
MM. Amer ptg today
MnU. 40 Amer ptrs
Farm composition no 1
Pearson. Mod renaissance
Pousette-Dart. Amer ptg
Farm still life
Getlein. Abraham Rattner
Figure and mask   IU
IU. Contemp Amer ptg, 1950 (col)
Pierson
WMAA. Four Amer expressionists
Figure with wings and mask
PPC. International ex, 1950
Figures waiting
UNESCO. 1860-1955
UNESCO. 1860-1959
WMAA. Four Amer expressionists
Fisherman
Pearson. Mod renaissance
Flying trapeze
Getlein. Abraham Rattner
Gargoyles no 5, Paris
IU. Contemp Amer ptg & sculp, 1961
Gothic enflamed
Getlein. Abraham Rattner
Heads
Getlein. Abraham Rattner
Industrial town   ATeS
ATeS. Collection
Job no 2, 1958
Getlein. Abraham Rattner (col)
Job no 9, 1959
Getlein. Abraham Rattner
Lake landscape
WMAA. Four Amer expressionists (col)
The last Don Quixote
WMAA. Four Amer expressionists
Martyr
Getlein. Abraham Rattner
Moses
Getlein. Abraham Rattner
IU. Contemp Amer ptg & sculp, 1959
Mother and child   MMA
Getlein. Abraham Rattner
Of the resistance
Getlein. Abraham Rattner
People on 6th avenue
Gruskin

Pier composition   MoKN
  CoS. New accessions USA, 1956
  IU. Contemp Amer ptg, 1951
Prairie landscape
  Getlein. Abraham Rattner
Prairie sky
  Getlein. Abraham Rattner
  IU. Contemp Amer ptg & sculp, 1955
  (col front)
  MiD. Coll in progress (col cover)
Prairie sky no 6   PPC
  PPC. International ex, 1955
  Read. Concise history
Red tapestry chair
  MnU. 40 Amer ptrs
Rome no 1, 1951-52
  Getlein. Abraham Rattner
Rome no 4, 1951
  IU. Contemp Amer ptg & sculp, 1953
  WMAA. Four Amer expressionists
Self-portrait, 1947
  Getlein. Abraham Rattner (col)
Self-portrait, 1957   MiD
  Getlein. Abraham Rattner
Song of Esther   WMAA
  Goodrich. Amer art (col)
  WMAA. Four Amer expressionists (col)
Still life with mirror
  Pearson. Mod renaissance
Still life with oysters
  UNESCO. 1860-1955
  UNESCO. 1860-1959
Storm composition no 4
  IU. Contemp Amer ptg & sculp, 1957
Temptation of St Anthony
  Getlein. Abraham Rattner
  IU. Contemp Amer ptg, 1949
Transcendence
  NBuA. Expressionism
Valley of dry bones—triptych
  WMAA. Four Amer expressionists
Window cleaner no 1, 1951
  WMAA. Four Amer expressionists
Window cleaner no 3, 1951
  Getlein. Abraham Rattner
Window cleaner, 1953
  UNESCO. 1860-1959
Window composition
  WMAA. Four Amer expressionists
  (col)
Woman cutting bread   MM
  CoS. New accessions USA, 1952
  MM. 100 Amer ptrs
Workman's lunch
  Getlein. Abraham Rattner
Yellow table   OkNU
  NUM. Art across America
RAUSCHENBERG, Robert, 1925-
Curfew
  IU. Contemp Amer ptg & sculp, 1959
  MMA. Sixteen
Double feature
  MMA. Sixteen
The magician
  MMA. Sixteen
Painting with red letter S   NBuA
  NBuA. Acquisitions 1959-1961
  PPC. International ex, 1958
Satellite
  MMA. Sixteen
Second time painting
  PPC. International ex, 1961/62
Summer storm
  MMA. Sixteen

Ravello by R. Morgan
Ravenel, Daniel, c 1734-1774
  Theus, J. Daniel Ravenel
Ravenel, Elizabeth Damaris
  Theus, J. Elizabeth Damaris Ravenel and
  her sister
Ravenel, Elizabeth Jane (Ravenel) 1734-1809
  Theus, J. Mrs Daniel Ravenel
Ravenel, Susanne. See Mazyck, Susanne
  (Ravenel)
The ravine by H. Hofmann
RAY, Man, 1890-
  Admiration of the orchestrelle for the
    cinematograph   MMA
  Pierson.
  Aerograph
    Baur. New art
    MMA. Abstract
  Black widow
    McCurdy
    MMA. Abstract
  Interior, 1915   PPhM
    PPhM. Gallatin coll
  Invention—dance
    Brown. Amer ptg
  Jazz   OCo
    Brown. Amer ptg
  Mime
    WMAA. Pioneers
  Promenade   CtY
    CtY. Soc Anonyme
  Rope dancer accompanies herself with her
    shadows   MMA
    Baur. New art (col)
    Hunter. Mod Amer ptg
    MMA. Abstract
    Pierson
  La rue Férou
    Jean. Surrealist ptg
  Taming of the shrew
    Baur. New art
  Through the Luxembourg
    Read. Concise history
RAY, Robert D. 1924-
  The Honorable Dorothy Eugenie Brett
    IU. Contemp Amer ptg & sculp, 1957
  Manzanillo, Mexico
    IU. Contemp Amer ptg & sculp, 1959
RAY, Ruth, 1919-
  The messenger
    NAD. Annual ex, 1960
  Nana
    NAD. Annual ex, 1955
  Navajo land
    NAD. Annual ex, 1948
  Survivors
    NAD. Annual ex, 1952
  What is man
    IU. Contemp Amer ptg & sculp, 1959
Ray by W. Sommer
A ray of hope by P. Santo
Raymond children, c 1840
  Unidentified artist. Joseph and Anna Ray-
  mond
Razing old Post office, New York by E.
  Fiene
Rea, Daniel, fl 1750
  Badger, J. Daniel Rea
Rea, Mrs Daniel
  Copley, J. S. Mrs Daniel Rea and child
Reaching waves by A. G. Dove

READ, Thomas Buchanan, 1822-1872
  Portrait of a cardinal   OCiM
  MiD. Travelers in Arcadia
Reade, Catharine Livingston. See Stuy-
  vesant, Catharine Livingston (Reade)
Reading by J. S. Sargent
Reading in the sun by W. Homer
Reading Le Figaro by M. Cassatt
Ready-to-wear by S. Davis
Ready-to-wear, Study for by S. Davis
Real estate agent offering valuable lots by
  F. W. Edmonds
Real numbers by Y. Tanguy
Reapers by M. Sterne
Reavey, Mrs George. See Pereira, Irene
  (Rice)
Re-awakening by W. Drewes
Rebecca by G. W. Flagg
Rebecca at the well by W. Allston
Rebecca at the well by Unidentified artist
Rebecca street by H. Scheuch
Rebound by E. Kelly
Receding red by I. R. Pereira
Reception in Miami by J. Levine
Recipe for bouillabaisse by S. Moy
The recitation by T. W. Dewing
Reclining figure by H. Warshaw
Reclining model by J. Pascin
Reclining nude by W. M. Chase
Reclining nude by E. L. Kirchner
Reclining woman with mandolin by M. Beck-
  mann
Reclining youth by L. A. Golub
Recollections by P. Mangravite
Reconstruction by J. Frankfurter
Reconstruction by B. Shahn
Recruit from civilization by F. Remington
Recruiting, Union square by J. Sloan
Recruits wanted by D. G. Blythe
Rectangles by I. R. Pereira
Red and black by S. Francis
Red and black by C. Still
Red and blue by J. Ferren
Red and blue by I. R. Pereira
Red and gold by F. W. Benson
Red and white parasols by M. B. Prender-
  gast
Red barge 1 by R. Crawford
Red barn by C. E. Burchfield
Red bird by E. J. Stevens
Red box by B. W. Tomlin
Red-breasted merganser by J. J. Audubon
Red-breasted warbler on apple blossom by
  C. E. Heil
Red bridge by J. A. Weir
Red, brown and black by M. Rothko
Red cabinet by C. Brown
Red Cap (pseud) See Ball, Elias
Red cap by H. Hofmann
Red cap by M. Weber
Red carpet by G. Tooker
Red cart by S. Davis

Red chair by S. Haley
Red chair with straw flowers by J. Binford
Red chimneys by C. H. Demuth
Red clock by K. Knaths
Red Cloud and Burning Heart by H. H.
  Cross
Red coffee pot by H. Katzman
Red cross by M. Hartley
Red dominant by J. M. Hanson
Red figure by S. W. Hayter
Red flow by K. R. Morris
Red forest by C. A. Morris
Red gateway by M. Dixon
Red-haired gentleman and his wife by J. S.
  Ellsworth
Red hand mirror by J. Sloan
Red house by H. Rose
Red in red by S. Francis
Red Jacket (Sagoyewatha) (Seneca Indian
  chief) 1751?-1830
  Haddoca, A. Red Jacket
  Mathies, J. L. D. Red Jacket
  Weir, R. W. Red Jacket
Red kimono on the roof by J. Sloan
Red landscape by W. A. Baziotes
Red lift by H. Hofmann
Red man—white man—black man by M.
  Tobey
Red mill by A. M. R. Moses
Red mill by Unidentified artist
Red Molly by L. Rivers
Red mule by E. F. Spruce
Red object by F. E. Conway
Red paint mill by J. Sloan
Red pastoral by J. E. Levi
Red quarry by K. Schrag
Red, red, not the same by P. Burlin
Red ribbon by I. G. Olinsky
Red rocks by R. O. Pozzatti
The red room by H. E. Niese
Red roses by J. Carroll
Red schoolhouse by G. H. Durrie
Red Sea terrace no 1 by T. Stamos
Red ship by R. A. Parker
Red skirt by R. B. Motherwell
Red sky by A. Gottlieb
Red snapper and still life by W. M. Chase
Red stairway by B. Shahn
Red still life by C. Brown
Red studio by R. Bennett
Red sun by M. Avery
Red sun—Brooklyn bridge by J. Marin
Red sweater by F. De Erdely
Red table by K. Knaths
Red-tailed hawk by J. J. Audubon
Red tapestry chair by A. Rattner
Red theme by P. Burlin
Red torso by J. Strombotne
Red trickle by H. Hofmann
Red vine by G. W. Bellows

Red vine, autumn, Dogtown by W. A. Kien-
busch
Red votive lights by L. MacIver
Red, white and brown by M. Rothko
Red, yellow and blue by I. R. Pereira
Red, yellow and white roses by H. Pippin
REDERER, Franz Joseph, 1899-
Alban Berg, Portrait of
IU. Contemp Amer ptg, 1949
Civic center, San Francisco
CSFP. Annual ex, 1946
Flowers
IU. Contemp Amer ptg, 1952
REDFIELD, Edward Willis, 1869-
Laurel run   OBY
Chew. 250 years of art
OYB. Catalogue 1951
Winter in the valley   PR
PR. Catalogue
Redhead ducks by F. W. Benson
Redlake by J. Tworkov
Redwood, William, 1734-1784
Stuart, G. William Redwood
Reed, Hezekiah Hutchins, fl 1825
Tuthill, A. G. D. Hezekiah Hutchins
Reed
REED, Orrel P. 1921-
Untitled, 1954
NNSG. Younger Amer ptrs
REED, Reuben Law, 1841-1921
Washington and Lafayette at the battle
of Yorktown   VWR
VWR. Amer folk art
VWR. Folk art (col)
Reed, Thomas, fl 1825
Tuthill, A. G. D. Thomas Reed
REEDER, Dickson
Walter Martin
OYB. Annual 1957
Reflected verticals by C. A. Morris
Reflection by I. R. Pereira
Reflection by H. Pittman
Reflection by W. W. Quirt
Reflection by R. Soyer
Reflection, self-portrait by J. McGarrell
Reflections by M. Avery
Reflections by H. Ballin
Reflections by T. D. Benrimo
Reflections by P. Cadmus
Reflections by H. Moller
Reflections by J. H. Twachtman
Reflections in a Roman river by Y. Johnston
Reflections number 6 by B. Margo
REFREGIER, Anton, 1905-
Boy drawing
PPC. Ptg in the U.S. 1949
Broken life   ATU
ATU. Coll of Amer art (col)
Feeding the hungry
Gruskin
Fire: 1906
Mendelowitz
Heir to the future
Larkin
Larkin rev ed
Picture of my young son
IU. Contemp Amer ptg, 1951

Shipbuilding in the 18th century
Pierson
The staircase   WMAA
Goodrich. Amer art
IU. Contemp Amer ptg, 1950
Pierson
Refugees by M. Siporin
Refugees by M. Weber
Regal lilies by S. C. Sears
Regal personages by C. Booth
Regatta by J. Jones
Regatta by M. Roberts
Regatta at Edgartown by F. S. Chapin
Region of Brooklyn bridge fantasy by J.
Marin
Region Weehawken, New Jersey by J. Marin
Regulus (Marcus Atilius Regulus) d 250
B.C.
West, B. Departure of Regulus
Rehearsal by L. Kester
Rehearsal of the Pas de Loup Orchestra
at the Cirque d'Hiver by J. S. Sargent
Rehearsal under the big top by B. Stahl
REHN, Frank Knox Morton, 1848-1914
Glittering moonlight   DC
NYG. Fine art
Rehoboth beach, Delaware
Peale, T. R. Bright house, Rehoboth
beach, Delaware
REICH, Don, 1931-
Texas landscape no 3   CSFP
IU. Contemp Amer ptg & sculp, 1961
REID, Robert, 1862-1929
The bather   CtY
CtY. Soc Anonyme
Reid, Samuel Chester, 1818-1897
Jarvis, J. W. Capt Samuel Chester Reid
REILLY, Frank Joseph, 1906-
Mount Overlook
NAD. Annual ex, 1956
REILLY, John William
Old man, Portrait of an
NAD. Annual ex, 1957
Transients
NAD. Annual ex, 1959
REINDEL, Edna, 1900-
Hiroshima
ICA. Annual ex, 1947-48
REINHARDT, Adolph Frederick, 1913-
Black and white, 1950
MNU. 40 Amer ptrs
Number 1, 1959
MnMW. 60 Amer ptrs
Number 2
Pousette-Dart. Amer ptg
Number 7A, 1953
WMAA. New decade
Number 11, 1949
McCurdy
MMA. Abstract
Number 12, 1952
PPC. International ex, 1955
Number 14, 1948
MnU. 40 Amer ptrs
Number 15   NBuA
NBuA. Acquisitions 1957-58
Number 18, 1948-49   WMAA
Pierson
WMAA. New decade
Number 18, 1950
Hess. Abstract ptg

REINHARDT, A. F.—*Continued*
  Number 19, 1953
    VR. Amer ptg, 1954
  Number 24, 1954
    Pierson
    WMAA. New decade
  Triptych
    Brussels. Exposition
  Untitled painting, 1945
    Hess. Abstract ptg
REINHARDT, Marnye   VR
  View into Maryland
    Pousette-Dart. Amer ptg
REINHARDT, Siegfried G. 1925-
  Adam and Eve
    WMAA. Young America 1960
  Exultation
    NAD. Annual ex, 1960
  The miracle
    WMAA. Young America 1960
  Pieta   MoSL
    CoS. New accessions USA, 1952
  Raising of Lazarus
    MnMW. Reality and fantasy
  Resistance
    IU. Contemp Amer ptg & sculp, 1957
  Sentinel
    Pousette-Dart. Amer ptg
    WMAA. Contemp Amer ptg, 1951
  Sentry
    MoSL. Contemporary Amer ptg
REISS, Wallace, 1926?-
  Bursting flowers
    WMAA. Contemp Amer ptg, 1955
Rejected suitor by L. M. Eilshemius
Relation within space by F. Ruvolo
Relational painting by F. Glarner
Relaxation by O. Foss
Relics of a den by G. W. Platt
Religious themes. See Biblical and re-
    ligious themes
Remains II by B. Chaet
Remember me by F. C. Watkins
Remember now the days of thy youth by
    P. S. Sample
Remembering by R. W. Anliker
Remembrance of things past by B. Ullrich
REMICK, Christian, b 1726
  Blockade of Boston, View of the   MSE
    Flexner. First flowers
REMINGTON, Frederic, 1861-1909
  Among the led horses
    Carlson. Gallery (col)
  Apaches are coming   NOR
    McCracken. Remington
  Apaches listening   NOR
    Carlson. Gallery (col)
    McCracken. Remington
  Army officer   NOR
    McCracken. Remington
  Attack on the supply train
    McCracken. Portrait of the old west
      (col)
  Breaking up the ice in spring   NOR
    McCracken. Remington
  Bringing home the new cook
    Carlson. Gallery (col)
  The captive Gaul   NOR
    McCracken. Remington

  Cavalry charge on the southern plains
                                            MM
    McCracken. Remington
    MM. 100 Amer ptrs
  Cavalry charge on the western plain MM
    Mendelowitz
  Charge of the Rough Riders at San Juan
    hill   NOR
    McCracken. Remington
  Dead men
    McCracken. Remington
  Death of Minnehaha
    McCracken. Portrait of the old west
  Dismounted: 4th troopers moving MWiS
    MWiS. Ex 4 and 7
  Downing the nigh leader
    McCracken. Remington
  End of the day   NOR
    McCracken. Remington
  Fight for the water hole   TxH
    Time. 300 years (col)
  General Leonard A. Wood on horseback
                                            NOR
    McCracken. Remington
  Ghost stories   NOR
    McCracken. Remington
  Halt—dismount
    McCracken. Remington
  Hauling in the gill net   NOR
    McCracken. Remington
  Head of a frontiersman
    McCracken. Portrait of the old west
      (col)
  Holding up the payroll
    Carlson. Gallery (col)
  How order no 6 came through
    McCracken. Portrait of the old west
  Howl of the weather   NOR
    McCracken. Remington
    Time. 300 year (col)
  The last march   NOR
    McCracken. Remington (col)
  Lost warrior
    McCracken. Remington
  Navajo raid
    McCracken. Remington
  An old time plains fight   NOR
    Carlson. Gallery (col)
    McCracken. Remington (col front)
  On the southern plains in 1860
    Carlson. Gallery (col)
  The outlier   NOR
    McCracken. Remington
  Pioneer and the Indian   ATeS
    ATeS. Collection
  The quarrel
    McCracken. Remington
  Recruit from civilization
    McCracken. Portrait of the old west
  The scout: friends or enemies?   MWiS
    McCracken. Portrait of the old west
    McCracken. Remington
    MWiS. Ex 4 and 7
    Rathbone
    Time. 300 years (col)
  The scream of shrapnel at San Juan hill,
    Cuba   CtY
    U.S. National Capital sesquicentennial
      com
  The sentinel   NOR
    Larkin
    Larkin rev ed
    McCracken. Remington
    NUM. Art across America

The snow trail   NOR
  McCracken. Remington
Snowbound on the overland stage
  Carlson. Gallery (col)
Sun dance   NOR
  McCracken. Remington
United States cavalry defending a posi-
  tion, 1895   NOR
  McCracken. Remington
Visitation of the buffalo gun
  McCracken. Remington
Waiting in the moonlight   NOR
  McCracken. Remington
Remington's studio by L. Carr
Reminiscence by H. Hofmann
Reminiscence of the Genesee river by J. W.
  Casilear
Reminiscent Italia by P. Zimmerman
Remnants by A. Brook
Remnants of an era by J. L. Meador
Remote field by M. Tobey
Removal of the Sphinxes by M. Beckmann
Remsen, Elizabeth (De Peyster) 1787-1826
  Unidentified artist. Mrs Hendrick Rem-
    sen
Remsen, Hendrick, 1762-1843
  Pollard, C. Residence of Hendrick Rem-
    sen
  Unidentified artist. Hendrick Remsen
Remsen, Mrs Hendrick. See Remsen, Eliza-
  beth (De Peyster)
Renaissance by N. J. Pousette-Dart
Renaldo and the enchanted garden by R. M.
  Farruggio
Renascence by B. Shahn
Rendezvous by F. Kleinholz
Rendezvous by A. J. Miller
Rendezvous by R. Philipp
Rendezvous by M. Siporin
Rendezvous in the Wind river mountains by
  A. J. Miller
Renganeschi's Saturday night by J. Sloan
Renunciation by P. Evergood
Repair shack interior by S. Wilson
Report from Rockport by S. Davis
Repose by B. Karfiol
Repose by S. Menkès
Repose by J. S. Sargent
Repose no 2 by M. Weber
The reprimand by W. Stuempfig
Republican automatons by G. Grosz
Request number by R. Philipp
Requiem by D. Fredenthal
Requiem by F. J. Kline
The rescue by W. R. Leigh
Residence of David Twining by E. Hicks
La résistance by R. B. Motherwell
Resistance by S. G. Reinhardt
RESNICK, Milton, 1917-
  Genie   WMAA
    Goodrich. Amer art (col)
  Page, 1959
    MnMW. 60 Amer ptrs
  Rubble
    Art since 1945
  Untitled painting, 1954
    CtY. Yale alumni

Resort beach by P. Evergood
Rest in air by J. McGarrell
Restaurants. See Hotels, restaurants, etc.
Resting by J. S. Sargent
Resting at the bazaar by M. Sterne
Restless horizon by C. A. Morris
Restrained flow by W. Lockwood
Resurrection by D. Aronson
Resurrection by A. P. Ryder
Resurrection by F. C. Watkins
Resurrection by J. Zajac
Retreat by W. T. Ranney
The return by F. C. Watkins
Return from Bohemia by G. Wood
Return of Jephthah by B. West
Return of Rip Van Winkle by J. Quidor
Return of the gleaner by W. Homer
Return of the prodigal by F. Castellon
Return of the warriors by C. M. Russell
Returning by R. Taylor
Returning from the Feria by H. G. Keller
Returning to the farm by G. H. Durrie
Revelation by Y. Kuniyoshi
Revelers by G. S. Ratkai
Revere, Paul, 1735-1818
  Copley, J. S. Paul Revere
  Quidor, J. Paul Revere
  Wood, G. Midnight ride of Paul Revere
Revere beach by M. B. Prendergast
Reverie by L. Kroll
Reverie by K. H. Miller
Reverse image by N. Carone
Review, 1948-49 by P. Guston
REVINGTON, Arthur
  The apparition
    Cheney. Expressionism 1948 ed
Revolving head by P. Tchelitchew
Revue by E. Shinn
The reward by T. Stamos
Reynolds, Lydia (Bartlett) 1770-1843
  Ames, E. Mrs Stephen Reynolds
Reynolds, Marcus Tullius, 1788-1864
  Ames, E. Marcus T. Reynolds
Reynolds, Sir Joshua, 1732-1792
  Stuart, G. Sir Joshua Reynolds
Rhett, William, b 1666
  Johnston, H. Col William Rhett
Rhode Island choir boy by Unidentified
  artist
Rhythms by L. Dabo
Rhythms by H. G. Keller
RIBA, Paul, 1912-
  Along the coast
    OYB. Annual 1952
  Sandpipers
    PPC. International ex, 1952
  Symbol of the sun and moon
    NAD. Annual ex, 1958
RIBAK, Louis Leon, 1903-
  At the beach   ATU
    ATU. Coll of Amer art
  White city no 3
    IU. Contemp Amer ptg & sculp, 1959

The **ribbon** of extremes by Y. Tanguy

Ricci, Geraldine. See Ricci, Jerri

RICCI, Jerri, 1916-
In the studio
NAD. Annual ex, 1953
Louisburg square, winter
NAD. Special ex, 1956

RICE, Henry Webster, 1853-1934
Landscape with mountains   MB
    MB. Ptgs in water color
Seascape   MB
    MB. Ptgs in water color
Sunset in the mountains   MB
    MB. Ptgs in water color

Rice field near Milan by Leonid

Rice Hope by C. Fraser

Rice line by M. Greenwood

Rich, Aphia Salisbury, fl 1833
Unidentified artist. Aphia Salisbury Rich
    and baby Edward

Richard, Elizabeth (Garland) 1700-1774
Copley, J. S. Mrs Paul Richard

RICHARDS, John, 1831-1889
Battle of Gettysburg, 1863
    U. S. National Capital sesquicentennial
    com

RICHARDS, William Trost, 1833-1905
June day   OCl
    Chew. 250 years of art
Lands End, Cornwall   OYB
    OYB. Catalogue 1951
Near Paradise, Newport, Rhode island
    MB
    MB. Ptgs in water color

RICHARDSON, Constance (Coleman)
1905-
French Canadian barn
    WiMiA. Amer ptg 1760-1960
Wyoming desert
    WiMiA. Amer ptg 1760-1960

RICHARDSON, Dean, 1931-
Child's toy
    MBIC. View 1960
Motorists   WMAA
    WMAA. Contemp Amer ptg, 1959/60
    WMAA. Young America 1960

Richardson, Mrs Edgar Preston. See Richardson, Constance (Coleman)

Richardson, Mrs Edward. See Richardson, Elizabeth (Poinsett)

Richardson, Elizabeth (Poinsett) b c 1751
Theus, J. Mrs Edward Richardson

Richardson, F. E.
Parcell, M. S. F. E. Richardson jr

Richardson, William, 1743-1786
Theus, J. Col William Richardson

Richardson memorial by H. Moore

Richardson's Columbian squirrel by J. J. Audubon

RICHARDT, Joachim Ferdinand, 1819-1895
Emporium of Indian curiosities   NCHA
    Jones. New-found folk art

Richmond Hill, Story of by P. Evergood

Richmond, Virginia by Unidentified artist

The **riddle** by I. R. Pereira

A **ride** for liberty: the fugitive slave by E. Johnson

The **rider** by M. B. Prendergast

Rider against blue hills by M. B. Prendergast

Riders by C. A. Morris

Riders in the hills by J. Sloan

Riders in the park by M. Avery

Ridge and forecast by R. Tam

Ridgely, Eliza, 1802-1867
Sully, T. Lady with a harp: Eliza Ridgely

Ridgely, Mary (Middleton) Vining, 1705-1761
Unidentified artist. Mrs Nicholas Ridgely

Ridgeway by J. Tworkov

Rigging by J. S. Sargent

Right and left by W. Homer

Riker's island prison, Study for mural at by B. Shahn

RILEY, Bernard
Newsboys
    NAD. Annual ex, 1959

Riley, James Whitcomb, 1849-1916
Sargent, J. S. James Whitcomb Riley

RIMMER, William, 1816-1879
Flight and pursuit (Pursuer and pursued)
    MB
Mendelowitz
Pierson
Richardson. Ptg in America

Rinaldo and Armida by B. West

RINDISBACHER, Peter, 1806-1834
Buffalo hunting in summer   MCH
    Rathbone
Buffaloes in winter   MCH
    Rathbone
Indian dance
    Rathbone
Indians hunting buffalo
    Rathbone
Indians returning from war   MCH
    Rathbone
Inside of an Indian tent   MCH
    Rathbone
War dance of the Sauks and Foxes
    McCracken. Portrait of the old west
    (col)
    Rathbone

Ring around the moon by T. D. Benrimo

Ringing the pig by W. S. Mount

Ringside seats by G. W. Bellows

Rio di San Barnaba, Venice by E. D. Boit

Rio di San Lorenzo, Venice by E. D. Boit

Rip Van Winkle (steamboat)
Bard, J. Hudson river steamboat Rip Van
    Winkle

Rip Van Winkle at Nicholas Vedder's tavern by J. Quidor

RIPLEY, Alden Lassell, 1896-
After the storm   MB
    MB. Ptg in water color
Winter morning
    NAD. Annual ex, 1949, 2d half

Rise of the full moon by A. G. Dove

Rishi calling up a storm by J. La Farge

Rising city by C. A. Morris

Rising moon by R. A. Blakelock

Rising moon by A. G. Dove

Rising of a thunderstorm at sea by W. Allston

Rising sun by H. Hofmann

Rising tide by A. G. Dove

A **risk** in each hand by Y. Tanguy

RITMAN, Louis
  Michigan landscape
    NAD. Annual ex, 1959
RITTENBERG, Henry R. 1879-
  Caroline Augusta   OYB
    OYB. Catalogue 1951
Ritual by J. Pollock
Ritual vessel-mirror by M. Graves
Riva San Biagio, Venice by M. B. Prender-
  gast
The river by L. Feininger
The river by L. Guglielmi
The river by C. S. Price
River bathers by G. Hartigan
River Eau Sucre by A. J. Miller
River effect, Paris by J. Marin
River flowing . . . flowing by Chen Chi
River front no 1, 1915 by G. W. Bellows
River in the Catskills by T. Cole
River men by J. Whorf
River movement—downtown by J. Marin
River night by C. A. Morris
River Rouge plant by C. Sheeler
River scene by T. Chambers
River scene by J. F. Kensett
River scene, lumberman, and logs in river
  by W. Homer
River scene, watering horses, by A. J. Mil-
  ler
River view from the plaza by C. F. Gaert-
  ner
River view with shepherd and animals by
  Unidentified artist
Riverbank by D. Park
Riverfront no 1 by G. W. Bellows
Rivers, Deborah. See Skaats, Deborah
  (Rivers)
RIVERS, Larry, 1923-
  Birdie with straw hat
    McCurdy
  Double portrait of Birdie   WMAA
    MMA. 12 Americans
    Pierson
  The final veteran
    NBuA. Acquisitions 1959-1961
  Head of Stevie
    MMA. 12 Americans
  Red Molly
    WMAA. Museum and its friends, 1958
  Saxophone player—Jay Cameron
    IU. Contemp Amer ptg & sculp, 1959
  Self figure   DC
    DC. 24 biennial ex, 1955
    MMA. 12 Americans
  Washington crossing the Delaware   MMA
    MMA. 12 Americans (col)
  Water mill prospect
    MMA. 12 Americans
Riverton yacht club, New Jersey by A. B.
  Serwazi
Rivington, James, 1724-1802
  Ames, E. James Rivington (after Stuart)
The road between by G. Seibert
Road from the cove by L. Kroll
Road in early spring by C. E. Burchfield
Road in Midi by J. S. Sargent
Road into Ranchos de Taos by A. Dasburg

Road roller by R. Kent
Road through the willows by L. Kroll
Road through the woods by D. Macknight
Road to Alcumenar by C. Voorhies
Road to Bonao by W. E. Heitland
Road to Danbury by M. Varga
Road to friendship by A. N. Wyeth
Road to Golgotha by J. P. Wheat
Road to Lamy by A. Dasburg
Road to Sparta by T. Stamos
Road to the West by G. Tattersall
The road with no turn by W. W. Quirt
Roads no 6 by H. Sterne
Roadside meeting by A. P. Ryder
Roanoke, Virginia
  Fransioli, T. A. St Andrew's church,
    Roanoke
Roar of the wooden horse by E. Isenburger
Roasting ears by T. H. Benton
Roasting the hump rib by A. J. Miller
Robbery of Europe by M. Beckmann
Robbins, Ammi Ruhamah
  Moulthrop, R. Rev Ammi Ruhamah Rob-
    bins
ROBBINS, Franklin
  The bride
    NAD. Annual ex, 1956
Robbins, Maria Louisa. See Davis, Maria
  Louisa (Robbins)
Robbins, Thomas, 1777-1865
  Moulthrop, R. Thomas Robbins
Robert Knapp (schooner)
  Bard, J. Hudson river schooner Robert
    Knapp
The Robert L. Stevens breaking ice in the
  Hudson river by J. Bard
Roberto by W. Kuhn
ROBERTS, Alice T. 1876-
  Ipswich sand dunes no 2
    PA. Annual ex, 1952
ROBERTS, Bishop, fl 1735-1739
  Charleston before 1739
    Davidson v 1
    Flexner. First flowers (detail)
Roberts, Henry Laurens, fl 1831
  Davis, J. H. Henry Laurens Roberts
Roberts, Mary W. fl 1823
  Unidentified artist. Mrs Mary W. Roberts
ROBERTS, Morton, 1927-
  Bar and grill
    OYB. Annual 1956
  The derelict
    NAD. Annual ex, 1954
  Regatta
    NAD. Annual ex, 1957
Roberts, Owen Josephus, 1875-1955
  Watkins, F. C. Justice Owen J. Roberts
ROBERTS, Priscilla W. 1916-
  Bird and rose
    NAD. Annual ex, 1949, 1st half
  The old shop window
    IU. Contemp Amer ptg & sculp, 1961
  Pipe and bowl
    IU. Contemp Amer ptg, 1949
  Plumage
    IU. Contemp Amer ptg, 1950
    PPC. Ptg in the U. S. 1949

ROBERTS, P. W.—*Continued*
Self-portrait
  IU. Contemp Amer ptg, 1951
  NAD. Annual ex, 1947, 1st half
  PPC. International ex, 1950
ROBERTS, Richard
Ohio evening   OYB
  OYB. Annual 1954
ROBERTSON, Archibald, 1765-1835
New York city from North river, View of
                    NNHS
  Larkin
  Larkin rev ed
Tidal mill
  Davidson v 1

Attributed works

The collect or fresh water pond
  Flexner. Light of western skies
ROBERTSON, Thomas
Composition no 30   MAP
  Rathbun
Robeson mill at the mouth of the Wissahickon by R. Smith
Robin by G. W. Bellows
Robin Hood cove, Georgetown, Maine by M. Hartley
Robinhood marina by W. Zorach
Robins, Margaret, fl 1745
Hesselius, J. Margaret Robins
Robinson, Alexander, fl 1795
Peale, C. W. Alexander and Angelica Robinson
Robinson, Angelica, fl 1795
Peale, C. W. Alexander and Angelica Robinson
Robinson, Annie, fl 1794
Unidentified artist. Annie Robinson
ROBINSON, Boardman, 1876-1952
The Dutch in the Baltic
  Larkin rev ed
Ethiopia saluting the colors
  Genauer (col)
Hannah Armstrong   ATU
  ATU. Coll of Amer art
Judson Stoddard   ATU
  ATU. Coll of Amer art
Moby Dick
  Cheney. Expressionism 1948 ed
Richard Bone   ICA
  Pierson
Stubb and Starbuck   GAtM
  GAtM. Holbrook collection
Wintry park
  Gruskin
Robinson, Faith. See Trumbull, Faith (Robinson)
ROBINSON, Florence Vincent, 1860?-1930
Versailles   MB
  MB. Ptgs in water color
Robinson, Mrs Henry
Sully, T. Mrs Henry Robinson
ROBINSON, J. C. fl 1848
An old lady   DN
  DN. Amer primitive ptgs, pt 1
An old man   DN
  DN. Amer primitive ptgs, pt 1
Robinson, Jane, fl 1826
Morse, S. F. B. Mrs Jane Robinson
ROBINSON, Jay, 1915-
Nice drums
  PPC. Ptg in the U. S. 1949

ROBINSON, Theodore, 1852-1896
Girl at the piano   OT
  Richardson. Ptg in America
Spring in Giverney
  CSB. Impressionism
  NUM. Art across America
Val d'Arconville   ICA
  Born
  Pierson
Watering pots   NBM
  Pierson
Willows   NBM
  Mendelowitz
Robinson, Tony
Speicher, E. E. Tony Robinson
Rochelle by R. Philipp
Rochester, New York
Belton, F. S. Rochester, New York
Unidentified artist. Mill of C. J. Hill & Son, Rochester, New York
The **rock** by P. Blume
Rock fluorescence by E. Loran
Rock formations by A. J. Miller
Rock landscape by K. L. Callahan
Rock of Independence by A. J. Miller
Rock painting by J. Ernst
Rock vista by G. W. Bellows
Rockbound forms by C. A. Morris
Rockefeller, John Davidson, 1839-1937
Sargent, J. S. John D. Rockefeller
Rockhill special by K. E. Fortess
ROCKMORE, Noel
Family group
  OYB. Annual 1953
Rockport by J. J. Jones
Rockport beach by S. Davis
Rockport harbor by M. Beck
Rockport window by J. Teyral
Rocks and pines by M. Beck
Rocks and rubble by W. Schock
Rocks and sea by C. S. Hopkinson
Rocks and sea, Small point, Maine by J. Marin
Rocks and water by H. Maril
Rocks in New England by M. J. Heade
Rocks in the sea by H. Wentz
Rockwell, Elizabeth de Long, fl 1865
Mason, B. F. Elizabeth de Long Rockwell
Rockwell, Simeon, fl 1867
Mason, B. F. Simeon Rockwell
Rockwell, Mrs Simeon, fl 1867
Mason, B. F. Mrs Simeon Rockwell
Rocky cliffs—Yosemite valley by W. Zorach
Rocky coast by W. Homer
Rocky coast by A. Walkowitz
Rocky farmyard by J. C. Atherton
Rocky field, Camp island, Maine by W. A. Kienbusch
Rocky hillside by H. More
Rocky landscape by E. H. Betts
Rocky moorland by B. West (attributed works)
Rocky mountains
Bierstadt, A. Rocky mountains
Blakelock, R. A. Rocky mountains

Egan, J. J. Distant view of the Rocky mountains
Miller, A. J. Lake scene, Rocky mountains
Miller, A. J. Wild scenery
Seymour, S. View near the base of the Rocky mountains
Seymour, S. View of the Rocky mountains on the Platte
Wenck, P. Rockies from Bear lake
Whittredge, W. In the Rockies
Rocky neck, Gloucester by S. Davis
Rocky neck (Gloucester) by K. Matthew
Rocky place by E. F. Spruce
Rocky shore by M. J. Heade
Rocky shore by W. Homer
Rococo table by H. Kallem
Rodeo by K. Evett
Rodeo in the Rockies by A. Blanch
Rodgers, Rebecca. See Codwise, Rebecca (Rodgers)
Rodin, Auguste, 1840-1917
Sargent, J. S. Auguste Rodin
Rodman, Mr, fl 1800
Malbone, E. G. Mr Rodman
ROESCH, Kurt Ferdinand, 1905-
Dice players
  IU. Contemp Amer ptg, 1951
Imagined music   NBuA
  NBuA. Acquisitions 1957-58
Odalisk
  IU. Contemp Amer ptg, 1952
Walk in town   PA
  Pousette-Dart. Amer ptg
ROESEN, Severin, c 1815-1871
Boy with still life   OYB
  OYB. Supplement 1959
Dutch lunch
  Frankenstein. After the hunt
Fruit on table
  NUM. Art across America
Still life with fruit and flowers
  Chew. 250 years of art
Rogers, Elizabeth (Gatfield) fl 1780
Unidentified artist. Mrs Leonard Rogers
Rogers, Helen
Speicher, E. E. Helen Rogers
ROGERS, Nathaniel, 1788-1844
Man in black coat
  OCl. Portrait miniatures
Rogers, Robert, 1758-1835
Allston, W. Robert Rogers
ROGOWAY, Alfred, 1905-
The family
  IU. Contemp Amer ptg & sculp, 1955
Summer
  IU. Contemp Amer ptg & sculp, 1953
Rogues' gallery by C. E. Burchfield
Roller skating rink by W. J. Glackens
Rolling power by C. Sheeler
Rollins, James S. fl 1871
Bingham, G. C. James S. Rollins, Study for portrait
Rolph, James, 1869-1934
Shahn, B. Gov James Rolph jr of California
Roman aqueduct by S. Drumlevitch
The **Roman** Campagna by T. Cole
The **Roman** Campagna by G. Inness

Roman Campagna by M. B. Prendergast
Roman head by A. B. Durand
Roman shop by E. Betsberg
Romanesque facade by A. Gottlieb
Romanscape by Z. Kachadoorian
ROMANO, Umberto, 1905-
Behold . . . man
  IU. Contemp Amer ptg, 1949 (col)
Ecce Homo
  Genauer (col)
Fragments and reconstruction
  NAD. Annual ex, 1956
Green clown
  IU. Contemp Amer ptg, 1950
I bear the children of tomorrow
  NAD. Annual ex, 1961
Romantic figure by E. Isenburger
Romantic landscape by E. Ames
Romantic landscape by T. Cole
Rome, Italy
Bierstadt, A. Arch of Octavius
Blume, P. Eternal city
Boit, E. D. St Peter's Rome
Gikow, R. Roman street scene
Healy, G. P. A. Arch of Titus
Pelin, B. Colosseum
Prendergast, M. B. Afternoon, Pincian hill, Rome
Prendergast, M. B. On the Corso, Rome
Prendergast, M. B. Pincian hill, Rome
Prendergast, M. B. Spanish steps, Rome
Rattner, A. Rome no 1, 1951-52
Rattner, A. Rome no 4
Sargent, J. S. Piazza Navona, Rome
Vanderlyn, J. View in Rome
Vedder, E. Rome
Rome—St Augustine by K. Zerbe
Romeyn, Harriet. See Stafford, Harriet (Romeyn)
RONALD, William, 1927?-
Seventy-seven   MnMW
  MnMW. 60 Amer ptrs
The visitor
  MnMW. Eighty works
RONDEL, Frederic, 1826-1892
Self-portrait
  WiMiA. Amer ptg 1760-1960
RONSON, David, 1923-
Marriage at Cana
  Pearson. Mod renaissance
Roof gossips by J. Sloan
Roof pattern by A. Parella
The **roof** playground by W. Zorach
Roofs: 23rd street, sunset by J. Sloan
Rooftops by A. G. Dove
The **room** by P. Guston
Room 8—hotel Flora, Cannes by R. B. Motherwell
Room in Brooklyn by E. Hopper
Room in New York by E. Hopper
Room interior no 1 by J. Cox
Room number VI by E. Cortor
Room 110 by Y. Kuniyoshi
Room 203 by I. L. Albright
Rooms by the sea by E. Hopper
Rooms for tourists by E. Hopper

Roosevelt, Franklin Delano, president U.S. 1882-1945
  Salisbury, F. O. Franklin D. Roosevelt
  Woolf, S. J. Franklin D. Roosevelt
  Woolf, S. J. Franklin D. Roosevelt—beginning of his office
Roosevelt, Samuel Montgomery, 1864-1920
  Lockman, D. M. Samuel Montgomery Roosevelt
Roosevelt, Theodore, president U.S. 1853-1919
  Sargent, J. S. Theodore Roosevelt
Roosters
  Avery, M. Pink cock
  Avery, M. Rooster's domain
  Hensel, H. Clown with rooster
  Knaths, K. Cock and glove
  Knaths, K. King cock
  Lebrun, R. Rooster on arm of the cross
  Luks, G. B. Mrs Gamley [with rooster]
  Spruce, E. F. Yellow rooster
  Zerbe, K. Rooster
  Unidentified artist. The cock
  Wilson, R. Pet rooster
Root-diggers by A. J. Miller
Roots by G. Prestopino
The rope by J. French
Rope dancer accompanies herself with her shadows by M. Ray
Rope walk interior by C. B. King
ROPES, George, 1788-1819
  Crowninshield's wharf, Salem, 1806 MSP
    Davidson v 1
  Launching the ship Fame at Salem MSP
    Davidson v 1
Roping a grizzly by C. M. Russell
Roping a wild one by C. M. Russell
Roque by P. S. Sample
Rosa, Salvator, 1615-1676
  Cole, T. Salvator Rosa sketching banditti
Rosa gallica by B. Connelly
Rosa Maria by A. Brook
Rosalie by W. Allston
Rosalind by I. G. Olinsky
ROSE, Herman, 1909-
  East New York
    MMA. Fifteen
  From Avenue A
    MMA. Fifteen
  Manhattan tops
    Pierson
  Red house
    MMA. Fifteen
ROSE, Iver, 1899-
  Flower women   MAP
    Gruskin
  Sharp drummer
    Genauer (col)
  Take my picture, mister
    NAD. Annual ex, 1955
  Three slickers   MSM
    CoS. New accessions USA, 1954
  A world I never made
    PPC. Ptg in the U.S. 1949
Rose, Johannes, 1694-1718
  Unidentified artist. Johannes Rose
Rose of the four winds by Y. Tanguy
Rose sequence by W. Brice
Roseate spoonville by J. J. Audubon

ROSEN, Charles, 1878-1950
  Two tugs   OT
    OT. Contemp Amer ptgs
Rosen, Katherine
  Bellows, G. W. Katherine Rosen
ROSENBERG, Charles D, fl 1858 and CAFFERTY, James H. 1819-1869
  Wall street, half past 2 o'clock, October 13, 1857
    U.S. National Capital sesquicentennial com
ROSENBERG, James N. 1874-
  Grey day in Adirondacks   GAtM
    GAtM. Holbrook collection
ROSENBERG, Samuel, 1896-
  Composition no 5, 1956
    PPC. International ex, 1958
  The dance   PGr
    Chew. 250 years of art
  Israel   PPC
    Gruskin
  Maine
    Chew. 250 years of art
  Moment in time
    IU. Contemp Amer ptg, 1952
  The patriarch   OYB
    OYB. Catalogue 1951
  The present
    PPC. Ptg in the U.S. 1949
  The season's turning
    PPC. International ex, 1955
  Street by the mill
    Chew. 250 years of art
  Time echoes
    IU. Contemp Amer ptg & sculp
    PPC. International ex, 1952
ROSENBORG, Ralph, 1911-
  Land of the bright sun
    IU. Contemp Amer ptg & sculp, 1955
  Landscape forms
    IU. Contemp Amer ptg & sculp, 1961
  Northern seascape
    IU. Contemp Amer ptg & sculp, 1959
  Subjective landscape   CtY
    CtY. Soc Anonyme
ROSENFELD, Edward, 1906-
  Kitchen sink   DP
    DP. Catalogue
ROSENTHAL, Doris
  Don Pasquale   IaDa
    IaDa. Silver jubilee
    Pearson. Mod renaissance
  Girl and bananas   OT
    Gruskin (col)
    OT. Contemp Amer ptgs
    Pearson. Mod renaissance
  Hotel corridor
    IU. Contemp Amer ptg, 1948
    OYB. Annual 1953
  Mexican church   ATU
    ATU. Coll of Amer art (col)
  Nixtamal y postole
    MM. Amer ptg today
  Tops   MMA
    Gruskin (col)
ROSENTHAL, Toby Edward, 1848-1917
  The cardinal's portrait   CSFP
    CSFP. Handbook (col)
  Seine Madonna   CSFP
    NYG. Fine art
Roses by W. Brice
Roses by M. Hartley

Roses on a palette by M. J. Heade
Roses with red chair by H. Pippin
Rosh Hashana by W. Pachner
Ross, Anna Helena Amelia. See Plumstead, Anna Helena Amelia (Ross)
ROSS, C. Chandler
  Autumn pleasures
    NYG. Fine art
  Eastern tranquillity
    NYG. Fine art (col)
  From my window
    NYG. Fine art
  Oriental simplicity
    NYG. Fine art (col)
  Prize flowers
    NYG. Fine art
  Tang horse
    NYG. Fine art
  Thoroughbreds
    NYG. Fine art
  Treasures from China
    NYG. Fine art
Ross, Elizabeth, 1751-1781. See Tyng, Elizabeth (Ross) 1751-1831
ROSS, Jamie, 1931-
  Uncompleted bridge   OYB
    OYB. Annual 1955
    OYB. Supplement 1959
Ross snow geese by B. Wilson
ROSSBACH, Lois, 1922
  Girl with bird   OCl
    CoS. New accessions USA, 1952
  Tired   OYB
    OYB. Annual 1955
    OYB. Supplement 1959
ROSSITER, Thomas Pritchard, 1817-1871
  Opening of the wilderness   MB
    MB. Karolik coll
  Picnic on the Hudson
    U.S. National Capital sesquicentennial com
ROSZAK, Theodore J. 1907-
  Carcass
    MnMW. Roszak
  Composition in an oval
    MnMW. Roszak
  Composition in white
    MMA. Abstract
  Fisherman's bride   WMAA
    MnMW. Roszak
  Florence
    MnMW. Roszak
  Forty-second street, 1936
    MNMW. Roszak
  Opposition within a circle
    MnMW. Roszak
  Peasant woman
    MnMW. Roszak
  Seated figure
    MnMW. Roszak
  Self-portrait
    MnMW. Roszak (col)
Rotating vision by F. Ruvolo
ROTH, Frank, 1936-
  Agincourt   NBuA
    NBuA. Acquisitions 1957-58
  Fragment of an empire   CSB
    WMAA. Young America 1960
  Hommage à Albert Camus
    WMAA. Young America 1960

ROTH, Jack, 1927-
  Untitled, 1954
    NNSG. Younger Amer ptrs
Rotherham, Yorkshire, England by T. H. Hinckley
ROTHKO, Mark, 1903-
  Archaic idol
    MMA. Contemp ptrs
  Astral image
    CSFP. Annual ex, 1947/48
  Baptismal scene   WMAA
    MMA. Rothko
  Birth of cephalopods
    Hess. Abstract ptg
  The black and the white
    MMA. New Amer ptg
    MMA. Rothko (col)
  Black over reds
    Art since 1945 (col)
    MMA. Rothko
    Read. Concise history
  Brown and black on plum
    Ponente. Mod ptg, 1960 (col)
  Earth and green
    Hunter. Mod Amer ptg (col)
  Entombment I, 1946   WMAA
    Goodrich. Amer art
  Green on blue   ATU
    NUM. Art across America
  Light, earth and blue
    MMA. Rothko
  Maroon on blue
    PPC. International ex, 1961/62
  Mural number 1, 1958, Sketch for
    MMA. Rothko (col)
  Mural number 6, 1958, Sketch for
    MMA. Rothko (col)
  Mural, section 3, 1959
    MMA. Rothko
  Mural, section 7, 1959
    MMA. Rothko
  Number 1, 1949
    MMA. Fifteen
  Number 2, 1954
    MMA. Rothko
  Number 4, 1948
    Hess. Abstract ptg
  Number 4A, 1947
    MnU. 40 Amer ptrs
  Number 7, 1960
    MMA. Rothko
  Number 8, 1952
    MMA. Rothko (col)
  Number 8, 1953
    MMA. Rothko
  Number 8, 1960
    MMA. Rothko
  Number 9, 1958
    MMA. Rothko
  Number 10, 1950   MMA
    Barr. What is mod ptg
    McCurdy
    MMA. Fifteen
    MMA. New Amer ptg (col)
    Newmeyer
    Pierson
    Read. Concise history (col)
  Number 12, 1948   DP
    MMA. Rothko
  Number 12, 1960
    MMA. Rothko

ROTHKO, Mark—*Continued*
Number 14, 1949
  Hess. Abstract ptg (col)
  MMA. Abstract
Number 14, 1960
  MMA. Rothko
Number 17, 1949
  MnU. 40 Amer ptrs
Number 18, 1948
  MMA. Rothko
Number 18, 1951
  MMA. Fifteen
Number 18, 1952
  MMA. Rothko (col)
Number 19
  IU. Contemp Amer ptg, 1951
Number 19, 1948   ICA
  MMA. Rothko
Number 19, 1958
  MMA. Rothko
Number 22, 1950
  MMA. Rothko
Number 24, 1947
  MMA. Rothko
Orange and yellow   NBuA
  Barker. From realism (col)
  Eliot. Art of our time
Orange over yellow
  Time. 300 years (col)
Painting   ICA
  Pierson
Red, brown and black   MMA
  MMA. Rothko
Red, white and brown   SwB
  Ponente. Mod ptg, 1960 (col)
Tan and black on red
  MMA. New Amer ptg
  MMA. Rothko
Three forms
  Cheney. Story 1958 ed
Untitled
  CSEP. Annual ex, 1948/49
Untitled, 1946
  MMA. Rothko
Vessels of magic   NBM
  Baur. Revolution
  Pierson
White and greens in blue
  MMA. Rothko (col)
  Ponente. Mod ptg, 1960 (col)
White center
  MnMW. 60 Amer ptrs
Yellow over purple
  Art since 1945
Rothmaler, Elizabeth, fl 1757
  Theus, J. Elizabeth Rothmaler
Rotting on the shore by Y. Kuniyoshi
Rough sea at Portofino, Italy by E. D. Boit
ROULAND, Orlando, 1871-1945
  William T. Evans   NJMo
  NJMo. Forty Years
  NJMo. Your Montclair art museum
Round table by C. Brown
Round table with fiasco and landscape by
  C. Brown
Round trip by H. Frankenthaler
Roundhouses at High Bridge by G. B. Luks
The **roundup** by C. M. Russell
Route 6, Eastham by E. Hopper
Rouvert, Edmond
  Peale, J. Edmond Rouvert

Rouvert, Jane
  Peale, J. Jane Rouvert
ROWELL, A. J.
  George Washington (miniature)   OYB
  OYB. Catalogue 1951
Rowing home by W. Homer
Rowland, Henry A. 1848-1901
  Eakins, T. Professor Henry A. Rowland
Roy, Ann. See Rutherfoord, Ann (Roy)
Royal palm trees by W. Homer
Royal psalmist by L. Douglass
Royall, Elizabeth, 1747-1775
  Copley, J. S. Mary and Elizabeth Royall
Royall, Sir Isaac, 1719-1781
  Feke, R. Sir Isaac Royall and his family
Royall, Mary Macintosh, 1745-1786
  Copley, J. S. Mary and Elizabeth Royall
ROWLEY, Reuben, fl 1825-1835
  Elijah Rathbone
  Jones. Rediscovered ptrs
  Eliza Betts Rathbone
  Jones. Rediscovered ptrs
Rubber plant by M. Hartley
Rubble by M. Resnik
RUBEN, Richard, 1924-
  Back of beyond V   CP
  CoS. New accessions USA, 1956
  Bird and ball
  IU. Contemp Amer ptg, 1952
  Deciduous circumstance
  NNSG. Younger Amer ptrs
  East of Easter
  VR. Amer ptg, 1958
RUBINGTON, Norman, 1923?
  Night and prophecy
  IU. Contemp Amer ptg & sculp, 1955
  Nude image no 5
  IU. Contemp Amer ptg & sculp, 1959
Ruby by F. Martin
Ruby flux by I. R. Pereira
Ruby-throated hummingbird by J. J.
  Audubon
Rudy: midget by J. Teyral
Rue Daguerre by L. MacIver
Rue de Crimee by B. Lamotte
La **rue** de la Santé by Y. Tanguy
Rue de l'Echaude by S. Davis
La **rue** de Nevers by A. Russell
Rue de Rivoli, Paris by T. Asplund
Rue des Rats by S. Davis
Rue du Singe qui Pêche by C. H. Demuth
La **rue** Férou by M. Ray
Rue Gabrielle by O. M. Pleissner
Rue Saint Denis by A. Russell
Rue Vercingetorix by S. Davis
RUELLAN, Andreé, 1905-
  Boy and gull
  NAD. Annual ex, 1948
  Children's mardi gras
  MM. Amer ptg today
  Pink masks
  IU. Contemp Amer ptg, 1950
  White shell
  IU. Contemp Amer ptg & sculp, 1957
        Portrait of the artist
  Speicher, E. E. Andrée Ruellan
Rufescent idlers by R. Bidner

RUFTY, Eleanor M. 1936-
  Bridge over Dock street
    VR. Amer ptg, 1958
Ruggles, Carl, 1876-
  Benton, T. H. Sun treader—Portrait of
    Carl Ruggles
Ruggles, Ellen (Bulkley) 1779-1865
  Ames, E. Mrs Philo Ruggles
Ruggles, Philo, 1765-1829
  Ames, E. Philo Ruggles
RUHTENBERG, Cornelis, 1923-
  Men building bridge
    NAD. Annual ex, 1960
  Staircase no 1, 1953
    VR. Amer ptg, 1954
Ruin at Daphne by E. W. Dickinson
Ruined wharf by K. Knaths
Ruins by S. Drumlevitch
Ruins, Brantone by C. Zerbe
Rum cay by W. Homer
Rumour by C. Howard
The runaway by D. G. Blythe
The runaway by D. E. Lee
Runaway horse by Unidentified artist
RUNGIUS, Carl, 1869-1959
  Moose
    NSP. Sportscapes
Running buffalo by A. J. Miller
RUNQUIST, Arthur, 1891-
  Bird   OrPA
    OrPA. Ptgs & sculptures
  Summer day
    OrPA. Ptgs & sculptures
Rural family by F. Martin
Rural happiness by H. Inman
Rural pattern by L. W. Coleman
Rural scene by R. Porter
Rush, Benjamin, 1745-1813
  Peale, C. W. Benjamin Rush
Rush, William, 1756-1833
  Eakins, T. William Rush and his model
  Eakins, T. William Rush carving his alle-
    gorical figure of the Schuylkill river
Rush hour by I. Norman
Rush hour, New York, 1915 by M. Weber
Rush the wind by W. W. Quirt
RUSSELL, Alfred, 1920-
  Diana and Callisto
    WMAA. New decade
  Finding of Queen Zenobia
    WMAA. New decade
  Painting no 24
    IU. Contemp Amer ptg, 1952
    Pousette-Dart. Amer ptg
  Prehistoric construction
    ICA. Annual ex, 1947/48
  La rue de Nevers   WMAA
    WMAA. New decade
  Rue Saint Denis
    MMA. Abstract
  Venus Anadyomene no 2
    IU. Contemp Amer ptg & sculp, 1953
Russell, Alicia Hopton, 1791-1840
  Malbone, E. G. Alicia Hopton Russell
Russell, Catherine A. b 1804
  Freeman, Mr. (attributed works) Cather-
    ine A. Russell (in her twelfth year)

RUSSELL, Charles Marion, 1864-1926
  At close quarters
    McCracken. Charles M. Russell (col)
  At the end of the rope
    Carlson. Gallery (col)
  Battle of the elks
    McCracken. Charles M. Russell
  Beauty parlor
    McCracken. Charles M. Russell
  Before the white man came
    McCracken. Charles M. Russell
  Big nose George
    McCracken. Charles M. Russell
  The bolter
    McCracken. Charles M. Russell (col)
  The brave's return
    McCracken. Charles M. Russell
  Bringing home the scalp
    McCracken. Charles M. Russell
  A bronc to breakfast
    McCracken. Charles M. Russell (col)
  Bucking bronco   ATeS
    ATeS. Collection
  Bucking bronco   MonH
    McCracken. Charles M. Russell
  Buffalo crossing the Missouri
    McCracken. Charles M. Russell
  The buffalo drive
    McCracken. Charles M. Russell
  Buffalo hunt (1)
    McCracken. Charles M. Russell
  Buffalo hunt (2)
    McCracken. Charles M. Russell (col)
  Call of the law
    McCracken. Charles M. Russell
  Canadian Mounted Police with prisoners
    McCracken. Charles M. Russell
  Capturing the grizzly
    McCracken. Charles M. Russell (col)
  Carson's men
    McCracken. Charles M. Russell (col)
  Caught with the goods
    McCracken. Charles M. Russell (col)
  The challenge
    Carlson. Gallery (col)
  Charles Russell and his friends   MonH
    McCracken. Charles M. Russell
  Charles Russell on Red Bird
    McCracken. Charles M. Russell
  Christmas at the line camp
    McCracken. Charles M. Russell
  The cinch ring
    McCracken. Charles M. Russell (col)
  Contemplation
    McCracken. Charles M. Russell
  Cowboy life
    McCracken. Charles M. Russell
  Crow scouts in winter
    McCracken. Charles M. Russell
  Custer's last stand
    McCracken. Charles M. Russell
  A dangerous cripple
    McCracken. Charles M. Russell (col)
  Dangerous territory
    McCracken. Charles M. Russell
  Deadline on the range
    McCracken. Charles M. Russell (col)
  Defiant culprit
    McCracken. Charles M. Russell
  Desperate stand
    McCracken. Charles M. Russell (col)

When shadows hint death
  McCracken. Charles M. Russell
When Sioux and Blackfeet meet
  McCracken. Charles M. Russell (col)
When the trail was long between camps
  Carlson. Gallery (col)
When tracks spell meat   OkTT
  McCracken. Charles M. Russell
When wagon trails were dim
  Carlson. Gallery (col)
When white men turn red
  McCracken. Charles M. Russell
White tails
  McCracken. Charles M. Russell
Wild horse hunters
  McCracken. Charles M. Russell (col)
Wild man's meat
  McCracken. Charles M. Russell
Wolf men
  McCracken. Charles M. Russell
Wounded buffalo
  McCracken. Charles M. Russell
York in the lodge of the Mandans
                                          MonH
  McCracken. Charles M. Russell
Russell, Daniel
  Unidentified artist. Daniel Russell
Russell, Edith Hammond. See Playfair, Edith
  Hammond (Russell) lady
Russell, Elizabeth. See Sullivan, Elizabeth
  (Russell)
RUSSELL, Frank J. 1921-
  Star watchers
    IU. Contemp Amer ptg & sculp, 1953
Russell, George Gordon. See Russell, Gor-
  don
RUSSELL, Gordon, 1932-
  Floating island
    IU. Contemp Amer ptg & sculp, 1957
  Mrs Besant takes action
    IU. Contemp Amer ptg & sculp, 1961
Russell, Jane Henrietta, fl 1844
  Stock, J. W. Jane Henrietta Russell
RUSSELL, Morgan, 1886-1953
  Four part synchromy, no 7, 1914-15
                                          WMAA
    Goodrich. Amer art
  Synchromie cosmique (Cosmic synchromy)
    Brown. Amer ptg
    Cheney. Primer 1958 ed
    WMAA. Pioneers
  Synchromy no 2 to light, 1912
    Read. Concise history
  Synchromy no 3, color counterpoint
                                          MMA
    Pierson
  Synchromy no 5, 1914
    Baur. Revolution
  Synchromy to form   MnMW
    McCurdy
    MMA. Abstract
  To form synchromy no 4, 1914
    Hess. Abstract ptg
  Synchromy to form: orange   NBuA
    NBuA. Acquisitions 1957-58
Russell, Rensselaer W. b 1803
  Freeman, Mr. (attributed works) Rens-
    selaer W. Russell
Russell, Sarah. See Sullivan, Sarah (Rus-
  sell)
Russell, Thomas, 1740-1796
  Malbone, E. G. Thomas Russell c 1796
  Malbone, E. G. Thomas Russell (Fearing
    coll)

RUSSELL, Warren E.
  The pioneers
    NAD. Annual ex, 1959
Russian ballet by M. Weber
Russian tea service by D. Bortin
RUSSO, Alexander Peter, 1922-
  Joyous landscape
    IU. Contemp Amer ptg & sculp, 1957
RUSSO, Michele, 1909-
  Gesturing figures
    OrPA. Ptgs & sculptures
Rustic dance by W. S. Mount
Rustic dance after a sleigh ride by W. S.
  Mount
The rustics by W. Homer
RUTA, Peter
  Garlics
    ICA. Annual ex, 1951
Rutgers, Anthony, 1675-1746?
  Unidentified artist. Anthony Rutgers
Rutgers, Elsje. See Vas, Elsje (Rutgers)
  Schuyler
Ruth and Naomi by Unidentified artist
Ruth Ann by R. F. Lahey
Ruth with cat by P. C. Lewis
RUTHENBERG, Cornelis, 1923-
  Girl in yellow jacket
    DC. 21 biennial ex, 1949
Rutherfoord, Ann (Roy) 1831-1908
  Hubard, W. J. Mrs John C. Rutherfoord
Rutherford, Margaret. See White, Margaret
  (Rutherford)
Ruth's zowie by W. De Kooning
Rutland, Vermont, View of by A. B.
  Durand
Rutter children, fl 1805
  Johnston, J. Edward and Sarah Rutter
RUVOLO, Felix, 1912-
  The aggressor
    IU. Contemp Amer ptg, 1949
  Atmospheric mood
    IU. Contemp Amer ptg, 1952
  Attraction   MnMW
    MnMW. 60 Amer ptrs
  Duel of the entomologist
    Genauer
  Hybrid
    IU. Contemp Amer ptg & sculp, 1961
  The informer
    CSFP. Annual ex, 1946
  Kaleidoscopic journey
    IU. Contemp Amer ptg, 1951
  Meeting of the three
    CSFP. Annual ex, 1952
  Metamorphosis
    ICA. Annual ex, 1947/48
  The monarch
    IU. Contemp Amer ptg, 1950
  Path in motion
    NBuA. Expressionism
  Relation within space
    IU. Contemp Amer ptg & sculp, 1953
  Rotating vision
    CSFP. Annual ex, 1950/51
  Transcendental   CSFM
    Pousette-Dart. Amer ptg
  Transcending motion
    ICA. Annual ex, 1951
  Undulating landscape
    MMA. Abstract

Ryan, Ann Elizabeth, fl 1803
  Malbone, E. G. Ann Elizabeth Ryan
Rydal falls, England by J. F. Kensett
RYDER, Albert Pinkham, 1847-1917
  The barnyard   NUM
    Goodrich. Ryder
  Blue marine
    Leepa
  By the tomb of the prophet
    Goodrich. Ryder
  The canal   ATeS
    ATeS. Collecton
    Goodrich. Ryder
  Christ appearing to Mary   DN
    Goodrich. Ryder (col)
  Constance   MB
    DC. Ryder (col front)
    Goodrich. Ryder (col)
    Goodrich. Ryder (detail)
    Larkin rev ed (col)
    Pierson
    WMAA. Ryder
  Country girl
    Goodrich. Ryder
  Curfew hour   MM
    Goodrich. Ryder
  Dancing dryads   DN
    Goodrich. Ryder
  Dead bird
    Barker. Amer ptg
    DC. Ryder (col)
    DP. Catalogue
    Goodrich. Ryder (col)
    Pierson
    Walker. Ptgs from America
  Death on a pale horse. See Race track
  Desdemona   DP
    DC. Ryder
    DP. Catalogue
    Goodrich. Ryder
  Diana
    DC. Ryder
    Goodrich. Ryder
  Evening glow—the old red cow   NBM
    Goodrich. Ryder
  Fishermen's huts   DP
    Born
    DP. Catalogue
  Flying Dutchman   DNC
    Baur. Revolution
    Cheney. Story 1958 ed
    Goodrich. Ryder (col)
    Pierson
    Walker. Ptgs from America (col)
  Forest of Arden
    Baur. Revolution
    Craven. Rainbow book (col)
    Craven. Treasury 1952 ed (col)
    Goodrich. Ryder (col)
    Goodrich. Ryder (detail)
    Pierson
    WMAA. Ryder
  Gay Head
    DP. Catalogue
    Goodrich. Ryder
  Grazing horse   NBM
    Goodrich. Ryder
    Pierson
    Time. 300 years (col)
  Homeward bound   DP
    DP. Catalogue
    Goodrich. Ryder

  Hunter's rest
    DC. Ryder
    Goodrich. Ryder
    MiD. Coll in progress
    WiMiA. Amer ptg 1760-1960
  In the stable   DN
    Goodrich. Ryder
  Joan of Arc   MWM
    DC. Ryder
    Goodrich. Ryder
    MWAA. Ryder
  Jonah   DNC
    Barker. Amer ptg
    DNC. Gellatly coll, 1954
    Goodrich. Ryder (col)
    Lewisohn
    Pierson
  King Cophetua and the beggar maid   DN
    Goodrich. Ryder
  Landscape   MM
    DC. Ryder
  Little maid of Arcady
    DC. Ryder
  Lone horseman
    Goodrich. Ryder
  Lone scout
    Goodrich. Ryder
  Lord Ullin's daughter. See The sea
  The Lorelei
    DC. Ryder
    Goodrich. Ryder
  The lovers   NPV
    Goodrich. Ryder
  Lovers' boat (Moonlight on the waters)
    DC. Ryder
    Goodrich. Ryder
  Macbeth and the witches   DP
    Cheney. Expressionism 1948 ed
    DC. Ryder (col)
    DP. Catalogue
    Goodrich. Ryder (col)
    Goodrich. Ryder (detail)
    Larkin
    Larkin rev ed
    Pierson
    WMAA. Ryder
  Marine
    DC. Ryder
    Goodrich. Ryder
  Mending the harness   DN
    DC. Ryder
    DC. 25 biennial ex, 1957
    Goodrich. Ryder
    Lewisohn
    WMAA. Ryder
  Moonlight   DNC
    Goodrich. Ryder
  Moonlight   NBM
    Goodrich. Ryder
  Moonlight at sea   DNC
    Cheney. Story 1958 ed
  Moonlight-marine   MM
    Bazin. History of art
    Craven. Treasury 1952 ed
    Goodrich. Ryder (col)
    MM. 100 Amer ptrs
    MM. 100 Amer ptrs (col detail)
    Pierson
  Moonlight on the sea   KW
    Goodrich. Ryder
    WMAA. Ryder
  Moonlight on the waters. See Lovers'
    boat

Moonlit cove   DP
  Cheney. Story 1958 ed
  DC. Ryder (col)
  DP. Catalogue
  Goodrich. Ryder
  NYG. Fine art
  Pierson
  UNESCO. 1860-1949
  UNESCO. 1860-1955
  UNESCO. 1860-1959
  WMAA. Ryder
Moonrise, marine
  Goodrich. Ryder
Night and clouds   MoSL
  MoSL. Handbook 1953
Night clouds   MoSL
  Cheney. Story 1958 ed
  Lewisohn
Noli me tangere. See Resurrection
Oriental camp   MAC
  DC. Ryder
  Goodrich. Ryder
Outward bound   DC
  Cheney. Expressionism 1948 ed
Passing song   DN
  Goodrich. Ryder
Pastoral study   DNC
  Barker. Amer ptg
  Goodrich. Ryder
  Pierson
The pasture   NoCR
  Goodrich. Ryder
  NoCR. Catalogue
Pegasus (The poet on Pegasus entering
  the realm of the Muses)   MWM
  Cheney. Expressionism 1948 ed
  DC. Ryder
  Goodrich. Ryder
  WMAA. Ryder
Perrette   MNS
  DC. Ryder
  Goodrich. Ryder
Pirates island   GAtM
  GAtM. Holbrook collection
  NUM. Art across America
  PPC. Amer classics
Poet on Pegasus entering the realm of the
  Muses. See Pegasus
The pond   MnMW
  Goodrich. Ryder
Race track (Death on a pale horse)   OCl
  Baur. Amer ptg
  Canaday
  Cheney. Expressionism 1948 ed
  Cheney. Story 1958 ed
  Craven. Rainbow book
  Craven. Treasury 1952 ed
  Goodrich. Ryder (col)
  Goodrich. Ryder (detail)
  Lee. Art then and now
  Lewisohn
  Myers. Art
  NAD. Amer tradition
  NBuA. Expressionism
  OCl. Handbook
  Pierson
  Riley. Your art heritage
  Robb. Art 1953 ed
  Roos
  Time. 300 years (col)
  WMAA. Ryder

Resurrection (Noli me tangere)   DP
  DP. Catalogue
  Goodrich. Ryder
  WMAA. Ryder
Roadside meeting   OYB
  Goodrich. Ryder (col)
  OYB. Catalogue 1951
  WMAA. Ryder
Sailing by moonlight
  Cheney. Story 1958 ed
The sea (Lord Ullin's daughter)   DN
  Goodrich. Ryder
Self-portrait
  DC. Ryder
  Goodrich. Ryder
  MiD. Coll in progress
  WiMiA. Amer ptg 1760-1960
Sentimental journey   NCa
  DC. Ryder
  Goodrich, Ryder
The sheepfold   NBM
  Goodrich, Ryder
The shepherdess   NBM
  Goodrich, Ryder
Shore scene   GAtM
  Goodrich, Ryder
Siegfried and the Rhine maidens   DN
  Barker. Amer ptg
  Bazin
  DC. Ryder
  DN. Mellon coll
  Goodrich. Ryder (col)
  Goodrich. Ryder (details)
  Mendelowitz
  MiD. Ptg in America
  Pierson
  Richardson. Ptg in America
  Roos
  Time. 300 years (col)
  Walker. Ptgs from America
  WMAA. Ryder
Smugglers' cove   MM
  Goodrich. Ryder
Spring   OT
  Goodrich. Ryder
Stag and two does (Stag drinking)
  CtY. Yale alumni
  Goodrich. Ryder
Story of the cross
  DC. Ryder (col)
  Goodrich. Ryder (col)
Summer's fruitful pasture   NBM
  Goodrich. Ryder
Sunset hour
  Goodrich. Ryder
The tempest   MiD
  DC. Ryder
  Goodrich. Ryder
  MiD. Treasures
  Pierson
  Richardson. Ptg in America (col)
Temple of the mind
  Cheney. Story 1958 ed
  DC. Ryder (col)
  Goodrich. Ryder (col)
  Goodrich. Ryder (detail)
  McCurdy
  NBuA. Catalogue of the ptgs
  Pierson
  WMAA. Ryder
Toilers of the sea   MAP
  Cheney. New world history
  Cheney. Story 1958 ed

RYDER, A. P.—*Continued*
Flexner. Amer ptg
Flexner. Short history
McKinney
NYG. Fine art
Rathbun (col)
Robb. Art 1953 ed
Robb. Harper history (col)
Roos
UNESCO. 1860-1949
UNESCO. 1860-1955
UNESCO. 1860-1959
Toilers of the sea   MM
Goodrich. Ryder (col)
Pierson
Time. 300 years (col)
WMAA. Ryder
Under a cloud
Cheney. Story 1958 ed
DC. Ryder
Goodrich. Ryder (col)
Time. 300 years (col)
WMAA. Ryder
Weir's orchard
DC. Ryder
Goodrich. Ryder
WMAA. Ryder
White horizon   ATeS
ATeS. Collection
White horse   NJP
Goodrich. Ryder
The windmill
Goodrich. Ryder
With sloping mast and dipping prow   DN
Goodrich. Ryder
Wood road
Goodrich. Ryder
   Portrait of the artist
Hartley, M. Albert Pinkham Ryder
Miller, K. H. Albert P. Ryder
RYDER, Chauncey Foster, 1868-1949
March wind
NYG. Fine art
Power line
NAD. Annual ex, autumn 1949
Rye bread by K. Knaths
Rynders, Barent, d 1726
Unidentified artist. Barent Rynders
Rynders, Hester (Leisler) 1673-1757?
Unidentified artist. Mrs Barent Rynders

S

S—1951 by J. D. Brooks
S.S. Del Sud, 1954 by R. Crawford
SAALBURG, Allen Russell, 1899-
Wild horses
NYG. Fine art
Sabbath by M. Weber
Sabbath phantoms by K. Seligmann
Sacco, Nicola, 1892-1927
Shahn, B. Sacco and Vanzetti in coffins
Sacco-Vanzetti series. See Shahn, B. The
Lowell committee; Passion of Sacco
and Vanzetti: Webster Thayer
SACHS, L. fl 1857
The Herbert children   DN
DN. Amer primitive ptgs, pt 1
Mendelowitz

Sacramento, California, View from water-
front by G. Tirrell
Sacred and profane by A. Bohrod
Sacred grove near Rome by G. Inness
The sacred red pipe—stone quarry by G.
Catlin
The sacrifice by A. Salemme
Sacrifice of Chronos by T. Stamos
Sacrifice of Isaac by R. Foster
Sacrifice of the hair by S. MacDonald-
Wright
The sad departure by Unidentified artist
Sad interior by M. Soyer
Saddled for the first time by G. Bartlett
SAFFER, Saraga Philip
Three queens
NAD. Annual ex, 1961
Sagamore by W. De Kooning
SAGE, Kay, 1898-
All soundings are referred to high water
CSFP. Annual ex, 1948/49
The answer is no
DC. 27 biennial ex, 1961
WMAA. Annual ex, 1958
Detour
ICA. Annual ex, 1959/60
In the third sleep
ICA. Annual ex, 1945/46
Man working
VR. Amer ptg, 1954
Nests of lightning
DC. 22 biennial ex, 1951
No one heard the thunder
Jean. Surrealist ptg
No passing   WMAA
CoS. New accessions USA, 1956
Goodrich. Amer art
Pierson
Small portrait
Pearson. Mod renaissance
Starlings caravan
CSFP. Annual 1950/51
A stranger passed
ICA Annual ex, 1947/48
Suspension bridge for swallows
IU. Contemp Amer ptg & sculp, 1959
Three thousand miles to the point of be-
ginning
ICA. Annual ex, 1951
Tomorrow is never   MM
Jean. Surrealist ptg
Unicorns came down to the sea
IU. Contemp Amer ptg, 1949
Pierson
Unusual Thursday
Pearson. Mod renaissance
Watching the clock   MMA
MMA. Soby collection
Sagebrush sport by C. M. Russell
Saguenay river, lower rapids by W. Homer
Sail loft by S. Davis
Sailboats by J. Whorf
Sailboats racing on the Delaware by T.
Eakins
Sailcloth by W. De Kooning
Sailing by T. Eakins
Sailing a dory by W. Homer
Sailing boats by T. Eakins

Sailing boats in a watering trough by W. Homer

Sailing by moonlight by A. P. Ryder

Sailing by moonlight by W. Zorach

Sailing in the mist by J. H. Twachtman

Sailing the catboat by W. Homer

Sailing vessels
  Bard, J. Hudson river schooner Robert Knapp
  Birch, T. Brig in a storm
  Birch, T. Marine view with ships
  Birch, T. New York harbor
  Birch, T. Off the Maine coast
  Birch, T. Seascape
  Birch, T. The United States and the Macedonian
  Birch, T. The Wasp and the Frolic
  Blunt, J. S. Boston harbor
  Blunt, J. S. Topsail schooner in sheltered waters
  Bradford, W. Ship Dashing Wave off Boston Light
  Bygrave, W. American clipper bark Zephyr in Messina harbor, Sicily
  Chambers, T. Boston harbor
  Corné M. F. The brig Charles of Boston
  Corné, M. F. The Constitution and the Guèrriere
  Corné, M. F. Letter-of-marque ship Mount Vernon of Salem
  Corné, M. F. Ship America hand-lining on the Grand Bank
  Eilshemius, L. M. Flying Dutchman
  Evans, J. The white squall
  Garneray, A. L. Lake Erie, Battle of
  Grant, G. Harbor traffic
  Gregory, A. V. The ship Ringleader
  Hashagen, A. Ship Arkansas leaving Havana
  Homer, W. Breezing up
  Homer, W. Gloucester schooners and sloop
  Homer, W. The wreck of the Iron Crown
  Lane, F. H. At the fishing grounds
  Lane, F. H. Brig Antelope in Boston harbor
  Lane, F. H. New England coast shipping
  Lane, F. H. New York harbor
  Lane, F. H. Owl's Head, Penobscot, Maine
  Lane, F. H. Ships in the ice off Ten Pound island, Gloucester
  Marin, J. Deep-sea trawlers, Maine
  Marin, J. Four-master off the Cape
  Marin, J. Headed for Boston
  Marin, J. The three master
  Marin, J. Two master becalmed, Maine
  Patterson, C. R. Furling the foresail
  Prendergast, M. B. Pretty ships
  Salmon, R. W. Plymouth sound, England
  Salmon, R. W. South Sea whale fishing
  Salmon, R. W. Storm at sea
  Salmon, R. W. (attributed works) Black Ball liner, New York
  Sanborn, P. Ship Charlotte W. White
  Thomas, J. The ship Nancy, homeward bound
  Unidentified artist. Five master
  Unidentified artist. Letter of marque ship Bethel of Boston
  Unidentified artist. Privateer hermaphrodite brig Rambler of Medford
  Unidentified artist. Privateer schooner Surprise of Baltimore capturing the British ship Star, 1815
  Unidentified artist. Ship Bavaria
  Unidentified artist. Ship Hercules of Salem, 1809
  Unidentified artist. The Southern Belle
  Unidentified artist. Whaling scene
  Unidentified artist. Whaling scene—Triton of New Bedford
  Wales, G. C. Clipper ship Competitor
  Walter, J. Arrival of the Great Western at New York, 1838
  West, B. F. Whaling scene: Ship Julien and Bark Richard
  Wight, J. H. (attributed works) U. S. Ship Constellation

A **sailor** by Unidentified artist

Sailors by Unidentified artist

Sailor's holiday by R. Brackman

Sailor's wedding by R. C. Woodville

Sails by R. Crawford

Sails by C. H. Demuth

Sails by A. G. Dove

St Andrew's church, Roanoke by T. A. Fransioli

The **St** Clair fire by C. F. Gaertner

St Cyr by E. Ewing

St Francis of Assisi by N. Carone

Saint-Gaudens, Augustus, 1848-1907
  Cox, K. Augustus Saint-Gaudens

St George by P. Jenkins

St George by J. La Farge

St George and the calla lilies by R. S. Du Casse

St George and the dragon by Holmead

St George and the dragon by B. West

St Germaine by W. G. Congdon

St John, Frank Jay
  Eakins, T. Frank Jay St John

St Lawrence river from the citadel, Quebec by A. Bierstadt

St Louis, Missouri
  Catlin, G. St Louis, 1836
  Hinchey, W. J. Dedication of the Eads bridge at St Louis, 1874
  Lewis, H. A street in St Louis
  Lewis, H. (attributed works) St Louis after the great fire
  Unidentified artist. Chouteau's pond, St Louis
  Wild, J. C. View of St Louis, c 1841

St Louis belle by A. M. Von Phul

St Louis cemetery, New Orleans by D. Herron

St Louis drawing room by K. Zerbe

St Louis post office mural by M. Siporin

St Malo from Dinard, low tide, Brittany by E. D. Boit

St Mark's, Venice by M. B. Prendergast

St Martin's summer by J. S. Sargent

Saint-Méry, Moreau de, fl 1797
  Sharples, J. Moreau de Saint-Méry

St Patrick's at night by W. Pach

St Paul persecuting the Christians by B. West

St Paul's restoration to sight by Ananias by B. West

St Paul shaking off the viper by B. West

St Peter's, Rome by E. D. Boit

St Peter's, Rome from the Palatine by F. Crowninshield

St Philip's, Charleston by K. Zerbe

St Rose by K. Fearing

St Thomas
  Carlsen, E. Entrance to the harbor of St Thomas

St Thomas church by P. S. Kramer

St Valentine by G. Hartigan

Ste Hilaire by J. Mitchell

Saints deposed by H. Mandel

Saks Fifth avenue window by G. L. K. Morris

Sala del Collegio, Ducal palace, Venice by W. P. P. Longfellow

Salem, Massachusetts
  Ropes, G. Crowninshield's wharf, Salem, 1806

Salem willows by M. B. Prendergast

SALEMME, Attilio, 1911-1955
  Assignation
    McCurdy
  Astronomical blessings are in order
    MBIC. Salemme (col)
  Caught in the equinox   MM
    Newmeyer
    Pierson
    WMAA. New decade
  Echo of a dream
    MBIC. Salemme (col)
  End of the game
    MBIC. Salemme (col)
  Good time
    MBIC. Salemme (col)
  Inquisition   WMAA
    Goodrich. Amer art (col)
    MBIC. Salemme (col)
    Pierson
    WMAA. New decade
  Lunar voyage
    IU. Contemp Amer ptg & sculp, 1955
    MBIC. Salemme (col)
  Madam X
    WMAA. New decade
  Mahatmas of the lunar shore
    NNSG. Younger Amer ptrs
  Night of the ritual
    MM. Amer ptg today
  The oracle   PPhM
    MBIC. Salemme (col)
  The sacrifice   WMAA
    Pousette-Dart. Amer ptg
    WMAA. Contemp Amer ptg, 1952
  Vintage of uncertainties
    MBIC. Salemme (col)

Salisbury, Elizabeth (Tuckerman) 1768-1851
  Stuart, G. Mrs Stephen Salisbury I

SALISBURY, Frank O. 1874-
  Calvin Coolidge   MWA
    MWA. Checklist of portraits
  Franklin D. Roosevelt
    NYG. Fine art

Salisbury, Stephen
  Goodridge, E. Stephen Salisbury

Salisbury, Mrs Stephen, 1st. See Salisbury, Elizabeth (Tuckerman)

SALMON, Robert W. fl 1800-1840
  Boston harbor from Constitution wharf
                                                MdAN
    Pierson
  Boston harbor: Long and Central wharves, 1832 (Dalton coll)
    Davidson v2
  The Constitution in Boston harbor
    Baur. Amer ptg (detail)
  Plymouth Sound, England   MB
    MB. Karolik coll
  Rainsford's island, Boston harbor   MB
    MB. Karolik coll
  South Sea whale fishing   MB
    Davidson v 1
    Pierson
  Storm at sea   MB
    MB. Karolik coll

Attributed works
  Black Ball liner, New York
    Davidson v 1

Salmon
  Audubon, J. J. Osprey and the otter and the salmon
  Homer, W. Ouananiche fishing: Lake St John, Quebec

Salmon river by W. Plate

Salmon trout and smelt by S. M. Brookes

Salome by J. Glasco

Salt fire by L. Mullican

Salt flats by K. Knaths

Salt marshes, Newport, Rhode Island by M. J. Heade

The salt sea by R. Tam

Salt shaker by S. Davis

Saltillo rooftops by E. Hopper

Saltimbanques by Y. Tanguy

Salto mortal by E. Frances

Saltonstall, Gurdon, 1666-1724
  Unidentified artist. Gurdon Saltonstall

SALTZMAN, William, 1916-
  Linear pattern
    CSFP. Annual ex, 1947/48

Salutat by T. Eakins

Salute to General Washington in New York harbor by L. M. Cooke

Salute to the robe trade by C. M. Russell

Sam Perryman by G. Catlin

SAMANT, Manmohan, 1926-
  Sun chariot
    PPC. International ex, 1961/62

SAMPLE, Paul Starrett, 1896-
  Barber shop
    Gruskin (col)
    NHMC. Paul Sample
  Beaver meadow   NHD
    NHMC. Paul Sample
  Country horse show
    PPC. Ptg in the U. S. 1949
  Day in bed
    NHMC. Paul Sample
  Delirium is our best deceiver
    NAD. Annual ex, 1947, 2d half
  East Charleston school   MWiC
    NHMC. Paul Starrett
  Freight cars in desert
    NHMC. Paul Sample

Going to town   IBM
    NHMC. Paul Sample
Hill beyond the bridge
    NHMC. Paul Sample
Iceland fishermen
    NSP. Sportscapes
Janitor's holiday   MM
    Pierson
Maple sugaring in Vermont
    Larkin
    Larkin rev ed
Milk sledge   OYB
    OYB. Catalogue 1951
Miners resting   NeL
    NHMC. Paul Sample
Real wealth   MB
    MB. Ptgs in water color
Remember now the days of thy youth
    NAD. Annual ex, 1953
Roque   NCa
    NHMC. Paul Sample
Spring song
    NHMC. Paul Sample
Sweet hour of prayer
    NHMC. Paul Sample
Two trout fishermen
    NSP. Sportscapes
Winter holiday
    NAD. Annual ex, spring 1950
Winter visitor
    NHMC. Paul Sample
Samson and the lion by P. Evergood
SAMSTAG, Gordon, 1906-
    Young man desiring position   InTH
    InTH. Catalogue
SAMUELSON, Paul F. 1924-
    Mansion doorway   OYB
    OYB. Annual 1949
    OYB. Catalogue 1951
San Barnaba by L. Bosa
San Diego zoo by H. G. Keller
SANBORN, Percy, fl 1860
    Ship Charlotte W. White   MeC
    Jetté. Amer heritage collection
The sanctified by J. C. Wayne
Sanctuary by J. S. Curry
Sanctuary by P. Guston
Sand and sea by D. MacKnight
Sand and sky by J. E. Levi
Sand barge by A. G. Dove
Sand dune by W. Homer
Sand dunes by W. M. Chase
Sand, sea and sky by M. Avery
Sand team by G. W. Bellows
Sandburg, Carl, 1878-
    Freeman, D. Carl Sandburg
Sandcart by G. W. Bellows
Sanders, John, 1714-1783
    Unidentified artist. John Sanders
Sanders, Robert, 1705-1765
    Unidentified artist. Robert Sanders
Sanderson, Mrs Luther. See Hall, Abigail
SANDERSON, William, 1905-
    Composition with fried egg   CoD
    CoS. New accessions USA, 1952
SANDGREN, Nelson, 1917-
    The abiding—summer and sea
    OrPA. Ptgs & sculptures

Sandpipers by P. Riba
Sandy by A. James
SANFORD, M. M.
    Washington at Princeton   NCHA
    Time. 300 years (col)
Sanford, Sarah Ingersoll (Olmstead) 1774-
    1838
    Jarvis, J. W. Mrs Benjamin Sanford
San Francisco, California
    Du Casse, R. S. San Francisco bay
    Firks, H. San Francisco, 1849
    Rederer, F. J. Civic center, San Francisco
    Sheeler, C. San Francisco, 1956
    Tobey, M. San Francisco street
    Unidentified artist. Telegraph hill, San
        Francisco, c 1849
San José mission
    Allen, T. Portal of the mission of San
        José, Texas
San Rafael, California by A. Bierstadt
Santa Maria della Salute by B. Perlin
Santa Maria Formosa, Venice by M. B.
    Prendergast
Santiago de Compostela, Spain by J. S. Sar-
    gent
Santiago de Cuba by W. Homer
SANTO, Patsy, 1894-
    A ray of hope   ATU
    ATU. Coll of Amer art (col)
Sapaque by L. Calcagno
Sappho by D. E. Lee
Sappington, Jane (Breathitt) b 1783?
    Bingham, G. C. Mrs John Sappington
Sappington, John, b 1775?
    Bingham, G. C. Dr John Sappington
Sarasate y Navascuez, Pablo Martín Meli-
    tón, 1844-1908
    Chase, W. M. Pablo de Sarasate
Sargasso sea by J. Skolle
Sargeant, Isabella. See Vallé, Isabella (Sar-
    geant)
Sargent, Emily, 1857-1936
    Sargent, J. S. Simplon pass: the lesson
Sargent, Epes, 1690-1762
    Copley, J. S. Epes Sargent senior
Sargent, FitzWilliam, 1768-1822
    Sargent, J. S. Dr FitzWilliam Sargent
SARGENT, Henry, 1770-1845
    Dinner party   MB
        Baur. Amer ptg (detail)
        Pierson
        Richardson. Ptg in America
        U.S. National Capital sesquicentennial
            com
    Tea party   MB
        Barker. Amer ptg
        Flexner. Light of distant skies
        Pierson
        Roos
SARGENT, John Singer, 1856-1925
    A. Lawrence Lowell   MCH
        McKibbin. Sargent's Boston
    Asher Wertheimer   ELT
        Craven. Treasury 1952 ed
        Mount. John Singer Sargent
    Atlas and Hesperides   MB
        McKibbin. Sargent's Boston
    Auguste Rodin
        Mount. John Singer Sargent
    A backwater, Chalcot
        NSP. Sportscapes

SARGENT, J. S.—*Continued*

Bailleul: tents   MB
  MB. Ptgs in water color
Battle front
  Mount. John Singer Sargent
La biancheria   MB
  MB. Ptgs in water color
Blonde model   MWiS
  MWiS. Ex 4 and 7
Boats at anchor   MWM
  UNESCO. 1860-1949
  UNESCO. 1860-1955
  UNESCO. 1860-1959
Boys on the beach   MWiS
  MWiS. Ex 4 and 7
The breakfast table: Sargent's sister
  Violet   MCH
  McKibbin. Sargent's Boston
Brook among rocks   MB
  MB. Ptgs in water color
Café on Riva degli Schiavoni, Venice
  Sweet
Capri girl
  Sweet
Carmela Bertagna   OCo
  Sweet
Carmencita   FPL
  Mount. John Singer Sargent
Carnation Lily, Lily Rose, Sketch for
  Mount. John Singer Sargent
Carolus-Duran   MWiS
  MWiS. Ex 4 and 7
Carrara: a quarry   MB
  MB. Ptgs in water color
Carrara: in a quarry   MB
  MB. Ptgs in water color
Carrara: little quarry   MB
  MB. Ptgs in water color
Carrara: Lizzatori I   MB
  MB. Ptgs in water color
Carrara: Lizzatori II   MB
  MB. Ptgs in water color
Carrara: M Derville's quarry   MB
  MB. Ptgs in water color
Carrara: marmo statuario   MB
  MB. Ptgs in water color
Carrara: quarry I   MB
  MB. Ptgs in water color
Carrara: quarry II   MB
  MB. Ptgs in water color
Carrara: Trajan's quarry   MB
  MB. Ptgs in water color
Carrara: wet quarries   MB
  MB. Ptgs in water color
Carrara: workmen   MB
  MB. Ptgs in water color
Cashmere shawl (Rose Marie Ormond)
   MB
  MB. Ptgs in water color
  McKibbin. Sargent's Boston
  Mount. John Singer Sargent
Charles M. Loeffler   MBI
  McKibbin. Sargent's Boston
Classic and romantic art (ceiling decora-
  tion)   MB
  McKibbin. Sargent's Boston
Cordova: interior of the cathedral   MB
  MB. Ptgs in water color
Corfu: a rainy day   MB
  MB. Ptgs in water color
Corfu: cypresses   MB
  MB. Ptgs in water color

Corfu: lights and shadows   MB
  MB. Ptgs in water color
Corfu: the terrace   MB
  MB. Ptgs in water color
Corner of the church of St Staë, Venice
  Mount. John Singer Sargent
The countess of Lathom   IBM
  Sweet
Courtyard, Tetuan
  Mount. John Singer Sargent
Cypresses
  Mount. John Singer Sargent
The Danaïdes (lunette)   MB
  MB. Ptgs in water color
  McKibbin. Sargent's Boston
Daniel J. Nolan   DC
  Mount. John Singer Sargent
Daphne   MB
  MB. Ptgs in water color
Daughters of Asher Wertheimer   ELT
  Upjohn
Daughters of Edward D. Boit   MB
  Larkin
  Larkin rev ed
  Larkin rev ed (col detail)
  McKibbin. Sargent's Boston (col)
  Mendelowitz
  Pierson
  Sweet
  Time. 300 years (col)
Decorations in the dome, Boston public
  library
  Pierson
Doctrine of the Trinity   MBP
  Pierson
Edmund Gosse
  Mount. John Singer Sargent
Egyptian girl
  Sweet
  Time. 300 years (col)
Eiger from Mürren   MB
  MB. Ptgs in water color
Elizabeth Chanler
  NAD. Amer tradition
Elsie Palmer   NBuA
  NBuA. Catalogue of the ptgs
Elsie Swinton   ICA
  Mount. John Singer Sargent
En route pour la pêche. See Oyster
  gatherers of Cancale
Evora, Portugal   MB
  MB. Ptgs in water color
Femme avec fourrures   MWiS
  MWiS. Ex 4 and 7
Festa della regata, Palazzo Barbaro
  McKibbin. Sargent's Boston
Figure study
  Mount. John Singer Sargent
FitzWilliam Sargent
  McKibbin. Sargent's Boston
  Mount. John Singer Sargent
Flora Priestley
  Mount. John Singer Sargent
Florence: Boboli gardens   MB
  MB. Ptgs in water color
Florence: Torre Galli   MB
  MB. Ptgs in water color
Florence: Torre Galli, wine bags   MB
  MB. Ptgs in water color
Francis Brooks Chadwick
  McKibbin. Sargent's Boston
Frederick Porter Vinton   RPS
  McKibbin. Sargent's Boston

La fumée d'ambre-gris   MWiS
    MWiS. Ex 4 and 7
Gabriel Fauré
    Mount. John Singer Sargent
Garden wall   MB
    MB. Ptgs in water color
Genoa: the university   MB
    MB. Ptgs in water color
Glacier streams—the Simplon   MSM
    MSM. Handbook
Gondolier
    Mount. John Singer Sargent
Gondolier (Nicola d'Inverno)
    Mount. John Singer Sargent
Gordon Fairchild holding a guinea-pig
    McKibbin. Sargent's Boston
Gourds   NBM
    Mount. John Singer Sargent
    Sweet
Henri Lefort
    Mount. John Singer Sargent
Henry James   ELP
    Mount. John Singer Sargent
Henry Lee Higginson   MCH
    McKibbin. Sargent's Boston
Herbert M. Sears on his yacht Constella-
    tion
    McKibbin. Sargent's Boston
Hillside   MB
    MB. Ptgs in water color
In the Generalife   MM
    Sweet
In the Luxembourg gardens
    Born
Italian head   NCa
    NUM. Art across America
El Jaleo   MBI
    McKibbin. Sargent's Boston
    Pierson
    Time. 300 years (col)
    UNESCO. 1860-1949
    UNESCO. 1860-1955
    UNESCO. 1860-1959
James Whitcomb Riley   InIJ
    InIJ. 105 ptgs
    PPC. Amer classics
John D. Rockefeller
    Mount. John Singer Sargent
Joseph Pulitzer   MCH
    Pulitzer v2
    Sweet
Judith Gautier
    Mount. John Singer Sargent
Lady Cholmondeley
    Mount. John Singer Sargent
Lady Sassoon
    Sweet
Lady with a blue veil (Sally Fairchild)
    McKibbin. Sargent's Boston
Lady Playfair   MCH
    McKibbin. Sargent's Boston
    Sweet
The lesson. See Simplon pass: the lesson
Louis de Fourcaud
    Mount. John Singer Sargent
Luxembourg gardens at twilight   MnMI
    Pierson
    Sweet
Mme Allouard-Jouan
    Mount. John Singer Sargent
Mme Buloz
    Mount. John Singer Sargent

Mme Paul Escudier   MWiS
    CtY. Yale alumni
    MWiS. Ex 4 and 7
    Sweet
Madame X (Madame Gautreau)   MM
    Craven. Treasury 1952 ed
    Flexner. Amer ptg
    Flexner. Short history
    Lee. Art then and now
    McKibbin. Sargent's Boston
    Mendelowitz
    Mount. John Singer Sargent
    Pierson
    Sweet (col cover)
    Taylor. Fifty centuries, 1954 ed (col)
    Time. 300 years (col)
Mlle Jourdain   MWiS
    MWiS. Ex 4 and 7
Man reading   PR
    PR. Catalogue
Mr and Mrs Isaac Newton Phelps Stokes
                                     MM
    Pierson
    Sweet
Mr and Mrs John W. Field   PA
    Pierson
    Sweet
Mrs Adrian Iselin
    Sweet
Mrs Alice Mason
    Sweet
Mrs Asher Wertheimer   ELT
    Sweet
Mrs Augustus Hemenway
    McKibbin. Sargent's Boston
Mrs Charles Edward Inches
    McKibbin. Sargent's Boston
Mrs Charles Gifford Dyer   ICA
    Canaday
    Lewisohn
    Pierson
    Richardson. Ptg in America
    Sweet
Mrs Charles Hunter   ELT
    Mount. John Singer Sargent
Mrs Charles Pelham Curtis
    McKibbin. Sargent's Boston
Mrs Daniel Sargent Curtis
    McKibbin. Sargent's Boston
Mrs Edward D. Boit
    McKibbin. Sargent's Boston
Mrs Edward D. Brandegee
    McKibbin. Sargent's Boston
Mrs Edward Livingston Davis and her
    son Livingston
    McKibbin. Sargent's Boston
Mrs Fiske Warren and her daughter
    Rachel
    McKibbin. Sargent's Boston
Mrs George Swinton   ICA
    Canaday
Mrs Henry White   DC
    DC. De gustibus
Mrs Hugh Hammersley
    Sweet
Mrs J. Montgomery Sears
    McKibbin. Sargent's Boston
Mrs John Joseph Townsend
    Mount. John Singer Sargent
Mrs John Lowell Gardner   MBI
    McKibbin. Sargent's Boston
Mrs Joseph E. Widener
    Mount. John Singer Sargent

SARGENT, J. S.—*Continued*
Mrs Jules Vallé
  Mount. John Singer Sargent
Mrs Knowles and her children   OYB
  OYB. Catalogue 1951
Mrs William Crowninshield Endicott DN
  McKibbin. Sargent's Boston
  Sweet
Mosquito net
  NBuA. Fifty ptgs
  Sweet
Muddy alligators   MWM
  Pierson
Nonchaloire (Sargent's niece, Rose Marie
    Ormond)   DN
  McKibbin. Sargent's Boston (col front)
Oyster gatherers of Cancale (En route
    pour la pêche)
  DC. Masterpieces
  McKibbin. Sargent's Boston (replica)
  NYG. Fine art (col)
  Sweet
Padre Sebastiano   MM
  Bazin
  Sweet
Pailleron children
  Sweet
Paul Helleu
  Mount. John Singer Sargent
Paul Helleu sketching and his wife NBM
  Sweet
Peter Augustus Jay at the age of three
  DC. Privately owned
Piazza Navona, Rome
  Sweet
Pink dress
  Mount. John Singer Sargent
Poperinghe: two soldiers   MB
  MB. Ptgs in water color
Ralph Curtis on the beach at Scheven-
    ingen, Holland
  McKibbin. Sargent's Boston
Reading   MB
  MB. Ptgs in water color
Rehearsal of the Pas de Loup orchestra
    at the Cirque d'Hiver
  Sweet
Repose   DN
  Bazin
  Craven. Treasury 1952 ed
Resting   MWiS
  MWiS. Ex 4 and 7
Rigging   MBM
  Sweet
Road in Midi   MWiS
  MWiS. Ex 4 and 7
Robert Louis Stevenson   OCiT
  Craven. Rainbow book
  McKinney
  Roos
  Sweet
  Time. 300 years (col)
Robert Louis Stevenson (Whitney coll)
  Cheney. Story 1958 ed
  CtY. Yale alumni
  Richardson. Ptg in America
Rose Marie Ormond. See Nonchaloire
St Martin's summer
  Mount. John Singer Sargent
Sally Fairchild. See Lady with a blue
    veil
Santiago de Compostela, Spain   MB
  MB. Ptgs in water color

Scuola di San Rocco, Venice
  Sweet
Self-portrait at twenty-one
  McKibbin. Sargent's Boston
Self-portrait aged thirty-six
  McKibbin. Sargent's Boston
  Mount. John Singer Sargent
Señor Subercaseaux in a gondola in Venice
  Sweet
Shadowed stream   MB
  MB. Ptgs in water color
Shallows
  MB. Ptgs in water color
Simplon pass: at the top   MB
  MB. Ptgs in water color
Simplon pass: avalanche track   MB
  MB. Ptgs in water color
Simplon pass: chalets   MB
  MB. Ptgs in water color
Simplon pass: crags   MB
  MB. Ptgs in water color
Simplon pass: fresh snow   MB
  MB. Ptgs in water color
Simplon pass: mountain brook   MB
  MB. Ptgs in water color
Simplon pass: the foreground   MB
  MB. Ptgs in water color
Simplon pass: the green parasol   MB
  MB. Ptgs in water color
Simplon pass: the lesson (Emily Sargent,
    Rose Marie and Reine Ormond) MB
  Canaday
  McKibbin. Sargent's Boston
  MB. Ptgs in water color
  Sweet
Simplon pass: the tease   MB
  MB. Ptgs in water color
Spanish boys at play. See Vianna do
    Castello, Portugal
Spanish soldiers   NBM
  Sweet
A staircase   MWiS
  MWiS. Ex 4 and 7
Street in Venice   MWiS
  MWiS. Ex 4 and 7
Suzanne Poirson
  Sweet
Time. 300 years (col)
Tents at Lake O'Hara   CtHW
  CtHW. Handbook
Theodore Roosevelt
  Mount. John Singer Sargent
Thomar, Portugal   MB
  MB. Ptgs in water color
Tyrolese crucifixion
  Taylor. Fifty centuries, 1954 ed (col)
Val d'Aosta, stepping stones
  Mount. John Singer Sargent
Val d'Aosta, a stream over rocks
  Mount. John Singer Sargent
Venetian bead stringers   NBuA
  NBuA. Catalogue of the ptgs
Venetian interior   MWiS
  MWiS. Ex 4 and 7
  Sweet
Venice: I Gesuati   MB
  MB. Ptgs in water color
Venice: La Dogana   MB
  MB. Ptgs in water color
Venice: La Salute   MB
  MB. Ptgs in water color
Venice: Under the Rialto bridge   MB
  MB. Ptgs in water color

Vernon Lee   ELT
  Mount. John Singer Sargent
Sweet
  Walker. Ptgs from America (col)
Vianna do Castello, Portugal (Spanish
  boys at play)
  MB. Ptgs in water color
Villa di Marlia: a fountain   MB
  MB. Ptgs in water color
Villa di Marlia, Lucca   MB
  MB. Ptgs in water color
Villa di Marlia: the balustrade   MB
  MB. Ptgs in water color
Villa Falconiere   MB
  MB. Ptgs in water color
Vines and cypresses   MB
  MB. Ptgs in water color
Violet at seven
  Mount. John Singer Sargent
Violet Sargent   MBI
  McKibbin. Sargent's Boston
White ships   NBM
  NYG. Fine art
The winds I   MB
  MB. Ptgs in water color
The winds II   MB
  MB. Ptgs in water color
The Wyndham sisters   MM
  Gardner 1959 ed
  McCurdy
  MM. 100 Amer ptrs
Sargent, Violet. See Ormond, Violet (Sar-
  gent)
Sargent family
  Unidentified artist. Sargent family
SARKISIAN, Paul, 1928-
Ancient facade   OYB
  OYB. Annual 1959
  OYB. Supplement 1959
SARKISIAN, Sarkis, 1909-
Archaic rock   OYB
  OYB. Annual 1955
  OYB. Supplement 1959
Self-portrait
  WiMiA. Amer ptg 1760-1960
SARTAIN, John, 1808-1897
  Men of progress: American inventors,
    1861 (after Christian Schuessele)
  U.S. National Capital sesquicentennial
    com
SASLOW, Herbert, 1920-
Oneness
  IU. Contemp Amer ptg & sculp, 1957
The processional
  IU. Contemp Amer ptg & sculp, 1955
Sassoon, Aline Caroline (de Rothschild)
  lady, d 1909
  Sargent, J. S. Lady Sassoon
Satan by W. H. Hahn
Sa-tan-ti addressing the Peace commission-
  ers by H. Stieffel
Satellite by R. Rauschenberg
Satisfaction in New Jersey by P. Evergood
SATO, Tadashi, 1923-
Composition, 1953-54   NBuA
  NBuA. Acquisitions 1954-57
  NNSG. Younger Amer ptrs
Composition no 10—three lines, 1957
                        NBuA
  NBuA. Acquisitions 1957-58

Sea form no 4
  IU. Contemp Amer ptg & sculp, 1961
Untitled   NNSG
  NNSG. Handbook
Saturday afternoon by Z. L. Sepeshy
Saturday again by G. Knee
Saturday night by W. De Kooning
Saturday night bath by H. Pippin
Saturday night in New York city by S.
  Shawkey
Saturday night on the ranch by L. Megargee
Saturday night, Sarasota, Florida by E.
  Shinn
Satyr by N. Carone
The Sauk and Fox slave dance by G. Cat-
  lin
Saul and the witch of Endor by B. West
SAVAGE, Edward, 1761-1817
Abiel Holmes
  DC. Privately owned
Abraham Whipple
  Larkin
  Larkin rev ed
Mrs Edward Savage   MWM
  MB. New England miniatures
Self-portrait   MWM
  Dickson. John Wesley Jarvis
The Washington family   DN
  DN. Mellon coll
  UNESCO. Prior to 1860
  UNESCO. Prior to 1860 3d ed
SAVAGE, Edward, 1761-1817, and PINE,
  Robert Edge, 1730-1788
Congress voting independence   PH
  U.S. National Capital sesquicentennial
    com
Savage, Elizabeth. See Heyward, Elizabeth
  (Savage)
SAVAGE, Eugene Francis, 1883-
Death of Europe
  NAD. Annual ex, 1949, 1st half
Savage, Sarah (Seaver) 1765-1861
  Savage, E. Mrs Edward Savage
Savage, Thomas, c 1606-1682
  Unidentified artist. Thomas Savage
Savannah by L. Dodd
Saved—a hard chase by A. F. Tait
Savo, Jimmy, 1896-1960
  Dehn, A. A. Jimmy Savo and rope
  Isenburger, E. Jimmy Savo
  MacIver, L. Jimmy Savo's shoes
  Miller, L. Jimmy Savo
SAVORY, Thomas C. fl 1837-1852
National lancers on Boston Common, 1838
  U.S. National Capital sesquicentennial
    com
Sawtooth Falls by A. Friedman
SAWYER, Belinda A., fl 1820
Fruit in a white bowl   VWR
  Ford. Pictorial folk art
SAWYER, Helen Alton, known as Henka,
  1900-
Carnival
  IU. Contemp Amer ptg, 1948
Dolores in blue costume
  NAD. Annual ex, 1949, 1st half
Valentine still life   OT
  OT. Contemp Amer ptgs
Saxe, John Godfrey, 1816-1887
  Mason, B. F. John Godfrey Saxe

Saxe, Sophia Newell (Sollace) fl 1841-1875
  Mason, B. F. Mrs John Godfrey Saxe
Saxophone player—Jay Cameron by L.
    Rivers
Say, Thomas, 1787-1834
  Wood, J. Thomas Say
Saying prayers by H. Pippin
Say's or western fox squirrel by J. J.
    Audubon
Scallop fleet by G. G. MacNutt
Scalp dance by G. Catlin
The scalplock by A. J. Miller
SCARLETT, Rolph, 1890-
  Blue lines
    IU. Contemp Amer ptg & sculp, 1953
  Pica Cotto
    MM. Amer ptg today
  Yellow above
    IU. Contemp Amer ptg, 1951
Scava by J. Heliker
Scene at rendezvous by A. J. Miller
Scene in the Catskills by F. E. Church
Scene on the Magdalene by F. E. Church
Scenery found by J. G. Chapman
Scent by J. Pollock
Scenting the breeze by A. J. Miller
SCHAMBERG, Morton L. 1882-1918
  Abstraction
    MMA. Abstract
  A girl, Study of
    WMAA. Pioneers
  Landscape   PPhM
    PPhM. Arensberg coll
  Machine   CtY
    Baur. Revolution
    CtY. Soc Anonyme
    McCurdy
    MMA. Abstract
    Pierson
  Mechanical abstraction   PPhM
    PPhM. Arensberg coll
  Still life, camera flashlight
    MnMW. Precisionist view
  Telephone   OCo
    Brown. Amer ptg
    Pierson
SCHANKER, Louis, 1903-
  Abstract no 1   NBM
    Pousette-Dart. Amer ptg
  Circle image
    NNSG. Younger Amer ptrs
  Circle image number 18
    IU. Contemp Amer ptg & sculp, 1955
  Circles in rectangles
    MnU. 40 Amer ptrs
  Crucifixion
    Rathbun
  Football
    MnU. 40 Amer ptrs
  Number 9, 1951
    PPC. International ex, 1952
  Sea grass
    IU. Contemp Amer ptg & sculp, 1957
SCHAPIRO, Miriam, 1923-
  The game
    IU. Contemp Amer ptg & sculp, 1961
  Summer's end
    WMAA. Annual ex, 1958
SCHARF, William, 1927-
  A share of fire
    IU. Contemp Amer ptg & sculp, 1961

Schatacook mountain, Housatonic valley,
    Connecticut by J. F. Crospey
SCHELL, F. Cresson
  Trolley-car excursion, 1896   DLC
    Davidson v2
SCHELL, Francis H.
  Election scene during the Harrison-Van
    Buren campaign, 1840
    Davidson v2
Schenectady, New York, 1832 by J. W. Hill
Schenk, Franklin L.
  Eakins, T. The Bohemian (Franklin
    Schenk)
SCHEUCH, Harry William, 1907-
  Rebecca street
    OYB. Annual 1952
  Soho portrait
    VR. Biennial ex, 1948
SCHLEETER, Howard B. 1903-
  Full moon
    NNSG. Younger Amer ptrs
Schleppengull, Colonel
  Copley, J. S. Colonels Hugo and Schlep-
    pengull
SCHMIDT, Katherine, 1898-
  Broe and McDonald listen in   WMAA
    Goodrich. Amer art
    Pierson
  Waiting for his turn   ATU
    ATU. Coll of Amer art (col)
SCHNAKENBERG, Henry Ernest, 1892-
  Button falls
    Gruskin
  Cat and kittens
    NYG. Fine art
  Conversation   WMAA
    Goodrich. Amer art
  Mrs James M. Osborn
    WMAA. Juliana Force
  A place to swim
    PPC. Ptg in the U.S. 1949
SCHOCK, William, 1913-
  Rocks and rubble
    IU. Contemp Amer ptg, 1950
Schock, Mrs William. See Janicki, Hazel
SCHOENER, Jason
  Down the ways
    OYB. Annual 1952
Scholar by W. Pachner
Schools and school teachers
  Durrie, G. H. Red schoolhouse
  Edmonds, F. W. New scholar
  Harvey, G. Extra-curricular activity under
    the Apostle oak, 1841
  Homer, W. Country school
  Johnston, D. C. Early New England
    schoolroom scene
  Pickett, J. Manchester valley
  Rosenthal, D. Don Pasquale
  Sample, P. S. East Charleston school
  Unidentified artist. Ceremonies at a young
    ladies' seminary, 1810-1820
  Unidentified artist. Schoolmaster and
    boys
  Unidentified artist. The schoolroom,
    c 1830
The schooner by C. H. Demuth
Schooner and scow by S. Wilson
Schooners at anchor, Key West by W.
    Homer

SCHRAG, Karl, 1912-
Black tree in bright light
  Gordon. Karl Schrag
Coast after sundown
  Gordon. Karl Schrag
Dark trees and sunny meadow
  Gordon. Karl Schrag
Edge of the town
  Gordon. Karl Schrag
Evening
  Gordon. Karl Schrag
Evening radiance
  Gordon. Karl Schrag
Evening sky
  Gordon. Karl Schrag
Flame and winter tree
  Gordon. Karl Schrag
Fragrance of grasses
  Gordon. Karl Schrag (col)
Heat wave
  Gordon. Karl Schrag
Iris
  Gordon. Karl Schrag
Montserrat   WMAA
  Gordon. Karl Schrag
Mountains and trees
  Gordon. Karl Schrag
Oropesa
  Gordon. Karl Schrag
The painter
  Gordon. Karl Schrag
Rainstorm
  Gordon. Karl Schrag
Red quarry
  Gordon. Karl Schrag
Self-portrait
  Gordon. Karl Schrag
Still life
  Gordon. Karl Schrag
Stillness and reflections
  Gordon. Karl Schrag
Summer thoughts in winter
  Gordon. Karl Schrag
Sun filled fields
  Gordon. Karl Schrag (col)
Sun sinking into the sea
  Gordon. Karl Schrag
Tree tops and veiled moon
  Gordon. Karl Schrag
Trees against the sky   NBM
  Gordon. Karl Schrag
Trees and sinking sun
  Gordon. Karl Schrag
Trees, light and movement
  Gordon. Karl Schrag
Waves of love and of the sea
  Gordon. Karl Schrag
Wild iris   CtHW
  Gordon. Karl Schrag
Wind, wave and tree
  Gordon. Karl Schrag
SCHRECKENGOST, Viktor, 1906-
Fish forms
  Pousette-Dart. Amer ptg
SCHREIBER, Georges, 1904-
From Arkansas   InTH
  InTH. Catalogue
SCHREYVOGEL, Charles, 1861-1912
My bunkie   MM
  McCracken. Portrait of the old west
   (col)
The silenced war whoop
  McCracken. Portrait of the old west
   (col)

SCHUCKER, Charles, 1908-
Ascensions
  WMAA. Contemp Amer ptg, 1955
The bridge   WMAA
  Goodrich. Amer art
  Pierson
Tree
  Baur. Nature
SCHUELER, Jon, 1916-
Evening
  Baur. Nature
Snow cloud and blue sky   WMAA
  Goodrich. Amer art
SCHUESSELE, Christian, 1824?-1879 and
  WEBER, Paul, 1823-1916
Skating at Kelly's dam, Germantown PH
  Chew. 250 years of art
SCHULDT, H.
Traffic halt, 1878   RPS
  Davidson v2
SCHULEIN, Julius Wolfgang, 1881-
Harbor
  IU. Contemp Amer ptg, 1952
Schuyler, **Anne (Van Rensselaer).** See Van
  Rensselaer, Anne
Schuyler, **Ariaantje.** See Van Rensselaer,
  Ariaantje (Schuyler)
Schuyler, **Catharina,** b 1703
  Unidentified artist. Catharina Schuyler
Schuyler, **Catherine (Van Rensselaer)** 1734-
  1803
  Unidentified artist. Mrs Philip Schuyler
Schuyler, **David Davidse,** 1669-1715
  Unidentified artist. David Davidse
  Schuyler
Schuyler, **Elizabeth Staats (Wendell)** d 1737
  Watson, J. (attributed works) Capt Jo-
  hannes Schuyler and his wife Eliza-
  beth Staats Wendell
Schuyler, **Elsje (Rutgers)** See Vas, Elsje
  (Rutgers) Schuyler
Schuyler, **Johannes,** 1668-1747
  Watson, J. (attributed works) Capt Jo-
  hannes Schuyler and his wife Eliza-
  beth Staats Wendell
Schuyler, **Mrs Johannes.** See Schuyler, Eliz-
  abeth Staats (Wendell)
Schuyler, **Johannes,** 1697-1741
  Unidentified artist. Johannes Schuyler
Schuyler, **Mrs John.** See Van Rensselaer,
  Anne
Schuyler, **Philip,** 1695-1745
  Unidentified artist. Col Philip Schuyler
Schuyler, **Mrs Philip** See Schuyler, Catherine
  (Van Rensselaer)
Schuyler, **Pieter,** 1657-1724
  Unidentified artist. Pieter Schuyler
Schuyler **family,** fl 1824
  Andrews, A. Schuyler family
Schuyler **family, Member of**
  Unidentified artist. Gentleman of the
  Schuyler family
  Unidentified artist. Little girl of the
  Schuyler family
The **Schuylkill,** View on the by J. Neagle
Schuylkill at Manayunk by F. Speight
Schuylkill county almshouse property, View
  of the by C. Hofmann

SCHWABACHER, Ethel K. 1903-
Dead leaves
Baur. Nature (col)
Morning   NBuA
NBuA. Acquisitions 1959-1961
Oedipus at Colonos no 2, 1959   WMAA
Goodrich. Amer art
Shannon
WMAA. Annual ex, 1958
SCHWARTZ, Lester O. 1912-
Circus fantasy
IU. Contemp Amer ptg, 1950
Cloistered island
IU. Contemp Amer ptg, 1948
SCHWARTZ, Manfred, 1909-
David the king no 1
Genauer
David the king no 2
Genauer
Finding of Moses
WMAA. Annual ex, 1955
SCHWARTZ, William Samuel, 1896-
De Profundis
IU. Contemp Amer ptg, 1948
Through my cosmic eye
IU. Contemp Amer ptg, 1950
Time and space   NJMo
NJMo. Forty years
NJMo. Your Montclair art museum
SCHWARZ, Joseph
Mourning the child   OYB
OYB. Annual 1955
Schweig, Martyl. See Martyl
Schweig, Suzanne. See Martyl
Scobie, James, fl 1804
Malbone, E. G. James Scobie
Scollay, Deborah, 1737-1794
Copley, J. S. Deborah Scollay
Scotch and Burgundy by H. Hofmann
Scotch day at Kennywood by J. Kane
SCOTT, John W. A. 1815-1890
Old covered wagon
Sears. Highlights
SCOTT, Peter Markham, 1909-
Pintails
NSP. Sportscapes
Scott's Bluff by A. J. Miller
Scott's Run, West Virginia by B. Shahn
The **scout** by C. M. Russell
The **scout**: friends or enemies? by F. Remington
Scouting party by W. T. Ranney
Scoyen, Peter, d 1832
Jarvis, J. W. Peter Scoyen
Scranton, William Worthington
Chase, W. M. William Worthington Scranton
Scrap by D. W. Ellis
The **scream** of shrapnel at San Juan Hill, Cuba by F. Remington
Screaming eagle by Unidentified artist
The **scullers** by P. S. Kramer
Sculling by K. Knaths
Sculling by W. Stuempfig
The **sculptor** by P. Guston
Sculptor's studio by J. J. Hammer
Sculptor's studio by T. H. Matteson
Sculpture by H. Holtzman
Scuola di San Rocco, Venice by J. S. Sargent

Sea captains carousing at Surinam by J. Greenwood
Sea cross by S. Etnier
Sea depth by E. Loran
Sea eagle by J. J. Audubon
Sea form by T. Sato
Sea grass by L. Schanker
Sea gulls by B. Benn
Sea gulls by J. Marin
Sea gulls by E. F. Spruce
Sea gulls by M. Sterne
Sea gulls by W. Thon
Sea horses—sea movement off Deer island, Maine by J. Marin
Sea nymph drawn by dolphins by J. La Farge
Sea piece—Boat fantasy by J. Marin
Sea sounds by G. R. Davis
Sea wall by C. Morris
Seal rocks, Farallones by A. Bierstadt
Seamstress by J. Lawrence
Seamstress by R. Soyer
Seaquake by W. Kamys
The **search** by K. L. Callahan
The **search** by S. E. Dickinson
The **search** by J. Pollock
Searching the Scriptures by W. M. Harnett
Searchlight, harbor entrance, Santiago de Cuba by W. Homer
Searle, John, fl 1822
Interior of the Park theater, New York, 1822   NNHS
Davidson v2
U.S. National Capital sesquicentennial com
Sears, Herbert Mason, 1867-1942
Sargent, J. S. Herbert M. Sears on his yacht Constellation
Sears, Mrs Joshua Montgomery. See Sears, Sarah (Choate)
SEARS, Richard
Towards integrating sculptural influence   CSFM
Pousette-Dart. Amer ptg
SEARS, Sarah Choate, 1858-1935
Regal lilies   MB
MB. Ptgs in water color
Portrait of the artist
Sargent, J. S. Mrs Joshua Montgomery Sears
Seascape
Avery, M. Advancing sea
Avery, M. Sand, sea and sky
Avery, M. Sea and dunes
Avery, M. Seascape
Avery, M. Sunset on a quiet sea
Baziotes, W. A. The sea
Bellows, G. W. Fog breakers—sea spume
Bellows, G. W. Seascape
Birch, T. Off the Maine coast
Birch, T. Seascape
Birch, T. Shipwreck
Carlsen, E. The surf
Chesney, L. Night sea
Darrah, S. T. Seascape
Davis, J. Painting of the ocean
Durfee, H. Seascape no II

Eilshemius, L. M. Flying Dutchman
Evans, J. The white squall
Galloway, Sea coming into the land
Gottlieb, A. Sea and tide
Graves, M. Sea and the morning redness
Graves, M. Sea, fish and constellation
Greene, B. The sea
Haseltine, W. S. Seascape
Hassam, C. Sunny blue sea
Homer, W. Backrush
Homer, W. Coast in winter
Homer, W. Early morning after a storm at sea
Homer, W. Eastern point, Prout's neck
Homer, W. Lost on the Grand Banks
Homer, W. Northeaster
Homer, W. On a lee shore
Homer, W. Summer squall
Homer, W. Sunlight on the coast
Homer, W. Weatherbeaten
Homer, W. Wreck of the Iron Crown
Jamieson, M. Off Hatteras no 2
Johnston, D. C. Ship smashing against rocks
Kensett, J. F. Sea and rocky shore
Kensett, J. F. and Huntington, D. Seascape, Newport
Marin, J. Boats, sea and rocks
Marin, J. Cape Split, Maine
Marin, J. Movement, boat and sea, Deer isle, Maine
Marin, J. My Hell raising sea
Marin, J. Rocks and sea, Small point, Maine
Marin, J. Sea after hurricane
Marin, J. Sea and gulls
Marin, J. Sea and rocks
Marin, J. Sea and sky
Marin, J. Sea piece
Marin, J. Sea with red sky
Marin, J. Seascape fantasy, Maine
Mattson, H. E. Atlantic
Mattson, H. E. Eventide
Nordfeldt, B. J. O. Sea and rocks
Pollock, J. Seascape
Remington, F. Hauling in the gill net
Remington, F. Howl of the weather
Rice, H. W. Seascape
Ryder, A. P. The sea
Singer, C. Stormy weather
Sterne, M. After the storm
Sterne, M. Sea, sand and wind
Tam, R. The salt sea
Unidentified artist. Whaling
Waugh, F. J. A bit of the Cape
Waugh, F. J. Breakers at floodtide
Waugh, F. J. Coast of Maine
Waugh, F. J. Great seas
Waugh, F. J. Open sea
Waugh, F. J. Pounding surf
Waugh, F. J. Surf under moonlight
Waugh, F. J. Windward shore
West, B. Seascape
Zajac, J. Seacoast
Zajac, J. Seascape
Seashore by L. B. La Farge
Seashore by M. B. Prendergast
Season ended by Y. Kuniyoshi
Season of mists by H. Lundeberg
The season's turning by S. Rosenberg
Seated boy by B. Otis

Seated boy in lavender overalls by W. Sommer
Seated figure by W. De Kooning
Seated figure by B. Greene
Seated figure by T. Roszak
Seated figure in garden by E. N. Bischoff
Seated figure of a young woman by W. M. Chase
Seated figure with gray by R. Goodnough
Seated figure, Yakshi by A. Hoener
Seated girl by H. Hofmann
Seated man by W. De Kooning
Seated man with object by N. J. Oliveira
Seated nude by B. Karfiol
Seated nude by K. S. Williams
Seated self-portrait by M. Marcus
Seated witness by S. W. Hayter
Seated woman by B. Currie
Seated woman by W. De Kooning
Seated woman by B. Greene
Seaver, Sarah. See Savage, Sarah (Seaver)
Seaweed by G. O'Keeffe
Sebastian, Saint, d 286
    Taubes, F. Phantasy on the martyrdom of St Sebastian
Sebastian river, Florida by M. J. Heade
SEBREE, Charles, 1914-
    The note
        ICA. Annual ex, 1951
SEBRON, Victor Valentin
    Sugar levee, New Orleans, 1853
        Davidson v2
Secluded by A. Nepote
Second allegory by B. Shahn
Second floor front by K. Zerbe
Second spring by B. Shahn
Second-story sunlight by E. Hopper
Second time painting by R. Rauschenberg
The second two-panel horizontal by A. Leslie
Second variation by E. Fiene
Secret by E. Friedensohn
The secretary's table by W. M. Harnett
Security of the mother by C. Walker
Sedation by J. Lawrence
Sedgwick, Katherine, 1820-1880
    Ingham, C. C. Katherine Sedgwick
Seed by C. A. Morris
Seed corn by A. N. Wyeth
The seed was in itself by K. L. Callahan
Seedling by T. Stamos
Seeking a future by P. Evergood
Seeking the trail by C. M. Russell
Seeking work by M. Weber
The seer by A. Gottlieb
The seesaw by W. Homer
Segment of Spain by B. Kamihira
Segment of the garden by C. La More
Segovia, Andrés, 1894-
    Stein, R. J. Hommage à Andrés Segovia
SEIBERT, Garfield, 1881-
    The road between
        IU. Contemp Amer ptg & sculp, 1959

SEIFERT, Paul A., 1840-1921
Jacob Bennett farm, Gotham, Wisconsin, c 1886
  Lipman. Primitive ptrs
Residence of Lemuel Cooper, Plain, Wisconsin
  Lipman. Primitive ptrs
Residence of Mr. E. R. Jones, Dodgeville, Wisconsin
  Lipman. Primitive ptrs
Wisconsin farm scene   NCHA
  Time. 300 years (col)
The **Seine** by M. Avery
The **Seine,** View of by H. D. Martin
Seine Madonna by T. E. Rosenthal
The **seiner** by S. M. Etnier
SEKULA, Sonia, 1918-
Succession of feelings
  IU. Contemp Amer ptg & sculp, 1953
Selectmen by A. James
Self figure by L. Rivers
Self-portraits
Adolphe, A. J. Self-portrait
Albright, I. L. Self-portrait, 1935
Allston, W. Self-portait
Ames, E. Self-portrait
Avery, M. Self-portait
Bascom, R. H. M. Self-portrait
Beckmann, M. Portrait of the artist with a saxophone
Beckmann, M. Self-portrait, 1912
Beckmann, M. Self-portrait, 1950
Beckmann, M. Self-portrait with a cigarette
Bellows, G. W. Self-portrait
Benton, T. H. Self-portrait, 1925
Betts, L. Self-portrait
Bingham, G. C. Self-portrait, 1877?
Bohrod, A. Self-portrait
Bouché, L. Self-portrait
Brackman, R. Self-portrait
Brown, M. Self-portrait
Carone, N. Self-portrait: head
Cassatt, M. Self-portrait
Catlin, G. Self-portrait, 1824
Chapman, J. G., Looking for good scenery
Chapman, J. G. Scenery found
Chase, W.M. Self-portrait
Copley, J. S. Copley family
Copley, J. S. Self-portrait (Hammond coll)
Copley, J. S. Self-portrait (miniature, Green coll)
Copley, J. S. Self-portrait (pastel, Du Pont coll)
Davis, E. P. Mr and Mrs Eben P. Davis
De Martini, J. Self-portrait
Dickinson, E. W. Self-portrait, 1941
Douché, T. S. Dr Jacob and Thomas Spence Douché
Dunlap, W. Self-portrait
Durrie, G. H. Self-portrait
Duyckinck, Gerrit. Self-portrait
Eakins, T. Self-portrait
Eichholtz, J. Self-portrait
Evergood, P. Self-portrait, 1943
Evergood, P. Self-portrait with divining rod
Evergood, P. Self-portrait with nude

Feke, R. Self-portrait
Fiene, E. Self-portrait
Fisher, Jonathan. Self-portrait
Frankenstein, J. P. The artist in his studio
Goldsmith, D. Self-portrait
Gorky, A. Artist and his mother
Gorky, A. Self-portrait, c 1937
Grosz, G. Self-portrait, 1938
Hancock, N. Self-portrait
Heliker, J. E. Self-portrait
Hesselius, G. Self-portrait
Hofmann, H. Self-portrait
Hopkinson, F. Self-portrait
Hovenden, T. Self-portrait
Hubard, W. J. Mann S. Valentine, 2nd, and the artist
Hubard, W. J. Self-portrait
Hunt, W. M. Self-portrait
Inman, H. Self-portrait
Isenburger, E. Self-portrait
James, A. Self-portrait, 1940
Jarvis, J. W. Self-portrait
Johnson, L. Self-portrait in ochre
Kearns, J. Self-portrait
Krans, O. Self-portrait
Kuniyoshi, Y. Self-portrait as a golf player
La Farge, J. Self-portrait
Levine, J. Self-portrait with muse
Lockman, D. M. Self-portrait
McGarrell, J. Reflection, self-portrait
Malbone, E. G. Self-portrait
Marcus, M. Seated self-portrait
Mattson, H. E. Self-portrait
Maurer, A. H. Self-portrait, 1897
Maurer, A. H. Self-portrait with hat
Meng, J. Self-portrait
Menkès, S. Self-portrait
Mintz, H. Self-portrait
Myers, J. Self-portrait
Page, W. Self-portrait
Peale, C. W. The artist in his museum
Peale, C. W. Self-portrait
Peale, C. W. Self-portrait in uniform
Peale, J. Self-portrait with his family
Peale, Rembrandt. Self-portrait
Peale, Rembrandt. Self-portrait, 1791, age 13
Peto, J. F. Self-portrait with rack picture
Phillips, J. Self-portrait, Versailles
Pickens, A. Actor and his family
Pippin, H. Self-portrait
Price, C. S. Head
Rattner, A. Self-portrait, 1947
Rattner, A. Self-portrait, 1957
Roberts, P. W. Self-portrait
Rondel, F. Self-portrait
Roszak, T. Self-portrait
Russell, C. M. Charles Russell on Red Bird
Russell, C. M. Self-portrait
Ryder, A. P. Self-portrait, c 1880
Sargent, J. S. Self-portrait at thirty-six
Sargent, J. S. Self-portrait at twenty-one
Sarkisian, S. Self-portrait
Savage, E. Self-portrait

Schrag, K. Self-portrait
Shahn, B. Self-portrait among church-goers
Sloan, J. Self-portrait
Smibert, J. Self-portrait (detail from Bermuda group)
Smith, R. Self-portrait, 1887
Smith, T. Self-portrait
Soyer, R. Self-portrait
Street, R. Likeness of himself
Sully, T. Self-portrait
Sully, T. Thomas Sully and Mrs Sully
Thayer, A. H. Self-portrait, c 1898
Tilyard, P. Artist in his studio
Tomlin, B. W. Self-portrait, 1932
Toole, J. Self-portrait
Troye, E. Edward Troye and an unidentified boy
Trumbull, J. Portrait of an artist, probably self-portrait
Trumbull, J. Self-portrait at 18 years
Trumbull, J. Self-portrait at about 56 years
Tuthill, A. G. D. Self-portrait
Vanderlyn, J. Self-portrait
Waldo, S. L. Self-portrait
Watkins, F. C. Self-portrait
Weir, R. W. Self-portrait
West, B. Self-portrait
West, B. Self-portrait in miniature, c 1756-57
Whistler, J. A. M. Self-portrait, c 1858
Whistler, J. A. M. Self-portrait, 1867
Whittredge, W. Self-portrait: the artist at his easel
Wood, G. Return from Bohemia
Wood, G. Self-portrait
Wright, J. Self-portrait of the artist and family
Wyeth, A. N. Self-portrait
Ziroli, N. Self-portrait

SELIGER, Charles, 1926-
Cross-section, plant life   NUM
  NUM. Root bequest
Don Quixote
  Read. Art now, 1948 ed
The kiss
  Read. Concise history
Mood indigo
  ICA. Annual ex, 1947/48
Winterscape
  MMA. Abstract
SELIGMANN, Kurt L. 1900-1961
Age of reason
  Pearson. Mod renaissance
The balcony I, 1949-50   WMAA
  Goodrich. Amer Art
  Pierson
Composition.
  Read. Art now
Effervescence no 3
  Pousette-Dart. Amer ptg
Envelopment (Rubezahl)
  IU. Contemp Amer ptg & sculp, 1961
Environment of the Chateau Argol
  Pearson. Mod renaissance
Fallen angels
  DC. 22 biennial ex, 1951
  ICA. Annual ex, 1957
  Pierson
The great waters
  ICA. Annual ex, 1947/48

High priest   IU
  IU. Contemp Amer ptg, 1951
  IU. 20th century
Magnetic mountain
  WMAA. Contemp Amer ptg, 1950
Mythomania
  IU. Contemp Amer ptg & sculp, 1957
One-eyed creature
  Pearson. Mod renaissance
Philemon and Baucis
  CSFP. Annual ex, 1948/49
  IU. Contemp Amer ptg, 1950
Sabbath phantoms   MMA
  Read. Concise history
Sleepwalkers' meeting
  IU. Contemp Amer ptg, 1952
Souvenir of America   NBuA
  NBuA. Contemporary ptgs
Sellers, Coleman
  Peale, C. W. Coleman Sellers
Sellers, Mrs Coleman. See Sellers, Sophonisba Angusciola (Peale)
Sellers, Sophonisba Angusciola (Peale) 1786-1859
  Peale, C. W. Sophonisba Peale Sellers
SELLSTEDT, Lars Gustaf, 1819-1911
Buffalo harbor from the foot of Porter avenue   NBuA
  NBuA. Catalogue of ptgs
  U.S. National Capital sesquicentennial com
Seme by S. Davis
SEMSER, Charles, 1922-
Butcher shop
  IU. Contemp Amer ptg & sculp, 1955
Semtua by N. Yamamoto
SENAT, Prosper Louis, 1852-1925
Street in Taormina   MB
  MB. Ptgs in water color
The **Senate** by W. Gropper
The **Senate**, Albany, 1850 by Unidentified artist
The **senator** by J. Hirsch
Send-off by A. Pickens
Seneca veterans of the war of 1812 by J. L. D. Mathies
SENNHAUSER, John, 1907-
Collage, no 3 (watercolor)
  WMAA. Annual ex, 1956
Synchroformic no 4, staccato
  WMAA. Contemp Amer ptg, 1949
Synchroformic 27
  Pousette-Dart. Amer ptg
Synchroformic no 28, étude in yellows
  IU. Contemp Amer ptg & sculp, 1953
Sentimental journey by A. P. Ryder
Sentimental moment by P. Guston
The **sentinel** by S. Greene
Sentinel by S. G. Reinhardt
The **sentinel** by F. Remington
Sentinels by A. Brook
Sentinels of the West by A. Dehn
Sentry by S. Reinhardt
Seoul, 1952 by F. H. Beaugureau
Separate tables by J. H. Davis
Separate worlds by W. W. Quirt
Separated by C. R. Bentley

SEPESHY, Zoltan L. 1898-
Aft deck no 2
  NAD. Annual ex, 1949, 2d half
Congregation
  PPC. Ptg in the U.S. 1949
Crucifixion, Sketch for
  NAD. Annual ex, 1955
Departing boat   IaDa
  IaDa. 30th anniversary
Driftwood
  Baur. Revolution
End of day   ATU
  ATU. Coll of Amer art
Fisherman's morning
  Gruskin (col)
Interlude
  NAD. Annual ex, 1951
January, Michigan farm, 1937
  MiC. Zoltan Sepeshy
Morning, 1940   MoSL
  MiC. Zoltan Sepeshy
Negro meeting, 1933
  MiC. Zoltan Sepeshy
On deck
  Pierson
Patterns
  MM. Amer ptg today
  MiC. Zoltan Sepeshy
Saturday afternoon   NBuA
  NBuA. Contemporary ptgs
Siesta
  CSFP. Annual ex, 1948/49
Sunday afternoon
  Gruskin
They wait   MoKN
  CoS. New accessions USA, 1950
  IU. Contemp Amer ptg, 1948
Where are the people I knew
  IU. Contemp Amer ptg, 1949
September 1, 1956 by J. Levee
September harvest by J. Wheat
September light by W. Kahn
September morn by W. De Kooning
September wind and rain by C. E. Burch-
  field
Serafina by A. Brook
The **sergeant's** coat by E. Ewing
SERGER, Frederick, 1889-
Pink fan   OYB
  OYB. Supplement 1959
A **serious** predicament by C. M. Russell
SERISAWA, Sueo, 1910-
Black-eyed susans
  PPC. International ex, 1952
Bouquet   ATeS
  ATeS. Collection
Figure
  CSFP. Annual ex, 1952
House of cards
  IU. Contemp Amer ptg, 1952
Mary, 1948
  IU. Contemp Amer ptg, 1950
The mountain
  WMAA. Annual ex, 1958
Pierrot
  PA. Annual ex, 1947
Puppet and child
  MM. Amer ptg today
Summer afternoon
  IU. Contemp Amer ptg & sculp, 1953

Sermon on the Mount by A. Dasburg
Serpentine by H. Hoffmann
SERRES, Dominique, 1722-1793
British fleet forcing the Hudson river
  passage, 1776
  Davidson v 1
SERWAZI, Albert B.
Riverton yacht club, New Jersey
  NAD. Annual ex, 1954
Still life at Christmas
  PPC. Ptg in the U.S. 1949
SESSLER, Alfred
The year eleven   OYB
  OYB. Annual 1961
Setting out the decoys by J. Whorf
Seurat's lunch by B. Shahn
Sevastopol by F. de Erdély
Seven A. M. by E. Hopper
Seven miles to Farmington by G. H. Durrie
Seven red squares by I. R. Pereira
Seven Sisters mountain by C. F. Miller
Seventy-seven by W. Ronald
Sewall, Margaret (Mitchell) 1664-1736
  Smibert, J. Mrs Stephen Sewall
Sewall, Samuel, 1652-1730
  Emmons, N. Samuel Sewall
Sewing machine by W. T. Murch
Sexton, Fred, 1907?-
Musical instruments
  CSFP. Annual ex, 1947/48
The **sexton** by A. N. Wyeth
SEYFFERT, Leopold, 1884-1956
Florence O. R. Lang   NJMo
  NJMo. Forty years
  NJMo. Your Montclair art museum
Seymour, Horatio, fl 1846
  Mason, B. F. Horatio Seymour
Seymour, Molly (Marsh) 1752-1826
  Earl, R. Mrs Moses Seymour and her
  son Epaphroditus
SEYMOUR, Samuel, 1797-1882
Cliffs of red sandstone near the Rocky
  mountains   CtY
  McDermott. Samuel Seymour
  Rathbone
Dog dance of the Kansas Indians   CtY
  Rathbone
Hills of the Trap formation   CtY
  McDermott. Samuel Seymour
Indians   WMAA
  Ford. Pictorial folk art
  McDermott. Samuel Seymour
Kiowa encampment   CtY
  McDermott. Samuel Seymour
Oto council
  McCracken. Portrait of the old west
  McDermott. Samuel Seymour
Pawnee council   CtY
  McDermott. Samuel Seymour
  Rathbone
View near the base of the Rocky moun-
  tains   CtY
  McDermott. Samuel Seymour
View of the Rocky mountains on the
  Platte   NNPL
  McCracken. Portrait of the old west
  Rathbone
View on the Arkansa near the Rocky
  mountains   CtY
  McDermott. Samuel Seymour

View parallel to the base of the mountains at the head of the Platte   CtY
McDermott. Samuel Seymour
War [dog] dance in the interior of a Konza lodge   CtY
McDermott. Samuel Seymour

Seymour, Thomas Youngs, 1757-1811
Turnbull, J. Capt Thomas Youngs Seymour

Shack by L. MacIver
Shackelford, Eliza (Pulliam) fl 1839
Bingham, G. B. Mrs Eliza Pulliam Shackelford

Shadow and substance by G. Mofchum
Shadow country by Y. Tanguy
Shadowed stream by J. S. Sargent
Shadows by J. Pollock
Shadows of evening by R. Kent
Shadows on the rock by K. L. Callahan
Shafer, William Anton
Hubard, W. J. William A. Shafer
Shaffer, Susan Angevine
Wood, G. Susan Angevine Shaffer
Shahah by P. Guston
SHAHN, Ben, 1898-
After Titian   WMAA
  WMAA. Sara Roby
Age of anxiety
  IU. Contemp Amer ptg & sculp, 1955
Allegory
  Rodman. Portrait of the artist
Anatomical man
  Rodman. Portrait of the artist
Anger
  ICA. Annual ex, 1959-60
Apotheosis (Mooney series)
  MMA. Shahn
Arch of Triumph
  Rodman. Portrait of the artist
Ave   CtHW
  CoS. New accessions USA, 1952
  Baur. New art (col)
  50 years of mod art
  ICA. Amer artists paint the city
  MnU. 40 Amer ptrs
  Pearson. Mod renaissance
  Read. Concise history (col)
Baling cotton (detail of Bronx Post Office mural)
  Soby. Ben Shahn
Bartolomeo Vanzetti (Sacco-Vanzetti series)
  MMA. Shahn
  Rodman. Portrait of the artist
Bartolomeo Vanzetti and Nicola Sacco. See Vanzetti and Sacco
Blind accordion player
  MnMW. Contemporary
  Rodman. Portrait of the artist
  Soby. Ben Shahn (col)
  WMAA. Neuberger collection
Blind botanist   KW
  Larkin rev ed (col)
  Pierson
Boy   MiA
  Rodman. Portrait of the artist
Brothers
  CanO. Hirshhorn coll
  Rodman. Portrait of the artist

Carnival
  Rodman. Portrait of the artist
  Soby. Ben Shahn
Carpenters (detail of mural for Social Security building)
  Rodman. Portrait of the artist
Cat's cradle in blue   PA
  CoS. New accessions USA, 1960
Cherubs and children   WMAA
  Rodman. Portrait of the artist
  Soby. Ben Shahn
Chicago
  PA. Annual ex, 1956
City of dreadful night
  PPC. International ex, 1952
Clown
  Shahn (col)
Composition with clarinets and tin horn   MiD
  Baur. New art
  CoS. New accessions USA, 1952
  MiD. Ptg in America
  MiD. Treasures
  Pousette-Dart. Amer ptg
  Richardson. Ptg in America
  WMAA. Museum and its friends, 1959
Contemporary American sculpture
  MnU. 40 Amer ptrs
Convention
  CSFP. Annual ex, 1950/51
  Rodman. Portrait of the artist
Conversations   WMAA
  Goodrich. Amer art
Cybernetics
  WMAA. Contemp Amer ptg, 1953
Death of a miner   MM
  MM. 100 Amer ptrs
  Rodman. Portrait of the artist
Death on the beach
  Soby. Ben Shahn (col)
Defaced portrait
  PPC. International ex, 1958
  Read. Concise history
The defendants (Mooney series)
  MMA. Shahn
Democracies fear peace offensive. See Spring
Demonstration in Paris (Sacco-Vanzetti series)
  MMA. Shahn
Dewey, Vandenberg and Taft
  Rodman. Portrait of the artist
East Twelfth street
  MMA. Shahn
  Rodman. Portrait of the artist (col)
Epoch   PPhM
  Baur. New art
  Canaday
  Newmeyer
Everyman   WMAA
  Goodrich. Amer art (col)
  Pierson
Farmer (detail of Bronx Post Office mural)
  MMA. Shahn
Father and child   MMA
  Baur. Revolution
  MMA. Shahn
  MMA. Soby collection
  Read. Art now, 1948 ed
  Rodman. Portrait of the artist (col)
  Shahn

SHAHN, Ben—*Continued*
Four and a half out of every five
  MiD. Coll in progress
Four piece orchestra
  Soby. Ben Shahn
Fourth of July orator
  MMA. Shahn
  Wight. Milestones
Frog monster
  Shahn
From that day on
  DC. 27 biennial ex, 1961
Girl jumping rope
  Rodman. Portrait of the artist
  Soby. Ben Shahn (col)
Handball   MMA
  Barr. What is mod ptg
  Baur. New art
  Faulkner. Art today, 1956
  Gardner 1959 ed
  Hunter. Mod Amer ptg (col)
  McCurdy
  Mendelowitz
  MMA. Masters (col)
  Robb. Art 1953 ed
  Rodman. Portrait of the artist
  Roos
  Soby. Ben Shahn (col)
Harpie
  Shahn (col)
Head (detail of Roosevelt mural)
  Rodman. Portrait of the artist
Head of a cretin
  Rodman. Portrait of the artist
Hebrew books, holy day books   MiD
  CoS. New accessions USA, 1956
Helix and crystal
  WMAA. Annual ex, 1957
Homeric struggle
  WMAA. Annual ex, 1952
Hunger
  Larkin
  Pearson. Mod renaissance
  Soby. Ben Shahn
India
  Rodman. Portrait of the artist
Industrial worker (detail of Bronx Post
  Office mural)
  MMA. Shahn
Inflation means depression   MMA
  Soby. Ben Shahn
Inside looking out   OYB
  OYB. Supplement
Italian landscape I   MnMW
  MMA. Shahn
  Rodman. Portrait of the artist
Italian landscape II
  MMA. Shahn
  Pearson. Mod renaissance
James Rolph jr of California (Mooney
  series)
  Soby. Ben Shahn
Jesus exalted in song
  MMA. Shahn
Labyrinth
  ICA. Annual ex, 1954
Labyrinth, detail no 2
  Pearson. Mod renaissance
Liberation
  Janson. Key monuments
  Janson. Picture history (col)
  Rodman. Portrait of the artist
  Soby. Ben Shahn (col)

The Lowell committee (Sacco-Vanzetti
  series)   WMAA
  Rodman. Portrait of the artist
  Soby. Ben Shahn
Lullaby   CSB
  CoS. New accessions USA, 1954
Lute no 2, 1957
  Shahn (col)
Man with wild flowers
  IU. Contemp Amer ptg & sculp, 1957
May 5
  Rodman. Portrait of the artist
Mine disaster   ICA
  PPC. Ptg in the U.S. 1949
Miners' wives   PPhM
  Flexner. Amer ptg
  Flexner. Short history
  Rodman. Portrait of the artist
Morning   DP
  MMA. Shahn
Mural at Roosevelt, New Jersey, Com-
  munity center
  MMA. Shahn
  Rodman. Portrait of the artist
  Soby. Ben Shahn
My son is innocent (Mooney series)
  Soby. Ben Shahn
Nearly everybody reads the Bulletin
  Canaday
  MMA. Shahn
  Rodman. Portrait of the artist
New York
  IU. Contemp Amer ptg, 1949
  MMA. Shahn
  Rodman. Portrait of the artist
Nocturne
  Rodman. Portrait of the artist
Nude reclining
  Rodman. Portrait of the artist
Ohio magic   CSFP
  CSFP. Annual ex, 1948/49
  CSFP. Handbook
  MMA. Shahn
Ohio skyline
  MMA. Shahn
Pacific landscape   MMA
  Rodman. Portrait of the artist
  Soby. Ben Shahn
The parable   NUM
  NUM. Art across America
Parade for repeal with Jimmy Walker
  (Prohibition series)
  MMA. Shahn
Passion of Sacco and Vanzetti (Sacco-
  Vanzetti series)   WMAA
  Baur. New art
  Baur. Revolution
  Canaday
  Goodrich. Amer art (col)
  McCurdy
  MMA. Shahn
  Pearson. Mod renaissance
  Pierson
Paterson
  Rodman. Portrait of the artist
Peter and the wolf
  Soby. Ben Shahn (col)
Picking cotton (detail of Bronx Post
  Office mural)
  Soby. Ben Shahn
The playground
  MiD. Coll in progress
  WiMiA. Amer ptg 1760-1960

The pool
CtY. Yale alumni
Rodman. Portrait of the artist
Portrait of myself when young   MMA
Rodman. Portrait of the artist
Soby. Ben Shahn (col)
Pretty girl milking a cow
Rodman. Portrait of the artist
Soby. Ben Shahn (col)
Reconstruction   WMAA
Lewisohn
Pierson
Rodman. Portrait of the artist
Soby. Ben Shahn
WMAA. Juliana Force
Red stairway   MoSL
Gruskin (col)
MMA. Contemp ptrs
MoSL. Handbook 1953
Myers. Art
Pierson
Riley. Your art heritage
Rodman. Portrait of the artist
Soby. Ben Shahn (col)
Time. 300 years (col)
Rena and Tom Mooney
Rodman. Portrait of the artist
Renascence
MMA. Shahn
Rodman. Portrait of the artist
Riker's island prison, Study for mural at
MMA. Shahn
Sacco and Vanzetti in coffins (detail)
Rodman. Portrait of the artist
Scotts Run, West Virginia   WMAA
Goodrich. Amer art
Mendelowitz
Myers
Soby. Ben Shahn (col)
Second allegory
IU. Contemp Amer ptg & sculp, 1953
(col)
Second spring
PPC. International ex, 1955
Self-portrait among churchgoers
Rodman. Portrait of the artist
Soby. Ben Shahn
Seurat's lunch
MMA. Shahn
Sing sorrow
Rodman. Portrait of the artist
Six   MdBM
MnMW. Expressionism 1900-1955
Social security murals (Federal Security
building, Washington)
MMA. Shahn
Soby. Ben Shahn (detail)
The song
CanO. Hirshhorn coll (col cover)
DC. 22 biennial ex, 1951
Sound in the mulberry tree   MNS
Baur. New art
NBuA. Expressionism
Rodman. Portrait of the artist
Speakeasy closed for violation (Prohibi-
tion series)
MMA. Shahn
Spring   NBuA
MMA. Contemp ptrs
MMA. Shahn
Munsterberg
NBuA. Contemporary ptgs
Rodman. Portrait of the artist
Time. 300 years (col)

Spring (Democracies fear peace offensive)
MMA. Shahn
Spring on Morton street
Rodman. Portrait of the artist
Still life
IU. Contemp Amer ptg & sculp, 1959
Still music   DP
DP. Catalogue
Study for Goyescas
Shahn (col)
Study for The Marriage of Heaven and
Hell
Shahn
Summertime   MAP
CoS. New accessions USA, 1950
Rodman. Portrait of the artist
Sunday football
MMA. Shahn
Sunday painting
Soby. Ben Shahn
The Supreme Court of California
(Mooney series)
MMA. Shahn
Susanna and the elders
Rodman. Portrait of the artist
Textile mill worker (Textile worker) de-
tail of Bronx Post Office mural)
MMA. Shahn
Rodman. Portrait of the artist
Textile mills (detail of Bronx Post Office
mural)
Soby. Ben Shahn
Three doors
Rodman. Portrait of the artist
Three men
MiD. Coll in progress
WiMiA. Amer ptg 1760-1960
Trouble
MMA. Shahn
Two witnesses, Mellie and Sadie Edeau
(Mooney series)   MMA
Rodman. Portrait of the artist
Soby. Ben Shahn (col)
Vacant lot   CtHW
CtHW. Handbook
Larkin
Larkin rev ed
Pierson
Rodman. Portrait of the artist
Soby. Ben Shahn
Vanzetti and Sacco   MMA
Cheney. Story 1958 ed
Soby. Ben Shahn (col)
Violin player   MMA
Biddle. Yes and no
MMA. Shahn
W.C.T.U. parade, 1933-34 (Prohibition
series)
Soby. Ben Shahn (col)
Walker greets Mooney (Mooney series)
Rodman. Portrait of the artist
Walker greets mother of Mooney
(Mooney series)
MMA. Shahn
Rodman. Portrait of the artist
Webster Thayer (Sacco-Vanzetti series)
MMA. Shahn
The welders   MMA
Larkin
Larkin rev ed
Pierson
Rodman. Portrait of the artist
Soby. Ben Shahn (col)

SHAHN, Ben—*Continued*
Willis avenue bridge
  Rodman. Portrait of the artist
  Soby. Ben Shahn (col)
Woman in chair
  Rodman. Portrait of the artist
World's greatest comics
  DC. Halpert collection
  Rodman. Portrait of the artist
  WMAA. Museum and its friends, 1958
Shakespeare on the lap of the muse of inspiration by E. G. Malbone
Shallows by J. S. Sargent
Shambattle by R. Wilt
Shanah by P. Guston
Shannon by E. K. Schwabacher
Shapes of landscape space by S. Davis
Shapiro, Mrs Harold. See Geller, Esther
Share croppers by E. Higgins
A **share** of fire by W. Schraf
Sharks
  Copley, J. S. Watson and the shark
  Homer, W. Shark fishing
SHARON, W. C.
Western landscape   DN
  DN. Amer primitive ptgs, pt 2
Sharp, Benjamin, 1858-1915
  Eakins, T. Oboe player (Benjamin Sharp)
SHARP, John, 1911-
Old South wharf
  IU. Contemp Amer ptg, 1952
Thompson-Neely house
  PPC. Ptg in the U. S. 1949
SHARP, Joseph Henry, 1859-
Young chief's mission   OYB
  OYB. Catalogue 1951
SHARP, William, 1819?-1885?
Railroad jubilee on Boston Common MB
  MB. Karolik coll
  Time. 300 years (col)
Sharp drummer by I. Rose
Sharp sea by G. Anderson
SHARPLES, James, 1751?-1811
Catharine Livingston Thorn Johnson
  WiMiA. Amer ptg 1760-1960
Isaiah Thomas   MWA
  Larkin
  Larkin rev ed
Moreau de Saint-Méry   MM
  Pierson
  Richardson. Ptg in America
SHARRER, Honoré Desmond, 1920?-
Country fair
  CSFP. Annual ex, 1946
  MMA. Fourteen
In the parlor
  MMA. Fourteen
Industrial scene
  Baur. Revolution
Rose Callahan and child
  WMAA. New decade
Tribute to the American working people WMAA
  WMAA. New decade
  WMAA. Sara Roby
Workers and paintings   MMA
  MMA. Contemp ptrs
  MMA. Fourteen (col)
  Pierson

Workers and paintings (study) MMA
  MMA. Fourteen
Shaumonekusse, chief of the Otoes by C. B. King
SHAW, Charles Green, 1892-
Force in space
  MMA. Abstract
Tonal rhapsody
  Pousette-Dart. Amer ptg
SHAW, Joshua, c 1777-1860
Indians sighting a ship
  Chew. 250 years of art
On the Susquehanna   MB
  MB. Karolik coll
Shaw, Lemuel, 1781-1861
  Hunt, W. M. Chief Justice Lemuel Shaw
SHAWKEY, Sigmund
Bus stop   OYB
  OYB. Annual 1960
Saturday night in New York city
  OYB. Annual 1952
Shaw's propeller no 2, 1960 by R. Crawford
She mourns by Y. Kuniyoshi
She walks among the ruins by Y. Kuniyoshi
The **she-wolf** by J. Pollock
SHEARER, Christopher High, 1846-1926
Smoky range, Allegheny mountains PR
  PR. Catalogue
The **Shed,** Woodruff stables, Jerome avenue, the Bronx, 1848 by J. A. S. Oertel
SHEELER, Charles, 1883-
Aerial gyrations
  WMAA. Museum and its friends, 1959
American interior
  NYG. Fine art
American landscape   MMA
  Barr. What is mod ptg
  Cheney. Story 1958 ed
  Flexner. Amer ptg
  Flexner. Short history
  Gruskin (col)
  McCurdy
Americana, 1931
  Baur. New art
  MnU. 40 Amer ptrs
  MnMW. Precisionist view
Architectural cadences   WMAA
  Baur. New art (col)
  Goodrich. Amer art (col)
  Larkin rev ed (col)
  Newmeyer
  Pierson
Artist looks at nature   ICA
  Born (col front)
  Time. 300 years (col)
Barn abstraction   PPhM
  Rosenblum
Barn reds
  Barker. From realism
Barn variation   ATeS
  ATeS. Collection
Basement room   MiD
  CoS. New accessions USA, 1946
Bird's nest
  CSFP. Annual ex, 1947/48
Bucks county barn   OCo
  Brown. Amer ptg
  Goodrich. Amer art
  MnMW. Precisionist view
  NYG. Fine art

Buildings at Lebanon
  CSFP. Annual ex, 1950/51
  ICA. Annual ex, 1951
Cactus   PPhM
  PPhM. Arensberg coll
Church street el, 1919   MMA
  Baur. New art
  Baur. Revolution
  Brown. Amer ptg
  Larkin
  Larkin rev ed
City interior   MWM
  Baur. New art
  Baur. Revolution
  Pierson
Classic landscape (Modern classic) (Ford
    coll)
  Baur. New art
  Born
  Hunter. Mod Amer ptg
  MiD. Ptg in America
  Pierson
  Richardson. Ptg in America
Classical landscape (Fleischman coll)
  MiD. Coll in progress
  WiMiA. Amer ptg 1760-1960
Composition around red
  IU. Contemp Amer ptg & sculp, 1959
  WMAA. Contemp Amer ptg, 1959/60
Connecticut farm buildings   NJN
  Born
Croton dam. See The web
Flower forms
  Cheney. Primer 1958 ed
Golden Gate   MM
  Eliot. Art of our time (col)
  Time. 300 years (col)
Home, sweet home   MiD
  MiD. Treasures
Impressionism (Lhasa)   OCo
  WMAA. Pioneers
Improvisation on a mill town
  DC. 21 biennial ex, 1949
  MM. Amer ptg today
Incantation   NBM
  Baur. Revolution
  CoS. New accessions USA, 1950
  Mendelowitz
  MnMW. Precisionist view
Interior   WMAA
  Chew. 250 years of art
  CSB. Illusion
  Roos
Landscape, 1915   MLL
  MnMW. Precisionist view
Landscape, 1925   PPhM
  PPhM. Arensberg coll
Macdougal alley
  NUM. Art across America
Manchester   MdBM
  CSFP. Annual ex, 1952
  MnMW. Precisionist view
  MnU. 40 Amer ptrs
  Pousette-Dart. Amer ptg
  WMAA. Contemp Amer ptg, 1949
Midwest   MnMW
  IU. Contemp Amer ptg & sculp, 1955
  MnMW. Precisionist view (col detail)
Modern classic. See Classic landscape
Offices   DP
  Bazin
  DP. Catalogue

On a Shaker theme
  MnMW. Precisionist view
Pertaining to yachts and yachting
                                           WMAA
  Pierson
  Riley. Your art heritage
  WMAA. Juliana Force
River Rouge plant   WMAA
  Brown. Amer ptg
  Goodrich. Amer art
Rolling power   MNS
  MnMW. Precisionist view
San Francisco, 1956   WMAA
  IU. Contemp Amer ptg & sculp, 1957
  WMAA. Sara Robie (col)
Skyline   KW
  MnMW. Classic tradition
Staircase, Doylestown
  McCurdy
Steam turbine   OYB
  OYB. Catalogue 1951
Steel—Croton   VR
  CoS. New accessions USA, 1954
  MnMW. Reality and fantasy
  VR. Amer ptg, 1954
Still life no I   OCo
  Roos
Still life, pitcher
  Brown. Amer ptg
Upper deck   MCH
  Baur. New art
  Baur. Revolution
  Brown. Amer ptg
  Larkin
  Larkin rev ed
  Mendelowitz
  Pierson
  Wight. Milestones
Water   MM
  ICA. Annual ex, 1945/46
  MM. 100 Amer ptrs
  Taylor. Fifty centuries, 1954 ed (col)
The web (Croton dam)
  ICA. Amer artists paint the city (col)
  WMAA. Museum and its friends, 1958
    (col)
Western industrial
  WMAA. Contemp Amer ptg, 1955
Wind, sea and sails
  DC. Halpert collection
Sheep
Avery, M. Sheep
Delano, G. C. Sheep on the desert
Elmer, E. R. Mourning picture
Hinckley, T. H. Cows and sheep in
  pasture
Hinckley, T. H. Great Blue hill and
  Neponset river
Hinckley, T. H. Noon
Homer, W. Shepherdess of Houghton
  farm
Moses, A. M. R. May: making soap,
  washing sheep
Putnam, W. B. Sheep in fog
Ryder, A. P. The shepherdess
Unidentified artist. The shepherd and his
  flock
Wall, A. B. Shepherd and his flock
The sheepfold by A. P. Ryder
Sheepshead shore by W. E. Heitland

SHEETS, Millard Owen, 1907-
Black horse   WMAA
  Pierson
Gift bearer
  Gruskin
Mazatlan women   ATeS
  ATeS. Collection
Tropical squall
  MM. Amer ptg today
SHEFFIELD, Isaac, 1798-1845
Connecticut sea captain   DN
  DN. Amer primitive ptgs, pt 2
James Francis Smith   CtNL
  NUM. Art across America
Shelburne woods, New Hampshire by D.
  Macknight
Sheldon, J. B. fl 1825
  Unidentified artist. J. B. Sheldon
Sheldon, Mrs J. B. fl 1825
  Unidentified artist. Mrs J. B. Sheldon of
  Unionville, Ohio
Shelf still life by C. Brown
The **shell** heap by W. Homer
Shell holes and observation balloon by H.
  Pippin
Shell of Mary by R. Lebrun
Shelocta, Pennsylvania by P. C. Elliott
Shelter of longing by L. W. Coleman
Shelves by D. E. Lee
Shenandoah valley by A. M. R. Moses
Shepard, Angeline Eliza, 1837-1919
  Unidentified artist. Angeline Eliza Shep-
  ard and her brother, Elisha Henry
  Shepard
Shepard, Elisha Henry, 1834-1852
  Unidentified artist. Angeline Eliza Shep-
  ard and her brother, Elisha Henry
  Shepard
The **shepherd** and his flock by Unidentified
  artist
The **shepherd** and his flock by A. B. Wall
The **shepherdess** by A. P. Ryder
Shepherdess of Houghton farm by W.
  Homer
Sherburne, Joseph, 1710-1779
  Copley, J. S. Joseph Sherburne
Sherburne, Mary. See Bowers, Mary (Sher-
  burne)
Sherburne, Mrs John. See Moffatt, Eliza-
  beth
Sherburne, Mrs Samuel. See Warner, Mary
Sheridan theatre by E. Hopper
Sherman, Ellen (Ewing)
  Healy, G. P. A. Mrs William T. Sherman
Sherman, Roger, 1721-1793
  Earl, R. Roger Sherman
SHERMAN, Sarai, 1922-
Arid land
  IU. Contemp Amer ptg & sculp, 1955
The centaurs
  WMAA. Contemp Amer ptg, 1959/60
Fête champêtre
  IU. Contemp Amer ptg & sculp, 1961
The forest
  IU. Contemp Amer ptg & sculp, 1959
Voyage to Matera
  WMAA. Contemp Amer ptg, 1955
Sherman, William Tecumseh, 1820-1891
  Healy, G. P. A. William T. Sherman
Sherman's march through Georgia by A. B.
  Carlin

Sherwood, Elizabeth (Moffatt) See Moffatt,
  Elizabeth
Shewell, Elizabeth. See West, Elizabeth
  (Shewell)
Shifting shadows by H. Nichols
Shim-a-co-che, Crow chief by A. J. Miller
Shimmering substance by J. Pollock
SHINN, Everett, 1876-1953
Bal Tabarin   WMAA
  McCurdy
Ballet dancer   GAtM
  GAtM. Holbrook collection
Curtain call
  Glackens
Dancer in white   OYB
  OYB. Accessions
  OYB. Supplement 1959
Early morning, Paris   ICA
  PA. Annual ex, 1955
  Pierson
Flight of the clowns
  NAD. Annual ex, 1947, 2d half
Green ballet   PW
  Chem. 250 years of art
  NUM. Art across America
Independence hall, Philadelphia
  Chew. 250 years of art
Knoedler's, 34th street
  PA. Annual ex, 1955
London Hippodrome   ICA
  Brown. Amer ptg
  PA. Annual ex, 1955
  Pierson
London Music Hall   MM
  MM. 100 Amer ptrs
Mark Twain
  MiD. Coll in progress
Paris Music Hall
  WiMiA. Amer ptg 1760-1960
Revue   WMAA
  Goodrich. Amer art
  Larkin (detail)
  Larkin rev ed (detail)
Saturday night, Sarasota, Florida
  NAD. Annual ex, spring 1950
Sleeping clown
  NSyE. The eight
Theatre
  PA. Annual ex, 1955
Theatre box   NBuA
  NBuA. Fifty ptgs
Trapeze, Winter garden, New York
  CtY. Yale alumni
  Time. 300 years (col)
Trenton, New Jersey Commission cham-
  bers murals
  Brown. Amer ptg
Winter scene   NJMo
  NJMo. Your Montclair art museum
SHINN, John Marion, 1849-1936
Old barn door
  Frankenstein. After the hunt
Shinnecock canal by G. Hartigan
Shinnecock hills by W. M. Chase
Shinnecock hills landscape by W. M. Chase
Ship chandlers' row by R. Spencer
Ship channel by J. W. Guerin
Ship Dashing Wave off Boston Light by
  W. Bradford

Ship graveyard by J. E. Levi
Ship smashing against rocks by D. C. Johnston
Ship unfurling sails by W. Homer
Shipbuilding in the 18th century by A. Refregier
Shippen, Anne. See Willing, Anne (Shippen)
Shippen, Edward, 1729-1806
  Jouett, M.H. Edward Shippen
  Stuart, G. Chief Justice Edward Shippen of Pennsylvania
Shippen, Jane (Galloway) See Galloway, Jane
Shippen, Mrs Joseph. See Galloway, Jane
Shipping out by J. Lawrence
Ships by J. Marin
Ships in ice off Ten Pound island, Gloucester by F. H. Lane
Ships of the plains by S. Colman
Shipwreck by T. Birch
Shipwreck by W. Snelgrove
Shipwreck at sea by R. W. Weir (attributed works)
Shipyard, Singapore by D. Teague
SHIRLAW, Walter, 1838-1909
  Dorothea A. Dreier
    CtY. Soc Anonyme
  Susannah and the elders   MB
    MB. Ptgs in water color
Shoeshine by G. Grosz
Shooting a cougar by A. J. Miller
Shooting birds by B. West (attributed works)
Shooting for the beef by G. C. Bingham
Shooting gallery by F. Martin
Shooting the rapids, Saguenay river by W. Homer
The shopper by K. H. Miller
Shoppers by W. J. Glackens
The shore by M. Beckmann
The shore by A. Brook
The shore by B. Perlin
Shore and surf, Nassau by W. Homer
Shore birds by M. Graves
Shore birds submerged in moonlight by M. Graves
Shore birds, Tomales bay by B. J. O. Nordfeldt
Shore flowers II by H. Durfee
Shore house by G. W. Bellows
Shore scene by A. P. Ryder
Shore scene by J. L. Smith
Shore tapestry by P. L. Dike
Shoremen by D. G. Blythe
Shoshone cliffs by E. Hopper
Shoshone female catching a horse by A. J. Miller
Shoshone Indian and his pet horse by A. J. Miller
Shoshone Indian preparing his meal by A. J. Miller
Shoshone Indian smoking by A. J. Miller
Shoshone Indians fording a river by A. J. Miller

Shovel hats by G. P. Du Bois
Shoveller duck by J. J. Audubon
Show window no 2 by K. H. Miller
The showcase by G. Hartigan
The shower by P. Cadmus
Shower in Colorado by A. A. Dehn
Shrewsbury river near Seabright, New Jersey by Unidentified artist
The shrine by P. Blume
The shrine by S. F. B. Morse
Shubrick, Sarah Alicia, fl 1801
  Malbone, E. G. Sarah Alicia Shubrick
SHULKIN, Anatol, 1899-1961
  Summer storm on Sunday afternoon
    Gruskin
  You can't come home again
    IU. Contemp Amer ptg, 1950
SHUMACHER, William Emile, 1870-1931
  Lendall Pitts   MiD
    MiD. Ports of the Pitts family
SIBLEY, Charles Kenneth, 1921-
  Blue evolution
    VR. Amer ptg, 1958
  Holiday
    NAD. Annual ex, 1953
SICARD, Pierre, 1900-
  Night over Los Angeles
    IU. Contemp Amer ptg & sculp, 1957
Sicilian altar by J. Kinigstein
Sicily by L. Dodd
The sick chicken by W. Homer
Side pull by A. Gottlieb
The sideboard by F. C. Watkins
The sidewalk by L. MacIver
Side-wheelers
  Anderson, E. A. Delta Queen and Packet Whisper
  Baumann, L. T. U.S. mail boat
  Catlin, G. Steamboat Yellowstone leaving St Louis
  Feininger, L. Side-wheeler
  Palmer, F. F. Champions of the Mississippi
  Palmer, F. F. Wooding up on the Mississippi
  Sebron, V. V. Sugar levee, New Orleans
  Unidentified artist. Belle Creole at New Orleans
The siding by P. Evergood
Siegfried by F. J. Kline
Siegfried and the Rhine maidens by A. P. Ryder
SIEGRIEST, Louis B. 1899-
  Virginia City building
    CSFP. Annual ex, 1950/51
SIEGRIEST, Lundy, 1925-
  Birds at rest
    CSFP. Annual ex, 1952
  Burning of the hearts
    VR. Amer ptg, 1958
  Desert landscape
    IU. Contemp Amer ptg & sculp, 1955
  Montezuma alarmed by evil signs
    WMAA. Young America 1957
  Mount Lassen
    IU. Contemp Amer ptg & sculp, 1961

SIEGRIEST, Lundy—*Continued*
Temple fragment   CSB
CoS. New accessions USA, 1956
Tenochtitlan
WMAA. Young America
Under the pier
IU. Contemp Amer ptg & sculp, 1953
Village above the river
Brussels. Exposition
Siena by M. B. Prendergast
Sierra Madre at Saltillo by E. Hopper
Siesta by L. Andersen
Siesta by D. E. Lee
Siesta by Z. L. Sepeshy
SIEVAN, Maurice, 1898-
Astoria boulevard   ATU
ATU. Coll of Amer art
Sifter of gold by Y. Tanguy
Sign of the sun by M. Tomkins
Signal by W. Lachowicz
Signal fire by C. M. Russell
Signing of the Declaration of Independence
by J. Trumbull
Signs and portents by J. Guerrero
Signs of the city by F. Hillsmith
Sigourney, Lydia Howard (Huntley) 1791-
1865
Alexander, F. Lydia Huntley Sigourney
Silence and evening light by G. Symonds
Silence broken by G. D. Brush
Silenced war whoop by C. Schreyvogel
Silent watcher by M. Cone
Silktown on the Passaic by O. F. Bluemner
Silliman, Benjamin, 1779-1864
Morse, S.F.B. Benjamin Silliman
SILSBEE, Martha, 1858-1929
Taormina and Mt Aetna   MB
MB. Ptgs in water color
Silver by K. Okada
Silver lake, New Hampshire by Unidentified
artist
Silver sea by W. Kahn
Silver square by J. Pollock
Silver tanks by N. Spencer
Silver tanks and moon by A. G. Dove
Silver vase by T. H. Benton
SILVERMAN, Miles
Poppies
OYB. Annual 1948
Silvers, Herbert Ferber. See Ferber, Her-
bert
Silvery night by F. D. Ogden
SIMKHOVITCH, Simka, 1893-
Two horses
Gruskin (col)
Simple confession by M. Greenwood
Simplon pass: at the top by J. S. Sargent
Simplon pass: avalanche track by J. S.
Sargent
Simplon pass: chalets by J. S. Sargent
Simplon pass: crags by J. S. Sargent
Simplon pass: fresh snow by J. S. Sargent
Simplon pass: the foreground by J. S.
Sargent

Simplon pass: the green parasol by J. S.
Sargent
Simplon pass: the lesson by J. S. Sargent
Simplon pass: mountain brook by J. S.
Sargent
Simplon pass: the tease by J. S. Sargent
SIMPSON, Merton D. 1928-
Poem—2
NNSG. Younger Amer ptrs
Sims, William Sowden, 1858-1936
Lockman, D. M. Admiral William Sowden
Sims
Sing Sing, 1856 by R. Havell
Sing sorrow by B. Shahn
SINGER, Clyde, 1908-
Big business
OYB. Annual 1948
Selections from the permanent collection
OYB
OYB. Supplement
Stormy weather   OYB
OYB. Catalogue 1951
Singer building by J. Marin
Singing men by J. Hirsch
Single handed by C. M. Russell
The sink by R. A. Mintz
Sinkler, Charles, fl 1802
Malbone, E. G. Charles Sinkler (?)
Sinkler, Margaret (Cantey) 1763-1821
Malbone, E. G. Mrs James Sinkler
SINTZENICH, Eugene, 1792-1848
Train leaving Auburn station at Roches-
ter, New York
Jones. Rediscovered ptrs
Sinzig, Ferdinand
Glackens, W. J. Ferdinand Sinzig
A Sioux, Head of by A. J. Miller
Sioux beggar's dance by G. Catlin
Sioux Indian at a grave by A. J. Miller
Sioux Indian guard by A. J. Miller
Sioux Indians by A. J. Miller
Sioux Indians attacking a Minnesota farm
by J. Stevens
Sioux Indians breaking up camp by S. East-
man
Sioux Indians pursuing a stag in their
canoes by G. Catlin
Sioux reconnoitering by A. J. Miller
A Sioux village by G. Catlin
SIPORIN, Mitchell, 1910-
Aging actress
Pousette-Dart. Amer ptg
Conflagration at the museum   OYB
OYB. Annual 1960
Dancers by the clock   WMAA
CoS. New accessions USA, 1952
Goodrich. Amer art
Pierson
The doll
ICA. Annual ex, 1951
Dream of a good life
Wight. Milestones (col)
End of an era
Rathbun
Fiesta in Trastevere
CSFP. Annual ex, 1952
OYB. Annual 1953

Order No 11   ATU
  ATU. Coll of Amer art
The refugees   MMA
  Pierson
Rendezvous
  WMAA. Contemp Amer ptg, 1955
St Louis Post office mural
  Larkin
  Larkin rev ed
Winter soldiers
  IU. Contemp Amer ptg, 1948
Sirens in voice by J. Tworkov
Si-roc-u-an-tua by A. J. Miller
Sisson, Charles H. fl 1850
  Chandler, J. G. Charles H. Sisson
SISSON, Laurence Philip, 1928-
  New England November
  IU. Contemp Amer ptg, 1952
Sissy by R. Henri
Sister Rebecca Cleaden by H. Ballin
The sisters by W. Allston
The sisters by A. Dehn
Sisters by W. Zorach
Sisters in red by Unidentified artist
Siva dance, Samoa by J. La Farge
Six by B. Shahn
Six o'clock by C. E. Burchfield
Six sketches of ladies by M. B. Prendergast
Sixth avenue and Thirteenth street by J.
  Sloan
Sixth avenue and Thirtieth street by J.
  Sloan
Sixth avenue elevated at Third street, 1928
  by J. Sloan
Skaats, Deborah (Rivers) fl 1794
  Trumbull, J. Mrs Bartholomew Skaats
Skating. See Games and sports—Skating
Sketch in Florida by W. Homer
Sketch of a child by W. M. Chase
SKINAS, John C. 1924-
  Composition I, 1953
  NNSG. Younger Amer ptrs
Skinner, Elizabeth (Van Cortlandt)
  Unidentified artist. Mrs William Skinner
Skinner, Otis, 1858-1942
  Luks, G. B. Otis Skinner as Colonel
    Bridau in The honor of the family
Skinner, Thomas Harvey, 1791-1871
  Morse, S. F. B. Rev Thomas Harvey
    Skinner
Skipping. See Games and sports—Skipping
  rope
Skirmish in The Wilderness by W. Homer
SKOLLE, John, 1903-
  Sargasso sea
  CSFP. Annual ex, 1946
The skull by H. L. McFee
Skunk cabbage by G. O'Keeffe
Sky after El Greco by C. H. Demuth
Sky and boats by V. Vytlacil
Sky festival by G. Wagner
Skylight by L. MacIver
Skylights by E. Hopper
Skyline by C. Sheeler
Skyline (New York) by K. Matthew
Skyrocket by M. Kantor

Skyscrapers (central panel of New York
  interpreted) by J. Stella
Slade, Alice, b 1767?
  Border limner. Alice Slade
Slade, Joseph, fl 1816
  Border limner. Joseph Slade
Slade, Philip, fl 1818
  Border limner. Philip Slade
Slaughtered animal by H. Bloom
Sleep by A. Fiene
Sleep and revelry by S. Amato
Sleeper by F. Bultman
Sleeper by P. Guston
Sleepers by J. Glasco
Sleepers by E. Melcarth
Sleeping by J. Carroll
Sleeping clown by E. Shinn
Sleeping effort by J. Pollock
Sleeping figure by J. Glasco
Sleeping figure by C. di Marca-Relli
Sleeping girl by Brook
Sleeping man by W. W. Quirt
Sleepwalker by W. A. Baziotes
Sleepwalkers' meeting by K. L. Seligmann
Sleighs
  Beckett, C. E. Furbish's dash to Montreal
  Birch, T. Sleigh ride in the country
  Clonney, J. G. Sleigh ride
  Ferrill, M. E. Sleighing scene, Lansing-
    burgh
  Keyes, C. A. Geo. S. Howe driving Rough
    and Ready
  Van Zandt, T. K. Judge Van Arnam in his
    sleigh
Sleight, Helena Jansen
  Vanderlyn, P. Helena Jansen Sleight
Sligo opposite Pittsburgh by R. Smith
Slip by E. Kelly
Sloan, Anna M. (Wall) d 1943
  Sloan, J. My wife in blue (Dolly)
SLOAN, John, 1871-1951
  Arachne   PPhM
    Canaday
  Backyards, Greenwich village   WMAA
    Canaday
    Craven. Treasury 1952 ed
    Goodrich. Amer art (col)
    Goodrich. John Sloan
    Mendelowitz
    PA. Annual ex, 1955
    Pierson
  Balancing rock, Gloucester harbor
    NUM. Art across America
  Big apple tree
    Goodrich. John Sloan
  Bleecker street Saturday night
    Brooks. John Sloan
  Carmine theatre
    CanO. Hirshhorn coll
  The Chama running red
    Brooks. John Sloan
    Goodrich. John Sloan
  Chinese restaurant
    Brooks. John Sloan
  The city from Greenwich village, 1922
    Goodrich. John Sloan (col)
    Gruskin (col)

SLOAN, John—*Continued*
Coffee line
  Brown. Amer ptg
Cornelia street
  WiMiA. Amer ptg 1760-1960
Corpus Christi, Santa Fe
  Goodrich. John Sloan
The cot
  Brooks. John Sloan
Dawn   ATU
  ATU. Coll of Amer art
Dust storm, Fifth avenue   MM
  MM. 100 Amer ptrs (col)
East entrance, City hall, Philadelphia, 1901
  Goodrich. John Sloan
Fifth avenue, 1909
  Goodrich. John Sloan
Girl in fur hat   CtNB
  Goodrich. John Sloan
Girl in window
  Goodrich. John Sloan
Gloucester trolley   NCa
  Goodrich. John Sloan
Hairdresser's window   CtHW
  Baur. New art (col)
  Baur. Revolution
  CtHW. Handbook
  DC. De gustibus
  Goodrich. John Sloan
Haymarket   NBM
  Baur. Revolution
  Brooks. John Sloan
  Brown. Amer ptg
  Goodrich. John Sloan
  Hunter. Mod Amer ptg (col)
  McCurdy
  WMAA. Juliana Force
Helen. See Tea for one
Hill, Main street, Gloucester
  MnU. 40 Amer ptrs
In the wake of the ferry   DP
  Cheney. Story 1958 ed
Kent Crane
  Brooks. John Sloan
Lafayette hotel, 1927   MM
  Brooks. John Sloan
  Time. 300 years (col)
Large white nude
  Goodrich. John Sloan
Little movie theater   OT
  Goodrich. John Sloan
Looking out on Washington square
  Goodrich. John Sloan
McSorley's back room
  Brooks. John Sloan
McSorley's bar   MiD
  Brooks. John Sloan
  Cheney. Story 1958 ed
  Craven. Treasury 1952 ed (col)
  Gruskin (col)
  MiD. Treasures
  NBuA. Fifty ptgs
  PA. Annual ex, 1955
  Robb. Harper history
  Wight. Milestones
McSorley's cats
  Goodrich. John Sloan
Main street, Gloucester
  Brooks. John Sloan

Model in dressing room
  Goodrich. John Sloan
  Time. 300 years (col)
Monument in the plaza
  Goodrich. John Sloan
My wife in blue (Dolly)
  Brooks. John Sloan
The necklace
  Goodrich. John Sloan
Nude and nine apples   WMAA
  Baur. New art
  Brooks. John Sloan
  Chew. 250 years of art
  Goodrich. Amer art (col)
  Goodrich. John Sloan (col)
  PA. Annual ex, 1955
Nude at foot of stairs
  Goodrich. John Sloan
Nude on the roof
  Brooks. John Sloan
Old clown making up   DP
  Bazin
  DP. Catalogue
  Lee. Art then and now
Picnic grounds   WMAA
  Brooks. John Sloan
  Goodrich. Amer art
  Goodrich. John Sloan
  Mendelowitz
  Pierson
Picnic on the ridge
  WiMiA. Amer ptg 1760-1960
Pigeons   MB
  Brooks. John Sloan
  Brown. Amer ptg
  Time. 300 years (col)
The Rathskeller (Soula's Rathskeller)
                                                        OCI
  Goodrich. John Sloan
  PA. Annual ex, 1955
Recruiting, Union square   OYB
  Chew. 250 years of art
  OYB. Supplement
Red hand mirror
  MnU. 40 Amer ptrs
Red kimono on the roof
  NSyE. The eight
Red paint mill
  Goodrich, John Sloan
Renganeschi's, Saturday night   ICA
  Goodrich, John Sloan
Riders in the hills   WMAA
  Goodrich. John Sloan
  Pousette-Dart. Amer ptg
Roof gossips   ATeS
  ATeS. Collections
Roofs: Twenty-third street, sunset
  CSFP. Annual ex, 1952
Savings bank
  Goodrich. John Sloan
Self-portrait   ATU
  ATU. Coll of Amer art
Self-portrait, 1924 (Fleischman coll)
  WiMiA. Amer ptg 1760-1960
Sixth avenue and Thirteenth street, 1907
  Brooks. John Sloan
  Brown. Amer ptg
  Goodrich. John Sloan
Sixth avenue elevated at Third street,
    1928   WMMA
  Baur. New art
  Craven. Rainbow book
  Flexner. Amer ptg

Flexner. Short history
  Goodrich. Amer art
  Goodrich. John Sloan
  Pierson
South Beach bathers   MnMW
  Baur. New art
  Goodrich. John Sloan
  Pierson
Spring planting
  Goodrich. John Sloan
  WMAA. Museum and its friends, 1958
Sunday in Union square
  Goodrich. John Sloan
Sunday, women drying their hair   MAP
  Brown. Amer ptg
  DC. 25 biennial ex, 1957
  Goodrich. John Sloan
  NYG. Fine art
Tea for one (Helen)
  Brooks. John Sloan
  Goodrich. John Sloan
Three A.M. 1909   PPhM
  Baur. New Art
  Goodrich. John Sloan (col)
  Larkin rev ed (col detail)
  Pierson
Wake of the ferry (Wake of the ferry
    boat II)   DP
  Brooks. John Sloan
  Canaday
  CSB. Impressionism
  DP. Catalogue
  Goodrich. John Sloan
  Larkin
  Larkin rev ed
  MiD. Ptg in America
  Myers. Art
  NYG. Fine art
  PA. Annual ex, 1955
  Pierson
  Richardson. Ptg in America
  Time. 300 years
The White way   PPhM
  Goodrich. John Sloan
  Gruskin (col)
Woman's work
  Brooks. John Sloan
Yeats at Petitpas'   DC
  Brooks. John Sloan
  Goodrich. John Sloan
  Pierson

Portrait of the artist
  Henri, R. John Sloan, 1906
SLOANE, Marian Parkhurst
Vermont hamlet   NJMo
  NJMo. Forty years
The sloop—Bermuda by W. Homer
Slow poke by R. Strang
Slowly toward the north by Y. Tanguy
Slums by J. Lawrence
Small personage by R. B. Motherwell
Small pine and snow by F. Heidel
Small portrait by K. Sage
Small town evening by R. V. Cassill
Smallwood, William, b 1732
  Peale, C. W. Gov William Smallwood
A smart turnout by unidentified artist
Smelt, Ann (Tyng) 1733-1756
  Copley, J. S. Ann Tyng
Smelt brook falls by M. Hartley

SMIBERT, John, 1688-1751
Artist's wife   MBH
  Flexner. First flowers
Benjamin Colman
  Flexner. First flowers
Bishop Berkeley and his family (Berkeley
    family; Berkeley group; Bishop
    Berkeley and his entourage; The Ber-
    muda group)   CtY
  CtY. Portrait index
  Flexner. First flowers
  Foote. John Smibert
  Gardner 1959 ed
  McKinney
  Mendelowitz
  Pierson
  Richardson. Ptg in America
  Robb. Harper history
  Roos
  U.S. National Capital sesquicentennial
    com
Continence of Scipio (copy of Poussin)
  Flexner. First flowers
Daniel Oliver
  Belknap
  Foote. John Smibert
Daniel, Peter and Andrew Oliver   MB
  Pierson
Ebenezer Turell
  Foote. John Smibert
Henry Collins
  Belknap
Jane Clark   MBH
  Belknap
  Flexner. First flowers
  MiD. Ptg in America
  Pierson
Joseph Wanton   RPHS
  Time. 300 years (col)
Lady Pepperrell
  Belknap
Mrs Daniel Oliver
  Belknap
Mrs James Lindall   MiD
  MiD. Ports of the Pitts family
  MiD. Treasures
Mrs John Erving
  Belknap
Mrs John Pitts   MiD
  MiD. Ports of the Pitts family
Mrs Nathaniel Cunningham   OT
  Belknap
Mrs Stephen Sewall   MSE
  Foote. John Smibert
  NUM. Art across America
Mrs Thomas Bulfinch   OCl
  OCl. Handbook
Nathaniel Byfield   MM
  Flexner. First flowers
  Pierson
  Roos
Peter Faneuil   DC
  DC. Masterpieces
Peter Faneuil   MBH
  ICA. From colony to nation
Self-portrait   NJMo
  NUM. Art across America
Self-portrait (detail from Bishop Berkeley
    and his family)   CtY
  Flexner. First flowers
  Roos
Three gentlemen
  Barker. Amer ptg

SMIBERT, John—*Continued*
Sir William Pepperrell   MSE
   Larkin
   Larkin rev ed
Smibert, Mary (Williams)
   Smibert, J. Artist's wife
Smibert, Mrs John. See Smibert, Mary
   (Williams)
SMIBERT, Nathaniel, 1734-1756
   Ezra Stiles   CtY
      CtY. Portrait index
      Foote. John Smibert
      Pierson
SMITH, Arthur Hall
   Wraith, wreath, and a final horn   VR
      CoS. New accessions USA, 1952
Smith, Benjamin, fl 1790
   Unidentified artist. Capt Benjamin Smith
Smith, Betsy. See Smith, Elizabeth Ann
SMITH, Charles William, 1893-
   Horizontal arrangement
      Read. Art now, 1948 ed
   Tall building
      Read. Art now, 1948 ed
Smith, De Mott, b 1839?
   Walton, H. De Mott Smith, aged 8
SMITH, Edith M. 1925-
   Continuum number 16
      IU. Contemp Amer ptg & sculp, 1955
   Diptych
      IU. Contemp Amer ptg & sculp, 1957
Smith, Elizabeth Ann, fl 1730
   Theus, J. Elizabeth Smith
Smith, Elizabeth (Oakes) fl 1845
   Paradise, J. W. Mrs Elizabeth Oakes
      Smith
Smith, Elizabeth (Storer) 1726-1788
   Copley, J. S. Mrs Isaac Smith
SMITH, Francis Hopkinson, 1838-1915
   Venice: canal scene I   MB
      MB. Ptgs in water color
   Venice: canal scene II   MB
      MB. Ptgs in water color
SMITH, Hassel Wendell, 1915-
   Number 4, 1960   NBuA
      NBuA. Acquisitions 1959-1961
SMITH, Houghton Cranford
   The Loma, New Mexico
      PPC. Ptg in the U.S. 1949
Smith, Isaac, 1719-1787
   Copley, J. S. Isaac Smith
Smith, J. Somers
   Allen, A. J. Somers Smith
SMITH, Jacob Getlar, 1895-
   Old blacksmith shop
      Gruskin
Smith, James Francis, b 1833?
   Sheffield, I. James Francis Smith
Smith, Jesse Kittredge, fl 1842
   Woolson, E. Jesse Kittredge Smith
SMITH, Joseph B.
   John street, New York, c 1768   NNMC
      Ford. Pictorial folk art
   Steamer Hartford, 1849 (Blair coll)
      Davidson v 1
SMITH, Joseph Lindon, 1863-1950
   Bergamo, Italy   MB
      MB. Ptgs in water color
   Critics: San Giorgio degli Schiavoni,
      Venice   MB
      MB. Ptgs in water color
   Shore scene   MB
      MB. Ptgs in water color

Smith, Judith. See Ladson, Judith (Smith)
SMITH, Judson De Jonge, 1880-
   Black and white
      WMAA. Contemp Amer ptg, 1953
   Portrait of the artist
      Dasburg, A. Judson Smith
SMITH, Lawrence Beall, 1902-
   Trio at the bar   ATU
      ATU. Coll of Amer art
SMITH, Leon Polk, 1906-
   Behold   ATU
      ATU. Coll of Amer art
   Full white
      PPC. International ex. 1961/62
Smith, Luther
   James, A. Luther Smith
Smith, Maria Catherine, fl 1693
   Smith, T. Maria Catherine Smith
SMITH, Mary, fl 1862
   Skating at the wide waters on the canal
      Jones. Rediscovered ptrs
Smith, Mrs Isaac. See Smith, Elizabeth
   (Storer)
Smith, Mary Ann, 1774-1825
   Malbone, E. G. Mary Ann Smith
Smith, Mary Jane, b 1836
   Stock, J. W. Mary Jane Smith
Smith, Mrs Noah, fl 1798
   Unidentified artist. Mrs Noah Smith and
      family
Smith, Nathan, 1762-1829
   Morse, S. F. B. Nathan Smith
SMITH, Russell, 1812-1896
   Academy of music, Philadelphia, Sketch
      for curtain
      Lewis, V. E. Russell Smith
   Aqueduct in the Pennsylvania canal over
      the Juniata, 1876
      Lewis, V. E. Russell Smith
   The aqueduct, Pittsburgh
      Lewis, V. E. Russell Smith
   L'Ariccia
      Lewis, V. E. Russell Smith
   Ben Cruachan
      Lewis, V. E. Russell Smith
   Birmingham from the top of Coal hill
      opposite Pittsburgh, 1834
      Lewis, V. E. Russell Smith
   Blockhouse as residence of Isaac Craig
      Lewis, V. E. Russell Smith
   Branch bank of the United States
      Lewis, V. E. Russell Smith
   Brighton, England
      Lewis, V. E. Russell Smith
   The Capitol from Mr Elliott's garden,
      1839
      Lewis, V. E. Russell Smith
   Chartiers creek near Pittsburgh, 1840
      Lewis, V. E. Russell Smith
   Chartiers creek on the Ohio river, 1872
      Lewis, V. E. Russell Smith
   Chew house   PA
      Lewis, V. E. Russell Smith
   Civita Vecchia
      Lewis, V. E. Russell Smith
   Cloud study
      Lewis, V. E. Russell Smith
   Curtain study for Edwin Booth: Dell
      scene from Boccaccio
      Lewis, V. E. Russell Smith
   Curtain study for the Brooklyn theatre:
      Francesca da Rimini
      Lewis, V. E. Russell Smith

Edgehill
  Lewis, V. E. Russell Smith
Edgehill road, Philadelphia
  Lewis, V. E. Russell Smith
Fort St Jean, Marseilles
  Lewis, V. E. Russell Smith
Grave of John Keats and the pyramid of
    Sestius
  Lewis, V. E. Russell Smith
In the falls of the Saco, Crawford's notch
  Lewis, V. E. Russell Smith
Lake George near Caldwell, New York
  Lewis, V. E. Russell Smith
Larry's creek, Westbranch, Susquehanna
  Lewis, V. E. Russell Smith
Looking up the Monongahela river from
    Coal hill   PPC
  Lewis, V. E. Russell Smith
Monongahela bridge after the freshet in
    1832
  Lewis, V. E. Russell Smith
Monongahela river opposite Pittsburgh,
    1837
  Lewis, V. E. Russell Smith
Near Manayunk
  Lewis, V. E. Russell Smith
Nelson's island showing Monument hill
    and Allegheny waterfront in 1840
                                         PPC
  Lewis, V. E. Russell Smith
North avenue, Pittsburgh
  Lewis, V. E. Russell Smith
Old courthouse in Philadelphia, 1835
  Lewis, V. E. Russell Smith
Old Holiday street theatre, Baltimore,
    1839
  Lewis, V. E. Russell Smith
Old trees at Ormsby farm   PPC
  Lewis, V. E. Russell Smith
Old Walnut street prison, Philadelphia in
    1835
  Lewis, V. E. Russell Smith
Oldest house at foot of Coal hill, opposite
    Market street   PPC
  Lewis, V. E. Russell Smith
Original tomb of Washington, 1836
  Lewis, V. E. Russell Smith
Powder magazine, Fort Duquesne, Penn-
    sylvania, 1832
  Lewis, V. E. Russell Smith
Robeson mill at the mouth of the Wissa-
    hickon
  Lewis, V. E. Russell Smith
Ruins of Fort Ticonderoga, Lake Cham-
    plain
  Lewis, V. E. Russell Smith
Scene on the Ohio
  Lewis, V. E. Russell Smith
Self-portrait, 1887
  Lewis, V. E. Russell Smith
Sligo opposite Pittsburgh
  Lewis, V. E. Russell Smith
Val Ticino, St Gothard route
  Lewis, V. E. Russell Smith
View of Pittsburgh from the salt works on
    Saw mill run
  Chew. 250 years of art
  Lewis, V. E. Russell Smith
Western university of Pennsylvania PPC
  Lewis, V. E. Russell Smith

Wingahocking at Shoemaker's lane, Ger-
    mantown, 1836
  Lewis, V. E. Russell Smith
Wissahickon
  Lewis, V. E. Russell Smith
Smith. Samuel, 1752-1839
  Peale, Rembrandt. Gen Samuel Smith
Smith, Sarah. See Keteltas, Sarah (Smith)
SMITH, Thomas, fl 1669-1693
  Maria Catherine Smith   MWA
    Flexner. First flowers
    Mendelowitz
  Self-portrait   MWA
    Barker. Amer ptg
    Belknap
    Flexner. First flowers (col)
    ICA. From colony to nation
    Larkin
    Larkin rev ed
    MWA. Checklist of portraits
    Pierson
    Richardson. Ptg in America
    Time. 300 years (col)
      Attributed works
  Thomas Savage
    Belknap (as Unidentified artist)
    Davidson v 1
    Flexner. First flowers
    Pierson
SMITH, Wallace Henderson, 1901-
  Hell gate bridge
    NYG. Fine art
SMITH, William Arthur, 1918-
  Calcutta
    NAD. Annual ex, 1960
  Les Halles
    NAD. Annual ex, 1953
  Montmartre impasse
    NAD. Annual ex, 1951
  Out back
    NAD. Annual ex, 1949, 2d half
    OYB. Annual 1953
Smith, William Howard, b 1832
  Stock, J. W. William Howard Smith
Smith family, Member of
  Jennys, W. Member of the Smith family
    of Suffield, Connecticut and Rutland,
    Vermont, c 1800
Smith and Dimon shipyard, New York by
    J. Pringle
Smith memorial by Unidentified artist
Smith's cove by S. Davis
Smithtown, Long Island, c 1860 by A. Milne
Smoke of a .45 by C. M. Russell
Smoking mirror by C. R. Bentley
Smoking them out by C. M. Russell
Smoky range, Allegheny mountains by C. H.
    Shearer
Smugglers' cove by A. P. Ryder
Smyth, Mary. See Hunter, Mary (Smyth)
Snack bar by I. Bishop
Snails by H. G. Keller
Snake Indian and his dog by A. J. Miller
Snake Indian camp by A. J. Miller
Snake Indian pursuing a Crow horse thief
    by A. J. Miller
Snake Indians by A. J. Miller

Snake Indians fording a river by A. J. Miller
Snake Indians shooting elk by A. J. Miller
Snake Indians—testing bows by A. J. Miller
Snakes
    Audubon, J. J. Mockingbird (with rattle-snake robbing nest)
    Curry, J. S. Hog killing a rattlesnake
    Curry, J. S. Hogs killing a snake
    Graves, M. Snake and moon
Snap shot by A. Blanch
Snap the whip by W. Homer
SNELGROVE, Walter, 1924-
    Shipwreck
        CSFP. Annual ex, 1950/51
SNOW, Jenny Emily, fl 1850
    Belshazzar's feast
        Ford. Pictorial folk art
Snow, Cape Cod by D. Macknight
Snow city by P. Evergood
Snow cloud and blue sky by J. Schueler
Snow drapery by G. H. Hallowell
Snow horse by W. Sommer
Snow in April by M. B. Prendergast
Snow on the mountain by S. Davis
Snow scene by J. H. Twachtman
Snow thaw by A. G. Dove
The **snow** trail by F. Remington
Snow, White mountains by D. Macknight
Snowbound on the overland stage by F. Remington
Snowscape by L. MacIver
Snowshoe dance of the Ojibbeway by G. Catlin
Snowy heron or white egret by J. J. Audubon
Snowy owl by J. J. Audubon
Snug harbor by P. Evergood
Snyder's Hollow by J. H. Lawman
Soap-locks or Bowery boys, New York by N. V. Calyo
Soaring by A. N. Wyeth
Social club by W. M. Harnett
Social security murals by B. Shahn
The **socialite** by K. J. Priebe
Soda fountain by W. J. Glackens
Soda jerker by P. Burlin
Soft night by A. Gorky
Softly falling snow by D. Macknight
Soho portrait by H. W. Scheuch
SOKOLE, Miron, 1901-
    Approaching night
        Gruskin
    The aquarium
        IU. Contemp Amer ptg, 1950
    Nostalgic night
        IU. Contemp Amer ptg, 1949
    Within the confines of window frame
        IU. Contemp Amer ptg, 1948
Solace by W. M. Harnett
Le **Soldat** du Chêne, an Osage chief by G. B. King (attributed works)
Soldier and bull by R. A. Nelson
Soldier's dream by M. Beckmann
Soldier's joy by T. H. Benton

Soldier's medal by A. Leslie
Solids into blue by C. A. Morris
Soliloquy by F. C. Watkins
Solitaire. See Games and sports—Cards
A **solitary** by A. James
Solitudes by L. Guglielmi
Solo by M. Weber
SOLOMON, Hyde, 1911-
    Vermont autumn   WMAA
        Baur. Nature
SOLOMON, Syd, 1907-
    Bird Key bay   OYB
        OYB. Annual 1957
        OYB. Supplement 1959
    Boca
        Pousette-Dart. Amer ptg
SOLOMON, Vita P.
    End of the day
        NAD. Annual ex, 1959
Solomon at the court of Sheba by P. Evergood
Solstice by K. Okada
Solstice rider by L. Mullican
Sombre vertical with lines by I. Bolotowsky
Some grow up by H. D. Pickering
Somebody tore my poster by Y. Kuniyoshi
Somerby, Joanna (Cotter) 1805-1886
    Jouett, M. H. Mrs Rufus Somerby
Somers, Mary. See Deas, Mary (Somers)
Something on the eight ball by S. Davis
Somewhere today by I. R. Pereira
SOMMER, William, 1867-1949
    Apples
        OCl. Sommer
    April cat
        OCl. Sommer
    Asleep on the path
        OCl. Sommer
    Bald **boy**
        OCl. Sommer
    Big horse
        OCl. Sommer
    Black horse
        OCl. Sommer
    Blue chair
        OCl. Sommer
    Blue horse
        OCl. Sommer
    Blue vase
        OCl. Sommer
    Bowl of apples
        OCl. Sommer
    A boy   ICA
        OCl. Sommer
    Brandywine
        OCl. Sommer
    Brandywine landscape
        OCl. Sommer
    Cows
        OCl. Sommer
    Cows resting
        OCl. Sommer
    Faith, hope, and **charity**
        OCl. Sommer
    Fruit bowl
        OCl. Sommer
    The goblet
        OCl. Sommer

Horses in the snow   OCl
  OCl. Handbook
  OCl. Sommer
June
  OCl. Sommer
Kitchen
  OCl. Sommer
Languid leisure
  OCl. Sommer
Little girl with apple
  OCl. Sommer
Little Mozart
  OCl. Sommer
Marvin
  OCl. Sommer
Meditation in space
  OCl. Sommer
One of the Dominskis
  OCl. Sommer
Orange door
  OCl. Sommer
Ornamatique
  OCl. Sommer
Pa's brainstorm
  OCl. Sommer
Patchwork cows
  OCl. Sommer
Pensive boy
  OCl. Sommer
Pink cow
  OCl. Sommer
Pompous boy
  OCl. Sommer
Portrait   OYB
  OYB. Catalogue 1951
Ray
  OCl. Sommer
Rose montage
  OCl. Sommer
Seated boy in lavender overalls
  OCl. Sommer
Snow horse
  OCl. Sommer
Spinach tree
  OCl. Sommer
Still life: the blue vase   OCl
  OCl. Sommer
Tess
  OCl. Sommer
Three horses in alarm
  OCl. Sommer
Tree forms
  OCl. Sommer
Turreted pitcher
  OCl. Sommer
Two yellow horses   OCl
  OCl. Sommer
Waiting in Bethlehem
  OCl. Sommer
Winter landscape, 1923
  OCl. Sommer
Winter landscape, c 1934
  OCl. Sommer
Sommernachtstraum by H. Hofmann
Son of a sharecropper by J. B. Turnbull
The song by B. Shahn
Song in the rain by C. E. Burchfield

Song of Esther by A. Rattner
Song of the guitar by W. W. Quirt
Song of the katydids by C. E. Burchfield
Song of the katydids on an August morning
  by C. E. Burchfield
Song of the marsh by C. E. Burchfield
Song of the talking wire by H. F. Farny
Song of the telegraph by C. E. Burchfield
SONNTAG, William Louis, 1869-1898
  The Bowery at night, c 1895   NNMC
  U.S. National Capital sesquicentennial
  com
  Morning in the Blue Ridge mountains
  Sears. Highlights
The soothsayer by F. S. Franck
Sorcerer's gear by R. Gorchov
Sorceress by D. Austin
Sorrow by S. Csoka
La sortie du bain by M. Cassatt
Sortie from Gibraltar by J. Trumbull
Sortie of the British garrison from Gibraltar
  by J. Trumbull
Sou'easter interim by K. Knaths
The soul leaving the body by W. W. Quirt
Soul of space by I. R. Pereira
Soula's Rathskeller by J. Sloan
Soult, Nicolas Jean de Dieu, duke of Dal-
  matia, 1769-1851
  Healy, G. P. A. Nicolas Jean de Dieu
  Soult, duke of Dalmatia, 1769-1851
Sound asleep and wide awake by D. C.   OYB
  Johnston
Sound in the mulberry trees by B. Shahn
Sound of blue light by N. Carone
Sound of flowers by M. Broderson
Sounds in the rock by T. Stamos
Source by M. Manigault
Source of the Romanche by L. Pitts
South American river by M. J. Heade
South Beach bathers by J. Sloan
South Boston pier by M. B. Prendergast
South of Scranton by P. Blume
South of Taxco by Martyl
South Sea whale fishing by R. W. Salmon
South window by R. F. Gates
Southern belle by A. Brook
The Southern Belle by Unidentified artist
Southern community by R. Gwathmey
Southern scene by R. Gwathmey
Southern souvenir by E. Cortor
Southern tier by M. H. Visser't Hooft
Southwest no 4 by W. Lockwood
Southwest no 9—riders by W. Lockwood
Southwest wind by C. Hassam
A southwester by J. Marin
Souvenir of America by K. L. Seligmann
Souvenir of Chicago by M. Beckmann
Souvenirs of the sea by A. Gottlieb
Sowing by R. Gwathmey
Sowing grain at Bishop hill by O. Krans

SOYER, Isaac, 1907-
  Employment agency   WMAA
    Baur. Revolution
    Goodrich. Amer art
    McCurdy
    Pierson
    WMAA. Juliana Force
  The model
    Gruskin (col)
  Office girls
    Bazin
SOYER, Moses, 1899-
  Dancer
    NAD. Annual ex, 1959
  Dancers
    NAD. Annual ex, 1961
  David Burliuk in his studio
    CSFP. Annual ex, 1948/49
  Four dancers
    OYB. Annual 1953
  Girl in orange sweater   WMAA
    Goodrich. Amer art
    Pierson
  New costume
    Gruskin (col)
  Sad interior
    Brown. Amer ptg
  Three dancers
    MM. Amer ptg today
SOYER, Raphael, 1899-
  The blue shawl
    CSFP. Annual ex, 1948/49
  Boheme girl
    CSFP. Annual ex, 1950/51
  Boy and girl
    NAD. Annual ex, spring 1950
  Brown sweater   WMAA
    Goodrich. Amer art
    Pierson
  Disorder
    NAD. Annual ex, 1949, 1st half
  Dressmaker's shop
    NAD. Annual ex, 1954
  Female figure   ATeS
    ATeS. Collection
  Figure in blue
    VR. Amer ptg, 1954
  Flower vendor
    NYG. Fine art
  Girl in a white blouse   MM
    MM. 100 Amer ptrs
  A group of artists
    NAD. Annual ex, 1956
  In the studio
    ICA. Annual ex, 1945/46
  Interior with figure
    IU. Contemp Amer ptg, 1949
  Lamplight
    Brown. Amer ptg
  Nude in profile
    WMAA. Contemp Amer ptg, 1950
  Office girls   WMAA
    Baur. Revolution
    Goodrich. Amer art (col)
    Mendelowitz
    Pierson
  Pensive girl   PPC
    CoS. New accessions USA, 1948
  Reflection
    WMAA. Museum and its friends, 1958
  Seamstress
    NAD. Annual ex, 1948
    WMAA. Annual ex, 1957

  Self-portrait   ATU
    ATU. Coll of Amer art
  Still life
    NAD. Annual ex, 1957
  Subway platform
    Gruskin
  Two sisters
    NAD. Annual ex, 1947, 1st half
    VR. Biennal ex, 1948
  Waiting for the audition
    DC. 22 biennial ex, 1951
  Waiting room   DC
    Larkin
    Larkin rev ed
    Pierson
  Young woman
    PPC. Ptg in the U.S. 1949
  Portrait of the artist
    Biddle, G. Raphael Soyer and his model
    Dickinson, S. E. Raphael Soyer
Space intangibles by M. Tobey
Space modulator by L. Moholy-Nagy
Space ritual no 3 by M. Tobey
Space, time, embrace by W. Pachner
Spad by G. L. Mueller
SPAGNA, Vincent, 1898-
  Air raid
    Gruskin
Spanish boys at play (Vianna do Castello,
    Portugal) by J. S. Sargent
Spanish cavalier by W. M. Chase
Spanish lace by E. Graham
Spanish soldiers by J. S. Sargent
Spanish steps, Rome by M. B. Prendergast
Sparhawk, Nathaniel, 1715-1776
    Copley, J. S. Nathaniel Sparhawk
Sparhawk, William Pepperrell. See Pepper-
    rell, Sir William, 2d bart
Sparking by J. Carlin
Sparking by F. W. Edmonds
Sparks, Mary Crowninshield (Silsbee) 1809-
    1887
    Alexander, F. Mrs Jared Sparks
Sparrows
    Evergood, P. Lily and the sparrows
    Graves, M. Preening sparrows
    Heil, C. E. Field sparrow on blackberry
Speakeasy closed for violation by B. Shahn
The **speaker** by W. Gropper
Spectator by H. Warshaw
Spectre of the sea by A. Gottlieb
The **spectrum,** a painting in four acts by
    B. Connelly
Speculation by J. Ernst
Speed—Lake Champlain by J. Marin
SPEICHER, Eugene Edward, 1883-
  Agnes Clark
    NAD. Annual ex, 1948
  Andrée Ruellan   ATeS
    ATeS. Collection
    CSFP. Annual ex, 1952
  A. Conger Goodyear, 1942   MMA
    NBuA. Eugene Speicher
  Babette, 1931   PPC
    NBuA. Eugene Speicher
  Begonias, 1947
    NBuA. Eugene Speicher
  Blue necklace   OT
    Larkin
    Larkin rev ed

Brigham's yard, Kingston   NUM
  NUM. Root bequest
Caim Lasher
  CSFP. Annual ex, 1947-48
Consuela
  NAD. Annual ex, 1947, 2d half
Farm news, 1944
  NBuA. Eugene Speicher
Farmer
  IU. Contemp Amer ptg, 1948
Flowers in pineapple pitcher, 1947
  NBuA. Eugene Speicher
Georgia O'Keeffe, 1908
  NBuA. Eugene Speicher
Graziana
  Bazin
Greek boy
  Baur. Revolution
  NBuA. Fifty ptgs
Green hat   FaW
  Lewisohn
Helen Rogers
  DC. 20 biennial ex, 1947
Henry Emerson Tuttle, 1945   CtY
  CtY. Portrait index
  NBuA. Eugene Speicher
Jean Bellows, 1940   ICA
  NBuA. Eugene Speicher
Jean in blue
  Gruskin (col)
Joyce   InIJ
  InIJ. 105 ptgs
Katharine   MB
  NBuA. Eugene Speicher
  WMAA. Juliana Force
Katharine Cornell as Candida, 1926
     NBuA
  NBuA. Eugene Speicher
  Pierson
Kathleen Colleti
  PPC. International ex, 1950
Lilya   OCiM
  Baur. Revolution
  NBuA. Eugene Speicher
Marianna   WMAA
  Goodrich. Amer art
  McCurdy
Mrs Ogden Phipps
  Time. 300 years (col)
The mountaineer
  NBuA. Eugene Speicher
  Pierson
Murray Bay landscape, 1933   WMAA
  NBuA. Eugene Speicher
Nancy, 1942
  NBuA. Eugene Speicher
Nude back   OCo
  CoS. New accessions USA, 1960
  NYG. Fine art
  WMAA. Museum and its friends, 1958
Patty
  NBuA. Eugene Speicher
Peach jacket   VR
  NBuA. Eugene Speicher
Pigtails, 1939   MoKN
  NBuA. Eugene Speicher
Polly   MM
  MM. 100 Amer ptrs
Portrait of a girl   WMAA
  Roos
Sara Grace Heath Butler   OYB
  OYB. Catalogue 1951

Steve
  NAD. Annual ex, 1952
Tony Robinson
  IU. Contemp Amer ptg, 1949
Tulips in a white pitcher   MoSL
  MoSL. Handbook 1953
Yvette von Kories
  PPC. Ptg in the U.S. 1949
SPEIGHT, Francis, 1896-
Cliffs at Manayunk
  NAD. Annual ex, 1952
End of the street   OYB
  OYB. Catalogue 1951
Schuylkill at Manayunk
  NAD. Annual ex, 1958
Spell by L. Feininger
Spell of Italy by H. G. Keller
Spencer, Ambrose, 1765-1848
  Ames, E. Ambrose Spencer, 1811
  Jarvis, J. W. Ambrose Spencer
SPENCER, Lilly Martin, 1822-1902
The war spirit at home, celebrating the
    victory of Vicksburg   NJN
  NJN. Early N.J. artists
  U.S. National Capital sesquicentennial
  com
SPENCER, Niles, 1893-1952
Above the excavation
  MnMW. Classic tradition
Apartment tower   WMAA
  Goodrich. Amer art
Blast furnace
  MnU. 40 Amer ptrs
City shapes   ATeS
  ATeS. Collection
City walls   MMA
  Baur. New art
  McCurdy
  MMA. Masters
  MnMW. Precisionist view
  Pierson
Corporation shed   OCo
  Brown. Amer ptg
The cove, Ogunquit   NJN
  Baur. New art
The desk   CSFM
  DC. 22 biennial ex, 1951
  MnMW. Precisionist view
Erie underpass   MM
  Baur, New art
  MM. 100 Amer ptrs
  MnU. 40 Amer ptrs
Green table   WMAA
  Baur. New art
  Goodrich. Amer art
  Pierson
In Fairmont   MMA
  Baur. New art (col)
  IU. Contemp Amer ptg, 1952
  Pierson
  Pousette-Dart. Amer ptg
In the cabin
  ICA. Annual ex, 1951
Near Avenue A   MMA
  Baur. Revolution
Pike county church
  VR. Biennial ex, 1948
Silver tanks
  PPC. Ptg in the U.S. 1949
Still life
  NYG. Fine art

SPENCER, Niles—*Continued*
  Two bridges
    Hunter. Mod Amer ptg (col)
    McCurdy
    MMA. Abstract (col)
    MnMW. Contemporary (col)
    WMAA. Neuberger collection (col)
  Wake of the hurricane   MnMW
    MnMW. Precisionist view (col)
  Watch factory   OYB
    OYB. Catalogue 1951
SPENCER, Robert, 1879-1931
  Ship chandlers' row   DP
    DP. Catalogue
Spencer, Sarah Louisa, b 1841
  Walton, H. Sarah Louisa Spencer
The **sphinx** and the Milky way by C. E. Burchfield
The **sphinx** on the seashore by E. Vedder
Spider's nightmare by O. Herford
The **spielers** by G. B. Luks
SPIERS, Harry, 1870-1947
  As the sunlight bursts   MB
    MB. Ptgs in water color
Spike's folly by W. De Kooning
Spinach tree by W. Sommer
Spindrift by A. N. Wyeth
The **spinet** by T. W. Dewing
Spirals by J. C. Atherton
Spirit bird by M. Graves
Spirit of air by I. R. Pereira
Spirit of the Indian by T. Moran
Spirit 3 by W. Hedrick
Spiritual decadence by E. Burkhart
Spiritual decay by E. Burkhart
Splatters and leaves by L. MacIver
Splicing the cable by R. Dudley
SPOHN, Clay Edgar, 1898-
  November 1951
    IU. Contemp Amer ptg & sculp, 1953
  Number 11-24-46
    CSFP. Annual ex, 1947/48
Spong, Hilda
  Chase, W. M. Hilda Spong
Sponge diver by W. Homer
Sponge fishermen, Bahamas by W. Homer
Spoonbills
  Audubon, J. J. Roseate spoonbill
Spooner, Rebecca. See Green, Rebecca (Spooner)
Sports, Barent
  Unidentified artist. Barent Sports of Albany
Sports. See Games and sports
Sportsman's still life by A. Pope
Sprague, Albert Arnold, 1835-1915
  Betts, L. Albert Arnold Sprague
Sprague, Jonathan, fl 1828
  Bosworth, S. Jonathan Sprague
Sprague, Mrs Jonathan. See Sprague, Melissa
SPRAGUE, Mark A.
  Arrangement
    ICA. Annual ex, 1951
Sprague, Melissa, fl 1828
  Bosworth, S. Melissa Sprague
Spring by J. Blair

Spring by M. Graves
Spring by J. E. Heliker
Spring by W. Homer
Spring by H. Lundeberg
Spring by H. E. Mattson
Spring by A. P. Ryder
Spring by B. Shahn
Spring by J. Stella
Spring by R. Strang
Spring by W. Zorach
Spring beauty by A. N. Wyeth
Spring blossoms by F. Crowninshield
Spring blossoms by W. Homer
Spring bonnet by J. Carroll
Spring: burning up fallen trees, a girdled clearing, Canada by G. Harvey
Spring cleaning by J. L. Howard
Spring festival by H. Pittman
Spring fishing by Unidentified artist
Spring flowers by L. Karp
Spring harvest by S. Chun
Spring idyll by K. Matthew
Spring in Central park by A. A. Dehn
Spring in France by M. Avery
Spring in Giverney by T. Robinson
Spring in the country by G. Wood
Spring in the valley by A. M. R. Moses
Spring in town by G. Wood
Spring is in the air by F. Kleinholz
Spring landscape by C. Hinkle
Spring landscape by S. Laufman
Spring landscape by G. Wood
Spring melody by N. Cikovsky
Spring mist by W. Thon
Spring night, Harlem river by E. Lawson
Spring no 1 by J. Marin
Spring no 1, 1913 by W. Zorach
Spring on Morton street by B. Shahn
Spring on Ninth avenue by L. Bosa
Spring orchard by M. Avery
Spring planting by J. Sloan
Spring shower, Connecticut valley by M. J. Heade
Spring song by E. P. Etting
Spring song by S. Moy
Spring song by P. S. Sample
Spring song by W. Stuempfig
Spring, twelve o'clock by I. R. Pereira
Springtime by J. E. Costigan
Springtime by H. B. Kayn
Springtime by D. Macknight
Springtime by D. W. Tryon
Springtime by F. C. Watkins
Springtime in Virginia by W. Homer
Springtime of delight by A. B. Davies
Sproat, David, 1734-1799
  Trumbull, J. David Sproat
Sprouting coconuts by R. Tam

SPRUANCE, Benton, 1904-
  Still life with horns
    PPC. Ptg in the U.S. 1949
SPRUCE, Everett Franklin, 1907-
  Angora goat
    Leeper. Everett Spruce
  Antelope mountain
    Leeper. Everett Spruce
  Arkansas landscape   DP
    Leeper. Everett Spruce
  Autumn landscape   TxD
    Leeper. Everett Spruce
  The beach   MdBM
    Leeper. Everett Spruce
  Bee keeper
    Leeper. Everett Spruce
  Big Bend
    Leeper. Everett Spruce
  Bird study
    Leeper. Everett Spruce
  Brushy hillside   WMAA
    Goodrich. Amer art
    Leeper. Everett Spruce
  Century plant   LaN
    DC. 21 biennial ex, 1949
    Leeper. Everett Spruce
  The cliff
    Leeper. Everett Spruce
  Cold day
    Leeper. Everett Spruce
  Dark mountains
    PA. Annual ex, 1947
  The desert   MiD
    Leeper. Everett Spruce
    PPC. Amer ptg in the U.S. 1949
  Desert at night
    CSFP. Annual ex, 1950/51
  Fence builders
    Leeper. Everett Spruce
  Fiddler
    Leeper. Everett Spruce
  Fish and birds   MnU
    Leeper. Everett Spruce (col)
  Fisherman
    IU. Contemp Amer ptg, 1950
    NBuA. Expressionism
  Goat
    MM. Amer ptg today
  Gull
    Leeper. Everett Spruce
  The hawk   MMA
    Leeper. Everett Spruce
    Pierson
  Kildeer
    Leeper. Everett Spruce
  Little canyon
    VR. Biennial ex, 1948
  Low tide
    Leeper. Everett Spruce
  Mending fence
    Leeper. Everett Spruce
  Night fisherman
    Leeper. Everett Spruce (col)
  Old tree   MnMW
    Leeper. Everett Spruce
  On the beach
    Leeper. Everett Spruce
  Padre island
    Leeper. Everett Spruce
  Pigeons on a roof   MM
    MM. 100 Amer ptrs

  Precipice
    Pousette-Dart. Amer ptg
  Red mule
    Leeper. Everett Spruce
  Rocky place
    IU. Contemp Amer ptg, 1952
  Sea gulls
    Leeper. Everett Spruce
  Surf fisherman
    Leeper. Everett Spruce
  The wave
    Leeper. Everett Spruce
  Wave breaking
    Leeper. Everett Spruce
  Waves
    Leeper. Everett Spruce
  Whippoorwill, sandpiper
    Leeper. Everett Spruce
  White cow
    Leeper. Everett Spruce
  White mountain
    Leeper. Everett Spruce
  Yellow rooster
    Leeper. Everett Spruce
Spruce tree in a landscape by C. W. Hudson
Squall off Christmas cove by M. Freedman
The **square** by P. W. Zimmerman
Square on the pond by A. G. Dove
Squash by Y. Kuniyoshi
The **squatters** by G. C. Bingham
Squirrels
  Audubon, J. J. Richardson's Columbian squirrel
  Audubon, J. J. Say's or western fox squirrel
  Copley, J. S. Boy with squirrel (Henry Pelham)
Stables by G. O'Keeffe
Staccato for dormers by R. L. Lancaster
Stacey hill, Stoddard, New Hampshire, View from by T. Doughty
Stacking alfalfa by O. M. Pleissner
Staff, distaff and rod by A. T. Mason
Stafford, Harriet (Romeyn) 1792-1848
  Ames, E. Mrs Spencer Stafford
Stafford, Spencer, 1772-1844
  Ames, E. Spencer Stafford
Stag and two does by A. P. Ryder
Stag at Sharkey's by G. W. Bellows
Stag drinking by A. P. Ryder
Stage fragment, Faust by G. L. Mueller
Stagecoaches
  Blythe, D. G. Stagecoach
  Boese, H. Stagecoach seventy-six of the Knickerbocker line
  Johnson, E. The old stagecoach
  Johnson, F. T. On Salt lake trail
  Peters, J. Good intent
  Remington, F. Snowbound on the overland stage
  Russell, C. M. Holding up the stage
  Shinn, E. Winter scene
  Stucker, F. Albany Schoharie stagecoach
  Tattersall, G. Road to the west
Stages of man by Unidentified artist
STAHL, Ben, 1910-
  Mother earth
    NAD. Annual ex, 1952
  Rehearsal under the big top
    NAD. Annual ex, 1948, 1st half

STAIGG, Richard Morell, 1817-1881
  Mrs Gerard Stuyvesant   NNHS
    Vail. Stuyvesant ports
The **staircase** by A. Refregier
Staircase by C. Ruhtenberg
A **staircase** by J. S. Sargent
Staircase, Doylestown by C. Sheeler
Staircase group by C. W. Peale
Stairs, Provincetown by C. H. Demuth
Stairway by J. Koch
Stamford harbor by L. Bouché
STAMOS, Theodoros, 1922-
  Corinth no 3, 1959
    MnMW. 60 Amer ptrs
  Death of the anarchist
    Pousette-Dart. Amer ptg
  East field
    PPC. International ex, 1961/62
  Echo
    MM. 100 Amer ptrs
  The emperor ploughs the fields   MiD
    MiD. Treasures
    WMAA. Contemp Amer ptg, 1950
  Field II
    CtY. Yale alumni
  Field III, 1954
    WMAA. New decade
  Flower eruption
    CSFP. Annual ex, 1950/51
    PPC. Ptg in the U.S. 1949
  Greek island
    NUM. Art across America
  Greek orisons   WMAA
    Faulkner. Art today, 1956
    Mendelowitz
    Pierson
    WMAA. New decade
  Heart of Norway spruce   DC
    DC. Masterpieces
    Eliot. Art of our time (col)
    Time. 300 years (col)
  High snow, low sun, no 3, 1957
    MMA. New Amer ptg (col)
  High snow, low sun, no 11, 1957
    Baur. Nature (col)
    Goodrich. Amer art (col)
  Levant for E. W. R.   NBuA
    NBuA. Acquisitions 1957-58
  Levant no 7
    IU. Contemp Amer ptg & sculp, 1961
  Lupine   DP
    Larkin rev ed
  Oriental beggar
    IU. Contemp Amer ptg & sculp, 1955
  Red Sea terrace no 1
    CoS. New accessions USA, 1960
  The reward   NUM
    NUM. Root bequest
  Road to Sparta
    WMAA. New decade
  Sacrifice of Chronos no 2, 1948   DP
    McCurdy
    MMA. Abstract
  Seedling   NUM
    MiA. Root coll
  Sounds in the rock   MMA
    Baur. Revolution
    MMA. Contemp ptrs
    Pierson

  Sun games no 2, 1958
    MMA. New Amer ptg
  Theatre
    IU. Contemp Amer ptg, 1950
  A walk in the poppies
    Barker. From realism
  White field no 2, 1957
    MMA. New Amer ptg
  World tablet   DP
    DP. Catalogue
Stampede of wild horses by A. J. Miller
Stampeded by C. M. Russell
Stampeding bulls by L. Corbino
STAMPER, Willson Y. 1910-
  Perfume counter
    NBuA. Expressionism
Standard with still life by S. Davis
Standing couple by D. Park
Standing figure by J. Davis
Standing figure by K. Finch
Standing in the need of prayer by C. M.
    Williamson
Standing male by W. De Kooning
Standing man and stick by N. J. Oliveira
Standing nude by B. Karfiol
Standing with reluctant feet where brook and
    river meet by J. Farnsworth
Standing woman by N. J. Oliveira
Standing woman with hat by N. J. Oliveira
Stanford, John, 1754-1834
  Jarvis, J. W. Rev John Stanford
STANLEY, A. R. fl 1840
  Eliza Wells   DN
    DN. Amer primitive ptgs, pt 1
Stanley, Sir Henry Morton, 1841-1904
  Healy, G. P. A. Sir Henry M. Stanley
STANLEY, John Mix, 1814-1872
  Assiniboin encampment on the upper Mis-
    souri   MiD
    Rathbone
  Bear's Paw
    WiMiA. Amer ptg 1760-1960
  Bois de Sioux river
    WiMiA. Amer ptg 1760-1960
  Buffalo hunt on the southern plains
        DNC
    McCracken. Portrait of the old west
    (col)
  Chinook burial grounds   MiD
    Rathbone
  Distributing goods to the Gros Ventres
    McCracken. Portrait of the old west
  Gov Stevens at Fort Benton
    McCracken. Portrait of the old west
  Indian telegraph   MiD
    Rathbone
  Indians playing cards   MiD
    Pierson
  Ko-kak-koo-kiss, a Towoccono warrior
        DNC
    Roos
  Osage scalp dance   DNC
    McCracken. Portrait of the old west
    (col)
    Rathbone
  Prairie encampment   MiD
    Rathbone
  Samuel Mountfort Pitts jr   MiD
    MiD. Ports of the Pitts family

Western landscape   MiD
  Larkin
  Larkin rev ed
  Rathbone
Stanley, Ruth. See Mix, Ruth (Stanley)
Stanton, Daniel
  Elliott, C. L. Daniel Stanton
Staples, Seth Perkins, 1776-1861
  Flagg, J. B. Seth Perkins Staples (after
    Waldo and Jewett)
The star by C. E. Burchfield
The star by M. Kopf
Star watchers by F. J. Russell
Starlings caravan by K. Sage
Starr, Abigail. See Taylor, Abigail (Starr)
Starr, Nathan, 1784-1852
  Jarvis, J. W. Nathan Starr jr (of Middle-
    town, Connecticut)
Starr King mountain, California by A. Bier-
  stadt
Starrucca viaduct, Susquehanna valley by
  J. F. Cropsey
Start of the hunt by Unidentified artist
Starting out after rail by T. Eakins
Startled by W. Homer
STASACK, Edward, 1929-
  Undersea mountain
    IU. Contemp Amer ptg & sculp, 1961
State street, Albany by J. Eights
The statesman by C. H. Pepper
Station of the Cross by H. Moller
Statue at Vaux-le-Vicomte by W. Gay
Statue of Liberty
  Moran, E. Unveiling the statue of Lib-
    erty, 1886
Steam room at Bayes Hot Springs by J.
  Brown
Steam turbine by C. Sheeler
Steamboats on the Ohio by T. P. Anshutz
Steamship Odin by L. Feininger
STEARNS, Junius Brutus, 1810-1885
  Children fishing   OYB
    OYB. Catalogue 1951
  Fisherman's still life   OT
    Pierson
Steel—Croton by C. Sheeler
Steel mill at night by A. H. Gorson
Steel structure by R. Marsh
Steel town madonna by S. Bookatz
STEELE, Gordon
  Construction no 2   OYB
    OYB. Annual 1960
STEELE, Theodore Clement, 1847-1926
  Early spring   InTH
    InTH. Catalogue
Steelworkers' noontime by T. P. Anshutz
Steep bridge by E. Berman
Steeplechase by L. Gatch
Steeplechase horses by R. J. Bové
Steeplechase park by R. Marsh
STEFANELLI, Joseph, 1921-
  Occasion
    WMAA. Annual ex, 1957
  Ponte Margherita
    IU. Contemp Amer ptg & sculp, 1961

Stein, Gertrude, 1874-1946
  Tomlin, B. W. Number 9: in praise of
    Gertrude Stein
STEIN, Ronald Jay, 1930-
  Hommage à Andrés Segovia
    PPC. International ex, 1958
STEIN, Walter, 1930-
  Boy holding lamb's head
    ICA. Annual ex, 1957
  The pillow
    IU. Contemp Amer ptg, 1952
STEINBERG, Saul, 1914-
  Gentleman hunter   NBuA
    NBuA. Acquisitions 1954-57
  Portrait of the artist
    Bouché, R. Saul Steinberg
Steinberg, Mrs Saul. See Sterne, Hedda
STEINITZ, Kaethe, 1889-
  Pine trees   CtY
    CtY. Soc Anonyme
Steinman, Mrs John F.
  Watkins, F. C. Mrs John F. Steinman
Stele by S. Davis
STELLA, Frank, 1936-
  Arundel castle
    MMA. Sixteen
  Die fahne hoch!
    MMA. Sixteen
  Marriage of reason and squalor
    MMA. Sixteen
  Tomlinson court park
    MMA. Sixteen
STELLA, Joseph, 1880-1946
  American landscape
    Janson. Picture history
  Battle of light, Coney island   CtY
    Baur. New art
    Baur. Revolution
    Brown. Amer ptg
    CtY. Soc Anonyme
    Hess. Abstract ptg
    Hunter. Mod Amer ptg (col)
    McCurdy
    MMA. Abstract
    NUM. Art across America
    Pierson
    WMAA. Juliana Force
    WMAA. Pioneers
  The bridge (Brooklyn bridge)   NJN
    Larkin (detail)
    Larkin rev ed
    Pierson
    Richardson. Ptg in America
    Time. 300 years (col)
  Brooklyn bridge   CtY
    Baur. Revolution
    Blesh
    Brown. Amer ptg
    Cheney. Primer 1958 ed
    Cheney. Story 1958 ed
    CtY. Soc Anonyme
    Gardner. 1959 ed
    Gruskin
    Janson. Key monuments
    MMA. Abstract
    Pierson
    Rosenblum
  Brooklyn bridge—Variation on an old
    theme
    Baur. New art (col)
    Goodrich. Amer art (col)
    ICA. Amer artists paint the city

STELLA, Joseph—*Continued*
Gas tank
  WMAA. Neuberger collection
The port from New York interpreted
                                 NJN
  Baur. Revolution
  Brown. Amer ptg
Skyscrapers (central panel of New York
  interpreted)   NJN
  Baur. New art
  Mendelowitz
Spring   CtY
  Baur. Nature
  Baur. New art
  MMA. Abstract
  Pierson
Voice of the nightingale
  NYG. Fine art
Stella by H. V. Olson
Stenographer by W. De Kooning
Stepping out by E. J. Kosa
Steps to the lighthouse by Y. Johnston
STERNBERG, Harry, 1904-
Mexican ruin
  PPC. Ptg in the U.S. 1949
STERNE, Hedda, 1916-   NBuA
Alaska 1
  NBuA. Acquisitions 1957-58
Grandfather
  ICA. Annual ex, 1947/48
M. R. D.
  IU. Contemp Amer ptg & sculp, 1961
New York
  ICA. Amer artists paint the city (col)
Number 32, 1952
  Pousette-Dart. Amer ptg
Roads no 6
  PPC. International ex, 1958
STERNE, Maurice, 1878-1957
After rain   DP
  DP. Catalogue
After the rain   MMA
  Time. 300 years (col)
After the storm
  IU. Contemp Amer ptg, 1950
  PPC. Ptg in the U.S. 1949
Bali bazaar   WMAA
  Goodrich. Amer art
  Pierson
Bazaar with coconut palms, Bali   MM
  MM. 100 Amer ptrs
Benares   DP
  DP. Catalogue
  WMAA. Pioneers
Benares on the Ganges
  NAD. Annual ex, 1957
Breadmakers   MB
  Baur. Revolution
  Pierson
Eggs with carafe
  Lewisohn
Expression of an impression   MM
  CoS. New accessions USA, 1952
  NAD. Annual ex, 1958
Girl in blue dress   MMA
  Cheney. Story 1958 ed
Higgins pier
  IU. Contemp Amer ptg, 1948
Maine coast   MB
  MB. Ptgs in water color
Mother and child   DP
  DP. Catalogue

Peasant girl
  Cheney. Primer 1958 ed
Plum girl
  NYG. Fine art
Provincetown seascape
  Lewisohn
Reapers   DP
  Cheney. Expressionism 1948 ed
  Cheney. Primer 1958 ed
Resting at the bazaar   MMA
  Baur. Revolution
  Brown. Amer ptg
  Gruskin
  McCurdy
Sea gulls
  Genauer (col)
Sea, sand and wind
  PA. Annual ex, 1949
Still life   MoSL
  MoSL. Handbook 1953
Summer shower
  IU. Contemp Amer ptg, 1949
Winding road
  Lewisohn
STERNER, Harold, 1895-
Beach scene with a newspaper   MB
  MB. Ptgs in water color
STETTHEIMER, Florine, d 1944
Family portrait no 2   MMA
  MnMW. Reality and fantasy
  Pierson
STETTINIUS, Samuel Enredy, 1768-1815
              Attributed works
Jane L. Van Reid   DN
  DN. Amer primitive ptgs
Mr and Mrs Wolfersberger
  Chew. 250 years of art
Wellington Van Reid   DN
  DN. Amer primitive ptgs, pt 1
Steuben, Friedrich Wilhelm Ludolf Gerhard Augustin, baron von, 1730-1794
  Earl, R. Baron von Steuben
Steve by E. E. Speicher
Stevedores in the hole by M. Petersen
Stevens, Ebenezer, 1751-1823
  Turnbull, J. Ebenezer Stevens
STEVENS, Edward John, 1923-
Isle of the gods
  IU. Contemp Amer ptg & sculp, 1953
The jungle
  IU. Contemp Amer ptg & sculp, 1959
Mad bull
  ICA. Annual ex, 1947/48
Red bird
  Pousette-Dart. Amer ptg
Voyage of the gods
  IU. Contemp Amer ptg, 1952
Stevens, Elizabeth (Allen) 1713-1778
  Copley, J. S. Elizabeth Allen Stevens
Stevens, Isaac Ingalls, 1818-1862
  Stanley, J. M. Gov Stevens at Fort Benton
STEVENS, John
Sioux Indians attacking a Minnesota farm
                            MnSH
  Ford. Pictorial folk art
Stevens, Sophie Candace. See Page, Sophie
  Candace (Stevens)
Stevens, Mrs William. See Stevens, Elizabeth (Allen)

STEVENS, William Lester, 1888-
Mill stream
NAD. Annual ex, 1947, 2d half
Stevenson, Mrs Andrew. See Stevenson,
Sarah (Coles)
Stevenson, Robert Louis, 1850-1894
Sargent, J. S. Robert Louis Stevenson
Stevenson, Sarah (Coles) fl 1841
Healy, G. P. A. Mrs Andrew Stevenson
Stevenson memorial angel by A. H. Thayer
Stew by C. H. Carter
STEWARD, Joseph, 1750-1822
John Phillips   NHD
Flexner. Light of distant skies
ICA. From colony to nation
Stewart, Charles, 1778-1860
Sully, T. Capt Charles Stewart
Stewart, Ira, fl 1846
Mason, B. F. Ira Stewart
Stewart, Isabella. See Gardner, Isabella
(Stewart)
Sticks and stones by J. L. Lasker
STIEFFEL, Hermann, b 1826
Fort Harker, Kansas   DNC
Rathbone
Fort Keough, Montana   DNC
Rathbone
Miles city, Montana   DNC
Rathbone
Sa-tan-ti addressing the Peace commis-
sioners at Council Grove   DNC
Rathbone
Wichita mountains from the Medicine
Bluffs   DNC
Rathbone
Yellowstone river near Fort Keough
                                        DNC
Rathbone
Stieglitz, Alfred, 1864-1946
Chase, W. M. Alfred Stieglitz
Stieglitz, Mrs Alfred. See O'Keeffe, Georgia
Stiles, Ezra, 1727-1795
Moulthrop, R. Ezra Stiles
Smibert, N. Ezra Stiles
STILL, Clyfford E. 1904-
1907—Y
NBuA. Still
1907-8—W
NBuA. Still
1938—N
NBuA. Still
1941—R
NBuA. Still
1943—J
NBuA. Still
1943—M
NBuA. Still
1944—A
NBuA. Still
1944—G
NBuA. Still
1944—N
NBuA. Still
1945—H
NBuA. Still
1945—R
NBuA. Still
1946—C
NBuA. Still
1946—E
NBuA. Still

1946—H
NBuA. Still
1946—L
NBuA. Still
1946—M
NBuA. Still
1946—T
NBuA. Still (col)
1947—F
NBuA. Still
1947—G
NBuA. Still
1947—H-No 1
NBuA. Still
1948—B
NBuA. Still
1948—D
NBuA. Still
1948—E
NBuA. Still
1948—S
NBuA. Still
1949—D
NBuA. Still
1950—A
NBuA. Still (col)
1950—B
NBuA. Still
1950—K
NBuA. Still
1950—M-No 1
NBuA. Still (col)
1951—D
NBuA. Still
1951—K
NBuA. Still
1954—S
NBuA. Still
1955—D
NBuA. Still
1955—H
NBuA. Still (col)
1956—H
NBuA. Still
1956—J
NBuA. Still
1957—D no 1
NBuA. Acquisitions 1959-1961 (col)
1957—G
NBuA. Still
1957—J
NBuA. Still (col)
Number 2, 1949
Art since 1945 (col)
Hunter. Mod Amer ptg (col)
MMA. New Amer ptg (col)
A painting
CSFP. Annual ex, 1948/49
Painting, 1947 (1)
MMA. Fifteen
Painting, 1947 (2)
MMA. Fifteen
Painting, 1949
MnMW. 60 Amer ptrs
Painting, 1951   MMA
McCurdy
MMA. New Amer ptg
Pierson
Read. Concise history
Red and black   NBuA
Eliot. Art of our time (col)
NBuA. Acquisitions 1957-58 (col cover)

STILL, C. E.—*Continued*
Untitled
　CSFP. Annual ex, 1950/51
Untitled   SwB
　Ponente. Mod ptg, 1960
Still harbor by C. A. Morris
Still life by S. Amato
Still life by M. Avery
Still life by J. Badger
Still life by W. A. Baziotes
Still life by W. F. Benson
Still life by G. Cope
Still life by A. Dasburg
Still life by S. Davis
Still life by W. De Kooning
Still life by C. H. Demuth
Still life by P. Dickinson
Still life by S. C. Edie
Still life by P. Evergood
Still life by J. F. Francis
Still life by M. Goldberg
Still life by A. Gorky
Still life by E. N. Griffith
Still life by W. M. Harnett
Still life by M. Hartley
Still life by L. E. Hess
Still life by C. R. Holty
Still life by E. Isenburger
Still life by M. Kantor
Still life by W. Keane
Still life by H. Lever
Still life by H. B. McCarter
Still life by H. L. McFee
Still life by A. H. Maurer
Still life by A. Ozenfant
Still life by A. C. Peale
Still life by M. A. Peale
Still life by Raphaelle Peale
Still life by S. M. Peale
Still life by W. Plate
Still life by A. Pope
Still life by M. Powers
Still life by M. Ramsey
Still life by K. Schrag
Still life by C. Sheeler
Still life by R. Soyer
Still life by M. Sterne
Still life by D. Teague
Still life by B. W. Tomlin
Still life by F. C. Watkins
Still life by M. Weber
Still life by J. A. Weir
Still life by T. Yerxa
Still life: apples by H. L. McFee
Still life at Christmas by A. B. Serwazi
Still life: balsam apples and turnips by
　Raphaelle Peale
Still life: book, pipe, beer stein by J. F.
　Peto
Still life, bread and peppers by M. Weber

Still life, camera flashlight by M. L. Scham-
　berg
Still life—crabapples in blue bowl by W. J.
　Glackens
Still life—delphinium by P. W. Zimmerman
Still life, Egyptian pot by M. Weber
Still life: fruit by M. Hartley
Still life—fruit and nuts by Raphaelle Peale
Still life, fruit and pottery by W. M. Chase
Still life, fruit in a monogrammed bowl,
　"R. P." by M. J. Peale
Still life in gold and green by S. Menkès
Still life in gray by R. Brackman
Still life in green by A. Leepa
Still life in primary colors by B. Browne
Still life in red, yellow, white and blue by
　A. Leepa
Still life in white by L. Blanch
Still life in winter by C. E. Burchfield
Still life, melons by R. Lebrun
Still life, New York by W. Drewes
Still life on a sewing machine by J. J. P.
　Meert
Still life—oranges by H. L. McFee
Still life: pear by A. H. Maurer
Still life: pipe, beer stein, book by J. F.
　Peto
Still life, pitcher by C. Sheeler
Still life: salt glaze pot, pipe and Le Figaro
　by W. M. Harnett
Still life—striped bass by W. M. Chase
Still life: the blue vase by W. Sommer
Still life with a green jar by H. L. McFee
Still life with apples by M. B. Prendergast
Still life with apples and chestnuts by J. F.
　Francis
Still life with ashtray by A. H. Maurer
Still life with banjo by L. Karp
Still life with black bottle by A. Blatas
Still life with blue vase by S. Menkès
Still life with bottles by C. Brown
Still life with bric-a-brac by W. M. Harnett
Still life with brushes and pottery by W. M.
　Chase
Still life with cake by Raphaelle Peale
Still life with cake, raisins and nuts by
　M. A. Peale
Still life with Christmas candy by J. Wilde
Still life with cockatoo by W. M. Chase
Still life with coffee pot by R. D'Arista
Still life with currants by J. Wilde
Still life with dead leaves by M. Marcus
Still life with decanter by H. L. McFee
Still life with derby by M. Avery
Still life with doily by A. H. Maurer
Still life with figure by R. Brackman
Still life with fish by W. M. Chase
Still life with fish by N. Vasilieff
Still life with fish—a skate by W. M. Chase
Still life with fish and pinwheel by M.
　Beckmann
Still life with fish bowl by J. Peale
Still life with fish, brass kettle, lemon and
　onions by W. M. Chase

Still life with flower and insects by T. R. Peale

Still life with flowers by M. Beckmann

Still life with flowers by S. Davis

Still life with flowers by M. Weber

Still life with fruit by H. G. Keller

Still life with fruit by J. Peale

Still life with fruit by Rubens Peale

Still life with fruit and flowers by S. Roesen

Still life with glasses and roses by C. Brown

Still life with grapes by J. Peale

Still life with herring by Raphaelle Peale

Still life with horns by B. Spruance

Still life with hourglass by H. Muller

Still life with ivy by H. L. McFee

Still life with Johnson's dictionary by Unidentified artist

Still life with landscape by C. Brown

Still life with lanterns by J. F. Peto

Still life with letter to Thomas B. Clarke by W. M. Harnett

Still life with lobster by N. Vasilieff

Still life with melon and grapes by S. M. Peale

Still life with melons by Unidentified artist

Still life with melons by B. Wood

Still life with milk bottle by W. Meigs

Still life with mirror by A. Rattner

Still life with nude by J. Floch

Still life with onion rolls by M. Goldberg

Still life with oysters by A. Rattner

Still life with palette by A. Gorky

Still life with palette by M. Weber

Still life with peaches by Raphaelle Peale

Still life with pears by A. H. Maurer

Still life with playbill by N. A. Brooks

Still life with portrait of the artist's daughter by J. F. Peto

Still life with raisin cake by Raphaelle Peale

Still life with red fish by L. Hartl

Still life with red plush and thistle by J. C. Bradley

Still life with saw by S. Davis

Still life with skull by A. Gorky

Still life with skull by F. Martin

Still life with skulls by J. Kirschenbaum

Still life with steak by Raphaelle Peale

Still life with strawberries by A. C. Peale

Still life with tankard by W. M. Harnett

Still life with thistles by M. Frary

Still life with three glasses by W. Glackens

Still life with two tables by M. Weber

Still life with vegetables by Raphaelle Peale

Still life with violin by W. M. Harnett (attributed works)

Still life with watermelon by J. Peale

Still life with watermelon by Raphaelle Peale

Still life with watermelon by Unidentified artist

Still life with white cloth by H. L. McFee

Still life with wine bottles and basket of fruit by J. F. Francis

Still life with yellow-green chair by P. Dickinson

Still music by B. Shahn

STILLMAN, William James, 1828-1901
Philosophers' camp in the Adirondacks (unfinished sketch)   MCoL
Jones. Rediscovered ptrs

Stillman sisters by A. H. Thayer

Stillness by J. Ernst

Stillness and reflections by K. Schrag

STOCK, Joseph Whiting, 1815-1855
Child in wicker basket (Baby in wicker basket)   DN
DN. Amer primitive ptgs, pt 1
Ford. Pictorial folk art
Fisherman with his dog   MSM
Lipman. Primitive ptrs
MSM. Handbook
Horace Wilson Eddy   VWR
Ford. Pictorial folk art
Jane Henrietta Russell
Ford. Pictorial folk art
Lipman. Primitive ptrs
Jasper Raymond Rand   NJN
Pierson
Luther Stock
Lipman. Primitive ptrs
Mary Jane Smith   VWR
VWR. Amer folk art (col)
VWR. Folk art (col)
Parsons family
Ford. Pictorial folk art
Wilcox children   DN
DN. Amer primitive ptgs, pt 2
William Howard Smith   VWR
VWR. Amer folk art (col)
VWR. Folk art (col)
Young hammerer   NCHA
Jones. New-found folk art

Attributed works

Mary Amidon   MSM
Ford. Pictorial folk art

Stock, Luther, b 1811
Stock, J. W. Luther Stock

Stock exchange, New York city by J. Marin

Stockton, California by A. D. Browere

STODDARD, Alice Kent
Leila   PR
PR. Catalogue

Stokes, Edith (Minturn) d 1937
Sargent, J. S. Mr and Mrs Isaac Newton Phelps Stokes

Stokes, Isaac Newton Phelps, 1867-1944
Lockman, D. M. I. N. Phelps Stokes
Sargent, J. S. Mr and Mrs Isaac Newton Phelps Stokes

Stokes, Mrs Isaac Newton Phelps. See Stokes, Edith (Minturn)

STOKES, John Stogdell, 1870-1947
Wedding in the Big Smoky mountains
Davidson v2

Portrait of the artist

Watkins, F. C. J. Stogdell Stokes

Stokes, Mrs M. S.
Eakins, T. Mrs M. S. Stokes

STOLTENBERG, Donald, 1927-
Blue building
MBIC. View 1960
STONE, William Oliver, 1830-1875
Eleazer Thompson Fitch   CtY
CtY. Portrait index
Samuel F. B. Morse   CtY
CtY. Portrait index
The stone by H. Bloom
Stone angel by B. Cross
Stone city by G. Wood
Stone cottage, Hanover, New Hampshire
by M. T. Chapin
Stone garden by Y. Ohashi
Stone in the tree by Y. Tanguy
Stone matrix by C. A. Morris
Stonehenge by W. W. Baumgartner
Stonington and the harbor, Maine by J.
Marin
Stonington harbor by J. Marin
Stony beach, Ogunquit by M. B. Prender-
gast
Store and gear by K. Knaths
Storer, Clement, fl 1829
Cole, J. G. Clement Storer
Storer, Ebenezer, 1730-1807
Dunkerley, J. Ebenezer Storer (possibly
after Copley)
Storer, Elizabeth. See Smith, Elizabeth
(Storer)
Storm by G. C. Bingham
Storm by A. Ippolito
Storm by M. Kantor
Storm by A. V. Tack
Storm by Y. Tanguy
Storm approaching Narragansett bay by
M. J. Heade
Storm at sea by R. W. Salmon
Storm at the Bahamas by W. Homer
Storm brewing by L. Feininger
Storm clouds in silver by A. G. Dove
Storm clouds, Maine by M. Hartley
Storm coming by J. L. Howard
Storm composition number 4 by A. Rattner
Storm departs by P. Fine
Storm-frightened animals by H. G. Keller
Storm-frightened horses by H. G. Keller
Storm in the mountains by A. Bierstadt
Storm over Narragansett bay by M. J.
Heade
Storm over Taos by J. Marin
Storm tide by E. H. Betts
Storm tide by R. Henri
Storm: waiting for the caravan by A. J.
Miller
Stormy sky, Venice by W. Barker
Stormy weather by W. H. Singer
Storrs, Constant, fl 1802
Jennys, W. Constant Storrs
Storrs, Mrs Constant, 1758-1839
Jennys, W. Mrs Constant Storrs
Story, Margaret
Bellows, G. W. Margarite
Story of the cross by A. P. Ryder

Stoughton, William, 1631-1701
Unidentified artist. William Stoughton
STOUT, Myron S. 1908-
Number 3, 1957
PPC. International ex, 1958
Stoutenburg, Jacobus, b 1696
Unidentified artist. Jacobus Stoutenburg
Stoutenburg, Margaret (Teller) b 1696
Unidentified artist. Mrs Jacobus Stouten-
burg
Stoves
Kuniyoshi, Y. Stove and bouquet
Wood, G. Dinner for threshers
Stowing sails, Bermuda by W. Homer
Strachan, Margaret. See Harwood, Margaret
(Strachan)
Strahmutchi by R. S. Du Casse
STRAND, Paul, 1890-
Circular forms
Brown. Amer ptg
Stranded boat by M. J. Heade
STRANG, Ray, 1893-
Horse power
Carlson. Gallery (col)
Native's return
Carlson. Gallery (col)
Slow poke
Carlson. Gallery (col)
Spring
Carlson. Gallery (col)
Waiting for the mail
Carlson. Gallery (col)
Water
Carlson. Gallery (col)
Wood gatherers
Carlson. Gallery (col)
Strange thing little Kiosai saw in the river
by J. La Farge
A stranger passed by K. Sage
Strata by J. E. Levi
Strategist by C. di Marca-Relli
STRATER, Henry, 1896-
Cape Nedick   ATU
ATU. Coll of Amer art
Colts at Soda Springs
NYG. Fine art
Winter in the Verde valley
NYG. Fine art
Strathmere by W. Stuempfig
Stratton, Barnard, b 1796
Willson, Mr. Barnard Stratton of Am-
herst, New Hampshire
Straw bridge by M. B. Prendergast
Strawberries and cherries by M. A. Peale
Strawbridge, James, fl 1802
Malbone, E. G. James Strawbridge
Stream and distant hills by B. West (at-
tributed works)
Street, Augustus Russell, 1791-1866
Jocelyn, N. Augustus Russell Street
STREET, Robert, 1796-1865
Likeness of himself   MB
MB. Karolik coll
The street by M. Beckmann
The street by P. Guston
The street by J. Levine
The street by L. MacIver
The street by B. Perlin

Street and bridge by S. Davis
Street by the mill by S. Rosenberg
Street corner by P. Evergood
Street corner incident by W. De Kooning
Street corner, Paris by F. Koester
Street crossing, New York by J. Marin
Street dance by B. Perlin
Street in Paris by L. Feininger
Street in Stillwater by C. Booth
Street in Tepoztlan, Mexico by K. Zerbe
The street is young with spring by L. Mac-
   Iver
Street movement, abstraction, New York by
   J. Marin
Street music by W. Stuempfig
A street, Perugia by F. Crowninshield
Street scene by P. Burlin
Street scene by G. Grosz
Street scene by R. Marsh
Street scene, Boston by M. B. Prendergast
Street scene in Seville by T. Eakins
Street scene in winter by C. Hassam
A street seeing by J. Marin
Street urchins by D. G. Blythe
The strenuous life by C. M. Russell
Striated forest by C. A. Morris
STRICKLAND, William, 1787-1854
   View on the Susquehanna
      McClintock

            Portrait of the artist
   Neagle, J. William Strickland
The strike—trout fishing by J. B. Sword
String composition number 50 by C. S. Fuller
String construction by C. S. Fuller
String music by M. Weber
String of pearls by E. Melcarth
String quartette by J. Levine
String trio by G. L. K. Morris
Strings of amber by Tseng Yu-ho
Strip tease by R. Marsh
Stripper by R. Marsh
Strolling by C. H. Demuth
STROMBOTNE, James, 1934-
   Execution
      IU. Contemp Amer ptg & sculp, 1961
   The group
      WMAA. Young America 1960
   Red torso
      WMAA. Young America 1960
   Three bathers
      WMAA. Contemp Amer ptg, 1959-60
Strong, Theodore, 1790-1869
   Ames, E. Theodore Strong
Strong woman and child by Y. Kuniyoshi
Structure by M. Tobey
The struggle by R. Goodnough
The struggle by R. S. Neuman
Strunsky house by L. MacIver
Stryker sisters by R. Earl
STUART, Duncan Robert, 1919-
   Matrix
      Pousette-Dart. Amer ptg

STUART, Gilbert, 1755-1828
   Benjamin West   ELNP
      Roos
   Caleb Whitefoord   NJMo
      NJMo. Forty years
      NJMo. Your Montclair art museum
   Charles Davis   NoCR
      NoCR. Catalogue
   David Humphreys   CtY
      CtY. Portrait index
   Edward Loftus   InIJ
      InIJ. 105 ptgs
   Edward Shippen of Pennsylvania   DC
      DC. Masterpieces
   Elizabeth Boardley   PA
      Roos
   Francis and Saunders Malbone
      Flexner. Light of distant skies
   Gabriel Manigault   NBuA
      NBuA. Catalogue of the ptgs
   George Washington   MWiS
      MWiS. Ex 4 and 7
   George Washington
      Taylor. Fifty centuries, 1954 ed (col)
   George Washington (Allibone type) OCiM
      OCiM. Guide
   George Washington (Athenaeum type)
                                    MB
      Craven. Rainbow book
      Craven. Treasury 1952 ed (col)
      Flexner. Amer ptg
      Flexner. Light of distant skies
      Flexner. Short history
      MB. Great Americans
      Mendelowitz
      NYG. Fine art
      Pierson
      Roos
      UNESCO. Prior to 1860
      UNESCO. Prior to 1860 3d ed
      UNESCO. Prior to 1860 5th ed
   George Washington (Athenaeum type)
                                    MoSL
      MoSL. Handbook 1953
   George Washington (Gibbs-Channing-
      Avery type)   MM
      NYG. Fine art
      Roos
      UNESCO. Prior to 1860
      UNESCO. Prior to 1860 3d ed
      UNESCO. Prior to 1860 5th ed
   George Washington (Lansdowne type) PA
      Flexner. Light of distant skies
      ICA. From colony to nation
      Pierson
      Time. 300 years (col)
   George Washington (Miller-Cake-J. Stew-
      art portrait)   PR
      PR. Catalogue
   George Washington (Vaughan type) DN
      DN. Mellon coll
      Flexner. Light of distant skies
      Pierson
   George Washington (Vaughan-Sinclair
      type)   DN
      DN. Mellon coll
   George Williams
      MdBMu. Rendezvous
   Henrietta Elizabeth Frederica Vane MNS
      NUM. Art across America
   Henry Knox   MB
      MB. Great Americans

STUART, Gilbert—*Continued*
  Horatio Gates
    Flexner. Light of distant skies
  Isaac Coffin
    Barker. Amer ptg
  Isaac de Abraham Touro   MSE
    MSE. Cat of ports, 1950
  James Heath   CtHW
    CtHW. Handbook
  James Madison   MAC
    ICA. From colony to nation
  James Monroe   MM
    ICA. From colony to nation
  James Monroe   PA
    Time. 300 years (col)
  James Ward   MnMi
    Roos
  John Adams
    Larkin
    Larkin rev ed
    Pierson
  John Henderson
    CLA. 35 ptgs
  John Quincy Adams (finished by T. Sully)
                                        MCH
    Time. 300 years (col)
  John Randolph   DN
    DN. Mellon coll
  John Young
    Chew. 250 years of art
  Joseph Coolidge   DN
    DN. Mellon coll
  Joseph de Jaudenes y Nebot   MM
    Pierson
  Josiah Quincy   MB
    MB. Great Americans
  Lawrence Yates   DN
    DN. Mellon coll
  Martha Washington   MB
    MB. Great Americans
    NYG. Fine art
  Mathilde de Jaudenes y Nebot   MM
    Larkin
    Larkin rev ed
    Pierson
  Mrs Charles Davis   NoCR
    NoCR. Catalogue
  Mrs Gabriel Manigault   NBuA
    NBuA. Catalogue of the ptgs
  Mrs George Plumstead   PA
    Flexner. Light of distant skies
  Mrs James Bard   NJMo
    NJMo. Forty years
  Mrs John Bannister and her son   RNR
    Pierson
  Mrs John Thompson Mason   OCl
    OCl. Handbook
  Mrs John Wickham
    DC. Privately owned
  Mrs Josiah Quincy
    DC. Privately owned
  Mrs Maria Barclay Young
    Chew. 250 years of art
  Mrs Perez Morton   MWM
    Larkin rev ed (col detail)
    Lee. Art then and now
    Pierson
    Robb. Art 1953 ed
    Robb. Harper history
    Roos
    Walker. Ptgs from America

  Mrs Richard Yates   DN
    Barker. Amer ptg
    Craven. Treasury 1962 ed
    DN. Mellon Coll
    Gardner 1959 ed
    McKinney
    Mendelowitz
    MoSL. 40 masterpieces
    Pierson
    UNESCO. Prior to 1860
    UNESCO. Prior to 1860 3d ed
    UNESCO. Prior to 1860 5th ed
    Walker. Ptgs from America
  Mrs Stephen Peabody   ATeS
    ATeS. Collection
  Mrs Stephen Salisbury I   MWM
    ICA. From colony to nation
  Nathaniel Bowditch
    Flexner. Light of distant skies
    CtY. Portrait index
  Oliver Wolcott   CtY
    CtY. Portrait index
  Petrus Stuyvesant   MNHS
    Vail. Stuyvestant ports
  Richard Yates   DN
    DN. Mellon coll
  Sir Joshua Reynolds   DN
    DN. Mellon coll
    Flexner. Light of distant skies
  The skater   DN
    Craven. Treasury 1952 ed
    Pierson
    Time. 300 years (col)
    Walker. Ptgs from America (col)
  Study head   MoSL
    MoSL. Handbook 1953
  Thomas Jefferson   MeB
    Myers. Art
    Upjohn
  Thomas Macdonough   DN
    DN. Mellon coll
  Two girls sewing
    CtY. Handbook
  Washington at Dorchester Heights
    Richardson. Ptg in America
  Webb sr   OYB
    OYB. Catalogue 1951
  William Cooper of Cooperstown
    CtY. Yale alumni
  William Ellery Channing
    Flexner. Light of distant skies
  William Redwood   RNR
    Roos
              Portrait of the artist
  Goodridge, S. Gilbert Stuart
  Neagle, J. Gilbert Stuart
  Peale, C. W. and Peale, Rembrandt. Gil-
    bert Stuart
STUART, James Reeve, 1834-1915
  Sword, pistols, and teacup   MB
    MB. Karolik coll
Stubb and Starbuck by B. Robinson
STUCKER, F.
  Albany Schoharie stagecoach
    Ford. Pictorial folk art
Studebaker, John Mohler, 1833-1917
  Powell, H. M. T. J. M. Studebaker in
    his wagon tire shop at Hangtown,
    California, 1853
Studio tapestry by L. Gatch
Studios
  Beckmann, M. Studio corner
  Bennett, R. Red studio

Burkhardt, H. G. Studio of G
Carr, L. Remington's studio
Chase, W. M. Alice in the Shinnecock studio
Chase, W. M. Duveneck in the studio
Chase, W. M. Self-portrait (Artist in his Fifth avenue studio) 1915
Chase, W. M. Tenth street studio
Demuth, C. H. Studio interior
Eakins, T. William Rush and his model
Eakins, T. William Rush carving his allegorical figure of the Schuylkill river
Eastman, W. Studio table
Frankenstein, J. P. The artist in his studio
Giacometti, A. The studio
Greene, B. The studio
Grosz, G. Model in the studio
Hamilton, J. M. Paul Wayland Bartlett in his Paris studio
Hofmann, H. Studio no 1 in grey
Hovenden, T. Self-portrait
Kaplan, J. Interior
Matteson, T. H. Sculptor's studio
Mintz, R. A. Artist's studio
Mommer, P. Studio interior
Pittman, H. Studio in Charleston
Ricci, J. In the studio
Rosenthal, T. E. The cardinal's portrait
Soyer, M. David Burliuk in his studio
Soyer, R. In the studio
Watkins, F. C. The studio
Weir, J. F. Artist's studio
Wood, G. Turner alley studio
The **study** by G. R. Davis
The **study** by G. L. Mueller
Study for a soldier by R. Lebrun
Study head by G. Stuart
Study in black and green by J. W. Alexander
Study in brown by N. E. Craig
Study in curves by W. M. Chase
Study in red—morning news at the camp by E. Johnson
Study in space V by L. Feininger
Study of a head after Couture by J. A. M. Whistler
Study of a house by J. La Farge
Study table by W. M. Harnett
STUEMPFIG, Walter, 1914-
  End of day   MAP
    CoS. New accessions USA, 1956
  Float on the Schuylkill
    CtY. Yale alumni
  Manayunk
    CSFP. Annual ex, 1947/48
    Time. 300 years (col)
  The railroad bridge
    MoSL. Contemporary Amer ptg
  The reprimand   PPhM
    CoS. New accessions USA, 1948
  Sculling   NJMo
    NJMo. Forty years
  Spring song
    Chew. 250 years of art
  Strathmere
    CSFP. Annual ex, 1950/51
  Street music   InIJ
    Bazin
    InIJ. 105 ptgs
  The tempest   OT
    OT. Contemp Amer ptgs

  Three alone
    PPC. International ex, 1952
  Thunderstorm II   MM
    MM. 100 Amer ptrs
  Pierson
    PPC. Ptg in the U.S. 1949
  Trajan and the children   NBuA
    NBuA. Contemporary ptgs
  Two houses   DC
    DC. 20 biennial ex, 1947
    Gruskin
    Mendelowitz
    Wight. Milestones (col)
  Via Partenope
    NAD. Annual ex, 1952
  The wall   PA
    MMA. Contemp ptrs
  West Wildwood   CSFP
    CoS. New accessions USA, 1950
    CSFP. Handbook
Stuka by G. L. Mueller
Stump speaking by G. C. Bingham
STURGIS, Katharine, 1904-
  Pigeon cove, Rockport, Massachusetts MB
    MB. Ptgs in water color
STURGIS, Mabel Russell, b 1865
  Heavy sea, Manchester   MB
    MB. Ptgs in water color
Sturtevant, Mrs Eugene. See Clark, Mary Rebecca
Stuyvesant, Augustus Van Horne, 1838-1918
  Baker, G. A. (attributed works). Augustus Van Horne Stuyvesant sr
  Williams, A. A. V. H. Stuyvesant
Stuyvesant, Catharine Livingston (Reade) 1775-1862
  Durand, A. B. Mrs Nicholas William Stuyvesant
Stuyvesant, Gerard, 1805-1859
  Hicks, T. Gerard Stuyvesant
Stuyvesant, Mrs Gerard. See Stuyvesant, Susan Rivington (Van Horne)
Stuyvesant, Gerardus, 1690-1777
  McIlworth, T. Gerardus Stuyvesant
Stuyvesant, Harriet LeRoy (Steward) 1842-1872
  Baker, G. A. (attributed works) Mrs A. V. H. Stuyvesant
  Fagnani, G. Mrs A. V. H. Stuyvesant
  Unidentified artist. Mrs A. V. H. Stuyvesant (as a child)
Stuyvesant, Margaret (Livingston) 1738-1818
  Unidentified artist. Mrs Petrus Stuyvesant
Stuyvesant, Nicholas William, 1722-1780
  McIlworth, T. Nicholas William Stuyvesant
  Unidentified artist. Nicholas William Stuyvesant
Stuyvesant, Nicholas William, 1769-1833
  Unidentified artist. Nicholas William Stuyvesant
Stuyvesant, Mrs Nicholas William. See Stuyvesant, Catharine Livingston (Reade)
Stuyvesant, Peter, 1592-1672
  Couturier, H. (attributed works) Governor Stuyvesant
  Unidentified artist. Governor Peter Stuyvesant
Stuyvesant, Peter Gerard, 1778-1847
  Unidentified artist. Peter Gerard Stuyvesant

Stuyvesant, Petrus, 1727-1805
  Stuart, G. Petrus Stuyvesant
STUYVESANT, Susan Rivington (Van Horne) 1812-1899
  The trumpeter   NNHS
  Vail. Stuyvesant ports
            Portrait of the artist
  Staigg, R. M. Mrs Gerard Stuyvesant
Stuyvesant family
  Unidentified artist. Gerard Stuyvesant family group
STYKA, Tadé, 1889-1954
  Tigers
  NSP. Sportscapes
Subercaseaux, Ramón, fl 1880
  Sargent, J. S. Señor Subercaseaux in a gondola in Venice
Subjective landscape by R. Rosenborg
Submerged by H. Hofmann
Substance and sustenance by N. Tschacbasov
Subterranean by R. Pousette-Dart
Suburb in Havana by W. De Kooning
Suburban figure by K. Finch
Subway by C. Enders
Subway by H. Koerner
Subway by G. Tooker
Subway lights by L. MacIver
Subway platform by R. Soyer
Subway scene by I. Bishop
Succession of feelings by S. Sekula
Succubus by P. Mangravite
Sudbury, Massachusetts, Old homestead at by Unidentified artist
Suddarth, Martha Morris, fl 1840
  Toole, J. Mrs Martha Morris Suddarth
Suddarth, Mary Jane. See Toole, Mary Jane (Suddarth)
Suddarth, Richard Pleasants, fl 1840
  Toole, J. Richard Pleasants Suddarth
Suddarth, Tempe McCutchen, fl 1840
  Toole, J. Tempe McCutchen Suddarth
Sudden windstorm over the Vega by H. G. Keller
Suffering softens stones by Y. Tanguy
Suede and tiger stripe by C. A. Morris
Sugar levee, New Orleans by V. V. Sebron
Sugar loaf mountain by A. Fisher
Sugar mill on Bayou Teche, Oliver plantation by A. Persac
Sugaring-off by A. M. R. Moses
Sugaring-off in Maple orchard by A. M. R. Moses
Suicide in costume by F. C. Watkins
Suicide of Judas by J. Brewton
Suites illimitées by Y. Tanguy
Sulking boy by G. B. Luks
SULLIVAN, Charles, 1794-1867
  Marietta earth works
    Ford. Pictorial folk art
Sullivan, Elizabeth (Russell) 1779-1854
  Malbone, E. G. Mrs John L. Sullivan
Sullivan, John Langdon, 1777-1865
  Malbone, E. G. J. L. Sullivan
Sullivan, Mrs John Langdon. See Sullivan, Elizabeth (Russell)
Sullivan, John Lawrence, 1858-1918
  Bellows, G. W. Introducing John L. Sullivan

SULLIVAN, Patrick, 1894-
  Fourth dimension
    MnMW. Reality and fantasy
Sullivan, Sarah (Russell) 1786-1831
  Malbone, E. G. Mrs Richard Sullivan
Sullivan street abstraction by G. C. Ault
Sully, Jane Cooper. See Darley, Jane Cooper (Sully)
Sully, Sarah (Annis) 1770-1867
  Sully, T. Thomas Sully and Mrs Sully
  Trumbull, J. Mrs Thomas Sully
SULLY, Thomas, 1783-1872
  Andrew Jackson, 1845   DN
    Time. 300 years (col)
  Andrew Jackson (Long coll)
    DC. Privately owned
  Charles Stewart   DN
    Pierson
  Elizabeth Wignall   OYB
    OYB. Catalogue 1951
  Fanny Kemble as Bianca   PA
    Flexner. Amer ptg
    Flexner. Light of distant skies
    Flexner. Sport history
  Frances Kemble, sketch   MB
    Larkin
    Larkin rev ed
  George Cadwalader
    Chew. 250 years of art
  Jean T. David   OCl
    Pierson
  John Biddle   MM
    NYG. Fine art
    UNESCO. Prior to 1860
    UNESCO. Prior to 1860 3d ed
  John Connelly   ATeS
    ATeS. Collection
  John Myers   MB
    MB. Karolik coll
  Lady with a harp: Eliza Ridgely   DN
    Flexner. Light of distant skies
    PA. Annual ex, 1955
    Pierson
  Levi Fletcher
    CtY. Yale alumni
  Mary Sicard David   OCl
    Pierson
  Miss C. Parsons as the Lady of the Lake
                                          KLU
    NUM. Art across America
  Mrs Edward Hudson   MiD
    MiD. Treasures
    PA. Annual ex, 1955
  Mrs Henry Robinson   InIJ
    InIJ. 105 ptgs
  Mrs James Montgomery   MM
    NYG. Fine art
    UNESCO. Prior to 1860
    UNESCO. Prior to 1860 3d ed
  Mrs John Boucher Morris
    MdBMu. Rendezvous
  Mrs John Redman Coxe
    Chew. 250 years of art
  Mother and son (Mrs William H. W. Darley and Francis Thomas Sully Darley)   MM
    Mendelowitz
    Pierson
  Passage of the Delaware (Washington at the passage of the Delaware)   MB
    Mendelowitz
    Pierson
    Richardson. Ptg in America
  Queen Victoria
    Taylor. Fifty centuries, 1954 ed (col)

Rebecca Cornell Biddle   NJMo
  NJMo. Your Montclair art museum
Samuel Coates
  Barker. Amer ptg
  ICA. From colony to nation
  Pierson
  Walker. Ptgs from America
Self-portrait   MM
  MdBMu. Rendezvous
Self-portrait   PH
  Roos
Thomas Biddle   PA
  PA. Annual ex, 1955
Thomas Handasyd Perkins   MBA
  Pierson
Thomas Jefferson   CtY
  CtY. Portrait index
Thomas Sully and Mrs Sully   CtY
  CtY. Portrait index
Torn hat   MB
  Roos
  UNESCO. Prior to 1860 3d ed
  UNESCO. Prior to 1860 5th ed
Victor René Value and his daughter Char-
  lotte   MB
  MB. Karolik coll
Washington at the passage of the Dela-
  ware. See Passage of the Delaware
William Edmonds Horner
  PA. Annual ex, 1955 (detail)
William Henry Hoffman
  MdBMu. Rendezvous (replica)
SULLY, Thomas, 1783-1872 and SULLY,
  Thomas Wilcocks, 1811-1847
Thomas Biddle   DN
  DN. Mellon coll
Sulphurous evening by C. E. Burchfield
Sultan's tomb, Fez, Morocco by G. O. Hart
Summit of Antelope valley by E. J. Kosa
Summer by V. Candell
Summer by A. G. Dove
Summer by O. Dozier
Summer by C. S. Du Back
Summer by S. Francis
Summer by P. Guston
Summer by W. Kahn
Summer by B. Karfiol
Summer by D. E. Lee
Summer by E. Magafan
Summer by R. Natkin
Summer by G. Peterdi
Summer by M. B. Prendergast
Summer by G. Prestopino
Summer by A. Rogoway
Summer by J. H. Twachtman
Summer by A. Walkowitz
Summer by M. Weber
Summer afternoon by C. E. Burchfield
Summer afternoon by R. Parker
Summer afternoon by S. Serisawa
Summer bounty by D. Nichols
Summer bouquet by H. V. Poor
Summer breezes by R. Philipp
Summer day by M. Beckmann
Summer day by R. Eshoo
Summer day by M. B. Prendergast
Summer day by A. C. Runquist
Summer day by J. H. Twachtman
Summer days by G. O'Keeffe
Summer 8, 1957 by M. Tobey
Summer flowers by A. B. Carles
Summer flowers with two chairs by H. Pip-
  pin
Summer holiday by J. Corbino
Summer house by M. Goldberg
Summer in the Catskills by T. Doughty
Summer landscape by S. Davis
Summer landscape by G. H. Durrie
Summer night by B. Browne
Summer night by W. Homer
Summer night, East side park by J. Myers
Summer night, Provincetown, Massachusetts
  by J. Whorf
Summer night, Riverside drive by G. W.
  Bellows
Summer orchard by A. G. Dove
Summer outing on the rocks by M. B. Pren-
  dergast
Summer shower by M. Sterne
Summer squall by W. Homer
Summer still life by E. Berman
Summer storm by Y. Johnston
Summer storm by Y. Kuniyoshi
Summer storm by R. Rauschenberg
Summer storm on Sunday afternoon by A.
  Shulkin
Summer thoughts in winter by K. Schrag
Summer twilight by S. Davis
Summer vista by K. Matthew
Summer wind by A. Brook
Summer's end by C. W. Rain
Summer's end by M. Schapiro
Summer's fruitful pasture by A. P. Ryder
Summertime by W. M. Chase
Summertime by M. Kantor
Summertime by J. Pollock
Summertime by B. Shahn
The sun by K. Knaths
Sun after rain by M. Phillips
Sun and rocks by C. E. Burchfield
Sun bath by J. Glasco
Sun bathers by W. Peirce
Sun chariot by M. Samant
Sun dance by G. Catlin
Sun dance by F. Remington
Sun filled fields by K. Schrag
Sun games by T. Stamos
Sun, isles and sea by J. Marin
Sun King and merganser by M. Peterson
Sun on the lake by B. Krauskopf
Sun setting through the catalpas by C. E.
  Burchfield
Sun sinking in Tyrzona by C. Cloar
Sun sinking into the sea by K. Schrag
Sun trap by J. W. Boynton
Sun treader—portrait of Carl Ruggles by
  T. H. Benton

Sun valley by Martyl

Sun worshipper by J. La Farge

Sun worshippers by C. M. Russell

Sun-a-get, a Pottawattomie chief by J. O. Lewis

Sunbath by J. Glasco

Sunburst by W. Thon

Sunday by A. M. R. Moses

Sunday afternoon by Z. L. Sepeshy

Sunday football by B. Shahn

Sunday in the country by G. H. Durrie

Sunday in Union square by J. Sloan

Sunday morning by G. Beal

Sunday morning by A. B. Durand

Sunday morning by H. Packman

Sunday morning breakfast by H. Pippin

Sunday morning in Gordon park, Cleveland by H. G. Keller

Sunday morning in the mines by C. C. Nahl

Sunday morning in Virginia by W. Homer

Sunday on Main street by E. Hopper

Sunday painters by A. A. Dehn

Sunday painting by B. Shahn

Sunday promenade by M. B. Prendergast

Sunday school room by A. N. Wyeth

Sunday sun by P. Cadmus

Sunday walk by E. D. Glackens

Sunday, women drying their hair by J. Sloan

Sunflower by R. F. Gates

Sunflower by K. Knaths

Sunflower by R. H. Laessig

Sunflower patterns by H. G. Keller

Sunflowers by H. G. Keller

Sunflowers and goldfinches by R. F. Gates

Sunken ledges by C. H. Woodbury

Sunlight and shadow by W. M. Chase

Sunlight and shadow by A. S. Wall

Sunlight on brownstones by E. Hopper

Sunlight on the coast by W. Homer

Sunlight on the Piazzetta, Venice by M. B. Prendergast

Sunny blue sea by C. Hassam

Sunny morning by F. C. Watkins

Sunny morning on the Hudson by T. Cole

Sunny side of the street by P. Evergood

Sunrise by R. A. Blakelock

Sunrise by S. Davis

Sunrise I, 1937 by A. G. Dove

Sunrise II, 1937 by A. G. Dove

Sunrise III, 1937 by A. G. Dove

Sunrise at Uponohu, Society islands by J. La Farge

Sunrise fishing in the Adirondacks by W. Homer

Sunrise in the stratosphere by D. Porter

Sun's path by H. G. Keller

Sunset by L. Feininger

Sunset by M. J. Heade

Sunset by J. Marin

Sunset by M. B. Prendergast

Sunset by G. Prestopino

Sunset and sea fog by M. B. Prendergast

Sunset and white trees by L. Harmon

Sunset, Black rock, Connecticut by M. J. Heade

Sunset by the river by Unidentified artist

Sunset, Casco bay by J. Marin

Sunset fires by L. Feininger

Sunset, Gloucester by L. J. Liberté

Sunset, High bridge by E. Lawson

Sunset hour by A. P. Ryder

Sunset in the fields by H. B. McCarter

Sunset in the mountains by H. W. Rice

Sunset: Lake Champlain by M. J. Heade

Sunset Mount Carmel, Connecticut by G. H. Durrie

Sunset on a quiet sea by M. Avery

Sunset on Long beach by M. J. Heade

Sunset over the marshes by M. J. Heade

Sunset, Saco Bay by W. Homer

Sunset: tropical marshes by M. J. Heade

Sunshine and shadow by G. Hetzel

Super table by S. Davis

Supplication by F. Castellón

Supplying camp with buffalo meat by A. J. Miller

The **Supreme** Court of California by B. Shahn

Surf at Ogunquit, Maine by E. Decombes

Surf birds by M. Graves

Surf fisherman by E. F. Spruce

Surf, Point Lookout by E. W. Dickinson

Surf reflected upon higher space by M. Graves

Surf, ten mile by I. E. Nordfeldt

Surf under moonlight by F. J. Waugh

Surgery by S. Radulovic

Surprise attack by C. M. Russell

Surprise party by M. Hoff

Surprised wader by P. Evergood

The **surround** by A. J. Miller

Surround of buffalo by Indians by A. J. Miller

Surveyor's wagon in the Rockies by A. Bierstadt

Surviving trace of something by W. A. Gaw

Survivor by G. Grosz

Survivors by R. Ray

Survivors by K. Zerbe

Susan by A. S. Andersen

Susanna and the elders by T. H. Benton

Susanna and the elders by B. Shahn

Susannah and the elders by W. Shirlaw

Suspended discs by G. L. K. Morris

Suspended forms by E. E. Boccia

Suspension bridge at Niagara falls by Unidentified artist

Suspension bridge for swallows by K. Sage

Suspension of forms by C. R. Holty

Susquehanna river

Cropsey, J. F. Starrucca viaduct, Susquehanna valley

Mifflin, L. The Susquehanna below Wrightsville, Pennsylvania, View of

Montalant, J. O. The Susquehanna
Shaw, J. On the Susquehanna
Strickland, W. View on the Susquehanna
Sutliff, Betsy (Mulford) 1792-1871
  Ames, E. Mrs Henry Sutliff
SUTTON, W. fl 1820
  Young girl with music book
    Ford. Pictorial folk art

Attributed works

Girl with a cat   MSM
  Ford. Pictorial folk art
Swamp country by A. Blanch
Swamp folk by A. Blanch
SWAN, Barbara, 1922-
  Interior
    MBIC. View 1960
Swan island by V. Flannery
Swans
  Audubon, J. J. Trumpeter swan
  Graves, M. Moor swan
  Jones, J. Landscape with swans
  Prendergast, M. B. The swans
  Whorf, J. Swans
Sweet hour of prayer by P. S. Sample
Swift, Joseph Gardner, 1783-1865
  Jarvis, J. W. Gen Joseph Gardner Swift
Swimming hole by T. Eakins
Swimming off West Washington market by
  R. Marsh
The swing by W. J. Glackens
Swing landscape by S. Davis
Swinging chairs by R. Marsh
Swimmers and sunbathers by M. Avery
SWINNERTON, James E. 1875-
  After the shower
    Carlson. Gallery (col)
  Deserted Navajo home
    Carlson. Gallery (col)
  Deserted Navajo trading post
    Carlson. Gallery (col)
  Grand Canyon
    Carlson. Gallery (col)
  Moonrise—northern Arizona
    Carlson. Gallery (col)
  Navajoland
    Carlson. Gallery (col)
Swinton, Elizabeth (Ebsworth)
  Sargent, J. S. Mrs George Swinton
Swinton, Elsie
  Sargent, J. S. Elsie Swinton
Swiss mountains by E. Decombes
SWORD, James Brade, 1839-1915
  A good day's work—return from duck
    hunt
    NSP. Sportscapes
  The strike—trout fishing
    NSP. Sportscapes
The sword by K. Davies
Sword, pistols, and teacup by J. R. Stuart
Les sylphides by G. R. Davis
Sylvan episode by D. Lutz
Sylvia by W. M. Paxton
Symbol of the sun and moon by P. Riba
Symbolical and allegorical themes
  Blashfield, E. H. Power of the law
  Cole, T. Voyage of life: Childhood
  Cole, T. Voyage of life: Youth
  Cooper, J. Allegorical figures

  Cox, K. The light of learning
  Eakins, T. William Rush carving his alle-
    gorical figure of the Schuylkill river
  Hunt, W. M. Anahita, the flight of night
  Hunt, W. M. Flight of night
  Kennedy, T. J. Symbolical painting
  La Farge, J. Athens
  Morse, S. F. B. Allegorical landscapes
  Pachner, W. Israel
  Pachner, W. Maternità
  Peale, Rembrandt. Court of Death
  Sargent, J. S. Classic and romantic art
  Shahn, B. Allegory
  Thayer, A. H. Florence protecting the
    arts
  Unidentified artist. Allegory of freedom
  Unidentified artist. Aurora
  Unidentified artist. Civil war—Symbolical
    panorama
  Unidentified artist. Columbia
  Unidentified artist. Miss Liberty
  West, B. Air, Water, Earth, Fire
Symbols by W. R. Garver
Symbols of our time by Ben-Zion
Symbols over the west by M. Tobey
SYMONDS, Gardner, 1863-1930
  Silence and evening light   OYB
    OYB. Catalogue 1951
Symonds, George Gardner. See Symonds,
  Gardner
Symphony by M. Oppenheimer
Symphony in brown and silver by J. A. M.
  Whistler
Symphony in white by J. A. M. Whistler
Symphony in white no 2 by J. A. M. Whistler
Synagogue by H. Bloom
Synagogue by S. Drumlevitch
Synagogue by J. Friebert
Synchroformic no 4, staccato by J. Senn-
  hauser
Synchroformic no 27 by J. Sennhauser
Synchroformic no 28, étude in yellows by
  J. Sennhauser
Synchromie cosmique by M. Russell
Synchromy by S. MacDonald-Wright
Synchromy in green and orange by S. Mac-
  Donald-Wright
Synchromy no 2 to light, 1912 by M. Russell
Synchromy no 3 by S. Macdonald-Wright
Synchromy no 3, color counterpoint by M.
  Russell
Synchromy to form by M. Russell
Synchromy to form: orange by M. Russell
Syracuse, New York
  Culverhouse, J. M. Clinton square, Syra-
    cuse, N.Y.

T

T by A. A. Gottlieb
T—1954 by J. D. Brooks
Tabb, Mrs John, fl 1850
  Hubard, W. J. Mrs John Tabb
Tabb, Maria Mason. See Hubard, Maria
  Mason (Tabb)
Tabb, Martha (Tompkins)
  Hubard, W. J. Mrs Henry Wythe Tabb

Table by A. Blanch
Table by J. P. Jones
Table of fruit by G. A. Keniston
Table with bottles and cheese by R. D'Arista
Table with cyclamens by J. Binford
Table with fish and scales by C. Brown
Table with glasses and napkin by C. Brown
Table with glasses and roses by C. Brown
Table-talk by G. Grosz
Tabletop by B. Dyer
Tabletop by K. Knaths
TACK, Augustus Vincent, 1870-1949
   Aspiration   DP
     DP. Catalogue
   Passacaglia   DP
     DP. Catalogue
   Storm   DP
     DP. Catalogue
   Voice of many waters   DP
     DP. Catalogue
Taft, Robert Alphonso, 1889-1953
   Shahn, B. Dewey, Vandenberg and Taft
Taft, William Howard, president U.S. 1857-1930
   Kendall, W. S. William Howard Taft
Tagert, Joseph, 1758-1849
   Neagle, J. Joseph Tagert
TAGUE, Robert Bruce, 1912-
   Attic windows
     NAD. Annual ex, 1955
Tah-ro-hon, an Iowa warrior by G. B. King
Tailer, Elizabeth. See Nelson, Elizabeth (Tailer)
TAIT, Arthur Fitzwilliam, 1819-1905
   American frontier life   CtY
     Rathbone
   Barnyard   OYB
     OYB. Catalogue 1951
   Buffalo hunt
     Davidson v2
   Duck shooting
     Davidson v2
   On the warpath
     McCracken. Portrait of the old west (col)
   Saved—a hard chase
     NSP. Sportscapes
   Striped-bass fishing
     Davidson v2
   Trappers at fault looking for the trail
     Rathbone
   Young buck and doe
     NSP. Sportscapes
TAIT, Arthur Fitzwilliam, 1819-1905 and
   GAY, Edward, 1837-1928
   Deer at the lake
     NSP. Sportscapes
TAIT, Arthur Fitzwilliam, 1819-1905 and
   HART, James McDougal, 1828-1901
      Attributed works
   The Burden family enjoying the Hudson river near Troy   NAI
     Jones. Rediscovered ptrs
Taj Mahal by W. G. Congdon
The Taj Mahal by E. S. Field
TAKAI, Teiji
   Metamorphosis
     WMAA. Contemp Amer ptg, 1959/60
Take my picture, mister by I. Rose

TAKEHITA, Natsuko
   Autumn landscape
     MM. Amer ptg today
Taking off by W. T. Murch
Taking sunflower to teacher by W. Homer
Taking the count, Study for head of referee by T. Eakins
Taking the hump rib by A. J. Miller
Talcott family, fl 1832
   Goldsmith, D. Talcott family
Tales of love by G. Ortman
Talk by W. W. Quirt
Tall building by C. W. Smith
The tall red by O. Osver
Tallmadge, Benjamin, 1754-1835
   Ames, E. Benjamin Tallmadge
Tallmadge, Mrs Benjamin, 1763-1805. See Tallmadge, Mary (Floyd)
Tallmadge, Mrs Benjamin, d 1838. See Tallmadge, Maria (Hallett)
Tallmadge, Elizabeth (Clinton) 1780-1825
   Ames, E. Mrs Matthias Burnett Tallmadge
Tallmadge, Maria (Hallett) d 1838
   Ames, E. Mrs Benjamin Tallmadge
Tallmadge, Mary (Floyd) 1763-1805
   Earl, R. Mrs Benjamin Tallmadge
Tallmadge, Matthias Burnett, 1774-1819
   Ames, E. Matthias Burnett Tallmadge
Tallmadge, Mrs Matthias Burnett. See Tallmadge, Elizabeth (Clinton)
Talmudic student by W. Gropper
Talpa by A. Dasburg
Talpa graveyard by V. I. Cuthbert
TAM, Reuben, 1916-
   The coast of fog
     WMAA. Contemp Amer ptg, 1959/60
   Dark wave
     IU. Contemp Amer ptg & sculp, 1953
     Pousette-Dart. Amer ptg
   Flounder   OYB
     OYB. Catalogue 1951
   Horizon conditions   NUM
     NUM. Root bequest
   Moon and shoals   MMA
     Pierson
   Noon on the reef
     DC. 21 biennial ex, 1949
   Ridge and forecast
     IU. Contemp Amer ptg & sculp, 1959
   The salt sea
     IU. Contemp Amer ptg & sculp, 1961
   Sprouting coconuts
     CSFP. Annual ex, 1952
     IU. Contemp Amer ptg, 1951
Tambourine by J. Myers
Taming of the shrew by M. Ray
Tampa fair by A. Blanch
Tamworth, View near; In the White mountains by T. Cole
Tan and black on red by M. Rothko
The Tanagra by T. P. Anshutz
Tang horse by C. C. Ross
Tangerine moon and wine dark sea by M. Avery
TANGUY, Yves, 1900-1955
   The armoire of Proteus
     MMA. Yves Tanguy
   At the fair
     MMA. Yves Tanguy

Black landscape. See The storm
The boat
    MMA. Yves Tanguy
Closed sea, wide world
    MMA. Yves Tanguy
Closing days
    CtY. Yale alumni
    MMA. Yves Tanguy (col)
Conversation
    MMA. Yves Tanguy
Dame à l'absence
    Genauer (col)
De mains pâles aux cieux lassés
    MnMW. Reality and fantasy
    PPC. International ex, 1950
Divisibilité indéfinie. See Indefinite divisibility
The doubter
    MMA. Yves Tanguy
L'eau nue
    MnU. 40 Amer ptrs
Elle viendra
    Pearson. Mod renaissance
Ennui and tranquillity
    Jean. Surrealist ptg
Extinction of the species
    MMA. Yves Tanguy
    Read. Art now, 1948 ed
Extinction of useless lights   MMA
    MMA. Yves Tanguy
Fear   WMAA
    CoS. New accessions USA, 1950
    Goodrich. Amer art (col)
    Mendelowitz
    MMA. Yves Tanguy (col)
Fear   NBuA
    Pierson
Five strangers   CtHW
    CtHW. Handbook
    MMA. Yves Tanguy
    Moderns and their world
Four o'clock in summer: hope
    Raynal. History v3 (col)
From one night to the other   CSFP
    CSFP. Annual ex, 1948/49
    CSFP. Handbook
Furniture of time   MMA
    Janson. Picture history (col)
    MMA. Soby collection
    MMA. Yves Tanguy (col)
Genesis
    Jean. Surrealist ptg (col)
    MMA. Yves Tanguy
Girl with red hair
    MMA. Yves Tanguy
The glance of amber
    Jean. Surrealist ptg
Gouache, 1931   MMA
    MMA. Yves Tanguy
He did what he wanted
    MMA. Yves Tanguy
Hérédité des caractères
    Pearson. Mod renaissance
Hunted sky
    MMA. Yves Tanguy
Illimited sequences
    PA. Annual ex, 1953
Indefinite divisibility (Divisibilité indéfinie)
    McCurdy
    MMA. Yves Tanguy (col)
    NBuA. Contemporary ptgs
    Pierson

Lady of eleven
    MMA. Yves Tanguy
A large picture which is a landscape
    MMA. Yves Tanguy (col)
The last days
    Cheney. Story 1959 ed
The lovers
    MMA. Yves Tanguy
Ma vie blanche et noire. See My life
    white and black
Le malheur adoucit les pierres. See Suffering softens stones
Mama, Papa is wounded   MMA
    MMA. Masters (col)
    MMA. Yves Tanguy (col)
    Myers
Mirage of time   MM
    MMA. Yves Tanguy
The mood of now   MMA
    MMA. Soby collection
    MMA. Yves Tanguy
The mountebanks
    IU. Contemp Amer ptg & sculp, 1955
Movements and acts
    MMA. Yves Tanguy
Multiplication of the arcs   MMA
    50 years of mod art
    Jean. Surrealist ptg
    McCurdy
    MMA. Yves Tanguy (col)
    Pierson
My life white and black (Ma vie blanche
    et noire)
    Bazin. History of art
    CSFP. Annual ex, 1947/48
    MMA. Yves Tanguy
Old horizon
    MMA. Yves Tanguy
Palace of the windowed rocks
    MMA. Yves Tanguy
The parallels   PPhM
    PPhM. Arensberg coll
The rapidity of sleep   ICA
    Jean. Surrealist ptg
    MMA. Yves Tanguy
    Pierson
Real numbers
    Jean. Surrealist ptg
Ribbon of extremes
    Jean. Surrealist ptg (col)
    MMA. Yves Tanguy
A risk in each hand
    MMA. Yves Tanguy
Rose of the four winds
    MMA. Yves Tanguy
    MnU. 40 Amer ptrs
La rue de la Santé
    Jean. Surrealist ptg
    MMA. Yves Tanguy
Saltimbanques
    MMA. Yves Tanguy
Shadow country
    Canaday
    MMA. Yves Tanguy
Sifter of gold
    MMA. Yves Tanguy
Slowly toward the north   MMA
    McCurdy
    MMA. Yves Tanguy (col)
Stone in the tree   ATeS
    ATeS. Collection
The storm (Black landscape)   PPhM
    MMA. Yves Tanguy
    PPhM. Arensberg coll

TANGUY, Yves—_Continued_
Suffering softens stones (Le malheur
  adoucit les pierres)   IU
  IU. Contemp Amer ptg, 1949
  IU. 20th century
  MMA. Yves Tanguy   PA
Suites illimitées
  Pousette-Darte. Amer ptg
Sun on cushion
  Read. Concise history
Time and again
  Rathbun
Tower of the sea   MoSLW
  MMA. Yves Tanguy
Transparent ones
  MMA. Yves Tanguy
Untitled, 1947   MMA
  MMA. Soby collection
Water-table
  Jean. Surrealist ptg
When they shoot me
  MMA. Yves Tanguy
Where are you
  Jean. Surrealist ptg (col)
  MMA. Yves Tanguy
Wine, honey and oil
  MMA. Yves Tanguy
The wish
  IU. Contemp Amer ptg & sculp, 1953
With my shadow
  MMA. Yves Tanguy
The witness
  MMA. Yves Tanguy
Your tapers taper
  Jean. Surrealist ptg
Tanguy, Mrs Yves. See Sage, Kay
Tanks by A. G. Dove
TANNER, Henry Ossawa, 1859-1937
Banjo lesson
  Larkin
  Larkin rev ed (detail)
TANNING, Dorothea, 1910-
Fête champetre
  CSFP. Annual ex, 1947/48
Juke box
  IU. Contemp Amer ptg & sculp, 1955
Eine kleine nachtmusik
  Jean. Surrealist ptg
Palaestra
  Baur. Revolution
Profanation of the host
  Jean. Surrealist ptg
A very happy picture
  ICA. Annual ex, 1947/48
Taormina
Croninshield, F. Taormina
Hotchkiss, T. H. Taormina, the island of
  Sicily
Senat, L. Street in Taormina
Silsbee, M. Taormina and Mt Aetna
Taos by J. Marin
Taos landscape, New Mexico by J. Marin
Taos plaza by A. Dasburg
Tapping a furnace by G. P. Ennis
TARBELL, Edmund Charles, 1862-1938
Girl crocheting   NCa
  Pierson
Josephine and Mercie   DC
  Larkin
  Larkin rev ed
Timothy Dwight   CtY
  CtY. Portrait index

Target with four faces by J. Johns
Tarkington, Booth, 1869-1946
  Betts, L. Booth Tarkington
Tarquinia by J. E. Heliker
Tarrasa by A. Yunkers
Tarring nets by J. E. Levi
Tasker, Levi B. fl 1830
  Davis, J. H. Levi B. Tasker
TATTERSALL, George
Road to the west
  Davidson v2
Tattle tale grey by D. Lord
Tattoo and haircut by R. Marsh
Tattooed by M. Tobey
TAUBES, Frederic, 1900-
Figure study
  IU. Contemp Amer ptg & sculp, 1957
Phantasy on the martyrdom of St Se-
  bastian
  PPC. Ptg in the U. S. 1949
Portrait of a painter
  Gruskin
Taurus by F. S. Okada
Taverns. See Hotels, restaurants, etc.
Taxco street by R. Thompson
Taxi by L. MacIver
Taxi dance hall by R. Marsh
Taxidermist's window by E. A. Chaves
TAYLOR, fl 1850
American slave market   CtC
  Davidson v 1
Taylor, Abigail (Starr) 1768-1845
  Earl, R. Mrs William Taylor and child
Taylor, Archibald, fl 1802
  Malbone, E. G. Archibald Taylor
Taylor, John 1742-1829
  Ames, E. John Taylor
TAYLOR, John Williams, 1897-
The levee no 2
  NAD. Annual ex, 1951
The ramparts   InIJ
  InIJ. 105 ptgs
Tin, sand and tide
  IU. Contemp Amer ptg, 1949
The tower
  IU. Contemp Amer ptg, 1948
Taylor, Mrs John Williams. See Ruellan,
  Andrée
Taylor, Maria. See Byrd, Maria (Taylor)
Taylor, Maxwell Davenport, 1901-
  Lockman, D. M. Gen Maxwell D. Taylor
Taylor, Nathaniel William, 1786-1858
  Emmons, A. H. Nathaniel William Taylor
TAYLOR, Richard, 1902-
Returning   MB
  MB. Ptgs in water color
Taylor, William, 1764-1841
  Earl, R. Col William Taylor
Taylor, Mrs William. See Taylor, Abigail
  (Starr)
TAYLOR, William Ladd, 1854-1926
Electric automobile, Boston, 1892
  Davidson v2
Taylor, Zachary, president U.S. 1784-1850
  Unidentified artist. Major General Zach-
  ary Taylor
TCHELITCHEW, Pavel, 1898-1957
Bathers
  Read. Art now

Blue clown   MMA
  MMA. Soby collection
Bull fight
  Myers
Burial of an acrobat   MWi
  McCurdy
Cabbage head   MMA
  MMA. Soby collection
Derby hill theme: Hiawatha   CtHW
  CtHW. Handbook
Fallen rider
  Bazin
Fatma   MoKN
  CoS. New accessions USA, 1958
  MoKN. Handbook
Fish bowl
  Wight. Milestones
The green lion   CSB
  CoS. New accessions USA, 1950
Head of winter   MMA
  MMA. Masters (col detail)
Hide-and-seek   MMA
  Canaday
  Mendelowitz
  MMA. Ptg and sculpture
  Newmeyer
Madame Bonjean   MMA
  MMA. Soby collection
The mirror
  CtY. Yale alumni
Revolving head
  Pousette-Dart. Amer ptg
The riddle of Daedalus
  ICA. Annual ex, 1947/48
Tree into hand and foot (study for Hide
  and seek)   MMA
  MMA. Masters
Twilight head
  IU. Contemp Amer ptg, 1949
  Roos
The whirlwind   MM
  MM. 100 Amer ptrs
Tea for one by J. Sloan
Tea party by H. Sargent
Tea time by W. M. Chase
TEAGUE, Donald, 1897-
  Mid-ocean
    NAD. Annual ex, 1947, 2d half
  Shipyard, Singapore
    NAD. Annual ex, 1952
  Still life
    NAD. Annual ex, 1949, 2d half
  Work stock
    NAD. Annual ex, 1946, 2d half
Team of horses by A. G. Dove
Teel, Henry
  Wyeth, A. N. Henry Teel
Teenagers by R. Gikow
Telegraph hill, San Francisco by Unidenti-
  fied artist
Telegraph pole by A. G. Dove
Telephone by M. L. Schamberg
Telephone habit by G. Baumgarden
Telephones by C. Browning
Television by S. Davis
Teller, Margaret. See Stoutenburg, Mar-
  garet (Teller)
Telling fortunes by G. B. Luks
The **tempest** by L. E. Kupferman
The **tempest** by D. Newman

The **tempest** by A. P. Ryder
The **tempest** by W. Stuempfig
Temple, Augusta Grenville, fl 1803
  Malbone, E. G. Augusta G. Temple
Temple, Elizabeth (Bowdoin) lady, 1750-
  1809
  Malbone, E. G. Lady Elizabeth Temple
  Trumbull, J. Sir John Temple and his
  family
Temple, Sir John, 8th bart, 1732-1798
  Trumbull, J. Sir John Temple and his
  family
Temple at Philae by H. R. Newman
Temple fragment by L. Siegriest
Temple gold medal nude by W. J. Glackens
Temple of Segesta with the artist sketching
  by T. Cole
Temple of the mind by A. P. Ryder
Temptation of St Anthony by J. Covert
Temptation of St Anthony by L. Guglielmi
Temptation of St Anthony by J. Muller
Temptation of St Anthony by H. Pippin
Temptation of St Anthony by A. Rattner
Temptation in Tonopah by F. Martin
10 A.M. by J. Koch
Ten cents a ride by L. Bouché
Ten miles to Salem by G. H. Durrie
10 P.M. by H. C. King
Ten shots ten cents by R. Marsh
The **tenant** by C. di Marca-Relli
Ten Broek, Christina, 1718-1801
  Unidentified artist. Christina Ten Broek
Tenement by G. Biddle
Ten Eyck, Catharina. See Van Zandt,
  Catharina (Ten Eyck)
Ten Eyck, Matthew, fl 1733
  Vanderlyn, P. Matthew Ten Eyck
Ten Eyck, Tobias, fl 1740
  Unidentified artist. Tobias Ten Eyck
Ten Eyck family, member of
  Unidentified artist. Girl of the Ten Eyck
  family
TENNEY, Ulysses Dow
  David Daggett   CtY
  CtY. Portrait index
Tennis. See Games and sports—Tennis
Tennyson by J. Johns
Tenochtitlan by L. Siegriest
Tension by moonlight by B. W. Tomlin
Tens-qua-ta-wa, the Shawnee prophet by
  J. O. Lewis
Tenth street studio by W. M. Chase
Tents at Lake O'Hara by J. S. Sargent
Tepees
  Catlin, G. Comanche village in Texas
  Catlin, G. Crow chief at his toilet
  Catlin, G. A Crow tepee
  Catlin, G. Sioux village
  Miller, A. J. Fort Laramie
  Miller, A. J. Large encampment north
    of the Cut rocks
  Miller, A. J. Shoshone Indian and his
    pet horse
  Stanley, J. M. Assiniboin encampment on
    the upper Mississippi

Terminal by S. Davis

Terminal by X. Gonzales

Terminal by E. Lanyon

Termination of a militia sham fight by D. C. Johnston

Terrace by J. Floch

Terrace at Windsor, View from the by B. West

Terrace, Central park by G. R. Beal

Terraced mound in a snow storm at sunset by J. J. Egan

TERRELL, Elizabeth, 1908-
  Fisherman   ATU
    ATU. Coll of Amer art

Terror by K. Zerbe

Terror in Brooklyn by L. Guglielmi

TERRY, Luther, 1813-1900
  Jacob's dream   NNHS
    MiD. Travelers in Arcadia

Tess by W. Sommer

Test-able by R. Crawford

TESTER, Jefferson, 1900-
  The critic
    ICA. Annual ex, 1945/46

Teton range by T. Moran

Texas landscape no 3 by D. Reich

Textile mill worker by B. Shahn

Textile mills by B. Shahn

Textile merchant by Unidentified artist

TEYRAL, Hazel (Janicki) 1918-
  Figures with mobiles
    IU. Contemp Amer ptg, 1950
  Fragment: three heads
    IU. Contemp Amer ptg, 1948
  Fragment: two figures
    IU. Contemp Amer ptg, 1949

TEYRAL, John, 1912-
  Algerian soldiers   OYB
    OYB. Catalogue 1951
  Night worker
    IU. Contemp Amer ptg, 1950
  Rockport window
    PPC. Ptg in the U.S. 1949
  Rudy: midget
    IU. Contemp Amer ptg, 1948

Teyral, Mrs John. See Teyral, Hazel (Janicki)

Thacher, Thomas, 1620-1678
  Pollard limner. Thomas Thacher, so-called

The Thames from Battersea bridge by J. A. M. Whistler

The Thames in ice by J. A. M. Whistler

Thanksgiving by D. E. Lee

Thanksgiving day by D. E. Lee

That red one by A. G. Dove

That which I should have done I did not do by I. L. Albright

Thatcher, Margaret Ann. See Walton, Margaret Ann (Thatcher)

Thatcher, Rhoda Ann. See Davis, Rhoda Ann (Thatcher)

That's my doll! by Unidentified artist

Thayendanegea. See Brant, Joseph

THAYER, Abbott Henderson, 1849-1921
  Florence protecting the arts   MeB
    Pierson

Margaret MacKittrick   InIJ
  InIJ. 105 ptgs

Meditation   OYB
  OYB. Catalogue 1951

Self-portrait (Blagden coll)
  CtY. Yale alumni

Self-portrait, c 1898   NAD
  NAD. Amer tradition

Stevenson memorial angel   DNC
  DNC. Gellatly coll, 1954
  Pierson

Stillman sisters   NBM
  Larkin
  Larkin rev ed

The virgin   DF
  Time. 300 years (col)

Young woman   MM
  Mendelowitz
  MM. 100 Amer ptrs

Young woman in a fur coat   CtNB
  NUM. Art across America

Thayer, Catherine M. See Wetherby, Catherine M. (Thayer)

Thayer, Deliverance, fl 1800
  Brewster, J. (attributed works) Deacon Eliphaz Thayer and his wife Deliverance

Thayer, Eliphaz, b 1750
  Brewster, J. (attributed works) Deacon Eliphaz Thayer and his wife Deliverance

Thayer, Sanford
  Elliott, C. L. Sanford Thayer

Thayer, Webster
  Shahn, B. Judge Webster Thayer

Thea by G. D. Brush

Theaters
  Cassatt, M. The loge
  Du Bois, G. P. Opera box
  Engel, T. The theatre
  Hopper, E. First row, orchestra
  Hopper, E. Sheridan theatre
  Hopper, E. Two on the aisle
  Searle, J. Interior of the Park theater, New York
  Shinn, E. Theatre
  Shinn, E. Theatre box
  Sloan, J. Carmine theatre
  Sloan, J. Little movie theater
  Smith, R. Old Holliday street theatre, Baltimore, 1839

THECLA, Julia
  I looked into a dream
    ICA. Annual ex, 1947/48
  Willow in the rain
    IU. Contemp Amer ptg, 1949
    PPC. Ptg in the U.S. 1949

Their only roof by H. Gottlieb

Theme and variations by A. Ozenfant

Theme of earth by W. Pachner

Theodore Roosevelt's cabin door by R. L. Goodwin

There is man in God by I. L. Albright

There were no flowers tonight by I. L. Albright

There were seven in eight by J. Pollock

Thetis bringing the armor to Achilles by B. West

Theus, Anne. See Lee, Anne (Theus)

THEUS, Jeremiah, 1719-1774
  Alexander Fraser
    Middleton. Jeremiah Theus

Barnard Elliott jr   SCGG
  Middleton. Jeremiah Theus
Charles Burnham Cochran
  Middleton. Jeremiah Theus
Christiana Broughton (copy of pastel by
    Henrietta Johnston)
  Middleton. Jeremiah Theus
Col Jones' grandchild (Sarah Jones)
  Middleton. Jeremiah Theus
Daniel Heyward
  Middleton. Jeremiah Theus
Daniel Horry
  Middleton. Jeremiah Theus
Daniel Ravenel   GST
  Middleton. Jeremiah Theus
  NUM. Art across America
Eleanor Ball
  Middleton. Jeremiah Theus
Elias Ball
  Middleton. Jeremiah Theus
Elizabeth Allen
  Middleton. Jeremiah Theus
Elizabeth Damaris Ravenel and her sister
  Middleton. Jeremiah Theus
Elizabeth Rothmaler   NBM
  Barker. Amer ptg
  Middleton. Jeremiah Theus
  Pierson
Elizabeth Smith
  Middleton. Jeremiah Theus
Gabriel Manigault   MM
  Middleton. Jeremiah Theus
Hutchinson boy
  Middleton. Jeremiah Theus
Isaac Holme
  Middleton. Jeremiah Theus
Isaac Motte (?)   DN
  Mendelowitz
James Habersham
  Middleton. Jeremiah Theus
Lionel Chalmers   MB
  Middleton. Jeremiah Theus
Little Alice Hayne
  Middleton. Jeremiah Theus
Mary Trusler
  Middleton. Jeremiah Theus
Maurice Keating
  Middleton. Jeremiah Theus
Mrs Algernon Wilson
  Middleton. Jeremiah Theus
Mrs Barnard Elliott jr
  Middleton. Jeremiah Theus
Mrs Daniel Heyward
  Middleton. Jeremiah Theus
Mrs Daniel Ravenel
  Middleton. Jeremiah Theus
Mrs Edward Richardson
  Middleton. Jeremiah Theus
Mrs Gabriel Manigault   MM
  Flexner. First flowers
  Middleton. Jeremiah Theus
Mrs Henry Izard
  Middleton. Jeremiah Theus
Mrs John Moore
  Middleton. Jeremiah Theus
Mrs Lionel Chalmers   MB
  Middleton. Jeremiah Theus
Mrs Paul Trapier III
  Middleton. Jeremiah Theus
Mrs Peter Manigault   SCCG
  Middleton. Jeremiah Theus
  Pierson

Mrs Rawlins Lowndes
  Middleton. Jeremiah Theus
Mrs Stephen Mazyck
  Middleton. Jeremiah Theus
Mrs Theus (traditionally Eva Rosanna
    Ainslie)
  Middleton. Jeremiah Theus
Mrs Thomas Grimball
  Middleton. Jeremiah Theus
Mrs William Hutson
  Middleton. Jeremiah Theus
Mrs William Lee
  Middleton. Jeremiah Theus
Mrs William Mazyck
  Middleton. Jeremiah Theus
Polly Ouldfield of Winyah   IBM
  Middleton. Jeremiah Theus
Ralph Izard as a boy
  Middleton. Jeremiah Theus
Rebecca Motte
  Middleton. Jeremiah Theus
Samuel Brailsford
  Middleton. Jeremiah Theus
Stephen Mazyck
  Middleton. Jeremiah Theus
Susannah Maybank
  Middleton. Jeremiah Theus
Thomas Grimball
  Middleton. Jeremiah Theus
William Mazyck
  Middleton. Jeremiah Theus
William Richardson   CtY
  CtY. Portrait index
  Middleton. Jeremiah Theus
William Wragg   MiD
  DC. Amer ptrs of the South
  Richardson. Ptg in America
Young William Branford
  Middleton. Jeremiah Theus

Theus, Mrs Jeremiah, fl 1755
  Theus, J. Mrs Theus (traditionally known
    as Eva Rosanna Ainslie)

They guard the night by R. Breinin
They pay to be seen by R. Marsh
They shall sail the seven seas by J. De Diego
They wait by Z. L. Sepeshy
THIBAULT, Aimée, 1780-1868
  Althea Lenox (?)   NNHS
    NNHS. Waldron Phoenix Belknap coll
  Lady of the Lenox family   NNHS
    NNHS. Waldron Phoenix Belknap coll
  Mrs Robert Maitland   NNHS
    NNHS. Waldron Phoenix Belknap coll
  Robert Lenox   NNHS
    NNHS. Waldron Phoenix Belknap coll
The **thicket** by D. Wingren
Thiers, Louis Adolphe, 1797-1877
  Healy, G. P. A. Louis A. Thiers
Thieves in the pantry by W. M. Harnett
Things and mess in classroom by J. Brown
Things I loved and did not keep by A. F.
    Radomski
Things on a table by H. L. McFee
Think of me, dear by L. Lewitin
The **thinker** by T. Eakins
Third avenue by F. J. Kline
Third avenue el by R. Crawford
Third avenue el by H. Gerardia
Third beach, Newport by J. F. Kensett
The **third** hand by H. Hofmann

Thirsty trapper by A. J. Miller
This architectural world by B. Greene
This is my playground by Y. Kuniyoshi
Thistles
  Ben-Zion. Large thistles
  Frary, M. Still life with thistles
Thomar, Portugal by J. S. Sargent
THOMAS, Howard, 1899-1959
  Fernandina
    Pierson
Thomas, Isaiah, 1749-1831
  Greenwood, E. A. Isaiah Thomas
  Sharples, J. Isaiah Thomas
THOMAS, J. fl 1810
  The ship Nancy, homeward bound   DN
    DN. Amer primitive ptgs, pt 2
THOMAS, John, 1927-
  Women on Victorian couch
    IU. Contemp Amer ptg & sculp, 1961
THOMAS, Mary Leath, 1905-1959
  We bought a fish   GAtM
    GAtM. Holbrook collection
THOMAS, Paul Middlebrook, 1875-
  Franklin Bowditch Dexter   CtY
    CtY. Portrait index
THOMPSON, A. E. fl 1847

Attributed works

Wetumpka bridge, Alabama   MB
  MB. Karolik coll
  Pierson
THOMPSON, Cephas, 1775-1856
  Girl with dove   VWR
    VWR. Folk art (col)
THOMPSON, Jerome B. 1814-1886
  Harvest in Vermont
    Born
  Peep show   MB
    MB. Karolik coll
  A picnic in the woods of New England   MB
    Pierson
  The picnic, near Mount Mansfield, Vermont   CSFD
    Pierson
THOMPSON, Ralston, 1904-
  The grudge   OYB
    OYB. Annual 1948
    OYB. Catalogue 1951
  Taxco street   OCiM
    CoS. New accessions USA, 1958
Thompson, Rosemary
  Watkins, F. C. Miss Rosemary Thompson
THOMPSON, Wordsworth
  Departing guests   NNHS
    NYG. Fine art (col)
Thompson-Neely house by J. Sharp
THON, William, 1906-
  After the fire
    IU. Contemp Amer ptg, 1948
  Aunt Thankful's farm
    Bazin
  The fountain
    IU. Contemp Amer ptg & sculp, 1951
  Light in autumn
    Time. 300 years (col)
  Maine quarry
    Pousette-Dart. Amer ptg
  Midnight quarry   WMAA
    Pierson

Night passage
  IU. Contemp Amer ptg, 1950
The outpost
  Gruskin (col)
Owl's head
  Genauer (col)
Padre Paolo of Pisa
  CSFP. Annual ex, 1948/49
Sea birds   MM
  Pierson
Sea gulls
  Gruskin (col)
Spring in Maine
  IU. Contemp Amer ptg, 1952
Spring mist
  IU. Contemp Amer ptg & sculp, 1955
Sunburst   OYB
  OYB. Annual 1956
  OYB. Supplement 1959
Vineyards in Tuscany
  NAD. Special ex, 1956
Thorndike sisters, fl 1841
  Unidentified artist. Thorndike sisters
Thornhill bar, Florida by W. Homer
Thornton, John, fl 1835
  Bingham, G. C. John Thornton
Thoroughbreds by C. C. Ross
Thorp, Aaron, fl 1826
  Ames, E. Aaron Thorp
Thorp, Mary (Dunn) fl 1826
  Ames, E. Mrs Aaron Thorp
THRALL, Donald, 1918-
  Entrance   OYB
    OYB. Annual 1951
    OYB. Catalogue 1951
The **thread** of life by G. C. Bingham
Threading light by M. Tobey
Threatened attack by A. J. Miller
Three by J. Pollock
3 A.M. by H. Maril
Three A.M., 1909 by J. Sloan
Three alone by W. Stuempfig
Three balls for five cents by J. Donaghy
Three bathers by D. Park
Three bathers by J. Strombotne
Three blues by J. Guerrero
Three boys on the shore by W. Homer
Three candidates for election by L. Gatch
Three children by J. F. Francis
Three children by W. M. Prior (manner of)
Three clowns by J. Berlandina
Three cows on hillside by M. Avery
Three dancers by Ben-Zion
Three dancers by M. Soyer
Three days of rain by C. E. Burchfield
Three doors by B. Shahn
Three doorways by M. Cone
Three figures by T. H. Benton
Three figures by J. Kramer
Three fishermen by R. Baker
Three forms by M. Rothko
Three friends by M. Avery
Three generations by C. M. Russell
Three gentlemen by J. Smibert
Three gold diggers by L. Carroll

Three horsemen by J. Corbino
Three horses in alarm by W. Sommer
Three jugs by M. Weber
Three kings by M. T. Kelly
Three literary gentlemen by M. Weber
The three-master by J. Marin
Three men by B. Shahn
Three men in a canoe by W. Homer
Three nudes by J. Marin
Three princesses by J. S. Copley
Three queens by S. P. Saffer
Three roses by A. Gorky
Three slickers by R. Iver
Three thousand miles to the point of begin-
ning by K. Sage
Three towers by J. C. Atherton
Three trees by R. A. Blakelock
Three trees by C. E. Burchfield
Three trees by J. Twachtman
Threshing wheat by T. H. Benton
Threshold to success by P. Evergood
Throop, Deborah (Goldsmith). See Gold-
smith, Deborah
Throop, Enos T. 1784-1874
    Ames, E. Enos T. Throop
Throop, George Addison, fl 1831
    Goldsmith, D. George Addison Throop
Throop, Mrs George Addison. See Gold-
smith, Deborah
Through a frosty moon by A. G. Dove
Through a glass darkly by A. Bohrod
Through Coleman Hollow up the Allegheny
    valley by J. Kane
Through the Luxembourg by M. Ray
Through the marshes by E. Berman
Through the pines, the ocean by W. Kien-
busch
Through the window by F. D. Duncan
Through the woods by S. Laufman
Through to the sea by F. D. Duncan
Throughway by H. Gramatky
Thunderclap by C. E. Burchfield
Thunderstorm II by W. Stuempfig
Thunderstorm in the Rocky mountains by A.
    Bierstadt
Thursby, Emma, 1845-1931
    Healy, G. P. A. Emma Thursby
THWAITES, Charles W. 1904-
    Portrait
        CSFP. Annual ex, 1946
Tibbits, George, 1763-1849
    Ames, E. George Tibbits
Tibbits, Sarah (Noyes) 1767-1846
    Ames, E. Mrs George Tibbits
Tiber below Perugia by G. Inness
Ticonderoga or Mount Defiance, View near
    by T. Cole
Tidal by G. Peterdi
Tidal mill by A. Robertson
Tidewater by C. H. Carter
Tidewater shapes by J. E. Levi

TIFFANY, Louis Comfort, 1848-1933
    Old New York, c 1878   NBM
        Baur. Revolution
        U.S. National Capital sesquicentennial
        com
Tigers
    Austin, D. The tiger
    Austin, D. Tigress with three cubs
    Hirshfield, M. Tiger
    Pippin, H. Blue tiger
    Styka, T. Tigers
Tight dally and loose latigo by C. M. Russell
The tightrope by D. Austin
Tightrope dancer by M. Beckmann
Tilden children, fl 1840
    Mason, B. F. Julia, Ann and Harriet Til-
    den
Tilghman, Henrietta Maria. See Goldsbor-
    ough, Henrietta Maria (Tilghman)
Tilghman, Mary
    Peale, C. W. Mary Tilghman
Tilghman, Richard, fl 1790
    Peale, C. W. Richard Tilghman
Tilghman, Tench, 1744-1786..
    Peale, C. W. Washington, Lafayette, and
    Tench Tilghman
TILLES, J. A. fl 1829
    Watch and fob   VWR
        VWR. Folk art (col)
Tilley, James, 1707-1765
    Copley, J. S. James Tilley, New England
    merchant
Tilted bowl by M. A. Haviland
Tilted horizon by J. Hultberg
Tilton family
    Davis, J. H. Tilton family
Tilyard, Charles Slade, 1820-1900
    Tilyard, P. Charles Slade Tilyard
TILYARD, Philip, 1787-1827
    Artist in his studio
        D.C. Amer ptrs of the South
    Charles Slade Tilyard
        MdBMu. Rendezvous
    First envoy from Santo Domingo   NBM
        DC. Amer ptrs of the South
    John Pendleton Kennedy
        DC. Privately owned
Timber line, Estes park, Colorado by G.
    Peirce
Time by W. Gropper
Time and again by Y. Tanguy
Time and eternity by J. Haberle
Time and space by W. S. Schwartz
Time clock by W. T. Murch
Time echoes by S. Rosenberg
Time enclosure by C. A. Morris
A time for fear by J. Ernst
Time is money by F. Danton
Time of change by M. Graves
Time of change by N. Meitzer
The time of fire by W. De Kooning
Time table by W. T. Wiley
Time, tide and town by K. Knaths
Times square, abstraction no 1 by A. Walko-
    witz
Times square, abstraction no 2 by A.
    Walkowitz

Timescape by J. Ernst
Tin by I. L. Albright
Tin, sand and tide by J. W. Taylor
Tioga point valley by J. O. Montalant
Tired by L. Rossbach
Tired violin by K. Knaths
TIRRELL, George, fl 1860
  View from waterfront, Sacramento, California
    Baur. Amer ptg
    Pierson
'Tis me O Lord by F. Martin
Tishcohan by G. Hesselius
Titian's goblet by T. Cole
Tittering female by W. W. Quirt
Tivoli by S. R. Gifford
To Edwin Booth by W. M. Harnett (attributed works)
To form synchromy by M. Russell
To Queequeg by P. Jenkins
To the ball by Y. Kuniyoshi
To the dock, Tadoussac by A. P. Lowrie
To the earth by R. W. Barnett
To the harbourmaster by J. Mitchell
To the rescue by W. Homer
To the sea by B. W. Tomlin
To the tomb by F. C. Watkins
To the yacht races by A. A. Abbot
To thine own self be true by S. M. Adler
TOBEY, Mark, 1890-
  Above the earth   ICA
    Baur. New art
    Cheney. Primer 1958 ed
  Agate world   WaS
    Cheney. New world history
    Cheney. Story 1958 ed
    Roberts. Mark Tobey (col)
  Allegro
    IU. Contemp Amer ptg & sculp, 1955
  Arena of civilization
    Roberts. Mark Tobey
  Awakening night   NUM
    Roberts. Mark Tobey (col)
  Broadway, 1936   MM
    Baur. New art
    Larkin rev ed (col)
    Pierson
  Burned over
    IU. Contemp Amer ptg, 1951
  Calligraphic
    Ponente. Mod ptg 1960 (col)
  Canals   WaS
    Read. Concise history
  Canticle   WMAA
    WMAA. Sara Roby
  City radiance
    Blesh
    ICA. Amer artists paint the city
    Ponente. Mod ptg, 1960
  Constellation
    Roberts. Mark Tobey (col)
  The cycle
    MnU. 40 Amer ptrs
  Dawn. See Prophetic light
  Desert town
    CSFP. Annual ex, 1952
  Drift for summer
    Baur. Nature
    MMA. Fourteen

Drums, Indian and word of God
  MMA. Fourteen
E pluribus unum   WaS
  MMA. Fourteen
  NBuA. Expressionism
Edge of August   MMA
  Baur. New art (col)
  MMA. Masters
  WMAA. Contemp Amer ptg, 1953
End of summer
  Roberts. Mark Tobey
Forms follow man   WaS
  Roberts. Mark Tobey (col)
Fossils
  Roberts. Mark Tobey
Fountains of Europe   MB
  Eliot. Art of our time (col)
  Pierson
  Time. 300 years (col)
Fragment of peace
  OCl. Some contemporary works
Genesis
  Roberts. Mark Tobey
Golden gardens
  OCl. Some contemporary works
Gothic
  UNESCO. 1860-1955
  UNESCO. 1860-1959
Harvest
  Ponente. Mod ptg, 1960 (col)
Horn pipe
  NBuA. Expressionism
Intersection
  Roberts. Mark Tobey (col)
Journey in white
  50 years of mod art
Lyric
  WMAA. Museum and its friends, 1959
Marriage   DP
  DP. Catalogue
Meditative series no 9, 1954
  Roberts. Mark Tobey (col)
  Seiberling
Neon thoroughfare
  ICA. Amer artists paint the city
  Roberts. Mark Tobey
New life (Resurrection)   WMAA
  Goodrich. Amer art (col)
New York
  MMA. Fourteen
New York tablet   NUM
  NUM. Root bequest
1951
  Art since 1945
Orpheus   WaS
  Pousette-Dart. Amer ptg
Pacific circle
  Roberts. Mark Tobey (col)
Pacific transition   MCH
  Pulitzer v2
Partitions of the city   NUM
  MiA. Root coll
Prehistoric playground
  CtY. Yale alumni
Prophetic light (Dawn)
  MnMW. 60 Amer ptrs
Red man—white man—black man NBuA
  NBuA. Contemporary ptgs
Remote field   MMA
  Larkin
  MMA. Fourteen

San Francisco street   MiD
  ICA. Amer artists paint the city
  Richardson. Ptg in America
  Time. 300 years (col)
Space intangibles
  Hess. Abstract ptg (col)
Space ritual no 3
  OCl. Some contemporary works
Structure, 1946
  Hess. Abstract ptg
Summer 8, 1957
  Roberts. Mark Tobey (col)
Symbols over the west
  PPC. International ex, 1958
Tattooed
  Roberts. Mark Tobey (col)
Threading light   MMA
  McCurdy
  Mendelowitz
Transit   MM
  Baur. New art
  MM. 100 Amer ptrs
  Time. 300 years
Tropicalism
  Art since 1945 (col)
  ICA. Annual ex, 1951
  Read. Concise history (col)
Tundra
  Baur. Revolution
  Hunter. Mod Amer ptg (col)
  IU. Contemp Amer ptg, 1949
  MMA. Fourteen
Universal field   WMAA
  Goodrich. Amer art
  MnU. 40 Amer ptrs
  Pierson
Untitled, 1960
  PPC. International ex, 1961/62
White journey
  Roberts. Mark Tobey (col)
Window
  ICA. Annual ex, 1954
Yellow harvest
  Roberts. Mark Tobey (col)
Tod, David
  Crawford, J. S. Gov David Tod
Todd, Robert Llewellyn, 1792-1825
  Jouett, M. H. Robert Llewellyn Todd
Tofellini by P. Guston
The **toilers** by M. Weber
Toilers of the sea by R. Kent
Toilers of the sea by A. P. Ryder
La **toilette** by M. Cassatt
Toiling hands by P. Evergood
Toledo I by P. M. Gish
Toledo blade by W. M. Harnett
Toledo, Spain, View of by H. Mintz
TOLEGIAN, Manuel J. 1912-
  Afternoon at Tony's   ATU
    ATU. Coll of Amer art
Toll rope by A. N. Wyeth
Tolling bell by P. Fine
Tolling bell by A. N. Wyeth
Tolman, Joseph Robertson, fl 1795
  Hathaway, R. Joseph Robertson Tolman
Tom Kenney comes home by F. A. Mechau
Tom Walker's flight by J. Quidor
Tomato patch by G. Fuller

Tomatoes, fruit, and flowers by Unidentified artist
Tombstone cutter by J. Levine
Tombstones by J. Lawrence
TOMKINS, Margaret, 1916-
  Fragrance of fear
    ICA. Annual ex, 1951
  Genesis
    WMAA. Annual ex, 1957
  Matriarchy
    VR. Biennial ex, 1948
  Sign of the sun
    OrPa. Ptgs & sculptures (col)
TOMLIN, Bradley Walker, 1899-1953
  Abstraction no 6, 1952-53   MCH
    Pulitzer v 1
  Armor must change
    Baur. Bradley Walker Tomlin
  Arrangement   IU
    Baur. Bradley Walker Tomlin (col)
    CoS. New accessions USA, 1950
    IU. Contemp Amer ptg, 1949 (col)
  Autocrats
    Baur. Bradley Walker Tomlin
    MnU. 40 Amer ptrs
  Burial   MM
    Baur. Bradley Walker Tomlin
    Baur. Revolution
    MM. 100 Amer ptrs
    WMAA. Juliana Force
  Death cry
    Baur. Bradley Walker Tomlin
  The goblet   DP
    Baur. Bradley Walker Tomlin
    DP. Catalogue
  Green
    Baur. Bradley Walker Tomlin
  Maneuver for position
    Baur. Bradley Walker Tomlin
  Number I
    IU. Contemp Amer ptg, 1951
  Number 1, 1949   WMAA
    Baur. Bradley Walker Tomlin (col)
    MnMW. 60 Amer ptrs (col)
    WMAA. New decade
  Number 1, 1951   NUM
    Mendelowitz
    MMA. Fifteen
    NUM. Root bequest
  Number 1, 1952-53
    Baur. Bradley Walker Tomlin
    WMAA. New decade
  Number 1, 1956   NUM
    NUM. Art across America
  Number 2, 1950
    Baur. Bradley Walker Tomlin
  Number 3, 1948
    Baur. Bradley Walker Tomlin
  Number 3, 1949
    Hess. Abstract ptg
    Pousette-Dart. Amer ptg
  Number 5, 1942
    Baur. Bradley Walker Tomlin
  Number 5, 1948
    NBuA. Expressionism
  Number 5, 1949
    Baur. Bradley Walker Tomlin
  Number 6, 1950
    Baur. Bradley Walker Tomlin
  Number 6, 1952
    Baur. Bradley Walker Tomlin

TOMLIN, B. W.—*Continued*
Number 7, 1950
  Baur. Bradley Walker Tomlin (col)
  Hess. Abstract ptg (col)
  MMA. Abstract
Number 7, 1951
  MnMW. Classic tradition
Number 8, 1949
  Baur. Bradley Walker Tomlin
  MnU. 40 Amer ptrs
Number 9, 1952   DP
  Baur. Bradley Walker Tomlin
Number 9: in praise of Gertrude Stein
      MMA
  Art since 1945 (col)
  Baur. Bradley Walker Tomlin
  Hunter. Mod Amer ptg (col)
  MMA. Fifteen
  MMA. New Amer ptg (col)
Number 10, 1949
  MMA. Fifteen
Number 10, 1952-53   NUM
  Baur. Bradley Walker Tomlin
  Baur. New art
  Faulkner. Art today, 1956
  Ponente. Mod ptg, 1960 (col)
  WMAA. New decade
Number 11, 1952-53   MM
  Baur. New art (col)
Number 12, 1949
  Baur. Bradley Walker Tomlin
  PPC. International ex, 1952
Number 13, 1952-53
  Pierson
Number 15, 1953
  MMA. New Amer ptg
Number 18, 1950
  Baur. Bradley Walker Tomlin
  Baur. New art
  McCurdy
Number 18, 1952-53
  Baur. Bradley Walker Tomlin
Number 20, 1949   MMA
  Baur. Bradley Walker Tomlin (col)
  Baur. New art
  MMA. Fifteen
  MMA. Masters (col)
  MMA. New Amer ptg
  Pierson
  Read. Concise history
Outward preoccupation (Still life)
  Baur. Bradley Walker Tomlin
  Gruskin
Red box
  Baur. Bradley Walker Tomlin
Self-portrait, 1932   WMAA
  Baur. Bradley Walker Tomlin
Still life   WMAA
  Baur. Bradley Walker Tomlin
  Goodrich. Amer art
  Pierson
Tension by moonlight
  Baur. Bradley Walker Tomlin
To the sea
  Baur. Bradley Walker Tomlin (col)
  Rathbun
Two figures and easel
  Baur. Bradley Walker Tomlin
Untitled
  CSFP. Annual ex, 1950-51
Tomlinson court park by F. Stella
Tomorrow and tomorrow by F. Martin

Tomorrow is never by D. Tanning
Tomorrow morning by J. Ernst
Tomorrow we'll be sober by H. Bacon
Tompkins, Daniel D. 1774-1825
  Ames, E. Daniel D. Tompkins
  Jarvis, J. W. Daniel D. Tompkins
Tompkins, Hannah (Minthorne) 1781-1829
  Ames, E. Mrs Daniel D. Tompkins
Tompkins children, fl 1809
  Ames, E. Children of Gov Daniel D. Tompkins
Tonal rhapsody by C. G. Shaw
Tondo no 8, 1948 by F. Glarner
TONEY, Anthony, 1913-
  Bathers
    WMAA. Contemp Amer ptg, 1955
  Bridge
    IU. Contemp Amer ptg, 1951
Tontine coffee house, New York by F. Guy
Tony's house by E. Hopper
TOOKER, George, 1920-
  Artist's daughter
    ICA. Annual ex, 1959/60
  Chess game
    WMAA. New decade
  Government bureau   MM
    Pierson
  Guitar
    WMAA. Annual ex, 1958
  The gypsy
    CSFP. Annual ex, 1952
  Highway
    ICA. Annual ex, 1954
  In the summerhouse   WMAA
    WMAA. Sara Roby
  Red carpet
    WMAA. New decade
  Sleepers   WMAA
    CSB. Illusion
  Subway   WMAA
    Goodrich. Amer art
    ICA. Amer artists paint the city
    McCurdy
    Mendelowitz
    Pierson
    Pousette-Dart. Amer ptg
    WMAA. New decade
  The window
    WMAA. Annual ex, 1957
Toole, Anne Leitch. See Toole, Nannie
Toole, George Henry, b 1837
  Toole, J. George Toole
Toole, Jennie, 1841-1917
  Toole, J. Jennie Toole
TOOLE, John, 1815-1860
  Capture of Major André
    O'Neal
  George Toole (1)
    O'Neal
  George Toole (2)
    O'Neal
  Jennie Toole (1)
    O'Neal
  Jennie Toole (2)
    O'Neal
  John Mann
    O'Neal
  Martha Morris Suddarth
    O'Neal
  Mary Jane Toole
    O'Neal

Nannie Toole
  O'Neal
Richard Pleasants Suddarth
  O'Neal
Self-portrait (1)
  O'Neal
Self-portrait (2)
  O'Neal
Skating scene   DN
  DN. Amer primitive ptgs, pt 2
Tempe McCutchen Suddarth
  O'Neal
Toole children
  O'Neal
Unknown sitter
  O'Neal
Vesuvius
  O'Neal
West Point
  O'Neal
Toole, Martha Jane. See Toole, Jennie
Toole, Mary Jane (Suddarth) 1817-1902
  Toole, J. Mary Jane Toole
Toole, Nannie, 1847-1862
  Toole, J. Nannie Toole
Toole children
  Toole, J. Toole children
Tops by D. Rosenthal
Topsail schooner in sheltered waters by
  J. S. Blunt
Torero and young girl by M. Cassatt
Torment, Puerto Rico by H. G. Keller
The tormentors by P. Guston
Torn hat by T. Sully
Torn in transit by J. Haberle
Torn sail by S. Wilson
The tornado by T. Cole
The tornado by J. S. Curry
Toro by L. Neiman
Torrey, Bethia. See Mann, Bethia (Torrey)
Torso and limbs by H. Bloom
The tortured ham by G. Grosz
The toss by F. Martin
Totem by J. Pollock
Tour of inspection by R. Crawford
Tournament by A. Gottlieb
Tournos by S. Davis
Touro, Isaac de Abraham, 1737-1782
  Stuart, G. Rev Isaac de Abraham Touro
Tousard, Anne-Louis de, 1749-1817
  Malbone, E. G. Col Anne-Louis de Tou-
  sard
TOVISH, Harold, 1921-
  Flayed arm
    MnMW. Reality and fantasy
Towards integrating sculptural influence by
  R. Sears
The tower by C. H. Demuth
The tower by K. Knaths
The tower by C. A. Morris
The tower by J. W. Taylor
The tower, Avallon by O. M. Pleissner
Tower of the sea by Y. Tanguy
Towers, Mrs John. See Towers, Susan
  (Coren)
Towers, Susan (Coren) fl 1796
  Peale, J. Mrs Susan Coren Towers

Town Gate tower II, 1925 by L. Feininger
Town hall (Zottelstedt) by L. Feininger
Town hall of Cammin by L. Feininger
Town house by F. Hillsmith
Town meeting by R. Haines
Town of Jim Thorpe, Pennsylvania by T.
  Asplund
Town on a river by Unidentified artist
Town square by S. Davis
Town square, Independence, Missouri by
  F. E. Warren
Townsend, Absolom, 1786-1861
  Ames, E. Absolom Townsend
Townsend, Catherine (Bronson)
  Sargent, J. S. Mrs John Joseph Town-
  send
Towson, Nathan, 1784-1854
  Peale, Raphaelle. Capt Nathan Towson
Toy battle by M. Jackson
Toy duck on wheels by L. MacIver
Toy in the sun by W. A. Baziotes
Toy world by W. A. Baziotes
Tracery of leaves by L. Lucioni
TRACY, John M. 1844-1892
  Grouse shooting (Hunter and two dogs)
    NSP. Sportscapes
  Pointers
    NSP. Sportscapes
Tracy, Patrick, 1711-1789
  Trumbull, J. Patrick Tracy
Traffic halt by H. Schuldt
Tragedy or Found drowned by L. M.
  Eilshemius
Tragedy is self-contained by W. W. Quirt
Tragic actor by B. Greene
Trail of the iron horse by C. M. Russell
Train leaving Auburn station at Rochester,
  New York by E. Sintzenich
Trajan and the children by W. Stuempfig
A tramp on Christmas day by A. M. R.
  Moses
Tramps hideout by D. G. Blythe
Trance by W. A. Baziotes
Tranquility by L. M. Eilshemius
Tranquility by M. Kantor
Tranquility by M. Weber
Tranquillity of previous existence by W. W.
  Quirt
Transcendental by F. Ruvolo
Transcending motion by F. Ruvolo
Transfiguration by A. Gottlieb
Transfluent lines by I. R. Pereira
Transforming gold by I. R. Pereira
Transients by J. W. Reilly
Transit by M. Tobey
Transition by K. L. Callahan
Transparent ones by Y. Tanguy
Transparent planes by I. R. Pereira
Transverse by J. Tworkov
Transverse parallels by I. R. Pereira
Transversion by I. R. Pereira
Transylvania university
  Jouett, M. H. Principal building of Tran-
  sylvania university

Trapeze, Winter garden, New York by E. Shinn

Trapier, Mrs Benjamin Foissin. See Heyward, Hannah Miles

Trapier, Elizabeth (Foissin) 1758-1836
  Theus, J. Mrs Paul Trapier III

Trapier, Hannah Miles (Heyward) See Heyward, Hannah Miles

Trapier, Mrs Paul, 1758-1835. See Trapier, Elizabeth (Foissin)

Trapier, Mrs Paul, fl 1801. See Shubrick, Sarah Alicia

Trapier, Sarah Alicia (Shubrick) See Shubrick, Sarah Alicia

The trapped by K. L. Callahan

The trapper by C. Deas

The trapper by R. Kent

Trappers by A. J. Miller

Trappers by A. M. R. Moses

Trappers by W. T. Ranney

Trappers and Indians communicating by signs by A. J. Miller

Trappers at fault looking for the trail by A. F. Tait

Trapper's bride by A. J. Miller

Trappers' encampment on the Big Sandy river by A. J. Miller

Trappers' return by G. C. Bingham

Trappers starting for the beaver hunt by A. J. Miller

Trapping beaver by A. J. Miller

Travelers meeting Minnetaree Indians by K. Bodmer

Treadmill by P. Evergood

Treasure map by H. Bloom

Treasures from China by C. C. Ross

TREBILCOCK, Paul, 1902-
  Mrs James M. Bovard
    PPC. Ptg in the U.S. 1949

Trecothick, Grizzell (Apthorp) fl 1748
  Feke, R. Mrs Barlow Trecothick

Tree by A. Leepa

Tree by L. MacIver

Tree by C. Schucker

Tree and sea, Maine by J. Marin

Tree forms by J. Marin

Tree house by D. Lord

Tree of foreboding by W. R. Keefe

Tree planting by G. Wood

Tree tops and veiled moon by K. Schrag

Trees by M. Avery

Trees by C. H. Demuth

Trees by S. Laufman

Trees against the sky by K. Schrag

Trees and barns, Bermuda by C. H. Demuth

Trees and sinking sun by K. Schrag

Trees in winter by G. H. Hallowell

Trees, light and movement by K. Schrag

TREIMAN, Joyce Wahl, 1922-
  Absolom
    WMAA. Young America 1957
  Arguing angels
    IU. Contemp Amer ptg & sculp, 1961
  Cactus and sundry
    IU. Contemp Amer ptg, 1952

Escape   ICA
  CoS. New accessions USA, 1952
  Pousette-Dart. Amer ptg
The human fold—flowering
  IU. Contemp Amer ptg & sculp, 1957
Nisus and Scylla
  ICA. Annual ex, 1957
Porch no 2
  WMAA. Annual ex, 1958
The wanderers
  IU. Contemp Amer ptg, 1951 (col front)

Trelawny, Edward John, 1792-1881
  West, W. E. Trelawny

Tremont street, Boston by P. Hardy

Tremont street, Boston by M. B. Prendergast

TRENHOLM, Portia Ash, 1813-1892
  Legareville, South Carolina   VWR
    VWR. Folk art (col)

Trenton, Battle of, 1776
  Trumbull, J. Battle of Trenton
  Trumbull, J. George Washington at the Battle of Trenton

Trenton falls, New York by J. F. Kensett

Trenton, New Jersey. Commission chambers murals by E. Shinn

The trial by J. Levine

Trial of John Brown by H. Pippin

Trial scene by D. G. Blythe

Triatic by S. Davis

Tribute to the American working people by H. Sharrer

Trinity by D. Aronson

Trinity by C. Howard

Trio by K. Evett

Trio by W. Kuhn

Trio by B. Utter

Trio at the bar by L. B. Smith

Tripoli, Bombardment of by M. F. Corne

TRISCOTT, Samuel Peter Rolt, 1846-1925
  English cottage   MB
    MB. Ptgs in water color

Triumph by J. Hirsch

Triumphant child by W. Quirt

TRIVIGNO, Pat, 1922-
  Andante
    Pearson. Mod renaissance
  The captives
    CSFP. Annual ex, 1952
    IU. Contemp Amer ptg, 1950
    Pearson. Mod renaissance
  Gothic sentinels
    Pearson. Mod renaissance
  Iberia
    IU. Contemp Amer ptg & sculp, 1961

TRIVILINI, Armond
  White wall
    NAD. Special ex, 1956

Trodden weed by A. N. Wyeth

Trojan gates by H. Frankenthaler

Trojan horse by J. De Diego

Trojan horse by M. H. Visser't Hooft

Trolley cars
  Glackens, W. J. The green car
  Hewes, M. The outing
  Prestopino, G. Trolley car
  Schell, F. H. Trolley excursion

Trombone player by R. J. Lee

Troost, Benoist, fl 1859
  Bingham, G. C. Dr Benoist Troost
Tropes de teens by S. Davis

Tropical landscape by M. J. Heade

Tropical squall by M. O. Sheets

Tropical sunset by F. E. Church

Tropical surf, Florida by K. Matthew

Tropicalism by M. Tobey

TROTTER, McKie, 1918-
  Two cities
    NNSG. Younger Amer ptrs
TROTTER, Newbold Hough, 1827-1898
  Held up by buffalo   DNC
    Davidson v 1
    Rathbone
The **trotter** by Unidentified artist

Trouble by B. Shahn

Trouble hunters by C. M. Russell

Trouble in Frisco by F. Martin

Trout
  Graves, M. Trout in stream
  Homer, W. Leaping trout
Trout fishing by P. R. Goodwin

Trout fishing, Lake St John, Quebec by W.
  Homer
Trout pool by W. Whittredge

TROYE, Edward, 1808-1874
  Edward Troye and an unidentified boy
                                          CtY
    CtY. Portrait index
  Richard Singleton
    Richardson. Ptg in America
Truax, Susanna, fl 1730
  Unidentified artist. Susanna Truax
The **truck** by W. Pachner

Trumbull, Eunice (Backus) 1749-1826
  Trumbull, J. Jonathan Trumbull jr with
    Mrs Trumbull and Faith Trumbull
Trumbull, Faith, 1769-1846
  Trumbull, J. Jonathan Trumbull jr with
    Mrs Trumbull and Faith Trumbull
Trumbull, Faith (Robinson) 1718-1780
  Trumbull, J. Jonathan and Faith Robin-
    son Trumbull
Trumbull, John, 1750-1831
  Trumbull, J. John Trumbull, poet and
    cousin of the artist

TRUMBULL, John, 1756-1843
  Alexander Hamilton   DN
    DN. Mellon Coll
    UNESCO. Prior to 1860 5th ed
  Alexander Hamilton   MB
    MB. Great Americans
    Sizer. John Trumbull
  Alexander Hamilton   MSE
    Pierson
  Attack on Quebec   CtY
    Sizer. John Trumbull
  Battle of Bunker's Hill   CtY
    Barker. Amer ptg
    CtY. Portrait index
    Lee. Art then and now
    Mendelowitz
    Pierson
    Robb. Harper hist
    Roos
    Sizer. John Trumbull
    U.S. National Capital sesquicentennial
      com
    Walker. Ptgs from America

  Battle of Princeton. See Death of General
    Mercer at the Battle of Princeton
  Battle of Princeton (preliminary composi-
    tion)   CtY
    Flexner. Light of distant skies
  Capture of the Hessians at Trenton (Bat-
    tle of Trenton)   CtY
    CtY. Portrait index
    Sizer. John Trumbull
    Time. 300 years (col)
  Christopher Gore
    MB. New England miniatures
  Daniel Morgan   CtY
    CtY. Portrait index
  David Sproat   NNHS
    NNHS. Waldron Phoenix Belknap coll
  Death of General Mercer at the Battle of
    Princeton (Battle of Princeton) CtY
    CtY. Portrait index
    Flexner. Light of distant skies
    Roos
    Sizer. John Trumbull
  Death of General Montgomery at the
    siege of Quebec   CtY
    CtY. Portrait index
    Flexner. Amer ptg
    Flexner. Light of distant skies
    Flexner. Short history
    Larkin
    Larkin rev ed
    Pierson
  Declaration of Independence at Phila-
    delphia, July 4, 1776   CtHW
    CtHW. Handbook
  Declaration of Independence, July 4, 1776
                                          CtY
    CtY. Portrait index
    Flexner. Light of distant skies
    Pierson
    Sizer. John Trumbull
    Time. 300 years (col)
  Ebenezer Stevens   CtY
    CtY. Portrait index
  Eleanor Parke Custis
    CtHW. Trumbull
  Falls of Niagara taken from the road two
    miles below Chippawa. See Pan-
    oramas of Niagara Falls
  George Washington   MM
    CtHW. Trumbull
  George Washington at the Battle of
    Trenton   CtY
    CtY. Portrait index (col)
  George Washington, detail of head of
    Washington at the battle of Trenton
                                          CtY
    Sizer. John Trumbull
  George Washington (Martha Washing-
    ton type)   MNS
    Sizer. John Trumbull
  Giuseppe Ceracchi   MM
    Sizer. John Trumbull
  Goldsbrow Banyar   NNHS
    Vail. Stuyvesant ports
  Harriet Chew   CtY
    Sizer. John Trumbull
  Jabez Huntington
    CtHW. Trumbull
  Jabez Huntington   MB
    Sizer. John Trumbull
  James Codwise   NNHS
    NNHS. Waldron Phoenix Belknap coll

TRUMBULL, John—*Continued*
Jeremiah and his son Daniel Wadsworth
    CtHW
  Pierson
Jeremiah Wadsworth
  Sizer. John Trumbull
John Adams   CtY
  Sizer. John Trumbull
John C. Calhoun   CtY
  CtY. Portrait index
John M. Trumbull, nephew
  Sizer. John Trumbull
John Trumbull, poet and cousin of the
  artist   MiD
  MiD. Treasures
  Sizer. John Trumbull
John Vernet and his family   CtY
  Larkin
  Larkin rev ed
  Pierson
Jonathan and Faith Robinson Trumbull
  ICA. From colony to nation
Jonathan Trumbull   CtY
  CtY. Portrait Index
Jonathan Trumbull jr with Mrs Trum-
  bull and Faith Trumbull   CtY
  Barker. Amer ptg
  CtY. Portrait index
  Flexner. Light of distant skies
  Pierson
  Sizer. John Trumbull
Jonathan Trumbull sr   CtY
  Sizer. John Trumbull
Mrs Bartholomew Skaats (Schaets) IBM
  CtHW. Trumbull
Mrs James Codwise   NNHS
  NNHS. Waldron Phoenix Belknap coll
Mrs John Trumbull, wife of the artist
    CtY
  Sizer. John Trumbull
Mrs Robert Lenox   NNHS
  NNHS. Waldron Phoenix Belknap coll
Mrs Stephen Minot   MB
  CtHW. Trumbull
Mrs Thomas Sully   MAC
  Sizer. John Trumbull
Mrs Trumbull on her deathbed
  Sizer. John Trumbull
Oliver Ellsworth   CtY
  CtY. Portrait
Panoramas of Niagara Falls (Falls of
  Niagara taken from the road two
  miles below Chippawa)   NNHS
  Born
  Sizer. John Trumbull
Patrick Tracy
  Sizer. John Trumbull
Portrait of an artist, probably self-portrait
    CtHW
  CtHW. Trumbull
Priam returning the body of Hector MBA
  CtHW. Trumbull
Ralph Izard   CtY
  CtY. Portrait index
Resignation of General Washington at
  Annapolis   CtY
  CtY. Portrait index
  Sizer. John Trumbull
Robert Benson   NNHS
  Flexner. Light of distant skies
Robert Lenox   NNHS
  NNHS. Waldron Phoenix Belknap coll

Rufus Putnam   CtY
  CtY. Portrait index
Self-portrait at 18 years
  Sizer. John Trumbull
Self-portrait at 21 years   MB
  MB. Great Americans
  Sizer. John Trumbull
Self-portrait at about 56 years
  Sizer. John Trumbull
Signing the Declaration of Independence
    NNPL
  Ford. Edward Hicks
Sir John Temple   NCa
  Flexner. Light of distant skies
Sir John Temple and his family   CtY
  Sizer. John Trumbull
Sortie from Gibraltar   OCiM
  CtHW. Trumbull
  ICA. From colony to nation
  OCiM. Guide
  Pierson
  Sizer. John Trumbull
Sortie from Gibraltar   CtY
  CtY. Portrait index
Sortie of the British garrison from Gibral-
  tar   MBA
  Richardson. Ptg in America
Surrender of General Burgoyne at Sara-
  toga   CtY
  CtY. Portrait index
  Sizer. John Trumbull
Surrender of Lord Cornwallis at York-
  town   CtY
  CtY. Portrait index
  Sizer. John Trumbull
Surrender of Lord Cornwallis at Yorktown
    DCap
  Richardson. Ptg in America
Surrender of Lord Cornwallis at York-
  town (Aiken coll)
  U.S. National Capital sesquicentennial
  com
Thomas Jefferson, detail from the Declara-
  tion of Independence   CtY
  Sizer. John Trumbull
Thomas Youngs Seymour   CtY
  Sizer. John Turnbull
Timothy Dwight   CtY
  CtY. Portrait index
View of Niagara from upper bank on
  British side   CtHW
  CtHW. Handbook
  CtHW. Trumbull
  Pierson
William Cochran
  CtHW. Trumbull

Portrait of the artist
Twibill, G. W. Col John Trumbull
Waldo, S. L. and Jewett, W. John Trum-
  bull

Trumbull, Mrs John. See Trumbull, Sarah
  Hope (Harvey)
Trumbull, John M. 1784-1859
  Trumbull, J. John M. Trumbull, nephew
Trumbull, Jonathan, 1710-1785
  Trumbull, J. Jonathan and Faith Robin-
  son Trumbull
  Trumbull, J. Jonathan Trumbull
Trumbull, Mrs Jonathan, 1718-1780. See
  Trumbull, Faith (Robinson)
Trumbull, Jonathan, 1740=1809
  Trumbull, J. Jonathan Trumbull jr with
  Mrs Trumbull and Faith Trumbull

Trumbull, Mrs Jonathan, 1749-1826. See Trumbull, Eunice (Backus)
Trumbull, Sarah Hope (Harvey) 1771-1824
  Trumbull, J. Mrs John Trumbull, wife of the artist
  Trumbull, J. Mrs Trumbull on her deathbed
The trumpeter by S. R. Van H. Stuyvesant
Trumpeter in the village by L. Feininger
Trumpeter swan by J. J. Audubon
Trusler, Mary, c 1723-1789
  Theus, J. Mary Trusler
Trussed sheep by A. Blaustein
Truth is upward by J. Carroll
TRYON, Dwight William, 1849-1925
  Springtime   DF
    Time. 300 years (col)
TSCHACBASOV, Nahum, 1899-
  The clown
    Genauer
    IU. Contemp Amer ptg, 1949
    Roos
  Family with flowers   OYB
    OYB. Supplement
  Flower still life
    IU. Contemp Amer ptg & sculp, 1955
  I, my own keeper
    IU. Contemp Amer ptg & sculp, 1957
  Lady with fan   OYB
    OYB. Catalogue 1951
  The monkey
    IU. Contemp Amer ptg, 1948
  The offering
    NAD. Annual ex, 1948
  Profiles no 8
    IU. Contemp Amer ptg & sculp, 1953
  Substance and sustenance
    IU. Contemp Amer ptg, 1950
TSENG Yu-ho, 1923-
  Aquarelle: collage
    IU. Contemp Amer ptg & sculp, 1959
  Strings of amber
    IU. Contemp Amer ptg & sculp, 1961
Tuberoses by C. H. Demuth
TUCKER, Allen, 1866-1939
  Washington crossing the Delaware
                                                WMAA
    Pierson
TUCKER, Joshua, b 1800
  South east view of Greenville, South Carolina
                                                VWR
    VWR. Folk art (col)
Tuckerman, Elizabeth. See Salisbury, Elizabeth (Tuckerman)
Tudor, Emma Jane. See Gardiner, Emma Jane (Tudor)
Tug by L. Feininger
Tugboat O. M. Pettit by J. Bard
Tuileries gardens by M. B. Prendergast
Tulip buds by W. Kuhn
Tulips by M. Beckmann
Tulips by A. Dasburg
Tulips by S. Greene
Tulips in a white pitcher by E. E. Speicher
Tully, William, 1785-1859
  Ames, E. William Tully
Tumbling waters by S. Nichols
Tundo no 21 by F. Glarner

Tundra by M. Tobey
Tunk mountains, autumn, Maine by J. Marin
Turbulent forest by C. A. Morris
Turell, Ebenezer, 1701?-1778
  Smibert, J. Rev Ebenezer Turell
Turf house on the plains by C. Wimar
Turkey by A. B. Carles
Turkey buzzards
  Audubon, J. J. Turkey buzzard
  Wyeth, A. Soaring
Turkey shoot by J. W. Ehninger
Turkey shoot by T. H. Matteson
Turkeys
  Audubon, J. J. Wild turkey
  Moses, A. M. R. Catching the Thanksgiving turkey
Turkish page by W. M. Chase
Turkish page by F. Duveneck
TURMAN, William T. b 1867
  Gravel pit   InTH
    InTH. Catalogue
TURNBULL, James Baare, 1909-
  Son of a sharecropper   ATU
    ATU. Coll of Amer art
Turner, John B.
  Wood, G. John B. Turner, pioneer
TURNER, Ross Sterling, 1847-1915
  Dawn   MB
    MB. Ptgs in water color
  A garden is a sea of flowers   MB
    MB. Ptgs in water color
Turner alley studio by G. Wood
Turning the stake boat by T. Eakins
The turnkey by J. Levine
Turreted pitcher by W. Sommer
Turtle creek valley by J. Kane
Turtles
  Homer, W. The turtle pound
  Homer, W. Rum cay
Tuscany by E. C. Clark
TUTHILL, Abraham G. D. 1776?-1843
  Alida Livingston Woolsey
    Frankenstein. Two journeyman ptrs
  Anna Miretta Vail
    Frankenstein. Two journeyman ptrs
  Benjamin West
    Frankenstein. Two journeyman ptrs
  Ezekiel Walton
    Frankenstein. Two journeyman ptrs
  George Larned
    Frankenstein. Two journeyman ptrs
  Hezekiah Hutchins Reed
    Frankenstein. Two journeyman ptrs
  Hiram Pratt
    Frankenstein. Two journeyman ptrs
  Jackson, Solon, Mary Elizabeth and Anna Miretta Vail
    Frankenstein. Two journeyman ptrs
  Lewis Cass
    Frankenstein. Two journeyman ptrs
  Melancthon Taylor Woolsey
    Frankenstein. Two journeyman ptrs
  Mary Elizabeth Vail
    Frankenstein. Two journeyman ptrs
  Mrs Ezekiel Walton
    Frankenstein. Two journeyman ptrs
  Mrs Melancthon Taylor Woolsey
    Frankenstein. Two journeyman ptrs
  Mrs Nathaniel Platt
    Frankenstein. Two journeyman ptrs

TUTHILL, A. G. D.—*Continued*
  Self-portrait
    Frankenstein. Two journeyman ptrs
  Sylvester, Julia, Jane and Catherine
    Larned
    Frankenstein. Two journeyman ptrs
  Thomas Reed
    Frankenstein. Two journeyman ptrs
  Thomas Vail (?)
    Frankenstein. Two journeyman ptrs
Tuttle, Esther, fl 1835
  Davis, J. H. Esther Tuttle
Tuttle, Henry Emerson, 1890-
  Speicher, E. E. Henry Emerson Tuttle
Tuttle, James, fl 1836
  Davis, J. H. James and Sarah Tuttle
Tuttle, Mrs James. See Tuttle, Sarah
Tuttle, Sarah, fl 1836
  Davis, J. H. James and Sarah Tuttle
  Davis, J. H. (attributed works) Mrs
    Tuttle
TWACHTMAN, John Henry, 1853-1902
  Blue brook water fall   OCiM
  Born
  Coast scene   PR
    PR. Catalogue
  Emerald pool   DP
    DP. Catalogue
  End of winter   DNC
    Cheney. Story 1958 ed
  Summer day   InIJ
    InIJ. 105 ptgs
  Footbridge at Bridgeport   MdH
    MdH. Catalogue 1940
  From the upper terrace   ICA
    Cheney. Story 1958 ed
  Hemlock pool   MAP
    Pierson
    Robb. Harper history
  Holly house, Cos Cob, Connecticut
                                     MWiC
    Pierson
  Horseneck brook, winter
    PPC. Amer classics
  Landscape   WMAA
  Born
  March woodlands   MoSL
    MoSL. Handbook 1953
  Rapids, Yellowstone park   MWM
    Cheney. Story 1958 ed
  Reflections   NBM
    Baur. Revolution
    McCurdy
  Sailing in the mist   PA
    Pierson
    Richardson. Ptg in America
  Snowbound   ICA
    Larkin
    Larkin rev ed
    Pierson
  Snow scene   DNC
    DNC. Gellatly coll, 1954
  Summer   DP
    DP. Catalogue
    Pierson
  Three trees   NBM
    Mendelowitz
  Venice   NB
    CSB. Impressionism
  The waterfall   MM
    MM. 100 Amer ptrs
  Wild cherry tree   NBuA
    NBuA. Catalogue of the ptgs

Twain, Mark. See Clemens, Samuel
    Langhorne
TWARDOWICZ, Stanley John, 1917-
  Lobster traps
    IU. Contemp Amer ptg, 1948
  Number 38, 1957-58
    IU. Contemp Amer ptg & sculp, 1959
  White on blue
    NNSG. Younger Amer ptrs
Tweedy, Miss, fl 1840
  Unidentified artist. Miss Tweedy of
    Brooklyn
Twentieth century baroque by R. O.
    Preusser
Twenty-cent movie by R. Marsh
27 December 1959 by C. di Marca-Relli
23 September, 1959 by C. di Marca-Relli
Twenty-two houses and a church by Un-
    identified artist
TWIBILL, George W. c 1806-1836
  John Trumbull
    Cowdrey v 1
Twilight by R. A. Blakelock
Twilight head by P. Tchelitchew
Twilight landscape by P. Evergood
Twilight travelling by A. B. Davies
Twin heads by A. H. Maurer
Twin pine by W. A. Kienbusch
Twin sisters by Unidentified artist
Two by D. Hare
Two by J. Pollock
Two acrobats by C. H. Demuth
Two armies before a city by Unidentified
    artist
Two bathers by L. M. Eilshemius
Two bathers by B. Karfiol
Two birds by C. S. Price
Two boats by W. Homer
Two bridges by N. Spencer
Two brown and white puppies by Unidenti-
    fied artist
Two circles by A. Liberman
Two cities by M. Trotter
Two citizens engaged in a conversation by
    G. C. Bingham
Two classical studies by H. Warshaw
Two-figure composition by W. W. Quirt
Two figures by B. Browne
Two figures by J. Glasco
Two figures and easel by B. W. Tomlin
Two figures at a desk by M. Avery
Two fishermen by K. Knaths
Two flags by J. Johns
Two girls by I. Bishop
Two girls by A. H. Maurer
Two girls in New England woodland by
    M. B. Prendergast
Two girls sewing by G. Stuart
Two grouse in underbrush of laurel by
    Rubens Peale
Two guides by W. Homer
Two heads by B. Greene
Two heads by A. H. Maurer
Two heads by C. S. Price

Two houses by W. Stuempfig
Two little girls in blue by Unidentified artist
Two-master becalmed, Maine by J. Marin
Two men by E. Johnson
Two musicians by S. M. Grode
Two musicians by M. Weber
Two Negroes by G. Biddle
Two nudes by E. Cortor
Two nudes by R. Diebenkorn
Two nudes before Japanese screen by H. Katzman
Two on the aisle by E. Hopper
Two sides of red by D. Von Schlegell
Two sisters by R. Beauchamp
Two sisters by A. H. Maurer
Two sisters by R. Soyer
Two standing figures by B. Karfiol
Two standing women by W. De Kooning
Two trout by W. Homer
Two trout fishermen by P. S. Sample
Two tugs by C. Rosen
Two up by I. R. Pereira
Two ventilators by A. Osver
Two witnesses by B. Shahn
Two women by M. Beckmann
Two women by W. De Kooning
Two women by B. Greene
Two women by S. Macdonald-Wright
Two women by E. G. H Pinney
Two women by W. W. Quirt
Two women in front of a mirror by M. Hirshfield
Two women on a wharf by W. De Kooning
Two women with still life by W. De Kooning
Two women's torsos by W. De Kooning
Two worlds by S. Francis
Two yellow horses by W. Sommer
Two young ladies by A. M. Von Phul
TWORKOV, Jack, 1900-
 Blue cradle
  MMA. New Amer ptg
 Cradle
  MMA. New Amer ptg
 Crest
  MnMW. 60 Amer ptrs
 Duo I, 1956   WMAA
  Goodrich. Amer art
 East barrier   NBuA
  NBuA. Acquisitions 1959-1961
 Flowering white
  Hess. Abstract ptg
 Green landscape   MbBM
  CoS. New accessions USA, 1954
  Hess. Abstract ptg
 Nausicaa
  PPC. International ex, 1952
 Pink Mississippi
  Art since 1945 (col)
  Hunter. Mod Amer ptg (col)
  Read. Concise ptg
 Redlake
  PPC. International ex, 1958
 Ridgeway
  IU. Contemp Amer ptg & sculp, 1961

Sirens in voice
 Pousette-Dart. Amer ptg
Transverse
 MMA. New Amer ptg (col)
Watergame
 Cheney. Story 1958 ed
The wheel   MMA
 Pierson
Tyler, Alice, fl 1842
 Healy, G. P. A. Alice Tyler
Tyler, John, president U.S. 1790-1862
 Healy, G. P. A. John Tyler
 Jarvis, J. W. John Tyler
Tyler, Mary Brown
 Bellows, G. W. Mrs T in cream silk
 Bellows, G. W. Mrs T in wine silk
Tynemouth sands by W. Homer
Tyng, Ann. See Smelt, Ann (Tyng)
Tyng, Elizabeth (Ross) 1751-1831
 Copley, J. S. Elizabeth Ross
Tyrol at Kufstein, Tyrol series, no 3 by J. Marin
Tyrolean mountains by J. Marin
Tyrolese crucifixion by J. S. Sargent

U

U. N. Conference room 3, 1956, Study for by S. Davis
U.S. mail boat by L. T. Bauman
U.S.S. Pensacola, 1946 by R. Crawford
Ud-je-jock, the Pelican by G. Catlin
UHLE, Bernard, b 1847
 An election day bonfire, Fifth and Chestnut streets, Philadelphia
  U. S. National Capital sesquicentennial com
ULBRICHT, John, 1926-
 La Veronica   CoD
 CoS. New accessions USA, 1954
ULLRICH, Beatrice, 1907-
 Remembrance of things past   ATU
 ATU. Coll of Amer art
Ulreich, Mrs Eduard Buk. See Nura
Ulreich, Nura (Woodson) See Nura
ULRICH, Charles Frederic, 1858-1908
 In the land of promise: Castle garden DC
 Davidson v2
  U. S. National Capital sesquicentennial com
The ultimate city by F. E. Warren
Ultra-marine by S. Davis
Ulysses by B. Newman
Umbrellas and parasols
 Prendergast, M. B. Dieppe
 Prendergast, M. B. Umbrellas in the rain, Venice
Umpferstedt by L. Feininger
Una and the lion by B. West
The unattainable by A. Gorky
Uncle Tom by H. Pippin
Uncle Tom and Little Eva by R. S. Duncanson
Uncompleted bridge by J. Ross
The undefeated by F. Martin

Under a cloud by A. P. Ryder
Under Cliff by T. Chambers
Under sea by E. Loran
Under the coco palm by W. Homer
Under the el by J. Levine
Under the falls, grand discharge by W. Homer
Under the greenwood by G. Inness
Under the horse-chestnut tree by M. Cassatt
Under the pier by L. Siegriest
Under the river by A. Pickens
Underpass by B. P. Arnest
Underpass by P. Blume
Underpass by S. Davis
Undersea mountain by E. Stasack
Undertow by W. Homer
Undulating arrangement by I. R. Pereira
Undulating fence by D. Macknight
Undulating landscape by F. Ruvolo
Unemployable by A. Friedman
Unexpected encounter by J. De Diego
Unformed figure by J. Pollock
Unicorns by A. B. Davies
Unicorns came down to the sea by K. Sage
UNIDENTIFIED artist
    See also Border limner; Freake limner; Gansevoort limner; Mason limner; Pierpont limner; Pollard limner
Abigail Hall
    MB. New England miniatures
Abraham and Isaac Pierson
Abraham Clark and his children   DN
    DN. Amer primitive ptgs pt 1
Abraham Van Cortlandt
    Belknap
Abram Gouverneur
    Belknap
Adam and Eve   DN
    DN. Amer primitive ptgs, pt 1
Adam Winne   DeWin
    Belknap
Adams family   VWR
    VWR. Folk art (col)
Adeline Harwood   DN
    DN. Amer primitive ptgs, pt 1
Adolphus Philipse   NNMC
    Belknap
Adoration of the Magi   NAI
    NAI. Hudson valley
Albert Crary
    Ford. Pictorial folk art
Allegory of freedom   DN
    DN. Amer primitive ptgs, pt 1
The all-seeing eye   CtHW
    Frankenstein. After the hunt
Alvah Cook   DN
    DN. Amer primitive ptgs, pt 1
American harvest (probably copy after Cropsey)
    Ford. Pictorial folk art
American madonna and child   NCHA
    Jones. New-found folk art
Angeline Eliza Shepard and her brother, Elisha Henry Shepard   CtHW
    CtHW. Handbook

Anna Cruger   NNMC
    Belknap
Anna Wendell Cuyler   NAI
    Jones. Rediscovered ptrs
Annie Robinson   DN
    DN. Amer primitive ptgs
Anthony Duane   NNHS
    NNHS. Waldron Phoenix Belknap coll
Anthony Rutgers
    Belknap
Anthony Van Schaick (formerly known as Sybrant Gozen Van Schaick)   NAI
    Belknap
    Jones. Rediscovered ptrs
    NAI. Hudson valley (as by Schuyler painter)
Aphia Salisbury Rich and baby Edward   DN
    DN. Amer primitive ptgs, pt 1
Apple gatherers   VWR
    Ford. Pictorial folk art
Ariaantje Coeymans. See Mrs David Verplanck
Ariaantje Schuyler Van Rensselaer   NAI
    Belknap
    NAI. Hudson Valley
Asahel Pomeroy
    ICA. From colony to nation
Attack of the rebel ram Manassas on the U.S.S. Pensacola, 1862   MeC
    Jetté. Amer heritage collection
Augusta, Maine, c 1825   MeC
    Jetté. Amer heritage collection
Augustus Cornelius Van Horne   NNHS
    Vail. Stuyvesant ports
Augustus Jay   NNHS
    Belknap
Aurora   DN
    DN. Amer primitive ptgs, pt 2
Baby in blue cradle   DN
    DN. Amer primitive ptgs, pt 2
Baby in pink and white   DN
    DN. Amer primitive ptgs, pt 1
Baby in red chair   VWR
    Lee. Art then and now
    Roos
    VWR. Amer folk art (col)
    VWR. Folk art (col)
    Walker. Ptgs from America
Baby reclining   DN
    DN. Amer primitive ptgs, pt 2
Baby with fruit   NCHA
    Jones. New-found folk art
Barbara Dean
    NYG. Fine art p20
Barclay children
    Belknap
Barent Rynders   NNHS
    Belknap
Barent Sports of Albany
    Belknap
Barn Bluff, Red Wing, Minnesota   NCHA
    Jones. New-found folk art
Basket of flowers   VWR
    VWR. Folk art (col)
Battle of White Oak swamp, Virginia 1862   NCHA
    Jones. New-found folk art
Beacon-on-the-Hudson
    Sears. Highlights
The Belle Creole at New Orleans
    U.S. National Capital sesquicentennial com

Belshazzar's feast NAI
NAI. Hudson valley
Benjamin Smith DN
DN. Amer primitive ptgs, pt 2
Bethlehem, Pennsylvania
Davidson v 1
Blue eyes DN
DN. Amer primitive ptgs, pt 1
Time. 300 years (col)
The bountiful board VWR
VWR. Folk art (col)
Bowl of fruit DN
DN. Amer primitive ptgs, pt 1
Ford. Pictorial folk art
Bowl of fruit (Halladay-Thomas coll)
Ford. Pictorial folk art
Boy and girl DN
DN. Amer primitive ptgs, pt 1
Boy and girl with dog MeC
Jetté. Amer heritage collection
Boy in blue coat DN
DN. Amer primitive ptgs, pt 2
Boy in plaid VWR
VWR. Folk art (col)
Boy of the De Peyster family NNHS
Belknap
Boy of the Hallett family ICA
Belknap
Boy with a toy drum NNHS
Ford. Pictorial folk art
Boy with finch VWR
Ford. Pictorial folk art
VWR. Folk art (col)
Boy with hammer and iron pot NCHA
Jones. New-found folk art
Boy with whip MeC
Jetté. Amer heritage collection
British privateers with French prizes in
New York harbor NNHS
Flexner. First flowers (col)
Brother and sister DN
DN. Amer primitive ptgs, pt 1
Buffalo hunter CSB
Baur. Amer ptg
Walker. Ptgs from America
Burning of Charles Town DN
DN. Amer primitive ptgs, pt 1
Burning of Old South church, Bath,
Maine DN
DN. Amer primitive ptgs, pt 2
Burning of the Tombs, New York
city NNMC
Ford. Pictorial folk art
By the fireside MMA
Lee. Art then and now
Cadwallader Colden family
Ford. Pictorial folk art
Caleb Heathcote NNHS
Larkin
Larkin rev ed
Caleb Kempton
Ford. Pictorial folk art
Camp Butler, Maryland, 1861 MB
MB. Karolik coll
Captain Carnes of Salem MSP
Davidson v 1
Captain Farnham of Farnham, Maine
MeC
Jetté Amer heritage collection
Captain George, Haverhill, Massachu-
setts NJP
NJP. Amer folk art

The cat DN
DN. Amer primitive ptgs, pt 1
Cat and kittens DN
DN. Amer primitive ptgs, pt 2
Catalina Schuyler NNHS
Belknap
Catalynje Post DN
Belknap
DN. Amer primitive ptgs, pt 1
Ford. Pictorial folk art
Catharina Schuyler DeWin
Belknap
Catharine Hendrickson DN
DN. Amer primitive ptgs, pt 1
Caught in the act
Ford. Pictorial folk art
Ceremonies at a young ladies' seminary,
1810-20
Davidson v2
Charlotte Marsteller DC
DC. Masterpieces
Cheese factory MeC
Jetté. Amer heritage collection
Cheney family DN
DN. Amer primitive ptgs, pt 2
Child and doll
Ford. Pictorial folk art
Child holding eyeglasses NCHA
Jones. New-found folk art
Child in blue
Belknap
Child in blue dress NJN
Ford. Pictorial folk art
Child in red dress
Ford. Pictorial folk art
Child with dog VWR
VWR. Folk art (col)
Child with rocking horse DN
DN. Amer primitive ptgs, pt 2
Child with wheelbarrow MeC
Jetté. Amer heritage collection
Children of Jacob Franks (1)
NNHS. Waldron Phoenix Belknap coll
Children of Jacob Franks (2)
NNHS. Waldron Phoenix Belknap coll
Christ and the woman of Samaria VWR
VWR. Folk art (col)
Christ at Emmaus NAI
Flexner. First flowers
Jones. Rediscovered ptrs
NAI. Hudson valley
Christ on the road to Emmaus, versions
I and II NAI
NAI. Hudson valley
Christina Ten Broek NAI
Belknap
Christmas party MB
MB. Karolik coll
A city of fantasy DN
DN. Amer primitive ptgs, pt 2
Civil war battle scene DN
DN. Amer primitive ptgs, pt 2
Civil war—Symbolic panorama NCHA
Jones. New-found folk art
The cock NCHA
Jones. New-found folk art
Columbia DN
DN. Amer primitive ptgs, pt 1
Coming storm
Sears. Highlights
Composite harbor scene with volcano DN
DN. Amer primitive ptgs, pt 1

UNIDENTIFIED artist—*Continued*
Contemplation VWR
 VWR. Folk art (col)
Coon hunt DN
 DN. Amer primitive ptgs, pt 1
The courtship MeC
 Jetté. Amer heritage collection
Creation scene
 Ford. Edward Hicks
Creole child
 Ford. Pictorial folk art
Crowning of King Jereboam NAI
 NAI. Hudson valley
Crow's nest from Bull hill. Hudson river
 looking toward West Point NCHA
Crucifixion MM
 Jones. New-found folk art
 Flexner. Light of distant skies
 Mendelowitz
Curls and scallops NCHA
 Jones. New-found folk art
Curse of gold
 Ford. Pictorial folk art
The dandy VWR
 VWR. Folk art (col)
Daniel LeRoy NNHS
 Vail. Stuyvesant ports
Daniel Russell
 Flexner. First flowers
Daniel Webster at his farm MB
 MB. Great Americans
 MB. Karolik coll
David Alling house and shop, Newark
 NJN
 Ford. Pictorial folk art
David Davidse Schuyler NAI
 Belknap
 NAI. Hudson valley
David, Joanna and Abigail Mason
 Pierson
David Porter MB
 MB. Great American
 MB. Karolik coll
David Provoost (?) NNHS
 Belknap
Deer hunt DN
 DN. Amer primitive ptgs, pt 1
Dennison hill, Southbridge, Massachusetts
 DN
 DN. Amer primitive ptgs, pt 2
De Peyster boy with deer NNHS
 Belknap
 Flexner. Amer ptg
 Flexner. First Flowers (col)
 Flexner. Short history
De Peyster girl with lamb (Margaret or
 Catherine) NNHS
 Belknap
 Flexner. First flowers
The domino girl DN
 DN. Amer primitive ptgs, pt 2
Dover baby NJN
 Ford. Pictorial folk art
Eagle and snake
 Ford. Pictorial folk art
Easton, Pennsylvania
 McClintock
Edward Brodnax VR
 Belknap
Edward Jaquelin II as a child
 Barker. Amer ptg
 Pierson

Edward Payson Crowell MSE
 MSE. Cat of ports, 1950
Egg salad MB
 MB. Karolik coll
Elizabeth Eggington CtHW
 CtHW. Handbook
 Pierson
Elizabeth Paddy Wensley
 Flexner. First flowers
 Pierson
Elizabeth Fenimore Cooper
 Ford. Pictorial folk art
 Time. 300 years (col)
Emblem of peace
 Ford. Pictorial folk art
End of the hunt (End of the fox hunt)
 DN
 Davidson v 1
 DN. Amer primitive ptgs, pt 1
 Flexner. First flowers
Enigmatic foursome NCHA
 Jones. New-found folk art
Eva and Catherina De Peyster
 Belknap
 Flexner. First flowers
Family burying ground DN
 DN. Amer primitive ptgs, pt 2
Fancy picture: fishing with waterfall MeC
 Jetté. Amer heritage collection
Farm scene ICA
 Ford. Pictorial folk art
Farmhouse in Mahantango valley DN
 DN. Amer primitive ptgs, pt 2
Fashionable inn, New York, c 1825 MoKN
 Ford. Pictorial folk art
Father and son
 Ford. Pictorial folk art
Finding of Moses NAI
 NAI. Hudson valley
Fire of the warehouse of Henry Webb
 and company, Baltimore, 1827 MdBH
 Davidson v2
The fish is on the other side
 Frankenstein. After the hunt
Five children of the Budd family DN
 DN. Amer primitive ptgs, pt 2
Five Points, New York, c 1829
 Davidson v2
Flag carried at the siege of Louisburg,
 1745 NNHS
 Flexner. First flowers
Flight into Egypt NAI
 Jones. Rediscovered ptrs
 NAI. Hudson valley
Flowers & fruit DN
 Brussels. Exposition
 DN. Amer primitive ptgs, pt 1
Flowers, butterfly, and book MB
 MB. Karolik coll
Fort Snelling, c 1838 (also attributed to
 Eastman) MnMI
 Davidson v 1
The four apostles writing the Gospels
 NAI
 NAI. Hudson valley
Fourth Pennsylvania cavalry, 1861 DN
 DN. Amer primitive ptgs, pt 2
Frances Parke Custis VLW
 Belknap
Fruit and flowers DN
 DN. Amer primitive ptgs, pt 1
Fruit and melon VWR
 VWR. Folk art (col)

Fruit in bowl   MeC
  Jetté. Amer heritage collection
Furniture shop and warehouse of Duncan
  Phyfe, Fulton street, New York   MM
  Davidson v 1
General Putnam's leap   NCHA
  Larkin
  Larkin rev ed
  Time. 300 years (col)
Gentleman farmer   VWR
  VWR. Folk art (col)
Gentleman from Montague, Massachu-
  setts   MeC
  Jetté. Amer heritage collection
Gentleman of the Beekman family (Wil-
  liam Beekman?)
  Belknap
Gentleman of the Hallett family (probably
  Joseph Hallett)   NNHS
  NNHS. Waldron Phoenix Belknap coll
Gentleman of the Schuyler family   NAI
  Belknap
George and Jane Bigelow
  Larkin
George Curwin   MSE
  Belknap
George Phillips   NNHS
  Belknap
  NNHS. Waldron Phoenix Belknap coll
George Washington family
  Kallir. Amer primitive ptgs
George Washington on white charger DN
  DN. Amer primitive ptgs, pt 1
George Washington, the Mason   DN
  DN. Amer primitive ptgs, pt 1
George Washington with horse   MeC
  Jetté. Amer heritage collection
Gerard De Peyster   NNHS
  Belknap
  NNHS. Waldron Phoenix Belknap coll
Gerard Stuyvesant family group   NNHS
  Vail. Stuyvesant ports
Gerrit Teunise Van Vechten (formerly
  known as Gerardus Beekman) NAI
  NAI. Hudson valley
Girl by the waterfall   VWR
  VWR. Folk art (col)
Girl in black pinafore   VWR
  VWR. Folk art (col)
Girl in blue
  Ford. Pictorial folk art
Girl in garden   VWR
  VWR. Folk art (col)
Girl in green   VWR
  Ford. Pictorial folk art
  VWR. Folk art (col)
Girl in red   MB
  MB. Karolik coll
Girl in ruffled collar   VWR
  VWR. Folk art (col)
Girl of the Ten Eyck family   NAI
  NAI. Hudson valley
Girl of the Van Rensselaer family
  Flexner. First flowers
Girl on balcony   VWR
  VWR. Folk art (col)
Girl with a gray cat   MB
  MB. Karolik coll
Girl with hoop   VWR
  VWR. Folk art (col)
Girl with the red shoes. See Magdalena
  Douw

Good Samaritan I, II, III, IV, V, VI
                                          VWR
  VWR. Folk art (col)
Governess and children   VWR
  Ford. Pictorial folk art
Gracie Beardsley Jefferson Jackman and
  her daughter   DN
  DN. Amer primitive ptgs, pt 2
Grapevine   VWR
  VWR. Folk art (col)
Gurdon Saltonstall   CtY
  CtY. Portrait index
Die gute mutter   MeC
  Jetté. Amer heritage collection
Hannah Alden   MeC
  Jetté. Amer heritage collection
Harlan Page   DN
  DN. Amer primitive ptgs, pt 1
Harmanus Wendell   NNMC
  Belknap
Harmony Child Wight
  Ford. Pictorial folk art
Haymakers   VWR
  Ford. Pictorial folk art
Headless horseman
  Ford. Pictorial folk art
Hendrick Remsen   NNHS
  NNHS. Waldron Phoenix Belknap coll
Henrietta Dorr, Chatham Center, New
  York   NJP
  NJP. Amer folk art
Henrietta Frances Cuthbert   VWR
  VWR. Folk art (col)
Henry A. Morehouse   VWR
  VWR. Folk art (col)
Henry Beekman
  Belknap
Henry Gibbs
  Larkin
Henry Wells   DN
  DN. Amer primitive ptgs, pt 1
High bridge across the Harlem river,
  c 1840   NNHS
  Davidson v2
High water in the bayou country   MoSL
  Rathbone
Hobby horse   DN
  DN. Amer primitive ptgs, pt 1
Home on the Mississippi, c 1850
  Davidson v 1
Horace Tuttle's livery stable   NCHA
  Jones. New-found folk art
Horses in a stream
  Sears. Highlights
Hudson river landscape   MeC
  Jetté. Amer heritage collection
Hudson river landscape with sailboats
                                          RPS
  Born
Hudson river scene   MMA
  Ford. Pictorial folk art
Hudson river view c 1800
  Ford. Pictorial folk art
Hunter family of Germantown, Pennsyl-
  vania   MeC
  Jetté. Amer heritage collection
Hunting scene   MM
  Ford. Pictorial folk art
In the heart of New Hampshire
  Sears. Highlights
Indian chief   DN
  DN. Amer primitive ptgs, pt 1

UNIDENTIFIED artist—*Continued*
Indian encampment   DN
  DN. Amer primitive ptgs, pt 2
Indian Treaty of Greenville, 1795 (Signing
  the Treaty of Greenville)   ICH
  Davidson v 1
  U. S. National Capital sesquicentennial
  com
Innocence   DN
  DN. Amer primitive ptgs, pt 1
Interior of a butcher shop, c 1840   NJN
  Davidson v2
The ironers   NCHA
  Jones. New-found folk art
Isaac blessing Jacob, versions I and II
                                                  NAI
  NAI. Hudson valley
Isaac De Peyster
  Belknap
Israel Munson   CtY
  CtY. Portrait index
J. B. Sheldon   DN
  DN. Amer primitive ptgs, pt 1
  Ford. Pictorial folk art
Jacob Franks
  Belknap
Jacob Myers
  Ford. Pictorial folk art
Jacob Von Kline   DN
  DN. Amer primitive ptgs, pt 2
Jacobus Stoutenburg   NNMC
  Belknap
  Flexner. First flowers
James A. De Peyster (?)   NNHS
  Pierson
James Lenox   NNHS
  NNSH. Waldron Phoenix Belknap coll
James Pierpont   CtY
  Larkin rev ed
Jane Goelet   NAI
  Belknap
  NAI. Hudson valley
Jean Macdonald Lee Myers   VWR
  VWR. Folk art (col)
Jeremias Van Rensselaer   NAI
  Belknap
Johannes De Peyster III   NNHS
  Belknap
  NNHS. Waldron Phoenix Belknap coll
Johannes Rose
  Belknap
Johannes Schuyler   NNHS
  Belknap
Johannes Wendell   NAI
  Belknap
  NAI. Hudson valley
John Cruger   NNMC
  Belknap
John Fitch
  Belknap
John Mix   VWR
  VWR. Folk art (col)
John Perrin   MSt
  Little. Country art
John Sanders
  Belknap
John Van Cortlandt   NBM
  Belknap
  NNHS. Waldron Phoenix Belknap coll
  Pierson
John Whorf with bow and arrow   NCHA
  Jones. New-found folk art

Jonathan Benham   DN
  DN. Amer primitive ptgs, pt 2
Joseph and Anna Raymond   DN
  DN. Amer primitive ptgs, pt 2
Joseph and his brethren   VWR
  VWR. Folk art (col)
Joseph interpreting Pharaoh's dream
                                                  MMA
  Ford. Pictorial folk art
Joseph interpreting Pharaoh's dreams
                                                  VWR
  VWR. Folk art (col)
Judd's hotel, Philadelphia, c 1825   DN
  DN. Amer primitive ptgs, pt 2
Judd's house, Southold, Long Island   MB
  MB. Karolik coll
Lady Berkeley
  Belknap
Lady from Hornell   MiD
  Jones. Rediscovered ptrs
Lady from Montague, Massachusetts MeC
  Jetté. Amer heritage collection
Lady in a white dress   MeC
  Jetté. Amer heritage collection
Lady in blue   VWR
  VWR. Folk art (col)
Lady in red   DN
  DN. Amer primitive ptgs, pt 1
Lady in white   DN
  DN. Amer primitive ptgs, pt 2
Lady in white bonnet   NCHA
  Jones. New-found folk art
Lady of the Beekman family (Mrs Wil-
  liam Beekman?)
  Belknap
Lady of the Hallett family (probably Mrs
  Joseph Hallett)   NNHS
  NNHS. Waldron Phoenix Belknap coll
Lady of the lake   VWR
  Ford. Pictorial folk art
Lady of the Van Rensselaer family
  NNHS. Waldron Phoenix Belknap coll
Lady Suffolk [a horse]   MeC
  Jetté. Amer heritage collection
Lady with a rose   MeC
  Jetté. Amer heritage collection
Lady with brown eyes   DN
  DN. Amer primitive ptgs, pt 2
Lady with curls   MeC
  Jetté. Amer heritage collection
Lady with lavender ribbons   VWR
  VWR. Folk art (col)
Lady with plumed headdress   DN
  DN. Amer primitive ptgs, pt 2
Land and seawater scape   MeC
  Jetté. Amer heritage collection
Landscape with figures   VWR
  VWR. Folk art (col)
Lavinia Van Vechten   NBM
  Belknap
Leaving the manor house   DN
  DN. Amer primitive ptgs, pt 2
Le Roy, New York   MeC
  Jetté. Amer heritage collection
Letter of marque ship Bethel of Boston
                                                  MBH
  Davidson v 1
  U. S. National Capital sesquicentennial
  com
Lexington battle monument   DN
  DN. Amer primitive ptgs, pt 1
Lincoln and his Cabinet, c 1860
  Kallir. Amer primitive ptgs

Little boy in red   MB
  MB. New England miniatures
Little Falls, New York   MeC
  Jetté. Amer heritage collection
Little girl and the cat   DN
  DN. Amer primitive ptgs, pt 2
Little girl of the Schuyler family
  Ford. Pictorial folk art
Little girl with a flower book   NCHA
  Jones. New-found folk art
Little girl with a snowberry
  Ford. Pictorial folk art
Littleton, New Hampshire   MB
  MB. Karolik coll
Lock Haven, Pennsylvania   MB
  MB. Karolik coll
Lowell Mason   MSE
  MSE. Cat of ports, 1950
Lucy Orcutt Leeds and her son
  Ford. Pictorial folk art
Lydia and Tabitha   VWR
  VWR. Folk art (col)
Magdalen Beekman
  Flexner. First flowers (here by Patroon
  painter)
Magdalena Bogardus   NAI
  Belknap
  NAI. Hudson valley
Magdalena Douw (Girl with the red
  shoes)   DeWin
  Belknap
  Mendelowitz
Mahantango valley farm   DN
  DN. Amer primitive ptgs, pt 1
The maid of the grove   MeC
  Jetté. Amer heritage collection
Making hay   VWR
  VWR. Folk art (col)
A man, Portrait of (formerly attributed
  to Badger)   DN
  Belknap
Man in a blue coat   MeC
  Jetté. Amer heritage collection
Man in red   DN
  DN. Amer primitive ptgs, pt 1
Man with blue eyes   DN
  DN. Amer primitive ptgs, pt 2
Mansion with soldiers   NCHA
  Jones. New-found folk art
Margarita Van Vechten (formerly known
  as Miss Beekman)   NAI
  NAI. Hudson valley (as by Schuyler
  painter)
Maria with dog under a tree   MeC
  Jetté. Amer heritage collection
Marine hospital, Chelsea, Massachusetts,
  1835-40
  U. S. National Capital sesquicentennial
  com
A mariner   NCHA
  Jones. New-found folk art
Marriage at Cana   NAI
  NAI. Hudson valley
Martha   DN
  DN. Amer primitive ptgs, pt 2
Martha   VWR
  VWR. Folk art (col)
Mary and David Dalzell of South Egre-
  mont, Massachusetts   NJP
  NJP. Amer Folk art
Mary Briggs   VWR
  VWR. Folk art (col)

Mary W. Roberts   MeC
  Jetté. Amer heritage collection
Maryland family   VWR
  VWR. Folk art (col)
Master Willoughby
  NYG. Fine art, p 16
  UNESCO. Prior to 1860
  UNESCO. Prior to 1860 3d ed
Meditation by the sea   MB
  MB. Karolik coll
  Mendelowitz
  Walker. Ptgs from America
Melons and other fruit   VWR
  VWR. Folk art (col)
The mill   VWR
  VWR. Folk art (col)
Mill of C. J. Hill & Son, Rochester,
  New York   NR
  Jones. Rediscovered ptrs
Mills residence, Ames, New York   MeC
  Jetté. Amer heritage collection
Miss Arnold knitting   DN
  DN. Amer primitive ptgs, pt 1
Miss Daggett   DN
  DN. Amer primitive ptgs, pt 1
Miss Dennison   DN
  Brussels. Exposition
  DN. Amer primitive ptgs, pt 1
Miss Liberty   VWR
  VWR. Folk art (col)
Miss Parke (possible Frances Parke)
  Belknap
Miss Tweedy of Brooklyn   MiD
  Ford. Pictorial folk art
  Pierson
Mr Briggs   VWR
  VWR. Folk art (col)
Mr Carpenter
  Ford. Pictorial folk art
Mr Denison
  DN. Amer primitive ptgs, pt 1
Mr Goodrich, Hancock, Massachusetts
                                        NJP
  NJP. Amer folk art
Mr Murray   DN
  DN. Amer primitive ptgs, pt 2
Mrs A. V. H. Stuyvesant (as a child)
  Vail. Stuyvesant ports
Mrs Abram Gouverneur
  Belknap
Mrs Anthony Van Schaick (formerly
  known as Mrs Sybrant Gozen Van
  Schaick)   NAI
  Jones. Rediscovered ptrs
  NAI. Hudson valley
Mrs Arnold holding an apple   DN
  DN. Amer primitive ptgs, pt 1
Mrs Barent Rynders   NNHS
  Belknap
Mrs Briggs   VWR
  VWR. Folk art (col)
Mrs Daniel Phoenix   NNHS
  NNHS. Waldron Phoenix Belknap coll
Mrs David Provoost (?)   NNHS
  Belknap
  Flexner. First flowers
Mrs David Ver Planck   NAI
  Belknap
  Jones. Rediscovered ptrs
  NAI. Hudson valley
Mrs Denison   DN
  DN. Amer primitive ptgs, pt 1

UNIDENTIFIED artist—*Continued*
Mrs George Washington (after C. W. Peale)
   Belknap
Mrs Hendrick Remsen   NNHS
   NNHS. Waldron Phoenix Belknap coll
Mrs Henry S. Low
   MB. New England miniatures
Mrs J. B. Sheldon of Unionville, Ohio
                      DN
   DN. Amer primitive ptgs, pt 1
   Flexner. Light of distant skies
Mrs Jacob Von Kline   DN
   DN. Amer primitive ptgs, pt 1
Mrs Jacobus Stoutenburg   NNMC
   Belknap
   Flexner. First flowers
Mrs Jan Jansen Bleecker
   Belknap
Mrs Johannes Van Brugh   NNHS
   Belknap
Mrs John Casey and daughter MoSL
   Ford. Pictorial folk art
   MoSL. Handbook 1953
Mrs John Nelson
   DC. Privately owned
Mrs Leonard Rogers   NNHS
   Belknap
Mrs Mann Page II and baby John VWC
   Belknap
   Flexner. First flowers
Mrs Murray   DN
   DN. Amer primitive ptgs, pt 2
Mrs Myers with baby
   Ford. Pictorial folk art
Mrs Nicholas Ridgely
   Belknap
Mrs Noah Smith and family
   ICA. From colony to nation
Mrs Petrus Stuyvesant
   Vail. Stuyvesant ports
Mrs Philip Schuyler   NNHS
   Belknap
Mrs Rip Van Dam   NNHS
   Belknap
Mrs Robert Elliston
   Belknap
Mrs Robert Lenox   NNHS
   NNHS. Waldron Phoenix Belknap coll
Mrs Robert Lenox (possibly a copy of Inman portrait)   NNHS
   NNHS. Waldron Phoenix Belknap coll
Mrs Robert Livingston
   Belknap
Mrs Robert Macbraire   NKS
   Belknap
Mrs Ruth Stanley Mix   VWR
   VWR. Folk art (col)
Mrs Samuel Browne jr   MB
   Belknap
Mrs Samuel Vetch   NNMC
   Belknap
Mrs Sheldon
   Ford. Pictorial folk art
Mrs Starke's brother of Troy NCHA
   Jones. New-found folk art
Mrs Sybrant Gozen Van Schaick. See Mrs Anthony Van Schaick
Mrs Thomas Lawrence   PH
   Belknap

Mrs Thomas Van Alstyne   NNHS
   Belknap
   Flexner. First flowers
   Pierson
Mrs Timothy Green
   MB. New England miniatures
Mrs William Axtell (possibly Mrs Abraham De Peyster jr)
   Belknap
Mrs William Goldborough and grandson
                 MdBH
   Belknap
Mrs William Skinner
   Belknap
Mrs William Van Bergen NNMC
   Belknap
Mrs Wynant Van Zandt   NNHS
   Belknap
   ICA. From colony to nation
Mohawk valley (formerly attributed to Durand)   NCHA
   Born
Morgan addressing his friends VWR
   VWR. Folk art (col)
Moses in the bulrushes   VWA
   Ford. Pictorial folk art
   VWR. Amer folk art
   VWR. Folk art (col)
Moses Levy   NNMC
   Belknap
   Flexner. First flowers
Mother and child c 1810   NCHA
   Time. 300 years (col)
Mother and child in white   DN
   DN. Amer primitive ptgs, pt 1
Mother and child in white   NCHA
   Jones. New-found folk art
Mother and child in Windsor chair DN
   DN. Amer primitive ptgs, pt 1
Mount Vernon
   Ford. Pictorial folk art
Mount Vernon (after aquatint by Francis Jukes)   NJN
   Ford. Pictorial folk art
Mountain landscape   MMA
   Born
Mounting of the guard   DN
   DN. Amer primitive ptgs, pt 1
Mourning picture   RPS
   Ford. Pictorial folk art
Mourning picture   VWR
   Ford. Pictorial folk art
Mourning picture—Elizabeth Farr VWR
   VWR. Folk art (col)
Mourning picture—left behind VWR
   VWR. Folk art (col)
Mourning picture—Philo Day VWR
   VWR. Amer folk art
   VWR. Folk art (col)
Mourning picture—Polly Botsford and her children   VWR
   VWR. Folk art (col)
Mourning picture sacred to the memory of Jerhusha Williams
   Jetté. Amer heritage collection
Mourning scene
   Ford. Pictorial folk art
Murder of Jane McCrea   NCHA
   Time. 300 years (col)
Musicians in the snow   MB
   MB. Karolik coll

The Narrows from Fort Hamilton, New
   York Harbor   NCHA
   Jones. New-found folk art
Nathan Hawley and family   NAI
   Jones. Rediscovered ptrs
The navigator   VWR
   VWR. Folk art (col)
The navigator's wife   VWR
   VWR. Folk art (col)
Negro child   NCHA
   Jones. New-found art
New England faces: husband and wife
                       NCHA
   Jones. New-found folk art
New England family group   MB
   MB. Karolik coll
New England farm in winter   DN
   DN. Amer primitive ptgs, pt 2
New England goddess   RPS
   Ford. Pictorial folk art
New England hillside   MB
   MB. Karolik coll
New England village   DN
   DN. Amer primitive ptgs, pt 1
New England village   MB
   MB. Karolik coll
New England village, possibly North-
   wood, New Hampshire   MSt
   Little. Country art
Nicholas William Stuyvesant   NNHS
   Flexner. First flowers
   Pierson
   Vail. Stuyvesant ports
Nicholson Broughton
   Pierson
Nitrate fleet at the Chinchas islands MSP
   Davidson v 1
Northwestern town   DN
   DN. Amer primitive ptgs, pt 2
Old homestead at Sudbury, Massachu-
   setts   MeC
   Jetté. Amer heritage collection
Old lady with a Bible   MB
   MB. Karolik coll
Old lady with a plaid shawl   MB
   MB. Karolik coll
Old mill
   Sears. Highlights
The old plantation   VWR
   VWR. Amer folk art (col)
   VWR. Folk art (col)
Oliver Wight
   Ford. Pictorial folk art
On the lake
   Ford. Pictorial folk art
Our flag in there
   Ford. Pictorial folk art
Out for a drive   NCHA
   Jones. New-found folk art
Outdoor scene with feasting and danc-
   ing   CtHW
   Ford. Pictorial folk art
Outing on the Hudson   VWR
   VWR. Folk art (col)
Oxbow (formerly attributed to Cole) OCl
   Born
Palisades
   Sears. Highlights
Paul and Virginia   VWR
   VWR. Folk art (col)
A peaceful village   DN
   DN. Amer primitive ptgs, pt 2

Pennsylvania Dutch lady   MB
   MB. Karolik coll
Pennsylvania hospital   VWR
   VWR. Folk art (col)
Pennsylvania mill with Conestoga wagon
                       NCHA
   Jones. New-found folk art
Peter Farrington   VWR
   VWR. Folk art (col)
Peter Stuyvesant   NNHS
   Davidson v 1
   Flexner. First flowers
   Richardson. Ptg in Amer
   Vail. Stuyvesant ports
Philip Schuyler   NNHS
   Belknap
Philipse manor at Yonkers, New York
   Davidson v 1
Picking flowers   NCHA
   Jones. New-found folk art
Picking flowers   VWR
   VWR. Folk art (col)
Pierre Van Cortlandt   NBM
   Belknap
   ICA. From colony to nation
   NNHS. Waldron Phoenix Belknap coll
Pieter Schuyler
   Belknap
   Flexner. First flowers
   Richardson. Ptg in America
Pieter Waldron
   Belknap
Pineapple   VWR
   VWR. Folk art (col)
Pink roses   DN
   DN. Amer primitive ptgs, pt 1
Pioneer's camp
   Ford. Pictorial folk art
The plantation   DN
   DN. Amer primitive ptgs, pt 1
Polly Maxon of Stephentown, New York
                       NJP
   NJP. Amer folk art
The Pool sisters   MeC
   Jetté. Amer heritage collection
Privateer hermaphrodite brig Rambler of
   Medford   MSP
   Davidson v 1
Privateer schooner Surprise of Baltimore
   capturing the British ship Star, 1815
                     MdBH
   Davidson v 1
Prodigal son gambling   DN
   DN. Amer primitive ptgs, pt 2
The prodigal son in misery   VWR
   VWR. Folk art (col)
The prodigal son receiving his patrimony
                     VWR
   VWR. Folk art (col)
The prodigal son reclaimed   VWR
   VWR. Folk art (col)
The prodigal son reveling with harlots
                     VWR
   VWR. Folk art (col)
Profile portrait of a lady   DN
   DN. Amer primitive ptgs, pt 1
Profile portrait of a man   DN
   DN. Amer primitive ptgs, pt 1
Profile portrait of lady in white cap DN
   DN. Amer primitive ptgs, pt 2
Prospectors   DN
   DN. Amer primitive ptgs, pt 2

UNIDENTIFIED artist—*Continued*
Quilting party   MMA
    Barker. Amer ptg
    Ford. Pictorial folk art
    Walker. Ptgs from America
Quilting party   VWR
    VWR. Amer folk art (col)
Raft on river   InBU
    U.S. National Capital sesquicentennial com
Railroad engine, the Star
    Ford. Pictorial folk art
Rebecca at the well   VWR
    VWR. Folk art (col)
Red mill   NCHA
    Jones. New-found folk art
Rhode Island choir boy
    Ford. Pictorial folk art
Richard Ward
    Belknap
    NNHS. Waldron Phoenix Belknap coll
Richmond c 1822
    Davidson v 1
Rip Van Dam   NNHS
    Belknap
River landing   MB
    MB. Karolik coll
River landscape   VWR
    VWR. Folk art (col)
River view with shepherd and animals
    Ford. Pictorial folk art
Robert Lenox (after Jarvis)   NNHS
    NNHS. Waldron Phoenix Belknap coll
Robert Livingston
    Belknap
Robert Macbraire   NKS
    Belknap
Robert Sanders
    Belknap
Runaway horse   WMAA
    Ford. Pictorial folk art
    Walker. Ptgs from America (col)
Running before the storm   MB
    MB. Karolik coll
Ruth and Naomi   VWR
    VWR. Folk art (col)
The sad departure   DN
    DN. Amer primitive ptgs, pt 2
A sailor   DN
    DN. Amer primitive ptgs, pt 2
Sailors   ICA
    Ford. Pictorial folk art
Samuel Hart
    MB. New England miniatures
Samuel Houston as Marius   TxA
    Roos
Samuel Mountfort Pitts sr (possibly by J. G. or L. E. Cole)   MiD
    MiD. Ports of the Pitts family
Samuel Vetch   NNMC
    Belknap
Sarah Alden   MeC
    Jetté. Amer heritage collection
Sarah Hobbs
    Flexner. Light of distant skies
The Sargent family   DN
    DN. Amer primitive ptgs, pt 1
    Time. 300 years (col)
Schoolmaster and boys   VWR
    VWR. Folk art (col)

The schoolroom
    U.S. National Capital sesquicentennial com
Screaming eagle   NCHA
    Jones. New-found folk art
Schuyler family girl
    Belknap
The Senate, Albany, 1850   NAI
    Jones. Rediscovered ptrs
The shepherd and his flock   VWR
    VWR. Folk art (col)
Ship Bavaria
    Davidson v 1
Ship Hercules of Salem, 1809   MSP
    Davidson v 1
Shrewsbury river near Seabright, New Jersey   MB
    MB. Karolik coll
Signing the Treaty of Greenville. See Indian Treaty of Greenville, 1795
Silas Ilsley   MeC
    MeC. Inaugural ex
    NUM. Art across America
Silver lake, New Hampshire
    Sears. Highlights
Sisters in red   DN
    DN. Amer primitive ptgs, pt 1
A smart turnout   CtHW
    CtHW. Handbook
Smith memorial
    Jones. New-found folk art
Son of Captain Samuel Hallett   ICA
    Belknap
Sophia Burpee   DN
    DN. Amer primitive ptgs
Southeast prospect of the city of New York c 1850   NNHS
    Born
The Southern Belle   MeC
    Jetté. Amer heritage collection
Spring fishing   VWR
    VWR. Folk art (col)
Stages of man   VWR
    VWR. Folk art (col)
Star spangled banner in the rocket's red glare over Fort McHenry, 1814   MdBH
    Davidson v2
Start of the hunt   DN
    DN. Amer primitive ptgs, pt 1
Stephen Decatur
    Ford. Pictorial folk art
Stephen Greenleaf jr
    Belknap
Still life with Johnson's dictionary
    CtY. Yale alumni
Still life with melons   DN
    DN. Amer primitive ptgs
Still life with watermelon   VWR
    VWR. Folk art (col)
Street in Brooklyn c 1840-60   MiD
    Ford. Pictorial folk art
    Pierson
    Richardson. Ptg in America
Street in winter; evening   MB
    MB. Karolik coll
Stylized landscape   DN
    DN. Amer primitive ptgs, pt 2
Stylized landscape   MeC
    Jetté. Amer heritage collection
Summer
    Sears. Highlights
Summer landscape: haymaking
    MB. Karolik coll

Sunset by the river
  Sears. Highlights
Susanna Truax   DN
  Belknap
  DN. Amer primitive ptgs, pt 1
Suspension bridge at Niagara Falls
  Baur. Amer ptg
Sybrant Gozen Van Schaick. See Anthony
  Van Schaick
Telegraph hill, San Francisco, c 1849
  U.S. National Capital sesquicentennial
  com
Textile merchant   DN
  DN. Amer primitive ptgs, pt 1
That's my doll!   NCHA
  Jones. New-found folk art
Theatre scenic backdrop   RPHS
  Ford. Pictorial folk art
Thomas Lawrence   PH
  Belknap
Thomas Savage   MWM
  Belknap
  Davidson v 1
Thomas Van Alstyne   NNHS
  Barker. Amer ptg
  Belknap
  Flexner. First flowers
  Larkin
  Larkin rev ed
  Pierson
Thorndike sisters
  MB. New England miniatures
Thrifty farm   NCHA
  Jones. New-found folk art
Tobias Ten Eyck   NAI
  Belknap
  NAI. Hudson valley
Tomatoes, fruit, and flowers   MB
  MB. Karolik coll
Tomb in memory of Richard Newhall
                                       MeC
  Jetté. Amer heritage collection
Town bridge   VWR
  VWR. Folk art (col)
Town on a river   NCHA
  Jones. New-found folk art
The trotter   DN
  DN. Amer primitive ptgs, pt 2
True cross   MMA
  Ford. Pictorial folk art
Twenty-two houses and a church   DN
  DN. Amer primitive ptgs, pt 1
Twin sisters   DN
  DN. Amer primitive ptgs, pt 1
Two armies before a city   NCHA
  Jones. New-found folk art
Two boys in green tunics   NCHA
  Jones. New-found folk art
Two brown and white puppies   MeC
  Jetté. Amer heritage collection
Two children with a deer
  Belknap
Two little girls in blue   NCHA
  Jones. New-found folk art
Two young girls, 1835   MeC
  Jetté. Amer heritage collection
A valley farm   DN
  DN. Amer primitive ptgs, pt 2
Van Schaick hatchment   NAI
  Jones. Rediscovered ptrs
  NAI. Hudson valley
Venice, c 1840   NCHA
  Jones. New-found folk art

Venus drawn by doves   VWR
  VWR. Folk art (col)
Victorian dairy farm, study in green
                                       NCHA
  Jones. New-found folk art
Victorian family   NCHA
  Jones. New-found folk art
Victorian landscape   MeC
  Jetté. Amer heritage collection
View of Baltimore, c 1840
  U.S. National Capital sesquicentennial
  com
View of Barnstable   MAP
  Born
View of the Palisades
  Sears. Highlights
View of the Schuylkill waterworks, Phila-
  delphia (after William Henry Bart-
  lett)   MiD
  Born
Village by the river   DN
  DN. Amer primitive ptg, pt 2
A village street, Massachusetts, c 1845
                                       MeC
  Jetté. Amer heritage collection
Virgin Mary with Holy Ghost
  Mendelowitz
Walker family, father and son   NJP
  NJP. Amer folk art
Walker family, mother and daughter
                                       NJP
  Ford. Pictorial folk art
  NJP. Amer folk art
Walking the puppy   NCHA
  Jones. New-found folk art
Wall painting from Connecticut
  Ford. Pictorial folk art
War horses   NCHA
  Jones. New-found folk art
Warren Crosby
  Ford. Pictorial folk art
Washington and his staff at Fort Cum-
  berland, Maryland, 1794
  Davidson v2
The Washington, first double decker on
  the Mississippi
  Born
Watchmaker with his tools   MSt
  Little. Country art
Watercolor class
  U.S. National Capital sesquicentennial
  com
Watercolor on a religious theme   VWR
  Ford. Pictorial folk art
Watermelon   MB
  MB. Karolik coll
Waterworks, Center square, Philadelphia
                                       PH
  Ford. Pictorial folk art
We go for the Union   DN
  DN. Amer primitive ptgs, pt 1
Wesleyan academy, Wilbraham, Massa-
  chusetts   MeC
  Jetté. Amer heritage collection
West Point, c 1850
  Ford. Pictorial folk art
West Point from above Washington valley
                                       MB
  MB. Karolik coll
Western frontier homestead   DN
  DN. Amer primitive ptgs, pt 2
Whaling   DN
  DN. Amer primitive ptgs, pt 2

UNIDENTIFIED artist—*Continued*
Whaling scene
  Davidson v 1
Whaling scene—Triton of New Bedford
  MeC
  Jetté. Amer heritage collection
Wheat stack   VWR
  VWR. Folk art (col)
Wife of Capt George, Haverhill, Massa-
  chusetts   NJP
  NJP. Amer folk art
Wilkes-Barre and the Wyoming valley
  McClintock (col)
William Stoughton   MCH
  Flexner. First flowers
  U. S. National Capital sesquicentennial
  com
William Van Bergen   NNMC
  Belknap
Winter scene
  Born
Winter sports on the farm   NCHA
  Jones. New-found folk art
A woman   ICA
  Ford. Pictorial folk art
Woman in a yellow dress (Pennsylvania)
  MeC
  Jetté. Amer heritage collection
Woman with apple   OYB
  OYB. Supplement
Woman with sewing box   VWR
  VWR. Folk art (col)
Woodcutting in winter   MB
  MB. Karolik coll
Woodman spare that tree   MoSL
  Ford. Pictorial folk art
Woodshed interior   MB
  MB. Karolik coll
Woodward children
  MB. New England miniatures (col)
Worth family mourning
  Ford. Pictorial folk art
Wynant Van Zandt   NNHS
  Belknap
Wyoming valley (Conyngham coll)
  McClintock
Wyoming valley in 1850 (Wyoming his-
  torical society)
  McClintock
Yellow coach   VWR
  VWR. Folk art (col)
Young girl in a red dress   MeC
  Jetté. Amer heritage collection
Young girl in white   VWR
  VWR. Folk art (col)
Young ladies' seminary, Virginia
  Flexner. Light of distant skies
Young man in a gray linen suit   NCHA
  Jones. New-found folk art
Young man wearing white stock   DN
  DN. Amer primitive ptgs, pt 1
Zachary Taylor   NNHS
  Ford. Pictorial folk art

The uninvited by G. Gutmann

Union square in spring by C. Hassam

Union square, night by M. Kantor

United States (frigate)
  Martens, J. W. Brooklyn Navy yard
    (Frigate USS United States)
The United States and the Macedonian by
  T. Chambers
United States Capitol
  Burton, C. The Capitol, Washington, 1824
United States cavalry defending a position
  by F. Remington
United States. Congress. House of repre-
  sentatives
  Morse, S. F. B. Old House of representa-
    tives, 1821-22
United States Military Academy, West
  Point
  Catlin, G. United States Military Acade-
    my, West Point
Universal field by M. Tobey
Universe by E. E. Wentz
Unknown Dane by W. M. Chase
Unmasked by R. Brackman
Unpainted horses by L. Bouché
Unscheduled stop by C. M. Russell
Untilled field by P. Bacon
Up the Hudson by G. W. Bellows
UPJOHN, Anna Milo
  Andrew Dickson White   CtY
  CtY. Portrait index
Upper deck by C. Sheeler
Upper House by W. Gropper
Upper pasture by M. Avery
Upright 3 by K. E. Fortess
Upright trees by A. Blanch
Uprooted tree by P. Pearlstein
Upside down table and mask by Y. Kuni-
  yoshi
Uptown by E. Model
URBAN, Albert, 1909-1959
  Painting, 1959   MMA
    MMA. Sixteen
  Painting 1959   NBuA
    NBuA. Acquisitions 1959-1961
  Painting, 1959 (Urban coll)
    MMA. Sixteen
  Phoenix no 2
    IU. Contemp Amer ptg & sculp, 1959
Urban by N. Lewis
Urban cathedral by J. Friebert
Urban landscape by A. Alcalay
Urchin's game by F. Martin
Urgent hour by G. Kamrowski
Uriel in the sun by W. Allston
Ursine park by S. Davis
Uruguay medicine man, South America by
  G. Catlin
Ut-Ha-Wah (Capt Vole) by W. J. Wilgus
UTLEY, Windsor, 1920-
  Aggressors
    OrPA. Ptgs & sculptures
UTTER, Bror, 1913-
  Pharmaceutic cabinet
    Pousette-Dart. Amer ptg
  Trio   TxF
    CoS. New accessions USA, 1954

V

V. J. day by V. Deezik
Vacant lot by B. Shahn
Vacationist by R. Gwathmey
Vagrants by C. A. Hall
Vail, Anna Miretta, fl 1840
 Tuthill, A. G. D. Anna Miretta Vail
Vail, Mary Elizabeth, fl 1840
 Tuthill, A. G. D. Mary Elizabeth Vail
Vail, Thomas, b 1760
 Tuthill, A. G. D. Dr Thomas Vail (?)
Vail children, fl 1818
 Tuthill, A. G. D. Jackson, Solon, Mary
 Elizabeth and Miretta Vail
Val d'Aosta, a stream over rocks by J. S.
 Sargent
Val d'Aosta, stepping stones by J. S.
 Sargent
Val d'Arconville by T. Robinson
Val Ticino, St Gothard route by R. Smith
Valentine, Mann Satterwhite, 1786-1865
 Hubard, W. J. Mann S. Valentine
Valentine, Mann Satterwhite, 1824-1892
 Hubard, W. J. Mann S. Valentine 2nd
 and the artist
The valentine by W. Allston
Valentine still life by H. A. Sawyer
Valhalla bridge by T. Donnelly
Vallé, Isabella (Sargeant)
 Sargent, J. S. Mrs Jules Vallé
The valley by E. Lawson
The valley by E. Ludins
Valley below by W. Lockwood
A valley farm by Unidentified artist
Valley landscape by J. Wilkinson
Valley of dry bones—triptych by A. Rattner
Valley of Mexico by C. W. Chapman
Valley ranch by P. L. Dike
Value, Charlotte Elizabeth, b 1830
 Sully, T. Victor René Value and his
 daughter Charlotte
Value, Victor René, 1790-1860?
 Sully, T. Victor René Value and his
 daughter Charlotte
Van Alen, Maria. See Van Alstyne, Maria
 (Van Alen)
Van Alen, Miss, fl 1720
 Vanderlyn, P. (attributed works) Miss
 Van Alen
Van Alstyne, Maria (Van Alen) fl 1695
 Unidentified artist. Mrs Thomas Van
 Alstyne
Van Alstyne, Thomas, 1688-1765
 Unidentified artist. Thomas Van Alstyne
Van Arnam, Judge, fl 1855
 Van Zandt, T. K. Judge Van Arnam in
 his sleigh
Van Bergen, Elinor (Van Dyke) fl 1720
 Unidentified artist. Mrs William Van
 Bergen
Van Bergen, William, fl 1720
 Unidentified artist. William Van Bergen
 of Catskill, New York
Van Brugh, Elizabeth. See Van Rensselaer,
 Elizabeth (Van Brugh)

Van Brugh, Margareta (Provoost) b 1673
 Unidentified artist. Mrs Johannes Van
 Brugh
Van Buren, Amelia C. fl 1889
 Eakins, T. Miss Van Buren
Van Buren, Martin, president U. S. 1782-
 1862
 Ames, E. Martin Van Buren
 Healy, G. P. A. Martin Van Buren
Van Cortlandt, Abraham, 1713-1746
 Unidentified artist. Abraham Van Cort-
 landt
Van Cortlandt, Anne (Stevenson) 1774-1821
 Ames, E. Mrs Pierre Van Cortlandt II
Van Cortlandt, Elizabeth. See Skinner,
 Elizabeth (Van Cortlandt)
Van Cortlandt, John, 1718-1747
 Unidentified artist. John Van Cortlandt
Van Cortlandt, Maria. See Van Rensselaer,
 Maria (Van Cortlandt)
Van Cortlandt, Philip, 1749-1831
 Ames, E. Philip Van Cortlandt
Van Cortlandt, Pierre, 1721-1814
 Unidentified artist. Pierre Van Cortlandt
Van Cortlandt, Pierre, 1762-1848
 Ames, E. Pierre Van Cortlandt II
Van Dam, Mrs Rip. See Van Dam, Sarah
 (Van Der Spiegel)
Van Dam, Rip, 1660?-1749
 Unidentified artist. Rip Van Dam
Van Dam, Sarah (Van Der Spiegel) 1663-
 1736
 Unidentified artist. Mrs Rip Van Dam
Van Dame, Bartholomew, fl 1836
 Davis, J. H. Bartholomew Van Dame
Vandenberg, Arthur Hendrick, 1884-1951
 Shahn, B. Dewey, Vandenberg and Taft
Vander Horst, Elizabeth. See Moore, Eliza-
 beth (Vander Horst)
VANDERLYN, John, 1775-1852
 Ariadne   PA
 Bazin
 Canaday
 Flexner. Amer ptg
 Flexner. Light of distant skies
 Flexner. Short history
 Larkin
 Larkin rev ed
 Mendelowitz
 MdBMu. Rendezvous
 Pierson
 Richardson. Ptg in America
 Roos
 Time. 300 years (col)
 Catherine H. Van Rensselaer   ATeS
 ATeS. Collection
 Death of Jane McCrea   CtHW
 Barker. Amer ptg
 CtHW. Handbook
 Flexner. Light of distant skies
 Pierson
 Falls of Niagara   NNPL
 Ford. Edward Hicks
 Falls of Niagara taken from under the
 Table rock   NNHS
 Born
 James Hillhouse   CtY
 CtY. Portrait index
 A lady and her son   NKS
 Pierson
 Richardson. Ptg in America

VANDERLYN, John—*Continued*
Marius amidst the ruins of Carthage
        CSFD
  Canaday
  Larkin rev ed (col detail)
  Pierson
Mrs Marinus Willett and child   MM
  Flexner. Light of distant skies
Niagara Falls   NKS
  Flexner. Light of distant skies
  Pierson
Panorama: palace and gardens of Ver-
  sailles (Panoramic view of the palace
  and gardens of Versailles)   MM
  Born
  Larkin rev ed (detail)
  Pierson
Robert R. Livingston   NNHS
  Larkin
  Larkin rev ed
  Pierson
Self-portrait   MM
  Mendelowitz
  Roos
Severyn Bruyn   NKS
  Larkin
  Larkin rev ed
Theodosia Burr
  DC. Privately owned
View in Rome   NKS
  Pierson
VANDERLYN, Pieter, 1687-1778
Helena Jansen Sleight   NKS
  Belknap

      Attributed works

Catherine De Peyster
  Belknap
Cornelius D. Wynkoop
  Belknap
Matthew Ten Eyck
  Belknap
Miss Van Alen   DN
  Belknap
  DN. Amer primitive ptgs, pt 1
Mrs Petrus Vas   NAI
  Belknap
  Flexner. First flowers
  Jones. Rediscovered ptrs
  NAI. Hudson valley
VAN DER POOL, James, 1765-1799
A woman, Portrait of   NJN
  Ford. Pictorial folk art

      Attributed works

A man, Portrait of   NJN
  Ford. Pictorial folk art
Vander Sluis, George J. 1915-
Grey and green
  IU. Contemp Amer ptg & sculp, 1961
Van Der Spiegel, Sarah. See Van Dam,
  Sarah (Van Der Spiegel)
VANDERSPRITT, John
Increase Mather   MBH
  Davidson v 1
Vanderveer, Jane (Herbert) fl 1819
  Williams, M. Mrs Jane Herbert Vander-
  veer
Vanderveer, John G, 1799-1883
  Williams, M. John G. Vanderveer
Vanderveer, Mrs John G. See Vanderveer,
  Jane (Herbert)

VAN DUZER, Clarence Eugene, 1920-
Pietà   OYB
  OYB. Annual 1956
  OYB. Supplement 1959
Van Dyke, Elinor. See Van Bergen, Elinor
  (Van Dyke)
Vane, Henrietta Elizabeth Frederica, fl 1783
  Stuart, G. Henrietta Elizabeth Frederica
  Vane
VAN EVEREN, Jan, 1875-1947
Abstraction   CtY
  CtY. Soc Anonyme
Van Horne, Augustus Cornelius, 1765-1853
  Unidentified artist. Augustus Cornelius
  Van Horne
Van Horne, David
  Dunlap, W. David Van Horne
Van Horne, Susan Rivington. See Stuy-
  vesant, Susan Rivington (Van Horne)
Vanishing city by A. Alcalay
Vanity by W. Auerbach-Levy
Vanity fair by H. Koerner
Vanity of an artist's dream by C. B. King
Van Ness, William W. 1776-1823
  Jarvis, J. W. William W. Van Ness
Van Reid, Jane L. fl 1810
  Stettinius, S. E. (attributed works) Jane
  L. Van Reid
Van Reid, Wellington, fl 1810
  Stettinius, S. E. (attributed works) Wel-
  lington Van Reid
Van Rensselaer, Anne, b 1719
  Watson, J. (attributed works) Anne Van
  Rensselaer
Van Rensselaer, Ariaantje (Schuyler) 1720-
  1763
  Unidentified artist. Ariaantje Schuyler
  Van Rensselaer
Van Rensselaer, Catherine, 1734-1803. See
  Schuyler, Catherine (Van Rensselaer)
Van Rensselaer, Catherine H.
  Vanderlyn, J. Catherine H. Van Rens-
  selaer
Van Rensselaer, Elizabeth (Groesbeek)
  1707-1729
  Watson, J. (attributed works) Mrs
  Stephanus (?) Van Rensselaer
Van Rensselaer, Elizabeth (Van Brugh)
  b 1712
  Duyckinck, G. (attributed works) Mrs
  Henry Van Rensselaer
Van Rensselaer, Mrs Henry. See Van Rens-
  selaer, Elizabeth (Van Brugh)
Van Rensselaer, Jacobus, 1713-1754?
  Watson, J. (attributed works) Gentleman
  of the Van Rensselaer family (prob-
  ably Jacobus Van Rensselaer)
Van Rensselaer, Jan Baptist, fl 1658
  Watson, J. (attributed works) Van Rens-
  selaer gentleman (known as Jan
  Baptist Van Rensselaer)
Van Rensselaer, Jeremias, 1705-1745
  Unidentified artist. Jeremias Van Rens-
  selaer
Van Rensselaer, Mrs Kiliaen, b 1680. See
  Van Rensselaer, Maria (Van Cort-
  landt)
Van Rensselaer, Mrs Kiliaen, 1720-1763. See
  Van Rensselaer, Ariaantje (Schuyler)
Van Rensselaer, Maria (Van Cortlandt)
  b 1680
  Watson, J. (attributed works) Mrs Kiliaen
  Van Rensselaer III

Van Rensselaer, Solomon, 1774-1852
Ames, E. Solomon Van Rensselaer
Van Rensselaer, Stephanus, 1707-1747
Watson, J. (attributed works) Gentleman
of the Van Rensselaer family (prob-
ably Stephanus Van Rensselaer)
Van Rensselaer, Mrs Stephanus (?). See
Van Rensselaer, Elizabeth (Groes-
beek)
Van Rensselaer, Stephen, 1764-1839
Ames, E. Stephen Van Rensselaer
Van Rensselaer family, Member of
Unidentified artist. Girl of the Van Rens-
selaer family
Van Rensselaer family, Member of, fl 1725
Unidentified artist. Lady of the Van
Rensselaer family
Van Schaick, Anthony, 1682-1756
Unidentified artist. Anthony Van Schaick
Van Schaick, Mrs Anthony, b 1685?
Unidentified artist. Mrs Anthony Van
Schaick
Van Schaick, Sybrant Gozen. See Van
Schaick, Anthony
Van Schaick hatchment by Unidentified
artist
Van Vechten, Gerrit Teunise, b 1703
Unidentified artist. Gerrit Teunise Van
Vechten
Van Vechten, Lavinia, fl 1720
Unidentified artist. Lavinia Van Vechten
Van Vechten, Margarita, b 1705
Unidentified artist. Margarita Van
Vechten
Van Zandt, Catharina (Ten Eyck) 1692-1772
Unidentified artist. Mrs Wynant Van
Zandt
VAN ZANDT, Thomas K. fl 1844-1870
Judge Van Arnam in his sleigh   NAI
Jones. Undiscovered ptrs
Van Zandt, Wynant, 1683-1757
Unidentified artist. Wynant Van Zandt
Vanzetti, Bartolomeo, 1889-1927
Shahn, B. Bartolomeo Vanzetti
Shahn, B. Sacco and Vanzetti in coffins
Shahn, B. Vanzetti and Sacco
VARGA, Margit, 1908-
Connecticut farm   ATU
ATU. Coll of Amer art
Country carnival
IU. Contemp Amer ptg, 1952
Road to Danbury
Gruskin (col)
Variation on a theme by S. Zingale
Variations by J. Xceron
Variations in pink and grey—Chelsea by
J. A. M. Whistler
Variations on a still life by B. Browne
Variations on a theme: the wreck by E.
Fiene
Variations on the Avignon Pietà, no 2 by W.
Pachner
Varick, Richard, 1753-1831
Inman, H. Col Richard Varick
Vartoosh, Portrait of by A. Gorky
Vas, Elsje (Rutgers) Schuyler, b 1674
Vanderlyn, P. (attributed works) Mrs
Petrus Vas
Vase and flowers by P. Evergood
Vase of flowers by C. S. Price
Vase of mixed flowers by M. J. Heade

Vase with flowers by W. Chaiken
Vases by A. Ozenfant
VASILIEFF, Nicholas, 1892?-
Black table
IU. Contemp Amer ptg & sculp, 1961
Girl with cat
IU. Contemp Amer ptg & sculp, 1955
Mrs V, Portrait of
IU. Contemp Amer ptg & sculp, 1953
On the porch   IU
IU. Contemp Amer ptg & sculp, 1957
IU. 20th century
Pink tablecloth   DC
CoS. New accessions USA, 1958
Still life with fish   IU
CoS. New accessions USA, 1956
Still life with lobster
PPC. International ex, 1952
VASS, Gene, 1922-
Deux personnages   NBuA
NBuA. Acquisitions 1957-58
Eleventh street   NBuA
NBuA. Acquisitions 1959-1961
Hell Gate tie
IU. Contemp Amer ptg & sculp, 1961
Vaudeville by C. H. Demuth
Vaudeville by J. Lawrence
Vaudeville musicians by C. H. Demuth
VAUGHAN, David A.
The welder
CSFP. Annual ex, 1946
VAVRUSKA, Frank, 1917-
Cows in a tropical landscape
ICA. Annual ex, 1947/48
VEDDER, Elihu, 1836-1923
Bed of the torrent Mugnone, near Flor-
ence
MiD. Coll in progress
WiMiA. Amer ptg 1760-1960
A corner of Capri
MiD. Travelers in Arcadia
Fiesole   MiD
MiD. Treasures
Ideal head
Pierson
Richardson. Ptg in America
Italian landscape   MB
MiD. Travelers in Arcadia
Lair of the sea serpent   MB
Pierson
Richardson. Ptg in America
The lost mind   MM
MiD. Travelers in Arcadia
Pierson
The philosopher   NJN
Mendelowitz
Rome   MeB
Pierson
The sphinx on the seashore
MiD. Coll in progress
Veiled bouquet by H. Pittman
Vellanti, Ailene
The mother
NAD. Annual ex, spring 1950
Venetian bead stringers by J. S. Sargent
Venetian girl by F. Duveneck
Venetian Gothic art building on the old Yale
campus by P. B. Wight
Venetian interior by J. S. Sargent
Veni, vidi, vici by D. Fredenthal

Venice
Boit, E. D. Rio di San Barnaba, Venice
Boit, E. D. Rio di San Lorenzo, Venice
Boit, E. D. Venice: afternoon on the Campo San Trovaso
Boit, E. D. Venice: afternoon on the Grand Canal
Boit, E. D. Venice: fisherman's quarter on the Giudecca
Boit, E. D. Venice: looking toward the Grand Canal
Boit, E. D. Venice: morning on the Grand Canal
Boit, E. D. Venice: off San Giorgio
Boit, E. D. Venice: showery morning on the Zattere
Chase, W. M. City streets, Venice
Chase, W. M. View of Venice
Congdon, W. G. Piazza San Marco
Congdon, W. G. Piazza, Venice
Congdon, W. G. Venice no 1
Congdon, W. G. Venice no 1, 1950
Congdon, W. G. Venice no 2
Inness, G. Venice: S. Giorgio Maggiore
Longfellow, W. P. P. Sala del Collegio, Ducal palace, Venice
MacIver, L. Venice, 1949
Moran, T. View of Venice
Prendergast, M. B. Bridge and steps, Venice
Prendergast, M. B. Bridge in Venice
Prendergast, M. B. Café Florian, Venice
Prendergast, M. B. Campo Santa Maria Formosa, Venice
Prendergast, M. B. Easter procession, St Mark's, Venice
Prendergast, M. B. Festival day, Venice
Prendergast, M. B. The Lagoon, Venice
Prendergast, M. B. Market place, Venice
Prendergast, M. B. Piazza di San Marco, Venice
Prendergast, M. B. Ponte della Paglia
Prendergast, M. B. Procession, Venice
Prendergast, M. B. Riva San Biagio, Venice
Prendergast, M. B. St Mark's Venice
Prendergast, M. B. Santa Maria Formosa, Venice
Prendergast, M. B. Sunlight on the Piazzetta, Venice
Prendergast, M. B. Umbrellas in the rain, Venice
Prendergast, M. B. Venice
Sargent, J. S. Cafe on Riva degli Schiavoni, Venice
Sargent, J. S. Corner of the church of St Staë, Venice
Sargent, J. S. Festa della regatta, Palazzo Barbaro
Sargent, J. S. Scuola di San Rocco, Venice
Sargent, J. S. Street in Venice
Sargent, J. S. Venice: La Digana
Sargent, J. S. Venice: I Gesuati
Sargent, J. S. Venice: La Salute
Sargent, J. S. Venice: under the Rialto bridge
Smith, F. H. Venice: canal scene I
Smith, F. H. Venice: canal scene II
Unidentified artist. Venice, c 1840
Whistler, J. A. M. Lagoon, Venice: Nocturne in blue and silver

Venice lace makers by H. Bacon
Venus. See Mythological themes
Verdant rise by R. Eshoo
Verde by C. Woods
Verdict of the people by G. C. Bingham
Verdure by H. Bayer
VERELST, Willem, fl 1734-1756
Oglethorpe presenting Tomo-Chi-Chi and the Indians to Lord Trustees of the colony of Georgia
Davidson v 1
VERES (Mrs Margo Clark)
Davy Emmet Crocky (Emmett Kelly) NSP. Sportscapes
Verge by R. Lytle
Verlaine, Paul
Lindner, R. Paul Verlaine
Vermilion cliffs by G. C. Delano
Vermont
Durand, A. B. View of Rutland, Vermont
Holt, H. Fading light, Stowe valley
Hopper, E. First branch of the White river, Vermont
Sloane, M. Vermont hamlet
Solomon, H. Vermont autumn
Thompson, J. B. Harvest in Vermont
Williams, F. B. Down from Mount Mansfield, Vermont
Vermont lawyer by H. Bundy
Vernal by S. Laufman
Vernet, John, fl 1806
Trumbull, J. John Vernet and his family
The **Veronica** by J. De Feo
La **Veronica** by J. Ulbricht
Verplanck, Ariaantje (Coeymans) 1672-1743
Unidentified artist. Mrs David Verplanck
Verplanck, Mrs David. See Verplanck, Ariaantje (Coeymans)
Verplanck, Eliza (Fenno) See Fenno, Eliza
Verplanck, Mrs Gulian Crommelin. See Fenno, Eliza
Verplanck, Samuel, 1739-1820
Copley, J. S. Samuel Verplanck
Versailles
Robinson, F. V. Versailles
Vanderlyn, J. Panorama: palace and gardens of Versailles
VERSTILLE, William, 1755-1803
Noah Webster
MB. New England miniatures
Solomon Ingraham
MB. New England miniatures
Vertical by W. P. Morehouse
Vertical by C. A. Morris
Vertical black by L. Calcagno
Vertical composition by F. Lebrun
The **very** great lion hunters by W. W. Quirt
A **very** happy picture by D. Tanning
Vessels of magic by M. Rothko
Vesuvius by J. Toole
Vetch, Margaret (Livingston) 1681-1758
Unidentified artist. Mrs Samuel Vetch
Vetch, Samuel, 1668-1732
Unidentified artist. Samuel Vetch
Veteran in a new field by W. Homer
Veteran's dream by C. Williamson
Via delle Corso, Rome by M. B. Prendergast

Via Partenope by W. Stuempfig
Via Porta Romana II by F. Bultman
Vianna do Castello, Portugal by J. S.
    Sargent
Vibration by S. Franks
VICENTE, Esteban, 1904-
    Composition, 1951
        Hess. Abstract ptg
    Composition no 6, 1959
        WMAA. Museum and its friends, 1958
    Growth, 1951
        Hess. Abstract ptg
    Number 3, 1952
        IU. Contemp Amer ptg & sculp, 1953
    Number 6
        IU. Contemp Amer ptg, 1952
    Number 9, 1959   MnMW
        MnMW. 60 Amer ptrs
VICKREY, Robert, 1926-
    Abandoned wharf
        IU. Contemp Amer ptg & sculp, 1959
    The barker
        IaDa. 30th anniversary
    Conversation
        Newmeyer
        WMAA. New decade
    Doorway
        ICA. Annual ex, 1951
    Fear   WMAA
        Pierson
        WMAA. Sara Roby
    Fear   PMB
        WMAA. New decade
    Gravel
        CSB. Illusion
    Halloween mask
        WMAA. New decade
    Hopscotch
        MiD. Coll in progress
        WiMiA. Amer ptg 1760-1960
    The labyrinth   WMAA
        Goodrich. Amer art
        McCurdy
        MnMW. Reality and fantasy
    Late afternoon   OYB
        OYB. Supplement 1959
    The poster
        IU. Contemp Amer ptg & sculp, 1955
Victim by S. W. Hayter
Victoria, queen of Great Britain, 1819-1901
    Sully, T. Queen Victoria
Victoria by W. Kuhn
Victorian building by Mingle
Victorian dairy farm, study in green by
    Unidentified artist
Victorian family by Unidentified artist
Victorian interior I, 1945 by H. Pippin
Victorian interior II, 1945 by H. Pippin
Victorian landscape by Unidentified artist
Victorian tapestry by P. L. Dike
VIDAR, Frede, 1911-
    Canal in Brooklyn
        IU. Contemp Amer ptg, 1949
    Manila no 4
        IU. Contemp Amer ptg, 1948
View from my window by E. Quincy
Vigil at the beach by T. C. Quirk
Villa dei misteri by A. Osver
Villa di Marlia: a fountain by J. S. Sargent

Villa di Marlia, Lucca by J. S. Sargent
Villa di Marlia: the balustrade by J. S.
    Sargent
Villa Falconiere by J. S. Sargent
Villa la Mouette by E. W. Dickinson
Villa Maria by C. Grant
Villa Rotunda by J. C. Atherton
The village by A. Blanch
Village above the river by L. Siegriest
Village church by L. Feininger
Village church by E. Ganso
Village church (Nieder-Reissen) by L.
    Feininger
Village dog by V. Candell
Village in the mountains by M. Kahn
Village, Maine by J. Marin
Village of the dead by G. Catlin
Village post office by T. W. Wood
A village street, Massachusetts, c 1845 by
    Unidentified artist
La Villette by W. J. Glackens
Vinal, John, 1736-1823
    Furness, J. M. John Vinal
Vinal, Mrs John
    Feke, R. Unknown woman (Mrs John
    Vinal?)
VINCENT, Andrew McDuffie, 1898-
    McKenzie motif   OrPA
        OrPA. Ptgs & sculptures
Vincent, Hannah. See Everett, Hannah
    (Vincent)
VINCENT, Tom, 1930-
    Crucifixion
        OYB. Annual 1959
Vines and cypresses by J. S. Sargent
Vineyards in Tuscany by W. Thon
VINSON, Charles
    Paper flowers and paper
        OYB. Annual 1954
Vintage of uncertainties by A. Salemme
Vinton, Frederick Porter, 1846-1911
    Sargent, J. S. Frederick Porter Vinton
Violet at seven by J. S. Sargent
The virgin by A. H. Thayer
Virgin Mary with Holy Ghost by Unidenti-
    fied artist
Virginia City building by L. B. Siegriest
Virginia deer by J. J. Audubon
Virginia in the grotto by P. Evergood
Virginia's constitutional convention of 1829-
    30 by G. Catlin
The virgins by J. Muller
Visa by S. Davis
Visione nobilissima by H. Hofmann
The visit by P. Guston
The visit by J. Koch
The visit by M. Weber
Visit to an Indian camp by A. J. Miller
Visitation of the buffalo gun by F. Reming-
    ton
Visiting neighbors by J. A. Weir
VISSER'T HOOFT, Martha H. 1906-
    Fish in bottle
        PPC. Ptg in the U.S. 1949

VISSER'T HOOFT, M. H.—*Continued*
Southern tier   NBuA
  NBuA. Acquisitions 1959-1961
Trojan horse
  IU. Contemp Amer ptg, 1952
Un **vista** by R. S. Neuman
Vita nova by L. Feininger
Vital storm by K. L. Callahan
Viterbo by J. E. Heliker
Viva Mexico by E. Berman
Vixen by D. Austin
Vocalization by J. K. Covert
VOGEL, Donald S. 1917-
Still life
  IU. Contemp Amer ptg & sculp, 1957
A **voice** from the cliffs by W. Homer
Voice of many waters by A. V. Tack
Voice of the desert by W. R. Leigh
Voice of the nightingale by J. Stella
Voices of spring by H. Hofmann
The **volante** at Habana by N. V. Calyo
Vollersroda by L. Feininger
Von Habermann, Hugo, fl 1875
Chase, W. M. Hugo Von Habermann
Von Hoesslin, Georg, fl 1878
Duveneck, F. George Von Hoesslin
Von Kline, Jacob, fl 1845
Unidentified artist. Jacob Von Kline
Von Kline, Mrs Jacob, fl 1845
Unidentified artist. Mrs Jacob Von Kline
Von Kories, Yvette
Speicher, E. E. Yvette Von Kories
Von Pfister, Alexander, fl 1803
Malbone, E. G. Alexander Von Pfister
VON PHUL, Anna Maria, 1786-1823
Boy in beaver hat   MoSLH
  Rathbone
Two young ladies   MoSLH
  Rathbone
Young gentleman of fashion   MoSLH
  Rathbone
VON SCHLEGELL, David, 1920-
Flayed hills
  IU. Contemp Amer ptg & sculp, 1957
Two sides of red
  MBIC. View 1960
VON WICHT, John G. F. 1888-
Harbor festivity   WMAA
  Pousette-Dart. Amer ptg
Paganini
  WMAA. Annual ex, 1948
Pertaining to harbour
  WMAA. Contemp Amer ptg, 1952
VON WIEGAND, Charmion
Eight allegories of fate
  WMAA. Annual ex, 1955
VON WITTKAMP, Andrew L. fl 1850
Black cat on a chair   MB
  MB. Karolik coll
VOORHIES, Charles, 1901-
Road to Alcumenar
  OrPA. Ptgs & sculptures
Vote for me by S. Raffo
Vox humana by J. D. Graham
The **voyage** by L. Feininger
The **voyage** by E. Giobbi
The **voyage** by R. B. Motherwell

Voyage of life: Childhood by T. Cole
Voyage of life: Manhood by T. Cole
Voyage of life: Youth by T. Cole
Voyage of the gods by E. J. Stevens
Voyage to Hell Gate from Communipaw by
  J. Quidor
Voyage to Matera by S. Sherman
Voyager's return by A. Gottlieb
Voyageurs by C. Deas
VYTLACIL, Vaclav, 1892-
Fish cleaner
  IU. Contemp Amer ptg, 1949
Fish composition
  DC. 21 biennial ex, 1949
Forest number 4
  IU. Contemp Amer ptg, 1951
Granada gardens
  IU. Contemp Amer ptg & sculp, 1957
Images of Pompeii   PA
  Pousette-Dart. Amer ptg
Sky and boats
  IU. Contemp Amer ptg, 1950
Wood interior   DP
  DP. Catalogue
Pierson
Wood interior   NJMo
  NJMo. Forty years

W

W. 1954 by A. Gottlieb
W. C. T. U. parade by B. Shahn
Waa-Na-Taa, chief of the Sioux by J. O.
  Lewis
Wade, Frances. See Bleecker, Frances
  (Wade)
Wade, James, 1789-1868
Ames, E. Dr James Wade
Wadsworth, Daniel
Trumbull, J. Jeremiah and his son Daniel
  Wadsworth
Wadsworth, Jeremiah, 1743-1804
Trumbull, J. Jeremiah and his son Daniel
  Wadsworth
Trumbull, J. Jeremiah Wadsworth
Wadsworth, Mrs Daniel. See Trumbull,
  Faith
WAGGUNO, fl 1858
Fruit and goldfinch   DN
  DN. Amer primitive ptgs, pt 1
WAGNER, Gordon
Sky festival   CoD
  Cos. New accessions USA, 1960
WAGNER, Jacob, 1852-1898
Neponset river, Milton   MB
  MB. Ptgs in water color
WAGNER, Joseph E. 1917-
Morning of November first   OYB
  OYB. Catalogue 1951
Wagner, Mrs Geoffrey. See Browning, Col-
  leen
Wagon boss by C. M. Russell
Wainwright, Rufus, fl 1840
Mason, B. F. Rufus Wainwright
Wainwright, Mrs Rufus, fl 1840
Mason, B. F. Mrs Rufus Wainwright

Wainwright children, fl 1840
Mason, B. F. Rufus and Gardner Wainwright
Waiter by G. P. Du Bois
Waiting by I. Bishop
Waiting by C. H. Demuth
Waiting by A. Gottlieb
Waiting figure by B. Greene
Waiting for a chinook by C. M. Russell
Waiting for a job by G. Grosz
Waiting for his turn by K. Schmidt
Waiting for the audition by R. Soyer
Waiting for the mail by R. Strang
Waiting for the stage by R. C. Woodville
Waiting in Bethlehem by W. Sommer
Waiting in the moonlight by F. Remington
Waiting room by R. Soyer
Wake of the ferry by J. Sloan
Wake of the hurricane by N. Spencer
Waking up by J. G. Clonney
Walden pond by L. E. Kupferman
Waldo, Cornelius, 1684-1753
Badger, J. Cornelius Waldo
Waldo, Mrs Cornelius. See Waldo, Faith (Savage)
Waldo, Deliverance Mapes, fl 1826
Waldo, S. L. Deliverance Mapes Waldo and her son
Waldo, Elizabeth. See Austin, Elizabeth (Waldo)
Waldo, Faith (Savage) 1683-1760
Badger, J. Mrs Cornelius Waldo
Waldo, George Mapes, 1827-1831
Waldo, S. L. Deliverance Mapes Waldo and her son
Waldo, Griselda (Oliver) b 1737
Copley, J. S. Mrs Samuel Waldo jr
Waldo, Samuel, 1696-1759
Feke, R. Gen Samuel Waldo
Waldo, Mrs Samuel. See Waldo, Griselda (Oliver)
WALDO, Samuel Lovett, 1783-1861
Andrew Jackson   MM
  Mendelowitz
Deliverance Mapes Waldo and her son
                                        MB
  MB. Karolik coll
James Gould   CtY
  CtY. Portrait index
  Pierson
Man with a watch fob   MB
  MB. Karolik coll
  Richardson. Ptg in America
Self-portrait   MiD
  MiD. Treasures
WALDO, Samuel Lovett, 1783-1861 and
  JEWETT, William, 1795-1873
Frederick Wolcott   CtY
  CtY. Portrait index
John Trumbull   CtY
  CtY. Portrait index
  Pierson
Lady in a dark blue dress   MB
  MB. Karolik coll
Waldron, Pieter, fl 1720
Unidentified artist. Pieter Waldron
Wales, Abby Langdon (Frothingham)
  fl 1820
Goodridge, S. Mrs Thomas B. Wales

WALES, George Canning, 1868-1940
Clipper ship Competitor   MB
  MB. Ptgs in water color
Racing to market   MB
  MB. Ptgs in water color
Wales, Mrs Thomas B. See Wales, Abby Langdon (Frothingham)
A walk in the poppies by T. Stamos
Walk-in-the-Water (steamship)
Mathies, J.L.D. Wreck of the steamer Walk-in-the-Water
Walk in town by K. F. Roesch
WALKER, Charles Howard, 1857-1936
Albert IV the Wise   MB
  MB. Ptgs in water color
Elizabeth of Tirol   MB
  MB. Ptgs in water color
Godfrey of Bouillon   MB
  MB. Ptgs in water color
Joanna of Castile   MB
  MB. Ptgs in water color
Philip the Good   MB
  MB. Ptgs in water color
Section of the Parthenon   MB
  MB. Ptgs in water color
Walker, Clara. See Allen, Clara (Walker)
WALKER, Clay, 1924-
Security of the mother   OYB
  OYB. Annual 1959
  OYB. Supplement 1959
WALKER, Gene Alden
Mal du pays
  PPC. Ptg in the U. S. 1949
Tetralogy portrait—Percy MacKaye
  NAD. Annual ex, 1949, 1st half
Young Aurora
  IU. Contemp Amer ptg, 1948
Walker, Lucretia Pickering. See Morse, Lucretia Pickering (Walker)
WALKER, William Aiken, 1838-1921
Charleston harbor from the Battery during the bombardment of Fort Sumter, April 13, 1861
  Davidson v2
Cotton picker's home
  Davidson v1
Dollarfish and sheepshead   MB
  MB. Karolik coll
Scene along the lower Mississippi, 1883
  Davidson v2
Walker family, fl 1790
Unidentified artist. Walker family, father and son of Middle Haddam, Connecticut
Unidentified artist. Walker family, mother and daughter of Middle Haddam, Connecticut
Walker greets Mooney by B. Shahn
Walker greets mother of Mooney by B. Shahn
WALKOWITZ, Abraham, 1880-
Bathers: eight foreground figures   MB
  MB. Ptgs in water color
Bathers: four foreground figures   MB
  MB. Ptgs in water color
Bathers: three foreground figures   MB
  MB. Ptgs in water color
Color symphony
  WMAA. Pioneers
Family group   MB
  MB. Ptgs in water color

WALKOWITZ, Abraham—*Continued*
New York
  Cheney. Primer 1958 ed
New York, 1917   WMAA
  Goodrich. Amer art
New York, improvisation, 1913   WMAA
  McCurdy
Oriental head
  Cheney. Expressionism 1948 ed
People in the park   DP
  Cheney. Story 1958 ed
Rocky coast   MB
  MB. Ptgs in water color
Summer   MM
  Brown. Amer ptg
Three dance abstractions: Isadora Duncan
                     CtY
  CtY. Soc Anonyme
Times square, abstraction no 1   MB
  MB. Ptgs in water color
Times square, abstraction no 2   MB
  MB. Ptgs in water color
WALL, A. Bryan, d 1937
Shepherd and his flock   PW
  Chew. 250 years of art
WALL, Alfred S. fl 1835-1890
Sunlight and shadow   PPC
  Chew. 250 years of art
WALL, William Allen, 1801-1885
New Bedford in 1807
  Davidson v 1
WALL, William Coventry, 1810-1886
Homestead mill near Pittsburgh
  U. S. National capital sesquicentennial
  com
Pittsburgh after the fire of 1845 (Ruins of
  Pittsburgh)   PPC
  Chew. 250 years of art
  Davidson v2 (detail)
WALL, William Guy, 1792-1864
Hudson river from West Point   CtNL
  NYG. Fine art
View from Fishkill, New York   NNHS
  Born
View near Fishkill   NNPL
  Larkin
  Larkin rev ed
View near Fort Montgomery   NNHS
  Flexner. Light of distant skies
View of Ogdensburg
  Jones. Rediscovered ptrs
The **wall** by J. Erickson
The **wall** by R. Gleitsman
The **wall** by L. Grebenak
The **wall** by W. T. Murch
The **wall** by W. Stuempfig
Wall of spikes by E. Berman
Wall street, half past 2 o'clock, October 13,
  1857 by J. H. Cafferty and C. D.
  Rosenberg
Wall with green door by G. O'Keeffe
WALLER, Frank, 1842-1923
Metropolitan museum in Fourteenth
  street, 1881   MM
  Davidson v2
  Larkin
  Larkin rev ed
Wallscape by J. L. Lasker
Walsh, Ann, 1800-1811
  Ames, E. Ann Walsh

WALSH, Edward
Fort Erie from Buffalo creek, site of the
  city of Buffalo, c 1810   NNPL
  Davidson v2
WALTER, Joseph, 1783-1856
Arrival of the Great Western at New
  York, 1838   NNPL
  Davidson v1
  U.S. National Capital sesquicentennial
  com
WALTERS, S.
A Collins line steamship
  Davidson v 1
WALTERS, Susane, fl 1852
Memorial to Nicholas Catlin   DN
  DN. Amer primitive ptgs, pt 1
Walton, Cornelia (Beekman) 1708-1786
  Wollaston, J. Mrs William Walton
Walton, Ezekiel, fl 1811
  Tuthill, A. G. D. Gen Ezekiel Walton
Walton, Mrs Ezekiel, fl 1811
  Tuthill, A. G. D. Mrs Ezekiel Walton
WALTON, Henry, fl 1842
De Mott Smith, aged 8
  Jones. Rediscovered ptrs
Emeline Boynton, aged 32
  Jones. Rediscovered ptrs
Harriet Elizabeth Boynton, age 2 years
  Jones. Rediscovered ptrs
Henry Boynton, age 39
  Jones. Rediscovered ptrs
Sarah Louisa Spencer   VWR
  VWR. Folk art (col)
View of Ithaca, Tompkins county, New
  York, 1838
  Jones. Rediscovered ptrs
Walton, Mrs Jonathan. See Walton, Mar-
  garet Ann (Thatcher)
Walton, Margaret Ann (Thatcher) d 1843
  Ames, E. Mrs Jonathan Walton
Walton, Mrs William. See Walton, Cornelia
  (Beekman)
Wanamaker block by F. J. Kline
Wandelaer, Pau de, fl 1725
  Gansevoort limner. Pau de Wandelaer
The **wanderer** by W. Day
The **wanderers** by J. W. Treiman
Wandering Jew by P. Burlin
Wanderlust by P. Bacon
Wanton, Joseph, 1705-1780
  Smibert, J. Joseph Wanton
Wapiti by W. J. Hayes
Wapping on Thames by J. A. M. Whistler
War among the arthropods by F. Carbone
War dance of the Sauks and Foxes by P.
  Rindisbacher
War [dog] dance in the interior of a Konza
  lodge by S. Seymour
War horses by Unidentified artist
War news from Mexico by R. C. Woodville
War prisoners by L. Eades
War series: another patrol by J. Lawrence
The **war** spirit at home: celebrating the
  victory at Vicksburg by L. M. Spencer
Warblers
  Heil, C. E. Bay-breasted warbler on apple
  blossom
  Heil, C. E. Chestnut-sided warbler on
  barberry

WARD, Charles Caleb, fl 1870
Circus is coming
Davidson v2
Ward, Hugh C. fl 1870
Bingham, G. C. Hugh C. Ward
Ward, James, 1769-1859
Stuart, G. James Ward
Ward, Richard, 1689-1763
Unidentified artist. Richard Ward
Warehouse by R. Morgan
Warehouse mannequins by W. De Kooning
Warmth of memory by L. W. Coleman
WARNER, Catherine Townsend, 1785-1828
Mourning picture—George Washington
VWR
VWR. Folk art (col)
Warner, Elizabeth (Pitts) See Pitts, Elizabeth
Warner, Mary, 1757-1780?
Blackburn, J. Mary Warner
Copley, J. S. Mary Warner
Warner, Mary MacPhedris (Osborne) fl 1761
Blackburn, J. Mrs Jonathan Warner
WARRE, Henry J. 1819-1898
Fort Vancouver, 1845
U.S. National Capital sesquicentennial com
WARREN, Ferdinand E. 1899-
Lunar magic   OYB
OYB. Annual 1954
OYB. Supplement
Night baseball game Cardinals vs. Dodgers
GAtM
GAtM. Holbrook collection
Town square, Independence, Missouri
DC. 21 biennial ex, 1949
The ultimate city
NAD. Annual ex, 1951
Warren, Gretchen (Osgood)
Sargent, J. S. Mrs Fiske Warren and her daughter Rachel
WARREN, Harold Broadfield, 1859-1934
Aegina from the Acropolis, Athens   MB
MB. Ptgs in water color
Corner of the Parthenon, Athens   MB
MB. Ptgs in water color
The Parthenon, Athens   MB
MB. Ptgs in water color
The Propylaea, Athens   MB
MB. Ptgs in water color
Warren, James, 1726-1808
Copley, J. S. James Warren
Warren, Joseph, 1731-1775
Copley, J. S. Joseph Warren
Warren, Mercy (Otis) 1728-1815
Copley, J. S. Mrs James Warren
Warren, Rebecca. See Brown, Rebecca (Warren)
Warrior by C. di Marca-Relli
Warriors' long trail by C. M. Russell
WARSHAW, Howard, 1920-
Blue hands
NNSG. Younger Amer ptrs
Child's skull
CtY. Yale alumni
Reclining figure
IU. Contemp Amer ptg, 1951
Spectator
MAA. Contemp Amer ptg, 1953

Two classical studies
PPC. International ex, 1955
The witnesses
IU. Contemp Amer ptg & sculp, 1959
Warwick mine, exit no 1 by A. Frasconi
Wase, Phillip
Bellows, G. W. Mr and Mrs Phillip Wase
Wash day by A. M. R. Moses
Washburn, Cadwalader
Chase, W. M. Cadwalader Washburn
Washerwomen by E. Melcarth
Washington, Bailey
Peale, J. Surgeon Bailey Washington, U.S.N.
Washington, George, president U.S. 1732-1799
Ames, E. George Washington
Bingham, G. C. Washington crossing the Delaware, 1872
De Grailly, V. Washington's headquarters, Newburgh-on-the-Hudson
Heath, J. (after G. Stuart) George Washington
Hicks, E. Washington crossing the Delaware
Kemmelmeyer, F. George Washington reviewing the western army at Fort Cumberland
Leutze, E. Washington crossing the Delaware
Peale, C. W. George Washington
Peale, C. W. Washington, Lafayette and Tilghman at Yorktown
Peale, Rembrandt. George Washington
Peale, Rembrandt. George Washington (porthole portrait)
Pickett, J. George Washington under the Council tree
Reed, R. L. Washington and Lafayette at the battle of Yorktown
Rivers, L. Washington crossing the Delaware
Rowell, A. J. George Washington
Sanford, M. M. Washington at Princeton
Smith, R. Original tomb of Washington, 1836
Stuart, G. George Washington
Stuart, G. George Washington (Athenaeum type)
Stuart, G. George Washington (Lansdowne type)
Stuart, G. George Washington (Miller-Cake-J. Stewart portrait)
Stuart, G. George Washington (Vaughan type)
Stuart, G. Washington at Dorchester Heights
Sully, T. Passage of the Delaware
Trumbull, J. George Washington
Trumbull, J. George Washington (Martha Washington type)
Trumbull, J. George Washington (detail of head of Washington at the Battle of Trenton)
Trumbull, J. George Washington at the Battle of Trenton
Trumbull, J. Resignation of Gemeral Washington at Annapolis
Unidentified artist. General Washington on white charger

Washington, George, president U.S.—_Continued_
  Unidentified artist. George Washington family
  Unidentified artist. George Washington with horse
  Unidentified artist. Washington and his staff at Fort Cumberland, Md. 1794
  Unidentified artist. Washington, the Mason
  Warner, C. T. Mourning picture—George Washington
  Willson, M. A. George Washington on horseback
  Wright, J. George Washington
Washington, Martha (Dandridge) Custis, 1732-1802
  Stuart, G. Martha Washington
  Unidentified artist. Mrs George Washington (after C. W. Peale)
Washington family
  Savage, E. The Washington family
Washington, D.C.
  Boit, E. D. The Capitol, Washington
  Burton, C. United States capitol, 1824
  Heriot, G. The Capitol after the British assault on Washington, 1815
  Latrobe, B. H. East front of the President's house with the addition of the north and south porticos, 1807
  Matthew, K. Capitol reflections
Washington arch, spring by C. Hassam
Washington crossing the Delaware by L. Rivers
The **Washington,** first double decker on the Mississippi by Unidentified artist
Washington monument, Washington square, N.Y. by A. S. Mira
Washington square by W. J. Glackens
Washington square, New York by D. Kingman
Washington's tomb by F. Guy
Washington's tomb at Mount Vernon by W. De Grailly
Washington's tomb at Mount Vernon by W. M. Prior
Washington's tomb, Mt Vernon by W. H. Bartlett
The **Wasp** and the Frolic by T. Birch
Watch and fob by J. A. Tilles
Watch factory by N. Spencer
Watching by A. Gottlieb
Watching for the smoke signal by C. M. Russell
Watching the cargo by G. C. Bingham
Watching the clock by K. Sage
Watching the settlers by C. M. Russell
Watchmaker with his tools by Unidentified artist
Water by C. Sheeler
Water by R. Strang
Water fan by W. Homer
Water front by E. Ludins
The **water** girl by C. M. Russell
Water lily by M. J. Heade
Water mill prospect by L. Rivers
Water of the flowery mill by A. Gorky
Water-table by Y. Tanguy
Water waltz by J. Guerin
Waterbury bridge: number one by D. Margules

Waterfall by A. G. Dove
Waterfall by A. Gorky
Waterfall by B. Miller
Waterfall by M. B. Prendergast
The **waterfall** by J. H. Twachtman
Waterfall, Morse pond by M. Hartley
Waterfront (New York) by K. Matthew
Watergame by J. Tworkov
The **watering** place by A. Fisher
Watering pots by T. Robinson
Watermelon by Unidentified artist
Watermelon and fruit by J. Peale (attributed works)
Watermelon and fruit by Raphaelle Peale
WATERS, E. A.
  Lady of the lake   VWR
    Ford. Pictorial folk art
Waters, John, 1774-1844
  Malbone, E. G. John Waters
Waters, Joseph Gilbert, 1796-1878
  Osgood, C. Joseph Gilbert Waters
Waterton, Charles, 1782-1865
  Peale, C. W. Charles Waterton
Waterworks, Center square, Philadelphia by Unidentified artist
WATKINS, Franklin Chenault, 1894-
  Angel   MiD
    MMA. Watkins
  Angel posed
    MMA. Watkins
  The angel will turn a page in a book   DP
    DP. Catalogue
    MMA. Watkins
  Autumn recollections   DP
    DP. Catalogue
  Beloved dead   ATeS
    ATeS. Collection
    MMA. Watkins
    Pousette-Dart. Amer ptg
  Birth of spring
    Chew. 250 years of art
  Blue chair   MoKN
    MMA. Watkins
  Boris Blai   MMA
    Cheney. Story 1958 ed
    MMA. Watkins
  Crucifixion
    MMA. Watkins
  Death
    Baur. New art
    MMA. Watkins
    PPC. International ex, 1950
  Death, Study for
    MMA. Watkins
  Death in the orchard
    MMA. Watkins
  Descent no 1, 1947
    MMA. Watkins
  Dr George Kamperman
    Baur. Revolution
  Fanciful meeting long ago
    MMA. Watkins
  Fire eater   PPhM
    Baur. New art (col)
    Gruskin
    MMA. Watkins
    NYG. Fine art
    Pierson
    Wight. Milestones
  Flowers in Pennsylvania Dutch teapot
    WiMiA. Amer ptg 1760-1960

Gabriel   MM
  MM. 100 Amer ptrs
Henry P. McIlhenny
  MMA. Watkins
J. Stogdell Stokes   PPhM
  MMA. Watkins
Joseph G. Butler   OYB
  OYB. Supplement 1959
Justice Owen J. Roberts   PPhUn
  Baur. New art
  MMA. Watkins
  Pierson
Make the monkey jump
  IU. Contemp Amer ptg & sculp, 1959
Misses Maude and Maxine Meyer de
  Schauensee
  MMA. Watkins (col)
Mrs C. E. Etnier
  MMA. Watkins
Mrs John F. Steinman
  MMA. Watkins
Mrs Joseph S. Clark jr
  PA. Annual ex, 1954
Musician
  MMA. Watkins
Negro spiritual
  MMA. Watkins
Paul P. Cret
  MMA. Watkins
The picnic
  MMA. Watkins
Prudence
  PPC. Ptg in the U.S. 1949
R. Sturgis Ingersoll
  MMA. Watkins
Remember me
  MMA. **Watkins**
Resurrection   IBM
  MMA. Watkins
Resurrection (McIlhenny coll)
  MMA. Watkins (col)
Resurrection no 1, 1947
  MMA. Watkins
Resurrection no 2, 1947
  MMA. Watkins
Resurrection, Study for, 1947
  MMA. Watkins
The return
  MMA. Watkins
Robert Raeburn White, esq
  Gruskin
Rosemary Thompson
  MMA. Watkins
Self-portrait
  WiMiA. Amer ptg 1760-1960
The sideboard   WMAA
  Goodrich. Amer art (col)
Soliloquy   WMAA
  Baur. New art
  Goodrich. Amer art
  MMA. Watkins
  Pierson
Solitaire   MNS
  MMA. Watkins
  Time. 300 years (col)
Springtime   CSB
  MMA. Watkins
Still life   MiD
  MiD. Treasures
Still life (Wenger coll)
  MMA. Watkins
The studio   NBuA
  MMA. Watkins
  NBuA. Contemporary ptgs

Suicide in costume   PPhM
  Canaday
  MMA. Watkins
Sunny morning
  WiMiA. Amer ptg 1760-1960
Thomas Raeburn White
  Baur. New art
  MMA. Watkins
  Richardson. Ptg in America
To the tomb
  MMA. Watkins
WATKINS, Mary Bradley
  The blue and the strawberry roan   DP
  DP. Catalogue
Watson, Sir Brook, bart, 1735-1807
  Copley, J. S. Brook Watson
Watson, Elizabeth (Oliver) 1737-1767
  Copley, J. S. Mrs George Watson
Watson, Elkanah, 1758-1842
  Ames, E. Elkanah Watson
  Copley, J. S. Elkanah Watson
Watson, Mrs George. See Watson, Elizabeth
  (Oliver)
WATSON, John, 1685-1768
  Lewis Morris of New Jersey   NBM
    Belknap
    Flexner. First flowers
    Pierson
  William Burnet   NNHS
    Belknap
  William Burnet   NAI
    NAI. Hudson valley

Attributed works

  Anne Van Rensselaer   NNHS
    Belknap
  Gentleman of the Van Rensselaer family
    (probably Jacobus Van Rensselaer,
    also known as Kiliaen Van Rensselaer)
                           NAI
    Belknap
  Gentleman of the Van Rensselaer family
    (probably Stephanus Van Rensselaer)
                          NNHS
    Belknap
    NNHS. Waldron Phoenix Belknap coll
  Johannes Schuyler and his wife Elizabeth
    Staats Wendell   NNHS
    Belknap
    Pierson
  Mrs Kiliaen Van Rensselaer   NNHS
    Belknap
    NNHS. Waldron Phoenix Belknap coll
  Mrs Stephanus(?) Van Rensselaer
    Belknap
  Van Rensselaer gentleman (known as Jan
    Baptist Van Rensselaer)   NAI
    Belknap
    NAI. Hudson valley
WATSON, Robert, 1923-
  The bridge
    CSFP. Annual ex, 1952
  The guardian
    NAD. Annual ex, 1955
  Interior
    IU. Contemp Amer ptg & sculp, 1955
Watson and the shark by J. S. Copley
Watts, Francis O. fl 1805
  Brewster, J. Francis O. Watts with bird
WAUGH, Frederick Judd, 1861-1940
  A bit of the Cape
    NYG. Fine art (col)
  Breakers at floodtide   OYB
    OYB. Catalogue 1951

WAUGH, F. J.—*Continued*
Coast of Maine   NJN
  NYG. Fine art
Great seas   InTH
  InTH. Catalogue
Open sea
  NYG. Fine art
Pounding surf   PPC
  NYG. Fine art
Surf under moonlight   PR
  PR. Catalogue
Windward shore   IaIU
  NYG. Fine art
WAUGH, Samuel B. 1814-1885
Immigrants' arrival at New York, 1847
                                NNMC
  Davidson v2
The **wave** by W. De Kooning
The **wave** by M. Hartley
The **wave** by C. A. Morris
The **wave** by G. O'Keeffe
The **wave** by E. F. Spruce
Wave breaking by E. F. Spruce
Wave motif by E. Kelly
Waves by E. F. Spruce
Waves of love and of the sea by K. Schrag
Waving the flag by G. Grosz
Wayland, Francis, 1826-1904
  Weir, J. F. Francis Wayland
WAYNE, June C. 1918-
The advocate
  IU. Contemp Amer ptg & sculp, 1955
The ladder
  ICA. Annual ex, 1951
Law court
  IU. Contemp Amer ptg & sculp, 1953
The messenger
  IU. Contemp Amer ptg & sculp, 1957
The sanctified
  CSFP. Annual ex, 1952
Ways and means by S. Davis
Wayside inn by A. F. Bellows
We bought a fish by M. L. Thomas
We gather together by M. Kahn
We go for the Union by Unidentified artist
Weaning the calf by W. Homer
Weary by E. Higgins
Weary by W. Homer
Weather vane by A. G. Dove
Weather vane and sofa by Y. Kuniyoshi
Weatherbeaten, or Stormbeaten by W.
  Homer
Weatherbee, Mrs
  Fuller, G. Old age (Mrs Weatherbee)
Weavers of a spell by H. Janicki
The **web** (Croton dam) by C. Sheeler
Webb, Mr. fl 1791
  Stuart, G. Webb sr
Webb, Clifton, 1893-
  Bellows, G. W. Robin (Portrait of Clifton
    Webb)
Webb, James Watson, 1802-1884
  Chase, W. M. Gen James Watson Webb
Webb, Samuel Blachley (or Blatchley) 1753-
  1807
  Peale, C. W. Samuel B. Webb

Webber, Mrs Jeremiah
  Blythe, D. G. Mrs Jeremiah Webber and
    son
WEBBER, John, fl 1750-1793
View in Nootka sound   CtY
  U.S. National Capital sesquicentennial
    com
WEBER, Hugo, 1918-
Dark stretch
  NNSG. Younger Amer ptrs
WEBER, Max, 1881-1961
Acrobats
  Goodrich. Max Weber
  WMAA. Museum and its friends, 1959
Adoration of the moon   WMAA
  Baur. New art
  Goodrich. Amer art (col)
  Goodrich. Max Weber (col)
  NJN. Weber
  Pierson
After an ice storm   DP
  DP. Catalogue
Alone   FaW
  Goodrich. Max Weber
The antique   CtY
  CtY. Soc Anonyme
At the lake
  Goodrich. Max Weber
At the mill   NJN
  Goodrich. Max Weber
  NJN. Weber
Avenue of trees
  MnU. 40 Amer ptrs
Bach orchestra
  NJN. Weber
The bathers [1]
  Goodrich. Max Weber
The bathers [2]   MdBM
  NJN. Weber
Beautification   MM
  MM. 100 Amer ptrs
  Taylor. Fifty centuries, 1954 ed (col)
Beautification   InBU
  NUM. Art across America
Blue New York
  NJN. Weber
Broken tree
  Cheney. New world history
Chinese restaurant   WMAA
  Baur. New art
  Goodrich. Amer art (col)
  Goodrich. Max Weber
  Hunter. Mod Amer ptg (col)
  Larkin
  Larkin rev ed
  McCurdy
  Mendelowitz
  MMA. Abstract (col)
  NBuA. Expressionism
  NJN. Weber
  Pierson
  Rathbun
  Rosenblum
  WMAA. Juliana Force
The comb
  PA. Annual ex, 1956
Composition—three figures
  Brown. Amer ptg
Composition with three figures
  Brown. Amer ptg
  Goodrich. Max Weber
Conversation
  Pearson. Mod renaissance

A cup of tea
  Goodrich. Max Weber
Dauntless bird
  IU. Contemp Amer ptg, 1949
  Pousette-Dart. Amer ptg
Decoration with cloud   MMA
  Baur. Revolution
  Cheney. Story 1958 ed
Deserted farm   OCl
  OCl. Handbook
Drapeau   GAtM
  GAtM. Holbrook collection
Draped head   DP
  DP. Catalogue
Early American abstract
  CtY. Yale alumni
Eight figures
  Pearson. Mod renaissance
Family reunion
  Goodrich. Max Weber
  IU. Contemp Amer ptg, 1951
  Pearson. Mod renaissance
Figure study   NBuA
  NBuA. Acquisitions 1959-1961
  NJN. Weber
Figure with bird
  DC. 27 biennial ex, 1961
Flower piece   TxF
  UNESCO. 1860-1949
  UNESCO. 1860-1955
  UNESCO. 1860-1959
Flute soloist
  Roos
The forest
  Barker. From realism
Friendship
  Goodrich. Max Weber
Geranium   MMA
  Baur. New art
  Goodrich. Max Weber
  McCurdy
  MMA. Masters (col)
  MMA. Ptg and sculpture
  Pierson
  Raynal. History v3 (col)
Gesture
  Baur. Revolution
  Cheney. Expressionism 1948 ed
  Flexner. Amer ptg
  Flexner. Short history
  Goodrich. Max Weber
  NJN. Weber
Good news
  Goodrich. Max Weber
Good news
  NBuA. Expressionism
Grand central terminal
  DC. De gustibus
Group of figures
  Goodrich. Max Weber
Guitar player   IBM
  Genauer (col)
The harem
  NJN. Weber
Hasidic dance
  Baur. New art
  Baur. Revolution
  Goodrich. Max Weber
  MMA. Contemp ptrs
  Pierson
  WMAA. Museum and its friends, 1958
Head of a woman
  NJN. Weber

Heads
  NJN. Weber
Interior of the fourth dimension
  NJN. Weber
Interior with figures
  WMAA. Annual ex, 1958
Interior with men
  Blesh
Invocation
  Biddle. Yes and no
Joel's cave
  NJN. Weber
Landscape, 1928   NJN
  NJN. Weber
Latest news   MoKN
  Time. 300 years (col)
Leaning figure
  IU. Contemp Amer ptg & sculp, 1959
Mothers and children
  Lewisohn
Multiple portrait
  IU. Contemp Amer ptg & sculp, 1961
Muses
  Goodrich. Max Weber
Music   NBM
  CoS. New accessions USA, 1950
  Goodrich. Max Weber
  Lee. Art then and now
  Munsterberg
Music of the Orient
  IU. Contemp Amer ptg & sculp, 1957
Musical evening   CLA
  CLA. 35 ptgs
New York
  MMA. Abstract
  NBuA. Fifty ptgs
New York at night
  Brown. Amer ptg
  MMA. Abstract
  MnMW. Classic tradition
La Parisienne
  NJN. Weber
Pleasures of summer
  Goodrich. Max Weber
The rabbi
  Brown. Amer ptg
  Goodrich. Max Weber
Red cap   WMAA
  Larkin
  Larkin rev ed
Refugees   KW
  Goodrich. Max Weber
  NJN. Weber
Repose no 2, 1950
  NJN. Weber
Rush hour, New York
  Goodrich. Max Weber
  Hess. Abstract ptg
  MMA. Abstract
  Pierson
  Rosenblum
Russian ballet
  Goodrich. Max Weber
Sabbath
  NJN. Weber
Seeking work
  Gruskin (col)
  McCurdy
Solo
  NJN. Weber
Still life   ATeS
  ATeS. Collection
Still life   ICA
  CoS. New accessions USA, 1946

WEBER, Max—*Continued*
Still life, bread and peppers
  NJN. Weber
Still life, Egyptian pot
  Brown. Amer ptg
Still life with flowers
  NYG. Fine art
  UNESCO. 1860-1949
  UNESCO. 1860-1955
  UNESCO. 1860-1959
Still life with palette
  CSFP. Annual ex, 1952
  Goodrich. Max Weber
Still life with two tables
  Goodrich. Max Weber
String music
  Goodrich. Max Weber
  MnMW. Contemporary (col)
  WMAA. Neuberger collection
Summer   WMAA
  Bazin
  Goodrich. Amer art
  NYG. Fine art
  UNESCO. 1860-1949
  UNESCO. 1860-1955
  UNESCO. 1860-1959
Three jugs   DP
  Cheney. Primer 1958 ed
Three literary gentlemen   MLL
  Baur. New art (col)
  Baur. Revolution
  Goodrich. Max Weber
  IU. Contemp Amer ptg, 1948
  Pierson
The toilers
  NJN. Weber
Tranquility
  Baur. New art
  Goodrich. Max Weber
  Pierson
The trio   WMAA
  DC. Halpert collection
  IU. Contemp Amer ptg & sculp, 1953
  WMAA. Sara Roby
Two musicians   MMA
  Brown. Amer ptg
  MMA. Contemp ptrs
  NJN. Weber
  Read Concise history
The visit
  Baur. Revolution
  Goodrich. Max Weber
Whither now
  Wight. Milestones
Wind orchestra
  Goodrich. Max Weber
Winter twilight   CSB
  Cheney. Story 1958 ed
  Goodrich. Max Weber
  Gruskin
  Pearson. Mod renaissance
  Pierson
  Robb. Art 1953 ed
  Robb. Harper history
Woman carrying picture   MnMW
  Goodrich. Max Weber
Woman holding tablet
  MnU. 40 Amer ptrs
Women and tents
  WMAA. Pioneers
Young model
  Pearson. Mod renaissance
Zinnias   NJN
  NJN. Weber

WEBER, Paul, 1823-1916
  The artist sketching his friends
    Chew. 250 years of art
WEBER, Paul, 1823-1916 and SCHUES-
  SELE, Christian, 1824?-1879
  Skating at Kelly's dam. Germantown PH
    Chew. 250 years of art
Webster, Daniel, 1782-1852
  Healy, G. P. A. Daniel Webster
  Unidentified artist. Daniel Webster at his
    farm
Webster, Noah, 1758-1843
  Verstille, W. Noah Webster
Wedding dress by B. Kamihira
Weddings
  Krimmel, J. S. Country wedding
  Lee, D. E. Country wedding
  Stokes, J. S. Wedding in the Big Smoky
    mountains, 1872
  Woodville, R. C. Sailor's wedding
WEDIN, Elof, 1901-
  Black harbor, a grey moon   MNS
    CoS. New accessions USA, 1954
Weeds by N. Ziroli
Weeping girl by F. Martin
Weighing cotton by T. H. Benton
Weights of the Pacific by L. Mullican
WEINER, Bernard M. 1924-
  Bronx light   OYB
    OYB. Annual 1958
    OYB. Supplement 1959
WEIR, John Ferguson, 1841-1926
  Artist's studio   CtY
    Weir. Recollections
  Forging the shaft (replica)   MM
    Weir. Recollections
  Forging the shaft: a welding heat   MM
    Pierson
  Francis Wayland   CtY
    CtY. Portrait index
  Gun foundry, Cold Spring, New York
    (Gun factory)
    Baur. Revolution
    U.S. National Capital sesquicentennial
    com
    Weir. Recollections
  Russell H. Chittenden   CtY
    CtY. Portrait index
  Samuel Wells Williams   CtY
    CtY. Portrait index
  The Theological of Yale university (Bacon,
    Barbour, Day, Dwight, Fisher, Harris)
        CtY
    CtY. Portrait index
  View of the Highlands from West Point
        NNHS
    Born
    Weir. Recollections

Portrait of the artist
  Alexander, J. W. Professor John Fergu-
    son Weir
WEIR, Julian Alden, 1852-1919
  Building a dam, Shetucket   OCl
    OCl. Handbook
  The green bodice   MM
    MM. 100 Amer ptrs
  Miss De L   DC
    DC. 25 biennial ex, 1957
  Pan and the wolf   DP
    DP. Catalogue

Red Bridge   MM
  Pierson
Still life   InIJ
  InIJ. 105 ptgs
Visiting neighbors   DP
  DP. Catalogue
  Larkin
  Larkin rev ed
  Pierson
Willimantic, Connecticut   ATeS
  ATeS. Collection
Willimantic thread mill   NBM
  Born
Windham village   MoSL
  MoSL. Handbook 1953
WEIR, Robert Walter, 1803-1889
  Bianca   MB
    MB. Karolik coll
  Red Jacket   NCHA
    Jones. Rediscovered ptrs
  Self-portrait   NNHS
    Weir. Recollections
  View of the Hudson from West Point
    Sears. Highlights (col)

            Attributed works
  Shipwreck at sea   NAI
    Jones. Rediscovered ptrs
Weir by J. E. Levi
The weir and the island by W. A. V. Kien-
  busch
Weir's orchard by A. P. Ryder
WEISMANN, Donald L. 1914-
  Ground-air control   OYB
    OYB. Annual 1957
    OYB. Supplement 1959
WEISS, Hugh, 1925-
  Italian village
    IU. Contemp Amer ptg & sculp, 1953
Welcome home by L. Bosa
Welcome home by J. Levine
Weld, Mrs. Henry T. See Hoffman, Harriet
  Emily
The welder by D. A. Vaughan
Welders by B. Shahn
Wellfleet, Cottages at by E. Hopper
WELLS, Cady, 1904-
  The idols
    IU. Contemp Amer ptg & sculp, 1953
  Interlunar sea
    ICA. Annual ex, 1947/48
  Landscape from above
    IU. Contemp Amer ptg, 1952
  Penitente
    WMAA. Annual ex, 1949
Wells, Eliza, fl 1840
  Stanley, A. R. Eliza Wells
Wells, Henry, fl 1845
  Unidentified artist. Henry Wells
Welsteed, William, fl 1753
  Copley, J. S. Rev William Welsteed
WENCK, Paul
  Grand Canyon, Arizona
    NYG. Fine art
  Rockies from Bear lake
    NYG. Fine art
Wendell, Elizabeth Staats. See Schuyler,
  Elizabeth Staats (Wendell)
Wendell, Harmanus, 1678-1732
  Unidentified artist. Harmanus Wendell
Wendell, Johannes, b 1714?
  Unidentified artist. Johannes Wendell

Wenona's leap by S. Eastman
Wensley, Elizabeth (Paddy) b 1641
  Unidentified artist. Elizabeth Paddy
    Wensley
Wentworth, Frances Deering (Wentworth)
  Lady, 1746-1813
  Copley, J. S. Lady Frances Wentworth
Wentworth, Hannah. See Atkinson, Hannah
  (Wentworth)
WENTZ, Evelyn E.
  Universe   OYB
    OYB. Annual 1951
WENTZ, Harry, 1876-
  Rocks in the sea   OrPA
    Pierson
Wertheimer, Asher, 1844-1918
  Sargent, J. S. Asher Wertheimer
Wertheimer, Mrs Asher
  Sargent, J. S. Mrs Asher Wertheimer
Wertheimer, The Misses
  Sargent, J. S. Daughters of Asher Wert-
    heimer
WERTZ, Harry
  Fisherman in red hat and shirt
    NSP. Sportscapes
WESCOTT, Paul, 1904-
  The harbor   OYB
    OYB. Annual 1959
    OYB. Supplement 1959
Wesleyan academy, Wilbraham, Massachu-
  setts by Unidentified artist
WEST, Benjamin, 1738-1820
  The Adrian Hope family group   MB
    Pierson
  Agrippina and her children mourning over
    the ashes of Germanicus
    Evans. Benjamin West
  Agrippina landing at Brundisium with the
    ashes of Germanicus   CtY
    Evans. Benjamin West
  Flexner. Light of distant skies
  Air, Water, Earth, and Fire (Dome of the
    Royal academy of arts, London)
    Evans. Benjamin West
  The angel of the Lord announcing the
    resurrection to the Marys at the
    sepulchre   NMB
    Evans. Benjamin West
  The apotheosis of Nelson
    Evans. Benjamin West
  The appeal of Coriolanus
    Evans. Benjamin West
  The archangel Gabriel
    Evans. Benjamin West
  Arthur Middleton, his wife and son PPhM
    Canaday
  The ascension of our Saviour   ELT
    Evans. Benjamin West
  The battle of Crécy   ELB
    Evans. Benjamin West
  Belisarius and the boy   MiD
    Evans. Benjamin West
  Benjamin Franklin drawing electricity
    from the sky
    ICA. From colony to nation
  Charles Willson Peale   NNHS
    Roos
  The choice of Hercules   ELV
    Evans. Benjamin West
  Christ healing the sick in the temple
    Evans. Benjamin West
  Christ on the Mount of Olives
    Evans. Benjamin West

WEST, Benjamin—*Continued*
Christ rejected by the Jews   PA
  Evans. Benjamin West
  Flexner. Light of distant skies
Cleombrotus ordered into banishment by
  Leonidas II, king of Sparta   ELT
  Canaday
Conference of the treaty of peace with
  England, 1783   DeWin
  Davidson v 1
  Richardson. Ptg in America
The conversion of St Paul   MNS
  Evans. Benjamin West
The conversion of St Paul (St Paul's
  church, Richmond, Virginia)
  Evans. Benjamin West
Cupid and Psyche   DC
  Evans. Benjamin West
Cyrus liberating the family of Astyges
                                 ELB
  Evans. Benjamin West
Death of Epaminondas   ELK
  Evans. Benjamin West
Death of General Wolfe   CanO
  Canaday
  Davidson v 1
  Flexner. Light of distant skies
  ICA. From colony to nation
  Janson. Key monuments
  Larkin
  Larkin rev ed
  Lee. Art then and now
  Robb. Harper history
  U.S. National Capital sesquicentennial
    com
  Walker. Ptgs from America
Death of General Wolfe   ELK
  Evans. Benjamin West
Death of Lord Nelson, 1808
  Evans. Benjamin West
Death of Lord Nelson, 1811
  Evans. Benjamin West
Death of Socrates
  Evans. Benjamin West
  Flexner. Light of distant skies
Death of the Chevalier Bayard   ELK
  Evans. Benjamin West
Death on a pale horse (sketch)   PPhM
  Canaday
Death on the pale horse, c 1783   PPhM
  Evans. Benjamin West
  Pierson
Death on the pale horse, 1802   PPhM
  Evans. Benjamin West
Death on the pale horse, 1817   PA
  Barker. Amer ptg
  Evans. Benjamin West
  Flexner. Light of distant skies
  PA. Annual ex, 1955
Departure of Regulus   ELK
  Evans. Benjamin West
The destruction of the beast and the false
  prophet   MnMI
  Evans. Benjamin West
Diana, wife of Thomas Wyld of Sheen
                                 NJMo
  NJMo. Forty years
Diomed and his horses stopped by the
  lightning of Jupiter
  Evans. Benjamin West
Elijah convincing the false prophets of
  Baol   MAC
  Evans. Benjamin West

Elizabeth Peale   PA
  Evans. Benjamin West
  Flexner. First flowers
An English gentleman   PW
  Chew. 250 years of art
General Kosciusko   OOb
  NUM. Art across America
General Monk receiving Charles II on the
  beach of Dover
  WiMiA. Amer ptg 1760-1960
Guy Johnson   DN
  DN. Mellon coll
  Evans. Benjamin West
  Flexner. Light of distant skies
  Janson. Picture history
  Time. 300 years (col)
Hagar and Ishmael   MM
  Evans. Benjamin West
Hector parting with his wife and child at
  the Scæan gate   NNHS
  Evans. Benjamin West
Jane Galloway   PH
  Flexner. First flowers
Juno receiving the cestus from Venus
  Evans. Benjamin West
King Edward III entertaining his prison-
  ers after the battle of Calais
  Evans. Benjamin West
King Lear   MB
  Evans. Benjamin West
Landscape with cow
  Flexner. First flowers
  Ford. Pictorial folk art
  Pierson
Mr and Mrs John Custance   MoKN
  MoKN. Handbook
Mrs Samuel Boudé   DN
  DN. Amer primitive ptgs, pt 2
Mrs West and her son Raphael   OCl
  Evans. Benjamin West
  OCl. Handbook
Musidora
  MdBMu. Rendezvous
Narcissus
  Chew. 250 years of art
Omnia vincit amor   MM
  Evans. Benjamin West
Penn's treaty with the Indians   PA
  Barker. Amer ptg
  Canaday
  Davidson v 1
  Evans. Benjamin West
  Flexner. Amer ptg
  Flexner. Light of distant skies
  Flexner. Short history
  Mendelowitz
  MiD. Ptg in America
  Pierson
  Richardson. Ptg in Amer (col)
  Roos
  Time. 300 years (col)
  U.S. National Capital sesquicentennial
    com
Penn's treaty with the Indians   NNPL
  Ford. Edward Hicks
Peter denying Christ
  Evans. Benjamin West
Prodigal son
  Taylor. Fifty centuries, 1954 ed (col)
Project for a monument: The apotheosis
  of Nelson   NNCo
  Evans. Benjamin West
Queen Philippa interceding for the bur-
  gesses of Calais   MiD
  Evans. Benjamin West

Raising of Lazarus, 1780   CtHW
    Evans. Benjamin West
Raising of Lazarus (study) 1776
    Evans. Benjamin West
Return of Jephthah   ATeS
    ATeS. Collection
Rinaldo and Armida
    Evans. Benjamin West
Robert Fulton   NCHA
    ICA. From colony to nation
    Mendelowitz
St George and the dragon   PR
    PR. Catalogue
St Paul persecuting the Christians MNS
    Evans. Benjamin West
St Paul's restoration to sight by Ananias
                                  MNS
    Evans. Benjamin West
St Paul shaking off the viper   ELT
    Evans. Benjamin West
Samuel Boudé   DN
    DN. Amer primitive ptgs, pt 2
Saul and the witch of Endor   CtHW
    CtHW. Handbook
    ICA. From colony to nation
    MiD. Ptg in America
    Richardson. Ptg in America
Saul and the witch of Endor   ELT
    Evans. Benjamin West
Seascape
    Flexner. First flowers
Self-portrait, 1756   CtY
    CtY. Portrait index
    Flexner. First flowers
    Pierson
Self-portrait, c 1770   DN
    Evans. Benjamin West (col)
Self-portrait c 1795
    Canaday
Self-portrait (Blaustein coll)
    MdBMu. Rendezvous
Stephen Carmick
    Chew. 250 years of art
Thetis bringing the armor to Achilles
                                  CtNB
    Evans. Benjamin West
Thomas Astle   MeC
    MeC. Inaugural ex
Thomas Mifflin   PH
    Flexner. First flowers (col)
    Pierson
Una and the lion   CtHW
    Evans. Benjamin West
Venus lamenting the death of Adonis PPC
    Evans. Benjamin West
View from the terrace at Windsor ELT
    Evans. Benjamin West
William Henry   PH
    Flexner. First flowers
Woodcutters in Windsor Great park InIJ
    Evans. Benjamin West
    Flexner. Light of distant skies
    InIJ. 105 ptgs

        Attributed works
Bagshot heath, Surrey   MB
    MB. Ptgs in water color
Conway castle, North Wales   MB
    MB. Ptgs in water color
Lake in wooded country: sunset   MB
    MB. Ptgs in water color
Meadow and hills: sunset   MB
    MB. Ptgs in water color

Moorland landscape   MB
    MB. Ptgs in water color
Mountain landscape with cattle   MB
    MB. Ptgs in water color
Parkland and trees   MB
    MB. Ptgs in water color
Ploughland and distant hills   MB
    MB. Ptgs in water color
Rainstorm on the moors   MB
    MB. Ptgs in water color
Rocky moorland   MB
    MB. Ptgs in water color
Shooting birds   MB
    MB. Ptgs in water color
Stream and distant hills   MB
    MB. Ptgs in water color
Winding road with trees: sunset   MB
    MB. Ptgs in water color
Wolseley Park house, Staffordshire MB
    MB. Ptgs in water color
Wooded landscape with castle   MB
    MB. Ptgs in water color

        Portrait of the artist
Allston, W. Benjamin West
Delanoy, A. Benjamin West
Pratt, M. Benjamin West
Stuart, G. Benjamin West
Tuthill, A. G. D. Benjamin West
West, Benjamin, 1739-1809
Malbone, E. G. Benjamin West
West, Mrs Benjamin. See West, Elizabeth
    (Shewell)
WEST, Benjamin Franklin, 1818-1854
Whaling scene: Ship Julien and Bark
    Richard   MSP
    U.S. National Capital sesquicentennial
    com
West, Elizabeth (Shewell) fl 1765
Pratt, M. Mrs Benjamin West
West, B. Mrs West and her son Raphael
WEST, William Edward, 1788-1857
Edward John Trelawny
    MiD. Travelers in Arcadia
    Richardson. Ptg in America
Muses of painting, poetry and music DC
    DC. Amer ptrs of the South
West by A. Ippolito
West Chester courthouse by H. Pippin
West Chester, Pennsylvania by H. Pippin
West church, Boston by M. B. Prendergast
West 57th street in 1902 by R. Henri
West Hartford, 1907 by W. J. Glackens
West Point, New York
Chambers, T. View of West Point
De Grailly, W. View from West Point
Eilshemius, L. M. West Point, New York
Toole, J. West Point
Unidentified artist. West Point, c 1850
Unidentified artist. West Point from
    above Washington valley
Whittredge. W. West Point on the Hud-
    son, View of
West point, Prout's neck by W. Homer
West rock, New Haven by G. H. Durrie
West Sand lake by J. H. Hidley
West side docks by R. Henri
West Wildwood by W. Stuempfig
The **west** wind by W. Homer
Westchester hills by W. J. Hays

Western air by R. B. Motherwell
Western festival by A. W. Garrett
Western frontier homestead by Unidentified artist
Western industrial by C. Sheeler
Western landscape by T. Moran
Western landscape by W. C. Sharon
Western landscape by J. M. Stanley
Western landscape by W. Whittredge
Western log cabin by A. J. Miller
Western roadstead by L. Feininger
Western sea by L. Feininger
Western sunset by A. Bierstadt
Western university of Pennsylvania
  Smith, R. Western university of Pennsylvania
WESTON, Harold, 1894-
  The arena   DP
    DP. Catalogne
  Loneliness   DP
    DP. Catalogue
Westward the course of empire takes its way by E. Leutze
Westwood children, fl 1805
  Johnston, J. Westwood children
Westwood hillside by C. C. Allen
Wet day, Paris by M. B. Prendergast
Wetherby, Catherine M. (Thayer) 1828-1912
  Wetherby, I. A. Catherine M. Thayer
WETHERBY, Isaac Augustus, 1819-1904
  Catherine M. Thayer   NNHS
    Ford. Pictorial folk art
  Mary Eliza Jenkins
    Ford. Pictorial folk art
    Pierson
Wetherby, Mrs Isaac Augustus. See Wetherby, Catherine M. Thayer
Wetmore, Prosper M.
  Elliott, C. L. Prosper M. Wetmore
Wetumpka bridge, Alabama by A. E. Thompson (attributed works)
WEYGANDT, C. E. c 1860
  Easton
  McClintock
Whalers and whaling
  Salmon, R. W. South Sea whale fishing
  Unidentified artist. Whaling
  Unidentified artist. Whaling scene
  Unidentified artist. Whaling scene—Triton of New Bedford
  West, B. F. Whaling scene: Ship Julien and Bark Richard
Wharf in winter by S. Wilson
Wharf players, moonlight by C. F. Gaertner
Wharves by R. A. Florsheim
What a catch by J. G. Clonney
What are they going to do next (Disaster of the soul series) by J. De Diego
What atomic war will do to you by B. Deutsch
What is man by R. Ray
WHEAT, John Potter, 1920-
  Road to Golgotha
    NAD. Annual ex, 1949, 1st half
  September harvest
    UNESCO. 1860-1959
Wheat farmers by J. J. Jones

Wheat stack by Unidentified artist
The wheel by J. Tworkov
Wheeler, Catherine Sears. See Hardy, Catherine Sears (Wheeler)
Wheeler, Dora, b 1858
  Chase, W. M. Miss Dora Wheeler
Wheeler, Permelia Redmon
  Orear, L. R. Permelia Redmon Wheeler
WHEELOCK, Merrill Greene, 1822-1866
  On the Hudson   MB
    MB. Ptgs in water color
Wheels of victory by P. Evergood
Wheelwright, John, 1594-1679
  Foster, J. John Wheelwright (?)
Wheelwright, Mary Cabot
  Duveneck, F. Mary Cabot Wheelwright
Whelan's pier, Roslyn by P. Gerry
When autumn is here by H. Pushman
When guns were slow by C. M. Russell
When guns were their passports by C. M. Russell
When horseflesh comes high by C. M. Russell
When horses turn back there's danger ahead by C. M. Russell
When law dulls the edge of chance by C. M. Russell
When meat was plentiful by C. M. Russell
When shadows hint death by C. M. Russell
When Sioux and Blackfeet meet by C. M. Russell
When the trail was long between camps by C. M. Russell
When they shoot me by Y. Tanguy
When tracks spell meat by C. M. Russell
When wagon trails were dim by C. M. Russell
When white men turn red by C. M. Russell
Where are the people I knew by Z. Sepeshy
Where are you by Y. Tanguy
Where sun and rain mate: landscape near Pali, Oahu, Hawaii by B. L. Culwell
Where will you spend eternity by C. Cloar
Wherefore now ariseth the illusion of a third dimension by I. L. Albright
Which is which by J. D. Chalfant
Which way to Sunbury? by A. Brook
Whipper, William, fl 1835
  Prior, W. M. (manner of) William Whipper
Whipple, Abraham, 1753-1819
  Savage, E. Abraham Whipple
Whipple, Catherine (Moffatt) 1723-1823
  Copley, J. S. Mrs William Whipple
Whippoorwills
  Audubon, J. J. Chuck-Will's widow
  Spruce, E. F. Whippoorwill, sandpiper
The whirlwind by P. Tchelitchew
WHISTLER, James Abbott McNeil, 1834-1903
  Arrangement in black (F. R. Leyland) DF
    Pearson, H. The man Whistler
  Arrangement in black and brown: the fur jacket   MWM
    Pearson, H. The man Whistler
    Sweet
  Arrangement in black and white: the young American (Maud)   DF
    Pearson, H. The man Whistler

Arrangement in flesh-color and black. See
  Théodore Duret
Arrangement in grey and black (Artist's
  mother)
    Barr. What is mod ptg
    Canaday
    Cheney. Story 1958 ed
    Craven· Rainbow book
    Flexner. Amer ptg
    Flexner. Short history
    Janson. Key monuments
    Janson. Picture history
    Newmeyer
    Pearson, H. The man Whistler
    Roos
    Sweet
    UNESCO. 1860-1949
    UNESCO. 1860-1955
    UNESCO. 1860-1959
Arrangement in grey and black no 2, 1872.
  See Thomas Carlyle
Arrangement in pink and purple   OciM
    Bazin
    Sweet
Arthur Jerome Eddy   ICA
    Sweet
The artist in his studio   ICA
    Lewisohn
    Sweet
Artist's mother. See Arrangement in grey
  and black
At the piano
    Cheney. Story 1958 ed
    Rewald. History of impressionism
Battersea Reach   DC
    DC. Masterpieces
The Chelsea girl
    Sweet
Chelsea shop   ICA
    Sweet
Cicely Alexander (Miss Alexander; Har-
  mony in grey and green   ELT
    Canaday
    Cheney. Story 1958 ed
    Gardner 1959 ed
    Gregory. The world of Whistler
    Pearson, H. The man Whistler
Coast of Brittany: alone with the tide
                                     CtHW
    CtHW. Handbook
    Pierson
Comte Robert de Montesquiou-Fezensac
    Gregory. The world of Whistler
Courbet at Trouville, Harmony in blue
  and silver   MBI
    Rewald. History of impressionism
Cremorne gardens no 2   MM
    Sweet
The doorway, Venice
    Sweet
Falling rocket. See Nocturne in black and
  gold
Fire wheel. See Nocturne in black and
  gold
Frederick R. Leyland. See Arrangement
  in black
The fur jacket. Arrangement in black
  and brown
Gold scab
    PPC. Amer classics
Golden screen: caprice in purple and gold
  no 2, 1865   DF
    Cheney. Story 1958 ed

Grey and silver, Battersea Reach   ICA
    Sweet
Grey note—mouth of the Thames. See
    Little Scheveningen: grey note
Harmony in blue and silver. See Courbet
  at Trouville
Harmony in grey and green. See Cicely
  Alexander
Harmony in red: Lamplight
    Pearson, H. The man Whistler
Henry Graves, the printseller
    Sweet
Jo. See The little white girl
Jo in "Before the mirror." See The little
  white girl
Lady of the Lange Lijsen
    Pierson
    Sweet
Lagoon, Venice: nocturne in blue and sil-
  ver   MB
    Baur. Amer ptg
Last of Old Westminster   MB
    Pierson
    Richardson. Ptg in America
Lillian Woakes   DP
    DP. Catalogue
Little Rose of Lyme Regis   MB
    Cheney. Story 1958 ed
    Riley. Your art heritage
Little Scheveningen: grey note (Grey note
    —mouth of the Thames)   MB
    MB. Ptgs in water color
    Pearson, H. The man Whistler
The little white girl (Jo; Jo in "Before
  the mirror"; Symphony in white no 2,
  1864)   ELT
    Cheney. Story 1958 ed
    Craven. Treasury 1952 ed (col)
    Gregory. The world of Whistler
    Pearson, H. The Man Whistler
    Sweet
    UNESCO. 1860-1949
    UNESCO. 1860-1955
    UNESCO. 1860-1959
Mme Camille D'Avouille   MAP
    Sweet
Marine   OCiM
    Cheney. Story 1958 ed
Miss Alexander. See Cicely Alexander
Music room   DF
    Pierson
Nocturne in black and gold (The falling
  rocket)   MiD
    MiD. Treasures
    Pierson
    Richardson. Ptg in America (col)
    Sweet
Nocturne in black and gold (Fire wheel)
    Roos
Nocturne in blue and gold. See Old Bat-
  tersea bridge
Nocturne in blue and green   ELT
    Cheney. Story 1958 ed
Nude   OYB
    OYB. Supplement 1959
Old Battersea bridge (Nocturne in blue
  and gold)   ELT
    Cheney. New world history
    Cheney. Story 1958 ed
    Janson. Picture history
    Robb. Harper history
    Roos

WHISTLER, J. A. M.
Old Battersea bridge—*Continued*
  Sweet
  Time. 300 years (col)
  Upjohn
Old Battersea bridge (Symphony in brown
  and silver)   MAP
  Pierson
  Sweet
The Pacific
  Lee. Art then and now
Portrait of Mrs Whistler. See Harmony
  in red: lamplight
La princesse du pays de la porcelaine DF
  Pearson, H. The man Whistler
  Pierson
Richard Canfield   OCiM
  Cheney. Story 1958
Rosa Corder
  Gregory. The world of Whistler
  Pearson, H. The man Whistler
Self-portrait, c 1858   DF
  Rewald. History of impressionism
Self-portrait, 1867   MiD
  MiD. Treasures
  Sweet
Study of a head after Couture
  Sweet
Symphony in brown and silver. See Old
  Battersea bridge
Symphony in white no 1. See The white
  girl
Symphony in white no 2. See The little
  white girl
The Thames from Battersea bridge OYB
  OYB. Supplement 1959
The Thames in ice   DF
  Born
Théodore Duret (Arrangement in flesh-
  colour and black)   MM
  Cheney. Story 1958 ed
  Mendelowitz
  MM. 100 Amer ptrs
  Pierson
  Sweet
  Taylor. Fifty centuries, 1954 ed (col)
Thomas Carlyle (Arrangement in grey
  and black no 2)   ScG
  Cheney. New world history
  Cheney. Story 1958 ed
  Craven. Treasury 1952 ed
  ICA. Sargent, Whistler and Mary Cas-
  satt
  McCurdy
  Richardson. Ptg in America
  Robb. Harper History
  Roos
  Time. 300 years (col)
  Walker. Ptgs from America
Variations in pink and grey—Chelsea
      DF
  Walker. Ptgs from America
Wapping on Thames
  CtY. Yale alumni
  Sweet
The white girl   DN
  Canaday
  McKinney
  NYG. Fine art
  Pierson
  Rewald. History of impressionism
  Sweet (col)
  UNESCO. 1860-1955
  UNESCO. 1860-1959

The young American (Maud Franklin).
  See Arrangement in black and white
Young girl in blue
  Bazin (col detail)
    Portrait of the artist
  Chase, W. M. James Abbott McNeill
    Whistler
  Whistler, J. A. M. Artist in his studio
Whistling boy by W. M. Chase
Whistling boy by F. Currier
Whistling boy by F. Duveneck
WHITAKER, Frederic, 1891-
Pro Deo, pro populo
  NAD. Annual ex, 1947, 2d half
WHITCOMB, Susan, fl 1847-1852
Mount Vernon (Residence of General
  Washington)   VWR
  Flexner. Light of distant skies
  VWR. Folk art (col)
White, Alden Perley, 1856-1933
Noyes, W. F. Alden Perley White (copy)
White, Andrew Dickson, 1832-1918
Upjohn, A. M. Andrew Dickson White
WHITE, Charles, 1918-
Hampton institute mural design   NJN
  Larkin (detail)
  Larkin rev ed (detail)
White, Charlotte. See Poor, Charlotte
  (White)
WHITE, Doris A.
Quiet street   OYB
  OYB. Annual 1960
White, John, fl 1835
Bascom, R. H. M. Rev John White
WHITE, John Blake, 1781-1859
General Marion in his swamp encampment
  inviting a British officer to dinner
  Cowdrey v 1
White, Margaret (Rutherford) fl 1883
Sargent, J. S. Mrs Henry White
WHITE, Richard A. 1917-
Untitled, 2-27-59, 1950
  NNSG. Younger Amer ptrs
White, Thomas Raeburn, 1875-1959
Watkins, F. C. Thomas Raeburn White
White and gold by K. Okada
White architecture by C. Demuth
White bench by W. M. Chase
White bird by W. A. Baziotes
White, black and red by F. Mitchell
White callas by A. B. Carles
White Canadian barn by G. O'Keeffe
White castles on the Missouri by C. Wimar
White catamount by D. Austin
White center by M. Rothko
White city no 3 by L. L. Ribak
White cloud by J. R. Cox
White cloud by H. V. Poor
White cockatoo by W. M. Chase
White cockatoo by J. Pollock
White cow by E. F. Spruce
White cows by D. Burliuk
White factory by P. Blume
White field by T. Stamos
White flower by E. N. Bischoff
White flower by J. Carroll

White flower by G. O'Keeffe
White forms by F. J. Kline
White front by J. Albers
White garden by R. Pousette-Dart
The white girl by J. A. M. Whistler
White Hall plantation, Louisiana, c 1790 by C. Colomb
White horizon by A. P. Ryder
White horizontal by J. Pollock
White horse by G. W. Bellows
White horse by T. H. Benton
White horse by A. P. Ryder
White horses at the sand pit by H. G. Keller
White house by R. Breinin
White iris by G. O'Keeffe
White journey by M. Tobey
White landscape by G. Peterdi
White light by J. Pollock
White light by W. W. Quirt
White lilac by S. Menkès
The white line by S. Francis
White lines by I. R. Miller
White lines by I. R. Pereira
White mare with foal by C. S. Price
White mist to greens by W. Meigs
White moon by M. Avery
White morning by I. Cavat
White morning by A. Dasburg
White mountains
    Cole, T. Notch of the White mountains
    Cole, T. View of Monte Video
    Cole, T. View of the White mountains
    Cropsey, J. F. White mountains in autumn
    Fisher, A. White mountains
    Macknight, D. Winter in the White mountains
    Marin, J. White mountain country, Dixville Notch
    Marin, J. White mountain country, New Hampshire
    Marin, J. White mountains, autumn
    Smith, R. In the falls of the Saco, Crawford's notch
    Spruce, E. F. White mountain
White nude with apple by A. B. Carles
White numbers by J. Johns
White Oak swamp, Virginia, Battle of, 1862
    Unidentified artist. Battle of White Oak Swamp, Virginia, 1862
White on black by J. Pollock
White on blue by S. J. Twardowicz
White painting by L. Calcagno
White painting by P. Guston
White painting by W. Ivey
White pelicans in Florida by G. Harvey
White pitcher by G. F. Hacker
White pitcher with field flowers by Ben-Zion
The white place in shadow by G. O'Keeffe
White Plume by A. J. Miller
White portico by J. A. Oneto
White rectangle by I. R. Pereira

White reverie by R. Pousette-Dart
White river at Sharon by E. Hopper
White rocks, Nova Scotia by J. E. Heliker
White sails by E. Lewandowski
White sands by C. R. Bentley
White shell by A. Ruellan
White ships by J. S. Sargent
The white squall by J. Evans
White still life by S. M. Adler
White structures by H. N. Cook
White table by B. Chaet
White tablet by C. A. Morris
White tails by C. M. Russell
White target by J. Johns
White town, Azemmour, Morocco by D. Macknight
White vase by K. Knaths
White violets and abandoned coal mine by C. E. Burchfield
White violets and coal mine by C. E. Burchfield
White wall by A. Trivilini
White water ahead by C. S. Chapman
The White way by J. Sloan
Whitefield, George, 1714-1770
    Wollaston, J. George Whitefield preaching
Whitefoord, Caleb, fl 1782
    Stuart, G. Caleb Whitefoord
Whitehouse, Hannah Goodwin. See Moulton, Hannah Goodwin (Whitehouse)
Whitehouse family
    Healy, G. P. A. Boating party on the Thames
The Whiteside church by A. M. R. Moses
Whitestone bridge by R. Crawford
Whither now by M. Weber
Whitman, Walt, 1819-1892
    Eakins, T. Walt Whitman
Whitney, Eben, fl 1807
    Woodside, J. A. Eben Whitney
Whitney, Eli, 1765-1825
    Morse, S. F. B. Eli Whitney
WHITNEY, L.
    American landscape   NJN
    Barker. Amer ptg
    Ford. Pictorial folk art
    Mendelowitz
    Pierson
Whittemore, Mrs John Howard, fl 1899
    Cassatt, M. Portrait of a grand lady (Mrs John Howard Whittemore)
Whittemore, Mary Anne. See Low, Mary Anne (Whittemore)
Whittemore, Rebecca Tufts, fl 1811
    Greenwood, E. A. Rebecca Tufts Whittemore
Whittemore, William, 1761-1842
    Williams, H. William Whittemore
WHITTREDGE, Worthington, 1820-1910
    Apples   MB
    MB. Karolik coll
    Boating party in Central park
    Born
    Camp meeting   MM
    Mendelowitz
    U.S. National Capital sesquicentennial com

WHITTREDGE, Worthington—*Continued*
Crossing the ford, Platte river, Colorado
                                    NNCe
  Rathbone
Crow's nest   MiD
  Pierson
Deer, Mount Storm park, Cincinnati
                                 MWM
  Barker. Amer ptg
  Baur. Amer ptg
  Pierson
Drachenfels
  Sears. Highlights
Home by the sea   MAP
  Pierson
House on the sea   CLA
  Born
In the Rockies
  Rathbone
Landscape   OCiM
  OCiM. Guide
Long's peak, Colorado   MB
  MB. Karolik coll
Old homestead by the sea   MB
  MB. Karolik coll
On the Platte river   MB
  MB. Karolik coll
Outskirts of the forest   MB
  MB. Karolik coll
Self-portrait: the artist at his easel
  WiMiA. Amer ptg 1760-1960
Trout pool   MM
  Richardson. Ptg in America
View of West Point on the Hudson MB
  MB. Karolik coll
Western landscape
  WiMiA. Amer ptg 1760-1960
Whoa Emma by D. G. Blythe
Whorf, John, fl 1784
  Unidentified artist. John Whorf with bow
    and arrow
WHORF, John, 1903-1959
Algerian scene   MB
  MB. Ptgs in water color
Algerian street scene   MB
  MB. Ptgs in water color
Birches   MB
  MB. Ptgs in water color
Brightening Seine
  NYG. Fine art
Edge of the east water
  NSP. Sportscapes
Keeper of the bell   OYB
  OYB. Catalogue 1951
River men   MB
  MB. Ptgs in water color
Sailboats   MB
  MB. Ptgs in water color
Setting out the decoys
  NSP. Sportscapes
Summer night, Provincetown, Massachu-
  setts   MB
  MB. Ptgs in water color
Swans   MB
  MB. Ptgs in water color
Winter by the sea
  NYG. Fine art
Winter, North end, Boston   MB
  MB. Ptgs in water color
Why not use the L by R. Marsh
Wichita mountains from the Medicine Bluffs
  by H. Stieffel

Wickham, Catherine (Fry) See Fry, Cath-
  erine
Wickham, Elizabeth S. (McClurg)
  Stuart, G. Mrs John Wickham
Wickham, Mrs Samuel. See Fry, Catherine
WICKWIRE, Jere Raymond, 1883-
  William Lyon Phelps   CtY
  CtY. Portrait index
Widener, Ella (Pancoast)
  Sargent, J. S. Mrs Joseph E. Widener
The widow by H. Hensel
The widow by J. E. Levi
The widow by H. Pittman
Widow Magee by G. B. Luks
WIEGHARDT, Paul, 1897-
  Oganda
    IU. Contemp Amer ptg & sculp, 1957
  Quiet colors
    IU. Contemp Amer ptg & sculp, 1955
WIGFALL, Benjamin L. 1931?-
  Chimneys
    Pousette-Dart. Amer ptg
WIGHE, A.
  Rural court scene, 1849   RPS
    Davidson v2
Wight, Harmony Child
  Unidentified artist. Harmony Child Wight
Wight, Oliver, fl 1786
  Unidentified artist. Oliver Wight
WIGHT, Peter Bonnett, 1838-1925
  Venetian Gothic art building on the old
    Yale campus   CtY
    Weir. Recollections
Wignall, Elizabeth, fl 1814
  Sully, T. Elizabeth Wignall
Wilcocks, Maria. See Ellis, Maria (Wil-
  cocks)
WILCOX, Lucia, 1906-
  60-340
    PPC. International ex, 1961/62
Wilcox children, fl 1845
  Stock, J. W. Wilcox children
WILD, John Casper, 1806?-1846
  Cincinnati, 1835
    Davidson v2
  Dubuque, Iowa   ICH
    Rathbone
  Fort Snelling   MnSH
    Rathbone
  View of Davenport, Iowa and the Missis-
    sippi   IaDA
    Rathbone
  View of St Louis, c 1841   ICH
    Rathbone
The wild bunch by I. L. Albright
Wild cherry tree by J. H. Twachtman
Wild flowers by H. R. Newman
Wild flowers by W. Williams
Wild flowers and grasses by H. L. McFee
Wild geese by W. Homer
Wild horse hunters by C. M. Russell
Wild horses by A. J. Miller
Wild horses by A. R. Saalburg
Wild iris by K. Schrag
Wild man's meat by C. M. Russell
The wild one by D. Fink
Wild roses by M. Hartley
Wild scenery by A. J. Miller
Wild turkey by J. J. Audubon

Wild West by G. W. Platt

WILDE, John, 1919-
Apotheosis of Marie-Henri Beyle
Pierson
WMAA. Annual ex, 1955
Further festivities at the Contessa San-
severini's
IU. Contemp Amer ptg, 1952
MnMW. Reality and fantasy
Green peppers
IU. Contemp Amer ptg & sculp, 1961
The pseudolucànus reconsidered
IU. Contemp Amer ptg & sculp, 1955
Still life with Christmas candy   MiD
CoS. New accessions USA, 1954
Still life with currants
IU. Contemp Amer ptg & sculp, 1959
Wildeworld
IU. Contemp Amer ptg & sculp, 1957
With a few of my favorites
IU. Contemp Amer ptg & sculp, 1953
(col)
Work reconsidered
MM. Amer ptg today
Wildeworld by J. Wilde

WILES, Irving Ramsey, 1861-1948
John Gellatly   DNC
DNC. Gellatly coll 1954
Wiley, John, fl 1771
Williams, W. John Wiley, his mother and
sisters
WILEY, William Thomas, 1937-
Firecrackers sold here
WMAA. Young America 1960
Peaceable kingdom   CSFM
IU. Contemp Amer ptg & sculp, 1961
Time table
WMAA. Young America 1960
WILGUS, William John, 1819-1853
Ut-Ha-Wah (Capt Cole)   CtY
CtY. Portrait index
WILKES, Max S.
Girl resting
PA. Annual ex, 1949
Wilkes-Barre and the Wyoming valley by
Unidentified artist
WILKINSON, Jack, 1913-
Valley landscape
OrPA. Ptgs & sculptures
Wilkinson, Jemima, fl 1773
Mathies, J. L. D. Jemima Wilkinson: the
Publick Universal Friend
Will Schuster and blackman going shooting
for rail by T. Eakins
Willett, Mrs Marinus, fl 1800
Vanderlyn, J. Mrs Marinus Willett and
child
William, Otho Holland, 1749-1794
Peale, Raphaelle. Otho Holland William
William Rush carving the allegorical figure
of the Skuylkill river by T. Eakins
Williams, Lady, fl 1783
Earl, R. Lady Williams and child
WILLIAMS, Alyn, b 1865
Augustus Van Horne Stuyvesant   NNHS
Vail. Stuyvesant ports
Williams, Ann (Wray) 1780-1817
Jarvis, J. W. Mrs John Williams jr
Williams, Charles K. fl 1846
Mason, B. F. Chief Justice Charles K.
Williams
Williams, Elisha, 1694-1755
Moulthrop, R. Elisha Williams

WILLIAMS, Frederick Ballard, 1871-1956
Down from Mount Mansfield, Vermont
NJMo
NJMo. Forty years
Williams, George, 1778-1852
Stuart, G. George Williams
WILLIAMS, Henry, 1787-1830
Unknown man   MB
MB. New England miniatures
William Whittemore
MB. New England miniatures
Williams, Jerhusha
Unidentified artist. Mourning picture
sacred to the memory of Jerhusha
Williams
Williams, John, 1752-1806
Jarvis, J. W. Gen John Williams
Williams, John, 1783-1858
Jarvis, J. W. Col John Williams, jr
Williams, Mrs John. See Williams, Ann
(Wray)
WILLIAMS, Keith Shaw, 1905-1951
Seated nude
NAD. Annual ex, autumn 1949
Williams, Mary Goddard, fl 1876
Duveneck, F. The crimson gown
WILLIAMS, Micah, fl 1815
John G. Vanderveer   VWR
VWR. Folk art (col)
Mrs Jane Herbert Vanderveer   VWR
VWR. Folk art (col)
Williams, Norman, fl 1867
Mason, B. F. (attributed works) Norman
Williams
Williams, Mrs Oliver E.
Prendergast, M. B. Mrs Oliver E. Wil-
liams
Williams, Pamela. See Brown, Pamela
(Williams)
Williams, Rose Adèle (Cutts) Douglas
Healy, G. P. A. Mrs Stephen A. Douglas
Williams, Samuel, d 1841
Allston, W. Samuel Williams
Williams, Samuel Wells, 1812-1884
Weir, J. F. Samuel Wells Williams
Williams, Susan. See Proudfit, Susan (Wil-
liams)
WILLIAMS, Virgil
Winnowing grain in California, 1872
Davidson v2
WILLIAMS, Walter, 1920-
Poultry market   WMAA
Pierson
Wild flowers
WMAA. Annual ex, 1957
WILLIAMS, William, fl 1740-1794
Conversation piece
Flexner. First flowers
David Hall
Flexner. First flowers
Deborah Hall   NBM
Barker. Amer ptg
Flexner. First flowers (col)
Larkin
Larkin rev ed
Pierson
Husband and wife in a landscape (Master-
piece)   DeWin
Mendelowitz
Richardson. Ptg in America
John Wiley, his mother and sisters
Flexner. First flowers
Pierson

WILLIAMS, William—*Continued*
Masterpiece. See Husband and wife in a landscape
William Denning family
  Flexner. First flowers
  ICA. From colony to nation
  U.S. National Capital sesquicentennial com
William Hall   DeWin
  Pierson

Williams, William Stoddard, 1762-1829
  Jennys, W. Dr William Stoddard Williams

WILLIAMSON, Clara (McDonald) b 1875
Autumn outing
  PPC. International ex, 1955
First Texas Central railroad
  Kallir. Amer primitive ptgs
Night hunters
  IU. Contemp Amer ptg & sculp, 1957
Standing in the need of prayer   TxD
  Ford. Pictorial folk art
  IU. Contemp Amer ptg & sculp, 1953
Veteran's dream   TxD
  Lipman. Primitive ptrs

Williamson, Thomas, 1771-1846
  Hubard, W. J. Thomas Williamson

Williamstown, Massachusetts by A. M. R. Moses

Willie Gee by R. Henri

Willimantic, Connecticut, 1923 by J. A. Weir

Willimantic thread mill by J. A. Weir

Willing, Anne (Shippen) 1710-1791
  Feke, R. Mrs Charles Willing

Willis avenue bridge by B. Shahn

Willoughby, Master by Unidentified artist

Willow in the rain by J. Thecla

Willow-Swamp, Minnesota by B. J. O. Nordfeldt

Willow tree by A. G. Dove

Willows by T. Robinson

WILLSON, Mr. fl 1822
  Barnard Stratton of Amherst, New Hampshire   NCHA
  Jones. New-found folk art

WILLSON, Mary Ann, fl 1810-1826
General Washington on horseback RPS
  Brussels. Exposition
  Lipman. Primitive ptrs
Mermaid
  Lipman. Primitive ptrs
Pelican   RPS
  Lipman. Primitive ptrs
Prodigal son reclaimed by his father
  Lipman. Primitive ptrs

Wilson, Mrs Algernon. See Wilson, Sarah Procter (Daniell)

WILSON, Bryan, 1927-
Hawk and quail
  IU. Contemp Amer ptg & sculp, 1961
Ross snow geese
  Mendelowitz
  PPC. International ex, 1958

WILSON, Mary R. fl 1820
Fruit in yellow bowl   VWR
  VWR. Folk art (col)

WILSON, Milton, 1923-
The Great Goot
  OrPA. Ptgs & sculptures (col)

WILSON, Reginald, 1909-
Pet rooster   ATU
  ATU. Coll of Amer art

Wilson, Sarah Proctor (Daniell)
  Theus, J. Mrs Algernon Wilson

WILSON, Solomon, 1896-
Drugstore
  NAD. Annual ex, 1951
East wind
  Gruskin
Fishermen's festival
  IU. Contemp Amer ptg, 1948
Floats and markers
  NAD. Annual ex. 1953
Last stop
  IU. Contemp Amer ptg, 1950
Old boats and beach
  IU. Contemp Amer ptg & sculp, 1955
The pier
  IU. Contemp Amer ptg, 1949
Repair shack interior
  DC. 21 biennial ex, 1949
Schooner and scow   OYB
  OYB. Accessions
  OYB. Supplement 1959
Torn sail
  PPC. Ptg in the U.S. 1949
Town square
  IU. Contemp Amer ptg, 1951
Wharf in winter
  OYB. Catalogue 1951

WILT, Richard H. 1915-
Birthday cake   MiD
  CoS. New accessions USA, 1952
Circus triptych   OYB
  OYB. Annual 1953
Shambattle   OYB
  OYB. Catalogue 1951

WIMAR, Carl, 1828-1862
The Adam Lemp Brewery   MoSL
  MoSL. Handbook 1953
Attack on an emigrant train, 1856 MiA
  Davidson v 1
Buffalo dance   MoSL
  McCracken. Portrait of the old west (col)
  MoSL. Handbook 1953
  Pierson
  Rathbone (col)
Buffalo hunt   MoSLW
  McCracken. Portrait of the old west
  Rathbone
Buffaloes crossing the Yellowstone
                                          MoSLW
  Rathbone
Buttes on the Missouri   MoSLH
  Rathbone
Captive charger   MoSL
  Davidson v 1
  Rathbone
  Roos
Cottonwoods on the Missouri   MoSLH
  Rathbone
Indian camp fire
  Rathbone
Indians approaching Fort Benton MoSLW
  Born
  Davidson v 1
  Rathbone
Medicine bag   MoSL
  Rathbone
On the warpath
  WiMiA. Amer ptg 1760-1960

Studies of a quartered buffalo   MoSL
  Rathbone
Turf house on the plains
  Rathbone
  Time. 300 years (col)
White castles on the Missouri   MoSLH
  Rathbone
Wimar, Charles Ferdinand. See Wimar,
  Carl
Wind, clouds and water by A. G. Dove
Wind clouds at sundown by L. Feininger
Wind from the sea by A. N. Wyeth
The wind of the sun by I. R. Pereira
Wind on land and sea, Maine by J. Marin
Wind orchestra by M. Weber
Wind river chain by A. J. Miller
Wind river country, Wyoming by A. Bier-
  stadt
Wind river mountain by A. J. Miller
Wind river mountains, Wyoming, View from
  by A. Bierstadt
Wind rose by M. Hoff
Wind, sea and sails by C. Sheeler
Wind, wave and tree by K. Schrag
Windham village by J. A. Weir
Winding road by M. Sterne
Winding road with trees: sunset by B. West
  (attributed works)
The windmill by A. P. Ryder
The window by C. Browning
The window by H. Hofmann
The window by R. A. Mintz
The window by H. E. Niese
The window by M. Tobey
The window by G. Tooker
Window by the alley by C. E. Burchfield
Window cleaner by A. Rattner
Window cleaner no 3, 1951 by A. Rattner
Window composition by A. Rattner
Window with flowers by B. Connelly
Window in the Union club by G. P. Du Bois
Window shade by L. MacIver
Windows by T. Yerxa
Windows, Paris by E. W. Dickinson
Windward shore by F. J. Waugh
Windy corner by J. Myers
Windy day—Lowe's point by W. Zorach
Wine, honey and oil by Y. Tanguy
Wing, Halsey, fl 1832
  Mason, B. F. Halsey Wing
Wing, Mrs Halsey, fl 1832
  Mason, B. F. Mrs Halsey Wing
Wingaersheek beach by E. L. Novotny
Wingaersheek marsh by J. C. Pellew
Wingahocking at Shoemaker's lane, German-
  town by R. Smith
Winger web by R. Koppe
WINGREN, Dan, 1923-
  The thicket
  PPC. International ex, 1955
Wings of the morning by H. E. Mattson
Winne, Adam, fl 1730
  Unidentified artist. Adam Winne

WINNER, William E. c 1815-1883
  Crazy Nora   PH
    Chew. 250 years of art
Winnowing grain by E. Johnson
Winona Falls by A. H. Wyant
Winslow, Benjamin, 1783-1863
  Malbone, E. G. Benjamin Winslow
Winslow, Isaac, 1707-1777
  Blackburn, J. Winslow family
  Copley, J. S. Mr and Mrs Isaac Winslow
  Feke, R. Isaac Winslow
Winslow, Jemima (Debuke) 1732-1790
  Blackburn, J. Winslow family
  Copley, John S. Mr and Mrs Isaac Wins-
    low
Winslow, Joshua, 1727?-1801
  Copley, J. S. Joshua Winslow
Winsted, Connecticut, 1877 by S. E. Harvey
WINTER, Andrew, 1892-1958
  Bleak weather
    NAD. Annual ex, autumn 1949
  Breeches buoy
    NAD. Annual ex, 1949, 1st half
WINTER, C.
  Minstrel show   MB
    MB. Karolik coll
Winter by T. Birch
Winter by E. Lawson
Winter by R. Kent
Winter by H. Moller
Winter by G. Prestopino
Winter, a view of Monhegan, Maine by R.
  Kent
Winter afternoon by G. W. Bellows
Winter along the mills by G. Kachmer
Winter: an impediment in travelling by G.
  Harvey
Winter bouquet by C. E. Burchfield
Winter by the sea by J. Whorf
Winter, Central park, New York by E. Law-
  son
Winter coast by W. Homer
Winter cottonwoods east, V by G. O'Keeffe
Winter, Dirigo island by W. A. Kienbusch
Winter dunes by L. MacIver
Winter farm scene by G. H. Durrie
Winter forms by J. Maxwell
Winter holiday by P. S. Sample
Winter Hudson by J. C. Atherton
Winter idyl by B. Crane
Winter in the Catskills by D. E. Lee
Winter in the country, a cold morning by
  G. H. Durrie
Winter in the country, distant hills by G. H.
  Durrie
Winter in the country, getting ice by G. H.
  Durrie
Winter in the country, the old grist mill by
  G. H. Durrie
Winter in the valley by E. W. Redfield
Winter in the Verde valley by H. Strater
Winter journey by H. Koerner
Winter landscape by T. Doughty
Winter landscape by G. H. Durrie
Winter landscape by H. G. Keller
Winter landscape by W. Sommer

Winter landscape; gathering wood by G. H. Durrie
Winter landscape with skaters by F. R. Gignoux (attributed works)
Winter moonlight by C. E. Burchfield
Winter morning by A. L. Ripley
Winter nightfall in the city by C. Hassam
Winter, North end, Boston by J. Whorf
Winter on the river by E. Lawson
Winter port by E. D. Lewandowski
Winter rhythm by L. Pytlak
Winter road by L. Dodd
Winter rooftops by A. Osver
Winter scene by J. S. Blunt
Winter scene by G. H. Durrie
Winter scene by E. Shinn
Winter scene in Brooklyn by F. Guy
Winter scene in New England by G. H. Durrie
Winter scene in New Jersey by F. R. Gignoux
Winter scene, Jones' inn by G. H. Durrie
Winter scene on the Hudson by J. F. Cropsey
Winter scene outside of Bristol, Pennsylvania by T. Birch
Winter scene: the red fox by J. Hope
Winter shapes by K. Mattern
Winter silence by F. D. Ogden
Winter soldiers by M. Siporin
Winter solstice by C. E. Burchfield
Winter sports by F. R. Gignoux
Winter sun by H. Lundeberg
Winter trees by R. Gleitsmann
Winter twilight by C. E. Burchfield
Winter twilight by M. Weber
Winter visitor by P. S. Sample
Winter wharf by K. Knaths
Winter without snow by W. Zorach
Winter wood by L. Gatch
Winter's day by W. A. Lewis
A winter's day by A. M. R. Moses
Winter's dreamland by K. Matthew
Winter's end by W. E. Baum
The winters passed by C. Booth
Winter's playground by R. Gwathmey
Winterscape by C. Seliger
Winthrop, Hannah (Fayerweather) 1727-1790
  Copley, J. S. Mrs John Winthrop
Winthrop, John, 1714-1779
  Copley, J. S. Professor John Winthrop
Winthrop, Mrs John. See Winthrop, Hannah (Fayerweather)
Winthrop, Katherine. See Browne, Katherine (Winthrop)
Winthrop, Thomas Lindall, 1760-1841
  Malbone, E. G. Thomas L. Winthrop
Wintry park by B. Robinson
Wires down by C. E. Burchfield
Wisconsin
  Cikovsky, N. Wisconsin landscape
  Curry, J. S. Wisconsin landscape

Seifert, P. A. Jacob Bennett farm, Gotham, Wisconsin, c 1880
Seifert, P. A. Residence of E. R. Jones, Dodgeville, Wisconsin, 1881
Seifert, P. A. Residence of Lemuel Cooper, Plain, Wisconsin, 1879
Seifert, P. Wisconsin farm scene
Wisdom and destiny by H. G. Keller
Wise bird by G. S. Ratkai
The wise men by M. Dixon
The wish by Y. Tanguy
Wissahickon by R. Smith
Witchery by F. E. Conway
With a few of my favorites by J. Wilde
With my shadow by Y. Tanguy
With sloping mast and dripping prow by A. P. Ryder
With the Staatszeitung by W. M. Harnett
Within autumn by F. D. Duncan
Within the confines of window frame by M. Sokole
The witness by Y. Tanguy
Witness the whatless by P. Burlin
The witness tree by J. H. Fitzgerald
The witnesses by H. Warshaw
Woakes, Lillian
  Whistler, J. A. M. Miss Lillian Woakes
WOELLFER, Emerson S. 1914-
  Birds and orange sky
    Pierson
  Napoli forio
    IU. Contemp Amer ptg & sculp, 1959
WOISERI, L. J. Boqueta de, fl 1805
  New Orleans, 1803
    Davidson v2
Wolcott, Abigail. See Ellsworth, Abigail (Wolcott)
Wolcott, Frederick, 1767-1837
  Waldo, S. L. and Jewett, W. Frederick Wolcott
Wolcott, Oliver, 1760-1833
  Catlin, G. Oliver Wolcott
  Stuart, G. Oliver Wolcott
Wolf men by C. M. Russell
WOLFE, Jack, 1925?-
  Crucifixion
    WMAA. Young America 1957
  Purlieu
    MBIC. View 1960
Wolfe, James, 1727-1750
  West, B. Death of General Wolfe
Wolfe, Thomas Clayton, 1900-1938
  Gorsline, D. W. Thomas Wolfe
Wolfersberger, Elizabeth
  Stettinius, S. E. (attributed works) Mr and Mrs Wolfersberger
Wolfersberger, Philip
  Stettinius, S. E. (attributed works) Mr and Mrs Wolfersberger
Wolfert's will by J. Quidor
WOLFF, Robert Jay, 1905-
  Erewhon
    IU. Contemp Amer ptg & sculp, 1957
WOLLASTON, John, fl 1736-1767
  Abraham Barnes   DC
    DC. Amer ptrs of the South
  Children of Warner Lewis
    Barker. Amer ptg

George Whitefield preaching   ELNP
U. S. National Capital sesquicentennial
com
Mrs Daniel Blake
Flexner. First flowers
Mrs Samuel Gouverneur   DeWin
Mendelowitz
Mrs Warner Lewis   VWC
Pierson
Mrs William Allen   NBM
Belknap
Mrs William Axtell (?)   NNHS
ICA. From colony to nation
Mrs William Walton   NNHS
Belknap
Philip Philipse   NNMC
Larkin
Larkin rev ed
Sir William Johnson   NAI
NAI. Hudson valley
Thomas Appleford   NNHS
NNHS. Waldron Phoenix Belknap coll
Warner Lewis   VWC
Pierson
Warner Lewis II and Rebecca   VWS
Pierson
Wolseley Park house, Staffordshire by B.
West (attributed works)
Wolverene by J. J. Audubon
Wolves
Audubon, J. W. Gray wolf or white American
wolf
Kuhn, R. Wounded wolves
Price, C. S. Wolves
Woman by I. L. Albright
A **woman** by W. M. Chase
Woman by W. De Kooning
A **woman** by T. Eakins
A **woman** by W. M. Prior (attributed works)
Woman by W. W. Quirt
Woman I, stage 1. Summer, 1950 by W.
De Kooning
Woman I, stage 2 by W. De Kooning
Woman I, stage 3 by W. De Kooning
Woman I, stage 4 by W. De Kooning
Woman I, stage 5 by W. De Kooning
Woman I, stage 6 by W. De Kooning
Woman (Green) by W. De Kooning
Woman and bicycle by W. De Kooning
Woman and checkerboard by R. Diebenkorn
Woman and man by B. Greene
Woman and table by P. Wonner
Woman arranging her hair by M. B. Prendergast
Woman arranging her veil by M. Cassatt
Woman as landscape by W. De Kooning
Woman at piano by P. Evergood
Woman at Samaria by H. Pippin
Woman at work by J. Lawrence
Woman carrying picture by M. Weber
Woman cutting bread by A. Rattner
Woman dressing by B. Greene
Woman driving geese by W. Homer
Woman drying her hair by H. Katzman
Woman feeding birds by A. Blanch

Woman holding tablet by M. Weber
Woman in a white room by M. Hoff
Woman in a window by R. Diebenkorn
Woman in a yellow dress by Unidentified
artist
Woman in black by M. Cassatt
Woman in black by W. M. Chase
Woman in chair by B. Shahn
Woman in doorway by C. E. Burchfield
Woman in landscape by W. De Kooning
Woman in white by W. M. Chase
Woman, ocher by W. De Kooning
Woman of Iowa by P. Evergood
Woman of sorrows by W. W. Quirt
Woman of the crucifixion by R. Lebrun
Woman on sofa by W. J. Glackens
Woman on trapeze by K. Zerbe
Woman reading by M. Cassatt
Woman reclining by M. Cassatt
Woman sewing by W. Homer
Woman sitting by W. De Kooning
The **woman** taken in adultery by H. Pippin
Woman watering plant by B. Currie
Woman with a dog by M. Cassatt
Woman with a fan by W. Jennys
Woman with a letter by G. Biddle
Woman with a purple hat by J. Binford
Woman with apple by Unidentified artist
Woman with black cat by G. Luks
Woman with cigarette by G. P. Du Bois
Woman with fighting dogs by J. Kirschenbaum
Woman with flower by W. Homer
Woman with folded arms by B. Greene
Woman with forget-me-nots by F. Duveneck
Woman with green face by M. Avery
Woman with plants by G. Wood
Woman with sewing box by Unidentified
artist
Woman with walking stick by C. H. Demuth
Woman's work by J. Sloan
Women admiring a child by M. Cassatt
Women and sea by J. Marin
Women and tents by M. Weber
Women forms and sea by J. Marin
Women on Victorian couch by J. Thomas
Women's dance by D. E. Brett
Wonderful object by F. Martin
WONG, Frederick
Rain on Park south   OYB
OYB. Annual 1960
WONNER, Paul, 1920-
Landscape II, 1953
NNSG. Younger Amer ptrs
Woman and table
IU. Contemp Amer ptg & sculp, 1961
WOOD, Bernardine, 1924-
Still life with melons
IU. Contemp Amer ptg & sculp, 1957
Wood, Caroline Matilda. See Burnham,
Caroline Matilda (Wood)

WOOD, Grant, 1892-1942
Adolescence
  Baur. New art
  IaDa. Wood
  KLU. Wood
American Gothic   ICA
  Baur. New art (col)
  Baur. Revolution
  Canaday
  Cheney. Story 1958 ed
  Craven. Treasury 1952 ed
  Faulkner. Art today, 1956
  Flexner. Amer ptg
  Flexner. Short history
  Gardner 1959 ed
  IaDa. Wood
  Lee. Art then and now
  Lewisohn
  McCurdy
  Mendelowitz
  Newmeyer
  NYG. Fine art
  Pierson
  Richardson. Ptg in America
  Roos
  Taylor. Fifty centuries, 1954 ed (col)
  Time. 300 years (col)
  UNESCO. 1860-1949
  UNESCO. 1860-1955
  UNESCO. 1860-1959
  Wight. Milestones
Currants
  KLU. Wood
Daughters of revolution
  Barr. What is mod ptg
  Baur. New art
  Walker. Ptgs from America
Fall plowing
  KLU. Wood
Iowa cornfield   IaDa
  IaDa. Wood
  NUM. Art across America
Italian farmyard
  KLU. Wood
John B. Turner, pioneer
  KLU. Wood
Midnight ride of Paul Revere   MM
  Canaday
  Craven. Rainbow book
  Craven. Treasury 1952 ed
  MM. 100 Amer ptrs
  Pierson
  Time. 300 years (col)
Nan
  KLU. Wood
Old sexton's place
  KLU. Wood
Parson Weems' fable
  Baur. New art
  KLU. Wood
Return from Bohemia   IBM
  KLU. Wood
Self-portrait, 1932
  IaDa. Wood
  KLU. Wood
Spring in the country   InTH
  Bazin
Spring in town   InTH
  IaDa. Wood
  InTH. Catalogue
  KLU. Wood

Spring landscape
  NYG. Fine art
  UNESCO. 1860-1949
Spring turning
  KLU. Wood
Stone City   NeO
  IaDa. Wood
  NYG. Fine art (col)
Susan Angevine Shaffer
  KLU. Wood
Tree planting
  IaDa. Wood
Turner alley studio
  IaDa. Wood
Woman with plants   IaCR
  Baur. New art
  Craven. Treasury 1952 ed (col)
  UNESCO. 1860-1949
  UNESCO. 1860-1955
  UNESCO. 1860-1959
Young corn
  KLU. Wood
  MnMW. Reality and fantasy
Wood, Horatio C.
  Eakins, T· Dr Horatio C. Wood
WOOD, Joseph, 1778-1832
Thomas Say   CtY
  CtY Portrait index

Attributed works
Oliver Hazard Perry
  MB. New England miniatures
WOOD, Leonard, 1860-1927
  Remington, F. Gen Leonard Wood
WOOD, Thomas Waterman, 1823-1903
Moses, the Baltimore news vendor CSFP
  CSFP. Handbook
Negress   CSFP
  CSFP. Handbook
New England country store, 1873
  Davidson v 1
Village post office   NCHA
  Barker. Amer ptg
  Pierson
Wood, Zipporah. See Ames, Zipporah
  (Wood)
The **wood-boat** by G. C. Bingham
Wood-boatmen on a river by G. C. Bingham
Wood for winter by G. H. Durrie
Wood gatherers by R. Strang
Wood interior by V. Vytlacil
Wood of the Holy Cross by R. Le Brun
Wood road by A. P. Ryder
Wood rose by E. I. Maurice
Woodbridge, Nathaniel Shaw
  Earl, R. Nathaniel Shaw Woodbridge and
    his daughter Mary
WOODBURY, Charles Herbert, 1864-1940
Canal scene, Holland   MB
  MB. Ptgs in water color
Sunken ledges   MB
  MB. Ptgs in water color
Woodbury, Mrs Charles Herbert. See Woodbury, Marcia Oakes
WOODBURY, Marcia Oakes, 1865-1913
Triptych   MB
  MB. Ptgs in water color
The **woodchopper** by W. Homer
The **woodcutter** by W. Homer
Woodcutters in Windsor Great park by B. West

Woodcutting in winter by Unidentified artist

Wooded landscape with castle by B. West (attributed works)

Wooden box of catawba grapes by W. M. Harnett

Wooden horses by R. Marsh

Wooden Indian by M. Manigault

Woodgatherers: autumn afternoon by G. Inness

Wooding up the Mississippi by F. F. Palmer

Woodland scene by W. T. Aldrich

Woodland scene by E. W. Dickinson

Woodland stream by J. F. Cropsey

Woodland vista by G. Inness

Woodlands, seat of William Hamilton, near Philadelphia by W. Groombridge

Woodman spare that tree by Unidentified artist

Woodpeckers
Audubon, J. J. Ivory-billed woodpecker
Audubon, J. J. Pileated woodpecker
Audubon, J. J. Woodpeckers
Dove, A. G. Woodpecker
Graves, M. Woodpeckers

Woodpile by H. Moller

WOODS, Conrad, 1932?-
Verde
    IU. Contemp Amer ptg & sculp, 1959

Woods at sunset by R. A. Blakelock

Woods in winter by W. L. Palmer

Woodshed by A. N. Wyeth

Woodshed interior by S. M. Green

Woodshed interior by Unidentified artist

WOODSIDE, John Archibald, 1781-1852
Children in a courtyard—the origin of drawing (copy of ptg by J. Paul)
    Chew. 250 years of art
Country fair
    Barker. Amer ptg
    Davidson v 1
    Flexner. Light of distant skies
    U.S. National Capital sesquicentennial com
Eben Whitney   MeC
    Jetté. Amer heritage collection

Woodsman and fallen tree by W. Homer

Woodsman in winter by G. H. Durrie

Woodstock art conference by H. Hering

Woodstock pastoral by J. Levine

WOODVILLE, Richard Caton, 1825-1856
Card players   MiD
    Cowdrey v 1
    Pierson
First step   NNHS
    NYG. Fine art
Mexican news
    Cowdrey v 1
Politics in an oyster house   MdBW
    Mendelowitz
    MiD. Ptg in America
    Pierson
    Richardson. Ptg in America
    Roos
Robert Gilmor II   MdBM
    MdBMu. Rendezvous
Sailor's wedding   MdBW
    Davidson v 1
    Larkin

Larkin rev ed

Waiting for the stage
    DC. Amer ptrs of the South
War news from Mexico   NAD
    Baur. Amer ptg
    Pierson

Woodward, Mary. See Hutson, Mary (Woodward)

WOODWARD, Stanley Wingate, 1890-
Along the North shore   MB
    MB. Ptgs in water color

Woodward children, fl 1830
Unidentified artist. Woodward children

WOODWELL, Joseph R. 1843-1911
Farmhouse at Scalp Level   PW
    Chew. 250 years of art

The wool winder by C. Gray

WOOLF, S. J.
Franklin D. Roosevelt—beginning of his office
    NYG. Fine art

Woolsey, Alida Livingston, fl 1817
Tuthill, A. G. D. Alida Livingston Woolsey

Woolsey, Melancthon Taylor, fl 1817
Tuthill, A. G. D. Capt Melancthon Taylor Woolsey

Woolsey, Mrs Melancthon Taylor, fl 1817
Tuthill, A. G. D. Mrs Melancthon Taylor Woolsey

WOOLSON, Ezra, fl 1842
Jesse Kittredge Smith   MSt
    Little. Country art

WOOLWORTH, Charlotte A. fl 1865
Little dog   WMAA
    Ford. Pictorial folk art

Woolworth building by J. Marin

Woolworth building in construction by J. Marin

Word, Mrs William Shaw
Eakins, T. Mrs William Shaw Word

Work reconsidered by J. Wilde

Work stock by D. Teague

Workers and paintings by H. Sharrer

Workers' victory by P. Evergood

Workman's lunch by A. Rattner

A world I never made by I. Rose

World of wires by A. Osver

World tablet by T. Stamos

World's Columbian exposition—the fountains at night by W. Homer

World's greatest comics by B. Shahn

Worship at Eleusis by L. E. Kupferman

Worth family mourning by Unidentified artist

Worthy of liberty by C. W. Peale

Wounded animal by J. Pollock

Wounded beast by J. Pollock

Wounded buffalo by C. M. Russell

Wounded deer by C. Codman

Wounded gull by M. Graves

Wounded ibis by M. Graves

Wounded scoter by M. Graves

Wounded sea gull by M. Graves

Wounded wolf by R. Kuhn

Wragg, Elizabeth. See Manigault, Elizabeth (Wragg)

Wragg, Mary (du Bosc) fl 1708
   Johnston, H. Mrs Samuel Wragg
Wragg, Samuel, 1769-1842
   Malbone, E. G. Samuel Wragg
Wragg, William, fl 1740
   Theus, J. William Wragg
Wraith, wreath, and a final horn by A. H. Smith
Wray, Ann. See Williams, Ann (Wray)
The **wreck** by B. Greene
The **wreck** by W. Homer
Wreck of the Ancon in Loring bay, Alaska by A. Bierstadt
Wreck of the Iron Crown by W. Homer
Wreck of the St Christopher by J. De Martini
The **wreck,** or girl with red stockings by W. Homer
Wrecked building by C. Cloar
Wrecked schooner by W. Homer
Wrestlers. See Boxers and wrestlers
Wright, Henry Parks, 1839-1918
   Beckwith, J. C. Henry Parks Wright
WRIGHT, James Henry, 1813?-1883

Attributed works

U.S. Ship Constellation   MB
   MB. Karolik coll
WRIGHT, Joseph, 1756-1793
   George Washington   OCl
   OCl. Handbook
   George Washington   PH
   Pierson
   Self-portrait of the artist and family PA
   MiD. Ptg in America
   Pierson
   Richardson. Ptg in America

Attributed works

Benjamin Franklin   CtY
   CtY. Portrait index
Wright, Stanton MacDonald-. See MacDon-
   ald-Wright, Stanton
Written in stone by C. A. Morris
Wyalusing by E. C. Frank
Wyalusing by J. O. Montalant
Wyan, Mary Gay. See Nelson, Mary Gay (Wyan)
WYANT, Alexander Helwig, 1836-1892
   Falls of the Ohio and Louisville   KyLS
   Barker. Amer ptg
   Forest stream, a study from nature   MnMI
   Born
   Lake George
   Sears. Highlights
   Mohawk valley   MM
   Pierson
   Richardson. Ptg in America
   Mountain brook, Adirondacks   NBuA
   NBuA. Catalogue of the ptgs
   An old clearing   MM
   Bazin
   Pierson
   On the upper Hudson
   Sears. Highlights
   Winona Falls   MoSL
   MoSL. Handbook 1953
Wyckoff, Alexander Robertson, fl 1810
   Jarvis, J. W. Alexander Robertson Wyckoff

Wyckoff, George
   Bentley, L. George Wyckoff jr
Wyer, Alice, fl 1805
   Malbone, E. G. Alice Wyer
WYETH, Andrew Newell, 1917-
   Afternoon   WiMiA
   IU. Contemp Amer ptg
   NHMC. Andrew Wyeth
   Albert's son
   WMAA. Contemp Amer ptg, 1959/60
   Arthur Cleveland   DeW
   NHMC. Andrew Wyeth
   NUM. Art across America
   Benjamin's house   CSFP
   CSFP. Handbook
   Blackberry picker
   Gruskin
   Brown Swiss
   PPC. International ex, 1958
   Chambered nautilus
   Time. 300 years (col)
   Christina Olsen
   Canaday
   CtY. Yale alumni
   NHMC. Andrew Wyeth
   Christina's world   MMA
   Baur. New art (col)
   Baur. Revolution
   McCurdy
   Mendelowitz
   MMA. Masters
   NHMC. Andrew Wyeth
   Pierson
   The cloisters
   NHMC. Andrew Wyeth
   PPC. Ptg in the U.S. 1949
   Coot hunter   ICA
   NHMC. Andrew Wyeth
   A crow flew by   MM
   MM. 100 Amer ptrs
   Time. 300 years (col)
   Edge of the field   MeC
   MeC. Inaugural ex
   General Knox mansion   OYB
   OYB. Catalogue 1951
   Goose river   NJMo
   NJMo. Forty years
   Hay ledge
   ICA. Annual ex, 1959/60
   Henry Teel
   NHMC. Andrew Wyeth
   Hoffman's slough
   Baur. New art
   House on Teel's island
   NAD. Annual ex, 1947, 2d half
   The hunter   OT
   OT. Contemp Amer ptgs
   John Olsen's funeral   CtNB
   NHMC. Andrew Wyeth
   Karl
   Baur. New art
   Cheney. Story 1958 ed
   NHMC. Andrew Wyeth (col)
   Pierson
   McVey's barn   CtNB
   Baur. New art
   IU. Contemp Amer ptg, 1949
   Man from Maine
   PA. Annual ex, 1952
   Pousette-Dart. Amer ptg
   Memorial day   MB
   MB. Ptgs in water color
   Mr River's garden   MB
   MB. Ptgs in water color

Mother Archie's church   MAP
  NHMC. Andrew Wyeth
Nicholas
  PPC. International ex, 1955
Northern point   CtHW
  Baur. New art
  CtHW. Handbook
  Larkin rev ed
  Seiberling
  WMAA. Museum and its friends, 1959
Raccoon
  ICA. Annual ex, 1959/60
Road to friendship   MeR
  NHMC. Andrew Wyeth
Seed corn
  NHMC. Andrew Wyeth
Self-portrait   NAD
  Bazin
The sexton
  NHMC. Andrew Wyeth
Soaring   MB
  NHMC. Andrew Wyeth
  Pierson
  WMAA. Museum and its friends, 1958
Spindrift   NHMC
  NHMC. Andrew Wyeth
Spring beauty
  Barker. From realism
Sunday school room
  NAD. Annual ex, spring 1950
Toll rope
  PPC. International ex, 1952
Tolling bell   ATeS
  ATeS. Collection
Trodden weed
  Chew. 250 years of art
Wind from the sea
  ICA. Annual ex, 1954
  NHMC. Andrew Wyeth
Woodshed
  NHMC. Andrew Wyeth
Young America   PA
  Eliot. Art of our time (col)
  MM. Amer ptg today
  Time. 300 years (col)
WYETH, Newell Convers, 1882-1945
Buttonwood farm   PR
  PR. Catalogue
Wyld, Diana, fl 1766
  West, B. Diana, wife of Thomas Wyld of
    Sheen
WYLIE, Theophilus Adam
  Political scene in early Bloomington InBU
  Pierson
Wyndham sisters by J. S. Sargent
Wynkoop, Cornelius D. 1734-1792
  Vanderlyn P. (attributed works) Cornelius
    D. Wynkoop
Wyoming
  Albright, I. L. Roaring fork, Wyoming
  Bierstadt, A. Jenny lake, Wyoming
  Bierstadt, A. Wind river country, Wyo-
    ming
  Moran, T. Cliffs of the Green river, Wyo-
    ming
  Richardson, C. C. Wyoming desert
Wyoming valley by E. A. Christie
Wyoming valley by J. F. Cropsey
Wyoming valley by G. Grunewald
Wyoming valley by T. Hill
Wyoming valley by E. D. Lewis
Wyoming valley in 1850 by Unidentified ar-
  tist

X

X—1955 by H. Hofmann
X-1000 by N. J. Oliveira
XCÉRON, Jean, 1890-
  Beyond white
    IU. Contemp Amer ptg, 1951
    IU. 20th century
  Genesis
    IU. Contemp Amer ptg & sculp, 1953
  Ikon no 386   NNSG
    NNSG. Handbook
  Multiform
    IU. Contemp Amer ptg
  Painting 290
    IU. Contemp Amer ptg, 1950
  Painting 341, 1951   WMAA
    Pousette-Dart. Amer ptg
    WMAA. Contemp Amer ptg, 1952
  Painting 388
    IU. Contemp Amer ptg & sculp, 1957
  Radar   GAtM
    GAtM. Holbrook collection
  Variations
    PPC. International ex, 1950
Xmas morning by R. Philipp

Y

Yacht by L. Feininger
The **yacht** America leaving Boston harbor
  for England by J. E. Butterworth
Yacht race by L. Feininger
Yaddo by J. V. Harvey
Yaddo gardens by L. Gatch
Yale university
  Wight, P. B. Venetian Gothic art building
    on the old Yale campus
YAMAMOTO, Noriko, 1919-
  Semtua
    WMAA. Young America 1960
Yankee peddler by J. W. Ehninger
Yankee peddler at work by A. B. Durand
Yaquima bay, Oregon by M. M. Albright
Yates, Catherine (Brass) b 1735
  Stuart, G. Mrs Richard Yates
Yates, Helen Maria. See Paige, Helen Maria
  (Yates)
Yates, Joseph Christopher, 1768-1837
  Ames, E. Joseph C. Yates
  Malbone, E. G. Joseph Yates
Yates, Lawrence Reid, d 1796
  Stuart, G. Lawrence Yates
Yates, Richard, 1732-1808
  Stuart, G. Richard Yates
Yates, Mrs Richard. See Yates, Catherine
  (Brass)
Yates family, fl 1834
  Manchester, M. M. Conversation piece:
    A Yates family portrait
Ye Boston baked beans by H. E. Coville
Ye knights of old by W. M. Harnett
Yeamans, Mary. See Martin, Mary (Yea-
  mans)
The **year** eleven by A. Sessler
Yeats at Petitpas' by J. Sloan

YEKTAI, Manoucher, 1922-
Blue table
MnMW. 60 Amer ptrs
Yellow curtain
IU. Contemp Amer ptg & sculp, 1955
Yell of triumph by A. J. Miller
Yellow above by R. Scarlett
Yellow arc by C. A. Morris
Yellow blinds by C. H. Carter
Yellow-breasted chat by J. J. Audubon
Yellow chair by H. Pittman
Yellow coach by Unidentified artist
Yellow curtain by M. Yektai
The **yellow** fan by A. Brook
Yellow harvest by M. Tobey
Yellow hat by E. Manville
Yellow jacket by M. Avery
Yellow light by C. A. Morris
Yellow lines by I. R. Pereira
Yellow marsh, Sandwich by D. Macknight
Yellow meadow by M. Avery
Yellow oblongs by I. R. Pereira
Yellow over purple by M. Rothko
Yellow pitcher by H. L. McFee
Yellow, plus and minus by S. Chermayeff
Yellow river by W. De Kooning
Yellow room by F. C. Frieseke
Yellow rooster by E. F. Spruce
Yellow roses by W. M. Chase
Yellow seascape by R. Diebenkorn
Yellow sheep by I. Kriesberg
Yellow sky by M. Avery
Yellow sky by J. Hultberg
Yellow table by A. Rattner
The **Yellowstone** and Missouri rivers by K. Bodmer
Yellowstone park
Bierstadt, A. Geyser, Yellowstone park
Moran, T. Mist in the Yellowstone
Twachtman, J. H. Rapids, Yellowstone park
Yellowstone river near Fort Keough by H. Stieffel
YERXA, Thomas, 1935-
Atlantic
NAD. Annual ex, 1954
City child   OYB
NAD. Annual ex, 1957
OYB. Annual 1957
OYB. Supplement 1959
Still life
NAD. Annual ex, 1952
Windows
WMAA. Annual ex, 1958
Yesterday by I. L. Albright
Yesterday by R. O. Pozzatti
YEWELL, George Henry, 1830-1923
The bootblack   NNHS
MiD. Travelers in Arcadia
York by E. Kelly
York family by J. H. Davis
York in the lodge of the Mandans by C. M. Russell
Yosemite Falls
Zorach, W. Yosemite Falls

Yosemite valley
Bierstadt, A. In the Yosemite valley
Bierstadt, A. Valley of the Yosemite
Hahn, W. Yosemite valley
Hill, T. Bridal veil and El Capitan, Yosemite valley
Zorach, W. Rocky cliffs—Yosemite valley
YOST, Fred
Cape May wharf
OYB. Annual 1948
You can buy whiskey for twenty-five cents a quart by J. Lawrence
You can't come home again by A. Shulkin
Youle's shot tower, East river shore by J. F. Cropsey
YOUNG, Art
Trees
Brown. Amer ptg
Young, John, 1762-1840
Stuart, G. Judge John Young
Young, Mrs John. See Young, Maria (Barclay)
Young, Maria (Barclay) d 1811?
Stuart, G. Maria (Barclay) Young
Young America by A. N. Wyeth
Young American artist by J. D. Prendergast
Young artist, Portrait of by F. Knight
Young Aurora by G. A. Walker
Young birds by C. S. Price
Young boy by J. W. Jarvis
Young buck and doe by A. F. Tait
Young chief's mission by J. H. Sharp
Young Christ by D. Aronson
Young clown by W. Kuhn
Young colonial by R. Feke
Young corn by G. Wood
Young crow by C. E. Heil
Young couple drinking by P. Mangravite
Young Daniel Webster and the Constitution by B. Faulkner
Young gander ready for flight by M. Graves
Young gentleman of fashion by A. M. Von Phul
Young girl by J. Carroll
Young girl by E. Decombes
Young girl by W. Jennys (attributed **works**)
Young girl by A. H. Maurer
Young girl by Unidentified artist
Young girl in a red dress by Unidentified artist
Young girl in blue by J. A. M. Whistler
Young girl in flower by R. Feke
Young girl in green bonnet by M. Cassatt
Young girl in white by Unidentified artist
Young girl with music book by W. Sutton
Young girls by M. Cassatt
Young hammerer by J. W. Stock
Young hunter by C. W. Hare
Young hunter in woods by W. Homer
Young Joseph by D. Aronson
Young ladies' seminary, Virginia by Unidentified artist
Young lady by G. Duyckinck (attributed works)
Young lady in pink by E. G. Malbone
Young lovers by P. Mangravite

Young man by T. Eakins
Young man by Raphaelle Peale
Young man by W. M. Prior
Young man alone with his face by P. Burlin
Young man desiring position by G. Samstag
Young man from Arkansas by J. Farnsworth
Young man in a gray linen suit by Unidentified artist
Young man of the sea by J. Marin
Young man wearing white stock by Unidentified artist
Young men by the sea by M. Beckmann
Young merchants by W. Page
Young model by M. Weber
Young musician by D. G. Blythe
Young Omahaw, War Eagle, Little Missouri and Pawnees by C. B. King
Young owl and moth by M. Graves
Young pianist by A. Brook
Young woman by J. Chapin
Young woman by R. Soyer
Young woman by A. H. Thayer
Young woman in a fur coat by A. H. Thayer
Young woman in pink dress by T. Eakins
Young woman in white by R. Henri
Young woman of the Flathead tribe by A. J. Miller
Young woman reading by M. Cassatt
Young woman with bird by R. Brackman
Young woman with gloves by W. Brice
Young women picking fruit by M. Cassatt
Young worshipper of the truth by M. Hartley
YOUNGERMAN, Jack, 1926-
  Aquitaine   MMA
    MMA. Sixteen
  Aztec III
    MMA. Sixteen
  Big black
    MMA. Sixteen
  Coenties slip
    MMA. Sixteen
  "Cuba Si"
    PPC. International ex, 1961/62
  Delfina   NBuA
    NBuA. Acquisitions 1959-1961
  Naxos
    PPC. International ex, 1958
  Ram
    MMA. Sixteen
Your tapers taper by Y. Tanguy
Youth by B. Greene
Youth playing fife by T. Eakins
Yule log by V. Candall
Yuma, Arizona by L. M. Eilshemius
YUNKERS, Adja, 1900-
  Composition in black and ochre   NNSG
    NNSG. Handbook
  Gosier II
    IU. Contemp Amer ptg & sculp, 1961
  Tarrasa
    PPC. International ex, 1958
  Tarrasa XIII, 1958   WMAA
    Goodrich. Amer art
  Untitled I, 1960
    MnMW. 60 Amer ptrs
Yvanka by B. Greene

Z

Zagorin, Mrs Perez. See Sharrer, Honoré Desmond
ZAJAC, Jack, 1929-
  The anglers
    IU. Contemp Amer ptg, 1952
  Bird in the sun no 2, 1955
    WMAA. Young America 1957
  Resurrection
    WMAA. Young America 1957
  Seacoast   CLA
    CoS. New accessions USA, 1954
  Seascape
    PPC. International ex, 1955
ZALMAR, 1925-
  Landscape with potted plant in foreground
    IU. Contemp Amer ptg, 1951
ZELIFF, A. E. fl 1850
  Barnyard   DN
    DN. Amer primitive ptgs, pt 1
Zen Buddist by X. Gonzales
Zenka of Bohemia by R. Henri
ZERBE, Karl, 1903-
  Aging harlequin
    Baur. Revolution
  Apartment no 2
    Pousette-Dart. Amer ptg
  At night
    Pearson. Mod renaissance
  The birdcage   InIJ
    InIJ. 105 ptgs
  Boston daily
    NAD. Annual ex, 1948
  Canal street no 2
    IU. Contemp Amer ptg & sculp, 1957
  China Town no 1   MAP
    CoS. New accessions USA, 1954
  Collection X, no 2
    CSFP. Annual ex, 1952
  East of Lexington
    DC. 21 biennial ex, 1949
  Felix Adler
    Pearson. Mod renaissance
  Fortune seller
    IU. Contemp Amer ptg, 1949 (col)
  Gloucester alley   NBuA
    NBuA. Contemporary ptgs
  Golden hat
    IU. Contemp Amer ptg, 1948
  Good angel tenanted
    IU. Contemp Amer ptg & sculp, 1959
  Good Friday
    IU. Contemp Amer ptg, 1950
    Pearson. Mod renaissance
  Harlem   MMA
    Pierson
  Harlequin   WMAA
    Goodrich. Amer art
    Gruskin (col)
    Pierson
  The inventor
    IU. Contemp ptg & sculp, 1953
  Kokoschka, 1949
    MnMW. Expressionism 1900-1955
  Landscape with letters
    IC. Annual ex, 1954
  Landscape with scrap metal III   IU
    IU. Contemp Amer ptg & sculp, 1955
    IU. 20th century
    WMAA. Annual ex, 1955

ZERBE, Karl—*Continued*
Melancholia
  ICA. Annual ex, 1947/48   ICA
  Roos
Night
  MeC. Inaugural ex
Park street, Boston   DP
  DP. Catalogue
The parrot and decanter
  ICA. Annual ex, 1945/46
Pastorale   MM
  MM. 100 Amer ptrs
Rome—St Augustine
  Pearson. Mod renaissance
Rooster   GAtM
  GAtM. Holbrook collection
Ruins, Brantone   OYB
  OYB. Catalogue 1951
St Louis drawing room
  Wight. Milestones
St Philip's, Charleston   MoSL
  MoSL. Handbook 1953
Second floor front   NUM
  NBuA. Expressionism
  PPC. Ptg in the U.S. 1949
Street in Tepoztlan, Mexico   MB
  MB. Ptgs in water color
Survivors
  IU. Contemp Amer ptg, 1951
  PA. Annual ex, 1949
Terror
  Cheney. Story 1958 ed
Woman on trapeze   IBM
  Genauer
ZEREGA, Andrea Pietro, 1917-
In Montgomery county
  IU. Contemp Amer ptg & sculp, 1953
Zeretelli by M. Beckmann
ZIMMERMAN, Paul Warren, 1921-
Reminiscent Italia
  OYB. Annual 1950
The square
  NAD. Annual ex, 1954
Still life—delphinium
  IU. Contemp Amer ptg & sculp, 1961
ZINGALE, Santos, 1908-
Variation on a theme
  IU. Contemp Amer ptg & sculp, 1953
Zinnias by H. Katzman
Zinnias by M. Weber
Zinnias, larkspur and daisies by C. H. Demuth
Zion canyon by D. Macknight
Zirchow VII by L. Feininger
Zirchow VII by L. Feininger
ZIROLI, Nicola, 1908-
Self-portrait   OYB
  OYB. Annual 1955
  OYB. Supplement 1959
Weeds
  OYB. Annual 1956

ZOGBAUM, Rufus F. 1849-1925
Admiral Dewey at Manila bay, 1898
  U.S. National Capital sesquicentennial com
Zone by P. Guston
ZORACH, Marguerite (Thompson) 1888-
Hound
  Cheney. Expressionism 1948 ed
Moonset and sunrise
  WMAA. Pioneers

Portrait of the artist
Biddle, G. Woman with a letter
ZORACH, William, 1887-
The artist's son
  Baur. William Zorach
Five islands, Maine
  NYG. Fine art
Interior and exterior
  Baur. William Zorach
Leo Ornstein (Piano concert)
  Baur. William Zorach
  WMAA. Pioneers
  WMAA. Zorach
Mirage—ships at night
  Baur. William Zorach
  WMAA. Zorach
Morning glow, autumn
  Baur. William Zorach
  WMAA. Zorach
Piano concert. See Leo Ornstein
Popham beach no 1, Maine
  Baur. William Zorach
Robinhood marina
  Baur. William Zorach
  WMAA. Zorach
Rocky cliffs—Yosemite valley
  Baur. William Zorach
The roof playground
  Baur. William Zorach
Sailing by moonlight   DP
  DP. Catalogue
Sisters
  Baur. William Zorach
Spring no 1, 1913
  Baur. William Zorach
  WMAA. Zorach
Windy day—Lowe's point
  Baur. William Zorach
  WMAA. Zorach
Winter without snow   MB
  MB. Ptgs in water color
Yosemite Falls
  Baur. William Zorach
Yosemite Falls I
  Baur. William Zorach
Yosemite Falls II
  Baur. William Zorach
  WMAA. Zorach
Zorach, Mrs William. See Zorach, Marguerite (Thompson)
Zsissly. See Albright, Malvin Marr

DATE DUE

Demco, Inc. 38-293